P9-CBE-434

2914.24

University Casebook Series

May, 1989

ACCOUNTING AND THE LAW, Fourth Edition (1978), with Problems Pamphlet (Successor to Dohr, Phillips, Thompson & Warren)

George C. Thompson, Professor, Columbia University Graduate School of Business.
Robert Whitman, Professor of Law, University of Connecticut.
Ellis L. Phillips, Jr., Member of the New York Bar.
William C. Warren, Professor of Law Emeritus, Columbia University.

ACCOUNTING FOR LAWYERS, MATERIALS ON (1980)

David R. Herwitz, Professor of Law, Harvard University.

ADMINISTRATIVE LAW, Eighth Edition (1987), with 1983 Problems Supplement (Supplement edited in association with Paul R. Verkuil, Dean and Professor of Law, Tulane University)

Walter Gellhorn, University Professor Emeritus, Columbia University.
Clark Byse, Professor of Law, Harvard University.
Peter L. Strauss, Professor of Law, Columbia University.
Todd D. Rakoff, Professor of Law, Harvard University.
Roy A. Schotland, Professor of Law, Georgetown University.

ADMIRALTY, Third Edition (1987), with Statute and Rule Supplement

Jo Desha Lucas, Professor of Law, University of Chicago.

ADVOCACY, see also Lawyering Process

AGENCY, see also Enterprise Organization

AGENCY—PARTNERSHIPS, Fourth Edition (1987)

Abridgement from Conard, Knauss & Siegel's Enterprise Organization, Fourth Edition.

AGENCY AND PARTNERSHIPS (1987)

Melvin A. Eisenberg, Professor of Law, University of California, Berkeley.

ANTITRUST: FREE ENTERPRISE AND ECONOMIC ORGANIZATION, Sixth Edition (1983), with 1983 Problems in Antitrust Supplement and 1988 Case Supplement

Louis B. Schwartz, Professor of Law, University of Pennsylvania.
John J. Flynn, Professor of Law, University of Utah.
Harry First, Professor of Law, New York University.

BANKRUPTCY, Second Edition (1989)

Robert L. Jordan, Professor of Law, University of California, Los Angeles.
William D. Warren, Professor of Law, University of California, Los Angeles.

BANKRUPTCY AND DEBTOR–CREDITOR LAW, Second Edition (1988)

Theodore Eisenberg, Professor of Law, Cornell University.

BUSINESS ORGANIZATION, see also Enterprise Organization

BUSINESS PLANNING, Temporary Second Edition (1984)

David R. Herwitz, Professor of Law, Harvard University.

BUSINESS TORTS (1972)

Milton Handler, Professor of Law Emeritus, Columbia University.

CHILDREN IN THE LEGAL SYSTEM (1983) with 1988 Supplement

Walter Wadlington, Professor of Law, University of Virginia.
Charles H. Whitebread, Professor of Law, University of Southern California.
Samuel Davis, Professor of Law, University of Georgia.

CIVIL PROCEDURE, see Procedure

CIVIL RIGHTS ACTIONS (1988), with 1988 Supplement

Peter W. Low, Professor of Law, University of Virginia.
John C. Jeffries, Jr., Professor of Law, University of Virginia.

CLINIC, see also Lawyering Process

COMMERCIAL AND DEBTOR–CREDITOR LAW: SELECTED STATUTES, 1988 EDITION

COMMERCIAL LAW, Second Edition (1987)

Robert L. Jordan, Professor of Law, University of California, Los Angeles.
William D. Warren, Professor of Law, University of California, Los Angeles.

COMMERCIAL LAW, Fourth Edition (1985)

E. Allan Farnsworth, Professor of Law, Columbia University.
John Honnold, Professor of Law, University of Pennsylvania.

COMMERCIAL PAPER, Third Edition (1984)

E. Allan Farnsworth, Professor of Law, Columbia University.

COMMERCIAL PAPER, Second Edition (1987) (Reprinted from COMMERCIAL LAW, Second Edition (1987))

Robert L. Jordan, Professor of Law, University of California, Los Angeles.
William D. Warren, Professor of Law, University of California, Los Angeles.

COMMERCIAL PAPER AND BANK DEPOSITS AND COLLECTIONS (1967), with Statutory Supplement

William D. Hawkland, Professor of Law, University of Illinois.

COMMERCIAL TRANSACTIONS—Principles and Policies (1982)

Alan Schwartz, Professor of Law, University of Southern California.
Robert E. Scott, Professor of Law, University of Virginia.

COMPARATIVE LAW, Fifth Edition (1988)

Rudolf B. Schlesinger, Professor of Law, Hastings College of Law.
Hans W. Baade, Professor of Law, University of Texas.
Mirjan P. Damaska, Professor of Law, Yale Law School.
Peter E. Herzog, Professor of Law, Syracuse University.

COMPETITIVE PROCESS, LEGAL REGULATION OF THE, Third Edition (1986), with 1987 Selected Statutes Supplement

Edmund W. Kitch, Professor of Law, University of Virginia.
Harvey S. Perlman, Dean of the Law School, University of Nebraska.

UNIVERSITY CASEBOOK SERIES—Continued

CONFLICT OF LAWS, Eighth Edition (1984), with 1987 Case Supplement

Willis L. M. Reese, Professor of Law, Columbia University.
Maurice Rosenberg, Professor of Law, Columbia University.

CONSTITUTIONAL LAW, Eighth Edition (1989)

Edward L. Barrett, Jr., Professor of Law, University of California, Davis.
William Cohen, Professor of Law, Stanford University.
Jonathan D. Varat, Professor of Law, University of California, Los Angeles.

CONSTITUTIONAL LAW, CIVIL LIBERTY AND INDIVIDUAL RIGHTS, Second Edition (1982), with 1987 Supplement

William Cohen, Professor of Law, Stanford University.
John Kaplan, Professor of Law, Stanford University.

CONSTITUTIONAL LAW, Eleventh Edition (1985), with 1988 Supplement (Supplement edited in association with Frederick F. Schauer, Professor of Law, University of Michigan)

Gerald Gunther, Professor of Law, Stanford University.

CONSTITUTIONAL LAW, INDIVIDUAL RIGHTS IN, Fourth Edition (1986), (Reprinted from CONSTITUTIONAL LAW, Eleventh Edition), with 1988 Supplement (Supplement edited in association with Frederick F. Schauer, Professor of Law, University of Michigan)

Gerald Gunther, Professor of Law, Stanford University.

CONSUMER TRANSACTIONS (1983), with Selected Statutes and Regulations Supplement and 1987 Case Supplement

Michael M. Greenfield, Professor of Law, Washington University.

CONTRACT LAW AND ITS APPLICATION, Fourth Edition (1988)

Arthur Rosett, Professor of Law, University of California, Los Angeles.

CONTRACT LAW, STUDIES IN, Third Edition (1984)

Edward J. Murphy, Professor of Law, University of Notre Dame.
Richard E. Speidel, Professor of Law, Northwestern University.

CONTRACTS, Fifth Edition (1987)

John P. Dawson, late Professor of Law, Harvard University.
William Burnett Harvey, Professor of Law and Political Science, Boston University.
Stanley D. Henderson, Professor of Law, University of Virginia.

CONTRACTS, Fourth Edition (1988)

E. Allan Farnsworth, Professor of Law, Columbia University.
William F. Young, Professor of Law, Columbia University.

CONTRACTS, Selections on (statutory materials) (1988)

CONTRACTS, Second Edition (1978), with Statutory and Administrative Law Supplement (1978)

Ian R. Macneil, Professor of Law, Cornell University.

COPYRIGHT, PATENTS AND TRADEMARKS, see also Competitive Process; see also Selected Statutes and International Agreements

COPYRIGHT, PATENT, TRADEMARK AND RELATED STATE DOCTRINES, Second Edition (1981), with 1988 Case Supplement, 1987 Selected Statutes Supplement and 1981 Problem Supplement

Paul Goldstein, Professor of Law, Stanford University.

COPYRIGHT, Unfair Competition, and Other Topics Bearing on the Protection of Literary, Musical, and Artistic Works, Fourth Edition (1985), with 1985 Statutory Supplement

Ralph S. Brown, Jr., Professor of Law, Yale University.
Robert C. Denicola, Professor of Law, University of Nebraska.

CORPORATE ACQUISITIONS, The Law and Finance of (1986), with 1988 Supplement

Ronald J. Gilson, Professor of Law, Stanford University.

CORPORATE FINANCE, Third Edition (1987)

Victor Brudney, Professor of Law, Harvard University.
Marvin A. Chirelstein, Professor of Law, Columbia University.

CORPORATE READJUSTMENTS AND REORGANIZATIONS (1976)

Walter J. Blum, Professor of Law, University of Chicago.
Stanley A. Kaplan, Professor of Law, University of Chicago.

CORPORATION LAW, BASIC, Third Edition (1989), with Documentary Supplement

Detlev F. Vagts, Professor of Law, Harvard University.

CORPORATIONS, see also Enterprise Organization

CORPORATIONS, Sixth Edition—Concise (1988), with Statutory Supplement (1988)

William L. Cary, late Professor of Law, Columbia University.
Melvin Aron Eisenberg, Professor of Law, University of California, Berkeley.

CORPORATIONS, Sixth Edition—Unabridged (1988), with Statutory Supplement (1988)

William L. Cary, late Professor of Law, Columbia University.
Melvin Aron Eisenberg, Professor of Law, University of California, Berkeley.

CORPORATIONS AND BUSINESS ASSOCIATIONS—STATUTES, RULES AND FORMS (1988)

CORPORATIONS COURSE GAME PLAN (1975)

David R. Herwitz, Professor of Law, Harvard University.

CORRECTIONS, SEE SENTENCING

CREDITORS' RIGHTS, see also Debtor-Creditor Law

CRIMINAL JUSTICE ADMINISTRATION, Third Edition (1986), with 1988 Case Supplement

Frank W. Miller, Professor of Law, Washington University.
Robert O. Dawson, Professor of Law, University of Texas.
George E. Dix, Professor of Law, University of Texas.
Raymond I. Parnas, Professor of Law, University of California, Davis.

CRIMINAL LAW, Fourth Edition (1987)

Fred E. Inbau, Professor of Law Emeritus, Northwestern University.
Andre A. Moenssens, Professor of Law, University of Richmond.
James R. Thompson, Professor of Law Emeritus, Northwestern University.

CRIMINAL LAW AND APPROACHES TO THE STUDY OF LAW (1986)

John M. Brumbaugh, Professor of Law, University of Maryland.

CRIMINAL LAW, Second Edition (1986)

Peter W. Low, Professor of Law, University of Virginia.
John C. Jeffries, Jr., Professor of Law, University of Virginia.
Richard C. Bonnie, Professor of Law, University of Virginia.

CRIMINAL LAW, Fourth Edition (1986)

Lloyd L. Weinreb, Professor of Law, Harvard University.

CRIMINAL LAW AND PROCEDURE, Seventh Edition (1989)

Ronald N. Boyce, Professor of Law, University of Utah.
Rollin M. Perkins, Professor of Law Emeritus, University of California, Hastings College of the Law.

CRIMINAL PROCEDURE, Third Edition (1987), with 1988 Supplement

James B. Haddad, Professor of Law, Northwestern University.
James B. Zagel, Chief, Criminal Justice Division, Office of Attorney General of Illinois.
Gary L. Starkman, Assistant U. S. Attorney, Northern District of Illinois.
William J. Bauer, Chief Judge of the U.S. Court of Appeals, Seventh Circuit.

CRIMINAL PROCESS, Fourth Edition (1987), with 1988 Supplement

Lloyd L. Weinreb, Professor of Law, Harvard University.

DAMAGES, Second Edition (1952)

Charles T. McCormick, late Professor of Law, University of Texas.
William F. Fritz, late Professor of Law, University of Texas.

DECEDENTS' ESTATES AND TRUSTS, Seventh Edition (1988)

John Ritchie, late Professor of Law, University of Virginia.
Neill H. Alford, Jr., Professor of Law, University of Virginia.
Richard W. Effland, late Professor of Law, Arizona State University.

DISPUTE RESOLUTION, Processes of (1989)

John S. Murray, President and Executive Director of The Conflict Clinic, Inc., George Mason University.
Alan Scott Rau, Professor of Law, University of Texas.
Edward F. Sherman, Professor of Law, University of Texas.

DOMESTIC RELATIONS, see also Family Law

DOMESTIC RELATIONS, Successor Edition (1984) with 1988 Supplement

Walter Wadlington, Professor of Law, University of Virginia.

EMPLOYMENT DISCRIMINATION, Second Edition (1987), with 1988 Supplement

Joel W. Friedman, Professor of Law, Tulane University.
George M. Strickler, Professor of Law, Tulane University.

EMPLOYMENT LAW (1987), with 1987 Statutory Supplement and 1988 Case Supplement

Mark A. Rothstein, Professor of Law, University of Houston.
Andria S. Knapp, Adjunct Professor of Law, University of California, Hastings College of Law.
Lance Liebman, Professor of Law, Harvard University.

ENERGY LAW (1983) with 1986 Case Supplement

Donald N. Zillman, Professor of Law, University of Utah.
Laurence Lattman, Dean of Mines and Engineering, University of Utah.

ENTERPRISE ORGANIZATION, Fourth Edition (1987), with 1987 Corporation and Partnership Statutes, Rules and Forms Supplement

Alfred F. Conard, Professor of Law, University of Michigan.
Robert L. Knauss, Dean of the Law School, University of Houston.
Stanley Siegel, Professor of Law, University of California, Los Angeles.

ENVIRONMENTAL POLICY LAW 1985 Edition, with 1985 Problems Supplement (Supplement in association with Ronald H. Rosenberg, Professor of Law, College of William and Mary)

Thomas J. Schoenbaum, Professor of Law, University of Georgia.

EQUITY, see also Remedies

EQUITY, RESTITUTION AND DAMAGES, Second Edition (1974)

Robert Childres, late Professor of Law, Northwestern University.
William F. Johnson, Jr., Professor of Law, New York University.

ESTATE PLANNING, Second Edition (1982), with 1985 Case, Text and Documentary Supplement

David Westfall, Professor of Law, Harvard University.

ETHICS, see Legal Profession, Professional Responsibility, and Social Responsibilities

ETHICS AND PROFESSIONAL RESPONSIBILITY (1981) (Reprinted from THE LAWYERING PROCESS)

Gary Bellow, Professor of Law, Harvard University.
Bea Moulton, Legal Services Corporation.

EVIDENCE, Sixth Edition (1988 Reprint)

John Kaplan, Professor of Law, Stanford University.
Jon R. Waltz, Professor of Law, Northwestern University.

EVIDENCE, Eighth Edition (1988), with Rules, Statute and Case Supplement (1988)

Jack B. Weinstein, Chief Judge, United States District Court.
John H. Mansfield, Professor of Law, Harvard University.
Norman Abrams, Professor of Law, University of California, Los Angeles.
Margaret Berger, Professor of Law, Brooklyn Law School.

FAMILY LAW, see also Domestic Relations

FAMILY LAW Second Edition (1985), with 1988 Supplement

Judith C. Areen, Professor of Law, Georgetown University.

FAMILY LAW AND CHILDREN IN THE LEGAL SYSTEM, STATUTORY MATERIALS (1981)

Walter Wadlington, Professor of Law, University of Virginia.

FEDERAL COURTS, Eighth Edition (1988)

Charles T. McCormick, late Professor of Law, University of Texas.
James H. Chadbourn, late Professor of Law, Harvard University.
Charles Alan Wright, Professor of Law, University of Texas, Austin.

UNIVERSITY CASEBOOK SERIES—Continued

FEDERAL COURTS AND THE FEDERAL SYSTEM, Hart and Wechsler's Third Edition (1988), with the Judicial Code and Rules of Procedure in the Federal Courts (1988)

Paul M. Bator, Professor of Law, University of Chicago.
Daniel J. Meltzer, Professor of Law, Harvard University.
Paul J. Mishkin, Professor of Law, University of California, Berkeley.
David L. Shapiro, Professor of Law, Harvard University.

FEDERAL COURTS AND THE LAW OF FEDERAL–STATE RELATIONS, Second Edition (1989)

Peter W. Low, Professor of Law, University of Virginia.
John C. Jeffries, Jr., Professor of Law, University of Virginia.

FEDERAL PUBLIC LAND AND RESOURCES LAW, Second Edition (1987), with 1984 Statutory Supplement

George C. Coggins, Professor of Law, University of Kansas.
Charles F. Wilkinson, Professor of Law, University of Oregon.

FEDERAL RULES OF CIVIL PROCEDURE and Selected Other Procedural Provisions, 1988 Edition

FEDERAL TAXATION, see Taxation

FOOD AND DRUG LAW (1980), with Statutory Supplement

Richard A. Merrill, Dean of the School of Law, University of Virginia.
Peter Barton Hutt, Esq.

FUTURE INTERESTS (1958)

Philip Mechem, late Professor of Law Emeritus, University of Pennsylvania.

FUTURE INTERESTS (1970)

Howard R. Williams, Professor of Law, Stanford University.

FUTURE INTERESTS AND ESTATE PLANNING (1961), with 1962 Supplement

W. Barton Leach, late Professor of Law, Harvard University.
James K. Logan, formerly Dean of the Law School, University of Kansas.

GOVERNMENT CONTRACTS, FEDERAL, Successor Edition (1985)

John W. Whelan, Professor of Law, Hastings College of the Law.

GOVERNMENT REGULATION: FREE ENTERPRISE AND ECONOMIC ORGANIZATION, Sixth Edition (1985)

Louis B. Schwartz, Professor of Law, Hastings College of the Law.
John J. Flynn, Professor of Law, University of Utah.
Harry First, Professor of Law, New York University.

HEALTH CARE LAW AND POLICY (1988)

Clark C. Havighurst, Professor of Law, Duke University.

HINCKLEY, JOHN W., JR., TRIAL OF: A Case Study of the Insanity Defense (1986)

Peter W. Low, Professor of Law, University of Virginia.
John C. Jeffries, Jr., Professor of Law, University of Virginia.
Richard C. Bonnie, Professor of Law, University of Virginia.

INJUNCTIONS, Second Edition (1984)

Owen M. Fiss, Professor of Law, Yale University.
Doug Rendleman, Professor of Law, College of William and Mary.

UNIVERSITY CASEBOOK SERIES—Continued

INSTITUTIONAL INVESTORS, (1978)

David L. Ratner, Professor of Law, Cornell University.

INSURANCE, Second Edition (1985)

William F. Young, Professor of Law, Columbia University.
Eric M. Holmes, Professor of Law, University of Georgia.

INTERNATIONAL LAW, see also Transnational Legal Problems, Transnational Business Problems, and United Nations Law

INTERNATIONAL LAW IN CONTEMPORARY PERSPECTIVE (1981), with Essay Supplement

Myres S. McDougal, Professor of Law, Yale University.
W. Michael Reisman, Professor of Law, Yale University.

INTERNATIONAL LEGAL SYSTEM, Third Edition (1988), with Documentary Supplement

Joseph Modeste Sweeney, Professor of Law, University of California, Hastings.
Covey T. Oliver, Professor of Law, University of Pennsylvania.
Noyes E. Leech, Professor of Law Emeritus, University of Pennsylvania.

INTRODUCTION TO LAW, see also Legal Method, On Law in Courts, and Dynamics of American Law

INTRODUCTION TO THE STUDY OF LAW (1970)

E. Wayne Thode, late Professor of Law, University of Utah.
Leon Lebowitz, Professor of Law, University of Texas.
Lester J. Mazor, Professor of Law, University of Utah.

JUDICIAL CODE and Rules of Procedure in the Federal Courts, Students' Edition, 1988 Revision

Daniel J. Meltzer, Professor of Law, Harvard University.
David L. Shapiro, Professor of Law, Harvard University.

JURISPRUDENCE (Temporary Edition Hardbound) (1949)

Lon L. Fuller, late Professor of Law, Harvard University.

JUVENILE, see also Children

JUVENILE JUSTICE PROCESS, Third Edition (1985)

Frank W. Miller, Professor of Law, Washington University.
Robert O. Dawson, Professor of Law, University of Texas.
George E. Dix, Professor of Law, University of Texas.
Raymond I. Parnas, Professor of Law, University of California, Davis.

LABOR LAW, Tenth Edition (1986), with 1986 Statutory Supplement

Archibald Cox, Professor of Law, Harvard University.
Derek C. Bok, President, Harvard University.
Robert A. Gorman, Professor of Law, University of Pennsylvania.

LABOR LAW, Second Edition (1982), with Statutory Supplement

Clyde W. Summers, Professor of Law, University of Pennsylvania.
Harry H. Wellington, Dean of the Law School, Yale University.
Alan Hyde, Professor of Law, Rutgers University.

LAND FINANCING, Third Edition (1985)

The late Norman Penney, Professor of Law, Cornell University.
Richard F. Broude, Member of the California Bar.
Roger Cunningham, Professor of Law, University of Michigan.

LAW AND MEDICINE (1980)

Walter Wadlington, Professor of Law and Professor of Legal Medicine, University of Virginia.

Jon R. Waltz, Professor of Law, Northwestern University.

Roger B. Dworkin, Professor of Law, Indiana University, and Professor of Biomedical History, University of Washington.

LAW, LANGUAGE AND ETHICS (1972)

William R. Bishin, Professor of Law, University of Southern California.

Christopher D. Stone, Professor of Law, University of Southern California.

LAW, SCIENCE AND MEDICINE (1984), with 1989 Supplement

Judith C. Areen, Professor of Law, Georgetown University.

Patricia A. King, Professor of Law, Georgetown University.

Steven P. Goldberg, Professor of Law, Georgetown University.

Alexander M. Capron, Professor of Law, University of Southern California.

LAWYERING PROCESS (1978), with Civil Problem Supplement and Criminal Problem Supplement

Gary Bellow, Professor of Law, Harvard University.

Bea Moulton, Professor of Law, Arizona State University.

LEGAL METHOD (1980)

Harry W. Jones, Professor of Law Emeritus, Columbia University.

John M. Kernochan, Professor of Law, Columbia University.

Arthur W. Murphy, Professor of Law, Columbia University.

LEGAL METHODS (1969)

Robert N. Covington, Professor of Law, Vanderbilt University.

E. Blythe Stason, late Professor of Law, Vanderbilt University.

John W. Wade, Professor of Law, Vanderbilt University.

Elliott E. Cheatham, late Professor of Law, Vanderbilt University.

Theodore A. Smedley, Professor of Law, Vanderbilt University.

LEGAL PROFESSION, THE, Responsibility and Regulation, Second Edition (1988)

Geoffrey C. Hazard, Jr., Professor of Law, Yale University.

Deborah L. Rhode, Professor of Law, Stanford University.

LEGISLATION, Fourth Edition (1982) (by Fordham)

Horace E. Read, late Vice President, Dalhousie University.

John W. MacDonald, Professor of Law Emeritus, Cornell Law School.

Jefferson B. Fordham, Professor of Law, University of Utah.

William J. Pierce, Professor of Law, University of Michigan.

LEGISLATIVE AND ADMINISTRATIVE PROCESSES, Second Edition (1981)

Hans A. Linde, Judge, Supreme Court of Oregon.

George Bunn, Professor of Law, University of Wisconsin.

Fredericka Paff, Professor of Law, University of Wisconsin.

W. Lawrence Church, Professor of Law, University of Wisconsin.

LOCAL GOVERNMENT LAW, Second Revised Edition (1986)

Jefferson B. Fordham, Professor of Law, University of Utah.

MASS MEDIA LAW, Third Edition (1987)

Marc A. Franklin, Professor of Law, Stanford University.

UNIVERSITY CASEBOOK SERIES—Continued

MENTAL HEALTH PROCESS, Second Edition (1976), with 1981 Supplement

Frank W. Miller, Professor of Law, Washington University.
Robert O. Dawson, Professor of Law, University of Texas.
George E. Dix, Professor of Law, University of Texas.
Raymond I. Parnas, Professor of Law, University of California, Davis.

MUNICIPAL CORPORATIONS, see Local Government Law

NEGOTIABLE INSTRUMENTS, see Commercial Paper

NEGOTIATION (1981) (Reprinted from THE LAWYERING PROCESS)

Gary Bellow, Professor of Law, Harvard Law School.
Bea Moulton, Legal Services Corporation.

NEW YORK PRACTICE, Fourth Edition (1978)

Herbert Peterfreund, Professor of Law, New York University.
Joseph M. McLaughlin, Dean of the Law School, Fordham University.

OIL AND GAS, Fifth Edition (1987)

Howard R. Williams, Professor of Law, Stanford University.
Richard C. Maxwell, Professor of Law, University of California, Los Angeles.
Charles J. Meyers, late Dean of the Law School, Stanford University.
Stephen F. Williams, Judge of the United States Court of Appeals.

ON LAW IN COURTS (1965)

Paul J. Mishkin, Professor of Law, University of California, Berkeley.
Clarence Morris, Professor of Law Emeritus, University of Pennsylvania.

PATENTS AND ANTITRUST (Pamphlet) (1983)

Milton Handler, Professor of Law Emeritus, Columbia University.
Harlan M. Blake, Professor of Law, Columbia University.
Robert Pitofsky, Professor of Law, Georgetown University.
Harvey J. Goldschmid, Professor of Law, Columbia University.

PLEADING AND PROCEDURE, see Procedure, Civil

POLICE FUNCTION, Fourth Edition (1986), with 1988 Case Supplement

Reprint of Chapters 1–10 of Miller, Dawson, Dix and Parnas's CRIMINAL JUSTICE ADMINISTRATION, Third Edition.

PREPARING AND PRESENTING THE CASE (1981) (Reprinted from THE LAWYERING PROCESS)

Gary Bellow, Professor of Law, Harvard Law School.
Bea Moulton, Legal Services Corporation.

PROCEDURE (1988), with Procedure Supplement (1988)

Robert M. Cover, late Professor of Law, Yale Law School.
Owen M. Fiss, Professor of Law, Yale Law School.
Judith Resnik, Professor of Law, University of Southern California Law Center.

PROCEDURE—CIVIL PROCEDURE, Second Edition (1974), with 1979 Supplement

The late James H. Chadbourn, Professor of Law, Harvard University.
A. Leo Levin, Professor of Law, University of Pennsylvania.
Philip Shuchman, Professor of Law, Cornell University.

PROCEDURE—CIVIL PROCEDURE, Fifth Edition (1984), with 1988 Supplement

Richard H. Field, late Professor of Law, Harvard University.
Benjamin Kaplan, Professor of Law Emeritus, Harvard University.
Kevin M. Clermont, Professor of Law, Cornell University.

PROCEDURE—CIVIL PROCEDURE, Fourth Edition (1985), with 1988 Supplement

Maurice Rosenberg, Professor of Law, Columbia University.
Hans Smit, Professor of Law, Columbia University.
Harold L. Korn, Professor of Law, Columbia University.

PROCEDURE—PLEADING AND PROCEDURE: State and Federal, Fifth Edition (1983), with 1988 Supplement

David W. Louisell, late Professor of Law, University of California, Berkeley.
Geoffrey C. Hazard, Jr., Professor of Law, Yale University.
Colin C. Tait, Professor of Law, University of Connecticut.

PROCEDURE—FEDERAL RULES OF CIVIL PROCEDURE, 1988 Edition

PRODUCTS LIABILITY (1980)

Marshall S. Shapo, Professor of Law, Northwestern University.

PRODUCTS LIABILITY AND SAFETY, Second Edition, (1989)

W. Page Keeton, Professor of Law, University of Texas.
David G. Owen, Professor of Law, University of South Carolina.
John E. Montgomery, Professor of Law, University of South Carolina.
Michael D. Green, Professor of Law, University of Iowa

PROFESSIONAL RESPONSIBILITY, Fourth Edition (1987), with 1989 Selected National Standards Supplement

Thomas D. Morgan, Dean of the Law School, Emory University.
Ronald D. Rotunda, Professor of Law, University of Illinois.

PROPERTY, Fifth Edition (1984)

John E. Cribbet, Professor of Law, University of Illinois.
Corwin W. Johnson, Professor of Law, University of Texas.

PROPERTY—PERSONAL (1953)

S. Kenneth Skolfield, late Professor of Law Emeritus, Boston University.

PROPERTY—PERSONAL, Third Edition (1954)

Everett Fraser, late Dean of the Law School Emeritus, University of Minnesota.
Third Edition by Charles W. Taintor, late Professor of Law, University of Pittsburgh.

PROPERTY—INTRODUCTION, TO REAL PROPERTY, Third Edition (1954)

Everett Fraser, late Dean of the Law School Emeritus, University of Minnesota.

PROPERTY—REAL AND PERSONAL, Combined Edition (1954)

Everett Fraser, late Dean of the Law School Emeritus, University of Minnesota.
Third Edition of Personal Property by Charles W. Taintor, late Professor of Law, University of Pittsburgh.

PROPERTY—FUNDAMENTALS OF MODERN REAL PROPERTY, Second Edition (1982), with 1985 Supplement

Edward H. Rabin, Professor of Law, University of California, Davis.

PROPERTY—PROBLEMS IN REAL PROPERTY (Pamphlet) (1969)

Edward H. Rabin, Professor of Law, University of California, Davis.

UNIVERSITY CASEBOOK SERIES—Continued

PROPERTY, REAL (1984), with 1988 Supplement

Paul Goldstein, Professor of Law, Stanford University.

PROSECUTION AND ADJUDICATION, Third Edition (1986), with 1988 Case Supplement

Reprint of Chapters 11–26 of Miller, Dawson, Dix and Parnas's CRIMINAL JUSTICE ADMINISTRATION, Third Edition.

PSYCHIATRY AND LAW, see Mental Health, see also Hinckley, Trial of

PUBLIC REGULATION OF DANGEROUS PRODUCTS (paperback) (1980)

Marshall S. Shapo, Professor of Law, Northwestern University.

PUBLIC UTILITY LAW, see Free Enterprise, also Regulated Industries

REAL ESTATE PLANNING, Third Edition (1989), with Problem and Statutory Supplement

Norton L. Steuben, Professor of Law, University of Colorado.

REAL ESTATE TRANSACTIONS, Revised Second Edition (1988), with Statute, Form and Problem Supplement (1988)

Paul Goldstein, Professor of Law, Stanford University.

RECEIVERSHIP AND CORPORATE REORGANIZATION, see Creditors' Rights

REGULATED INDUSTRIES, Second Edition, (1976)

William K. Jones, Professor of Law, Columbia University.

REMEDIES, Second Edition (1987)

Edward D. Re, Chief Judge, U. S. Court of International Trade.

REMEDIES, (1989)

Elaine W. Shoben, Professor of Law, University of Illinois.
Wm. Murray Tabb, Professor of Law, Baylor University.

RESTITUTION, Second Edition (1966)

John W. Wade, Professor of Law, Vanderbilt University.

SALES, Second Edition (1986)

Marion W. Benfield, Jr., Professor of Law, University of Illinois.
William D. Hawkland, Chancellor, Louisiana State Law Center.

SALES AND SALES FINANCING, Fifth Edition (1984)

John Honnold, Professor of Law, University of Pennsylvania.

SALES LAW AND THE CONTRACTING PROCESS (1982)

Reprint of Chapters 1–10 of Schwartz and Scott's Commercial Transactions.

SECURED TRANSACTIONS IN PERSONAL PROPERTY, Second Edition (1987) (Reprinted from COMMERCIAL LAW, Second Edition (1987))

Robert L. Jordan, Professor of Law, University of California, Los Angeles.
William D. Warren, Professor of Law, University of California, Los Angeles.

SECURITIES REGULATION, Sixth Edition (1987), with 1988 Selected Statutes, Rules and Forms Supplement and 1988 Cases and Releases Supplement

Richard W. Jennings, Professor of Law, University of California, Berkeley.
Harold Marsh, Jr., Member of California Bar.

SECURITIES REGULATION, Second Edition (1988), with Statute, Rule and Form Supplement (1988)

Larry D. Soderquist, Professor of Law, Vanderbilt University.

SECURITY INTERESTS IN PERSONAL PROPERTY, Second Edition (1987)

Douglas G. Baird, Professor of Law, University of Chicago.
Thomas H. Jackson, Professor of Law, Harvard University.

SECURITY INTERESTS IN PERSONAL PROPERTY (1985) (Reprinted from Sales and Sales Financing, Fifth Edition)

John Honnold, Professor of Law, University of Pennsylvania.

SENTENCING AND THE CORRECTIONAL PROCESS, Second Edition (1976)

Frank W. Miller, Professor of Law, Washington University.
Robert O. Dawson, Professor of Law, University of Texas.
George E. Dix, Professor of Law, University of Texas.
Raymond I. Parnas, Professor of Law, University of California, Davis.

SOCIAL RESPONSIBILITIES OF LAWYERS, Case Studies (1988)

Philip B. Heymann, Professor of Law, Harvard University.
Lance Liebman, Professor of Law, Harvard University.

SOCIAL SCIENCE IN LAW, Cases and Materials (1985)

John Monahan, Professor of Law, University of Virginia.
Laurens Walker, Professor of Law, University of Virginia.

TAX, POLICY ANALYSIS OF THE FEDERAL INCOME (1976)

William A. Klein, Professor of Law, University of California, Los Angeles.

TAXATION, FEDERAL INCOME (1989)

Stephen B. Cohen, Professor of Law, Georgetown University

TAXATION, FEDERAL INCOME, Second Edition (1988)

Michael J. Graetz, Professor of Law, Yale University.

TAXATION, FEDERAL INCOME, Sixth Edition (1987)

James J. Freeland, Professor of Law, University of Florida.
Stephen A. Lind, Professor of Law, University of Florida and University of California, Hastings.
Richard B. Stephens, late Professor of Law Emeritus, University of Florida.

TAXATION, FEDERAL INCOME, Successor Edition (1986), with 1988 Legislative Supplement

Stanley S. Surrey, late Professor of Law, Harvard University.
Paul R. McDaniel, Professor of Law, Boston College.
Hugh J. Ault, Professor of Law, Boston College.
Stanley A. Koppelman, Professor of Law, Boston University.

TAXATION, FEDERAL INCOME, VOLUME II, Taxation of Partnerships and Corporations, Second Edition (1980), with 1988 Legislative Supplement

Stanley S. Surrey, late Professor of Law, Harvard University.
William C. Warren, Professor of Law Emeritus, Columbia University.
Paul R. McDaniel, Professor of Law, Boston College.
Hugh J. Ault, Professor of Law, Boston College.

UNIVERSITY CASEBOOK SERIES—Continued

TAXATION, FEDERAL WEALTH TRANSFER, Successor Edition (1987)

Stanley S. Surrey, late Professor of Law, Harvard University.
Paul R. McDaniel, Professor of Law, Boston College.
Harry L. Gutman, Professor of Law, University of Pennsylvania.

TAXATION, FUNDAMENTALS OF CORPORATE, Second Edition (1987)

Stephen A. Lind, Professor of Law, University of Florida and University of California, Hastings.
Stephen Schwarz, Professor of Law, University of California, Hastings.
Daniel J. Lathrope, Professor of Law, University of California, Hastings.
Joshua Rosenberg, Professor of Law, University of San Francisco.

TAXATION, FUNDAMENTALS OF PARTNERSHIP, Second Edition (1988)

Stephen A. Lind, Professor of Law, University of Florida and University of California, Hastings.
Stephen Schwarz, Professor of Law, University of California, Hastings.
Daniel J. Lathrope, Professor of Law, University of California, Hastings.
Joshua Rosenberg, Professor of Law, University of San Francisco.

TAXATION, PROBLEMS IN THE FEDERAL INCOME TAXATION OF PARTNER-SHIPS AND CORPORATIONS, Second Edition (1986)

Norton L. Steuben, Professor of Law, University of Colorado.
William J. Turnier, Professor of Law, University of North Carolina.

TAXATION, PROBLEMS IN THE FUNDAMENTALS OF FEDERAL INCOME, Second Edition (1985)

Norton L. Steuben, Professor of Law, University of Colorado.
William J. Turnier, Professor of Law, University of North Carolina.

TAXES AND FINANCE—STATE AND LOCAL (1974)

Oliver Oldman, Professor of Law, Harvard University.
Ferdinand P. Schoettle, Professor of Law, University of Minnesota.

TORT LAW AND ALTERNATIVES, Fourth Edition (1987)

Marc A. Franklin, Professor of Law, Stanford University.
Robert L. Rabin, Professor of Law, Stanford University.

TORTS, Eighth Edition (1988)

William L. Prosser, late Professor of Law, University of California, Hastings.
John W. Wade, Professor of Law, Vanderbilt University.
Victor E. Schwartz, Adjunct Professor of Law, Georgetown University.

TORTS, Third Edition (1976)

Harry Shulman, late Dean of the Law School, Yale University.
Fleming James, Jr., Professor of Law Emeritus, Yale University.
Oscar S. Gray, Professor of Law, University of Maryland.

TRADE REGULATION, Second Edition (1983), with 1987 Supplement

Milton Handler, Professor of Law Emeritus, Columbia University.
Harlan M. Blake, Professor of Law, Columbia University.
Robert Pitofsky, Professor of Law, Georgetown University.
Harvey J. Goldschmid, Professor of Law, Columbia University.

TRADE REGULATION, see Antitrust

TRANSNATIONAL BUSINESS PROBLEMS (1986)

Detlev F. Vagts, Professor of Law, Harvard University.

UNIVERSITY CASEBOOK SERIES—Continued

TRANSNATIONAL LEGAL PROBLEMS, Third Edition (1986) with Documentary Supplement

Henry J. Steiner, Professor of Law, Harvard University.
Detlev F. Vagts, Professor of Law, Harvard University.

TRIAL, see also Evidence, Making the Record, Lawyering Process and Preparing and Presenting the Case

TRUSTS, Fifth Edition (1978)

George G. Bogert, late Professor of Law Emeritus, University of Chicago.
Dallin H. Oaks, President, Brigham Young University.

TRUSTS AND SUCCESSION (Palmer's), Fourth Edition (1983)

Richard V. Wellman, Professor of Law, University of Georgia.
Lawrence W. Waggoner, Professor of Law, University of Michigan.
Olin L. Browder, Jr., Professor of Law, University of Michigan.

UNFAIR COMPETITION, see Competitive Process and Business Torts

UNITED NATIONS LAW, Second Edition (1967), with Documentary Supplement (1968)

Louis B. Sohn, Professor of Law, Harvard University.

WATER RESOURCE MANAGEMENT, Third Edition (1988)

The late Charles J. Meyers, formerly Dean, Stanford University Law School.
A. Dan Tarlock, Professor of Law, II Chicago-Kent College of Law.
James N. Corbridge, Jr., Chancellor, University of Colorado at Boulder, and
    Professor of Law, University of Colorado School of Law.
David H. Getches, Professor of Law, University of Colorado School of Law.

WILLS AND ADMINISTRATION, Fifth Edition (1961)

Philip Mechem, late Professor of Law, University of Pennsylvania.
Thomas E. Atkinson, late Professor of Law, New York University.

WORLD LAW, see United Nations Law

WRITING AND ANALYSIS IN THE LAW (1989)

Helene S. Shapo, Professor of Law, Northwestern University
Marilyn R. Walter, Professor of Law, Brooklyn Law School
Elizabeth Fajans, Writing Specialist, Brooklyn Law School

University Casebook Series

EDITORIAL BOARD

DAVID L. SHAPIRO
DIRECTING EDITOR
Professor of Law, Harvard University

EDWARD L. BARRETT, Jr.
Professor of Law, University of California, Davis

ROBERT C. CLARK
Professor of Law, Harvard University

OWEN M. FISS
Professor of Law, Yale Law School

JEFFERSON B. FORDHAM
Professor of Law, University of Utah

GERALD GUNTHER
Professor of Law, Stanford University

THOMAS H. JACKSON
Dean of the School of Law, University of Virginia

HARRY W. JONES
Professor of Law, Columbia University

HERMA HILL KAY
Professor of Law, University of California, Berkeley

PAGE KEETON
Professor of Law, University of Texas

ROBERT L. RABIN
Professor of Law, Stanford University

CAROL M. ROSE
Professor of Law, Northwestern University

SAMUEL D. THURMAN
Professor of Law, Hastings College of the Law

REAL ESTATE PLANNING

Cases, Materials, Problems,
Questions and Commentary

on the

Planning of Real Estate Transactions

THIRD EDITION

By

NORTON L. STEUBEN
Professor of Law
University of Colorado
School of Law

Westbury, New York
THE FOUNDATION PRESS, INC.
1989

COPYRIGHT © 1974, 1980 THE FOUNDATION PRESS, INC.
COPYRIGHT © 1989 By THE FOUNDATION PRESS, INC.

                    615 Merrick Ave.
                    Westbury, N.Y. 11590

All rights reserved
Printed in the United States of America

Library of Congress Cataloging-in-Publication Data

Steuben, Norton L.
    Real estate planning: cases, materials, problems, questions, and
commentary on the planning of real estate transactions / by Norton
L. Steuben.—3rd ed.
        p.   cm. — (University casebook series)
    Includes index.
    ISBN 0–88277–713–0
    1. Vendors and purchasers—United States—Cases. 2. Real estate
business—Law and legislation—United States—Cases. 3. Real estate
development—Law and legislation—United States—Cases. 4. Real
estate development—Finance—Law and legislation—United States—
Cases.   I. Title.   II. Series.
KF665.A4S7 1989
346.7304'37—dc19
[347.306437]   89–1601
                                                                  CIP

To Judith, Sara and Marc.

*

PREFACE

One of the purposes of this book is to familiarize the student with the art of the planner—to develop the student's skill in using legal concepts to accomplish objectives in a transactional setting. The use of concepts to achieve desired results is considered in many of the courses in the law school curriculum. It, however, is given, at most, equal time with the development of the student's understanding of the concepts and the analytic tools employed in the subject area. The primary focus of these materials is the development of the student's ability to use concepts to achieve desired results.

It is assumed that by the time a student is enrolled in a planning course the student has received some exposure to many of the areas of the law considered in the course. This is not to say that in order to master these materials and successfully complete a planning course a student must have been exposed to all of the areas considered or that any course is necessarily a prerequisite to a planning course and a student's use of this book. The book is designed to provide the student with a basic understanding of most of the areas of the law considered, with liberal citation to various materials for outside reading. For this reason, among others, excerpts from articles and treatises and expositive treatment of some areas have taken, in part, the place of the more traditional case and question technique.

It, however, would be less than candid to say that no prior exposure is necessary. In my years of teaching a real estate planning course I have found that the development of the student's ability to use concepts and the coverage of the materials is affected by the amount of prior exposure to the various areas considered in the course.

The art of the planner is not solely the use of concepts to achieve objectives. It includes the ability to anticipate problems which may arise in the future and to presently devise methods of solving or avoiding the problems. Many courses in the law school curriculum attempt to involve the student in anticipation of problems and planning for their solution or avoidance but, at best, as a secondary matter. My experience has been that a planning question, as a class hypothetical or an examination question in a course in substantive area, frequently provides a frustrating experience for the student and a less than satisfying result for the professor. This book attempts to assist in the development of the student's skill in problem anticipation, solution and avoidance by frequently asking, in a variety of ways, how a particular transaction might be handled to solve or avoid the problem which is being considered at that point in the materials. In addition, the book demonstrates the ripple effect of a decision made with respect to one aspect of a transaction by following the consideration of that aspect with a discussion of the effects the decision which was made might have on other aspects of the transaction.

Lastly, the materials seek to develop the student's appreciation of the fact that, in a planning context, he is creating, to a greater or lesser extent, the facts which in the future may lead a colleague or, heaven forbid, a court to reach the result which he and his clients presently contemplate.

When a planning question is asked in a course in a substantive area the answer is arrived at in terms of the course content, the best income tax, property, corporate, partnership, securities, etc. result. The best income tax result, however, may promote the worst transactional result because of the impact the steps taken to produce the income tax result have on the corporate, property or security aspects of the transaction. From the standpoint of the planner, the best result is that which maximizes the achievement of the objectives of the parties to the transaction. The book attempts to assist the student in developing the skill of cutting across legal categories to arrive at the best result in a transactional sense. For this reason, the book adopts a transactional approach. It deals with the acquisition of real estate in Division I, the disposition in Division II, financing in Division III and development and operation in Division IV. In each area the attempt is made to integrate the discussion of legal categories so that, for example, the student is made aware of both the property attributes and the income tax consequences of an option. The use of a transactional approach means that the same concept, or at least attributes thereof, may be relevant to the subject matter contained in more than one division. An attempt is made to maintain each division as an integrated whole. The problem of the overlap of concepts among the divisions is handled in two ways. First, frequent cross references are made within and among divisions. Second, concepts are developed to a point which enables the student to use the concept in the context of the transaction being considered. The further development of the same concept takes place when further development is needed for use in a different transactional setting. For example, subordination is considered in a somewhat summary manner in Division I when dealing with the acquisition of real estate and is developed more fully in Division III when dealing with financing.

These materials attempt to give the student a realistic appreciation of an area of practice. Hopefully, as a result of their use, the student will realize that the practitioner dealing with a real estate problem needs more than an understanding of property and mortgages, just as the practitioner dealing with a business problem needs more than a familiarity with corporations. One of the results of this and other objectives of the book is to provide the student with some, and I use the word "some" advisedly, exposure to the variety of substantive legal concepts and analytic tools involved in the typical real estate transaction thus possibly easing some of the demand on student time in the second and third years of law school.

The detailed problems presented in the supplement to the book are designed to be used in conjunction with the consideration of each division. Problem #1 deals with acquisition, Problem #2 with disposition and so on. The problems are composites of situations I and others faced in practice with the names changed to protect the innocent and facts added to highlight certain facets and satisfy, for lack of a better phrase, the intellectual curiosity of the author. I have found that they serve to further the objectives of the book and that the students have not obtained the "solutions" from former students. Actually, there are no "official" solutions to problems of this kind. The problems are really exercises in informed judgment.

The material contained in each division of the book goes beyond that necessary to analyze the problem associated with that division. For example, even though a corporation is involved in Problem #2, Division II considers the disposition of assets by a partnership as well as by a corporation. The book has been designed to permit the teacher to play his own tune, whatever that may be, on the instrument. In addition, because of the limitations of time and space and a belief that a student in an advanced course should do some of his own research rather than just reading excerpts, the book contains many questions, short problems and references to a variety of other sources.

Division IV departs somewhat from the pure transactional approach of the first three divisions. This was necessitated by the nature of Division IV. There are a myriad of problems which can arise in the operation of real estate and I have attempted to choose from among them the ones which are most typically encountered.

The book is designed to be used in a three-hour course on a semester basis or a two-hour course in each of two quarters on a quarter basis. Only selected footnotes from reprinted material and cases have been reproduced and, in many instances, the footnotes have been omitted entirely. Reproduced footnotes have been renumbered and the numbering has included my footnotes to reprinted material. My footnotes to, and insertions within, reprinted material have been placed in brackets. I have changed, in most places, references to the 1939 and 1954 Internal Revenue Code, the Model Business Corporation Act, and state enactments of the Uniform Partnership Act, the Uniform Limited Partnership Act and the Revised Uniform Limited Partnership Act appearing in the material and cases reprinted to the corresponding sections of the Internal Revenue Code of 1986, the Revised Model Business Corporation Act, the Uniform Partnership Act, the Uniform Limited Partnership Act and the Revised Uniform Limited Partnership Act.

Many people have played an important part in the development and preparation of these materials. The training and exposure provided me by my associates and partners in Hodgson, Russ, Andrews, Woods and

Goodyear of Buffalo, New York and the experience gained as counsel to Ireland, Stapleton, Pryor & Pascoe, P.C. of Denver, Colorado contributed substantially. Both the encouragement and criticism of my colleagues on the faculty of the University of Colorado School of Law helped immeasurably. The assistance and comments provided by my research assistants, Margaret Brown, Paul Gaide, Rienne Hartman, Virginia Schaeffer and Robynne Thaxton have been valuable. The "feed-back" from the professors and students who have used the book, hopefully, has made this edition a better pedagogical tool. The contributions of Marjorie Brunner of the secretarial staff at the University of Colorado School of Law were much more than simply those of a secretary. Marge made sure that the little things that make a book a good book got done. For what is of value in the pages that follow the above share a great deal of the credit; for its shortcomings, I am responsible.

NORTON L. STEUBEN

Boulder, Colorado
January, 1989

ACKNOWLEDGMENTS

It is with appreciation that acknowledgment is made to the publishers and authors who gave permission for the reproduction of excerpts from the following materials:

American Bankruptcy Law Journal

Cohen, Shareholder Advances: Capital or Loans?

American Law Institute—American Bar Association

Revised Model Business Corporation Act.

Revised Uniform Limited Partnership Act.

Uniform Partnership Act.

Uniform Limited Partnership Act.

Banking Law Journal

Haggerty, Procedures, Forms and Safeguards in Construction Lending With a Permanent Takeout.

Bankers Magazine

Spellman, A Banker's Tour Through the Second Mortgage Market.

Brooklyn Law Review (Fred B. Rothman & Company)

Colbourn, A Guide to Problems in Shopping Center Leases.

California Law Review (Fred B. Rothman & Company)

Comment, Uniform Vendor and Purchaser Risk Act: Effect on California Law.

Comment, Subordination of Purchase-Money Security.

Hetland, The California Land Contract.

Justin Sweet and Lesly Sweet, Architectural Cost Predictions: A Legal and Institutional Analysis.

J. Sweet, Owner-Architect-Contractor: Another Eternal Triangle.

University of California at Los Angeles Law Review

Asimow, The Interest Deduction.

Callaghan and Company

McQuillan, The Law of Municipal Corporations.

Case Western Reserve Law Review

Abrams, Imposing Liability for "Control" Under Section 7 of the Uniform Limited Partnership Act.

ACKNOWLEDGMENTS

Benfield, Money, Mortgages, and Migraine—The Usury Headache.

Chicago Bar Record

Committee on Real Property Law, Drafting of Real Estate Sales Contracts.

University of Cincinnati Law Review

Editorial Note, Judicial Attitude Toward Executive Compensation.

Note, Section 351 of the Internal Revenue Code and "Mid-Stream" Incorporations.

University of Colorado Law Review

Comment, Securities Regulation: Corporate Spin-Offs as a Device for Public Distribution Without Registration.

Comment, Colorado Real Estate Broker Listing Agreements.

Fiflis, Land Transfer Improvement: The Basic Facts and Two Hypotheses for Reform.

Colorado Lawyer

Smith, The Investment Interest Limitation Under the Tax Reform Act of 1986.

Columbia Law Review

Kreidmann, Dividends—Changing Patterns.

Note, Interplay of Rights of Stockholders Dissenting From Sale of Corporate Assets.

Note, The Duty of a Public Utility to Render Adequate Service: Its Scope and Enforcement.

Rohan, The Model Condominium Code—A Blueprint for Modernizing Condominium Legislation.

De Paul Law Review

Kratovil, Mortgages—Problems in Possession, Rents and Mortgagee Liability.

Wolfe and DeJong, The S Corporation as an Alternative Form of Business Organization After ERTA, TEFRA and the Subchapter S Revision Act of 1982.

University of Florida Law Review

Anderson, The Mortgagee Looks at the Commercial Lease.

Hillman, Indissoluble Partnerships.

Foundation Press, Inc.

Cary, Cases and Materials on Partnership Planning.

ACKNOWLEDGMENTS

Fordham Law Review

Kessler, Share Repurchases Under Modern Corporation Laws.

Harvard Law Review Association

Note, Lessor's Covenants Restricting Competition: Drafting Problems.

Note, Zoning Variances.

Siegel, When Corporations Divide: A Statutory and Financial Analysis.

Hastings Law Journal

Note, Contract and Conditional Zoning: A Tool for Zoning Flexibility.

University of Illinois Law Forum

Baum, Lessor's Covenants Restricting Competition.

Bernard & Perlstadt, Sale and Leaseback Transactions.

Davis, Tax Consequences of Leasing Transactions.

Faletti, Financing the Shopping Center.

Kranzsdorf, Problems of the Developer.

Indiana Law Journal (Fred B. Rothman & Company)

Note, Allocating Tenant Tort Liability Through the Fire Insurance Policy.

Insurance Counsel Journal

Kent, The Architect's Duty: Owner-Contractor Disputes Involving Allegations of Architect's Fault.

International Council of Shopping Centers Report

Gunning, On Submitting Mortgage Applications.

Investment Bankers Association of America

A Primer on State Securities Regulation.

Journal of the Bar Association of the District of Columbia

Stambler & Stein, The Real Estate Broker—Schizophrenia or Conflict of Interests.

Journal of Corporate Taxation

Snyder and Gonick, Affiliated Corporate Groups for Real Estate Investments: The Syndication Vehicle of the Future?

ACKNOWLEDGMENTS

Journal of Real Estate Taxation

Sexton, Cutting a Path Through Section 751—Parts I, II and III.

Tucker, Real Estate Depreciation: A Fresh Examination of the Basic Rules.

Van Dorn, Planning Tax-Free Like-Kind Exchanges of Real Estate.

Journal of Taxation

Faber, Planning Opportunities for Avoiding Collapsible Corporation Treatment.

Rabinowitz, Realty Syndication: An Income Tax Primer for Investor and Promoter.

Seago, The Treatment of Start-Up Costs Under Section 195.

Tucker, An Analysis of Real Estate Investment Strategies Under the New Tax Law.

Journal of Taxation of Investments

August and Silow, S Corporation vs. Partnership for Real Estate Ventures.

University of Kentucky Law Journal

Note, Application of the Cost and Value Theories in Measuring Contractor's Liability.

Los Angeles Bar Bulletin

Leon, Subordination: The Handy Test of Fairness.

Wayte, Drafting a Lease Which is Mortgageable.

Marquette Law Review

Aiken, "Subject to Financing" Clauses in Interim Contracts for Sale of Realty.

Mercer Law Review

Hall, Use of Limited Partnership to Invest in Depreciable Realty.

Miami Law Review

Stanley, The Real Estate Investment Trust: Legal and Economic Aspects.

National Real Estate Investor

Blumberg, Short-Term Funds Through Interim Financing.

New York University Institute on Federal Taxation

Dean, Redemptions: Liquidating and Non-Liquidating Kinds of Distributions.

ACKNOWLEDGMENTS

Kaster, Co-ops and Condominiums—The Sponsor's Viewpoint.

Mandell, Tax Aspects of Sales and Leasebacks as Practical Devices for Transfer and Operation of Real Property.

North Carolina Law Review

Christopher, Options to Purchase Real Property in North Carolina.

Ohio State Law Journal

Dunbar, Drafting the Liquidated Damage Clause—When and How.

Oklahoma Bar Association Journal

Simes, The Improvement of Conveyancing: Recent Developments.

University of Oregon Law Review

Platt, Valid Spot Zoning: Creative Tool for Flexibility of Land Use.

Practical Lawyer

Anderson, Liquidated Damage Problems in Construction Contracts.

Berger, The Condominium-Cooperative Comparison.

Clarke, Problem Claims under Business Interruption Policies.

Garfinkel, The Negotiation of Construction and Permanent Loan Commitments—Parts 1 and 2.

Kroll, The Why and How of Real Estate Syndications Regulation Aspects.

Practical Real Estate Lawyer

Leidner, An Overview of Mechanics' Liens and Future Advance Mortgages.

Practical Tax Lawyer

Megaard, Structuring Business Sales and Acquisitions.

Practicing Law Institute (Real Estate Closings Workshop)

Pedowitz, The Lawyer and the Title Company.

Real Estate Review

Gunning, The Wrap-Around Mortgage . . . Friend or U.F.O.?

Williford, The Unique Characteristics of Partnerships.

Real Property, Probate and Trust Journal (Copyrights held by The American Bar Association)

Gunning & Roegge, Contemporary Real Estate Financing Techniques: A Dialogue on Vanishing Simplicity.

Hershman, Usury and "New Look" in Real Estate Financing.

ACKNOWLEDGMENTS

Note, Ground Leases and Their Financing.

Rutgers-Camden Law Journal

Hutchins, What Exactly is a Loan Participation?

Southern California Law Review (William S. Hein & Company, Inc.)

Lefcoe & Schaffer, Construction Lending and the Equitable Lien.

University of Southern California Tax Institute (Matthew Bender & Company)

Voeglin, Use of Options in Tax Planning.

Tax Court Memorandum Decisions (Commerce Clearing House, Inc.)

Aurora Village Shopping Center, Inc. v. Commissioner.

Joseph Sheban v. Commissioner.

Tax Law Review

Cannon, The Apportionment of Real Estate Taxes Between Purchaser and Seller Under Section 164(d) of the 1954 Code.

Fleischer, The Tax Treatment of Expenses Incurred in Investigation for a Business or Capital Investment.

Greenbaum, The Basis of Property Shall Be the Cost of Such Property: How is Cost Defined?

Little, Partnership Distributions Under the Internal Revenue Code of 1954.

Lokken, The Time Value of Money Rules.

Tax Lawyer

Kronovet, Characterization of Real Estate Leases: An Analysis and Proposal.

Kurtz & Kopp, Taxability and Straw Corporations in Real Estate Transactions.

Taxes

Bluhm, Tax Considerations in Financing Real Estate Transactions.

Holzman, The Tax Consequences of a Loss.

Lipton, Fun and Games with Our New PALs.

Lubick, Personal Holding Companies—Yesterday, Today and Tomorrow.

Merritt, How the Proceeds of Use and Occupancy, or Business Interruption Insurance are Taxed.

ACKNOWLEDGMENTS

Temple Law Quarterly

Warm, Some Aspects of the Rights and Liabilities of Mortgagee, Mortgagor and Grantee.

Tulane Law Review

Nathan, The "In Rem" Mortgage.

Tulane Tax Institute (Bobbs-Merrill Company, Inc.)

Borini, What's New Under Section 531?

Vanderbilt Law Review

Bearman, Caveat Emptor in Sales of Realty—Recent Assaults Upon the Rule.

Virginia Law Review (Fred B. Rothman & Company)

Spencer, Powers of Direction and Determination Under Construction Contracts.

Washington University Law Quarterly

Cook, Straw Men in Real Estate Transactions.

Neuhoff, Mortgaging Out and Related Problems.

West Publishing Company

Revised Model Business Corporation Act.

Revised Uniform Limited Partnership Act.

Uniform Partnership Act.

Uniform Limited Partnership Act.

Willamette Law Review

Mylan, Installment Sales Revision Act of 1980.

The Yale Law Journal (Fred B. Rothman & Company)

Comment, Enhancing the Marketability of Land: The Suit of Quiet Title.

Fuller, Partnership Agreements for the Continuation of an Enterprise After the Death of a Partner.

Johnstone, Title Insurance.

Manning, The Shareholder's Appraisal Remedy: An Essay for Frank Coker.

*

SUMMARY OF CONTENTS

DIVISION I. ACQUISITION OF REAL ESTATE

DIVISION II. DISPOSITION OF REAL ESTATE

DIVISION III. FINANCING THE ACQUISITION AND DEVELOPMENT OF REAL ESTATE

TABLE OF CONTENTS

DIVISION III. FINANCING THE ACQUISITION AND DEVELOPMENT OF REAL ESTATE

DIVISION IV. DEVELOPMENT AND OPERATION OF REAL ESTATE

*

TABLE OF CASES

The principal cases are in italic type. The cases cited in the illustrative material or text material are in roman type. Where the United States, the Commissioner or Helvering is the plaintiff, the title of the case is set out herein under the name of defendant. References are to Pages.

TABLE OF STATUTES

a. INTERNAL REVENUE CODE SECTIONS

TABLE OF STATUTES

b. REVISED MODEL BUSINESS CORPORATION ACT SECTIONS

c. UNIFORM PARTNERSHIP ACT SECTIONS

d. UNIFORM LIMITED PARTNERSHIP ACT SECTIONS

e. REVISED UNIFORM LIMITED PARTNERSHIP ACT SECTIONS

REAL ESTATE PLANNING

*

Division I

ACQUISITION OF REAL ESTATE

---

1. THE ACQUIRING ENTITY

---

a. GENERAL OBSERVATIONS

One of the initial problems faced in considering the acquisition and development of real estate is determining what type of entity to use for the acquisition and development. This subdivision is devoted to a consideration of the factors bearing on the choice of an entity.

SETTING UP THE REAL ESTATE VENTURE: AN OVERVIEW

Gerald J. Robinson
3 The Journal of Real Estate Taxation 28 (1975).
[footnotes omitted]

* * *

Choice of Owning Entity

A real estate entrepreneur unable to finance an acquisition from his own funds instinctively thinks of "bringing in a few partners." But soon after interest is aroused in prospective participants, the question arises as to whether they really wish to be "partners" in the legal sense. If they do, they must decide whether their partnership will be a general partnership or a limited partnership. If they do not, their remaining choice generally is limited to ownership through a corporation or as tenants in common. The ownership vehicle chosen is important, since the form of ownership of real estate has significant legal, practical, and tax implications.

Tabular Comparison of Owning Entities

The table which follows presents a bird's-eye view of the principal similarities and differences in the forms of real estate ownership.

1

Characteristic	Corporation	Corporation Taxed "Like Partnership"	General Partnership	Limited Partnership	Tenancy In Common	Real Estate Investment Trust	Individual
Number of Owners	Unlimited	[In general] not more than [35] individuals	Practically, small group	Unlimited	Practically, small group	Not less than 100	One
Limited Liability	Yes	Yes	No	General Partners— No Limited Partners— Yes	Partial	Partial	No
Ownership Interest Freely Transferable	Yes	Yes, subject to "consent"	No	Partially	Yes	Yes	Yes
"Double" Tax	Yes	No	No	No	No	No	No
"Pass Through" of Tax Losses	No	Yes	Yes	Yes	Yes	No	Yes
Special Tax Problems	Possible penalty taxes	Disqualification	None	"Association" status	None	Disqualification	None

Corporation vs. Partnership

The virtue most often associated with owning real estate through a corporation is that a corporation, unlike a partnership, insulates its owners from personal liability. Secondary virtues are that stock in a corporation, unlike an interest in a partnership, is readily transferable, and that while the death or bankruptcy of a partner terminates a partnership it does not affect the continued existence of a corporation.

The difficulty with attributing these virtues solely to a corporation is that they may either be illusory or have counterparts in a partnership. Limited liability through corporate ownership may be largely illusory if lenders, as they often do, demand personal guaranties of corporate loans by stockholders. On the other hand, the substantial equivalent of limited liability can be obtained for a partnership by exculpatory provisions in mortgages and comprehensive liability insurance. Indeed, a limited partnership with a corporation as its sole general partner can provide essentially the same limited liability as a corporation. Moreover, partnership interests can be made transferable by contract, just as the transfer of stock can be, and often is, restricted by a stockholders' agreement. And a partnership agreement can provide for the continuation of a partnership on the death or bankruptcy of a partner so as to provide the counterpart of continuity enjoyed by stockholders in a corporation.

In short, in most cases a real estate partnership can be molded to provide substantially the same legal and practical benefits as a real estate corporation. And even when it cannot, the parties often may consider the differences to be insignificant. In either event, the choice of the ownership vehicle then will hinge on tax considerations. It is in the tax area that the divergence between the corporate and partnership forms of ownership become most marked.

It is relatively easy to transfer property to a corporation or a partnership without incurring tax, though occasionally * * *, unexpected snares may be encountered. And it is equally difficult to dispose of property owned either by a corporation or partnership without paying tax, though a partnership presents less danger of costly tax blunders. The major tax difference between the two forms of ownership occurs during the period of operation between acquisition and disposition. Here the "double" tax problem of corporations and the "conduit" feature of partnerships take on controlling significance.

Corporation vs. Partnership—Operation

A corporation is a separate taxable entity. [The income of the corporation is taxed to the corporation.] * * *

If its income is distributed as dividends to its stockholders, they must pay a second tax on the amount distributed to them at their individual rates * * *. On the other hand, income from property owned directly by an individual is taxed only once [to the individual]. By virtue of the "conduit" feature of partnerships, partners are placed in essentially the same position as individuals. The partnership itself is not subject to tax, and the individual partners pick up their share of partnership income * * *. They report their share of partnership income on their individual returns regardless of whether it is distributed to them, and the character of the partnership's income as ordinary income, capital gain, etc., carries over to them.

On first impression then, it appears that the "double" tax produced by corporate ownership makes corporations an expensive tax luxury. But this is not necessarily so. One or more of [the following] factors may actually make the corporate form of ownership * * * no more costly as a tax vehicle than individual or partnership ownership.

* * *

[1] Dividend payments are not deductible by a corporation. But a corporation can deduct reasonable salaries and other compensation, even if paid to stockholders. To the extent the corporation's income can be reduced or eliminated by such deductible payments, the "double" tax is avoided. If all of a corporation's profit can be paid to stockholders as salary, the tax consequences of corporate operation are much the same as they would be if the property was owned directly by an individual or through a partnership.

[2] Under certain limited circumstances, a corporation may make a "Subchapter S" election which, in effect, permits the corporation to partially take on the conduit feature of a partnership. If this election can be made, the "double" tax is avoided.

Unfortunately, these factors favoring corporate ownership require considerable qualification. * * *

[R]educing or eliminating the "double" tax by salary payments to stockholders is not always a trouble-free procedure. Compensation payments by a corporation are deductible only to the extent they are "reasonable." The Service carefully scrutinizes salary payments to stockholders and often disallows excessive payments. The amount disallowed is treated as a dividend, nondeductible to the corporation and taxable to the stockholder. The result is that the corporation's income is increased by the amount disallowed and the stockholder pays the same tax on this amount as he would if it were salary. So while the payment of corporate earnings to stockholders as salary may mitigate the "double" tax problem, it is a solution subject to constraints. As a practical matter, if owners need more income from property than can be withdrawn from the corporation as "reasonable compensation," they probably will be saddled with a double tax if they chose the corporate form of ownership.

While determining the desirability of corporate ownership of real estate may require delicate balancing of competing factors if the property is producing taxable income, no such refined judgment is normally required if the property is generating tax losses. At least if the losses are substantial and continuing, corporate ownership is clearly undesirable in most cases. Losses incurred by a corporation may be carried back or forward to offset the corporation's own income in other years, but, except for Subchapter S corporations, such losses do not "pass through" to the stockholders. Consequently, stockholders generally do not receive any benefit on their personal returns from losses generated by property owned by a corporation. Since the deduction for depreciation often causes real estate to show tax losses even though it may be producing a cash return, the absence of this pass through characteristic frequently encourages individual or partnership ownership rather than corporate ownership.

Corporations Taxed "Like Partnerships"

As indicated above, the "double" tax often imposed on corporate income may be a substantial deterrent to corporate ownership of real estate. This deterrent is eliminated if the corporation can operate under a Subchapter S election. The general effect of the election is to absolve the corporation from the payment of corporate tax and to tax its stockholders in much the same manner as if they were partners, while the status of the corporation under state law remains unchanged.

* * *

To qualify for the election the corporation must be a "small business corporation." This is defined as a domestic corporation with the following characteristics: (1) no more than [thirty-five] stockholders; (2) all stockholders must be individuals, [certain trusts] or estates; (3) no stockholder may be a nonresident alien; (4) the corporation[, generally,] must have only one class of stock; and (5) it must not be a member of an "affiliated group." Most real estate corporations could readily meet these requirements. * * *

Even assuming the double tax deterrent to corporate ownership can be eliminated and the pass-through of losses achieved by a Subchapter S election, the question still remains whether a Subchapter S corporation is a desirable vehicle for owning real estate. While the statute is relatively simple in concept, it is relatively complex in application and often may place significant constraints on operations. Consequently, an intelligent decision as to the desirability of Subchapter S corporation ownership requires a reasonably intimate knowledge of the mechanics of the statute.

Limited Partnerships

Limited partnerships are widely used as vehicles for raising equity capital for real estate ventures. Their attraction is that they combine the limited liability feature of an investment in corporate stock with the tax advantages of a partnership, discussed above.

The use of limited partnerships for the ownership of investment real estate often requires relatively sophisticated tax planning. * * *

Joint Ventures and Syndications

When real estate entrepreneurs propose a "joint venture" or "syndication" they usually are using these terms in their generic sense. Generically, the term "joint venture" refers to a combination of the capital and skills of independent parties for the purpose of carrying out a venture which neither could handle alone. "Syndication" usually refers to the raising of equity funds from private investors.

Legally, the term "joint venture" has a specific meaning. It refers to a type of special purpose partnership for a particular undertaking. It usually is carried out under a joint venture contract containing provisions analogous to those found in a general partnership agreement.

For tax purposes, joint ventures normally are treated as partnerships. As a consequence, the joint venture itself is not subject to tax and the joint venturers report their "distributive share" of the joint venture's income and deductions on their own returns. Since a joint venture normally is treated as a partnership for income tax purposes, * * * tax [considerations support] carrying out the venture as a general partnership. Similarly, there usually is no significant business reason for favoring a joint venture over a partnership for the ownership of real estate. Indeed, since a partnership is subject to a more highly developed body of law than a joint venture, it may assure the parties more certainty as to their rights and obligations.

When equity funds are to be raised from private investors, the legal form which the "syndication" should take generally is governed by the factors previously discussed. In most instances the limited partnership will be found to be the best form of organization for syndication.

Tenancy in Common

Under the tenancy in common form of ownership, each cotenant owns an undivided interest in the entire property. In the absence of an agreement among the cotenants, each may deal with his undivided interest as he pleases.

When a [number] of investors acquire property as tenants in common, [they] normally enter [into] a cotenancy agreement to establish management rights, provide for the sharing of profits and losses, and deal with related matters. In content and scope, such agreements often resemble partnership agreements. But the tenancy in common form of ownership is sometimes regarded as more desirable than a general partnership because, unlike a partner, a cotenant generally cannot act or contract on behalf of any or all his cotenants without their authorization. Moreover, one tenant in common generally is not liable for debts contracted by another without his authorization, even though the debt is incurred in connection with the property. Consequently, the tenancy in common generally affords an insulation from liabilities created by co-venturers not found in a general partnership.

If no substantial business activity is contemplated, as where raw land is to be acquired and held for investment, the tenancy in common is an attractive ownership vehicle. But if substantial business activities are to be engaged in, the requirement for unanimous action by multiple owners can be cumbersome. While this problem often can be solved by provisions in a cotenancy agreement, other problems may remain. For example, the death or incompetency of one of the tenants in common may jeopardize the ability to pass title quickly.

From the income tax viewpoint, the threshold question is whether the tenancy in common will be recognized as such or treated as a partnership. If the tenancy in common is recognized as such for tax purposes, each cotenant can compute and report his share of income or loss without reference to the partnership provisions. On the other hand, if the tenancy in common is treated as a partnership, computations are made at the partnership level and each tenant reports his distributive share of "partnership" income or loss. In most cases the distinction is academic, except for the need to file a partnership return and make elections at the "partnership" level. Under the regulations, a tenancy in common is not treated as a partnership merely because the property owned is maintained, kept in repair, and rented. However, tenants in common may be treated as partners if they actively carry on a trade or business. For example, if cotenants owning an apartment building lease space and provide services to occupants either directly or through an agent, they will be treated as partners.

If the tenancy in common is recognized as such, each cotenant reports his proportionate share of gross income from the property and deducts his proportionate share of expenses. If a cotenant pays more than his proportionate share of expenses, he can deduct only his proportionate share. The excess is treated as an advance to his cotenants for which he is entitled to reimbursement.

A cotenant's basis for his interest is determined under the general basis rules. The amount realized on a sale or other disposition of the entire property is allocated among the cotenants in proportion to their interests in legal title, absent proof of beneficial ownership in different proportions.

Individual Ownership

When an individual acquires property without equity contributions by others, his choice as to the form of ownership is limited to individual ownership in his own name or ownership through a corporation of which he is the sole stockholder. This choice is normally controlled by the same factors which control the choice between a partnership and a corporation, discussed above. However, it should be observed that where the property is of relatively small value, the use of a corporation may be undesirable because of administrative burdens. A separate set of books must be maintained for the corporation, and an often-annoying number of state and federal returns and reports must be prepared and filed.

* * *

Public Financing—Real Estate Investment Trusts and Limited Partnerships

* * * A REIT is a special taxpayer classification created by the Internal Revenue Code for real estate activities. Designed to somewhat resemble a mutual fund, it eliminates the "double" taxation associat[ed] with the corporate form of ownership. But being strictly a creation of the Internal Revenue Code, the REIT is a creature whose tax life is completely and continuously dependent on compliance with the Code's requirements for "qualification." And the qualification provisions are replete with myriad definitions, limitations, and exceptions which often place severe restraints on operating flexibility. Basically, the REIT is [a corporation or] an unincorporated trust managed by one or more trustees with 100 or more beneficiaries with transferable shares. It avoids tax on income which it distributes to its beneficiaries if it meets an array of requirements relating to its organization, the type of assets it owns, the type of income it receives, and the percentage of its income it distributes. [A substantial percentage] of its assets must be "real estate assets," cash, and government securities. There are three separate percentage limitations applicable to the sources of its income. These limitations are designed to insure that the trust's income is primarily from passive real estate investment. The trust does not avoid tax unless it distributes [almost all] of its income each year.

As a result of the requirement for 100 or more "shareholders," REITs are not suitable for small syndications. Most REITs are publicly owned and tend to concentrate their investments either in real estate mortgages or equity interests in real estate. Each of these types of REITs has its own special set of tax problems.

The public limited partnership is [similar to] the private limited partnership in both its legal and tax structures. [One of] the differences, of course, is in the number of limited partners, which in the public limited partnership often runs into many hundreds. [Potential income tax differences include statutory treatment of a public limited partnership as a corporation, and greater limitations on the use and availability of losses generated by a public limited partnership.] Unlike the REIT, the public limited partnership[, if not treated as a corporation,] affords its investors the "pass through" of losses, a benefit sorely missed by the owners of REIT shares during periods of adversity. On the other hand, the REIT affords its owners the ability to dispose of their shares easily, a benefit not normally enjoyed by the owners of limited partnership interests. * * *

When participation in a real estate venture is offered to the public, compliance with federal and state securities laws is required. This usually is an elaborate undertaking.

NOTE

1. As the foregoing brief excerpt indicates there are many possible choices of entity for the acquisition and development of real estate. The joint venture form is typically used for a single limited life project. In this context, the joint venture is defined by an agreement between two or more entities or individuals relating to the sharing of income and expenses, etc., with respect to a specific project. In an extended form it may amount to a partnership. See Maller, *Financing Ideas: Real Estate Joint Ventures—Legal and Business Concepts,* 13 Real Est.L.J. 177 (1984).

    a. Joint tenancy is also a possible choice but it is not particularly amenable to large commercial or residential developments. The right of survivorship usually is not appropriate. Even without the survivorship problem, title and conveyancing difficulties militate against its use. Of course, for the sole individual, individual ownership is a possibility. See generally Solomon and Smith, *Detouring The Tax Reform Act of 1976: Tax Shelter Proprietorships,* 32 U.Miami L.Rev. 1 (1977).

    b. See generally Friedman, *Choosing Between Corporate and Partnership Entities for Real Property Depends on Its Use,* 11 Tax'n Law. 366 (1983); Kaplan and Ritter, *Partnerships and S Corporations: Has the Tax Gap Been Bridged?,* 1 J.Ps.Tax'n 3 (1984); Mullaney and Blau, *An Analytic Comparison of Partnerships and S Corps as Vehicles for Leveraged Investments,* 59 J.Tax'n 142 (1983); August and Silow, *S Corporation vs. Partnership for Real Estate Ventures,* 1 J. Tax'n Inv. 91 (1984); Eustice, *Subchapter S Corporations and Partnerships: A Search for the Pass Through Paradigm (Some Preliminary Proposals),* 39 Tax L.Rev. 345 (1984); Bowers, Bonn, Cuff, Smith and Sharp, *Choice of Entity: A Primer,* 1 # 1 Prac. Tax Law.

79 (1986); Liveson, *Partnerships vs. S Corporations: A Comparative Analysis in the Light of Legislative Developments,* 5 J.Ps.Tax'n 142 (1988).

2. Regardless of which entity is chosen there are certain problems basic to the organization and operation of any entity. The participants must decide on the amount and form of each one's contribution, the effect of a failure to make that contribution, the manner of compensation of the promoters and/or managers, the allocation of profits, losses and distributions, the form, manner and limitation of management and control of the entity and if, how and when interests in the entity may be transferred. See generally Leon, *Designing The Real Estate Joint Venture to Work,* 3 # 1 Real Est.Rev. 33 (1973); *Multiple Use Land Development: Real Property and Tax Problems,* 7 Real Prop., Prob. & Tr. J. 585 (1972).

3. The form of the entity under state law may not be determinative for income tax purposes. For example, a tenancy in common, joint tenancy or joint venture may be a partnership for income tax purposes. See Sections 761 and 7701(a)(2); Reg.Sec. 307.7701–(c); Rev.Rul. 75–374, 1975–2 C.B. 261; Note, *The Fine Line Between Partnership and Co–Ownership,* 1975 Utah L. Rev. 495; Weidner, *The Existence of State and Tax Partnerships: A Primer,* 11 Fla.St.U.L. Rev. 1 (1983); Halpern and Joszef, *Partnership Classification Under the Internal Revenue Code,* 17 Tax Adviser 172 (1986). Or, a limited partnership or a trust may be treated as an association taxable as a corporation. See Section 7701(a)(3) and Reg.Secs. 301.7701–1(c), 301.7701–2, 3, 4.

4. As noted in the above excerpt, while the tenancy in common may have some advantages in terms of a "simple" means of acquisition and holding of real estate by more than one person, it is not frequently employed for commercial and residential rental projects because of the problems which may result from the death or incompetency, arbitrariness and right of partition of one of the tenants in common. When available under state law, a land trust is sometimes used to acquire and hold the real estate. The investors are then beneficiaries of the essentially passive trust. If available, and properly used, this approach can result in the benefits of the tenancy in common while eliminating some of its disadvantages. The following case illustrates a use of the land trust which does not avoid the beneficiaries being treated as partners for income tax purposes.

CLYDE W. GROVE

54 T.C. 799 (1970)

[footnotes omitted]

Opinion

SCOTT, Judge. Respondent determined a deficiency in petitioners' income tax for the calendar year 1964 in the amount of $2,153.59.

The only issue for decision is whether an amount received by petitioners as profit from the construction and sale of 18 condominium units pursuant to an agreement entitled, "Joint Venture Agreement," is ordinary income or capital gain. * * *

Clyde W. Grove (hereinafter referred to as petitioner) and two other individuals on June 3, 1963, entered into an agreement with Edward Talaczynski and Edward Holzrichter and their wives entitled,

"Joint Venture Agreement," under which an 18–unit condominium was to be built on certain property in Chicago owned by Talaczynski and Holzrichter and their wives and upon completion the units were to be sold. The parties agreed that the property should be valued at $50,000 and petitioner and the two other individuals who owned no interest in the land were to put up $50,000 in cash. The agreement provided in part as follows:

1.   John Balik will invest the sum of $25,000.00 for which he shall have a ⅙th interest in said venture; Clyde Grove will invest $12,500.00 for which he shall have a 1/12 interest in said venture and Carl Holzrichter shall invest $12,500.00 for which he shall have a 1/12 interest in said venture. Edward Talaczynski and Edward Holzrichter, shall each have a one-third interest in said venture.

2.   The property in questions [*sic*] shall be conveyed by Edward Holzrichter and spouse and Edward Talaczynski and spouse, hereinafter referred to as parties of the first part, to a Trustee, under a land trust, and the beneficial interest under the trust shall be as follows:

Edward Talaczynski and Thelma Talaczynski, jointly ⅓rd.
Edward Holzrichter and Carol Holzrichter, jointly ⅓rd.
John Balik and Josephine Balik, jointly ⅙th.
Clyde Grove and Charity Grove, jointly 1/12th.
Carl Holzrichter and Lelia Holzrichter, jointly 1/12th.

3.   The construction of said project shall be in charge of Edward Talaczynski who shall have the final decesion [*sic*] as to type and nature of construction of the project, except that he shall consult and discuss plans and construction with the other members of this venture. Sales shall be in charged [*sic*] of Edward Holzrichter, who shall negotiate sales and managing for all units. Both parties herein shall perform their duties at no additional compensation, other than their share in the profits of this venture.

* * *

7.   Upon the completion of the project, and after payment of all expenses and a return to each individual of his initial investment, then the profits shall be divided by the parties in accordance with their prorated shares, previously indicated, herein.

8.   This shall not be deemed a partnership nor are the parties herein to be deemed partners, but rather this is a legal joint venture entered into by the parties for this sole venture to be known as "Windsor Condominiums."

* * *

10.   No party hereunder shall transfer his interest herein without the full consent of all other parties.

In 1964 the condominium, known as Windsor Court Condominium # 1 was completed and the 18 units were sold for $378,951.19. The cost of construction was $270,601.34, leaving a gross profit, of $108,349.85 from which operating expenses of $15,314.36 were paid leaving a net profit of $93,035.49. During 1964 the amount of $20,250 was distributed to petitioner from the venture, leaving a credit balance in his capital account of $2.96. Petitioners on their 1964 Federal income tax return reported a long-term capital gain of $7,750 from "Windsor Court Corp." which they arrived at by showing a "gross sales price" of $20,250 from which they subtracted a "cost" of $12,500, showing a resulting gain of $7,750.

Respondent in his notice of deficiency determined that petitioners' "gain of $7,752.96 from Windsor Courts Condominium # 1 for 1964 is taxable as ordinary income."

Petitioner takes the position that he made an investment of $12,500 in a capital asset because he held either a "beneficial interest" in a real estate investment trust, receipts from which are taxable under section 857, I.R.C.1954, or a capital investment similar to stock in a corporation.

Respondent takes the position that the joint venture in which petitioner invested should be considered for Federal income tax purposes as a partnership under section 761, that the partnership was in the trade or business of building condominiums for sale to customers, thereby deriving ordinary income from the gain from the sales, and that under section 702(b) the income constitutes ordinary income to petitioners.

A mere reading of sections 856 and 857 shows that petitioner's $12,500 investment was not in a "Real Estate Investment Trust." One of the many requirements which was not met is that more than 100 persons hold an interest in the trust. Only five persons held an interest in the Windsor Court Condominium project.

The real question here is whether, as respondent contends, the "Joint Venture Agreement" created a joint venture which is considered a partnership under Federal tax laws or a trust or other association taxable as a corporation. If we conclude that the "joint venture" is to be considered a partnership, then we must decide whether the partnership was in the trade or business of building and selling condominiums so that its income would be ordinary income to the partners under section 702(b).

Section 761(a) defines a partnership for tax purposes as including a syndicate, group, pool, joint venture, or other unincorporated organization through or by means of which any business, financial operation or venture is carried on and which is not a corporation or trust or estate within the meaning of the Internal Revenue Code.

Petitioners argue without citation of any specific provision of the Revenue Code or the regulations, that with their $12,500 they purchased in 1963 a 12½ percent beneficial interest in a trust and received the $20,250 in 1964 in "liquidation" of this interest or as a "liquidating dividend." Section 641 deals with the taxation of estates and trusts. Section 1.641(a)–0 of the Income Tax.Regs. specifically provides that this section has "no application to any organization which is not to be classified for tax purposes as a trust under the classification rules of

Secs. 301.7701–2, 301.7701–3 and 301.7701–4." Section 1.761–1(a), Income Tax.Regs., issued under section 761, I.R.C.1954 defining partnerships, also refers to sections 301.7701–2, 301.7701–3, and 301.7701–4, Proced. & Admin.Regs. A consideration of these sections of the regulations shows that petitioners' $12,500 was not invested in a trust as defined therein.

The characteristics separating a trust from a partnership are centralization of management, continuity of life, free transferability of interests and limited liability. In the instant case the venture involving the parties had no centralization of management for although the construction and sales functions were delegated to two individuals of the group, those individuals had to consult with the remainder of the parties to the agreement. There was no free transferability of interest since each party was prohibited without the consent of the other parties from transferring the interest which he had in the proposed venture. The agreement does not specifically state the extent of the liability of the individuals for losses. There is nothing in the record indicating any agreement that the parties were not to share losses and we conclude that the parties had agreed to share losses in the same ratio as they were to share gains. The function of the venture was to construct and sell the condominiums at a profit. In our view the functions of the venture were those of a partnership and not those of a trust.

Section 702(b) states:

The character of any item of income, gain, loss, deduction, or credit included in a partner's distributive share under paragraphs (1) through (8) of subsection (a) shall be determined as if such item were realized directly from the source from which realized by the partnership, or incurred in the same manner as incurred by the partnership.

Since petitioner in this case intended to and did enter into a joint venture, it is the character of the profits in the hands of the joint venture or partnership that determines whether the income constitutes capital gain or ordinary income to petitioner.

In Barham v. United States, an unreported case (M.D.Ga.1969, 23 AFTR2d 1347), the Court stated that where a joint venture holds real estate for the primary purpose of selling it to customers in the ordinary course of business the character of the income from the property sold is determined from the standpoint of the joint venture rather than from the standpoint of each individual member. The trade or business of the partnership is separate and distinct from the intent or motivation of the partners in forming the partnership. Raymond Bauschard, 31 T.C. 910 (1959), affd. 279 F.2d 115 (C.A. 6, 1960), and Freeland v. Commissioner, 393 F.2d 573 (C.A. 9, 1968), affirming a Memorandum Opinion of this Court.

* * *

In the instant case we find that it was the intent of each of the parties that the property be developed and the condominiums completed by the joint venture for sale to customers in the ordinary course of the trade or business of the joint venture. We, therefore, hold that the joint venture in which petitioner was a participant held the property for sale to customers in the ordinary course of its trade or business and find that petitioners are not entitled to capital gains treatment on the income received from the venture.

Decision will be entered for respondent.

NOTE

1. In some situations, the beneficiaries of an Illinois Land Trust may not be personally liable for the debts of the trust. If this was the situation in the above case, would it cast any doubt on the court's conclusions with respect to limited liability?

    a. Was there a specific finding of fact on this question, one way or the other?

2. The death or withdrawal of the holder of an interest in an Illinois Land Trust does not, in and of itself, terminate the trust or cause its dissolution. In addition, the trustee holds title to the real estate and a conveyance of the real estate requires only his signature. What effect do these facts have on the continuity of life aspect?

    a. The interest of a beneficiary is considered personalty rather than realty and such interest is usually represented by a "certificate of ownership" which is freely transferable. Transferability, however, can be limited by express provision in the agreement and certificate much like the transferability of stock in a closely held corporation. See *Sheridan v. Park National Bank of Chicago,* 97 Ill.App.3d 589, 52 Ill.Dec. 921, 422 N.E.2d 1130 (1981); *In re Preston,* 52 B.R. 296 (Bkrtcy.M.D.Tenn.1985).

    b. Generally the trustee can not dispose of the real estate without authorization by the holders of 51% of the beneficial interests in the trust.

    c. The beneficiaries of the trust, rather than the trustee, have full power and control over the operation and management of the real estate.

    d. See Turner, *Some Legal Aspects of Beneficial Interests Under Illinois Land Trusts,* 39 U.Ill.L.Rev. 216 (1945); Peckron, *Tax Consequences of Land Trusts,* 16 Haw.B.J. 3 (1981); Haswell and Levine, *The Illinois Land Trust: A Fictional Best Seller,* 33 De Paul L.Rev. 277 (1984).

3. Apparently, the individual in charge of construction had the "final decision", and authority over the sales aspects was vested in another person. How "centralized" does centralized management have to be?

4. In *Clyde W. Grove* what was the structure of the entity with which the court was concerned? Were the rights and relations of the participants in the entity exclusively governed by the terms and provisions of the trust agreement? Or, were the participants the beneficiaries of a land trust whose rights and relations *inter se* were governed by a separate agreement among them? If the participants had desired, might they have entered into a partnership agreement and had the partnership hold the sole beneficial interest in the land trust which held the land to be developed? Are there substantive differences, tax or otherwise, among the three ways of structuring the entity as described above?

5. If the court had held that the entity was a "trust," it would have further held that the "trust" should be treated as an association taxable as a

corporation since the holders of the interests in the "trust" were "associates" with "an objective to carry on business for profit." See Reg.Sec. 301.7701–(2)(a) (2). Would this holding have made any difference in the result of the case?

6. In general, the use of the land trust, if available under state law, may avoid some of the problems associated with holding real estate as tenants in common, while permitting the investors the "benefits" of treatment, for income tax purposes, as individuals rather than as partners or shareholders when the real estate, to be held by the trust, is to be acquired and held for investment purposes and the investors will engage in few, if any, activities with respect to the real estate. See generally Schwind, *Land Trusts: A Real Estate Syndication Device*, 101 Tr. & Est. 650 (1962); McKillop, *The Illinois Land Trust in Florida*, 13 U.Fla.L.Rev. 173 (1960); Arntson, *The Virginia Land Trust—An Overlooked Title Holding Device for Investment, Business and Estate Planning Purposes*, 30 Wash. & Lee L.Rev. 73 (1973).

b.   THE PARTNERSHIP FORM

CASES AND MATERIALS ON PARTNERSHIP PLANNING
William L. Cary
Excerpt from 34–78
Foundation Press, Inc. (1970).
[footnotes omitted]

* * *

The considerations governing the decision whether to incorporate or operate in partnership form * * * [i]n their probable order of importance * * * are:

(1) Insulation from liability provided by the corporate form; the liability of a stockholder is said to be limited to his investment whereas all of the property of a general partner is subject to the claims of the firm's creditors, if its assets are insufficient to provide payment in full.

(2) The federal income tax rates applicable to the owners, and to the corporation; and to a limited extent state taxes on incorporated business and individuals.

(3) Continuity of existence, or duration of the firm—which for all practical purposes may be perpetual in the case of a [corporation]; ordinarily death or withdrawal is said to dissolve the partnership, though a partnership agreement may provide that the firm shall be continued by the surviving partners or by them and the estate of the deceased partner.

(4) Centralization of management in one person or selected persons, rather than in all the general partners.

(5) Free transferability of interest; this merely requires the endorsement and delivery of corporate stock; by the sale of a partnership interest the assignee has limited rights and does not become a partner.

(6) Access to capital, through issuing new shares or finding a new partner.

Each of these will be discussed, but *not* in the order of importance.

Let us analyze each of the stated advantages indicated above, raising functionally the major problems which counsel faces in relation to partnerships.

(a) Insulation from Liability—The Element of Risk

(1) Limited liability is not always as significant as one might assume at the outset. In the case of the close corporation shareholders frequently must pledge their own credit in borrowing funds. Nevertheless, it is true that general creditors furnishing trade credit or employees having wage claims are usually not able to reach the assets of the investors but are limited to the amount of the corporation's capital. * * * Furthermore, the "partners" can generally be protected from tort liability if they have incorporated.

There seems to be no way for partners to avoid liability except through the avenue of limited partnership. For this reason insurance is widely used as a protection from the business risks. Every partner is an agent of the partnership for the purposes of its business and the act of every partner binds the firm, with some exceptions. (See § 9 [of the Uniform Partnership Act.]) Furthermore, a partnership is bound by a partner's wrongful act or breach of trust. (See §§ 14 and 15.) * * *

But what if a partner specifically advised an outsider that he personally would not be responsible for any additional orders? This was the case in National Biscuit Company v. Stroud, 249 N.C. 467, 106 S.E.2d 692 (1959). Stroud, one of the two partners of Stroud's Food Center, advised an agent of the plaintiff that he would not be responsible for any more bread sold to his partnership. The Supreme Court, with one dissent, concluded that the co-partner's purchase of additional bread bound the firm and also Stroud, saying:

> "Freeman as a general partner with Stroud, with no restrictions on his authority to act within the scope of the partnership business so far as the agreed statement of facts shows, had under the Uniform Partnership Act 'equal rights in the management and conduct of the partnership business.' Under G.S. § 59–48(h) Stroud, his co-partner, could not restrict the power and authority of Freeman to buy bread for the partnership as a going concern, for such a purchase was an 'ordinary matter connected with the partnership business,' for the purpose of its business and within its scope, because in the very nature of things Stroud was not, and could not be, a majority of the partners. * * *"

What if Freeman's authority, or the scope of [his] activities, had been limited in the partnership agreement? Under what circumstances would Stroud and the firm be insulated from liability? (See § 9.)

* * *

(2) If * * * the members decide to organize a limited partnership in order to insulate some of them from liability, §§ 7 and 10 of the Uniform Limited Partnership Act are relevant. Strict compliance with filing provisions is required in order to achieve protection. See Vidrick-

sen v. Grover, 363 F.2d 372 (9th Cir.1966). * * * [W]hat if one of those furnishing capital in our partnership wanted to be a limited partner and yet sought maximum controls without subjecting himself to liability? What if he is dictatorial because of his personality and because his money is carrying the venture? How far could you advise him to go? [See §§ 7 and 10 of the Uniform Limited Partnership Act and §§ 302 and 303 of the Revised Uniform Limited Partnership Act.]

* * *

(3) There are special problems of liability arising (i) from the relations of the partners, *inter se,* and (ii) from the relation of former and incoming partners to creditors. Under (i) the first question is how losses are to be shared in the absence of agreement. This is answered in § 18(a) i.e., generally, in accordance with the sharing of profits.

* * *

With respect to (ii), the problems arise when one partner is added or another has dropped out of the firm. In the latter case the partnership is dissolved. Because of the continuing nature of many partnerships an *Incoming* partner is liable for the obligations of the firm but only out of partnership property. (§ 17.) (See further in this connection § 41.) The *Outgoing* partner also has problems of liability. He is still liable for debts incurred by the old partnership while he was a member. As to those incurred after his retirement, liability may depend on whether the outsider is on notice of his retirement. (See § 35.) If these results do not conform with the parties' wishes, they may be altered by contractual arrangements.

* * *

Another problem concerns the possibility that a creditor may not be able to reach *all* the partners. May he recover a judgment against less than all the partners, since in many jurisdictions their *contractual* (as distinguished from tort) liability is *joint* but not several? There have been enactments in some states outside the partnership act which provide that a judgment based on service against one partner is collectible against him and also the partnership itself, but not from the personal estates of the partners who were not served.

Finally, what about the personal creditors of the partners themselves? § 40(h) provides that "partnership creditors shall have priority on partnership property and separate creditors on individual property."

(b) Centralized Management—The Control Problem

Centralized management obviously is related to insulation from liability, since the act of every partner binds the partnership—with reservations to be discussed below. For this reason it is said that even small businesses may wish to incorporate in order to vest responsibility in one or several persons. This of course may not always be true where each of the founders want to have an interest in the operations as well as the ownership of the partnership.

The traditional starting point is that all partners (other than limited ones) have an equal voice in the management and conduct of the firm. (§ 18(e).) Thus each one of them has the sweeping power to bind his co-partners.

* * *

"[E]ven if the partners agree among themselves that the powers of management shall be exclusively in a selected few, this agreement will be ineffective as against an outsider who had no notice of it." * * * They are jointly and *severally* liable in the event of tort or breach of trust (see §§ 13, 14, and 15(a)). There are a few exceptions where a single partner has no authority to act: for example, assigning of partnership property to creditors; disposing of the goodwill; making it impossible to carry on the ordinary business of a partnership; confessing a judgment; submitting a claim or liability to arbitration (all listed in § 9(3)).

Generally the vote of the majority of partners controls (§ 18(h)). There may be a contractual provision providing for control by majority in interest (whether of earnings or capital contribution of the partners). However, there must be unanimous approval for action contrary to the terms of the partnership agreement. Gifford, in Changing a Partnership into a Corporation, 16 Vand.L.Rev. 351, at 359 (1963), has made the statement as follows:

> * * * Although partnership government is sometimes conceived as involving a dispersion of control and a structure in which all of the partners participate in making many decisions and corporate government is often conceived as centering exclusive control over operations of the business in the board of directors, neither form must conform to such conceptions in all circumstances. Thus the government of a partnership can be concentrated in the hands of managing partners or of an executive committee, voting power can be distributed among the partners in the forms of weighted votes and non-voting partners, and separate classes of partners, resembling the separate classes of stock sometimes found in corporations, can be established. The government of a corporation, on the other hand, need not be centralized but may be diffused by the use of high quorum requirements on the board of directors or for stockholders' meetings and of extra-majority voting requirements, and agreements among stockholders can often obligate such stockholders to vote for specified action. * * *

* * *

The statements Gifford makes * * *, however, relate to operation of the partnership *inter se*. The limitations on a partner's activity are not likely to be effective as against outside parties without notice. [See generally Hillman, *Power Shared and Power Denied: A Look at Participatory Rights in the Management of General Partnerships,* 1984 U.Ill.L.Rev. 865.]

Fiduciary Responsibility

In connection with the operation of a partnership and its management, there is a further question of duty or responsibility as fiduciaries. Thus partners must make full disclosure to their colleagues, maintain records, refrain from competing with the partnership and exercise due care in their business operations. Indeed, it is the standard, applied to joint ventures and co-partners by Justice Cardozo, that has been widely quoted and carried over into the corporate field.

> Joint adventurers, like co-partners, owe to one another, while the enterprise continues, the duty of the finest loyalty. Many forms of conduct permissible in a workaday world for those acting at arm's length, are forbidden to those bound by fiduciary ties. A trustee is held to something stricter than the morals of the market place. Not honesty alone, but the punctilio of an honor the most sensitive, is then the standard of behavior. As to this there has developed a tradition that is unbending and inveterate. Uncompromising rigidity has been the attitude of courts of equity when petitioned to undermine the rule of undivided loyalty by the "disintegrating erosion" of particular exceptions. * * * Only thus has the level of conduct for fiduciaries been kept at a level higher than that trodden by the crowd. It will not consciously be lowered by any judgment of this court. Cardozo, J. in Meinhard v. Salmon, 249 N.Y. 458, 464, 164 N.E. 545, 546–547, 62 A.L.R. 1 (1928).

* * *

(c) Access to Capital—Ownership

Obviously, a partnership may not offer shares to the general public but can only expand its capital by finding more general or limited partners. On the other hand, it is a gross over-simplification to say that the same firm, by incorporating, can raise capital from outsiders with much greater facility. Just because a business has a certificate of incorporation, it does not follow that the public will buy its shares. Furthermore, if the principal participants have to sign the firm's note, there is little difference between the partnership and corporate form in raising money through debt. At the level of a small business the importance of access to outside capital may often be overemphasized.

As already indicated, the partners with the capital in the classical situation typically make the principal contribution to the firm. Does it remain their specific property? * * * If it does not, then what provisions have to be made in order to ensure that the man with experience does not ask for dissolution on the next day and demand a substantial share of the partnership assets? * * * Thus, the plan of contribution also raises the question of rights in the event of dissolution—in the absence of agreement. * * * [I]t is said in § 24 that the property rights of a partner are:

(1) His rights in specific partnership property (he is co-owner with his partners holding as a tenant in partnership (§ 25); this is a very special type of interest, with ownership primarily in the partnership)

(2) His interest in the partnership (i.e., his share of the profits and surplus; this is personal property), and

(3) His right to participate in the management.

The division of profits is of course the basis upon which investors might be willing to participate. Some of them may or may not insist on some form of control. The percentage of profits can be worked out by contract and need not be in the same proportion as losses. Just as profits can be divided in accordance with the wishes of the *partners,* so may individual participants in a *corporation* insist on special provisions and rights for the capital which they contribute; these may be spelled out through different classes of shares containing provisions tailored to the wishes of the parties. Of course, a partner may not compete for payment with outside creditors who have priority even as to loans (§ 40). Limited partners who have made advances to the firm, however, may share, with creditors upon a pro rata basis (ULPA § 13) [and Rev. ULPA §§ 107 and 804. Under the Rev. ULPA a general partner also may lend money to the partnership and share with creditors on a pro rata basis.]

* * *

(d) Transferability of Interest

This attribute of a corporation, permitting the free transfer of shares, is often claimed to be one of the special advantages of incorporating a small business. It makes it possible for an investor to retire and get back his contribution (or some part of it) without having to undermine the company or force its dissolution. He simply lets someone else take over and stand in his shoes. In a small business, however, this may be more theoretical than real. For example, what if a small stockholder in a closely held company wants to convert his investment into cash? Who is there to buy it? Perhaps the public as such would not be interested; possibly his "partners" in the corporation may be buyers, but he is at their mercy unless an agreement obligating them or the corporation to purchase his shares was made in advance.

In this connection the assumption should not be made that in all close corporations the parties want free transferability. * * * [T]here is often a group of persons joining together to form a company who want to remain close and who do not wish to admit any stranger. For this reason, in the corporate field much effort is devoted to designing, drafting and developing buy-sell restrictions that effectively keep the shares from being freely transferable. Thus it is only in the event that the parties are looking toward subsequent access to capital or disposition of their shares to the public that transferability is an important reason for incorporation.

Despite the foregoing reservations about the virtues of transferability even in a closely held company, it is quite clear that a partnership involves many more obstacles. In the first place, transfer without consent of a partner's interest offers the assignee limited rights. It does not of itself dissolve the partnership (§ 27; but see § 29). In the absence of an agreement it does not entitle the assignee to interfere in the management or administration of the affairs of the continuing partnership, to require any information or account of partnership transactions, or to inspect its books. (§ 27.) It merely gives him the right to receive the profits to which the assignor would otherwise be entitled. Furthermore, no person may become a member of a partnership without the consent of all the other partners (§ 18(g)). Thus in general, it is safe to conclude that where counsel and his client have not looked ahead and drafted a reasonable solution for the parties in the event of his retirement or death, a partnership arrangement under the terms of the Uniform Partnership Act would not offer a satisfactory solution.

(e) Continuity

Continuity of life is tied directly with transferability of interest, discussed above. The corporation continues to exist in contemplation of law despite the death or withdrawal or transfer of interest on the part of any of its officers, directors, shareholders or employees. The continuity of corporate life provides stability but not always enduring vitality to the enterprise. Some businesses in corporate form may be entirely dependent upon the efforts of a single person and may practically lose all meaning and value upon his death or retirement. The loss of a key owner can cripple or destroy a business—whether partnership or corporation. This distinction between legal and economic continuity is of great practical significance.

On the other hand, it has been truly said that aside from the hazard of unlimited liability, the greatest danger in the operation of a partnership is the possibility of chaos in the business on the death or retirement of a partner. The two provisions that create the most problems in this area are found in § 31. (See also § 32.) It provides that dissolution is caused by the express will of any partner "when no definite term or particular undertaking is specified," or by the death or bankruptcy of any partner. In this connection a distinction should be drawn between dissolution and winding up the business. § 29 defines dissolution as a change in the relation of the partners caused by any partner ceasing to be associated in carrying on the business. Dissolution in turn may entail the termination of the active conduct of the business and the liquidation of the business assets and liabilities. Thus there are several different words used in connection with the dissolution process. For example, the partnership is not *terminated* on dissolution but continues until the *winding up* of partnership affairs is completed. *Liquidating* the partnership appears to be much the same as winding it up.

Death or Withdrawal of a Partner

One of the major areas for counsel is to provide a satisfactory solution in the event of the death or withdrawal of a partner. Professor A.R. Bromberg, in Partnership Dissolution—Causes, Consequences, and Cures, 43 Tex.L.R. 631, at 668 (1965), concludes that proper contractual provisions can usually ensure that dissolution will not force termination of the business. As he puts it, "With (advance agreement), the partnership may be given virtually as much continuity as a corporation." [It is possible for the remaining partners of a general partnership to continue the "business" of the partnership after its dissolution as a result of the withdrawal, death or bankruptcy of a partner. The withdrawal, death or bankruptcy of a limited partner will not cause the dissolution of a limited partnership. In addition, the dissolution of a limited partnership can be avoided, in most cases, on the withdrawal, death or bankruptcy of a general partner if these occurrences are properly planned for and provided for in the partnership agreement. See §§ 9(1)(g) and 20 of the ULPA and §§ 402 and 801 of the Rev. ULPA.] If in the case of three partners, one with experience, the others with capital, the agreement provided that the business should continue and payments should be made to the partner or his estate or his beneficiaries, what are the problems that must be considered in the event of retirement or death?

May the executor consent to the continuance of the business without authority in the will? May he exercise any control? To what extent will the estate be liable? Does this depend on the form of the payments? May the agreement specify whether the payments are income or capital gain to the retiring partner, the estate or the beneficiaries, and a deduction to the partnership? Are the partner, estate, or the beneficiaries liable to creditors subsequent to retirement or death? To the extent of the partnership interest only? Are the executor, or the beneficiaries, personally liable for debts when the surviving partners continue the business? May the estate be a limited partner? Should the agreement be specific as to the rights of the surviving partners and of the decedent's estate? Should a value be fixed; if so, how? Should a buy-sell agreement be prepared? If so, should the * * * [surviving partners] be bound to purchase or be given a first option? Is the value more difficult to fix than the value of shares of a closely held [corporation]? * * *

* * * [A] variety of contractual arrangements can be made in connection with the death or retirement of a participant, whether he be a shareholder or partner. In the case of the close corporation, there is of course freedom of transferability of shares as compared with the inflexibility inherent in conveying a partnership interest. Yet it may be of little practical value if there is no buyer. Therefore, in order to protect the decedent's widow or the retiring participant himself, the agreement can provide that the corporation (or its shareholders) or the partnership shall be under a duty to buy his interest. Alternatively,

the restriction or agreement may take the form of an option running to the surviving shareholders or partners, or to the corporation (or in some cases to both shareholders and company).

Purchase agreements in turn raise the question of fixing a value (the price formula). Whether the business is incorporated or not, the valuation problems of a small enterprise are much the same. * * *

NOTE

1. Are there substantial and unavoidable differences between the small partnership and the close corporation? If so, what are they?

    a. If you number the tax treatment as one of the prominent differences which must be taken into account in the choice of entity, is this a case of the tail wagging the dog?

2. A substantial difference lies in the "continuity of life" concept. To some extent, however, the "continuity of life" inherent in the corporate form can be obtained in both the general partnership and limited partnership forms by the use of a continuation agreement. Since the useful life of real estate improvements is typically thirty to fifty years and at least some of the participants will want to treat their partnership interests as continuing investments, the partnership agreement should provide, in certain instances, for the "continuation of the partnership" after the withdrawal, death or bankruptcy of a general partner.

3. The withdrawal, death or bankruptcy of a limited partner will not cause the dissolution of a limited partnership and one can provide for continuity of a limited partnership pursuant to Sections 9(1)(g) and 20 of the U.L.P.A. and Sections 402 and 801 of the Revised U.L.P.A. in the event of the withdrawal, death or bankruptcy of a general partner. On the other hand, providing for the continuity of a general partnership in the event of the withdrawal, death or bankruptcy of a partner is somewhat problematic. No problem arises if the withdrawing partner or the successor or representative of the deceased or bankrupt partner accepts the terms of the continuation agreement (i.e., the method of, and amount provided for, the repurchase of the partnership interest). If, however, the withdrawing partner or the successor or representative of the deceased or bankrupt partner refuses to honor the continuation agreement, the chances are that the withdrawing partner or the successor or representative of the deceased or bankrupt partner can cause the dissolution of the partnership.

INDISSOLUBLE PARTNERSHIPS
Robert W. Hillman
37 University of Florida Law Review 691, 721 to 728 (1985).
[footnotes omitted]

* * *

WHAT CAN PARTNERS DO? THE PLANNING PERSPECTIVE

Although the UPA renders all partnerships freely dissolvable, stability is sometimes an important objective of business partners. Given the apparent conflict between the free dissolution posture of the

UPA and the desire of some partners to stabilize their relationships, the question becomes: What can partners do, short of incorporation, to eliminate or minimize the risk of premature dissolution?

Some measure of stability may be provided through effective business planning. Unlike corporations, partnerships are stabilized, to the degree possible, largely through contract rather than statute. This requires individuals forming a partnership to recognize the fragile nature of their form of business association. Facilitating sensible planning is the high degree of cooperation that normally exists at the inception of a partnership. Too frequently, however, partnerships are established informally and without any measurable degree of planning; in such cases, the opportunity to address major issues is more theoretical than real.

Probably the most important method of achieving some degree of stability is the establishment of a fixed partnership term. This will not render a partnership indissolvable, but, in many cases, it will increase the "costs" assigned to a partner desiring a premature, wrongful dissolution.[1] However, when those "costs" become acceptable to a dissatisfied partner, that partner effectively enjoys the option, and often the incentive, to dissolve the partnership in violation of the partnership agreement. Accordingly, more than a simple agreement concerning the term of the partnership may be necessary to provide meaningful disincentives to dissolution.

Sometimes, partnership agreements establish a fixed term and include a provision rendering ineffective attempts to dissolve before the expiration of the term. While this is clear evidence of the intent of the partners, it nevertheless is meaningless in light of the distinction drawn under partnership law between the power and the right to dissolve. It is both ironic and unfortunate that the same statute which subordinates most of its norms to contrary agreements among the partners also precludes any attempt by partners to waive by agreement their powers of dissolution.

Even a clearer expression of intent may prove ineffective. Suppose, for example, a partnership agreement establishes a term, provides that no partner has the power to dissolve prior to the expiration of that term, and adds that if any partner attempts to dissolve or otherwise withdraw, the partnership agreement may be specifically enforced against that partner. Two obstacles face the non-breaching partner seeking to enforce such an agreement. First, the UPA does not permit a waiver of the power of dissolution. Second, even though contracting parties freely agree to a provision giving the non-breaching party the

[1. The costs of a wrongful dissolution, as provided in Section 38(2) of the U.P.A., include (a) damages for breach of the agreement, (b) the value of the breaching partner's partnership interest will not include such partner's share of the value of the goodwill of the partnership and (c) if the business of the partnership is continued, the payment to the breaching partner of the value of such partner's partnership interest may be deferred and paid in installments if secured by a bond approved by the court.]

right to secure specific enforcement of the agreement, most courts do not view such provisions as binding. This type of an agreement, if properly drafted, may render specific performance of the non-partnership contract more likely, but it cannot insure the availability of the remedy in the event of a breach.

Enforceability problems should not deter partners otherwise desiring the remedy of specific performance from including appropriate provisions in their agreement. A specific enforcement clause can only increase the possibility that equitable relief will be available, particularly if a court * * * treats partnership dissolution as a problem of remedies rather than a question of partnership law. Further, a well drafted clause tailored to the peculiar circumstances of the partnership and including a statement indicating why specific performance is appropriate will focus the partners' attention at an early stage on their expectations for the duration of the venture. Used in this fashion, the agreement serves both to spell out the rights and responsibilities of the parties, and to educate the partners by providing them with the occasion to evaluate carefully their mutual expectations.

Partners may also attempt by agreement to alter the consequences of dissolution. For example, a partnership agreement may provide for a continuation of the business following a dissolution and the deferred payout, often on an installment basis, of the dissolving partner's interest. Such an understanding, which is generally referred to as a continuation agreement, strikes a balance between stability and liquidity interests. Continuation agreements, however, are most appropriately utilized in anticipation of either the death of a partner or the dissolution of a partnership which is terminable at will. Used more broadly as a response to the premature and wrongful dissolution of a fixed term partnership, such agreements normally leave the continuing partner in a position inferior to that resulting from imposition of the wrongful dissolution sanctions of the UPA.

More meaningful stability provisions are found in the covenants not to compete often included in partnership agreements. These devices are particularly common in partnerships among professionals, although they also appear in other contexts. Typically, such covenants provide that, in the event of a premature dissolution, the dissolving partner is precluded from engaging in activities, in a defined area, which will compete with those of the partnership. The clauses, which are used in both fixed term and terminable at will partnerships, often restrict activities following the withdrawal from a partnership for any reason. Breach of a covenant not to compete may give the protected partner the option of either seeking damages or pursuing injunctive relief. Such clauses, which occasionally are accompanied by liquidated damages provisions, may present, if enforceable, significant disincentives to dissolution. For this reason, noncompetition covenants, together with agreements establishing a term, constitute the principal contractual means of providing some stability to partnerships.

* * *

NOTE

1. While Professor Hillman recognizes the current difficulty, if not the impossibility, of guaranteeing the continuity of a general partnership, he suggests that permitting partners to agree on the continuity of a partnership for a term of years would be a worthwhile and meaningful reform of the U.P.A.

"What effect, then, is to be given an agreement concerning life of a partnership? The issue of duration is easily understood by those negotiating a partnership agreement. Admittedly, partners may have difficulty identifying the types of future disputes that may lead one or more partners to become dissatisfied. Most partners, however, understand that serious differences may arise and are in a position to evaluate their relative interests in stability, risk-aversion, and liquidity. The duration question is a fundamental matter on which the law should facilitate bargaining.

"Because an agreement concerning duration is normally reached as a method of stabilizing a partnership, it should be given just that effect. If permitted to bargain effectively on this issue, partners most concerned with the adverse consequences of an early dissolution could pay the price for, and enjoy the benefits of, stability. Partnership law can facilitate this objective by denying a partner the unilateral power to dissolve a partnership by express will prior to the expiration of the term previously accepted by that partner. An agreement concerning duration, in short, should effectively deny a partner the power to unilaterally cause a premature dissolution through an expression of will. If cause exists, the dissatisfied partner may seek a decree of dissolution." Hillman, *Indissoluble Partnerships,* 37 U.Fla.L.Rev. 691, at 731 (1985).

2. How should the partnership agreement provide for the "continuity of life" of the partnership in the event of the withdrawal, death or bankruptcy of a partner?

> a. Should the partners agree that the partnership will continue for a period regardless of such occurrences (such occurrences will not cause the dissolution or winding-up of the partnership); making provision for the installment "payout" of the interest of the withdrawing, etc. partner, or
>
> b. Should they agree that the remaining partners will or may agree in a defined manner to reform the partnership after dissolution brought about by such occurrences; making provision for the installment "payout" of the interest of the withdrawing, etc. partner?

3. Does the manner in which continuity is provided for make any substantive difference? Cf. *Fairway Development Co. v. Title Ins. Co. of Minn.,* 621 F.Supp. 120 (N.D. Ohio 1985).

> a. Will an agreement to continue, rather than reform, a general partnership be effective in light of Sections 29–33 of the U.P.A.? Might one have a better chance of continuing the life of a limited partnership? See Sections 2(1)(a) XIII, 9(1)(g) and 20 of the U.L.P.A., and Sections 401 and 801(4) of the Rev.U.L.P.A. See generally Bromberg, Crane and Bromberg on Partnership, 1968, page 418 and Bromberg, *Partnership Dissolution—Causes, Consequences, and Cures,* 43 Tex.L.Rev. 631 (1965). Cf. *Estate of Martha B. Watt,* 51 CCH Tax Ct.Mem. 60 (1985), aff'd, 823 F.2d 483 (11th Cir.1987).
>
> b. Can the partners agree to reform in certain situations and continue in others?

3. Cf. Hillman, *The Dissatisfied Participant in the Solvent Business Venture: A Consideration of the Relative Permanence of Partnerships and Close Corporations,* 67 Minn.L.Rev. 1 (1982); Hillman, *Misconduct as a Basis for Excluding or Expelling a Partner: Effecting Commercial Divorce and Securing Custody of the Business,* 78 Nw.U.L.Rev. 527 (1983).

4. Consider in the context of choosing between continuing and reforming the partnership the following:

a. The ability of a withdrawing partner to ignore an installment payout provision in the continuation agreement and demand immediate payment of the value of the partner's partnership interest.

b. The rights of pre-existing creditors against present partnership assets. Does Section 41 of the U.P.A. provide any help in analyzing this situation? The rights of current creditors against the assets of the partnership prior to the occurrence giving rise to the continuation or reformation. For example, the ability of a current partnership creditor to recover partnership assets paid to a withdrawing partner or the estate of a deceased partner prior to the creditor extending credit to the partnership.

c. The rights of a judgment creditor of a withdrawing partner against the assets of the partnership after the withdrawal, where the withdrawing partner is paid out by a share of profits over a period of years.

d. The rights of a trustee in bankruptcy of a bankrupt partner against the assets of the partnership. See Kaster and Cymbler, *The Impact of a General Partner's Bankruptcy Upon the Remaining Partners,* 21 Real Prop., Prob. & Tr.J. 539 (1986). Cf. Leta and Jones, *Selected Bankruptcy Considerations in Drafting Real Estate Documents,* 1984 Utah L.Rev. 227.

e. The rights of an executor of a deceased partner with regard to the assets of the partnership if, pursuant to the continuation agreement, the deceased partner's interest is to be paid out by a share of profits over a period of years.

f. The possibility that the Internal Revenue Service might treat the assets of the partnership as being distributed to the partners on the occurrence of the withdrawal, death or bankruptcy of a partner, see Section 708 of the Internal Revenue Code of 1986,—resulting in the partners recognizing gain to the extent that the money distributed exceeds the partners' bases in their partnership interests. See Sections 731 and 751; *Austin v. United States,* 461 F.2d 733 (10th Cir.1972), and Reg.Sec. 1.708–1(b)(1)(iv). Cf. Parker and Lee, *Constructive Cash Distributions in a Partnership: How and When They Occur,* 41 J.Tax'n 88 (1974). The Internal Revenue Service has held that contributions by new partners to a partnership in exchange for more than 50 per cent of the capital and profits interests in the partnership do not result in a termination of the partnership under Section 708(b)(1). See Rev.Rul. 75–423, 1975–2 C.B. 260. See generally Birkeland and Postlewaite, *The Uncertain Tax Ramifications of a Terminating Disposition of a Partnership Interest—The Constructive Termination of a Partnership,* 30 Tax Law. 335 (1977); Swisher, *Tax Pitfalls of Unexpected Partnership Terminations,* 66 A.B.A.J. 1010 (1980); Cleveland and Berryman, *Tax Treatment Upon Termination of a Partnership May Be Uncertain, But Planning Opportunities Exist,* 2 J.Ps.Tax'n 35 (1985); Birkeland and Postlewaite, *Constructive Termination of a Partnership—A Fresh Look,* 39 Tax Law. 701 (1986). Cf. Seago and Horvitz, *Some Subtle Effects of the Partnership Constructive Distribution Rules,* 58 Taxes 97 (1980).

g. The effect of the agreement on the question of whether the partnership has the corporate aspect of "continuity of life" in determining whether the entity is taxed as a corporation or a partnership. See Reg.Sec. 301.7701–2(b)(1). Cf. *Richard H. Foster,* 80 T.C. 34 (1983), aff'd in part, vacated in part, 756 F.2d 1430 (9th Cir.1985).

5. For more on the rights of creditors see Comment, *Partnership Creditors v. Creditors of the Individual Partners,* 24 Baylor L.Rev. 557 (1972); Hanley, *Partnership Bankruptcy Under the New Act,* 31 Hastings L.J. 149 (1979); Axelrod, *The Charging Order—Rights of a Partner's Creditor,* 36 Ark.L.Rev. 81 (1982). See also Mandan Security Bank v. Heinsohn, 320 N.W.2d 494 (N.D.1982), which held partners individually liable on their guaranties of a partnership debt, when the foreclosure of a mortgage on partnership real property resulted in an amount less than the principal amount of the debt, even though neither the partnership nor the partners would have been liable for any deficiency under the state antideficiency statute. For a discussion of the rights of a withdrawing partner when the business is continued after dissolution see *Schoeller v. Schoeller,* 497 S.W.2d 860 (Mo.App., 1973), and Note, *Settlement of Former Partner's Account When the Business is Continued After a Dissolution,* 39 Mo.L.Rev. 632 (1974).

6. At this point, certain of the fundamental income tax concepts relative to the organization and operation of a partnership should be considered.

THE UNIQUE TAX CHARACTERISTICS OF PARTNERSHIPS

Jerry S. Williford
13 # 2 Real Estate Review 28 (1983).

* * *

The Partnership as Both Entity and Aggregate

Partnerships are not subject to taxation but serve as conduits through which income, gains, losses, and credits pass through to each partner based on that partner's pro rata share of these items. Each partner is treated as if he owned an undivided interest in the specific property. The concept of a partnership as the aggregate of each partner's ownership of undivided interests in the property is referred to as the "aggregate" theory.

On the other hand, the partnership is sometimes also treated as a separate entity. In accordance with the "entity" theory, the partnership has its own taxable year, and the partnership may engage in a transaction with a partner who acts in other than his capacity as a partner. Furthermore [a number of elections for income tax purposes are made by] the partnership [rather than by the partners] * * *.

The Partnership Agreement

Usually there is a written partnership or joint venture agreement, although the income tax regulations do not require a partnership to have a written agreement. In fact, the regulations specifically state that the agreement can be oral. However, the partners of a partnership based on an oral agreement have the burden of proving the terms of the particular partnership. The terms of a limited partnership or one containing special partner allocations must be written.

The income tax regulations concerning amendments to a partnership agreement are liberal. The regulations allow a partnership agreement applying to a particular year to be amended up to the time for filing that year's tax return, not including any extensions (i.e., up to the fifteenth day of the fourth month following the partnership's year-end).

* * *

Treatment of Property Contributions to Partnerships

The Internal Revenue Code provides that no gain (or loss) may result to either the partnership or the partner when the partner contributes property, including cash, to the partnership in exchange for a partnership interest. Also, the holding period of the partnership interest includes the holding period of the property contributed.

The partnership's basis in the contributed property is the contributing partner's basis in the property. Thus, there is a "carryover" basis. The partner's basis in the partnership interest he receives is generally the same as the basis he had in the property contributed.

* * *

Distributions From Partnerships

Generally, distributions of property, including cash, by partnerships to partners do not result in either gain or loss to either the partnership or partner. However, if the cash distribution exceeds the partner's basis in the partnership, gain results. Furthermore, the relief of liabilities is treated as a "deemed" distribution of cash. Thus, gain can occur in connection with a reduction of liabilities even though no actual cash is distributed. Consequently, a reduction of a partner's interest in the partnership may result in an unexpected gain. Since a partner generally shares in liabilities based upon his loss-sharing percentage of ownership, a reduction in his loss-sharing percentage results in a reduction in his share of liabilities. This reduction is treated as a deemed distribution of cash. To the extent the deemed distribution exceeds his basis, the partner has a gain.

When a partner receives a distribution of property other than cash, his basis in the property is generally the same as the basis of the property to the partnership (plus any gain recognized) unless the distribution is in liquidation of his interest. This reflects the carryover basis rule of contributions. If the distribution is in liquidation of the partner's interest, the basis of the property is generally the same as the basis of his partnership interest. This is known as the substituted basis concept.

As to the holding period, there are two rules. If the property received is not in liquidation of the partner's interest, the holding period includes the time the partnership held the property. However, if the distribution is in liquidation of the partner's interest in the partnership, the holding period becomes the holding period of his partnership interest.

Special Allocations

One of the major advantages of using the partnership form of ownership is the ability of the partnership to allocate income, gains, losses, and credits specially among the partners. Special allocations are not available to corporations or even to Subchapter S corporations.

For any special allocation to be recognized by the Internal Revenue Service, it must have "substantial economic effect." The * * * term * * * generally means that the special allocation must affect the amount of cash the partners will ultimately receive. Generally, for the special allocation to stand up, * * * liquidating partnership distribution must be based * * * on the capital account balances of the partners. Thus, he who receives a greater share of losses gets a lesser share of the cash. Looking at it another way, he who deducts the losses must actually bear the losses or pay for the losses by receiving less cash. There is no such thing as sharing in the losses "for tax purposes only."

* * *

Recently, tax advisers have recommended the use of a "gain chargeback" provision in the partnership agreement in order to prevent the trading of losses for cash. This provision specifies that the partner who received the special allocation of losses receive a greater than proportionate share of the gain on sale of the partnership assets. Thus, that partner's capital account is "charged back" so as to increase his capital account balance as if he had never received a special loss allocation.

* * *

Retroactive Allocations

Often, upon the admission of a partner, the partnership attempts to allocate retroactively to the new partner, losses from the beginning of the year. This practice is generally prohibited by the [Internal Revenue Code]. Generally, a partner may be allocated losses (or income) only from the date he is admitted into the partnership or purchases his interest. * * *

Special Basis Election

The partnership provisions of the Internal Revenue Code provide a unique election for certain partners to receive a basis adjustment to their share of the assets of the partnership. This election, generally referred to as a Section 754 election, usually occurs in two situations: when someone purchases a partnership interest and when someone acquires the interest of a partner who has died.

The Code allows the partnership to elect to adjust the new partner's share of the partnership assets to his purchase price (or, if the partner has acquired the estate of a deceased partner, to the value for estate tax purposes). This provision appears to be based on the aggregate theory discussed earlier, rather than on the entity theory. The law permits the new partner to increase his basis inside the partnership so as to reflect what he paid for the interest (or the value on which estate taxes were paid). The step-up must be allocated among the assets (e.g., land, building, etc.). To the extent the step-up is allocated to depreciable property, the new partner is able to obtain higher depreciation. * * *

It should be noted that the partnership must elect to make this adjustment. * * * Also, it should be noted that once the partnership makes the election, it is binding on all subsequent transfers. This binding election usually presents no problem, but it could if the value of the partnership assets falls below the partnership's basis in the assets. In that case, the adjustment would result in a step-down rather than a step-up in the basis of the partnership assets.

It should also be noted that whether or not the partnership makes the election, the partner's basis in his partnership interest is the amount that he paid for it. The election merely allows the basis of his partnership interest to be spread among the specific assets inside the partnership.

Dealings Between Partner and Partnership

The Internal Revenue Code allows a partner to deal with the partnership as if he were any outside party. Payments made to a partner for the use of capital (interest) or for services (e.g., a management fee) are called "guaranteed payments." * * *

The section of the Internal Revenue Code dealing with transactions between a partner and the partnership also contains a provision that prohibits the partner from deducting a loss on the sale or exchange of property between the partner and partnership if the partner owns more than 50 percent of the partnership, either directly or indirectly. This same section requires that gains from the sale of certain assets between the partnership and a partner owning more than [5]0 percent of the partnership shall be ordinary income.

Sale and Exchange of Partnership Interests

A partnership interest is generally a capital asset, so that a sale of an interest results in either a capital gain or loss. However, if partnership property includes property that, if sold at a gain, would produce ordinary income (e.g., inventory), all or a portion of any gain on the sale of the partnership interest may be ordinary income. In addition to inventory, other examples of such property are unrealized rent receiv-

ables and depreciation recapture. These assets in the partnership that would produce ordinary income are known as "hot assets."

* * *

Inadvertent Terminations

An often overlooked rule in the partnership tax laws is the provision that causes a partnership to be deemed terminated if there is a sale or exchange of 50 percent or more of the partnership interests within a twelve-month period. If the partnership is deemed terminated, the property is deemed to be distributed to the partners who recontribute it to the new partnership. In some cases, this can result in some added problems for the partners and partnership, and this situation should be avoided if at all possible.

* * *

NOTE

1. Generally, partners recognize no gain or loss on the contribution of property including money to the partnership in exchange for an interest in the partnership. See Section 721. The partners' bases in their partnership interests as a result of the contributions are equal to the amount of money contributed and the adjusted basis of the contributed property to the partners. See Section 722. The partnership's basis in the contributed property is equal to its adjusted basis to the contributing partners. See Section 723. The contribution of property to a partnership in exchange for a partnership interest is not a disposition of that property for the purpose of depreciation recapture under Sections 1245 and 1250. See Sections 1245(b)(3) and 1250(d)(3). Since the partnership's basis in contributed property is equal to the property's adjusted basis in the hands of the contributor, problems may arise when the fair market value of the property is greater or less than its adjusted basis. While economically the contribution of the partner may be measured by the fair market value of the property, the income tax effects stemming from the ownership of the property by the partnership will be governed by its adjusted basis. The Internal Revenue Code requires that the income, gain, loss, and deduction with respect to property contributed to a partnership by a partner shall be shared among the partners so as to take account of the variation between the basis of the property to the partnership and its fair market value at the time of contribution. See Section 704(c). For example, if the basis of the property to the partnership is $10 and the fair market value of the property is $50, the first $40 of taxable gain recognized on the disposition of the property by the partnership must be allocated to the partner who contributed the property. See Jones and Jackson, *How to Handle Property Contributions to a Partnership Under Mandatory Allocations,* 64 J. Tax'n 205 (1986); Comment, *Contributions of Property to a Partnership: A Primer (and Beyond),* 33 U.Fla.L.Rev. 33 (1980); Marich and McKee, *Sections 704(c) and 743(b): The Shortcomings of Existing Regulations and the Problems of Publicly Traded Partnerships,* 41 Tax L.Rev. 627 (1986); Orbach and Raymond, *A Practical and Policy Examination of Secs. 704(b), 704(c) and 743(b),* 19 Tax Adviser 174 (1988). Section 707(a)(2)(B) treats a contribution to a partnership combined with a distribution to the contributor as a sale rather than a contribution if, in substance, the two transactions when viewed together amount to a sale. See Hirschfeld, *When is an Acquisition of a Partnership Interest a Disguised Sale by the Partners?,* 58 J. Tax'n 346 (1983);

Hoskins and Bower, *Partner vs. Nonpartner Distinctions After the Deficit Reduction Act of 1984*, 2 J.Ps. Tax'n 99 (1985); Antonio, *When Will a Transfer to a Partnership be Treated as a Sale Under New Sec. 707?*, 63 J. Tax'n 32 (1985); Burke, *Disguised Sales Between Partners and Partnerships: Section 707 and the Forthcoming Regulations*, 63 Ind.L.J. 489 (1988). The contribution of a partnership interest for a partnership interest in a new partnership may be tax-free to the contributor under Section 721. See Rev.Rul. 84–115, 1984–2 C.B. 118.

      a.   Services are not considered property for the purposes of Section 721. See Reg. Secs. 1.721–1(b)(1) and (2). Therefore, if a partner receives an interest in partnership capital in return for services, the partner will be taxed at ordinary rates on the value of that interest unless the interest is subject to a substantial risk of forfeiture or a restriction which never lapses, as defined under Section 83. If the interest in partnership capital received in return for services is subject to a restriction which never lapses, the recipient partner will be subject to tax on the difference between the value of the interest received, taking into account the restriction which may reduce or eliminate such value, and the purchase price, if any, paid for the interest. See Reg.Secs. 1.721–1(b)(1) and (2) and *Hensel Phelps Construction Company v. Comm'r*, 703 F.2d 485 (10th Cir.1983). But see McGuire, *The Concept of Fair Market Value in the Measurement of Income*, 10 J. Real Est. Tax'n 111 (1983), for some suggested limits on the taxation of a partnership interest received in return for services. See generally Egerton and Jans, *Partnership Interest for Services: The Plight of the Service Partner Revisited*, 1 J.Ps.Tax'n 47 (1984); Comment, *Section 83 Applied to Partnership Transactions: The Road to Certainty in Planning and Controlling the Tax Consequences of Exchanges of Partnership Interests for Services*, 13 Fla.St.U.L.Rev. 325 (1985); Hortenstine and Ford, *Receipt of a Partnership Interest for Services: A Controversy that Will Not Die*, 65 Taxes 880 (1987). An interesting case dealing with an attempt to side-step the receipt of a partnership interest for services is *Stafford v. United States*, 435 F.Supp. 1036 (M.D.Ga.1977), reversed, 611 F.2d 990 (5th Cir. 1980), on remand, 552 F.Supp. 311 (M.D.Ga.1982), reversed, 727 F.2d 1043 (11th Cir.1984). In this case a partnership interest was received in return for a letter of intent to enter into a lease and make a mortgage loan. The letter of intent had been personally obtained by the recipient of the partnership interest. In the initial decision, the district court held that the letter of intent was property for the purposes of Section 721. The Fifth Circuit Court of Appeals reversed and remanded the district court's decision indicating some doubt whether a letter of intent to make a mortgage loan and enter into a lease was property for the purposes of Section 721. In addition, even if it was, the court was not convinced that the letter of intent, and not the taxpayer's services, constituted the sole consideration for the partnership interest he received. On remand the district court concluded that the letter of intent, while valuable, was not enforceable and therefore did not constitute property for the purposes of Section 721. See Witt, *New Decision Raises Additional Hurdle to Partnership Nonrecognition Treatment*, 59 J.Tax'n 36 (1983). The Eleventh Circuit Court of Appeals reversed and remanded the district court's second decision. The Eleventh Circuit held that the letter of intent was property for the purposes of Section 721 and remanded for a determination whether the taxpayer received the interest in the partnership for services, for the letter

of intent, or for both. See George and Fireman, *Stafford Revisited: Government's Litigating Position Rejected by Eleventh Circuit,* 1 J.Ps. Tax'n 244 (1984). If the recipient of the partnership interest had received an interest in the partnership in return for an agreement to secure the lease and mortgage for the partnership, would there be any question with respect to whether he had received a partnership interest for services? Does the *Stafford* case indicate a planning technique which might, in an appropriate situation, be used to avoid some of the problems inherent in the receipt of a partnership interest for services?

It had been generally thought that if the "services" partner received only an interest in profits and no interest in capital that the partner would not be taxed on receipt of the interest, since the income accruing as a result of the interest would be taxed to the partner as it was earned by the partnership. See Reg.Sec. 1.721–1(b); Comment, *Taxation of the Service Partner: A Need For Clarification,* 6 Ga.L.Rev. 781 (1972); Note, *Income Regulation of Future Interests In Partnerships Profits and Losses—Taxation—Federal Income Tax—Diamond v. Commissioner (T.C.1970),* 9 San Diego L.Rev. 373 (1972); Lane, *Sol Diamond: The Tax Court Upsets The Service Partner,* 46 S.Cal.L.Rev. 239 (1973); but see *Sol Diamond,* 56 T.C. 530 (1971), aff'd, 492 F.2d 286 (7th Cir.1974).

b. While the Court of Appeals for the Seventh Circuit in *Diamond v. Commissioner of Internal Revenue,* 492 F.2d 286 (7th Cir.1974), agreed with the Tax Court and the Internal Revenue Service that the receipt of an interest in profits in return for services might be taxable, it quite carefully limited its holding to situations in which the interest in profits had a determinable market value at the time of its creation. The court stated:

"There must be wide variation in the degree to which a profit-share created in favor of a partner who has or will render service has determinable market value at the moment of creation. Surely in many if not the typical situations it will have only speculative value, if any.

"In the present case, taxpayer's services had all been rendered, and the prospect of earnings from the real estate ＊ ＊ ＊ was evidently very good. The profit-share had determinable market value.

"If the present decision be sound, then the question will always arise, whenever a profit-share is created or augmented, whether it has a market value capable of determination. ＊ ＊ ＊ " 492 F.2d at 290.

Mr. Diamond received the interest in profits on February 18, 1962, and sold the interest on March 8, 1962 for $40,000, which the court found to be the market value of the interest. As the court points out, it may be in the typical case that an interest in profits received for services on formation of a partnership will have a speculative value at best and therefore the recipient of the interest in profits will not be taxed upon its receipt. Cf. *Vestal v. United States,* 498 F.2d 487, petition for rehearing denied, 498 F.2d 495 (8th Cir.1974). Cowan, *Receipt of a Partnership Interest for Services,* 32 N.Y.U.Inst.Fed. Tax'n 1501 (1974); Robinson, *The Tax Implications of Exchanging a Partnership Interest for Services: An Analysis,* 51 J.Tax'n 16 (1979); Rosenberg, *Tax Consequences of Exchanging a Partnership Interest for Services,* 13 Tax Adviser 132 (1982); Robinson, *Diamond's Legacy—A New Perspective on the Sol Diamond Decision,* 61 Taxes 259 (1983); Egerton and Jans, *Partnership Interest for Services: The Plight of the Service Partner Revisited,* 1 J.Ps.Tax'n 47 (1984); Lewis, *Receipt of Partnership Interest for Services Not Always Subject to Immediate Tax,* 15 Tax'n Law. 158 (1986). While there were some indications that the Internal Revenue Service would not attempt to tax an interest in profits received for services where the services were to be rendered in the future by a partner, the interest was received early in the life of the partnership and the partnership's income stream was not determinable at the time of the receipt. See *GCM Discloses IRS View of Profits Interest for Services,* 57 J.Tax'n 91 (1982). Recent cases indicate that the Internal Revenue Service is pursuing the issue. See *St. John v. United States,* 53 A.F.T.R.2d 84–718 (D.Ill.1983); *Kenroy, Inc.,* 47 CCH Tax Ct.Mem. 1749 (1984); *George Kobor v. United States,* 62 A.F.T.R.2d 88–5047 (C.D.Cal.1987); Bower and Shapleigh, *St. John: New Standards To Be Applied to Partners' Profits Interest,* 63 Taxes 14 (1985); Comment, *Receipt of a Partnership Profits Interest for Services: St. John v. United States and a Suggested Solution,* 5 Va.Tax Rev. 127 (1985).

2. A partnership must use as its taxable year (in order of priority) the taxable year of the partners owning a majority of partnership profits and capital, the taxable year of its principal partners, or the calendar year. A partnership can use a different taxable year if it can establish a business purpose for its use. In addition, a partnership may elect to use a different taxable year than those described above if the partnership is willing to pay for the privilege and the deferral period of the taxable year elected, the period between the beginning of the elected year and the close of the first taxable year which the partnership would have been required to use had the election not been made, is, in general, not greater than three months. See Sections 444 and 7519; Morris, *Fiscal Years of S Corporations and Partnerships After the Revenue Act of 1987,* 66 Taxes 134 (1988); Newland and Klinger, *The Costs of Electing a Fiscal Year Under New Section 444,* 68 J.Tax'n 206 (1988); Strauss and Bush, *Fiscal–Year Nonconformity,* 19 Tax Adviser 253 (1988); Cohen and Millman, *New Rules for Taxable Years of Partnerships and S Corporations Provide Greater Flexibility,* 5 J.Ps.Tax'n 126 (1988).

3. The Internal Revenue Service can audit a partnership, make changes in partnership "items" and litigate the validity of those changes at the partnership, rather than the partner, level despite the fact that, for income tax purposes, partnerships are conduits—the income tax results of the operation of a partnership are reported by the partners. The partners must treat partnership "items" the same as those items are treated on the partnership information return or notify the Internal Revenue Service of any difference in treatment. Small partnerships of ten or fewer partners each of whom is a natural person (and not a nonresident alien) or an estate are not subject to audit at the partnership level if each partner's share of any partnership "item" is the same as his share of every other "item." Small partnerships, however, can elect to be audited at the partnership level. See Sections 6031, 6046A and 6221 through 6232. See also Caplin and Brown, *Partnership Tax Audits and Litigation After TEFRA,* 61 Taxes 75 (1983); Palmer, *TEFRA Treats Partnerships as Separate Entities Under its New Procedural Rules,* 58 J.Tax'n 34 (1983); Boles, *All Partnerships Subject to More Effective Audits as a Result of Changes Made by TEFRA,* 11 Tax'n Law. 354 (1983); Cohen, *Operating Under the New Partnership Audit Rules,* 41 N.Y.U.Inst.Fed.Tax'n 16–1 (1983); Borison, *Rights and Obligations of Partners Under TEFRA When Their Partnership is Audited,* 1 J.Ps.Tax'n 107 (1984); Ausness, *Partnership Level Proceedings: Policies,*

Procedures and Planning, 72 Ky.L.J. 89 (1983–84); Lewis and Brown, *Partnership Audits and Litigation Under TEFRA,* 42 N.Y.U.Inst.Fed.Tax'n 3–1 (1984).

4. Section 709 requires that the organization and, if any, the syndication expenses of a partnership must be capitalized. Section 709(b) then permits the amortization of organization expenses, as defined in 709(b)(2), over a period of sixty months. This treatment is similar to that provided by Section 248 for the organization expenses of a corporation. Syndication expenses, once capitalized, cannot be amortized and cannot be written off on termination and liquidation of the partnership. If the syndication expenses are paid using proceeds derived from the sale of limited partnership interests, the bases of the limited partners in their partnership interests are not reduced by the amount of the syndication expenses. As a result, on termination and liquidation of the partnership the limited partners may recognize a loss equal to the syndication expenses. See Reg.Sec. 1.704–1(b)(2)(iv)(i)(2) and Rev.Rul. 85–32, 1985–1 C.B. 186. See generally *Martin H. Fishman,* 51 CCH Tax Ct.Mem. 738 (1986); Winston, *Partnership Syndication Costs—The Problem That Will Not Go Away,* 63 Taxes 742 (1985); Comment, *Internal Revenue Code Section 709: To Deduct, Amortize, or Capitalize, That is the Question,* 65 Neb.L.Rev. 385 (1986).

5. The income tax results of the disposition of a partnership interest may vary depending on whether the interest is sold back to the partnership or sold to a third party (which may include the other partners). If the interest of a partner is sold back to the partnership, Section 736 applies. In this context, if the partnership agreement contains no provision for payment with respect to the partner's share of goodwill, the payments allocated to goodwill and unrealized receivables in excess of any basis allocated to the selling partner's interest in those assets are ordinary income to the partner, see Section 736(a) and (b)(2) and, depending on the method of payment, are deductible by the remaining partners or result in a reduction in the remaining partners' distributive shares of partnership income. To the extent the proceeds received from the partnership are allocated to assets other than the above, under Section 736(b)(1) any gain recognized by the selling partner is treated as capital gain except to the extent the proceeds are allocated to substantially appreciated inventory, in which case the excess over allocated basis would be treated as ordinary income. See Section 731(c) and 751(b).

a. In the event that the remaining partners purchase the interest of the selling partner, Section 741 applies. The gain recognized by the selling partner will be treated as capital gain except to the extent the proceeds are allocable to his interest in unrealized receivables and/or substantially appreciated inventory, and gain with respect to these assets will be treated as ordinary income. The remaining partners will acquire a cost basis in the purchased partnership interest under Section 1012. The line between the repurchase of a partnership interest by the partnership and its purchase by the remaining partners is quite thin. The parties should clearly indicate their intent in the documents effectuating the transaction. If the nature of the transaction is left unclear, the Internal Revenue Service and the courts may consider it other than that contemplated by the parties. Cf. *Bernard D. Spector,* 71 T.C. 1017 (1979), reversed and remanded, 641 F.2d 376 (5th Cir.1981), in which the disposition of a partnership interest was treated by the Tax Court as a sale to the other partners rather than as a repurchase by the partnership despite contrary indications in written documents. In *David B. Sloan, Jr.,* 42 CCH Tax Ct.Mem. 1606 (1981), the disposition of a partnership interest was held to be a repurchase by the partnership rather than a sale to the remaining partners despite the fact that the payments were made by the remaining partners rather than the partnership. See Moore, *The Sloan Doctrine—New Twist in the Partnership Interest Sale/Redemption Question?,* 14 Tax Adviser 613 (1983).

   b.   For a discussion of unrealized receivables and substantially appreciated inventory, see Division II, pages 486 to 493 infra. For a more detailed discussion of the income tax results of the disposition of a partnership interest, see Division II, pages 547 to 550 and Division IV, pages 1086 to 1100 infra; Hewitt and Pennell, *Partnership Taxation: Interest Shifts, Basis Adjustments and Unrealized Receivables,* 38 J.Tax'n 219 (1973); Barrie, *The Liquidation of a Partner's Interest,* 61 A.B.A.J. 762 (1975); Nash, *How to Evaluate the Tax Consequences When a Partner Retires or Sells His Interest,* 4 Tax'n Law. 28 (1975); Solomon, *How Use of Section 736 Enhances Planning in Liquidating Partnership Interests,* 51 J.Tax'n 347 (1979); Cleveland, *Retirement Payments to Partners: Timing of Recognition of Income,* 57 J.Tax'n 86 (1982); Robinson and Shiff, *Structuring a Partner's Retirement to Achieve Best Results for Partners and Partnership,* 16 Tax'n Law. 38 (1987); Palmer, *Breaking Up is Hard to Do: Redemption of Partnership Interests Under Section 736,* 66 Taxes 914 (1988). If capital gains are subject to tax at ordinary rates, the differences between the application of Section 736 and the application of Section 741 are not substantial. Under Section 736 the selling partner, if the interest is being purchased on the installment basis, might achieve a longer deferral of the recognition of gain. The remaining partners might have available deductions or reductions in income with respect to part of the payments made to the selling partner. A purchase by the remaining partners governed by Section 741 will result in strict installment treatment of the selling partner and elective special additions to the bases of partnership property for the remaining partners.

   6.   In prior years, in order to encourage investments in partnerships, the promoters of the partnerships sometimes attempted to retroactively allocate some or all of the expenses incurred by the partnership during the partnership's fiscal year to partners (generally limited partners) who purchased their partnership interests during the same year but after the expenses were incurred. The desired result is simply illustrated by a partner who purchases a one-sixth interest in the partnership at the start of the last quarter of the year being allocated one-sixth of the total expenses for the year. The ability to deduct one-sixth of all of the expenses might be a major inducement to a prospective investor to invest in the partnership. In *Norman Rodman,* 32 CCH Tax Ct.Mem. 1307 (1973), the taxpayer purchased on Nov. 5 a 22% interest in a calendar year partnership. The partnership return showed a loss for the year and the taxpayer was allocated 22% of it. Subsequent adjustments by the Internal Revenue Service changed the loss to a profit and the Internal Revenue Service proposed to tax the taxpayer on 22% of the full year's income, pointing to the tax return as evidence that an allocation of 22% of the full year's income and loss had been allocated to the taxpayer. The Tax Court agreed that such an allocation was made and could be made. The decision of the Tax Court on this issue, however, was reversed and remanded by the Second Circuit in *Rodman v. Commissioner,* 542 F.2d 845 (2d Cir.1976). Subsequent to the reversal by the Second Circuit the Internal Revenue Service issued Rev.Rul. 77–119, 1977–1 C.B. 177, which, in effect, follows the decision of the Second Circuit. See *Cecil R. Richardson,* 76 T.C. 512 (1981), affirmed, 693 F.2d 1189 (5th Cir.

1982); *Mahoney v. United States,* 48 A.F.T.R.2d 81–6131 (Ct.Cl.Tr.J.Op.1981); *Williams v. United States,* 680 F.2d 382 (5th Cir.1982); Lee and Parker, *Retroactive Allocations to New Partners: An Analysis of the Area After Rodman,* 40 J. Tax'n 166 (1974); McGuire, *Retroactive Allocations Among Partners: The Rodman Decision,* 52 Taxes 325 (1974); Cowan, *Allocating the Tax Shelter Retroactively: The Rodman Case,* 2 J. Real Est. Tax'n 5 (1974); Koff and Hammer, *Retroactive Allocations: The Case Against Rodman,* 2 J. Real Est. Tax'n 18 (1974); Anderson and Bloom, *Of Battles Yet to be Fought: The Allocation of Partnership Deductions,* 2 J. Real Est. Tax'n 32 (1974); Weidner, *Yearend Sales of Losses in Real Estate Partnerships,* 1974 U.Ill.L.F. 533.

Whatever may have been the merits of a retroactive allocation under the Internal Revenue Code, Congress, in large measure, eliminated the possibility of making retroactive allocations through the amendment of Sections 704(a), 706(c)(2) and 761 by the Tax Reform Act of 1976. The key amendment was the amendment of Section 706(c)(2)(B) which added after the words "with respect to a partner whose interest is reduced" the parenthetical clause (whether by entry of a new partner, partial liquidation of a partner's interest, gift, or otherwise). As a result of this amendment, when a new partner "buys-in", the distributive shares of income, gain, loss, deduction, or credit of the partners whose interests were reduced by the purchase by the new partner must be determined by taking into account the reduced partners' varying interests in the partnership during the taxable year. See Section 706(d)(1). In determining, under Section 706(d)(1), the allocation of income, loss, etc. to an incoming partner, the partnership may either allocate on a daily basis or separate the partnership year into two (or more) segments and allocate income, loss, etc. in each segment among the persons who were partners during that segment. The amendments to Sections 704(a) and 761 make clear that the required allocation can not be overriden by a contrary provision in the partnership agreement.

The amendments discussed above left open some limited possibilities for retroactive allocations. See Cowan, *Retroactive Partnership Allocations: New Restrictions Do Not Bar the Technique,* 46 J. Tax'n 332 (1977). For example, allocating on the segment of the year basis may be favorable to an investor who "buys-into" an accrual basis partnership near the end of the first quarter when most of the deductible expenses had been paid or incurred early in the first quarter. Allocating on a daily basis may be favorable to an investor who "buys-into" a cash basis partnership after the deductible expenses are incurred but before they are paid. See generally *Cecil R. Richardson,* 76 T.C. 512 (1981), affirmed, 693 F.2d 1189 (5th Cir.1982); Hess, *Retroactive Allocations Among Contemporaneous Partners—Are They Still Valid?,* 58 Taxes 290 (1980); Sexton and Charyk, *Prospective Partnership Allocations: Part 1 (Normal Allocations),* 7 J.Real Est.Tax'n 62 (1979).

Subsection (d) was added to Section 706 in 1984. Section 706(d)(1) expressly requires that a partner's distributive share of income, gain, etc. shall be determined by any method prescribed by the regulations which takes account of the varying interests of the partners during the year. Section 706(d)(2) requires, in the case of a partnership which uses the cash method of accounting, a form of economic accrual of certain deductible items. For allocation purposes, the items are assigned to the day in the year to which they are attributable regardless of the time of payment. If items are attributable to a prior year, they are assigned to the first day of the year of payment; if attributable to a future year, they are assigned to the last day of the year of payment. Any portion of an item allocated under these rules to a person who is not a partner must be capitalized. Section 706(d)(2) eliminates the technique used by cash method partnerships of delaying payment of deductible items until most or all of the investors have been brought into the partnership and, in this way, attempting to give the investors the full benefit of the deduction of these items. Section 448, added by the Tax Reform Act of 1986, provides that C corporations, partnerships which have C corporations as partners and tax shelters, as defined in Section 461(i)(3), cannot use the cash method of accounting. C corporations and partnerships which have C corporations as partners are excepted from Section 448 if their average annual gross receipts for the prior 3 taxable years was $5,000,000 or less.

The amendments to Sections 706(c) and (d) do not precisely deal with the situation in which an investor purchases a previously established but unsold partnership interest. In this situation it might be argued that the investor's purchase does not have the effect of reducing the interests of the partners who had previously acquired their interests and, therefore, Sections 706(c)(2)(B) and 706(d)(1) do not apply. It is doubtful that this analysis would be accepted for a year after the first year of the partnership since it would seem unlikely that the I.R.S. or the courts would accept an allocation of income, loss, etc. to no one for the first year. Even during the first year it appears likely that these phantom interests would be disregarded. Cf. Rev.Rul. 77–310, 1977–2 C.B. 217, and Rev.Rul. 77–311, 1977–2 C.B. 218, and see *John M. Moore,* 70 T.C. 1024 (1978), and *Louis R. Gomberg,* 39 CCH Tax Ct.Mem. 1147 (1980).

7. While the 1976 and 1984 amendments to the Internal Revenue Code, for all practical purposes, eliminated the use of retroactive allocations, special allocations continue to be permitted. To be respected, however, such allocations must have a "substantial economic effect or be in accord with the partners' interests in the partnership." To illustrate the use of a special allocation one might assume a developer who has most of the real estate needed for a shopping center project but needs a few additional acres to get the project off the ground. The developer approaches the owner of the additional acreage and offers to exchange a small, 5%, interest in a partnership which will own and operate the project for the additional acres. The developer, to make the investment more attractive, and because the developer has plenty of losses from other projects, suggests that 25% of the partnership's losses be allocated to the owner of the 5% interest in the partnership. Other than the loss allocation, all items of income, profit, gain, and cash flow are shared 95% by the developer and 5% by the owner of the additional acres. Is the special allocation valid? The following case addresses this question.

JOHNIE VADEN ELROD v. COMMISSIONER

87 T.C. 1046 (1986).
[footnotes omitted]

STERRETT, Chief Judge: Respondent determined by notice of deficiency dated April 7, 1983 deficiencies in the Federal income taxes of petitioner for the taxable years ended * * * December 31, 1977 through December 31, 1980 as follows:

Taxable Year	*Deficiency*
1977	$138,016.00
1978	127,258.00
1979	158,030.00
1980	162,616.00

After concessions, the issue remaining for decision * * * [is] whether petitioner is entitled to a special allocation of partnership losses.

Findings of Fact

* * *

Petitioner, Johnie Vaden Elrod (Elrod), resided in Arlington, Virginia at the time he filed his petition in this case. He filed Federal income tax returns for all of the taxable years in issue with the Internal Revenue Service Center in Memphis, Tennessee.

* * *

Special Allocation of Partnership Losses. On August 19, 1977, a Certificate of Limited Partnership and Limited Partnership Agreement were executed with respect to the formation of EWH [Woodbrige Associates (EWH)] as a Virginia limited partnership, in accordance with the provisions of the Virginia Uniform Limited Partnership Act. The partnership was formed with [Earnest W.] Hahn[, Inc. (Hahn)] as its general partner, holding a 95–percent partnership interest, and petitioner as its limited partner, holding a 5–percent partnership interest. The stated purpose of the partnership was to "acquire and develop certain real property in Prince William County, Virginia," consisting of 100 acres of land "as a regional shopping center."

* * * The partnership agreement stated that petitioner and Hahn each agreed to convey to EWH their respective interests in the 100–acre parcel, as the site of the proposed shopping center. It also stated that petitioner was to be paid 95 percent of the fair market value of this 100–acre parcel by EWH, and the remaining 5–percent value was deemed a contribution of capital.

Petitioner and Hahn valued petitioner's capital contribution at $175,000, and petitioner's partnership capital account was credited with this amount. Petitioner's adjusted basis with respect to the 5–percent interest was $7,500. Petitioner did not make any additional capital contributions of cash or property to the partnership during any of the taxable years in issue. However, petitioner's total adjusted basis in EWH included adjustments with respect to certain partnership liabilities.

The partnership agreement required the maintenance of partner capital accounts. It also provided that petitioner was to receive a distributive share of 5 percent of partnership profits and a special allocation of 25 percent of partnership losses. Upon liquidation of the partnership, proceeds were to be distributed in accordance with the partners' capital account balances and partnership assets were to be distributed in accordance with the Uniform Limited Partnership Act as then in effect in Virginia. There was no provision in the partnership agreement that required petitioner upon liquidation to restore any deficit in his capital account. In the event of petitioner's death, Hahn was to purchase petitioner's partnership interest at the agreed-upon price of $175,000, the value of petitioner's capital contribution to the partnership.

The partnership agreement contained the following provisions:

Article 2

Partnership Property

Section 2.1 *Acquisition of Land.* * * * Hahn and Elrod are, concurrently with the execution of this Partnership Agreement and recordation of the Certificate of Limited Partnership, conveying their respective interests in the Land to this Partnership, and the Partnership is assuming and agrees to pay and perform any and all obligations with respect to the Land as provided for in certain promissory notes and deeds of trust in favor of United Virginia Bank and Elrod respectively.

Section 2.2 *Title to Property.* The Property of the Partnership shall be held in the name of the Partnership.

Article 3

Partnership Capital

Section 3.1 *Capital Contribution by Limited Partner.* * * * The Partnership is paying Elrod a purchase price, which Hahn and Elrod agree represents the value of a ninety-five (95%) percent undivided interest in the land. The value of the remaining five (5%) percent undivided interest in the land is being conveyed by Elrod as a contribution to the capital of the Partnership at an agreed value of $175,000.00. No interest shall be payable on such contribution by Elrod.

* * *

Section 3.5 *Capital Accounts.* The Partners shall have separate capital accounts to which their respective shares of Profit and Loss of the Partnership shall from time to time be credited or charged and withdrawals therefrom and all distributions of capital shall be in amounts from time to time agreed upon by the Partners, it being understood and agreed that all such distributions shall be in proportion to the respective Partner's Partnership Interest as provided in Section 4.1.

* * *

Article 4

Partnership Interests * * *

Section 4.1 *Partnership Interests.* The interest of each Partner in the Partnership, hereinafter referred to as the "Partnership Interest" of such Partner, shall be as follows:

Hahn 95%
Limited Partner 5%

* * *

Section 4.3 *Profit and Loss.* * * * The Profit and Loss of the Partnership shall be allocated to each Partner in proportion to each Partner's Partnership Interest; provided, however, that in consideration of Elrod having made the land available to the Partnership at extremely costly damage to the residue of the Elrod property, and Elrod's contribution of the value of a five (5%) [percent] undivided interest in the Land, Hahn and Elrod agree that so long as Elrod remains a Limited Partner in this Partnership, he shall be allocated twenty-five (25%) percent of any and all losses (for tax purposes) accruing to the Partnership. The remainder of such losses (for tax purposes), if any, shall be allocated to Hahn.

* * *

Section 11.2 *Proceeds of Liquidation.* The proceeds from the liquidation of Partnership assets shall be divided in the following order:

1. The expenses of liquidation and the debts of the Partnership other than debts owing to the Partners shall be paid.

2. Such debts as are owing to the Partners, including loans and advances made to or for the benefit of the Partnership shall be computed. Such amounts shall be paid after offsetting capital deficits, if any, against the amount owing to the Partners.

3. The balance in each Partner's capital account shall be paid after crediting or debiting such Profit and Loss as shall have accrued from the date of last posting to these accounts.

Subject to the foregoing, the business and affairs of the Partnership shall be wound up and its assets distributed in the manner provided in the Uniform Limited Partnership Act as the same may be in effect at the time in the State of Virginia.

Section 11.3 *Gain or Loss.* Any gain or loss arising out of the disposition of Partnership assets during the course of liquidation shall be credited or debited to the Partners in the same proportions as Profit and Loss were distributed prior to liquidation.

Section 11.4 *Distribution.* After all of the debts of the Partnership have been paid, the Partners may elect, by mutual agreement, to distribute the assets of the Partnership in kind. The Partners shall evaluate such assets and distribution shall then proceed as if the assets were being distributed in cash.

* * *

EWH operated at a loss during all of the taxable years in issue. The following amounts were reported on the Federal income tax returns filed by EWH and petitioner, for the 1977 through 1980 taxable years, with respect to EWH partnership losses and their allocation to petitioner:

	EWH Partnership Losses	*Petitioner's Capital Contributions*	*Petitioner's Capital Account as of Beginning of Year*	*Losses Allocated to Petitioner*	*Losses Deducted by Petitioner*	*Petitioner's Capital Account as of End of Year*
1977	$106,275	$175,000	—	$ 26,569	—	$148,431
1978	314,371	—	$148,431	78,593	78,593	69,838
1979	449,797	—	69,838	112,449	112,449	(42,611)
1980	612,036	—	(42,611)	153,009	163,009	(195,620)

*   *   *

Ultimate Findings of Fact

*   *   *

The special allocation to petitioner of 25 percent of partnership losses cannot be respected to the extent that it created deficit capital account balances that petitioner had no obligation upon liquidation to restore.

Opinion

*   *   *

Special Allocation of Partnership Losses. The * * * issue for decision is whether petitioner is entitled to a special allocation of 25 percent of partnership losses with respect to his partnership interest in **EWH.** In the notice of deficiency, respondent determined deficiencies in petitioner's Federal income taxes for the 1977 through 1980 taxable years based on the dissallowance of the special allocation for lack of substantial economic effect. Respondent argues that petitioner's distributive share of partnership loss is limited to 5 percent, consistent with petitioner's capital interest in the partnership and distributive share of profits. Respondent also has determined that, in any event, the total amount of losses deductible by petitioner is limited to his $132,500 basis in [his] partnership [interest]. Petitioner argues that the special allocation set forth in the partnership agreement should be respected for Federal income tax purposes and disagrees with respondent's determination of his partnership basis. * * *

a. *Petitioner's Basis in the Partnership.* Petitioner's distributive share of partnership loss is deductible to the extent of his basis in [his] partnership [interest]. Sec. 704(d). Therefore, before we discuss whether the special allocation of partnership loss may be respected, we first must determine petitioner's basis * * * based upon the adjusted basis of property deemed contributed by petitioner to the partnership. Sec. 722.

Petitioner and Hahn have agreed that the purchase price of the 100–acre parcel constitutes only 95 percent of its fair market value. The remaining 5–percent value, $175,000, was deemed to be a contribution of capital by petitioner to the partnership and was so reflected in petitioner's partnership capital account. As of the formation of **EWH,** petitioner's adjusted basis in this 5–percent interest in the land equaled $7,500.

Petitioner's basis in the partnership also must be increased by his share in certain partnership liabilities. Sec. 752. In 1977, **EWH** executed a promissory note in the amount of $1,800,000 to the Virginia National Bank for the development of the shopping center site. At trial, petitioner conceded that, because Hahn was personally liable for the satisfaction of this note, as a limited partner petitioner is not entitled to any increase in his partnership basis with respect to this partnership debt. Secs. 752 and 1.752–1(e), Income Tax Regs.

EWH also executed a promissory note in the amount of $2,500,000 to petitioner with respect to the purchase of the 100–acre parcel. We note that petitioner contends that he also is not entitled to any increase in his partnership basis with respect to this note, on the belief that the note does not constitute a fixed and unconditional obligation of **EWH**. We disagree, * * * and state that this note constitutes a valid debt issued pursuant to the completed sale of petitioner's land. Therefore, as a limited partner, petitioner is entitled to share in this nonrecourse liability * * *.

We conclude that as of 1977 petitioner's total basis in the partnership equaled * * * $7,500 for the land deemed contributed plus [his share of] the nonrecourse partnership debt * * *. Petitioner did not make any additional capital or cash contributions to the partnership and he does not present any other arguments to increase his partnership basis for any of the taxable years in issue. Therefore, under section 704(d), the total amount of partnership losses deductible by petitioner for all of the taxable years in issue cannot exceed [his total basis in the partnership as of 1977].

b. *Special Allocation.* The partnership agreement provides that petitioner's distributive shares of partnership profits and losses are 5 percent and 25 percent, respectively. Section 4.3 of the partnership agreement provides that the special allocation was made "in consideration of Elrod having made the land available to the Partnership at extremely costly damage to the residue of the Elrod property * * * "

In general, a partner's distributive share of income, gain, loss, deduction, or credit shall be determined by the terms of the partnership agreement. Section 704(a). However, this general rule is limited by the provisions of section 704(b), as follows:

SEC. 704. PARTNER'S DISTRIBUTIVE SHARE.

* * *

(b) Determination of Distributive Share.—A partner's distributive share of income, gain, loss, deduction, or credit (or item thereof) shall be determined in accordance with the partner's interest in the partnership (determined by taking into account all facts and circumstances), if—

* * *

(2) the allocation to a partner under the agreement of income, gain, loss, deduction, or credit (or item thereof) does not have substantial economic effect.

In determining whether the special allocation is to be respected, the sole test for all of the taxable years in issue here is whether the special allocation has "substantial economic effect."

Respondent argues that the special allocation to petitioner lacks substantial economic effect. Petitioner argues that the special allocation satisfies the test for substantial economic effect, as interpreted by *Miller v. Commissioner,* a Memorandum Opinion of this Court which states as follows:

> If a partner's allocation of an item of income or deduction is reflected in his capital account and if the liquidation proceeds of the partnership are distributed in accordance with the capital account balances, the allocation has substantial economic effect. [Citations and footnote omitted. T.C. Memo. 1984–336, 48 T.C.M. 409, 411, 53 P–H Memo T.C. par. 84,336, at 1304–84 (1984).]

In *Miller,* the special allocation was not respected partly because the partnership agreement provided that liquidation proceeds were to be distributed in accordance with the partners' ownership interests rather than their capital account balances. There was no further discussion with respect to any additional elements of the substantial economic effect test. However, even where these first two requirements are met, there is a third requirement, which provides that where a partner's capital account registers a deficit attributable to a special allocation that partner must have the obligation upon liquidation to restore such deficit. *Ogden v. Commissioner,* 84 T.C. 871, 884 (1985), affd. per curiam 788 F.2d 252 (5th Cir.1986); *Goldfine v. Commissioner,* 80 T.C. 843, 852 (1983).

The parties do not dispute that the first two requirements of the substantial economic effect test are met. Sections 3.5 and 11.2—11.5 of the EWH partnership agreement provide for the maintenance of partners' capital accounts and for liquidation proceeds to be distributed in accordance with the capital accounts. However, there is no express provision in the agreement that establishes an obligation upon liquidation for petitioner to restore any deficit in his capital account balance. The so-called "capital accounts" analysis examines whether the partner to whom a special allocation is made for tax purposes also bears the economic burdens and benefits of the special allocation. *Allison v. United States,* 701 F.2d 933, 938 (Fed.Cir.1983); *Hamilton v. United States,* 231 Ct.Cl. 517, 532–533, 687 F.2d 408, 417–418 (1982); *Goldfine v. Commissioner, supra* at 851. Absent such an obligation to restore a deficit in a capital account attributable to a special allocation, the other partner or partners would bear part of an economic burden resulting from such special allocation. *Ogden v. Commissioner,* 84 T.C. at 884–885.

The General Explanation of the Tax Reform Act of 1976 prepared by the Staff of the Joint Committee on Taxation explains the meaning of "substantial economic effect" as "whether the allocation may actually affect the dollar amount of the partners' share of the total partnership income or loss, independent of tax consequences." The explanation continues, in a footnote, that—

> The determination of whether an allocation may actually affect the dollar amount of the partners' shares of total partnership income or loss, independent of tax consequences, will to a substantial extent involve an examination of how these allocations are treated in the partners' capital accounts for financial (as opposed to tax) accounting purposes; this assumes that these accounts actually reflect the dollar amounts that the partners would have the rights to receive upon the liquidation of the partnership. [Staff of Joint Comm. on Taxation, 94th Cong., 2d Sess., General Explanation of the Tax Reform Act of 1976, 95 & n. 6 (1976), 1976–3 C.B. (Vol. 2) 1, 107.]

Respondent has determined deficiencies in petitioner's Federal income taxes for the 1977 through 1980 taxable years. In 1977 and 1978, petitioner maintained positive capital account balances, and in 1979 and 1980, petitioner's capital accounts registered deficits. The absence of express language in the partnership agreement of an obligation upon liquidation to restore a deficit in a partner's capital account is not necessarily fatal to the validity of a special allocation. *Frink v. Commissioner,* T.C. Memo. 1984–669, affd. with respect to the allocation of partnership losses and revd. and remanded on another issue 798 F.2d 106 (4th Cir.1986).

As of the end of each of the 2 years in which petitioner maintained positive capital account balances, no other partners could bear more than their share of any economic burden or benefit attributable to the special allocation to petitioner. Therefore, with respect to the 1977 and 1978 taxable years, the special allocation does not lack substantial economic effect. However, to the extent that the special allocation creates a deficit in petitioner's capital account in the 1979 and 1980 taxable years, the absence of the obligation upon liquidation to restore such deficit is fatal here. In these years the other partners in the partnership could have borne more than their share of any economic burden attributable to the special allocation if the partnership had liquidated as of the end of either year. Therefore, the special allocation lacks economic effect in 1979 and 1980 to the extent that it creates a deficit in petitioner's capital account balance in each of these years.

Accordingly, we conclude that for the 2 years in which petitioner maintained positive capital account balances, 1977 and 1978, the special allocation to petitioner is to be respected. However, for the 2 years in which petitioner's capital account balances registered deficits, 1979 and 1980, the special allocation lacks economic effect and is not to be respected to the extent that any deficit in each year is attributable to the special allocation.

Decision will be entered under Rule 155.

NOTE

1. The Internal Revenue Service and the courts, when faced with the question whether an allocation has substantial economic effect, have concluded that, in order to have substantial economic effect, at the minimum an allocation must affect the partners' capital accounts and the partners must share on liquidation of the partnership and on liquidation of their interests in the partnership in accord with their capital accounts. Sharing in accord with capital accounts appears to include having the obligation to make up any deficits existing in the capital accounts. See Ltr.Ruls. 8133028, 8139005, 8247003 and 864200; *Boynton v. Comm'r,* 649 F.2d 1168 (5th Cir.1981); *Holladay v. Comm'r,* 649 F.2d 1176 (5th Cir.1981); *Allison v. United States,* 701 F.2d 933 (Fed.Cir.1983); *Morton S. Goldfine,* 80 T.C. 843 (1983); *James E. Miller,* 48 CCH Tax Ct.Mem. 409 (1984); *Mary K.S. Ogden,* 84 T.C. 871 (1985), affirmed, 788 F.2d 252 (5th Cir.1986). The courts, however, consistent with the *Elrod* case, when considering taxable years unaffected by the regulations issued under Section 704(b), have concluded that the absence of an obligation to make up a deficit in a capital account is not fatal to an allocation so long as the capital account is not in deficit. See *Phillip A. Dibble,* 49 CCH Tax Ct.Mem. 32 (1984).

2. Would the *Elrod* case have been decided differently if the regulations issued under Section 704(b) had been fully applicable to the years at issue in that case?

     a. The regulations under Section 704(b) require that an allocation have economic effect and that the economic effect be substantial when compared with the income tax effect of the allocation. See Reg.Sec. 1.704–1(b)(2)(iii).

         1. In order for an allocation to have an economic effect it must affect the partners' capital accounts which have been properly established and maintained, the partners must share in liquidation of the partnership, and the amount received by partners on liquidation of their interests by the partnership must be determined, according to the balances in their capital accounts and any deficits in capital accounts must be made up upon liquidation. See Reg.Sec. 1.704–1(b)(2)(ii); Bailis and Hartung–Wendel, *Meeting the Economic Effect Test Under Section 704(b) Regulations,* 3 J.Ps.Tax'n 311 (1987); Cuff, *Drafting a Partnership Agreement to Comply with the "Economic Effect" Regulations,* 5 J.Ps.Tax'n 3 (1988).

             (i) If a partnership agreement contains a "qualified income offset," allocations to a partner who is not obligated to restore a deficit balance in his capital account will be respected to the extent partnership allocations and distributions do not cause the partner's capital account to become less than zero. In determining whether partnership allocations will cause the partner's capital account to become less than zero, the partner's capital account must be reduced by, among other things, distributions that, as of the end of the year, are reasonably expected to be made to the partner to the extent such distributions exceed offsetting increases in the partner's capital account which are reasonably expected to occur during or prior to the year in which the distributions are reasonably expected to be made.

(ii) A "qualified income offset" provides that a partner who unexpectedly receives an adjustment, allocation or distribution which causes his capital account to become less than zero will be allocated items of income and gain in an amount and manner sufficient to eliminate the deficit balance "as quickly as possible."

(iii) See Reg.Sec. 1.704–1(b)(2)(ii)(d); Charyk, *Working With a "Qualified Income Offset"*, 14 J. Real Est.Tax'n 81 (1986).

2. In determining whether the economic effect is substantial, the existence of an economic effect is assumed and it is compared with the income tax effect. For example, in a two person partnership, if all of the tax-free income of the partnership is allocated to the partner subject to a high income tax rate and all of the taxable income is allocated to the partner subject to a low income tax rate at a time when it is known or can be reasonably assumed that the taxable and tax-free income will be in the same or similar amounts, the allocation will be deemed not to have a substantial economic effect. See Reg. Secs. 1.704–1(b)(2)(iii) and 1.704–1(b)(5) Ex. (7)(i). The substantiality of the economic effect is determined by assuming that the effect will occur without regard to the probability of such occurrence. Therefore, in the real estate area, an allocation of depreciation, even if coupled with a gain-chargeback, will pass the substantiality test since a corresponding decrease in the depreciable property's value is assumed. See Reg.Sec. 1.704–1(b)(2)(iii)(c); Shapleigh and Hoskins, *How to Satisfy the Substantiality Requirement Under the Section 704(b) Regulations*, 3 J.Ps.Tax'n 291 (1987).

b. In order for a partner's capital account to have been properly established and maintained, it must be increased by:

1. The amount of money contributed by the partner to the partnership;

2. The fair market value of property contributed by the partner to the partnership (net of liabilities secured by such contributed property that the partnership is considered to assume or take subject to under Section 752);

3. Allocations to the partner of partnership income and gain (or items thereof).

Similarly, a partner's capital account must be decreased by:

1. The amount of money distributed to the partner by the partnership;

2. The fair market value of property distributed to the partner by the partnership (net of liabilities secured by such property that such partner is considered to assume or take subject to under Section 752);

3. Allocations to the partner of expenditures of the partnership described in Section 705(a)(2)(B) (and certain other adjustments); and

4. Allocations of partnership loss and deduction (or items thereof).

See Reg.Sec. 1.704–1(b)(2)(iv); Serling and Gardarian, *Selected Aspects of Partnership Capital Accounting—Liabilities, Promissory Notes, and Revaluations Under Section 704(b) Regulations,* 5 Va.Tax.Rev. 455 (1986); Miller, *Disproportionate Partnership Capital Accounts,* 44 N.Y.U.Inst.Fed. Tax'n 22–1 (1986); Marich, *Substantial Economic Effect and the Value Equals Basis Conundrum,* 42 Tax L.Rev. 509 (1987).

    c.   The use of nonrecourse debt (partnership debt for which no partner bears the economic risk of loss), particularly in the real estate area, presents a special problem in determining whether the allocation of deductions attributable to the use of such debt, such as depreciation, will be respected by the Internal Revenue Service. If the nonrecourse debt is in excess of the adjusted basis or properly computed (for the purposes of the regulations) book value of the property which secures the debt, the allocation of deductions attributable to the debt cannot have an economic effect on the partners since the economic burden which corresponds to the allocation is borne by the creditor. See Reg.Sec. 1.704–1(b)(4)(iv)(a). In general, the regulations define nonrecourse deductions for a partnership's taxable year as the amount of deductions attributable to nonrecourse debt which equals the net increase, if any, during that taxable year, in the amount by which the nonrecourse debt of the partnership exceeds the adjusted basis or book value of the property which secures the debt. (The excess of the debt over the adjusted basis or book value of the property is referred to in the regulations as minimum gain.) See Reg.Secs. 1.704–1(b) (4)(iv)(b) and (c). The regulations provide, however, that an allocation of nonrecourse deductions will be respected if:

    1.   Properly determined capital accounts are maintained for the partners and the partners share upon liquidation of the partnership, and upon liquidation of their interests in the partnership, in accord with the amount in their capital accounts;

    2.   The allocation of nonrecourse deductions among the partners is reasonably consistent with allocations, which have substantial economic effect, of some other significant item attributable to the property securing the nonrecourse debt (other than the minimum gain recognized by the partnership);

    3.   Either the partners must be obligated to make up any deficits in their capital accounts or the partnership agreement must provide that, if there is a net decrease in partnership minimum gain allocable to the disposition, or deemed disposition, of partnership property subject to one or more nonrecourse debts of the partnership during a taxable year, all partners with a deficit capital account balance at the end of the year will be allocated, before any other allocation is made, items of income and gain for such year in the amount and proportions needed to eliminate such deficits as quickly as possible; and

    4.   All other material allocations and capital account adjustments under the partnership agreement are recognized and respected under the regulations.

See Reg.Secs. 1.704–1(b)(4)(iv)(d) and (e); Mahaffey, *Allocation of Losses Attributable to Nonrecourse Debt: Impact of Treasury Regulations,* 15 Colo. Law. 2191 (1986); Presant and Loffman, *The Final Partnership Nonrecourse Debt Allocation Regulations,* 65 Taxes 67 (1987); Wheelwright and Boyle, *Safe Harbor Provided for Partnership Allocations Based on Nonre-*

course Debt, 15 Tax'n Law. 216 (1987); Brumbaugh and Coleman, *Nonrecourse Debt Regulations Resolve Most Special Allocation Issues,* 4 J.Ps. Tax'n 21 (1987); Cuff, *Final Regulations on Allocating Nonrecourse Deductions are Deceptively Simple,* 66 J.Tax'n 166 (1987); Cash, Dickens and White, *Allocations of Nonrecourse Debt Deductions,* 18 Tax Adviser 730 (1987).

d.   It appears that the "qualified income offset" and nonrecourse debt provisions are applicable to allocations made to limited partners since limited partners, in the usual case, will not be required to make up any deficits in their capital accounts upon liquidation of the partnership or of their interests in it.   Cf. Reg.Sec. 1.704–1(b)(5) Exs. (15), (16), (20), (22).

Compliance with the "qualified income offset" and, to some extent, the nonrecourse debt regulations might be avoided by having the limited partners agree to make up any deficits in their capital accounts.   What economic risks do the limited partners take in agreeing to make up deficits in their capital accounts?   See Gazur, *Partner Beware: Evaluating the Economic Risks Presented by an Obligation to Restore a Deficit Capital Account Balance,* 3 Tax L.J. 179 (1986); Teitelbaum, *The Impact on Partners of Allocations That Have Substantial Economic Effect,* 4 J.Ps. Tax'n 112 (1987).

e.   See generally Haist and Petrini, *Final Regulations Further Tighten Partnerships' Ability to Make Special Allocations,* 64 J.Tax'n 200 (1986); Volet and Millman, *Testing Partnership Allocations Under the New Final Substantial Economic Effect Regulations,* 64 J.Tax'n 194 (1986); Welch, *A Practical Guide to Achieving Substantial Economic Effect in Partnership Allocations,* 3 J.Ps.Tax'n 3 (1986); Charyk, *The Final Section 704 Partnership Allocation Regulations—Real Estate Partnership Concerns,* 13 J.Real Est.Tax'n 315 (1986); Hoskins and Bower, *An Analysis of the Final Regulations Under Sec. 704(b),* 17 Tax Adviser 328 (1986); Wiesner and Massoglia, *Section 704(b) Final Regulations Pose "Substantial" Interpretative Problems,* 17 Tax Adviser 472 (1986); Franke, *The End of the Debate: The Final Regulations of Partnership Allocations Under 704(b),* 10 Rev.Tax'n Indiv. 299 (1987); Moore, *Guidelines for Coping with the Final Section 704(b) Regulations,* 3 J.Tax'n Inv. 283 (1986); Stevens and Heick, *What Real Estate Practitioners Need to Know About Partnership Allocations,* 3 # 3 Prac.Real Est.Law. 23 (1987); Tureen, *Achieving Real Estate Developer's Tax Objectives Under Section 469 and Economic Objectives Under Section 704(b),* 65 Taxes 478 (1987); Sloan and Naponick, *Special Allocations of Bottom–Line Profits and Losses in Real Estate Partnerships Under the Final 704(b) Regulations,* 38 U.Fla.L.Rev. 698 (1986); Kuller, McKee, Whitman and Nelson, *The Section 704(b) Regulations,* 45 N.Y.U.Inst.Fed.Tax'n 22–1 (1987).

3.   What if a general partnership agreement contains a special allocation of, or the general partner of a limited partnership receives a special allocation of, depreciation and the partnership agreement does not impose on the general partners or partner an obligation to make up any capital account deficit nor contain a qualified income offset provision, will the allocation have a substantial economic effect?   The Supreme Court of Texas in *Park Cities Corp. v. Byrd,* 534 S.W.2d 668 (Tex.Sup.Ct.1976), indicates that it will, via a somewhat circuitous route.   In this case the partnership agreement allocated substantially all of the losses resulting from the construction and operation of a large apartment complex to the general partner in a limited partnership which owned the

complex. There was only one limited partner. At the time of the death of the general partner, the general partner's capital account had a deficit of almost 2 million dollars as a result of the allocation of substantially all of the losses of the partnership to the general partner. Since over the years, the general partner had made various contributions to the partnership to take care of actual cash losses, the parties agreed that the deficit in the general partner's capital account resulted from the allocation to the general partner of substantially all of the depreciation taken by the partnership on the apartment complex.

Since the partnership was dissolved by the death of the general partner, the question arose on termination of the partnership and distribution of its assets whether the executors of the estate of the general partner were obligated to pay to the partnership the amount of the deficit in the capital account of the general partner. The trial court and intermediate appellate court agreed with the executors that the estate of the general partner was not obligated to pay to the partnership the amount of the deficit in the general partner's capital account since none of the deficit resulted from an actual withdrawal by, or distribution to, the general partner. The Supreme Court of Texas reversed stating, "[i]t seems that these parties would not intend that Mrs. Byrd [the general partner] should receive the entire tax benefit from the nearly $2,000,000 in partnership losses and never be required to suffer any actual financial loss as a result of those allocations." 534 S.W.2d at 674. What comes first, the chicken or the egg?

4. As the *Elrod* case indicates, even if the allocation of losses has substantial economic effect, pursuant to Section 704(d) a partner will not be able to personally use those losses unless the partner has a basis in his or her partnership interest sufficient to cover the losses allocated to the partner.

REALTY SYNDICATION: AN INCOME TAX PRIMER FOR INVESTOR AND PROMOTER

Martin J. Rabinowitz
29 Journal of Taxation 92 (1968).
[footnotes omitted]

* * *

Basis of Partnership Interest

In general, the basis for a partner's interest in a partnership is his original cost (or other tax basis) for that interest, plus his share of partnership liabilities. Each partner's basis is increased annually by his share of partnership income. Basis is reduced annually by any distributions received from the partnership and the partner's share of partnership losses. However, a partner is not permitted to deduct his share of the partnership's losses in an amount greater than his basis for his interest in the partnership, at the end of the partnership year in which the loss occurred. In general, a partner's share of partnership liabilities is determined in accordance [with how the partner bears the economic risk of loss for those liabilities. In the usual case, a general partner bears the economic risk of loss for recourse liabilities in accord with] his ratio for sharing partnership losses. However, in the case of a no personal liability mortgage (or in any case in which no partner [bears the economic risk of loss]) the partner's share is[, in general,] determined in accordance with the ratio for sharing *profits*.

The basis provisions have particular importance to [partnerships developing, owning and operating real estate] because: (1) they are typically financed with mortgages substantially in excess of the cash investment; (2) they frequently generate tax losses during their early years; and (3) distributions of cash in excess of taxable income are common.

In determining basis, each partner adds to basis his share of partnership liabilities. These liabilities include his share of mortgage liabilities of the partnership. Consequently, the [partner's] basis is increased by his share of the partnership's mortgage liabilities and he may deduct losses in excess of his cash investment. In the case of a limited partnership, the limited partners' share of mortgage liabilities will be limited to their required capital contributions, except in the case of the "no personal liability" mortgage [with respect to which no partner bears an economic risk of loss], in which case liabilities are [generally] considered as shared by all partners in the same ratio as partnership profits.

*   *   *

Since a partner's basis includes his share of partnership liabilities, any reduction of those liabilities is treated as a distribution of money to him. For example, each amortization payment made by the partnership reduces the mortgage liability and results in a constructive distribution. Conversely, any refinancing of the partnership's mortgage which increases the outstanding principal balance would increase his basis to the extent of his share thereof. This permits the tax-free distribution to partners of the proceeds of the mortgage refinancing.

*   *   *

At some point, however, mortgage amortization payments will exceed annual depreciation deductions, resulting in more taxable income than cash flow. This unhappy state of affairs (taxable income without a corresponding receipt of cash) is generally avoided through a refinancing of the mortgage or sale of the partnership property. [An additional possibility is the incorporation of the partnership.] *   *   *

NOTE

1. The ability of a partner to include a share of partnership liabilities in the basis of the partner's partnership interest, as was the result in the *Elrod* case, supra, pages 38 to 46 frequently allows the partner to deduct partnership losses and receive tax-free cash flow distributions from the partnership in amounts greatly in excess of the partner's investment in the partnership. See Katz, *Inclusion of Liabilities in the Basis of a Partnership Interest and Related Issues,* 41 N.Y.U.Inst.Fed.Tax'n 13–1 (1983); Levine, *Structuring Real Estate Loans to Preserve Investors Tax Benefits (Part 1),* 1 # 5 Prac.Real Est.Law. 55 (1985); *(Part 2),* 1 # 6 Prac.Real Est.Law. 75 (1985); Burke and Friel, *Allocating Partnership Liabilities,* 41 Tax L.Rev. 173 (1986); Postlewaite and Bialosky, *Liabilities in the Partnership Context—Policy Concerns and the Forthcoming*

Regulations, 33 UCLA L.Rev. 733 (1986); Heitner and Berg, *Losses and the Partner: Toward a Rational Basis Standard*, 3 J.Ps.Tax'n 195 (1986); Schmalz, *The Effect of Partnership Liabilities on Basis, At-Risk Amounts, and Capital Accounts*, 5 J.Ps.Tax'n 291 (1989). The amount of a nonrecourse liability shared by partners as an addition to the bases of their partnership interests is probably limited to the fair market value of the real estate and improvements securing the liability. See Section 752(c) and cf. *Fortune Odend'hal*, 80 T.C. 588 (1983), affirmed, 748 F.2d 908 (4th Cir.1984); *Warner R. Waddell*, 86 T.C. 848 (1986); Rev.Rul. 84–5, 1984–1 C.B. 32.

2. In general, a partner bears the economic risk of loss for a partnership liability to the extent that the partner would bear the economic burden of discharging the obligation represented by the liability if the partnership were unable to do so. See Reg.Sec. 1.752–1T(d)(3)(A).

3. The considerations relevant to determining whether and when a limited partner can add a share of partnership liabilities to the basis of his or her partnership interest are discussed at pages 70 to 87 supra.

4. Even if a partner has enough basis in his or her partnership interest to permit the partner, under Section 704(d), to personally use the partnership losses allocated to him or her, the personal use of those losses may be prevented by the application of the at-risk rules of Section 465 or the limitations on the use of passive losses provided by Section 469. The at-risk and passive loss concepts are considered at pages 149 to 166 infra. In fact, had the at-risk rules applied to the taxpayer in the *Elrod* case, pages 38 to 46 supra, he would not have been able to personally benefit from the partnership losses allocated to him in an amount greater than his basis in the real estate which he contributed to the partnership.

5. For a discussion of financing and refinancing techniques see generally Division III.

6. For an examination of the problems arising on the incorporation of a partnership, see Division IV, pages 1149 to 1153 infra.

(i) THE LIMITED PARTNERSHIP

If a general partnership is an attractive entity to use for the ownership, development and operation of real estate then, in many cases, a limited partnership may prove irresistible. While having many of the advantages of a general partnership, a limited partnership does not share some of the disadvantages. Some of the investors may have limited liability. Since the death, insanity, etc. of a limited partner will not cause the dissolution of the entity, and the avoidance of dissolution and/or the continuation of the business upon the death, etc. of a general partner can be planned for, continuity of life is more likely. Management, at least in a day to day sense, is centralized in the general partner or partners. Limited partnership interests may be made transferable. The major cost which is exacted for the advantages listed above is that the limited partners can not take part in control of the enterprise without subjecting themselves to liability as general partners. The following excerpt discusses the tests which have been employed to determine whether a limited partner has participated in control.

IMPOSING LIABILITY FOR "CONTROL" UNDER SECTION 7 OF THE UNIFORM LIMITED PARTNERSHIP ACT

Norman Abrams
28 Case Western Reserve Law Review 785 (1978).
[some footnotes omitted]

* * *

I. Existing Tests for Control Under Section 7

A. *The Quantitative Power Test*

The quantitative power test derives from an analysis of the earliest section 7 cases decided under the ULPA. One of the first cases to deal explicitly with the problem of control was Holzman v. DeEscamilla.[2] The general partner was a tenant farmer who had formed a limited partnership with two investors to cultivate his land. Within a year the partnership became insolvent, and the creditors sought to recover from the limited partners. The court held that the limited partners had exercised control and were liable as general partners. It noted that the limited partners often decided what crops were to be planted, sometimes against the wishes of the general partner, DeEscamilla. Particularly telling was the fact that the general partner could not write checks on the enterprise without the cosignature of one of the two limited partners. * * *

A similar analysis was used by the courts in two subsequent cases to determine whether a limited partner could be held generally liable. In each instance, the court looked to the limited partner's participation in the affairs of the partnership. In Silvola v. Rowlett,[3] a creditor of a partnership, which operated an auto dealership, brought an action against the limited partner when the venture went into bankruptcy. Although the limited partner acted as a foreman in the repair shop and advised the general partner from time to time on enterprise affairs, the court concluded that final decisions on all matters were made by the general partner. "[S]ole control and management," the court noted, "rested with the [general partner]," and "the activities of the [limited partner] were at all times subject to such control."[4] The implication of this holding is that the limited partner was not personally responsible for wasting partnership assets and consequently, should not be held liable to partnership creditors.

In Grainger v. Antoyan,[5] the limited partner served as the sales manager of the partnership and as such sold new cars and had limited charge of that department. The court examined the extent of the limited partner's participation and concluded that he did not conduct himself in a manner which would make him liable as a general partner.

2. 86 Cal.App.2d 858, 195 P.2d 833 (1948).

3. 129 Colo. 522, 272 P.2d 287 (1954).

4. Id. at 528, 272 P.2d at 290.

5. 48 Cal.2d 805, 313 P.2d 848 (1957).

The court found that the evidence "clearly demonstrates that defendant had no control over prices, purchases, the extension of credit, wages, salaries, employment, or the funds of the * * * firm, and that he in fact did not take part in the control of the * * * firm's business." [6]

These early cases caused considerable difficulty for both courts and commentators since the cases appear to turn on the nature of the limited partner's participation in the enterprise. The courts made no express attempt to seek any causal relationship between the limited partner's participation and the harm suffered by creditors, although this element is present in each case. The cases suggest instead that courts were measuring the extent of a limited partner's participation. The implication is that at some point the sum of the limited partner's acts in the partnership crossed an imaginary line between controlling and noncontrolling participation. The courts seem to have been looking to some quantitative test of control.

The quantitative test has proven to be impractical because of the difficulty of measuring participation. For example, how many acts are needed to constitute control? What kinds of acts are significant? Has a partner performed an act of control if he insists that the general partners purchase a particular kind of typewriter for the partnership offices? If so, how is this to be compared to another act in which a limited partner forces the general partner to plant crops ill-suited to the climate as in *Holzman?* In addition, the same act can mean entirely different things in different circumstances. A limited partner who plants a particular crop on a 200 acre plot will have greater effect on partnership affairs if the partnership farms only 200 acres than he will if it farms ten times that acreage. Every partnership is unique. On the basis of this fact alone, it has been suggested that any effort to establish a consistent measure of control is doomed to failure.

[It has been suggested] that the characterization of types of participation may offer a solution. Thus, it might be possible to conclude that a limited partner has exercised control if he has done "anything which would affect the partnership's relations to third parties." This approach helps identify the kind of acts on which one might base liability, but only restates the basic question. At what point can an act be said to affect third parties? How direct must the effect be? How extensive must the effect be? A limited partner affects third parties if he buys a typewriter. Is he to become generally liable to all creditors because he affected this one third party? If not, the same measurement problem arises. Thus, this approach offers little increased predictability.

The danger of a quantitative test is that it will operate to force courts to rely almost entirely on equitable considerations. It offers no definitive reason for concluding that a certain amount of power is permissible but that a little more is not. To avoid case-by-case determinations, courts would have to adopt the kind of arbitrary, technical

6. Id. at 813, 313 P.2d at 853.

distinctions the draftsmen of the ULPA explicitly set out to avoid.

* * *

B. *The Day-to-Day Powers Test*

In the wake of the initial efforts to resolve the "control" dilemma, courts in two cases [7] attempted to refine the quantitative test by developing what may be characterized as a day-to-day powers test. As in the quantitative power cases, the courts which employed the day-to-day powers analysis looked to the limited partner's role in partnership operations. But the courts attempted to avoid the problem of measuring the limited partner's participation as a method of determining general liability. Instead, under the day-to-day powers test, a limited partner exercises control sufficient to subject himself to section 7 liability if his participation constitutes the day-to-day exercise of power over the operation of partnership affairs on a continuous basis.

In Weil v. Diversified Properties,[8] the general partner in a real estate venture sued the limited partners to establish their general liability to partnership creditors. The limited partners had taken away his day-to-day control when the partnership was on the verge of insolvency. The court held that the partners were bound by the terms of the agreement which provided that "day-to-day management of the business of [the] partnership" [9] was reserved to the general partner. The court also concluded that the limited partners did not subject themselves to general liability when they attempted to salvage the business of the partnership because their actions did not amount to the normal day-to-day course of business activities within the meaning of the partnership agreement. By the time the general partner gave up his responsibility for management of the partnership to the limited partners, "funds coming in were far from sufficient to meet current obligations, and no partnership account was being accumulated." [10] The court concluded that "this clearly was not a normal day-to-day business question; it involved the very ability of the enterprise to survive."[11] The implication is that by the time the limited partners intervened, there was really nothing left over which normal day-to-day control could be exerted.

It is reasonable to assume that if the case had come before the court on the complaint of one of the partnership creditors the court would have held much the same way:

> Certainly common sense dictates that in times of severe financial crisis all partners in such an enterprise, limited or general, will become actively interested in any effort to keep the enterprise afloat and many abnormal problems will arise that are not under

---

7. Weil v. Diversified Properties, 319 F.Supp. 778 (D.D.C.1970); Gast v. Petsinger, 228 Pa.Super.Ct. 394, 323 A.2d 371 (1974).

8. 319 F.Supp. 778 (D.D.C.1970).

9. Id. at 781.

10. Id.

11. Id.

any stretch of the imagination mere day-to-day matters of managing the partnership business. This is all that occurred in this instance.[12]

A similar analysis was undertaken in Gast v. Petsinger,[13] where the limited partners served as engineering consultants on a number of partnership projects. A creditor sued, claiming that this participation was sufficient to establish general liability. As in *Weil*, the partnership agreement vested control of day-to-day operations in the general partner. This was, the court observed, "[c]onsistent with statutes regulating limited partnership * * *."[14] The case was remanded to determine whether the limited partners, who formally were serving only as consultants, had sufficient influence to control day-to-day operations:

> It is not apparent from the face of the record that the technical skills and training of [the limited partners] did by virtue of their retention as "Project Managers" place them in a position where their "advice" did influence and perhaps, control the decision of the General Partner, whose particular expertise is unknown.[15]

If the general partners were incapable of making informed business judgments concerning partnership affairs and were deferring instead to the decisions of the limited partners, then they would have been subject to general liability. As the court noted: "The 'control' a partner has in the day-to-day functions and operations of the business is the key question. Does the limited partner have decisionmaking authority that may not be checked or nullified by the general partner?"[16]

The *Gast* court seemed to suggest that occasional consultation by a limited partner is permissible under the control rule. This would provide a limited partner with much more certainty as to the kind of control he could exercise under the ULPA than would a quantitative test. It would also seem to assure limited partners more freedom to participate in the partnership decisionmaking process. The rule implied in *Weil*, on the other hand, may be less extensive. The court's emphasis on the fiscal crisis which precipitated the intervention of the limited partners would suggest that such action is permissible only in unique circumstances. Under this approach occasional participation without a showing of absolute necessity might subject a limited partner to general liability.

A test which conditions general liability solely on the exercise of day-to-day powers, as the court adopted in *Gast*, would provide a much more workable standard for establishing liability than the less refined quantitative powers test. If a limited partner assumes powers that are usually attributable to a general partner on an ongoing basis, he will become generally liable. If, however, he exercises authority only occasionally, his limited liability will likely remain unimpaired. Problems

---

12. Id.

13. 228 Pa.Super.Ct. 394, 323 A.2d 371 (1974).

14. Id. at 398, 323 A.2d at 373.

15. Id.

16. Id. at 402, 323 A.2d at 375.

might arise when a court has to determine when participation has become frequent enough to constitute day-to-day control, but for the most part the range of uncertainty would be less extensive than under a purely quantitative test.

This test has a number of disadvantages, however. It would seem to lead to a just result in the case of the limited partner who insisted that the partnership buy a particular typewriter. Read literally it would also seem to protect the limited partners in *Holzman,* if the one and only decision they interjected into enterprise operations was their choice of a particular crop. Suppose, for example, a limited partnership is formed to purchase and operate real estate properties. The partnership agreement provides that purchases are to be made by majority vote of all partners, both limited and general. Over a period of five years the partnership acquires two apartment houses. The investments turn out to be unwise. It is questionable whether the limited partners would be held to have exercised control under the tests of either *Weil* or *Gast.* Yet it seems hard to deny that they are as responsible for creditor losses as the general partners. Confronted with these facts, the *Gast* court would probably be less likely to interpret section 7 as it did. It would be clearly inequitable to deny a creditor the right to recover against a limited partner who made occasional management decisions but had not assumed ongoing day-to-day control if those decisions played some role in the subsequent insolvency of the partnership. The day-to-day powers test, therefore, would seem to confer broader powers on the limited partners than the draftsmen may have intended.

A problem shared by both the day-to-day powers test and the quantitative powers test is that neither considers the relationship between the limited partner's activities and the creditor's losses. A creditor might recover from a limited partner whose participation had not affected the creditor in any way. On the other hand, a creditor might be denied recovery even though the limited partner's activities were directly responsible for the losses he has suffered. The result in either instance would be arbitrary and inequitable.

This problem arises because both tests operate on the assumption that a limited partner who exercises the kind of powers usually reserved to general partners is effectively a general partner and should be treated like one. However, it is submitted that the rules for determining the creditors to whom a general partner will be liable should not apply to a limited partner who controls. A general partner in any partnership is liable to all those who transact business with the enterprise while he is associated with it. While the decisions made by a general partner who joins an operating partnership can have a devastating effect on the ability of prior creditors to recover on partnership obligations outstanding at the time he becomes a general partner, the Uniform Partnership Act (UPA) limits his liability to prior creditors to the amount of any contribution he makes to the partnership.

If a limited partner who exercises control is treated as if he joined the partnership on the day he began to exercise control, he would also be liable to prior creditors only to the extent of his contribution to the partnership. This result would seem to be improper for two reasons. First, if new general partners were liable to prior creditors, partnerships would find themselves hardpressed to obtain needed management skills. The exigencies of commerce require that an enterprise be able to obtain managers capable of responding to changing conditions and markets. The UPA rule recognizes this fact. The same rationale should not serve to limit the liability of a limited partner who participates in control. His participation comes only by virtue of his investment association with the enterprise. There is no reason to believe that he brings with him any special skills, managerial or otherwise, that are likely to benefit the partnership or its creditors. Thus, the need for special encouragement and protection is gone.

Second, the UPA approach can be justified by the fact that a general partner is treated as if he exercises management authority on a continuous basis whether or not he actually does so. To escape liability to future creditors, he must cease all association with the partnership. A limited partner, on the other hand, is in a position to exercise management powers whenever he chooses, maintaining a passive position at all other times without having to disassociate himself from the enterprise. Thus, a limited partner, unlike a general partner, is in a position to exercise a single act of control. If the UPA rule were applied to this limited partner, he might, by his single act, bankrupt the partnership without incurring personal liability.

In fact, it can be argued that prior creditors have dealt with the enterprise on the understanding that, because an individual has claimed the status of a limited partner in the filing certification or elsewhere, he would not be managing partnership affairs. Of all the individuals in the world who might assume control of a partnership, a creditor has at least some right to expect that those who specifically represented that they would not assume control can be relied upon not to do so. To deny a creditor the right to recover from a limited partner whose decisions prevented recovery from the partnership would seem to be contrary to the equitable principles the draftsmen sought to infuse into the ULPA.

On the other hand, if prior creditors are permitted to recover, a limited partner will be treated as if he had become a general partner before he began to exercise control. Unless liability is linked to some form of causation, there is no other way to determine at what point this liability arose.

Such logic would prevent a court from disallowing the claims of subsequent creditors. This, too, could produce an inequitable result. Subsequent creditors should not be permitted to argue that they have been harmed by activities undertaken before they decided to transact business with a particular enterprise. Otherwise, once a limited partner exercises control, he might discover that he has subjected himself to liability to all subsequent creditors of the partnership, even though he may have ceased active participation and even though any effects of his participation may long since have been rendered benign. Having once exercised control, he could never be sure his liability to future creditors would cease until he terminated his association with the partnership altogether. This would be true even though his control may have caused the partnership no harm. It may even have benefited the partnership and improved opportunities for creditor recovery. Partnership insolvency may come several years later. It may be entirely unrelated to anything the limited partner may have done, but unless a court is willing to look directly at the relationship between particular acts of control and the harm they have caused, inequitable consequences may result.

C.   *The Specific Reliance Test*

The search for a defensible rule has led a number of courts and commentators to conclude that the draftsmen might have intended section 7 to protect creditor reliance. General liability would arise whenever the acts of a limited partner have given a creditor a reasonable basis for concluding that he is actually a general partner. Since the creditor has a right to assume that all general partners are generally liable, the limited partner has a duty to make sure that he has given no one cause to adopt such an erroneous belief.

Reliance considerations are referred to in the official commentary to the ULPA, although not specifically in connection with section 7. In two of the early control cases, courts indicate a willingness to entertain reliance claims. In Silvola v. Rowlett,[17] the defendant limited partner had been employed as a foreman in the partnership repair shop and had purchased parts without the knowledge or consent of the general partner. Nonetheless, the court determined that the limited partner had not taken part in control, reasoning that the plaintiff could not have relied on the limited partner being generally liable because he had had actual knowledge of the defendant's limited partner status. In Rathke v. Griffith,[18] the limited partner had cosigned several documents with the general partners and had negotiated contracts with third parties on two occasions. These activities, the court concluded, had been conducted under the direction of the general partners. The limited partner's testimony that he had never "in any sense managed the affairs of the concern or had the power to initiate and control execution of policy"[19] was uncontradicted. The court added: "[I]t is not alleged that respondent ever relied on Mr. Griffith's position as a general partner, or in fact even understood that Mr. Griffith was anything other than a limited partner."[20]

* * *

17. 129 Colo. 522, 272 P.2d 287 (1954).

18. 36 Wash.2d 394, 218 P.2d 757 (1950).

19. Id. at 407, 218 P.2d at 764.

20. Id. at 408, 218 P.2d at 764.

Commentators were quick to perceive the advantages of a reliance standard for section 7 control.[21] The simple justice of the principle is undeniable. Reliance is after all one of the basic equitable tools of the common law. Then, too, the principle of reliance seems to correspond with the essential outlook of the ULPA draftsmen. As has been observed, the entire drafting process can be characterized as an attempt to eliminate the arbitrary decisions of pre-ULPA courts and infuse notions of equity into the interpretations of limited partnership problems. Creditor reliance is the basic thrust of many sections of the ULPA, and it is specifically identified as an underlying principle of the statute in the draftsmen's Official Comment to section 1.

Most appealing to commentators, however, was recognition of the fact that investing partners would enjoy more freedom to participate in enterprise management if a reliance standard was read into section 7 than they would under a more arbitrary quantitative power test.[22] It seemed to offer a limited partner, as a quantitative test could not, some ability to predict whether the acts he was undertaking were the type that might subject him to general liability under the control rule. Because a reliance standard looks to the relationship between the limited partner and particular creditors, a limited partner need never fear that his participation in and of itself might be considered control.

There are, however, a number of strong arguments against reading a reliance standard into the control test of the ULPA. A reliance standard would provide limited liability for a limited partner acting as an undisclosed principal. Thus, even where the limited partner would be liable under any objective standard, he would be able to manage the enterprise behind the cloak of his limited partner status and avoid general liability.

A second objection to a reliance interpretation is that section 7, * * *, makes no mention of reliance. Yet a limited partner's general liability in several other sections of the ULPA is made specifically dependent upon a showing of reliance. If the draftsmen intended to impose a reliance standard for measuring control, one would expect to find evidence of their intent in the specific terminology of section 7. Professor Alan Feld has suggested that this oversight can be attributed to the fact that "the ULPA is the product of a less rigorous tradition of draftsmanship, which saw no need to spell out the precise meaning of the control test."[23] This "realistic answer" is unpersuasive and even Feld seemed to reject it.[24] If the draftsmen neglected to include a reliance standard in section 7 because of tradition, how can one explain the obvious care they took to spell it out elsewhere? In fact, the more plausible conclusion is that one of the reasons the draftsmen saw no need to define control is that they did not intend control to turn on the presence of reliance.

---

21. Feld, *The "Control" Test for Limited Partnerships,* 82 Harv.L.Rev. 1471, 1478–80 (1969), 56 Mich.L.Rev. 285 (1957).

22. See Feld, supra note [21] at 1479.

23. Feld, supra note [21] at 1480.

24. Id.

Related, and possibly more telling, is the fact that application of a reliance test to the control rule of section 7 does not correspond with the common sense meaning of the word. The dictionary, that great source of common sense meanings, informs us that one who has control has the power to direct and regulate.[25] Introduction of a reliance element into control rule adjudications would seem to sidestep the obvious intent of the draftsmen. Taken to its logical extreme, it would mean that a limited partner could exercise day-to-day control without running the risk of general liability as long as no one except the general partners were aware of his activities. At the other extreme, if everyone were aware of his limited status, the rule would permit a limited partner to run every aspect of the business without running the risk of general liability. No commentator has been willing to carry section 7 this far.

D.   *The Estoppel Test*

Consequently, some commentators have found themselves in the uncomfortable position of endorsing two separate tests for the same rule. On one hand, they recognize that one who controls an enterprise in the sense that he directs its affairs and regulates its activities should be liable to creditors. On the other hand, they are unwilling to deny the principle that one who induces another to deal with an enterprise to that person's detriment should assume the responsibility for his loss. The problem, of course, is that it is hard to accept the notion that a single rule in a logically drafted statute could have been intentionally designed to facilitate two distinct interpretations serving two separate, though admittedly related, purposes.

Recognizing this problem, Feld attempted to reconcile the two tests into a single logical construct.[26] He suggested that the draftsmen may have designed section 7 to function on an estoppel, rather than on a specific reliance, basis. Feld reasoned that the draftsmen omitted a reliance test from section 7 because they were looking not to specific incidents of reliance but to the kinds of participation on which reliance might reasonably be based. Under this view a limited partner would be held generally liable to a creditor if he controlled the day-to-day affairs of the enterprise because his activities, if known to a creditor, would have been sufficient to lead him to believe that the limited partner was actually representing himself as a general partner. When such conduct could be shown, the limited partner would be estopped from asserting that a particular creditor was unaware of his participation in the enterprise and therefore could not be said to have relied on his general liability.[27]

25. Webster's Third New International Dictionary 496 (unabr. version 1970).

26. Feld, supra note [21] at 1480. Other commentators have apparently failed to perceive that estoppel and actual reliance are not identical.

27. Feld, supra note [21] at 1480.

Feld's approach is ingenious. It creates a single test capable of serving both concerns. However, the Feld test poses a number of problems. Suppose a limited partner orders a typewriter for the enterprise on his own accord. He tells the typewriter salesman that he is a general partner in the partnership. Under a specific reliance test he would be liable to the typewriter company but not to any other partnership creditor. Should all partnership creditors be permitted to recover even if the limited partner never makes another partnership decision? Feld insisted that individual creditors need not demonstrate specific reliance. They need only demonstrate that "liability-creating activities" can be attributed to the limited partner.[28] Yet it would be hard to deny that recovery by any other creditor on these facts alone would be arbitrary and unfair. And if these activities are not sufficient to establish a reason to impose liability, how much "liability-creating" conduct is necessary? In addition to measurement problems, the test also raises creditor identification problems. Feld suggested that any creditor can recover if he can show that a limited partner acted as if he were a general partner.[29] Thus, one act or series of acts undertaken at a particular point in time, after which the limited partner ceased to perform any management role in the partnership, would be sufficient to subject him to liability to all future creditors. This would follow even though the decision he may have made could not be said to have harmed them in any way. The consequence is to convert the best features of the reliance test, fairness and simplicity, into the worst feature of the quantitative power test, open-ended liability.

The final and possibly most significant argument against adopting either the specific reliance test or the estoppel test for determining control under section 7 is that to do so would duplicate another provision of the statutory scheme capable of providing creditors with the same protection. This conclusion, however, is not readily obvious from analysis of the ULPA. In fact, nothing in the ULPA, except possibly section 7, would protect a creditor who erroneously concluded that a particular partner was a general partner. This has led commentators to conclude that the draftsmen must have meant section 7 to serve this purpose. The assumption implicit in this approach is that the ULPA incorporates within its provisions an independent, internally coherent scheme of statutory regulation. Yet the statute itself indicates that the draftsmen intended the ULPA to function in conjunction with the UPA.

The ULPA expressly provides that the relations between partners must be understood in the broad context of both statutes. Section 1 of the ULPA states that a limited partnership is a partnership composed of both general partners and limited partners. The Official Comment to section 1 indicates that the draftsmen conceived of limited partners as being members of the partnership, not partners, in spite of their name. Section 9 of the Act provides in part that "a general partner

---

28. Id.   **29.** Id.

shall have all the rights and powers and be subject to all the restrictions and liabilities of a partner in a partnership without limited partners. ∗ ∗ ∗"[30] The obvious purpose of the ULPA is to provide a framework for creating limited partners and for resolving problems that may arise from their relations with general partners and with creditors. At the same time, it is clear that the draftsmen contemplated that limited partnership problems concerning general partners exclusively or the relationship between general partners and partnership creditors were to be resolved within the framework of the UPA. Thus, one may reasonably conclude that, where the problem at issue involves an individual who may be either a limited partner or a general partner or both, the draftsmen intended to provide courts with recourse to the provisions of both statutes as needed to obtain equitable resolution of the controversy.

The draftsmen state in the Official Comment to section 1 of the ULPA that a limited partner in a partnership may become a general partner in the same manner that any individual may become a partner in an enterprise. Thus, when a controversy arises because a limited partner has begun to act like a general partner, it is not unreasonable to look to the UPA for the proper rule of law. Section 16(1) of the UPA specifically deals with the rights of creditors who have transacted business with an individual on the mistaken assumption that he is a partner in an enterprise or with an enterprise on the mistaken assumption that a particular individual was generally liable for the obligations of the enterprise. Section 16, entitled "Partner by Estoppel," provides:

(1) When a person, by words spoken or written or by conduct, represents himself, or consents to another representing him to anyone, as a partner in an existing partnership or with one or more persons not actual partners, he is liable to any such person to whom such representation has been made, who has, on the faith of such representation, given credit to the actual or apparent partnership, and if he has made such representation or consented to its being made in a public manner he is liable to such person, whether the representation has or has not been made or communicated to such person so giving credit by or with the knowledge of the apparent partner making the representation or consenting to its being made.

(a) When a partnership liability results, he is liable as though he were an actual member of the partnership.

(b) When no partnership liability results, he is liable jointly with the other persons, if any, so consenting to the contract or representation as to incur liability, otherwise separately.[31]

---

30. [ULPA] § 9 [(1916)].

31. UPA § 16(1). This approach appears to have been adopted in J.C. Wattenberger & Sons v. Sanders, 191 Cal.App.

2d 857, 13 Cal.Rptr. 92 (1963), although it has been cited as a case reading reliance into § 7. ∗ ∗ ∗

There is nothing in either the UPA or the ULPA which would preclude application of UPA section 16(1) to a situation in which a limited partner takes on the appearance of a general partner. As the Official Comment to section 1 of the ULPA seems to indicate, there is nothing in his status as a limited partner which could be said to confer a special privilege of nonliability. Nor is there anything arising from his special contractual relationship with the enterprise that would seem to dictate the necessity of a special provision in the ULPA to protect creditors who act on the mistaken assumption that he is something other than a limited partner. Therefore, it seems unlikely that the draftsmen, who had just completed the UPA, would have had any reason to duplicate their prior efforts or could be said to have intended to do so.

There is nothing in the UPA that would enable a creditor to recover from a limited partner whose business judgment was responsible for the insolvency of the partnership. Under the UPA, if no question of reliance is at issue, a creditor may recover from an individual only by demonstrating that he participated as a partner in the enterprise. To do this he must convince a court that an arrangement existed among the individuals in question making each the agent of the other. This may be achieved by presenting evidence of a written or oral agreement to this effect or by demonstrating that an implied contract can be inferred from the manner in which the affairs of the enterprise were conducted. If a limited partner participates in the partnership in a manner authorized by the terms of the partnership agreement, the provisions of the UPA alone will be of little assistance to a creditor, regardless of whether his participation assumes the indicia of control over enterprise affairs. The creditor will be unable to point to any agreement, written or oral, in which participants could be said to have agreed to share the risk of any losses occasioned by the operations of the enterprise. Nor will he be able to point to any course of conduct which can be said to demonstrate the existence of any arrangement other than that contemplated by the partnership agreement. By granting individuals the right to distribute risk so that some enjoy limited liability while others do not, the ULPA creates a situation in which the status of a limited partner serves to protect him from the justified, reasonable claims a creditor would otherwise seek to assert under the UPA. Indeed, if one concludes that section 7 of the ULPA was designed to protect creditors' reliance, creditors will lose the right to protect themselves from a limited partner whose conduct in the enterprise, unbeknownst to them, destroyed the partnership's ability to meet its contractual obligations.

That the draftsmen of the ULPA intended to protect creditors from limited partners who manage partnership affairs is clear. In the Official Comment to section 1, the draftsmen listed two basic assumptions which they intended to incorporate into limited partnership arrangements:

First: No public policy requires a person who contributes to the capital of a business, acquires an interest in the profits, and some degree of control over the conduct of his business, to become bound for the obligations of the business; provided creditors have no reason to believe at the times their credits were extended that such person was so bound.

Second: That persons in business should be able, while remaining themselves liable without limit for the obligations contracted in its conduct, to associate with themselves others who contribute to the capital and acquire rights of ownership, provided that such contributors do not compete with creditors for the assets of the partnership.[32]

Commentators favoring a reliance interpretation of section 7 have noted the draftsmen's statement in the first assumption that creditors should be able to recover from those who erroneously lead them to believe they are generally liable for partnership obligations. No commentator, however, has considered section 7 in terms of the draftsmen's second assumption. One element of this assumption is that "persons in business should be * * * liable without limit for the obligations contracted in its conduct. * * *"[33] One who merely contributes capital to a venture is not a "person in business," but if he contributes capital and makes decisions affecting the conduct of partnership affairs, he is a "person in business" as much as any general partner. His status as a limited partner should not protect him from the obligations his conduct has created.

This means that creditors have two separate rights. They can rely on those who represent themselves as being generally liable. And, under the second assumption, creditors can also recover from those who manage the partnership whether or not they ever made representations to anyone. Since creditors can recover on a reliance claim under UPA section 16(1), the statutory scheme would be sufficient to provide both forms of protection envisioned by the draftsmen if section 7 is given its common sense meaning. By contrast, if section 7 is interpreted simply as a reliance provision, a significant loophole would be created. When a limited partner imposes his own business judgment on partnership affairs, he should be liable to those creditors whose ability to recover from the enterprise is thereby impaired. No other provision of either the UPA or the ULPA is suited to this task. If it is read out of section 7, it is read out of the statutory scheme entirely.

II. The Effects Test

A. *The Rule and Its Justification*

Simply stated, an effects test would make limited partners generally liable to those creditors who have been harmed because of limited partner participation in partnership affairs. In applying the test, a

---

32. [ULPA] § 1, Official Comment.   **33.** ULPA § 1, Official Comment (1916).

court would have to examine what a limited partner had actually done and ask whether those activities, either alone or in conjunction with the activities of other partnership participants, could be said to have caused the harm suffered by partnership creditors.

This test looks to the nature of the limited partner's partnership activities, without attempting to characterize them as more—or less—characteristic of those undertaken by general partners. Because it derives its basic premises from the common sense meaning of section 7, it adopts the most significant element of the quantitative and day-to-day powers tests. The test also functions to prevent a limited partner from secretly controlling partnership affairs without risking liability for the consequences. In this way the two major weaknesses of the specific reliance test are avoided. And yet by introducing a causation element, the rule offers courts the same benefits previous courts sought by utilizing a reliance factor in their deliberations. Like reliance, causation is a tool of historically proven value with which courts are familiar and which they know how to use. Like reliance, it is grounded in the essentially equitable notion that those whose acts or omissions bring harm to another should bear the burden for the damage that results.

There is at least as much justification for introducing causation into section 7 as for introducing reliance. Read independently of the rest of the statute, the control rule of section 7 seems to make no distinction between acts of control which harm creditors and those which do not. A different result obtains, however, when section 7 is interpreted in light of the express dictates of section 28(1). Section 28 is entitled "Rules of Construction" and states that "[t]he rule that statutes in derogation of the common law are to be strictly construed shall have no application to this act." In effect, this provision instructs courts to interpret the statute in a manner that will avoid arbitrary determinations. In other words, a participant in a limited partnership should not be held liable unless he has done something to justify such a result. Therefore, in interpreting section 7, a court should consider whether the activities of the limited partner have produced any injury to partnership creditors. If not, the imposition of liability would be arbitrary.

* * *

NOTE

1. How might a situation in which a limited partner possessed certain specialized talents which would constitute a valuable asset in the operation of the partnership be handled?

    a. For example, what if one of the limited partners was an architect and the partnership desired his services during the design and construction stage of a real estate development?

    b. Could the partnership hire him as the architect for the project, or as a consultant to the general partners, without violating the "control" test?

c. See generally, Feld, *Comment: The "Control" Test For Limited Partnerships*, 82 Harv.L.Rev. 1471 (1969); O'Neal, *Comments on Recent Developments in Limited Partnership Law*, 1978 Wash.U.L.Q. 669 (1978); Comment, *"Control" in the Limited Partnership*, 7 J. Marshall J.Prac. & Proc. 416 (1974); Comment, *Partnership: The Viability of the Estoppel Theory in Relation to Third Parties Dealing with Limited Partnerships*, 33 Okla.L.Rev. 170 (1980); Burn, *The Potential Liability of Limited Partners as General Partners*, 67 Mass.L.Rev. 22 (1982); Freedberg, *The Shield of the Limited Partnership*, 28 N.Y.L.Sch.L.Rev. 561 (1983); Basile, *Limited Liability for Limited Partners: An Argument for the Abolition of the Control Rule*, 38 Vand.L.Rev. 1199 (1985); Note, *Limited Partnership Control: A Reexamination of Creditor Reliance*, 60 Ind.L.J. 515 (1985); Buxbaum and Etlin, *Limited Partners' Liability for Impermissable Control Activity Under the Revised California Limited Partnership Statute*, 16 Sw.U.L.Rev. 535 (1986).

d. If a limited partner takes part in management and, as a result, becomes liable to creditors as a general partner, does the limited partner then acquire the rights of a general partner in the management of the limited partnership? See *Roeschlein v. Watkins*, 686 P.2d 1347 (Colo.App. 1984).

2. To a greater or lesser extent, depending on the amount of risk of loss of limited liability limited partners decide to incur, limited partners are at the mercy of the general partner. For an examination of steps being taken, and which may be taken, to protect the limited partner see Comment, *Proposed Regulation of Limited Partnership Investment Programs*, 6 U.Mich.J.L.Ref. 465 (1973); Roulac, *Resolution of Limited Partnership Disputes: Practical and Procedural Problems*, 10 Real Prop., Prob. & Tr.J. 276 (1975); Hooker, *The Power of Limited Partners to Remove and Replace the General Partner of a Limited Partnership*, 19 Tex.Tech L.Rev. 1 (1987).

a. With the growth of public ownership of limited partnership interests in real estate ventures various regulatory bodies have promulgated regulations seeking to protect the limited partners. See Mosburg, *Regulation of Tax Shelter Investments*, 25 Okla.L.Rev. 207 (1972), and Division III, pages 888 to 892 infra. Common among these regulations are requirements that a majority in interest of the limited partners have the right to: (1) Amend the partnership agreement, (2) Dissolve the partnership, (3) Remove the general partner or partners, and/or (4) Continue the business with a substituted general partner. Does the granting of these rights to, or the exercise of these rights by, the limited partners violate the "control" test of Section 7 of the U.L.P.A.? See Comment, *Partnership: Can the Rights Required To Be Given Limited Partners Under New Tax Shelter Investment Regulations Be Reconciled With Section 7 Of The Uniform Limited Partnership Act?*, 26 Okla.L.Rev. 289 (1973).

b. The frequent use of the limited partnership form as an investment vehicle and the syndication of limited partnership interests have resulted in considerable attention being drawn to the relationship between the general partner and the limited partners and the position of limited partners in a limited partnership. See generally Volz and Berger, *The Limited Partnership Agreement*, 22 Prac.Law. 35 (Sept.1976); Kratovil and Werner, *Fixing Up the Old Jalopy—The Modern Limited Partnership Under the ULPA*, 50 St. John's L.Rev. 51 (1975); Comment, *Procedures and Remedies in Limited Partners' Suits for Breach of the General Partner's*

Fiduciary Duty, 90 Harv.L.Rev. 763 (1977); Basile, *Admission of Additional and Substitute General Partners to a Limited Partnership: A Proposal for Freedom of Contract,* 1984 Ariz.St.L.J. 235; Reynolds, *Loyalty and the Limited Partnership,* 34 U.Kan.L.Rev. 1 (1985); Kaster and Cymbler, *The Impact of a General Partner's Bankruptcy Upon the Remaining Partners,* 21 Real Prop., Prob. & Tr.J. 539 (1986); Montgomery, *The Fiduciary Duties of General Partners,* 17 Colo.Law, 1959 (1988).

3. The Revised Uniform Limited Partnership Act approved by the Commissioners on Uniform State Laws in 1976 and amended in 1985 seeks to clarify the control problem by enumerating the activities in which a limited partner can engage without being held to have participated in control. See Section 303(b). These activities include: (i) being a contractor, agent or employee of the partnership or of a general partner or being an officer, director or shareholder of a corporate general partner; (ii) consulting with, and advising, a general partner on partnership business; (iii) being a surety for the partnership; (iv) bringing or pursuing a derivative action; (v) requesting or attending a meeting of partners; (vi) voting on an amendment to the partnership agreement; (vii) voting on matters including: dissolution of the partnership, sale, exchange, lease, mortgage or pledge of substantially all of the partnership's assets, the partnership's incurring indebtedness other than in the ordinary course of business, changes in the nature of the partnership's business, admission or removal of a general or limited partner, a transaction involving an actual or potential conflict of interest between a general partner and the limited partnership or the limited partners and other matters relating to the business of the partnership which the partnership agreement provides are subject to the vote of the limited partners. In addition, the Revised Act makes it clear that engaging in activities, or having the right to engage in activities, other than those listed above does not necessarily mean that the limited partners, as a result, have participated in control. See Section 303(c). Engaging in, or having the right to engage in such activities, must be shown to constitute participation in control of the business. See Section 303(a). Even if a limited partner participates in control, the Revised Act limits the liability of the limited partner. The limited partner is liable only to persons who transact business with the limited partnership reasonably believing, based upon the limited partner's conduct, that the limited partner is a general partner. See Section 303(a). This limitation requires that a person asserting the liability of a limited partner have knowledge of his participation in control. Therefore, the limited partner's liability, incurred as a result of his participation in control, is restricted to those persons who transact business with the limited partnership with actual knowledge of his participation and a reasonable belief, derived from the conduct of the limited partner, that the limited partner is a general partner.

The Revised Act permits the partnership agreement to grant all or a specified group of the limited partners the right to vote (on a per capita or other basis) on any matter. See Section 302. This right to vote, however, cannot be extended beyond the matters described above without the limited partners possibly incurring liability as a result of participating in control of the business. In the absence of a provision to the contrary in the partnership agreement, the written consent of all limited partners is required for the addition of new limited partners. See Section 301(b)(1). The Revised Act provides that a limited partner's interest in the partnership is personal property and assignable, in whole or in part, unless otherwise provided in the partnership agreement. See Sections 701 and 702. The assignee is only entitled to become, or exercise the rights of, a limited partner upon the consent of all partners or in those instances in which the assignor gives the assignee those rights in accordance with authority provided in the partnership agreement. See Section 704(a). Article 10 of the Revised Act grants limited partners the right to bring derivative actions on behalf of the limited partnership. See generally, Symposium *Limited Partnership Act,* 9 St. Mary's L.J. 441 (1978); Shapiro, *The Need For Limited Partnership Reform: A Revised Uniform Act,* 37 Md.L.Rev. 544 (1978); Hecker, *The Revised Uniform Limited Partnership Act: Provisions Affecting the Relationship of the Firm and Its Members to Third Parties,* 27 U.Kan.L.Rev. 1 (1978); Kessler, *The New Uniform Limited Partnership Act: A Critique,* 48 Fordham L.Rev. 159 (1979); Hecker, *Limited Partners' Derivative Suits Under the Revised Uniform Limited Partnership Act,* 33 Vand.L.Rev. 343 (1980); Comment, *Investor Protection and the Revised Uniform Limited Partnership Act,* 56 Wash.L.Rev. 99 (1980); Donnell, *An Analysis of the Revised Uniform Limited Partnership Act,* 18 Am.Bus.L.J. 399 (1981); Mann, *Investors Need the Revised ULPA,* 11 # 2 Real Est.Rev. 93 (1981); Hecker, *The Revised Uniform Limited Partnership Act: Provisions Governing Financial Affairs,* 46 Mo.L.Rev. 577 (1981); Comment, *Limited Partnership, Model Agreement and Certificate with Commentary,* 26 S.Tex.L.J. 15 (1986); Closen, *Limited Partnership Reform: A Commentary on the Proposed Illinois Statute and the 1976 and 1985 Versions of the Uniform Limited Partnership Act,* 6 N.Ill.U.L.Rev. 205 (1986).

a. The Revised Uniform Limited Partnership Act grants to limited partners certain rights to participate in the management of the partnership and be an employee of the partnership without being held to have participated in control. Yet, Section 469 of the Internal Revenue Code, which is discussed on pages 154 to 166, infra, in providing for limitations on the use of passive losses, seems to assume that in the usual case a limited partner cannot materially participate in the trade or business of the partnership. See Section 469(h)(2) and Reg.Sec. 1.469–5T(e)(2). There are, however, exceptions to this rule. See Reg.Sec. 1.469–5T(e)(2). Is a limited partner who is employed by the partnership an exception to the rule? See Priv.Ltr.Rul. 8810079.

b. In the case of a 10% or more limited partner in a partnership operating rental real estate, would the exercise by the limited partner of the rights granted by the Revised Uniform Limited Partnership Act amount to active participation in the limited partnership in order for the limited partner to claim the $25,000 offset for passive losses and credits provided by Section 469(f)? See Section 469(i)(6)(C). Cf. Reg.Sec. 1.469–5T(e)(2); Priv.Ltr.Rul. 8810079.

4. The income tax treatment of a limited partnership and its limited and general partners is similar to the treatment, discussed earlier, accorded a general partnership and its partners. There are, however, two significant determinations which are of particular importance when considering the treatment of a limited partnership. These determinations are: (i) the computation of the basis of a limited partner in his or her partnership interest; and (ii) whether the limited partnership will be classified, for income tax purposes, as an association taxable as a corporation. The next excerpt explores these considerations.

USE OF LIMITED PARTNERSHIP TO INVEST IN DEPRECIABLE REALTY

Ellsworth Hall, III
21 Mercer Law Review 481 (1970).
[footnotes omitted]

*   *   *

Federal Income Tax Characteristics of Limited Partnerships

*   *   *

Basically, a limited partnership is treated for federal income tax purposes the same as an ordinary partnership with general and limited partners being treated identically. Thus, if the project shows a profit for tax purposes, there will be no tax at the partnership level and each partner will report his share of the income on his individual return. If the income item in question were long term capital gain at the partnership level, it will retain that characteristic on the individual returns. Net losses also generally pass through and may be deducted by the partners; however, in this respect the nature of a limited partnership causes a special problem.

The Basic Problem

In the case of either type of partnership and either general or limited partners, *a partner is not permitted to deduct his share of partnership losses if they exceed his basis in his partnership interest.* Moreover, "cash flow" distributed to a partner in excess of his basis will result in taxable gain.

For a general partner in a real estate venture this rule is unlikely to pose much of a problem since a general partner's basis includes not only his investment in the partnership *but also his share of the partnership debts* due to the fact that a general partner is liable for such debts. Thus, the general partner is permitted to include his share of the mortgage loan in his partnership basis. On the other hand, a limited partner is not liable for such debts and is not ordinarily permitted to add any portion of the debt to his basis. In the case of an investment which consistently produces a tax loss, this rule, when applicable, will soon preclude the limited partner from deducting his share of losses, because a partner's basis is reduced by his share of all losses incurred. Since the investment by the partners is usually relatively small (the bulk of the funds being furnished by the mortgage lender), the limited partner's basis will soon be reduced to zero, and he will be precluded from taking further losses and, as stated, will realize gain on the distribution of "cash flow".

However, where none of the partners [bear an economic risk of loss] with respect to a partnership liability (as in the case of a mortgage on real estate acquired by the partnership without the assumption by the partnership or any of the partners of any liability on the mortgage), then all partners, including limited partners, [generally] share such liability * * * in the same proportion as they share the profits. [See Reg. Sec. 1.752–1T(a)(2).]

Therefore, where the *attractiveness of the investment depends upon the ability of the limited partner to deduct losses,* [*or to receive tax free cash flow distributions*] *it is absolutely* essential that no personal liability exists. Any procedure that will preclude personal liability will do the job; however, the most obvious one would be [an "in rem" mortgage discussed infra at pages 776 to 782. * * *

Alternatively, the loan can be closed in the name of some other entity, such as a nominee corporation, and title transferred to the limited partnership without any assumption of liability.

[While a limited partner can add a share of an in rem or nonrecourse liability to the partner's basis in his or her partnership interest, the application of the at-risk rules, Section 465, may prevent the partner from taking advantage of the additional basis provided by the share of the liability in order to personally deduct the partner's share of partnership losses in excess of the partner's investment in the partnership. With respect to an activity involving real property, a partner will not be able to take advantage of his or her share of a partnership's nonrecourse liability in order to deduct a share of partnership losses in excess of the partner's investment unless the liability constitutes qualified nonrecourse financing. See Section 465(b)(6). In general, qualified nonrecourse financing is real estate financing, other than convertible debt, provided by the government or a person unrelated to the partnership who is actively and regularly engaged in the business of lending money. The at-risk rules are examined in detail at pages 150 to 153 infra.]

*   *   *

[A]nother approach to the problem that can be used, even though the mortgage loan cannot be obtained without "personal" liability [is, at the point the limited partners'] * * * bases are in danger of becoming exhausted, the limited partners, for a valid consideration, each agree to become liable to the lender for the repayment of a certain portion of the mortgage loan, such portion being large enough to cover each partner's anticipated share of the tax losses [or cash flow distribution]. The limited partners should be allowed to increase their bases [in their partnership interests if they are ultimately liable for the repayment of each one's portion of the mortgage loan and will acquire no rights against the general partners, the partnership and its property in the event they are actually required to repay the mortgage loan]. Moreover, a limited partner who is unwilling to become liable as a general partner may not object to this sort of "piece-meal" liability. Whether a sophisticated investor would look with favor on this approach is another question.

Avoidance of Being Taxed as "Association"

If the problem of being permitted to add the mortgage to the basis is the first hurdle that must be overcome to utilize the limited partnership effectively, the second is the avoidance of characterization as an "association" for tax purposes. The revenue code expressly provides that the term "corporation" includes an "association" which is subjected to taxation as a corporation * * *.

Treasury Regulations Sections 301.7701–2 through 301.7701–4 sets forth the criteria which govern in determining whether an organization is an association, a partnership, or a trust. While recognizing that other factors may be significant in some cases, the Regulations set forth six characteristics ordinarily found in a corporation:

(1) Associates;

(2) An objective to carry on business and divide the gain therefrom;

(3) Continuity of life;

(4) Centralization of management;

(5) Liability for corporate debts limited to corporate property;

(6) Free transferability of interests.

The Regulations then go on to state that, since the first two characteristics are possessed by both partnerships and corporations, only the last four will be considered. "An unincorporated organization shall not be classified as an association unless such organization has more corporate characteristics than non-corporate characteristics. * * * For example, if a limited partnership has centralized management and free transferability of interests, but lacks continuity of life and limited liability, and if the limited partnership has no other characteristics which are significant in determining its classification, such limited partnership is not classified as an association." [See Reg. Sec. 301.7701–2(a)(5).]

Basically then, determining whether or not a limited partnership retains its partnership status depends upon a finding that it does not possess more than two of the last four characteristics. (The proviso " * * * has no other characteristics which are significant * * * " is not defined in the Regulations, but should be kept in the back of the mind of the draftsman.)

Continuity of Life. This, of course, refers to the corporate characteristic of continuing in existence, regardless of what happens to its shareholders. The rule set forth is not entirely clear. However, this regulation concludes: "Accordingly, a general partnership subject to a statute corresponding to the Uniform Partnership Act and a limited partnership subject to a statute corresponding to the Uniform Limited Partnership Act both lack continuity of life." Thus, in a state in which the Uniform [Limited] Partnership Act applies, [and, in most instances, where the Revised Uniform Limited Partnership Act applies] the draftsmen should be careful that the partnership agreement does not purport to grant any greater continuity of life than the statute affords. * * *

Centralization of Management. What is referred to here is the corporate characteristic of being governed by a board of directors. The regulations, after stating at one point that any organization in which less than all the members have exclusive authority to make the management decisions possesses this characteristic, nevertheless conclude: "In addition, limited partnerships subject to a statute corresponding to the Uniform Limited Partnership Act, generally do not have centralized management, but centralized management does exist in such a limited partnership if substantially all the interests in the partnership are owned by the limited partner." [This same statement can be made about limited partnerships subject to the Revised Act.] Although "substantially all" is not defined in the regulations, two examples are set forth in which the regulations state centralized management does exist. In one example the general partners contributed three per cent of the capital and in the other they contributed six per cent. Since the limited partners typically contribute most of the capital in a real estate venture, this characteristic may be difficult to avoid. In any event there would seem to be nothing that can be done from a drafting standpoint to improve this situation.

Limited Liability. The regulations state that this characteristic exists if there is *no member* who is personally liable for the debts of the organization. However, if the general partner in a limited partnership has no substantial assets (other than his interest in the partnership) which could be reached by a creditor of the organization *and* is a mere dummy acting as the agent of the limited partners the limited partnership will be found to have limited liability. The Regulations expressly state that if a corporation is a general partner, it will be deemed to have personal liability if it has substantial assets, other than its partnership interest, that can be reached by the partnership's creditors. Obviously, the safe course to take here is to have at least one financially responsible general partner. * * *

Free Transferability of Interest. An organization has this characteristic, say the Regulations, if all members or those owning substantially all of the interests in it have the power, without the consent of other members, to substitute for themselves a person who is not a member of the organization.

Under the Uniform Limited Partnership Act [and the Revised Act], a limited partner has the right to assign his interest (which basically gives the assignee the right to receive the monies to which the assignor was entitled but confers no other rights) but does not have the right to make the assignee a "substituted limited partner" without the consent of all members or an express power to do so set forth in the partnership certificate. It seems clear from the language of the Regulation that this power does not constitute free transferability. A general partner has the same [limitations on the ability] to transfer his interest that he would have as a partner in a general partnership. Thus, unless some peculiar local law grants the right to transfer a general partnership interest, general partnership interests do not possess this characteristic. In any event, * * * the draftsman [might] make sure that this corporate characteristic does not exist by expressly making all partnership interests non-transferable except with unanimous consent of all members.

* * *

Structuring the Partnership Agreement

The general partner, or partners, should obviously be the real estate developer(s) who conceived the project, who will then be in a position to exercise professional management control without interference from the limited partners. To be sure, the developer will be exposed to unlimited liability, a burden not to be lightly undertaken; however, the form of organization and terms of the agreement can at least partially ameliorate this. First, * * * if the applicable corporate law poses no bar, a corporation may usually be the sole general partner. * * * Moreover, the partnership agreement can afford some relief, for example by providing that the general partners can advance funds to the partnership to meet excess construction costs or operating losses as loans, re-payable from cash flow and/or from proceeds of the sale of the project. Also, the agreement should absolve a general partner from liability to partners [for] any type [of] decisions made in good faith. * * *

The investor-limited partner, although forbidden to take part in the management of the business, may nevertheless be granted some control in the partnership agreement over those things which affect him most vitally. For example, the agreement may provide that the project may not be sold nor the mortgage refinanced, * * * without the consent of a majority or more of the limited partners.

* * *

NOTE

1. As pointed out in the above excerpt one of the attractive income tax features of the partnership form of entity is the ability of the partner to increase the basis in his or her partnership interest by the partner's share of the liabilities of the partnership.

a. For a general partner this result is authorized by Section 752(a), Reg. Sec. 1.752–1T(a)(1) and Section 705(a)(1). If personal liability is present the partner's share of the liability is the portion of the economic risk of loss for such liability that is borne by such partner. In the usual general partnership, the partner's portion of the economic risk of loss is defined by the partner's share of the losses of the partnership. See Reg. Sec. 1.752–1T(a)(1)(iii).

b. The income tax effect of this increase in basis in a partnership interest enables the partner to take advantage of partnership losses and receive tax free cash flow distributions in an amount in excess of the partner's actual contributions to the partnership. This is magnified in the typical real estate partnership since most of the financing of the partnership is generally in the form of mortgage loans.

c. The repayment of a liability is treated as a distribution of money by the partnership to the partners. See Section 752(b). The repayment will, therefore, reduce the basis of a partner in his partnership interest, see Section 705(a)(2), and if that basis has already been reduced by the distribution of losses and/or cash flow, the amount of the partner's share of any repayment which exceeds his basis in his partnership interest will result in taxable gain. See Section 731(a)(1). This result, however, might be avoided by refinancing.

d. The above discussion of the effect of partnership liabilities on the adjusted basis of a general partner in the partner's partnership interest, with respect to the "flow through" of partnership losses, assumes that the partnership liability under consideration is a recourse liability.

2. Since limited partners are not usually liable for the losses of a partnership, the advantages of an increase in basis are not available to them if personal liability is present. If, however, no partner bears the economic risk of loss—there is no personal liability with respect to a partnership loan or loans—the regulations in general permit all partners, both general and limited, to increase their bases in their partnership interests by a share of the loan or loans determined in accord with the percentages in which they share profits. See Reg. Secs. 1.752–1T(a)(2) and 1.752–1T(e). Therefore, in general, for a limited partner to be in a position to realize the full income tax benefits of the partnership entity, there should be no personal liability for the partnership's mortgage loans. See Banoff, *Tax Distinctions Between Limited and General Partners: An Operational Approach*, 35 Tax L.Rev. 1 (1979). In the case of a loan which is partially recourse and partially nonrecourse, the limited partners can add their shares of the nonrecourse portion to their bases in their partnership interests. See Reg.Sec. 1.752–1T(j)(2); Rev.Rul. 84–118, 1984–2 C.B. 120.

a. This concept is an extension of the *Crane v. Comm'r,* 331 U.S. 1, 67 S.Ct. 1047, 91 L.Ed. 1301 (1946), doctrine. The partnership will acquire a basis in real estate equal to any cash paid for it and any mortgage liability, assuming the liability does not exceed the fair market value of the real estate, incurred on its purchase and/or with respect to the construction of any improvements on it, even if there is no personal liability for the mortgage loan. The liability is included as part of the partnership's cost basis under Section 1012, see pages 368 to 373 infra. See Division III, pages 709 to 713 infra for some possible limitations on this concept. Reg. Secs. 1.752–1T(a)(2) and 1.752–1T(e) take this concept one step further and provide for an increase in the partners' bases in their partnership interests.

1. It is interesting to note that although the partnership will not acquire an increased basis on refinancing the partners will.

b. The Internal Revenue Service has attempted to limit the instances in which partners can obtain increased bases as a result of the partnership incurring nonrecourse debt. See e.g., Rev.Rul. 72–135, 1972–1 C.B. 200, holding that nonrecourse loans by a general partner to a limited partnership were not loans but, rather, a contribution to capital by the general partner. See also Ltr.Rul. 8140017. But see *Dillingham v. United States,* 48 A.F.T.R. ¶ 81–5815 (W.D.Okl.1981), which treats a nonrecourse loan made by a general partner as a liability of the partnership. See generally Montgomery, *Should Unpaid Advances by a General Partner Be Treated as Debt or as Equity?*, 2 J.Ps.Tax'n 137 (1985). The regulations provide that if a partner makes a nonrecourse loan to the partnership, the partner is considered as bearing the economic risk of loss for that loan unless the partner's interest in the partnership is 10% or less and the loan constitutes qualified nonrecourse financing within the meaning of Sec. 465(b)(6). See Reg.Sec. 1.752–1T(d)(3)(B). For an examination of the type of debts which will, and will not, be treated as liabilities for partner basis purposes, see Caruthers, *True Debt: Leveraging in Real Estate Limited Partnership Tax Shelters*, 4 J. Real Est.Tax'n 5 (1976). For example, treatment as a liability for the purpose of Section 752(a) will be denied when the principal of the debt exceeds the value of the real estate which was acquired through the use of the debt or by which the debt is secured and when the taxpayer is unable to demonstrate that the fair market value of the real estate acquired in return for the debt was at least equal to the principal amount of the debt. Cf. *Fortune Odend'hal*, 80 T.C. 588 (1983), affirmed, 748 F.2d 908 (4th Cir.1984); *Brountas v. Comm'r*, 692 F.2d 152 (1st Cir.1982); Rev. Rul. 77–110, 1977–1 C.B. 58; Rev.Rul. 77–125, 1977–1 C.B. 130. In addition, the question has been raised whether the guarantee of an otherwise nonrecourse loan by the general partner of a limited partnership causes the loan to be treated as other than nonrecourse thereby depriving the limited partners of the ability to add their shares of the loan to the bases in their limited partnership interests. The answer of the Claims Court was "no." See *Raphan v. United States*, 3 Cl.Ct. 457 (1983). The answer of the Internal Revenue Service was "yes." See Rev.Rul. 83–151, 1983–2 C.B. 105; Reg.Sec. 1.752–1T(a)(1)(ii). See generally Wallach and Heller, *Does Partner Guarantee of Nonrecourse Debt Prevent Increase in Limited Partners' Bases?* 60 J. Tax'n 206 (1984). Congress finally resolved the issue in favor of a "yes" answer by indicating in the Conference Committee Report accompanying the Tax Reform Act of 1984 that *Raphan v. United States* is not to be followed for the purposes of applying Section 752 or the regulations thereunder. See H.R.Rep. 98–861, 98th Cong., 2d Sess. (1984), pp. 868–869. In addition, subsequent to the enactment of the Tax Reform Act of 1984, the Court of Appeals for the Federal Circuit reversed the part of the decision of the Claims Court in *Raphan v. United States*, 3 Cl.Ct. 457 (1983). See *Raphan v. United States*, 759 F.2d 879 (Fed.Cir.1985). See generally Cuff, *Effect of Partner Liability for Nonrecourse Indebtedness*, 68 J. Tax'n 100 (1988).

c. Permitting a limited partner to increase the basis in his or her partnership interest by the partner's share of the nonrecourse liabilities of a limited partnership has come in for increasing criticism in recent years. The concept is not, however, without its defenders. See generally Epstein, *The Application of the Crane Doctrine to Limited Partnerships*, 45 S.Cal.L. Rev. 100 (1972); Perry, *Limited Partnerships and Tax Shelters: The Crane Rule Goes Public*, 27 Tax L.Rev. 525 (1972); Gallagher, *Fiscal Alchemy and the Crane Rule: Alternative Solutions to the Tax Shelter*, 8 Conn.L.Rev. 607 (1976); Weidner, *Realty Shelters: Nonrecourse Financing, Tax Reform, and Profit Purpose*, 32 Sw.L.J. 711 (1978); Heitner and Berg, *Losses and the Partner: Toward a Rational Basis Standard*, 3 J.Ps.Tax'n 195 (1986); Crim and Brenneman, *Channeling Partnership Losses: Constant Underpinnings and Inconsistent Interpretations*, 64 Taxes 747 (1986).

d. As indicated above, in the context of determining the deductibility of a partner's share of partnership loss, Section 465, the at-risk limitation, which applies to real estate partnerships, may limit the effects of Reg.Sec. 1.752–1T(e) and the *Crane* doctrine by requiring that a partner not only have enough basis in the partner's partnership interest, but also that the partner's "amount at risk" be equal to or greater than the partner's share of partnership loss. The at-risk concept as it applies to real estate partnerships is considered at pages 150 to 153, infra. See generally Coven, *Limiting Losses Attributable to Nonrecourse Debt: A Defense of the Traditional System Against the At–Risk Concept,* 74 Calif.L.Rev. 41 (1986); Eisenstadt and Giroux, *Real Estate Now Subject to At–Risk Rules; Rehab Credit Reduced by Tax Reform Act,* 15 Tax'n Law. 242 (1987); Maples, *Limited Partner Obligations and At–Risk Amounts: The Tax Court Speaks But Not Too Clearly,* 18 Tax Adviser 117 (1987).

3. When the liabilities of a partnership are recourse liabilities, limited partners have sought to increase the bases of their partnership interests by making commitments to contribute to partnership capital amounts equal to their shares of the recourse liabilities, by giving their personal recourse notes to the partnership, by guaranteeing or assuming the liabilities of the partnership, or a portion thereof, and by securing their liabilities under the commitments to contribute to capital, personal recourse notes, guarantees or assumptions by letters of credit. The Internal Revenue Service has, at times, challenged the increased basis in a partnership interest resulting from one or more of the techniques described above.

The questions usually faced in litigation with respect to an increased basis in a limited partnership interest purportedly derived through the use of one or more of the methods described above include the following: (1) how definite does the partner's obligation to make the contributions to capital or pay the promissory note have to be, and (2) can a guaranty or assumption of partnership recourse liabilities ever result in an increase in the basis of a partnership interest.

SIDNEY J. GEFEN v. COMMISSIONER

87 T.C. 1471 (1986).
[Some footnotes omitted]

STERRETT, Chief Judge: * * * The deficiencies resulted from respondent's determination that petitioners were not entitled to deduct losses and interest expenses attributable to an investment by petitioner Lois I. Gefen in a limited partnership. After concessions, the issues for decision [include] * * * whether petitioner Lois I. Gefen was entitled to include in her partnership basis her allocable share of partnership liabilities; and whether petitioner Lois I. Gefen was at risk within the meaning of section 465 for her allocable share of the partnership's recourse indebtedness.

Findings of Fact

* * *

The Partnership

Dartmouth Associates (the Partnership) was formed in 1976 by Integrated Resources, Inc. (Integrated), as a limited partnership under the Uniform Limited Partnership Act of the State of Connecticut. * * *

The general partners of the Partnership were IR–Oak Corporation (IR–Oak), a wholly owned subsidiary of Integrated, and Bernard Kaplan, the president of Underwriters' Service Agency, Inc., also a wholly owned subsidiary of Integrated. IR–Oak and Bernard Kaplan contributed in cash $5,060 and $506, respectively, as their capital contributions to the Partnership. Donald Olsen, the initial limited partner, contributed in cash $506 as his capital contribution to the Partnership.

In July of 1977, the Partnership acquired, and commenced the business of owning and leasing, computer equipment. * * *

Commencing in September of 1977, the Partnership distributed a confidential private placement memorandum (the Confidential Memorandum) and offered for sale to a limited number of qualified investors limited partnership interests aggregating a 98.8 percent interest in the Partnership. Pursuant to this offering, the limited partners other than the initial limited partner contributed $499,928 as their aggregate capital contribution to the Partnership.

* * *

Petitioner's Interest in the Partnership, the Limited Partner Guarantee, and Petitioner's Obligation to Make Additional Contributions to the Partnership

Petitioner Lois I. Gefen (petitioner) acquired her interest in the Partnership by paying $24,996.50 (4.94 percent of the Partnership's aggregate capital contributions) in cash to the Partnership in October of 1977. She was a limited partner in the Partnership on December 31 of each of the Partnership taxable years 1977 through 1983. At all times relevant to this proceeding, she had a 4.94 percent interest in the Partnership's capital, profits, and losses.

As a condition to her admission to the Partnership as a limited partner, petitioner was required to and did execute and deliver to the Partnership a Limited Partner Guarantee (the Guarantee). The Guarantee stated that petitioner assumed personal liability for her pro rata share (4.94 percent) of the Partnership's recourse indebtedness of $1,030,000. In pertinent part, the Guarantee reads as follows:

Dartmouth Associates
Limited Partner Guarantee

WHEREAS, the undersigned is a limited partner of Dartmouth Associates, a Connecticut limited partnership (the "Partnership") and

WHEREAS, The Partnership is personally liable under certain circumstances to Sun Life Insurance Company of America (the "Lender") for an aggregate amount of $1,030,000 (the "Recourse Amount") under the terms, and subject to the conditions and limitations, of Section 5 of a Security and Loan Agreement (the "Loan Agreement"), dated as of June 15, 1977, as amended, between the Lender and the Partnership, such Recourse Amount constituting a portion of the indebtedness of the Partnership under the Loan Agreement.

WHEREAS, each of the limited partners (the "Limited Partners") of the Partnership, as a condition to their admission as Limited Partners, are required by the Partnership personally to guaranty a pro rata portion of the Recourse Amount.

NOW, THEREFORE, in consideration of the premises and for other good and valuable consideration, receipt of which is hereby acknowledged and subject to the conditions set forth below, *the undersigned assumes personal liability for repayment of a portion of the Recourse Amount* and guarantees to the Lender as follows:

1. Subject to the provisions of, and conditions and limitations set forth in, Paragraph 4 below, Section 5 of the Loan Agreement and Section 5(c) of the Limited Partnership Agreement (the "Partnership Agreement") of the Partnership, the undersigned hereby *unconditionally guarantees to the Lender, its successors and assigns, the due and prompt collection, in accordance with the terms thereof,* of up to $101,764 of the Recourse Amount per Unit of Limited Partnership Interest in the Partnership purchased by the undersigned.

2. This undertaking shall operate as a continuing guarantee and shall remain in full force and effect until January 1, 1982. *The undersigned's obligation hereunder is not contingent upon similar undertakings by other Limited Partners.* The Lender may demand the undersigned's performance in whole or in part without regard to the undersigned's rights against co-guarantors, but in any event, the undersigned shall not be obligated for more than the product of (a) that portion of the Recourse Amount demanded by the Lender at the time of default and (b) the undersigned's percentage interest in the profits and losses of the Partnership.

*   *   *

4. *If the assets of the Partnership securing the Recourse Amount pursuant to the terms of the Loan Agreement shall not be sufficient to repay the Recourse Amount to the Lender, when due, then, and in such event, the undersigned agrees to make additional capital contributions to the Partnership, subject, as to the time and amount thereof, to the provisions of paragraphs 1 and 2 hereof and in accordance with Section 5(c) of the Partnership Agreement. The obligations of the undersigned to make additional capital contributions shall not in any way derogate from the right of the Lender to proceed to enforce this Guarantee directly against the undersigned without first proceeding against the Partnership.* It is understood and agreed that the obligation of the under-

signed hereunder and under the Partnership Agreement shall be limited to any deficiency remaining with respect to the Recourse Amount after the Lender shall have exhausted all its rights, powers and remedies under the Loan Agreement with respect to the assets of the Partnership initially securing the Recourse Amount. In addition, the aggregate of the amount of additional capital contributions the undersigned shall be obligated to make and any amounts paid by the undersigned hereunder directly to the Lender shall in no event exceed the undersigned's proportionate share of the Recourse Amount based upon the undersigned's share of profits and losses in the Partnership.

*   *   *

*   *   *

6. The undersigned hereby authorizes the General Partners of the Partnership to act for and on behalf of the undersigned in all dealings with the Lender and co-guarantors and acknowledges that the General Partners of the Partnership may act for the Lender or co-guarantors in enforcing the obligations of the undersigned. In the event the undersigned defaults in the payment of his obligations hereunder, the General Partners may institute legal action to enforce such payment, and the undersigned hereby pledges to the General Partners his right to all Partnership distributions after the date of such default as security for payment of his obligations hereunder.

*   *   * [Emphasis added.]

Petitioner also was obligated under Section 5(c) of the Amended and Restated Limited Partnership Agreement (the Limited Partnership Agreement) to make a Special Contribution to the Partnership under certain circumstances. Section 5(c) of the Limited Partnership Agreement reads as follows:

(c) The Special Contribution of each Partner signatory to the counterpart of this Agreement shall be as specified in the Schedule of Partners' Contributions attached to this counterpart and shall be made by each such Partner pursuant to special calls therefor made on or before January 1, 1982 by the General Partner, such calls not to exceed, in any event, an aggregate amount equal to the product of such Partners's [sic] Distribution Percentage and $1,030,000. All Special Contributions by a Limited Partner shall be subject to the conditions and limitations of, and shall be in accordance with, the provisions of a certain Limited Partner Guarantee executed by such Limited Partner and a certain Security and Loan Agreement, dated as of June 15, 1977, between the Partnership and Sun Life Insurance Company of America, as amended.

*   *   *

Under the terms of the Limited Partnership Agreement, petitioner had no right to reimbursement from either the Partnership or the general partners for amounts paid by her to the Partnership as a Special Contribution or to Sun Life pursuant to the limited partner Guarantee. Section 6(f) of the Limited Partnership Agreement provided that limited partners had no right to withdraw or reduce their Special Contributions to the Partnership once made, and Section 7(d) of the Limited Partnership Agreement provided that the general partners were not liable to the limited partners for any loss or liability incurred in connection with any matter, except for losses or liabilities attributable to the willful misconduct or gross negligence of a general partner.

* * *

Opinion

We must decide whether petitioner is entitled to deduct her distributive share of Partnership losses and interest expenses for the years in question. Petitioner bears the burden of proof with respect to the original deficiencies and respondent bears the burden of proof with respect to the increased deficiencies in the amended answer. Rule 142(a); *Welch v. Helvering*, 290 U.S. 111, 115 (1933); *Reiff v. Commissioner*, 77 T.C. 1169, 1173 (1981).

* * *

Petitioner * * * asserts that she was entitled to include in her basis in her Partnership interest her allocable share (4.94 percent) of the Partnership's recourse and nonrecourse liabilities and that she was at risk within the meaning of section 465 for an amount sufficient to permit her to deduct her distributive share of Partnership losses and interest expenses for each of the years in question. For the reasons set forth below, we find for petitioner.

* * *

Basis

Respondent * * * argues that petitioner's basis in her Partnership interest is limited to her cash contribution to the Partnership, and that petitioner therefore is limited to that extent in the amount of her distributive share she can deduct. [W]e disagree.

Section 752(a) provides:

Any increase in a partner's share of the liabilities of a partnership, or any increase in a partner's individual liabilities by reason of the assumption by such partner of partnership liabilities, shall be considered as a contribution of money by such partner to the partnership.

Section 722 provides that a contribution of money by a partner to the partnership increases the partner's basis in the partnership.

Section 752(c) provides:

For purposes of this section, a liability to which property is subject shall, to the extent of the fair market value of such property, be considered as a liability of the owner of the property.

* * *

Petitioner had a 4.94 percent interest in the capital, profits, and losses of the Partnership at all relevant times since she became a partner in October of 1977. The Partnership's indebtedness was genuine. Petitioner assumed personal liability for her pro rata share (4.94 percent) of the Partnership's recourse indebtedness pursuant to the Limited Partner Guarantee, and she was obligated under the Limited Partnership Agreement to make a Special Contribution to the Partnership in an amount not greater than $50,882.[34] Moreover, under the terms of the Limited Partnership Agreement, petitioner had no right to reimbursement from either the Partnership or the general partners for amounts paid by her to the Partnership as a Special Contribution or to Sun Life pursuant to the Limited Partner Guarantee.[35] Petitioner was therefore not a mere guarantor of her pro rata share of the Partnership's recourse indebtedness, but was ultimately liable for it, because there was no primary obligor against whom she had a remedy to recover amounts paid by her to the Partnership as a Special Contribution or to Sun Life pursuant to the Limited Partner Guarantee. See *Abramson v. Commissioner*, 86 T.C. 360, 366 n. 10 (1986); *Smith v. Commissioner*, 84 T.C. 889, 908 (1985); *Brand v. Commissioner*, 81 T.C. 821, 828 (1983).

Under these circumstances * * * petitioner [is entitled] to include in her basis in her Partnership interest her allocable share (4.94 percent) of the Partnership's recourse and nonrecourse liabilities.[36]

At Risk Issue

Respondent's final contention is that petitioner was not "at risk" within the meaning of section 465 for any amount in excess of her cash contribution to the Partnership during any of the years in question. In

---

34. Under the terms of the Limited Partner Guarantee and the Limited Partnership Agreement, petitioner was personally liable for the repayment of her pro rata share of the Partnership's recourse indebtedness to Sun Life in two ways: first, if the Partnership defaulted on its obligation to Sun Life, and if Sun Life brought an action against the Partnership to enforce the obligation, petitioner would be required by the Partnership, pursuant to Section 5(c) of the Limited Partnership Agreement, to make her Special Contribution to the Partnership of up to $50,882 (which amount would then be applied by the Partnership to the debt owed to Sun Life); in the alternative, if Sun Life chose not to proceed against the Partnership for repayment of the debt, Sun Life could proceed directly against petitioner, pursuant to the terms of the Limited Partner Guarantee, and require her to pay up to $50,882, her pro rata share (4.94 percent) of the Partnership's recourse indebtedness.

35. Section 6(f) of the Limited Partnership Agreement expressly provided that limited partners had no right to withdraw or reduce their Special Contributions to the Partnership once made, and Section 7(d) of the Limited Partnership Agreement provided that the general partners were not liable to the limited partners for any loss or liability incurred in connection with any matter, except for losses or liabilities attributable to the willful misconduct or gross negligence of a general partner.

36. Respondent argues, however, that in *Brown v. Commissioner*, T.C. Memo. 1980–267, affd. without published opinion 698 F.2d 1228 (9th Cir.1982), and *Block v. Commissioner*, T.C. Memo. 1980–554, we held that a direct assumption by a limited partner of partnership recourse indebtedness does not entitle the limited partner to increase his basis in his partnership interest. Those cases are distinguishable from this case, however, because neither of them involved, as this case does, a direct assumption by a limited partner of partnership recourse indebtedness coupled with an obligation under the partnership agreement to make additional capital contributions to the partnership.

support of this contention, respondent argues that (1) under the Limited Partner Guarantee, petitioner was a mere guarantor and not ultimately liable for her pro rata share of the Partnership's recourse indebtedness, and (2) petitioner was protected against the loss of any amount in excess of her cash contribution to the Partnership by the Lloyd's of London insurance policy [insuring that the leased equipment had residual value] and [the ultimate lessee's] credit rating. For the reasons set forth below, we hold for petitioner on this issue.

Section 465(a) provides that in the case of certain taxpayers engaged in an activity to which section 465 applies, losses from the activity for a taxable year will be allowed up to the aggregate amount that the taxpayer is "at risk" for such activity at the close of such taxable year. Section 465(b)(1) provides that a taxpayer is at risk for money contributed to the activity, and section 465(b)(2) provides that a taxpayer is at risk for amounts borrowed for use in the activity to the extent that the taxpayer is personally liable for the repayment of such amounts. However, section 465(b)(4) provides that "a taxpayer shall not be considered at risk with respect to amounts protected against loss through nonrecourse financing, guarantees, stop loss agreements, or other similar arrangements." Petitioner concedes that section 465 applies to her investment in the Partnership.

Petitioner entered into legally enforceable contracts that made her personally liable for her pro rata share of certain Partnership indebtedness that was incurred and used by the Partnership to acquire the Computer Equipment. These agreements consist of the Limited Partner Guarantee and the Limited Partnership Agreement, and they were executed by petitioner in October of 1977. Under the Limited Partner Guarantee, petitioner assumed direct liability to Sun Life for her pro rata share of the Partnership's recourse indebtedness, and she consented to be sued directly by Sun Life for the portion of the indebtedness she assumed, regardless whether Sun Life first proceeded against the Partnership. In the event Sun Life proceeded against the Partnership for the recourse indebtedness, however, petitioner was obligated under the Limited Partnership Agreement to make a Special Contribution to the Partnership in an amount sufficient to pay her pro rata share of the indebtedness, and she had no right to reimbursement for any amounts paid by her to Sun Life pursuant to the Limited Partner Guarantee or to the Partnership as a Special Contribution.[37] As a result, contrary to respondent's assertion, petitioner was not a mere guarantor of her pro rata portion of the Partnership's recourse indebtedness, but was ultimately liable for it, because there was no primary obligor against whom she had a remedy to recover amounts paid by her to Sun Life pursuant to the Limited Partner Guarantee or to the Partnership as a Special Contribution. See *Abramson v. Commissioner*, supra at 366 n. 10; *Smith v. Commissioner*, supra at 908; *Brand v. Commissioner*, supra at 828. Petitioner was therefore at risk within

37. See notes 34 and 35, *supra*.

the meaning of section 465 for the full amount of her pro rata share of the Partnership's recourse indebtedness to Sun Life. See *Abramson v. Commissioner, supra* at 375–376.[38]

Respondent argues, however, that because [the ultimate lessee of the equipment] was a strong credit risk and not likely to default on its lease obligations during the years in question, petitioner was protected against loss and was therefore not at risk within the meaning of section 465 for her pro rata share of the Partnership's recourse indebtedness. We reject this argument because we perceive nothing in section 465 or its legislative history that requires an owner of property to enter into a transaction with a party that is a poor credit risk in order to be "at risk" within the meaning of section 465.

We also reject respondent's assertion that petition[er] was protected against loss by the Lloyd's of London insurance policy. The insured period under the Lloyd's policy did not commence until August 1, 1980, and the policy therefore provided no protection against loss for anyone during the years in question.

Petitioner entered into legally enforceable contracts that made her personally and ultimately liable for her pro rata share of the Partnership's recourse indebtedness to Sun Life. The Partnership incurred its recourse indebtedness to Sun Life for the purpose of acquiring the Computer Equipment, and petitioner was not protected against loss with respect to her share of this indebtedness. Consequently, petitioner was at risk within the meaning of section 465 for her proportionate share ($50,882) of the Partnership's recourse indebtedness to Sun Life.[39]

38. "A limited partner who assumes personal liability on a loan to the partnership (made by a bank or other lender), but who obtains the general partner's agreement to indemnify him against some or all of any loss arising under such personal liability, is at risk only with respect to the excess of the amount of the indebtedness over the maximum amount covered by the indemnity agreement." S.Rept. No. 94–938 (1976), 1976–3 C.B. (Vol. 3) 49, 87 n. 5. It follows that a limited partner such as petitioner, who assumed personal liability on a loan to the Partnership, which was made by a bank or other lender, and who had no agreement with anyone to indemnify her against any loss arising with respect to such liability, was at risk for the full amount of the indebtedness. Not only did petitioner not have an agreement with the general partners to indemnify her against loss arising under the Limited Partner Guarantee, but, as already noted, the Limited Partnership Agreement expressly provided that the general partners were not liable to the limited partners for any loss or liability incurred in connection with any matter, except for losses or liabilities attributable to the willful misconduct or gross negligence of a general partner.

39. As a result of petitioner's cash contribution to the Partnership and her assumption of her pro rata share of the partnership's recourse indebtedness, petitioner was at risk in the partnership's leasing activity at the close of each of the taxable years in question for an amount sufficient to permit her to deduct all of the claimed losses and interest expenses.

| | December 31, | | |
	1977	1978	1979
Amount at risk	$75,878.50*	$54,986.50**	$27,254.50**
Claimed losses and interest expenses	20,892.00	27,732.00	11,121.00
Excess amount at risk	$54,986.50	$27,254.50	$16,133.50

* Cash contribution of $24,996.50 plus proportionate share of recourse indebtedness, $50,882.

** Amount at risk as of end of immediately preceding taxable year, reduced by losses claimed by petitioners with respect to immediately preceding taxable year. See sec. 465(b)(5).

NOTE

1. Was Mrs. Gefen permitted to increase her basis in her partnership interest by her share of the partnership's recourse liability because she was "obligated to make [a contribution in that amount] under the partnership agreement" or because her guaranty of her share of the recourse liability amounted to an "increase in [her] individual liabilities by reason of the assumption [of her share] of partnership [recourse] liabilities"?

    a. The Tax Court in footnote 36 appears to indicate that the increased basis resulted from the combination of the reasons stated above. But, are not each of the reasons stated above an independent justification for an increase in the basis of a partnership interest, each of which should stand or fall on its own account? What does her agreement to contribute to the partnership an amount equal to her share of the recourse liability have to do with her guaranty of her share of the recourse liability?

    b. If Mrs. Gefen was called upon to contribute to the partnership an amount equal to her share of the recourse liability might she also have been called upon to honor her guaranty? Might one say that the combination of the agreement to contribute and the guaranty provided assurance to the court that no matter whether the lender, on the partnership's default in payment of the loan, looked directly to the guarantors or looked first to the assets of the partnership, assuming the assets of the partnership prior to the limited partners' capital contributions were not enough to pay the remaining amount due on the loan, that Mrs. Gefen would be obligated to pay an amount which, at the minimum, was equal to her share of the difference between the remaining amount due on the loan and the value of partnership assets? But, would not this state of facts be ultimately true if she were just a guarantor or had just made the agreement to contribute? Possibly not, since if the lender had first looked to the partnership it might have collected the difference between the amount remaining due on the loan and the value of the assets of the partnership from the general partners and, as a result, Mrs. Gefen would owe nothing as a guarantor. On the other hand, if she and the other limited partners had only agreed to make the special contributions, the lender would have had to look to the assets of the partnership for payment which probably would have required foreclosure and the lender may have conditioned the availability of the loan on it having the ability to simply look to the guarantors for payment.

    c. Regardless of the purpose of combining the guaranty with the agreement to contribute, if Mrs. Gefen had been required to pay some amount under either status, would she ultimately have been out of pocket, at the minimum, an amount equal to her share of the difference between the amount remaining due on the loan at the time of default and the value of the assets of the partnership, with no right to reimbursement from the partnership or the other partners? Is this the fact which substantively distinguishes this case from *Brown v. Comm'r,* 75 T.C. 172 (1980), and *Block v. Comm'r,* 41 CCH Tax Ct.Mem. 546 (1980)? It appears that Mrs. Gefen had the ultimate liability for payment of a portion of the indebtedness to the Sun Life Insurance Company. This was not true in either *Brown v. Comm'r,* supra or *Block v. Comm'r,* supra. In both of those cases the taxpayer, as a guarantor of the partnership's indebtedness, would have been subrogated, on payment of the guarantee, to the rights of the creditor against the partnership. See Bobrow and Boyle, *Section 752 and Limited*

Partners: The "Ultimate Liability" Doctrine as Applied to Partnership Recourse Indebtedness, 4 J.Ps.Tax'n 172 (1987); Priv. Ltr. Rul. 8702006. Cf. *Pritchett v. Comm'r,* 827 F.2d 644 (9th Cir.1987), reversing 85 T.C. 580 (1985).

d.   If the partnership made all of the payments due prior to January 1, 1982 on the liability to Sun Life, would the additional basis which Mrs. Gefen obtained in her partnership interest ever have actually cost her anything? If not, is the additional basis "free" basis? While limited partners may assume or guarantee partnership recourse liabilities and agree to make additional contributions to a partnership for the primary purpose of acquiring additional bases in their partnership interests, it is well to remember that if the partnership does not pay the liabilities, the limited partners may be required to. See *F.D.I.C. v. Van Laanen,* 769 F.2d 666 (10th Cir.1985). On the other hand, since a limited partner's liability may be limited to the amount necessary to produce enough basis to permit the partner to take personal advantage of the partner's share of partnership losses, the limited nature of the liability may present enforcement problems to the creditor. Cf. Barnett, *Limited Guarantees: Variations, Limitations, and Lamentations,* 104 Banking L.J. 244 (1987).

2.   It appears that limited partners are not entitled to increase their bases in their partnership interests if they simply guarantee recourse liabilities of the partnership. See *Richard C. Brown,* 40 CCH Tax Ct.Mem. 725 (1980); *Danoff v. United States,* 499 F.Supp. 20 (M.D.Penn.1979); Priv.Ltr.Rul. 8504005. Cf. *Hugh M. Brand,* 81 T.C. 821 (1983); Note, *The Tax Treatment of a Partner's Contingent Liability,* 6 Va.Tax Rev. 221 (1986). They may, however, be able to increase their bases if they guarantee or assume nonrecourse liabilities of the partnership. See *George F. Smith, Jr.,* 84 T.C. 889 (1985), and *Edwin D. Abramson,* 86 T.C. 360 (1986). Cf. Priv. Ltr. Ruls. 8636003 and 8636004.

3.   The Internal Revenue Service has issued temporary regulations under Section 752 which are consistent with the holding of the Tax Court in *Sidney J. Gefen v. Comm'r,* supra, pages 77 to 84.

a.   The temporary regulations provide that partners, including limited partners, can add their shares of the nonrecourse liabilities of the partnership to their bases in their partnership interests. The partners' shares of nonrecourse liabilities are determined, in general, in accordance with their interests in partnership profits. See Reg. Sec. 1.752–1T(e).

1.   The partners' interests in partnership profits, for the purpose of determining their shares of the nonrecourse liabilities of the partnership, include their shares of minimum gain, see page 48, and their shares of gain which would be allocated under Sec. 704(c), see page 31, or, in the same manner as under Sec. 704(c), on revaluation of partnership property. See Reg. Sec. 1.752–1T(e)(1).

2.   If more than a 10% partner makes a no personal liability loan to a partnership, the full amount of the loan is allocated to the lending partner. See Reg. Sec. 1.752–1T(d)(3)(i)(B).

b.   The partners' shares of the recourse liabilities of the partnership, however, are equal to the portions, if any, of the economic risk of loss for the recourse liabilities that are borne by each of the partners. See Reg. Sec. 1.752–1T(d).

1.   A partner bears the economic risk of loss for a partnership liability to the extent the partner would bear (without right of reim-

bursement) the economic burden of discharging the obligation represented by the liability (by a payment to a creditor or a contribution to the partnership) if the partnership was unable to do so. See Reg. Secs. 1.752–1T(a)(1)(ii) and (iii) and 1.752–1T(a)(3).

2. Therefore, a limited partner in the position of Mrs. Gefen in *Sidney J. Gefen v. Comm'r*, supra, pages 77 to 84, can add her share of the partnership's recourse liability to her basis in her partnership interest. In addition, a general partner in a limited partnership in which the limited partners bear none of the economic risk of loss for a partnership recourse liability can add 100% of that liability to the basis in the general partner's partnership interest.

c. A partnership liability is a recourse liability to the extent that any partner bears the economic risk of loss for that liability. See Reg. Sec. 1.752–1T(a)(1)(i). If no partner bears the economic risk of loss for a partnership liability, the liability is a nonrecourse liability of the partnership. See Reg. Sec. 1.752–1T(a)(2)(i).

d. An economic risk of loss is an obligation to make a payment to a creditor or a contribution to a partnership (without right of reimbursement) in order to discharge a liability of a partnership if the partnership is unable to do so. See Reg. Sec. 1.752–1T(d)(3).

4. See generally Katz, *Inclusion of Liabilities in the Basis of a Partnership Interest and Related Issues*, 41 N.Y.U.Inst.Fed.Tax'n 13–1 (1983); Volet and Millman, *Liability Assumption Under Section 752: An Analysis of the Underlying Theory*, 60 J.Tax'n 374 (1984); Winston, *Basis and At–Risk Consequences of a Partner's Assumption of Partnership Debt*, 2 J.Tax'n Inv. 15 (1984); Levine, *Structuring Real Estate Loans to Preserve Investors' Tax Benefits (Part 1)*, 1 # 5 Prac.Real Est.Law. 55 (1985); *(Part 2)*, 1 # 6 Prac.Real Est.Law. 75 (1985); Postlewaite and Bialosky, *Liabilities in the Partnership Context—Policy Concerns and the Forthcoming Regulations*, 33 UCLA L.Rev. 733 (1986); Heitner and Berg, *Losses and the Partner: Toward a Rational Basis Standard*, 3 J.Ps.Tax'n 195 (1986); Maples, *Limited Partner Obligations and At–Risk Amounts: The Tax Court Speaks But Not Too Clearly*, 18 Tax Adviser 117 (1987); Schmalz, *The Effect of Partnership Liabilities on Basis, At–Risk Amounts, and Capital Accounts*, 5 J.Ps.Tax'n 291 (1989).

REVENUE PROCEDURE 89–12

1989–7 Internal Rev.Bull. 22

Section 1. Purpose

.01 This revenue procedure specifies the conditions under which the Internal Revenue Service will consider a ruling request that relates to classification of an organization, for federal tax purposes, as a partnership. * * *

.02 Organizations covered by this revenue procedure include both those formed as partnerships and other organizations seeking partnership classification. * * *

Any reference to a "limited partnership" includes an organization formed as a limited partnership under applicable states law and any other organization formed under a law that limits the liability of any member for the organization's debts and other obligations to a determinable fixed amount. References to "general partners" and "limited partners" apply also to comparable members of an organization not designated as a partnership under controlling law and documents: the "general partners" of such an organization will ordinarily be those with significant management authority relative to the other members. * * *

.03 The provisions of this revenue procedure are not intended to be substantive rules for the determination of partner and partnership status and are not to be applied upon audit of taxpayers' returns.

* * *

Sec. 2. Background

.01 Section 7701(a)(2) of the Code defines the term "partnership" to include a syndicate, group, pool, joint venture, or other unincorporated organization, through or by means of which any business, financial operation, or venture is carried on, and which is not, within the meaning of the Code, a trust or estate or a corporation. Sections 301.7701–2 and 301.7701–3 of the Procedure and Administration Regulations set forth rules for determining whether an organization is classified, for federal tax purposes, as a partnership or as an association taxable as a corporation.

* * *

Sec. 3. Information to be Submitted

* * *

.03 Required General Information * * *

(9) A description of the relationships, direct and indirect, between the limited partners and the general partners that suggest that the general partners, individually or in the aggregate, may not at all times act independently (because of individual or aggregate limited partner influence or control).

Such relationships include: (a) ownership by limited partners of 5 percent or more of the stock or other beneficial interests in a general partner; (b) control by limited partners of 5 percent or more of the voting power in a general partner; (c) ownership of 5 percent or more of the stock or other beneficial interests in any general partner and in any limited partner by the same person or persons acting as a group; and (d) control of 5 percent or more of the voting power in any general partner and in any limited partner by the same person or persons acting as a group. For purposes of the preceding sentence, a person shall be considered to own any beneficial interest owned by a related person and shall be considered to control any voting power controlled by a related person; a person shall be treated as related to another person if they bear a relationship specified in section 267(b) or section 707(b)(1) of the Code. The relationships defined in the first sentence of this section 3.03(9) may also include a debtor-creditor relationship and an employer-employee relationship.

(10) A representation of the net worth (based on assets at current fair market value) of each general partner, excluding interests in the

partnership, a description of all general partner assets and liabilities arising from transactions with the partnership or with a person related to any general partner under section 267(b) or section 707(b)(1) of the Code, and a description of all other partnerships in which any of the general partners has an interest.

* * *

Sec. 4. Provisions Applicable to Limited Partnerships

The Service will ordinarily consider a ruling request that relates to classification of a limited partnership as a partnership, for federal tax purposes, only if the conditions in this section 4 are satisfied. Section 4.05, however, relates solely to the corporate characteristic of continuity of life described in section 301.7701–2(b) of the regulations. Similarly, section 4.06 relates solely to the corporate characteristic of centralization of management described in section 301.7701–2(c). Therefore, failure to satisfy section 4.05 or section 4.06 will preclude a specific ruling that continuity of life or centralized management is lacking, but will not necessarily preclude the issuance of a partnership classification ruling. Section 4.07 provides a safe harbor, generally applicable to a limited partnership with at least one corporate general partner, that relates to the corporate characteristic of limited liability described in section 301.7701–2(d).

.01 Unless exempted by section 4.02 below or the provisions of this section 4.01, the interests (including limited partnership interests) of all the general partners, taken together, in each material item of partnership income, gain, loss, deduction, or credit must be equal to at least 1 percent of each such item at all times during the existence of the partnership, and the partnership agreement must expressly so provide. If the 1-percent standard will not be satisfied because of a temporary allocation required under section 704(b) of the Code, section 704(c), or corresponding Income Tax Regulations (a qualified income offset or minimum gain chargeback, for example), this will generally not be considered a violation of this section 4.01, but the ruling request must describe any such allocation and explain why the allocation is required under section 704(b) or (c), as appropriate. Any other temporary nonconformance with the 1-percent standard will be considered a violation of this section 4.01 unless it is demonstrated that the general partners' interest in net profits and losses over the anticipated life of the partnership is material. For this purpose, a profits interest generally will not be considered material unless it is substantially in excess of 1 percent and will be in effect for a substantial period of time during which it is reasonably expected that the partnership will generate profits. For example, a 20-percent interest in profits that begins 4 years after partnership formation and continues for the life of the partnership would generally be considered material if the partnership is expected to generate profits for a substantial period beyond the 4 years.

.02 If the limited partnership has total contributions exceeding $50 million, the general partners need not meet the 1-percent standard in section 4.01. However, except for a temporary allocation or nonconformance specified in section 4.01, the general partners' aggregate interest at all times in each material item must be at least 1 percent divided by the ratio of total contributions to $50 million, and the partnership agreement must expressly incorporate at least the computed percentage. For example, if total contributions are $125 million, the interest in each material item must be at least .4 percent, that is, 1 percent divided by 125/50. In no event, however, other than as a result of a temporary allocation or nonconformance specified in section 4.01, may the general partners' aggregate interest at any time in any material item be less than .2 percent.

.03 Unless section 4.04 applies, the general partners, taken together, must maintain a minimum capital account balance equal to either 1 percent of total positive capital account balances for the partnership or $500,000, whichever is less. Whenever a limited partner makes a capital contribution, the general partners must be obligated to contribute immediately capital equal to 1.01 percent of the limited partner's capital contribution or a lesser amount (including zero) that causes the sum of the general partners' capital account balances to equal the lesser of 1 percent of total positive capital account balances for the partnership or $500,000. If no limited partner capital account has a positive balance, the general partners, taken together, need not have a positive capital account balance to satisfy this section 4.03: Capital accounts and the value of contributions are determined by application of the capital accounting rules in section 1.704–1(b)(2)(iv) of the regulations.

.04 If at least one general partner has contributed or will contribute substantial services in its capacity as a partner, apart from services for which guaranteed payments under section 707(c) of the Code are made, then the general partners need not meet the capital account standard in section 4.03. However, the partnership agreement must expressly provide that, upon the dissolution and termination of the partnership, the general partners will contribute to the partnership an amount equal to: (a) the deficit balances, if any, in their capital accounts; or (b) the excess of 1.01 percent of the total capital contributions of the limited partners over the capital previously contributed by the general partners; or (c) the lesser of (a) or (b). Those services that do not relate to day-to-day operations in the partnership's primary business activity, such as services relating to organization and syndication of the partnership, accounting, financial planning, and general business planning, and those that are in the nature of investment management will be closely scrutinized to determine if they are in fact substantial services. In making this determination, the Service will consider the nature of the partnership and its activities.

.05 For a limited partnership formed in a state with a statute corresponding to the Uniform Limited Partnership Act or the Revised Uniform Limited Partnership Act, in the case of the removal of a general partner, the partnership agreement may not permit less than a majority in interest of limited partners to elect a new general partner to continue the partnership or the Service will not rule that the partnership lacks continuity of life.

.06 Limited partner interests, excluding those held by general partners, may not exceed 80 percent of the total interests in the partnership, or the Service will not rule that the partnership lacks centralized management. In addition, the Service will consider all the facts and circumstances, including limited partner control of the general partners (whether direct or indirect, in determining whether the partnership lacks centralized management.

.07 If the net worth of corporate general partners at the time of the ruling request equals at least 10 percent of the total contributions to the limited partnership and is expected to continue to equal at least 10 percent of the total contributions throughout the life of the partnership, then, for advance ruling purposes, the partnership will generally be deemed to lack limited liability. In the case of a limited partnership in which the only general partners are corporations that do not satisfy the safe harbor described in the preceding sentence, close scrutiny will be applied to determine whether the partnership lacks limited liability. In that connection, it must be demonstrated either that a general partner has (or the general partners collectively have) substantial assets (other than the partner's interest in the partnership) that could be reached by a creditor of the partnership or that the general partner individually and collectively will act independently of the limited partners.

NOTE

1. Why was the foregoing issued as a Revenue Procedure rather than as a Revenue Ruling? Provision 1.03 indicates that the rules contained in Rev.Proc. 89–12 are not intended to be substantive nor are they to be applied on audit of returns. Yet, if the structure of a limited partnership complies with the rules set out in provisions 4.01 to 4.07 and the limited partnership was formed in a state with a statute corresponding to the Uniform Limited Partnership Act or the Revised Uniform Limited Partnership Act, is there a significant chance that the limited partnership will be found to possess the corporate characteristic of centralized management or limited liability or continuity of life? One can expect many limited partnerships, especially those seeking public investors, to comply with Rev.Proc. 89–12 since the stakes involved in the failure to achieve partnership treatment are much too high to be left to chance.

2. The rules contained in provisions 4.01 4.02, 4.03 and 4.04 in general require that the general partner have at least a one percent interest in each item of partnership income, gain, loss, deduction or credit and have a one percent or $500,000, whichever is the lesser, interest in capital. It might be said that these requirements affect the determination whether centralized management is present since, lacking such an interest, the general partner might be said to be acting as a representative of the limited partners similar to the position of the board of directors of a corporation. See Reg.Sec. 301.7701–2(c)(4).

3. It is possible that a limited partnership can be treated, for tax purposes, as a partnership, even if it does not comply with the rules contained in Rev. Proc. 89–12?

a. Can the corporate attribute of centralized management be avoided if the limited partners directly or indirectly, individually or in the aggregate, own more than 80% of the interests in the limited partnership or more than 20% of the interests in the general partner or any affiliates? See Rev.Proc. 72–13, 1972–1 C.B. 735.

1. If so, how much more? Can the limited partners' interests in the partnership ever exceed 99%? If the limited partners controlled more than 50% of the interests in the general partner, might there be concerns with respect to participation in control under the U.L.P.A. or the Revised U.L.P.A.? See pages 117 to 125, infra.

b. Can the corporate attribute of limited liability be avoided if the net worth of a corporate general partner is less than the amount specified in Rev.Proc. 89–12?

1. If so, how much less? At what point can it be said that a corporate general partner is inadequately capitalized or is a "sham" for state law purposes?

4. Rev.Proc. 89–12 takes the position that the net worth of a corporate general partner is to be determined without taking into account the value of its interests in the limited partnership.

a. What is the rationale for excluding, in the computation of corporate net worth for the purpose of determining whether the corporation meets the test set out in provision 4.07 of Rev.Proc. 89–12, the fair market value of the corporation's interests in the limited partnership?

5. See generally with respect to the classification problem Fox and Wilson, *Treasury Restrictions Concerning the Tax Classification of Business Entities: Recent Developments,* 1 J.Corp.Tax'n 28 (1974); Sexton, *Qualifying as a Partnership for Tax Purposes,* 32 N.Y.U.Inst.Fed.Tax'n 1447 (1974); Hyman and Hoffman, *Partnerships and "Associations": A Policy Critique of the Morrissey Regulations,* 3 J.Real.Est.Tax'n 377 (1976); Fisher, *Classification Under Section 7701—The Past, Present, and Prospects for the Future,* 30 Tax Law. 627 (1977); Peel, *Definitions of a Partnership: New Suggestions on an Old Issue,* 1979 Wis.L.Rev. 989; Hecker, *The Tax Classification of Limited Partnerships Revisited,* 88 Com.L.J. 537 (1983); Lee, *Entity Classification and Integration: Publicly Traded Partnerships, Personal Service Corporations and the Tax Legislative Process,* 8 Va.Tax Rev. 57 (1988). With respect to the classification of a limited partnership with a corporate general partner see generally Weiler, *Limited Partnerships with Corporate General Partners: Beyond Rev.Proc. 72–13,* 36 J.Tax'n 306 (1972); Fraser, *Taxing the Limited Partnership as a Corporation,* 50 Taxes 333 (1972); Welter, *Limited Partnerships with a Corporate General Partner—Rev.Proc. 72–13,* 3 Tax Adviser 329 (1972). But see *Curtis W. Kingbay,* 46 T.C. 147 (1966), in which the Internal Revenue Service and the Tax Court treated as a partnership a limited partnership with a sole corporate general partner which had made a nominal investment in the partnership and was 100% owned and controlled by the limited partners.

Sections 301.7701–2(a) and (c) of the regulations treat the Revised Uniform Limited Partnership Act as a statute corresponding to the Uniform Limited Partnership Act. Therefore, a limited partnership formed pursuant to the Revised Act, in most cases, will be classified as a partnership for income tax purposes. The regulations, however, warn that the ability of limited partners to remove a general partner, under certain circumstances, may result in the attribute of centralized management being present. If, however, the right of removal is substantially restricted, i.e., removal for gross negligence or self-dealing, the right of removal will not result in centralized management being present. See generally Banoff, *Can Tax Practitioners Support the Revised ULPA?*, 60 Taxes 97 (1982).

6. Section 7704 of the Internal Revenue Code treats certain publicly traded partnerships as corporations for income tax purposes. Publicly traded partnerships are partnerships in which the interests are (a) traded on an established securities market or (b) readily tradeable on a secondary market. Publicly traded partnerships will be treated as corporations unless ninety percent or more of partnership income is passive-type income. For the purposes of Section 7704 only, passive-type income includes: (a) Interest or dividends; (b) Certain rents from real property; (c) Gain from the sale or other disposition of real property; (d) Income and gains from specified natural resource activities; (e) Any gain from the sale or other disposition of a capital or Section 1231(b) asset held for the production of income as described in (a) through (d) above; and (f) Income and gains from certain activities involving commodities. Section 7704 does not, until the first tax year beginning after December 31, 1997, apply to partnerships which were in existence on December 17, 1987.

The Internal Revenue Service has excluded from treatment as a publicly traded partnership any "private placement" partnership. If all the interests in a partnership were issued in a transaction (or transactions) which was not registered under the Securities Act of 1933 and either the partnership does not have more than 500 partners or the initial offering price of a unit of partnership interest is at least $20,000 and the partnership agreement provides that no unit of partnership interest may be subdivided for resale into a smaller unit worth less than $20,000, the partnership is a private placement partnership. In addition, if the sum of percentage interests in partnership capital or profits sold or disposed of during the taxable year does not exceed 5%, in some circumstances, and 2%, in other circumstances, of the total interests in partnership capital or profits, the partnership will not be treated as a publicly traded partnership. See Notice 88–75, 1988–27 I.R.B. 29. See Haney and Holmes, *Publicly Traded Partnerships After the Revenue Act of 1987*, 66 Taxes 331 (1988); Reir, *Section 7704—Another Nail in the Tax Shelter Coffin*, 17 Real Est. L.J. 67 (1988); Banoff, *Avoiding Publicly Traded Partnership Status: Living and Dying with Notice 88–75*, 66 Taxes 561 (1988).

7. See generally Kanter, *Real Estate Tax Shelters*, 51 Taxes 770 (1973); McGuire, *Limited Partnerships: Steps That Can Be Taken To Overcome Problems in the Area*, 34 J.Tax'n 235 (1971); Ben–Horin, *Real Estate Syndications, Limited Partnerships*, 24 U.S.Cal.Tax Inst. 71 (1972); Weidner, *Realty Shelter Partnerships in a Nutshell*, 8 Ind.L.Rev. 899 (1975); Coleman and Weatherbie, *Special Problems in Limited Partnership Planning*, 30 Sw.L.J. 887 (1976); Rhodes, *Real Estate Limited Partnerships: Selected Tax Considerations*, 72 Nw. U.L.Rev. 346 (1977); Warren, *The Requirement of Economic Profit in Tax Motivated Transactions*, 59 Taxes 985 (1981).

c. THE CORPORATE FORM

If the considerations taken into account in making the choice of an entity for the acquisition, development and operation of real estate were limited to nontax considerations, it might be asserted with substantial justification that the preferred entity is a corporation. "The concept of limited liability is commonly acknowledged to be the most important nontax factor in selecting a form of business organization. In a sole proprietorship, the owner is personally liable for the debts of his business. Similarly, in a general partnership, all of the partners are jointly liable for the partnership's obligations to the full extent of their individual assets. In a limited partnership, however, the limited partners are shielded from personal liability to partnership creditors if they are true limited partners and they do not participate in the management of the business.

"The corporate shareholder's potential liability, on the other hand, is generally limited to the amount of his investment, regardless of his management activity. ＊ ＊ ＊ Thus, where the principal investors intend to be active in managing the business, and the venture involves a relatively high degree of risk, limited liability may well be the key nontax consideration favoring use of the corporate vehicle.

"A second nontax factor to consider when selecting a business entity is the ease of forming that entity. The formation of a proprietorship requires literally nothing more than establishing a business bank account. Similarly, there are no legal formalities required to establish a general partnership. Although a written partnership agreement, which defines the relative rights and duties of the partners, is not legally required, the absence of such an agreement often proves disastrous in later years. ＊ ＊ ＊

"A written partnership agreement is essential in the formation of a limited partnership, however, and a certificate outlining the terms of the agreement must be filed with the appropriate state office.

"The formation of a corporation is also relatively routine in most cases. All that is necessary is the filing of articles of incorporation, the drafting of bylaws, and the documenting of the organizational meeting of the directors. ＊ ＊ ＊

"Other traditional corporate characteristics, such as transferability of interests, continuity of existence, and centralized management, also serve as significant nontax considerations. While corporate shares and limited partnership interests may be freely transferred or assigned (subject in the latter case to the terms of the underlying partnership agreement) without affecting the existence of the respective entities, transfer of a general partnership interest usually necessitates execution of a new partnership agreement. Similarly, although a corporation or limited partnership continues as a separate legal entity despite the death, retirement, legal incompetence or bankruptcy of a shareholder or limited partner, any of these events causes a formal dissolution of a general partnership. Finally, centralized management is absent in the case of a general partnership because all partners normally have management rights and responsibilities. The management rights of a limited partner, on the other hand, must be substantially restricted to prevent the imposition of personal liability for partnership debts. * * * The management of a corporation is usually less cumbersome because it is centralized in a board of directors elected by shareholders.

"A final nontax consideration that should not be overlooked is the annual maintenance cost of the business form being considered. The corporate form is subject to various operational costs, such as qualification to do business in other states, preparation of annual reports, documentation of corporate actions taken by the shareholders or the board of directors, and payment of franchise taxes to one or more states. This degree of formality, along with its accompanying cost, is not required for either type of partnership, although major partnership decisions should certainly be documented.

"In summary, the nontax characteristics of a C or an S corporation are at least conceptually more attractive than those of a general partnership. On a nontax basis, the limited partnership is somewhat of a hybrid vehicle; although the limited partnership resembles the corporate form in most respects, a general partner in a limited partnership will find his interest governed by the general partnership rules.

"It should be emphasized, however, that these conceptual nontax differences between corporations and partnerships can be, and often are, minimized or eliminated entirely to meet the needs of a particular enterprise. For example, corporate organizational documents or shareholder agreements can be drafted to restrict shareholder rights to an extent not mandated by state law, such as by limiting the transfer of shares to outsiders. Alternatively, a partnership agreement can be drafted that incorporates the desired corporate characteristics into the partnership. However, such drafting should be undertaken with some degree of restraint in order to avoid transforming the entity into an association taxable as a corporation [or attempting to include corporate attributes which are not achievable under the governing partnership statute]." [40]

NOTE

1. While it has been asserted that the C corporation, at least when used as part of a group of corporations which file a consolidated return, might be the syndication vehicle of the future, one might conclude that the income tax disadvantages of the C corporation form outweigh the advantages when the purpose of the inquiry is to choose one entity for a limited number of investors in a single rental real estate project. See Snyder and Gonick, *Affiliated Corporate Groups for Real Estate Investments: The Syndication Vehicle of the Future?*, 14 J.Corp.Tax'n 15 (1987).

2. The income tax advantages and disadvantages of the C corporation include the following:

a. While the income tax rates imposed on corporations having taxable income in the lower brackets may be less than the income tax rates

40. Wolfe and DeJong, *The S Corporation as an Alternative Form of Business Organization After ERTA, TEFRA and the* Subchapter S Revision Act of 1982, 32 De Paul L.Rev. 811, 813–815 (1983).

imposed on individuals having taxable income of a similar amount, the income tax rate imposed on corporations whose taxable income places them in the highest bracket is higher than the income tax rate imposed on individuals having the same amount of taxable income.

b. Corporate income is subject to double taxation. The income is taxed to the corporation when recognized by it. The income is then taxed to the shareholders of the corporation when distributed to them as dividends or in liquidation of the corporation.

c. If a corporation distributes appreciated property as a dividend, in repurchase of its shares or in liquidation, the corporation must recognize the gain inherent in the property. See Sections 311(b) and 336. A distribution of appreciated property by a partnership is, in general, tax free. See Section 731.

d. An advantage of the use of a corporation is the ability to dispose of the assets of, or interests in, the corporation without recognition of gain or loss. The reorganization sections of the Code may be used to accomplish a tax-free disposition of the participants' interests. This may be accomplished by a Section 368(a)(1)(A) merger, or a Section 368(a)(1)(B) stock for stock exchange. A tax-free disposition of the assets of a corporation may be accomplished by a Section 368(a)(1)(C) exchange of stock for assets. In other than the corporate form nonrecognition may be available only in the case of a like-kind exchange of assets.

e. The alternative minimum tax is imposed on both individuals and corporations. The alternative minimum tax imposed on individuals is 21% of alternative minimum taxable income in excess of an exemption amount which varies with the taxpayer's filing status and is phased out as the taxpayer's alternative minimum taxable income increases. Alternative minimum taxable income is computed by adjusting taxable income, limiting the amount of certain "regular" deductions and adding to income, certain tax preferences. The corporate alternative minimum tax is 20% of a corporation's alternative taxable income in excess of $40,000 which amount is phased out as the corporation's alternative minimum taxable income increases. As with individuals, a corporation's alternative minimum taxable income is computed by adjusting taxable income, limiting the amount of certain "regular" deductions and adding to income, certain tax preferences. In the case of a C corporation one of the significant adjustments may be the addition to alternative minimum taxable income of 50% of the amount by which the adjusted book income of the corporation exceeds its alternative taxable income as computed prior to making this adjustment. This adjustment is replaced, after December 31, 1989, with an adjustment based on the earnings of the corporation. The corporate and individual alternative minimum taxes are discussed in detail at pages 485 to 486 infra.

f. Corporations are subject to Section 291 which, in general, requires that a corporation reduce the benefit to it of certain tax preference items by a specified percentage of such items. See Zwick, *Benefits of Corporate-Owned Real Estate Reduced by New Sec. 291*, 15 Tax Adviser 450 (1984); Dentino, *The Unveiling of Section 291 With a Focus on the Disposition of Real Property by Corporations*, 11 J.Corp.Tax'n 258 (1984). Section 291 will apply to an S corporation only if the S corporation was a C corporation within the prior three years. Section 291 is coordinated with the corporate alternative minimum tax provisions so that the same item will not be counted under both Section 291 and the alternative minimum tax provisions.

g. Certain tax free fringe benefits are available to participant-employees of a corporation while they are not available to participant-employees in noncorporate forms. Tax free fringe benefits such as term life insurance, Section 79, accident and health insurance, Section 106, and certain benefits therefrom, Section 105, and meals and lodging, Section 119, (if the terms of the various applicable sections are complied with) are available to shareholder-employees. The position of the Internal Revenue Service is that these benefits are not available to participant-employees in noncorporate entities. See Reg. Sec. 1.707–1(c); Rev.Rul. 56–362, 1956–2 C.B. 100; Rev.Rul. 69–184, 1969–1 C.B. 256; Rev.Rul. 72–596, 1972–2 C.B. 395. But see *Armstrong v. Phinney,* 394 F.2d 661 (5th Cir.1968). The benefit to the participants of these fringes may be calculated at the participants' effective tax rates since the cost thereof is deductible to the corporation, assuming total compensation is reasonable. The fringe benefits provided to a shareholder who owns more than 2% of the stock of an S corporation are treated, for tax purposes, the same as they would be if the S corporation was a partnership or other noncorporate entity. See generally Starr and Perine, *To What Extent Can Partners and S Corporation Shareholders Receive Nontaxable Fringe Benefits?,* 67 J. Tax'n 40 (1986). The use of a corporation assures that the compensation paid to shareholder-employees, if reasonable and for ordinary and necessary real estate management services, is deductible. Whereas, as a result of Section 707(c) and *Pratt v. Comm'r,* 550 F.2d 1023 (5th Cir.1977), affirming, 64 T.C. 203 (1975), it may be held that under certain circumstances such as when compensation is based on a percentage of the income of a partnership compensation paid for management services performed by partners is not deductible by the partnership.

h. The taxable year of a corporation, other than certain personal service corporations, does not have to be tied to the year of its principal shareholders or be the calendar year. In fact, Priv.Ltr.Rul. 8003010 indicates that a corporate partner may adopt a different fiscal year than the partnership in which it is a member. A partnership, however, must use (in order of priority) the same fiscal year as the partners owning the majority of profits and capital, the same fiscal year as all of its principal partners or the calendar year. An S corporation must use the calendar year. A partnership and an S corporation can use a different taxable year if a business purpose for its use can be established. In addition, a partnership and an S corporation may elect to use a taxable year different than the required years described above if the entity is willing to pay a toll for the privilege and the deferral period of the taxable year elected, the period between the beginning of the elected year and the close of the first taxable year which the entity would have been required to use had the election not been made, is, in general, not greater than three months.

i. Lastly, the at-risk rules, the limitations on the deduction of passive losses and the limitations on the deduction of interest have limited application to corporations.

[1] "*The At–Risk Rules*

"Section 465 of the Code was designed to prevent taxpayers from deducting losses (primarily of the 'tax shelter' variety) beyond their economic investment in an activity, including amounts borrowed where the taxpayer is personally liable for repayment of the debt. [The Tax Reform Act of 1986] adds real estate holdings to these at-risk rules, but creates an exception for 'certain qualified third party nonrecourse financing' by banks and certain other persons in the business of lending money. Seller or promoter financing is not within the exception, on the asserted ground that the property could be overvalued, creating artificially high debt and losses, notwithstanding stringent penalties in the Code for such a scheme. While the financing must be true debt and not disguised equity, a qualified third-party lender apparently may continue to have certain types of equity interests in the real estate joint venture other than convertible debt.

* * *

"Corporations are generally not subject to the at-risk rules, nor are their shareholders. In 1978, Congress amended the at-risk provision to apply to certain closely held corporations. Corporations with five or fewer shareholders owning more than 50 percent of the stock (personal holding company definition) are within the at-risk rules because of a potential abuse by small groups who might attempt to use tax losses as an offset against accumulated earnings, enhancing the value of their stock. In 1980, the Treasury extended this concept to consolidated returns to prevent the creation of losses through a nominally capitalized subsidiary corporation and the consequent offset of these losses against income of other members of the affiliated group. However, the consolidated regulations limit this at-risk rule to the general provision in Section 465(a)(1)(B), so that there is no at-risk rule for the non-closely held corporation.

" * * * [T]he partnership, with non-third-party financing, would be subject to the at-risk rules unless the losses were offset by income. Any excess losses would not be deductible currently. [A] consolidated corporate group, with ten shareholders in the parent corporation, would not be a closely held corporation, and the losses generated by [one of the] corporation[s] would be offset by income of [other corporations in the group]. Corporate real estate syndications must therefore have a large enough group to avoid the at-risk rules; partnerships will generally not avoid the new [1986 Tax Reform Act] restrictions.

[2] "*Passive Activity Loss Rules*

"The passive activity loss rule[, Section 469,] operates in the context of a * * * partnership to convert all losses and credits to passive status, notwithstanding the fact that the activity itself would otherwise be a 'trade or business.' Ten shareholders holding equal amounts of stock bypass the closely held corporation threshold[, five or fewer shareholders owning more than 50%,] in the passive activity rules. [T]here is a potential trap in the 'personal service corporation' definition under Section 469, where the * * * corporation's 'principal activity' is the performance of personal services, 'substantially' performed by *employee-owners* (with expansive attribution rules), but only where they own (by value) more than 10 percent of the [corporation's] stock. Thus, if the shareholders ＊ ＊ ＊ perform substantial services for the corporation, they could cause the ＊ ＊ ＊ losses to fall under the passive loss restrictions of Section 469. This distinction between personal services and capital investment may require the resurrection of old Section 1348 (maximum tax of 50 percent on 'personal service income') and its interpretations of the line between the two types of sources of income, triggering, perhaps, another role reversal posture by the government and taxpayers. ＊ ＊ ＊

"Thus, in a partnership, passive losses are offset only against passive income, specially defined to exclude services and portfolio investment type income. Interesting classification questions arise under these rules, requiring conventional structuring of real estate and other transactions to be reconsidered. For example, passive activity includes all rental activity, whether or not the taxpayer 'materially participates' in the activity. There is a limited exception that may apply to noncorporate ＊ ＊ ＊ partners, which allows up to [a] $25,000 offset of nonpassive income with losses and credits from real estate activities, with respect to activities in which the individual actively participates. The Senate Finance Committee Report states that operation of a hotel, where substantial services are provided, is not a rental, but rather a service activity. Therefore, losses from an office building held by a limited partnership arguably may not be offset against income from a hotel run by the partnership. This results in the hotel income being taxed, with the office building losses carried forward and offset against net passive income in a subsequent year, or held in a suspension account until either the partnership sells the office building or the partner sells his or her *entire* partnership interest. By the same token, investment income, such as interest or dividend income, a classic type of passive income, is converted by the new passive loss rules into active income, so that tax shelter losses (and economic losses as well) cannot offset this type of income. The Senate Report once again creates the possibility of role reversal by taxpayers and government, including treating activity by a 'dealer' in real estate as nonrental or active, thus allowing losses from those activities to be deductible, apparently, however, only if they pass the material participation test. [The non-closely held corporation which avoids being classified as a personal service corporation, i.e., 11 shareholders owning equal amounts of the corporation's stock, can use its passive losses against any of its income. In addition, a closely held corporation, which is not a personal service corporation, can use its passive losses against its active income.]

[3] "*The Interest Deduction Limitation—Section 163(d)*

"[The Tax Reform Act of 1986] expand[ed] the limitation on interest deductions, particularly for limited partnerships. Under prior law, it was unclear whether interest incurred to purchase an interest in a limited partnership was deemed 'investment' interest, and therefore, deductible only to the extent of 'investment' income. The Act provides that such interest is akin to interest incurred by a passive investor in corporate stock, since limited partnership interests ＊ ＊ ＊ closely resemble 'securities.' Therefore, interest on indebtedness attributable to the purchase of such an interest is now deductible as investment interest in the year paid to the extent of investment income, unless the interest expense is taken into account under the passive loss restrictions in Section 469. [In addition, it is possible that debt incurred by a partnership may be incurred for investment rather than trade or business purposes. If the debt is incurred for investment purposes, the deduction of the interest paid or incurred on the debt may be limited under Section 163(d).]

"Despite the congressional analogy that limited partners are similar to corporate investors, the Section 163(d) limitations are not applicable to debt incurred by corporations * * *. Here again, the policy underlying this distinction is that corporate losses are not passed through to investors, although they may be offset within a corporate group or fall within the more liberal carryback and carryforward net operating loss deduction rules (as assumed "business" losses) even in a single corporation. However, the rationale for inhibiting the mismatching of income and expense (where, for example, the limited partnership has no current income) may equally apply to a highly leveraged real estate investment by one or a group of corporations.

"Thus, * * * [the partners in a] partnership * * * [can] deduct [the partnership's investment] interest [only] to the extent of [their] net [investment] income (determined without interest expense) * * *. Any shortfall in [investment] income would result in a disallowance of interest to that extent, with a carryover to future years. * * *

"However, the Conference Committee Report, in effect, places the partnership [investment] interest deduction limitation within the passive activity loss rules, which may result in the [deduction for the] interest * * * being disallowed because [the partners do not have enough passive income against which to deduct the interest]. * * * Corporations do not have to run the gauntlet of the definitional and other timing aspects in Section 163(d), but, most significantly, limited partnerships that pass muster under that provision find themselves faced by other new restrictions on all deductions (as described previously), not applicable to corporations (other than those that are closely held [or are personal service corporations])."

Snyder and Gonick, *Affiliated Corporate Groups for Real Estate Investments: The Syndication Vehicle of the Future,* 14 J.Corp. Tax'n 15, 37–43 (1987).

3. The corporate and income tax treatment of corporate distributions, both dividends and redemptions, is treated at length in Division IV, pages 1100 to 1120 infra. Division IV also considers the problems involved in the organization of a corporation and shareholder loans to it, see pages 1120 to 1153 infra. See generally North, *Organizing the Closely Held Corporation,* 32 N.Y.U.Inst. Fed.Tax'n 697 (1974).

4. See generally Baker and Berkowitz, *Sheltering a Corporate Investor,* 57 Taxes 211 (1979); Price, *Using "Collapsing" Corporations to Maximize Returns from Development Ventures,* 7 J. Real Est. Tax'n 260 (1980); McEntee, *Use of Controlled Corporation in Real Estate Development,* 58 Taxes 520 (1980); McGrady and Weaver, *Why Set Up a Corporation To Own Real Estate?,* 10 # 3 Real Est.Rev. 89 (1980); Day, *Corporate Investment in Real Estate Ventures— Special Considerations for Special Allocations Under Section 704: "The Price is Right,"* 10 J.Corp.L. 313 (1985); Spradling, *A Feasibility Analysis of the C Corporation Form for Closely Held Businesses After the Tax Reform Act of 1986,*

65 Taxes 740 (1987); Glickman, *Choosing a Corporate Tax Structure*, 74 A.B.A.J. 75 (1988).

5. While the use of a C corporation to acquire, develop, own and operate a rental real estate project may be appropriate in certain somewhat special situations, the use of an S corporation for a rental real estate project is a definite possibility in many relatively typical situations.

S Corporation vs. Partnership for Real Estate Ventures

JERALD D. AUGUST AND MARK L. SILOW
1 Journal of Taxation of Investments 91 (1983).
[footnotes omitted]

* * *

[S]hareholders in an S corporation report items of income, deduction (including items of tax preference), loss, and credit realized by the corporation on their individual returns in a manner similar to partners in a partnership. All tax items of an S corporation are allocated to the shareholders on a daily basis in proportion to stock ownership. * * * However, since important differences remain between the taxation of S corporations and partnerships, the tax adviser may often find that real estate investments should continue to be held in partnership form. This recommendation will most likely be made where real estate is to be acquired with nonrecourse financing or if certain equity participants cannot qualify as shareholders in an S corporation.

Eligibility

In order to elect Subchapter S status, a corporation must meet the statutory definition of a "small business corporation"

1. A corporation created or organized in the United States,

2. Which is not an ineligible corporation, e.g., a member of an affiliated group, a DISC or a former DISC, etc.,

3. Has 35 or fewer shareholders, each of whom is either an individual, decedent's estate, estate in bankruptcy of an individual, or eligible trust,

4. Has no nonresident alien shareholder, and

5. Has only one class of stock.

* * *

[T]he [permitted] number of shareholders * * * was apparently intended to correspond to the private placement exemption under federal securities laws. However, this represents an oversimplification of Regulation D under Section 4(2) of the Securities Act of 1933 since the number of purchasers in an exempt issue pursuant to this regulation is limited to thirty-five plus certain "accredited investors." Thus, since it is possible for a real estate syndication to satisfy the Regulation D safe harbor while still offering more than thirty-five interests for sale, use of an S corporation for large real estate syndications will be unavailable. * * *

A more important limitation on S elections concerns the shareholder-eligibility requirements. * * *[A]n S corporation may not have as a shareholder a nonresident alien, partnership, corporation, nongrantor trust or trust that does not otherwise meet the definition of a qualified Subchapter S trust. These restrictions on eligible shareholders certainly favor use of a partnership for conducting investment programs since partnerships are generally free from any similar restraints. * * *

* * * [While] an S corporation may have no more than one class of stock, Section 1361(c)(4) provides that differences in voting rights among shares are permitted. This will be of benefit in structuring management control of the corporation for those that are actively involved in the affairs of the business. For example, a small percentage of the total interest in the venture can be issued to the developer or entrepreneur in the form of voting stock, while the balance of the shares are nonvoting and issued to private investors who provide the venture capital. * * *

Despite the flexibility provided in issuing voting and nonvoting stock, an S corporation is still prohibited from issuing stock carrying a dividend or liquidation preference. This prevents equity participants in an S corporation from making special allocations of cash flow or establishing distribution priorities, as is frequently done in the partnership area. * * * Debt instruments, if properly qualified, will not cause the S corporation to have a prohibited second class of stock, even though such obligations may otherwise constitute equity for other tax purposes. Under Section 1361(c)(5)(B), the issuance of "straight debt" will not result in violation of the one class of stock limitation regardless of the corporation's ratio of debt to equity. Straight debt is defined as a written unconditional promise to pay on demand or on a specified date a sum certain in money. In addition, the interest rate and interest payment dates must not be contingent on profits, the borrower's discretion, or "similar factors." However, * * * a rate of interest dependent on the prime rate or factors other than those related to the debtor corporation will not violate the interest rate provision. Finally, this type of instrument cannot be convertible into stock or issued to a person who would otherwise be ineligible to hold shares in an S corporation.

* * *

Certainty of Entity Tax Status

In choosing between an S corporation and a partnership for purposes of structuring a real estate transaction, it is essential that the form of entity selected be classified as such for federal income tax purposes. For example, if a partnership is held to be an association taxable as a corporation for federal income tax purposes, the consequences could be disastrous. * * * The regulations identify four characteristics that generally distinguish a corporation from a partnership: continuity of life, centralization of management, limited liability, and free transferability of interests. An unincorporated organization, such as a partnership, will be classified for federal tax purposes as a corporation if such organization has a preponderance of these four corporate characteristics. Accordingly, the decision whether to proceed as a corporation or as a partnership may depend on how many of these four corporate characteristics have to be retained for business (i.e., nontax) purposes, and at what risk. Clearly, by electing Subchapter S status, all four of these corporate characteristics can be retained while the entity tax status is assured, so long as the corporation or any shareholder does not act in a manner which would cause a termination of the S election.

Limited Liability

Probably the most attractive corporate characteristic to both investors and promoters is limited liability. * * * Although a limited partner has no liability to creditors of the partnership in excess of his capital contribution, the regulations provide that a limited partnership subject to a statute corresponding to the ULPA generally does not have the corporate characteristic of limited liability since the general partner is personally liable for the obligations of the partnership. However, where the general partner has no "substantial assets" (other than his interest in the partnership) that could be reached by a creditor of the partnership and where he is merely a "dummy" acting as an agent of the limited partners, the requisite personal liability does not exist.

* * *

With an S corporation, limited liability can be generally assured for both the investors and promoters without the need to retain any substantial net worth in the corporation or a particular shareholder and without jeopardizing the entity's "association" status.

Continuity of Life

* * * Under the ULPA, the retirement, death, or insanity of a general partner dissolves the partnership, unless the business is continued by the remaining general partners if so provided in the certificate of limited partnership or with the consent of all the partners. * * * In addition, * * * a partnership will terminate for tax purposes if more than 50 percent of the total interests in partnership capital and profits are sold or exchanged within a twelve-month period. * * *

As in the case of corporations in general, an S corporation will remain in existence in perpetuity, regardless of the fortunes or fates of any of its shareholders. Moreover, the ownership of stock in an S corporation may be freely exchanged without the risk of termination, provided, however, that the transferees are not ineligible shareholders. Restrictive shareholder agreements and legended share certificates can protect against ineligible shareholders.

Centralization of Management

* * * [A] limited partnership subject to a statute corresponding to the ULPA will ordinarily be deemed to have centralized management if substantially all of the interests in the partnership are owned by the limited partners. Although centralized management will be deemed to exist in the typical syndicated limited partnership since substantially all of the partnership interests are ordinarily owned by the limited partners, the limited partners will be afforded little, if any, role in the management of the affairs of the partnership. * * *

Unlike limited partners whose limited liability may be jeopardized by active participation in management, the shareholders of an S corporation may actively engage in the affairs of the corporation without jeopardizing entity tax status. Indeed, in many closely held corporations, shareholders often impose their own set of restrictions to ensure the centralization and continuity of management. Such restrictions are most frequently contained in shareholder agreements, voting trust agreements, or irrevocable proxies. In addition, the ability to issue voting and nonvoting common stock will add to the flexibility in the structuring of control of S corporations.

Free Transferability of Interests

* * *

In order to avoid the corporate characteristic of free transferability, many limited partnership agreements prohibit the transfer of a limited partner's interest without the consent of the general partner and/or grant a right of first refusal to the nonselling limited partners. Additional restrictions may relate to the ability of a general partner to transfer his general partnership interest. * * *

Again, an S corporation offers both the investors and promoters the flexibility of free transferability without jeopardizing the organization's intended tax status as a pass-through entity as long as transfers are not made to ineligible shareholders.

Entity Formation

* * * [T]ax-free incorporations or contributions by controlling shareholders may * * * be made to an S corporation pursuant to Section 351(a). Basically, this provision allows for nonrecognition of gain or loss where one or more persons transfers property to a corporation solely in exchange for stock or securities provided that immediately after the exchange, such person or persons, as a group, are in "control" of the transferee corporation. The definition of "control" is provided under Section 368(c), which requires ownership of at least 80 percent of the voting and nonvoting shares of stock. * * *

Under Section 351(d)(1), stock or securities issued in exchange for services rendered or to be rendered are not considered to be issued in return for property under Section 351(a). However, an individual who receives stock in a corporation in exchange for services is still counted in determining whether those receiving stock or securities in exchange for property, as a group, satisfy the control requirement. Accordingly, the issuance of more than 20 percent of the corporation's stock to a service provider (i.e., promoters) will cause the transaction to fall outside of Section 351(a), resulting in gain or loss recognition to contributors of property.

In contrast to the control group requirement under Section 351(a), partners transferring property to a partnership generally are afforded nonrecognition treatment under Section 721. This is because Section 721 does not require that the transferors of property to the partnership be "in control" of the partnership immediately following the transfer. The absence of a control requirement under Section 721 gives the partnership the advantage of being able to admit additional partners after entity formation without tax cost. * * *

With respect to contributions of mortgaged real estate to a new or existing entity, the rules governing S corporations (or regular corporations) are disadvantageous when compared with the rules in the partnership area. In particular, Section 357(c) provides that a shareholder transferring appreciated property subject to a liability is required to recognize gain in the event the liability exceeds the property's adjusted basis. However, gain recognition on a similar transfer may be avoided under the partnership rules since a partner-contributor's basis in his partnership interest includes his proportionate share of the liability taken subject to (or assumed) by the partnership under Section 752(a).

* * *

Conduit Rules for S Operations

* * * [E]ach shareholder reports on his individual return his pro rata share (allocated daily) of each corporate item of income, loss deduction, or credit incurred by the S corporation during its taxable year. Generally, an item must be separately stated for all shareholders if its treatment could affect the tax liability of any shareholder of the corporation. * * * The remaining items affecting the liability of any shareholder ("nonseparately computed income or loss") are passed through to the shareholders on an aggregate basis. The pass-through rules * * * are * * * similar to the rules for reporting partnership items under Section 702(a). * * *

As in the case of a partnership, the character of any item of corporate income, loss, deduction, or credit that a shareholder must take into account in computing his tax liability is to be determined as if such item were realized directly from the source by the corporation and incurred in the same manner as incurred by the corporation.

* * *

Any election affecting the computation of tax items passed through to the shareholders from an S corporation is to be made at the corporate level. Such elections include method of accounting (Section

446), electing out of the installment sale provision (Section 453), involuntary conversions (Section 1033), method of depreciation (Sections 167 and 168), inventory method (Section 472), additional first-year depreciation (Section 179), and selection of taxable year (Section 1378). Exceptions to the rule requiring tax elections to be made at the corporate level are essentially the same as those contained in the partnership area, including the discharge of indebtedness income (Section 108), limitation on interest on investment indebtedness (Section 163(d)), deduction and recapture of mining exploration expenditures (Section 617), and taxes paid or incurred to foreign countries and U.S. possessions. * * *

Although an S corporation may adopt any permissible method of accounting, it is automatically placed on the cash method for purposes of deducting payments (e.g., interest or compensation) made to a * * * shareholder who is on the cash method of accounting. The effect of Section 267(e) may be material in the real estate area since many real estate programs are designed to generate significant tax losses for the benefit of their investors as a result of the accrual of fees and interest payable to related parties. * * *

Under the partnership rules, * * * if [a] transaction is governed by Section 707(a), [Section 267(e) will control] * * *. However, if the payment is considered a guaranteed payment under Section 707(c), the recipient must include such payment in income in the year in which the payment is deductible to the partnership according to its method of accounting. * * *

Basis Adjustments for S Operations

Paralleling the adjustments to the basis of a partnership interest under Section 705(a), Section 1367 requires a shareholder to adjust his stock basis for his proportionate share of the current year's tax items. First, increases to basis will result from the pass-through of separately and nonseparately computed income, including tax-exempt income. Decreases to basis will arise on the pass-through of separately and nonseparately computed items of deduction and loss. Once stock basis is reduced to zero, a shareholder cannot claim additional deductions or losses which are passed through for reporting on a current basis. However, if the shareholder has advanced monies to the corporation, he can reduce his debt basis (but not below zero) in order to claim additional deductions. If debt basis has been reduced by the pass-through of losses and deductions, Section 1367(b)(2)(B) directs that any subsequent net increase to basis restore the basis of debt before any portion is allocated to increase stock basis.

* * * [A]ny loss or deduction that is disallowed to a shareholder because of insufficient stock and debt basis will be allowed in the succeeding taxable year if basis is increased either as a result of additional contributions or the pass-through of income items. This carryforward of excess losses continues for an indefinite period as long

as the corporation's S election remains in effect. In the event of termination, an excess loss may be used against available stock basis on the last day of the corporation's "post-termination transition period."

* * *

Distributions

Section 1368 permits an S corporation that has no accumulated earnings and profits to make distributions of cash or property, to the extent of fair market value, to its shareholders without tax cost if such amounts can be absorbed against the distributee's stock basis. Any amounts in excess of basis are treated as gain from the sale or exchange of stock under Section 301(c)(3). Although no particular set or ordering rules directly appears in Section 1367, the Committee Reports direct that adjustments first be made with respect to the pass-through of corporate-level items prior to accounting for distributions. Because property distributions by an S corporation will be applied against a shareholder's stock basis at fair market value, it is obvious that many distributions will result in a shareholder-level tax under the S rules which would otherwise result in nonrecognition to a partner-distributee under Section 731. However, a partner, unlike an S shareholder-distributee, will not obtain a fair market value basis in the property received. Of course, a carryover of the partnership's adjusted basis may be preferable if the property has depreciated in value.

For S corporations with accumulated earnings and profits, distributions are first permitted to be recovered tax-free against a shareholder's adjusted stock basis to the extent of the corporation's accumulated adjustments account (AAA). [The AAA] is defined in Section 1368(e)(1) as an S corporation's post–1982 accumulated gross income less deductible expenditures and prior distributions allocable to the account. Under a three-tier priority rule set forth in Section 1368(c), distributions of AAA are received as a tax-free return of capital and, if in excess of stock basis, as gain from the sale or exchange of stock. Distributions in excess of AAA are taxed as dividend income to the extent of the corporation's accumulated earnings and profits. Finally, any distributions in excess of the AAA and accumulated earnings and profits constitute a nontaxable return of stock basis, with any further excess as gain from the sale or exchange of stock. It is important to note that * * * an S corporation will not generate earnings and profits in a current reporting period unless acquired from another corporation * * *.

Since the presence of Subchapter C earnings and profits may be critical to an S corporation in avoiding a termination of its election or a current tax on passive investment income, as discussed below, * * * an S corporation may elect on a yearly basis to treat distributions as first being made from the second-tier or accumulated earnings and profits account bypassing AAA. * * *

Stock Basis Hurdle

* * *

Perhaps the most significant limitation on the use of an S corporation for real estate investments is the inability of a shareholder to include any portion of corporate-level debt in stock basis * * *. Thus, in order for an S corporation's shareholder to increase stock basis with respect to borrowed funds, such person must first directly borrow the monies from the lender and then contribute them to the corporation in the form of either debt or equity. In a closely held S corporation, this hurdle may represent only a strict adherence to form if the lender requires the personal guarantees of the investors. However, in the context of a venture with many investors, each of whom is to be equally responsible for the repayment of the debt, personal borrowing may prove to be impractical.

This restriction on obtaining stock basis for corporate debt has the obvious effect on limiting the amount of deductions that a shareholder may otherwise claim, both on a current basis and over the entire life of the project. This limitation is in sharp contrast with the operation of Section 752(a) which permits a partner to include his proportionate share of partnership liabilities in the basis for his partnership interest.

* * *

A second limitation on the use of S corporations for real estate ventures is the absence of a rule permitting special allocations of items of income and loss between shareholders. As previously mentioned, a shareholder in an S corporation is allocated his pro rata share (computed daily) of corporate-level items of income, deduction, loss, and credit. In contrast, partners in a partnership may by agreement specially allocate items of partnership income and loss, provided such allocations have "substantial economic effect." In many real estate limited partnerships, special allocations are employed to allocate substantially all of the partnership's tax losses and cash flow to the investor-limited partners, at least until their equity contributions have been recovered. Moreover, in the case of contributed property, the partners [must], by agreement, allocate the depreciation and gain or loss on sale in such a manner as to take into account the variation between fair market value and basis in the contributed property as of the date of funding.

Although not expressly permitted, one potential method for obtaining a de facto special allocation of tax items in an S corporation would be through the use of straight debt. By first segregating the portion of the venture capital into a straight debt instrument, the stock could then be issued in a manner reflecting the desired ratios for sharing profits and losses. Since no allocation of tax items is made to holders of straight debt even if recharacterized as equity for other purposes, this would have the effect of creating a special allocation of the items realized by the corporation and passed through in proportion to stock ownership. * * *

A second alternative to achieving a special allocation of loss or deduction generated by the venture would be to form a partnership comprised of two S corporations. The two corporations, as partners, would then enter into a partnership agreement providing for the special allocation of tax items realized by the partnership. A partnership of S corporations to obtain a special allocation of tax items may be particularly useful for real estate syndications whereby the investors would be placed in one S corporation and the promoter-managers in a second. However, care must be exercised to ensure that the shareholders of both corporations (or at least the corporation receiving the special allocation) are eligible under Subchapter S rules.

Passive Income Limitations

*   *   *

[A] newly electing S corporation may derive all of its income from passive sources without fear of a termination. However, a *   *   * passive income termination rule is [provided] for S corporations with Subchapter C accumulated earnings and profits. In addition, [a] corporate-level tax [is imposed] on the passive investment income of certain S corporations with Subchapter C accumulated earnings and profits.

The *   *   * termination rule for passive investment income is contained in Section 1362(d)(3). Pursuant to this section, an S corporation will forfeit its election if it has (1) three consecutive taxable years (as an S corporation) during which its passive investment income exceeds 25 percent of its gross receipts, and (2) Subchapter C earnings and profits as of the close of each of such three consecutive years. *   *   * Thus, an S corporation without Subchapter C earnings and profits may derive 100 percent of its receipts from rents, maintain its Subchapter S election, and avoid application of both the personal holding company and accumulated earnings taxes. *   *   * [The] definition of "passive investment income" *   *   * includes gross receipts derived from royalties, rents, dividends, interest, annuities, and sales and exchanges of stock or securities. *   *   *

Obviously, rents will constitute the largest single item of passive investment income for S corporations owning real estate. Pursuant to the regulations promulgated under former Section 1372(e)(5), *   *   * the term "rents" is broadly defined as amounts received for the use of, or right to use, real or personal property. The regulations further provide that payments for the use or occupancy of rooms or other space for which significant services are also rendered to the occupant, such as for the use or occupancy of rooms in hotels, boarding houses, or apartment houses furnishing hotel services, do not constitute "rents" provided such services are not customary to rentals of that type. This requirement of "noncustomary" services has been consistently used by the courts in finding that rents constitute passive investment income for Subchapter S corporations operating office buildings, shopping malls, or other commercial facilities despite the presence of significant "customary" services.

In addition to the risk of termination faced by an S corporation engaged in leasing of real estate and having Subchapter C earnings and profits, * * * Section 1375 imposes a corporate-level tax on excess net passive income of an S corporation for each taxable year in which it derives 25 percent of its gross receipts in the form of passive investment income. The rate of tax is the highest corporate rate set forth under Section 11 * * * and is applied against the lesser of the corporation's taxable income or excess net passive income. * * *

As previously discussed, to avoid both a passive investment income tax and termination of its election, S corporations with Subchapter C earnings and profits may engage in a cleansing distribution of accumulated earnings and profits account. Such a distribution can avoid the presence of Subchapter C earnings and profits at the end of the relevant tax year. Moreover, since S corporations with accumulated earnings and profits may also have AAA, an election under the special procedure * * * contained in Section 1368(e) may have to be made in order to make current distributions out of the accumulated earnings and profits instead of AAA. * * *

Distributions of Appreciated Property

Pursuant to Section 1363(d), an S corporation realizes gain, including recapture amounts, on the distribution [including a distribution in liquidation,] of appreciated property (other than its own obligations) to a shareholder in the same manner as if the asset were sold to a third party at fair market value. Gain not subject to recapture will be characterized by reference to the S corporation's activities (e.g., capital assets, Section 1231 property, inventory, or "dealer" property). Since the conduit rules governing the operations of an S corporation require that items of income be allocated among the shareholders for reporting on their individual returns, the distributee-shareholder will be able to obtain a full step-up in basis for the acquired asset while being charged with the gain and recapture only to the extent of his proportionate stock interest. * * *

It is also important to note that gain recognized under Section 1363(d) may also generate a passive investment income tax under Section 1375 if the assets distributed are appreciated stock of another corporation. Moreover, distributions of appreciated property (including appreciated stock or securities) could also trigger a corporate-level [income tax on built-in gain] under Section 1374 [if the S corporation had previously been a C corporation or had received any assets from a C corporation in which it had a carryover basis]. Furthermore, Section 1239 may recharacterize part or all of the gain as ordinary income if the shareholder-distributee's actual and constructive stock ownership renders the S corporation [a controlled] entity under Section 1239(b)(2). The tax consequences of the distribution to the shareholder-distributee are not completed, however, until the distribution rules under Section 1368 are applied. This may result in additional income if the value of the property is allocated to accumulated earnings and profits and/or exceeds the distributee's stock basis (after prior adjustment for current S operations).

In contrast to Section 1363(d)'s general prescription of gain recognition, a distribution of property from a partnership to a partner will not trigger gain unless it is deemed to be disproportionate with respect to the partner-transferee's interest in certain partnership assets under Section 751(b). Moreover, gain realized on a hypothetical sale under Section 751(b) is taxed to either the distributee or nondistributee partner instead of being allocated among all partners, as is applicable to shareholders under Subchapter S. An additional benefit in the partnership area is the ability to make basis adjustments for gain or loss as a result of the distribution of partnership property. No equivalent adjustments are available to shareholders in an S corporation. Finally, distributions of property will generally not be taxable to a partner-distributee under Section 731(a). The distributee will generally inherit the partnership's adjusted basis and holding period in the assets, in further contrast to the distribution rules under Subchapter S.

* * *

Sale of Assets by S Corporation

If an S corporation realizes gain from the sale or exchange of [its assets] the [gain] will be allocated to the shareholders in proportion to stock ownership and passed through for reporting on their individual tax returns. Because items of gross income increase stock (or debt) basis under Section 1367(a)(1) (Section 1367(b)(2)(B)), the proceeds from asset sales may be distributed to the shareholders without additional tax cost provided the distributions are not allocated to accumulated earnings and profits. * * *

Assuming an asset sale will result in * * * gain, consideration must be given to the application of a corporate-level * * * tax under Section 1374 * * *. [If an S corporation was formerly a C corporation or had received assets from a C corporation in which the S corporation took a carryover basis, a corporate level tax at the maximum rate is imposed on any gain which existed prior to the conversion of the C corporation to S corporation status or the conveyance of the assets by the C corporation to the S corporation (built-in gain). In order to be subject to the corporate level tax the built-in gain must be recognized by the S corporation, through sale or distribution, within ten years after the date on which the conversion from C corporation to S corporation took place or the date of the conveyance by the C corporation to the S corporation. The amount of gain reported by the shareholders of the S corporation is reduced by the amount of the corporate tax imposed.]

Generally, the same results are obtained for sales of appreciated [property] by partnerships except that no tax is ever imposed at the entity level. * * *

NOTE

1. Note that while the Real Estate Investment Trust is not available for the closely held venture because of the 100 beneficial owners requirement, the Subchapter S election is not available if there are more than 35 shareholders.

In an interesting attempt to avoid the Subchapter S limitation on the number of shareholders, at a time when only 15 shareholders were permitted, a single business operated by 30 individuals was transferred to three separate corporations each corporation having 10 shareholders. The corporations then formed a partnership for purpose of operating the business. Treating this arrangement as entered into solely for the purpose of tax avoidance, the I.R.S. took the position in Rev.Rul. 77–220, 1977–1 C.B. 263, that the three corporations will be treated as one corporation for the purpose of the Subchapter S limitation on the number of shareholders. Might the I.R.S. have reached the same result by relying on Section 7701(a)(3) and the regulations thereunder?

2. While it has been said that an S corporation is an incorporated partnership for income tax purposes, this is only true in the sense that both the partnership and the S corporation are, in general, treated as conduits. As pointed out in the preceding excerpt, there are substantial differences between these two forms of entity. In fact, except for the special provisions of Subchapter S, Sections 1361–79, such a corporation is governed by the corporate sections of the Internal Revenue Code.

3. The classification of debt as equity is only one of the problems arising under the one class of stock requirement. The use by the stockholders of an S corporation of various voting control devices may also lead to a finding of two classes of stock. See Comment, *Voting Rights And The Single Class Of Stock Requirement Of Subchapter S*, 10 Hous.L.Rev. 869 (1973). But see *Parker Oil Co. Inc.*, 58 T.C. 985 (1972), acq. 1973–2 C.B. 3, and Rev.Rul. 73–611, 1973–2 C.B. 312, permitting variation in voting rights through shareholders' agreements. See Comment, *Subchapter S and the One–Class–Of–Stock Rule: How Far Will the Service Retreat?*, 40 Brooklyn L.Rev. 315 (1973).

Since an S corporation, pursuant to Section 1361(c)(4), may have differences in voting rights among the shares of the common stock of the corporation without violating the one class of stock limitation, it would appear that shareholder agreements which accomplish substantially the same purpose ought to be treated in the same manner. Under Section 1361(c)(4) neither the issuance of nonvoting stock to key employees, see Ltr.Rul. 8528049, nor the execution of a stock purchase agreement by the shareholders of an S corporation, see Rev.Rul. 85–161, 1985–2 C.B. 191, will violate the one class of stock rule. See generally Proctor, *The One Class of Stock Requirement After the Subchapter S Revision Act of 1982*, 14 Cumb.L.Rev. 439 (1984); Blau, Rohman and Lemons, *Shareholder Agreements and the Single Class of Stock Requirement*, 68 J.Tax'n 238 (1988). In *Paige v. United States*, 36 A.F.T.R.2d 75–5408 (D.C.Cal.1975), affirmed, 580 F.2d 960 (9th Cir.1978), the corporation issued one class of common stock. The California Commissioner of Corporations, however, in issuing a permit to the corporation authorizing it to sell and issue its stock imposed certain conditions on the stock to be issued for property as opposed to cash. The court held that the imposition of such conditions created a second class of stock. In *Lafayette Distributors, Inc. v. United States*, 397 F.Supp. 719 (W.D.La.1975), the Commissioner did not make the argument that a voting trust established by some of the stockholders of a corporation in order to obtain control of the corporation created a second class of stock. The Commissioner asserted, however, that the trust was an ineligible stockholder. After a review of the legislative history of Subchapter S and some of the cases bearing on this issue the court concluded that the voting trust should not be considered a stockholder and that the regulations which so provided were clearly inconsistent with the statute. See Note, *Voting Trust Does Not Disqualify An Electing Corporation*, 50 Tul.L.Rev. 979 (1976). Pursuant to the amendments made by the Tax Reform Act of 1976 a voting trust is now an eligible shareholder of a Subchapter S corporation.

The question has arisen whether the bankruptcy of a shareholder in a Subchapter S corporation terminates the election. In *CHM Co.*, 68 T.C. 31 (1977), certain shareholders filed petitions under Chapters XI and XII and were appointed debtors-in-possession, and in *Dan E. Mason*, 68 T.C. 163 (1977), affirmed, 646 F.2d 1309 (9th Cir.1980), nonacq. 1978–1 C.B. 2, the sole shareholder filed a petition in straight bankruptcy and the trustee later abandoned the stock of the corporation. The Tax Court's answer in both cases was that the Subchapter S election was not terminated. See also *In re Weisser*, 44 A.F. T.R.2d ¶ 79–5854 (M.D.Fla.1979). Section 1361(c)(3) now permits the estate of an individual in bankruptcy to be a shareholder in a Subchapter S corporation.

4. An election to be an S corporation can be made at any time during the year preceding the taxable year for which the election is effective. All persons who are shareholders of the electing corporation on the day the election is made must consent to the election. An election to be an S corporation for the current taxable year can be made during the first two and one-half months of the year if: (1) the electing corporation met the requirements for Subchapter S on each day of the taxable year prior to the day of election, and (2) each person who held stock in the corporation during the taxable year before the election consented to the election. See Section 1362(b).

A Subchapter S election can be revoked by the consent of the shareholders holding more than one-half of the shares of stock of the corporation on the day that the revocation is made. See Section 1362(d)(1). If the revocation is made on or before the 15th day of the third month of a taxable year, it will be effective for that whole year. If the revocation is made after two and one-half months have passed, it will be effective for the following taxable year. If, however, the revocation specifies an effective date that is on or after the date on which the revocation is filed, the specified date will be the effective date. See Section 1362(d)(1)(D).

A Subchapter S election will terminate at any time the electing corporation ceases to qualify as an S corporation. See Section 1362(d)(2). The termination is effective on the date that the corporation ceases to qualify. If the termination occurs during a taxable year, that year is divided into two short years. See Section 1362(e). The tax items of the corporation for the termination year are allocated pro rata between the two short years. If, however, all of the shareholders consent, the allocation can be made according to the actual amounts incurred in each of those short years rather than pro rata. The normal Subchapter S provisions apply to the short year during which the corporation was subject to Subchapter S.

If a termination of S corporation status is inadvertent and caused by the corporation's ceasing to qualify as an S corporation, the Commissioner can permit the election to continue uninterrupted for a period specified by the Commissioner upon reasonably prompt steps being taken by the corporation and its shareholders to again qualify the corporation for Subchapter S treatment and agreement by the corporation and shareholders to make the adjustments required by the Commissioner. See Section 1362(f). If the inadvertent termination rule is not available, once an election has been terminated a new election cannot be made for five taxable years unless the Commissioner consents to an earlier election. See Section 1362(g). If an election is terminated, and if the corporation has accumulated earnings and profits, the corporation is granted a period of time (roughly one year) to distribute cash to its shareholders up to the amount of their accumulated adjustments accounts without causing dividend treatment. See Sections 1371(e) and 1377(b).

5. In determining the availability and treatment of employee fringe benefits, the same limitations and principles which apply to partnerships and partners apply to S corporations and to persons who own (or are deemed to own) more than two percent of the corporation's outstanding stock or more than two percent of the total combined voting power of the stock of the corporation. See Section 1372. See generally Starr and Perine, *To What Extent Can Partners and S Corporation Shareholders Receive Nontaxable Fringe Benefits?*, 65 J.Tax'n 40 (1986).

6. The basis of a partner in his partnership interest will, in general, include the partner's share of the liabilities of the partnership. The basis of a shareholder in an S corporation will not. The shareholder, however, will be able to include in his basis the amount of any liability owed him by the corporation. This difference in basis computation may be a significant factor in the choice of entity since losses and tax free cash flow are only available to the participants to the extent of their bases in the entity. Since most of the investment in a real estate development venture is generally in the form of mortgage loans a partner, at least initially, will have a greater basis than a shareholder in an S corporation. In the "right" situation, however, the shareholder of an S corporation may be able to include in his basis the amount of a corporate liability which he has guaranteed. The "right" situation is when the creditor has primarily looked to the liability of the guarantor. See *Selfe v. United States*, 778 F.2d 769 (11th Cir.1985); August, *"Selfe" Reflections: The Search for Basis for S Shareholder Guarantees of Corporate Indebtedness*, 3 J.Ps.Tax'n 260 (1986); Pope and Duvall, *Shareholder Guarantee of S Corporation Debt: Is There Basis After "Selfe?"*, 65 Taxes 330 (1987). But see *Estate of Daniel Leavitt*, 90 T.C. 206 (1988).

7. While the inability of shareholders to add their shares of S corporation liabilities to their bases in their interests in an S corporation, the inability to provide for shifting and special allocations of the profits and losses of an S corporation, and the potential recognition of gain on current and liquidating distributions of property by an S corporation may discourage the choice of an S corporation for use as the operating entity in a rental real estate venture, might the entity used during the acquisition and/or construction period be an S corporation?

a. Are there any advantages to be gained from the use of an S corporation during the acquisition and/or construction period? When does the greatest exposure to liability exist? Are cash flow distributions generally made during the construction period? Would the losses incurred, for tax purposes, during this period exceed the contributions of the participants?

b. If the choice is made to use an S corporation during the acquisition and construction period and an entity other than a corporation is to be used as the operating entity, what problems should be considered?

1) How will the ownership of the improved real estate be transferred from the S corporation to the entity, such as a partnership, to be used for operating?

a) Might the S corporation sell the improved real estate to the investors and the investors transfer it to a partnership? Might the S corporation sell the improved real estate to a partnership made up of the investors?

b) Might the S corporation distribute the improved real estate as a dividend to the investors who are its shareholders and the investors transfer it to a partnership? Or, might the S corporation distribute the improved real estate to a partnership made up of the investors?

c) Might the S corporation be liquidated and, as part of the liquidation, transfer the improved real estate to the investors who were the shareholders and the investors transfer it to a partnership? Or, as part of the liquidation might the S corporation transfer the improved real estate to a partnership made up of the investors?

2) Might the S corporation and the partnership simply enter into a long-term lease of the improved real estate?

a) Should more or less than a fair market rent be charged?

b) What might be the result if a nominal rent was charged?

3) Might the S corporation contribute the improved real estate to the partnership in return for an interest in the partnership?

8. See generally Mullaney and Blau, *An Analytic Comparison of Partnerships and S Corps as Vehicles for Leveraged Investments,* 59 J.Tax'n 142 (1983); Crumbley and Dickens, *Partnership Tax Treatment for Real Estate Corporations,* 13 # 2 Real Est.Rev. 36 (1983); Yelen, *Choosing the S Corporation as the Preferred Entity,* 42 N.Y.U.Inst.Fed.Tax'n 13–1 (1984); Shaw and August, *An Analysis of the Subchapter S Revision Act: Eligibility, Election, Termination,* 58 J.Tax'n 2 (1983); Shaw and August, *Subchapter S Revision Act Makes Significant Changes in Taxing S Corporation Operations,* 58 J.Tax'n 84 (1983); Shaw and August, *Subchapter S Revision Act: Distributions, Taxable Years and Other Changes,* 58 J.Tax'n 300 (1983); Miller, *A Walking Tour Through S–Land,* 10 J.Real Est.Tax'n 235 (1983); Coven and Hess, *The Subchapter S Revision Act: An Analysis and Appraisal,* 50 Tenn.L.Rev. 569 (1983); August and Schwimmer, *Integration of Subchapter C with Subchapter S After the Subchapter S Revision Act—Part 1,* 12 J.Corp.Tax'n 107 (1985); *Part II,* 12 J.Corp.Tax'n 269 (1985); *Part III,* 12 J.Corp.Tax'n 323 (1986); Wright, *Using S Corporations in Leveraged Ventures Where the Investors Anticipate Early Losses,* 15 Tax'n Law. 98 (1986); Rowland, *Distributions of Cash and Property by S Corporations Require Careful Planning,* 4 J.Ps.Tax'n 34 (1986); Ackerman, *Benefits of S Corporation Election for Closely Held Corporations Under the Tax Reform Act of 1986,* 65 Taxes 372 (1987); Volpi, *S Corporations Before and After the TRA,* 18 Tax Adviser 365 (1987); August, *Corporate–Level Taxes on S Corporations After the Tax Reform Act of 1986,* 4 J.Ps.Tax'n 91 (1987); Kramer and Kramer, *New Section 1374 Tax Reduces the Attractiveness of an S Corpora-*

tion Election for Closely Held Corporations, 65 Taxes 653 (1987); Billings and Ryan, *Making the S Election With Built–In Gain,* 14 J.Corp.Tax'n 283 (1988); Kristan, *Planning Around the Built–In Gains Tax,* 18 Tax Adviser 865 (1987); Smith, *S Corporation Built-in Gains: An Analysis of Section 1374 After the Tax Reform Act of 1986,* 39 U.Fla.L.Rev. 1117 (1987).

d.   THE LIMITED PARTNERSHIP WITH A CORPORATE GENERAL PARTNER

The corporate form and the partnership form offer certain advantages to the real estate developer. Combining the forms in a limited partnership with a corporate general partner may provide the best of all possible worlds or the worst, depending on the care taken in organizing the entity. For example, if properly organized, the use of this form of entity will insure limited liability for all individual participants in the venture. The corporation will be liable for the debts of the partnership. In addition, a corporate general partner is not as fallible as an individual general partner: it cannot die, become incompetent, become married or divorced. The corporate general partner might, however, become bankrupt or be dissolved, and its life is no longer than the period provided in its certificate of incorporation. The individual participants in the entity may have a substantial voice in whether bankruptcy or dissolution occurs. Stock in the corporate general partner may be disposed of without resulting in the dissolution of the partnership. Centralized management will be present in the board of directors and officers of the corporate general partner.

Initially, one should consider whether a corporation can become a partner. The Uniform Limited Partnership Act defines a limited partnership as a partnership formed by two or more "persons." The Uniform Partnership Act defines "persons" to include corporations. The definition of a limited partnership contained in the Revised Uniform Limited Partnership Act is similar to that contained in the U.L. P.A., and the Revised U.L.P.A. defines "persons" to include corporations. Therefore, in states which have statutes corresponding to the U.L.P.A., the Revised U.L.P.A. and the U.P.A., corporations are permitted to be partners. The question then becomes whether, under the corporate statutes of the state, a corporation has the power to become a partner. The Revised Model Business Corporation Act specifically grants this power to a corporation. See Rev.M.B.C.A. Section 3.02. Therefore, in states which have adopted this or a similar provision, a corporation has the power to become a partner. If, however, neither this nor a similar provision has been adopted, there may be some question whether a corporation can be a partner. The participation in a partnership by a corporation may be said to conflict with the statutory requirement of board control of corporate activities especially if there is more than one general partner. Or, it may be said to be an action which subjects corporate assets to risks and liabilities not contemplated by the shareholders at the time of investment. Neither of these reasons seems particularly persuasive in the case of a corporation which is the sole general partner of a limited partnership.

Assuming that a corporation can be the sole general partner of a limited partnership, can the individual participants, who will be the limited partners, also be the stockholders, officers and directors of the corporate general partner without being held to have participated in "control"? There are apparently a couple of answers to this question.

DELANEY, JR. v. FIDELITY LEASE LIMITED
Supreme Court of Texas, 1975.
526 S.W.2d 543.

DANIEL, Justice. The question here is whether limited partners in a limited partnership become liable as general partners if they "take part in the control of the business" while acting as officers of a corporation which is the sole general partner of the limited partnership. The trial court, by summary judgment, held that under such circumstances the limited partners did not become liable as general partners. The court of civil appeals affirmed with a dissent and a concurring opinion. 517 S.W.2d 420. We reverse and remand the case for trial on the merits.

Fidelity Lease Limited is a limited partnership organized under the Texas Uniform Limited Partnership Act, Article 6132a, to lease restaurant locations. It is composed of 22 individual partners, and a corporate general partner, Interlease Corporation. Interlease's officers, directors and shareholders were W.S. Crombie, Jr., Alan Kahn, and William D. Sanders, who were also limited partners of Fidelity. In February of 1969, plaintiffs Delaney, et al. entered into an agreement with the limited partnership, Fidelity, acting by and through its corporate general partner, Interlease, to lease a fast-food restaurant to the partnership. In accordance therewith, plaintiffs built the restaurant, but Fidelity failed to take possession or pay rent.

Plaintiffs brought suit for damages for breach of the lease agreement, naming as defendants the limited partnership of Fidelity Lease Limited, its corporate general partner Interlease Corporation, and all of its limited partners. On plaintiffs' motion the cause against the limited partners individually, insofar as it relates to their personal capacities and liabilities, was severed from the cause against Fidelity and Interlease. In this severed cause, the trial court granted a take nothing summary judgment for the limited partners. Plaintiffs appealed only as to limited partners Crombie, Kahn, and Sanders. Plaintiffs sought to hold these three individuals personally liable under Section 8 of Article 6132a, alleging that they had become general partners by participating in the management and control of the limited partnership.

Pertinent portions of the Texas Uniform Limited Partnership Act, Article 6132a, provide:

"Sec. 8.   A limited partner shall not become liable as a general partner unless, in addition to the exercise of his rights and powers as a limited partner, he *takes part in the control of the business.*

" *   *   *

"Sec. 13.   (a) A person may be a general partner and a limited partner in the same partnership at the same time.

"(b) A person who is a general, and also at the same time a limited partner, shall have all the rights and powers and be subject to all the restrictions of a general partner; except that, in respect to his contribution, he shall have the rights against the other members which he would have had if he were not also a general partner."   (Emphasis added.)

It was alleged by plaintiffs, and there is summary judgment evidence, that the three limited partners controlled the business of the limited partnership, albeit through the corporate entity.   The defendant limited partners argue that they acted only through the corporation and that the corporation actually controlled the business of the limited partnership.   In response to this contention, we adopt the following statements in the dissenting opinion of Chief Justice Preslar in the court of civil appeals:

"I find it difficult to separate their acts for they were at all times in the dual capacity of limited partners and officers of the corporation.   Apparently the corporation had no function except to operate the limited partnership and Appellees were obligated to their other partners to so operate the corporation as to benefit the partnership.   Each act was done then, not for the corporation, but for the partnership.   Indirectly, if not directly, they were exercising control over the partnership.   Truly 'the corporation fiction' was in this instance a fiction."   517 S.W.2d at 426–27.

Thus, we hold that the personal liability, which attaches to a limited partner when "he takes part in the control and management of the business," cannot be evaded merely by acting through a corporation. See Bergeson v. Life Ins. Corp. of America, 170 F.Supp. 150, 159 (D.Utah 1958), modified on other grounds, 265 F.2d 227 (10th Cir.) cert. den., 360 U.S. 932, 79 S.Ct. 1452, 3 L.Ed.2d 1545 (1959); Strang v. Thomas, 114 Wis. 599, 91 N.W. 237 (1902); 68 C.J.S. Partnership § 478, p. 1029 (1950); 60 Am.Jur.2d Partnership § 381, pp. 262–63 (1972).

The defendant limited partners also contend that the "control" test enumerated in Section 8 of Article 6132a for the purpose of inflicting personal liability should be coupled with a determination of whether the plaintiffs relied upon the limited partners as holding themselves out as general partners.   Thus, they argue that, before personal liability attaches to limited partners, two elements must coincide: (1) the limited partner must take part in the control of the business;   and (2) the limited partner must have held himself out as being a general partner having personal liability to an extent that the third party, or plaintiff, relied upon the limited partners' personal liability.   See

Vulcan Furniture Mfg. Corp. v. Vaughn, 168 So.2d 760 (Fla.Dist.Ct.App. 1964); Silvola v. Rowlett, 129 Colo. 522, 272 P.2d 287 (1954); Rathke v. Griffith, 36 Wash.2d 394, 218 P.2d 757 (1950). They observe that there is no question in this case but that the plaintiffs were in no way misled into believing that these three limited partners were personally liable on the lease, because the lease provided that the plaintiffs were entering into the lease with "Fidelity Lease, Ltd., a limited partnership acting by and through Interlease Corporation, General Partner."

We disagree with this contention. Section 8 of Article 6132a simply provides that a limited partner who takes part in the control of the business subjects himself to personal liability as a general partner. The statute makes no mention of any requirement of reliance on the part of the party attempting to hold the limited partner personally liable.

Crombie, Kahn, and Sanders argue that, since their only control of Fidelity's business was as officers of the alleged corporate general partner, they are insulated from personal liability arising from their activities or those of the corporation. This is a general rule of corporate law, but one of several exceptions in which the courts will disregard the corporate fiction is where it is used to circumvent a statute. Pacific American Gasoline Co. of Texas v. Miller, 76 S.W.2d 833 (Tex. Civ.App.1934, writ ref'd). See also Drye v. Eagle Rock Ranch, Inc., 364 S.W.2d 196, 202 (Tex.1962), and Pace Corporation v. Jackson, 155 Tex. 179, 284 S.W.2d 340 (1955). That is precisely the result here, for it is undisputed that the corporation was organized to manage and control the limited partnership. Strict compliance with the statute is required if a limited partner is to avoid liability as a general partner. See Hamilton on Business Organizations, 19 Texas Practice § 215, at p. 206. See also "The Limited Partnership With a Corporate General Partner * * *", Comment, 24 S.W.Law J. 285, 291–292 (1970). It is quite clear that there can be more than one general partner. Assuming that Interlease Corporation was a legal general partner, a question which is not before us and which we do not decide, this would not prevent Crombie, Kahn, and Sanders from taking part in the control of the business in their individual capacities as well as their corporate capacities. In no event should they be permitted to escape the statutory liability which would have devolved upon them if there had been no attempted interposition of the corporate shield against personal liability. Otherwise, the statutory requirement of at least one general partner with general liability in a limited partnership can be circumvented or vitiated by limited partners operating the partnership through a corporation with minimum capitalization and therefore minimum liability. We hold that the trial court erred in granting summary judgment for the defendants, Crombie, Kahn, and Sanders. If, upon trial on the merits it is found from a preponderance of the evidence that either of these three limited partners took part in the control of the business, whether or not in his capacity as an officer of Interlease

Corporation, he should be adjudged personally liable as a general partner.

NOTE

1. The three limited partners involved in the above case were also the president, vice president and treasurer, and constituted all of the directors and shareholders of the corporate general partner.

2. The lower appellate court in *Delaney, Jr. v. Fidelity Lease Limited,* 517 S.W.2d 420 (Tex.Civ.App., 1974), in affirming the trial court's summary judgment in favor of the defendants, analyzed the "control" test in terms of whether there was, or could have been, reliance on the personal liability of the limited partners. See Note, *Absent Creditor Reliance, A Limited Partner Who is a Director of the Corporate General Partner is Not Personally Liable for Partnership Obligations,* 6 Tex.Tech.L.Rev. 1171 (1975). Obviously, the Texas Supreme Court rejected the use of the reliance analysis. See Note, *Liability of Limited Partners Participating in the Management of the Sole Corporate General Partner,* 29 Sw.L.J. 791 (1975). The Texas Supreme Court's rejection of the reliance analysis appears somewhat in conflict with recent trends in the area. For example, Section 303(a) of the Revised Uniform Limited Partnership Act adopts a form of the reliance test in imposing liability on a limited partner who takes part in "control."

3. Which analysis of the control test did the Texas Supreme Court adopt?

a. Would it have come to a different conclusion if the corporate general partner was adequately capitalized? Apparently not, since it appears that the corporation was adequately capitalized and the plaintiffs did not allege any deception, misrepresentation or inadequate capitalization of the corporation. See Note, *Liability of Limited Partners Participating in the Management of the Sole Corporate General Partner,* 29 Sw.L.J. 791, 797, 798–99 (1975).

b. Since the adequacy of the capitalization of the corporate general partner was not considered to be of substantial relevance by the court, one might then infer that in its analysis of the control test the court adopted a fairly broad direct or indirect participation in management approach in concluding that the use of the corporate general partner "circumvented" the policy of Sec. 7 of the U.L.P.A. See generally Note, *Limited Partners Who Control Corporate General Partner Are Subject to Personal Liability as General Partners,* 7 Tex.Tech.L.Rev. 745 (1976). In this context any substantial participation by a limited partner in the management of the corporate general partner might be unwise if the limited partner wanted to maintain limited liability status.

c. If the Revised Uniform Limited Partnership Act had been in effect in Texas at the time of *Delaney Jr. v. Fidelity Lease Limited,* would the Texas Supreme Court have reached a different result? In order for limited partners to be liable, Section 303(a) of the Revised Act requires a form of reliance by creditors unless the limited partners' participation in control of the business is substantially the same as the exercise of the powers of a general partner. If the limited partners are the only shareholders, officers and directors of the sole corporate general partner, is their participation in control the same as a general partner? Consider the result if the limited partnership act, effective in Texas, also provided that a limited partner could act as an officer, director or shareholder of a corporate general partner without being held to have taken part in control of the business. Does this mean that the limited partners can own 100% of the stock and make up the board and officers of a sole corporate general partner?

If the limited partners own 100% of the stock and make up the board of directors and officers of the sole corporate general partner, might the limited partners be considered materially or actively participating in the activities of the limited partnership for the purpose of avoiding, in whole or in part, the passive loss limitations of Section 469?

In Rev.Rul. 88–23, 1988–15 I.R.B. 7, the Internal Revenue Service held that the Revised Uniform Limited Partnership Act as adopted in Texas corresponds to the Uniform Limited Partnership Act for the purposes of Reg. Sec. 301.7701–2 in determining whether a limited partnership should be treated as a partnership or as an association taxable as a corporation.

4. A fact situation very similar to that in *Delaney, Jr. v. Fidelity Lease Ltd.* was presented to the Washington Court of Appeals in *Frigidaire Sales Corp. v. Union Properties, Inc.,* 14 Wash.App. 634, 544 P.2d 781 (1976). The Washington Court of Appeals disagreed with the Texas Supreme Court's analysis of the control test stating, "[t]he underlying purpose of the control prohibition * * * is not furthered, however, by prohibiting limited partners from forming a corporation to act as the sole general partner in a limited partnership. A third party dealing with a corporation must reasonably rely on the solvency of the corporate entity. It makes little difference if the corporation is or is not the general partner in a limited partnership. In either instance, the third party cannot justifiably rely on the solvency of the individuals who own the corporation.

"We hold that limited partners are not liable as general partners simply because they are active officers or directors, or are stockholders of a corporate general partner in a limited partnership." at 544 P.2d 785.

The Supreme Court of Washington affirmed the decision of the Court of Appeals.

FRIGIDAIRE SALES CORP. v. UNION PROPERTIES, INC.

Supreme Court of Washington, 1977.
88 Wash.2d 400, 562 P.2d 244.
[footnotes omitted]

HAMILTON, Associate Justice. * * *

Petitioner entered into a contract with Commercial Investors (Commercial), a limited partnership. Respondents, Leonard Mannon and Raleigh Baxter, were limited partners of Commercial. Respondents were also officers, directors, and shareholders of Union Properties, Inc., the only general partner of Commercial. Respondents controlled Union Properties, and through their control of Union Properties they exercised the day-to-day control and management of Commercial. Commercial breached the contract, and petitioner brought this suit against Union Properties and respondents. The trial court concluded that respondents did not incur general liability for Commercial's obligations by reason of their control of Commercial, and the Court of Appeals affirmed.

We first note that petitioner does not contend that respondents acted improperly by setting up the limited partnership with a corporation as the sole general partner. Limited partnerships are a statutory form of business organization, and parties creating a limited partnership must follow the statutory requirements. In Washington, parties may form a limited partnership with a corporation as the sole general partner. * * *

Petitioner's sole contention is that respondents should incur general liability for the limited partnership's obligations under [Section 7 of the U.L.P.A.] because they exercised the day-to-day control and management of Commercial. Respondents, on the other hand, argue that Commercial was controlled by Union Properties, a separate legal entity, and not by respondents in their individual capacities.

Petitioner cites Delaney v. Fidelity Lease Ltd., 526 S.W.2d 543 (Tex. 1975), as support for its contention that respondents should incur general liability under [Section 7 of the U.L.P.A.] for the limited partnership's obligations. That case also involved the issue of liability for limited partners who controlled the limited partnership as officers, directors, and shareholders of the corporate general partner. The Texas Supreme Court reversed the decision of the Texas Court of Civil Appeals and found the limited partners had incurred general liability because of their control of the limited partnership. See Delaney v. Fidelity Lease Ltd., 517 S.W.2d 420 (Tex.Civ.App.1974), rev'd, 526 S.W.2d 543 (Tex.1975).

We find the Texas Supreme Court's decision distinguishable from the present case. In *Delaney,* the corporation and the limited partnership were set up contemporaneously, and the sole purpose of the corporation was to operate the limited partnership. The Texas Supreme Court found that the limited partners who controlled the corporation were obligated to their other limited partners to operate the corporation for the benefit of the partnership. " 'Each act was done then, not for the corporation, but for the partnership.' " Delaney v. Fidelity Lease Ltd., 526 S.W.2d 543, 545 (Tex.1975), quoting from the dissenting opinion in Delaney v. Fidelity Lease Ltd., 517 S.W.2d 420, 426 (Tex.Civ.App.1974). This is not the case here. The pattern of operation of Union Properties was to investigate and conceive of real estate investment opportunities and, when it found such opportunities, to cause the creation of limited partnerships with Union Properties acting as the general partner. Commercial was only one of several limited partnerships so conceived and created. Respondents did not form Union Properties for the sole purpose of operating Commercial. Hence, their acts on behalf of Union Properties were not performed merely for the benefit of Commercial.

* * * The Texas Supreme Court was concerned with the possibility that limited partners might form the corporate general partner with minimum capitalization:

In no event should they be permitted to escape the statutory liability which would have devolved upon them if there had been no attempted interposition of the corporate shield against personal liability.   Otherwise, the statutory requirement of at least one general partner with general liability in a limited partnership can be circumvented or vitiated by limited partners operating the partnership through a corporation with minimum capitalization and therefore minimum liability.

Delaney v. Fidelity Lease Ltd., supra at 546.

However, we agree with our Court of Appeals analysis that this concern with minimum capitalization is not peculiar to limited partnerships with corporate general partners, but may arise anytime a creditor deals with a corporation.   See Frigidaire Sales Corp. v. Union Properties, Inc., supra 14 Wash.App. at 638, 544 P.2d 781.   Because our limited partnership statutes permit parties to form a limited partnership with a corporation as the sole general partner, this concern about minimal capitalization, standing by itself, does not justify a finding that the limited partners incur general liability for their control of the corporate general partner.   See A. Bromberg, Crane and Bromberg on Partnership § 26 at 146–47 (1968).   If a corporate general partner is inadequately capitalized, the rights of a creditor are adequately protected under the "piercing-the-corporate-veil" doctrine of corporation law.
* * *

Furthermore, petitioner was never led to believe that respondents were acting in any capacity other than in their corporate capacities. The parties stipulated at the trial that respondents never acted in any direct, personal capacity.   When the shareholders of a corporation, who are also the corporation's officers and directors, conscientiously keep the affairs of the corporation separate from their personal affairs, and no fraud or manifest injustice is perpetrated upon third persons who deal with the corporation, the corporation's separate entity should be respected.   * * *

For us to find that respondents incurred general liability for the limited partnership's obligations under [Section 7 of the U.L.P.A.] would require us to apply a literal interpretation of the statute and totally ignore the corporate entity of Union Properties, when petitioner knew it was dealing with that corporate entity.   There can be no doubt that respondents, in fact, controlled the [partnership].   However, they did so only in their capacities as agents for their principal, the corporate general partner.   Although the corporation was a separate entity, it could act only through its board of directors, officers, and agents. * * * Petitioner entered into the contract with Commercial.   Respondents signed the contract in their capacities as president and secretary-treasurer of Union Properties, the general partner of Commercial.   In the eyes of the law it was Union Properties, as a separate corporate entity, which entered into the contract with petitioner and controlled the limited partnership.

Further, because respondents scrupulously separated their actions on behalf of the corporation from their personal actions, petitioner never mistakenly assumed that respondents were general partners with general liability. See Frigidaire Sales Corp. v. Union Properties, Inc., 14 Wash.App. 634, 641–42, 544 P.2d 781 (1975); Delaney v. Fidelity Lease Ltd., 517 S.W.2d 420 (Tex.Civ.App.1974); Feld, *The "Control" Test for Limited Partnerships*, 82 Harv.L.Rev. 1471 (1969). Petitioner knew Union Properties was the sole general partner and did not rely on respondents' control by assuming that they were also general partners. If petitioner had not wished to rely on the solvency of Union Properties as the only general partner, it could have insisted that respondents personally guarantee contractual performance. Because petitioner entered into the contract knowing that Union Properties was the only party with general liability, and because in the eyes of the law it was Union Properties, a separate entity, which controlled the limited partnership, there is no reason for us to find that respondents incurred general liability for their acts done as officers of the corporate general partner.

The decision of the Court of Appeals is affirmed.

WRIGHT, C.J., and ROSELLINI, STAFFORD, UTTER, HOROWITZ, BRACHTENBACH and DOLLIVER, JJ., concur.

NOTE

1. If the Washington Supreme Court had been faced with a situation in which a corporation was formed specifically for the purpose of acting as the corporate general partner of a limited partnership, would it have followed the decision of the Texas Supreme Court in *Delaney v. Fidelity Lease Ltd.,* 526 S.W.2d 543 (Tex.1975)?

    a. If the corporate general partner was adequately capitalized, would this produce a different result?

    b. If the parties dealing with the limited partnership relied on the liability of the corporate general partner and had no reason to assume that the limited partners, who were also shareholders, directors and/or officers of the corporate general partner, were themselves general partners, would this affect the result?

2. Might the result reached by a court be affected if, in addition to being the general partner of the limited partnership, the corporation leased certain property, such as land or furnishings, to the limited partnership?

3. In *Western Camps, Inc. v. Riverway Ranch Enterprises,* 70 Cal.App.3d 714, 138 Cal.Rptr. 918 (1977), the California Second District Court of Appeals, faced with a situation similar to that presented in *Delaney,* supra, and *Frigidaire,* supra, followed the reasoning of the Washington Court of Appeals in *Frigidaire Sales Corp. v. Union Properties, Inc.,* 14 Wash.App. 634, 544 P.2d 781 (1976), affirmed, 88 Wash.2d 400, 562 P.2d 244 (1977).

4. In view of the control question under the U.L.P.A. and Revised U.L.P.A., should the limited partners own all of the stock and act as officers and/or directors of the corporate general partner?

5. Turning to the considerations involved in the classification of the entity for tax purposes, if the limited partners were considered liable, as if they were general partners, because of their control over the corporate general partner and the lack of adequate capitalization of the corporate general partner, could it be said that both limited liability and centralized management were absent, and that the entity must be treated for income tax purposes as a partnership? See *Zuckman v. United States*, 524 F.2d 729 (Ct.Cl.1975).

6. If the bankruptcy of the corporate general partner will result in the dissolution of the partnership, does this conclusively establish that the partnership does not possess the attribute of continuity of life?

a. Cannot any corporation become bankrupt, thereby terminating its existence as then constituted? Yet, we say that a corporation has continuity of life.

b. Even if the limited partners do not control the corporation, they probably have the ability to furnish capital to it in order to avoid its bankruptcy.

1. Can the same be said of their ability to furnish capital to an individual general partner in order to avoid the individual general partner's bankruptcy?

2. Are there any substantial differences in this context between an individual general partner and a corporate general partner, particularly if the corporate general partner was formed for, and acted solely as, the general partner of one specific limited partnership?

7. See generally Wiggin, *Reappraising the Tax Status of Corporate General Partners*, 3 # 2 Real Est.Rev. 100 (1973); Sexton and Osteen, *Classification as a Partnership or as an Association Taxable as a Corporation*, 24 Tul.Tax Inst. 95 (1975); Comment, *Piercing the Veil of the Corporate General Partner in the Hybrid Limited Partnership: A Suggested Remedy for Inequitable Conduct by Limited Partners*, 17 Suffolk U.L.Rev. 949 (1983).

8. While the position taken by the Internal Revenue Service in Rev.Proc. 89–12, supra, pages 87 to 91, with respect to the treatment of a limited partnership with a corporate general partner is somewhat restrictive, the courts have required somewhat less in order for the limited partnership to be classified as a partnership.

PHILLIP G. LARSON v. COMM.
66 T.C. 159 (1976), acq. 1979–1 C.B. 1.
[footnotes omitted]

TANNENWALD, Judge.

* * *

Other issues having been disposed of by mutual agreement of the parties, the sole issue remaining for decision is whether the limited partnerships involved in this proceeding constitute associations taxable as corporations within the meaning of section 7701(a)(3).

* * *

Findings of Fact

* * *

Phillip G. Larson, * * * petitioner was a limited partner in Mai–Kai Apartments (hereinafter Mai–Kai), a limited partnership formed under the laws of the State of California. During the taxable year 1970, petitioner was also a limited partner in Somis Orchards (hereinafter Somis), a limited partnership formed under the laws of the State of California.

* * *

Grubin, Horth & Lawless, Inc. (hereinafter GHL), a California corporation, the sole general partner of both Mai–Kai and Somis, was formed April 2, 1968, primarily to organize so-called "real estate syndications" as limited partnerships under the laws of the State of California. GHL kept its books on the basis of a fiscal year ending March 31. GHL had a paid-in capital of $21,300. From its incorporation to March 31, 1974, its capital and surplus ranged between a maximum of $49,593 at the close of the fiscal year 1970 to a minimum of $18,764 as of the close of the fiscal year 1974. Cash on hand was generally negligible. GHL organized both Mai–Kai and Somis and managed and administered the partnership properties. * * *

Mai–Kai was formed on or about November 26, 1968, under the limited partnership provisions of California Corporations Code sections 15501–15531, for the purpose of owning and operating a student apartment complex in Arcata, Calif., known as the Mai–Kai Apartments. Upon the formation of Mai–Kai, GHL transferred to Mai–Kai, as a contribution to its capital, the right to acquire the Mai–Kai Apartments under a contract negotiated by Legrand Capital Corp., GHL's predecessor in interest.

* * *

GHL was not required to make any further capital contributions to Mai–Kai. The limited partnership interests in Mai–Kai were divided into 10 "units" of $9,500 per "unit." All of the "units" were sold to a total of eight limited partners. The total capital contribution to Mai–Kai by the limited partners was $95,000 in cash. GHL's total capital contribution to Mai–Kai was reflected and carried at zero ($0) on Mai–Kai's books and records.

* * *

After its formation, Mai–Kai purchased the Mai–Kai Apartments from Century Land Co., a California corporation, for a purchase price of $450,000. The purchase price was paid by the execution of a promissory note dated November 17, 1968, in the amount of $450,000 in favor of Century Land Co. The promissory note was secured by a deed of trust upon the Mai–Kai Apartments dated November 17, 1968, which was given to Century Land Co. by Mai–Kai to secure payment of the purchase price. Pursuant to section 580b of the California Code of Civil Procedure, in the event of default by Mai–Kai under the promissory note no money judgment would lie against Mai–Kai, and Century Land

Co.'s remedy would be limited to requiring the sale of the Mai–Kai Apartments pursuant to the deed of trust, with the proceeds to be applied to the promissory note.

The Mai–Kai partnership agreement and certificate provided, in pertinent part:

AGREEMENT OF LIMITED PARTNERSHIP

3. *Term.*

The partnership shall commence as of December 1, 1968 and shall continue for a period of thirty three (33) years * * * unless sooner terminated as hereinafter provided for, or unless extended for such longer term as may be determined by the election of the Limited Partners entitled to sixty per cent (60%) or more of the profits of the partnership allocable to the Limited Partners.

* * *

5. *Capital Contributions.*

(a) GRUBIN, HORTH & LAWLESS, INC. shall transfer and contribute to the partnership its right to acquire the [apartments] * * *.

The General Partner shall not be required to make any capital contribution other than its right to acquire the real property * * *.

(b) * * * The total capital contribution of the Limited Partners shall be Ninety Five Thousand Dollars * * *.

6. *Rights, Duties and Obligations of the General Partner.*

(a) The partnership business shall be managed by the General Partner. In addition to those powers granted to the General Partner by law the General Partner shall have the power to execute leases, incur obligations on behalf of the partnership in connection with the business, and execute on behalf of the partnership any and all instruments necessary to carry out the intentions and purposes of the partnership, including the power to dispose of the real property or other assets of the partnership for full and adequate consideration. The General Partner shall devote such time to the business of the partnership as shall be necessary to accomplish the purposes set forth herein.

(b) *Management and Brokerage Fees.* In addition to its share of the profits and cash flow distributions, * * * the General Partner shall receive and be entitled to the following fees:

(1) A monthly management fee equal to five per cent (5%) of the gross receipts of the partnership business during each month. * * *

(2) The General Partner may obtain financing or refinancing for the partnership property on behalf of the partnership, and if successful, the General Partner shall be entitled to a mortgage loan fee not to exceed two per cent (2%) of the total amount of each loan.

(3) The General Partner shall also be entitled to reimbursement for all reasonable out-of-pocket expenses incurred by it in the management and operation of the partnership business.

* * *

7. *Withdrawal of Capital.*

No Limited Partner may withdraw his capital contribution to the partnership without the consent of the General Partner. * * *

8. *Rights, Duties, Obligations of the Limited Partners.*

(a) Except as otherwise expressly provided herein, no Limited Partner shall participate in the management of the partnership business.

(b) A Limited Partner shall have the right to withdraw his capital account upon the termination of the partnership * * *.

* * *

10. *Profits, Losses and Distributions.*

(a) *Profits.* The net profits of the partnership shall be equal to the taxable income of the partnership as shown in the partnership tax information tax return filed in accordance with the requirements of the Internal Revenue Code.

Except as provided in Paragraph 11 below, profits shall be divided as follows:

(1) Twenty Per Cent (20%) to the account of the General Partner.

(2) Eighty Per Cent (80%) to the accounts of the Limited Partners * * *.

(b) *Losses.* All losses of the partnership shall be allocated entirely to the Limited Partners in proportion to their capital contributions, subject however to the limitation of liability of each Limited Partner to the amount of his individual investment in the partnership. All losses of the partnership in excess of the total capital contributions of the Limited Partners shall be borne entirely by the General Partner.

(c) *Distributions.* Subject to the provisions of Paragraph 11 below, in the event of the sale of the real property, or the liquidation of the partnership, the net proceeds realized from such sale, * * * or the proceeds of any liquidation, as the case may be, and the cash flow of the partnership shall be distributed as follows:

(1) Twenty Per Cent (20%) to the General Partner.

(2) Eighty Per Cent (80%) to the Limited Partners * * *.

* * *

(e) The General Partner shall distribute the cash flow of the partnership at convenient intervals, but not less frequently than quarterly.

11. *Limitation on Allocations and Distributions to General Partner.*

Notwithstanding Paragraph 10 above, it is agreed that the General Partner shall not participate in the cash flow or profits of the project until such time as a Limited Partner (assuming 50% tax bracket) has been returned his initial investment through a combination of cash flow and operating losses * * *. For the purpose of this computation, the total after-tax investment for the Limited Partners shall be considered to be $47,500. From said amount shall be deducted 100% of the cash distribution to the Limited Partners and 50% of operating losses * * *. Added thereto shall be 50% of profits. When the after-tax investment of $47,500 has thus been reduced to zero, it will be considered that the Limited Partners have been returned their after-tax investment and thereafter the General Partner will participate in all future cash flow and profits * * *.

* * *

15. *Assignment of Partners' Interests.*

(a) *General Partner.* The General Partner shall not assign, mortgage, encumber or sell its interest as General Partner in the partnership or enter into any agreement as a result of which any firm, person or corporation shall become interested with it in the partnership * * *.

(b) *Limited Partners Right to Receive Income.* The right of a Limited Partner to receive any income from the partnership shall not be transferred, sold or assigned without the prior written consent of the General Partner. The General Partner shall not unreasonably withhold such consent.

(c) *Transfer of Capital Interest—Limited Partner.* The capital interest of a Limited Partner may not be transferred, sold or assigned by such Limited Partner except in accordance with the following provisions:

A Limited Partner who desires to sell or transfer his capital interest in the partnership shall serve written notice on the General Partner * * *. If the General Partner, within ten (10) days following receipt of such notice, in good faith determines that the purchase price offered by the proposed transferee is less than the then fair market value of the interest to be transferred, the General Partner shall have the option to notify the proposed transferor within said ten day period, that the transferor cannot effect a transfer of the interest unless he first offers the interest to the remaining Limited Partners. * * *

In the event that (i) the General Partner does not exercise its option or (ii) the remaining Limited Partners do not elect to purchase the entire interest of the proposed transferor, the transferor may effect the transfer of his interest to the proposed transferee except that as a condition precedent to the admission of the proposed transferee, such person shall execute and acknowledge such instruments as the General Partner shall deem necessary or desirable to effect such admission and to confirm the agreement of the person being admitted to be bound by all of the terms and provisions of this agreement as the same have been amended. The transferee shall pay all reasonable expenses in connection with his admission as a substituted limited partner.

* * *

17. *Termination.*

Notwithstanding anything to the contrary contained herein, the partnership shall terminate upon any of the following events:

(a) A disposition of [sic] the partnership of its entire interest in the real property.

(b) The adjudication of bankruptcy of the General Partner or otherwise as provided by the Uniform Limited Partnership Act, unless the business is continued by a General Partner elected in place thereof.

(c) A determination by the election of Limited Partners entitled to sixty per cent (60%) or more of the profits of the partnership allocable to the Limited Partners that the partnership shall terminate.

(d) The removal of the General Partner by the vote of Limited Partners entitled to sixty per cent (60%) or more of the profits of the partnership allocable to the Limited Partners. In such event, there shall be a distribution of assets * * * unless the Limited Partners, by an affirmative vote of Limited Partners owning 100% of the profits in the partnership allocable to the Limited Partners, elect to form a new partnership to continue the partnership business.

* * *

* * *

In the case of Mai–Kai, GHL, thus had a 20–percent "subordinated" participation interest in operating profits, cash flow, and net proceeds upon the sale of partnership assets. GHL's participation interest in Mai–Kai became unsubordinated after December 31, 1972.

* * *

During 1973 Mai–Kai did not generate a profit or cash flow to be distributed to either the limited partners or to the general partner.

For each of the taxable years 1968 to 1973, inclusive, Mai–Kai reported losses on its U.S. Partnership Income Tax Returns as follows:

Year	Loss	Year	Loss
1968	$91,595	1971	$11,169
1969	38,030	1972	8,378
1970	23,491	1973	12,520

On his individual U.S. income tax returns, the petitioner deducted his distributive shares of the losses reported by Mai–Kai. Respondent disallowed said deductions on the ground that Mai–Kai was an association taxable as a corporation within the meaning of section 7701(a)(3).

Somis Orchards was formed on or about November 1, 1969, under the limited partnership provisions of California Corporations Code sections 15501–15531 for the purpose of acquiring, holding, operating, improving, leasing, selling, and otherwise managing approximately 265 acres of citrus groves and related assets in Ventura County, Calif.

The citrus groves were purchased from Kaiser Aetna in 1969 for a total purchase price of $3,620,000. * * *

The citrus groves were part of a 10,000 acre property owned by Kaiser Aetna known as Rancho Las Posas. At the time of their acquisition by Somis Orchards the citrus groves were planted with lemons, grapefruit, and oranges. The property was suitable, however, for possible future residential or commercial use. Kaiser Aetna, the seller of the property, had begun the formulation of an overall master plan for the development and marketing of the entire Rancho Las Posas property. A part of the consideration paid by Somis Orchards to Kaiser Aetna for the citrus groves related to Kaiser Aetna's agreement to enhance the value of the citrus groves through Kaiser Aetna's development of the comprehensive master plan and commencement of sales and marketing activities. Somis contracted with Kaiser Aetna to have the citrus groves remain in Kaiser Aetna's master plan and for the citrus groves to be managed by Kaiser Aetna in the interim.

GHL's capital contributions to Somis consisted of the transfer to the partnership of GHL's rights to acquire the citrus groves under the purchase contract negotiated by GHL. In addition, GHL assigned to Somis the management contract negotiated by GHL for management of the citrus groves by Kaiser Aetna.

A total of 44 limited partners contributed $420,000 in cash to Somis. Each limited partner also executed a series of promissory notes reflecting annual contributions to be made by the limited partners during the 8 years following the formation of Somis. Of the total 44 limited partners in Somis, 26 joined the partnership in 1969, making capital contributions totaling $265,000. The remaining 18 limited partners joined the limited partnership in 1970.

* * *

The partnership agreement and certificate signed by GHL and the Somis limited partners were generally similar to those of Mai–Kai, with the following material differences:

(1) The initial 15–year term could be extended by a 51–percent vote of limited partners.

(2) The general partner could not sell or pledge more than 45 percent of the partnership's assets or refinance the property without the approval of 51 percent of the limited partnership interests.

(3) The general partner was allowed additional compensation for organizational services, and an "incentive" fee equal to a percentage of cash flow in excess of a stated amount.

(4) Profits, proceeds from sales of assets, and liquidation proceeds were allocated, 15 percent to the general partner and 85 percent to the limited partners. The general partner had no interest in cash flow.

(5) Fifty-one percent of the limited partnership interests could elect to terminate the partnership. The same percentage could vote to remove the general partner, in which event the partnership would terminate unless 51 percent of the limited partnership interests elected to form a new partnership to continue the business. On removal, the general partner would be paid the value of its interest, as determined by arbitration.

(6) The limited partners acknowledged the general partner's receipt of a real estate broker's commission in connection with the acquisition of the real property.

(7) The rights of the parties were contingent on approval by the State department of corporations of the sale of the limited partnership interests.

(8) The agreement could be amended by a 51–percent vote of limited partners.

* * *

In the case of Somis, GHL had a 15–percent "subordinated" participation interest in operating profits and net proceeds upon the sale of partnership assets. GHL did not have a participation interest in Somis' cash flow. * * *

During the taxable years 1969 to 1973 inclusive, Somis operated at a loss. The following schedule sets forth the annual losses as reported by Somis on its U.S. Partnership Income Tax Returns:

Year	Loss	Year	Loss
1969	$185,820	1972	$267,335
1970	595,853	1973	229,621
1971	373,220		

On their respective individual and corporate U.S. income tax returns, the petitioners deducted their distributive shares of the losses reported by Somis. Respondent disallowed said deductions on the ground that Somis was an association taxable as a corporation within the meaning of section 7701(a)(3).

* * *

No limited partner in Somis or Mai–Kai was a stockholder of GHL, with the exception of Harris E. Lawless, who at all pertinent times held a 1.905–percent limited partnership interest in Somis and owned 23.125 percent of the stock of GHL. Neither Somis nor Mai–Kai issued certificates to the limited partners representing shares in the partnerships. During the period 1968 to 1973, no meetings of the limited partners in Mai–Kai were held, nor were any decisions with respect to either Mai–Kai or Somis referred to the limited partners for their vote or approval. Meetings of the Somis partners were held in December of 1972 and 1973 to allow Kaiser Aetna to inform them of progress in obtaining master plan approval for the planned city development covering the land owned by Somis.

Pursuant to the provisions of the California Corporate Securities Law (Cal.Corp.Code secs. 25000 et seq.), and prior to the formation of Somis, GHL applied for and secured from the California Corporations Commissioner a permit authorizing it to offer for sale, negotiate for the sale of, and sell security interests (or subscriptions therefor) in Somis.

Offering circulars, prepared by GHL, were distributed by GHL to prospective limited partners in Somis and Mai–Kai. The circulars advertised the limited partnership interests as "tax-sheltered real estate investments," and contained extensive descriptions of the underlying real property, the investment terms, and the anticipated return on the proposed investments.

Of the 42 limited partnership "units" sold in Somis, 17 were sold by two employees of GHL, Robert L. Horth and Alan J. Parisse, without commission, Horth and Parisse held restricted brokers' licenses issued by the National Association of Security Dealers (hereinafter NASD), which authorized them to sell mutual funds, limited partnership interests, and similar investments but not to sell stocks, bonds, or other corporate securities. Eleven and one-half of the Somis limited partnership "units" were sold by Robert Schmidt (a shareholder and director of GHL but not an employee), who was paid a commission on his sales by GHL. Schmidt also held a restricted NASD broker's license. The remaining 13½ Somis limited partnership "units" were sold by a total of nine financial planners holding restricted NASD brokers' licenses, all of whom were paid a commission by GHL.

All of the Mai–Kai limited partnership "units" were sold to investors by Robert L. Horth and Alan J. Parisse (as GHL employees) under their restricted NASD brokers' licenses. No commissions were paid to Horth or Parisse on said sales.

OPINION

Petitioners owned limited partnership interests in Mai–Kai and Somis, two real estate ventures organized under the California Uniform Limited Partnership Act, Cal.Corp.Code secs. 15501 et seq. (West Supp. 1976) (hereinafter referred to as CULPA). The partnerships incurred losses during the years in issue, and petitioners deducted their distributive shares of such losses on their individual tax returns. Respondent disallowed those deductions on the ground that the partnerships were associations taxable as corporations, as defined in section 7701(a)(3), and not partnerships as defined in section 7701(a)(2). Petitioners allege that the partnerships fail all of the tests of corporate resemblance established by respondent's regulations (sec. 301.7701–2, Proced. & Admin.Regs.); respondent contends that all those tests are satisfied. Both sides agree that the regulations apply and are controlling, and our opinion and decision are consequently framed in that context; the validity of respondent's regulations is not before us. In our previous (now withdrawn) opinion dated October 21, 1975, we concluded that respondent should prevail. Upon reconsideration, we have come to the opposite conclusion and hold for petitioners.

The starting point of the regulations' definition of an "association" is the principle applied in Morrissey v. Commissioner, 296 U.S. 344 (1935), that the term includes entities which resemble corporations although they are not formally organized as such. Morrissey identified several characteristics of the corporate form which the regulations adopt as a test of corporate resemblance. For the purpose of comparing corporations with partnerships, the significant characteristics are: continuity of life; centralization of management; limited liability; and free transferability of interests. Other corporate or noncorporate characteristics may also be considered if appropriate in a particular case. An organization will be taxed as a corporation if, taking all relevant characteristics into account, it more nearly resembles a corporation than some other entity. Sec. 301.7701–2(a)(1), Proced. & Admin.Regs.; see and compare Bush # 1, 48 T.C. 218, 227–228 (1967), and Giant Auto Parts, Ltd., 13 T.C. 307 (1949). This will be true only if it possesses more corporate than noncorporate characteristics.

The regulations discuss each major corporate characteristic separately, and each apparently bears equal weight in the final balancing. * * * This apparently mechanical approach may perhaps be explained as an attempt to impart a degree of certainty to a subject otherwise fraught with imponderables. In most instances, the regulations also make separate provision for the classification of limited partnerships. Petitioners rely heavily on those provisions, while respondent seeks to distinguish them or to minimize their importance.

1. Continuity of Life

* * * A corporation possesses a greater degree of continuity of life than a partnership, since its existence is not dependent upon events personally affecting its separate members. Because of their more intimate legal and financial ties, partners are given a continuing right to choose their associates which is denied to corporate shareholders. A material alteration in the makeup of the partnership, as through the death or incapacity of a partner, either dissolves the partnership relation by operation of law or permits dissolution by order of court. Uniform Partnership Act, secs. 31 and 32 (hereinafter referred to as UPA). Partners are then free to withdraw their shares from the business, though they may agree to form a new partnership to continue it. A partner is also given the right to dissolve the partnership and withdraw his capital (either specific property or the value of his interest) at will at any time (UPA sec. 31(2)), although he may be unable to cause the winding up of the business and may be answerable in damages to other partners if his act breaches an agreement among them (UPA secs. 37 and 38(2)). The significant difference between a corporation and a partnership as regards continuity of life, then, is that a partner can always opt out of continued participation in and exposure to the risks of the enterprise. A corporate shareholder's investment is locked in unless liquidation is voted or he can find a purchaser to buy him out.

In a partnership subject to the Uniform Limited Partnership Act (hereinafter referred to as ULPA), this right of withdrawal is modified. A limited partner can withdraw his interest on dissolution (ULPA sec. 16), but he can neither dissolve the partnership at will (ULPA sec. 10) nor force dissolution at the retirement, death, or insanity of a general partner if the remaining general partners agree to continue the business in accordance with a right granted in the partnership certificate (ULPA sec. 20). CULPA section 15520 further provides that a new general partner can be elected to continue the business without causing dissolution, if the certificate permits.

The sole general partner in the limited partnerships involved herein was a corporation, whose business was the promotion and management of real estate ventures. As a practical matter, it is unlikely that either Mai–Kai or Somis would have been dissolved midstream and the partners afforded an opportunity to withdraw their investments. Petitioners argue that the partnerships nevertheless lacked continuity of life because they could be dissolved either at will by, or on the bankruptcy of, the general partner. We turn first to the effect of bankruptcy of GHL.

California Uniform Partnership Act section 15031(5) (West Supp. 1976) (hereinafter referred to as CUPA) provides that a partnership is dissolved on the bankruptcy of a partner. CUPA section 15006(2) makes that act applicable to limited partnerships unless inconsistent with statutes relating to them. CULPA nowhere provides for dissolution or nondissolution in the event of bankruptcy. Section 15520, which merely covers dissolution and countervailing action by the remaining partners under certain circumstances, does not provide for such event. * * *

CUPA section 15031(5) therefore applies. Since the bankruptcy of GHL would bring about dissolution by operation of law, each limited partner would be entitled to demand the return of his contribution (CULPA sec. 15516). Somis and Mai–Kai simply do not satisfy the regulations' test of continuity, which requires that the "bankruptcy * * * of *any member* will *not* cause a dissolution of the organization." (Emphasis supplied.)

The fact that under the agreements involved herein a new general partner might be chosen to continue the business does not affect this conclusion. Respondent seizes upon this aspect of the agreements to argue that the limited partners could anticipate the bankruptcy of GHL and elect a new general partner. But this element does not detract from the hard fact that if GHL became bankrupt while it was the general partner of Somis and Mai–Kai, there would at best be a hiatus between the event of bankruptcy and the entry of a new general partner so that, from a legal point of view, the old partnerships would have been dissolved. Moreover, at least in the case of Mai–Kai, a vote of 100 percent of the limited partners was required to elect a new general partner. Glensder Textile Co., 46 B.T.A. 176 (1942), held that such contingent continuity of life did not resemble that of a corporation. Respondent's regulations * * * incorporate this conclusion.

We hold that the partnerships involved herein do not satisfy the "continuity of life" test as set forth in respondent's regulations. We recognize that our application of respondent's existing regulations to the event of bankruptcy results in a situation where it is unlikely that a limited partnership will ever satisfy the "continuity of life" requirement of those regulations. But the fact that the regulations are so clearly keyed to "dissolution" (a term encompassing the legal relationships between the partners) rather than "termination of the business" (a phrase capable of more pragmatic interpretation encompassing the life of the business enterprise) leaves us with no viable alternative. In this connection, we note that respondent is not without power to alter the impact of our application of his existing regulations. See Morrissey v. Commissioner, supra.

* * *

2. Centralized Management

In the corporate form, management is centralized in the officers and directors; the involvement of shareholders as such in ordinary operations is limited to choosing these representatives. In a general partnership, authority is decentralized and any partner has the power to make binding decisions in the ordinary course (UPA sec. 9). In a limited partnership, however, this authority exists only in the general partners (ULPA secs. 9 and 10), and a limited partner who takes part in the control of the business loses his limited liability status (ULPA sec. 7). From a practical standpoint, it is clear that the management of both Mai–Kai and Somis was centralized in GHL. The sole general partner was empowered by law as well as by the partnership agreements to administer the partnership affairs. However, respondent's regulations specify that—

In addition, limited partnerships subject to a statute corresponding to the Uniform Limited Partnership Act, generally do not have centralized management, but centralized management ordinarily does exist in such a limited partnership if substantially all the interests in the partnership are owned by the limited partners. [Sec. 301.7701–2(c)(4), Proced. & Admin.Regs.]

In other words, even though there may be centralized administration by a general partner, the "centralization of management" test will not be met if the general partner has a meaningful proprietary interest. See Zuckman v. United States, 524 F.2d 729 (Ct.Cl.1975). In specifying this additional condition, respondent has adopted the theory of Glensder Textile Co., supra, that managing partners with such interests in the business are not "analogous to directors of a corporation" because they act in their own interests "and not *merely* in a representative capacity for a body of persons having a limited investment and a limited liability." (46 B.T.A. at 185; emphasis added.) It is thus necessary to look to the proprietary interest of GHL in order to determine whether the additional condition imposed by respondent's regulations has been met.

Unlike the taxpayers in Zuckman v. United States, supra, petitioners herein have failed to show that the limited partners did not own all or substantially all the interests in the partnerships involved herein within the meaning of the regulations. GHL's interest in Mai–Kai and Somis were subordinated to those of the limited partners. Petitioners have not attempted to demonstrate that GHL's capital interests had any present value during the years in issue, and it is clear that, because of the subordination provisions, it had no present right to income during those years. Petitioners would have us look to the anticipated return on the partnership properties in future years to determine that GHL had a substantial proprietary stake in the business independent of its management role. They have not, however, proved by competent evidence that such a return could in fact be expected, relying instead on unsupported projections; nor have they shown that any such future profit would be reflected in the present value of GHL's interest. Although there was testimony that GHL expected profits from the subordinated interests when the limited partnerships were liquidated, we are not convinced that the possibility of such income at an indefinite future date had value during the years at issue. GHL reported gross income of $906,930.89 from fiscal 1969 to fiscal 1974, out of which only $118 represented a partnership distribution (from a partnership not involved herein).

Furthermore, the limited partners in Somis and Mai–Kai possessed the right to remove GHL as the general partner. Thus, GHL's right to participate in future growth and profits was wholly contingent on satisfactory performance of its management role, and not at all analogous to the independent proprietary interest of a typical general partner. In Glensder Textile Co., supra, our conclusion that centralization of management was lacking rested not only on the fact that management retained a proprietary interest but also on the fact that the limited partners could not "remove the general partners and control them as agents, as stockholders may control directors." 46 B.T.A. at 185.

Petitioners argue that such power of removal and control could be given to limited partners under ULPA, that CULPA (which makes specific reference to such power) is a statute corresponding to ULPA, and that accordingly respondent's regulation requires a decision in their favor on this issue. In our opinion, the regulation was not intended to provide a blanket exemption from association status for ULPA limited partnerships, regardless of the extent to which the partners by agreement deviate from the statutory scheme. It states only that a limited partnership in an ULPA jurisdiction *generally* will lack centralized management. * * * We have repeatedly held that an organization is to be classified by reference to the rights and duties created by agreement as well as those existing under State law. Bush # 1, 48 T.C. at 228; Western Construction Co., 14 T.C. 453, 467 (1950), affd. per curiam 191 F.2d 401 (9th Cir.1951); Glensder Textile Co., 46 B.T.A. at 183. The effect of such organic laws as ULPA (and CULPA) is to provide a rule which governs in the absence of contrary agreement. Where the theme is obscured by the variations, it is the latter which set the tone of the composition. Neither ULPA nor CULPA requires that the limited partners be given the right to remove the general partner; in fact, ULPA does not even mention such a possibility. By reserving that right, the limited partners in Mai–Kai and Somis took themselves out of the basic framework of ULPA and hence out of the shelter of the regulation, which is based on *Glensder*.

We conclude that Somis and Mai–Kai had centralized management within the meaning of respondent's regulations.

3. *Limited Liability*

Unless some member is personally liable for debts of, and claims against, an entity, section 301.7701–2(d)(1), Proced. & Admin.Regs., states that the entity possesses the corporate characteristic of limited liability. The regulation provides that "in the case of a limited partnership subject to a statute corresponding to the Uniform Limited Partnership Act, personal liability exists with respect to each general partner, except as provided in subparagraph (2) of this paragraph." The first sentence of subparagraph (2) establishes a conjunctive test, under which a general partner is considered not to have personal liability only "when he has no substantial assets (other than his interest in the partnership) which could be reached by a creditor of the organization *and* when he is merely a 'dummy' acting as the agent of the limited partners." (Emphasis added.) In other words, personal liability exists if the general partner *either* has substantial assets *or* is not a dummy for the limited partners. We do not agree with respondent's assertion, made for the first time in connection with the motion for reconsideration, that the regulation should be read disjunctively. Although the purpose of subparagraph (2) was ostensibly to delineate the conditions under which personal liability of a general partner *does not exist,* practically all the remaining material in the subparagraph outlines the conditions under which such personal liability does exist. In several examples, personal liability is said to exist, either because the general partner has substantial assets or because he is not a dummy for the limited partners. See Zuckman v. United States, supra. In no instance is there a suggestion that both conditions established by the first sentence of subparagraph (2) need not be satisfied.

In so concluding, we are mindful that in Glensder Textile Co., supra, the apparent source of the language in the regulations, the term "dummy" was arguably considered applicable to any general partner without substantial assets risked in the business. The opinion in *Glensder* states (46 B.T.A. at 183):

> If, for instance, the general partners were not men with substantial assets risked in the business *but* were mere dummies without real means acting as the agents of the limited partners, whose investments made possible the business, there would be something approaching the corporate form of stockholders and directors. * * * [Emphasis added.]

Thus, lack of substantial assets seems to be considered the equivalent of being a dummy—an equivalence which respondent apparently sought to avoid by using the word "and" in his existing regulations.

While it may be doubtful that GHL could be considered to have had substantial assets during the years in issue, we find it unnecessary to resolve this question since it is clear that GHL was not a dummy for the limited partners of Somis and Mai–Kai. Respondent contends that GHL fell within the "dummy" concept because it was subject to removal by the limited partners, and thus was subject to their ultimate control. While it is true that a mere "dummy" would be totally under the control of the limited partners, it does not follow that the presence of some control by virtue of the power to remove necessarily makes the general partner a "dummy." It seems clear that the limited partners' rights to remove the general partner were designed to give the limited partners a measure of control over their investment without involving them in the "control of the business"; the rights were not designed to render GHL a mere dummy or to empower the limited partners "to direct the business actively through the general partners." Glensder Textile Co., 46 B.T.A. at 183. Moreover, the record indicates that the limited partners did not use GHL as a screen to conceal their own active involvement in the conduct of the business; far from being a rubber stamp, GHL was the moving force in these enterprises. With a minor exception, the persons controlling GHL were independent of and unrelated to the limited partners.

In view of the foregoing, we conclude that personal liability existed with respect to GHL, and the partnerships lack the corporate characteristic of limited liability.

4. *Transferability of Interests*

A stockholder's rights and interest in a corporate venture are, absent consensual restrictions, freely transferable by the owner without reference to the wishes of other members. A partner, on the other hand, can unilaterally transfer only his interest in partnership "profits and surplus," and cannot confer on the assignee the other attributes of membership without the consent of all partners (UPA secs. 18(g), 26, and 27). Respondent's regulations recognize and rely upon this distinction.

The regulations state that if substantially all interests are freely transferable, the corporate characteristic of free transferability of interests is present. Since we have concluded, for the purposes of this case, that the limited partners should be considered as owning substantially all the interests in Mai–Kai and Somis * * * we turn our attention to the question whether their interests were so transferable.

A transferee of a limited partnership interest may become a substituted limited partner with the consent of all members or under a right given in the certificate. CULPA sec. 15519. The partnership certificates of Mai–Kai and Somis are silent in this regard. However, when the provisions of the agreements relating to transferability and the power of an assignee to obtain a judicial amendment of the partnership certificate (see CULPA secs. 15502(1)(a)X and 15525) are taken into account, it would appear that the agreements rather than the certificates should be considered the controlling documents herein. Indeed, petitioners do not seek to draw any solace from the certificates, positing their arguments as to lack of transferability on the agreements themselves.

Both partnership agreements permit the assignment of a limited partner's income interest with the consent of the general partner, which may not unreasonably be withheld. Petitioners have not suggested any ground on which consent could be withheld. The requirement of consent, circumscribed by a standard of reasonableness, is not such a restriction on transfer as is typical of partnership agreements; nor is it the sort referred to by the regulations. In our opinion, the limited partners' income rights were freely transferable. See Outlaw v. United States, 494 F.2d 1376, 1384 (Ct.Cl.1974).

Petitioners also argue that transferability is limited by the requirement that, in the event of a proposed assignment, a limited partner's capital interest first be offered to other members under certain circumstances. While an assignment for less than fair market value could be prevented in this manner, there was no requirement that such an offer be made if an interest was to be sold to a third party at fair market value. Thus, there was no "effort on the part of the parties to select their business associates," as is characteristic of the usual partnership arrangement. J.A. Riggs Tractor Co., 6 T.C. 889, 898 (1946). We think that these interests possessed considerably more than the "modified" form of free transferability referred to in subparagraph (2) of the regulation.

In sum, an assignee for fair consideration of a limited partner's interest in Somis or Mai–Kai could acquire all of the rights of a substituted limited partner within the framework of the agreement and governing State law, without discretionary consent of any other member. Any restrictions or conditions on such a transfer were procedural rather than substantive. The right of assignment more closely resembles that attending corporate shares than that typically associated with partnership interests. Mai–Kai and Somis therefore possessed the corporate characteristic of free transferability of interests. * * *

5. *Other Characteristics*

Both parties have identified other characteristics of Mai–Kai and Somis which they allege are relevant to the determination whether those entities more closely resemble partnerships or corporations. Some of these are within the ambit of the major characteristics already discussed. Petitioners point to the fact that, unlike a corporate board of directors, GHL as manager lacked the discretionary right to retain or distribute profits according to the needs of the business. This argument is in reality directed to the issue of centralized management. The same is true of respondent's analogy between the limited partners' voting rights and those of corporate shareholders. To be sure the partnership interests were not represented by certificates but this factor conceivably is more properly subsumed in the transferability issue. See Morrissey v. Commissioner, 296 U.S. at 360. Moreover, those interests were divided into units or shares and were promoted and marketed in a manner similar to corporate securities—an additional "characteristic" which we have not ignored (see Outlaw v. United States, supra), but which we do not deem of critical significance under the circumstances herein. Similarly, we do not assign any particular additional importance to the fact that the partnerships have not observed corporate formalities and procedures (Morrissey v. Commissioner, supra; Giant Auto Parts, Ltd., 13 T.C. 307 (1949)) or that, unlike general partners, limited partners were not required personally to sign the partnership certificates. Finally, respondent argues that the limited partnerships resemble corporations because they provide a means of pooling investments while limiting the liability of the participants. Cf. Helvering v. Combs, 296 U.S. 365 (1935). As it relates to the facts of this case, this point is subsumed in our earlier discussion. To the extent that it presages an attempt to classify *all* limited partnerships as corporations, it is in irreconcilable conflict with respondent's own regulations.

6. *Conclusion*

The regulations provide that an entity will be taxed as a corporation if it more closely resembles a corporation than any other form of organization. They further state that such a resemblance does not exist unless the entity possesses *more* corporate than noncorporate characteristics. If every characteristic bears equal weight, then Mai–Kai and Somis are partnerships for tax purposes. We have found that they possess only two of the four major corporate characteristics and that none of the other characteristics cited by the parties upsets the balance. On the other hand, if the overall corporate resemblance test, espoused by *Morrissey* and adhered to by the regulations, permits us to weigh each factor according to the degree of corporate similarity it provides, we would be inclined to find that these entities were taxable as corporations. Each possessed a degree of centralized management indistinguishable from that of a pure corporation; the other major factors lie somewhere on the continuum between corporate and partnership resemblance. Were not the regulations' thumb upon the scales, it appears to us that the practical continuity and limited liability of both entities would decisively tip the balance in respondent's favor. However, we can find no warrant for such refined balancing in the regulations or in cases which have considered them. See Zuckman v. United States, 524 F.2d 729 (Ct.Cl.1975); Outlaw v. United States, supra; Kurzner v. United States, 413 F.2d 97, 105 (5th Cir.1969) ("four equally weighted procrustean criteria"); secs. 301.7701–2(a)(3) and 301.7701–3(b)(2), Proced. & Admin.Regs., example (2). Cf. Estate of Smith v. Commissioner, 313 F.2d 724, 736 (8th Cir.1963) ("substantially greater noncorporate characteristics both in number *and in importance*") (emphasis added). Only in connection with free transferability of interests do the regulations recognize a modified and less significant form of a particular characteristic.

Our task herein is to apply the provisions of respondent's regulations as we find them and not as we think they might or ought to have been written. See and compare David F. Bolger, 59 T.C. 760, 771 (1973). On this basis, petitioners must prevail.

Reviewed by the Court.

Decisions will be entered under Rule 155.

NOTE

1. The two concurring opinions variously joined in by five judges and the five dissenting opinions variously joined in by six judges have been omitted above. The Tax Court followed its *Larson* decision in *Daniel S. Chaffin*, 35 CCH Tax Ct.Mem. 590 (1976), which involved facts almost identical to those present in *Larson*.

2. As the above opinion indicates, the Tax Court had originally held in favor of "association" status and then withdrawn that opinion and issued the one set out above. After the Tax Court had issued its original opinion and before the opinion's withdrawal the Court of Claims issued its opinion in *Zuckman v. United States,* 524 F.2d 729 (Ct.Cl.1975). This case also involved the classification, for income tax purposes, of a limited partnership with a sole corporate general partner. The Court of Claims held that the limited partnership should be treated as a partnership since it possessed none of the four major characteristics described in the Regulations. The limited partnership, in this case, was formed for the purpose of constructing and operating an apartment complex. The sole corporate general partner, which was a wholly owned subsidiary of the individual developer's wholly owned corporation, was capitalized at $500 and had no substantial assets other than its interest in the partnership. At the minimum, the corporate general partner owned about a 62% interest in the partnership and the individual developer, as a limited partner, owned about a 22% interest. The remaining 16% was distributed among 10 other persons and entities. The partnership agreement provided that a limited partner could not transfer his interest and constitute his assignee a substituted limited partner without the consent of the corporate general partner. It also provided that the business would not be continued on withdrawal of the general partner.

a. On the basis of the above facts the Court of Claims held that: (i) Continuity of life was not present since the state had adopted the U.L.P.A. and, therefore, the bankruptcy of the sole corporate general partner would cause the dissolution of the partnership. The control of the corporate general partner by the individual developer and an agreement by the corporate general partner not to voluntarily cause the dissolution of the partnership did not affect the court's holding; (ii) Centralized management was not present since the corporate general partner held a 62% interest in the partnership. The court refused to attribute the corporate general partner's interest to the individual developer who was a limited partner. If it had done so, the individual would have been treated as owning 84% and, as a result, the limited partners would have held 100% of the interests in the partnership and the corporate general partner would have been simply a "representative" of the limited partners; (iii) Limited liability was not present since, if the corporation was a "dummy", the individual developer would have been personally liable, if it was not a dummy, then it would have been personally liable; and (iv) While the limited partnership interest of the individual developer was freely transferable because of his control over the corporate general partner, the interest of the corporate general partner was not freely transferable since its transfer would cause the dissolution of the partnership unless 100% of the limited partners consented.

3. Could the court in *Zuckman v. United States* be faulted for being overly literal?

a. Certainly the partnership would be dissolved upon the bankruptcy or withdrawal of the corporate general partner, but, were not those occurrences substantially within the control of the limited partner who owned over one half of the limited partnership interests and directly or indirectly controlled over 84% of all of the interests in the entity? Cf. Rev. Rul. 77–214, 1977–1 C.B. 408. In many states a corporation can be dissolved upon the vote of a majority of its shareholders, and as long as a majority of the shareholders of a corporation desire and have the financial ability to avoid its bankruptcy by additional investment the possibility of the corporation becoming bankrupt is slight.

b. It is really so unusual in determining the "substance" of the ownership of an entity to attempt to determine who actually controls the entity? The question to be decided is whether the corporate general partner acts as the representative of the limited partners similar to the board of directors of a corporation. If the limited partners control 100% of the stock of the corporation, how else does it act? In *Zuckman v. United States*, however, there were limited partners who owned about 16% of the partnership who did not participate in the control of the corporate general partner. As to them the corporate general partner was not solely a representative. It is quite clear, however, under the regulations, that the entity is not required to be identical to the corporate form but only more nearly resemble it than a partnership. Reg. sec. 301.7701–2(a). In addition, it might be reasonably suggested that in many corporations the board of directors can be said to "represent" the holder or holders of a majority interest.

c. Quite clearly under the Texas Supreme Court's analysis in *Delaney, Jr. v. Fidelity Lease Limited*, 526 S.W.2d 543 (Tex.1975), if the individual developer in *Zuckman v. United States*, J.H. Kanter, took part in the actual management of the corporate general partner he would not have been able to claim limited liability. In fact, *Zuckman v. United States* probably presented the very case the court in *Delaney, Jr. v. Fidelity Lease Limited* was worried about; limited partners participating in management through a corporation which was not adequately capitalized. Certainly, the *Delaney, Jr. v. Fidelity Lease Limited* analysis, or one which arrived at unlimited liability for all limited partners by reasoning that a corporate general partner which is inadequately capitalized is merely an agent of the limited partners, would result in the absence of the attribute of limited liability. But, if one is prepared to accept the reliance analysis of the control test and postulate that even an inadequately capitalized corporate general partner might not be disregarded under the U.L.P.A. or the Revised U.L.P.A., it is difficult to see why, for income tax purposes, if the total capitalization of the corporate general partner in an entity such as that present in *Zuckman v. United States* is only $500, limited liability does not exist. Here again, it is resemblance not identity which is the general test to be applied.

d. Assuming, as the court does, that if the interests of both the individual developer and the corporate general partner were freely transferable, free transferability could be said to exist and that the interest of the individual developer was freely transferable because of his control over the corporate general partner, it would seem to be a short step to conclude that the interest of the corporate general partner was also, as a practical matter, freely transferable through the transfer of the stock of the corporation. The transfer of the stock of the corporation apparently would not cause the dissolution of the partnership. While it might be asserted that even after the transfer of stock the corporate general partner would remain the same entity, it could also be argued that the individual developer had the ability to freely transfer directly or indirectly about 84% of the interests in the entity. Cf. Rev.Rul. 77–214, 1977–1 C.B. 408.

e. Consider again, however, whether the court in *Zuckman v. United States* was being overly literal or was the decision of the court prompted in part by the Internal Revenue Service attempting to use one set of regulations to kill a number of different and possibly incompatible birds? See generally Hyman and Hoffman, *Partnerships and "Associations": A Policy Critique of the Morrissey Regulations,* 3 J. Real Est.Tax'n 377 (1976).

4. How would the entities in *Zuckman v. United States* and *Larson* have fared under Rev.Proc. 89–12, 1989–7 I.R.B. 22, pages 87 to 91 supra?

a. It appears from the facts given that the entity in *Zuckman v. United States* might have failed the net worth, the control of the general partner by the limited partners and the capital account tests described in Rev.Proc. 89–12 but may have complied with the ownership by the general partner of interests in the limited partnership test.

b. The entities in *Larson* presumably would have failed the net worth test but may have complied with the control of the general partner by the limited partners test. The entities may have failed to comply with the required interest and capital account of the general partner in the partnerships.

5. If the Tax Court had been faced with the facts present in *Zuckman v. United States,* using the analysis which it adopts in *Larson,* would it have classified the entity in *Zuckman v. United States* as a corporation or a partnership?

a. It would have found that the entity did not possess the attribute of continuity of life since the bankruptcy of the corporate general partner would dissolve the entity.

b. It may have found that the entity did not possess the attribute of centralization of management since the corporate general partner had a substantial interest in the partnership.

    1. This conclusion, however, might turn on how receptive the Tax Court would have been to the control argument. As may be remembered, in *Zuckman v. United States* a limited partner who owned over one half of the limited partnership interests indirectly owned 100% of the stock of the corporate general partner. Noting the Tax Court's somewhat less literal analysis in *Larson* and its concern with respect to the validity of the regulations as applied, it may have been receptive to the control argument.

c. Considering the language of the Tax Court in *Larson* one might come to the conclusion that it would have found limited liability present in *Zuckman v. United States.* The corporate general partner had insubstantial assets and *Zuckman v. United States* may have been a case in which a limited partner, owning over one half of the limited partnership interests, used the corporate general partner "as a screen to conceal [his] own active involvement in the conduct of the business."

d. The result as to transferability would appear to be in some doubt.

    1. The Tax Court in *Larson* found free transferability since the consent of the corporate general partner to the transfer of a limited partnership interest could not be unreasonably withheld. In *Zuckman v. United States* the requirement of the consent of the corporate general partner to the transfer of a limited partnership interest was not so modified.

    2. The result, however, might turn on the Tax Court's receptiveness to the argument that as a practical matter 84% of the interests in

the partnership were freely transferable. Although the Tax Court's opinion does not indicate that it was prepared to depart that far from a literal analysis, might it have found this to be a "modified" form of free transferability?

e. Assuming that the Tax Court might have found that the attributes of centralized management or free transferability and limited liability were present in *Zuckman v. United States,* were there any other corporate factors present in that case which the Tax Court might have deemed significant in order to tip its determination toward corporate classification? See Rev.Rul. 79–106, 1979–1 C.B. 448.

f. Since the Tax Court in *Larson* seemed to feel that, if it was free to apply a *Morrissey v. Comm'r,* 296 U.S. 344, 56 S.Ct. 289, 80 L.Ed. 263 (1935), "resemblance" test, it would conclude that the entities in *Larson* should be classified as corporations, how would it have felt if faced with the entity in *Zuckman v. United States*?

6. Can the Internal Revenue Service challenge the validity of the regulations as applied to cases such as *Zuckman v. United States* and *Larson*?

a. This approach might be seen as less than "sporting," but the parties are hardly engaged in a tennis match and it is not inconceivable that a court might provide that its decision only be applied prospectively.

1. In fact, might one say that there was a note of warning in the Tax Court's decision in *Larson*?

2. On the other hand, the Court of Claims in *Zuckman v. United States* seemed to feel that the applicable regulations as drafted and applied were valid.

b. Might amendment of the applicable regulations be another alternative?

1. Consider whether the following would affect the results in *Larson* or *Zuckman v. United States:*

a. Reg. sec. 301.7701–2(b)(1) providing in part that if the * * * bankruptcy of any member will cause the *termination* of the organization, continuity of life does not exist.

b. Reg. sec. 301.7701–2(d)(2) providing in part that personal liability does not exist * * * with respect to a general partner when he has no substantial assets * * * *or* when he is merely a "dummy". * * *

2. The applicable regulations might also be amended to provide that the various attributes have different weights in determining whether an organization is classified as a partnership or a corporation, or to provide that an entity needs three out of four to be classified as a partnership. In 1982 the Internal Revenue Service proposed certain amendments to Regulation Section 301.7701–2 which, if adopted, would have had the effect of classifying as a corporation any entity with associates and a joint profit objective if no member of the entity was personally liable for the debts of the entity under local law. Apparently, such an entity would be so classified even though it lacked the attributes of transferability, continuity of life and centralized management. In I.R. 82–45, 1983 *P.–H. Fed. Taxes* ¶ 54,703, the Internal Revenue Service announced the withdrawal of these amendments. In 1988, the Internal Revenue Service ruled that a limited liability

company (no member of the company was personally liable for the debts of the company under local law) can be treated as a partnership for tax purposes since the company lacked the corporate characteristics of continuity of life and free transferability. See Rev.Rul. 88–76, 1988–38 I.R.B. 26. See generally Comment, *Wyoming Limited Liability Company: A Viable Alternative to the S Corporation and the Limited Partnership*, 23 Land & Water L.Rev. 523 (1988).

3. Early in 1977 the Treasury proposed amended regulations which gave more weight to the general resemblance test and required that the general partner have a substantial interest in the partnership. The proposed regulations were withdrawn the same day they were filed and the Treasury has announced that they will not be reproposed. See Reichler, *Implications of the IRS' Withdrawal of its Proposals to Amend the Kintner Regs.*, 46 J. Tax'n 138 (1977).

c. In considering the possibilities under subparagraphs a. and b. above, does the following quote from *Morrissey v. Comm'r* provide any assistance?

"As the statute merely provided that the term 'corporation' should include 'associations,' without further definition, the Treasury Department was authorized to supply rules for the enforcement of the Act within the permissible bounds of administrative construction. Nor can this authority be deemed to be so restricted that the regulations, once issued, could not later be clarified or enlarged so as to meet administrative exigencies or conform to judicial decision." 296 U.S. at 354–55, 56 S.Ct. at 294 (1935).

d. Lastly, the Internal Revenue Service might continue to litigate in the appropriate case. Do you feel confident, even after *Zuckman v. United States* and *Larson*, that any limited partnership with a sole corporate general partner will be classified as a partnership?

1. Using the Tax Court's analysis in *Larson* consider the result which might be reached if the facts relating to the limited partnership were similar to those present in *Larson* with respect to the centralization of management and transferability of interest determinations and similar to those present in *Zuckman v. United States* with respect to the limited liability determination.

7. See generally Fox and Halperin, *A Corporate General Partner in Limited Real Estate Partnerships*, 3 J. Real Est. Tax'n 425 (1976); Livsey, *Limited Partnerships with a Sole Corporate General Partner: The Impact of Larson and Zuckman*, 54 Taxes 132 (1976); Mendenhall and Ferguson, *What Risks Now for Partnership Treatment of Shelters? Lessons of Larson, Zuckman*, 45 J. Tax'n 66 (1976); Felton, *A Larson–Zuckman Checklist for Partnership Tax Classification of U.L.P.A. Real Estate Shelters*, 11 U.Rich.L.Rev. 743 (1977); Note, *The Failure of the Kintner Regulations: A Tax Identity Crisis*, 8 U.Tol.L.Rev. 500 (1977); Note, *The Recent Larson Opinions Concerning IRS Attempts to Classify Limited Partnerships as Corporations*, 14 Am.Bus.L.J. 419 (1977); Horwood, *The Corporate Nominee/General Partner*, 37 N.Y.U.Inst.Fed.Tax'n 14–1 (1979).

8. As noted above, in the close situation when the analysis of the major attributes produces a 2:2 standoff, such as in *Larson*, the courts and the Internal Revenue Service may look to other factors to tip the scales one way or the other. The Internal Revenue Service has indicated what other factors will not be considered relevant in this context.

REVENUE RULING 79–106.

1979–1 Cum.Bull. 448.

*   *   *

Advice has been requested whether the factors described below will be considered "other factors" that are significant in determining the classification of arrangements formed as limited partnerships for purposes of the regulations under section 7701 of the Internal Revenue Code of 1954.

*   *   *

Section 301.7701–2(a)(1) of the Procedure and Administration Regulations lists six major characteristics ordinarily found in a pure corporation which, taken together, distinguish it from other organizations. These are (i) associates, (ii) an objective to carry on business and divide the gains therefrom, (iii) continuity of life, (iv) centralization of management, (v) liability for corporate debts limited to corporate property, and (vi) free transferability of interests. Whether a particular organization is to be classified as an association must be determined by taking into account the presence or absence of each of these corporate characteristics.

In addition to the major characteristics, section 301.7701–2(a)(1) of the regulations provides, in part, that "other factors" may be found in some cases which may be significant in classifying an organization as an association, a partnership or a trust.

The Internal Revenue Service will follow, in classifying organizations under section 7701 of the Code, the decision of the United States Tax Court in Larson v. Commissioner, 66 T.C. 159 (1976), *   *   * in which the court held that two real estate syndicates organized under the California Uniform Limited Partnership Act were partnerships for federal income tax purposes. In *Larson,* the court, while not concluding that additional "factors" are never relevant, found that some of the following "factors" were elements of the major characteristics and that the other "factors" were not of critical importance for purposes of classifying the partnerships.

(1) The division of limited partnership interests into units or shares and the promotion and marketing of such interests in a manner similar to corporate securities,

(2) the managing partner's right or lack of the discretionary right to retain or distribute profits according to the needs of the business,

(3) the limited partner's right or lack of the right to vote on the removal and election of general partners and the right or lack of the right to vote on the sale of all, or substantially all, of the assets of the partnership,

(4) the limited partnership interests being represented or not being represented by certificates,

(5) the limited partnership's observance or lack of observance of corporate formalities and procedures,

(6) the limited partners being required or not being required to sign the partnership agreement, and

(7) the limited partnership providing a means of pooling investments while limiting the liability of some of the participants.

Accordingly, as a result of the *Larson* case, the Service will not consider the factors enumerated above as "other factors" that have significance (independent of their bearing on the six major corporate characteristics) in determining the classification of arrangements formed as limited partnerships.

NOTE

1. If one or just a few of the participants in a venture were going to be active and the other participants were content to be limited partners, should the active participants form a corporation and have the corporation act as the sole general partner? None of the individual participants would be personally liable. How would the active participants obtain the benefits of the pass through of losses and tax-free cash flow distributions?

a. While the active participants might lose some of the income tax benefits of the partnership form, they would gain the income tax benefits of the corporate form, such as employee fringe benefits, nonapplicability of Section 163(d), the limitation on the deduction of investment interest and the availability of the reorganization sections for nonrecognition of gain on disposition of the assets of, or their interests in, the corporation.

b. Consider, in view of: (1) The net worth safe harbor for a corporate general partner provided by Rev.Proc. 89–12, 1989–7 I.R.B. 22; (2) The fact that a corporation, other than an S corporation and certain closely-held corporations, is not subject to the "at risk" provision, Section 465; (3) The fact that corporations, other than S corporations, certain closely-held corporations and personal service corporations, are not subject to the limitations on the use of passive losses provided by Section 469; and (4) The fact that a corporation, other than an S corporation, is not subject to the limitation on the deductibility of investment interest under Section 163(d), whether the corporate general partner, in a limited partnership which owns real property, should own and lease to the partnership all of the personal property to be used in conjunction with the real property? For example, the activity of the limited partnership might be leasing offices in an office building on a furnished basis. See generally Richelson, *Effect of the Tax Reform Act of 1976 on Corporate Partners Not Personally Liable for Partnership Liabilities*, 55 Taxes 177 (1977). One should note, however, that a C corporation and a partnership with a C corporation as a partner cannot use the cash method of accounting unless the average annual gross receipts of the entity for the three-taxable-year period ending with the immediately prior taxable year do not exceed $5,000,000. A tax shelter, as defined in Section 461(i)(3), cannot use the cash method of accounting regardless of the amount of its gross receipts. See Section 448.

2. See generally Fisher, *Classification Under Section 7701—The Past, Present, and Prospects for the Future*, 30 Tax Law. 627 (1977); Comment, *Tax Classification of Limited Partnerships*, 90 Harv.L.Rev. 745 (1977); Comment,

Tax Classification of Limited Partnerships: The I.R.S. Bombards the Tax Shelters, 52 N.Y.U.L.Rev. 408 (1977); Hyman and Hoffman, *Partnerships and "Associations": A Policy Critique of the Morrissey Regulations,* 3 J. Real Est. Tax'n 377 (1976); Comment, *The Viability of a Tax Shelter Vehicle: Limited Partnership with a Corporation as Sole General Partner,* 49 Miss.L.J. 469 (1978); Horwood, *The Corporate Nominee/General Partner,* 37 N.Y.U.Inst.Fed.Tax'n 14–1 (1979); Day, *Corporate Investment in Real Estate—Special Considerations for Special Allocations Under Section 704: The Price is Right!,* 10 J.Corp. Law 313 (1985).

    3. The next step, once it is determined that a limited partnership can have a corporate general partner, is to ask whether the corporate general partner can be an S corporation. As should be apparent from the preceding materials, the limited partners may be restricted in their ownership and control of the corporate general partner. Therefore, the stockholders of the corporate general partner may differ from the limited partners. An S election by the corporate general partner is one way of, to some extent, equalizing the tax treatment of the stockholders of the corporation and the limited partners.

    4. Even if a limited partnership with a sole S corporation general partner is treated as a partnership, the treatment, for income tax purposes, of the shareholders of the corporate general partner still may be different than the treatment of the limited partners since, for example, as described earlier, the shareholders' bases in their interests in the corporation may be computed differently than the bases of the limited partners in their partnership interests. This may affect the amount of loss which can be passed through to the shareholders and the amount of tax-free cash flow distributions they can receive. See pages 108 to 109 supra.

    5. The shareholders of the S corporation general partner also could own limited partnership interests and, in this capacity, receive a share of losses, and tax-free cash flow. If this approach was chosen, would the entity be treated, for tax purposes, as a partnership pursuant to the rules set out in Rev.Proc. 89–12?

e. LIMITATIONS ON THE USE OF LOSSES

    As previously pointed out in these materials, in order for a partner's and an S corporation shareholder's share of the losses of their respective entities to be "passed through" for use by the partner and the S corporation shareholder, the partner must have a basis in the partner's partnership interest, and the S corporation shareholder must have a basis in the shareholder's stock and the debt of the corporation owed to the shareholder equal to or in excess of the amount of the partner's and the S corporation shareholder's share of the losses of their respective entities. If the partner's or the S corporation shareholder's basis is less than the partner's or the shareholder's share of the losses of their respective entities, the excess of the losses of the entity over the partner's or the S corporation shareholder's basis is suspended at the entity level and is subsequently available to the partner or the S corporation shareholder when the partner or the shareholder acquires additional basis.

    Even if the partner and the S corporation shareholder have sufficient basis to permit the partner's and the shareholder's share of the losses of their respective entities to be passed through to the partner and the shareholder, there exist additional limitations on the partner's and the S corporation shareholder's personal use of the losses on their respective income tax returns. First, under Section 465, the partner and the S corporation shareholder must have an "amount at-risk" equal to, or greater than, the partner's or the S corporation shareholder's share of the losses. If the partner's or the S corporation shareholder's amount at-risk is less than the partner's or the shareholder's share of the losses, the excess loss is suspended at the partner or shareholder level and, in general, may be used when the partner or the shareholder acquires an additional amount at-risk. Secondly, under Section 469, even if the partner and the S corporation shareholder have a sufficient basis and amount at-risk, the partner or the S corporation shareholder might not have a sufficient amount of the type of income (in general, passive) against which the partner's or shareholder's share of the losses might be used. For example, assuming that the partner and the S corporation shareholder are each individuals and that their shares of the losses of their respective entities are classified as passive activity losses under Section 469, in general, the partner's and the S corporation shareholder's shares of the losses can only be used against passive activity income derived by the partner or the S corporation shareholder. If the partner's or the S corporation shareholder's passive activity losses exceed the partner's or the shareholder's passive activity income, the excess passive activity loss is suspended at the partner or the shareholder level and may, in general, be used against passive activity income derived by the partner or the S corporation shareholder in the future.

(i)   THE AT-RISK LIMITATIONS

The at-risk limitations, in general, suspend the deduction of any loss to the extent the loss exceeds the "aggregate amount with respect to which the taxpayer is at risk * * * at the close of the taxable year." See Section 465(a)(1). A loss is defined as the excess of the otherwise allowable deductions for the taxable year derived from an activity over the income received or accrued from the activity for the taxable year. See Section 465(d). A disallowed loss is carried over indefinitely to succeeding years and treated as a deduction derived from the activity, subject to the at-risk limitations, in the succeeding years. See Section 465(a)(2).

The at-risk limitations apply to individuals, including partners and shareholders in S corporations. They generally do not apply to a C corporation unless the C corporation is closely held; that is, five or fewer individuals owning 50% or more in value of the corporation's outstanding stock.

In determining the amount of loss deductible under the at-risk limitations, the crucial factor is the taxpayer's amount at-risk for the activity which gives rise to the loss. A taxpayer is at risk for an activity to the extent of the money and the adjusted basis of other property contributed by the taxpayer to the activity. The taxpayer is also at risk for amounts borrowed for use in the activity if the taxpayer is either personally liable for the repayment of the borrowed amount or has pledged property not used in the activity as security for the borrowed amounts. In the latter case, the amount at risk cannot exceed the fair market value of the taxpayer's interest in the pledged property. In general, borrowed or other amounts are not considered at risk to the extent that a taxpayer is "protected against loss by nonrecourse financing, guarantees, stop loss agreements or other similar arrangements." See Section 465(b)(4); Weldon T. Peters, 89 T.C. 423 (1987).

The amount at risk generally will fluctuate each year as a result of business operations. A taxpayer's amount at risk in an activity is increased by the taxable income which he derives from the activity and reduced by the amount of money withdrawn from the activity by, or on behalf of, the taxpayer. In addition, the amount at risk is reduced by the amount of loss from the activity allowed as a deduction to the taxpayer.

The proposed regulations, see Prop.Reg.Sec. 1.465–22(a), provide that a partner's amount at risk is not increased by the amount the partner is required to contribute to the partnership under the partnership agreement or as a result of a note given to the partnership by the partner until the contribution or note is actually paid. See e.g. Priv. Ltr.Rul. 8702006. On the other hand, as seen earlier in Sidney J. Gefen, 87 T.C. 1471 (1986), see pages 77 to 84, a limited partner's guarantee and assumption of a share of a partnership's recourse liability, coupled with the limited partner's agreement to contribute to the partnership on call by the general partners an amount equal to the partner's share of the partnership's recourse liability, resulted in the limited partner being permitted to include her share of the liability in determining her at-risk amount. See also Priv.Ltr.Rul. 8636003, as modified by Priv.Ltr.Rul. 8636004.

In the case of an activity involving real estate an exception to the at-risk limitations is provided for third-party nonrecourse commercial financing. A taxpayer is considered at risk with respect to qualified nonrecourse financing which is secured by the real property used in the activity. Under Section 465(b)(6), "qualified nonrecourse financing" is defined as financing which meets four tests. First, it must be borrowed by the taxpayer with respect to the activity of holding real property. The activity of holding real property includes personal property and services which are incidental to making real property available as living accommodations. Second, it must be borrowed either from a "qualified person," or be a loan from any federal, state, or local government or government instrumentality, or be guaranteed by any federal, state, or local government. Third, except as otherwise provided in the regulations to be issued, no person may be personally liable for the payment of the financing. Finally, the financing must not be convertible debt.

A "qualified person" is any unrelated person actively and regularly engaged in the business of lending money other than a person from whom the taxpayer acquired the property or a person related to such person. The lender or any person related to the lender must not receive any fee in connection with taxpayer's investment in the property.

While a related person generally cannot be a qualified person, under the statute, financing from a related person can be treated as qualified nonrecourse financing if such financing is "commercially reasonable and on substantially the same terms as loans involving unrelated persons." See Section 465(b)(6)(D)(ii). The terms of nonrecourse financing are commercially reasonable if the financing is represented by a written, unconditional promise to pay on demand or on a specified day or days a sum or sums certain of money and the interest rate is a reasonable rate of interest.

A partner's share of any qualified nonrecourse financing of a partnership is determined by the partner's share of the nonrecourse liabilities of the partnership. The financing must be qualified nonrecourse financing with respect to both the partnership and the partner. For the purpose of determining whether partnership borrowings qualify with respect to a partner, the partner is treated as the borrower. The amount for which all partners are treated as at risk under this rule cannot exceed the total amount of the qualified nonrecourse financing at the partnership level.

NOTE

1. In the context of the development of residential rental, commercial and industrial real estate, so long as the financing of the development is qualified nonrecourse financing there is little reason to be concerned about the at-risk limitations.

    a. In fact, the lender providing the financing might even have, or acquire, an interest in the borrower as long as the financing is commercially reasonable and on substantially the same terms as loans involving unrelated parties.

    b. If, however, the seller of the real estate to be developed takes back a nonrecourse purchase money note and mortgage of the buyer or takes back a recourse purchase money note and mortgage and the buyer is a limited partnership or a lender makes a recourse loan to a limited partnership, the at-risk limitations may be applicable.

        1. None of the financing described above is "qualified nonrecourse financing."

        2. In the latter two situations the at-risk limitations would apply in determining whether the limited partners can add a share of the financing to their at-risk amounts.

3. In these instances it becomes important to determine if, and how, the financing can be used to increase the at-risk amount of the buyer or the limited partners of the buyer or borrower.

2. Presently, a question exists whether the at-risk amount of a limited partner can be increased by the limited partner guaranteeing a portion of the partnership's recourse liabilities. Cf. Ltr.Rul. 8504005; *Hugh M. Brand,* 81 T.C. 821 (1983). The rights which the limited partner acquires against the partnership and the general partner(s) in the event the limited partner must honor the guarantee can be said to be a form of stop loss agreement. See *Weldon T. Peters,* 89 T.C. 423 (1987).

a. If, however, the partnership liabilities, which are guaranteed by the limited partner, are nonrecourse liabilities, the limited partner's guarantee may result in an increase in the limited partner's at-risk amount. Cf. *George F. Smith, Jr.,* 84 T.C. 889 (1985), and *Edwin D. Abramson,* 86 T.C. 360 (1986). When the partnership liabilities are nonrecourse, the limited partner who guarantees the liabilities is the only person who has personal liability. As opposed to a situation in which the partnership liabilities are recourse liabilities, when the liabilities are nonrecourse, the guaranteeing party can be considered as akin to a primary obligor, and at the least, the guaranteeing limited partner has no one to look to for reimbursement if the limited partner is called upon to make good on the guarantee.

3. If the liabilities of the limited partnership are recourse liabilities and each of the limited partners guarantees and assumes his share of the liabilities, agreeing not to look to the general partner(s) or the partnership for reimbursement if the guarantee and assumption must be honored, and each of the limited partners agrees to make a capital contribution to the partnership upon the call of the general partner in the amount of his share of the recourse liabilities, each of the limited partners may be able to add his share of the recourse liabilities to his at-risk amount. In this instance, as in the one described above, it can be said, as a result of the agreements made by the limited partners, that the limited partners are, in substance, the ultimate obligors. See *Sidney J. Gefen,* 87 T.C. 1471 (1986); *Marcus W. Melvin,* 88 T.C. 63 (1987); *Pritchett v. Comm'r,* 827 F.2d 644 (9th Cir.1987); Priv.Ltr.Ruls. 8636003; 8636004; 8702006. Cf. Bobrow and Boyle, *Section 752 and Limited Partners: The "Ultimate Liability" Doctrine as Applied to Partnership Recourse Indebtedness,* 4 J.Ps.Tax'n 172 (1987).

4. See generally Winston, *Basis and At–Risk Consequences of Partner's Assumption of Partnership Debt,* 2 J.Tax'n Inv. 15 (1985); Gotliboski and Lowe, *Determining a Limited Partner's Amount At Risk After Abramson and Pritch-ett,* 3 J.Ps.Tax'n 328 (1987); Eisenstadt and Geroux, *Real Estate Now Subject to At–Risk Rules: Rehab Credit Reduced by Tax Reform Act,* 15 Tax'n Law. 242 (1987); Maples, *Limited Partner Obligations and At–Risk Amounts: The Tax Court Speaks But Not Too Clearly,* 18 Tax Adviser 117 (1987); Hirsch, *Extension of At–Risk Rules to Real Estate Leaves Many Issues Unclear,* 4 J.Ps.Tax'n 226 (1987); Schmalz, *The Effect of Partnership Liabilities on Basis, At–Risk Amounts and Capital Accounts,* 5 J.Ps.Tax'n 291 (1989).

(ii) LIMITATIONS ON THE USE OF PASSIVE ACTIVITY LOSSES

Even if the taxpayer has sufficient basis in his interest, assuming the taxpayer is a partner or an S corporation shareholder, so that his full share of losses can be passed through to him and has an at-risk amount equal to, or greater than, his share of losses, the limitations on the use of passive activity losses provided by Section 469 may prevent the taxpayer's personal use of those losses in whole or in part to offset income which is not from passive activities.

FUN AND GAMES WITH OUR NEW PALS
Richard M. Lipton
64 Taxes 801 (1986)

Overview.—The purpose of Section 469 is to disallow the utilization of deductions from passive activities to offset income that is not from passive activities, e.g., salaries, interest, dividends and "active" business income. ＊ ＊ ＊

If an activity constitutes a passive activity within the meaning of Section 469, losses from such activity can be used[, in general,] to offset the income only from other passive activities in which the taxpayer has an interest. Any unutilized losses are carried forward indefinitely and can be used in subsequent years against income from all passive activities. ＊ ＊ ＊ Losses from passive activities can be utilized against "nonpassive" income only after the taxpayer has disposed of his interest in the activity.

The most difficult portion of the passive activity rule concerns the definitions of "activities" which are "passive." Passive activities are generally any trade or business in which the taxpayer does not materially participate and any rental activity. For purposes of this rule, legal entities are disregarded in determining what constitutes a separate activity.

＊ ＊ ＊

Taxpayers Subject to the [Passive Activity Loss] (PAL) Limitations.—The PAL limitation applies to individuals, estates, trusts, certain closely held C corporations and personal service corporations. The application of the PAL rule to individuals effectively includes all businesses conducted through partnerships (both general and limited) and S corporations.

The most significant trap for the unwary in connection with the taxpayers subject to the PAL limitation may involve the application to closely held C corporations. For purposes of this provision, a C corporation is considered to be closely held if it is subject to the at-risk limitations, which generally apply to corporations with five or fewer shareholders who own more than 50 percent of the [value of the] stock of the corporation. In light of the general rule that C corporations are not subject to the PAL limitations, the special rule for certain closely held C corporations could lead to unexpected surprises. For example, if a corporation that is actively engaged in business purchases the building in which it is located and leases extra rooms in the building to unrelated tenants, the utilization of the loss, if any, from such rental activity by the corporation could depend upon whether the corporation is closely held, and not upon the corporation's trade or business.

* * *

Definition of an Activity.—If a taxpayer is subject to the PAL rule, the next step is to determine the "activities" in which the taxpayer is engaged. It is important to note that "activity" is not defined in Section 469. Instead, the Senate Finance Committee Report ("Finance Report") merely states that an activity consists of "undertakings" that consist of an integrated and interrelated economic unit, conducted in coordination with or reliance upon each other, and constituting an appropriate unit for the measurement of gain or loss.

Several aspects of this definition of an activity must be highlighted. First, the definition is *not* based on legal entities. Thus, a single partnership could be involved in several activities. In particular, separate buildings will generally be treated as separate rental activities. This disregard for legal entities will prove to be a significant problem in connection with the allocation of items of income or deductions.

* * *

What establishes an activity? The limited guidance in the Finance Report indicates that providing two or more substantially different products or services generally results in two or more activities. Thus, two retail stores which provide different products (e.g., a clothing store and a grocery store) would be treated as separate activities. On the other hand, the appliance and clothing sections of a department store are treated as one activity. But the mere fact that two or more enterprises have common management is disregarded for purposes of this aspect of the PAL rule. Thus, there is no clear guidance with respect to this question other than a general facts and circumstances test.

The only practical problem addressed in either the Finance Report or the report of the Conference Committee ("Conference Report") involves the situation in which one activity could be viewed as "incidental" to another. For example, the Conference Report indicates that a laundry in an apartment building would generally be incidental to, and therefore part of, the rental activity, but even this exception depends upon the level of services provided. The implication of the Conference Report is that a self-service laundromat in an apartment building would be viewed as part of the rental activity, but a laundromat with an attendant might not be. The problem becomes even more severe in common situations, such as a flower shop in an office building, which presumably would be treated as a separate activity even if it were owned by the owners and managers of the building.

Definition of a Passive Activity.—Once a taxpayer has determined each of the activities in which he is engaged (if he is able to do so), the taxpayer must then determine whether or not each such activity is a "passive" one which is subject to the PAL rule. There are basically two types of passive activities: (i) any activity which involves the conduct of a trade or business in which the taxpayer does not materially participate and (ii) any rental activity.

Material Participation.—An activity is a passive activity if the taxpayer does not materially participate in such activity. A taxpayer is treated as materially participating in an activity only if the taxpayer is involved in the operations of the activity on a basis which is *regular, continuous and substantial.* The actions of a taxpayer's spouse are imputed to the taxpayer.

Neither Section 469 nor the Reports define what constitutes "regular, continuous and substantial" involvement in an activity. However, the Finance Report provides several examples [which] indicate [that] the level of activity required for material participation is so high that the test effectively requires full-time involvement in an activity.

* * *

Congress's intention in defining a passive activity was to limit satisfaction of the material participation test to situations in which personal services are provided to a significant extent. A taxpayer is most likely to have materially participated in an activity if such activity is the taxpayer's principal trade or business.

* * *

Material Participation by Entities.—As indicated previously, the PAL rule applies to certain types of entities as well as to individuals. In the case of an entity, there are several artificial rules that must be applied in order to determine whether the material participation test is satisfied.

In the case of a closely held corporation or a personal service corporation, the material participation test is applied in what appears to be a reasonable manner. A closely held corporation or a personal service corporation is treated as materially participating in an activity if (a) one or more shareholders holding stock representing more than 50 percent (by value) of the outstanding stock of the corporation materially participate in the activity, or (b) the requirements of Section 465(c)(7) (C) (determined without regard to clause (iv)), which relates to businesses with certain full-time, nonowner employees [who participate in the activity], are satisfied. Thus, the basic application of the material participation test in the case of corporations subject thereto involves review of the activities of the shareholders and other principals of such corporations.

This logical approach in the case of corporations subject to Section 469 should be compared with the rules applicable to estates and trusts. In the case of an estate or trust, material participation is determined on the basis of the actions of the executor or fiduciary in his capacity as such. The actions of the beneficiary of the estate or trust are not considered. It seems very odd that material participation by a beneficiary of an estate or trust is not looked at; this is either an error in the statute or a very significant loophole.

Material Participation by Limited Partners.—One of the few rules in Section 469 that is relatively clear is that any interest in an activity as a limited partner will be treated as a passive activity. This rule is based on the reasoning that (i) under state law a limited partner does not participate in a business and therefore (ii) every interest of a limited partner must be held solely as an inactive investment. This logic notwithstanding, Congress recognized that an inflexible rule concerning limited partners could lead to abuse. As a result, Congress also authorized regulations to address situations in which limited partnership interests will not be treated as passive activities.

The effect of this special rule concerning limited partners is to create a consistent matrix in which the activities of an individual are referred to in order to determine whether the individual materially participates in an activity; mere labels are not sufficient. The problem which arises, however, is that there is little guidance in making this determination. By making the application of this rule—even in the case of limited partners in certain circumstances—subject to a facts and circumstances test, Congress has basically invited significant future litigation.

Rental Activities.—In contrast to the material participation test that applies to most businesses, the absolute rule that every rental activity will be treated as a passive activity appears at first blush to be relatively easy to apply. This appearance is misleading, however, since the definition and scope of a rental activity are mystifyingly vague.

a. Definition of a Rental Activity.—A rental activity is any activity where payments are principally for the use of tangible property. An activity is not treated as a rental activity if it involves substantial services. Thus, for example, a hotel, a nursing home or a car-rental business generally would not be treated as a rental activity. In contrast, an apartment lease or a bareboat charter would generally be treated as a rental activity.

b. Scope of a Rental Activity.—The definition of a rental activity is obviously very narrow. The scope of a rental activity is also narrow. Activities which immediately precede the rental activity, are conducted by the same persons or take place in the same location, or are associated with but do not involve renting tangible property, generally are not considered to be part of the rental activity. For example, real estate construction and development is treated as being a different activity than renting the constructed building.

c. Separate Rental Activities.—Not only is the scope of a rental activity very narrow, the determination of what constitutes a separate "activity" is also made in a narrow framework. Generally, a rental activity is defined with respect to rental property that is at one location. Thus, each separate building would be treated as a separate rental activity.

Portfolio Income.—After a taxpayer has identified all of the activities in which he has an interest and has determined whether each such activity is a passive activity (whether as a result of the activity being a rental activity or because the taxpayer does not materially participate in the activity), the next step is to determine the income or loss of each separate passive activity. The first determination that must be made involves separation of the portfolio income from each activity, since the income or loss of a passive activity must be determined without taking into account any portfolio income.

Portfolio income generally consists of income from investments other than investments in trades or businesses. Thus, portfolio income includes interest, dividends, royalties and annuities not derived in the ordinary course of a trade or business. Likewise, any gain or loss attributable to the disposition of property that produces such income would be treated as portfolio income. Thus, gain on the sale of shares of stock or a bond held by a partnership as an investment would generally give rise to portfolio income.

There are several special rules concerning portfolio income. First, in determining portfolio income, expenses and interest properly allocable to investments are taken into account, i.e., portfolio income is determined on a net basis. * * *

Second, income or loss on the sale of a passive activity is *not* treated as portfolio income. * * *

Third, the Finance Report contains a number of special rules that apply to certain types of investments. * * * [I]ncome of a type generally regarded as portfolio income is not treated as such if it is derived in the ordinary course of a trade or business. Thus, the interest income of a bank would not be treated as portfolio income. Likewise, interest income on an installment sale made in the ordinary course of a trade or business would not be treated as portfolio income. * * * [A]ny income, gain or loss attributable to an investment of working capital is treated as not derived in the ordinary course of a trade or business. Thus, if a partnership that has significant losses earns interest on its working capital, the partnership would be treated as having portfolio income, which would have to be reported as such by the individual partners.

* * *

Congress authorized regulations that would prevent taxpayers from structuring income-producing activities so as to shelter portfolio income. Specifically, regulations are expected to address the treatment of (i) ground leases that produce income without significant expenses, (ii) related party leases or subleases, and (iii) activities that previously generated active business losses that the taxpayer intentionally seeks to treat as passive at the time when they generate income. * * *

One other special rule that is worthy of note involves closely held C corporations. If a closely held C corporation has "net active income," the passive activity loss of such corporation is allowed as a deduction against the corporation's net active income. Net active income is determined by eliminating the portfolio income of the closely held C corporation. Thus, a closely held C corporation is allowed to utilize its PALs and any passive activity credits to offset all income other than portfolio income.   *   *   *

Determination of Income.—After the portfolio income of an activity has been determined, a taxpayer can finally determine whether such activity has incurred a gain or a loss for the taxable year. This calculation involves the same rules as are generally applied under the Internal Revenue Code.

There is one significant aspect of the determination of gain or loss for an activity that is different than one usually encounters in making such determination for other taxable entities. For purposes of the PAL rule, legal entities are disregarded. Thus, instead of calculating all of the income and deductions of a partnership, it is necessary for PAL purposes to calculate the income and loss of each activity conducted by that partnership. For example, if a single partnership owns two real estate projects, or a real estate project in which is located a grocery store operated by the partnership, it would be necessary to determine the income or loss of each separate activity.

*   *   *

Treatment of PALs.—Assume for the moment that a taxpayer has been able to negotiate the above maze of steps and that he has finally reached the point where he has calculated the income or loss of an activity in which he has an interest, and has determined that such activity is a passive activity. If the taxpayer has invested in only one activity and it is profitable, or if all of the taxpayer's passive activities are profitable, the taxpayer will simply treat the passive activity income the same as other types of income, i.e., the taxpayer will pay tax on this income.

What if the taxpayer's passive activity results in a loss, i.e., a PAL. In that case, the first question is whether the taxpayer has any income from other passive activities during the taxable year. If so, the PAL from one or more activities can be utilized to offset the taxable income from other passive activities. In essence, PALs are "netted" against the income from all passive activities in order to determine whether the taxpayer's passive activities resulted in a net gain or loss for the taxable year. Thus, the PAL for any taxable year is the amount by which the aggregate losses from all passive activities for the taxable year exceed the aggregate income from all passive activities for such year.

If the netting of all of the taxpayer's income and losses from passive activities during the taxable year results in a net loss, such loss cannot be used to offset the taxpayer's income from other sources.

Instead, the loss is carried forward and treated as a loss that can be utilized against income from passive activities in subsequent years.

* * *

Passive activity credits ("PACs") are treated similarly. A PAC is the amount by which the sum of the credits from all passive activities in the taxable year exceeds the taxpayer's regular tax liability for the taxable year allocable to all passive activities in which the taxpayer has an interest. Like PALs, PACs can be utilized only against the tax liability of passive activities in subsequent years, and can never be carried back.

* * *

Special PAL Exceptions.—There are two types of activities that are excepted from the general rules disallowing the utilization of PALs against income that is not generated by passive activities. These exceptions involve [working] interests in oil and gas properties and rental real estate losses incurred by certain individuals.

* * *

Rental Real Estate Losses.—There is a limited exception to the disallowance of PALs for losses and credits incurred by certain individuals from rental real estate activities in which the taxpayer actively participates. Such losses and credits are allowed in an amount not to exceed the equivalent of $25,000 in losses, with a phase out of such allowance for taxpayers with adjusted gross income in excess of $100,000.

In order to take advantage of this rule the taxpayer must first determine the amount of his losses from rental real estate activities in which the taxpayer actively participates. The special rule is applied by first netting the taxpayer's income and losses from all of the taxpayer's rental real estate activities in which the taxpayer actively participates. If there is a net loss for the taxable year, the taxpayer's net income from other passive activities is then applied against such loss. Only if there is a loss after (i) netting rental real estate activities and (ii) offsetting the resulting loss against passive income can the taxpayer utilize such loss to offset other income.

The definition of "active participation" in a rental real estate activity is not the same as material participation for PAL purposes. Active participation can occur without regular, continuous and substantial involvement in operations if the taxpayer participates in the activity in a significant and *bona fide* sense. Such participation could involve, for example, making management decisions or arranging for others to provide services. For example, a taxpayer who owns and rents out an apartment may be treated as actively participating even if he hires a rental agent, so long as the taxpayer participates in the decision-making process. Such participation could include approving new tenants, deciding on rental terms, and approving capital and repair expenditures.

* * *

There arc two important exceptions * * *. First, a limited partner [may not be able to] satisfy the active participation test to the extent of [his] limited partnership interest. Second, an individual is not treated as actively participating with respect to any interest in any rental real estate activity if at any time during the taxable year (or shorter relevant period that the taxpayer holds an interest in the activity) the taxpayer's interest is less than 10 percent of all interests in the activity. The determination of what constitutes a taxpayer's "interest in an activity" is not specified in Section 469, and this is a possible problem area in the application of this provision.

If a taxpayer has rental real estate losses that are eligible for this special provision, the amount of the loss that can be utilized is limited to $25,000. * * *

The amount of the loss that can be utilized is phased out for taxpayers with adjusted gross income over $100,000. The amount is reduced by 50 percent of the amount by which the taxpayer's adjusted gross income exceeds $100,000. * * *

Disposition of Passive Activities.—* * * [S]uspended PALs (but not suspended PACs) may be utilized by a taxpayer when the taxpayer disposes of his entire interest in the activity in a transaction in which all gain or loss is recognized. An abandonment of an interest in an activity is treated as a fully taxable disposition.

Upon such a disposition, any loss from the activity (including previously suspended losses) is not treated as a PAL and is allowable as a deduction against income in the following order: (1) to offset income or gain from the passive activity for the taxable year (including any gain recognized upon the disposition); (2) to offset net income or gain for the taxable year from any other passive activities in which the taxpayer has an interest; and (3) to offset any other income or gain.

* * *

There are special rules for certain types of dispositions. First, the allowance of losses on the disposition of a taxpayer's entire interest in a passive activity does not apply if the transferee is related to the taxpayer within the meaning of Section 267(b) or 707(b)(1). This provision is necessary to prevent taxpayers from simply selling interests in passive activities to related parties in order to obtain the benefit of otherwise suspended losses. Similarly, like-kind exchanges are not treated as dispositions for PAL purposes.

Second, if an interest in an activity is transferred by reason of the death of a taxpayer, PALs may be utilized only to the extent that [they are greater than the amount by which] the basis of the property in the hands of the transferee exceeds its adjusted basis immediately before the death of the taxpayer. The effect of this rule is to eliminate losses in an amount equal to the "step-up" in the basis of assets at death. * * * It should be noted that to the extent the loss exceeds the step-up in basis, the loss is allowed only to the taxpayer who incurred it, i.e., the decedent.

Third, in the case of a disposition by gift, the basis of the interest immediately before the transfer is increased by the amount of PALs allocable to such interest, and the PALs are not allowable as a deduction. The amount of the step-up is limited by the fair market value of the property. * * *

Finally, in the case of an installment sale of an entire interest in an activity, PALs are allowed in the same ratio to all losses as the ratio of the gain recognized on the sale bears to the gross profit. The rules which accelerate the recognition of gain due to depreciation recapture will generally accelerate the recognition of PALs as well.

As noted previously, although suspended PALs are recognized upon the disposition of property, PACs are not so recognized. Instead, PACs are carried forward to be utilized against future passive activity income. This could lead to harsh results if the PACs had reduced the basis of the taxpayer's interest in the passive activity. In order to avoid this effect, the transferor may elect to increase the basis of transferred property immediately before the transfer by an amount equal to the portion of any unused credit which reduced the basis of such property for the taxable year in which the credit arose. Thus, the taxpayer will be placed in the same position as if the PACs had never been available.

* * *

NOTE

1. Assume an S corporation constructs, manages and maintains an apartment development consisting of fourteen identical three-story buildings, each containing twenty apartments and the development covers an entire city block. Are the shareholders of the S corporation engaged in three activities (construction, real estate rental and maintenance) or forty-two activities?

a. If the S corporation constructs, manages and maintains two identical apartment buildings at either end of a city block and a shopping plaza which is not owned by the S corporation is located between the two buildings, are the shareholders of the S corporation engaged in three activities (construction, real estate rental and maintenance) or six activities (two construction, two real estate rental, and two maintenance)?

b. If the S corporation constructs, manages and maintains a high-rise apartment building which includes (i) a cafeteria (owned and operated by the S corporation), (ii) an attended parking garage (also owned and operated by the S corporation), (iii) a gift shop (operated by an unrelated lessee), and (iv) a day-care center in which the S corporation has a one-half interest, how many activities are the shareholders of the S corporation engaged in? See Lipton, *Fun and Games With Our New Pals,* 64 Taxes 801, 808–09 (1986).

c. See generally Notice 88–94, 1988–35 I.R.B. 25.

2. In many cases, the general partner of a limited partnership which owns and operates rental real estate receives substantial payments from the partnership as compensation for managing the partnership and its real estate. Can the general partner, during the partnership's early years, use his share of the

losses of the partnership to offset the income he derives from the fees paid him by the partnership?

    a. Is the answer different if the general partner is a C corporation wholly-owned by one individual?

    3. An individual owns two office buildings which he actively manages and a hotel and a nursing home each of which are managed and operated by a national chain. Can the individual use the losses derived from the office buildings against the income produced by the hotel and the nursing home? See Lipton, supra, page 810.

    4. If the general partner of a limited partnership which owns and operates rental real estate has a 3% interest in profits, losses and cash flow until the limited partners receive back their investments plus 10% per annum and then the general partner's interest increases to 60%, can the general partner use his 3% share of the early losses of the partnership against his other income from active trades or businesses?

    a. Is it significant that, based on the current financial projections of the partnership, the present discounted value of the general partner's interest in the partnership is about 50% of the present discounted value of the limited partners' interest in the partnership?

    5. A limited partner is given an opportunity to demonstrate material participation in an activity. See Section 469(h)(2). Can a limited partner demonstrate active participation in an activity involving the rental of real estate? See Section 469(i)(6)(C).

    a. Can a limited partner materially participate in the business of a limited partnership without violating the control test? Can a limited partner actively participate without violating the control test? See pages 53 to 69 supra.

    b. If a limited partner becomes so involved in the operation of the business of a limited partnership that the limited partner is treated as liable as a general partner for the debts of the partnership, is the limited partner treated as a limited partner or a general partner for the purposes of Section 469, particularly Sections 469(h)(2) and 469(i)(6)(C)? Cf. *Roeschlein v. Watkins*, 686 P.2d 1347 (Colo.App.1983).

    6. Low-income housing credits equivalent to $25,000 in losses can be used without regard to whether the taxpayer claiming the credits actively participates. The availability of low-income housing credits, however, is phased out ratably as the taxpayer's adjusted gross income increases from $200,000 to $250,000. See Section 469(i)(3)(B) and Section 469(i)(6)(B).

    7. The activity of holding real estate for rental involves holding the real estate for use by tenants and deriving income principally from the tenants' use of the real estate. The activity of holding real estate for rental does not include the following activities.

    a. Short-term rentals. On the average, the period during which each tenant or customer uses the real estate is seven days or less. For example, the operation of a parking lot might qualify under this exception. See Reg. Sec. 1.469–1T(e)(3)(ii)(A).

    b. Significant Personal Services. On the average, the period during which each tenant or customer uses the real estate is greater than seven days but less than thirty days and significant personal services are provided to the lessees. Only personal services performed by individuals are considered significant personal services. For example, the operation of a hotel might qualify under this exception. See Reg.Sec. 1.469–1T(2)(5)(iv).

c. Extraordinary Personal Services. This activity involves the lessee's use of real estate in excess of thirty days in situations in which the lessee receives extraordinary personal services. For example, the operation of a nursing home or boarding school might qualify for this exception. See Reg.Sec. 1.469–1T(e)(3)(v).

d. Rentals Incidental to Nonrental Activities. In order to qualify for this exception (i) the principal purpose for holding the real estate must be investment and gross rental income must be less than two percent of the lesser of the basis or fair market value of the real estate, or (ii) the principal purpose for holding the real estate must be use in trade or business, the real estate must have been used in the trade or business during at least two of the last five years, and the gross rental income must meet the two percent test, or (iii) the real estate must be held primarily for sale to customers in the ordinary course of a trade or business and the rental income recognized only in the year of sale, or (iv) the real estate must be used for lodging which is excluded under Section 119. See Reg. Sec. 1.469–1T(e)(3)(iv).

e. Nonexclusive Use. If real estate is made available during business hours for nonexclusive use by customers, the real estate will not be considered held for rental. For example, the operation of a golf course might qualify for this exception. See Reg.Sec. 1.469–1T(e)(3)(ii)(E).

f. Property Made Available for Use in Nonrental Activity. If a taxpayer owns an interest in a partnership, S corporation or joint venture which is conducting a nonrental activity, it does not constitute holding real estate for rental when the real estate is provided by the taxpayer for use in the nonrental activity in the taxpayer's capacity as an owner. See Reg.Sec. 1.469–1T(e)(3)(vii).

When an activity is excepted from classification as an activity involving rental real estate under one of the exceptions described above and the activity qualifies as a trade or business, the taxpayer usually must demonstrate material participation in the activity in order for the taxpayer's share of the losses of the activity to be treated as active rather than passive losses.

8. The income from self-developed rental property and self-rented property is treated by the Internal Revenue Service as active income. See Reg.Secs. 1.469–2T(f)(5) and 1.469–2T(f)(6). Self-developed rental property is real estate which is rented while awaiting sale and is sold within twelve months after first being used in the rental activity and is real estate with respect to which the taxpayer materially or significantly participated during any year in providing services for the purpose of enhancing the value of the real estate. If real estate qualifies as self-developed rental property, the income from its sale is also treated as active income. Self-rented property is real estate which is rented to an activity in which the taxpayer materially participates. On the other hand, net income from an activity which holds nondepreciable real estate for rental, subject to the exceptions described above, will be treated as portfolio income. Real estate is treated as nondepreciable if less than thirty percent of the unadjusted basis of the real estate is subject to the allowance for depreciation under Section 167. See Reg.Sec. 1.469–2T(f)(3). An example of the foregoing would be the income derived by a lessor from a ground lease.

9. In order to be considered as materially participating in an activity, a taxpayer, who is an individual, must meet one of seven tests.

a. The taxpayer must participate in the activity for more than 500 hours during the taxable year. See Reg.Sec. 1.469–5T(a)(1). Any participation is counted except work which is not of a type usually done by an owner and one of the principal purposes for such work is the avoidance of Section 469, and work which is performed in the taxpayer's capacity as an investor. Participation by the taxpayer's spouse is treated as participation by the taxpayer.

b. The taxpayer's participation must be substantially all the participation in the activity by all individuals, including nonowners. See Reg.Sec. 1.469–5T(a)(2).

c. The taxpayer's participation in an activity must be more than 100 hours during the taxable year and the taxpayer's participation must not be less than the participation of any other individual, including nonowners. See Reg.Sec. 1.469–5T(a)(3).

d. The taxpayer's aggregate participation in significant participation activities (S.P.A.) must exceed 500 hours during the taxable year. S.P.A. are activities with respect to each one of which the taxpayer participates more than 100 hours during the year and are activities in which the taxpayer does not materially participate without the application of this rule. See Reg.Sec. 1.469–5T(a)(4). The amount of a taxpayer's gross income from each S.P.A. equal to the net income thereof is treated as active income if all of the taxpayer's S.P.A., taken together, generate net income for the taxable year.

e. A taxpayer is treated as materially participating in an activity if the taxpayer materially participated in that activity for any five of the preceding ten taxable years. See Reg.Sec. 1.469–5T(a)(5).

f. A taxpayer is treated as materially participating in any personal service activity in which he materially participated for any three prior taxable years. A personal service activity is a trade or business in which capital is not an income-producing factor. See Reg.Secs. 1.469–5T(a)(6) and 1.469–5T(d).

g. A taxpayer will be treated as materially participating in an activity if the facts and circumstances so warrant. The following, however, will not be taken into account: (i) The satisfaction of any other participation standard in the Internal Revenue Code; (ii) Participation in management of an activity if the management services performed are exceeded by those performed by another individual; and (iii) Participation in an activity for 100 or less hours during a year. See Reg.Sec. 1.469–5T(b)(2).

10. A limited partner will be treated as materially participating only if the limited partner (1) participates in the activity for more than 500 hours during the year, (2) materially participated in the activity for any five taxable years during during the preceding ten taxable years, or (3) materially participated in a personal service activity for any three preceding years. See Reg.Sec. 1.469–5T(e)(2).

11. The income and loss from publicly traded partnerships are accorded special treatment under Section 469(k). The income from a publicly traded partnership is treated as portfolio income and its losses can only be used to offset income from the same publicly traded partnership and upon a complete

disposition of the partner's entire interest in the publicly traded partnership. For the purposes of Section 469, publicly traded partnerships are partnerships in which the interests are (1) traded on an established securities market or (2) readily tradeable on a secondary market. See page 93 supra.

12. See generally Tureen, *Achieving Real Estate Developers' Tax Objectives Under Section 469 and Economic Objectives Under Section 704(b)*, 65 Taxes 478 (1987); Westin, *Shooting Pool in the Dark: Coping With the Passive Loss Rules*, 11 Rev.Tax'n Indiv. 139 (1987); Turner, *Defining the Scope of a Passive Activity*, 65 Taxes 594 (1987); Goldberg, *The Passive Activity Loss Rules: Planning Considerations, Techniques, and a Foray Into Never–Never Land*, 15 J.Real Est.Tax'n 3 (1987); Lipton and Serling, *Passive Activity Loss Limitations Can Have Unexpected Impact on Corporations*, 68 J.Tax'n 20 (1988); McKeown and Streer, *Preserving the Benefit of the Rental Real Estate Activity Loss Exception*, 66 Taxes 214 (1988); August, *How Do the Passive Activity Loss Rules Apply to S and C Corporations?*, 5 J.Ps.Tax'n 218 (1988); Peroni, *A Policy Critique of the Section 469 Passive Loss Rules*, 62 S.Cal.L.Rev. 1 (1988).

f.　THE REAL ESTATE INVESTMENT TRUST

An entity which might be used for the acquisition and ownership of real estate is specifically described by the Internal Revenue Code as the real estate investment trust. The word "trust" may be a misnomer since there is no requirement that an entity qualifying for real estate investment trust status under the Internal Revenue Code need be a trust under local law. The excerpts from the following article discuss the particular attributes of this form of entity and its possible uses.

THE REAL ESTATE INVESTMENT TRUST: LEGAL AND ECONOMIC ASPECTS
Carol MacMillan Stanley
24 University of Miami Law Review 155 (1969).
[footnotes omitted]

* * *

General Background of the REIT
* * *

There are two basic types of REITs—equity trusts and mortgage trusts. Equity trusts are primarily engaged in the ownership of all categories of real property, which may or may not be subject to encumbrances. Their main source of income is from rentals. Mortgage trusts, on the other hand, invest their assets in long or short term mortgages or other liens against real property. The mortgage trusts' income is derived principally from interest earned on the mortgages and from discounts and commissions on mortgage purchases.

Qualifying Requirements of the Internal Revenue Code

A.　Status

Except for the REIT provisions, a real estate association could be taxed as a corporation. * * * To escape this corporate qualification and the resultant imposition of double taxation the realty association must therefore adhere strictly to the statutory requirements. For example, the REIT * * * [may be incorporated] and must be managed by one or more trustees. * * *

The beneficial ownership of the trust must be represented by transferable shares or certificates of such interest and must be held by 100 or more persons. Even though the shares are transferable, however, the trustee may retain the power to refuse to transfer shares in order to maintain the requirements of REIT status.

Although the language of the Code does not use the word "passive," this requirement is deduced from the rule that a REIT may not hold any property primarily for sale to customers in the ordinary course of business. Whether or not property is held primarily for sale to customers depends on an interpretation of the facts and circumstances in each case. [The holding of property for sale to customers in the ordinary course of business, however, will not result in the disqualification of an REIT. The REIT will be subject to a 100 percent penalty tax on its profits from the sale of such property unless the property is "foreclosure property," see Section 856(e), or, (1) it has been held by the REIT for at least four years, (2) the total expenditures made by the REIT with respect to such property during the four year period prior to sale do not exceed 20 percent of the net selling price of the property, (3) the REIT does not sell more than five properties during the taxable year, and (4) if the property is land or improvements not acquired through foreclosure, the property had been held by the REIT for rent for a period of at least four years.]

The qualified REIT must not also qualify as a section 542 personal holding company. Thus, if more than half of the value of the REIT's outstanding stock is owned directly or indirectly by five or less individuals, the association would qualify as a personal holding company but not as a REIT.

B. *Income Requirements*

According to section 856(c), 75 percent of gross income must be derived from rents from real property, [interest on obligations secured by mortgages on real property or on interests in real property, gain from the sale or other disposition of real property, which is not property held for sale to customers in the ordinary course of trade or business, dividends or other distributions on and] gain from the sale or other disposition of transferable shares (or transferable certificates of beneficial interest) in other real estate investment trusts which meet all requirements, * * * abatements and refunds of taxes on real property[, income and gain derived from foreclosure property, certain commitment fees, unless based on income or profits of any person and qualified temporary investment income.]

Another 20 percent of gross income must be derived from dividends, interest, rents from real property and gain from the sale or other disposition of stock, securities, and real property (including interests in real property, interests in mortgages on real property [which is not property held for sale to customers in the ordinary course of trade or business]), abatements and refunds of taxes on real property[, income and gain derived from foreclosure property and certain commitment fees, unless based on income or profits of any person.] A maximum of 5 percent of gross income is not restricted as to source.

Less than 30 percent of the gross income can be from sales of stock or securities held for less than * * * [six months, property held for sale to customers in the ordinary course of trade or business] and real property held for less than four years (excluding involuntary conversions [and foreclosure property]). It must be noted that loss from the sale or other disposition of property subject to this 30 percent limitation is not netted with gain from the sale or other disposition of such property.

C. Asset Requirements

At the close of each quarter of the taxable year at least 75 percent of the value of the total assets of the trust must be represented by one or more of the following: real estate assets, cash and cash items (including receivables) and government securities. The receivables must not include those purchased from another person, but must arise in the ordinary course of the trust's operation. The character of the remaining 25 percent of the value of the total assets is not restricted. The ownership of securities under the 25 percent limitation is limited to an amount not greater in value than 5 percent of the value of the total assets, and to not more than 10 percent of the outstanding voting securities of any one issue.

The complexity of the above requirements is slightly alleviated by the provision that if a discrepancy exists immediately after the acquisition of any security or other property which is wholly or partly the result of such acquisition, the REIT shall not lose its status for such quarter; but the discrepancy must be eliminated within thirty days after the close of such quarter in order to qualify for REIT treatment during such quarter.

D. Rents from Real Property and the Independent Contractor

Section 856(d) and the regulations pertaining thereto give special, detailed treatment concerning "rents from real property." Rents from real property, as required by the 95 percent and 75 percent gross income tests of section 856(c), generally means the gross amounts received for the use of, or the right to use, real property of the REIT [and charges for services customarily furnished in connection with the rental of real property]. Apportionment is required where rent may also be received for personal property such as furnishings [and the rent attributable to such property exceeds 15 percent of the total rent for the taxable year attributable to both the real and personal property leased.] Any amount of rent which depends in whole or in part on the income or profits derived by any person from such property must also be excluded [except for rents received from a tenant which derives substantially all of its income with respect to the property leased from the REIT from the subleasing of substantially all the property so long as the rents the tenant receives from the subtenants qualifies as "rents from real property." The exclusion of rents based on the income or profits of a tenant] however, does not necessarily preclude use of a fixed percentage or an escalator provision. Nevertheless, any arrangement devised must conform with normal business practices and is not to be used as a means of basing the rent on income or profits.

Also excluded from rents of real property is any amount received from a corporation in which the REIT owns 10 percent or more of the voting stock [or 10 percent or more of the total number of shares of all classes of stock]. If the REIT receives rent from a non-corporate entity and the trust owns a 10–percent or more interest in its assets or net profits, the rent does not qualify. Moreover, any amount received with respect to any real [or personal] property from which the REIT receives money as a result of its furnishing services[, other than services customarily furnished in connection with the rental of real property,] to the tenants is also excluded. The income will qualify as rent from real property only if an independent contractor manages or operates the property and the REIT receives no dividend therefrom. [The type of services or management which must be performed by an independent contractor are those which would turn the rent into "active" rent. For example, the services or management required in the operation of a hotel must be performed by an independent contractor.] * * *

An independent contractor is defined as a person or a corporation who does not own more than 35 percent of the shares in the REIT. Likewise, a 35–percent owner of the REIT must not have more than a 35–percent interest in the independent contractor.

Taxation of the Trusts and Shareholders

A. *Taxation of the Trust*

The special tax benefits applicable to the REIT are not available unless the trust pays to its shareholders dividends in the amount of 95 percent of its REIT taxable income for such taxable year, and the trust complies with certain record-keeping requirements. If the association fails to meet the requirements for the taxable year, it will be subject to tax as a corporation, regardless of its classification. [An REIT will not be disqualified for failure to meet the distribution requirement if such failure is not due to fraud and if the failure is cured by a deficiency dividend distribution when the failure to meet the distribution requirement is "determined." The REIT, however, will be subject to a 4% excise tax on the excess of the required distribution for the year (defined in Section 4981(b)) over the actual distribution for the year.]

[In general,] after deducting dividends paid, the REIT is subject to the imposition of the normal tax as prescribed by section 11. * * * [If the] net long-term capital gain [of an REIT exceeds] the sum of its net short-term capital loss and its deduction for dividends paid (determined with reference to capital gains dividends only)[, the REIT may be entitled to determine its tax using the alternative tax described in Section 857(b)(3)].

B.   Taxation of Shareholders

[T]o the extent the trust designates any dividend or part thereof as a capital gain dividend, the shareholders rather than the trust are taxed on the long-term capital gain. Notice to shareholders of the amount of any capital gain dividends must be given within thirty days after the year of payment[, or 120 days after a "determination" is made that the net capital gain for a taxable year is greater than that originally reported by the REIT.]

Where a share or interest in a REIT is held for [six months] or less, any loss on the sale or exchange of the share or interest, to the extent of any capital gain dividend received in the [six-month] period, is a long-term capital loss.

The REIT trustees are permitted a twelve-month period after the taxable year closes to pay to the shareholders additional dividends; provided, however, that the declaration thereof occurs before the time for filing the return. [Note, however, the deficiency dividend procedures discussed above.]

Operational Considerations

A.   Federal Regulations

* * * A REIT [probably] cannot qualify for a private offering since there must be at least one hundred participants. It may qualify for the intrastate offering exemption, however, if it constitutes an investment company required to be registered under the Investment Company Act of 1940. This exemption provides that the trust will not be required to register under the act if it invests exclusively in fee interests in real estate or mortgage[s] or liens secured by real estate, and is not engaged in the business of issuing face amount certificates of the installment type or periodic payment plan certificates. A trust which invests to a substantial extent in securities of other real estate investment trusts or companies engaged in the real estate business or in other securities might not qualify under this exemption.

B.   State Laws

The REIT [in the form of a business trust or similar entity] cannot be used if the state law does not recognize such a form, or at least does not recognize it for the holding of realty or the collection of rentals. Despite the fact that state law may preclude a business trust from going into some jurisdictions, an interstate operation can still be carried on in other jurisdictions. * * *. [Since, however, a REIT can operate in the corporate form, whether a state recognizes the business trust or a similar entity is not a serious problem.]

* * * [T]rusts which seek to sell their shares in their own and in other states must familiarize themselves with the applicable state securities laws.

C. Conduit Theory

The REIT is only the conduit, i.e., the funnel through which each individual certificate holder receives income and pays his own tax, just as a partnership is a conduit through which each partner pays his own tax. * * * If capital gain is passed to the holder or the beneficiary of the certificates, it is [treated by] them as capital gain. The tax-free flow available by reason of depreciation may be passed on to the beneficiary without immediate tax impact, but whether this is in fact done is a policy decision to be made by the trustees. It may be wiser to use this cash flow for reinvestment rather than distribution.

In addition, the trust offers the same degree of limited liability formerly possessed by the corporation but denied to the general partnership.

* * *

D. Permitted Activity

The misconception that the REIT must have "passive income" has deterred many realtors from considering the REIT. The word "passive" does not actually appear in the Code or regulations. There are also certain activities which, according to lay usage, would be considered "active," but which are not so considered within the terminology of the Code. Such activities include the construction of buildings on property with the participation of outside contractors, architects, and engineers, and ownership of an office building [or residential rental real estate and the provision of services customarily furnished in connection with the rental of real property. If greater management and services are required, such as a hotel,] an independent contractor [must be] employed to manage it. As to the latter, the independent contractor must employ all of the building's employees on its own payroll, even though the trust has a right to pay the contractor on a "cost-plus" basis for his services. The price, of course, must be reasonable. The prohibition of a 35–percent cross-identity of ownership must be observed. Moreover, because of the amendment to permit trustees to be officers or directors of the independent contractor, there can now be a close working relationship between the trustee and the managing agent.

* * *

NOTE

1. Even though the 100 or more beneficial owners requirement serves to eliminate the REIT as an entity for use by the closely held venture, its availability as a participant, investor or lender should not be overlooked.

2. As is true with many special status entities under the Internal Revenue Code, the operational rules for a REIT are quite complex. See generally Aldrich, *Real Estate Investment Trusts: An Overview,* 27 Bus.Law. 1165 (1972); Nad and Friedman, *Income Tax Problems of Real Estate Investment Trusts,* 1 Real Est.L.J. 368 (1973); Mirsky and Auerbach, *R.E.I.T.'s: Problems and Possible Solutions,* 3 Tax Adviser 714 (1972); Zivan, *Won't You Be My Partner? A Complex Question For a Real Estate Investment Trust,* 27 Tax Law. 53 (1973); Kelley, *Real Estate Investment Trusts,* 4 J.Real Est.Tax'n 161 (1977); Allen, *REIT Provisions Substantially Changed by TRA; Greater Complexity, More Workable,* 46 J.Tax'n 114 (1977); Mirsky and Yates, *REITs: Tax Planning Under the '76 Act,* 8 Tax Adviser 196 (1977); Halpern, *Real Estate Investment Trusts and the Tax Reform Act of 1976,* 31 Tax Law. 329 (1978); Rosenberg, *REIT's Emerge as Source of Real Estate Finance and Investment,* 16 # 3 Real Est.Rev. 41 (1986); Galler, *Tax Reform Act of 1986 Changes Affecting Real Estate Investment Trusts,* 18 Tax Adviser 178 (1987); Mai and Grunfield, *The New Uses of Real Estate Investment Trusts,* 33 Prac.Law. 27 (Mar.1986).

3. Questions have arisen concerning the qualification of certain payments as rents or interest, under the REIT provisions. For example, the Internal Revenue Service has ruled that percentage rentals received by a REIT in an amount equal to the excess of a certain fixed percentage of the tenant's gross sales for each lease-quarter-year over the fixed monthly rent for the same period can be treated as rent. See Rev.Rul. 74–198, 1974–1 C.B. 171. See also Rev.Rul. 76–413, 1976–2 C.B. 213. In the context of a "wrap-around" mortgage made by a REIT, the Internal Revenue Service has ruled that when the REIT is not liable for the mortgage obligation wrapped around the only interest includible in the REIT's income is that paid on the amount actually loaned to the borrower by the REIT. See Rev.Rul. 75–99, 1975–1 C.B. 197. In addition, Sections 856 and 857 were amended in 1974 to permit a REIT without affecting its qualification to hold, for a limited period, generally at most two years, "foreclosure property," property which was acquired by the REIT because the mortgagor or lessee was in default or about to default. However, unqualified income received by the REIT from the property will be subject to corporate tax at the highest rate provided.

4. The Tax Reform Act of 1986 liberalized the REIT requirements in a number of ways, which included the following: (1) A pre-existing entity can qualify for REIT status if, at the time it seeks to qualify, it does not have any earnings and profits which were accumulated in a non-REIT year; (2) A REIT can have a "qualified REIT subsidiary"; (3) A REIT can temporarily, for a one-year period, invest new equity capital and the proceeds of publicly offered debt securities in nonqualifying assets; (4) As mentioned above, a REIT can perform certain general services with respect to its real estate assets so long as the performance of those services will not turn the income from the real estate into "active" income; (5) As mentioned above, a REIT can receive as "qualified rents," rents based on the net income or profits of a prime tenant so long as the prime tenant's rental income qualifies as "rents from real property"; (6) The amount which a REIT is required to distribute can be reduced by certain types of noncash income of the REIT which, in total, exceeds 5% of the REIT's

taxable income; (7) The safe harbor rules, under which sales of assets by a REIT which meet the conditions of such rules are not treated as prohibited transactions, have been broadened; and (8) A REIT can treat as "qualified" income the income it derives from certain shared appreciation mortgages which it holds.

g. COOPERATIVES AND CONDOMINIUMS

The cooperative and the condominium are not technically forms of acquiring entity. They can be described as methods of organization and marketing. If, however, one of these methods of organization is desired, it should be planned for from the outset and the appropriate steps taken.

The development of a multi-residential building is planned. If a condominium is to be the approach used, the sponsor, which could be a corporation, partnership, limited partnership, etc., will sell to the purchaser a fee interest in a unit in the building together with an undivided interest or right of use in all common areas. The organization of the condominium and the sale of the units must comply with state statutes providing for, and regulating, the condominium form of ownership. The interest sold to the purchaser can be conceived of, in traditional property terms, as a fee interest in a three dimensional unit of space. Generally, the sponsor of a cooperative, which again could be any one of a variety of entities, sells the building to a corporation usually formed pursuant to the provisions of a state's corporate statutes providing for cooperative corporations. The cooperative corporation then sells shares in the corporation to the "tenants." The shares usually entitle each purchaser to the use and occupancy, or lease, of a unit in the building together with the use of all common areas. In simplistic terms, the shareholders of a cooperative have the right to use and occupy all common areas, in common with all other shareholders.

The following excerpt describes a variety of ways in which a sponsor might structure the development and sale of a condominium or a cooperative project.

CO–OPS AND CONDOMINIUMS—THE SPONSOR'S VIEWPOINT
Lewis R. Kaster
28 N.Y.U. Institute on Federal Taxation 99 (1970).
[footnotes omitted]

* * *

Business Factors

* * * A co-op project always involves the sale to a single corporation of residential property, part of which may be devoted to producing commercial income. A condominium plan generally involves sales to numerous individuals and the plan may include solely commercial property, solely residential property or a combination of both.

* * *

Capital Gain

If real estate is held by a sponsor "primarily for sale to customers in the ordinary course of his * * * business" he is a dealer and his sale profit will be [treated] as ordinary income. * * *

Condominium Plans

Some typical condominium situations are as follows:

Condominium Sponsor Buys, Builds, and Sells

Case 1. The sponsor buys the land for this project, and constructs and sells the condominium units. This is as classic a case for dealer status as that of the builder of single family homes. The sponsor's profit is ordinary income.

Sponsor Buys Land, Holds, and Sells to Related Entity

Case 2. The sponsor buys the land, holds it for more than [the period required for long-term capital gains] and "sells" it on a deferred payment plan to a corporation or limited partnership at a profit. The profit reflects in part the land's estimated value when developed. The sponsor has a substantial interest in the corporation or partnership, and an investment group owns the balance of the equity. The owning entity builds the condominium units using the sponsor's contracting corporation as general contractor, and a sales agent sells the units.

Depending upon whether the sponsor is a dealer in land and, in any case, upon whether this land can be characterized as a capital asset, part or all of his land profit may be capital gain.[41] If the land is a capital asset the Commissioner may assert that part of the payments for the land represent compensation for the contractor's services rendered in building the project. But, if the deferred purchase price is not unreasonably high, and if the dealer stigma has not attached to the parcel in issue, capital gains may result with respect to the bulk of the land profit. The owning entity's gain on resale will be dealer income.

Sponsor Owns Improved Property and Sells as Condominium

Case 3. The sponsor has owned and rented the improved property for a number of years, and the real estate may be properly characterized as a Section 1231 asset. The sponsor decides to sell the building to the occupants via a condominium plan. He makes the minimal repairs and alterations required to make the sale and arranges the mortgage financing.

---

41. [Unless the purchaser partnership is a "controlled" partnership under Section 707(b)(2) of the Internal Revenue Code of 1986, as amended.]

Business or Investment

This presents the question whether the numerous unit sales involved in the disposition of the property constitute a "business," or are merely an orderly liquidation of an investment which entitles the sponsor to report his profit as capital gain. If this were the sponsor's only property, and he sold it to an unrelated third party investor, the profit would surely be capital gain. But in that case it is likely that the profit would be less than the "retail" sale price to the occupants. The multiple sales inherent in a condominium project do not necessarily require the conclusion that the sponsor is a dealer. But it is likely that the Commissioner would argue for dealer characterization of the sale profit.

In subdivision sales cases where the taxpayer did not acquire the land for resale and proved that subdivision was the only reasonable way to dispose of the property, the additional profit from multiple sales rather than a single sale apparently has not deterred courts from finding a capital gain under the "liquidation of investment" theory.

*   *   *

Co-op Plans

Some of the more common co-op plans involve the following patterns:

Sponsor Owns Property as Investment:

Case A. As in Case # 3 under the condominium discussion, the apartment building but for the sale would have been characterized as a Section 1231 asset of the sponsor. The co-op sponsor, in contrast to the sponsor of the condominium, may assert that he is making but a single sale to a corporation and that a single sale is not a "business" and thus Section 1221(1) has no application. If the transfer of the Section 1231 property to the co-op may be characterized for tax purposes as a single sale, then the capital gain result in this hypothetical case is clear.[42] Even if the transfer is somehow characterized as multiple *sales of stock* by the sponsor to the individual purchasers of co-op stock, the "liquidation of investment" rationale might support capital gains characterization.

Application of Section 1221

The Commissioner might find that the sponsor's activities in this situation come within the Section 1221(1) definition of "dealer" activity. The argument would be as follows: The co-op corporation is formed by the sponsor's attorneys, and the sponsor acts for the "co-op" as well as for himself in setting the terms of the sale. Furthermore, the sponsor chooses the sales agent for the stock of the co-op corporation. While

---

42. [Unless, of course, the controlled corporation problem, Section 1239, rears its ugly head.]

the sponsor's lawyers [may] arrange for "independent" counsel to represent the co-op in connection with the offering, * * * such counsel generally do not negotiate price or other substantial terms of purchase.

The Commissioner might conclude: (a) the co-op is the sponsor's alter ego until after the closing and (b) the substance of the transaction is that the co-op having issued all its stock to the sponsor, along with any purchase money note, the sponsor via his sales agent has sold the stock to the "customers." Therefore, his overall activity constitutes a "business" despite the "single sale" and "liquidation of investment" arguments.

New York attorneys may well find fault with part of this argument on the grounds that the co-op corporation is represented by the most powerful independent counsel in the state—the Attorney General—who scrupulously reviews each proposed offering prior to sale to insure not only full disclosure but fairness. * * * Certainly in cases where the tenants have formed committees to negotiate with the sponsor in respect of the co-op plan, the sponsor cannot be characterized as dealing with himself in respect of the sale to the co-op corporation.

* * *

Sponsor Buys Land, Uses Related Corporation for Improvements, Sells to Co-op Corporation

Case B. Sponsor buys the land, employs a related corporation to construct the building at a nominal profit or buys an existing building and employs a related corporation to renovate it at a nominal profit and then sells to the co-op corporation at a price reflecting the construction profit and the value of the land as improved.

The Service would characterize the entire profit as ordinary income. However, there are technical arguments to support a contrary view. It must be remembered that Section 1221(1) requires the existence of a "business" and "customers" and that the property be sold in the ordinary course of that business. This presents the question, "What is the sponsor's business?"

Construction Business

It might be said that he is in the construction business, despite the fact that the related corporation is an independent contractor, a separate entity whose activity may not be attributed to the sponsor. However, if the attribution of such activity were the sole bar to a decision that the sale profit was ordinary income, * * * [probably] a court would characterize the construction corporation as the sponsor's agent or alter ego and that its activity would be attributed to him. The next step of finding that the sale was part of the ordinary course of that business would not be a farfetched conclusion.

However, if an unrelated general contractor were employed to construct the building for a fixed price, no basis would exist for characterizing the sponsor as being in the "construction" business with respect to this building.

Real Estate Business

The Commissioner may contend that the sponsor is in the business of selling real estate. Yet, a number of cases, most of which involve unimproved land, have held that the sale of a single asset clearly acquired for resale to a single party is not a "business." * * *

* * * [But if] construction activity does not put the sponsor in "business" [and] if the sale to the co-op corporation does not constitute a "business" because it is a single sale to a single customer, a basis exists for capital gains characterization for the sponsor's profit.

However, if the court thought that the taxpayer's activities did constitute a "business" the "sale of stock" argument, discussed above in Case A, might be asserted to support a decision that the profit was ordinary income. In that event, it is clear that the sponsor could not claim that such sales represented a liquidation of an investment, rather than a "business."

Application of Section 482

If the sponsor's sale in this case cannot be characterized as a dealer transaction, the Commissioner may resort to Section 482 to allocate part of the gain to the construction corporation on the grounds that part of the gain is income earned as general contractor. This could produce some ordinary income to the construction corporation and a dividend to the sponsor.

Sponsor Sells to Unrelated Corporation

Case C. The sponsor in Case A is willing to reduce his profit if he can avoid the dealer problem and be sure of capital gains. He, therefore, contracts to sell the property to unrelated corporation S.H. which is in the real estate business. The price is materially less than the anticipated sale price to the co-op and materially more than would be paid by an investor-landlord. S.H. then proceeds with the co-op plan. S.H. makes a contract down payment and agrees to a closing date proximate to, or simultaneous with, its anticipated closing of the co-op offering. If in Case A the sponsor has ordinary income exposure, will he now be "home-free" because he is not dealing directly with the co-op?

If S.H.'s obligation to close its purchase of the property is not conditioned on its resale of the property to the co-op, and its liability for damages in case of default is represented by a significant down payment or is backed up by its general financial responsibility, the transaction should be treated as a *bona fide* sale. However, if the facts suggest S.H. is merely a convenient middleman taking no risk, the sponsor may have gained little by producing S.H. as the purported independent purchaser.

Sponsor's Retained Interest in the Land

One variation in sales technique used in both co-op and condominium plans involves the sponsor's retention of an interest in the land. This may be an interest as ground lessor or sub-lessor. In such cases tax counsel have been mindful that the Service might contend that the payment for the "building" constitutes "advance rent" to the sponsor, as lessor, or sub-lessor, rather than being sales proceeds.

In transactions where the land interest has been carved out, the lease often includes various provisions to substantiate the conclusion that full beneficial ownership of the improvement has been conveyed to the lessee. Such provisions have included the theoretical right of the co-op or the condominium unit owner to remove the building on expiration of the lease. * * *

Basis Allocation Problems

If the lease rental in the above "carve-out" situation is based on the value of the land as improved, there is authority, that would require the sponsor to allocate part of the cost of the building to the retained interest in the land. The net effect of reducing the basis that may be deducted in computing gain on sale of the improvement is to increase the seller's gain. The rationale requiring such an allocation is that the lease payments reflect the value of the building, thus part of the cost of the building should be reflected in the basis of the reversion. [See Gordon P. Connolly, 34 CCH Tax Ct.Mem. 1379 (1975). See also *Urbanek v. United States,* 2 Cl.Ct. 574 (1983), aff'd, 731 F.2d 870 (F.Cir. 1984).] The Commissioner might assert, as an alternative to the basis argument, that to the extent that the rental exceeds a fair rental on unimproved land, the sales proceeds include the value of the landlord's position in the ground lease. [In Lakeside Garden Developers, Inc., 35 CCH Tax Ct.Mem. 1294 (1976), aff'd sub. nom., Murry v. Comm., 601 F.2d 892 (5th Cir.1979), the Commissioner asserted that the present value of the "excessive" rent required to be paid by purchasers of condominium units for the use of "carved-out" recreational facilities should be considered part of the consideration received by the developer from the sale of the units. The Tax Court rejected this assertion. See also William Friedman, 36 CCH Tax Ct.Mem. 841 (1977); Harry T. Mangurian Jr., 38 CCH Tax Ct.Mem. 366 (1979). The attack on the required lease of "carved-out" recreation facilities by purchasers of condominium units has been more successful on other fronts. Putting Buckley Towers Condominium, Inc. v. Buchwald, 533 F.2d 934 (5th Cir. 1976), together with Miller v. Granados, 529 F.2d 393 (5th Cir.1976), it might be said that, in the proper case, requiring the purchasers of condominium units to enter into a lease of "carved-out" recreational facilities would be held, by at least the Fifth Circuit Court of Appeals, to be a "tying arrangement" violating the Sherman and Clayton Acts. See Imperial Point Colonnades Condominium, Inc. v. Mangurian, 549 F.2d 1029 (5th Cir.1977). See generally Avila South Condominium Ass'n, Inc. v. Kappa Corp., 347 So.2d 599 (Fla.1976).]

Common Recreational Facilities

Another problem of basis allocation exists with respect to recreational facilities constructed by the sponsor as part of a condominium project where each unit owner has an undivided interest in the facilities. However, there is substantial authority to support the proposition that part of the cost of these common facilities may be allocated to each condominium unit in determining the gain on sale of such units.

Carved Out Lease

There is a problem of basis allocation where the sponsor of a condominium or co-op plan carves out and retains a lease of the recreational or commercial facilities. In essence this is similar to allocation of basis in a sale-leaseback transaction. In general, such a lease is valuable if the rental is below market. In this case, the sponsor may have to allocate part of the overall basis of the project to the lease or include the value of the lease in the "amount realized" from the sale. This has the effect of increasing his gain on the sale of the residential space. Probably the basis allocation should be made in relation to date-of-sale fair market values of the lease and the interest which has been sold.

* * *

Shares and Shareholders

Unsold Shares

In certain co-op deals a special capital gains problem exists where shares relating to some apartments have not been sold by the co-op by the time when the closing takes place, and the sponsor receives these shares in partial payment of the purchase price of the real estate.

* * *

Sale and/or Section 351 Transaction Characterization

The issue is whether the shares are an "amount realized" on the sale of the real estate to the co-op or have been received as part of the consideration in a Section 351 exchange. If the former, any gain inherent in the value of the shares will be characterized in the same way as the other "amounts realized" from the sale. If the Section 351 characterization applies, the shares may have a low basis, and the profit on their resale may be dealer income. To the extent that the sponsor agrees to accept unsold shares from the co-op as part of the consideration for the transfer of the property, it is arguable that he has sold part of the real estate for cash (and in some cases, purchase money notes) and that he has exchanged part of the real estate for shares as part of a Section 351 transaction with the other shareholders who have purchased for cash.

If the transaction is treated as part sale and part Section 351 exchange in which the shares are the sole consideration received by the sponsor, the sponsor will have a substituted basis for the shares under Section 358(a)(1) representing a proportionate part of his basis of the real estate. Upon his sale of these shares at a price in excess of basis, there will be a profit which might be dealer income.

Liquidation of Investment

Depending on the circumstances relating to why the shares were "unsold," the "liquidation of investment" concept might form the basis for a capital gain decision in favor of the sponsor. For example, if there had been no buyers for the shares, this would suggest that sale of the shares was merely a continuation of his liquidation efforts. * * *

However, if in anticipation of the co-op plan he had kept the apartments vacant so as to avoid having a tenant as a "ready" buyer, his holding several blocks of stock for sale might be characterized as a business rather than a reasonable effort to realize the value of an investment through normal liquidation efforts. Thus, reliance on the "liquidation" theory as a separate argument, might be unwise where the sponsor had held out the shares for future sale.

Some sponsors arrange for third parties to purchase "unsold shares" in bulk at a discount so as to have a single sale rather than multiple sales. In this respect the discussion under Case C is equally applicable.

* * *

Leasehold Co-op—Taxes Assessed on Building Value

Although the tenant-stockholder in a co-op is entitled to deduct a proportionate part of the real estate taxes assessed against the co-op's interest in the real estate, he gets no deduction for leasehold rent paid by the co-op. If a co-op is built on a leasehold estate and the lease requires payment of all real estate taxes assessed against the entire property, the issue is whether the taxes relating to the building are to be characterized as leasehold rent or as real estate taxes. [See Rev.Rul. 78–31, 1978–1 C.B. 76]

Lease Term and Useful Life

Where a co-op acquires a ground lease and constructs a building, it is the Service's position that the real estate taxes assessed against the building and paid by the co-op will be considered deductible taxes only if the lease term is longer than the useful life of the building. A problem exists where the basic lease term is shorter than the useful life of the building, and there are several renewal options.

* * *

Probably the proper criterion for deciding whether renewal terms should be taken into account * * * is the "reasonable certainty" test developed with respect to the issue whether renewals should be considered in ascertaining the period over which cost of a leasehold should be amortized.[43] Apparently the Service has never ruled on this issue. In view of the desirability of providing the tenant-stockholder with the maximum tax deductions, it behooves the sponsor to provide the co-op with a ground lease having a basic term longer than the useful life of the building. * * *

NOTE

1. Is an interest in a cooperative realty or personalty? Is the sale of an interest in a cooperative governed by the U.C.C., or is it the sale of an interest in real estate? See Note, *Legal Characterization of the Individual's Interest in a Cooperative Apartment: Realty or Personalty?*, 73 Colum.L.Rev. 250 (1973).

a. If it is governed by the U.C.C., is it covered by Article 2 or Article 8?

b. See Comment, *Cooperative Apartments and the U.C.C.*, 29 Wash. & Lee L.Rev. 189 (1972); *Silverman v. Alcoa Plaza Associates*, 37 A.D.2d 166, 323 N.Y.S.2d 39 (1971); *State Tax Commission v. Shor*, 84 Misc.2d 161, 378 N.Y.S.2d 222 (1975), affirmed, 53 A.D.2d 814, 385 N.Y.S.2d 290 (1976), affirmed, 43 N.Y.2d 151, 371 N.E.2d 523 (1977); Office of Comptroller of Currency, Interpretive Ltr. # 117, P.H. Control of Banking, ¶ 3964 (1979); *Matter of Carmer*, 71 N.Y.2d 781, 525 N.E.2d 734, 530 N.Y.S.2d 88 (1988).

c. Is the stock in a cooperative considered a security under the Securities Act of 1933? Compare *1050 Tenants' Corp. v. Jakobson*, 365 F.Supp. 1171 (S.D.N.Y., 1973), with *Forman v. Community Services, Inc.*, 366 F.Supp. 1117 (S.D.N.Y., 1973).

The Second Circuit Court of Appeals, while recognizing that there were distinctions between *1050 Tenants Corp. v. Jakobson* and *Forman v. Community Services, Inc.*, affirmed the decision of the District Court in *1050 Tenants Corp. v. Jakobson* and reversed the decision of the District Court in *Forman v. Community Services, Inc.* The Court of Appeals concluded in both cases that a share of stock in a nonprofit cooperative was a security subject to the Securities Acts. See *1050 Tenants Corp. v. Jakobson*, 503 F.2d 1375 (2d Cir.1974), and *Forman v. Community Services, Inc.*, 500 F.2d 1246 (2d Cir.1974). The Court of Appeals found the necessary element of "profit" through: (1) The benefit to the shareholders of reduced carrying charges as a result of rent received by the cooperative through its commercial leases, (2) The tax savings available to the shareholders as a result of being able to personally deduct their share of the cooperative's deductible expenses and (3) The opportunity to acquire housing for an amount lower than the going rate for comparable apartment facilities. In addition, in *1050 Tenants Corp. v. Jakobson*, it was possible for the shareholders to sell their stock at a price greater than the cost to the shareholders of the stock.

The Supreme Court in *United Housing Foundation, Inc. v. Forman*, 421 U.S. 837, 95 S.Ct. 2051, 44 L.Ed.2d 621 (1975), rehearing denied, 423 U.S.

---

43. [Should Section 178 of the Internal Revenue Code, as amended, be applied by analogy?]

884, 96 S.Ct. 157, 46 L.Ed.2d 115 (1975), reversed sub nom. the decision of the Second Circuit in *Forman v. Community Services, Inc.* The Court held that the Securities Acts did not apply simply because the tenants purchased interests called "stock" since the shares of stock purchased had none of the characteristics which, in the commercial world, fall within the ordinary concept of a security. In addition, the Court disposed of the "investment contract" approach, taken by the Second Circuit, based on the following reasons. (1) There is no basis in law for the view that the ability to claim certain deductions constitutes profit. The benefits are nothing more than that available to any homeowner. (2) The low rent results from substantial subsidies provided by the State of New York. It does not result from the managerial efforts of others, and it no more embodies the attributes of profits than do welfare benefits, food stamps or other government subsidies. (3) The rent from the commercial facilities is far too speculative and insubstantial to bring the transaction within the Securities Acts. The commercial facilities were established not as a means of returning a profit but for the purpose of making essential facilities available for tenants. By statute the facilities can only be incidental and appurtenant to the housing project. The commercial facilities made the project a more attractive housing opportunity, but the possibility of a rental reduction does not amount to an expectation of profit.

The Supreme Court, however, did not have to face the possibility that a tenant might sell the stock in the cooperative corporation at a profit since that was not possible under the facts present in *United Housing Foundation, Inc. v. Forman.* It was possible in *1050 Tenants Corp. v. Jakobson,* and was the basis of the distinction made by the District Court between that case and *United Housing Foundation, Inc. v. Forman.* Subsequent to the Supreme Court's decision in *United Housing Foundation, Inc. v. Forman* the District Court in *Grenader v. Spitz,* 390 F.Supp. 1112 (S.D.N.Y. 1975), held that "stock" in a cooperative housing corporation amounted to "securities" under the Securities Acts when the tenants could sell the stock at a profit.

The plaintiff's victory in *Grenader v. Spitz* was short-lived. The Second Circuit reversed the District Court essentially relying on the Supreme Court's decision in *United Housing Foundation, Inc. v. Forman.* It also questioned whether the District Court's and its decision in *1050 Tenants Corp. v. Jakobson* had any validity after *United Housing Foundation, Inc. v. Forman.* See *Grenader v. Spitz,* 537 F.2d 612 (2d Cir.1976), cert. denied, 429 U.S. 1009, 97 S.Ct. 541, 50 L.Ed.2d 619 (1976).

2. Is the sale of a condominium unit the sale of a security under the Securities Act of 1933?

a. Does it make any difference if the purchaser occupies the unit as his permanent place of abode rather than merely using it part of the year as his vacation home and for the rest of the year putting the unit in the "rental pool" operated by the developer? See Division III, pages 893 to 897 infra; *S.E.C. v. Marasol Properties,* CCH Fed.Sec.L.Rep. ¶ 94,159 (1973 Trans.Bin.) (D.D.C.1973); Ellsworth, *Condominiums are Securities?,* 2 Real Est.L.J. 694 (1974); Clurman, *Are Condominium Units Securities?,* 2 # 1 Real Est. Rev. 18 (1972); Rosenbaum, *The Resort Condominium and the Federal Securities Laws—A Case Study in Governmental Inflexibility,* 60 Va.L.Rev. 785 (1974); Minahan, *State and Federal Regulation of Condominiums,* 58 Marq.L.Rev. 55 (1975); Yurow, *Resort Condominiums: Rental and*

Time Sharing Programs; Tax and Securities Problems, 33 N.Y.U.Inst.Fed. Tax'n 1193 (1975).

3. See generally Anderson and Cody, *Tax Considerations of the Condominium Sponsor and Purchaser,* 3 J. Real Est.Tax'n 299 (1976); Fink, *Conversion to Condominiums: Existing Rental Units; How to Treat Capital Gain; Handling Existing Mortgage; Co–Ops to Condominiums,* 33 N.Y.U.Inst.Fed.Tax'n 1141 (1975); Kaster, *Residential Co-ops and Condominiums Development Projects and Conversions Promoter's Tax Techniques,* 38 N.Y.U.Inst.Fed.Tax'n 13–1 (1980); Miller, *Can a Straight Condominium Conversion Produce a Capital Gain? An Analysis,* 54 J. Tax'n 8 (1981); Livsey, *Minimizing the Tax Consequences of Condominium Conversions and Other Real Property Development,* 39 N.Y.U.Inst.Fed.Tax'n 28–1 (1981); Leibowicz, *Conversions to Cooperative and Condominium Ownership of Real Estate,* 16 Tax Adviser 14 (1985); Comment, *Tax Aspects of Choosing Between a Cooperative or Condominium Conversion,* 12 Cumb.L.Rev. 453 (1982); Gordon, *Condominiums and Cooperatives: Planning for Acquisition and Disposition,* 49 N.Y.U.Inst.Fed.Tax'n 16–1 (1986).

In Rev.Rul. 80–216, 1980–2 C.B. 239 the Internal Revenue Service took the position that Section 1237, which in certain circumstances provides for limited capital gain treatment on the sale of subdivided realty, does not apply to the conversion of apartments into condominium units and the sale of the units to the public. See Bolling and Carper, *Capital Gains in Condominium Conversions? Internal Revenue Code Section 1237,* 13 Real Est.L.J. 45 (1984). In Priv. Ltr.Rul. 8204031, however, the Internal Revenue Service took the position that Rev.Rul. 80–216 does not preclude capital gain treatment of condominium conversions under applicable sections of the Code other than Section 1237. A cooperative corporation, when converting from the cooperative to the condominium form of ownership, generally recognizes no gain or loss, under Section 216(e), on the distribution in liquidation of the units and common areas to the shareholders. The shareholders, on receipt of the units in exchange for their stock, in general, do not recognize any gain, according to Priv.Ltr.Rul. 8810034.

While the cooperative form of ownership has been present in the United States for a number of years, the condominium form, in common law jurisdictions, is of relatively modern vintage. As indicated above, the cooperative form of ownership requires the creation of a cooperative corporation under state law and the sale of shares in the corporation to the "tenants". The management of the corporation and the relationship between it and the tenants and the relationships among the tenants inter se are governed by the certificate of incorporation and bylaws of the corporation and the tenants' "leases". The organization, management, operation and relationships present in the condominium form of ownership are not that easily described. Since 1950, all of the states have adopted condominium statutes in one form or another. The following excerpt, while particularly dealing with the Uniform Condominium Act (Uniform Act) and the Model Condominium Code (Model Code), provides a good overview of the organization, management and operation of, and the relationships present in, the condominium form of ownership.

THE "MODEL CONDOMINIUM CODE"—A BLUEPRINT FOR MODERNIZING CONDOMINIUM LEGISLATION
Patrick J. Rohan
78 Columbia Law Review 587 (1978).
[footnotes omitted]

* * *

Legislative Philosophy: The Goals of the Model Code

Brevity and Flexibility

For a number of reasons, it is important that condominium statutes be succinct, leaving the details to individual project draftsmen. First, condominiums may be developed in widely varying forms, and it may not be possible to fit every project into a complex legislative scheme; as a consequence, a complex statute might prevent both developers and would-be purchasers from accomplishing perfectly legitimate purposes. Second, a court faced with litigation involving a broad and detailed statute may assume that it has such a complex internal structure that any departure from the letter of the law would wreak havoc with the scheme. Third, condominium project documents are themselves extremely complex; the purchaser often completes the transaction without thoroughly understanding the rights and obligations involved. With a relatively simple statute, the courts are free to resolve disputes with a view to the equities of particular circumstances, just as they do with common-law forms of concurrent ownership.

* * *

In general, [the Model Code] sets forth only those elements deemed essential for a sound project, and these requirements for basic residential developments are separated from the more complex rules necessary to regulate intricate or high-rise projects. Thus—borrowing a page from the income tax treatment of trusts—the Model Code provides a modicum of statutory principles to govern "simple" projects, those with a fixed number of residential units and no major amenities or other complicating factors. Most residential condominiums, such as apartment house or "garden apartment" developments of 200–300 units, fall within this "simple" category. Other condominium ventures are classified as "complex" and are subject to additional statutory controls. The designation "complex" would apply to residential condominiums to be built in sections (staged developments); projects that include membership in an umbrella organization that owns large-scale amenities; mixed-use condominiums; commercial condominiums; condominiums involving "air rights"; leasehold condominiums; "time sharing"; "rental pools"; and other complicated arrangements.

The division of projects into "simple" and "complex" categories achieves several results. First, as discussed above, it makes possible a simplified statutory scheme for the basic type of projects, giving the courts ample flexibility to resolve disputes and easing the purchaser's understanding of his rights and responsibilities under the law. Second, the designation "complex" serves as a warning signal for buyers, general practitioners, and institutional lenders, alerting them to the fact that the project contains unusual or intricate aspects not found in the garden variety condominium.

Certainty and Marketability of Title

As with all forms of real estate, it is essential to ensure certainty and marketability of title to condominium units. In general, this goal is fostered by keeping statutory requirements to a minimum and leaving to project draftsmen the filling in of details. Title companies, attorneys, and lenders can then determine more easily whether project documents conform to the enabling legislation. The goal of title certainty is also furthered by liberally construing condominium instruments and by giving the courts power to reform instruments which do not conform to statutory requirements.

The Uniform Act provides for liberal construction and severability, but unfortunately uses certain terms which may increase the confusion and uncertainty in title transfer. One such term is "unconscionability"; experience with this term in the Uniform Commercial Code has demonstrated that it is not easily defined. The same conclusion is warranted with respect to the Uniform Condominium Act. "Unconscionability" is defined, in part, by a disparity between actual value and market price; in the condominium field, however, market prices of individual units may fluctuate widely without in fact affecting the owner's proportional interest in the project. By allowing the owner to avoid his purchase contract based upon such a misleading finding of "unconscionability," the Uniform Act lessens the certainty of title transfer. The Uniform Act also minimizes the importance of project by-laws and favors keeping them off the record. Often, however, the unit purchaser must look to the by-laws to determine his rights and obligations, since the recorded declaration may contain little useful information.

By contrast, the Model Code requires that by-laws and their amendments be recorded. This requirement will make it more probable that the prospective purchaser will work with an attorney, who can evaluate the legality of by-laws or amendments, their consistency with other project documents, and their conformity with the applicable condominium statute. The Model Code also provides for liberal construction of condominium documents, and gives the courts broad "cy pres" authority to conform documents to statutory requirements.

* * *

Treatment of Development Problems—Meeting the Practical Concerns of the Developer

Phased Projects

Developers often seek to build lateral condominium projects in stages, with the ultimate number and type of units left to market demand. Such projects present a number of problems: conforming to the applicable enabling statute, setting prices relative to percentage interest in the common elements, and estimating maintenance expenses. * * *

The Model Code authorizes the developer to build in successive stages and consolidate the stages into one unified condominium, subject to certain safeguards: (1) he must make public at the outset the maximum and minimum number of units he intends to build, their respective percentage interests, and a timetable for the completion of each stage; and (2) each successive stage must be comparable in quality and design and must contain no facilities that could radically increase the monthly assessment of units in prior sections. This approach balances the developer's need to build to meet actual demand and the purchaser's need for certainty. The Uniform Act, however, goes much farther; it allows the developer broad latitude in adding or subtracting land from the project and thus tips the scale too far in the developer's favor.

"Stepped–Down" Common Charges on Unsold Units

A second problem for developers of lateral projects arises from the general rule (of the first generation statutes) that common charges on *all* the units accrue as soon as the declaration is recorded—an event which usually occurs when the first unit is conveyed. In a high-rise project, this rule causes little trouble, since all the units are constructed and made available for sale at one time. In a lateral project, however, some units may still be unbuilt when the first ones are ready for sale. The result is a heavy financial burden for the developer, who is assessed the full amount due from all the unsold (even unbuilt) units.

Developers have countered this requirement in two ways. The developer may reserve the right to have no common charges assessed at all for a specified period after the declaration is filed, and to maintain the project's "public" areas at his own expense. Since the unoccupied units require no servicing and put no demand on the public areas, the cost of maintenance is, in fact, much lower during this period than after all units are sold. Alternatively, the developer may stipulate that he will be obligated to pay only a small percentage of the common charges allocated to unbuilt or unsold units with a guarantee to unit purchasers that their charges will be no higher than was projected in the offering literature for the project's first year of operation.

The Model Code approves both of these techniques. The Uniform Act, however, allows only the first option.

Use of the Power of Attorney

High-rise condominium projects—the model for first generation statutes—present few difficulties for the draftsmen, and those that do arise are normally encountered in the early stages of construction, long before any unit titles have closed. Moreover, since a high-rise building must be completed before any units are conveyed and occupied, the project documents can be perfected before the first unit closing. Just the opposite, however, is true of lateral condominium construction, and particularly staged developments. A number of problems may arise as the project is being built. Engineering, zoning, subdivision, or environmental requirements may change; rock, underground streams, or other natural impediments to construction may be encountered; declaration or by-law provisions may be found to be unworkable or invalid; institutional lenders, title companies, governmental agencies, or private mortgage insurers may change their requirements. Developers must, of course, be able to respond to these changed circumstances.

The Model Code allows the developer to take a power of attorney from each unit buyer, giving him authority to amend the condominium documents (offering plan, declaration, by-laws, house rules, filed maps, and plans), provided that no such amendment shall: (1) alter the percentage interest of units already sold or subject to a binding contract; or (2) significantly increase the annual budget of the condominium or alter the project's appearance and amenities. Such authority would facilitate compliance with the requirements of the condominium legislation, governmental agencies, institutional lenders, and title insurance companies. The limitations placed on its exercise would provide adequate safeguards against abuse. Moreover, the Model Code enables purchasers to sue for injunctive relief or rescission in the event of a radical departure from the project's original design and substantive content. In contrast, perhaps the single greatest flaw of the Uniform Act is that it gives the developer all but blanket authority to expand or contract a project (as long as such options are properly disclosed in the project's documentation), and prohibits the use of a power of attorney. This approach ignores the vital function served by the power of attorney in the condominium field to date and undermines all agreements between sponsor and unit purchaser, no matter how sound.

Protection of the Purchaser

The Need for a Supervising Agency

Condominium unit purchasers (and sometimes even their counsel) do not make a careful study of the project documents or offering plan. Moreover, the use of a prospectus-type document may lead the unwary purchaser to assume—even when contrary statements are contained in the offering plan—that a governmental agency has approved the project and the offeror. Accordingly, the most effective protection for the consumer may be the ongoing scrutiny of a regulatory agency charged with protecting consumer interests and the prospects for the project.

On the other hand, several factors already work to protect the consumer. Most developers do not seek to shortchange the public. Market forces and institutional lenders also play a significant role in keeping the project within the mainstream of what is generally available in the locality. Moreover, there is a danger that complex or financially burdensome requirements imposed upon the developer will have the adverse effect of increasing the cost of condominiums relative to other forms of development. There will also be buyer resistance if onerous and little-understood responsibilities are placed on the shoulders of individual unit owners when they later offer their units for resale.

The Model Code attempts to balance the two goals of protecting the consumer and minimizing complexity and cost. It mandates the establishment of a state review agency with authority to require full disclosure by the developer. Such an agency will have the expertise to ferret out the "sleepers" in condominium project documents and to keep promotional puffing within the bounds of decency. It can also take suitable counter-measures, including legislative recommendations against abusive tactics.

While the Uniform Act provides for such state review agencies, it does not require them. Given the role review agencies can play in protecting the consumer, their establishment should be mandatory.

Protecting the Purchaser Against Incomplete or Faulty Construction

1. *Down Payment Security and Construction Warranties.* In the case of condominium purchases—as in any real estate transaction in which the improvements are yet to be constructed—purchasers' down payments should be characterized as trust funds and held in escrow. While this approach may increase the developer's cost of construction and consequently the purchase price, it is necessary if the purchaser's down payment is to be safeguarded. Both the Uniform Act and the Model Code require such escrow accounts. Both proposed statutes also require that the developer give a construction warranty to all purchasers. * * *

2. *Performance Bonds.* The posting of a performance bond also protects purchasers against the developer's failure to complete construction; it is particularly important where large-scale amenities (such as ski lifts or golf courses) remain to be completed and where the failure to complete will lower the value or increase the monthly maintenance cost of units already conveyed. In many jurisdictions, however, such a bond is prohibitively expensive, and in some it is not available at all. In such a case, an exception to the performance bond requirement should be available, since developers will otherwise avoid the condominium form. The Model Code allows for such exceptions. The Uniform Act does not require a performance bond, although it does establish various warranties of quality.

3. *Priority of Liens.* If the developer defaults on his construction loan, it may be extremely important (from the point of view of those

who have already purchased their units) that the lender move expeditiously to foreclose on the construction mortgage. As discussed earlier, the developer is responsible for paying the common charges on unsold units during this period; the condominium, through the board of managers, has a lien for unpaid charges. In the case of a default on the construction loan, the developer will also default on his common charge payments. If the defaulting developer owns a sufficient number of units to control the board of managers, he and the bank may together be able to take advantage of the earlier purchasers. The developer will prevent the board from enforcing its lien; the lender, on its part, will delay in foreclosing on the construction loan. As a result, the burden of carrying the common charges is placed on the other unit purchasers.

The Uniform Act attempts to remedy this situation by giving the condominium's previous six months' common charges priority over the lien of any mortgagee. This type of provision may, however, have the side effect of discouraging lenders from financing condominium projects altogether or leading them to require that the developer deposit the six months' charges in an escrow account. The Model Code takes a less stringent approach, limiting the preference over an institutional lender's first mortgage to three months' common charges.

Developer Control and Privileges

It is desirable that the developer turn over control of the project to the unit purchasers as early as possible. At the same time, however, the developer and construction lender must retain sufficient control to complete construction and to market the balance of the project.
*   *   *

The Model Code requires that control be transferred to the unit purchasers at the earliest possible date, but also allows the developer to retain control of the board of managers for a longer period in phased projects and to exercise certain veto powers over operation of the property independently of his representation on the board of managers. Thus, for example, the developer is permitted to retain a sales office, signs, and a working easement over the completed portions of the project. Where the project's documentation so provides, the developer may veto extraordinary expenditures or any changes in the declaration or by-laws that would impair or revoke his retained rights. He may also lease unsold units pending their eventual sale.

The Uniform Act sets forth extensive limitations upon the developer's control of the board of managers; unlike the Model Code, it fails to recognize the needs of the builder and the construction lender for protection from overbearing unit purchasers.

Controlling Developer Abuses in the Use of Long–Term Management Contracts and Recreational Leases

Experience has demonstrated that condominium purchasers need protection from unscrupulous developer "gimmicks" in two particular areas: the long-term management contract and the recreational lease.

1. *Management Contracts.* Since the initial management contract is arranged when the developer is in control of the board of managers, it offers the unscrupulous developer an opportunity to take advantage of the unit owners by contracting with a controlled company for an unreasonable amount of compensation (or by not requiring that management services actually be performed).

Both the Uniform Act and the Model Code limit the developer's freedom to negotiate such contracts. The Model Code limits the term of the initial contract to three years (to commence upon closing of title to the first unit). The contract remains subject to revision throughout the initial term if the agreed compensation is found to be "exorbitant" or if the managing agent fails to provide customary services, and can be cancelled for cause at any time. Once control of the board of managers has passed to the unit owners, it may renew the contract. The Uniform Act's provisions are similar.

2. *Recreational Leases.* Developers frequently retain ownership of the project's recreational facilities or amenities by renting them to the unit owners under a long-term net lease (requiring that the lessee pay the lessor an agreed amount and, in addition, pay all expenses of operating and maintaining the facility). Commonly, the developer sets the reserved rental at many times his cost for the land and facilities.

* * *

The Uniform Act also bars this form of recreational lease, but sanctions it in a more sophisticated form: the developer may designate a particular amenity as a common element for a specified period, after which it reverts to the developer. This should not be countenanced, since it allows the unscrupulous developer to do indirectly that which he cannot do directly, merely by foregoing rental payments in the interim period.

Risk of Loss and Title Insurance Coverage

* * * As a matter of policy, the risk of loss should be placed on the seller until the purchaser obtains either title or possession, because the purchaser lacks insurance until that point, and because the unit itself is insured under the development's master casualty policy. In light of these considerations, the Model Code places the risk of loss on the seller until the transfer of title or possession. The Uniform Act does not address this question. Knowledgeable attorneys in the condominium field usually also insist that the purchaser's title insurance policy cover any loss due to a later finding that the project was not properly constituted. Such riders frequently are issued by title insurers at no additional cost. The Model Code requires that such a provision be included in the purchaser's title insurance. Here again, however, the Uniform Act is silent.

* * *

Protection of the Unit Owner

The condominium purchaser ultimately acquires title to his unit and becomes exposed to an entirely different set of risks than those created by the developer's marketing program and the law of vendor-purchaser. After passage of title, he becomes obligated for his share of any expenditures, however extreme, that may be sanctioned by a majority vote of the owners. The individual owner is also placed at a disadvantage by flaws in prevailing statutes and practices, as well as the nearly absolute control over the common areas vested in the project's board of managers.

Special Assessments and Extraordinary Increases in Common Charges

Under almost all first generation condominium statutes, a unit owner's common charges are determined by a majority vote of the owners, regardless of the rate of increase over the prior year's common charges and irrespective of whether the increment represents increased maintenance costs, affirmative (capital) improvements, or a combination of the two. Such an open-ended obligation is, of course, particularly problematic for owners living on fixed incomes. * * *

The Model Code authorizes project draftsmen to include in the by-laws a ceiling on annual increases in common charges and/or special assessments (other than for emergencies), unless approved by ninety percent of the unit owners. The Model Code does not, however, *require* such a provision, and in its absence any assessment would merely have to meet the voting requirement set by the applicable first generation statute—generally a majority vote. The Uniform Act authorizes a majority of the unit owners (or such greater number as the project documents specify) to rescind any special expenditure voted by the board of managers.

Amendment of House Rules

Just as the first generation statutes place no direct restraints on the majority's assessments, they also allow the majority to amend the "house rules" in such a way as to alter substantially the character of the development or ownership rights previously granted. For example, the controlling group could vote to acquire additional land for parking or recreational facilities, impose a minimum age requirement for residents, restrict the right to lease, impose a right of first refusal on a sale, or ban animals. * * *

Neither the Uniform Act nor the Model Code regulates the content of house rules or the manner of their adoption and revision. The Model Code does, however, authorize draftsmen to include certain rights (for example, the right to keep pets) in the project's documentation, and to specify that those rights cannot be changed without a unanimous or overwhelming vote. There is no analogous provision in the Uniform Act.

Alteration of the Common Elements

Under the first generation condominium statutes, the board of managers has plenary authority with respect to the common areas. Substantial alterations may, however, lead to a degree of dissatisfaction—where, for example, a wooded picnic area is paved to make way for a basketball court, or where an in-ground swimming pool is filled in to avoid maintenance headaches. To prevent such excesses, the Model Code authorizes (but does not require) the draftsman to list in the by-laws those common elements or amenities that cannot be altered without the unanimous consent of the constituent owners. There is no corresponding provision in the Uniform Act.

* * *

Provisions Governing Eminent Domain and Dissolution

Several problems arise with respect to the termination of a condominium, whether the end comes through the governmental power of eminent domain or, more commonly, by voluntary dissolution.

1. *Eminent Domain.* The Model Code contains detailed provisions concerning the substantive and procedural aspects of eminent domain. It authorizes the board of managers to represent the interests of the unit owners in the common elements. Where all or part of an individual unit is taken, however, the owner has the right to appear through counsel of his own choosing. The Model Code also authorizes the inclusion in project documents of provisions respecting issues such as reallocation of the percentage interest of truncated or severed units and special assessments where the condemnation award does not cover the full cost of restoration. The Uniform Act contains similar provisions for reallocating percentage interests in the project.

2. *Dissolution.* Upon voluntary dissolution of a condominium, the owners vote to dissolve, sell the property, and divide the proceeds according to each owner's percentage interest. Such action may follow a casualty loss, where the owners may find dissolution preferable to undertaking large-scale repairs. Dissolution may also provide a valuable means of salvaging a failing project, which then can be reconstituted in a more workable format.

Where a unanimous—or near-unanimous—vote is required for dissolution, however, one or two unit owners can block a reasonable reorganization plan, or even blackmail other participants as the price of their cooperation. Consequently, the Model Code authorizes dissolution on a vote of not more than seventy-five percent of the unit owners, a figure which is still sufficiently high to prevent precipitous or self-serving dissolutions. The Uniform Act, by contrast, allows the project documentation to prescribe any voting requirement, including unanimous or near-unanimous margins.

The Model Code and Uniform Act also differ in their treatment of unit valuation. The Model Code distributes the proceeds on dissolution in proportion to each unit's undivided percentage interest in the project. The Uniform Act, however, requires that the association appoint an independent appraiser to determine the relative fair market value of each unit. This method of compensation undermines the integrity of each owner's percentage interest in the project, particularly where the respective interests were originally based upon square footage. Over time, the market demand for units of particular sizes may vary; other units may rise in value because their owners put in valuable fixtures.

Clarification of the Powers of the Board of Managers

Authority of the Board to Borrow Money

* * * Since condominiums occasionally need substantial loans to meet sudden increases in operating costs or to finance large-scale improvements or renovations, the board's funding flexibility should be increased by legislation clearly authorizing it to incur debt. At the same time, of course, the unit owner must be protected. Project documentation should at least be required to state whether the board of managers is authorized to borrow money, and if so, under what conditions. The statute should also clarify the personal liability of unit owners for any debt incurred and should provide a means of transferring such liabilities on resale. Finally, the statute should require the board to notify all purchasers on resale of any outstanding loans and of the terms governing repayment.

These matters are included in the Model Code, but are not specifically treated in the Uniform Act. * * *

Authority to Litigate and to Engage in Arbitration

1. *Litigation.* There is little question that a condominium board of managers may bring suit on a matter that directly concerns the internal operations of the project itself. Recent cases, however, have raised the question whether the board may sue on behalf of the unit owners—and pay the expenses of such suits—where the project's "well-being" is concerned: where, for example, the validity of a zoning variance or an environmental decision is at stake which controls property adjoining the condominium.

The Uniform Act grants litigating authority to the board in rather general terms; the board may institute, defend, or intervene in litigation or administrative proceedings on behalf of two or more unit owners on "matters affecting the condominium." This characterization of the proper type of litigation, however, is not specific enough to guide the board; it does not adequately define what a "matter affecting the condominium" is.

Under the Model Code, the Board may bring any suit it deems necessary and proper to protect the interests of all (or substantially all) the unit owners. This authority can be limited or taken away by a duly enacted by-law; the by-laws might, for example, limit the amount of legal fees the board can incur without the unit owners' approval. Moreover, the owners are protected against frivolous litigation through their power to surcharge the board for litigation expenses improperly incurred. Finally, the Model Code specifically authorizes the board to represent the unit owners on all matters concerning the units and the common elements (including construction defects) and to settle any such litigation out of court.   •

2. *Arbitration.* * * * Experience over the past decade has indicated, that arbitration of internal condominium disputes may be beneficial to all parties. In the absence of legislative authorization, it is not clear whether the unit owner's right to resort to the courts to question actions of the board or of the majority of unit owners could be taken away through an arbitration clause contained in the condominium's declaration or by-laws. Accordingly, the Model Code authorizes the inclusion of arbitration provisions in the project's initial documentation or in an amendment of the declaration or by-laws. The Uniform Act contains no parallel provision.

Enforcement Procedures

Both the Uniform Act and the Model Code empower the board of managers to levy fines upon unit owners who violate the provisions of the declaration, by-laws and house rules. The Model Code also authorizes the board to add the fine to the succeeding month's common charges and to place a lien on the unit for non-payment of common charges if the levy is not met. Finally, the board is authorized to notify the unit mortgagee of any such default in payment of common charges; many unit mortgages stipulate that a default on the condominium obligations also constitutes a default under the mortgage which empowers the lender to accelerate payment of the mortgage debt. The Model Code expressly sanctions such mortgage provisions.

* * *

NOTE

1. See generally with respect to the formation and operation of condominiums, Roth and Isaacson, *The Leasehold Condominium,* 8 # 1 Real Est.Rev. 59 (1978); Thomas, *The New Uniform Condominium Act,* 64 A.B.A.J. 1370 (1978); Judy and Wittie, *Uniform Condominium Act: Selected Key Issues,* 13 Real Prop., Prob. & Tr.J. 437 (1978); Laughlin, *Practical Look At Condominium Legal Documents,* 52 Fla.B.J. 716 (1978); Catalina, *Wisconsin's Condominium Statute,* 8 Real Est.L.J. 258 (1980); *A Symposium on Condominium Law and Practice in Colorado,* 11 Colo.Law. 2734 (1982); Garfinkel, *The Uniform Condominium Act,* 28 # 8 Prac.Law. 43 (1982).

2. Once an appreciation of the manner in which the condominium and cooperative forms may be organized and used is acquired, the next consideration is how to make the choice between them.

THE CONDOMINIUM—COOPERATIVE COMPARISON

Curtis J. Berger
Practical Lawyer, January, 1965, V. 11, no. 1, at 37.

* * *

Advantages of Condominium

Separate Financing. Condominium's most striking advantage for the potential consumer stems from the availability of separate financing. The first purchasers of a cooperative apartment are tied to the financing arrangements of the blanket mortgage. * * *

But consider the consumer who can and who wishes to make a substantial down payment. For example, the older consumer with accumulated savings (often the equity in the house he seeks to replace) may wish a comparatively debt-free shelter; condominium should have an especial appeal for him. * * *

Individual mortgages also facilitate the resale transaction. Take these comparable situations: A cooperative apartment and a condominium unit each have an original value of $50,000; 80 per cent financing is available; the cash needed is $10,000. Ten years later the owner is ready to sell; the value of his unit has risen to $60,000; the mortgage attributable to his unit has been reduced to $30,000. The condominium seller, if he (or his prospect) is able to get 80 per cent refinancing, needs a buyer who can raise $12,000. By contrast, unless the blanket mortgage is refinanced, the cooperative seller must either find a buyer who can raise $30,000 or defer full receipt of his equity.

* * *

Less Financial Interdependence. Condominium also lessens the financial interdependence that is a risk of every adventure in community ownership. In both the stock-cooperative and condominium, the members bear severally the common expenses, and each member must hope that his fellows will do their share. Stipulate a vibrant economy, healthy reserves, a well-situated and well-cared-for project and a reasonable balance of supply and demand, and our concern for financial interdependence is academic. Should an owner default, a replacement would be readily available to assume his share of the burden. There is no assurance, however, of the permanence of satisfactory conditions. Unsatisfactory conditions, moreover, breed further delinquency by stepping up the need for new members at a time when their supply is shrinking.

This risk is the larger in the stock-cooperative, where the common obligation includes real estate taxes and debt service, items comprising in the typical cooperative 60 to 70 per cent of the annual budget. To be sure, a condominium does not eliminate this risk, for its members are assessed for the upkeep of the common areas. Moreover, in computing the degree of risk, we must still consider real estate taxes as a joint burden, even though the condominium budget does not include them.

* * * [I]t is debt service, the largest expense of home ownership, that distinguishes the relative interdependence of the cooperative and condominium. In the cooperative debt service is fairly immutable; should a default be imminent, the blanket mortgagee must be persuaded to defer his claim—a step he will take reluctantly, if at all, and only in great stress, after reserves are exhausted and the surviving cooperators seem unable to manage. In the condominium, by contrast, the unit mortgagee whose debtor is in trouble can make new arrangements with the debtor or a potential buyer without compromising the status of his other mortgages in the project. It is this advantage of unit mortgaging—flexibility and, by inference, more ready negotiability of debt service—that enhances the security of the condominium for its occupants.

* * *

Disadvantages of Condominium

* * *

Higher Costs. We should also not be surprised if the unit mortgage bears a fractionally higher interest rate than the blanket mortgage of the stock-cooperative—the price the condominium owner pays, so to speak, for the privilege of mortgage flexibility and the reduced risk of financial interdependence. * * *

The unit owner will also have to watch carefully his property tax obligation, lest this exceed the taxes allocable for an equivalent cooperative apartment. In theory, the total assessed value of 100 condominium units should be identical to the assessed value of the project's carbon image in cooperative form. * * * But tax assessors are intensely practical human beings, and, faced with the insistent demand for ever larger tax base and given the awareness that individual condominium owners may be less able to protect themselves in the clinches than the monolithic cooperative corporation, one should not be surprised if some tax assessors react like intensely practical human beings. [In In re Summit House Real Property Assessment Appeals, 349 A.2d 505 (Pa.Cmwlth.1975) the court held that condominium units are to be assessed and taxed as separate parcels of real estate and the valuation of each unit should be based on the value of the unit as a separate parcel rather than assessing and valuing the unit at a proportion of the fair market value of the entire building. In this case the condominium unit owners demonstrated that the total assessed value of all the units together would exceed the assessed value of similar rental apartment buildings. Whereas, in Condominium Owners 5–7 Slade Ave. v. Supervisor of Assessments of Baltimore County, 283 Md. 29, 388 A.2d 116 (1978) the court held that the units in a condominium could not be separately valued, the condominium must be valued as a whole.]

Casualty insurance costs may also run higher in the condominium, at least initially, because of duplicated coverage. In addition to the master policy carried by the project for its full insurable value, the unit owners also will be paying for insurance to secure their individual mortgagees. Eventually, some of this excess premium cost should disappear through the fashioning of more sophisticated insurance arrangements than we now have—tailored for the special needs of the condominium.

More Personal Liability. Apart from the prospect of higher closing and carrying costs, the unit owner faces several forms of personal liability not the concern of the cooperator. These include liability on the unit mortgage, on real estate taxes * * * on uninsured tort claims for accidents occurring in the common areas, and on contract claims against the condominium association. This contract liability springs from the principle that each member of an association is jointly and severally liable for the debts of the association—a liability that is not relieved under our present law even after the unit owner pays his pro-rata share of the association debt.

While it may be possible to avoid this liability by turning to the corporate form of operating entity, such a move may churn up a complex of tax problems that had better lie buried; moreover, the use of a corporation tends to blur the distinction between the cooperative and condominium entities. * * *

Difficulty of Financing Improvements. This leads to a final disadvantage of the condominium: the difficulty of financing major improvements to the common areas. Unlike the cooperative, which may use its equity to finance capital outlays, the condominium cannot give the improvement contractor the security of either a real estate mortgage or a mechanic's lien. Unless the condominium venture can raise the needed cash (through reserves, special assessments, or short-term unsecured borrowing), the contractor must depend ultimately either upon the financial responsibility of the condominium members or upon their equity positions in the separate units. * * *

NOTE

1. For a comparison of the condominium with conventional subdivision home ownership see Krasnowiecki, *Townhouse Condominiums Compared to Conventional Subdivision With Homes Association,* 1 Real Est.L.J. 323 (1973), and Krasnowiecki *Townhouses with Homes Associations: A New Perspective,* 123 U.Pa.L.Rev. 711 (1975).

2. The condominium owners association is usually liable for tortious injuries incurred by third parties in common areas. As noted in the preceding excerpt, the association is usually unincorporated. Is the association liable for injuries suffered in a common area by the owner of a unit who is a member of the association? The California Second District Court of Appeal in *White v. Cox,* 17 Cal.App.3d 824, 95 Cal.Rptr. 259 (1971), held that the association was liable. See Note, *Condominiums—Member of Unincorporated Association of Condominium Owners Permitted to Bring Personal Injury Action Against Association for Negligent Maintenance of Common Areas,* 40 Fordham L.Rev. 627 (1972).

   a. Are the individual owners of units who are members of the association personally liable to parties negligently injured in common areas? If there is joint and several liability for the full amount of the judgment obtained, an owner could be liable for an amount in excess of the value of his unit and all the units could be subject to a judgment lien if only one of the owners failed to pay his share of the judgment. But see *Dutcher v. Owens*, 647 S.W.2d 948 (Tex.1983), which limits a unit owner's liability to a pro rata amount of the judgment rather than imposing joint and several liability. See also Note, *Condominium Law—Allocation of Tort Liability—Unit Owner's Liability for Tort Claims Arising from Common Elements Due to Negligence of Owner's Association Limited to Proportionate Ownership in Common Elements*, 15 St. Mary's L.J. 663 (1984). If ownership of the common areas is vested in the association, incorporation of the association might solve the unit owners' liability problem. Incorporation, however may not be desirable for other reasons. Some states have resolved the liability problem through statute. "Enactments in Alaska and Washington provide that as to an individual unit owner's tort liability, a judgment against the association may be satisfied by payment of his proportionate share of the expense. Statutes in Florida, Mississippi and New Jersey go even farther. In these states the unit owners have no liability for torts caused by the condominium association. In Idaho, a statute provides that a unit owner's liability for torts in the common areas is limited to his pro rata share of the common areas multiplied by the amount of the judgment. The Massachusetts provision requires that claims involving common areas and facilities must be brought first against the organization of owners. Any judgment in excess of the association's assets constitutes a lien on the individual owners' apartments. The amount of each lien is computed by taking the balance due and multiplying it by the percentage interest in the common areas. Once the lien is satisfied, the individual owner's title is clear." Note, *White v. Cox: Tort Actions Against the Condominium Association—Implications for the Individual Owner*, 8 Cal.W.L.Rev. 536, 544 (1972). See also Lawrence, *Tort Liability of a Condominium Unit Owner*, 2 Real Est.L.J. 789 (1974); Jackson, *Why You Should Incorporate a Homeowners Association*, 3 Real Est.L.J. 311 (1975); Comment, *Living in a Condominium: Individual Needs Versus Community Interests*, 46 U.Cin.L.Rev. 523 (1977); Note, *Judicial Action and Condominium Unit Owner Liability: Public Interest Considerations*, 1986 U.Ill.L.Rev. 255; Freyfogle, *A Comprehensive Theory of Condominium Tort Liability*, 39 U.Fla.L.Rev. 877 (1987).

b. The use of the corporate form for the association in order to avoid the personal liability of the unit owners raises a number of income tax problems. First of all, is the corporation a taxable entity; if it is, can it be considered an agent of the unit owners? If it is a taxable entity and is not an agent, it may then be taxed on the amounts it receives from its members as dues and assessments and any investment income it earns. It, rather than the members, will deduct, if deductible, any expenses it incurs—i.e., real estate taxes on any property owned by the corporation— and it is the position of the Internal Revenue Service that the annual assessments paid to the association by its members are not deductible by the members as real property taxes, under Section 164(a). See Rev.Rul. 76–495, 1976–2 C.B. 43. In addition, amounts expended by the corporation for improvement of commonly owned property might be considered dividends to the members.

If the corporation is a taxable entity and not an agent, some problems might be avoided by making sure that the income from membership dues and assessments does not exceed the corporation's expenditures during the year.

For example, the corporation could return to the members prior to the end of the year, pursuant to a pre-existing agreement, any unexpended funds. See Rev.Rul. 70–604, 1970–2 C.B. 9. If, however, the corporation acquires, through the expenditure of membership dues or assessments, a capital asset which it must depreciate or cannot expense, the problems are not solved by balancing expenditures and income. The membership dues and more plausibly the assessments might be said to be contributions to capital and therefore not income. See Rev.Rul. 74–563, 1974–2 C.B. 38; *Wisconsin Dept. of Rev. v. Lake Wis. Country Club,* 123 Wis.2d 239, 365 N.W.2d 916 (1985). Whether the dues or assessments can be considered as contributions to capital may depend on the uses to which such dues or assessments are put. See Rev.Rul. 75–370, 1975–2 C.B. 25; Rev.Rul. 75–371, 1975–2 C.B. 52; *The Edison Club,* 34 CCH Tax Ct.Mem. 79 (1975), affirmed 535 F.2d 1241 (2d Cir.1975). Cf. *Concord Village, Inc.,* 65 T.C. 142 (1975); *Washington Athletic Club v. United States,* 40 A.F.T.R.2d 77–5074 (W.D.Wash.1977).

Finally, the corporation might try to achieve tax exempt status. The Internal Revenue Service, however, has not been prone to grant such status. See Rev.Rul. 74–17, 1974–1 C.B. 130; but see Rev.Rul. 72–102, 1972–1 C.B. 149; Rev.Rul. 74–99, 1974–1 C.B. 131; Rev.Rul. 69–281, 1969–1 C.B. 155. For a general exploration of the problems dealt with above see Snowling, *Federal Taxation of Homeowners' Associations,* 28 Tax Law. 117 (1974); Brauer, *Federal Income Taxation of the Condominium Management Corporation,* 52 Taxes 196 (1974); Garrett, *The Taxability of Condominium Owners' Associations,* 12 San Diego L.Rev. 778 (1975); Brandzel and Silverstone, *Achieving Tax–Exempt Status for Condo Associations,* 6 # 3 Real Est.Rev. 78 (1976); Frank, *IRS Takes Harsh Position on Exempting Condominium and Homeowner's Associations,* 44 J.Tax'n 306 (1976); Saltzman, *Federal Income Tax Considerations for Community Associations,* 16 Tax Adviser 724 (1985).

Section 528 of the Internal Revenue Code removes some of the problems discussed above for those condominium and homeowners' associations which are eligible for, and chose to elect, the application of this section. Two types of associations qualify for the election; condominium management associations and residential real estate management associations. Cooperative housing corporations can not make the election. Both types of eligible associations must meet several requirements in order to qualify to make the election.

First, the association must be organized and operated to provide for the acquisition, construction, management, maintenance and care of property held by the association or commonly held by members of the association. The association may maintain areas that are privately owned by members of the association and which affect the overall appearance and structure of the project and property owned by a governmental unit and used for the benefit of residents of the unit but only if there is a covenant of appearance applying on the same basis to all property in the project, there are pro rata annual mandatory assessments on all members of the association for maintaining this property, and membership in the association is compulsorily tied to every person's ownership of property in the project.

Second, certain income and expenditure tests must be met.

1. At least 60 percent of the association's gross income for each taxable year must consist solely of membership dues, fees, or assessments from owners of residential units (in the case of condominium

management associations) or residences or residential lots (in the case of residential real estate management associations).

a. Assessments for capital improvements that otherwise would not be treated as income to the association and would be treated as capital contributions are not treated as income for the purposes of the 60 percent test.

b. Fixed annual membership dues or fees and assessments that vary depending upon the need of the association to pay for acquisition, construction, management, maintenance, improvements, real property taxes, and so forth, with respect to the common property are treated as income.

c. If an association owns mortgaged property, assessments to pay principal and interest on the mortgage debt are treated as income.

d. In order to be treated as income for the purposes of the 60 percent test, association receipts must be derived from members in their capacity as owner-members and not in a capacity such as customers for services provided by the association. For example, payments by owner-members for maid service, secretarial service and cleaning do not qualify.

2. At least 90 percent of the expenditures of the association for each taxable year must be to acquire, construct, manage, maintain, care for, or improve association property.

a. Qualifying expenditures include both current and capital expenditures with respect to association property.

b. Investments or transfers of funds to be held to meet future costs are not taken into account as expenditures. For example, transfers to a sinking fund account for the replacement of a roof is not treated as an expenditure.

Third, no part of the net earnings of the association may inure to the benefit of any private shareholders or individuals.

In the case of condominium management associations, substantially all of the units of the condominium project must be used by individuals for residences. In the case of residential real estate management associations, substantially all the lots or buildings in the subdivision or development must be used by individuals for residences.

If an association elects to be taxed under Section 528, the association is not taxed on "exempt function income"—membership dues, fees, and assessments received from owners of condominium housing units (in the case of condominium management associations) or owners of real property (in the case of residential real estate management associations). For example, assessments for the current management, maintenance and care of association property, and assessments to finance current or future capital improvements to association property are considered exempt function income.

The association is taxed on income that is not exempt function income including interest earned on amounts set aside in a sinking fund for future improvements, amounts paid by persons who are not members of the association for use of the association's facilities, such as tennis courts, swimming pools, and golf courses and amounts paid by members for special use of association facilities the use of which is not available to all members as a result of having paid membership dues, fees, or assessments required to be paid by all members. For example, if membership assessments do not entitle a member to use the association's party room or swimming pool, amounts paid for their use are taxable.

In computing the association's taxable income, deductions are allowed for expenses directly connected with the production of taxable income; a specific annual deduction of $100 is allowed and no Section 172 net operating loss deduction is allowed. The association's taxable income is subject to tax at a flat 30% rate. See generally Boles, *Homeowners Associations: Improved Tax Status Under the Tax Reform Act of 1976,* 4 J.Real Est.Tax'n 348 (1977); Cowan, *Tax Reform on the Home Front: Cooperative Housing Corporations, Condominiums, and Homeowners Associations,* 5 J.Real Est.Tax'n 101 (1978); Comment, *Taxation of Homeowners Associations Under the Tax Return Act of 1976,* 36 Wash. & Lee L.Rev. 299 (1979); Campbell–Bell, *Homeowners Associations—Is Tax Exemption Worth the Effort?,* 20 Real Prop., Prob., & Tr.J. 647 (1985).

3. See generally Hyatt, *Condominium and Home Owner Associations: Formation and Development,* 24 Emory L.J. 977 (1975); Jackson, *A Developer's Guide to Homeowners' Associations,* 7 # 3 Real Est.Rev. 79 (1977); Jackson, *How Homeowners' Associations Solve Their Enforcement Problems,* 8 # 1 Real Est.Rev. 80 (1978); Hyatt, *Community Associations: How to Draft Documents That Work,* 7 Real Est.L.J. 26 (1978).

4. A decision by a developer to operate and market through the use of the condominium or cooperative does not eliminate the choice of entity problem for the developer.

    a. What problems will the developer face if the entity chosen is a corporation?

        1. How can the "double tax" problem be solved?

        2. Is a Subchapter S election possible, and does it solve this problem?

    b. If the choice is a partnership or a limited partnership, will the presence of "dealer" partners affect the treatment of gain to the investor partners?

        1. See *Riddell v. Scales,* 406 F.2d 210 (9th Cir.1969).

        2. Does the possibility that partners may be able to add their shares of partnership liabilities to basis and that allocations of income and loss can vary from interests in capital and can change during the life of the partnership and that, in all likelihood, no gain or loss will be recognized on liquidation of the partnership justify giving up some of the corporate attributes such as limited liability, centralized management, free transferability and continuity of life?

    c. If the venture involves financial assistance from the government, particularly in the low- and moderate- income housing area, the choice of entity and the various attributes of the entity chosen may be dictated to a greater or lesser extent by the federal or state laws and regulations relating to such financial assistance. See Division III, pages 775 to 776 infra.

5. The foregoing materials dealing with cooperatives and condominiums are by design fairly general in scope. There are a great many more considera-

tions and problems which must be taken into account when organizing, developing, financing, marketing and operating the condominium or cooperative. See generally *Symposium on the Law of Condominiums*, 48 St. John's L.Rev. 677 (1974); Minahan, *State and Federal Regulation of Condominiums*, 58 Marq.L.Rev. 55 (1974); Committee on Condominium and Cooperative Ownership of Apartments, *Lawyer Counseling Considerations in Representing Condominium Purchasers*, 10 Real Prop., Prob. & Tr.J. 464 (1975); Geis, *Representing the Condominium Developer: Tending the Paper Jungle*, 10 Real Prop., Prob. & Tr.J. 471 (1975); Walter, *Condominium Government: How Should the Laws be Changed?*, 4 Real Est.L.J. 141 (1975); Fink, *Condominium Taxation*, 53 Taxes 742 (1975); Nicholson, *Condominium Insurance: Old Problems, New Concerns*, 6 Colo.Law. 783 (1977); Jackson, *Attorneys for Lenders: What You Should Check in Condominium and PUD Documentation, Part 1*, 4 # 1 Barrister 47 (1977); *Part 2*, 4 # 2 Barrister 55 (1977); Thomas, *Guiding the Condominium Developer Through the Control Period*, 6 Real Est.L.J. 132 (1977); Whitman, *Financing Condominiums and Cooperatives*, 13 Tulsa L.J. 15 (1977); Fisher, *The Model Real Estate Cooperative Act: A Critique*, 12 Real Est.L.J. 53 (1983); Goldberg, *Cooperative Tax Implications*, 42 N.Y.U.Inst.Fed.Tax'n 25–1 (1984).

2.　MEANS OF ACQUISITION

Once the form of entity to be used to acquire the real estate has been chosen and organized, the usual next step is to consider the means of obtaining the real estate. This subdivision contains a discussion of various means of acquiring real estate and some of the factors which should be considered when using these means of acquisition.

a.　THE OPTION

OPTIONS TO PURCHASE REAL PROPERTY IN NORTH CAROLINA

Thomas W. Christopher
44 North Carolina Law Review 63 (1965).
[footnotes omitted]

* * *

I.　Definitions and Nature

An option to buy real property is a right acquired by contract to accept or reject a present offer to sell. An option creates a unilateral obligation upon the prospective vendor (maker) to sell on the conditions agreed, but creates no obligation on the optionee or holder (prospective buyer) to buy. It does give the latter the right to exercise the option at his election. If the holder does not exercise his election by an acceptance, he loses only the consideration paid for the option. In effect, an option to buy land amounts to a conditional contract to sell, although it is important to bear in mind that there are material differences between an option and a contract for sale of land. An option does not create an "interest" in the property, but is, in effect, an offer to convey; this is true even though the offer is binding. Thus, an optionee has no legal or equitable "interest" as such in the land. * * * While an option does not create an "interest" in the property, it does establish a right that the courts will enforce. * * *

II. Distinguished From Contract for Sale

* * * The name that the parties give the written agreement does not determine whether it is an option or a contract for sale; rather, the nature of the obligations that are imposed is the determining factor. An agreement by which one party binds himself to purchase and the other to sell is a "contract for sale." * * *

III. First Refusal

The right of "first refusal" in a lease, deed, or other agreement may be a binding promise, and it is something like, yet strictly speaking not, an option. It is not an offer, and it creates no power of acceptance. The typical situation is where *A* agrees that *B* shall have a right of first refusal at the same price and terms as those of an offer made by a third person that *A* is willing to accept. *A* is not obligated to sell to anyone, and *B* has no power to accept unless *A* is willing to accept an offer by a third party. If there is consideration for *A*'s promise, then a valid unilateral contract exists. For the agreed period, *B* has a right that *A* not sell to anyone else at any price without first offering the property to *B* at the same price, and this right is enforceable at law and in equity.

* * *

IV. Requirements and Form

An option to purchase real property must be definite and certain in its terms. It must adequately describe the property and state the financial and other terms of the agreement. It is not necessary that it specify the obligations of each party as such, as long as these are clear from the context. * * *

An option for land must be in writing, and the general requirements of the writing are the same as for a contract for sale. Thus, a later amendment to the memorandum must be signed by the party to be charged. * * * The party to be charged (thus, the defendant) must sign the memorandum, although the position of the signature on the instrument is not important as long as it is affixed for the purpose of signing. * * * It is not necessary that the plaintiff sign. Of course, both parties should sign, for at the time of the making of the agreement it is not known which party will be suing.

An option may be cancelled by the parties by parol or abandoned by acts or matters in pais. Acceptance of the offer by the optionee may be by parol, except when the option agreement provides otherwise.

Death or insanity of the owner of the land does not terminate the option if there is consideration, as the obligations of the option are not personal. The courts sometimes speak of options as covenants running with the land. * * *

What is the effect on the option if improvements on the property are destroyed prior to acceptance? The general rule appears to be that the owner is not required to replace the improvements, and the optionee is not entitled to an abatement of the option price. This is because an optionee does not have an interest in the land, and acceptance does not relate back to the date of the offer.

* * *

A statement of the price to be paid for the land is an essential ingredient of the option. Normally this is accomplished merely by stating the price and the terms, but it may be enough if the option provides a manner in which the price may be fixed with certainty. * * * But merely to state "at a price to be agreed on" is usually held to be invalid. It may be satisfactory to provide for the price to be fixed by arbitration if the terms of the arbitration arrangements are specified, but some courts will not grant specific performance in such cases. * * *

The terms of payment need not be set out in great detail, but they should be clear. Where no terms are stated, it would seem that the contract should be interpreted to mean payment in cash, since this would be in accord with common practice.

Must there be consideration for an option? If there is no consideration, the maker is free to withdraw the offer at any time prior to acceptance; but if the optionee properly accepts prior to a withdrawal of the offer and within the time provided, the maker is bound. Notice of the withdrawal must be given to the optionee, and oral notice is sufficient. * * * If there is consideration and the option is otherwise valid, the maker is bound for the time of the option and cannot withdraw the offer.

* * * At law, * * * a seal [may, in some states, be] enough to make a valid contract. Would the seal be sufficient in equity, for example, in an action for specific performance? Equity generally looks beyond form and ordinarily will refuse to exert its powers in aid of a sealed instrument except when there is a valuable consideration. Thus, in the absence of such consideration, specific performance may be denied. But options to purchase do not come within this rule. Equity will enforce options under seal even though there is no valuable consideration. The reasoning is as follows: The seal is enough to keep the option open; an acceptance within the time provided [results in] a bilateral contract * * *, and in an action for specific performance, "the consideration is not restricted to the seal or the nominal amount usually present in these bargains, but extends to and includes the purchase price agreed upon."

A nominal amount of money is sufficient to support specific performance of an option. * * *

V. Estoppel

Consideration makes an option, which is otherwise sufficient, irrevocable for the time provided. An option may also be irrevocable due to an estoppel. In fact, estoppel may in certain cases take the place of both consideration and a writing.

* * * Thus, if the plaintiff-optionee fails to tender within the time specified in the option because of a request of the defendant-maker, and if the plaintiff-optionee was ready, willing, and able to tender within the time and forbore solely at the defendant's request, then the defendant cannot be heard to say that his promise was oral or that it was without consideration.

* * *

VII. Rule Against Perpetuities

As a rule, future interests in land reserved in the grantor are not subject to the Rule Against Perpetuities, for the reversion, the resulting trust, the power of termination, and the possibility of reverter are not covered by the rule. A grantor may also retain an interest of sorts by reserving an option in the land, and in theory this would seem to be similar to other types of retained interests, but it is settled [at least in most jurisdictions] that the option contract is subject to the Rule Against Perpetuities. It makes no difference whether the grantor keeps the option and parts with the land, or keeps the land and gives an option. If the option to purchase land is in gross, and thus is not appendant to a leasehold estate, and if it can be exercised beyond the period of the rule, it is void. * * *

VIII. Exercise of Option

Except where the agreement provides otherwise, an oral acceptance of a valid option to purchase land binds the maker when the optionee sues the maker, since the person being charged has signed a memorandum. But an oral acceptance does not bind the optionee where the maker is suing him, since the person to be charged is the optionee and a written acceptance signed by him is necessary under the Statute of Frauds. It is usually held that the acceptance must in fact be received by the maker for the bilateral contract to come into effect. The acceptance must be unqualified; variation of the terms thereof constitutes merely a new offer.

A. Time of Essence

If no time limit for acceptance is stated, courts generally hold that the option must be exercised within a reasonable time. * * * If a duration for the option is specified then time is of the essence. This means that a thirty-day option must be exercised within thirty days. Normally, time is not of the essence in a contract for the sale of land. However, since an option, unlike a contract for sale, is unilateral, it is construed strictly in favor of the maker; therefore the optionee must adhere strictly to all the terms, including the time limit. However, an extension of time for acceptance granted by the maker for his own convenience, even though orally given, may be binding on him.

* * *

B. Tender

Whether tender is necessary in order to constitute acceptance depends on the agreement; keep in mind that the option is construed in favor of the maker. Where tender is construed to be a condition of acceptance, strict adherence is necessary. In one case, the option stated that "$2,000 of [the purchase price] * * * is to be paid 1 April, 1905," and the court held that tender of 2,000 dollars was necessary for acceptance. * * *

If tender is not a condition of acceptance, it follows that it is not necessary for acceptance. * * * Where an option read that the lessee "may at any time during the term of this lease elect to purchase said property at the sum of $6,700," the court held that tender of the purchase price was not necessary for acceptance and need only be made when the owner tenders the deed. * * *

Even when tender is required, it may be excused in certain situations. The optionee is not required to do a vain thing; thus, tender is not necessary if the maker has given notice that he will not honor the option, or if the property has been sold to a third party. The maker, for his own benefit, may waive tender (or other requirement, including the time), even by parol. In such case, notice of acceptance without tender is sufficient to bind the bargain.

* * * Payments made as consideration for the option ordinarily are not considered part of the purchase price.

IX. Encumbrances

What is the effect of the maker's inability to give good title because of encumbrances? If the option provides that the maker is obligated to give whatever title he has, or is obligated only if he has good title, then, of course, the optionee cannot hold him beyond such agreement. If the option is for a consideration and it provides that on acceptance the maker will give good title, a breach because of an encumbrance should give the optionee an action for damages. In some circumstances, it seems that the optionee may deduct from the amount of the tender the value of the encumbrance * * *.

When the encumbrance is discovered after exercise of the option, the rules of contract for sale should apply. In a situation where the vendor seeks to enforce the contract, with the vendee's pleading lack of good title as a defense for refusal to perform, the contract will be enforced if the encumbrance can be removed before delivery of the deed is required by using a portion of the purchase price; otherwise the vendee is not bound to accept an encumbered title.

X. Option As An Encumbrance

An option itself is an encumbrance on land, but if the option is revocable, then the encumbrance can be removed by the maker's revocation.

XI. Right to Assign

A revocable option, which is nothing more than an offer, gives the optionee no interest in the land which is assignable. If the option is irrevocable, then the optionee has sufficient interest in the land to enable him to assign the option in the absence of an agreement to the contrary. Such right is not dependent on the use of the word "assigns." If the assignee gives notice to the maker and performs all conditions precedent, specific performance will be granted.

*   *   *

Since an option for the sale of land must be in writing, it follows that an assignment must also be in writing. However, the Statute of Frauds is not available as a defense to the maker in a suit by the assignee. If the option gives a privilege of credit, this privilege is ordinarily considered personal and therefore not assignable. Likewise other provisions of a personal nature are not assignable.

No special form or words of art are required for assignment of an option, but the assignment must comply with the general requirements for assigning a contract concerning land. Thus, informal language may be sufficient. Whether the assignment must be written on the original instrument is an open question, with some authority in the affirmative. As between the parties and as to those with notice (as by recording), however, it would seem that a separate instrument should suffice. Where the assignment is a gift to the assignee and the option instrument is delivered to him, there is no apparent reason why the gift should not be enforced as between the assignee and the original maker (grantor-owner). In regard to notice to the maker and to third parties, the recording laws are applicable, and a maker is not liable to an assignee until he has actual or constructive notice of the assignment.

*   *   *

XII. Remedies for Breach

On valid acceptance by the optionee, the relationship between the parties is that of vendor and vendee in a contract for sale of land, normally a bilateral contract. For breach of the contract for sale, an aggrieved party generally may at his election sue for damages or seek specific performance. Rescission or restitution lies for fraud, duress, mistake, undue influence, mental incompetence, or default by one party, and, also, of course, by mutual consent. Damages and specific performance are remedies based on an affirmation of the contract, and they are therefore not inconsistent, whereas rescission, since it destroys the contract, is inconsistent with any remedy affirming it. If an election is made to sue for damages rather than specific performance, and third parties are affected, the actor may not be allowed to change his mind and later seek specific performance.

An option contract is specifically enforceable between the parties without recording, as are other instruments. Options are subject to the recording statutes in general. * * *

NOTE

1. In what circumstances should a developer initially acquire an option rather than enter into a contract of purchase?

    a. The optionor can not compel the optionee to specifically perform. Can the vendor under a contract of purchase require the vendee to specifically perform?

        1. A brief discussion of this problem appears in Division II, pages 410 to 413 infra.

    b. See generally Temkin, *Too Much Good Faith in Real Estate Purchase Agreements? Give Me an Option*, 34 U.Kan.L.Rev. 43 (1985).

2. Since an option is not generally regarded as an interest in land, whereas a contract of purchase, if recorded, normally is, under which means of acquisition:

    a. Does the prospective purchaser have standing to apply for a zoning change, planned unit development or variance?

        1. See page 327 infra.

        2. If an optionee does not have standing, but an option is used as the means of acquisition for other reasons, how can the standing problem be handled?

    b. Does an optionee, upon exercise of the option, have a claim with an earlier priority than a judgment creditor of the optionor with respect to a judgment lien which arose during the period after the date of execution of the option but before acceptance and delivery of title?

        1. Does the result depend on whether the option was recorded? Or, does the recording of the option have no effect?

        2. If the judgment creditor's lien is prior to the rights of an optionee, how can this problem be avoided, if the option method of acquisition is chosen?

        3. For example, might the option provide that the purchase price will be reduced by the amount of any such lien? What if the amount of the lien is greater than the purchase price?

3. If there is consideration for the option, neither the death nor insanity of the optionor will terminate it. However, what if the optionor becomes bankrupt before acceptance by the optionee? Can the trustee in bankruptcy of the optionor reject the option? If the trustee can, will the optionee have a claim against the bankrupt estate or a lien against the real estate for the consideration paid for the option? See Countryman, *Executory Contracts in Bankruptcy: Part I,* 57 Minn.L.Rev. 439, 460–474 (1973), and Section 365 of the Bankruptcy Code.

4. See generally Bovell, *Preparing an Option on Unimproved Property,* 22 # 3 Prac.Law. 43 (1976); Haymes, *The Crucial Role of Option Agreements,* 8

2 Real Est.Rev. 19 (1978); Brown, *An Examination of Real Estate Purchase Options,* 12 Nova L.Rev. 147 (1987); Newman, *How to Draft Option Contracts (with Form) (Part 1),* 4 #5 Prac.Real Est.Law. 35 (1988); *(Part 2),* 4 #6 Prac.Real Est.Law. 29 (1988).

5. As in most matters, the acquisition and holding of an option are not without tax implications.

USE OF OPTIONS IN TAX PLANNING
Harold S. Voegelin
1965 Southern California Tax Institute 729.
[footnotes omitted]

* * *

The Holding of an Option

Few tax problems are raised by a taxpayer passively holding an option. There is, however, one problem that may trip the unwary if some degree of care is not taken, and this problem arises when the optionee wishes to have the optionor extend the terms of the option. For example, the optionor may have granted an option to buy property for a period [shorter than the required holding period for capital gains (hereinafter referred to as the "required holding period")]. The property increases in value and the optionee wishes to sell the option. If he does, however, * * * he may be selling a capital asset, but it will not be one which he has held for more than [the required holding period] and thus the long-term capital gain provisions will not apply. The solution appears simple: Buy a short-term extension from the optionor.

* * * [T]he Commissioner has argued that the extension effected a termination of the old option and the grant of a new one. He has yet to be successful.

* * * [A]lthough the extension alone is apparently not sufficient to extinguish the old option and create a new one, additional variations in the extended option draw it nearer to that result; and * * * the sole reason for extending the option should not be to create a tax advantage to the optionee but rather the standard "business purpose" doctrine should dictate documenting the optionee's nontax, business reasons for the extension, such as continuing negotiations for financing, negotiations with developers, uncompleted economic survey, etc. Additionally, it may be well to make the extension for more than just enough days necessary to go beyond the [required] holding period. If that is not done, the Commissioner may argue that an actual sale of the option took place prior to the extension, notwithstanding the fact that title passed later.

Disposition of Option by Exercise or Lapse

In the great majority of cases the original optionee either lets the option lapse or exercises it, rather than effecting a conveyance of the option. Usually there are no problems created by the exercise except when the time of the exercise and completion of the sale is vague, which upon occasion can create important holding period problems for either optionor or optionee. In the usual instance, the exercise of the option merely sets off a series of further steps ultimately resulting in transfer of ownership of the optioned property to the optionee at a subsequent date. However, this result can be varied by agreement between the parties, so that unclear drafting of the option contract may leave the issue in doubt as to what the parties intended.

[Section 1234 of the] Code [and the regulations issued thereunder are] quite specific on the effect of a lapse of an option to both the optionor and optionee. [Regulation Section 1.1234–1(b) states] that

> "If the holder of an option to buy or sell property incurs a loss on failure to exercise the option, the option is deemed to have been sold or exchanged on the date that it expired. Any such loss to the holder of an option is treated under the general rule of paragraph (a) of this section. [In general,] any gain to the grantor of an option arising from the failure of the holder to exercise it is ordinary income."

The general rule in paragraph (a) referred to in the above quotation is that the character of the gain or loss from the sale or exchange of an option is determined by noting whether the property that is the subject of the option would be a capital asset in the hands of the optionee or not and, of course, whether or not the option was held for [the required holding period].

* * *

Obviously knowing the above rules will provide flexibility in the use of options. Assume a taxpayer has an option covering what in his hands would be a capital asset and the option runs for a period longer than [the required holding period] (as it should to provide flexibility to the optionee in the event of an increase in value of the property and the intention to sell the option rather than the property is involved). Assume the value of the underlying asset declines so that the intention not to exercise the option is formed prior to holding the option for [the required holding period]. A failure to sell the option within the [required holding] period will leave the optionee with a long-term loss, whereas a short-term loss was readily available merely by selling the option. Or, on the other hand, the option may have increased in value prior to the expiration of the [required] holding period and the optionee, realizing that an option is an asset and like any other asset can be the subject of an option, should sell an option on the option, rather than make an immediate conveyance of his option in order to take advantage of the current demand for the underlying property without generating a short-term capital gain.

There is little tax planning the optionor can do, of course, since under present law he has an ordinary gain on the lapse of the option, regardless of the subject matter.

Disposition of Option by Surrender to Optionor

The regulations, not surprisingly, do not answer all possible problems. For example, it may not be uncommon for an optionor to change his mind regarding sale of an asset, particularly if an increase in value has occurred. Having so changed his mind, he arranges with the optionee to cancel the option for a price. [The position can be taken] that since there [is] no sale or exchange, the gain [is] ordinary income to optionee. [Section 1234] merely holds that [a] sale or exchange is deemed to have occurred upon a loss *to the optionee*. Without more, it would appear that the basic rules of sale or exchange of a capital asset must apply if capital gain is desired. Under the circumstances there can be little doubt that the only safe route [to capital gain treatment] when your client has been offered a cancellation of an option contract at a profit is the sale of the option to a third party who can then sell or otherwise dispose of it to the optionor. * * *

As to the optionor who pays the optionee to obtain a release of the option, the Commissioner takes the position that this constitutes a capital expenditure which merely increases the optionor's cost basis for his property. Query, though, whether it is not arguable that the amount is properly amortizable over the remaining term of the option, particularly where the release is not being obtained in order to accomplish a sale of the property, similar to the rule for a lessor's payment to lessee to cancel a lease?

Disposition of Option by Sale

Another manner of generating gain to the optionee where the hoped for increase in value has occurred is through a sale of the option. The basic problem encountered many times by the taxpayer-optionee is that through lack of planning he is deemed to have exercised the option and then sold the underlying asset, rather than having sold the option itself. Obviously the difference may well be that of long- or short-term capital gain. * * *

To avoid the problems presented in [determining whether the option or the underlying property has been sold] the following suggestions might be noted:

(1) Have an unambiguous document of assignment [of the option].

(2) Give notice of the assignment to the optionor.

(3) Have the option exercised only by the assignee-buyer.

(4) Have any warranties by the optionee made purely in his role of optionee.

(5) Have payment upon exercise made direct to the optionor.

* * *

NOTE

1. If an extension of an option is dictated by "business reasons," the probable result is that the optionee will compute the holding period of the option including both the original period and the extension.

    a. If the original period was less than the required holding period, the price paid for the option was $500 and it is extended for an additional period equal to the original period (the combined periods being longer than the required holding period) for another payment of $500, what is the optionee's basis in the option?

    b. If, after a period of time greater than the required holding period, the optionee's financing falls through and the optionee sells the option to a third party for $1,200, what is the amount of the optionee's gain?

        1. Can it be argued that the optionee has $100 of long term capital gain and $100 of short term?

            a. If the underlying property appreciated during the option period, would determining which period the appreciation occurred in make any difference?

            b. What if all the appreciation occurred in the second period? Cf. *Carl E. Koch*, 67 T.C. 71 (1976).

        2. In *Paul D. Dunlap*, 74 T.C. 1377 (1980), the taxpayer asserted that it had bought ten separate options, one of which would lapse each year for the next ten years. The Internal Revenue Service claimed that one ten year option had been acquired. The Tax Court, after examining the agreement, agreed with the taxpayer that ten separate options had been acquired and the taxpayer could deduct the cost of the option which had lapsed. Unfortunately, the Eighth Circuit Court of Appeals, with one dissent, reversed the Tax Court and held that, in effect, one ten-year option had been purchased and there could be no lapse of the option until ten years had passed without its exercise. See *Dunlap v. Comm'r*, 670 F.2d 785 (8th Cir.1982).

2. A taxpayer holds an option having a term substantially longer than the required holding period. The taxpayer planned to use the real estate under option for an apartment house project. As a result of matters beyond the taxpayer's control the apartment house project must be abandoned and the taxpayer has no further use for the optioned real estate. The required holding period will be satisfied in another two months. What steps should the taxpayer take if:

    a. The optioned real estate has decreased in value resulting in the value of the option being substantially less than the taxpayer paid for the option and the taxpayer anticipates recognizing a substantial amount of long-term capital gain from other sources during the four months left in the current year?

    b. The optioned real estate has increased in value resulting in the value of the option being substantially more than the taxpayer paid for the option and the taxpayer anticipates recognizing a substantial amount of long-term capital loss from other sources during the four months left in the current year?

b. THE CONTRACT OF PURCHASE

The excerpt from the following article, although discussing the acquisition of real estate and the contract of purchase with particular reference to shopping center development, is generally applicable to the acquisition of real estate with respect to almost any commercial, residential rental or industrial real estate development.

PROBLEMS OF THE DEVELOPER

Norman M. Kranzdorf
1965 University of Illinois Law Forum 173.
[footnotes omitted]

* * *

Obtaining the Property

A. Selection of the Site

The very first problem for the private developer is the location of an appropriate site for [the] development. Unfortunately, the majority of locations are chosen merely on the basis that they exist. Very few are selected with any great degree of sophistication. The [site] * * * should be analyzed and researched by one of the market research companies presently engaged in the field. This type of scientific analysis involves a study of the retail market, population growth, expendable income, cars per family, purchasing power, etc.

An extremely important aspect of the physical site will be its ease of accessibility. Two types of accessibility should be considered. The first is the major road pattern leading from the economic market and the people to the site. Such analysis is often subject to traffic count and license plate checks to ascertain the road patterns and travel habits of the local population. Before any site is selected, a careful study should be made of projected and proposed roads in the area. What today is a major arterial highway can well turn into a side street after new highway construction. * * * [N]ew highways [are always being built], and while these highways may adversely affect some existing sites, they will undoubtedly open up new areas and new opportunities for developers. A careful· study should be made of the local, state, and federal plans for the whole area surrounding a proposed site.

The second type of access which should concern the developer is the immediate access from the highways into the [site]. The ideal site will be bounded on at least three sides by public highways or streets. It should be possible * * * to turn easily into the site without crossing heavily travelled or unprotected streets. The developer should inquire into the availability of traffic lights, acceleration lanes, and deceleration lanes. Along major highways many good locations have been ruined by the placing of concrete median barriers down the middle of a two- or four-lane highway. This barrier prohibits traffic from making a left turn into the [site].

B. The Contract of Purchase

When a site has been selected and it is determined that it is suitable for [the] complex, the lawyer is faced with his first major task. The average form-type contract of sale is useless to the lawyer representing a [commercial, residential rental or industrial real estate] developer. Mere "good and marketable title" is not enough; the property must be in a district appropriately zoned and without restrictions which would effectively limit or restrict the development. Naturally, intensive title searches and reports must be made to ascertain any defects in title or restrictions which would limit the flexibility of the builder. Care must be taken to insure that the premises may be used for any lawful purpose without setbacks or building restrictions. The mere presence of restrictions does not necessarily preclude the use of a given piece of land for a * * * development. However, a developer must be adequately advised as to the limitations and restrictions. He can then guide himself in the proper planning and leasing of the [development].

The contract of purchase for [the] site should take into account many of the problems facing the developer in the construction and planning of the [development]. In addition to the ordinary covenants of title and other necessary protections against easements, encroachments, etc., the * * * developer should be protected with clauses covering the following:

Zoning. Before taking title, the premises should be finally and effectively zoned (without further right of appeal) in full compliance with all planning board, subdivision, zoning board and other requirements so that the entire site may be used for [the purposes of the development], including the right to use all other areas for the purpose of parking motor vehicles. This covenant should also extend to the buyer's right to satisfy himself that he will have unlimited ingress and egress from all abutting streets. Such permits for ingress and egress should be obtained prior to settlement.

Utilities. The buyer should have ample time to satisfy himself that all utilities, including water, gas, electricity, and sanitary and storm sewer lines, are available at the perimeter of the site and are sufficient in capacity to serve the needs of the contemplated [development]. An investigation should be conducted to ascertain whether or not abutting streets are fully paved or are scheduled for major repairs or improvements. Aside from the problem of disrupting [the development], there is the question of major taxes and assessments for such new improvements.

Test Borings. Prior to the date of settlement, the buyer should have the right to enter upon the premises and test the soil and sub-soil conditions to ascertain whether or not any unusual or adverse conditions exist. If the same are found to adversely affect the construction of the necessary ∗ ∗ ∗ buildings, the buyer should have the right to terminate the agreement. Many times a developer learns that a piece of land he thought to be "cheap" has turned out to be extremely costly after draining creeks, filling ditches, and sinking abnormal foundations.

Condemnation and Taxes. Special care should be taken to ascertain the status of past, present, and future tax assessments in regard to the premises. All assessments for both confirmed and unconfirmed improvements should be the liability of the seller, and the buyer should not be burdened by any special assessments up to the date of settlement.

NOTE

1. See generally Thau, *Turning Raw Land Into Pay Dirt,* 2 # 1 Real Est. Rev. 73 (1972).

2. The preceding excerpt discussed, in general terms, the considerations faced by the vendee acquiring real estate through the use of a contract of purchase. The vendee's concerns, however, do not end there. A great number of particular pitfalls may be encountered using this means of acquisition.

DRAFTING OF REAL ESTATE SALES CONTRACTS

Committee on Real Property Law
35 Chicago Bar Record 247 (1954).

∗ ∗ ∗

1. *Parties.* ∗ ∗ ∗

a. *Seller.* The holder of title should agree to sell, otherwise specific performance in the event of default would not be possible. A careful buyer asks to see current evidence of title and insists, where possible, that the title holder disclosed by such evidence execute the contract. ∗ ∗ ∗

If title is held by a trustee, the buyer's attorney should examine the will or the trust agreement under which the trustee acts ∗ ∗ ∗ to determine whether the trustee has power to sell and ∗ ∗ ∗ to ascertain the pertinent provisions of the trust, if any, relative to the manner of executing contracts. The sales contract should indicate the source of the trustee's authority and should be executed by the trustee.

A trustee under an ordinary land trust might refuse to sign the sales contract. In [this event] the buyer should be sure that the persons having the power of direction and all the beneficiaries sign. ∗ ∗ ∗ The buyer [should examine] the trust agreement[,] if the sales contract is to be executed by persons other than the trustee, [in order to determine] the beneficiaries [and] to ascertain the names of the persons with power under the trust to sign the contract.

If the title is held by a corporation, the buyer should be satisfied by examination of the charter and by-laws [and corporate resolutions] that the corporate officers who sign the agreement have power [and authority] to do [so]. If the property constitutes all or substantially all of the property of the corporation and the sale is not in the usual course of the corporation's business, * * * [a majority] of the shareholders must approve the sale. * * * [See Section 12.02 of the Revised Model Business Corporation Act.] If the seller is a foreign corporation, the pertinent statutes of the state of incorporation should be examined.

If the title is in a partnership, the buyer should be sure * * * that all partners sign or that the person who signs for the partnership has full authority to act.

* * *

b. *Buyer.* From the standpoint of the seller, the importance of the identity of the party who signs the contract as buyer is largely a matter of credit or ability to pay the price and has little pertinence to the legal phases of the transfer of title.[44] * * *

2. *Price.* Except for situations where the property is encumbered with a mortgage which is to remain in force after the sale is completed or where the seller is to receive a purchase money mortgage[,] the provisions relating to price are simple and require no explanation. * * *

Whe[n] property is to be sold subject to an outstanding mortgage the contract should specify whether [the] purchaser shall or shall not assume the mortgage. In the absence of a special provision in the contract, it is the general rule that if a gross price is stated in the contract and purchaser takes title subject to an outstanding mortgage for which he receives credit against the purchase price, purchaser impliedly assumes the mortgage. * * * If the seller is the original mortgagor or is otherwise liable under the outstanding mortgage, he will remain liable * * * regardless * * * whether the mortgage is assumed by the purchaser[. H]e[, however,] will become secondarily liable after the sale and any material modification of the mortgage contract granted to the purchaser by the mortgagee without the approval of the seller [will, in whole or in part,] release the seller from [the liability.] * * * [The extent of the release of the seller may be determined by whether the purchaser assumed or took subject to. See Division III, pages 628 to 637 infra.]

If the sales contract specifies a price for the equity interest only and the purchaser agrees to accept title subject to an outstanding mortgage, * * * it is a question of fact * * * whether the purchaser has assumed the mortgage. If * * * the seller is liable on the outstanding mortgage, his position would be improved by requiring the purchaser to assume the mortgage. On the other hand, [the] purchaser may be unwilling to assume the outstanding mortgage[,] and if satisfactory to the seller, the contract and the deed should specifically state that the purchaser [does] not assume the outstanding mortgage.

44. [The seller, however, has power and authority considerations when selling to a corporation, trust or a partnership.]

* * * [A] purchase money mortgage [generally] creates a first lien on the interest acquired by a purchaser free of prior judgments against the purchaser and dower rights. If such a mortgage is to be taken, the contract should make adequate provision therefor[,] and it is desirable that the contract specify in some detail the form and the terms of such mortgage.

3. *Quality of Title and Legal Description.* * * * Some attorneys * * * feel that it is desirable, and necessary in order for a contract to be technically correct, to provide [specifically] in the contract that the seller agrees to convey fee simple title to the land. In view of the fact that [in most cases] the parties do intend [the conveyance of] fee simple title * * * it might be desirable for the contract to [so] state instead of relying on a rule of construction to reach that * * * result. * * *

A contract should, if possible, contain the legal description of the property being sold. [The] description will either * * * define the location and give the dimensions of the property to be conveyed or will enable the parties to obtain that information by reference to a plat. The legal description should be the same as that appearing in the caption of the seller's title policy, Torrens Certificate or abstract. If the legal description is not available[,] the property must be definitely located and the dimensions given by reference to existing monuments such as street or road intersections and the like. Where the property is described by street number[,] the city, county and state should also be specified and the property located and dimensions given by reference to monuments. * * *

[If there is] a question * * * whether the improvements are located on the land described or a question as to the location and size of the land, either a survey should be procured before the contract is executed or provision should be made in the contract for the furnishing of satisfactory evidence, by survey or otherwise, showing the location and size of the land and the location of improvements with respect to the property lines.

* * *

Because disputes may arise as to whether certain items are or are not included in the sale, whenever the sale includes items such as carpeting, refrigerators, stoves, blinds and so forth which might be personal rather than real property, it [is] advisable that such items be [specifically] described in the contract and [the contract contain] a provision * * * to the effect that such items are included in the sale. * * * [W]here the items to be included in the sale are clearly personal property, * * * the contract [should] provide for a bill of sale conveying such items.

4. *Form of Deed.* The usual types of deeds are warranty, special warranty and quitclaim. * * * A special warranty deed obligates the grantor only with respect to the particular matters specified in the deed. A quitclaim deed * * * [in most states] merely conveys the

right, title and interest, if any, of the grantor at the time the deed is made. A quitclaim deed can, however, be drawn so as to convey an interest subsequently acquired by the grantor. * * *

If the contract does not provide for a warranty deed, the attorney for a buyer must be cautious because[,] even though he is furnished with evidence of good record title, there may be title defects against which a title guarantee policy, Torrens Certificate or abstract examination may not protect such as mechanics' lien claims not shown of record and easements of certain types * * *.

5. *Title Exceptions.* [T]his section of the contract [indicates] the seller['s] * * * intention to convey a title subject to specified encumbrances, commonly called exceptions. The enumeration of specific exceptions implies an agreement that the title [is] free of all others and the buyer may refuse to accept the title where the encumbrances are different or more onerous than those excepted. * * *

6. *Prorating.* The following items are customarily adjusted or prorated:

a. *General Taxes.* The contract normally provides for prorating taxes on the basis of the most recently [levied] taxes. If * * * protection against increases or decreases in the unascertained taxes [is desired], the contract should so provide. If the parties wish to contest the amount of the tax[es], the contract should provide for the handling of [the] contest, the allocation of attorney's fees and the distribution of any recovery or tax savings.

* * *

b. *Special Assessments.* [Many of t]he printed forms of contract commonly in use provide that the purchaser * * * take[s the real estate] subject to installments not due under special assessments. The buyer [has] reasonable grounds for the contention that special assessments for local improvements which have been completed should be paid by [the] seller inasmuch as such improvements are considered in determining the purchase price of the property. * * *

c. *Rent.* In the absence of an agreement in the sales contract, rent belongs to the title holder on the date when the rent is due. The contract[, therefore,] should provide for adjustment of rent at the closing date. Special conditions must be inserted in the contract to cover rentals to be paid in the future on percentage leases. The contract should provide that all tenants' deposits held by the seller [are to] be transferred to the purchaser[.] * * * [T]he seller may wish some protection against claims resulting from misuse or loss of [the] deposits by the purchaser. * * * [T]he purchaser should be charged with the amount of unpaid rentals at date of closing as collectibility of such rentals by the seller after sale would be difficult.

d. *Insurance Premiums.* Most contracts provide for assignment of existing insurance and adjustment of insurance premiums. The purchaser should inform himself as to the amount and type of insurance in effect at the time of signing the contract as he may * * * wish to stipulate the amount, if any, of such insurance which is to be assigned. It has been suggested that in some cases the insurers may be unwilling to accept an assignment of existing insurance to the purchaser. Accordingly the contract could provide for cancellation by the seller of any such insurance. * * *

f. *Miscellaneous Adjustments.* * * * [T]he parties may desire to adjust the following items:

(a) Utility, [water and sewer] charges.

(b) Janitor's salary, vacations, welfare and other contributions. (Under many union contracts the vacations are based on a fiscal year and not the calendar year.)

(c) F.H.A. Insurance refunds. (Such refunds are normally payable to the original borrower after all loans in the group in which the original loan was made have been paid.)

(d) Decorating.

(e) Inspection fees.

(f) Bond premiums in connection with curb permits or other bonds posted with public authorities.

(g) Fuel and supplies on hand.

* * *

g. *Date of Prorations.* Most contracts provide for proration as of the date of delivery of deed. If the transaction is to be closed in escrow or there are other reasons calling for a different adjustment date, the contract should specify such date.

7. *Furnishing Evidence of Title, Title Clearance and Remedies in the Event of Default.*

(a) * * * [T]itle is [generally] evidenced by abstract, title policy or report on title or Torrens Certificate. "Good Title" is [in most cases] defined as one free of encumbrances. * * * Such a title does not necessarily have to be a perfect record title * * *.

(b) * * * [W]here an abstract is to be furnished as evidence of title * * * the seller * * * furnish[es to the buyer, within a specified period of time or within a reasonable time, an abstract of title] * * * covering the date of the contract[.] The buyer * * * [has] the abstract examined and furnish[es] the seller with a statement in writing[,] within a specified time[,] stating his objections to the title. Needless to say, many disputes arise between attorneys representing seller and buyer as to whether titles as shown in abstracts are, as a matter of law, defective. It should be noted that even though an abstract shows good record title there are defects in title such as forgery and lack of capacity on the part of the seller which would not be disclosed in an abstract.

(c) * * * A contract providing for the showing of title by policy or report should contain a provision that such policy or report shall be "conclusive evidence of good title as therein shown" * * * so that there can be no dispute ⁕ ⁕ ⁕ that such policy or report is to be accepted as evidence of title.

(d) The provisions of a contract [which govern] the mechanics of furnishing the policy or report and clearing of objections are important. ⁕ ⁕ ⁕ [T]he seller [may be obligated to] deliver a policy or preliminary title report to the purchaser or his agent within 15 or 20 days [after the execution of the contract]; and ⁕ ⁕ ⁕ the seller [may] have 60 days from the date of the report or policy to cure or remove defects. ⁕ ⁕ ⁕ [U]nder normal circumstances the times [mentioned] above are probably adequate[. I]f the title is complicated, [however,] more time may be needed to furnish title evidence or to clear objections. ⁕ ⁕ ⁕

(e) ⁕ ⁕ ⁕ [Usually the] contract ⁕ ⁕ ⁕ provide[s] that [the] guarantee policy or report on title ⁕ ⁕ ⁕ furnished to the buyer "show ⁕ ⁕ ⁕ title in seller (or grantor)." This provision is adequate unless the conveyance is not going to be made directly to the buyer from the seller or party in title. For example, the seller may himself be buying under a contract and may not be able to cause a conveyance to be made by the title holder directly to the [buyer]. Under such conditions the contract should specify the name of the party in whom title is to be shown and should contain appropriate provisions [insuring] that the buyer can be satisfied that the title will not be encumbered or become subject to other defects by virtue of the fact that the title is to pass through an intermediate party before it vests in the buyer. ⁕ ⁕ ⁕

⁕ ⁕ ⁕

(g) The matter of clearing objections to the title is[,] in the first instance[,] directly related to the substantive provisions of the contract. If care is exercised in the drafting of a contract[,] the attorney for the seller will see to it that the seller does not agree to convey more than he has in the way of title and will be sure that the contract notes all of the incurable objections to which the title is subject. ⁕ ⁕ ⁕

(h) There are, of course, situations [in which] known title defects ⁕ ⁕ ⁕ will have to be cured. Common examples are (1) [an] old trust deed where notes are lost, (2) claims against unprobated estates of decedents through whom title is derived, (3) conveyances by minors or incompetents, (4) outstanding dower claims, (5) old contract interests, and (6) restrictions on use. Certain objections of this type can be waived by a title guarantee company upon the furnishing of indemnity or by a temporary deposit of the purchase price[. O]ccasionally they can be waived upon the furnishing of satisfactory evidence[,] which does not appear of record[,] indicating that the objection is no longer valid. ⁕ ⁕ ⁕

(i) ⁕ ⁕ ⁕

Most of the forms of contract in common use contain no provisions relative to the clearing of objections disclosed by survey or inspection of the property and in all probability no form could cover adequately all types of title defects disclosed by survey or inspection. It might be desirable[, however,] to incorporate ⁕ ⁕ ⁕ provisions relative to the clearing of such defects[,] although as a practical matter the buyer can simply refuse to accept title so long as [such] defects exist.

(j) A contract need not [necessarily] contain provisions as to the remedies of the parties in the event of default because [the] remedies are well defined by law and in equity[. I]t is[, however,] advisable to provide for disposition of the earnest money. [T]he forms of contract generally in use [in most cases do] provide certain and somewhat different remedies for seller and purchaser. In the case of [the] seller, it is generally provided that if [the] purchaser defaults, "then at the option of seller, the earnest money shall be forfeited as liquidated damages and the contract shall then become null and void." This provision * * * does not [necessarily eliminate] the other remedies of the seller, namely, to enforce the contract specifically by action in equity, to sue at law for damages sustained by reason of purchaser's default (generally the difference between the market value of the premises and the contract price) or to * * * tender [the] deed and sue at law for the purchase price. The contract should provide that in case of any * * * suit [brought by the] seller * * * the earnest money [can be applied] on account of his claim without prejudice to his right of action. * * *

Despite [appropriate] provisions in the contract, a seller may encounter difficulty * * * clearing his title of the possible interest of a defaulted contract purchaser. The courts[, in] certain circumstances, [have] imposed stringent conditions upon the right of a contract seller to forfeit a purchaser's interest * * *.

Accordingly, both title guarantee companies and lawyers are reluctant to waive a contract purchaser's interest even though the contract provides that the seller can[, without notice,] terminate the contract upon default. [A s]eller may minimize the risk of the occurrence of this problem by signing only one copy of the contract and by providing that [the] signed contract [is to] be deposited with the broker or with some other person who, in seller's opinion, will retain possession of the contract and deliver it to the seller in the event of default. If the contract is deposited with a reliable escrowee and [is] returned to seller [upon] purchaser's default, the subsequent cancellation of the contract by [the] seller will ordinarily be sufficient to remove subsequent title difficulties in [the event] the defaulted purchaser * * * thereafter attempt[s] to becloud the title. * * *

From the standpoint of a buyer, most form contracts are inadequate. Under the terms of such contracts, in the event of seller's default, the buyer may terminate the contract and obtain a refund of the earnest money or he may accept the title in a defective condition, subject to his right to deduct from the purchase price the amounts of ascertainable liens. [If] this type of contract [is used,] a seller might simply fail to cure title defects if he concludes that he has made an improvident deal and the buyer may have no adequate remedy if he obtains a refund of the earnest money because the seller [could] then contend that the buyer was barred from further action by virtue of obtaining [the] refund. It would seem that sales contracts should contain a provision [which entitles] the buyer[,] in the event of default[,] * * * to the return of his earnest money without prejudicing any of his other rights. * * *

8. *The Fire Clause.* * * *

No one form of fire clause will be adequate for every type of transaction. The [terms] of the fire clause in a given transaction are dependent upon such factors as the nature, value and use of the improvements. [The nature of the] transaction may permit the use of a simple fire clause[. On the other hand,] a [very] detailed clause may be appropriate [for] another transaction. In the last analysis, the purpose of the fire clause is accomplished if it * * * provide[s] a *definite* and *ascertainable* basis for determining the respective rights of the parties in the event of loss or damage during the pendency of a real estate transaction.

9. *Notices and Demands.* Most of the form contracts in common use contain a clause to the effect that all notices and demands shall be in writing and that the mailing of a notice by registered mail to the party entitled to notice at an address specified in the contract shall be sufficient notice. * * * The contract should specify that notices become effective upon the deposit * * * in the United States mail or [upon the expiration of] a specified number of days after mailing[,] and it might be desirable to provide for written notice in the event a party makes an election provided for in the contract. * * * [N]otices are sent by registered mail so that proof of mailing will be available[,] if needed.

* * *

[I]t has been held in some cases that notice of forfeiture or termination is necessary even though the contract provides that the seller may terminate for the buyer's default without notice.

* * * In addition[,] it would seem desirable[,] if the contract is to be terminated because of a claimed default, that some notice of the termination be given to the defaulting party. * * *

10. *Broker's Commission.* * * *

[P]rovisions in the contract of sale purporting to limit the broker's right to a commission may not be effective [since] the broker is not a party to the contract. Such matters appropriately should be the subject of a separate written agreement between the seller and the broker.

* * *

11. *Provision for Escrow.* There are many situations where it is important to the seller or the buyer, or to both, that a sale of real estate be closed through escrow. Creation of an escrow with deposit of deed and purchase price as promptly as possible after execution of the sales contract will protect the buyer against the death or incapacity of the seller. [Will it protect the buyer against the trustee in bankruptcy of

the seller rejecting the contract? See Countryman, *Executory Contracts in Bankruptcy: Part I,* 57 Minn.L.Rev. 439, 460–474 (1973) and Section 365 of the Bankruptcy Code. If both the deed and the purchase price are deposited in escrow, is the purchase agreement still an executory contract?]

[The escrow] will assure the seller that the sale price is available. It will protect the buyer against the gap between the effective date of the title evidence and the actual date of the closing. In this connection[,] * * * bear in mind that deeds are not effectively registered in Torrens until the new certificate is issued. * * *

* * * [I]t is desirable to prepare the complete escrow agreement in conjunction with the contract and attach it to the contract as an exhibit and as an incorporated part of the contract.

* * *

12. *Sales of Property Registered Under the Torrens Act.* Some * * * contract forms provide that where the premises are registered under the Torrens System * * * the seller is to furnish "A Torrens Certificate accompanied by Torrens Title Tax search" or that "an Owner's Duplicate Certificate of Title issued by the Registrar of Titles * * * or a certified copy thereof, etc." shall be furnished.

The "Certificate of Title" is * * * found in the bound register book at the Registrar's Office * * * and, of course, cannot be furnished by the seller. From the standpoint of the seller[,] * * * providing that the Owner's Duplicate [must] be furnished to the buyer prior to the closing is undesirable because it is dangerous for the owner to [give up] possession [of the Duplicate]. * * * Furthermore[,] in many instances the Owner's Duplicate does not show the true state of the title since there may be many items registered [o]n the Certificate that do not appear on the Owner's Duplicate. Also[,] there are some instances whe[n] the seller may not * * * be able to exhibit the Duplicate Certificate; for instance, whe[n] he is purchasing the property under contract and the Duplicate Certificate is held by his vendor. Under such circumstances[,] a certified copy of the Certificate could be obtained but[,] as a practical matter, a certified copy is seldom (if ever) furnished and there is no reason for incurring the expense and delay which would be involved in procuring [it]. If the provisions of the contract with reference to the furnishing of evidence of title are not complied with by the seller, the buyer would have the right to claim a default and to rescind the contract. Therefore[,] the contract should contain provisions [which] the seller can comply with and [which] will afford the buyer protection. [For example, it could be] provide[d] that the Seller furnish a tax search within a specified time and that the purchaser be given an opportunity to examine the Duplicate Certificate at a designated place. [In addition, the contract should] provide that the Duplicate [is to] be delivered to the purchaser or surrendered to the Registrar at closing for the purpose of [transferring] title. The Certificate is, of course, always [available] for public inspection.

Steuben—Cs.Real Est.Plan. 3d Ed. UCB—10   * * *

Because original instruments are always retained by the Registrar many lawyers representing buyers are of the opinion that the contract should provide that the deed [will] be executed in duplicate so that the purchaser may have an executed copy in his possession.

* * *

If[,] under the terms of the contract[,] the seller is only required to furnish a tax search and produce the Duplicate Certificate for inspection, unless the contract provides that the transaction [will] be closed through escrow, it should provide that the transaction [will] be closed at the Registrar's Office. The buyer can then examine the Certificate of Title [when] the deed is delivered and the consideration paid and determine [whether] the title is good in the seller subject only to the exceptions specified in the contract.

* * *

14. *Possession.* In the absence of a contract provision to the contrary, the right to possession of real property passes to the buyer at the time of the delivery of the deed from the seller to the buyer.

* * *

Sometimes the seller of a residence needs the proceeds of the sale to finance the purchase of another residence. This will require that the seller deliver [the] deed to the buyer and obtain the proceeds of the sale before he completes his purchase of the new residence and becomes entitled to possession of the new residence. Under these circumstances, a seller may require [the postponement of] delivery of possession of the [transferred] residence * * * until a date when he can obtain possession of the new residence[.] * * * [The] date [of possession of the new residence may be] subsequent to the [date] when the buyer * * * received [the] deed [to the old residence] and parted with the purchase price. If this factor is present in a contemplated transaction, the contract should provide for the rights and obligations of the seller and the buyer after the delivery of the deed.

[T]he [contract may provide that the] seller is to be charged for the privilege of retaining possession subsequent to the delivery of the deed[.] * * * [If] the date when the seller agrees to deliver possession * * * is subsequent to the date of the delivery of the seller's deed, many contracts provide that a portion of the purchase price [is to] be held in escrow by a disinterested party subsequent to the closing of the transaction * * * as a guarantee of the seller's agreement to deliver possession at the future date.

* * *

15. *Merger of Contract in Deed.* It is a general rule of law that an executory contract for the sale of land, which requires the vendor to perform no acts other than the production of documentary evidence relating to the validity and character of his title and the execution and delivery of a deed conveying the character of title stipulated * * *, becomes merged in the deed and the covenants and stipulations contained in the contract are thereby extinguished. However, this general rule * * * does not apply to those provisions in the antecedent

contract which the parties did not intend to be incorporated in the deed or which are not necessarily performed or satisfied by the execution and delivery of the deed, for example, the vendor's promise to deliver possession at a given date or his undertaking to make specified repairs. A contract containing collateral or supplementary promises remains in force after the delivery of the deed until fully performed. [Good practice requires, however, that provisions which are intended by the parties to survive the delivery of the deed should be clearly indicated in the contract of purchase.] * * *

NOTE

1. Can a third party lender obtain a purchase money mortgage? See Division III, pages 595 to 600 infra.

a. If this can be done, as between the vendor who takes back a mortgage for part of the purchase price and a third party lender who, in return for the note and mortgage of the vendee, provides a portion or all of the cash payment paid by the vendee to the vendor, which one has priority?

b. Should the priority question be resolved in the purchase contract? Does the fact that the third party lender is not a party to the purchase contract affect your answer?

2. What "encumbrances" might be excepted under the title exceptions clause of the contract?

a. Should anything other than liens and mortgages be considered?

1. What about leases, rights of third parties in possession, special taxes and assessments, general taxes, private restrictions on use and enjoyment, zoning and building restrictions or ordinances, roads and highways, party walls or similar limitations on fee ownership, easements of necessity, implication or utility easements?

2. Municipalities, at times, have the power to form and delineate a special assessment or improvement district well before the improvement is made and the assessment entered. The lien of the assessment may relate back to the date of the enactment forming the district or may arise at the time of formation of the district. How can it be determined whether the real estate which is the subject of the contract is part of a special assessment or improvement district? Chances are that prior to entry of the assessment, if then, it will not appear as a matter of record.

3. Under the Comprehensive Environmental Response, Compensation and Liability Act as amended by the Superfund Amendments and Reauthorization Act ("Superfund"), if hazardous substances have been disposed of on real estate, the owner of the real estate is absolutely liable for all cleanup and remedial actions which may be undertaken by the United States, a state or local government, or any other person. As a result of the absolute liability imposed under Superfund, a potential buyer of real estate will certainly want to know, before completing the acquisition of the real estate, whether hazardous substances have been disposed of on the real estate to be acquired. If such disposal has occurred, arrangements can be made, prior to the acquisition of the real estate, with respect to how the costs of cleanup

will be shared, if at all. See Berz and Spracker, *The Impact of Superfund on Real Estate Transactions,* 2 # 2 Prob. & Prop. 49 (1988), Fitzsimmons and Sherwood, *The Real Estate Lawyer's Primer (and More) to Superfund: The Environmental Hazards of Real Estate Transactions,* 22 Real Prop., Prob. & Tr. J. 765 (1987); Burkhart, *Lender/ Owners and CERCLA: Title and Liability,* 25 Harv.J.Leg. 317 (1988); Last, *Superfund Liability Traps Affecting Developers and Lenders,* 3 #3 Nat.Res't & Env't 10 (1988).

b. Section 2–306 of the Uniform Land Transactions Act provides that, unless a deed specifically limits warranties by disclaiming, the warranties specified in Section 2–306 are implied.

3. If the title exceptions clause lists certain exceptions but the vendor is required to convey title through the use of only a quit-claim deed, what are the vendee's rights if title is subject to an encumbrance not excepted and more onerous than those excepted?

a. Is a title exceptions clause needed when the form of conveyance is to be a quit-claim deed?

b. The Uniform Land Transactions Act adopts, in Section 2–304(d), the rule that a contract provision requiring that the vendor convey by only a quit-claim deed does not of itself reduce the vendor's obligation to provide marketable title. Such a provision does, however, limit the vendee's remedy for lack of marketable title to rescission, which must occur before the deed is accepted.

c. For a general discussion of the application of the Uniform Land Transactions Act to contracts and conveyances see Balbach, *The Uniform Land Transactions Act: Articles 1 and 2,* 11 Real Prop., Prob. & Tr.J. 1 (1976); Maggs, *Remedies for Breach of Contract Under Article Two of the Uniform Land Transactions Act,* 11 Ga.L.Rev. 275 (1977).

4. The liquidated damages concept is discussed in Division II, pages 413 to 418 infra.

a. If, under the contract, the vendor retains all of his usual remedies in the event of the vendee's default, what is the consideration for a liquidated damages provision?

5. Even though a vendor would prefer that a contract of purchase not be recorded, would this be acceptable to a vendee?

a. There are legitimate reasons for each party's preference. What are the reasons? How can this conflict be resolved, generally accomplishing each party's desires?

6. The risk of loss problem is more fully discussed in Division II, pages 418 to 423 infra. The real estate broker considerations are also discussed in Division II at pages 395 to 405 infra.

7. Rather than adding the complexities of an escrow, can the gap between the date of the title evidence and the actual date of closing be handled by providing that the title evidence must be brought down to date at closing, and that any title insurance policy be dated as of the date of closing?

8. When the real estate being acquired is improved and currently in use there are a number of provisions which should be contained in the purchase contract in addition to the various provisions discussed in the above excerpt. For example, the contract should contain provisions describing all inventory

and equipment included in the sale and the working order thereof, the utility service facilities of the property and the adequacy thereof, the seller's rent roll and sources of income, and the utility, repair, maintenance and insurance costs. See generally Halper, *Representation Clauses in Apartment House Sales Contracts*, 7 # 4 Real Est.Rev. 46 (1978); Ridloff, *How to Prepare a Contract of Sale for Commercial Real Property*, 25 # 5 Prac. Law. 11 (1979); Hollyfield, *Avoiding Contract of Sale Disputes by Thoughtful Drafting*, 1 # 3 Prac. Real Est. Law. 11 (1985); Garfinkel, *A Basic Purchase Agreement*, 5 #1 Prac.Real Est.Law. 27 (1988).

9.   Unless the acquisition of the real estate is closed at the end of the real estate tax year, there will be an allocation of real estate taxes. The income tax implications of the allocation are described in the following excerpt.

NOTE

THE APPORTIONMENT OF REAL ESTATE TAXES BETWEEN PURCHASER AND SELLER UNDER SECTION 164(d) OF THE 1954 CODE

Allan T. Cannon
12 Tax Law Review 433 (1957).
[footnotes omitted]

* * *

Before discussing the apportionment of real property taxes where section 164(d) is applicable, a comment on section 164(a) is appropriate. This latter section * * * states, "Except as otherwise provided in this section, [real property taxes] shall be allowed as a deduction [for the taxable year within which] paid or accrued * * *."

In the ordinary circumstances, a cash basis taxpayer, regardless of when the tax becomes a lien under local property law, may take a deduction only when he pays the tax and has not sold the property. An accrual basis taxpayer has an election under the * * * Code. He may either take the deduction when the tax becomes a lien, at which time * * * it accrues in a lump sum, or he may elect under section 461(c) to prorate the taxes in equal amounts over the property tax year. * * *

It can be readily seen that if a taxpayer does not elect to accrue ratably under section 461(c) the tax will continue to be treated as accruing at some definite moment determined by local law. Thus, all the existing uncertainties and variations arising out of the character of local law will continue if the taxpayer does not elect. * * *

Section 164(d)(1). This section was enacted in order to provide the purchaser and seller of real estate a definitive guide in regard to the apportionment of real estate taxes. The section has a dual function in that it provides for a method of allocation of taxes between parties to the sale of real property, and it limits the deduction each may take for taxes to the portion as computed.

Thus, the tax is prorated between the seller and buyer by allocating the real estate taxes over the real property year in which the respective parties held the property. The seller is entitled to a deduction for his allocable share of the taxes up to but not including the day of the sale. The buyer is entitled to a deduction for his allocable share of the taxes from the day of sale. It should be noted that regardless of any agreement between the seller and purchaser of the property regarding the allocation of real property taxes, the taxes must be apportioned as stated in section 164(d). The taxes deemed paid by the seller will not be considered part of the selling price, and the taxes apportioned to the buyer shall not be capitalized as part of the cost of the property but shall be deducted as a tax under section 164. Of course, if the buyer elects to capitalize under section 266 (relating to the capitalization of certain carrying charges) he may do so notwithstanding section 164(d). [In addition, in certain situations the buyer may be required to capitalize pursuant to the requirements of section 263A.]

To illustrate, S is the seller and B the buyer. Taxes for the real property year July 1, 19[86] to June 30, 19[87] become payable and a lien arises by reason of local property law on January 1, 19[87]. S sells the property to B on September 30, 19[86]. The amount of taxes are $3,650. B pays the taxes as they fall due. If S and B are on a cash basis, S will deduct $910 as his share of the taxes, and B will deduct $2,740 as his share. S held the property from July 1, for the tax year, until September 29, the day before the sale, or 91 days. Nine hundred and ten dollars is $91/365$ths, and the complementary amount $2,740, or $274/365$ths, is deductible by B. * * *

[T]his example is the usual case, reflecting the terms of the closing agreement of the parties, and the usual way businessmen would apportion the taxes due between the two parties.

If S was on a cash basis and B was on an accrual basis, assume B elects under section 461(c) to accrue taxes ratably each month. B's taxable year—his reporting year for income tax purposes—ended on December 31, 19[86]. For the income tax year ended December 31, 19[86], B will be allowed to deduct and accrue $930 for real estate taxes (from September 30, 19[86] to December 31, 19[86]). On January 1, 19[87] B will accrue $1,810 ($3,650 minus $1,840) and will carry this item as an asset in the nature of a deferred charge to be written off over the following six months. On July 1, 19[87] he will start accruing again on a monthly basis.

Suppose in the above example S's taxable year for federal income tax purposes also ends on December 31, 19[86]. [S] is on a cash basis and is allowed to deduct items in the year in which they are paid. As of December 31, 19[86] the real estate taxes were not due and have not been paid. Is S entitled to the deduction for his share of the tax as allocated under section 164(d)? Is S entitled to an additional deduction for the amount he paid in January, 19[86] for taxes for the year July 1, 19[85] to June 30, 19[86]? The answer is yes in both instances. Assuming the amount of taxes is the same in the real property tax years ending June 30, 19[86] and June 30, 19[87], i.e., $3,650, S would be entitled to a deduction of $3,650 and $910 in his tax return for the year ended December 31, 19[86]. This indicates how strategic timing of a sale and payment for real estate can create considerable tax savings.

It is important to note that the taxes are apportioned over the "real property tax year" as stated in section 164(d)(1). There is no certain method of determining the real property tax year because it is fixed in each case by the law of the situs of the property. The Regulations define the real property tax year as the period which, under the law imposing the tax, is regarded as the period to which the tax imposed relates. The time when the tax rate is determined, the time when the assessment is made, the time when the tax becomes a lien, and the time when the tax becomes due or delinquent do not necessarily determine the real property tax year. The method used by the parties to the sale as to allocation of the taxes is disregarded in determining what the real property tax year is. Where one or more local governmental units (the state, the village, the town, etc.) impose a tax on real property, the real property tax year for each tax must be determined for purposes of apportioning the taxes under section 164(d)(1).

For example, the real property tax year ends December 31, 19[86]; taxes become a lien on November 1, 19[85], the preceding year. On November 15, 19[85] S sells to B. B does not sell the property in 19[86]. S does not get a deduction for his proportion of taxes; he cannot deduct in 19[85] any part of the tax for the real property year of 19[86], even though the lien accrued while he was the owner of the property. B receives the benefit of all of 19[86] "real property tax year" taxes. S may take a deduction for his pro rata share of the taxes which were a lien in 19[84] for the 19[85] real property tax year—$318/365$ths for January 1, 19[85] to November 14, 19[85]. For 19[85] B takes a deduction of $47/365$ths for November 15, 19[85] to December 31, 19[85]. The above assumes, of course, that S and B file their returns on a calendar year basis and pay or accrue taxes when they are due.

Special rules. Ordinarily, a cash basis taxpayer may deduct real property taxes only in the year in which they are paid. An exception is provided, however, for taxes of the real property tax year in which a sale occurs. Where the seller is on a cash basis and the buyer is liable for the tax under state law, the seller is treated as having paid his pro rata share of the tax on the date of sale. If the buyer is on a cash basis and under state law the seller is liable for the tax, the buyer is considered as having paid his pro rata share of the tax on the date of sale. If neither buyer nor seller is liable for the real property tax under state law, the party who holds the property at the time when the tax lien attaches is considered to be liable.

Section 164(d)(2)(A) applies to a purchaser only when the tax is payable prior to the sale. In addition, if the tax is payable before the sale but has not been paid, section 164(d)(2)(A) does not apply to any purchaser who does not pay the tax.

Thus, *S* and *B* are both on a cash basis. The real property tax year ends December 31, 19[86]; taxes become a personal liability on June 30, 19[86] and are payable September 30, 19[86], *S* sells the property to *B* on May 31, 19[86]. How are the taxes to be apportioned and when are they deductible? *S* may deduct $^{150}/_{365}$ths of the tax for January 1 to May 30, and *B* will get a deduction for $^{215}/_{365}$ths for May 31 to December 31. *S* will take his deduction as of May 31, the date of sale, because the "other party" was liable for the taxes and section 164(d)(2)(A) will apply. *B*, however will be allowed a deduction only when he pays the taxes, as determined under section 164(d)(1).

As illustrated in the Regulations * * * [w]here the original property owner pays the taxes for the year, let us say, in April, and the property is sold * * * in June and then again in September, each subsequent purchaser is entitled to take the deduction for his allocable share of the taxes as of the date of sale.

* * *

Where property is sold and the seller or the purchaser computes his tax on an accrual basis and either one does not elect to accrue taxes under section 461(c), he is treated as if the *Supplee* [45] decision were still applicable. However, in order to eliminate inequities where a taxpayer may not be able to take any deduction because of his method of accounting, section 164(d)(2)(B) provides that the portion of any tax which is treated as imposed on the taxpayer and which may not be deducted by him for any taxable year by reason of his method of accounting shall be treated as having accrued on the date of sale.

To clarify, assume the real property tax year ends December 31, 19[86]. There is no personal liability for the taxes, but taxes are assessed November 30, 19[86] and are payable on that date. *S* is on an accrual basis but has not elected to accrue taxes under section 461(c). The property is sold June 30, 19[86]. What may *S* deduct for his share of the taxes and as of what date is it accrued? Because of *S*'s method of accrual accounting, he ordinarily could not deduct any part of the tax for 19[86] because he sold the property prior to November 30, the date when he could have accrued it. Under section 164(d)(1) $^{180}/_{365}$ths of the 19[86] tax for January 1 to June 29 is considered imposed on *S,* and under section 164(d)(2)(D) the tax is considered accrued as of June 30, 19[86] and is deductible by *S* as of that time.

* * *

NOTE

1. Assume that the real property tax year ends on May 1st, the taxes become a lien on the prior November 15th, and the seller is on the cash basis. The seller pays the taxes on November 15th and deducts the full amount of the taxes on his income tax return for the year ending December 31st. On

45. [Magruder v. Supplee, 316 U.S. 394, 62 S.Ct. 1162, 86 L.Ed. 1555 (1942). Real estate taxes are deductible by the seller and not by the purchaser if the seller is on accrual basis for income tax purposes and prior to sale the taxes are a lien against the property or seller is personally liable for the taxes.]

February 1st the seller sells the property and as part of the proration at closing the purchaser reimburses the seller for the real property taxes for the period from February 1st to May 1st. How should the seller treat this receipt? Is it income to the seller in the current year to the extent the deduction of that portion of the real estate taxes was of "tax benefit"? See Section 111. Or, should the seller file an amended return for the prior year and reduce his deduction for real estate taxes by the amount reimbursed to him by the purchaser?

c. THE LAND CONTRACT

One of the major distinctions between an option and a purchase contract is that an option generally gives the purchaser the choice whether to go through with the actual purchase while the seller retains the option payment whether or not the purchaser chooses to purchase. If a purchase contract is used, assuming all conditions are met, the purchaser must purchase, and the seller must sell. In the usual purchase contract the date set for closing generally occurs fairly soon after the date of execution of the contract. At closing, the deed to the property is delivered to the purchaser and cash, and/or a note and mortgage are delivered to the seller or to the seller and the lender. The purchaser normally takes possession of the property on, or shortly after, closing.

Although a land contract can be used as a security device, see pages 600 to 610 infra, it also can be used as a means of acquisition, a marketing contract. A land contract may be conceived of as a contractual right given to the purchaser to use the property prior to closing, subject to certain conditions. In addition, the purchaser will have the right, upon full performance of the conditions of the contract including making installment payments of the purchase price for a period of one to several years, to compel the seller to convey the real estate to the purchaser. The use of the land contract as a means of acquisition has the advantages of giving possession of the real estate to the purchaser prior to closing, permitting a longer period of time to elapse between the date of the execution of the contract and closing and, to some extent, permitting installment payment of the down payment and, possibly, the full purchase price of the real estate. One of the problems in the use of a land contract as a means of acquisition is whether the land contract should be considered a security device or simply a marketing contract. If the land contract is considered a security device, the question is then whether it should be enforced according to its terms. This question is considered at pages 601 to 609 infra.

THE CALIFORNIA LAND CONTRACT

John R. Hetland
48 California Law Review 729 (1960).
[footnotes omitted]

*   *   *

Except for the proof of damage difficulties, most of the remedial problems * * * arise because the security device is read into the contract. Liquidated damages, for example, legitimately belong in the marketing contract. Specific performance without judicial sale or redemption is proper under the marketing instrument, and certainly * * * anti-deficiency legislation has no application to the marketing contract. * * *

It is easy in most cases to separate the earnest money contract from the security device. The early writers seemed to have assumed some general differences between earnest money and installment contracts. Perhaps this is about as specific as the distinction can be, i.e., a vague purpose test, leaving the precise definition to be resolved as a question of intent in each case.

Compare the general distinction with some of the legislative and proposed legislation distinctions which, supposedly, require more specificity. [Some states] define the security instrument as one having five or more installments; [certain] legislative proposals include more than one payment and more than two payments after the initial payment; and a proposal for model legislation would draw the line where a part of the purchase price was due, in the absence of default, more than one year after execution of the contract. Any of these tests will work in the overwhelming majority of cases, but these are the cases where the purpose is so clear that precise definition is not required in the first place.

Instead of an arbitrary, mechanical division the distinction should lie in the purpose for which the parties are using the contract. Actually, the problem is the same as the problem of separating a mortgage from an absolute conveyance or an option to repurchase. In the land contract as in the mortgage cases, the problem actually becomes whether or not the "equity of redemption" should be avoided. Certainly no one would say the mortgage problem should be decided by defining the mortgage in terms of its appearance. And because the same issue is to be decided, i.e., the applicability of the security debtor's protective devices, in making the installment-marketing distinction, the approach should be the same. Arbitrary lines and mechanical distinctions simply invite mechanical evasion devices. And mechanical lines are of too much aid in the borderline cases; they prevent the court from looking at the real issue, intent.

Intent may be evidenced by several factors including time, change of possession, number of installments, percent payable under the contract, other financing involved, and so on, but the issue remains intent.

The court has had little trouble with it in other contexts and it will have little difficulty with it here once it confirms that making the distinction is imperative. * * *

A short summary of the position of the land contract today [if it is construed as a security device] is that it offers far more disadvantages than advantages to both buyer and seller. Its disadvantages to one are not offset by commensurate advantages to the other.

Limiting the choice to a power of sale mortgage or a deed of trust on the one hand and an installment land contract on the other, the disadvantages of the contract to the vendor include the time and expense of quieting title and of regaining possession by action and the possibility of having to make restitution, an additional investment in possibly overencumbered property. The quick, certain and relatively inexpensive solution of these problems by a sale under the power leaves little to recommend the contract. The contract, moreover, [usually] offers no deficiency judgment advantage over the purchase money mortgage or deed of trust * * *.

The disadvantages to the buyer are equally discouraging. The transfer of his interest frequently is restricted by covenants against assignment. Obsolete, or perhaps overly conservative, opinion among lenders that his interest is subject to more rapid termination upon default makes his interest poor collateral if he needs security to raise additional money. Upon completion of his payments under an installment contract, a purchaser faces the possibility of receiving either a defective title or no title whatever. And if the vendor is adjudicated bankrupt, if title has passed to the vendor's heirs or if the vendor is under a legal disability, the purchaser can look forward to frustrating litigation before obtaining his deed upon completion of his payments.

Despite all of this, it would be naïve to assume that the contract is not still the preferable device to some. Thus, abstract comparison of the advantages and disadvantages of the contract overlooks, again, people. Undeniably the land contract remains attractive to several of the large developers because the low (in comparison to rental value) installment payments make it unlikely that the defaulting purchaser will do anything other than leave the property, with sufficient prodding, thus making it again available for sale without litigation or even an extrajudicial sale. In other words, the risk of an occasional clouded title or of an occasional ejectment action is more than offset by the advantages of old-fashioned private enforcement which, while theoretically barred, remains an excellent remedy against an uninformed purchaser. And undoubtedly the land contract offers far greater opportunity for unconscionable manipulation by those so inclined. * * *

It is important to the lawyer advising the individual seller to know that the notion that the land contract is the seller's most favorable security device is simply no longer true, just as it is important for the lawyer advising the developer or builder to be aware of the extent of the risk involved in preferring the land contract. And certainly anyone representing a buyer, either at the litigation or contracting stages, must be aware of all of the remedies and defenses available. ＊ ＊ ＊

NOTE

1. The use of a land contract as a marketing device may be said to involve no more than an "earnest money" contract or purchase agreement which grants possession prior to closing and/or permits the payment of the "equity" portion of the purchase price in installments prior to closing and/or provides for an extended period of time between execution and closing. In this context, however, the distinction between a purchase agreement and a land contract becomes somewhat blurred.

a. Is the label given the instrument of any real importance? Or, is the relevant concern to the planner whether a court might construe the instrument to be a security device? Cf. Jones, *Drafting the Installment Contract,* 62 Chi.B.Rec. 97 (1980); Cathey, *The Real Estate Installment Sale Contract: Its Drafting, Use, Enforcement and Consequences,* 5 U.Ark. Little Rock L.J. 229 (1982).

1. In some states, no matter how the instrument is construed, a land contract will be enforced according to its terms. See Cunningham and Tischler, *Disguised Real Estate Security Transactions As Mortgages in Substance,* 26 Rutgers L.Rev. 1, 7–8 (1972). See generally Lewis and Reeves, *How the Doctrine of Equitable Conversion Affects Land Sale Contract Forfeitures,* 3 Real Est.L.J. 249 (1975); Nelson and Whitman, *Installment Land Contracts—The National Scene Revisited,* 1985 B.Y. U.L.Rev. 1; Cane, *Equity and Forfeitures in Contracts for the Sale of Land,* 4 U.Haw.L.Rev. 61 (1982); Comment, *Forfeiture Clauses in Land Installment Contracts: Time for Equitable Foreclosure,* 8 U.Puget Sound L.Rev. 85 (1984). See also *Miller v. American Wonderlands, Inc.,* 275 N.W.2d 399 (Iowa 1979), in which the failure to pay $10.48 caused the forfeiture of the vendee's interest in approximately $30,000 of property. Cf. *Borchert v. Hecla Mining Co.,* 109 Idaho 482, 708 P.2d 887 (1985).

b. The Interstate Land Sales Full Disclosure Act requires that a contract which does not provide for the delivery of a warranty deed within 180 days from the date of the contract contain: (1) A description of the land being sold which would meet recording requirements, (2) A provision for notice of default to buyer and a twenty-day period to cure the default, and (3) In the event of a forfeiture, a clause requiring the seller to refund to the buyer any amounts the buyer has paid in excess of 15 percent of the purchase price, unless the seller can demonstrate that the actual damages, resulting from the default, were greater than the 15 percent. See Catalina, *Interstate Land Sales—Tightening Consumer Protection,* 10 Real Est.L.J. 72 (1981).

2. It appears that a land contract used as a marketing device can be rejected by the trustee of a bankrupt vendor. See Countryman, *Executory Contracts in Bankruptcy: Part I,* 57 Minn.L.Rev. 439, 460–474 (1973). But see Weintraub and Resnick, *What is an Executory Contract? A Challenge to the Countryman Test,* 15 U.C.C.L.J. 273 (1983). If, however, the agreement is regarded as an "installment land contract," a security device, for the purposes of Section 365 of the Bankruptcy Code and the vendee is in possession, the vendee has two alternatives if the vendor's trustee in bankruptcy rejects. The

vendee can leave and claim a lien on the property for any portion of the purchase price paid. See Section 365(j). Or, the vendee can elect to remain in possession of the property and continue to make payments under the agreement. See Section 365(i). When the vendee has completed making the payments called for by the agreement, the trustee must deliver title to the property. See generally Orr and Klee, *Secured Creditors Under the New Bankruptcy Code,* 11 U.C.C.L.J. 312, 338–342 (1979); Shanker, *The Treatment of Executory Contracts and Leases in the 1978 Bankruptcy Code,* 25 Prac.Law. 11 (Oct. 1979); Krasnowiecki, *The Impact of the New Bankruptcy Reform Act on Real Estate Development and Financing,* 53 Am.Bankr.L.J. 363 (1979); Fogel, *Executory Contracts and Unexpired Leases in the Bankruptcy Code,* 64 Minn.L. Rev. 341 (1980); Epling, *Treatment of Land Sales Contracts Under the New Bankruptcy Code,* 56 Am.Bankr.L.J. 55 (1982); Leta and Jones, *Selected Bankruptcy Considerations in Drafting Real Estate Documents,* 1984 Utah L.Rev. 227; Pedowitz, *The Effect of Bankruptcy or Insolvency on Real Estate Transactions—An Overview,* 20 Real Prop., Prob. & Tr.J. 25 (1985); Andrew, *Real Property Transactions and the 1984 Bankruptcy Code Amendments,* 20 Real Prop., Prob. & Tr.J. 47 (1985); Leta, *New Real Estate Issues Under the 1984 Bankruptcy Amendments,* 1 # 4 Prac.Real Est.Law. 13 (1985); Solomon, *Real Estate Aspects of the 1984 Amendments to the Bankruptcy Code,* 58 N.Y.St.B.J. 23 (1986).

d. THE GROUND LEASE

A ground lease also may be used to acquire real estate. It can be conceived of as similar to a security device in that, on default in the payment of rent, the lessor can use ejectment, etc., to recover the property and can retain the rental payments made to that point in time. On the other hand, a ground lease is different than a security device since at the end of the term of the lease the lessor gets the property back even if the lessee has made all of the payments called for by the lease.

The primary advantage of a ground lease is that its use defers the cost of acquiring the property outright, substituting an agreement to pay rent for a period of years. The developer's "front end" investment in the property is eliminated, or at least substantially decreased, and the developer is permitted to pay the acquisition cost of the property in payments spread over the term of the lease.

Despite the fact that the developer does not own the property, in the usual case the developer may depreciate any improvements which the developer constructs on the property. Since less "front money" or initial cash investment is required the leverage of the developer is increased. All of the developer's equity investment can be put into depreciable improvements. The combination of the increased leverage and the deductions for depreciation, interest on the financing of the improvements and rent make a ground lease an attractive means of acquisition.

FINANCING THE SHOPPING CENTER
Richard Faletti
1965 University of Illinois Law Forum 151.
[footnotes omitted]

* * *

Ground Lease

A device which has become exceedingly popular in recent years as a method of keeping equity investment at a minimum is the ground lease of undeveloped real property. The principal advantage of leasing the land rather than owning it is that the developer need not provide the cash otherwise required to buy the land. Hence, the ground lease constitutes a form of equity financing. Since land is not a depreciable asset for income tax purposes, the ownership of land does not provide any cash flow through noncash depreciation charges. The ground rental paid under a ground lease, however, provides a deductible item for income tax purposes. The developer who takes a ground lease should also acquire the right to mortgage the underlying fee; otherwise he will have to forego any thoughts of permanent mortgage financing of [improvements] * * * unless he is able to procure a leasehold mortgage. * * *

Until recently there was a great deal of reluctance on the part of most landowners to subordinate their fee simple interests in real property to a developer's mortgage. Recently, however, landowners have appreciated that this device enables them to achieve a return on real property in a manner which would avoid [the recognition of] a large [amount of gain] if the real estate were sold * * *.

The ground lessee-developer usually pays to the landowner [a percentage] of the agreed value of the real property as the rental under the ground lease. In some cases this rental may go as high as 12 per cent of the value of the leased land. * * * The ground lease is usually a net lease, so it is typical for the ground lessee-developer to pay all real estate taxes and assessments. Ground rent is usually not paid until the [development is constructed] and open for business with rent-paying tenants. For this reason the ground lessor is justified in imposing reasonable time limitations on the developer for the completion of the [development]. * * *

1. *Principal Terms of Subordinated Ground Lease.* * * *

The developer under a ground lease usually obligates himself to construct the [development], and in order to do this he [usually] requires the right to place a mortgage on the land and improvements, both with respect to interim financing and permanent mortgage financing after construction. The ground lessor-landowner must be required to join in the mortgage or trust deed (but not in the execution of the mortgage note) and must permit the land to be included as the security so fondly desired by the mortgage lender. If the land cannot be included in the mortgage, then the ability of the developer to obtain permanent mortgage financing is severely curtailed.

The hazard to the ground lessor-landowner in permitting a mortgage to be placed on his land by the ground lessee can be reduced [in the context of a shopping center or office building] by requiring the ground lessee to agree to enter into long term leases with tenants having AAA–1 credit ratings, the rentals of which are adequate to cover debt service requirements on the permanent mortgage, real property taxes, and operating expenses. The developer should be willing to agree that the term of his mortgage will not extend beyond the term of the ground lease. The landowner is entitled to require that the permanent mortgage provide that the mortgage lender will give the landowner at least 30 days notice of default by the ground lessee-developer, so that the landowner himself will have an opportunity to cure any default.

The developer should allow himself ample time in making any commitments to the landowner as to the time of commencement of construction of the [development]. Depending upon his degree of experience, anywhere from two to five years might be required for proper planning, leasing, and financing before ground can be broken[.]

*   *   *

To attain the greatest flexibility, the ground-lessee developer should attempt to procure the right to mortgage the leased premises in parcels so that if necessary [the development can be constructed] in stages. The ground lease should specifically require the landowner to execute all documents which may be required by the mortgage lender, as well as to execute any form of subordination of the fee simple interest in the land in whatever form the mortgage lender may require.

The ground lessee's right to mortgage the fee simple interest in the underlying land and the ground lessor's corollary obligation to join in the mortgage of the fee should run throughout the term of the lease and should include any refunding or extensions of the original mortgage. The ground lessor is entitled to be protected against the possibility of the developer overburdening his real property with mortgage financing. This may be achieved either by limiting the right of the ground lessee to make mortgage arrangements only with financial institutions or, in the alternative, by providing a percentage of value or aggregate dollar limit to be secured by [the] mortgage, such as two-thirds of the appraised value of the land and buildings.

Since a ground lease may have a term from 50 to 99 years, it is important that the ground lessee be granted the right of assignment of the lease, together with a release from all liability under the ground lease in the event of an assignment. The right of assignment exists unless expressly prohibited by the lease, but of more concern to the developer is a release from future liability in the event an assignment is made. It is the rare real estate developer who is willing to keep himself tied to a personal liability under a lease for a great many years after he has assigned it and during which period he is out of possession and control of the premises.

Of primary importance to the developer is his right to depreciat[e] the buildings erected on the leased ground. * * * [S]ince the ground lessee has assumed the cost of construction, he should be entitled to * * * depreciat[e] the buildings for income tax purposes. This right should be confirmed in the lease.

The handling of insurance proceeds in the event of a casualty or of an award received as the result of a condemnation proceeding are also important to the developer since they will be of concern to the mortgage lender when the developer seeks mortgage financing, and to [certain types of tenants] when he seeks to lease out the [development]. The ground lease should protect the ground lessee's right to all insurance proceeds and should place upon him the responsibility to repair any casualty damage. * * *

In the event of a total condemnation, the ground lease should provide for a fair allocation of the award between the parties. The ground lessee-developer should have some flexibility in the case of a partial condemnation to make a decision whether he can continue operating the [development] with the remainder of the property. If the condemnation clause in the ground lease is too much in favor of the ground lessor-landowner, it will severely hamper the ground lessee in granting to [certain of the] tenants the type of condemnation clauses that they (particularly the chain stores [in a shopping center development]) will require in their leases with him.

Because the real property is leased for many years in the future, a use which is not even anticipated at the time the ground lease is [entered into] may become the highest and best use of the land at some future period. Accordingly, the section of the ground lease dealing with the use of the leased premises should be as broad as the ingenuity of counsel permits.

Other lease provisions which should be considered are the right of the ground lessee to demolish existing structures on the land, if any; excuse of performance by the ground lessee in the event of acts of God or other events of *force majeure;* freedom on the part of the ground lessee to negotiate the occupancy leases from the * * * tenants [of the development]; questions of lease renewal options; rights to purchase the fee at a fixed price or a price subject to appraisal; rights of first refusal to purchase the fee; and options to purchase or rights of first refusal with respect to any adjoining real property owned by the landowner. The ground lessee-developer should also retain the right to make any alterations to the * * * buildings [in the development] after they are constructed.

So that the tenants of the [development] can be assured of the quiet enjoyment of the premises to be leased by them, the ground lessor-landowner should be required to keep all such tenants in possession of their premises as long as they are complying with their subleases, irrespective of what may happen to the basic ground lease.

* * *

2. *Unsubordinated Ground Lease.* * * * [I]nstitutional mortgage lenders have become more willing in the past few years to advance funds against a mortgage of a ground leasehold interest without requiring subordination of the fee by the landowner. * * *

The distinction between the subordinated ground lease and the unsubordinated ground lease is that [in] the latter [case] the landlord does not permit the fee simple title to the land to be mortgaged by the ground lessee-developer as security for his mortgage loan. However, the leasehold interest will be conveyed as security for a mortgage loan. The annual ground rent payments as well as the depreciation charges on the [development] constructed on the leasehold * * * are deductible by the developer for income tax purposes. As a result, the developer can achieve an economic advantage he would not enjoy if he owned the land.

* * *

Since the mortgage lender has as security a lesser estate in the land, and accordingly bears a greater risk, many additional safeguards are necessary in the unsubordinated ground lease in order to afford the mortgage lender the protection he demands and requires. In advancing funds against the security of a lien against a ground leasehold interest, most institutional lenders are concerned with the problem of a default by the ground lessee-developer resulting in a termination of the leasehold interest, thereby effectively depriving the mortgagee of its entire security interest. As a result, the mortgage lender is interested in seeing that the events of default which result in termination of the ground lease be limited as much as possible, and in any event that the lender itself be given ample opportunity to cure such defaults. At a minimum, there should be a requirement in the ground lease providing as conditions precedent to any termination that (1) the lessor-landowner gives 60 days notice of default to the ground lessee, and (2) if the default is not cured within 30 days thereafter, a 30-day notice of default to the mortgage lender.

If at all possible, events of default beyond the reasonable control of the ground lessee-developer, such as acts of God or *force majeure,* should not result in automatic termination of the ground lease. By giving the mortgage lender all possible opportunity to make good any defaults of the ground lessee, or to assume the position of the ground lessee, the ground lessor is acting in his own best interests. If the institutional lender steps into the picture in place of the original ground lessee-developer, the landowner usually will have acquired a tenant of substantially greater financial strength.

It is helpful if the ground lessor-landowner grants the ground lessee-developer a continuing power of attorney to execute the many documents which may be required by the lender, the title company, or the subtenants. In many cases the signature of the ground lessor-landowner will be required for the purposes of easements or dedications, estoppel certificates, offset statements, or attornment agreements. * * *

The mortgage lender will also be concerned about options on the part of the ground lessee-developer to purchase the fee simple interest in the realty. Safeguards should be provided in the ground lease so that upon the purchase of the underlying fee by the developer, a merger of * * * the leasehold interest [into the fee interest] would not result in destroying the leasehold mortgage.

Not only will the mortgage lender want the ground lessee-developer to have the unrestricted right to mortgage the leasehold and to assign the leasehold without further liability, but it will want those rights itself in the event of foreclosure of the leasehold mortgage or in the event of its assumption of the leasehold interest. The ground lease must contain an unlimited right of assignment without requiring the ground lessor's consent so that the lease can be conveyed to a purchaser at a foreclosure sale. The lease must also prohibit modifications or surrender without the consent of the mortgage lender. Most importantly, the ground lease should contain a negative covenant on the part of the ground lessor not to mortgage the fee simple interest.

In drafting the unsubordinated ground lease, foresight is also required in connection with problems which may arise in negotiating occupancy leases with the * * * tenants of the [development]. The * * * tenant who anticipates the prospect of not having any lease at all if the ground lessee-developer defaults with respect to any of his obligations under the ground lease will feel insecure. Accordingly, the ground lease should provide that the ground lessor will not disturb the possession of the * * * subtenants in the event of default by the ground lessee-developer, and that the ground lessor, or any of his successors, will assume the obligations of the ground lessee-developer to the * * * subtenants under the respective subleases. In turn, the lease with the * * * subtenant should provide that such tenant will agree to continue as a tenant under any successor to the interest of the ground lessee-developer.

* * *

NOTE

1. The financial differences between ownership of the land in fee simple by a developer and ownership of a term of years under a ground lease can be illustrated by a comparison of the results of the first year's operation of a development under both scenarios.

	Purchase	Lease
Total Cash Required	$4,000,000	$3,000,000
Provided by Mortgage	2,700,000	1,900,000
Equity Investment	$1,300,000	$1,100,000
Gross Rents	$ 800,000	$ 800,000

	Purchase	Lease
Operating Expenses	290,000	290,000
Mortgage Interest and Amortization	311,000	219,000
Leasehold Rent		100,000
Cash Flow	$ 199,000	$ 191,000
Percentage Return on Equity	15%	17%
Gross Rents	$ 800,000	$ 800,000
Operating Expenses	290,000	290,000
Mortgage Interest	297,000	209,000
Leasehold Rent		100,000
Depreciation	95,000	95,000
Taxable Income	$ 118,000	$ 106,000
Tax-free Cash Return (Cash flow less taxable income)	$ 81,000	$ 85,000
Tax-free Cash Return on Equity	6.2%	7.7%

The foregoing table was suggested by a table appearing in Faletti, *Financing the Shopping Center,* 1965 U.Ill.L.F. 151 at page 158.

    a. As is obvious from the comparison, the developer's return on equity and tax-free cash return on equity, using the ground lease alternative, exceed the returns derived by the developer when the purchase alternative is used.

    b. The reasons for the financial results produced by the ground lease alternative include: (1) The smaller equity investment of the developer under the ground lease alternative, (2) The deductibility, for income tax purposes, of the ground rent, (3) The fact that the amount of the developer's equity which is invested in the land under the purchase alternative is not depreciable, and (4) The fact that the amount paid by the developer which is applied to the amortization of the principal of a mortgage is not deductible and the developer is required to borrow less money under the ground lease alternative.

    2. If the development financier is prohibited by state or federal law or regulation from lending on the security of a leasehold interest, *must* the fee interest be subordinated?

    a. Might the improvements be "severed" from the land, thereby enabling the financier to take a mortgage in fee in the improvements?

    1. What problems might such an approach create? How can these problems be solved? For example, if the improvements are severed from the land, can the lessee "sell" the improvements for income tax purposes? See Rev.Rul. 70–607, 1970–2 C.B. 9. Cf. Priv. Ltr.Rul. 8433003.

    b. Might the lessor agree that, if there was a default on the leasehold mortgage, he would defer any claim for rent under the lease until the leasehold mortgage was paid in full?

    1. Would this approach permit the financier to take a leasehold mortgage as security? See Division III, pages 610 to 615 infra.

    c. See generally Halper, *Introducing the Ground Lease,* 15 # 3 Real Est.Rev. 24 (1985); Halper, *Mortgageability of the Unsubordinated Ground Lease, Part II,* 16 # 1 Real Est.Rev. 48 (1986); *Part III,* 16 # 2 Real Est. Rev. 72 (1986); *Part IV,* 16 # 3 Real Est.Rev. 64 (1986); *Part V,* 16 # 4 Real Est.Rev. 60 (1986).

d. The problems involved in the subordination of the lessor's interest are considered briefly in this Division I, see pages 252 to 256 infra and in more detail in Division III, see pages 637 to 649 infra. See also Note, *Purchase Money Subordination Agreements in California: An Analysis of Conditional Subordination,* 45 S.Cal.L.Rev. 1109 (1972); Bovell, *The Subordinated Ground Lease,* 23 Prac.Law. 41 (Sept. 1977); McNamara, *Subordination Agreements as Viewed by Sellers, Purchasers, Construction Lenders, and Title Companies,* 12 Real Est.L.J. 347 (1984).

3. Do all the tenants of the ground lessee have to have AAA–1 credit ratings to protect the lessor and the development financier? In fact, in a normal commercial setting, would this type of tenant composition make sense?

a. Should the lessor and financier be satisfied if the rental received by the ground lessee from tenants with AAA–1 credit ratings covers debt service, real property taxes and operating expenses?

4. If the lessor is willing to release the lessee from liability under the lease upon an assignment of the lease by the lessee, should not the person or entity to whom the lessee proposes to assign be subject to the approval of the lessor?

a. If so, how can this desire on the part of the lessor be achieved and yet leave the lessee the flexibility he desires with respect to assignment of the lease? See generally Todres and Lerner, *Assignment and Subletting of Leased Premises: The Unreasonable Withholding of Consent,* 5 Fordham Urb.L.J. 195 (1977); Kehr, *The Assignability of Commercial Leases,* 9 Real Est.L.J. 197 (1981). See *Kendall v. Ernest Pestana, Inc.,* 40 Cal.3d 488, 709 P.2d 837, 220 Cal.Rptr. 818 (1985), which holds that a lessor must have a reasonable basis on which to refuse to consent to an assignment of a lease even though the lease does not permit the lessee to assign. See also *Tucson Medical Center v. Zoslow,* 147 Ariz. 612, 712 P.2d 459 (1985).

b. See Thompson, *Some Tax Problems on Mid–Stream Modifications and Terminations of Leases,* 4 J.Real Est.Tax'n 214 (1977).

5. A ground lease is treated as a passive activity under Section 469. See Section 469(c)(2). As a result, any losses realized by the lessor from the ground lease will be treated as passive losses unless the ground lease is excepted from treatment as the holding of property for rent, under Reg. Sec. 1.469–1T(e)(3), or the lessor actively participates, both of which seem unlikely in the typical ground lease situation. The net income of a lessor derived from a ground lease, however, is treated as portfolio income if less than thirty percent of the unadjusted basis of the real estate subject to the ground lease is depreciable property. See Reg. Sec. 1.469–2T(f)(3).

If the ground lessor agrees in the lease to defer the lessee's payment of the ground rent until the lessee completes construction of the real estate improvements and the lease provides that the lessor will collect the deferred rent plus interest over the five years following completion of construction, when will the deferred ground rent plus interest be treated as income to a cash basis lessor and deductible by a cash basis lessee? See Section 467; Hamilton and Comi, *The Time Value of Money: Section 467 Rental Agreements Under the Tax Reform Act of 1984,* 63 Taxes 155 (1985); Shenkman, *Impact of the Deferred Rent Provisions of TRA '84 on Real Estate Leasing,* 13 J.Real Est.Tax'n 51 (1985); Allison, *New Rules Increase Exposure of Lessors to Tax on Rents That Will Not Be Received Until Later,* 64 J.Tax'n 8 (1986); Whitesman, *Section 467: Tax Planning for Deferred Payment Leases,* 5 Va.Tax Rev. 345 (1985); Reeves,

Section 467: Its Application to and Effect on Leases Containing Stepped or Deferred Rents, 13 J.Real Est.Tax'n 346 (1986).

6. If the rent payable pursuant to a ground lease amortized the value of the real estate at an interest rate of 11% over the term of the lease and the lessee had an option to purchase for $10 at the end of the term or an option to renew indefinitely at a rental of $10 a year, might the lease be called a mortgage for income tax and other purposes? See Division III, pages 616 to 618 infra, and generally Cunningham and Tischler, *Disguised Real Property Security Transactions as Mortgages in Substance,* 26 Rutgers L.Rev. 1 (1972); Dreier, *Real Estate Leasing Transactions,* 32 N.Y.U.Inst.Fed.Tax'n 1655 (1974); Morris, *Taxation of Leases: Profits and Pitfalls,* 30 Sw.L.J. 435 (1976); Kronovet, *Characterization of Real Estate Leases: An Analysis and Proposal,* 32 Tax Law. 757 (1979); Simonson, *Determining Tax Ownership of Leased Property,* 38 Tax Law. 1 (1984); Lucas, *The Lyon Dethroned: Federal Income Taxation Characterization of Leases and Leasebacks,* 15 Cumb.L.Rev. 431 (1984–85). The Financial Accounting Standards Board in the *Statement of Financial Accounting Standards No. 13, Accounting for Leases,* paragraph 25 at page 24, provides that a ground lease shall not be treated for accounting purposes by the lessee as a lease but rather as a purchase coupled with a financing device if the lease contains an option allowing the lessee to purchase the leased property for a price which is sufficiently lower than the expected fair value of the property at the date the option becomes exercisable, that exercise of the option, at the inception of the lease, appears to be reasonably assured, or the lease transfers ownership of the property to the lessee by the end of the lease term. The Securities and Exchange Commission, Release No. 33–5812, CCH Fed.Sec.L.Rep. ¶ 80,988, ('76–'77 Tr.Bin.), The Comptroller of Currency, P–H Fed.Control Banking ¶ 9680 and the Federal Reserve Board, P–H Fed.Control Banking ¶ 9686 require compliance with the Statement of Financial Accounting Standards No. 13 in financial reports submitted to them. Finally, consider whether, if the developer acquires a ground lease rather than a fee interest, the developer will be considered as engaged in the "activity of holding real property" for the purpose of being considered at risk with respect to qualified nonrecourse financing, under Section 465(b)(6). A lease of real property having a term greater than 30 years has been considered the equivalent of a fee. See Rev.Rul. 60–43, 1960–1 C.B. 687, and *Century Electric Co. v. Comm'r,* 192 F.2d 155 (8th Cir.1951). A lease with a term of less than 30 years might not amount to the "holding of real property". Cf. *Standard Envelope Mfg. Co.,* 15 T.C. 41 (1950); *May Dept. Stores Co.,* 16 T.C. 547 (1951); *Capri, Inc.,* 65 T.C. 162 (1975).

7. The Bankruptcy Code sets out the rights of the parties to a lease and the trustee in bankruptcy upon the bankruptcy of either the lessor or the lessee. " * * * Under the prior Bankruptcy Act, specific forfeiture clauses in leases that provide for automatic or optional termination on the bankruptcy of a party [were] generally effective and enforceable. Under the Code, lessors and secured parties will no longer be able to rely on forfeiture clauses for protection in bankruptcy cases. The Code specifically provides, with certain exceptions, that a forfeiture clause is ineffective to terminate or modify an unexpired lease * * * in a case under Title 11. The result is that all * * * unexpired leases become property of the estate and are subject, with exceptions, to being assumed or assigned by the bankruptcy trustee.

"If the debtor is not in default under an * * * unexpired lease, usually the trustee may assume that * * * lease subject to the approval of the court. The power of the trustee to assume the * * * lease is a federal right that is not affected by a provision in the contract or under nonbankruptcy law designed to prevent assumption.

"If there is a default under an ∗ ∗ ∗ unexpired lease of the debtor, other than a default under a forfeiture clause, the trustee may assume ∗ ∗ ∗ the lease only if the default is cured, damages relating to the default are paid, and adequate assurance of future performance under the ∗ ∗ ∗ lease is provided. With one exception, case law will determine exactly what constitutes 'adequate assurance.'

"Of course, if the default occurs before the commencement of the bankruptcy case and is a 'material breach,' the [lease] may be treated as terminated under nonbankruptcy law. The [other party] undoubtedly will be required to take action recognizing the default or it will be waived. However, if the default is properly noticed, the result may be that the contract is terminated and nothing will pass into the bankruptcy estate for the trustee to assume.

"Whether or not there is a default under an ∗ ∗ ∗ unexpired lease, the trustee has sixty days after the order for relief to assume the ∗ ∗ ∗ lease or it is rejected in a liquidation case. Before confirmation of a plan in a reorganization case, there is no statutory time limit within which the trustee must decide whether to assume or reject the ∗ ∗ ∗ unexpired leases of the debtor. However, a party to a [lease] may request the court to fix a specific time within which the trustee must decide.

"In the ordinary case, rejection of an ∗ ∗ ∗ unexpired lease constitutes a breach as of the commencement of the case. In that event, the creditor's claim for damages arising from the breach is not entitled to priority and is limited to a statutory maximum. If the ∗ ∗ ∗ unexpired lease is assumed before being breached or rejected, the Code describes various administrative priorities accorded to damages from the rejection.

"The trustee may assign ∗ ∗ ∗ unexpired leases of the debtor. However, if the trustee desires to assign an ∗ ∗ ∗ unexpired lease of the debtor, the trustee must first assume the ∗ ∗ ∗ unexpired lease. Even if there is no default to be cured, before the assignment may be made, the trustee must provide adequate assurance of future performance by the assignee. ∗ ∗ ∗ An express antiassignment clause will be ineffective to prevent the trustee from assigning an ∗ ∗ ∗ unexpired lease. This means that a secured party or lessor may be forced into a financial relationship with a complete stranger. ∗ ∗ ∗ The assignment of an ∗ ∗ ∗ unexpired lease relieves the trustee and the estate from any liability arising from a breach that occurs after the assignment.

"There are a number of special provisions in the Code that remedy inadequacies in provisions of the Bankruptcy Act with respect to particular aspects in the rejection of ∗ ∗ ∗ unexpired leases. In the event of a bankruptcy in which the debtor is the lessor, if the trustee rejects the lease, then the lessee may either treat the lease as terminated or remain in possession for the balance of the term of the lease. A lessee who remains in possession may offset damages arising from rejection of the lease against rent reserved under the lease for the balance of the term, but that is the exclusive remedy for those damages." Orr and Klee, *Secured Creditors Under the New Bankruptcy Code,* 11 U.C.C.L.J. 312, 338–342 (1979). See also Shanker, *The Treatment of Executory Contracts and Leases in the 1978 Bankruptcy Code,* 25 Prac.Law. 11 (Oct. 1979); Halper, *Bankruptcy Cancellation Clauses Under the Bankruptcy Reform Act,* 9 # 3 Real Est.Rev. 75 (1979); Fogel, *Executory Contracts and Unexpired Leases in the Bankruptcy Code,*

64 Minn.L.Rev. 341 (1980); Simpson, *Leases and the Bankruptcy Code: The Protean Concept of Adequate Assurance of Future Performance,* 56 Am.Bankr.L.J. 233 (1982); Ehrlich, *The Assumption and Rejection of Unexpired Real Property Leases Under the Bankruptcy Code—A New Look,* 32 Buffalo L.Rev. 1 (1983); Comment, *Landlord's Bankruptcy: An Analysis of the Tenant's Rights and Remedies Under Bankruptcy Code Section 365(h),* 35 Rutgers L.Rev. 631 (1983); Pedowitz, *The Effect of Bankruptcy or Insolvency on Real Estate Transactions— An Overview,* 20 Real Prop., Prob. & Tr.J. 25 (1985); Andrew, *Real Property Transactions and the 1984 Bankruptcy Code Amendments,* 20 Real Prop., Prob. & Tr.J. 47 (1985); Leta, *New Real Estate Issues Under the 1984 Bankruptcy Amendments,* 1 # 4 Prac.Real Est.Law. 13 (1985).

8. See generally Underberg, *Ground Leasing Makes Dollars and Sense for Developers,* 1 # 2 Real Est.Rev. 38 (1971); Halper, *To Buy or Not to Buy,* 13 # 2 Real Est.Rev. 78 (1983); Nelson and Schnall, *An Introduction to Ground Leases,* 4 # 1 Prac.Real Est.Law. 21 (1988).

9. The ground lease as a financing device, the sale and leaseback and the leasehold mortgage are considered in Division III.

e. SELECTED CONSIDERATIONS WITH RESPECT TO THE MEANS OF ACQUISITION

There are certain considerations which must be taken into account in working with any of the means of acquisition which have been discussed to this point. The following materials deal with some of the significant considerations.

(i) FINANCING CONDITIONS AND SUBORDINATION

When real estate is being acquired, there is always the possibility that financing will be required to (1) purchase the property and/or (2) develop the property. Therefore, when acquiring real estate one must consider whether financing is necessary and, if necessary, provide that the availability or receipt of the financing is a condition precedent to the purchaser's obligation to consummate the acquisition. Once it is determined that financing is necessary to acquire or develop, or both, the considerations involved in drafting the "subject to financing" clause become quite important.

"SUBJECT TO FINANCING" CLAUSES IN INTERIM CONTRACTS FOR SALE OF REALTY
Ray J. Aiken
43 Marquette Law Review 265 (1960).

A. Practical Considerations.

* * * Seldom, if ever, does the clause relating to the purchaser's financing requirements spell out more than a short suggestion of the various considerations involved in modern mortgage financing. Indeed, it is as common to see the simple phrase, "subject to financing", inserted randomly in the contract as it is to find any more definitive provision.

* * *

What is, * * * very commonly unrealized by the parties (if not by the brokers) is that "financing" is a term of broad scope, involving a multitude of complexities. There are, for example, the following minimum considerations:

1. What amount is sought to be borrowed? [46]

2. What repayment rate, extending over how long a period of time, is contemplated? [47]

3. What interest rate, and what initial "service" or "discount" charges will be acceptable? [48]

4. Is the contemplated loan to be "conventional", or are FHA or VA loan guarantee benefits to be sought? [49]

46. Specifying the amount in the statement of contingency may afford inadequate protection. In Day v. Kerley, 146 A.2d 571 (D.C.Mun.1958), the contract called for a $13,000 G.I. mortgage, apparently to be arranged for by broker, with seller paying the prevailing discount and service charges. On broker's testimony that buyer had orally authorized him to obtain a $12,000 loan, buyer was estopped, as against seller, from pleading the condition. Much the same result was produced in Probst v. Di Giovanni, 232 La. 811, 95 So.2d 321 (1957), where a contract condition of $35,000 financing at 6% over not to exceed 10 years was held waived by purchaser's letter stating that a $32,000, 15–year commitment was acceptable. The case arose, however, because seller sought to plead the condition in defense of broker's action for commission. In Zigman v. McMackin, 6 A.D.2d 907, 177 N.Y.S.2d 723 (1958), a seller's contention that purchaser was obligated to accept offered financing in any amount reasonably close to the stipulated "not more than $10,000" was rejected. Louisiana strictly enforced the stated loan amount in Savich v. Ruiz, 32 So.2d 415 (La.App.1947). The contract was subject to a $4,000 loan, and the lender to which application was made refused to approve over $3,800. Seller offered to post additional security to bring the loan up to the contract amount. Purchaser held entitled to refuse, and to recover down payment. Much the same type of situation was similarly handled in Antonini v. Thrifty–Nifty Homes, 76 So.2d 564 (La. App.1955), and in Slack v. Munson, 61 So. 2d 618 (La.App.1952).

No case discovered involves an attempted judicial construction of a "subject to financing" clause, lacking any statement of amount of mortgage intended, as to that particular feature.

47. Reese v. Walker, 151 N.E.2d 605 (Ohio Mun.1958), where the contract was "Contingent on securing necessary financing." Purchaser rejected a $10,800, 6.6% 12

year loan, offered in response to his application for a 6% 15–year loan. "The clause would mean to a layman: 'If we can borrow the money we need to finance the purchase on terms we can repay * * *'. Financing in its ordinary meaning connotes more than simply the face amount of a loan. It includes the interest rate, the term, the rate of repayment, and other terms and conditions. It means a loan on terms that the borrower can repay. Under the contract as executed, only the buyers can determine what financing they need. Having signed the contract without specifying what financing was 'necessary financing', the seller is in no position to complain if the buyers state they need a loan with repayments at a certain rate. * * *"

48. Doerflinger Realty Co. v. Maserang, 311 S.W.2d 123 (Mo.App.1958) was a suit by brokers directly against purchasers, who had countermanded payment on their earnest money check. The purchase offer was "subject to their ability to procure a cash loan * * * as per application for same now on file with Doerflinger Realty Co." The application in question specified a 5%, 20–year, $20,000 loan; but agents of the broker emphatically insisted, in their conversations with purchasers, that 5% money was unavailable. There were evidences that purchaser's mother-in-law did not approve of the property, and purchaser himself cited his health as his excuse for withdrawal. Nevertheless, the court held the broker's oral statements that 5% money was unavailable to constitute an effective rejection of purchaser's application, defeating the condition precedent of the main contract, despite the fact that a commitment satisfying the application was obtained well in advance of the contract closing date. "Nothing in the sale contract required them to seek a loan elsewhere or under different terms or under a different application."

49. Schwartz v. Baker, 99 N.E.2d 498 (Ohio App.1950) is a somewhat enigmatic decision on an equally enigmatic clause:

5. What special security-protection provisions (tax and insurance reserves, mortgage life insurance, mortgage repayment insurance, ordinary or special acceleration provisions, etc.) are acceptable, and are they to be deemed part of the specified repayment rate? [50]

6. By whose effort is such loan to be arranged and procured; if by the purchaser (with or without the broker's assistance), what potential sources of the money shall be applied to,[51] and within what span of time? [52]

"$6,900 cash, Bal. of $11,000 thro (sic) FHA, this offer is subject to $10,000 loan." The trial court received extrinsic evidence to the effect that purchasers intended to include non-FHA financing, since FHA guaranties were known to be unavailable on the transaction. On this proof, and the evidence that purchaser made no attempt to procure non-FHA financing, vendor was permitted to enforce the liquidation of damages against the earnest money deposit.

Equally obscure is Johnson v. Graham, 35 So.2d 278 (La.App.1948), where a contract "subject to my ability to secure a loan on the above described property in the amount of $7,100" was alleged, in the pleadings, to have been intended to stipulate the prevailing terms for FHA loans. In any event, the purchaser applied for FHA loan guaranty, and the property was approved for only $6,000. Purchaser then suggested, by letter, that vendor accept a second mortgage for $1,100; and vendor responded with an offer to loan the entire $7,100 on FHA terms. At this point, purchaser withdrew, and broker returned his deposit. The trial court dismissed the vendor's action against the broker on the theory that the contract contemplated third-party financing, not vendor-financing. The appellate court reversed, commenting that "The proviso * * * did not name any specific loan agency." It would probably have been more to the point to state that the proviso did not require that the loan pass FHA appraisal; and that, even had it done so, the purchaser's letter could constitute a waiver. The issue of substitution of vendor for third-party financing, however, is reserved for discussion below.

50. Aside from the purely practical consideration that such special security devices add materially to the cost of the loan, and may render it prohibitive, Fry v. George Elkins Co., 162 Cal.App.2d 256, 327 P.2d 905 (1958) held that a purchaser was not entitled to reject offered financing simply because he objected to a 2% prepayment penalty clause, where his contract was "conditioned upon buyer obtaining $20,000 loan at 5% for 20 years." Buyer evidently decided, after entering into the contract, to migrate to Hawaii. Noting this fact, and the fact that, "It is a matter of common

knowledge that the lending policies of different classes of financial institutions vary greatly", a trial court finding that buyer's application to two banks (ignoring the broker's suggestion that a savings and loan would consider the application) did not constitute good faith, was affirmed. Presumably, the only safe course is expressly to exclude special security devices in the statement of the condition.

51. Kelley v. Potomac Development Corp., 81 A.2d 81 (D.C.Mun.App.1951), involved the failure to explicate, on a printed form of contract, which party was to procure the financing. "(T)he purchaser is to assume, give, place, take title subject to, a first deed of trust secured on the premises. * * *" Decision: "We think the evidence permitted the trial court to conclude that the loan was to be obtained by the (purchaser)."

See also Fry v. George Elkins Co., note 50, supra. Hannah v. Yanke (unreported, Cir.Ct., Milwaukee County, Wis., 1957) ruled similarly on a case where purchaser applied to a savings and loan, was rejected on the ground that the property was insufficient security, and then withdrew. "This one effort to secure a loan does not sustain the (trial) court's conclusion that a bona fide effort was made to secure a loan." Suspect though they may be, the decisions demonstrate the hazard involved in failure to explicate the extent of search which will satisfy the contract. * * *

Callahan v. Siebert, 95 N.J.L. 243, 113 A. 914 (1920) construed the condition rather literally in purchaser's favor. "A further condition of this agreement being that the vendee is to negotiate either the reinstatement of the loan of $5,000 in full in his own name from the present Building and Loan Ass'n * * * or to negotiate from some other association a mortgage of said amount under like conditions. * * *" Purchaser applied to the existing mortgage-holder for reinstatement, which was approved only on condition that purchaser undertake to expend $200 in repainting the building. He refused, but made no effort to procure financing elsewhere. On

---

52. See note 52 on page 248.

7.   If a lender should indicate a willingness to make a mortgage loan, assuming that the interim contract specifies no minimum acceptable terms, may the purchaser refuse the offered loan on the ground that its terms are onerous, without violating the agreement (i.e., must the terms be "satisfactory to purchaser," "reasonably satisfactory to purchaser" or merely "reasonable")? [53]

suit to recover down payment, the court ruled the provisions of the contract to be alternative, and held the purchaser not required to accept the obligation of repainting, nor to seek elsewhere for acceptable financing.   It may have been significant that time was declared to be of the essence of the agreement, and only three days remained during which purchaser might have attempted to procure other financing.   The decision does not specifically comment on the point.

Doerflinger Realty Co. v. Maserang, supra note 48, is the only case discovered in which a purchaser whose application to a named lender was refused was expressly relieved of any obligation to apply elsewhere.   Kovarik v. Veseley, discussed at length in the text below, held that the named lending institution was not "of the essence," but did not affirmatively suggest a duty on purchaser to make further inquiry.   Such duty, however, appears to be implicit in the decision, since the case suggests that the condition could be satisfied at any time prior to the stated closing date. In this respect, is Sorota v. Baskin, 334 Mass. 123, 134 N.E.2d 428 (1956) distinguishable?   The contract was there contingent upon sellers' ability to procure extensions of existing mortgages.   Seller made one unsuccessful attempt to do so, and returned the deposit.   "We hold that the defendants were not required as a matter of law to do any more than they did, and particularly they were under no duty to endeavor to procure the extensions up to the date of performance of the agreement."

Margolis v. Tarutz, 265 Mass. 540, 164 N.E. 451 (1929) and Meyer v. Custom Manor Homes, Inc., 4 App.Div.2d 488, 167 N.Y.S.2d 112 (1957) both demonstrate that a contract obligating the seller to procure the financing, but not specifying the extent of his required diligence, may involve seller in the same sort of difficulty.   In both cases, seller assumed, erroneously as it developed, that the worst consequence of his lack of diligence would be return of the down payment.

52.   The express time-allotment for procurement of financing has been enforced strictly, even in the absence of any provision declaring it "of the essence."   Masson v. Vella, 94 So.2d 454 (La.App.1957) involved a loan approval issued one day after expiration of the 60–day procurement period.   "Since the loan was unavailable during the contract period, this contract then became null and void."   In Hodorowicz v. Szulc, 16 Ill.App.2d 317, 147 N.E.2d 887 (1958), the contract was conditional upon purchasers selling their house, and sellers were given an option to cancel if it was unsold by March 5, 1955.   The sale was not effected until May, and purchasers repudiated the contract.   Reasoning that the contract was initially unenforceable because of the precedent condition, and that sellers had an option of withdrawal after March 5, the court held that the contract lacked mutuality after March 5, and that "there was never a mutually binding and enforceable contract and agreement in effect between the parties."

The time-of-procurement limitation is one aspect of the condition which appears to be for the benefit of both parties.   Woodlark Const. Corp. v. Callahan, 275 App.Div. 857, 89 N.Y.S.2d 67 (1949); Kenney v. Wedderin, 220 La. 285, 56 So.2d 550 (1951); Baker v. Fell, 135 Tex. 375, 144 S.W.2d 255 (1940).   But the financing contingency itself is for purchaser's benefit only, and may be waived by him within the time limitation.   Nyder v. Champlin, 401 Ill. 317, 81 N.E.2d 923 (1948); Morrison v. Mioton, [163 La. 1065, 113 So. 456 (1927)].

53.   In Antonini v. Thrifty Nifty Homes, supra, note 46, the contract specified merely "ability of purchaser to borrow *   *   * $6250 by mortgage loans or loan."   A homestead Association refused to loan over $4,000, but vendor offered to loan the difference at 8% for 1½ years.   "We do not think plaintiff was obligated to accept * * * A fair interpretation of the contract * * * would be that the contract would be enforceable provided purchaser could secure the $6250 loan on the usual and customary terms and conditions, to be repaid over a period of years, such as loans made by any homestead, the FHA, or other long term lending institution."   Lach v. Cahill, 138 Conn. 418, 85 A.2d 481 (1951), construed "mortgage in the sum of $12,000" as meaning "suitable mortgage." Cf. Reese v. Walker, supra, note 47 which upheld the buyer's right to reject a variance of .6% in interest rate, and 3 years in

8. What is the consequence of a prospective lender's withdrawal, after tentative commitment, from his agreement to loan, assuming that neither party to the interim contract foments such withdrawal? [54]

To answer any of these important questions on the basis of an interim contract which merely recites that the transaction is "subject to financing" is to undertake an herculean feat of construction. Whenever it occurs, however, that one of the parties seeks to enforce the contract, and the other takes refuge in the indefinite financing "contingency", the only alternative to judicial construction of the clause is to declare the unenforceability of the sale, frequently in the face of an agreement that is in all other respects unmistakable in its provisions.

repayment period, without discussing whether such mortgage was "usual and customary" or not. The test there was stated to be buyers' determination in good faith "what kind of a loan they need," largely determined by "terms that the borrower can repay." The last-mentioned aspect arose in a different context in Real Estate Management, Inc. v. Giles, 293 S.W.2d 596 (Tenn.App.1956), where a contract was "contingent upon buyer's being able to purchase" two tracts of land owned by third persons. The trial court held that buyer's failure to purchase the other tracts was due to his failure to offer a price for them which was both within his means and "within the bounds of reason," and therefore enforced the contract in favor of seller. In reversing, the court asked, rhetorically, "Did Freeman, a successful businessman, by using the words 'able to purchase,' have reference to his financial ability? Did he intend to unconditionally obligate himself to purchase the * * * tracts at prices he might consider excessive * * * Or * * * is it not reasonably apparent that (he) had reference to his being able to acquire the tracts at prices acceptable to him? The latter appears to be * * * the more logical and reasonable construction." Kovarik v. Vesely, discussed in the text infra, describes the right to select the terms of financing as being "left to the discretion of the buyers." Cf. Callahan v. Siebert, supra, note 51, where buyers were held justified in rejecting a loan because coupled with a $200 repainting requirement; and Fry v. George Elkins Co., supra, note 50, where buyers were held not entitled to reject a loan because coupled with a 2% prepayment penalty clause.

The impact of this problem upon the question of the bona fides of the purchaser in seeking financing is inescapable, and becomes the touchstone of the entire legal problem arising out of these clauses.

54. In re King's Estate, 183 Pa.Super. 190, 130 A.2d 245 (1957) presented such a problem, but failed to resolve it because the plaintiff purchaser failed to plead or argue the point on either trial or appeal. The contract condition was "subject to the securing of a mortgage in the amount of $5,500." A loan association approved an application conforming to the contract, but cancelled the application upon notification that Mr. King had died. At the attempted "closing," seller offered to take Mrs. King's note and mortgage. She sought return of the down payment on the theory that the contract was fatally indefinite, in that it specified no mortgage terms, and was unsuccessful. "It seems to us that the appellant would have been on more substantial grounds had she * * * directed her action at the recovery of the deposit on the basis of her inability to obtain financing * * *"

A comparable, and more provoking circumstance arose in Brandes v. Oram Constr. Corp., 5 Misc.2d 710, 158 N.Y.S.2d 897 (1956). Purchaser had made application for a GI loan. While the same was pending, he withdrew it stating that he had learned that he would require an operation, that his financial circumstances had taken a turn for the worse, and that he anticipated that his future income would be less than that stated in the application and insufficient to permit him to carry the loan. Seller challenged the action as a breach of the agreement. Held, for buyer. "He acted wisely and prudently in withdrawing the application." Cf. Fry v. George Elkins Co., supra, note 50, where buyer decided that he would probably move to Hawaii; and Kelley v. Potomac Development Corp., supra, note 51, where buyer's marriage plans apparently went awry. Suppose buyer simply performs a reanalysis of his future budgetary aspects, and informs lender that his original estimates had been over-optimistic? Is the buyer's assumption of his continued good health the only aspect of the matter which he may correct without penalty?

Cases may arise under such clauses, it is true, which are entirely too plain for argument. On the one hand, the "subject to financing" clause may spell out with uncommon attention to detail the particular financing requirements envisioned by the parties, specifically declare each element thereof as being "of the essence," and positively state that, unless each such element is satisfied, the agreement shall be null and void. Any litigable question arising under such a clause would necessarily be either a straight question of fact, or would arise under some aspect of the law of waiver or estoppel. On the other hand, regardless of the indefiniteness of the clause itself, it could occur that, after diligent inquiry, the purchaser would find it impossible to obtain any amount of financing from anyone on any terms whatever. In such cases, the only legal problem which can arise with respect to the clause is whether it should be construed to express a contingency at all, or whether it was simply inserted for some incidental purpose, not affecting the primary obligations to buy and sell.[55]

* * *

B. Legal Considerations.

The legal problems presented by contracts of this type fall into three categories:

(1) Arguments concerned with the issue whether the clause is susceptible of construction at all;

55. Inexpert draftsmanship of the clause occasionally suggests the applicability of Williston's rule: " * * * if * * * (the parties) * * * intend that the debt shall be absolute, and fix upon the future event as a convenient time for payment merely * * * then the debt will not be contingent; and, if the future event does not happen as contemplated, the law will require payment to be made within a reasonable time." 3 Williston, Contracts, (Rev. ed.) § 799, p. 2246. The rule was applied in Noord v. Downs, 51 Wash.2d 611, 320 P.2d 632 (1958), in permitting seller to collect on a demand note taken in lieu of earnest money, which expressed itself to be payable "on approval of loan to mortgagor by Lincoln Fed. Sav. for purchase of home etc." There appeared to be ample evidence in the case, however, from which the same result might have been reached on a theory of purchaser's waiver of the condition. The appellate court indulges in unabashed fact-finding when it says " * * * the reference to the approval was meant to fix a convenient time for repayment and not to embody a condition limiting the liability of the defendants." It is difficult to perceive, except in cases involving waiver of the condition by purchaser, how a reference to uncertain purchase-money financing could be intended as any-

thing but a conditioning of the obligation. Prima facie, at least, that would seem to be the reasonable connotation of the reference. * * * To the same effect is Pegg v. Olson, 31 Wyo. 96, 223 P. 223 (1924), where the contract provided that the balance of price, after down payment, was to be paid "as soon as C.S. Olson * * * can get a loan through from the government * * *." Substantially identical language relating to sale of purchaser's property, however, was held to express a condition precedent in Biggs v. Bernard, 98 Ohio App. 451, 130 N.E.2d 152 (1954). Declaring that "The essential thing is for the court to look at the contract from the standpoint of the parties at the time they executed it, and the purpose they had in view in doing so," the Kentucky court, in Hawkins & Chamberlain v. Mathews, 242 Ky. 732, 47 S.W.2d 547 (1932) ruled conditional a contract providing terms of payment "as follows: At least $1,500 plus an amount of not less than $6,000 obtained on loan in a building and loan association secured by a first mortgage, to be paid in cash; balance evidenced by notes bearing interest at 6% per annum * * *". Buyers' down payment was returned when the $6,000 mortgage could not be obtained. * * *

(2) Problems of evidence, procedure, and "rules of construction";

(3) Problems of appropriate remedy.

In the first category, the specific questions most obvious for consideration are:

(1) Does such a contract, assuming some degree of failure to explicate the details of the financing contingency, satisfy the requirements of the statute of frauds?

(2) Regardless of the foregoing inquiry, is the contract sufficiently definite and certain to be enforceable, simply as a contract?

In the second category, such main questions arise as:

(1) To what degree are express statements of the details of financing "material" to the contingency?

(2) Which party—vendor or purchaser—has the burden of proof respecting fulfillment or nonfulfillment of the contingency?

(3) What varieties of evidence are competent on the question of the parties' intention in using the ambiguous language of contingency, and of what may judicial notice be taken?

In the third category, the following problems must be faced:

(1) To what extent is the liquidation of damages, customarily provided, enforceable, and by what means?

(2) Are equitable remedies, especially the decree of specific performance, available?

It is true, of course, that many of these questions raise legal problems of far broader scope and application than are immediately involved in the "subject to financing" clause. The same problems arise under an infinite variety of contracts, and their answers are strongly analogous if not identical in principal. * * *

NOTE

1. A purchaser is able to pay for the property in cash. The purchaser, however, is unwilling to go through with the transaction if development financing is not available. Can a "subject to financing" clause be drafted which complies with all of the factors listed in the preceding excerpt?

a. For example, is it practical at the time of acquisition of the real estate to specify precisely the amount of development financing required?

b. How can the foregoing and other problems which might be encountered be handled so as to meet the criteria described in the excerpt, and, at the same time, permit the purchaser some latitude in dealing with development financiers without, in effect, giving the purchaser an option?

c. Sections 2–201, 2–202 and 2–203 of the Uniform Land Transactions Act deal with the considerations applicable to the formal requirements, indefiniteness and open price terms of contracts for the conveyance of real estate. The requirement that the written memorandum contain all the material terms of the agreement is rejected. The only essential term of the writing is a description of the land. The test for sufficiency of the writing is that the writing must be "sufficient to indicate that a contract to convey has been made by the parties." If the parties intend to enter into a binding agreement, the agreement is an enforceable agreement despite missing terms if there is any reasonably certain basis for granting a remedy. If the price of the real estate is left open in an agreement which is nevertheless intended by the parties to be binding, the agreement will not be defeated on the ground of "indefiniteness" or that "an agreement to agree is unenforceable." Rather, the intention of the parties will be followed. See generally Balbach, *Uniform Land Transactions Act: Articles 1 and 2,* 11 Real Prop., Prob. & Tr.J. 1 (1976).

2. In the event the seller retains an interest in the property such as the mortgagee under a purchase money mortgage, or as the lessor under a ground lease, the development financier may, and in most cases will, require subordination of the seller's interest to the security interest held by the development financier.

SUBORDINATION: THE HANDY TEST OF FAIRNESS
Marvin Leon
42 Los Angeles Bar Bulletin 264 (1967).
[footnotes omitted]

* * *

Many times, buyers[,] purchasing land on credit for development purposes, desire to secure as part of the purchase agreement the seller's promise to subordinate purchase money financing to future construction and permanent loans. This agreement, commonly known as subordination, is typically negotiated by the buyer at a time when he is not fully informed as to the exact nature of the financing he will ultimately require. Thus, buyers historically have sought inclusion in land purchase agreements [and subordination agreements] of the broadest and most vague subordination terms. Sellers[,] on the other hand, concerned about the inherent dangers of subordination, generally attempt to negotiate stringent limits on the subordination provisions.

On occasion, sellers who have agreed to subordination in return for an increased purchase price or other concessions have refused to complete the sale of their land [or subordinate their retained interest upon the buyer's request]. Their buyers have thus been required to sue for specific performance. Sellers[,] defending such suits[,] have at times attempted to justify their refusal * * * on the grounds * * * that the subordination clause contained in the land purchase contract [or the subordination agreement itself] was too indefinite and uncertain and[,] therefore, the entire agreement was not one which could be specifically enforced. [As a result, t]he Courts have * * * been concerned with the question of whether the [terms and conditions] of the future loans to which the purchase money loan was to be subordinated were stated with sufficient clarity to be specifically enforceable.

It is not surprising then that * * * counsel concerned with the drafting of subordination clauses [and agreements] were encouraged to take great care to clearly spell out the maximum interest rate of the future loan or loans, the maximum amount thereof, the terms of payment thereof, and the terms and conditions of the note and deed of trust evidencing the new loan. Failing clear and definite provisions in those respects, the subordination clause and[,] therefore[,] the entire contract to purchase the land [or the subordination agreement] would be held unenforceable. * * *

[I]t appeared that the case law had gone so far as to develop an objective standard against which all subordination provisions contained in land purchase contracts [and subordination agreements] might be tested. * * *

However, the * * * decision of the California Supreme Court in Handy v. Gordon [65 C.2d 578, 55 Cal.Rptr. 769, 422 P.2d 329 (1967)] * * * established a new test which must be considered in determining the question of whether the provisions concerning subordination in a land purchase contract [or subordination agreement] make the contract [or agreement] unenforceable, to-wit, the test of fairness. The intrusion of this fairness test into the subordination field will certainly create consternation among developers, lenders and title insurers.

In *Handy* the defendant-seller had agreed to sell approximately 320 acres of land for a minimum down payment plus a $1,200,000 purchase money trust deed on which no payments were to be made for three years. The sales contract provided that the seller would subordinate the purchase money trust deed to later loans to be obtained by the buyer for construction and permanent financing. The construction financing was to have a final maturity date of not more than six years and an interest rate of not more than 7% per annum. The permanent financing was to have a final maturity date of not more than thirty-five years and an interest rate of not more than 6.6% per annum. The maximum amount of the loan depended upon the total number of lots into which the property was to be divided. However, minimum and maximum amounts per lot were agreed to.

When the seller refused to close the sale the plaintiff-buyer sued for specific performance. [T]he defendant-seller contended (i) that the subordination provisions were too indefinite to be enforceable, and (ii) that as a matter of law, the contract was not, as to the defendant-seller, just and reasonable. The Trial Court granted the defendant's motion for judgment on the pleadings. On appeal, the Appellate Court discussed only the issue of whether the subordination provisions of the land sale agreement were uncertain, as a matter of law[,] * * * [and found that the provisions met the certainty test]. The Appellate Court did, however, sustain the decision of the Trial Court on an entirely unrelated ground, finding that [other provisions of] the agreement [having nothing to do with subordination were] uncertain * * *.

The California Supreme Court, in affirming the decision of both the Trial and Appellate Courts, did not even consider the portions of the agreement found to be uncertain by the Appellate Court and on which the Appellate Court relied as the basis for its decision. The Supreme Court turned its attention [only] to the subordination provisions. The Court gave lip service to the certainty test * * * concluding that the test of certainty had been met. But[,] the Court then went on to find that the subordination clause was, as to the defendant-seller, unjust, unreasonable and unfair, and therefore, the purchase agreement was held unenforceable, as a matter of law. In the Court's opinion, a reasonable subordination clause must contain terms that define and *minimize* the risk that the seller's security will be destroyed or impaired by the later loans to which it is subordinated. Among the reasons cited to sustain the Court's holding of unfairness were the following[.]

There were no limits provided as to the borrower's use of the funds[. As a result,] the seller was without assurance that the * * * proceeds of the development loans would actually be used to improve the land that represented the seller's security. [Since t]he loan amounts [were] expressed as absolutes in dollars, there was no assurance that the new loans would not exceed the value of the proposed new improvements to the land, and[, as a result], the seller's security would be impaired. [Lastly, since] a substantial down payment [was not provided for], the subordination agreement could have the effect of placing the * * * defendant[-seller] in the position of receiving nothing for his land. For those reasons, the Court concluded that the contract was not [fair] and reasonable. * * *

We believe it unfortunate that the Court has introduced the test of fairness in subordination cases. Buyers, lenders and title insurers can now never be sure that a defaulting seller will not raise the defense that the buyer has negotiated too favorable a purchase [or subordination] agreement, and[,] therefore, that the agreement is unenforceable. Subjective equity tests will replace objective standards. Further, it now appears that the proceeds of development * * * loans [to which retained interests will be subordinated must] be applied [to] improving the purchased property or the subordination provisions [or subordination agreements] will be unenforceable * * *. We question how title companies will police that requirement so as to assure themselves of the application of loan funds and thus be able to issue title insurance as to the priorities of the new loan. * * *

It further appears that the amount of the * * * subordinating loans must not exceed the value that the new improvements [constructed with the proceeds of the subordinating loans] add to the secured property, or the subordination provision[s or subordination agreement] will be unfair and[,] therefore[,] unenforceable. This means that buyers cannot pay loan fees and commissions out of loan proceeds. Additionally, we must be concerned with providing evidence to lenders and title insurers to prove that the value of the new improvement[s] is equivalent to the amount of the [subordinating] loan[s]. * * *

It is also implied by [the decision in] *Handy* that a substantial down payment must exist to make [the] subordination provision[s or subordination agreement] reasonable, just and fair. Such a requirement could have a deleterious effect on developers who must husband capital for the contingencies which commonly occur in construction. * * *

If, in fact, the concept of fairness, as applied to subordination, is stretched to its ultimate limits, no subordination clause, however carefully drawn, is safe from attack, because subordination, in and of itself, is dangerous to the seller and[,] therefore[,] inherently unfair. [The interest of s]ellers who subordinate can be [terminated] if the superior loans are not paid, and [the sellers do not have the cash necessary] to cure the defaults. Even if the subordinating seller has [the] means, he can be exposed to substantial additional costs and liability to cure foreclosures of superior encumbrances. * * *

[W]e suggest that it may well be the duty of concerned counsel to advise their buyer-clients to request only the most reasonable of subordination provisions [and agreements]. In this connection, buyers should be advised to agree to stringent limitations of the amounts, terms and use of [the] proceeds of the subordinating loan[s]; to make [a] substantial proportional down payment of the purchase price; to provide for interim payments on the purchase money financing; to agree to a substantial payment to the seller at or about the time the subordinating loan is placed of record; to describe in as much detail as possible the proposed improvements to be placed on the property; to secure the specific agreement of the seller that points and loan fees and commissions can be paid from the proceeds of the subordinating loan; to agree to pay [to] the seller[, in reduction of the principal balance of the] purchase money [loan], the excess, if any, of construction and permanent loan amounts over actual development costs * * *; and[,] under no circumstances[,] to attempt to impose on the seller unjust, vague or indiscriminate subordination terms.

One must now constantly remember the motto that *too good a deal may be no deal at all.*

NOTE

1. Is the foregoing discussion of subordination applicable to the subordination of the lessor's interest in a ground lease?

2. If a clause providing for subordination or a subordination agreement satisfies the criteria listed in the excerpt from Professor Aiken's article at pages 245 to 251, will it satisfy the tests described in the preceding excerpt?

3. Can a subordination clause which is both certain and fair be drafted? Consider this question from the standpoint of permitting the purchaser maximum flexibility while fairly protecting the seller's interests. Cf. *Stenehjem v. Kyn Jin Cho,* 631 P.2d 482 (Alaska 1981).

   a. Is there any reason not to limit the purchaser's use of the proceeds of the development financing?

      1. Consider the income tax effects of a distribution to the investors in the purchaser of the excess proceeds of the loan. See generally Bell, *Negotiating the Purchase–Money Mortgage,* 7 # 1 Real Est.Rev. 51 (1977).

b. Is it practical to limit the amount of the loan, to which the seller's interest will be subordinated, to a percentage of the fair market value of the improvements financed through the use of the subordinating loan or to a percentage of the value of the property plus improvements, made and to be made, less the amount of the seller's retained interest?

1. If so, does it matter what the purchaser does with any excess proceeds of the loan, assuming the improvements are constructed?

c. If the purchaser's use of the proceeds of the development financing is to be restricted, what uses should it be restricted to?

1. For example, can the purchaser pay the loan commitment fees out of the proceeds of the loan? Cf. *Kennedy v. Betts,* 33 Md.App. 258, 364 A.2d 74 (1976); *Peoples Bank & Trust Co. v. L & T Developers Inc.,* 434 So.2d 699 (Miss.1983).

4. For a more detailed discussion of subordination see Division III, pages 637 to 649 infra. See generally Korngold, *Construction Loan Advances and the Subordinated Purchase Money Mortgagee: An Appraisal, A Suggested Approach, and the ULTA Perspective,* 50 Fordham L.Rev. 313 (1981); McNamara, *Subordination Agreements as Viewed by Sellers, Purchasers, Construction Lenders, and Title Companies,* 12 Real Est.L.J. 347 (1984); Halper, *Planning and Construction Clauses in a Subordinated Ground Lease,* 17 Real Est.L.J. 48 (1988).

(ii) THE USE OF THE NOMINEE OR STRAW MAN

The acquiring entity, at times, may use a nominee, agent or straw man to carry out certain transactions. For example, a nominee may be used to obtain options on, or acquire, the real estate in order to avoid disclosure of the identities of the principals involved in the acquisition and/or development. In addition, a nominee may be used to secure financing for the acquisition and/or development of the real estate in order to avoid the personal liability of the principals or in order to avoid the application of the usury laws.

STRAW MEN IN REAL ESTATE TRANSACTIONS
Robert N. Cook
25 Washington University Law Quarterly 232 (1940).
[footnotes omitted]

* * *

The * * * straw man may be a natural person, partnership, corporation, or other legal entity. While he may be used to hold title to any type of property, consideration will be given only to certain problems arising from conveyances of land to a straw man. * * *

A. Settlor v. Straw Man
* * *

Following a legitimate conveyance to a straw man, he may refuse to reconvey on demand. If the agreement to convey as directed was oral, then the court must either enforce the Statute of Frauds or create an exception to the statute. It is clear that relief need not be granted.

Most states require a trust of land to be in writing and to be properly signed. In these states, by decision or statute, constructive and resulting trusts need not be in writing because they are created by law. Therefore, the question which arises in an action to enforce an oral trust is whether the court should impose a resulting trust upon the grantee for the benefit of the grantor. The Uniform Trusts Act, and a number of courts, state that a resulting trust for the settlor's benefit arises whenever an oral trust is not enforceable because of the Statute of Frauds. The English decisions and a few of the American state courts have held that upon the grantee's refusing to reconvey on demand a resulting trust for the benefit of the grantor arises. This trust is based on the fact that the original conveyance resulted from the oral promise to hold to the use of the grantor. Other American courts have enforced the oral trust whenever the grantee has permitted the grantor to enter into or to remain in possession and to make valuable improvements, on the theory that part performance takes the oral trust out of the Statute of Frauds. There is decided conflict in the cases as to whether entering into or remaining in possession is in itself sufficient.

*   *   *

B. Settlor's Creditors v. Straw Man

*   *   *

When the transfer of legal title to the straw man was not fraudulent, then the existing creditors [of the grantor] cannot have it set aside. Later, the solvent grantor may become insolvent unless land held by the straw man can be reached by the grantor's creditors. If the passive trust was in writing signed by the grantee, then the Statute of Uses would execute the trust to give the grantor legal title. It is only when the trust is not in writing that the problem of reaching the land arises. Obviously, if the court imposes a resulting or a constructive trust for one of the reasons previously enumerated, the creditors could reach the legal interest through the debtor's equitable interest. But when the court has previously held that the debtor had no equitable interest, is it going to deny relief to his creditors? If the straw man is an honest person, he will stand ready to convey on demand. Thus, to refuse to aid the debtor's creditors to reach this land is to make the Statute of Frauds a means of defrauding. *   *   * [R]ecognizing the true owner as the beneficial or equitable owner would solve this problem.

*   *   *

C. Settlor v. Purchasers from Straw Man

When the owner of land, who is not in possession, conveys by absolute deed to a straw man who orally agrees to reconvey on demand but does not record his deed, there may arise the question whether a bona fide purchaser for valuable consideration from the straw man receives title as against the real owner. In those states where the straw man is trustee under a constructive trust for the benefit of the true owner, the equitable interest of the real owner would be extinguished by a transfer of the legal title to a bona fide purchaser for value. If the grantor has no equitable interest[,] then clearly the purchaser with or without notice would prevail.

The more difficult problem arises when there is a written agreement to reconvey, and neither the deed to the straw man nor the written agreement is recorded. In such a case the grantor would receive legal title under the Statute of Uses and the straw man would have no interest in the land. Only if the purchaser can bring himself within the protection of the recording acts would he be entitled to the land. The written agreement would be similar to an unrecorded deed from the grantee to the grantor. Consequently, all persons protected under a particular recording act would prevail as against this unrecorded written instrument or deed. The fact that the record may indicate that the grantor had title would not be material because his subsequent deed, though unrecorded, would transfer this title to the grantee as to those protected by the recording act.

If the real owner is not in possession and the deed to the straw man is recorded, then clearly all persons protected by the recording act would take free of any unrecorded written agreement or unrecorded deed of reconveyance.

The most difficult case arises when the grantor remains in possession and has either an equitable interest or legal title under an unrecorded deed. It is immaterial whether the deed to the straw man is recorded since bona fide purchasers for value would be entitled to protection in either case provided the grantor's possession was not constructive notice of his equitable or legal interest. In those states where the possession of one claiming an interest in the land is not constructive notice of his claim to those persons protected under the recording act, such persons would have rights superior to the grantor's. If possession does constitute constructive notice, is the possession by the grantor such notice? On this point the courts are divided. Some state that the grantor's possession is never notice of his claim; others that it is always notice; others that it is notice only after a reasonable time has elapsed. In any case, if it can be shown that upon inquiry being made the grantor would have denied having any interest in the land, then the purchaser would prevail. The grantor's ability to testify in an action brought by the grantee's purchaser that he would have disclosed his interest if asked (though in fact he probably would not have done so) gives him an unfair advantage and tends to promote perjury. Therefore, the bona fide purchaser for value from the straw man should be protected in all cases when the real owner or his tenant remains or enters into possession *after a voluntary conveyance to a straw man under an oral trust to convey as directed.*

* * *

D.   Settlor v. Creditors of Straw Man

Whenever the owner of land conveys bare legal title to a straw man under an oral trust to convey as directed, it is probable that the straw man's creditors will seek to have the land sold to pay their claims. For purposes of analysis it will be assumed that the true owner is not in possession, that he has an equitable interest in the land, that the deed to the straw man has been recorded, that the conveyance was not to defraud creditors, and that the straw man has three classes of creditors. The creditors of the straw man or grantee are, first, those who extended credit prior to the deed to the straw man, second, those who extended credit subsequent to such deed but without relying on title in him, and third, those who did rely on title in the straw man at the time of granting credit.

*   *   *

General and judgment creditors of the straw man who never relied on his title will not be protected. The doctrine of estoppel is applied in some states to subordinate the equitable interest to the right of all those who relied on title in the straw man; other states protect those relying only if the straw man, *with the express or implied consent of the real owner,* represented that he owned the land.

If the grantor has only a moral right to the land, either because the transfer was fraudulent or because the agreement to reconvey was oral, then all creditors of the straw man would have rights superior to those of the original grantor so long as the straw man retained title. Even those who extended credit prior to the conveyance could reduce their claims to judgment and have the land sold. Seldom would this happen, however, because the grantee would reconvey to the "true owner" before a lien could be secured. This reconveyance would raise the question whether it was fraudulent and voidable if the straw man was insolvent.

Whether a reconveyance by a straw man to the original grantor is fraudulent as to the straw man's creditors depends upon the attitude of the court toward moral consideration. If a transfer to prefer one creditor over another is fraudulent, then a transfer to discharge a moral debt would likewise be fraudulent. If such a transfer is not voidable for fraud, the court must then determine whether a moral debt is equivalent to a legal debt. At least one court considers a moral obligation to be the same as a legal debt and the reconveyance not fraudulent. Those courts which sustain a reconveyance to a fraudulent grantor, whether or not the straw man's creditors relied, on the ground that the rights of the fraudulent grantor's creditors are superior to the rights of the straw man's creditors aid the fraudulent grantor because his creditors will likely never benefit. However, there is a tendency to protect creditors of the straw man who have relied on his ownership as against the grantor.   *   *   *

Purchase-money trusts

One of the most numerous resulting trusts is the purchase-money trust. It arises from the paying of the purchase price and taking title in the name of a third person who is not related by blood or marriage so as to raise a presumption of a gift. This type of resulting trust may be used because the real purchaser desires to conceal his identity to purchase the land, or to defraud his creditors, or to limit his liability by having a note and mortgage executed by the third person, or for numerous other possible reasons.

It was early decided in New York that the courts had made a mistake when they recognized purchase-money trusts. This type of resulting trust was evidently used frequently to defraud existing and future creditors. Therefore[,] a statute was enacted abolishing the purchase-money trust and making the third person or straw man a trustee for the creditors of the real purchaser. If there are no creditors, the third person retains both legal and equitable title. This is no hardship on the real owner if the third person is a dummy corporation organized and controlled by him for the purpose of holding title to land. Those persons who cannot afford a dummy corporation can still take title in the name of a third person and rely on his moral duty to convey as directed. In either case there is always the danger that the straw man's creditors may have the land sold to satisfy their claims, since a conveyance to the real owner would be set aside in New York as fraudulent, provided the straw man would be left insolvent. However, the New York courts have construed the statute to give an equitable interest to the one paying the price if there has been part performance, conversion of the realty into personalty by a sale, a written trust, or a confidential relationship between the one paying the price and the grantee.

Some New York banks, real estate dealers, and others, have dummy corporations take title to land purchased by them. In addition to enabling the real purchaser to use the land in ways that would not have been permissible if title had been taken in his or its own name, there is no liability under deficiency judgments rendered against the dummy corporation on notes signed by it. If title is taken in the name of such dummy corporation and the note and mortgage duly signed by it, and title is then transferred to * * * the real purchaser, a deficiency judgment could not reach any of [the real purchaser's] assets. But should the [real purchaser] * * * neglect to have title transferred to itself[,] then a deficiency judgment against the dummy corporation would reach other land held for the [real purchaser] * * * and this could not be prevented by a conveyance of title to the [real purchaser] * * * prior to the entering of the judgment. Thus the effect would be almost the same as if the [real purchaser] * * * had signed the note except that the liability would be restricted to the land held in the name of the dummy corporation. If the dummy corporation which executes notes and mortgages immediately transfers title to the [real purchaser] * * * after the note and mortgage have been sold, there will arise the question whether one who secures a deficiency judgment against the dummy corporation under a prior or subsequent note can reach the land thus transferred to the [real purchaser]. * * * Since under the New York statute the dummy corporation and the [real purchaser] * * * are separate legal entities with legal and equitable title in the dummy corporation prior to the conveyance to the [real purchaser] * * * the problem is really the usual one which arises in every case involving fraudulent conveyances—was the conveyance fraudulent as to the plaintiff?

If the [real purchaser] * * * required the dummy corporation to execute a written memorandum stating that it held title as trustee for the [real purchaser,] * * * then the [real purchaser] * * * would have the legal interest under the Statute of Uses, assuming the trust was passive. If the trust was active, then the [real purchaser] * * * would have only the equitable interest. If the dummy corporation was solvent at the time of executing the memorandum, then the gift would not be fraudulent; if the corporation would be left insolvent, then the gift would be fraudulent. The problems are the same as in conveyance of legal title to the [real purchaser]. * * *

Statutes in some states raise a presumption that the title was placed in the name of the third person in order to defraud creditors of the real purchaser. Where this presumption is rebutted, or where there is no statute, the equitable interest of the real purchaser would be prior in time to the rights of creditors of the third party. Being prior in time, only the creditors of the third party who relied should be protected.

If the real purchaser desires to conceal his identity from the vendor, he will have the straw man, who is now an agent for an undisclosed principal, buy the land in [the straw man's] name with money furnished by his principal. From the purchaser's point of view, the transaction is simply a purchase-money trust; from the vendor's point of view the transaction is a contract with or conveyance to the agent of an undisclosed principal.

If A, the agent of P, the undisclosed principal, represents to the vendor, V, that A is buying the property for X, it is clear that a conveyance to A or a contract with A made because of the misrepresentation can be set aside for fraud. Not only would the contract be induced by fraud but there would be such a mistake as to the identity of the purchaser that the contract would be wholly void for want of two parties, unless A was personally bound, in which case it would be voidable by V. This result would follow whether or not V would have sold to P. Usually there are additional factors in this type of case to justify rescission and a right to a reconveyance.

When P knows that V will not sell to him at any price he may employ A to buy the land in A's name. If V owns other land in the neighborhood and P desires to use the land purchased from V in such a way as to reduce the market value of the land retained, then V would be entitled to relief because of the fraud and actual damage. In this type of case there is generally a misrepresentation as to the identity of the real purchaser and as to how the land will be used.

A more difficult problem arises when V does not own other land in the neighborhood and would not suffer any pecuniary loss if P used the land for purposes other than those declared by A. If V had no objection to selling to P at the price paid by A, then the right of V to dispose of his property to whom he pleases has not been damaged. If, however, V [objected] * * * to selling to P at any price and P or A knew this fact, in most states V would be entitled to rescind the contract or to a reconveyance of title if a deed has been executed and delivered to A. So long as title has not been transferred to a bona fide purchaser for value or one entitled to the protection of the recording act, there is no reason why a court should not compel a reconveyance. But, if V learns the identity of the real purchaser before executing and delivering the deed, a conveyance to the real purchaser or his agent would constitute a waiver of the right to compel a reconveyance. The vendor should have rescinded the contract and refused to convey.

Although V may have objected to selling to P at any price, he would have no grounds for rescission or for a reconveyance if at the time of the contract neither A nor P knew this fact. It is permissible for an agent to represent that he is not acting for any one so long as this is not done to induce third persons to deal with him when it is known by the agent or his principal that these persons would not deal with the principal. Consequently, in all of these cases involving the use of a straw man to purchase land for one to whom the vendor would not sell at any price, the validity of the transactions depends upon whether the principal or his agent knew that the vendor would not sell to the principal and whether the agent represented that he was not acting for P. Of course, if A said he was acting for X, then the case would come under those considered earlier. If A can buy from V the land desired by P without representing that he is agent for one other than P and without expressly or impliedly representing that he is not acting for P, the transaction is perfectly valid and free from fraud. Thus the duty is placed upon the owner of the property to inquire of the one seeking to buy whether he is acting for himself or for an undisclosed principal and the name of such undisclosed principal.

* * *

There remains to be considered the case where V is willing and perhaps eager to sell to P, but at a price far in excess of the price asked of others. This type of case may arise from the reputed wealth of P, or from the fact that V knows P needs his land and intends to refuse to sell unless he receives a very high price for it. P may be a factory that intends to buy rural land at the price of such land for farming purposes. All the owners are willing to sell to P, but if they knew all the facts they would demand a higher price. Therefore, P employs a straw man to buy this land, not recording any deeds until all the desired land has been secured. Then the straw man conveys to *P*. The vendors immediately seek to have their deeds set aside on the ground that *A* said he was buying the land for himself, and that he was not buying the land for *P*.

The first question that must be decided is the market value of the land. It may be contended that the price expected from *P* was the true value of the farming land because it was suitable for industrial use. This argument assumes that *P* must have this particular land. Usually *P* does not need the particular land and found it suitable for industrial use because of the low cost per acre. The price of the land is one of the factors that must be considered in determining whether it is suitable for industrial use. If the value of the land for farming purposes is $100 per acre and this price was used to determine the location of a factory, it can hardly be said that the owners of the land should be entitled to $200 per acre. If the courts should treat a purchase by *A* for *P* as fraudulent, entitling *V* to rescind, would this promote the public welfare? If not, should this fact influence the court in determining what is or is not fraudulent? The decisions on this point have treated misrepresentations as to the identity of the real purchaser as not fraudulent where *V* had no objection to selling to the real purchaser but simply wanted a higher price.

NOTE

1. Can the arrangement between the straw and the developer be structured so that the developer has the ability to regain title to the property from a bona-fide purchaser from the straw? Or, will the developer never regain title, if the purchaser from the straw is a bona-fide purchaser?

    a. Obviously, if the developer is in possession of the property and the straw's deed reconveying the property and the agreement to reconvey the property are recorded, the developer is in the best position to regain title from a purchaser from the straw.

        1. Although this approach might be appropriate if the straw is being used to avoid the personal liability of the developer with respect to the financing of the development, is it practical when the developer is using the straw to preserve its anonymity in the acquisition process?

2. Is the analysis proposed in the preceding excerpt applicable to a situation in which the straw is merely acquiring an option to purchase rather than a fee interest?

    a. Might the developer find this situation easier to control while still achieving the objectives sought through the use of the straw?

        1. What steps should be taken to protect the developer in this situation?

3. Does the use of the straw to acquire more than one parcel or option add further complications? If so, what complications?

    a. Is there a way of handling these complications other than using a new straw for each acquisition?

4. Personal liability also may be avoided by the use of an "in rem" mortgage. Division III, pages 776 to 782 infra, discusses the "in rem" mortgage.

5. If the straw is a corporation controlled by the developer, a number of problems are avoided. After the corporation acquires the property and/or negotiates and executes the financing documents, however, a partnership or another form of entity may be used for development and operation of the property. In this regard, a number of income tax problems must be considered.

TAXABILITY AND STRAW CORPORATIONS IN REAL ESTATE TRANSACTIONS

Jerome Kurtz and Charles G. Kopp
22 Tax Lawyer 647 (1969).
[footnotes omitted]

* * *

Tax Problems—Introduction

The use of corporate straws raises troublesome and confusing tax problems. The confusion and doubts seem unwarranted as a policy matter and result more from historical development than careful analysis.

* * *

In deciding whether a straw is a taxable entity, the courts have sometimes discussed the problem in terms of whether the real owners of the property derive any advantage from using a corporation and, if they do, the conclusion that the corporation is an entity which is taxable on the income from the property is presumed to follow. This analysis may well lead to erroneous conclusions for * * * the real question is not whether the use of a corporation to hold title is advantageous to the owners—presumably it always is, otherwise they would not use this form—but rather whether the corporation beneficially owns the property.

* * *

To put the question in perspective, the straw corporation may be compared with an individual straw. If title to real estate is put in the name of an individual straw, there is no doubt that the real owner alone is taxable on the income from the property and not the straw. This result has nothing to do with the question whether the straw exists—he obviously does—or whether he might be paying taxes on some other income which he has, or whether he might, in fact, have income from fees which he charges for acting as a straw in this particular transaction, or whether the beneficial owner gains some non-tax advantage by using the straw. The only question is whether the straw is taxable on the income from the real estate, and this depends on whether the income is his.

* * *

Unfortunately, not all courts have adopted this analysis. The reason they have not is perhaps best explained by a look at history.

Historical Development

Although many cases dealing with straw corporations were decided prior to 1943, the logical starting point for any discussion of the subject is the Supreme Court's 1943 opinion in Moline Properties, Inc. v. Commissioner. In that case, Moline Properties, Inc. sought to have its corporate existence ignored as merely fictitious for tax purposes and to have the gain on sales of real property titled in its name treated as the gain of its sole shareholder.

The facts in *Moline* were as follows: Moline Properties, Inc. was organized in 1928 at the suggestion of the second mortgagee of certain Florida realty owned by one Thompson, who was at all times Moline's sole stockholder and president. Under the mortgagee's plan, Thompson conveyed the property to the corporation, which assumed the outstanding mortgages on the property, in exchange for all but the qualifying shares of stock. Thompson then transferred the stock to a voting trustee appointed by the second mortgagee as security for an additional loan to himself.

From 1928 to 1933, the activities of the corporation consisted of the assumption of a certain obligation of Thompson to the original creditor, the defense of certain condemnation proceedings, and the institution of a suit to remove restrictions imposed on the property by a prior deed. The expenses of the suit were paid by Thompson. In 1933, the loan which occasioned the creation of the corporation was repaid through a refinancing, and control of the corporation was returned to Thompson. In 1934, the corporation leased a portion of the property for a rental of $1,000.

The refinanced mortgage debt was paid in 1936 by means of a sale of a portion of the property titled in the corporation. The remaining property titled in the corporation's name had been sold in three parcels, one each in 1934, 1935 and 1936, the proceeds being received by Thompson and deposited in his bank account.

The corporation had no activity after the sale of the last property in 1936 but was not dissolved. It kept no books and maintained no bank account during its existence, and owned no assets other than those referred to above. The sales made in 1934 and 1935 were reported on the corporation's income tax returns, a small loss being reported in 1934 and a gain of over $5,000 being reported for 1935. Subsequently, Thompson filed a claim for refund on the corporation's behalf for 1935, and sought to report the 1935 gain on his individual return. He reported the gain on the 1936 sale.

The Supreme Court held that the corporation could not be disregarded for tax purposes in this case, and set forth the following principle which has been stated over and over again in later cases:

> "The doctrine of corporate entity fills a useful purpose in business life. Whether the purpose be to gain an advantage under the law of the state of incorporation or to avoid or to comply with

the demands of creditors or to serve the creator's personal or undisclosed convenience, so long as that purpose is the equivalent of business activity or is followed by the carrying on of business by the corporation, the corporation remains a separate taxable entity."

Applying the foregoing principle to the facts in the case, the Supreme Court said:

"The petitioner corporation was created by Thompson for his advantage and had a special function from its inception. At that time it was clearly not Thompson's alter ego and his exercise of control over it was negligible. It was then as much a separate entity as if its stock had been transferred outright to third persons. The argument is made by petitioner that the force of the rule requiring its separate treatment is avoided by the fact that Thompson was coerced into creating petitioner and was completely subservient to the creditors. But this merely serves to emphasize petitioner's separate existence. * * * Business necessity, i.e., pressure from creditors, made petitioner's creation advantageous to Thompson."

Although the decision in this case may have been correct—after all Thompson had, for tax purposes, treated the corporation as the taxpayer by filing corporate returns showing all the income and expenses of the property and paying tax—the language of the opinion is at the root of the trouble in this area.

Problems with Moline Approach

Evidence of the difficulties stemming from *Moline* can be seen in cases such as Paymer v. Commissioner. In that case, two parcels of income-producing real estate owned by two partners were transferred respectively to two newly organized corporations in order to prevent possible attachment of the real estate by creditors of one of the partners. The partners each received half of the stock of the grantee corporations. The corporate minutes expressly stated that the corporations received the property as mere titleholders and that the full beneficial ownership and control and rights to profits remained in the two partners. The corporation had no further meetings and no office or bank accounts.

Six years after incorporation, one of the corporations (Raymep) obtained a loan from an insurance company and, as part security for the loan, executed an assignment of all the lessor's rights in two leases on the property and expressly covenanted that it was the sole lessor.

The second corporation (Westrich) never had any activity after it took title to the real estate.

The Court of Appeals for the Second Circuit held that the second corporation was a passive dummy that could be disregarded for tax purposes but that Raymep, which engaged in the financing transaction, was not a mere dummy and should not be disregarded for tax purposes. The court said:

> "We think that Raymep was active enough to justify holding that it did engage in business in 1938. The absence of books, records and offices and the failure to hold corporate meetings are not decisive on that question. Though Raymep was organized solely to deter creditors of one of the partners, it apparently was impossible or impracticable to use it solely for that purpose when it became necessary or desirable to secure the above mentioned loan in a substantial amount. * * *

> "Westrich, however, was at all times but a passive dummy which did nothing but take and hold the title to the real estate conveyed to it. It served no business purpose in connection with the property and was intended to serve only as a blind to deter the creditors of one of the partners."

The *Paymer* court did not face the question of the relevance of the corporate resolutions indicating that the corporations were acting as nominal title holders. The activity of Raymep does not seem inconsistent with its role as a straw. Being the record title holder, it might well be required to execute financing documents in that capacity. The business activity test set forth in *Paymer* which is derived from *Moline* seems entirely inappropriate where the corporate records clearly indicate from the outset that the corporation is a straw and its subsequent activities are consistent with its role as a straw. * * *

The Agency Approach

* * *

The foundation for the agency approach to the problem actually goes all the way back to *Moline*. In that case the Supreme Court, while setting forth the test discussed above, pointed out that there was no contract of agency nor the usual incidents of an agency relationship in the case before it. This language naturally suggested that the Court might not have taxed the income to the corporation had it been shown that the corporation was acting pursuant to an agency contract with its shareholder.

A few years after *Moline,* in National Carbide Corporation v. Commissioner of Internal Revenue, the Supreme Court had the opportunity to consider a case firmly grounded on the agency theory. In that case, a parent corporation had entered into a contract with three of its subsidiaries under which the parent agreed to make available to the subsidiaries certain assets, executive management and working capital in return for which the subsidiaries agreed to turn over to the parent all of their profits from operations except a nominal amount. The Supreme Court held that ownership and control of a subsidiary does not constitute an agency relationship for tax purposes, that the contractual arrangements were entirely consistent with a corporation-sole stockholder relationship whether or not any agency relationship existed (and with other relationships as well), and that the subsidiaries were all taxable on their entire net income.

The Court went on to state, however:

"What we have said does not foreclose a true corporate agent or trustee from handling the property and income of its owner-principal without being taxable therefor * * *. If the corporation is a true agent, its relations with its principal must not be dependent upon the fact that it is owned by the principal, if such is the case. Its business purpose must be the carrying on of the normal duties of an agent."

The dicta in *Moline* and *National Carbide* have been followed in several instances by the Tax Court. In two cases decided after *Moline*, but before *National Carbide*, the Tax Court held against the Commissioner on the theory that the titleholding corporation was an "agent" of the beneficial owner and was, therefore, not taxable on the income received from the property held in its name. First, in *Worth Steamship Corporation*, the Tax Court held that a corporation with record title to a steamship and an agreement to operate the ship for a joint venture owning the vessel was not taxable on the net income earned from operating the ship. The fees paid to the "agent" corporation for managing the ship's operations were reported by the corporation as its income and a tax paid thereon. In addition to a complete set of documents clearly stating that the corporation was merely holding title for the beneficial owners rather than for itself, the record in this case indicated that the beneficial owners of the vessel were not all shareholders of the titleholding corporation. One of the three joint venturers held no stock in the corporation. * * *

[Second,] in *Caswal Corporation*[,] the Tax Court held that a corporation was not taxable on the rental income from real property titled in its name because it was acting only in a fiduciary capacity (in this case called a "trustee" rather than an "agent" because the documents in the case described the corporation as "trustee" rather than "agent" for the beneficial owners) in collecting and remitting net rentals to its shareholders, the beneficial owners of the property.

The court's approach to the problem was as follows:

"We need not say here * * * that the separate entity of petitioner is to be disregarded. * * * We shall assume that it was an existing and functioning corporation which was operated for the purpose of acting as fiduciary. As such, its existence separate from that of stockholders or trust beneficiaries is to be respected. But neither do we feel free to disregard the trust instrument or its effect upon the relationship of the parties. * * *

"That petitioner did not actually engage in any business in its own right also seems clear. The mere collection and transmittal of the rents, with such incidental activities as negotiating with tenants and keeping the property in repair, do not on this record justify dignifying petitioner's operations as engaging in business, any more than would have been the case if an unrelated corporate fiduciary had done the same. * * * Petitioner's business, if any, was acting as fiduciary, not owning and operating an enterprise."

Problems of Proof

There are, of course, considerable difficulties facing courts in applying the agency approach in certain situations. These difficulties involve making factual determinations as to whether activities performed by a corporation are performed in the capacity of beneficial owner or in the capacity of agent for the beneficial owner. Closely held corporations are controlled directly by their shareholders, just as agents are controlled by their principals. Therefore, where the shareholders of a closely held corporation argue that the corporation is in reality their agent, it is difficult to establish an agency relationship since there are few meaningful criteria available for determining the capacity in which the corporation really is acting. Many facts relied upon in support of an agency relationship are also consistent with a shareholder-corporation relationship.

The proof questions, however, only seem difficult where the stock of the corporation purporting to act as an agent as to property is owned by the beneficial owners of the property. There is little difficulty in making this determination where the beneficial owners have no interest in the stock of the corporation. * * *

* * * It seems appropriate that the taxpayer be faced with a substantial burden of proof where he claims that a corporation is not the beneficial owner of property titled in its name. But the burden of proof should not be insurmountable—the presumption should not be conclusive against him. Where the corporate documents are clear from the beginning that the corporation is an agent and where its activities are consistent with its agent's role, the agency should be recognized. Moreover, an agent may well have activities in connection with the property, such as signing documents incident to its role as title holder.

The burden of proof problem could be more easily met by individuals wishing to use corporate straws if they used corporate straws in which they had no interest as shareholders. * * *

SUMMARY AND RECOMMENDATIONS

To summarize, the basic problem of straw corporations should not be a theoretical one of whether a corporation should be ignored for tax purposes or whether it should be viewed as a taxable entity where the shareholder-owners chose to use the corporate form to hold legal title for non-tax reasons, but rather should be one of proof of who owns the property. * * *

It is believed * * * that a taxpayer should be relatively safe in having the income or loss from real estate taxed directly to him where he transfers record title to a corporation formed to act as an *agent* for himself, the beneficial owner.

In the "agency" approach, the importance of carefully drawn documents clearly describing the limited purposes, duties and powers of the corporate agent or nominee and the control and beneficial ownership in the principal cannot be overstated. A straw corporation should be recognized as such if (1) it sets forth in its articles of incorporation that its corporate powers are limited to holding title to property on behalf of others and not itself, (2) it executes appropriate agreements and corporate resolutions spelling out clearly that the corporation's sole business is acting as agent and nominal titleholder for the beneficial owners, (3) under the terms of its agreements with the beneficial owners, the corporation has no discretionary authority to act with respect to the property titled in its name but may act only upon written direction from the beneficial owners, (4) the corporation agrees by contract to terminate the agency relationship upon notice from the beneficial owners and to retransfer legal title to such owners at their direction, (5) all income and expenses with respect to the property are paid to and out of the beneficial owners' bank account, the only funds passing through the straw corporation's bank account being the fees it receives for acting as nominal titleholder and executing specific documents on behalf of the beneficial owners, and amounts which it pays out for professional fees, etc., incurred as a result of conducting its business as an agent, and (6) all other corporate documents are consistent with the proposition that the straw corporation has no interest in, or duties or responsibilities toward, the property except to perform purely ministerial tasks at the direction of the real owners. And, as a final and important step in avoiding difficult proof problems concerning the tax status of the straw corporation as an agent, the shareholders of the straw corporation should be different from and independent of the beneficial owners of the property.

* * *

NOTE

1. See generally Kalb and Lapidus, *Nominee Corporations: Legislation Is the Only Solution*, 5 J.Real Est. Tax'n 142 (1978); Kaster, *Real Estate Nominees*, 55 Taxes 696 (1977); Stogel and Jones, *Straw and Nominee Corporations in Real Estate Tax Shelter Transactions*, 1976 Wash.U.L.Q. 403; Miller, *The Nominee Conundrum: The Live Dummy Is Dead, but the Dead Dummy Should Live*, 34 Tax L.Rev. 213 (1979); Horwood, *The Corporate Nominee/General Partner*, 37 N.Y.U.Inst.Fed.Tax'n 14–1 (1979); Falk, *Nominees, Dummies and Agents: Is It Time for the Supreme Court to Take Another Look?*, 63 Taxes 725 (1985).

2. If the straw corporation is considered a non-entity or an agent, the deductible expenses, if any, paid while the real estate is being acquired and the construction financing obtained are deductible by the developer. If, however, the straw corporation is considered an entity and not an agent, the expenses, if deductible, must be deducted by the straw corporation, and the payment of

these expenses by the developer may be considered capital contributions by the developer to the straw corporation.

a. Any income received from the real estate during this period is taxed to the developer if the straw corporation is considered a non-entity or an agent. Cf. *Louis Steinmetz*, 32 CCH Tax Ct.Mem. 969 (1973). If the straw corporation is considered an entity and not an agent, it is treated as having received the income and any payment to the developer of the income may be considered a dividend. See e.g., *Preferred Properties, Inc.*, 35 Tax Ct.Mem. 68 (1976); *Carver v. United States*, 412 F.2d 233 (Ct.Cl. 1969). For a discussion of the income tax treatment of dividends see Division IV, pages 1112 to 1115 infra.

b. The reconveyance of the real estate by the straw corporation to the developer is not a taxable event if the straw corporation is a non-entity or agent. If it is an entity and not an agent, the reconveyance may be considered a liquidation of the straw corporation. If the reconveyance is considered a liquidation, the corporation will recognize income to the extent the value of the real estate exceeds the corporation's basis in it and the developer will recognize income to the extent the value of the real estate less the liabilities to which it is subject exceeds the basis of the developer in his interest in the straw corporation. The value of the real estate less the liabilities to which it is subject can be greater than the developer's basis in his interest in the corporation in a situation in which the real estate consists of a number of contiguous parcels separately acquired, and development financing for the project to be placed on the real estate has been arranged and closed. See *David F. Bolger*, 59 T.C. 760 (1973), app. dis. without opinion, (2d Cir.1974), in which the Tax Court found straw corporations to be entities and not agents but did not reach the liquidation issue since it found that the fair market value of the real estate was equal to the liabilities to which it was subject. See Lurie, *Bolger's Building: The Tax Shelter that Wore No Clothes*, 28 Tax L.Rev. 355 (1973).

3. If the stockholders of the straw corporation are not the participants in the developer or the developer itself, does this state of facts raise the spectre of some of the problems discussed in the preceding excerpt from Cook, *Straw Men in Real Estate Transactions*, at pages 256 to 263 supra?

a. Is an agreement to reconvey real estate to the developer an executory contract which could be avoided by a trustee in bankruptcy of the straw?

4. If the straw corporation is formed for the purpose of avoiding the personal liability of the developer, or the participants in the developer, for the acquisition or development financing, would the developer, or the participants in the developer, want the straw corporation considered the developer's agent?

a. Can a straw corporation be considered an agent of a developer for income tax purposes, but not for general agency purposes?

1. Can an agreement be drafted which would produce this result? If so, how?

b. One use of a straw corporation suggested earlier in these materials, see pages 114 to 115 supra, is to hold the real estate during the construction period to avoid the personal liability of the developer for any liabilities which might arise during construction. If used in this context, the corporation certainly will not be considered a nonentity for income tax purposes. Will the use of the agency approach accomplish the purpose of avoiding personal liability? Might the use of the corporation for the entire construction period push the agency approach too far, even in an income tax sense?

5. If applicable state or federal laws or regulations do not permit a lender to make an "in rem" mortgage (the lender, in the event of default, will collect the debt only out of the property taken as security), are the laws or regulations satisfied by the personal liability of a straw corporation?

    a. If a state usury statute limits the interest that can be charged to individuals, including partnerships, and the developer is a partnership, can the usury limitation be avoided by making the loan to a straw corporation? See Division III, pages 804 to 812 infra.

6. Despite the suggestion in the above excerpt that taxpayers should be relatively safe if the straw corporation is formed to act as an agent, the cases decided and rulings issued prior to 1981, favored the government especially when the developer, or the participants in the developer, owned the stock in, or controlled, the corporation. See e.g. *Carver v. United States,* 412 F.2d 233 (Ct. Cl.1969); *Dave Stillman,* 60 T.C. 897 (1973); *Sam C. Evans,* 33 CCH Tax Ct. Mem. 1192 (1974), affirmed, 557 F.2d 1095 (5th Cir.1977); *Collins, III v. United States,* 386 F.Supp. 17 (S.D.Ga.1974), affirmed mem., 514 F.2d 1282 (5th Cir. 1975); *William Strong,* 66 T.C. 12 (1976), affirmed, 553 F.2d 94 (2d Cir.1977); *Maclin P. Davis, Jr.,* 66 T.C. 260 (1976), affirmed, 585 F.2d 807 (6th Cir.1978); *John Ogiony,* 38 CCH Tax Ct.Mem. 125 (1979), affirmed, 617 F.2d 14 (2d Cir.1980); Priv.Ltr.Rul. 7751012; Priv.Ltr.Rul. 7950003; Priv.Ltr.Rul. 8142004. There were, however, a few cases and rulings which recognized the "nominee" status of the corporation. See e.g. *Jacqueline, Inc.,* 37 CCH Tax Ct.Mem. 937 (1978); *Van Sickle Development Co., Inc.,* 37 CCH Tax Ct.Mem. 707 (1978); *Milbrew, Inc.,* 48 CCH Tax Ct.Mem. 1485 (1984); Rev.Rul. 75–31, 1975–1 C.B. 10; Rev.Rul. 76–26, 1976–1 C.B. 10.

7. After a long period, marked by a lack of success in persuading the Internal Revenue Service and the courts, as illustrated above, that a corporation formed for the purpose of avoiding usury limits or personal liability or maintaining anonymity should be ignored or treated as an agent, the Tax Court finally found what it felt were the appropriate facts on which to base a holding that a corporation was an agent. In *Joseph A. Roccaforte, Jr.,* 77 T.C. 263 (1981), the taxpayers conceded that a corporation, formed to avoid usury limits, was too active to be ignored for income tax purposes. The Tax Court, however, was persuaded that the corporation should be treated as an agent of the taxpayers' limited partnership. The operation of the corporation and its relationship with the limited partnership, in the opinion of the Tax Court, complied with five of the six factors necessary to constitute the corporation a true agent as described by the Supreme Court in *National Carbide Corporation v. Comm'r,* 336 U.S. 422, 69 S.Ct. 726, 93 L.Ed. 779 (1949). The five factors complied with were the following: (1) The corporation operated in the name and for the account of the limited partnership; (2) The limited partnership was bound by the actions of the corporation; (3) All the money received by the corporation was transmitted to the limited partnership; (4) The corporation's receipt of income was attributable to the services of employees of, and assets belonging to, the limited partnership; and (5) The corporation's business purpose was carrying on the normal duties of an agent. The sixth factor which required that the corporation's relations with the limited partnership not be dependent on the fact that it was owned by the limited partnership was not complied with since the stock of the corporation was owned by the participants in the limited partnership. The Tax Court felt that each of the factors was

entitled to equal weight and since five of the six had been complied with the corporation should be treated as an agent of the limited partnership.

Unfortunately, the Fifth Circuit Court of Appeals disagreed with the analysis of the Tax Court and reversed its decision in *Roccaforte v. Comm'r*, 708 F.2d 986 (5th Cir.1983). The Fifth Circuit Court of Appeals held that the six factors are not all of equal weight. The fifth and sixth factors—business purpose to act as an agent and relations not dependent on ownership—are mandatory prerequisites to treatment as an agent. Since the corporation was owned by the participants in the limited partnership and the taxpayers could not establish that the agency relationship was an arm's length arrangement, the corporation could not be treated, for income tax purposes, as a true agent.

Subsequent to the Fifth Circuit Court of Appeals' decision in *Roccaforte v. Comm'r*, supra, the United States Claims Court indicated its agreement with the Fifth Circuit by holding that a corporation was not an agent when it was controlled by the limited partnership for which it acted, see *Vaughn v. United States*, 3 Cl.Ct. 316 (1983), affirmed, 740 F.2d 941 (Fed.Cir.1984), and was an agent when, while owned by certain members of the limited partnership for which it acted, it was not controlled by the partnership, see *Raphan v. United States*, 3 Cl.Ct. 457 (1983), affirmed, 759 F.2d 879 (Fed.Cir.1985). In *Florenz R. Ourisman*, 82 T.C. 171 (1984), a case which was not appealable to the Fifth Circuit Court of Appeals, the Tax Court, with some dissent, reaffirmed its analysis and followed its decision in *Joseph A. Roccaforte, Jr.*, 77 T.C. 263 (1981). The decision of the Tax Court in *Florenz R. Ourisman*, supra, however, was reversed by the Fourth Circuit Court of Appeals using the same analysis that the Fifth Circuit had used to reverse the Tax Court's decision in *Joseph A. Roccaforte, Jr.*, supra. See *Ourisman v. Comm'r*, 760 F.2d 541 (4th Cir.1985).

The Tax Court, however, continued to follow the analysis it had adopted in *Roccaforte v. Comm'r*, supra, in cases which were appealable to Circuit Courts of Appeal other than the Fourth or Fifth Circuit, and its position was finally accepted by the Sixth Circuit Court of Appeals in *Jesse C. Bollinger, Jr.*, 48 CCH Tax Ct.Mem. 1443 (1984), affirmed, 807 F.2d 65 (6th Cir.1986), affirmed, ___ U.S. ___, 108 S.Ct. 1173, 99 L.Ed.2d 357 (1988). In cases which were appealable to the Fourth and Fifth Circuits the Tax Court continued to find for the taxpayers in cases in which the corporation was not literally controlled by the partnership. The Fourth and Fifth Circuits, however, rebuffed the Tax Court's efforts in this regard holding that control by a partnership included a situation in which a general partner who owned, at the minimum, 54% of the partnership also owned 50% of the corporation, while the other 50% of the corporation was owned by the spouse of the general partner. See *Gary R. Frink*, 49 CCH Tax Ct.Mem. 386 (1984), reversed on this issue, 798 F.2d 106 (4th Cir.1986), vacated and remanded, ___ U.S. ___, 108 S.Ct. 1264, 99 L.Ed.2d 476 (1988), and *George v. Comm'r*, 803 F.2d 144 (5th Cir.1986), vacated and remanded, ___ U.S. ___, 108 S.Ct. 1264, 99 L.Ed.2d 476 (1988). The Supreme Court, however, on appeal of *Comm'r v. Jesse C. Bollinger, Jr.*, supra, determined that the Tax Court's original position in *Roccaforte v. Comm'r*, supra, was correct.

COMMISSIONER v. BOLLINGER

Supreme Court of the United States, 1988.
—— U.S. ——, 108 S.Ct. 1173, 99 L.Ed.2d 357.

* * *

Justice SCALIA delivered the opinion of the Court.

Petitioner the Commissioner of Internal Revenue challenges a decision by the United States Court of Appeals for the Sixth Circuit holding that a corporation which held record title to a real property as agent for the corporation's shareholders was not the owner of the property for purposes of federal income taxation. 807 F.2d 65 (1986).

* * *

I

Respondent Jesse C. Bollinger, Jr., developed, either individually or in partnership with some or all of the other respondents, eight apartment complexes in Lexington, Kentucky. (For convenience we will refer to all the ventures as "partnerships.") Bollinger initiated development of the first apartment complex, Creekside North Apartments, in 1968. The Massachusetts Mutual Life Insurance Company agreed to provide permanent financing by lending $1,075,000 to "the corporate nominee of Jesse C. Bollinger, Jr." at an annual interest rate of eight percent, secured by a mortgage on the property and a personal guaranty from Bollinger. The loan commitment was stuctured in this fashion because Kentucky's usury law at the time limited the annual interest rate for noncorporate borrowers to seven percent. Ky.Rev.Stat. §§ 360.010, 360.025 (1972). Lenders willing to provide money only at higher rates required the nominal debtor and record title holder of mortgaged property to be a corporate nominee of the true owner and borrower. On October 14, 1968, Bollinger incorporated Creekside, Inc., under the laws of Kentucky; he was the only stockholder. The next day, Bollinger and Creekside, Inc., entered into a written agreement which provided that the corporation would hold title to the apartment complex as Bollinger's agent for the sole purpose of securing financing, and would convey, assign, or encumber the property and disburse the proceeds thereof only as directed by Bollinger; that Creekside, Inc., had no obligation to maintain the property or assume any liability by reason of the execution of promissory notes or otherwise; and that Bollinger would indemnify and hold the corporation harmless from any liability it might sustain as his agent and nominee.

Having secured the commitment for permanent financing, Bollinger, acting through Creekside, Inc., borrowed the construction funds for the apartment complex from Citizens Fidelity Bank and Trust Company. Creekside, Inc., executed all necessary loan documents including the promissory note and mortgage, and transferred all loan proceeds to Bollinger's individual construction account. Bollinger acted as general contractor for the construction, hired the necessary employees, and paid the expenses out of the construction account. When construction was completed, Bollinger obtained, again through Creekside, Inc., permanent financing from Massachusetts Mutual Life in accordance with the earlier loan commitment. These loan proceeds were used to pay off the Citizens Fidelity construction loan. Bollinger hired a resident manager to rent the apartments, execute leases with tenants, collect and deposit the rents, and maintain operating records. The manager deposited all rental receipts into, and paid all operating expenses from, an operating account, which was first opened in the name of Creekside, Inc., but was later changed to "Creekside Apartments, a partnership."

* * *

Following a substantially identical pattern, seven other apartment complexes were developed by respondents through seven separate partnerships. For each venture, a partnership executed a nominee agreement with Creekside, Inc., to obtain financing. (For one of the ventures, a different Kentucky corporation, Cloisters, Inc., in which Bollinger had a 50 percent interest, acted as the borrower and titleholder. For convenience, we will refer to both Creekside and Cloisters as "the corporation.") * * * The corporation had no assets, liabilities, employees, or bank accounts. In every case, the lenders regarded the partnership as the owner of the apartments and were aware that the corporation was acting as agent of the partnership in holding record title. The partnerships reported the income and losses generated by the apartment complexes on their partnership tax returns, and respondents reported their distributive share of the partnership income and losses on their individual tax returns.

The Commissioner of Internal Revenue disallowed the losses reported by respondents, on the ground that the standards set out in National Carbide Corp. v. Commissioner, 336 U.S. 422 (1949), were not met. * * *

II

For federal income tax purposes, gain or loss from the sale or use of property is attributable to the owner of the property. * * * The problem we face here is that two different taxpayers can plausibly be regarded as the owner. Neither the Internal Revenue Code nor the regulations promulgated by the Secretary of the Treasury provide significant guidance as to which should be selected. It is common ground between the parties, however, that if a corporation holds title to property as agent for a partnership, then for tax purposes the partnership and not the corporation is the owner. Given agreement on that premise, one would suppose that there would be agreement upon the conclusion as well. For each of respondents' apartment complexes, an agency agreement expressly provided that the corporation would "hold such property as nominee and agent for" the partnership, App. to Pet. for Cert. 21a, n. 4, and that the partnership would have sole control of and responsibility for the apartment complex. The partnership in each instance was identified as the principal and owner of the property during financing, construction, and operation. The lenders, contractors, managers, employees, and tenants—all who had contact with the development—knew that the corporation was merely the agent of the partnership, if they knew of the existence of the corporation at all. * * *

The Commissioner contends, however, that the normal indicia of agency cannot suffice for tax purposes when, as here, the alleged principals are the controlling shareholders of the alleged agent corporation. That, it asserts, would undermine the principle of Moline Properties v. Commissioner, 319 U.S. 436 (1943), which held that a corporation is a separate taxable entity even if it has only one shareholder who exercises total control over its affairs. * * *

The parties have debated at length the significance of our opinion in National Carbide Corp. v. Commissioner, supra. In that case, three corporations that were wholly owned subsidiaries of another corporation agreed to operate their production plants as "agents" for the parent, transferring to it all profits except for a nominal sum. The subsidiaries reported as gross income only this sum, but the Commissioner concluded that they should be taxed on the entirety of the profits because they were not really agents. We agreed, reasoning first, that the mere fact of the parent's control over the subsidiaries did not establish the existence of an agency, since such control is typical of all shareholder-corporation relationships, id., at 429–434; and second, that the agreements to pay the parent all profits above a nominal amount were not determinative since income must be taxed to those who actually earn it without regard to anticipatory assignment, id., at 435–436. We acknowledged, however, that there was such a thing as "a true corporate agent . . . of [an] owner-principal," id., at 437, and proceeded to set forth four indicia and two requirements of such status, the sum of which has become known in the lore of federal income tax law as the "six National Carbide factors":

> "[1] Whether the corporation operates in the name and for the account of the principal, [2] binds the principal by its actions, [3] transmits money received to the principal, and [4] whether receipt of income is attributable to the services of employees of the principal and to assets belonging to the principal are some of the relevant considerations in determining whether a true agency exists. [5] If the corporation is a true agent, its relations with its principal must not be dependent upon the fact that it is owned by the principal, if such is the case. [6] Its business purpose must be the carrying on of the normal duties of an agent." Id., at 47 (footnotes omitted).

* * *

The Commissioner contends that * * * two National Carbide factors are not satisfied in the present case. To take the last first: The Commissioner argues that here the corporation's business purpose with respect to the property at issue was not "the carrying on of the normal duties of an agent," since it was acting not as the agent but rather as the owner of the property for purposes of Kentucky's usury laws. We do not agree. It surely was not acting as the owner in fact, since respondents represented themselves as the principals to all parties concerned with the loans. Indeed, it was the lenders themselves who required the use of a corporate nominee. Nor does it make any sense to adopt a contrary-to-fact legal presumption that the corporation was the principal, imposing a federal tax sanction for the apparent evasion of Kentucky's usury law. To begin with, the Commissioner has not established that these transactions were an evasion. Respondents assert without contradiction that use of agency arrangements in order to permit higher interest was common practice, and it is by no means clear that the practice violated the spirit of the Kentucky law, much less its letter. It might well be thought that the borrower does not generally require usury protection in a transaction sophisticated enough to employ a corporate agent—assuredly not the normal modus operandi of the loan shark. That the statute positively envisioned corporate nominees is suggested by a provision which forbids charging the higher corporate interest rates "to a corporation, the principal asset of which shall be the ownership of a one (1) or two (2) family dwelling." Ky.Rev.Stat. § 360.025(2) (1987)—which would seem to prevent use of the nominee device for ordinary home-mortgage loans. In any event, even if the transaction did run afoul of the usury law, Kentucky, like most States, regards only the lender as the usurer, and the borrower as the victim. * * *

Since the Kentucky statute imposed no penalties upon the borrower for allowing himself to be victimized, nor treated him as in pari delictu * * * the United States would hardly be vindicating Kentucky law by depriving the usury victim of tax advantages he would otherwise enjoy. * * *

Of more general importance is the Commissioner's contention that the arrangement here violate[s] the fifth National Carbide factor—that the corporate agent's "relations with its principal must not be dependent upon the fact that it is owned by the principal." The Commissioner asserts that this cannot be satisfied unless the corporate agent and its shareholders principal have an "arm's-length relationship" that includes the payment of a fee for agency services. The meaning of National Carbide's fifth factor is, at the risk of understatement, not entirely clear. Ultimately, the relations between a corporate agent and its owner-principal are always dependent upon the fact of ownership, in that the owner can cause the relations to be altered or terminated at any time. Plainly that is not what was meant, since on that interpretation all subsidiary-parent agencies would be invalid for tax purposes, a position which the National Carbide opinion specifically disavowed. We think the fifth National Carbide factor—so much more abstract than the others—was no more and no less than a generalized statement of the concern, expressed earlier in our own discussion, that the separate entity doctrine of Moline not be subverted.

In any case, we decline to parse the text of National Carbide as though that were itself the governing statute. As noted earlier, it is uncontested that the law attributes tax consequences of property held by a genuine agent to the principal; and we agree that it is reasonable for the Commissioner to demand unequivocal evidence of genuineness in the corporation-shareholder context, in order to prevent evasion of Moline. We see no basis, however, for holding that unequivocal evidence can only consist of the rigid requirements (arm's-length dealing plus agency fee) that the Commissioner suggests. Neither of those is demanded by the law of agency, which permits agents to be unpaid family members, friends, or associates. See Restatement (Second) of Agency §§ 16, 21, 22 (1958). It seems to us that the genuineness of the agency relationship is adequately assured, and tax-voiding manipulation adequately avoided, when the fact that the corporation is acting as agent for its shareholders with respect to a particular asset is set forth in a written agreement at the time the asset is acquired, the corporation functions as agent and not principal with respect to the asset for all purposes, and the corporation is held out as the agent and not principal in all dealings with third parties relating to the asset. Since these requirements were met here, the judgment of the Court of Appeals is

Affirmed.

* * *

NOTE

1. Did the Supreme Court in *Comm'r v. Bollinger* hold that the taxpayer had satisfied all six of the *National Carbide* factors, or that satisfaction of four out of six is sufficient for agency status, or did the Supreme Court fashion a new test which it found the taxpayer had satisfied?

2. A nominee or agent corporation may be used for at least three different purposes. First, it can be used to avoid usury limits as it was in *Comm'r v. Bollinger*. Second, it can be used to avoid a "principal" having to undertake personal liability for development financing. See *Gary R. Frink*, 49 CCH Tax Ct.Mem. 386 (1984), affirmed in part, reversed in part, 798 F.2d 106 (4th Cir. 1985), vacated and remanded, ___ U.S. ___, 108 S.Ct. 1264, 99 L.Ed.2d 476 (1988). Third, a nominee or agent corporation can be used to avoid disclosure of the identity of the "real principal." In addition, a nominee or agent corporation might be used to achieve a combination of the purposes listed above.

   a. Can a nominee or agent corporation be used for any one of the purposes listed above and still satisfy the rationale of the Supreme Court in *Comm'r v. Bollinger?*

      1. How did the Supreme Court answer the assertion, which is sometimes made, that a corporation used to avoid usury limits cannot be an agent since, if it is an agent, the loan should be treated as indirectly made to the principal which would result in a violation of the usury laws?

2. Can a corporation which is used to avoid the personal liability of a limited partnership for development financing qualify as an agent of the partnership for income tax purposes? Is not a principal liable for the debts incurred on the principal's behalf by an agent? See *Gary R. Frink*, 49 CCH Tax Ct.Mem. 386 (1984), affirmed in part, reversed in part, 798 F.2d 106 (4th Cir.1986), vacated and remanded, ___ U.S. ___, 108 S.Ct. 1264, 99 L.Ed.2d 476 (1988).

a. Would a lender agree to look solely to the personal liability of a corporate agent even though the lender knew the corporation was acting on behalf of a limited partnership to enable the limited partnership to avoid incurring personal liability?

b. In order for the acts of the corporation to "bind" the limited partnership, as required by the second factor listed in *National Carbide Corporation v. Comm'r*, 336 U.S. 422, 69 S.Ct. 726, 93 L.Ed. 779 (1949), or for the corporation to function as an agent for all purposes and be held out as an agent and not a principal in all dealings with third parties, does the limited partnership have to undertake personal liability for the financing or just be the entity which repays the financing?

3. Can a corporation which is used to avoid the disclosure of the identity of the principal comply with the first *National Carbide Corporation* factor, operate in the name and for the account of the principal, and can the corporation be held out as an agent and not a principal in all dealings with third parties?

4. Is it easier, and possibly safer in an income tax context, to have one or more members of the law firm which represents the limited partnership be the stockholders of the agent corporation?

a. Might a law firm which does a substantial amount of real estate development work be well advised to have one or more agent corporations available for use by their clients at some nominal charge?

b. Can the same "agent" corporation be used for different clients?

5. Is the alternative of using a law firm's agent corporation better or worse than using an unrelated third party straw man or a corporation owned by an unrelated third party?

a. Is using a law firm's agent corporation as safe, in a common law context, as having the limited partnership actually control the nominee corporation?

6. See generally Seto and Glimcher, *When Will a Related Corporate Nominee Be a Partnership's Agent?*, 68 J. Tax'n 380, 384 (1988); Riess, *Supreme Court Provides Safe Harbor for Use of Straw Corporation*, 16 J.Real Est.Tax'n 99 (1989).

(iii) CAVEAT EMPTOR WITH RESPECT TO TITLE

An area of concern when considering the means of acquisition of the real estate is what, in fact, the acquiring entity receives when it is conveyed "marketable title." The following excerpts present a general consideration of the *caveat emptor* problem in the acquisition of real estate.

CAVEAT EMPTOR IN SALES OF REALTY—RECENT ASSAULTS UPON THE RULE

Leo Bearmen, Jr.
14 Vanderbilt Law Review 541 (1960).
[footnotes omitted]

* * *

Warranty of Marketable Title

* * * Here the settled rule is that, absent an agreement to the contrary, the vendor of real property must give his vendee a marketable title. To the extent that the courts are stiffening the requirements of marketable title, they are supplying the vendee with an implied warranty, not so much of quality, as of fitness of the land for a particular purpose.

A. *Private Covenants and Restrictions*

The law has been quite consistent * * * in holding that the existence of a private restriction upon the use of the land is enough to prevent the land from being marketable. * * * Some courts have added to the general rule the requirement that in order to make the title unmarketable the private covenant or restriction must impose greater restrictions upon the use of the land than those already imposed by statute or ordinance.

* * *

B. *Easements*

The presence of easements has generally had the same effect upon marketable title as have private restrictions. An existing easement will prevent title from being marketable, unless the easement is visible, open, and notorious. The same rule applies when the contract to convey states that the property will be free from encumbrances. The reasoning is sensible; there is an assumption that the vendee who must be aware of the obvious easement and who has nevertheless signed has impliedly consented to except the easement from the guarantee of no encumbrances. The longstanding rule places a burden upon the vendee to visit the property site before he buys, a burden which is slight and quite reasonable. * * *

* * *

C. *Zoning Restrictions*

Zoning regulations are also connected with the concept of marketable title, and as zoning itself has become more prevalent in this country, the cases have begun to settle the law as to the effect of zoning restrictions upon the covenant to convey [free] from encumbrances or with a marketable title. Here the general rule * * * is that the mere existence at the time of the contract of a zoning ordinance applicable to the property sold is not enough to render the title unmarketable or encumbered, since these zoning restrictions are matters of public record and the vendee is presumed to have contracted subject to them. If, however, the buyer is purchasing property which is at the time being used in violation of a zoning ordinance, this will render the title unmarketable because the buyer is also purchasing a lawsuit. Furthermore, an existing violation may be grounds for rescission notwithstanding the fact that the contract provides that the conveyance is made subject to all restrictions and easements of record.

* * *

D. The English Doctrine of "Permitted Use"

With the exception of a few cases * * * courts in this country have not since 1945 greatly increased vendor vulnerability in the marketable title area. One reason of course is that the rules applicable to private restrictions and latent easements had by that time already stiffened the requirements of marketable title. To a marked degree it is only in the area of zoning laws which are on the books but not yet violated at contract time that the * * * vendor has usually been able to argue caveat emptor with success. The * * * vendor may well be unable to find protection even in this narrow area, however, if the American judges decide to adopt from their English brethren the concept of "permitted use" and its possible effect upon marketable title.

In England, under the Town and Country Planning Act of 1947, local planning authorities have the power, subject to approval by the Minister of Town and Country Planning, to enter into agreements with anyone interested in a parcel of land, with a view to restricting or regulating the development of use of the land, either permanently or for a stated period; and these agreements may be enforced against subsequent title holders. In that country it is a general rule that the vendor of land must disclose to his vendee all matters affecting title to land, though he need not make such disclosures when they relate merely to the land's quality. Defects which are characterized as "nonmaterial" or "patent" have been held not to be matters affecting title and so do not require disclosure. The argument is made that, since under the Town and Country Planning Act of 1947 the "permitted or authorized use" of the land is now the most important factor which the potential vendee will consider before buying, and since the "permitted use" is not always obvious because it can be temporarily varied for a stated period, the "permitted use" of the land given by the local planning authorities is both material and latent. Therefore it is a matter affecting title which must be disclosed to the vendee under penalty of rescission, even though there is no actual violation of the "permitted use" because another use is temporarily being allowed. At the basis of this argument lies the interesting theory that, after the "permitted use" concept was imposed by the Town and Country Planning Act of 1947, there are no longer in England fee simples in land, but only fee simples in the use of the land; consequently the very existence of a "permitted use" on the land and not just a violation of this "permitted use" becomes a question of title which must be disclosed to the vendee. The validity of this theory has apparently not yet been tested in the English courts, but its possible impact upon the general American rule concerning the effect of zoning regulations on marketable title is most significant.

American courts may not—even in the face of increasing zoning—reject the ancient concept of a fee simple in land for the fee simple in the use of the land. Nevertheless the argument could be made * * * that the use [of the land] permitted by zoning * * * is close enough to the English concept of "permitted use" so that it becomes a matter affecting title, just as, it is argued, the "permitted use" is. Therefore, even if the * * * [proposed use] is not in actual violation of the zoning regulation, the * * * vendor would have a duty under risk of rescission to disclose to the vendee all currently existing zoning ordinances which affect the * * * land involved in the transaction. This duty to disclose on the part of the * * * vendor would also lay the foundation for a cause of action in fraud on behalf of the vendee when any incomplete disclosure is made, based on the theory that the vendor said nothing when he had a clear duty to speak. This would reverse the present rule discussed earlier which places no such duty of disclosure on the vendor in the absence of an actual zoning violation because the mere existence of the zoning regulation is not a matter affecting title. Absent the duty to disclose, of course, there can be no cause of action against the vendor in fraud for silence.

Thus far, the discussion [of the reduction of] the caveat emptor concept has centered around the extension of a contract or implied contract theory of warranty and marketable title. This is not the whole story, for the courts have been arriving at substantially the same results through expansion of longstanding rules in another field, that of torts, and particularly in the areas of fraud and of negligence.

* * *

NOTE

1. Can a purchaser rescind a contract for the purchase of certain real estate if, after the contract is signed, the local governing body with jurisdiction changes the zoning of the real estate preventing the purchaser's proposed use which use the seller knew of at the time of execution of the contract?

a. What if the seller knew, but the contract did not mention the proposed use?

b. Does the result depend on whether either one or both of the parties knew of the potential zoning change?

c. If the change in zoning is in conformity with the Master Plan adopted for the community prior to the execution of the contract, should knowledge be presumed? On whose part should knowledge be presumed, purchaser, seller, or both? If the seller had actual knowledge and the purchaser did not, would this make a difference? Cf. *DeMeo v. Horn,* 70 Misc.2d 339, 334 N.Y.S.2d 22 (Sup.Ct.1972); *Garrison v. Berryman,* 225

Kan. 644, 594 P.2d 159 (1979); Note, *Vendor's Misrepresentation of Local Zoning Status of Property Not Ground for Rescission,* 26 Mercer L.Rev. 349 (1974).

d. Can this problem be avoided by providing in the contract that appropriate zoning is a condition precedent to the purchaser's duty to close? If, at the time set for closing, the real estate is inappropriately zoned, can the purchaser, in addition to not going through with the purchase, recover his "earnest money" payment? What does the answer to this question turn on?

2. If, after execution of the contract, the City Council formed a special assessment or improvement district including the subject real estate but no improvements were made or assessments entered prior to closing, does this action by the City Council render the title not marketable?

a. Does the answer to this question turn on whether the lien for the assessment arose at, or related back to, the time of the formation of the district?

3. Section 2–306 of the Uniform Land Transactions Act implies certain warranties of title unless the contrary is provided in a deed. The warranties implied are that the real estate is free from all encumbrances, the buyer will have quiet and peaceable possession of, or right to enjoy, the real estate conveyed, the seller has the power and right to convey the title which he purports to convey, and the seller will defend the title to the real estate conveyed against all persons lawfully claiming it.

In addition, Section 2–309 of the Uniform Land Transactions Act provides certain warranties by the seller as to the quality of the real estate to be conveyed. Among the warranties provided by Section 2–309 is that a seller in the business of selling real estate warrants to a purchaser of residential real estate who intends to occupy part or all of such real estate as a residence that the existing use of the real estate, the continuation of which is contemplated by the parties, does not violate applicable law at the earlier of the time of conveyance or delivery of possession. Residential real estate is defined to include real estate containing not more than 3 acres, not more than 4 dwelling units, and no non-residential uses for which the purchaser will be the lessor.

3. POWER TO ACQUIRE AND THE AUTHORIZATION OF THE ACQUISITION

This subdivision deals with two problems. The first is whether the acquiring entity has the "power" to acquire real estate. If the entity has the power to acquire real estate, the second is how is the acquisition authorized by the participants in the entity.

Absent a provision in a partnership agreement to the contrary, a partnership and a limited partnership have the power to acquire real estate. See Section 8(3) of the Uniform Partnership Act. The power of a trust to acquire real estate is governed by the state statutes regulating the operations of trusts, where business and/or land trusts are permitted, and the provisions of the trust agreement governing the operation of the specific trust under consideration. Corporations governed by the Revised Model Business Corporation Act have the power to acquire real estate and to mortgage it. See Section 3.02(4) and (5).

Does it make any difference, if a corporation is formed under the Revised Model Act, that the corporation has nothing in its certificate of incorporation which gives it the power to purchase and mortgage real estate?

With respect to the authorization of an acquisition of real estate, there are two independent yet related inquiries to be made. First, who can bind the entity to a third party with respect to the acquisition of real estate? It is generally accepted that the shareholders of a corporation, the beneficiaries of a trust (with the possible exception, in some cases, of an Illinois Land Trust) and the limited partners of a partnership (see Section 10 of the Uniform Limited Partnership Act and Article 3, particularly Section 303, of the Revised Uniform Limited Partnership Act) cannot obligate their entities for the acquisition of real estate from a third party. On the other hand, a general partner, in many circumstances, may be able to bind a partnership. (See Sections 9(1) and 18(e) of the Uniform Partnership Act.) Second, if the trustee of a trust, an officer of a corporation and a general partner, at times, can bind their respective entities, in what situations are their acts alone sufficient to bind their entities, and when must additional steps be taken to authorize them to bind their respective entities?

LAWER v. KLINE

Supreme Court of Wyoming, 1928.
39 Wyo. 285, 270 P. 1077.

BLUME, C.J. This was an action for rent, brought by H.C. Lawer against E.A. Kline, David Kline, and Morris Kline, copartners doing business under the firm name of Kline's. * * * The plaintiff recovered judgment for the sum of $1,699.94, less a deduction of $416.06, and the costs of the action. From the judgment so rendered, the defendants appeal. * * * The partnership conducted a clothing business in the town of Riverton. The term during which it was to last does not appear, but it seems to have been unlimited as to time.

* * *

1. The main question herein is * * * whether or not the lease of January 8, 1923, was binding on the partnership. Counsel for defendant contend that it was void, for the reason that the person signing had no authority to bind the partnership or the other members of the partnership to a lease for a term of years. * * *

* * * [I]n the English courts in 1856 in the case of Sharpe v. Milligan, 22 Beav. 606, 52 Eng.Reprint, 1242, one of the partners had executed a lease for the partnership to last for the period of twenty-one years, and the master of the rolls said on this point as follows:

> " * * * I am disposed to concur in the argument that, where persons simply enter into an agreement to carry on a partnership of which the term is not fixed, one of those partners would not have authority within the scope of the partnership contract to take a lease for twenty-one years and to bind the other partners."

It may be noted that the master of rolls based his reason apparently upon the ground that a partner had no right to make a lease beyond the term for which the partnership was to last. He would not presume that one formed for a term which was not fixed would last for twenty-one years. The case is of doubtful authority in favor of the defendants, for the reason that leases for twenty-one years are, perhaps, somewhat unusual in case of partnerships, while leases of five years are not, and it is not unlikely that the master of rolls might have presumed, in case of a partnership formed for an indefinite period of time, that it would continue for at least five years.

* * *

Some of the cases distinctly uphold the implied authority of one partner to execute leases of the character in question here. * * *

The case of Stillman v. Harvey, 47 Conn. 26, decided in 1879, involved a lease for seven years, which was taken over by one of the partners for the partnership, but where the agreement of the other partner was not obtained. The court said:

> "The purchase of the right to use a brewery for the period of about seven years by a member of a partnership formed for the purpose of brewing, and which was without limitation as to time, is so directly in the line and so necessary to the prosecution of its business, that if it be effected by one partner his act and signature will bind the partnership to the contract. * * *."

The case of Seaman v. Ascherman, 57 Wis. 547, 15 N.W. 788, involved an agreement made by one partner on behalf of a commercial partnership to enter into a lease for five years. The court held the agreement binding, saying in part as follows:

> "The rule of law is that a firm is liable prima facie for the act of one partner in its behalf necessarily done for carrying on the partnership business in the ordinary way, although such act was not authorized by the other partners. 1 Lindley on Part. 236. In such matters each partner is the general agent of the firm, and the above rule has its foundation in the law of agency. It was certainly necessary to the carrying on of the business of the defendants in the ordinary way that they should have a proper building in which to transact it. * * *"

In the case of Woolsey v. Henke, 125 Wis. 134, 103 N.W. 268, the lease was for a term of five years and was entered into for the partnership by its manager, Henke, one of the partners. The court said in part:

> "The respondents urge, as an obstacle to this conclusion, that there is no finding of fact that Henke had any authority, as a partner, to bind the firm to the making of a lease. The evidence is uncontradicted that the business involved was the editing and publishing of a local newspaper. We have no hesitation in holding that the leasing of premises in which to conduct it is within the general scope of such a business, and hence that there exists prima

facie authority in a partner to bind the firm therefor. Stillman v. Harvey, 47 Conn. 26; Seaman v. Ascherman, 57 Wis. 547, 15 N.W. 788."

* * *

The review of these cases * * * shows, we think, that the decided weight of authority is to the effect that a partner has implied authority to execute leases of the character here under discussion, when they are necessary and appropriate to carry on the business of the partnership, and that such leases are binding upon it, unless of course, the partner who signs has no actual authority, and the want thereof is known to the lessor. Such holding seems to simply carry to its logical conclusion the general rule that each partner has implied authority to bind the firm and each member thereof by contracts in the firm name which are within the scope of the firm business as that is ordinarily conducted. Aside from these authorities, however, we must further bear in mind section 9 of the Uniform Partnership Act, which was adopted in this state in 1917, * * * and which reads in part as follows:

"Every partner is an agent of the partnership for the purpose of its business, and the act of every partner, including the execution in the partnership name of *any instrument,* for apparently carrying on in the usual way the business of the partnership of which he is a member binds the partnership, unless the partner so acting has in fact no authority to act for the partnership, in the particular matter, and the person with whom he is dealing has knowledge of the fact that he has no such authority."

* * * Those who drafted * * * [section 9] doubtless had in mind the conflicting authorities on that point, and seem to have definitely settled the dispute in favor of what we have stated to be the prevailing view. The controlling point in this case, accordingly, seems to be as to whether or not the lease in question is within the limitation expressed in the section; namely, that it was executed to carry on the business of the partnership in the usual way. We think it is. The partnership needed *some* lease to carry on its business. We do not think that leases lasting for five years are at all out of the ordinary, as is indicated in the case above cited. Past transactions may be taken into consideration in determining this point. Maasdam v. Van Blokland, 123 Or. 128, 261 P. 66. And, as we have seen, the partnership had a lease lasting for five years previous to the time that the lease in question was taken. In fact, leases lasting only a short time could, in the nature of things, not be satisfactory unless perchance in those cases in which a partnership is formed for only a short and definite period of time. We conclude that David Kline had implied authority to execute the lease in question, which was binding upon the partnership in the absence of knowledge by plaintiff of his actually limited power.

If, however, we are wrong in the foregoing conclusion, still the defendants in error, must be held to have ratified the lease in question through E.A. Kline, who at least had authority to sign it. The partnership had the benefit of the lease for the period of two years without in any way questioning it. The claim that E.A. Kline supposed that the new lease was upon the same terms as the old one is without merit. It is altogether unreasonable to think that he, who claimed to be executive head of the partnership, should not, during all that time, have made some inquiry into the actual terms embodied therein. Further than that, it stands undisputed that in October, 1924, plaintiff sent him a copy of the lease, and he admits that he read it, but he made no objection to it whatever.

* * *

NOTE

1. Does this case indicate that a general partner in a partnership which deals in real estate can bind the firm to acquire real estate without authorization by the other partners?

    a. The argument can be made that the real estate is necessary to carry on the business of the partnership. However, there is quite a difference between signing a five-year lease and taking title to the same property.

    b. Does it make any difference if the real estate purchased is for the office of the firm rather than for development and/or sale?

        1. Is it significant that, for income tax and accounting purposes, real estate acquired for the firm's office is considered a capital asset by the partnership, while real estate acquired for development and/or sale is considered inventory?

2. If a partnership agreement provides that the partnership can acquire real estate only upon majority vote of its partners and a potential seller of real estate has knowledge of that fact, a partner, without authorization, cannot bind the partnership to acquire real estate from the knowledgeable seller. (See Sections 9 and 18 of the Uniform Partnership Act.) The trustee of a trust may be able to bind the trust to acquire property from a third party unless the provisions of the state statutes regulating the trust or the instrument creating the trust provide to the contrary. If the provisions of the trust limit the trustee's authority, a trustee, unless the trustee's actions are properly authorized, will be unable to bind the trust to acquire real estate from a third party with knowledge of the provisions. One of the major officers of a corporation may be able to bind the corporation to acquire real estate from a third party if such act is within the scope of the officer's authority. See Sections 8.40, 8.41 and 8.42 of the Revised Model Business Corporation Act. This clearly would be the case if the by-laws of the corporation gave the officer the authority to acquire real estate.

STERLING v. TRUST CO. OF NORFOLK
Special Court of Appeals of Virginia, 1928.
149 Virginia 867, 141 S.E. 856.

CHRISTIAN, J. * * * [T]he Trust Company of Norfolk was appointed special commissioner of the court to sell a certain lot of the infant, Roberta G. Sterling, located on Monticello avenue in the city of Norfolk.

The trust company employed J.W. Borum, a real estate agent, to assist it in the sale. J.L. Elliott, secretary treasurer and general manager of the Elliott Motor Company, became interested in the purchase of said property. Negotiations between Charles Webster, trust officer of the trust company, and J.L. Elliott, resulted in an option given to the Elliott Motor Company by letter dated the 25th day of November, 1925, to purchase the property at $700 per front foot until the 7th day of December, 1925.

The Elliott Motor Company was incorporated for the purpose of doing a general automobile and garage business. Its capital stock is $15,000, divided into 150 shares of the par value of $100 each. M.T. Elliott owns 75 shares, R.B. Elliott, his wife, 5 shares, and J.L. Elliott, his brother, 70 shares. These three persons, with E.G. Elliott, the wife of J.L. Elliott, compose the board of directors. Its officers are M.T. Elliott, president, J.L. Elliott, secretary treasurer, and general manager.

On the 30th day of November, 1925, J.L. Elliott determined to exercise the option for the purchase of the property, and so informed Charles Webster, the trust officer of the plaintiff. Webster thereupon dictated the following letter of acceptance for signature:

"Norfolk, Va., November 30, 1925.

"Trust Company of Norfolk, Special Commissioner, Norfolk, Va.—Dear Sir: We offer to purchase the property adjoining the Elliott Motor Corporation on the south, situated west side of Monticello avenue, fronting about 32 feet on Monticello avenue and running back to Webster court, at a price of $700 per foot, Monticello frontage; payable one-third cash, balance one year with right to anticipate deferred payment with interest at date of payment.

"Yours truly, Elliott Motor
Corporation,
"J.L. Elliott, Secretary–
Treasurer."

J.L. Elliott next morning delivered the letter to Webster, who immediately turned the same over to Hugh C. Davis, attorney for the trust company, for the purpose of submitting the offer to the court for confirmation. Davis called up W.P. McBain, an attorney who represented Elliott corporation when requested by it, and exhibited the draft of the decree of confirmation to him for approval. McBain knew nothing of the offer nor had he been employed to represent the Elliott Motor Corporation, but after a conversation over the phone with Surles, assistant manager, he approved the decree, which was entered by the court on the 4th day of December, 1925.

M.T. Elliott, president and largest stockholder, was out of the state when the letter was written, and during the time the court proceedings were in progress, and did not return to Suffolk, his home, until the 7th or 8th of December.

It is true that he had discussed the matter of the purchase with his brother, J.L. Elliott, but had never agreed thereto. When J.L. Elliott told him on his return what had occurred, M.T. Elliott refused to purchase the property because his brother had no authority to make the offer to purchase same. Thereupon J.L. Elliott, with his attorney, McBain, called upon the trust company and explained the situation and requested it to release his corporation from the offer, and agreed to pay personally all the costs and expenses. The trust company replied that it did not know what it would do; that it would have to consult Davis, its attorney, as he held a lien upon the Sterling lot that he wanted paid.

Shortly thereafter, the court upon application from the trust company [ordered] the Elliott Motor Corporation to appear and show cause why the property should not be resold at its cost and risk. Upon the filing of [Elliott Motor Corporation's] answer * * * the court referred the matter to Commissioner Wells for a report thereon. The commissioner took the evidence of all parties to this transaction, and from the evidence it appears that M.T. Elliott never had any negotiation with the trust company in reference to this purchase. The only person connected with the transaction, outside of his brother, that ever mentioned the matter to him, was Borum, the real estate agent, who suggested about the time the offer was made that the corporation should purchase the property, and M.T. Elliott said he would talk with his brother about it.

Borum claimed that the above conversation took place the day the offer was made, and that M.T. Elliott must have acted upon his suggestion and authorized the offer to purchase. Elliott denied that he ever acted upon the said suggestion if it was ever made.

Commissioner Wells reported to the court that:

> "On the whole case your commissioner is of opinion, and so reports, that J.L. Elliott had authority to make the offer on behalf of Elliott Motor Corporation, as set forth in the letter of November 30, 1925, and that after said offer was accepted by this court in its decree of December 4, 1925, it became and was binding on Elliott Motor Corporation."

The commissioner called for the by-laws of the corporation when examining the witnesses, and was informed that they had been misplaced but would be produced; they were produced and filed with the exceptions of the corporation to the report of Commissioner Wells. This is mentioned here because the real basis of his conclusion in the report is stated therein as follows:

> "So, if it be true of this corporation that authority had to be given to its officers by resolutions of its board of directors (there being no by-laws in existence) it is not clear how it could transact any business whatsoever. The truth of the matter is, that although the organization was corporate in form, it was in reality a partnership, made up of the two Elliotts, and either one had power to bind the organization."

Upon the filing of the report of Commissioner Wells, the Elliott Motor Corporation excepted to the same, and upon consideration of said report with the exceptions thereto and argument of counsel, the learned chancellor was of opinion that J.L. Elliott was not authorized to purchase the property for or on behalf of the Elliott Motor Corporation, and that said corporation was not bound thereby * * *. From the above opinion and decree the trust company appealed, and its appeal is before this court for consideration.

* * *

The real question in this case is, Did J.L. Elliott, as secretary-treasurer and general manager, have authority to purchase real estate for the Elliott Motor Corporation? The corporation is organized to do a general automobile business, and while it might be desirable to own the property adjoining that in which its business is conducted, still the purchase of real estate for about $22,000 when its entire paid in capital amounts to $15,000, could scarcely be considered to be within the scope of the business J.L. Elliott was employed to conduct, and therefore by virtue of the offices he holds he had no authority to bind the corporation for this purchase.

Commissioner Wells was of the opinion that because there were only three stockholders and they [were] members of the same family, that it was a corporation in name only and not in law. The statute of Virginia permits only three persons to form and conduct business as a corporation, and there is no inhibition upon their being members of the same family, nor limitation upon the amount of stock each shall severally own. Persons dealing with corporations are affected with notice of its charter and the statutes of the state regulating its power and duties.

Section 3789, Virginia Code, vests all the powers of the corporation in the president and directors as board of directors, and provides that it may consist of three persons * * *.

In the case of Taylor v. Sutherlin–Meade Co., 107 Va. 787, 791, 60 S.E. 132, 134 (14 L.R.A.[N.S.] 1135), the Supreme Court set out the meaning and scope of the above statute by the following quotation:

"The board of directors have the widest of powers. All of the various acts and contracts which a corporation may enter into are entered into by and through the board of directors. The board of directors make or authorize the making of the notes, bills, mortgages, sales, deeds, liens and contracts generally of the corporation. They appoint the agents, direct the business, and govern the policy and plans of the corporation. The directors elect the officers * * *."

The statute in Virginia having fixed the agency to conduct the business of the corporation, the office of president nor secretary-treasurer of itself confers no power to bind the corporation or control its property. The officer's power as an agent must be sought in the organic law of the corporation, in a delegation of authority from it, directly or through its board of directors, formally, expressed or implied from a habit or custom of doing business. Crump v. U.S. Mining Co., 7 Grat. (48 Va.) 352, 56 Am.Dec. 116; Hodges, Ex'r, v. Bank, 22 Grat. (63 Va.) 60.

The powers of the corporation being delegated by law to the board of directors, there is considerable difference among the authorities whether they can delegate their authority outside of the ordinary business of the corporation, such as authority to mortgage its property or to purchase real estate, to its officers or a committee from its own number. In Iowa, it has been held that a committee of directors authorized "to do all acts necessary for the prosperity of the society in the intervals of the meeting of the board" have not power to purchase real estate. Tracy v. Gutherie County Ag. Soc., 47 Iowa 27; Thompson on Corporations, §§ 3954–3957.

* * *

One of the main purposes of incorporation is to limit the powers of its agents and vest those powers in a board of directors who act jointly in meeting assembled. M.T. Elliott and his wife knew that the law afforded their capital input this protection, and that he was at liberty to discuss the purchase of the real estate with his brother or Borum without binding the Elliott Motor Corporation unless the statute of Virginia was impotent. He had a perfect right * * * to refuse to purchase this property until the proposition was submitted to the board of directors. He misled no one to his injury by standing upon his legal rights.

* * *

The purchase of the lot in question was for the purpose of enlarging the business of the Elliott Motor Corporation, and was therefore a matter of policy and planning the business of the corporation, which in law depended solely for its determination upon the discretion and judgment of its board of directors.

From the law and facts above set forth, we are of opinion that the decree appealed from is clearly right and will be affirmed.

Affirmed.

* * *

GEORGE J. KIEBLER REALTY CO. v. MILLER

Court of Appeals of Ohio, Lucas County, 1927.
29 Ohio App. 130, 163 N.E. 51.

WILLIAMS, J. July 14, 1922, articles of incorporation were issued to the George J. Kiebler Realty Company, located at Toledo, Ohio. These articles show that the corporation was formed for the purpose of buying, selling, and dealing in real estate, * * * and the doing of all things incident thereto, including the constructing, erecting, and maintaining of buildings and other structures thereon, and the purchasing, holding, using, and mortgaging of such real estate. Shortly thereafter the organization of the corporation was completed, and George J.

Kiebler was elected a member of the board of directors and president of the corporation. Among the regulations adopted by the stockholders was the following:

"The president shall preside at all meetings of stockholders and directors, sign the records thereof and all certificates of stock, deeds, mortgages, and other similar papers, and perform generally all the duties usually performed by presidents in like companies, and such further duties as may be from time to time required of him by the stockholders and directors."

From the time George J. Kiebler was elected president, he was not only president, but the active managing agent of the corporation and had charge of the buying and selling of real estate. The following contract was entered into March 31, 1926, by the parties:

"Toledo, Ohio, Mar. 30, 1926.

"Received of A.L. Miller (purchaser) $50.00 account purchase of lot No. 20 Glenview to the city of Toledo, Lucas county, Ohio, this day by him agreed to be purchased at a price of $9,000.00, balance to be paid as follows: $2,000.00 in cash, purchaser to assume $5,000.00 mortgage at Home Bldg. & Sav. Co. & to give back second mortgage for balance payable 10% per month, interest 6%, when warranty deed is furnished, together with statement or opinion of title showing property clear and free from material defect or incumbrance, subject to taxes and assessments due and payable after June, 1926, payment.

"If this proposition is accepted by the owner it shall constitute a binding contract for the purchase and sale of said property upon these terms.

"If the owner fails to accept this proposition upon the terms above set forth, the said deposit of $50.00 shall be returned to the purchaser without any liability upon the part of Geo. J. Kiebler Co. to either party.

"Geo. J. Kiebler, Agent,
"By Herbert Sitzenstock.

"A.L. Miller, Purchaser.

"Accepted and conveyance agreed to be made: The Geo. J. Kiebler Realty Co. by Geo. J. Kiebler, Owner."

* * *

After this contract was entered into, a warranty deed was executed by the Geo. J. Kiebler Realty Company, by Geo. J. Kiebler, president, and Herbert Sitzenstock, secretary, under date of April 20, 1926, purporting to convey the property so sold to the purchaser. Thereupon the deed, with an opinion of title, which was approved by counsel for the purchaser as showing a clear title, was tendered to the purchaser, who refused to accept the deed and carry out the contract. Thereupon an action was brought in the court of common pleas of [the] county by the company against the purchaser for specific performance of the contract. Upon trial, the prayer of the petition was denied, and the plaintiff appealed the cause to this court.

It is contended here that the contract was insufficient in form to bind the defendant, A.L. Miller. The agreement quoted constituted a valid, subsisting and enforceable contract between the parties to this action, and, as to form, was sufficient in law to be binding upon both.

It is also contended that the plaintiff corporation, the Geo. J. Kiebler Realty Company, could only sell real estate, and execute and deliver a deed to the purchaser therefor, by lawful action of the board of directors, authorizing and approving such sale, and that the deed, in not reciting authority for that purpose from the board of directors, is defective.

The deed of a corporation which is in due form carries with it a presumption of authority for its execution. Cincinnati, H. & D.R. Co. v. Harter, 26 Ohio St. 426; Bank v. Flour Co., 41 Ohio St. 552, 557. However that may be, under the regulation adopted by the stockholders, quoted above, the president of the company was expressly authorized to sign deeds and similar papers and such authorization would carry with it the power to have his own signature acknowledged before a notary public and to perform the other things incidental to the signing and complete execution thereof.

The plaintiff corporation, being a corporation engaged in the buying and selling of real estate, the president, who is also managing officer of the corporation, as George J. Kiebler was, would have power to make sales of real estate without having each separate transaction expressly authorized or ratified by the board of directors. The sale of the property in question by the president, and the consummation thereof by the execution of proper instruments, was within the authority of that officer, he being also managing officer of the corporation in charge of its business of buying and selling real estate, which was, so to speak, the stock in trade of the corporation. The deed tendered, if it had been accepted, would have conveyed good title to the purchaser, and the plaintiff corporation fully performed its part of the contract.

The plaintiff is therefore entitled to specific performance. Decree accordingly.

NOTE

1. Is *Sterling* distinguishable from *Kiebler Realty*?

a. What if the by-laws of the corporation in *Sterling* had given the secretary-treasurer and general manager the same authority given the president in *Kiebler Realty*?

b. Would the result in *Kiebler Realty* have been different if the by-law provision pertaining to the authority of the president had only contained the first two lines of the provision as quoted in the opinion, ending with the word "directors"?

c. Would the court in *Kiebler Realty* have come to the same result if the president had bought real estate for a new office for the corporation, rather than selling some of the corporation's "inventory"?

2. The authority of the officers of a corporation to bind the corporation is considered in Division II, pages 437 to 442 infra and Division III, pages 879 to 881 infra.

3. As pointed out above, the second inquiry which must be made when determining if an entity is bound to acquire real estate is whether the individual purchasing the real estate for the entity has been properly authorized to do so. For example, a partnership agreement could restrict the authority of a general partner. The partnership agreement might provide that the acquisition of property can only be made upon a majority vote of the general partners. Subject to applicable state statutory regulation, a trustee might be limited by the terms of a trust agreement providing, if there is more than one trustee, that the acquisition of property by the trust can only be made upon the approval of a majority of the trustees, or the trust agreement might provide that the acquisition of property can be made only upon the affirmative vote of the holders of a majority of the beneficial interests in the trust (i.e. the Illinois Land Trust). Subject to any limitation provided in the articles of incorporation, under the Revised Model Business Corporation Act the board of directors manages the corporation. (See Section 8.01 of the Revised Model Business Corporation Act.) Therefore, in general, the acquisition of real estate is subject to the approval of a majority of the board of directors or of the executive committee of the corporation if such authority has been delegated to the executive committee. (See Section 8.25 of the Revised Model Business Corporation Act.) It appears that, even in the case where property is acquired and a purchase money mortgage given to the seller or to a lender which provided part of the purchase price, all that is necessary under the Revised Model Business Corporation Act is approval by the board of directors. (See Section 12.01 of the Revised Model Act.) Consider whether only director approval is necessary, under Section 12.01, when the mortgage given in return for part of the purchase price of the property is, in effect, a disposition of the property. For example, consider a situation in which the directors of a corporation knew at the time of the giving of the mortgage that the corporation would be unable to make the payments on the mortgage and that foreclosure was a certainty. Division II, pages 433 to 447 infra and Division III, pages 876 to 882 infra consider further the steps necessary to authorize an act by a partnership, trust or corporation.

4. TITLE PROTECTION

When acquiring real estate, the acquiring entity is concerned with the state of its title to the real estate. There are a variety of ways of assuring title to the acquired real estate. The commonly used techniques of assuring title are considered in this subdivision.

a. TITLE INSURANCE

One of the common ways of assuring title to real estate is through the use of title insurance. The following materials present many of the considerations, problems and pitfalls involved in the use of title insurance.

TITLE INSURANCE

Quintin Johnstone
66 Yale Law Review 492 (1957).

* * *

Title Insurance Protection

* * * [I]n some areas contracts of sale customarily provide that the seller shall pay some or all of the cost of a policy insuring title in the buyer. These contracts frequently give the seller the alternatives of providing either a title insurance policy or an abstract showing marketable title in the seller. In other areas the buyer pays the entire cost of title insurance coverage, if he wants insurance.

Applicants for a title insurance policy are interested in obtaining the insurance coverage, but they are sometimes more interested in what the company examination of title discloses. This is perhaps partly at the base of the prevailing philosophy of title insurance companies—stressing the service of risk delineation rather than risk coverage. In many contracts of sale the buyer agrees to buy only if the seller's title is one that a named title insurance company will insure subject to no more than the standard exceptions. Or contract purchasers may have agreed to buy only if the title is marketable, depending on the title insurance examination report for this determination; and if the title is not marketable, the seller will want to know what defects must be cleared to make it so. If the applicant is planning to erect a church, a factory or a liquor store on the premises, he will of course be anxious to know if there are restrictive covenants against such usage or easements inconsistent with the type of building he proposes to erect. If the property is to be mortgaged with a life insurance company, the title insurance examination report may be used to determine whether the title is sufficiently unencumbered to meet the legal standards set for life insurance investments. It is not unusual for title policies applied for never to be issued, for the examination report of the title insurance company may disclose a title that the buyer is not obligated to accept.

Risk Coverage

Title insurers argue that theirs is a dual system of title protection—combining a thorough title examination with the insurance of losses from some potential defects. Their critics assert that title insurance companies are not in fact insurers since they except any risks apparent after the title has been examined. Although this assertion is overbroad, the risks assumed by title insurers compared to most other kinds of insurers are very slight, and title companies except most risks disclosed by the title examination. All policies contain printed general exceptions, and in addition, defects in the particular title are excluded from coverage in a separate schedule.

* * *

Risks Usually Covered by Title Insurance Policies

Errors in the title examination. These include any negligence or fraud by an employee or agent of the company in making the title search and analyzing its results. The most common error is negligently failing to note a title defect appearing in the public records. Another common error is the failure to recognize defects that should be disclosed by a survey or other inspection of the premises whenever such examinations are actually made by the company or acceptable independent surveyors.

A few known defects. These are occasionally covered, particularly in mortgagees' policies, if they are trivial or probably unenforceable because of estoppel or a statute of limitations. Examples of this kind of occasional coverage are setback requirements, restrictive covenants, easements, possibilities of reverter, rights of re-entry and slight encroachments made by improvements on neighboring land.

Defects that would be disclosed by an examination which the company intentionally does not make. Some companies make only partial examinations and assume the risks of any defects that a complete examination would disclose. For example, in the eastern part of the United States insurance is often written on a search that goes back only sixty years. It is thought that there are few defects older than sixty years, and that it is unduly expensive to search for them.

*   *   *

Some hidden defects not disclosed by a competent examination of public records, physical inspection of the premises, or survey. Since the protection of the recording acts prevents most of these defects from being risks to the insured, there is no risk for the insurer. But the recording acts do not eliminate all such defects, and title insurance policies usually protect against some, including: a recorded instrument, appearing to be valid, but void because it was forged, never properly delivered, or executed by a person without capacity; any judgment that from the records appears valid but which is void for lack of jurisdiction; a deed incorrectly stating that the grantor is unmarried, if the fact of his marriage does not appear elsewhere in the records; failure of any public records to disclose an instrument or claim that need not be recorded under the recording acts, including the claim of an heir or devisee unknown at the time of examination; errors in the public records made by public officials, to the extent they are not protected against by the recording acts, including failure to put on record and failure to make a correct copy; errors resulting from the practice of some tax offices of promptly showing taxes as paid upon receipt of a payment check, then altering this record if the check is returned for lack of sufficient funds.

Marketability. This risk is generally covered in mortgagees' policies and often in owners' policies. One of the risks involved in insuring marketability is correctly anticipating the judicial meaning that will be given to this vague concept, for courts have been far from consistent in their interpretations of "marketable title."

Risks Usually Not Covered in Title Insurance Policies

Defects disclosed by the title examination. Defects of this sort are generally not covered, and when found are listed as exceptions in the policy.

Defects that physical inspection and survey of the premises would disclose. Defects of this kind are usually not covered in owners' policies, but ordinarily are in mortgagees' policies. They include such possible interests as adverse possession and unrecorded leases and easements that would be disclosed by an inspection of the premises. They also include the defects that surveys would disclose, including encroachments, incorrect boundary lines and setback violations.

Defects created subsequent to the date of the policy. * * *

Defects of which the insured was aware or which he assumed prior to the date of the policy. The general insurance doctrines of misrepresentation and concealment by the insured also apply to title insurance.

Restrictions of any government police power regulation on the use and enjoyment of the premises. These include building, fire and zoning ordinances. The apparent reasons for the limitation are that these regulations are difficult to ascertain, and that they are frequently ambiguous or of dubious constitutionality. But the limitation has been rationalized on the grounds that title policies insure titles, and police power regulations involve paramount government rights of a non-title character.[56]

Title to personal property, even when affixed to the realty. * * *

Some hidden defects not disclosed by a competent examination of public records, physical inspection of the premises or survey. More risky defects of this sort often are expressly excepted. They include mechanics' and materialmen's liens which are effective as liens without being recorded at the date of the policy; and dower, curtesy, community property and homestead rights of the insured's spouse. Some companies except tax titles because of the limited rights acquired at tax sales and the frequent errors in tax title proceedings. Mechanics' and materialmen's liens are often covered in mortgagees' policies if a physical inspection of the premises shows no sign of recent construction, or—when there has been recent construction—if there is satisfactory evidence of payment, if lien waivers or releases are secured, or if security is posted for payment of any unpaid construction costs.

The Scope of Coverage

Under a title insurance policy only one premium is paid by the insured—at the time the policy goes into effect. The insurance is not

56. [Will this rationalization be affected if the "permitted use" concept, discussed at pages 281 to 283 supra, gains wide acceptance?]

written for a fixed term, but coverage—up to the face amount of the policy—continues as long as the insured can suffer any loss from the risks covered. Insurance under a mortgagee's policy ends when the debt is paid or the mortgage released. But mortgagees' policies usually provide that protection continues if the mortgagee becomes an owner of the property through foreclosure or purchase in settlement of the mortgage debt. Insurance under an owner's policy ends when the insured conveys all his interest in the property, except that an insured grantor remains covered for his continued liability under title covenants, unless, as is occasionally possible, he has assigned the policy. Title policies uniformly contain subrogation clauses for the protection of the insurer; and mortgagees' policies contain salvage clauses providing that if the insurer pays the full amount of the debt to the insured mortgagee, the mortgage and indebtedness shall be assigned to the insurer.

Mortgagees' policies usually cover assignees of the mortgage, but owners' policies do not cover grantees of the insured, and assignments to grantees are seldom permitted by title insurers. Thus, each new grantee must take out a title policy, if he wishes title insurance coverage. He can secure some of the advantages of his grantor's policy, however, if there are title covenants in his deed.

Liability for Negligence

In addition to its liability under the policy, the company may be liable for negligence in performing title search and examination. If the opinion is in error due to negligence in the search or analysis of the facts disclosed by the search, the company is liable, provided the customer detrimentally relied on the opinion. Ordinarily under such circumstances the customer will claim under the policy, but it could be more advantageous for him to bring a tort action for negligence. This would be the case if a negligent search had been made but no policy issued, if it had been issued on the wrong tract, or if the policy had been issued after the reliance and it contained an exception to a defect not appearing in the examination report. A tort action would also be better if the loss from the reliance were greater than the face amount of the policy.

* * *

NOTE

1. When a title company prepares an abstract of title of a certain parcel of real estate for a party to a transaction the company usually guarantees that the abstract contains all matters appearing in the public records affecting title to the real estate, with limited exceptions.

a. If the title company neglects to include in the abstract an item which appears in the public records and constitutes a defect in title, is it liable to the party relying on the abstract? See *Williams v. Polgar*, 391 Mich. 6, 215 N.W.2d 149 (1974); Note, *Recovery Allowed for Negligent Misrepresentation Absent Privity of Contract*, 21 Wayne L.Rev. 137 (1974);

Kubicek and Kubicek, *Selected Topics in Examination of Abstracts of Title,* 26 Drake L.Rev. 1 (1976–77). See also *First American Title Insurance Company, Inc. v. First Title Service Company of the Florida Keys, Inc.,* 457 So.2d 467 (Fla.1984), further proceedings, 458 So.2d 822 (Fla.1987).

b. When a title company issues a title insurance policy on certain real estate, instead of merely providing an abstract of title of the real estate, has it materially increased its potential liability? If so, how? Cf. *Heyd v. Chicago Title Insurance Company,* 218 Neb. 296, 354 N.W.2d 154 (1984).

    1. Why do most purchasers and mortgagees prefer title insurance policies rather than guaranteed abstracts of title?

c. See generally Curtis, *Title Assurance In Sales of California Residential Realty: A Critique of Title Insurance and Title Covenants with Suggested Reforms,* 7 Pac.L.J. 1 (1976); Palomar, *Title Insurance Companies' Liability for Failure to Search Title and Disclose Record Title,* 20 Creighton L.Rev. 455 (1987).

2. In *Southern Title Guaranty Co. v. Prendergast,* 478 S.W.2d 806 (Tex.Civ. App.1972), affirmed, 494 S.W.2d 154 (1973), the insureds purchased a parcel of real estate for $10,233. A title insurance policy in the face amount of $10,233 was obtained by the insureds at the time of purchase. A year later, the insureds agreed to sell the real estate for $25,000. The purchaser refused to carry out the agreement because a 10% undivided interest in the real estate was found outstanding in a third party by the purchaser's title insurance company, and as a result, the title insurance company refused to issue to the purchaser a policy insuring against the defect. The insureds sued their title insurance company for breach of contract. The jury determined that there had been a breach and that the insureds had been damaged to the extent of $14,800. The trial court awarded judgment to the insureds in the full amount of the face value of the policy. The Court of Appeals reversed and remanded because the measure of damages had been improperly computed. The Court of Appeals held that the liability of the title insurance company should be measured by the difference, at the date of the insureds' purchase of the real estate, between the amount they paid and the value of the real estate with the defective title. Would the insureds have been better off if they had sued the insurer in tort for negligence? Would the same facts which established the breach of contract have established the insurer's negligence? Cf. *Red Lobster Inns of America, Inc. v. Lawyers Title Insurance Corporation,* 656 F.2d 381 (8th Cir.1981).

a. If real estate is appreciating in value, how can the owner avoid damages being limited to the face amount of the title insurance policy obtained on purchase, or less, in the event that insurer breaches the contract? Can the owner obtain an increase in the face amount of the policy which reflects the appreciation of the real estate? Even if the owner can obtain an increase in the face amount of the policy, does it make sense to do so? If the appropriate point in time for measuring damages is the date of purchase, it might not do the owner any good.

    1. On the other hand, if the owner did not increase the face amount of the policy would a co-insurance provision, as described in excerpts from *The Lawyer and The Title Company* beginning at page 302 infra, further limit the owner's recovery in the event of a partial loss? It would appear that title insurance companies should not have it both ways; measuring damages as of the date of purchase and then further limiting damages under the co-insurance provision.

b.   In *Overholtzer v. Northern Counties Title Ins. Co.*, 116 Cal.App.2d 113, 253 P.2d 116 (1953), the court faced essentially the same measure of damages issue as was present in *Southern Title Guaranty Co. v. Prendergast*, 478 S.W.2d 806 (Tex.Civ.App.1972), affirmed, 494 S.W.2d 154 (1973). The court in *Overholtzer*, however, came to a different conclusion stating, "[t]he [plaintiffs] also object to the method used in computing damages in the present case. As already pointed out, the trial court fixed damages as of the date the policy was issued and limited the damages to the diminution in the value of the property caused by the easement measured by the use to which the property was then devoted. The court found that at the date of purchase the property was used for agricultural purposes and that for such purpose the property without the easement was worth $3,000, but with the easement was worth but $2,000, hence allowed $1,000 as damages. The [trial] court also found that the [plaintiffs] purchased the property and an adjoining parcel for an industrial use, and devoted the two parcels to such use. It also found that the easement depreciated the value of the property as actually used by the [plaintiffs] at least $15,000. This finding, repudiated as a measure of damages by the trial court by its findings and judgment, is based on the highly questionable testimony of one witness, a mill operator, not versed in real estate operations.

"The findings present the question as to the proper time for the valuation of the property for purposes of damages in such cases—is it the diminution in the market value of the property caused by the defect and measured at the time of purchase, market value being measured by the use to which the property is then devoted, or is it the diminution in value as of the time of the discovery of the defect measured by the use to which the property is then being used? In either event, maximum liability is measured by the face amount of the policy.

"It seems quite apparent to us that liability should be measured by diminution in the value of the property caused by the defect in title as of the date of the discovery of the defect, measured by the use to which the property is then being devoted. When a purchaser buys property and buys title insurance, he is buying protection against defects in title to the property. He is trying to protect himself then and for the future against loss if the title is defective. The policy necessarily looks to the future. It speaks of the future. The present policy is against loss the insured 'shall sustain' by reason of a defect in title. The insured, when he purchases the policy, does not then know that the title is defective. But later, after he has improved the property, he discovers the defect. Obviously, up to the face amount of the policy, he should be reimbursed for the loss he suffered in reliance on the policy, and that includes the diminution in value of the property as it then exists, in this case with improvements. Any other rule would not give the insured the protection for which he bargained and for which he paid.

"There may be some conflict in the authorities on this subject but the weight of authority and the better reasoned cases support the views above expressed. * * * There may be a few cases contrary, but most of them involved distinguishable factual situations. * * *

"We believe the majority rule is sound and should have been followed in the present case." 253 P.2d 125–26. See also *Fohn v. Title Insurance Corp. of St. Louis*, 529 S.W.2d 1 (Mo.1975); *Sullivan v. Transamerica Title*

Insurance Co., 35 Colo.App. 312, 532 P.2d 356 (1975); *Hartman v. Shambaugh,* 96 N.M. 359, 630 P.2d 758 (1981).

3. The standard American Land Title Association policy excepts defects which arise subsequent to the date of the policy. Since the title company's report and binder will be issued prior to closing, how can the gap in title protection between the date of the report and the closing date be avoided?

a. Another gap problem is present in the situation in which the acquiring entity purchases the real estate and constructs improvements on it. Both the development financier and the acquiring entity want the title insurance to cover at least the cost of the improvements which do not exist on the date of acquisition, and protect against any defects in title arising during the construction period. Cf. *National Mortgage Corporation v. American Title Insurance Company,* 299 N.C. 369, 261 S.E.2d 844 (1980).

1. A new title insurance policy could be issued every time there was a draw under the construction loan, but this is quite cumbersome and may be quite expensive. Is there a better way to solve this problem? If so, how? See Division III, page 669 infra.

4. If a special assessment or improvement district including the subject real estate is formed before the issuance of the title report but no improvements are made or assessments entered prior to the issuance of the policy and the lien for the assessment arises at the time of the formation of the district or relates back to it, is the failure of the title insurance company to except such a lien a breach of the contract? Or, in policy terms is this a defect created subsequent to the date of the policy or a governmental restriction? See *Butcher v. Burton Abstract Title Co.,* 52 Mich.App. 98, 216 N.W.2d 434 (1974), cert. denied, 419 U.S. 998, 95 S.Ct. 314, 42 L.Ed.2d 273 (1974); *Cummins v. United States Life Title Ins. Co. of New York,* 40 N.Y.2d 639, 389 N.Y.S.2d 319, 357 N.E.2d 975 (1976); *Edwards v. St. Paul Title Ins. Co.,* 39 Colo.App. 235, 563 P.2d 979 (1977).

5. The preceding excerpts from the article by Professor Johnstone describe the matters which a title insurance policy will cover and those which it will not, and touch, to some extent, on the representation of the acquiring entity in obtaining and reviewing a title insurance policy. Being aware of the coverage of the title insurance policy and making sure it covers the real estate being acquired are not, however, the only responsibilities when representing the acquiring entity with respect to the title insurance policy.

THE LAWYER AND THE TITLE COMPANY

James Pedowitz
Real Estate Closings Workshop 127, 128–146.
(Practicing Law Institute, 1970).

* * *

The title policy when received, should be scrutinized carefully. The attorney should satisfy himself that the description contained in Schedule "A" of the policy is exactly the description of the premises that he wants insured. * * * If an appurtenant easement is to be insured, that easement should be specifically included in Schedule "A" as being insured within the policy. The reference to an easement in Schedule "B" as an exception to the policy does not mean that it is being insured. Title to any property beyond the lines of the premises described and lands in streets on which the premises abut, or the right to maintain any vaults, ramps or other structures or improvement or any rights or easements in the streets are excluded, unless specifically included as insured in the policy, with the sole exception that the policy, unless otherwise excepted, insures the ordinary rights of access and egress belonging to abutting owners.

*   *   *

The standard form of title policy contains co-insurance provisions. If vacant land is to be improved, or improved property altered, the client should be advised as to the implications of the co-insurance provisions. Co-insurance will only apply in case of a partial loss and after a subsequent alteration or improvement to the property, the cost of which exceeds 20% of the face amount of the policy. In such event the company will only be obligated to pay such proportion of the loss as 120% of the face amount of the policy bears to the policy amount plus the cost of the improvement. For example[, if] the policy amount is $10,000 and subsequent to the issuance of the policy an alteration is made to the property costing $5,000 and there is a partial loss, the company will then be obligated to pay only 80% of the loss. The computation is made as follows: 120% of the policy amount is $12,000. The policy amount plus the cost of the improvement is $15,000, the resulting fraction is ⅘ or 80%. Obviously where the cost of the alteration or improvement substantially exceeds the amount of the policy, these co-insurance provisions may cut down the protection very substantially unless the policy amount is later increased by paying the additional premium for the increase and having the policy endorsed to show the increase.

At any time[,] prior to knowledge of a claim with respect thereto, arrangements can be made for the title policy to be increased as of its original date by the payment of the difference between the premium for the new amount of the policy and the present premium for a policy in the original amount.

The Title Report. Let us now consider the title report itself. *   *   * The title report will become the binder which will subsequently determine the exact contents of the title policy. The certificate, on its face, provides that it will be null and void: (1) if the fees therefor are not paid; (2) if the prospective insured, his attorney or agent, makes an untrue statement with respect to a material fact or suppresses or fails to disclose a material fact with respect thereto, and (3) when the policy is issued.

*   *   *

It is well to caution that the title certificate specifically states that no search has been made for [security interests in personal property] because the policy will not insure title to personal property. [Security interests, including purchase money security interests,] are only reported when they are properly filed and indexed against real property in the Register's Office of the County in which the property is located, or, if there is no Register's Office therein, then in the County Clerk's Office thereof. Where a block system is used, only such [security interests] as are indexed against the proper block are returned. In some cases, the personal property is an essential and important part of the overall transaction. Under those circumstances, * * * a separate [U.C.C.] search at additional charge [should be done.]

The following explanation of several of the more common types of title exceptions found in a title report may assist the lawyer in dealing with them: * * *

Federal Estate Tax

Affidavits are acceptable to show that an estate is non-taxable for Federal Estate Tax purposes provided that they show the gross amount of the estate including all property, both real and personal, and wheresoever situate to be less than [the value of the Unified Credit Against Estate Tax to which the estate is entitled.] In a number of cases the affidavit may also be acceptable notwithstanding the fact that the gross estate is in excess of [the value of the Unified Credit] where a full disclosure is made: (1) of the amount of the gross estate; (2) the nature and amount of the deductions applicable to the estate and; (3) where the figures show that the net estate is substantially less than [the value of the Unified Credit]. In this type of situation the title company must consider the probabilities that some or all of the deductions will be disallowed, thereby making the estate subject to tax.

Where property was held by tenants by the entirety and the property is being sold or has been sold by the surviving tenant, the Internal Revenue Service has ruled that a purchaser for value from such surviving tenant takes the property free of the lien of Federal Estate Tax due from the estate of the deceased spouse (Rev.Rul. 56–144). In such cases the Internal Revenue Service may not even entertain an application for a release of lien on the ground that it is unnecessary. * * *

Section 6325 of the Internal Revenue Code * * * provides for the issuance of certificates of release of Federal Tax Liens under certain circumstances. The lien of Federal Estate Tax may be released upon appropriate request before the filing of an estate tax return, * * * or before an assessment is made. The application for such a release must show the value of the property to be released, the value of the gross estate, the value of the real estate included in the gross estate, the name and address of the purchaser or transferee, if obtainable, and such other information regarding the death, charges and expenses of the administration as will support a determination that there are or will be sufficient assets in the estate with which to discharge the full liability for tax that might be asserted.

* * *

In those cases where the tax ha[s] in fact been fixed and paid and a final determination made that there are no additional assessments or any additional liability for tax, the originals or photostat copies of the receipts and correspondence with the Internal Revenue Service showing such payments should be exhibited to establish that the entire tax has in fact been fixed and paid. It is also advisable, though not essential, to have an affidavit either from the attorney or executor or administrator who is fully familiar with the estate tax liability of the estate that will summarize the correspondence and affirmatively state that all of the taxes and additional assessments, if any, including interest, have been paid and that there is no further tax liability on behalf of the estate.

In summary, Federal Estate Tax can be disposed of either by: (1) affidavit; (2) release (recorded in the County Clerk's Office) or; (3) proof as to the amount of the estate tax liability and that the taxes have been paid in full.

Contiguity

* * * In any case where two abutting parcels are being acquired, or a parcel is being acquired that abuts a parcel already owned, or proposed to be acquired by the same client, it is appropriate and often essential to ask for contiguity insurance between the parcels. Ordinarily, a survey is also required in connection with contiguity insurance. In some cases if the adjoining parcel was not insured by the same company there may be a small additional charge for the additional work that may be required for the examination of the adjoining parcel. However, the price is very small compared to the problems that may be avoided at some future date when new construction is contemplated and it is disclosed that a strip or gore exists between the parcels that were believed to be contiguous. * * * [I]n the absence of specific contiguity insurance the title policy only insures the premises particularly described in the policy, subject to all of the conditions and exceptions contained therein.

Land Now or Formerly Under Water

Title companies generally refuse to insure land actually under water. In many cases they also refuse to insure land formerly under water. In analyzing a title report containing such exceptions, it is well to consider what the effect is of the exceptions in your particular case. Unless limited, the exceptions may exclude coverage as to the entire premises included within the title policy. Accordingly, wherever possible, it is important to determine what specific portion of the premises is affected by the exception. In order to make such a determination it may be essential to have a current survey showing what is true upland. It is also important to show proof that the lands were not artificially filled. Old surveys or Coast and Geodetic maps may also help to show the maximum extent of the encroachment of the waters. Whenever possible and practicable it is important to have the exception * * * limited to some specific line shown on a survey.

It may also be appropriate at this time to [consider] accretion, avulsion and erosion. Natural accretion can be insured in most cases.

It is important to be able to establish that it was entirely natural and not artificially induced nor artificially created. Accretion is the slow and most imperceptible addition to land from water. Erosion on the other hand is the gradual eating away of land in an imperceptible fashion. This results in a loss of title. * * *

However, loss of land as a result of storm or other sudden and violent actions is called avulsion and does not result in loss of title. In such cases the owner may re-fill. * * *

Questions Involving Jurisdiction Notwithstanding an Order or Judgment of the Court

Title companies are often criticized when they raise an objection with respect to an action or proceeding, notwithstanding the fact that an order or judgment was signed and entered by an appropriate court. * * * The fact is, however, that there have been a number of instances where titles have been held unmarketable despite a prior judicial approval of the procedure followed. * * *

* * *

There will always be some differences of opinion between a lawyer and the title company. These differences do not arise as a result of caprice or from a desire to be difficult.

A determination of the marketability or unmarketability of a title is a very specialized and difficult task.

Judgments, Federal Liens, etc.

These liens fall roughly into two categories: (1) those cases where because of similarity of name, or otherwise, the lien *may* affect; and (2) those cases where the lien definitely affects the property.

Category (1) can normally be disposed of by a specific affidavit, stating unequivocally that the lien in question does not affect the premises, and is not against the individual of that or similar name in our chain of title. It is often helpful to show in addition, that the address shown in the lien as that of the debtor is one at which our party never resided, or did business.

Of course, the more uncommon the name, the greater particularity will be required to establish that the lien does not in fact apply to our party.

In those cases where the lien in fact affects, it must be discharged of record. This should be done in advance of the closing and the title company notified in order to avoid needless delay at closing. In many cases, though, the owner cannot discharge the lien in advance of closing because he does not have the necessary funds and intends to use the proceeds of the closing to satisfy the lien or liens. When it is anticipated that this will be the case, an appropriate provision permitting this should be included in the contract. * * *

In many cases, a sum in an amount more than sufficient to discharge the lien is deposited with the title company at closing, with a request that the lien be omitted from, or its collection out of the premises insured against, in the policy. There may be many reasons for such a procedure—i.e., there may have been difficulty in locating the party who is to give the discharge—or, it is hoped that some additional time may be effectively utilized to work out a more favorable settlement—or, the lien may become outlawed by a statute of limitations in the near future—the lien may in fact have been paid, but no satisfaction obtained,—etc., etc. Normally, the title company will accede to such request to omit the lien when it knows the lien will be discharged of record within a few days, or so long as it knows that it can effectively control a prompt satisfaction of record in the event of an unanticipated emergency. Normally, though, when a deposit is accepted, the procedure as to fee insurance is to except the lien, but insure that it will not be enforced against or collected out of the insured premises. * * *

A title company may resist being asked to hold such funds for any extended period of time, even though only insuring against collection. Actually, when the company does so without the consent of the proposed insured, they can expect a fair share of future embarrassment, pressure and name-calling, even though their position may be technically correct. When a lien is excepted, but there is insurance against collection, there is normally no recourse against the title company who has insured against collection until there is a direct attempt to enforce collection. When re-selling a property with such a condition, the contract should except lien whose collection has been insured against, and provide that the existence of the particular lien shall not be deemed an objection to title so long as the "X" Title Company (which has so insured) will insure against its collection out of the subject premises.

* * *

Federal liens are a special headache because the six (6) year statute of limitations set forth in Section 6502 of the Internal Revenue Code * * * cannot be relied upon. It is subject to various means of being tolled by instruments and actions taken by the taxpayer and/or government, none of which are of record. In addition, the time required to obtain a satisfaction is much greater than other liens. In further addition, there have been cases where the government has been less than cooperative[,] notwithstanding tender of the full amount originally required, because of other items due or pending against the same taxpayer, or because of their own clerical errors, etc. For these reasons, title companies may be reluctant to accept any escrow deposits as to federal liens unless there is a letter from [the] Internal Revenue [Service] stating unequivocally that a release will be forthcoming on receipt of a specific amount, or that the lien has in fact been paid and that a release will be furnished. * * *

In summary, the title company wants all liens that are known to be of record affecting the property discharged of record in advance of closing or as promptly thereafter as possible. A lawyer for a purchaser or lender should want exactly the same thing.

Mechanics Liens

What has been said above as to other forms of liens applies equally to statutory mechanics liens * * *. In addition, there is the additional complication that in the enforcement of mechanics liens all have equality and there are no priorities among [them]. * * *

It is the obligation of the owner to clear mechanics liens from the record. When a title company agrees to hold an escrow to cover a mechanics lien for an extended period, it must take the risk that a foreclosure may be commenced and that additional liens with equal priority may be filed * * *. Accordingly, such escrows are usually resisted—except for short periods sufficient to permit bonding, deposit or payment.

* * *

Restrictive Covenants

* * *

Restrictive [c]ovenants are negative easements, clearly recognized by a vast body of law and subject on occasion to the most stringent enforcement. Those that are commonly enforced as running with the land fall broadly into three classes * * *. The first class is the so-called "general scheme", created when an owner divides his tract and in the deeds to different purchasers imposes uniform covenants restricting the use to which the grantees can put the property. In some cases the general scheme is imposed in the form of a declaration by the common owner in advance of his conveyance wherein it is clearly stated that it is intended for the benefit of the entire tract. * * * [General scheme] covenants are enforceable by any grantee or subsequent owner against any other within the tract on the theory that there is mutuality of covenant. The second class covers those cases in which a covenant is imposed by a grantor for the benefit of his neighboring lands. In this category, the subsequent owners of the retained lands can enforce the covenant against the subsequent owners of the land on which the covenant was imposed; although separate owners of the restricted lands cannot enforce against each other. * * * The third broad class of enforceable covenants covers those cases where there are mutual agreements between owners of neighboring lands in which the restrictions are imposed for the mutual benefit of the land of all of the covenantors. In this category too, all of the subsequent owners can enforce against each other. * * *

In recent years we have also seen numerous covenants created as a condition to, or in connection with[,] a re-zoning. * * *

The question most frequently asked of the title company is whether they will insure against the enforcement of covenants found of record with respect to an existing violation or with respect to a contemplated violation. Only rarely, however, has the inquirer taken the trouble to determine whether or not there is any basis in fact or in law for such an assurance.

The lawyer who requests some form of affirmative insurance from the title company is in a much better position, and much more likely to have his request complied with if he has first analyzed the particular set of restrictive covenants in the light of the above principles, and prepared a basis or argument in favor of his request. Affirmative insurance is not normally given on a strict casualty basis. It is freely given in those cases where it appears that the covenant does not run with the land within the general classes defined * * * supra, or where it can be fairly clearly established that it is a personal covenant and the imposer no longer has any interest to protect; or that it would clearly not be enforced by a court of equity. * * *

In those cases where it appears that the covenant may in fact have been of a class that was originally enforceable there may yet be valid reasons making the likelihood of present enforcement slim. The lawyer who can demonstrate that there has been a distinct change of neighborhood rendering the possibility of enforcement by a court of equity unlikely has a much better chance of obtaining the desired affirmative insurance than the lawyer who has made no effort to determine a possible basis for defense against enforcement of the covenant other than the fact that he or his client find it burdensome. In considering change of neighborhood, the important consideration is whether or not there was any change of neighborhood within the restricted area. A change of neighborhood across the street, unaffected by restrictions[,] may have no bearing whatsoever on the decision of the court. * * *

If the request is for affirmative insurance with respect to a violation or proposed violation of setback, it is important to be able to show how other properties in the same block on both sides of the street are set back. Where there has been a street widening subsequent to the creation of the covenant, set-backs are usually measured from the old street line. With respect to existing violations, it is important to determine how long the violation has existed undisturbed. * * *

In those cases where affirmative insurance with respect to restrictive covenants is given, there is usually an additional minimum charge of [a percent] * * * of the title premium unless [the property] was previously so insured, or [the restrictive covenant is] clearly within a court of appeals decision [invalidating] the same restrictions, or pertains to existing completed buildings or improvements. When the affirmative insurance in a fee or leasehold policy is on vacant land, the policy must be written in an amount to include the contemplated improvement.

* * *

Survey Exceptions

When survey protection is not requested or arranged for, the title report and policy will contain an exception: "Any state of facts which an accurate survey might show."

Some contracts are "subject to any state of facts that an accurate survey might show." In that case, the prospective purchaser is contracting to buy a parcel that may be thoroughly unmarketable. If the contract provides that it is "subject to any state of facts which an accurate survey might show provided that the title is not rendered unmarketable thereby" then the provision might just as well have been left out of the contract since for all practical purposes it is meaningless. Of course, if the contract is made subject to the state of facts shown on a specific survey which is exhibited at the time of closing and initialed by the parties, then the purchaser is agreeing to accept the state of facts shown on that survey notwithstanding that it might disclose an unmarketable condition. An attorney should only accept such a provision in a contract after he has carefully studied the survey and come to the conclusion that the state of facts shown thereon is acceptable to his client notwithstanding the fact it may involve unmarketability.

Unless encroachments come within the "de minimus" rules, they usually affect marketability. Where the encroachment of adjoining buildings on [the] premises is slight, a purchaser will not be permitted to reject title, although in some cases, an abatement in the purchase price [may be] * * * decreed.

* * *

Projections and encroachments of roof cornices, show windows, window trim, fire escapes, entrance steps and cellar doors on a street render the title technically unmarketable but ordinarily do not discourage a willing buyer or lender.

If the encroachment by [the subject] premises on adjoining premises has continued in excess [of the period required for the "ripening of adverse possession"] * * * and disabilities have not tolled the running of the statute of limitations, a prescriptive right for the wall to remain can be established. In almost every case where there is such an encroachment of an exterior wall on adjoining premises for over [the required period], a title company will affirmatively insure that notwithstanding the encroachment, the wall may remain undisturbed so long as it stands.

* * *

Party Walls. The mere fact that a wall is a party wall does not authorize a purchaser to reject title. * * * However, a party wall agreement may be a technical encumbrance but one that does not ordinarily discourage a willing buyer or lender. * * *

Variations between fences and the record lines of title where trivial, will not discourage a willing buyer or lender. Where they are more than trivial they may give rise to questions of prescriptive easements and claims of adverse possession. In many cases a title company will refuse to insure portions of land which lie beyond fence lines. In order to dispose of this type of exception it is best to advise the title company as to who erected the fence, when it was erected and to exhibit proofs showing that no adverse claims of right or title are being made as to the portion of the property that is "out of possession." These proofs can be by affidavit of the adjoining owner.

In discussing surveys, it should be kept in mind that in some areas there are differences in standards; some of the old surveys in the area having used "local standards" as distinguished from the ordinary "US standards." Surveys may also disclose errors which are contained in filed maps. In a number of cases they will disclose differences of opinion among surveyors as to the location of streets, property lines, monuments, etc.

It is not at all unusual for the courses on a current survey to be somewhat different from the courses contained in the record description. In most cases, this merely results from the current surveyor using a different "North" point [than] the previous surveyor. The simplest method of checking whether or not this is so, is to determine whether the angles within the lot lines are all the same both on the current survey and in the old record description. If they are, the difference is only in the north point and is unimportant. If the angles vary, there may be a real question which may require boundary line agreement or correction deeds.

Affidavits

Many of the exceptions in a title company report can be omitted on "satisfactory proof by affidavit, etc." The sufficiency of the affidavits that are submitted are in some cases a matter of contention between the lawyer and the title company. An affidavit should be concise, but complete. Many lawyers properly take pride of authorship in affidavits composed by them. In some cases, that pride of authorship is so strong that they resist requests for appropriate changes or additions.

In any case where time permits and the affidavit is not of a routine type, it is advisable to submit a draft form to the title company in advance of the execution of the affidavit. This permits the title reader or counsel to make appropriate suggestions for changes, additions or deletions. It also avoids the embarrassment of having to go back to the client for a supplementary affidavit after the client has already signed an affidavit prepared by you. It is unfair, and in many cases unlawful, to request the title company to prepare the affidavits. They are not permitted to practice law and should not be encouraged to do so.

NOTE

1. As should be obvious from the foregoing, the representative of the purchaser or the mortgagee does not have to accept the title certificate, report and title insurance policy as initially submitted by the title insurance company.

There are many steps which can and should be taken to eliminate exceptions, etc. See Bagley and Shumbob, *Getting the Right Title Insurance Endorsements,* 4 # 4 Prac.Real Est.Law. 19 (1988).

2. While a co-insurance provision may be contained in the standard form in some states such as New York, it is not present in other states. If, however, a co-insurance provision is contained in a title insurance policy, it intensifies the "gap" problems occurring in a construction situation as discussed at page 301 supra.

3. If, in addition to the real estate, personal property and/or fixtures are being acquired and are of major concern, should the title company's search be relied on, or should a separate search be made by the firm doing U.C.C. searches?

a. If two separate searches are made, how should fixtures be treated? Is it conceivable that the title company might claim that an item was personal property and the U.C.C. search company claim the same item was a fixture?

4. See generally Thau, *Protecting the Real Estate Buyer's Title,* 3 # 4 Real Est.Rev. 71 (1974); Rooney, *Title Insurance: A Primer for Attorneys,* 14 Real Prop., Prob. & Tr.J. 608 (1979); Taub, *Rights and Remedies Under a Title Policy* 15 Real Prop., Prob. & Tr.J. 422 (1980). For a discussion of the difference between "marketable title" and "insurable title" see *Kirkwall Corp. v. Sessa,* 60 A.D.2d 563, 400 N.Y.S.2d 349 (1977), reversed, 48 N.Y.2d 709, 422 N.Y.S.2d 368, 397 N.E.2d 1172 (1979). In addition, in *Fairway Development Co. v. Title Ins. Co. of Minn.,* 621 F.Supp. 120 (N.D.Ohio 1985), it was held that a successor partnership to a partnership dissolved on the death of a general partner is not a party to a title insurance policy issued to the dissolved partnership, and therefore, the successor partnership cannot make a claim under the policy. To avoid the result of this case a partnership agreement for a real estate partnership should contain a provision which provides for the continuation of the partnership in the event of the death of the general partner, etc. rather than a provision which provides for the reformation of the partnership after dissolution caused by the death of the general partner, etc.

b. REGISTRATION

Although title registration is not generally available in the United States, in those areas in which it is available it may provide an effective means of title protection for the acquiring entity. The following excerpts consider some of the fundamental concepts present in a title registration system.

LAND TRANSFER IMPROVEMENT: THE BASIC FACTS AND TWO HYPOTHESES FOR REFORM

Ted J. Fiflis
38 University of Colorado Law Review 431 (1966).
[footnotes omitted]

*   *   *

Title Registration

* * * Although recording acts exist in all states but Louisiana, title registration exists in only [a handful of] states today. The first act was passed in Illinois in 1895, but it was held to be unconstitutional under the state constitution. A new Illinois act was passed in 1897. All of the others were enacted within the next twenty years.

* * *

[I]n each of the states where title registration is utilized, it is used principally to assure titles to large subdivisions, to clear faulty titles, and to prevent loss of title through adverse possession.

Prevention of loss by adverse possession or prescription is often the purpose of registering timber and mining lands where squatters are a constant problem. But this feature of title registration is also useful in urban centers where open plazas are now being constructed. Thus, title to the Prudential Center in Boston was registered, one of the reasons being protection against loss by adverse possession or prescription.

* * *

Efficacy of the Systems of Title Protection

Under title registration, once title is registered, conveyancing is quicker and cheaper, and the title is safer than under recording. Some writers feel that although title registration is better than recording, with or without title insurance, the superiority is so slight as to be inconsequential. Others assert that once title is registered, the superiority of title registration over recording is indisputable. All would agree that the expense and time delay of transition from recording to title registration (initial registration) is the major difficulty with the system. * * *

Title Risks

Risks Under Title Registration Acts. Under the title registration system, with some exceptions, matters affecting title to the registered parcel must appear on the certificate of title in order to be valid against a *bona fide* purchaser. One can readily see that title registration must afford better protection than recording, since most instruments not registered are given no effect against a *bona fide* purchaser under the registration system, whereas many matters may remain unrecorded under the recording system and, nevertheless, be fully effective. Title registration gives additional protection in that all matters with a few exceptions, which appear on the records, are given conclusive effect.

The few items which, even though not noted on the certificate of title, are still good against a *bona fide* purchaser, generally fall within the following categories:

(a) Rights arising under the laws of the United States which are not required by federal law to be registered in order to be valid against subsequent purchasers or encumbrancers;

(b) Certain general and special tax assessments;

(c) Leasehold interests of less than a certain term under which the tenant is in actual occupation;

(d) Public highways;

(e) Interests of persons deprived of their rights by the decree of initial registration, for a certain period varying from thirty days to two years;

(f) Rights of appeal from the decree of initial registration.

Other less common statutory exceptions are subsisting easements and rights of parties in possession under deed or contract for deed. Several other interests have been held by judicial decision to retain their validity even though not noted on the certificate of title. For example, rights of parties in possession at the time of transfer, who were also in possession at the time of initial registration, are generally not cut off unless these parties were given proper notice on initial registration. Another defect not specifically excepted is that caused when there are two unrelated registered owners of interests in the same land. Also, the purchaser under a registered conveyance describing land which was never registered may not be protected.

This is not to say these are risks to be assumed by a purchaser. These exceptions are the items not fully protected against by examination of the certificate of title. Of the specified exceptions, most of them can be determined conclusively by further action, such as examination of additional records, inspection of the premises, and inquiry of occupiers. Thus, federal tax liens which would be good against purchasers, general taxes, and special assessments, are a matter of record in most states. Short term leasehold interests where the tenant is an occupier, and other possessory interests, may be determined by inquiry of persons occupying the premises. And for other exceptions, although loss may result, it may be that indemnity will be provided from the indemnity fund.

* * *

Conversion from Recording to Title Registration

Upon consideration of the four factors: title risks, remedies and other non-substantive matters, expense, and time delay, for the typical transaction, it seems that conveying a registered title is safer, less expensive and quicker, than conveying a recorded title, or a recorded title with title insurance. Hence, it seems that the general assumption must be correct that the materially significant drawbacks to the registration system must be in the process of converting from recording to registration, i.e., initial registration.

The Problems of Initial Registration

So far we have assumed, in considering the problems of title registration, that the land being dealt with has been put on the register at some prior time. Now we consider the problems arising from the processes necessary to initially register the land.

The typical registration proceeding in the United States consists of a judicial determination of the state of the title to the parcel, and then, placing the property on the register. The proceeding is initiated by the filing of a petition by the intending registrant, payment of a statutory fee, payment of additional fees for examination, publication, and other miscellaneous matters, and the giving of notice to specified classes of persons. In many states the notice consists of publication plus service by mail. The minimum notice period varies * * *. The requisite parties to the proceeding usually consist of adjoining owners and persons having or claiming an interest in the land. These parties may be persons in possession or persons having some form of record interest. Typically, the statute provides that the judge hearing the matter may appoint a title examiner and require the parties to present the examiner with an abstract of title. * * *

[In some states,] no survey is required if a plat of the subdivision is on file with the county recorder. * * * [A]n inspector is employed [at times] by the registrar to examine the premises for encroachments and occupiers. He [usually] reports to the title examiner. In [other states] the petitioner must supply a survey, complying with very strict standards * * *. Surveyors must make a plan of the lot, tying it to specific markers on the ground, which in turn are related to control points.

Contesting parties present their evidence to the examiner. The examiner may indicate what defects should be cured and what persons should be made additional parties. After any necessary actions are taken, the examiner reports his findings and conclusions as to the ownership and state of the title to the judge who may accept or revise them as he sees fit. If the judge determines that the petitioner is the owner, he will enter a decree so indicating, and giving the state of the title. Thereafter, the administrator of the registration system takes over. He will usually prepare the certificate of title which goes into the public records, and the duplicate certificate which is delivered to the petitioner.

For initial registration, the important factors to consider are costs and time delay. * * *

* * *

NOTE

1. Many of the states which have a registration act or have adopted enabling legislation permitting local adoption of a registration ordinance have

provided an indemnity fund for losses occurring as a result of the administration of the registration system.

    a. Is there any reason to obtain title insurance if the parcel being acquired is registered or is being put into registration?

    b. Are there situations in which, even though title insurance on the parcel is obtained, the parcel also might be registered?

        1. If so, in what situations would this occur?

  2. A quiet title action may be considered an alternative to title registration, at least in the context of clearing title defects.

    a. What are the differences? If the choice is available, when would quiet title be used and when would title registration be used?

        1. See Division II, pages 423 to 426 infra for a discussion of the quiet title concept.

  3. See generally Yzenbaard, *The Consumer's Need for Title Registration,* 4 N.Ky.L.Rev. 253 (1977); Sclar, *Minnesota Simplifies Land Registration,* 11 Real Est.L.J. 258 (1983); Comment, *The Torrens System of Title Registration: A New Proposal for Effective Implementation,* 29 UCLA L.Rev. 661 (1982); Comment, *Possessory Title Registration: An Improvement of the Torrens System,* 11 Wm. Mitchell L.Rev. 825 (1985); Bostick, *Land Title Registration: An English Solution to an American Problem,* 63 Ind.L.J. 55 (1987).

c. MARKETABLE TITLE ACTS

Some states have adopted marketable title acts. The provisions of these acts in some respects provide a form of assurance of title to an acquiring entity. A general discussion of the Model Marketable Title Act is contained in the excerpts from the following article.

THE IMPROVEMENT OF CONVEYANCING: RECENT DEVELOPMENTS
Lewis M. Simes
34 Journal of the Oklahoma Bar Ass'n 2357 (1963).

* * *

Let us now consider the content of the Model Act. What is its most basic feature? It is that, if one has an unbroken chain of record title of at least forty years duration, with no defects in that record chain of title, and no recorded instrument during that period which purports to divest the title, then that person has a marketable title. Instruments prior to the first deed recorded at the beginning of this period, and interests created prior to that time, are extinguished as a matter of law.

* * *

[U]nder the Model Marketable Title Act, the recorded instrument prior to the first one in the forty year period is a nullity. It cannot be asserted as a basis of claim even if discovered. The second essential of the Model Act is that, if one has an interest or claim which he wishes to preserve, he can do so by recording a notice before the forty year period has run on the adverse chain of title.

It should also be noted that the Marketable Title Act is not a statute of limitations. The person whose interest is barred may never have had any cause of action. He did, however, have a right to protect his claim by filing a notice. In a way the Marketable Title Act functions somewhat like a recording act, in that one must record a notice of claim to preserve the claim. But unlike a recording act, the filing of the notice determines validity, not mere priority.

Does the Marketable Title Act mean that, if one has a forty year chain of record title as described in the Act, he has a title which he could force on a vendee in a bill for specific performance of a land contract? The answer is: generally yes, but not universally so. First, it should be noted that the Act refers to an unbroken chain of title of record to "*any interest* in land." Of course, if the chain is of a record title to an interest less than a fee simple absolute, the title may not be marketable. Furthermore, the Model Act * * * provides certain exceptions to the operation of the statute. But if none of the exceptions are found to exist, and if the chain of title is in fee simple absolute, the forty year chain would be commercially marketable.

What then does the Marketable Title Act accomplish for the lawyer and for the public? It means that the record to be examined is shorter. The cost of the abstract should be less. The time consumed in preparing a title opinion is reduced, and thus the lawyer's labors are decreased. Moreover the parties to the real estate transaction will find that the time element is substantially reduced for them. Their land deal can be closed more promptly. As to title defects prior to the forty year period, the Model Act functions as curative legislation. Thus, instead of a fly-specker insisting on a quiet title suit before the title can be approved, we find that the Act simply wipes out the defect. All this works equally to the advantage of the lawyer who investigates the title and to the title insurance company which insures it.

Now, having indicated in a general way what the Act *does* accomplish, I wish to add a word of warning indicating what it will *not* do. First, it is obvious that, as a curative act, it will not cure defects quickly; the period is forty years. For such minor defects as defective acknowledgments or formal defects in records of judicial sales, a curative act or statute of limitations with a shorter period is needed. Someone may say, then why not enact a marketable title act with a much shorter period? The answer is, if we do so, people will constantly be finding it necessary to file notices to preserve perfectly valid interests. And the records will be cluttered with such notices. But experience has shown that, if a longer period, such as forty years, is employed, very few claims will be filed. For if a person has a valid claim, he is likely to assert it in less than forty years, and will consider it unnecessary to file a notice. Hence, although a marketable title act should employ a rather long period, it should be supplemented by curative acts in which much shorter periods are used.

Second, the Marketable Title Act does not cure any defects which are embodied in the recorded instruments necessary to establish the forty year chain of title. Thus, suppose [43 years ago] *A* convey[ed] a piece of land to *B* in fee simple on a common law condition subsequent and the deed [was] at once recorded. *A* thus retain[ed] a right of entry for breach of condition. Then, [33 years ago] *B* convey[ed] to *C* in fee simple absolute, and the deed [was] at once recorded. Now *C* wishes to sell, but he finds that, even under the Marketable Title Act, he is still subject to *A*'s right of entry. For, in order to establish his chain of record title under the Act, *C* must go back to the first deed, 40 or more years back. He cannot stop with the deed from *B* to him [33 years ago] for that is less than 40 years back. So he must go back to the next deed, which is the deed [43 years ago] from *A* to *B*. That deed contains the right of entry in favor of *A*. And although it has been more than forty years since that deed was recorded, *C* must rely on that deed. Hence, his title is subject to the right of entry in *A*. But if he waits until [another 7 years pass] and nothing more is recorded, he can start with the deed in fee simple absolute * * * from *B* to *C;* and thus * * * the right of entry in *A* is extinguished.

Third, it is not quite correct to say that the Model Act means we are to have only forty year abstracts and only title examination of a forty year record. * * * [For example, if the] last instrument on record concerning the title in question had been recorded considerably more than forty years prior to the time when [an] abstract [is] ordered. * * * [T]he abstractor [must] abstract the last instrument recorded prior to forty years back. For that was what the Act calls the "root of Title." And since there was no recorded instrument exactly forty years back, the search should have continued until an instrument from which the title in question could be traced, was found.

Furthermore, even prior to the last recorded instrument more than forty years back, there may be instruments coming within the statutory exceptions. Thus, the Model Act, Section 6, excepts the interest of a reversioner who has a right to possession at the expiration of a lease; any easement[,] or interest in the nature of an easement, the existence of which is clearly observable by physical evidence of its use; or any interest of the United States. * * *

Now, having summarized what the Act will do and what it will not do, I should like to take up certain critical and difficult points involved in the functioning of the Act.

(1) What is the effect of the possession of an owner who fails to record a notice within the forty year period? Suppose, for example, *A* has a good record title in fee simple absolute to a farm which he acquired in 1920, the deed to him having been recorded on that date.

A so-called wild deed from *X* to *Y* covering the same land was recorded in 1921. If *A* had not been in possession, the expiration of the forty year period with respect to *Y*'s deed would have occurred in 1961, and *A* would then have lost his title by reason of his failure to file a notice within that period. But Section 4(b) of the Model Act saves him. It reads in part as follows: "If the same record owner of any possessory interest in land has been in possession of such land continuously for a period of forty years or more, during which period no title transaction with respect to such land appears of record in his chain of title, and no notice has been filed by him * * *, and such possession continues to the time when marketability is being determined, such period of possession shall be deemed equivalent to the filing of the notice immediately preceding the termination of the forty year period." Thus, *A* 's title is preserved by the possession. Though *Y* can show a 40 year record title, it is subject to *A* 's title, since *A* 's title is still good.

(2) What about title by adverse possession? If the period of adverse possession is wholly prior to the forty year period, then the title by adverse possession is extinguished. Thus[,] suppose *C* can show a chain of record title running back more than forty years. He claims through a deed from *A* to *B* recorded [43 years ago] and a deed from *B* to *C* recorded [23 years ago]. But *X* claims that he acquired a title by adverse possession, the period of which ended [48 years ago]. The title by adverse possession is wiped out. That is made clear by Section 3 of the Act, which declares that the owner of the forty year record title shall hold it "free and clear of all interests, claims or charges whatsoever, the existence of which depends upon any act, transaction, event or omission that occurred prior to the effective date of the root of title."

On the other hand, suppose all or a part of the necessary period for title by adverse possession is subsequent to the period relied on for a marketable title under the Act. Thus, assume again that *C* can show a chain of record title as follows: *A* conveyed to *B* by deed which was recorded [43 years ago], and *B* conveyed to *C* by deed which was recorded [23 years ago]. *X* entered into possession holding adversely from [48 to 33 years ago], the period for title by adverse possession being ten years.

If the requirements for title by adverse possession are otherwise met, *X* got a title at the expiration of ten years after his possession began, or [38 years ago]. This is good against *C* 's forty year record title, because a part of the period accrued during the time which *C* would rely on for a title under the Marketable Title Act. If we do not give *Y* a title under these facts, then we must modify or abolish basic doctrines as to title by adverse possession. Of course, in our case, where *C* 's chain of title involved a conveyance to him recorded [23 years ago], *C* could rely on that deed as his "root of title" [after 17 more years had passed] and [following] that [point in time], *X* 's title by adverse possession, which accrued prior to [the conveyance from *B* to *C*] would be extinguished.

It must be conceded that in this case and in the situation already discussed, where the owner stays in possession for forty years after the record[ing] of the deed to him without filing any notice, we are giving effect to facts extrinsic to the record, and thus tending to weaken the effect of the forty year record itself. But the only satisfactory alternative would be to abolish completely the doctrine of title by adverse possession, and to give no special significance to the possession of a record owner for forty years or more. Such an alternative would seem to be entirely too drastic. After all, the situations discussed are unlikely to arise; and generally, when they do arise, the actual state of the possession at the time the question comes up will give notice of these unrecorded claims.

(3) What is the effect of two entirely independent chains of record title? Suppose *A*, being the grantee in a regular chain of record title, conveyed to *B* [43 years ago] the deed being at once recorded. Then [41 years ago] *X* conveyed to *Y* and the deed was at once recorded. Then assume further another conveyance [33 years ago] in each chain of the title. That is to say, *B* conveyed to *C* [33 years ago] and the deed was at once recorded; *Y* conveyed to *Z* [33 years ago] and the deed was at once recorded. Now at the present time, * * * by the terms of the Act it can be said that both *C* and *Z* have marketable record titles, since each chain is more than forty years in length. It cannot be said that anything appearing of record purports to divest either chain, since an interest in order to divest must be connected with the same chain of title. But by the terms of Section 2(d) of the Act, each chain is subject to "any title transaction which has been recorded subsequent to the effective date of the root of title from which the unbroken chain of title of record is started." Hence neither chain of title extinguishes the other and, the rights of the parties are settled by common law principles. Since *Z*'s chain of title starts with a wild deed, unconnected with any owner, *C* should win. But if *B* had not made a conveyance to *C* * * * and no notice had been filed on his behalf, then [40 years after the conveyance from *X* to *Y*] the chain of title starting with *A* would be extinguished under the Marketable Title Act, and *Z* would have a good title.

(4) What is the effect of a quitclaim deed in the chain of record title? The answer is: it is just like any other link in the chain. For purposes of the recording acts, nearly all states treat quitclaim deeds just like other deeds of conveyance. To make the Marketable Title Act work, we must do the same thing. This, in fact, is expressly provided in the definition of "title transaction", Section 8(f) of the Act.

* * *

The objection which may be made is that the Model Act extinguishes vested rights, and therefore takes property without due process, under the 14th amendment to the Federal constitution, or under similar provisions in state constitutions. * * *

[F]iling a notice once in forty years, is so simple and easy of accomplishment, that one can expect courts to recognize the constitutionality of such legislation. This, of course, is on the assumption that the Marketable Title Act provides a reasonable time after the Act takes effect in which to record notice of claims which have been in existence for forty years or more.   In the Model Act, * * * a period of two years after the effective date of the Act is allowed for recording notices of claims regardless of the length of time the claims have been in existence, or the length of time which has elapsed since the instrument of claim was recorded.

* * *

NOTE

1.   If a state has a registration system in effect, is there any reason for its legislature to adopt a Marketable Title Act?

a.   What about the reverse situation?   If the state legislature has enacted a Marketable Title Act, is there any reason for it to adopt a registration system?

b.   Does a Marketable Title Act address different problems than title registration?

2.   Professor Simes' article was written shortly after the enactment of the Oklahoma Marketable Record Title Act.   For a recent look at the operations of the Act see Hicks, *The Oklahoma Marketable Record Title Act,* 9 Tulsa L.J. 68 (1973).   See generally Slicker, *Real Estate: Marketable Title Acts,* 92 # 2 Case & Com. 3 (1986).

5.   UTILITIES

A matter of concern in carrying out of the acquisition of real estate for development is the availability of utilities.   An industrial park cannot be developed if electricity is not available.   An apartment house cannot be constructed and leased if sewer and water are not available. It is, of course, important, when planning the development of an office building, to know that telephone service will be available, and in planning the development of a shopping plaza, the availability of bus service and other forms of public transportation will be of concern.

NOTE:

THE DUTY OF A PUBLIC UTILITY TO RENDER ADEQUATE SERVICE: ITS SCOPE AND ENFORCEMENT

62 Columbia Law Review 312 (1962).
[footnotes omitted]

* * *

In committing its property to a public use, a utility does not profess to serve all persons, wherever situated.   Generally, the duty to offer service extends as far as but no further than the company's undertaking, a concept that varies according to the nature of the services to be performed, the duration of the obligation, and the geographical area to be served.   A utility's undertaking is normally defined by the terms of a franchise, charter, or certificate of public convenience and necessity. Continued service to an area or individual over a period of time will also give rise to an implied contract imposing an obligation to serve, and a utility may, of course, expand its undertaking through express contracts.

Once imposed, the duty to serve can not be extinguished by the unilateral action of the utility. Under any other rule, a segment of the public that has relied on a virtual monopoly to provide vital services could be irretrievably deprived of them at the whim of the utility. When two or more competing utilities have been enfranchised to serve the same area, the need for such a rule is less compelling, but the courts and commissions have nevertheless held that contracts dividing territory between competing utilities are void, even when no detriment to the public can be shown.

A utility's undertaking to provide service to a geographical area does not necessarily commit it to provide service under all circumstances to all potential customers within the area. Several considerations, which will be discussed below, may excuse a utility from its service obligation to particular consumers. Similarly, a utility may be justified in refusing to offer any service at all to a portion of its area of dedication. Thus, a utility may be excused for economic or other reasons from extending service to an area within its undertaking that has not previously been served, or it may be allowed to discontinue or abandon service to an area presently receiving service. The power to require extensions and to allow abandonments and discontinuances has been entrusted to the state and federal regulatory agencies, subject to review by the courts.

Extensions. The need for an extension of service typically arises when an area undergoes substantial economic development in the form of residential or industrial construction. In the early stages of development, the demand for service may be very slight, and the investment in utility facilities necessary to satisfy the demand extremely costly. In this situation, some accommodation must be made between the service needs of potential consumers and the revenue requirements of the utility under an equitable rate structure.

The due process guarantee of the Constitution precludes a state from requiring excessive expenditures for the extension of service when the effect of an order would be to compel the company to devote its property to a public use without just compensation. However, few extension cases actually assume constitutional dimensions, the essential inquiry more often being whether an extension order complies with judicial and statutory standards of reasonableness. The significant factors to be considered in determining whether an order is reasonable include the amount of demand, the cost of providing service, the immediate and prospective revenues collectible from the proposed extension, and the impact of the extension on the financial condition of the utility.

When present demand is extremely low and the probability of an increased future demand is so low that the cost of extending service will be likely to far exceed any possible yield from investment, no extension will be required even though no serious detrimental effect on the utility's over-all operation is threatened. Since the burden of the loss incurred by the extension would have to be borne for an indefinite period by the remainder of the consuming public, the interests of the few who seek service are sacrificed.

A more typical and difficult problem is presented when a sizeable increase in presently low demand can be expected to produce profits within the foreseeable future, but the cost of the newly extended service can not be covered by reasonable charges for a considerable length of time. Clearly the fact that present demand is insufficient to assure an immediate fair return on the investment does not in itself justify a refusal to serve, and when the losses resulting from initial operation of new facilities can be borne by the utility without disabling it from earning a fair return on all of its property or endangering its ability to serve the community, an extension order will normally be upheld.

* * *

The likelihood of a rise in demand may also place a utility in the dilemma of choosing between building facilities to satisfy future demand, the cost of which may now be prohibitive, and providing facilities to meet present demand, which may shortly become obsolete. * * *

The most difficult problem occurs when demand may be expected to reach such a level as to establish clearly a substantial need for service, but of insufficient dimensions to support a reasonable return on the extension expenditures at any time. The principle is often stated that a utility is not at liberty to serve only the profitable areas within its undertaking; thus, the final determination must rest on a balancing of the utility's ability to sustain a continuing loss in one segment of its operations against the service needs of a considerable body of the public.

Implicit in the foregoing analysis is the assumption that the utility can bear the burden of an extension under its present rate schedule or that economic conditions are such that a general rate increase is a feasible solution. Unfortunately, this is not always the case. When rates are already extremely high, * * * a rate increase imposes undue financial hardship on present consumers or forces them to use less convenient facilities. When a more acceptable alternative form of service is available, a rate increase may result in a lessening of demand and possibly a decrease in total revenue. Thus, extension orders are highly impractical when the utility is not prospering.

Some courts, on the theory that proof of a need for service within a utility's area of dedication is sufficient in itself to justify an extension order, maintain that rate considerations are not relevant in service proceedings. To encumber every service proceeding with all of the complications necessarily involved in a formal rate proceeding undoubtedly would create considerable confusion and delay. On the other hand, an extension order occasionally raises the need for full-scale reconsideration of rate schedules and structures, and time might be saved by resolving rate issues during the service proceeding. Perhaps the most workable solution would be to have the commission ignore rate questions unless the proposed extension involves large sums of money in relation to the company's total investment; if it does, some examination should be made. However, once a complainant has demonstrated the need for service within the company's area of dedication, a heavy burden should be placed on the utility to show that the proposed extension necessitates an inquiry into rate considerations.

* * *

NOTE

1. The problems and considerations discussed in the preceding excerpts become more complex when it is recognized that one utility company may provide more than one type of service and the franchise area for each type of service may be different.

a. For example, one utility company may offer both electric and gas service and another may offer only electric service. The gas service franchise area of the first company may include the electric service franchise area of the second company.

b. A real estate development occurs near the borderline between the two companies' electric service franchise areas. The development is within the second company's electric service franchise area and well within the first company's gas service franchise area. The development requires both electric and gas service, and neither company has service facilities in close proximity to the development. The facts indicate that a reasonable future return can be obtained as a result of an extension of electric service or of both gas and electric service but not solely gas service.

1. Should the state public utilities authority permit the company providing solely electric service to serve the development and deny a request that the other company extend its gas service?

2. Should it permit the company providing both gas and electric service to serve the development even though the development is in the other company's electric service franchise area?

3. Compare *Town of Fountain v. Public Utilities Commission,* 167 Colo. 302, 447 P.2d 527 (1968), with *Public Utilities Commission v. Home Light & Power Co.,* 163 Colo. 72, 428 P.2d 928 (1967), and *Public Utilities Commission v. Poudre Valley Rural Electric Ass'n,* 173 Colo. 364, 480 P.2d 106 (1970).

2. Frequently, municipalities provide certain utility services such as sewer and water. A municipality may not be subject to the jurisdiction of the state public utilities authority, but it is subject to the jurisdiction of the courts. Quite often, the question presented is when can a municipality be compelled to extend its water and sewer services to developments in properly-zoned areas within the municipal boundaries.

THE LAW OF MUNICIPAL CORPORATIONS
Eugene McQuillan
Sec. 35.35(e) at 471 (3rd Ed.1970).
[footnotes omitted]

The view has been expressed that a municipality distributing water to its inhabitants is under a duty to supply water to all the inhabitants of the community who apply for the service and tender the usual rates, which obligation includes the establishment of a distribution plant adequate to serve the needs of the municipality, and the enlargement of the system to meet the reasonable demands of a growing community. [It is generally accepted, however,] that in determining whether to extend its existing service, a municipality exercises its discretionary powers, which are not subject to review by the courts in the absence of bad faith. A municipality which owns its water [treatment plant and distribution system] cannot be compelled by mandatory injunction to extend a water main, since the municipality is invested with discretion in regard to such governmental functions; and such discretion, * * * exercised in good faith, cannot be controlled by mandatory injunction. Mandamus, also, has been denied where the cost of the extension, in view of the maximum current revenue of the municipality, was excessive. * * *

On the other hand, while the municipality [may] exercise discretion as to the extension of its water system, governed largely by the extent of the need and economic considerations, the discretion must be fairly and reasonably exercised. Denial of an extension for a newly developed tract, or the imposition of conditions to the grant of an extension, must not be unreasonable, arbitrary or an abuse of discretion, otherwise mandamus will lie to compel the extension. A city may also be compelled to make improvements in its water system.

NOTE

1. Does a municipality have any discretion with respect to the extension of services when its ordinances require such services?

    a. For example, assume the municipal ordinances prohibit the use of septic tanks and wells within the municipal boundaries. A proposed real estate development is to be located just within the municipal boundaries in a properly zoned area, but city water and sewer facilities, at present, are not available in the area.

        1. Can the municipality refuse to extend water and sewer facilities for the reason that the cost of the extension is excessive when compared with the revenue which can be obtained while prohibiting the use of septic tanks and wells for the development.

2. Municipalities can refuse to extend services to a proposed development to be located within their boundaries if the development is not permitted by the zoning of the area within which the development will be situated.

    a. Cf., *Corcoran v. Bennington*, 128 Vt. 482, 266 A.2d 457 (1970); Note, *Zoning—Pre-existing Use—Refusal of Municipality to Act on Application for Sewer and Water Services—Reliance by Officers on Invalid Zoning Ordinance No Bar to Mandamus,* 35 Alb.L.Rev. 421 (1971).

3. In the prior consideration of private utilities it was indicated that a utility might not be required to serve an area within its franchise if the utility demonstrated that neither now nor in the future would the utility be able to earn a fair return from its service to the area. Can a municipality avoid serving an area within the municipal boundaries for the same reason if it also can be shown that the present and future demand for service in the area will be sufficient to enable the municipality to recover the costs associated with the extension of service?

4. What steps, if any, can be taken if it can be shown that the present and future demand for service in an area will provide a handsome return to the municipality, but the municipality presently does not have the money necessary to fund the extension or add necessary capacity to its treatment plant?

a. Can a court compel a municipality to issue municipal bonds to fund the extension or the addition to the treatment plant?

b. Might a developer possessing enough capital offer to provide the money for the extension or the addition?

1. Should the developer provide the money as a loan or a contribution to the municipality?

2. If the developer provides the money as a contribution, should the developer be entitled to recover some of the contribution if another developer in the area to which service was extended benefits from the extension?

c. If the developer provides the money as a contribution to the municipality, can the developer take a charitable deduction for the amount of the contribution or must the developer treat the contribution as a "cost" of the development? See Division IV, page 997 infra.

5. Equal protection and due process have set limits, in appropriate cases, on the discretion of municipalities with respect to decisions involving the furnishing, quantity and quality of municipal services. See *Hawkins v. Shaw,* 437 F.2d 1286 (5th Cir.1971); Fessler and Haar, *Beyond the Wrong Side of the Tracks: Municipal Services in Interstices of Procedure,* 6 Harv.C.R.–C.L.L.Rev. 441 (1971); Comment, *Equal Protection in the Urban Environment: The Right to Equal Municipal Services,* 46 Tul.L.Rev. 496 (1972).

6. See generally Comment, *Control of the Timing and Location of Government Utility Extensions,* 26 Stan.L.Rev. 945 (1974).

6.   ZONING

Of particular concern in the acquisition of real estate for development is the zoning of the real estate to be acquired. For example, it would be foolhardy to attempt to construct a shopping plaza in an area zoned for agricultural use or an apartment house in an area zoned for single family residence or an office building in an area zoned for multiple family residences. In short, before many steps are taken with respect to the real estate under consideration, the developer should be certain that the real estate is properly zoned for the contemplated development or, if not, that there exists a significant probability that, in one way or another, the use of the real estate for the contemplated development will be permitted by the local government. If the real estate is appropriately zoned, minor problems such as setbacks and height restrictions may be of concern. If, however, the area is not properly zoned, there are a number of alternatives which the developer might pursue. Among these alternatives are (1) obtaining a variance, (2) obtaining a rezoning or, where authorized by state statute and permitted by local ordinances, (3) obtaining planned unit development status.

a.   VARIANCES

NOTE:

ZONING VARIANCES

74 Harvard Law Review 1396 (1961).
[footnotes omitted]

State acts authorizing local legislative bodies to pass zoning ordinances generally allow the granting of "variances"—the exemption of individual property from some of the restrictions set out in the ordinance. Normally this is done when the literal enforcement of these restrictions would result in "unnecessary hardship." This practice, which had its inception in the pioneer New York zoning legislation and is included in the Standard Zoning Enabling Act, was originally thought necessary to protect the zoning ordinance from constitutional objection; but today the prime purpose of the variance is to benefit the community and the individual property owner by assuring that property capable of being put to commercial, industrial, or residential use will not lie idle.

Two types of permission are subsumed under the term variance: that relating to the dimensions of the property, for example, allowing modification of the yard, area, or height restrictions; and that concerned with the use to which the property is put, for example, permitting a commercial establishment in a residential zone. That the former type is included within an authorization to grant variances is clear; as to the latter there is more doubt. While a few state enabling acts make specific provisions for "use" variances, the statutes of most states are indefinite, and the courts have differed as to whether use variances are authorized. In almost all states, however, nonconforming uses in existence when the zoning ordinance was passed are permitted to continue, creating substantially the same effect as a use variance; this result is probably necessary to prevent the zoning ordinance from being confiscatory.

The institution usually charged with the responsibility of granting variances is a board of appeal or adjustment created by the local legislative body pursuant to the zoning enabling act. Like any other administrative board, its actions must be governed by intelligible standards set out by the state legislature and perhaps further defined by the municipality. Although there are a few early decisions to the contrary, an ordinance authorizing a board to grant variances upon a showing of "unnecessary hardship" is not an undue delegation of power, especially since the decisions of the board are made subject to judicial review so as to assure that the standards will be followed. In some jurisdictions the local legislative body will itself undertake the task of deciding whether individual pleas for variances will be granted, sometimes upon the recommendation of a board. Judicial review remains available under such an arrangement.

*   *   *

In order to have standing to request a variance from a board of appeals the petitioner is generally required, if he does not already have a legal interest in the property, to have made a binding contract to acquire such an interest. Thus even the holder of an option to purchase the land does not qualify, since he is not bound to exercise the option. It is true that he may be able to make use of a variance granted to his vendor, since it is generally held that the benefit of a variance is not confined to the person who obtains it.   *   *   *

Most ordinances require the board to give public notice of its proceedings, usually in a newspaper of general circulation. Some also require personal notice to "parties in interest." If "parties in interest" is broadly interpreted, the potentially large number of persons whose identity and whereabouts may have to be ascertained will make this procedure burdensome; personal notice to the applicant and to adjacent property owners should suffice. If proper notice is not given, the board's order may be set aside on appeal, but failure to receive proper notice may be waived by appearance before the board.

Because of the effect that a variance may have on other property owners, most ordinances provide for public hearings. Although these hearings are usually conducted in an informal manner without rigid rules of procedure, the applicant normally has the right to cross-examine witnesses. In addition, the board may act on facts known to it though not produced at the hearing; for example, it often makes its own examination of the premises. Any such independent findings, if significant and capable of rebuttal, should be disclosed at the hearing; at least they should be contained in the record and thus open to attack on appeal.

Generally the board must reduce its decision to writing, setting forth findings of fact and the reasons for the action taken. In order to facilitate review and provide guidance for prospective applicants, the board cannot merely state, but must elaborate upon, the highly generalized language of the statute, and if the grounds of the decision cannot be determined from the record the board's order may be set aside or remanded.

The board may not reopen a case and set aside its former decision unless there are significant new factors to be considered. The successful applicant should be able to rely on the finality of the proceedings;

similarly, adversely affected property owners should be protected from being repeatedly called upon to oppose a variance previously denied. * * * A prior refusal based on a determination that a reasonable use of the land can be made within the terms of the ordinance should also preclude an applicant from obtaining a variance for a purpose different from that for which he had earlier applied. The fact that the purpose is different is not relevant to a determination of reasonable usability, and therefore the question facing the board would be the same as in the previous proceeding. If, however, the prior denial was based solely on a finding that the type of variance sought would have a serious detrimental effect on the public, a request for a different type should not be barred. Here the board would be facing a different question—whether the new variance proposed would be detrimental to the public.

* * *

Standards for Granting Variances

A. *The Primary Consideration: Fostering the Use of Land*

In most jurisdictions a variance will be granted if there is "unnecessary hardship." Since the main purpose of allowing variances is to prevent land from being rendered useless, "unnecessary hardship" can best be defined as a situation where in the absence of a variance no feasible use can be made of the land. Analysis of this standard requires an examination of the circumstances under which land will remain idle.

Often an applicant desires to use his property for a business purpose not permitted by the ordinance or seeks a dimensional variance for property which is either being used now for a permitted business purpose or contemplated to be so used. If in the absence of a variance a fair return cannot be earned on the property or excessive costs would be required to comply with the ordinance, the owner will probably not use the land. If in addition the possibility of sale at a fair profit, or at least not at an excessive loss, to one who will be able to comply is remote, the land will lie idle. These circumstances make out a strong case for granting a variance on the ground of "unnecessary hardship."

* * *

The courts often say that "mere financial hardship" is not sufficient ground to justify the granting of a variance. But this is an oversimplification, since factors leading to the nonuse of land—inability to earn a fair return, added expense in utilizing the property, or inability to sell at a fair price—are all of an economic nature. The statement that mere financial hardship is not sufficient is significant only where, although a fair return can be made if the ordinance is complied with, the petitioner wishes to make a greater profit on the property. In such a case, because the land can and will be used in compliance with the zoning ordinance, the variance should be denied.

* * *

B. Countervailing Considerations

Although the prime purpose of the variance procedure is to assure that the land will be used, thereby benefiting the community and the individual property owner, in some circumstances competing considerations arise which courts and boards consider more important to the community than fostering the use of land.

1. The Requirement of Uniqueness. The conditions rendering the land unusable must be unique to the property for which a variance is sought. This requirement is often made explicit in the enabling act. To allow a variance when the conditions are not unique would probably result in like demands from all the neighboring landowners similarly affected. If their requests were granted the board would be in effect rezoning the area under the guise of the variance procedure. The result of such action would be to undermine the function of the local legislative body whose task it properly is to make the basic value judgments involved in zoning an area. Preventing the usurpation of this function is properly considered of greater significance than permitting the nonuse of land which may result from an adherence to the uniqueness requirement. * * *

2. The "Self–Imposed Hardship" Doctrine. There are several situations in which, despite the fact that the land could not be used in the absence of a variance, some courts will not allow a variance because the "hardship" was "self-imposed." The most frequent instance occurs when the applicant has purchased the property after the passage of the zoning ordinance. The courts which refuse to grant a variance under this circumstance maintain that they will not undertake to aid people who by their own actions place themselves in a position where they need a variance. It is further argued that people should not be allowed to make speculative purchases of restrictively zoned property. * * *

A second situation in which this doctrine is sometimes applied occurs where the owner of a large tract of land uses or disposes of part of it in a lawful manner that results in a conforming use on the remainder being rendered unfeasible. * * *

Another application of this doctrine occurs when construction is undertaken in violation of the zoning ordinance. If the land is capable of being used in a conforming manner, there is good reason to deny a variance, for otherwise parties would be encouraged to violate the zoning ordinance and present a *fait accompli* to the board. * * * If the violation is minor and inadvertent, of area or height, and a large investment is involved, the grant of a variance might be proper.

In some cases where construction is undertaken without permission of the board and in significant violation of the zoning ordinance, there may nevertheless be adequate grounds for granting a variance if the land and the use are such that a variance would have been granted if the owner had applied for one before beginning construction. * * *

Other penalties, such as fines, are adequate [to encourage a prior request of a board.]

A final example of the doctrine may be found where a corporation's powers are so limited by its charter that it can use the land only for a prohibited purpose. The appeals board does not have power to remove the restriction, but it could relieve the situation by granting a variance. But it seems proper that variances are not allowed in this situation, since they would encourage incorporation for limited purposes to avoid the zoning scheme. * * *

3. Effect on the Public. The zoning ordinances make it clear that the denial of a variance is also required if the use for which it is sought would be detrimental to the public welfare.

A few courts have implicitly interpreted the public welfare language in the statute to sanction granting of variances when it was found that it would be best for the community. In stressing such factors as the need for a second such business in the city, the number of medical offices in the vicinity, or the lack of a service station for several blocks, these courts have generally failed to consider the essential purpose of a variance—to insure that land not usable under the restrictions of the ordinance will not lie idle. Where the land is usable the board's function is to enforce the ordinance. For it to determine what is good for the community would require value judgments properly left to a more representative institution, the local governing body. Therefore, the majority of courts are correct in declaring that, aside from the beneficial effect of rendering land usable which might otherwise lie idle, only the possible detrimental effects on the public—e.g., the possibility of increased fire hazards, enlarged traffic problems, inordinately reduced property values, or serious alteration of the essential character of the neighborhood—should be considered in the granting of a variance.

* * *

NOTE

1. For the purpose of determining whether an "unnecessary hardship" exists, how is a fair return on the property or a fair price for the property computed?

a. The same parcel of property may have a number of different values depending on its use. It may have one value if used for agricultural purposes and quite another if used for industrial use. A fair return might be obtained if the value of the property for agricultural purposes is used as the basis for computation. The same return, however, might be inadequate if the value for industrial purposes is used.

1. Should the computation of fair return be based on the value of the parcel at its highest and best use even though the property is not zoned for that use? What if the return on the property is fair when computed using its value as presently zoned?

2. If the property is not usable at all under its present zoning, how should fair return be computed? Should it be computed using the

property's value at its highest and best use or using its value when used in conformity with the next less restricted zoned use? Cf. *Nash v. Board of Adjustment of the Township of Morris,* 96 N.J. 97, 474 A.2d 241 (1984).

a. For example, if the property is presently zoned for agricultural use but cannot be so used, should fair return be computed on the basis of an industrial use or on the basis of use for single family residences if that use is the next less restricted use permitted under the zoning ordinances?

b. Does the value of the property as assessed for real property tax purposes make any difference?

3. See generally *Duncan v. Village of Middlefield,* 23 Ohio St.3d 83, 491 N.E.2d 692 (1986).

2. If a legitimate use is totally excluded from a community by reason of the zoning ordinance, there is some possibility that a court might consider this an invalid exercise of police power and hold the zoning ordinance invalid on its face. In recent years some courts have, upon a showing of complete exclusion of a legitimate use, required the municipality to demonstrate the relationship between the exclusion and the health, safety, morals or general welfare of its citizens. If the municipality succeeds in showing a relationship more substantial than that usually required to sustain an ordinance which solely defines use areas, the ordinance, in most situations, will be upheld. See Note, *Legitimate Use Exclusions Through Zoning: Applying a Balancing Test,* 57 Cornell L.Rev. 461 (1972); Comment, *Exclusionary Zoning: A Question of Balancing Due Process, Equal Protection and Environmental Concerns,* 8 Suffolk U.L.Rev. 1190 (1974); Mytelka and Mytelka, *Exclusionary Zoning: A Consideration of Remedies,* 7 Seton Hall L.Rev. 1 (1975); Comment, *Challenging Exclusionary Zoning: Contrasting Recent Federal and State Court Approaches,* 4 Fordham Urb.L.J. 147 (1975); Comment, *Exclusionary Zoning—Does a Zoning Ordinance with Racially Discriminatory Effects Violate the Constitution?,* 7 Loy.U.Chi.L.J. 141 (1976); Mayo, *Exclusionary Zoning, Remedies, and the Expansive Role of the Court in Public Law Litigation,* 31 Syracuse L.Rev. 755 (1980).

Similar to the exclusion of legitimate uses from a community by reason of a zoning ordinance is the attempt by some communities to limit their growth by use of zoning ordinances or related legislation. See generally Kellner, *Judicial Responses to Comprehensively Planned No–Growth Provisions: Ramapo, Petaluma, and Beyond,* 4 Envtl. Aff. 759 (1975); Comment, *General Welfare and "No–Growth" Zoning Plans: Consideration of Regional Needs by Local Authorities,* 26 Case W.Res.L.Rev. 215 (1975); Zumbrun and Hookano, *No–Growth and Related Land–Use Legal Problems: An Overview,* 9 Urb.Law. 122 (1977).

3. At times, to ameliorate any hardship which the grant of a variance may cause to neighboring landowners, the granting body may impose special conditions on the applicant as a condition of the granting of the variance.

4. In addition to variances, some enabling statutes authorize and zoning ordinances permit the granting of conditional use permits by the local government. The purpose of a conditional use permit is to authorize, subject to certain conditions, a use of property which is not permitted in the zone in which the property is located. A conditional use permit differs from a variance in that the permitted use is usually personal to the grantee and is limited in time to a defined period such as the term of the grantee's use of the subject property. Standards for the granting of conditional use permits are established

by the enabling statute and/or local ordinance and may vary from locality to locality. The standards may be specifically described or may amount to a general welfare standard, except that the standard cannot amount to a grant of legislative discretion to an administrative agency. Special conditions also may be imposed on the grantee of a conditional use permit.

5. See generally Bryden, *The Impact of Variances: A Study of Statewide Zoning,* 61 Minn.L.Rev. 769 (1977); Newbern, *Zoning Flexibility: Bored of Adjustment?,* 30 Ark.L.Rev. 491 (1977); Rosenzweig, *From Euclid to Eastlake— Toward a Unified Approach to Zoning Change Requests,* 82 Dick.L.Rev. 59 (1977); Kratovil, *Zoning: A New Look,* 11 Creighton L.Rev. 433 (1977); Comment, *Zoning for the Regional Welfare,* 89 Yale L.J. 748 (1980); Krasnowiecki, *Abolish Zoning,* 31 Syracuse L.Rev. 719 (1980); Patrick, *Land Use Regulation: A Handbook for the Eighties,* 17 Urb.Law. 324 (1985); Brooks, *Zoning Since Euclid v. Amber,* 21 Real Prop., Prob. & Tr.J. 409 (1986); Reynolds, *Self– Induced Hardship in Zoning Variances: Does a Purchaser Have No One But Himself to Blame?,* 20 Urb.Law. 1 (1988); Comment, *Replacing the Hardship Doctrine: A Workable, Equitable Test for Zoning Variances,* 20 Conn.L.Rev. 669 (1988).

b. REZONING

VALID SPOT ZONING: A CREATIVE TOOL FOR FLEXIBILITY OF LAND USE

George M. Platt
48 Oregon Law Review 245 (1969).
[footnotes omitted]

* * *

A Hypothetical Case

* * *

The owner of an undeveloped corner lot has an opportunity to develop it as a supermarket. The difficulty is that the lot is located in the center of a city district which for some years has been zoned exclusively for single-family residence use, one of the most restrictive of the urban-use classifications. No other commercial developments exist within a quarter of a mile in any direction of the lot except for legal nonconforming uses on the other three corners of the intersection where the lot is located. The neighborhood is completely developed with substantial single-family homes in prime condition. The sale of the lot for residence purposes has been made very difficult because of the nonconforming uses on the other three corner lots of the intersection and steadily increasing car, truck, and bus traffic through the intersection. One of the intersecting streets on which the lot is located has become a principal thoroughfare leading to a distant industrial area, although this was not anticipated at the time the district was zoned for single-family residential use.

The owner of the lot normally has three alternatives in seeking a use change. He may seek a use variance, or a conditional use permit, both through administrative channels of the municipal government, i.e., a zoning board of appeals or a planning commission; or he may seek rezoning of his lot to a less restrictive use by applying for amendment of the zoning ordinance by the municipal decision makers.

* * *

The Guidelines

The facts stated in the hypothetical case * * * represent one of the less complicated cases of small-area rezoning. Adding one or two additional facts will demonstrate the typically more difficult situation facing decision makers. For instance, the residents of the area may be so far from the nearest existing grocery store that there is not sufficient and convenient service for the needs of the district's residents. Or there may be a "strip" or "ribbon" commercial-use district creeping along either side of the principal street or road leading toward the lot in question, indicating a change of conditions since the original zoning and a need for reconsideration of the earlier zoning decision. Or, instead of being in the heart of the residential zone, the lot may be on its edge, abutting a less restricted use district.

* * *

The Abstract Guidelines. The most pervasive of the rules as to whether a given case of rezoning is valid or invalid appears in the generalization that the zoning ordinance amendment (or, for that matter, the original zoning ordinance), will be upheld if it is reasonable and within the scope of the police power, i.e., if the amendment is in the interests of the general health, safety, convenience, morals, and welfare of the community at large. This, of course, is the principle announced in Village of Euclid v. Ambler Realty Co. to which state courts throughout the country have religiously subscribed. Another extension of this rule, again announced in *Euclid,* is that if the issue of validity is "fairly debatable" the action of the local decision makers will be allowed to stand. * * * The decision makers, then, need to recognize the individual factors which make up the judicially stated abstractions. A number of specific rules of this more practical kind may be articulated from the large body of small-area rezoning cases. * * *

The Specific Guidelines. Most of the specific guidelines suggested below are in the broad sense related to an overriding general concept: If the facts demonstrate that conditions in a given use district have materially changed since the original zoning, there is a reasonable certainty that the rezoning of an appropriate small area within the existing district in response to this change will be upheld by the courts.

Effect of Size of Area. * * *

One is tempted to generalize a rule that the larger the area is, the greater the chances are that its rezoning will be upheld. Only rarely do courts indicate that such a rule influences their decisions. It seems, however, that courts are more favorably inclined to approve rezoning when the spot is large—at least a few score acres. Nonetheless, this judicial "inclination" cannot be relied on as determinative. The decision makers, then, are well advised to look to other, more important factors in calculating the ultimate validity of the rezoning under consideration.

The decision makers can be fairly certain that their decision to grant an application for rezoning of a small area will meet with a friendly attitude in the courts should one or more of the following factors be identifiable in the situation surrounding the application.

(1) The area is to be rezoned for a service business in a residential neighborhood under circumstances indicating a real need for the service.

(2) The existing zone classification has resulted in the complete loss of value of the land to the owner.

(3) The area is located near other rezoned small areas in the same use district or is located in close proximity to other less restrictive use zones.

(4) The area will be used by a public utility to provide area-wide service.

(5) The area is significantly affected by increased traffic or is located on existing transportation facilities.

(6) Rezoning of the area will have a demonstrably favorable impact on tax revenues and other economic goals of community-wide interest.

This list, though probably not exhaustive, encompasses the elements appearing most often in the cases. In applying the foregoing list, decision makers should be aware that not all are equally persuasive. For instance, guidelines (5) and (6), as will be seen in the expanded discussion below, are plus factors in upholding a rezoning ordinance, but are by no means solely determinative of the issue. By contrast, if any one of the guidelines (1) through (4) appear in a given fact situation it usually will be determinative in favor of the rezoning.

* * *

(1) Rezoning the Small Area for Service Businesses in Residential Districts. The now well-established pattern of urban growth outward from an older central business area has produced needs in the new residential areas for more convenient service businesses. As a result, many of the recent rezoning cases have involved shopping centers, the advent of which has been described as a "retail revolution." The service businesses referred to in this guideline usually include such enterprises as grocery stores, drug stores, department stores, barber shops, beauty parlors, restaurants, dry cleaners, and gas stations.

* * *

The conditions which will serve as a solid support for service-business rezoning include such elements as growth in population of a particular area, distance of the residents in the area from existing business centers, and the desire to minimize traffic congestion in the older central business district. * * *

(2) Rezoning When the Small Area Has No Value Because of Existing Classification. Sometimes the value of a particular parcel of land is destroyed because it is entirely unsuitable for the zoned use. When this situation exists the owner of the land usually seeks either rezoning or a use variance based on grounds of "practical difficulties or unnecessary hardship."

Typical of the cases where small-area rezoning has been upheld because of loss of value of the property as originally zoned is [a situation where the] * * * facts showed that the parcel was located on a ravine which rendered the construction of single-family homes uneconomical, because without very expensive footings homes would be subject to excessive settling. The extra expense for footings would, however, be feasible and economically acceptable in constructing apartment buildings. * * * [T]he rezoning * * * [was allowed] on the ground that the parcel had no value at all under its single-family use classification.

* * *

Topographical difficulty is not, of course, the only reason why particular parcels are rendered valueless to the owner because of an existing zone. Rezoning of a parcel from residential to commercial business use was approved * * * where it was shown that the parcel fronted on a heavily traveled thoroughfare and was hedged in on two other sides by established commercial districts. The court found that these conditions rendered use for residential purposes impractical and would result in loss of all value to the owner if the zoning was not changed.

Decision makers should take close note that the basis for upholding small-area rezoning under this guideline is that the locus in question is rendered entirely valueless as zoned. * * * [M]ere enhancement in value of the property sought to be rezoned is an insufficient basis for granting rezoning.

* * *

(3) Rezoning the Small Area Because of Its Location in Relation to Other Rezoned Areas or Use Districts. The thread of changing conditions runs through both guidelines (1) and (2), discussed above, and this is also true * * * under guideline (3). However, in guideline (3) the emphasis is either upon the location of the particular property to be rezoned in relation to nearby or contiguous-use districts of a different and usually less restrictive classification, or upon the location of the property near small areas previously rezoned in the same use area.

* * *

[W]hen the locus actually abuts a less restrictive use district the case for small-area rezoning is even stronger. Cases in [this] category show the following kinds of fact patterns which * * * have [been] held to justify rezoning: where the locus is on the edge of a residential zone abutting a commercial zone; where the locus in a residential zone touches the edge of an approaching "strip" or "ribbon" commercial zone and becomes an extension of that zone; where the locus touches a less restricted zone comprising multi-storied apartment building use which has advanced steadily toward the locus over a twelve-year period.

Interestingly, when the locus abuts another less restricted zone, the fact that the contiguous less restrictive zone is not within the same municipal corporate limits does not change the operation of the guideline.   And there is no logical reason why it should. * * *

(4) Rezoning the Small Area for Public Utility Purpose.   The discussion under guideline (1) demonstrates that the kind of use—a service business—may lead readily to valid small-area rezoning when coupled with certain necessary supporting factors such as marked community growth and appropriate location of the area.   On occasion, the public utility presents a related situation in which the decision makers can feel relatively certain that granting a request for rezoning will meet with ultimate judicial approval. * * *

(5) Rezoning the Small Area Based on Traffic Patterns and Access to Transportation Facilities.   It is well-recognized that busy streets, railroads, airports, and rivers play an essential role in the location of businesses and industrial plants.   While it is rare that small-area rezoning will be upheld solely because of the effect of traffic or because of the proximity of the locus to transportation facilities, in most rezoning cases the effect of increased traffic on the locus or the effect of the location of the locus in relation to transportation facilities quite properly plays an important part in rezoning decisions.

* * *

This guideline is relevant, but nevertheless of less weight in comparison to the preceding four.   Instead of relying solely on the traffic factor, the decision makers should be sure facts also exist that bring at least one of the first four guidelines into consideration.

(6) Rezoning the Small Area to Improve Tax Base or Economy of a Community.   Occasionally in small-area rezoning cases, the proponent asserts that rezoning of a particular locus is justified because of a beneficial impact on local tax revenues, or employment, or other community economic goals.   Improvements in the tax base and especially in the economic picture * * * [are] material factors in the upholding of rezoning. * * *

Although economic factors may work in favor of rezoning the small area, * * * of the various guidelines set forth herein, the one dealing with economics carries the least weight.   Like guideline (5), dealing with traffic and transportation facilities, guideline (6) will provide support for rezoning, but will not usually suffice unless taken in conjunction with the criteria listed in guidelines (1) through (4).

* * *

NOTE

1. Where contract or conditional zoning is authorized by state statute and permitted by local ordinance or held a valid exercise of general zoning power by the courts, it adds some flexibility to the rezoning process.

"Contract or conditional zoning is the process of imposing, by private agreement, land use restrictions upon a parcel which are extrinsic to the rezoning amendment and which are imposed in conjunction with the passage of the amendment. Each term is only applicable to certain types of methods used to effectuate the process. The term *contract zoning* can only be properly applied to a situation in which the property owner provides consideration to the local governing body in the form of an enforceable promise to do or not to do a certain thing in regard to his property in return for the zoning legislation which he seeks or an enforceable promise by the city for such legislation. In this procedure the landowner's promise is not effective until the passage of the legislation.

"The term *conditional zoning* can only be properly applied to a situation in which a zoning ordinance is passed upon condition that a landowner perform a certain act prior to, simultaneously with, or after the passage of the zoning ordinance. In such a situation the passage or effectiveness of the legislation is conditional upon the landowner's act, and there is no enforceable contract. This absence of a promise which is enforceable as against the landowner distinguishes conditional from contract zoning.

"The land use restrictions imposed through contract or conditional zoning are generally of two types. The first type is a restriction directly limiting the use of the rezoned property. It may limit the property to a single use or it may place building size, open space, or similar restrictions on the landowner's use of the property. The other type of restriction requires some act on the part of the landowner. This may include requiring the landowner to make improvements on the property such as construction of a wall, or to dedicate other property for park or street purposes, or to make payment of money to meet street improvement or other expenses necessitated by the newly permitted use.

"Whatever type of agreement the city exacts from the landowner, its general purpose is usually for the benefit of the neighbors to ameliorate the hardship of the zoning change or for the benefit of the city as a whole to meet the need for increased city services caused by the zoning change. ＊ ＊ ＊" Note, *Contract and Conditional Zoning: A Tool for Zoning Flexibility,* 23 Hastings L.J. 825, 830–832 (1972).

See Comment, *Toward a Strategy for the Utilization of Contract and Conditional Zoning,* 51 J.Urb.L. 94 (1973); Peterson, *Flexibility in Rezonings and Related Governmental Land Use Decisions,* 36 Ohio St.L.J. 499 (1975); Freilich and Quinn, *Effectiveness of Flexible and Conditional Zoning Techniques—What They Can and What They Can Not Do for Our Cities,* 1979 Inst. Plan., Zoning, Eminent Domain 167; Comment, *Concomitant Agreement Zoning: An Economic Analysis,* 1985 U.Ill.L.Rev. 89; Wegner, *Moving Toward the Bargaining Table: Contract Zoning, Development Agreements, and the Theoretical Foundations of Government Land Use Deals,* 65 N.C.L.Rev. 957 (1987).

2. It is clearly demonstrated to the appropriate local body that: (1) There is a definite need for the facilities to be constructed on the parcel to be rezoned; (2) The parcel is essentially valueless as presently zoned; (3) The parcel is contiguous to areas zoned in the same or a similar manner to the requested

zoning; (4) Traffic patterns lead to the conclusion that the proper zoning for the parcel is that which is requested; and (5) The rezoning will have a positive effect on the economy of the area. The local body, following all required and proper procedures, denies the request.

a. How can the applicant for rezoning challenge the denial of the request? Can this determination be appealed to the courts? If so, on what basis?

1. Can a court compel a legislative body to legislate? See *Quinn v. Town of Dodgeville*, 122 Wis.2d 570, 364 N.W.2d 149 (1985).

b. Does the applicant have a better position on appeal if a variance rather than a rezoning is requested?

c. See Comment, *Judicial Review of Zoning Administration*, 22 Clev. St.L.Rev. 349 (1973); Comment, *Exhausting Administrative and Legislative Remedies in Zoning Cases*, 48 Tul.L.Rev. 665 (1974); Cunningham, *Reflections on Stare Decisis in Michigan: The Rise and Fall of the "Rezoning as Administrative Act" Doctrine*, 75 Mich.L.Rev. 983 (1977); Harris, *Rezoning—Should It Be a Legislative or Judicial Function*, 31 Baylor L.Rev. 409 (1979).

3. Other municipal codes and regulations, such as building codes, also must be complied with by the developer. In addition, with the adoption by various states and localities of environmental protection acts, the developer may be required to do or cause to be done an environmental impact study prior to beginning development or obtaining necessary approval from appropriate state, county or city agencies. The developer also may have to take the steps necessary to adequately protect the environment. See *Friends of Mammoth v. Mono County Bd. of Supervisors*, 8 Cal.3d 247, 502 P.2d 1049, 104 Cal.Rptr. 761 (1972). The National Environmental Policy Act of 1969, which is the "model" for many of the state and local statutes, requires environmental impact studies on all real estate projects which significantly affect the quality of human environment and involve major federal action. What does "significantly affect" mean and what is a "major" local, state or federal action? It might include financing or licensing. See Note, *Environmental Law—State and Federal Impact Statements—What Type of Activity Constitutes a Project of Major Action?*, 8 Land & Water L.Rev. 565 (1973); Note, *The Requirement For An Impact Statement: A Suggested Framework For Analysis*, 49 Wash.L.Rev. 939 (1974); Note, *What is "Major" in "Major Federal Action"?*, 1975 Wash.U.L. Q. 485; McGuire, *Emerging State Programs to Protect the Environment: "Little NEPA's" and Beyond*, 5 Envtl.Aff. 567 (1976); Comment, *The Developing Common Law of "Major Federal Action" Under the National Environmental Policy Act*, 31 Ark.L.Rev. 254 (1977).

With respect to the environmental concerns of the developer see generally Symposium, *Environmental Control: Guide or Roadblock to Land Development?*, 19 Vill.L.Rev. 703 (1974); Berger, *To Regulate, or Not to Regulate—Is That the Question? Reflections on the Supposed Dilemma Between Environmental Protection and Private Property Rights*, 8 Loy.L.A.L.Rev. 253 (1975); Mastriana, *Environmental Regulation Checklist for Shopping Center Development*, 9 Nat.Res.Law 81 (1976); Symposium, *Effect of Environmental Regulations on Real Property Development*, 11 Real Prop., Prob. & Tr.J. 455 (1976); Schwenke, *Environmental and Land Use Laws, Regulations and Permits: How They Affect Real Estate Transactions, Financing and Lawyers, and What To Do About It*, 14 Real Prop., Prob. & Tr.J. 851 (1979). In addition to environmental concerns, the developer may be required to comply with regulations designed to implement the conservation of energy or the use of alternative energy sources promulgated under the 1975 Energy Policy and Conservation Act or under similar statutes and ordinances.

4. For a case study of the most and least persuasive arguments used in rezoning hearings see Ordway and Weaver, *Preparing for a Zoning Ambush,* 7 # 1 Real Est.Rev. 40 (1977). For a description of the practices and procedures involved in preparing and submitting an application for a zoning change see Hollin, *Application for a Zoning Change: Practice, Problems, and Solutions,* 1978 Plan., Zoning & Eminent Domain Inst. 205; Phillips, *Winning the Rezoning,* 11 Colo.Law. 635 (1982).

c. PLANNED UNIT DEVELOPMENT

AMCON CORPORATION v. CITY OF EAGAN

Supreme Court of Minnesota, 1984.
348 N.W.2d 66.
[footnotes omitted]

AMDAHL, Chief Justice.

Plaintiffs appeal from an order and a judgment of dismissal entered on May 17, 1983, by the Dakota County District Court after having heard arguments of counsel and reviewed affidavits, files, records, and proceedings generated by plaintiffs' efforts to obtain rezoning of their property by defendant, City of Eagan (city).

* * * The original application for rezoning filed by Amcon Corporation and O–J Sporting Goods Company on September 23, 1981, was denied by the city on August 3, 1982. Plaintiffs then commenced an action in Dakota County District Court for declaratory relief or, in the alternative, damages in the amount of $5,000,000 for an unconstitutional taking.

* * *

The Eagan City Council subsequently agreed on March 1, 1983, to grant a planned development (PD) zoning classification to plaintiffs, but plaintiffs contended that an underlying roadside business (RB) classification was a necessary concomitant to the supplementary PD zoning. After a hearing held on March 3, 1983, the trial court concluded that RB zoning is not necessary to effectuate PD zoning. * * * The action was dismissed. Plaintiffs appeal from the lower court's denial of their request for a court order requiring the initiation of RB zoning for plaintiffs' land.

* * *

Plaintiff O–J Sporting Goods is an Illinois corporation qualified to do business in Minnesota and is the owner of 20 acres in the city of Eagan. Plaintiff Amcon Corporation is a Wisconsin corporation also qualified as a foreign corporation to do business in Minnesota. Plaintiffs plan a joint venture to develop the property, originally zoned as agricultural (A), into a high-rise hotel-office building complex. Their application for rezoning provided for two multistory office buildings and a 225–room hotel at a projected cost of between $30 and $40 million dollars.

Plaintiffs claim their rezoning application was a request for a change from agricultural to planned development with an underlying roadside business classification in case the planned development was not granted. * * *

Code § 11.20, subd. 8 (1983), describes the purpose and intent of the planned development district as being—

> [S]upplementary to *all* other zoning districts contained in this ordinance, the purpose of which is to encourage, under appropriate circumstances, a more creative, varied and efficient use of residential land in Eagan township. Where such supplementary zoning is approved *it shall be deemed supplementary and superimposed* over the *basic* zoning of the property under consideration * * *.

(Emphasis added). Applicants for PD zoning must submit a detailed "preliminary plan with data, drawings, exhibits, plans, specifications, time projections * * * financial information and any other materials that the Advisory Planning Committee and/or the Board of Supervisors shall deem necessary and appropriate * * *." The Advisory Planning Committee then reviews the applications to determine if the PD will

> (a) better adapt itself to its physical and esthetic [sic] setting and that of surrounding lands than does development of the *underlying* zoning district; (b) be feasible for the owner and developer economically to complete according to proposed plans; and (c) benefit the community at large to a greater degree than would development of the *underlying* zoning district.

(Emphasis added). No building permit will be issued without approval of the PD application. Upon approval and prior to construction the applicant must submit detailed final plans. If the PD zoning is approved but the [applicant] fails to comply with the approved plans, as determined upon an annual review, the superimposed planned development zoning will be revoked and "the land area within the planned development shall automatically revert to its prior *basic* zoning classification." Eagan City Code § 11.20, subd. 8. (Emphasis added).

Code § 11.20, subd. 3(a)(b) (1975), describes the permitted, conditional, and accessory uses of a parcel that is zoned agricultural. These basically include only agricultural pursuits and residential dwellings with no provision for any commercial activity that is not agriculturally related.

The permitted conditional and accessory uses within a roadside business district include a motel or hotel but apparently do not allow the construction of a multistory office complex.

A comprehensive guide plan has been adopted by the city. The accompanying maps approved by the city council on January 22, 1974, and in February 1980 designate plaintiffs' property as roadside business.

The comprehensive guide plan states that it is—

[M]eant to serve as a guide and as such, should possess a degree of flexibility * * *. Deviations, however, should not be justified solely on the grounds that the comprehensive plan is only a guide and is meant to be flexible. Where deviations are proposed by developers and others, the burden of proof * * * should be the responsibility of the person or persons proposing the revision.

Plaintiffs argue that to be consistent with its comprehensive plan the city must grant the underlying RB designation. The city claims that its code contains no such requirement.

* * *

The city insists that it has never granted new underlying classifications where PD zoning has been granted. Plaintiffs, on the other hand, present affidavits and depositions of persons who were involved with the drafting of the ordinance at issue.

[These affidavits and depositions indicate that] "[t]he PD was never contemplated to be supplementary or superimposed over A, agricultural lands, a nonzone classification. All land * * * at the inception of the first zoning ordinance was classified as A unless there already existed concentrated residential, or commercial or industrial uses * * *. Thereafter lands were zoned to a *basic* zoning classification of residential, commercial, or industrial. When PD was applied for * * * the underlying zoning for the PD [was established], predicated upon the proper use of the land." (Emphasis added).

* * *

In support of their claim that the agricultural zoning classification is meant to be a holding zone, plaintiffs describe the property as not suitable for residential purposes because it is surrounded by a major freeway (Interstate No. 494), a major road (Pilot Knob Road), and commercial and light industrial districts, and has a very high noise level by reason of being beneath the aircraft approach onto runway 29L. The property is not suitable for agricultural purposes because it is largely treed, sloping, and has a ravine running through it. Plaintiffs have been paying real estate taxes based on a commercial property designation by the Dakota County Assessor. Hence, plaintiffs argue, the underlying RB zoning (which would allow the planned hotel and restaurant) is the most appropriate basic classification for their property.

* * *

Essentially, this court is confronted with a policy determination by the city that it will never grant an underlying zoning classification along with planned development zoning * * *. We must determine if the city has abused its discretion and acted arbitrarily and capriciously * * *.

A. Policy behind planned development districts.

Zoning ordinances should always be considered in light of their underlying policies. *Lowry v. City of Mankato,* 231 Minn. 108, 42 N.W.2d 553 (1950). Planned development zoning is a modern non-Euclidean concept which seeks to meet current needs and also permit adjustment to changing demands by allowing a use which does not correspond to those permitted in any single type of district. * * * The uses allowed "must be in harmony with the surrounding neighborhood, must not jeopardize or reduce zoning standards in the area and should promote the general welfare of the community * * *. [T]he use and method * * * are strictly limited to the plan presented to and approved by the City Council." *Moore v. City of Boulder,* 29 Colo. App. 248, 251, 484 P.2d 134, 135 (1971). Planned development usually involves a single use on a relatively small tract. The biggest problem is the possibility of "spot zoning." The planned development district does not appear on the initial zoning map of a municipality but regulations authorize its future creation. * * * The necessity of filing plans with the planning commission, which reviews them and transmits a recommendation to the legislative authority which decides whether or not to create a PD district, is all calculated to insure the surrounding land is protected and the PD is consistent with a comprehensive plan. The ordinance authorizing the PD district's creation must articulate sufficient standards to guide and contain the discretion of the agency and to facilitate meaningful judicial review. * * *

There are just a few cases addressing planned development nationwide. In each of those cases, PD is treated much like any other zoning classification and no *underlying* district is mentioned. *See Dillon v. City of Boulder,* 183 Colo. 117, 515 P.2d 627 (1973) (denial of request to rezone from agricultural to PD was upheld); *Haws v. Village of Hinsdale,* 68 Ill.App.3d 226, 386 N.E.2d 122 (1979) (rezoning from commercial to F, planned development, found arbitrary and capricious and not justified by public welfare); * * *.

In *Moore* planned development was differentiated from other types of rezoning. The Colorado court stated that when a property owner obtains a classification to a broad category such as business the land can be used for a multitude of permitted purposes but PD zoning is much more restrictive. 29 Colo.App. at 251, 484 P.2d at 135.

* * * Certainly the property owner who is given both rezoning classifications is in a more favorable position than the one whose investments and planning are wholly at the mercy of approval or rejection by the city council. Appellants clearly want a "back-up zoning classification" as the city claims. The city obviously maintains greater control over the use of the land with the granting of only a PD classification. But if, as the city states, it would by law have to be responsive to a request for rezoning in light of its comprehensive guidelines, it is difficult to conceive a reason why the city would not be willing to grant the RB classification at the outset rather than requir-

ing future applications and possible litigation. The city has advanced absolutely no reason for the denial of RB zoning except to say it does not conform with the council practices and is not required under the city code. If the proposed plans are rejected or if they fail somehow, plaintiffs have no recourse but to begin again with new plans and thousands of dollars in legal expenses.

B. Relationship of PD zoning to the comprehensive plan.

* * *

The designation of land uses on * * * a master plan is generally viewed as advisory and the city is not unalterably bound by its provisions. However, the recommendations should be entitled to some weight, particularly where the plan has been adopted by the legislative body although not implemented. *See Sharninghouse v. City of Bellingham,* 4 Wash.App. 198, 203, 480 P.2d 233, 236 (1971).

The city's own comprehensive plan and map designate the property at issue as roadside business. * * *

The failure of the city to advance any rationale for not following its comprehensive plan and not granting the RB classification is strong evidence of arbitrary action. In *Dillon* the Colorado court overturned the denial of an application for rezoning because there was no evidence to support the denial. * * *

The ordinance is vague and equivocal as to what "basic" zoning means. The city's own comprehensive plan designates the property as RB. * * * The parcel of land is not suitable for agricultural or residential use and plaintiffs have been paying commercial real estate taxes. Under these particular facts, the refusal to grant an underlying RB rezoning without stating any justification for the refusal is arbitrary and capricious action.

We therefore remand to the Dakota County District Court for the issuance of an order directing the Eagan City Council to grant plaintiffs an underlying rezoning from agricultural in addition to the planned development zoning already granted.

Reversed and remanded.

NOTE

1. Why did the city and the developer incur the legal fees and spend the time necessary to take the above case to the Minnesota Supreme Court when the developer could have carried out the planned project under the PD zoning granted by the city?

　　a. Could the developer construct two multistory office buildings in an RB zone?

　　b. Would the city have as much control over the design and placement of the restaurant and hotel in an RB zone?

2. If the developer had constructed the project solely under the PD zoning and the underlying zone had remained A, would the developer have been able to sell, without any problems, the land and buildings to the Sheraton hotel

chain which proposed to add two wings to the hotel building and build a new restaurant having a nightclub atmosphere? In answering this question consider the following description of PD zoning.

"A Planned Development (PD) District is a modern concept somewhat novel to traditional rezoning. R. Anderson, American Law of Zoning, §§ 5.16 and 8.38. Rezonings usually result in a change in the use of certain land from one broad category to another, such as from residential to business. For example, once a property owner has been successful in obtaining a zoning for a business use, he may then use his land for any one of a multitude of permitted uses in the business zone without regard to the effect on contiguous zones.

"A PD rezoning also allows for change in use from the previous zoning, but it is much more restrictive. Millbrae Assn. for Residential Survival v. Millbrae, 262 Cal.App.2d 222, 69 Cal.Rptr. 251. Although its intent is to permit diversification of uses, such uses must be in harmony with the surrounding neighborhood, must not jeopardize or reduce zoning standards in the area and should promote the general welfare of the community. Further, the use and method for carrying out such use are strictly limited to the plan presented to and approved by the City Council. Changed conditions are not a prerequisite to the establishment of a PD District. The prime requisite to such an establishment is that it must be compatible with the existing zones from which it is carved. Beall v. Montgomery County Council, 240 Md. 77, 212 A.2d 751.

"The * * * ordinance providing for PD Districts requires a special review by the City Council of the proposed use, in addition to a site plan of the proposed development. The City Council may, in order to effectuate the purposes of a PD District, impose upon such a plan any reasonable conditions to insure that it will be compatible with the surrounding neighborhood. Once a PD District has been established, any change in the site plan or the approved use must be submitted to and approved by the City Council." *Moore v. City of Boulder,* 29 Colo.App. 248, 249, 484 P.2d 134, 135–136 (1971).

3. Why did the developer request that the underlying zone be changed to RB? If it could have constructed the two multistory office buildings, the restaurant and the hotel in a C (commercial) zone, would it not have been better off with the underlying zone being changed to a C zone?

4. Did the court hold that the underlying zone should be changed because the zone underlying a PD zone should always be compatible with the use permitted under the PD?

    a. Or, did the court simply treat the developer's request as an application for rezoning and find that the circumstances indicated that rezoning was appropriate and that the city had been arbitrary and capricious in refusing to rezone?

    b. In fact, was A zoning in this particular case anything more than simply a "holding" zone?

    c. Would the court have reached the same result if the property had been zoned RB and the developer had requested C zoning?

5. See generally Hanke, *Planned Unit Development and Land Use Intensity,* 114 U.Pa.L.Rev. 15 (1965); Krasnowiecki, *Planned Unit Development: A Challenge to Established Theory and Practice of Land Use Control,* 114 U.Pa.L. Rev. 47 (1965); Aloi, *Legal Problems in Planned Unit Development: Uniformity, Comprehensive Planning Conditions, and the Floating Zone,* 1 Real Est.L.J. 5 (1972); Sternlieb, Burchell, Hughes and Listokin, *Planned Unit Development*

Legislation: A Summary of Necessary Considerations, 7 Urb.L.Ann. 71 (1974); Note, *Using Planned Development Ordinances to Downzone: Sherman v. City of Colorado Springs Planning Commission,* 1985 B.Y.U.L.Rev. 359.

7. INCOME TAX TREATMENT OF THE ACQUISITION OF REAL ESTATE

a. INVESTIGATION EXPENSES

Prior to the acquisition of real estate for a development, a developer usually will incur certain costs with respect to the analysis and investigation of the real estate proposed for acquisition and in negotiation with the present owner of the real estate or a representative of the owner. The tax question which must be faced when these costs are incurred is, of course, how these expenses should be treated for income tax purposes.

THE TAX TREATMENT OF EXPENSES INCURRED IN INVESTIGATION FOR A BUSINESS OR CAPITAL INVESTMENT

Arthur Fleischer, Jr.
14 Tax Law Review 567 (1959).
[footnotes omitted]

* * * Investigatory expenses, those charges incurred by an individual or business entity in its search for prospective businesses or investments, might possibly be deducted as business or non-business expenses, business losses, or losses from a transaction entered into for a profit. * * *

Deduction as Business Expenses or Business Losses by Those in a Trade or Business

Investigatory expenses are deductible as trade or business expenses or business losses if they are incident to an existing trade or business. Thus[,] the cost of architectural plans for buildings not purchased or geologist fees for a survey may be expensed by a going business. And if an enterprise has actually been started and later abandoned, the taxpayer will secure a business loss.

* * *

It is perhaps easy to find that an expense by a corporation is pursuant to its trade or business. But not every corporate expenditure is in this category. Thus, a beer company which spent funds in exploring a real estate deal might, plausibly, be denied a tax deduction on the ground that such an outlay was not incident to its trade or business. On the other hand, expenses by the same company in investigating the ale field might be deductible because of the closer economic relationship between the two activities.

An individual may deduct his investigatory expenses if they are incident to his trade or business. For example, * * * an author and lecturer, * * * [would be] allowed to deduct lawyer's fees incurred in connection with negotiations for a possible television series. The negotiations for narrating travel films on television * * * [would be] considered incident to his trade * * * or business of being a lecturer. * * * [A] developer of commercial and residential real estate [might be able to] deduct * * * the cost of investigating an industrial development. The latter activity [might be] * * * regarded as part of the business of developing real estate, not as an exploration into a new field.

A promoter of business and investment enterprises should also be allowed to deduct investigatory expenses as incident to his trade or business. A promoter organizes, finances, manages, and deals in enterprises, and for bad debt purposes, this activity is regarded as the trade or business of promoting. Consequently, debts created incident to this business are treated as business bad debts. As investigatory expenses are a necessary part of promoter-activity, they should therefore be deductible as business expenses. However, the courts have apparently not extended the concept of promoting as a business from the field of bad debts to other areas where it logically belongs.

* * *

Deduction as a Loss from a Transaction Entered Into for a Profit

Section 165(c)(2) allows an individual to deduct losses incurred in any transaction entered into for a profit. This section was enacted so that an individual taxpayer might receive tax relief on losses from activities whose aim was profit-seeking. The primary problem which has arisen under this section is whether or not a taxpayer's motive in entering a particular transaction was to make a profit. However, where investigatory expenses are concerned, the inquiry shifts to whether or not a transaction has been entered into.

In Revenue Ruling 57–418, [1957–2 C.B. 143,] the Treasury indicated that investigatory expenses would be deductible only if the taxpayer actually enters into a transaction for a profit and later abandons it. Where a search ends in the successful acquisition of a business or investment, the expenses incurred therein must be capitalized. The Ruling revoked I.T. 1505, [I–2 C.B. 112,] where the Service held that the expenses of sending an agent to Europe to organize an export business were deductible. The agent's reports were unfavorable, and the idea of establishing the business was abandoned. The Service ruled that this was a transaction entered into for a profit and that upon abandonment of the enterprise, any expenses incurred by the taxpayer in the course of the transaction became a loss which was deductible in the year in which the enterprise was abandoned. In revoking I.T. 1505, the Service indicated that the activities were merely investigatory and that therefore no transaction for a profit had been entered into. In so limiting the transaction concept, Revenue Ruling 57–418 supposedly effected a change in Treasury policy. However, this new policy had already been adopted in Revenue Ruling 55–442, [1955–2 C.B. 529,] where preliminary expenses incurred in search of a camp site for the purpose of establishing a boys' camp were held non-deductible.

The phrase "a transaction entered into for a profit" means something more than investigating a prospective business or investment.

*   *   *

The cases seem to require the taxpayer to enter at least temporarily into the business he is investigating before he will be considered as having entered into a transaction for a profit; otherwise the taxpayer will be regarded as refusing to enter into a transaction after making a preliminary search. For a transaction may be investigated without being entered into; and there is no inference of entrance every time a new city is visited or negotiations are undertaken. Moreover, there is no entry even though the taxpayer makes bids for a business or investment which are rejected. A fortiori this is true if the taxpayer voluntarily refuses to purchase.

*   *   *

[The use of] Subchapter S [may help to secure a deduction for] investigatory expenses *   *   *. Because such an expense is incurred by a corporate entity, it is [arguably] deductible as a business loss. Furthermore, as a result of the operation of Subchapter S, this deduction may be passed on to the shareholders. Thus[,] the interposition of a corporate shell may convert an otherwise non-deductible item into a deductible one on the individual level.

*   *   *

Relationship of Investigatory Expenses to Capital Expenditures

The denial of deductibility [of] investigatory expenses may also result from a notion that it is improper to allow as a current expense an outlay which may benefit the taxpayer over a period of years. Where the search for a business or investment ends successfully, expenses incurred in acquiring the asset will be capitalized as part of the cost of the asset. These expenses may be recovered through [amortization,] depreciation or depletion deductions over the life of the acquired asset or on the sale or abandonment of the asset. Where the search results in the purchase of a business, investigatory expenses will be added to the cost basis of the business. Tax-savings will follow the sale or liquidation of the business.

Where a search ends unsuccessfully, there is, of course, nothing against which a taxpayer may capitalize his expenses. Therefore, a court may deny [a present] deduction [for] these outlays, on the theory that the same expense cannot be a present deduction if it is ordinarily a capitalizable item. Moreover, if a taxpayer subsequently acquires a business or investment after deducting investigatory expenses, he will have secured a present deduction for outlays that result in benefits enduring over a period of years.

The present all-or-nothing approach by the courts and Treasury is not a satisfactory way of handling the above suggested problems. The rationale for capitalizing investigatory expenses where a search ends successfully is that these costs secure an asset which will survive beyond the year in which the expense[s were] incurred. Therefore, the recovery of the search expenditures should somehow be related to the term of the taxpayer's possession of the acquired property. However, where no property is secured, such a justification for deferring a deduction of the investigatory expenses disappears. On the abandonment of the search, the expenses have resulted in no benefit to the taxpayer and should be deductible as a loss.

To prevent an immediate deduction for expenses which result in the securing of an asset, the taxpayer should be required to prove he has abandoned an unsuccessful search. Where a taxpayer continuously searches for a business, at what point is his search abandoned? Should a division be made on the basis of a shift in geographical area or nature of the investigated business? It is reasonably clear that when a search results in the acquisition of property, it should be regarded as abandoned. Those expenses directly related to the property acquired should be capitalized. On the other hand, expenses of the same general investigation, but unrelated to such property, should be deductible as the cost of an unsuccessful and separate investigation. Moreover, where a taxpayer clearly proves his abandonment of an investigation for a particular investment or business, deduction should then be allowed.

It is in between the successful search and the clear abandonment that problems lie. A particular search might be regarded as terminated when it is not carried on for a period of time. Or[,] perhaps a shift in the type of business investigated, the geographical area of search, or the partners in the venture will end a particular transaction. A fair solution to the time of abandonment problem will require the courts to evaluate all the facts of the case in determining whether a search has ended—the sort of assessment required in other areas of the tax law.

* * *

NOTE

1. For the purposes of Section 165(c)(2), when is "solely" investigation ended and a transaction entered into?

   a. If a newly formed noncorporate entity acquires an option to purchase a parcel of real estate, does some soil testing, finds the soil unsuitable for the type of development planned and permits the option to lapse, may the investigation expenses with respect to this particular parcel of real estate be deducted as a loss under Section 165(c)(2)?

   1. If the entity had not obtained the option but merely secured permission to test the soil from the owner of the real estate, are the expenses deductible under Section 165(c)(2)?

2. If there had been some leased dwellings on the real estate and during the option period the optionee was required to maintain the dwellings and had the right to and did collect the rent, would this improve the chances of deducting the investigation expenses under Section 165(c)(2)?

3. If the entity gave no consideration for the option, would the investigation expenses be deductible under Section 165(c)(2)?

b. If the entity referred to in a., above, did not have an option but, with the oral understanding that it had a right of first refusal to purchase the real estate, it assisted the owner of the property in obtaining the rezoning necessary for development and the entity then abandoned the project, would it succeed in claiming the investigation expenses it incurred as a deductible loss under Section 165(c)(2)?

JOHAN DOMENIE AND ANNE DOMENIE v. COMMISSIONER

34 CCH Tax Ct.Mem. 469 (1975).

QUEALY, Judge:

* * *

During the year 1970, Johan Domenie (hereinafter sometimes referred to as "petitioner") was employed as manager of Banco da Lavoura de Minas Gerais, S.A., a foreign bank doing business in New York City. Having accumulated some capital to invest, the petitioner resigned that position in the fall of 1970 in order to devote full time to the search for a business which he might acquire. In response to advertisements that he placed in the Wall Street Journal and the Business Journal, in January 1971 the petitioner was contacted by Bennett Applebaum, a Florida broker. After several letters, Applebaum introduced the petitioner to Michael Enelow (hereinafter sometimes referred to as "Enelow"). Enelow was interested in selling his interest in Commercial Distributors, Inc., a retail and wholesale distributor of ice machines and fountain equipment in Irwin, Pennsylvania, which is near Pittsburgh, Pennsylvania.

On January 31, 1971, petitioner flew to Pittsburgh to meet with Enelow and to make a preliminary investigation of the company. Finding it met his basic requirements, on his return to New York he requested the Chase Manhattan Bank to provide him with credit information concerning Commercial Distributors, Inc. He also obtained reports from Dun & Bradstreet on the history and status of the company.

Subsequently, the petitioner studied the company and its business thoroughly. He visited various establishments to acquaint himself with the products being sold by Commercial Distributors, Inc. He contracted with the accounting firm of Peat, Marwick, Mitchell & Co. to review briefly the accounting system of Commercial Distributors, Inc. Said review indicated that the rate of return on invested capital of $200,000 would be 15 percent.

By February 11, 1971, the petitioner had made his own detailed analysis of the financial statements of Commercial Distributors, Inc., provided him by Enelow. He made other trips to Irwin to become familiar with the operation of the business, its staff and customers. At the petitioner's request, the Chase Manhattan Bank provided him with a letter of introduction to the Western Pennsylvania National Bank in order to obtain necessary future financing for the business. During this period, the petitioner also investigated the housing and schooling conditions in the Pittsburgh area in preparation for the eventual move of his family there.

After an oral agreement was entered into by the parties, on March 1, 1971, at the petitioner's request, Peat, Marwick, Mitchell & Co. made a complete audit of Commercial Distributors, Inc. The petitioner also contracted with a Pittsburgh law firm to represent him in the acquisition. He prepared a memorandum to the firm outlining the details and he instructed them to establish a Pennsylvania corporation to acquire all the assets or the stock of Commercial Distributors, Inc.

During March most of the details of the acquisition were agreed upon. Preliminary drafts of the acquisition agreement, promissory note and a consulting agreement with Enelow were prepared and sent to the attorneys of Commercial Distributors, Inc. The petitioner met with suppliers of the products sold by Commercial Distributors, Inc., and among other things, arranged that a franchise with Commercial Distributors, Inc., be transferred to him or to a corporation controlled by him.

On March 24, 1971, the petitioner transferred $125,000 from his bank account in the Chase Manhattan Bank to his personal checking account in the Western Pennsylvania National Bank. Contemplating that his proposed corporation would be opening an account with that bank upon the signing of the contract of purchase, the petitioner, the other two officers of the new corporation (who were also officers of Commercial Distributors, Inc.) and the treasurer of the new corporation made out signature cards authorizing the bank to recognize any of the signatures in the payment of funds or in the transaction of any business.

Articles of incorporation and by-laws for the new corporation were prepared and forwarded to Harrisburg, Pennsylvania, where it was to be incorporated. Also, a corporate name was reserved.

The petitioner was physically present in Pittsburgh a total of 33 days during the period January 31, 1971 through April 14, 1971. During this time, he was personally active in the business. He worked on a daily basis with the sales managers of Commercial Distributors, Inc., deciding on a development program, travel plans and prices for special bids to hospitals, schools and major chain businesses. He prepared a special bid on a major project. He rearranged the inventory and worked with mechanics familiarizing himself with the physical aspects of the products that Commercial Distributors, Inc., was selling.

He went along on installation, maintenance and repair calls. He collected some accounts. He assisted in the preparation of a layout for a forthcoming equipment and dealer show. He worked with the company's accountant on revised accounting procedures to go into effect after the acquisition and prepared detailed budgets for 1971–1972. In addition, Enelow introduced him to friends, business acquaintances, and customers as the future owner of Commercial Distributors, Inc.

Early in April, the final drafts of the acquisition agreement, the promissory note and the consulting agreement were submitted to Enelow's attorneys. The closing date was set for April 30, 1971.

About this same time, the petitioner began hearing rumors that another venture of Enelow's, "Barnacle Bill's, Inc.," was encountering financial difficulty. Barnacle Bill's was in the same building as, and was subleasing space from, Commercial Distributors, Inc. It was also purchasing all of its restaurant equipment from Commercial Distributors, Inc., which resulted in increased sales for Commercial Distributors, Inc., during 1970. In addition, Barnacle Bill's owed Commercial Distributors, Inc., approximately $9,000.

The petitioner also discovered that certain misrepresentations had been made to him. Some of the inventory which showed up as stock in the inventory of Commercial Distributors, Inc., actually belonged to Barnacle Bill's. This reduced the total assets of Commercial Distributors, Inc., by approximately $13,000. Some equipment which had been leased to Commercial Distributors, Inc., had been sold by Commercial Distributors, Inc., for cash. Certain repurchased equipment financed by a bank had been resold by Commercial Distributors, Inc., for cash without notification or repayment to the bank.

Assessing these factors along with the information that Barnacle Bill's would be filing for bankruptcy, the petitioner decided to abandon the acquisition. He felt that since Enelow had a previous bankruptcy in 1966, this new bankruptcy would affect Enelow's credibility in the local market and this in turn would have an adverse effect on Commercial Distributors, Inc. All efforts to acquire the business were abandoned on April 16, 1971.

The petitioner did not purchase any property or options on property in connection with the acquisition of Commercial Distributors, Inc. No contracts or agreements were actually signed and no downpayment was made. Although the petitioner was introduced as the future owner of the business, he was never given any position or title therein. He never paid any bills on behalf of Commercial Distributors, Inc. No stationery or letterheads for the proposed new corporation were printed up and the new corporation was never actually incorporated.

When the parties terminated the agreement in April, the petitioner made a trip to Florida. The petitioner testified that the trip took place early in April either a little before or a little after the transaction was terminated. He also stated that the purpose was to meet with Bennett Applebaum to get other information about Enelow and his relationship with Commercial Distributors, Inc., and to explain to Applebaum the petitioner's doubts about the deal. The possibility of another distributorship was mentioned but not followed up on.

Petitioners claimed miscellaneous expenses on their 1971 return totaling $5,749 in connection with the acquisition of Commercial Distributors, Inc. Such expenses included:

Airline fares	$ 848.00	Gasoline	$ 157.00
Train fares	72.00	Miscellaneous	200.00
Car rentals	201.00	Legal fees	1,762.00
Hotels	697.00	Accounting fees	1,200.00
Tolls	85.00	Business Journal ad	25.00
Postage	32.00	Wall Street Journal ad	420.00
Stationery	50.00	Total	$5,749.00

The respondent has conceded that $4,951.50 was spent in connection with petitioner's effort to acquire the business. The respondent contends that $797.50 spent for the advertisements in the Business Journal and Wall Street Journal and for the air fare to Florida in April were not expenses in connection with that acquisition. In addition, the respondent contends that none of the $5,749 is deductible.

Opinion

The petitioner claims that the expenses incurred by him in connection with the proposed acquisition of Commercial Distributors, Inc., are deductible either as business expenses pursuant to section 162(a)(2) or as expenses incurred for the production of income pursuant to section 212(1) or as losses incurred in a transaction entered into for profit pursuant to section 165(c)(2).

* * * The petitioner's * * * expenses [incurred in connection with the proposed acquisition of Commercial Distributors, Inc. are not deductible under] section 162(a)(2) * * *.

The expenses in question were incurred in searching for and investigating Commercial Distributors, Inc., with a view to purchasing that business. At the time, the petitioner was not engaged in any business. The expenses incurred were preparatory to locating and purchasing a business. For that reason, such expenses are not deductible under section 162(a)(2). George C. Westervelt, 8 T.C. 1248 (1947); Morton Frank, 20 T.C. 511 (1953). See also John F. Koons, 35 T.C. 1092 (1961).

* * * [The expenses relating to the proposed acquisition also are not deductible under] section 212 * * *.

For the expenses to be deductible under section 212, the petitioner must have an existing interest in an income producing asset to which the expenses relate. See, Morton Frank, supra; Marion A. Burt Beck, 15 T.C. 642 (1950), affd. 194 F.2d 537 (1952); Stella Elkins Tyler, 6 T.C. 135 (1946). See also Caruso v. United States, 236 F.Supp. 88 (D.N.J.1964); section 1.212–1(g), Income Tax Regs. Until the transaction was completed and Commercial Distributors, Inc. was acquired there could be no production of income for the petitioner's benefit. Until that time the expenses were merely capital expenditures. Dwight A. Ward, 20 T.C. 332 (1953); Mid–State Products Co., 21 T.C. 696 (1954). The expenses were incurred to acquire a business which might in the future be productive of income for the petitioners. See McDonald v. Commissioner, 323 U.S. 57 (1944).

Lastly, the petitioner contends that the expenses in question are deductible as a non-business loss under section 165(c)(2). * * *

While admitting that the petitioner had the requisite "profit motive," the respondent takes the position that the negotiations between the petitioner and Enelow did not reach the "transaction" stage. In substance, the respondent would restrict that term to the actual consummation of a contract. With this, we cannot agree.

The losses claimed in this case were not expenses incurred in the search for a suitable business. Cf. Morton Frank, supra. The petitioner thought that he had found such a business. There had been a meeting of minds between the petitioner and the seller with respect to the basis upon which the petitioner would acquire that business. The expenses were incurred by the petitioner in preparing to consummate the purchase. While subsequent developments compelled the petitioner to abandon the transaction, this is not a bar to the deduction of such expenses as having been incurred in a transaction entered into for profit within the meaning of section 165(c)(2). Harris W. Seed, 52 T.C. 880 (1969); Charles T. Parker, 1 T.C. 709 (1943).

As a practical matter, the expenses incurred by the petitioner in this case are indistinguishable from the type of expenses incurred by the taxpayer in Harris W. Seed, supra. Without attempting to delineate precisely what stage of the negotiations gives rise to a "transaction," it is our opinion that petitioner comes squarely within the decision of this Court in Harris W. Seed, supra. Upon the development of facts which compelled the petitioner to abandon his plans for the purchase of Commercial Distributors, Inc., the petitioner is entitled to deduct the expenses incurred in connection therewith as a loss under section 165(c)(2).

However, the expenses of petitioners incurred in advertising in the Wall Street Journal and Business Journal were not a part of the expenses incurred in the attempted acquisition of Commercial Distributors, Inc., and are not deductible as part of the loss. Likewise, as to the expense of the trip to Florida when the agreements were terminated, the petitioner has failed to show that this expense was related to the attempted acquisition. We find that these expenses are not part of the deductible loss.

* * *

NOTE

1. If the taxpayer had not entered into the "oral agreement" referred to in the opinion but had taken the rest of the steps described in the opinion, would the Tax Court still have held the expenses deductible under Section 165(c)(2)?

    a. Was the "oral agreement" much more than the taxpayer's agreement to acquire Commercial Distributors, Inc. if he was satisfied with the results of his subsequent investigation and negotiations?

    b. Cf. Rev.Rul. 77–254, 1977–2 C.B. 63; Galvin, *Investigation and Start–Up Costs: Tax Consequences and Considerations for New Businesses,* 56 Taxes 413 (1978); Bradley, *Deductibility of a Partnership's Investigation and Start–Up Expenses,* 2 J.Ps.Tax'n 233 (1985).

    c. If the amount of the taxpayer's deduction, under Section 165(c)(2), exceeded the taxpayer's income, could the taxpayer treat the excess as a net operating loss which could be carried back and possibly forward? See *Malcolm C. Todd,* 77 T.C. 246 (1981), affirmed, 682 F.2d 207 (9th Cir.1982).

2. If the steps taken by the taxpayer amounted to a "transaction entered into for profit," why did not the taxpayer have an "existing interest" for the purposes of Section 212?

    a. Is the answer that the transaction entered into gave the taxpayer, at most, a right to acquire an interest rather than being the acquisition of an interest?

3. If a corporate taxpayer is involved, investigation expenses probably will be deductible under Section 165(a) if it abandons the project. The investigation expenses arguably are deductible in this situation since there is no trade or business requirement under Section 165(a), and the limitations provided in Section 165(c) apply to individuals and not to corporations. But see *International Trading Co.,* 57 T.C. 455 (1971), reversed and remanded, 484 F.2d 707 (7th Cir.1973), and *Richard R. Riss, Sr.,* 57 T.C. 469 (1971). In these cases the Tax Court read into Section 165(a) a requirement that, in order to be deductible, the loss must be incurred with respect to assets held for the business purposes of the corporation.

    a. Assuming that investigation expenses can be deducted by a corporation under Section 165(a) without meeting an "engaged in trade or business" test, if the corporate taxpayer is an S corporation, the loss may be passed through to its shareholders.

    b. Does this present a workable solution to the investigation expense problem, i.e., form an S corporation to do the investigation and incur the expenses?

        1. Are there any drawbacks to this solution? If so, what are they?

        2. Might the rationale of the Tax Court in *International Trading Co.* and *Richard R. Riss, Sr.* be extended to deny the deduction in this situation? For example, could the Internal Revenue Service argue, if the project was abandoned, that the corporation which did the investigating was never in a trade or business and therefore, it is not entitled to a deduction under Section 165(a)? Cf. *William B. Howell,* 57 T.C. 546 (1972), and *Arthur H. Eppler,* 58 T.C. 691 (1972). See Note, *The Deductibility of Corporate Losses on the Sale of Non–Business Property*

Under Section 165(a), 1974 U.Ill.L.F. 176; *W.L. Schautz Co. v. United States,* 567 F.2d 373 (Ct.Cl.1977); *Union Mutual Life Ins. Co. v. United States,* 420 F.Supp. 1181 (D.C.Me.1976), remanded, 570 F.2d 382 (1st Cir.1978).

3. Since, after the Subchapter S Revision Act of 1982, an S corporation is treated as almost a pure conduit for both income and deduction purposes, might the Internal Revenue Service assert that whether investigation expenses are deductible should be determined at the individual shareholder level, using Section 165(c), rather than at the corporate level, using Section 165(a)?

c. What problems must be solved if the project is not abandoned, and it is to be operated by an entity other than an S corporation? See pages 114 to 115.

4. Since individual partners report their shares of partnership losses, the "transaction entered into for profit" and trade or business limitations of Section 165(c) are applicable in determining whether a partner's share of the loss is deductible, although the determination whether the limitations are met may be made at the partnership level. See *Edwin A. Snow,* 58 T.C. 585 (1972), affirmed, 482 F.2d 1029 (6th Cir.1973), reversed, 416 U.S. 500, 94 S.Ct. 1876, 40 L.Ed.2d 336 (1974).

JOSEPH SHEBAN v. COMMISSIONER
29 CCH Tax Ct.Mem. 727 (1970).

HOYT, Judge. * * *

Joseph's [petitioner] primary source of income during the years 1964 and 1965 was a business in which he leased certain real properties located in Youngstown, Ohio, which were either owned by him individually, or owned by a partnership known as the Sheban Mining Company. Joseph and his brother, Karam Sheban, each owned a one-half interest in the partnership. At some time prior to the years in question the partnership abandoned its coal mining operations, and was thereafter solely concerned with the rental of the real properties which it owned.

Petitioner realized gross rental income from the following properties owned by him individually in the total amounts of $4,060 in 1964 and $6,032 in 1965:

Description	Year Acquired	Cost
House, Cleveland Street	1947	$ 1,500
Improvements	1957	1,427
Apartments, Lakewood & Thorn	1957	34,339
Two Frame Houses, Rayen Ave.	1958	10,000
Frame House and One Store, Wilson Ave.	1958	4,000

The partnership received gross rental income from the following properties which it owned in the total amounts of $32,899.53 in 1964 and $32,173.22 in 1965:

Description	Year Acquired	Cost
Brick Building, 2501 Market	1952	$47,652.22
Brick Building, 5000 Market	1955	43,944.00
Improvements	1959	1,544.02
Brick Building, 2503 Market	1957	87,784.15
Improvements	1958	12,014.94
Improvements	1959	4,571.05
Frame Apartments, 2501 Market	1948	6,400.00
Frame House, Ellsworth	1951	6,000.00
Frame House, E. LaClede	1953	12,000.00
Frame House, North Lima	1948	5,528.31
Frame House, Parmalee	[57]	[57]
Office Building	1953	5,190.69

At some undetermined time in 1964, petitioner became interested in purchasing the Angebilt Hotel of Orlando, Florida, which was the principal asset of the Hotel Holding Company, a Florida corporation. Petitioner's plan was to convert the hotel into a "senior citizen home." On October 1, 1965, petitioner obtained an option to purchase all of the outstanding stock of the Hotel Holding Company for approximately $1,200,000. The terms of the option agreement are not of record. In an effort to obtain financing for this venture, petitioner made trips to several cities, including New York, Chicago, and Pittsburgh. A finance agency in New York told petitioner that it would probably be able to arrange for the requisite financing. Petitioner subsequently gave this agency a deposit in the amount of $13,000, which was to be used as the agency's commission in the event the financing was obtained.

On January 5, 1966, petitioner and Hotel Holding Company executed a "Memorandum Agreement", which was also described as an "interim agreement." This agreement stated that the parties had agreed on that date to transfer ownership of the Company to petitioner as soon as he was able to obtain the requisite financing. This agreement further provided, in part, as follows:

5. [Petitioner] agrees to assume all taxes, assessments and operating expenses as of and henceforward from Jan. 1, 1966, all income to be derived from the operation of the Corporation and/or hotel henceforward from Jan. 1, 1966 and during the life of this interim agreement to accrue to the [petitioner] solely for the purpose of assuring the continuity of the operations of the Corporation and all its appertenances [sic].

6. All terms of the heretoforementioned Option Agreement are reinstated except that final payment shall be in full and except for Special Clauses 21, 23, and 24, the life of this Interim Agreement to be from this date forward, retroactive to January 1, 1966, until all titles

57. The record does not reveal either the cost of this property or the year in which it was acquired.

have been searched and final financial arrangements completed to the satisfaction of both parties.

7. Both parties agree to expedite in every manner possible, to co-operate with all the means at their disposal and to provide whatever information, records and/or exhibits that may [be] required by the Lender in order to conclude at the earliest possible date financial requirements essential to the final transfer of ownership by [the seller] to [petitioner].

Soon after the execution of this "Memorandum Agreement" in January of 1966 petitioner took over the operation and management of the hotel. After he had managed the hotel for several months, petition-er was informed that he would be unable to obtain the requisite financing he had previously anticipated. Petitioner thereupon aban-doned the venture. For reasons not disclosed by the record herein, the finance agency refused to return the petitioner's $13,000 deposit. Peti-tioner "had to sue them in Federal Court to get the money back."

In his income tax return for 1965 petitioner deducted $2,665 as a business expense for travel. This expense was incurred in connection with his attempted acquisition of the Hotel Holding Company stock and in investigating and attempting to secure financing for the above hotel venture. Respondent disallowed this deduction in full.

* * *

Opinion

The first issue which we shall consider is whether certain traveling expenses incurred by petitioner in 1965 constituted deductible business expenses under section 162. Petitioner incurred these expenses while attempting to acquire a hotel in Florida which he intended to convert into a "senior citizen home." Respondent contends that these expenses were not related to the petitioner's business of managing and leasing real property in which he had an interest. It is respondent's position that these traveling expenses were incurred by petitioner while investi-gating and attempting to establish a new trade or business. This Court has held that such preliminary expenses do not constitute deductible business expenses. George C. Westervelt, 8 T.C. 1248 (1947); Morton Frank, 20 T.C. 511 (1953).

Petitioner has failed to carry his burden of proving that his traveling expenses were connected with his business of managing and leasing rental properties. At the trial he merely stated that he intend-ed to convert the hotel into a "senior citizen home." He did not offer any evidence to show what type of home he had in mind or how it would have related to his existing business. It is possible that petition-er merely intended to operate an apartment building for aged citizens. If petitioner had so informed the Court, then he would have been in a better position to argue that he did not embark upon a new trade or business since his existing business included the management of apart-ment buildings. On the other hand, the "senior citizen home" which petitioner intended to establish may well have provided its occupants with food, nursing care, and other services outside the realm of petitioner's existing business. Also since the travel was in connection with efforts to obtain financing it might well be that the expense thereof should properly be regarded as part of the acquisition cost of the stock petitioner was seeking to purchase, rather than a deductible business expense. We need not decide that question here, however, as we conclude that even if this expense is regarded as a business expense rather than a capital expenditure, petitioner has failed to establish any connection between his 1965 business operation and his travel expenses that year; the presumption of correctness attaching to the respondent's determination has not been overcome as to this issue.

Petitioner also appears to be arguing that he is entitled to deduct the traveling expenses in the taxable year 1965 as a loss under section 165. However, section 165(a) clearly states that only those losses which are sustained during the taxable year are deductible. It is very clear in the instant case that petitioner did not sustain a loss in 1965; petitioner began to operate the Angebilt Hotel in January 1966 and continued to do so for several months; he did not abandon his efforts to acquire the hotel until late in 1966 when he first learned that he would be unable to obtain the necessary financing.

We therefore conclude and hold that the traveling expenses in issue herein are not deductible in 1965 either as an ordinary and necessary business expense under section 162 or as a loss under section 165.

* * *

<h2 style="text-align:center">NOTE</h2>

1. How broadly should the trade or business of a taxpayer be defined?

   a. The facts in *Sheban* indicate that the taxpayer was engaged in renting properties which included apartments, single family residences, multiple residences and, through a partnership, an office building. A senior citizens' home may be somewhat different in terms of operation, but is the difference any greater than that between a single family residence and an office building? If, however, Mr. Sheban's reference to a "senior citizens' home" meant a nursing home, it would be clear that he was proposing to enter a new business since, in addition to providing accommodations, substantial services are provided in the operation of a nursing home.

      1. Does the holding in *Sheban* indicate that a real estate developer, which has a history of developing shopping plazas and office buildings, cannot deduct, under Section 162, the expenses incurred in investigating the possibilities of developing a site for an apartment complex, if it abandons the project?

         a. If the developer can establish that its intent from the time of its formation was to develop real estate in general and this was the first opportunity for apartment development, can it now deduct the investigation expenses on abandonment? See Rev.Rul.

74–104, 1974–1 C.B. 70; *York v. Comm'r,* 261 F.2d 421 (4th Cir. 1958); *Malmstedt v. Comm'r,* 578 F.2d 520 (4th Cir.1978).

b. If the developer decides to abandon the project, how does it effectuate the abandonment? Is its intent to abandon sufficient? See *Morris W. Finley,* 33 CCH Tax Ct.Mem. 1012 (1974), holding that the mere intention to abandon is not enough. See Note, *When Can Abandonment Loss Deduction Be Claimed?,* 4 Tax'n Law. 360 (1976); *Chevy Chase Land Co. of Montgomery County, Md.,* 72 T.C. 481 (1979); *H.R. Hanover,* 38 CCH Tax Ct.Mem. 1281 (1979).

2. If the developer incurred the expenses investigating a site on which it proposed to build and operate a restaurant, could it deduct the expenses if that project was abandoned? Cf. *Martin F. Whitcomb,* 35 CCH Tax Ct.Mem. 793 (1976).

b. Can investigation expenses be deducted if the taxpayer is the parent holding company of a diverse conglomerate of manufacturing corporations and the expenses were incurred in investigating the acquisition of a corporation which manufactured a product different than that manufactured by any of the existing subsidiaries? Cf. *Union Mutual Life Ins. Co. v. United States,* 420 F.Supp. 1181 (D.C.Me.1976), remand, 570 F.2d 382 (1st Cir.1978).

1. If not, why not?

a. See generally Roth, *Trade or Business Requirement of Section 162 and the Deductibility of Expenses Incurred in Rental Real Estate Projects,* 57 Taxes 3 (1979).

2. Should the taxpayer in *Sheban* be allowed, in 1966, to deduct the travel expenses?

3. In addition to Sections 162, 165(a) and 165(c), as mentioned earlier in these materials, it has been asserted that the expenses of an individual incurred in the investigation of a business or investment opportunity which is abandoned are deductible under Section 212(1). This approach generally has met with a lack of success. The rationale is that in order to deduct expenses under Section 212(1) the taxpayer must have an "existing interest" in the property in connection with which the expenses were incurred. It is unlikely that a taxpayer engaging in the investigation of a business will have such an interest. See New York State Bar Association Tax Section, Committee on Deductibility of Legal Fees, *The Deductibility of Investigatory Expenses Incurred in Connection with Prospective Investments Which Are Not Undertaken,* 44 N.Y.St.Bar J. 235 (1972).

4. See generally Wilberding, *An Individual's Business Investigation Expenses,* 26 Tax Law. 219 (1973); Comment, *The Deductibility of Real Estate Acquisition and Construction Expenses,* 11 Cumb.L.Rev. 689 (1980).

b. TREATMENT OF ACQUISITION, HOLDING AND START–UP EXPENSES

If the developer determines to go ahead with a project after completing the investigation of it, the developer will incur a number of costs prior to the time the construction of the project is complete and it is in operation. For example, the developer will incur a number of costs related to the acquisition of the real estate, such as the legal fees for the acquisition. In addition, most, if not all, of the developer's investigation costs will now be regarded as acquisition costs. The developer will also incur holding costs such as taxes, interest on the purchase money financing of the real estate and, possibly, security costs. When the project goes into construction, the developer will incur a variety of construction costs, such as the costs of construction supervision, construction financing costs and some insurance costs. Throughout the entire period from acquisition to completion of construction and the beginning of operation the developer will incur start-up expenses, expenses that would have been deductible if the developer had been engaged in a trade or business, such as management fees, lease-up expenses and the cost of general insurance policies. The following materials deal with the treatment for income tax purposes of the above-described variety of expenses.

1. Acquisition and Holding Expenses

TAX ASPECTS OF REAL ESTATE DEVELOPMENTS AND REACQUISITIONS

Committee on Tax Aspects of Real Estate Transactions, 1 Real Property, Probate and Trust Journal 472 (1966).
[footnotes omitted]

* * *

Expenses of Acquisition. Generally, the expenses of a developer in acquiring real property must be capitalized and added to the basis for the property. Thus, the following acquisition expenses would have to be capitalized:

(a) Professional fees—i.e., architectural legal, civil engineering, appraisal and real estate brokerage fees.

(b) Purchase money financing fees such as loan service charges. Where unimproved and unproductive property is held for development, interest expense on the purchase money financing * * * may be deducted as an ordinary expense or may be capitalized pursuant to section 266. (See discussion under heading "Expense of Holding Real Property" infra.)

(c) Escrow fees, recordation fees, title search and title insurance fees.

To the extent the developer reimburses the seller for real property taxes paid by the seller for the period subsequent to the date of the sale such taxes are deductible under section 164(d).

Expense of Holding Real Property. Normally, expenses of holding property for development, such as real estate taxes for the period subsequent to acquisition and interest on purchase money financing, will be deductible against ordinary income. [These expenses, however, will have to be capitalized into the basis of the constructed improvements if incurred or paid during construction. See Section 263A(f).]

Loan points or loan discount paid at the time the loan originates is considered interest but must be amortized over the period of the loan by cash basis as well as accrual basis taxpayers. [Loan commitment fees are treated in a similar manner.] Generally, the developer will find it to his advantage to expense [the] items [which can be deducted such as interest on the purchase money financing and real estate taxes incurred in the period prior to beginning construction]. However, if the property is both unimproved and unproductive, section 266 permits the developers to elect to capitalize such expenses in lieu of deducting them. This election to capitalize rather than to expense is exercisable for each tax year and as to each type of item, e.g., the developer could elect to deduct 19[87] taxes and at the same time he could elect to capitalize the 19[87] interest expenditures on the purchase money mortgage. Likewise, for 19[88], the developer could make a new determination as to whether to expense or capitalize the interest expense and/or the real property tax expense.

In the event the property held by the developer is presently productive, e.g., it is subject to a grazing or parking lease, then section 266 would not permit the capitalization of the carrying expenses for the property and such expenses could only be capitalized if such was proper under sound accounting practices.

* * *

NOTE

1. For an in-depth consideration of the income tax treatment of construction period, prepaid and investment interest, points, loan service charges and commitment fees see Division III, pages 829 to 849 infra.

2. Assume that a taxpayer acquires two or more parcels with the intent of developing all of the parcels with one development, such as a shopping plaza.

    a. Does Section 266 permit a separate election with respect to each parcel?

    b. If one of the parcels has an improvement on it, which the taxpayer leases to a third party prior to development of the whole, can the taxpayer make a Section 266 election with respect to the unimproved parcels?

    c. If the taxpayer begins development on one of the parcels, can the taxpayer make a Section 266 election with respect to the parcels not under development?

    d. If the taxpayer does not plan to develop some of the parcels for a period of years, can it capitalize an allocable share of the carrying charges to avoid the limitations on the deductibility of investment interest under Section 163(d)? See Division III, pages 829 to 832 infra.

    e. See generally Byars and Rao, *Section 266 Carrying Charges: Tax Planning Opportunities,* 58 Taxes 787 (1980).

3. For the most part, as pointed out above, expenses incurred during the construction period with relation to the construction such as supervision and insurance expenses must be capitalized into the basis of the constructed improvements. In addition, Section 263A requires that interest and real estate taxes paid or incurred during the construction period also must be capitalized

into the basis of the constructed improvements. The capitalized costs are recovered through the depreciation of the improvements.

4. A related, yet distinct, consideration must be taken into account when a developer acquires improved real estate and makes "repairs" to the improvements. Must the "repairs" be capitalized and depreciated over the life of the improvements or the life of the "repairs," or may the cost of the "repairs" be currently deducted? See Sections 179; 263(f); Reg. sections 1.263(f)–1, 1.167(a)–11(d)(2) and 1.167(a)–11(f)(4)(ii)(c) and Shugerman, *Basic Criteria for Distinguishing Revenue Charges from Capital Expenditures in Income Tax Computations,* 49 Mich.L.Rev. 213 (1950).

5. See generally Sandison and Waters, *More on Tax Planning for Land Developers: Allocations, Deductions, Reporting Income,* 37 J.Tax'n 154 (1972); Tucker and Leahy, *The Deductibility of Costs Incurred by Real Estate Developers,* 1 J.Real Est.Tax'n 408 (1974). See e.g. *James E. Forkan,* 36 CCH Tax Ct. Mem. 798 (1977); *William H. Eggert,* 36 CCH Tax Ct.Mem. 1071 (1977); *Moss v. Comm'r,* 831 F.2d 833 (9th Cir.1987), and Division IV, pages 990 to 998 infra.

2.   *Start–Up Expenses*

For a number of years prior to the adoption of Section 195 the Internal Revenue Service attempted to disallow the deduction of ordinary and necessary expenses paid or incurred during the acquisition, holding and construction of real estate—the period before the real estate became productive. The Internal Revenue Service argued that these expenses, such as salaries and various fees which would normally be considered ordinary and necessary, were not deductible under Section 162 since they were "start-up expenses" incurred before the taxpayer was engaged in a trade or business. The expenses, as a result, had to be capitalized. Cf. *H.K. Francis,* 36 CCH Tax Ct.Mem. 704 (1977). This position was derived from two cases, *Richmond Television Corp. v. United States,* 345 F.2d 901 (4th Cir.1965), vacated and remanded on another issue, 382 U.S. 68, 86 S.Ct. 233, 15 L.Ed.2d 143 (1965), and *Madison Gas and Electric Co.,* 72 T.C. 521 (1979), affirmed, 633 F.2d 512 (7th Cir.1980), in which ordinary and necessary expenses incurred prior to the time when the taxpayer received a licence or franchise permitting it to engage in business were held not deductible under Section 162.

The Internal Revenue Service was relatively successful in persuading the Tax Court that current deductions for ordinary and necessary expenses paid or incurred prior to the beginning of actual business operations ought to be denied and the expenses capitalized. See e.g. *Richard C. Goodwin,* 75 T.C. 424 (1980); *Estate of W. Burgess Boyd,* 76 T.C. 646 (1981); *Walter D. Swigart,* 40 CCH Tax Ct.Mem. 1215 (1980); *John C. Graybeal,* 39 CCH Tax Ct.Mem. 734 (1979); *Malcolm C. Todd,* 77 T.C. 246 (1981), affirmed, 682 F.2d 207 (9th Cir.1982); *Richard H. Davis,* 45 CCH Tax Ct.Mem. 1070 (1983). The concept has been extended to deny deductions with respect to the amortization of a capitalized expenditure if the deductions are claimed during the start-up period. See *Alex Aboussie v. United States,* 779 F.2d 424 (8th Cir.1985). In addition, the Internal Revenue Service has taken the position that an ordinary and necessary expense, rent, paid on behalf of a partnership which was actively engaged in the business of owning, operating and developing real estate by a partner who was also actively engaged in the same business was not deductible by the partner or the partnership when the partnership had not yet begun to lease stores in the shopping center which it constructed on the leased land. See Priv.Ltr.Rul. 8037024. Cf. Carldon O. Haskins, 45 CCH Tax Ct.Mem. 359 (1982). But see Duffy v. United States, 690 F.2d 889 (Ct.Cl.1982). Finally, the Tax Court in Herschel H. Hoopengarner, 80 T.C. 538 (1983), denied the deduction of rent payments under Section 162, because the rent payments were start-up expenses, but permitted the deduction of the rent payments under Section 212(2) since the payments were ordinary and necessary expenses for the maintenance of property held for the production of income.

Contrary to the position of the Tax Court, some of the District Courts and the Claims Court were not willing to deny a current deduction for normal recurring expenses simply because a taxpayer had not yet completed construction or acquisition of its income-producing assets. See Blitzer v. United States, 684 F.2d 874 (Ct.Cl.1982); Berglund v. United States, 47 A.F.T.R.2d 81–819, (D.Minn.1982); United States v. Manor Care, Inc., 490 F.Supp. 355 (D.Md.1980); Brotherman v. United States, 6 Cl.Ct. 407 (1984). The dispute with respect to the treatment of start-up expenses was resolved, for the most part, with the enactment and subsequent amendment of Section 195.

THE TREATMENT OF START–UP COSTS UNDER SECTION 195

W. Eugene Seago
66 Journal of Taxation 362 (1987).
[some footnotes omitted]

* * *

According to Congress, as a result of *Richmond Television* and its progeny, the developer of a new business faced the prospect of incurring out-of-pocket expenses that could not be deducted. Moreover, because of the all-or-nothing outcome of the case, and the facts and circumstances nature of the controversy over when a business began or whether it was a new business, the start-up cost rules [resulted in] litigation.[58] Therefore, to encourage the formation of new business and to decrease litigation Congress enacted Section 195 in 1980.

[In] the 1980 version of Section 195 * * * Congress endorsed the continued deductibility of the costs of expanding a business [59] but made no attempt to set forth guidelines for distinguishing between old and new business. * * *

58. H.Rep't No. 96–1278, 96th Cong., 2d Sess. (1980); 1980–2 C.B. 709, 712.

59. *Id.*, 1980–2 C.B. at 712.

Under Section 195, expenditures are eligible for amortization over 60 months if all of the following conditions are satisfied and the taxpayer actually enters the trade or business. The expenditures:

1.   Are paid or incurred in connection with creating, or investigating the creation or acquisition of an active trade or business.

2.   Are incurred prior to the time business begins.

3.   Would be deductible if they were paid or incurred in connection with the expansion or operation of a presently existing trade or business in the same field.

In effect, the taxpayer was given an option (1) to elect to capitalize the * * * start-up costs and then amortize these costs over not less than 60 months, or (2) to deduct the costs, and upon examination by the IRS, argue that *Richmond Television* was wrongly decided or that the business had, in fact, already begun when the expenses were incurred. * * * There were, however, some problems with the original Section 195. First, Congress left open the possibility that other courts could disagree with *Richmond Television* * * *. Second, Section 195 did not apply to Section 212 expenses.

In 1982, the Court of Claims held in *Blitzer,* 684 F.2d 874 (Ct.Cl. 1982), that the trade or business requirement of Section 162 exists merely to distinguish business from personal expenses, and, if the taxpayer enters the business, the ordinary and necessary expenses were deductible regardless of when they were incurred. Congress in [amending Section 195 in] 1984 adopted its own rationale for start-up costs. "The Committee believes that start-up expenditures generally result in the creation of an asset which has a useful life which extends substantially beyond the year in which incurred." [60] Consistent with this theory, the 1984 amendments to Section 195 generally preclude any deduction for start-up costs, except through amortization.

The omission of Section 212 expenses from Section 195 produced an absurd result in *Hoopengarner,* 80 TC 538 (1983). There, the Tax Court held that because Section 212 has no trade or business requirement, the * * * test of *Richmond Television* was inapplicable and a deduction for [start-up] expenses was thus allowed. [I]n 1984, Congress * * * prevented a repeat of *Hoopengarner* by [denying] start-up deductions [with respect to a] venture which it is anticipated [will] become an active trade or business.[61] [T]he Committee Reports set forth a very low minimum activity to determine whether the trade or business [is] "active." Thus, active trade or business means that the taxpayer is actively conducting a trade or business. The definition of active trade or business may include a trade or business that is in many respects passive. For example, a business where property is regularly leased on a net lease basis is an active trade or business for this purpose.[62]

60. Senate Finance Committee, *Explanation of the Deficit Reduction Tax Bill of 1984,* p. 282.

61. Section 195(b)(1)(A)(iii).

62. *Supra* note [58], 1980–2 CB at 714.

Congress, therefore, intended to sweep into Section 195, costs that would be deemed investment expenses deductible under Section 212. Thus, in *Hoopengarner,* where the start-up costs of a real estate operation were incurred before the building was completed, the costs would not be currently deductible but would be subject to amortization.

  *   *   *

Under the first of two tests set forth in Section 195 [for purposes of identifying start-up costs, the] costs must relate to the investigation, creation or acquisition of an active trade or business. The second test which provides that the expense would have been deductible if it had been incurred in the operation of an active trade or business, merely prevents the amortization, as a start-up cost, of a capital expenditure, or the amortization of a nondeductible expense. Thus, the start-up cost rules do not affect the tax treatment of capital expenditures, regardless of whether the business is in the start-up period.

It is also clear from the judicial history that since capital expenditures, including organization costs, can be identified, start-up costs are largely residual costs. Moreover, once the entity begins operations, costs that are not identified with assets or future benefits become [deductible] expenses. It follows then, that start-up costs are identified by establishing when the active trade or business began, or was acquired, and only expenditures that occurred before that time are subject to the capital expenditure—start-up cost dichotomy. Thus, for example, * * * if operations have not yet begun, and a supervisor is nevertheless paid, the salary is a start-up cost; on the other hand, if the supervisor is planning an equipment layout, his salary may be a capital expenditure regardless of whether operations have begun.

  *   *   * Interest, taxes and research and development expenditures are excluded from the start-up cost definition of Section 195(c)(1). Sections 163, 164 and [263A] govern the treatment of interest and taxes.

  *   *   *

According to the 1980 Committee Reports, the "active" requirement is intended to preclude expenses related to mere investments. The House Ways and Means Committee Report provides guidance as to when a particular active business begins.

"Generally, it is anticipated that the definition of when a business begins is to be made in reference to the existing provisions for the amortization of organizational expenditures (Code Sections 248 and 709)." [63] If the activities of the [venture] have advanced to the extent necessary to establish the nature of its business operations, it will be deemed to have begun business. For example, the acquisition of operating assets which are necessary to the type of business contemplated may constitute the beginning of business, according to Reg. 1.248–1(a)(3).

  *   *   *

---

63. H.Rep't No. 96–1278, *supra* note [58], 1980–2 CB at 714.

Assuming that the Section 248 standards apply to the issue of when an active business begins, there are still problems in identifying when the nature of the business operations has been determined. For example, in a case such as *Richmond Television,* which required a license or permit, it could be reasoned that whether there would ever be a business would not be known until the station license had been granted; alternatively, the license is an operating asset, and the nature of the business is not determined until the license is granted. But where there is an almost certainty that the license would be granted, the nature of the business will be known as soon as the assets (other than the license) are acquired.

* * *

The fact that expenditures are incurred during the start-up period is only incidental, because the statute requires an answer to a hypothetical question: Would the expenditure be deductible if it were incurred by an active business? In determining whether the expenditure would be currently deductible, the likelihood that the expenditure will result in a future benefit regardless of whether the results of the expenditure is a conventional tangible asset (*e.g.,* buildings * * *) must be considered. Moreover, the start-up cost classification is a middle ground (not a toll charge on new business as is capitalization without amortization) and not a complete loss of revenue to the Treasury. Therefore, the courts should be receptive to suggestions as to how the expenditures might be classified as start-up costs. Conversely, it should be expected that the courts would be quicker to accept arguments that the business is a new one, rather than an expansion of a former business, and thus apply the start-up cost rules.

* * *

Business investigation expenditures are the costs of gathering the information for the decision as to whether to enter the particular business. These costs are within the ambit of start-up costs as defined in Section 195, assuming the taxpayer actually enters the business.

* * *

Expenditures during the investigating period present some difficult issues, some of which the Statute does not anticipate. First, as with any other start-up expenditure, they must be of the type that if they had been incurred in connection with the operation of an existing business they would have been deductible. Investigating expenses would not be incurred in the operation of a business, except by including expansion of an existing business as "operations." However, when "operation" is read to include expansion of an existing business, the investigating expenditures become eligible for amortization, even though the business is a new one.

[In addition] in order for the investigatory expenses to qualify for amortization, the right kind of interest must be acquired, *i.e.,* an interest which makes the taxpayer more than a passive investor.

* * *

[Finally, as] already discussed, [Section 195 provides that] once active business begins, no more start-up costs are accumulated. By drawing such a line, the Code raises the issue of whether the taxpayer could account for the start-up costs by the cash method, defer payment until the business has begun and then deduct the costs as operating expenses. Section 195(b), for its part, does not tie the start-up rules with any particular accounting method since it defines start-up costs in terms of amounts "paid or incurred."

NOTE

1. As pointed out in the preceding excerpts, Section 195 permits a taxpayer to elect to amortize start-up expenditures over a period of not less than 60 months beginning with the month the business begins or is acquired. Start-up expenditures are amounts paid or incurred in connection with (1) investigating the creation or acquisition of an active trade or business, (2) creating an active trade or business, or (3) any activity engaged in for profit and for the production of income before an active trade or business is begun, in anticipation of the activity becoming an active trade or business. The expenditures must be the type which would have been deductible in connection with the expansion of an existing trade or business in the same field.

a. Under Section 195, two requirements must be met in order to be eligible to elect to amortize start-up expenditures. First, the trade or business being investigated, created or anticipated must be active. The Senate Finance Committee Report indicates that, in the case of rental activities, there must be significant furnishing of services incident to the rentals to constitute an active business. The Report further indicates that, in general, the operation of an apartment complex, office building, or shopping center will constitute an active trade or business. See Senate Finance Committee Report No. 96–1036, P.L. 96–605, 96th Cong., 2d Sess. (1980). Second, the expenditures must be the type of expenditures which would have been currently deductible had the taxpayer been engaged in trade or business at the time they were incurred or paid. Therefore, expenditures which represent the costs of acquisition of assets are not subject to the election to amortize. See Rev.Rul. 81–150, 1981–1 C.B. 119. One might expect to see the Internal Revenue Service assert that many start-up expenses are actually paid or incurred to acquire an asset. See Rev.Rul. 81–160, 1981–1 C.B. 312 (commitment fees) and Rev.Rul. 81–161, 1981–1 C.B. 313 (rent-up fees and commitment fees).

b. In Annouc. 81–43, 1981–1 I.R.B. 52, the Internal Revenue Service set forth the procedure to be followed in making the election to amortize "start-up expenditures" under Section 195.

2. See generally Hartgraves and Bates, *Planning for Start–Up Expenditures Under the Provisions of the Miscellaneous Revenue Act of 1980,* 59 Taxes 433 (1981); Solomon and Weintraub, *Business Start–Up Expenses and Section 195: Some Unresolved Problems,* 60 Taxes 27 (1982); McGuire, *Preopening Expenses and Real Estate Development,* 9 J.Real Est. Tax'n 163 (1982); Jones and Fowler, *Preoperating Expenses: Sec. 195 Does Not Resolve Conflicting Judicial Views,* 14 Tax Adviser 471 (1983); Ludtke, Vitek and Witt, *Tax Aspects of the Formation and Initial Operations of a Real Estate Limited Partnership,* 39 Tax Law. 195 (1986); Bradley, *Deductibility of a Partnership's Investigation and Start–Up Expenses,* 2 J.Ps.Tax'n 233 (1986); Fowler, *The Continuing Saga*

of Start–Up Costs and Their Identification, 17 Tax Adviser 244 (1986); Lee, *Start Up Costs, Section 195, and Clear Reflection of Income: A Tale of Talismans, Tacked-on Tax Reform, and a Touch of Basics,* 6 Va.Tax.Rev. 1 (1986).

c.   THE ACQUIRING ENTITY'S BASIS

A number of the future income tax consequences of the acquisition of real estate are determined by the acquiring entity's basis in the real estate.   Basis is important for at least two reasons: (1) the basis in depreciable property situated on the real estate will determine depreciation deductions in future years; and (2) the basis in the real estate and improvements will determine gain or loss on a subsequent sale of the property.

THE BASIS OF PROPERTY SHALL BE THE COST OF SUCH PROPERTY: HOW IS COST DEFINED?
Maurice C. Greenbaum
3 Tax Law Review 351 (1948).
[footnotes omitted]

*   *   *

Purchase of Property

The acquisition of property for a specific amount of cash or its equivalent generally gives rise to little difficulty in making a cost determination upon the subsequent disposition or for purposes of computing depreciation.   Generally speaking, the term "cost" is taken to mean the value of the property parted with in exchange for the item purchased.   In a purchase for cash no valuation problem as to the property parted with is presented; the determination is generally thought to be a purely arithmetical problem.   As a corollary proposition it is equally well grounded that generally there is no realization of income upon the purchase of property at a price below the readily identifiable market value.   Similarly, an overpayment by the purchaser does not result in a recognizable loss.   The purchaser in such situations makes either a good or a poor business investment, but the determination of gain or loss on the transaction must await the date of sale or other disposition.   The foregoing, however, presupposes dealing in a free market where the parties trade with each other at arm's length.   If the circumstances are such as to indicate that the sales price was determined by other than market considerations, e.g., a donative or compensatory intent, the cost would be the market value at the time of purchase, and the differential existing at that time would be either a gift or compensation for services.

But even in the countless acquisitions of property for a stated amount of cash there can be a multitude of "cost" problems which may prove difficult of solution.   A problem frequently arises in determining the various elements to be considered as part of the cost of a given item of property.   *   *   *

Encumbered Property. The cost of property which is subject to an encumbrance has presented many problems of relative difficulty. If in connection with the acquisition of property, the purchaser personally assumes a mortgage obligation, his cost would clearly seem to include the face amount of the mortgage. The same result follows where the acquisition is consummated by means of a purchase money mortgage. In both instances the obligation of the purchaser constitutes additional consideration which is included in the total cost of the property. A distinction had been suggested, however, in those cases where property was acquired subject to a mortgage for which the purchaser or acquiring person assumed no personal liability. The possibility of such a distinction has been dispelled by the decision of the Supreme Court in Crane v. Commissioner [331 U.S. 1, 67 S.Ct. 1047, 91 L.Ed. 1301 (1946)].

Although the *Crane* case involved the question of the basis of devised property under section [1014], the rationale of the opinion is equally applicable to property acquired by purchase or exchange. The taxpayer in the *Crane* case had argued that the cost of the property was limited to her equity therein and that the amount realized on the sale of the property was the amount of cash received, without consideration of the face amount of the mortgage which was still an encumbrance. She conceded that the result would be otherwise had she been liable on the bond. But the Court expressly repudiated this distinction, and Vinson, C.J., writing for the majority of the Court, stated that she was the "owner" of the property and was as effectively benefited by the purchaser's taking the property subject to the mortgage as if she were personally liable.

* * *

The Court did not confine itself to the narrow question in the case but sought to provide a consistent analysis of the "cost" of property taken subject to a mortgage, the basis for depreciation of such property, and the "amount realized" when disposition is made of such property. The taxpayer did not quarrel with the position that the basis for depreciation and the basis for computing gain or loss were the same; the dispute was on the fundamental question of what "property" was acquired by Mrs. Crane and the "amount realized" when she disposed of that property. The result reached by the Court on these points was prompted in large part by the answer that was sought with reference to the proper basis for depreciation. The [Internal Revenue Service's] practice of long standing has been to allow depreciation on the basis of the equity plus the amount of the mortgage, and there was a desire to avoid upsetting this administrative policy. Furthermore, if Mrs. Crane's property interest were only [the] equity, the depreciation of such an interest would involve burdensome accounting problems of a continuing nature.

The result reached by the Court is probably a desirable one in the light of the past development of the law of mortgages and is in accord with the general views of tax practitioners. From the standpoint of the logic of the case, however, there is considerable difficulty in accepting the proposition stated by the majority that the "owner" of property is benefited to the same extent as if money were transmitted when a mortgage, for which the owner is not personally liable, remains a charge on the property. The difficulties that arise in determining the cost of encumbered property stem from the legal fiction that the mortgagor is always the "owner" of the property, despite the equitable interest therein which is lodged in the mortgagee. To use the mortgagor's equity alone as the basis for depreciation results in an unrealistic recoupment of capital, as was pointed out in the *Crane* case, but to avoid that result by concluding that a mortgagor-owner who is not personally liable for the debt is purchasing more than equity, might also be deemed unrealistic. Unfortunately, the development of tax law with reference to mortgage transactions has been disconnected. Despite objections that might be raised to a particular portion of the *Crane* decision, it represents an answer to one question of the "cost" of mortgaged property, which is a part of a possible unified pattern. In that respect it is a worthy contribution to tax jurisprudence.

Apportionment of Cost. Where property is bought for a lump sum and is subsequently disposed of in small units which are a part of the whole, other subsidiary cost problems are created. The cost could be described in the following manner: (1) the *entire* amount of the purchase price—the cost—must be returned before any gain is realized, or (2) the cost must be allocated among the particular portions of the purchased property and gain or loss computed on that basis as to each portion. It is now well grounded that property acquired as a single unit that is subsequently disposed of in portions of the whole, requires an apportionment of cost among the several portions. A fairly typical example of the application of this rule is found in cases where realty is purchased in a single unit and then sub-divided for resale. The subsequent disposition of a single lot results in either gain or loss. The allocation of cost among the several units must, however, be made on an equitable basis of relative value rather than on a basis of proportionate acreage. But the rule of apportionment may be impossible to apply in some instances, in which event the purchaser of the *en bloc* property may recover the cost of the whole of the property before he realizes any gain from the disposition.

To carry the allocation of cost problem one step further: instead of a single purchase of property that is later disposed of in smaller portions, suppose that the property is acquired at varying times and at varying prices. If the property is of a nature which allows identification of each separate unit purchased there is no difficulty. On the other hand, if the property is of such a nature that one unit may be exchanged indifferently for another unit, i.e., fungible property, a fundamental question of "cost" must be answered. In those cases where identification cannot be made definitely, two rules are generally applied in allocation of the cost of the particular item sold: (1) the average cost of the total number of units is taken as the cost basis on the disposition of a single unit, or (2) the cost of the first unit acquired is applied to the first disposition—more commonly known as the "first in, first out" or "fifo" rule.

*   *   *

NOTE

1. As discussed earlier, the acquisition by a partnership of real estate subject to a mortgage, even if neither the partnership nor the partners have personal liability for the debt secured by the mortgage, not only results in the inclusion of the unpaid principal balance of the mortgage in the partnership's basis for the real estate, but also has the effect of increasing the partners' bases in their partnership interests. See pages 74 to 87 supra and Division III, pages 709 to 713 infra. If, however, the nonrecourse mortgage is not "qualified nonrecourse financing" as defined by Section 465(b)(6), Section 465 will prevent a partner, for the purpose of determining the amount of the losses of a partnership which can be passed through to the partner, from adding the partner's share of the nonrecourse mortgage to the partner's at-risk amount. See pages 150 to 153 supra.

2. The Internal Revenue Service has labored over the years to minimize the effects of the *Crane* doctrine.

a. In *Manuel Mayerson,* 47 T.C. 340 (1966), acq., 1969–1 C.B. 21, the Tax Court included in the basis of the taxpayer the face amount of a 99-year purchase money note and mortgage. The taxpayer purchased real estate and improvements in exchange for the note and mortgage. The note and mortgage imposed personal liability on the taxpayer to the extent of $10,000 of the approximately $300,000 purchase price and set definite installment payment dates for the $10,000. The taxpayer had no personal liability for the balance of the note and mortgage and it could be paid at any time during the 99 years.

b. In *David Bolger,* 59 T.C. 760 (1973), acq., 1976–1 C.B. 1, the taxpayer's transactional pattern was as follows. The taxpayer would form a corporation with minimum capitalization. The corporation would then arrange to buy some real estate which a third party desired to lease. The corporation would buy the real estate plus improvements and enter into a long term lease with the third party. The corporation would obtain financing for the purchase equal to the purchase price of the real estate plus improvements and secure the financing by a mortgage on the real estate and improvements and an assignment of the lease. The corporation would then convey to the taxpayer the real estate and improvements subject to the mortgage and lease. The Tax Court held that the taxpayer's basis in the real estate and improvements included the principal balance of the mortgage despite the Commissioner's assertion that all the taxpayer received was a reversionary interest which, since it was not a present interest, could not be depreciated. See Lurie, *Bolger's Building: The Tax Shelter That Wore No Clothes,* 28 Tax L.Rev. 355 (1973).

c. In *Edna Morris,* 59 T.C. 21 (1972), where the shareholders of a corporation acquired notes secured by first and second mortgages on certain real estate and the corporation then purchased the real estate subject to the mortgages, the Tax Court refused to include the amount of the notes secured by the second mortgage in the basis of the corporation in the real estate. The Tax Court found that the value of the real estate did not exceed the principal amount of the notes secured by the first mortgage.

The Internal Revenue Service has had its greatest success in avoiding the effects of the *Crane* doctrine in situations like that in *Edna Morris* in which the fair market value of the assets subject to the mortgage is less than the amount of the mortgage. See e.g. *Leonard Marcus,* 30 CCH Tax Ct.Mem. 1263 (1971); *Estate of Franklin v. Comm'r,* 544 F.2d 1045 (9th Cir.1976); *David L. Narver, Jr.,* 75 T.C. 53 (1980), affirmed, 670 F.2d 855 (9th Cir. 1982); *Carol W. Hilton,* 74 T.C. 305 (1980), affirmed, 671 F.2d 316 (9th Cir. 1982); *Milbrew, Inc.,* 42 CCH Tax.Ct.Mem. 1467 (1981), affirmed, 710 F.2d 1302 (7th Cir.1983); *John C. Beck,* 74 T.C. 1534 (1980), affirmed, 678 F.2d 818 (9th Cir.1982); *Fortune Odend'hal,* 80 T.C. 588 (1983), affirmed, 748 F.2d 908 (4th Cir.1984); *John M. Elliott,* 84 T.C. 227 (1985). In addition, the Internal Revenue Service has had some success denying an increase in basis resulting from a nonrecourse liability when (1) the taxpayer cannot demonstrate that the fair market value of the assets acquired in exchange for the nonrecourse liability is equal to or greater than the amount of the liability to which they are subject, (2) the payment of the nonrecourse liability is so contingent that it is not treated as a liability for income tax purposes, and (3) it is doubtful that the value of the assets securing the liability plus the income produced by the assets will be sufficient to eventually pay the liability. See e.g. Rev.Rul. 79–432, 1979–2 C.B. 289; Rev.Rul. 80–42, 1980–1 C.B. 182; Rev.Rul. 81–278, 1981–2 C.B. 159; *CRC Corporation v. Comm'r,* 693 F.2d 281 (3d Cir.1982); *E.A. Brannen,* 78 T.C. 471 (1982); *Max E. Wildman,* 78 T.C. 943 (1982); *Werner Graf,* 80 T.C. 944 (1983); *Ernest J. Saviano,* 80 T.C. 955 (1983), affirmed, 765 F.2d 643 (7th Cir.1985); *Stuart I. Fox,* 80 T.C. 972 (1983), affirmed sub nom., 731 F.2d 230 (4th Cir.1984). Cf. *Brountas v. Comm'r,* 692 F.2d 152 (1st Cir.1982), reversing, 73 T.C. 491 (1979); *Warner R. Waddell,* 86 T.C. 848 (1986). See generally Avent and Grimes, *Inflated Purchase Money Indebtedness in Real Estate and Other Investments,* 11 J.Real Est.Tax'n 99 (1984); Comment, *Nonrecourse Liabilities as Tax Shelter Devices After Tufts: Elimination of Fair Market Value and Contingent Liability Defenses,* 35 U.Fla.L.Rev. 904 (1983). In the case of property acquired in part for a contingent debt, the purchaser's basis in the property may be increased only as the purchaser pays the contingent debt. See Priv.Ltr.Rul. 8646005. Cf. Sec. 453(g)(1)(C).

d. Section 1274(b)(3) provides that, in a potentially abusive situation, in determining the principal amount of a debt issued in return for property, the principal amount of the debt cannot exceed the fair market value of the acquired property. On the other hand, Section 7701(g) provides that, from the seller's standpoint, the amount realized from a sale of property includes the amount of *any* nonrecourse indebtedness to which the property is subject.

3. See generally Simmons, *Nonrecourse Debt and Basis: Mrs. Crane Where Are You Now?,* 53 S.Cal.L.Rev. 1 (1979); Halpern, *Liabilities and Cost Basis: Some Fundamental Considerations,* 7 J.Real Est.Tax'n 334 (1980); Gans, *Re-Examining the Sham Doctrine: When Should an Overpayment be Reflected in Basis?,* 30 Buffalo L.Rev. 95 (1981); Comment, *Federal Income Tax Treatment of Nonrecourse Debt,* 82 Colum.L.Rev. 1498 (1982); Cain, *From Crane to Tufts: In Search of a Rationale For the Taxation of Nonrecourse Mortgagors,* 11 Hofstra L.Rev. 1 (1982); Miller, *The Supreme Court Does It Again in Tufts—Right Answer, Wrong Reason,* 11 J.Real Est.Tax'n 3 (1983); Blackburn, *Important Common Law Developments for Nonrecourse Notes: Tufting It Out,* 18 Ga.L.Rev.

1 (1983); Zimmerman, *Crane and Tufts: Resolved and Unresolved Issues,* 12 Pepperdine L.Rev. 631 (1985) and Division III, pages 709 to 713 infra.

4. In certain circumstances, a subdivider may add the estimated costs of future improvements to the basis of property to be currently sold for the purpose of determining the gain or loss resulting from the sale. If the subdivider is contractually obligated to make the improvements and the costs thereof are not recoverable by the subdivider through depreciation, the estimated costs may be added to basis. See Rev.Proc. 75–25, 1975–1 C.B. 720. See also Rev.Rul. 76–247, 1976–1 C.B. 217. Cf. *Robert F. Haynsworth,* 68 T.C. 703 (1977).

d. ALLOCATION OF BASIS

The allocation of the basis of acquired real property between land and improvements is important in determining the future income tax consequences of the acquiring entity's dealings with the real property. For example, the acquiring entity can depreciate only depreciable property. In the usual situation, land is not treated as depreciable property. Therefore, the amount of the basis of the acquired real property allocated to land cannot be depreciated by the acquiring entity, while the amount allocated to improvements may be depreciated.

WORLD PUBLISHING CO. v. COMMISSIONER

United States Court of Appeals, Eighth Circuit, 1962.
299 F.2d 614.

BLACKMUN, Circuit Judge. * * *

The issue before us concerns the taxpayer's right to a deduction for depreciation of a portion of the price it paid when it purchased improved real estate subject to an outstanding lease to the tenant who had built the building on the property.

The facts are not in dispute: On June 29, 1928, George Warren Smith, Inc., was the owner of two mid-block lots in downtown Omaha. On that date Smith leased those lots to Farnam Realty Corporation. The lease was for a term of fifty years from July 1, 1928, and called for annual rentals averaging $28,500 but varying between $25,000 and $32,500 for specified decades. It required Farnam immediately to construct a "six (6) story, or more, and basement building" on the property at a cost of not less than $250,000. Farnam complied with this requirement.

On January 4, 1950, the taxpayer purchased as an investment Smith's entire interest in the property, including the lease, for $700,000. The deed recited that it was subject to the lease to Farnam. The parties have stipulated that "the remaining useful life of the building in January, 1950, was not greater than the unexpired term of the lease".

In its income tax return for each of the years in question the taxpayer asserted a deduction of $10,547.92 for "Depreciation and Amortization". This amount was determined by spreading $300,000 (constituting that part of its purchase price which the taxpayer claimed was allocable to the building) over the remaining years of the still outstanding lease. The Commissioner disallowed this deduction.

* * *

There is substantial, and uncontradicted, evidence in the record to support the $300,000 figure. A qualified appraiser testified that at the time of purchase the fair and reasonable value of the ground alone was $400,000 and the fair and reasonable value of the building alone was around $300,000. These valuation allocations correspond, too, with the full valuations thereof used for real estate assessment purposes at the time of the purchase. The witness also testified that in his opinion the probable value of the land alone at the expiration of the lease in 1978 would be approximately $400,000.

On these facts, uninfluenced by any decided lease cases, it would seem clearly to follow that the taxpayer is entitled to a deduction * * * for depreciation of the $300,000 portion of its 1950 purchase price allocable to the improvements on the real estate in question. See Detroit Edison Co. v. Commissioner, 1943, 319 U.S. 98, 101, 63 S.Ct. 902, 87 L.Ed. 1286. The building, as well as the land, was acquired and held by the taxpayer "for the production of income". The taxpayer's interest was one acquired by purchase and was not in any sense a derivative right acquired without investment on its part. By the stipulation, the building is a wasting asset and its complete exhaustion will have been effected before the end of the lease term. The taxpayer's spreading of the wasting portion of its purchase price over the entire remaining lease term by the straight-line method approximated the minimal deduction for the taxpayer.

Furthermore, for what it may be worth, the lessor, and consequently the taxpayer, in spite of a contrary suggestion at the trial by the Commissioner's counsel, clearly owned the building in more than a bare-legal-title sense. The lease recites that all buildings erected on the premises "shall, *at and upon the construction thereof, be and become* a part of the realty and upon the termination of this lease * * * shall pass to and *remain* the property of the Lessor". (Emphasis supplied.) Consistent with this are other provisions of the lease: the reference in the tax clause to the lessor's interest in the "land or improvements"; the lessor's right to amend and even reject plans and specifications for the building; the insurance protection afforded the lessor and its being named as insured; the lessor's right to subject the improvements as well as the ground to a mortgage lien; and the lessee's inability to alter the completed building beyond a $10,000 cost without the lessor's approval. * * * This is consistent, too, with the general law, evidently recognized in Nebraska, to the effect that, unless provided otherwise by contract, a building permanently affixed to the land becomes a part of it. * * *

But the Commissioner—and the Tax Court has agreed with him—has taken the position that the taxpayer here acquired no depreciable interest in the property; that what it acquired was the land, not a wasting asset, for which it received ground rental income; that the taxpayer has not shown that it held any interest in the building for the production of income; that it acquired only such interest as its grantor Smith had; and that Smith had no depreciable interest in the lessee-constructed building. He strenuously urges, as supporting authority, a line of cases, including one of our own, concerning the situation where a taxpayer, through *inheritance* or *devise* from a deceased lessor, comes into the ownership of tenant-improved property subject to an outstanding lease. * * *

The theories which find expression in these cases are (a) that the decedent had—and his successor has—no investment in the wasting asset and (b) that the heir or devisee could acquire no different interest than was possessed by the decedent. "The major thrust of the statute is toward an allowance for recovery of investment in a wasting asset". Goelet (District Court), p. 307 of 161 F.Supp. "Appellants fail to show how a depreciable interest in the building was supplied to them * * *". Goelet (2 Cir.), p. 882 of 266 F.2d. "All she [the taxpayer] could acquire by inheritance from her mother, the testatrix, was such interest as her mother had to devise". Schubert, p. 579 of 286 F.2d.

Are these inheritance-or-devise cases cited by the Commissioner proper or helpful precedent for a situation involving acquisition by purchase? In determining this, some comments about the death cases are perhaps in order:

A. They have provoked substantial criticism. * * *

B. The facts of certain of these cases possess some significance. In Goelet the district court emphasized that, although the taxpayer by the terms of the lease may have had "technical legal title to the building", this was not determinative but "beneficial ownership" was. In Schubert it appears from the majority opinion of the Tax Court, p. 1049 of 33 T.C., that under the lease the improvement was to become the property of the lessor only "upon the termination of the lease". In Friend, too, it is clear from the Board's opinion, p. 771 of 40 B.T.A., that the taxpayers "did not own the buildings" and did not "even claim that they are entitled to an allowance for depreciation in respect of the buildings." In Pearson, Moore, and Nee the appellate courts all concluded that no part of the estate tax valuation, which constituted basis, was attributable to the improvements and that the taxpayer's case, depending, as it did, on a basis to depreciate, consequently failed. And in our Nee case we concluded that the rentals were attributable solely to the land; that the building was not held by the testamentary trustee for the production of income; that the tenant had the right to remove the building and replace it; and that because of this right the title to the building may have been in the lessee (the trial court had held specifically that under the terms of the lease title to the building was in the lessee: D.C., 85 F.Supp. 840, 843; D.C., 92 F.Supp. 328, 329).

C. An alternative and forceful argument made by the taxpayer in some of these cases is that he is entitled to claim a deduction for amortization of the "premium value" of the lease. The argument was rejected in Schubert (4 Cir. and Tax Court), Friend (Tax Court) and Moore (Tax Court); see Martha R. Peters, 1945, 4 T.C. 1236, 1241–1242. It prevailed, however, in Moore [207 F.2d 265 (9th Cir.1953)] and necessarily by the Tax Court on remand in that case, T.C.Memo. 1955–219. It was avoided in Goelet, on the ground the point was not preserved below or in the administrative proceedings, and in Frieda Bernstein, 1954, 22 T.C. 1146, 1151–1152, affirmed, 2 Cir., 230 F.2d 603, on the ground of failure of proof. Moore demonstrates, however, that one circuit has afforded relief to a taxpayer who found himself with a newly acquired interest in property with a newly acquired basis which had no rational relationship to land value alone. This alternative argument was mentioned by the Tax Court in the present case and was again rejected; it is not particularly urged by the taxpayer on this appeal.

D. The cases themselves intimate, though perhaps by indirection, that the purchase situation is distinguishable. Thus, in Friend, the Seventh Circuit, at p. 960 of 119 F.2d, describes the testamentary trustees' position there as though "they have the same right to amortize such cost as if the purchase had made for cash" and, on p. 961 of 119 F.2d, denies a construction of the statute that would "place the petitioners in the position of a purchaser of the leaseholds [together with the reversions] for a valuable consideration". * * *

E. Finally, as a collateral comment on the cases, we cannot fail to observe that the depreciation provisions of the Internal Revenue Code draw no distinction between death-acquired property and purchased property. The basis they establish for depreciation is the same as the basis for determining gain. * * *

So much for these death cases. The situation before us, however, is that of a purchaser of the lessor's interest and is not that of the lessor's heir or devisee. No purchase case precisely in point has been found. We therefore start with three established propositions:

1. Where an owner of land erects a building on it and then leases it he is still entitled to recover the cost of the improvement by depreciation deductions. * * *

2. Where a lessee makes a capital improvement on leased property he is entitled to recover its cost by appropriate deductions for depreciation or for amortization. * * *

3. Conversely, in the situation just described, the lessor, having no investment in the lessee's improvements, is not entitled to a deduction with respect to them. 4 Mertens, § 23.90, where possible exceptions to this rule are noted.

To these may be added the result reached by the death cases cited above. We think, however, that the death cases do not govern the purchase situation. We reach this result because:

A. The taxpayer-purchaser by his purchase of the property has made an investment. He is not concerned with the identity, as between his vendor-lessor and the tenant, of the builder of the building. From this point of view, if he is entitled to the deduction where his vendor-lessor was the builder, he is entitled to a deduction where the tenant was the builder.

B. To allow the purchaser to depreciate in the one situation and to deny him depreciation in the other, especially where, as here, title to the building is in the lessor and then in the purchaser, seems to be illogical, to emphasize a historical fact not participated in or caused by the purchaser and not of any other considered economic consequence to him, and to exalt form over substance. This would be illustrated by identical buildings, one constructed by the lessor and one by the lessee, on adjoining identical lots, subject to otherwise identical leases, when both improved properties are sold to the taxpayer-purchaser. There seems to be no merit in allowing the taxpayer, as distinguished from the lessor, depreciation on the one but not on the other.

C. It is no answer to say that the lease rentals, averaging $28,500, constitute only ground rent. We are concerned here not with depreciation of rentals, but with depreciation of a portion of this taxpayer's investment in the income producing property he purchased.

D. Whatever may be the proper result in the inheritance or devise situation, as exemplified by our 1951 holding in the Nee case, and by the other cases cited above, we are not now willing to extend the philosophy of those cases to the purchase situation of the present litigation.

We regard Millinery Center Building Corporation v. Commissioner, 2 Cir., 1955, 221 F.2d 322, as of particular and helpful significance here. That taxpayer had leased land with an option to renew and, in accordance with the lease, had erected a substantial building on it. Title to the building was in the taxpayer but under the lease it would vest in the lessor at the end of the lease term or the lessor could then compel the taxpayer to remove it. During the lease period the taxpayer fully depreciated the cost of the building. Then it exercised its option to renew. When this was done, it bought the fee. The taxpayer sought to deduct the difference between its purchase price and the then value of the land, as unimproved, as a business expense. The Tax Court disallowed this; it also refused to accept the taxpayer's alternative contentions (a) that the difference should be amortized over the lease term and (b) that it should be depreciated over the remaining useful life of the building. 21 T.C. 817. Six judges dissented on the ground that some part of the purchase price should be allocated to the additional rights the taxpayer acquired in the building and should be recovered through depreciation. On petition for review the Second Circuit reversed on the depreciation issue. It said, p. 324 of 221 F.2d, "A third-party purchaser of such a fee would be entitled to allocate part of its cost to the building and to depreciate it as such". On the taxpayer's petition for certiorari the Supreme Court affirmed. 350 U.S. 456, 76 S.Ct. 493, 100 L.Ed. 545. The Commissioner did not seek review of the allowance of depreciation.

The taxpayer there occupied a position similar to that of the taxpayer here. The only fact differences were the taxpayer's additional posture as lessee and the lease's consequent extinguishment upon the purchase. These differences seem to us, however, of minor import.

That Farnam may have been taking depreciation with respect to its cost in the building need not concern us. Its right so to do is not here at issue. Despite the Ninth Circuit's observation, by way of dictum in the *Moore* case, p. 272 of 207 F.2d, that "A construction of the law to permit not only the lessee (who has a real economic interest) but also the taxpayer here to take depreciation on the same building would be somewhat anomalous", we fail to see the anomaly. What is significant is that each taxpayer has a separate wasting investment which meets the statutory requirements for depreciation. To allow each to recover his own, and separate, investment is not, as is suggested, to permit duplication at the expense of the revenues and is not to permit one taxpayer to depreciate another's investment. That each is concerned with the same building is of no relevance. Farnam has its lessee's cost of the structure and the present taxpayer has the portion of its purchase price attributable to the building. If two taxpayers own undivided interests in improved real estate, each may be entitled to depreciation. The situation here is not dissimilar.

This leaves only the question of proof. We could remand the case with instructions to the Tax Court to take further evidence as to that portion of the taxpayer's purchase price which was properly allocable to the building as distinguished from the land. We feel, however, that on this record the taxpayer has sufficiently established his $300,000 allocation. The Commissioner had his opportunity in the proceedings which have already taken place in the Tax Court to controvert the taxpayer's evidence. This he did not do but chose, instead, to rely on his basic thesis that the taxpayer had no investment which was entitled to depreciation.

The decision of the Tax Court is reversed with directions to recompute the taxpayer's deficiencies in accord with the views herein expressed.

NOTE

1. In *World Publishing Co.*, if the useful life of the improvements was equal to, or less than, the remaining term of the lease, what interest in the improvements did the lessor have which could have been sold to the purchaser?

a. The First Circuit, in *M. De Matteo Constr. Co. v. United States*, 433 F.2d 1263 (1st Cir.1970), a case similar to *World Publishing Co.*, denied the purchaser's claimed deduction of depreciation, holding that the lessor's reversion was too speculative to be valued and in any event was worth less than the value of the improvements.

b.   If the improvements have a useful life greater than the term of the lease, at the worst, will the purchaser eventually be entitled to claim depreciation?   See *Geneva Drive–In Theatre, Inc.,* 67 T.C. 764 (1977), affirmed, 622 F.2d 995 (9th Cir.1980).

c.   See generally Morris and Glicklich, *Some Incongruities in the Taxation of Leased Real Property,* 40 Tax Law. 85 (1986); Note, *Purchaser's Depreciation Rights in Property Subject to a Lease,* 82 Mich.L.Rev. 572 (1983).

2.   If the purchaser in *World Publishing Co.* had not purchased the fee but merely taken an assignment of the lease in return for $300,000, would it have been able to amortize the cost of the lease over the remaining term of the lease? Cf. Section 178(a).

a.   If so, what method would the taxpayer use to amortize its investment?

b.   Does it make any difference if the taxpayer acquires the fee for $400,000 and the lease for $300,000?   Does the $400,000 paid for the land represent its present value or its future value discounted to the present?

c.   Could the taxpayer in *World Publishing Co.,* at the time it purchased the real estate, have used a method of depreciation faster than straight-line?

3.   If a purchaser acquires several parcels of land and improvements, what is the basis on which it allocates its costs between the land and improvements?

a.   See generally Sandison and Waters, *Tax Planning for the Land Developer: Cost Allocations of Land and Improvements,* 37 J.Tax'n 80 (1972); Sandison and Waters, *More on Tax Planning for Land Developers: Allocations, Deductions, Reporting Income,* 37 J. Tax'n 154 (1972); *Cleveland–Sandusky Brewing Corp.,* 30 T.C. 539, 544–545 (1958); *Albert Maloney,* 34 CCH Tax Ct.Mem. 1237 (1975) (Issues 3 and 4), affirmed, 566 F.2d 1054 (6th Cir.1977); *Randolph Building Corporation,* 67 T.C. 804 (1977).   Cf. Rev.Rul. 79–432, 1979–2 C.B. 289; *Dennis N. Marks,* 49 CCH Tax Ct.Mem. 1222 (1985).

b.   When making an allocation, one must determine what are land costs and what are building costs, since "pure" land costs are not depreciable whereas the building costs are.   See Division IV, pages 990 to 998 infra; Henderson, *Land Cost Expenditures, Recent Trend Shows Many Such Costs Now Depreciable,* 38 J.Tax'n 78 (1973).   In Rev.Rul. 74–265, 1974–1 C.B. 56, the costs involved in landscaping, including ornamental trees and perennial shrubbery, an area immediately adjacent to a newly constructed apartment complex were considered depreciable and recoverable over the useful life of the buildings since the replacement of the buildings would destroy the landscaping.   The landscaping was done according to an architect's plan to conform it to the general design of the complex.   Cf. *Tunnell v. United States,* 512 F.2d 1192 (3d Cir.1975), vacating and remanding, 367 F.Supp. 557 (D.C.Del.1973).

c.   If the purchaser intends to demolish the acquired improvements, how much of the purchase price can be allocated to the improvements?

d.   If the purchaser intends to demolish the acquired improvements in a few years but, in the meantime, leases the improvements to a third party, can any portion of the purchase price be allocated to the improvements?

1. See Reg. Section 1.165–3(a), (b) and (c); and Division IV, pages 997 to 998 infra.

2. Section 280B prohibits the deduction of any demolition losses or expenses by either the owner or the lessee of real estate and requires that such amounts be treated as properly chargeable to the capital account with respect to the land on which the demolished structure stood.

e. DEPRECIATION AND INVESTMENT CREDITS

Once the cost of the real estate improvements has been established through allocation of the purchase price and/or the determination of the construction or renovation costs, the significance of the cost for income tax purposes must be analyzed. Appropriate considerations include whether and when depreciation is available, the choice of a method, or methods, of depreciating the improvements and whether the investment made in the improvements, or any part thereof, results in the entitlement to investment credits.

REAL ESTATE DEPRECIATION: A FRESH EXAMINATION OF THE BASIC RULES

Stefan F. Tucker
6 The Journal of Real Estate Taxation 101 (1979).
[footnotes omitted]

* * *

Who May Deduct Depreciation?

* * *

Generally, the owner of real property may deduct depreciation, but only if the property is used in a trade or business or held for the production of income. Depreciation may not be taken on a personal residence. Furthermore, depreciation is not allowable with respect to "inventory property" (that is, property held for sale to customers in the ordinary course of a trade or business).

The concept of holding property "for the production of income" has engendered significant litigation, and Revenue Agents continue to raise the issue in audits today. It is clear that if there is no intention that the property produce income at any time (and the property is not used in a trade or business), then no depreciation deduction will be allowed. On the other hand, it is not necessary that the property currently produce income, so long as it is held for the production of future income. * * *

[T]he mere ownership or possession of bare legal title is not sufficient for the allowance of the depreciation deduction; it must be shown that the owner has both the burdens and benefits of the property and will suffer "economic loss" with regard to the property. In this connection, the purchaser of real property is generally considered as having the burdens and benefits of ownership upon the earlier to occur of the date he takes title or takes possession. ＊ ＊ ＊

Depreciation: An Overview

＊ ＊ ＊

A building or other improvement acquired or constructed has a limited useful life. While the taxpayer cannot treat an expenditure for an improvement as a deduction in the year made, the taxpayer is permitted under the Code to take annual deductions for depreciation (or amortization in lieu of depreciation) during the useful life of the improvement.

Under ＊ ＊ ＊ the Code, depreciation is defined as "a reasonable allowance for the exhaustion, wear and tear (including a reasonable allowance for obsolescence)" of property. ＊ ＊ ＊

At this point, the ＊ ＊ ＊ Royal St. Louis, Inc. v. United States [578 F.2d 1017 (5th Cir.1978), case] is instructive, for it illustrates the precept that with regard to depreciation deductions, as is generally the case in the income tax realm, the form of the documentation (or transaction) makes the substance. In that case, the taxpayers, which constructed and owned the Royal Sonesta Hotel in New Orleans, entered into a lease pursuant to which the lessee-operator of the Hotel leased the Hotel, including furnishings and other equipment, from the taxpayers. The provisions of the lease as to the Hotel itself provided that the lessee was to keep and maintain the Hotel "in good rentable condition" or "in good condition and repair," in each case "reasonable" or "ordinary" "wear and tear excepted." However, as to the furnishings and equipment, they were to be maintained "in first class condition," with the lessee "replacing the same when necessary for such purpose." The circuit court therefore found that "the lease imposed upon the lessee the obligation to maintain the personal property so as to preclude economic loss by the lessors over the period of the lease." Based upon such finding, the court concluded that the lessors were not entitled to any depreciation deduction with respect to the furnishings or equipment.

So long as the purchaser has the burdens and benefits of ownership, it is not necessary that it have legal title. ＊ ＊ ＊

[A] life tenant [of property] is considered the owner of the property for depreciation purposes. Where there is a trust, the depreciation deduction will be apportioned between the income beneficiaries and the trustees in accordance with the provisions of the trust instrument; in the absence of such provisions, the deduction will be apportioned on the basis of the trust income allocable to each. Likewise, in the case of an estate, the depreciation deduction will be apportioned between the estate and the beneficiaries on the basis of the income allocable to each.

Joint tenants, tenants in common, and tenants by the entirety share the depreciation deduction in proportion to their respective interests in the property. In contrast, partners may allocate the depreciation deduction as they agree so long as such allocation is found, under Section 704(b)(2), to have substantial economic effect; otherwise, as provided in Section 704(b), such deduction will be allocated in accordance with the partners' interest[s] in the partnership, determined by taking into account all facts and circumstances.

Finally, where [a] lessee constructs improvements on property, the lessee is entitled to the annual deductions attributable to the cost thereof. [Regardless whether] the useful life of the improvements in the hands of the lessee is [greater than,] equal to or less than the remaining period of the lease, the lessee * * * take[s] depreciation deductions. * * *

What Property Is Depreciable?

* * *

In order for tangible property, whether personalty or realty, to be depreciable, it must be subject to wear and tear, to decay or decline from natural causes, to exhaustion, and to obsolescence.

Land is not depreciable. Accordingly, the costs of clearing, grading, landscaping, and planting grass and shrubs, except to the extent attributable to the improvements, have been held "inextricably associated" with the land, and not depreciable. On the other hand, the costs of clearing, grading, and terracing a mobile home park were found to be depreciable because the work was associated with the construction of the trailer pads and patios on the trailer lots. Private streets, sidewalks, curbs, gutters, and drains are not considered land.

Improvements to land, such as buildings or other structures, are depreciable. When the property acquired consists of both land and improvements added to the land, the basis for depreciation of the improvements must be determined by an appropriate allocation of values. Such allocation may be substantiated by various means, such as appraisals, assessed values, and prices contained in purchase contracts based on arm's-length negotiations. * * *

When Does Depreciation Commence?

* * *

Generally, the deduction for depreciation commences when the building is completed and ready for service or occupancy. This is true even though minor work is performed at a later time. As a concomitant, no depreciation deduction may be claimed with respect to a building under construction. By way of illustration, reference may be made to Revenue Ruling 76–428, [1976–2 C.B. 47] in which, for * * * depreciation purposes, a generator was first placed into service on the date on which (1) the necessary permits and licenses had been approved, (2) the critical tests for the various components had been completed, (3) the unit had been placed in the control of the taxpayer by the contractor, and (4) the unit had been synchronized into the taxpayer's power grid for its function, even though the unit would undergo further testing to eliminate any defects and to demonstrate reliability.

Where a home is converted, in whole or in part, to rental property or an office, the deduction for depreciation commences at the date the conversion occurs. If the business use of the home commences at the time of acquisition of the home, the depreciation will be based on an allocable share of the cost; however, if that business use begins at a later time, the deduction will be based on the lower of the allocable share of the cost or the fair market value at the time.

* * *

What Amount Is Depreciable?

* * *

Depreciation is computed from the basis, as adjusted, less the salvage value,[64] of the property. The determination of such basis is itself dependent on the means by which the property was acquired.

Property Acquired by Purchase or Constructed. Where the property is acquired by purchase or is constructed by the owner, the basis, under Section 1012 of the Code, is generally the cost of the property. Cost includes (1) nondeductible acquisition expenses, such as title charges, brokers' commissions, appraisal fees, surveys, attorneys' fees and payments to remove clouds on title; (2) apportioned costs at settlement not deductible by the purchaser, such as certain real estate taxes and nondeductible assessments; (3) indebtedness assumed by the purchaser or incurred in the purchase of the property; and (4) indebtedness to which the purchaser takes the property subject. Cost will not include (1) interest or real estate taxes deductible when paid or incurred at the time of settlement on the acquisition * * *; (2) indebtedness incurred or taken subject to at the time of acquisition which is found to exceed the fair market value of the property, in which case the fair market value will serve as a basis limitation; (3) highly speculative or contingent liabilities, until such time as they are in fact paid or become fixed; and (4) sham liabilities.

* * *

Adjusted Basis. Generally, as provided in Section 1016 of the Code, *adjusted basis* equals basis as determined above, subject to the following principal adjustments: First, such basis is *increased* for expenditures properly chargeable to capital account (that is, the cost of nondeductible property improvements or carrying charges as to which the appropriate election * * * is made). Second, such basis is *reduced* by receipts properly credited to capital account and by losses which directly affect [the] capital account (such as losses due to fire or other casualty). Third, such basis is *reduced* by depreciation allowed or allowable. In this connection, the real key is not what was "allowed" or taken, but what was "allowable." Therefore, if the taxpayer does

[64. Salvage value is not taken into account when the accelerated cost recovery system is used.]

not take the depreciation that could have been taken, the amount foregone is lost forever; the depreciation deduction cannot be deferred to a later year, and, nonetheless, the basis is reduced by the amount of depreciation that was allowable. The taxpayer cannot even argue that the depreciation would not have produced any tax benefit, so that it did not have to be taken in the given taxable year.

* * *

Salvage Value. * * * The salvage value is not the scrap value, but rather the estimated proceeds (less costs of removal) which will be realized upon the sale or other disposition of the property at the end of its useful life. With regard to real estate, [unless the accelerated cost recovery system is used,] salvage must be considered under all depreciation methods other than the declining balance methods. [Salvage is not considered in determining cost recovery (depreciation) under the accelerated cost recovery system. As] a practical matter, because the cost of razing a building may equal or exceed the estimated proceeds to be derived therefrom, salvage is usually not considered in determining the depreciation of a building.

What Is the Depreciable Life of the Property?

* * *

Depreciable property may be depreciated over its "useful life," which is the period of time during which the asset can reasonably be expected to be useful to the particular taxpayer, even though shorter than the estimated physical life of the property.

Under present law, the depreciation for real property may be determined under [Section 168, which provides for the accelerated cost recovery system, sets a 27½ year recovery period (useful life) for residential rental real property, a 31½ year recovery period for nonresidential real property, requires the use of the straight-line method to recover real property costs and prohibits the use of component depreciation for property eligible for treatment under Section 168. A taxpayer, however, can elect to use the alternate depreciation system, under Section 168, which sets a 40 year recovery period for both residential and nonresidential real property and requires the use of the straight-line method.]

* * *

Depreciation of * * * Real Property

* * *

[Under the accelerated cost recovery system, both new and used property are subject to the same recovery periods and the same methods of cost recovery. Residential rental real property and nonresidential real property, however, are treated differently with respect to the applicable recovery period. As mentioned above, residential rental real property is subject to a recovery period of 27½ years and nonresidential real property is subject to a recovery period of 31½ years. See Section 168(c).]

* * *

Residential rental [real] property. A building or structure is "residential rental [real] property" for a taxable year *only if* 80 percent or more of the gross rental income attributable thereto during such year is rental income from dwelling units. Any building or structure as to which the gross rental income test is not met during any taxable year cannot be considered residential rental [real] property.

If two or more buildings on a single tract (or contiguous tracts) of land are operated as an integrated unit, they may be treated as a single building. The actual operation, management, financing, and accounting will constitute evidence in determining whether such buildings are an integrated unit. * * *

Dwelling unit: A dwelling unit is a house or an apartment used to provide living accommodations in a building or structure but not including units in a hotel, motel, inn, or other establishment in which more than half of the units are used on a transient basis. A dwelling unit will be considered as used on a transient basis if, for more than half the days in which it is occupied on a rental basis during the taxable year, it is occupied by a tenant or series of tenants each of whom occupies it for less than thirty days.

There is no requirement that the dwelling unit be occupied subject to a lease. In fact, the regulations look to the actual occupants of the dwelling unit and not to the formalities of any lease or sublease. There is no reference in the regulations to a kitchen, sleeping accommodations, or the like in order for the unit to constitute a dwelling unit.

Gross rental income: Generally, "gross rental income" includes only the gross amounts received from the use of (or the right to use) real property. It is important to note that it is the *ratio* between gross rental income *from dwelling units* and gross rental income *from the total structure* that is of significance here. There are several calculations and special rules which must be taken into account in determining whether an amount is attributable to the use of real property, and, if so, whether that use is also a dwelling unit use.

If the rent is for both real and personal property (such as rent for a furnished apartment), that portion attributable to the personal property does not constitute gross rental income. An attribution of a portion of rental income to personalty in a tight situation may cause the entire building or structure not to be considered residential rental [real] property due to a failure to meet the gross rental income test.

If part of the rent is for a facility located outside a building, the total amount may constitute gross rental income from the building *only if* (1) the facility is of a kind customarily associated with the occupancy of a living accommodation, such as a parking lot or swimming pool, (2) it is principally for the benefit of the tenants of the building, and (3) where separate charges are made to the tenants for the use of the facility, at least 80 percent of the gross income from the facility is from such tenants. If the building owner cannot prove that at least 80 percent of the gross income from the facility is attributable to tenants, none of the income from the facility is gross rental income from the building.

Portions of rent attributable to the furnishing of services usually or customarily related to the use of real property constitute gross rental income from the building. Amounts attributable to the furnishing of heat and light, janitorial services, or trash collection would generally be considered gross rental income from the building, but amounts attributable to maid service would not. Amounts paid by tenants directly to independent contractors (such as amounts paid to public utilities for electricity, gas, or water) do not constitute gross rental income from the building.

In computing the gross rental income from a building, the rental at which a vacant unit is offered is not taken into account.

Rent supplement payments under Section 221(d)(3) and interest reduction payments under Section 236 of the National Housing Act made on behalf of tenants are taken into account as gross rental income from dwelling units.

The fair rental value of that portion of a building occupied by the owner is included in gross rental income from the building. However, if the portion occupied is for commercial purposes, such as the operation of a drugstore or commercial laundry, while the fair rental value of the space is gross rental income from the building, it is not considered gross rental income from a dwelling unit. On the other hand, space reserved in the building for a rental office, equipment, or occupancy by a resident manager, or for similar purposes, is not treated as occupied by the owner. Thus, the fair rental value of such space would not be considered as gross rental income from the building.

* * *

Changes in Depreciation Method

Even though a building may not qualify as residential rental [real] property for one year, it may qualify for the next year or years. The change from one [recovery period] to another because the 80 percent test is met in one year and not the next (or vice versa) is not considered a change in accounting method requiring the consent of the Service. * * * [A] statement containing the relevant facts as to the property must be attached to the taxpayer's return for the year in which the change is made. * * *

Extraordinary Obsolescence

* * *

[O]bsolescence is a factor in determining the * * * allowance for depreciation [(cost recovery)]. In this connection, focus is placed upon the normal progress of the art, economic changes, inventions, and current developments within the industry and the taxpayer's trade or business. Accordingly, in order for a taxpayer to take a deduction for extraordinary obsolescence, the taxpayer must be able to prove that there was a sudden termination of use or abnormal retirement of the property.

Because extraordinary obsolescence is in reality the reflection of a loss with respect to the property, the appropriate statutory provision is Section 165(a), allowing as a deduction "any loss sustained during the taxable year and not compensated for by insurance or otherwise." However, the pertinent regulation is Regulations Section 1.167(a)–8, which requires that, in order for the taxpayer to be able to take the loss deduction, it must show both (1) sudden termination or other abnormal retirement if the property is withdrawn from use earlier than the end of its useful life and (2) the permanent withdrawal of the building from use.

* * *

NOTE

1. As noted in the above excerpts, residential rental real property is subject to a recovery period of 27½ years rather than the 31½ years applicable to nonresidential real property.

     a. To be classified as residential rental real property, 80% or more of gross rental income must be from the rental of dwelling units. Will this test be of concern to a C corporation which has accumulated earnings and profits, owns an apartment complex and plans to elect Subchapter S treatment. See Sections 1362(d)(3) and 1375. If the corporation attempts to comply with the 80% test, will the rent it receives be classified as passive income?

2. Component depreciation, which cannot be used for real estate improvements eligible for treatment under the accelerated cost recovery system, indirectly accomplishes the same mission as "accelerated" methods—it affords larger deductions in the early years and smaller deductions in later years. The effect of using component depreciation is that the overall effective rate of depreciation for the entire property will be substantially greater than if the property was depreciated at one composite rate. For example, if a building costing one million dollars with a 40–year life is depreciated using the straight-line method, depreciation would amount to approximately $25,000 per year (¹⁄₄₀ × $1,000,000). If the component method was used, the following might result:

Description	Cost	Life	Approximate Annual Depreciation
Building	$ 600,000	40 years	$15,000
Wiring	60,000	15 years	4,000
Plumbing	45,000	15 years	3,000
Roofing	50,000	10 years	5,000
Heating	100,000	10 years	10,000
Paving	25,000	10 years	2,500
Ceiling	25,000	10 years	2,500
Air conditioning	50,000	10 years	5,000
Elevators	45,000	15 years	3,000
	$1,000,000		$50,000

As mentioned above, the use of the component method of depreciation is denied for any real estate improvement which is eligible for the accelerated cost recovery system. Presently, it is the rare real estate improvement which is not eligible for treatment under the accelerated cost recovery system.

3. Under Section 312(k), a corporation's earnings and profits must be computed using, in the case of real estate improvements, the straight-line method over a recovery period (useful life) of 40 years.

a. How would this affect the earnings and profits of a corporation which was the general partner of a limited partnership which owned and operated a residential rental real property development and computed its depreciation using a 27½ year life?

b. Would it make any difference if the corporation was an S corporation? See pages 101 to 116 supra. See Section 1371(c)(1).

c. Since the earnings and profits of a C corporation general partner must be computed using the straight-line method and a 40–year recovery period for the depreciation of real estate assets, the differences in income tax treatment between the limited partners and the shareholders of the C corporation general partner are accentuated if the limited partnership uses the accelerated cost recovery system to depreciate its real estate assets.

4. The accelerated cost recovery system also may be used to recover the cost of a substantial improvement to a building. To qualify as a substantial improvement at least 25% of the adjusted basis of the building must be added to the capital account for the building over a two-year period, and the improvement must be made at least three years after the building was first placed in service.

5. There are various investment credits available to the investor in real estate. The investment credits, however, are only available for investments in particular kinds of real estate.

a. Investment credits are available for certain rehabilitation expenses. The investment credit is 10% of the rehabilitation expenses if the structure being rehabilitated is at least 50 years old. The credit is 20% if the structure being rehabilitated is a certified historic structure. The 10% credit is only available for rehabilitation expenses with respect to nonresidential buildings. If the credits are taken, the straight-line method must be used to depreciate the rehabilitation expenditures and the adjusted basis of those expenditures must be adjusted downward by the full amount of the credit. Investment credits may be available, in certain instances, for rehabilitation done by a lessee. In order to qualify for the credit, the rehabilitated building must be a qualified rehabilitated building, as defined in Section 48(g)(1). While these credits are subject to the limitations on the use of passive activity credits provided by Section 469, credits equivalent to the $25,000 offset, provided by Section 469(i), are available regardless whether the taxpayer actively participates. The availability of the credits is phased-out ratably as the taxpayer's adjusted gross income increases from $200,000 to $250,000. See Sections 469(i)(3)(B) and 469(i)(6)(B).

b. See generally Selinger, *The Use of Real Estate Rehabilitation Credits by Limited Partnerships,* 10 J. Real Est. Tax'n 129 (1983); Pollack, *Claiming the Rehabilitation Credit Can Trigger 1245 and 1250 Recapture on Disposition,* 59 J.Tax'n 98 (1983); Kenost, *Tax Incentives for Qualified Rehabilitated Buildings and for Donations of Preservation Easements,* 41 N.Y.U.Inst.Fed.Tax'n 20–1 (1983); Hanslin, *Building Rehabilitation Tax*

Credits, 1 # 1 Prac.Real Est.Law. 43 (1985); Goodman, *Real Estate Tax Credits After the Tax Reform Act of 1986*, 16 Real Est.L.J. 172 (1987); Coughlin, *Using Historic Rehabilitation and Low–Income Housing Credits*, 2 # 2 Prac.Tax Law. 25 (1988); Sanders and Toolson, *Rehabilitation Tax Credits Under the TRA*, 19 Tax Adviser 411 (1988); Friedman and Ak-selrad, *The Rehabilitation Tax Credit: A Survivor in an Era of Tax Reform*, 45 N.Y.U.Inst.Fed.Tax'n 19–1 (1987).

c. In addition to the investment credits available for rehabilitation expenditures, Section 42 of the Code provides low-income housing credits which may be claimed by owners of residential rental projects which provide low-income housing. In general, a project provides low-income housing if at least 20% of the units in the project are occupied by individuals having incomes of 50% or less of the area median income (adjusted for family size) or 40% of the units are occupied by individuals having incomes of 60% or less of the area median income (adjusted for family size). The rent charged for the 20% or 40% of the units, as the case may be, cannot exceed 30% of the tenant's income. Section 8 subsidies are not taken into account when determining whether the rent paid meets this criteria.

The credits can be claimed annually for a period of 10 years. For projects placed in service after December 31, 1986 and, in general, before January 1, 1990, the maximum annual credit rate is 9% of the cost of construction, or rehabilitation, of the low-income housing units, unless the construction or rehabilitation was financed by tax exempt bonds or similar Federal subsidies. A maximum credit of 4% per year for 10 years can be claimed with respect to the cost of acquiring low-income housing units and with respect to the expenditures incurred in constructing and rehabilitat-ing low-income housing units if the construction or rehabilitation is fi-nanced by tax exempt bonds or similar Federal subsidies. In order to be eligible for either of the credits for construction or rehabilitation, the expenditures per low-income housing unit must exceed $2,000.

Congress set the credit rate to provide an annualized credit amount which equals 70% or 30%, as the case may be, of the present value of basis attributable to the eligible low-income units. The Treasury is directed to adjust the credit rate for taxable years beginning on or after January 1, 1988 so as to maintain the credit amounts at 70% and 30% of basis. While these credits are subject to the limitations on the use of losses and credits from passive activities, under Section 469, credits equivalent to the $25,000 offset, provided by Section 469(i), are available regardless whether the taxpayer actively participates in the operation of the rental housing and are phased-out ratably as the taxpayer's adjusted gross income increases from $200,000 to $250,000. See Sections 469(i)(3)(B) and 469(i)(6)(B).

The credits claimed in any one State during a taxable year cannot exceed a ceiling amount equal to $1.25 per resident of the State. The credits given for construction and rehabilitation expenditures financed with tax exempt bonds, however, do not reduce a State's credit authority. A State housing credit agency and a constitutional home rule city within a State may allocate credits, out of the State's credit authority, to projects within their respective jurisdictions. The allocation to a project can be less than the maximum amount of credits to which the project is entitled under Section 42.

d. See generally Callison, *New Tax Credit for Low–Income Housing Provides Investment Incentive,* 66 J.Tax'n 100 (1987); Goldstein and Edson, *The Tax Credit for Low Income Housing,* 17 # 2 Real Est.Rev. 49 (1987); Goodman, *Real Estate Tax Credits After the Tax Reform Act of 1986,* 16 Real Est.L.J. 172 (1987); Segal and Bird, *The New Low–Income Housing Credit,* 19 Tax Adviser 507 (1988); Blatter and Marty–Nelson, *An Overview of the Low Income Housing Tax Credit,* 17 U.Balt.L.Rev. 253 (1988).

e. The availability of both the rehabilitation and the low-income housing credits is subject to at-risk limitations. See Sections 42(k) and 46(c)(8).

1. In the case of the rehabilitation credits, if the rehabilitation is financed through the use of nonrecourse debt, the cost of the rehabilitated property will be reduced by the amount of such debt unless the debt is "qualified commercial financing."

a. In order to be "qualified commercial financing":

i. The rehabilitated property cannot have been acquired from a party related to the taxpayer.

ii. The amount of nonrecourse financing cannot exceed 80% of the cost of rehabilitation.

iii. The financing must be provided by federal, state or local government or instrumentalities thereof or guaranteed thereby, or provided by a person actively and regularly engaged in the business of lending money (such as a bank) who is not related to the taxpayer, the person from whom the property was acquired or a person related to such person or a person who receives a fee with respect to the taxpayer's investment in the property or a person related to such person.

iv. The financing cannot be convertible.

b. Whether a partner's share of nonrecourse financing is "qualified commercial financing" is determined at the partner level and a partner's share is determined according to the sharing of "general profits."

2. With respect to the low-income housing credit, if the financing, if any, is accomplished through the use of nonrecourse debt, the eligible costs of the housing will be reduced by the amount of such debt unless the debt is "qualified commercial financing."

a. In order to be "qualified commercial financing" the financing must meet the same test described above, with the following exceptions:

i. The 80% limitation does not apply.

ii. The lender can be related to the taxpayer.

iii. In certain circumstances the financing can be provided by a "qualified" nonprofit corporation.

f. CONTRIBUTION OF PROPERTY AS AN INDUCEMENT TO LOCATE OR DEVELOP

At times, a local governmental entity, a non-profit corporation, a profit-making entity or an individual will contribute money or property to an acquiring entity as an inducement to the entity to develop certain designated real estate. The income tax treatment of such a contribution is discussed in the following case.

FEDERATED DEPARTMENT STORES, INC. v. COMMISSIONER

United States Court of Appeals, Sixth Circuit, 1970.
426 F.2d 417, affirming, 51 T.C. 500 (1968).
Non-acq. 1971–2 Cum.Bull. 4.

COMBS, Circuit Judge. * * *

Commissioner's Appeal

The Commissioner's cross-appeal involves the treatment to be accorded certain payments made to taxpayer in the fiscal years 1963 and 1964 by the Sharpstown Realty Company. Sharpstown owned a 2500–acre tract of unimproved land in Houston, Texas, on 115 acres of which it contemplated constructing a shopping center with the remainder to be devoted to residential and commercial purposes. Sharpstown was of the view that its venture would be more successful if taxpayer would construct and operate a department store in the shopping center. As inducement, Sharpstown offered to convey ten acres in its shopping center area to taxpayer and also to pay taxpayer $200,000 per year for ten years. The agreement was executed and taxpayer constructed a department store in the shopping center at a cost of $1,956,339. Neither taxpayer nor its shareholders owned an interest in Sharpstown; neither Sharpstown nor its shareholders owned an interest in taxpayer.

In the fiscal years 1963 and 1964, taxpayer received payments from Sharpstown of $200,000 and $400,000, respectively. The Commissioner included these amounts in taxpayer's income for the years in question. The Tax Court, however, held these payments excludable from taxpayer's income under Section 118 of the Internal Revenue Code, 26 U.S. C.A. § 118(a). That section provides: "In the case of a corporation, gross income does not include any contribution to the capital of the taxpayer." This resulted in a reduction in the deficiencies originally assessed by the Commissioner, and it is from this holding by the Tax Court that the Commissioner appeals.

The narrow question presented is whether the payments received by taxpayer from Sharpstown were contributions to taxpayer's capital within the purview of Section 118. We agree with the Tax Court that they were.

The Commissioner argues that Section 118 cannot be used to exclude from taxpayer's income the payments in question because (1) the payments were motivated by Sharpstown's own financial interests rather than by concern for the general welfare of the community; and (2) Sharpstown is not a governmental unit or civic group which allegedly is a prerequisite to the applicability of Section 118.

The Senate Finance Committee Report (83rd Cong., 2d Sess., S.Rept. No. 1622 (1954)), contains the following comment on the purpose of Section 118:

"[Section 118] deals with cases where a contribution is made to a corporation by a governmental unit, chamber of commerce, or other association of individuals having no proprietary interest in the corporation. In many such cases because the contributor expects to derive indirect benefits, the contribution cannot be called a gift; yet the anticipated future benefits may also be so intangible as to not warrant treating the contribution as a payment for future services." * * *

Treasury Regulation Section 1.118–1 also provides that Section 118 does not apply to any money or property transferred to a corporation in consideration for goods or services to be rendered.

The payments by Sharpstown to taxpayer were admittedly made with the expectation that the existence of taxpayer's department store would promote Sharpstown's financial interests. However, this expectation was clearly of such a speculative nature that any benefit necessarily must be regarded as indirect. In all the cases relied on by the government, the contributions had a reasonable nexus with the services which it was the business of the recipient corporation to provide. Such is not this case. Under these circumstances, we agree with the Tax Court that any benefit expected to be derived by Sharpstown was so intangible as not to warrant treating its contribution as a payment to taxpayer for future services.

In a somewhat different factual setting, the Supreme Court has held that contributions received to induce a taxpayer to locate factories in a certain area are contributions to capital. Brown Shoe Co. v. Commissioner, 339 U.S. 583, 70 S.Ct. 820, 94 L.Ed. 1081 (1950). Although *Brown Shoe Co.* was decided before the enactment of Section 118, the legislative history of Section 118 makes it clear that it restates existing law as developed through administrative and court decisions. 3 U.S.Code Cong. & Ad.News 4825 (1954).

We do not agree with the Commissioner's assertion that Section 118 has no application unless the contribution is made by a governmental unit or civic group. The Senate Report referred to herein expressly states that Section 118 is also to apply to contributions made to a corporation by an association of individuals having no proprietary interest in the corporation. Our conclusion is not inconsistent with Treasury Regulation Section 1.118–1 as is contended by the Commissioner. In pertinent part, that regulation provides:

"Section 118 also applies to contributions to capital made by persons other than shareholders. For example, the exclusion applies to the value of land or other property contributed to a corporation by a governmental unit or civic group for the purpose of inducing the corporation to locate its business in a particular community. * * *"

The reference in the regulation to a governmental unit or civic group obviously is only one example of the applicability of Section 118 to a contribution made by a nonshareholder, and by express language is not intended to be exclusive of other possible applications.

The judgment of the Tax Court is affirmed.

NOTE

1. How indirect must the financial benefit to the contributor be?

    a. In *Federated Department Stores, Inc.,* if Sharpstown (an interesting name for a real estate developer) anticipated receiving income directly from the operations of Federated, i.e. rental of parking facilities, maintenance, utility charges, would the result of the case have been different?

    b. Would a contribution of funds by Ford Motor Company to one of its dealers, in order to enable the dealer to acquire real estate in a better location in which to operate the dealership, be considered a contribution to capital? See *John B. White, Inc.,* 55 T.C. 729 (1971), affirmed, 458 F.2d 989 (3d Cir.1972).

    c. See also *The May Department Stores Company,* 33 CCH Tax Ct. Mem. 1128 (1974), affirmed, per curiam, 519 F.2d 1154 (8th Cir.1975).

2. If Section 118 applies to a contribution of property to a corporation, what is the corporation's basis in the contributed property? See Section 362(c).

3. How should the contributor treat the contribution for income tax purposes?

    a. If the contributor is a shareholder in the corporation, the logical conclusion would be to increase the shareholder's basis in the stock of the corporation. But, might the conclusion change if the contribution was of real estate having a fair market value greater than its basis to an individual non-controlling shareholder? Might the shareholder have to recognize gain measured by the difference between the fair market value of, and the shareholder's basis in, the real estate? See Section 351. If the shareholder received no stock or securities or any other "property" of the corporation in exchange, could the shareholder simply increase the basis in his existing shares in an amount equal to his basis in the real estate? Cf. Reg.Sec. 1.118–1.

    b. If the contributor is a governmental entity or a non-profit corporation such as a chamber of commerce or industrial development corporation, it makes little difference in most cases how the contribution is treated for income tax purposes.

    c. If, however, the contributor is a real estate developer, the income tax treatment of the contribution can be very significant to the developer.

        1. Arguably, through making the contribution the developer has acquired a capital asset (the presence of the recipient). What, however, is the useful life of the asset? If the contribution was of a leasehold interest, the useful life is determinable. What is the developer's "cost" of the contribution?

        2. On the other hand, the asset acquired as a result of the contribution can be said to be the increased value of the developer's surrounding or adjacent real estate. In this context the "cost" to the developer of the contribution might be added to its basis in the

surrounding or adjacent real estate. See *Perlmutter,* 45 T.C. 311 (1965); *Cooper,* 31 T.C. 1155 (1959); Rev.Rul. 68–478, 1968–2 C.B. 330; Sandison and Waters, *Tax Planning for the Land Developer: Cost Allocations of Land and Improvements,* 37 J.Tax'n 80 (1972); Sandison and Waters, *More on Tax Planning for Land Developers: Allocations, Deductions, Reporting Income,* 37 J.Tax'n 154 (1972).

3. Finally, as was the case in *Federated Department Stores, Inc.,* the corporation receiving the contribution may act as a traffic generator for the development. Approached in this manner, the contribution by the developer is similar to an advertising expense which is currently deductible. See Reg.Sec. 1.162–1(a).

4. Section 118 speaks in terms of corporations. What if the recipient of the contribution is a partnership or a proprietorship? Because of the incidental benefits expected by the contributor, the contribution might not be treated as a gift. Private Ltr.Rul. 8038037 applied Section 118 by way of analogy to a partnership. The availability of Section 118 was limited to corporations, however, by G.C.M. 38944. Recently, G.C.M. 39228, in dealing with a contribution made to a shopping center owned by a partnership, held that Section 118 did not apply because of the direct benefit received as a result of the contribution rather than because the shopping center was owned by a partnership.

5. See generally Comment, *Contributions to the Capital of a Corporation: A Reexamination,* 44 U.Cin.L.Rev. 549 (1975); Frolik, *Section 118 and the Tax Treatment of Non–Shareholder Contributions to Capital,* 38 Ohio St.L.J. 499 (1977).

Division II

DISPOSITION OF REAL ESTATE

1. THE REAL ESTATE BROKER

Generally, one of the first steps when disposing of real estate is the hiring of a real estate broker. The history of the relationship between vendors and brokers has been marked by a great deal of litigation. Although there are a number of factors which might be said to have played a part in this, one which has certainly contributed is the somewhat cavalier attitude toward the relationship with the broker many times displayed by the vendor. As a matter of fact, the relationship is fairly complex and a great deal of care and forethought is required in its definition.

a. THE LISTING AGREEMENT

The document which establishes the relationship between the vendor and the broker is generally known as a listing agreement. There are a number of forms which a listing agreement may take. Listing agreements fall into three to four distinct categories.

COMMENT:

COLORADO REAL ESTATE BROKER LISTING CONTRACTS

35 University of Colorado Law Review 205 (1963).
[footnotes omitted]

* * *

* * * Normally, the landowner with land to sell, places the land in the hands of the broker, promising to pay the broker a commission for his services in finding a purchaser ready, willing and able to buy under the terms set forth by the owner. In return, the broker makes no promise except perhaps an implied promise to make diligent and faithful efforts to find such a purchaser. The agreement under which the parties initially establish their relationship is called a *listing contract*. This contract * * * ordinarily takes one of three basic forms, commonly referred to as *open, exclusive agency,* or *exclusive right to sell*.

A listing agreement does not give the broker authority to enter into a contract binding upon the owner; the broker is limited to finding a prospective purchaser for the owner's land and to negotiating a sale between the purchaser and the owner. The owner, though he may be obligated to pay a commission, is not obligated to sell to the prospective purchaser. In the event the owner desires to give the broker authority to sell, an agreement to that effect must be in writing. The writing will be strictly construed, and every doubt as to the broker's authority will be resolved against him and against any third person dealing with the broker under the written authority. Where the listing agreement is in writing, the fact that the instrument uses, in general terms, the phrase "to sell" does not extend the broker's authority but gives to the broker nothing more than the authority to find a purchaser.

From the owner's point of view, the most favorable listing would provide that the owner is bound to pay a commission only after (1) the broker has introduced him to the purchaser, (2) the purchaser has accepted his terms of sale, and (3) he has received the sale price from the purchaser in return for the land. From the broker's point of view, the most favorable listing would provide that, regardless of who sells the property, the broker is entitled to a commission. Unfortunately, not all listing contracts are so clearly defined.

Open Listing

The open listing is a transaction in which the owner employs the broker to procure a purchaser ready, willing and able to buy on the terms proposed by the owner. In return, the owner promises to pay the broker a specified commission for his services. This transaction is an offer for a unilateral contract creating in the broker the power of acceptance by actual rendition of the requested services. The listing is not exclusive, and the owner is free to sell the property through his own efforts or through those of another broker without being obligated to pay a commission to the first broker. Being an offer for a unilateral contract, the open listing is revocable at will at any time before performance. The owner is neither bound to give the broker a reasonable time within which to act, nor is he precluded from changing his mind. The only way the broker can earn a commission is to find a ready, willing and able purchaser before other agents or the owner himself finds such a purchaser and before the owner revokes the offer.

An open listing may be created either expressly or impliedly, and though it may be revoked at will, the owner in so doing must act in good faith. * * * The owner may not step in during the time of the listing and without justification prevent the broker from obtaining an offer from a prospect whom he has secured, so long as the broker, in good faith and within a reasonable period of time, has been attempting to secure the offer. The owner may not step in and persuade the broker's prospect to deal directly with the owner, nor may the owner take advantage of the broker's work of procuring a purchaser and escape payment of the commission by discharging the broker before or after consummating the sale himself with the broker's prospect. In the event the broker is unable to persuade the owner and the prospective purchaser to agree to terms within a reasonable time, the owner, or the owner through another broker, may negotiate with the same purchaser; and if the owner and purchaser reach an agreement, the owner is free to consummate the sale without being obligated to the original broker. Also, if the owner at the time negotiations are commenced has no knowledge that the broker previously conferred with the same party, he may sell the property to said purchaser without being obligated to the broker. * * *

* * * [I]n the absence of bad faith, * * * the only way in which a broker under an open listing is entitled to any compensation is by full performance. Though the rule may seem harsh to the broker, a contrary rule would be equally harsh to the landowner, and at the same time be contrary to the owner's offer. When an owner and broker enter into an open listing agreement, the owner's offer of compensation is conditional upon the achievement of a specified result, i.e., procuring a purchaser ready, willing and able to buy the property. The owner's position is such that he receives no benefit until this condition is met. The owner's offer is not one in which part of the requested consideration can be given or tendered before all of the requested consideration is given or tendered. Furthermore, if this rule were not followed, it would not be economically feasible for the owner to exercise the reserved right to employ other brokers. By employing several brokers, under any theory of part performance, it is conceivable that the costs for brokerage services could exceed the purchase price of the property if it were necessary that the owner compensate all brokers who unsuccessfully rendered time, money and effort to find a purchaser.

It is necessary to distinguish between an open listing and a situation in which the owner merely "lists" his property with the broker. In the latter situation, there is no contract of employment as the owner makes no promise or offer of any kind to the broker. The owner merely invites the broker to submit offers from prospective purchasers that may or may not be accepted, and if not accepted, regardless of the reason, the owner incurs no liability to the broker. * * *

Exclusive Agency

An exclusive agency is an agreement between the owner and broker providing that, during the life of the contract, the owner will not sell the property to a purchaser procured by another agent. This arrangement reserves in the owner the privilege of selling the property himself without being obligated to the broker for payment of the commission, while at the same time leaving the broker with assurance that his commission will not be defeated by a sale through another broker. It is not necessary that the listing contract expressly stipulate the reservation by the owner of the right to sell the property himself as it is an implied condition unless expressly negated.

A problem, common to both the open listing and the exclusive agency listing, is the requirement of notification by the owner to the broker in the event the property is sold before the broker has procured a purchaser. * * * Though there is authority both ways, the better reasoned view requires notification. The theory of those jurisdictions not requiring notice is that once the property is sold, all agency relationships terminate and the authority to find a purchaser is automatically revoked regardless of notice to the agents. In contrast to this theory is the basic rule of agency providing that if an agent's authority is terminated by events known to the principal of which he has reason to know are unknown to the agent, the principal has the duty of informing the agent of the termination within a reasonable time. An application of this rule places a duty on the owner to notify the agent, and a failure to do so subjects him to liability to the broker for damages incurred by such failure. The injustice of the "no notification" view is obvious. It is unjust for the owner to permit the uninformed broker to expend additional money, time and effort in an attempt to fulfill the owner's desires, and, after doing so, to receive no compensation because the owner, without any notice to the broker, had attained the desired end by other means.

The requirement of notice may also be beneficial to the owner. A broker with an exclusive agency or open listing is fully aware of the competition in the race to find a purchaser. Consequently, the very nature of the listing discourages the broker from expending money, time and effort on advertising and other means in an attempt to reach the desired result. However, with continuous assurance that the property is available, the broker's position is less hazardous, and added efforts to procure a purchaser can be undertaken until notification is received that the property has been sold.

Exclusive Right of Sale or Exclusive Sale

An exclusive sale listing (also referred to as exclusive right of sale) is similar to an exclusive agency in all respects except that, in the exclusive sale, the broker is given the sole and exclusive right to sell the principal's property during the period of the listing. Regardless of who arranges a sale, whether it be the owner, another agent, or the listing broker himself, if it be during the period of the contract, the broker is entitled to a commission. In order for the listing to be construed as an exclusive right of sale, the agreement must expressly negate the owner's right to sell the property himself; if no such stipulation be made, the court will construe it as an exclusive agency. This construction is justified in that the exclusive right of sale is a harsh contract that takes away the owner's right to sell his own property without his having to reward someone else.

The * * * case of Garrett v. Richardson [149 Colo. 449, 369 P.2d 566 (1962)] sheds considerable light on the proposition that the broker with an exclusive sale listing, who has made good faith efforts to procure a purchaser, is entitled to a commission for services if he has procured a purchaser during the life of the contract, even though the owner has made an attempt to revoke the listing. In this case, the owners signed and delivered to the broker a ninety day exclusive sale listing. The broker spent time, money and effort in advertising and showing the property to prospective purchasers, but was unsuccessful in his attempts to find a purchaser. Prior to the termination of the ninety day period, the owners, in writing, extended the listing and reduced the price of the home. During the extension period, the broker procured an offer from a party with whom he had been negotiating. Since the offer was not totally in accord with the terms proposed by the owners in the extension, the owners declined to accept. At the same time, the owners notified the broker that the property was no longer for sale and requested that the broker take the property off the market. The broker refused and continued his efforts to find a purchaser. Two weeks later he procured a second offer to purchase from the same party. The offer was in complete accord with the terms proposed by the owners in the extended listing agreement. The owners again refused to accept the offer and the broker commenced an action for the recovery of the commission. The trial court concluded that prior to the time that the broker had procured a ready, willing and able purchaser, the listing agreement was an executory agreement on both sides, and the owners had the right and privilege to revoke the agreement prior to the expiration date without obligation. The Colorado Supreme Court reversed the judgment and remanded the cause with directions to enter judgment as prayed for in the complaint.

* * * The Colorado Supreme Court stated that at the time of [the execution of the] listing agreement, due to a lack of consideration by the broker, the exclusive listing contract is not binding on the owner and does not become binding until the broker renders some service in procuring a purchaser. Once the broker manifests assent to the offer by spending time and money in his effort to find a purchaser, then the offer of the owner becomes a binding and legal obligation according to its terms and irrevocable during the stated period. The court promptly recognized the theoretical difficulties of the decision, and attempted to justify it with the following statement:

> The theoretical difficulties, formidable as they seem, are outweighed by considerations of practical justice. This rule avoids hardship to the offeree, and yet does not hold the offeror beyond the terms of his promise. It is true by such terms he was to be bound only if the requested act was done; but this implies that he will let it be done, that he will keep his offer open until the offeree who has begun can finish doing it. At least this is so where the doing of it will necessarily require time and expense.

This decision, though it may be justifiable * * *, raises both theoretical and practical difficulties. First, is the exclusive sales listing a bilateral contract, a unilateral contract, or a combination of both? * * * The Colorado court states that the listing at its inception is an offer for a unilateral contract [in] which the broker makes no express promise, but in which the owner expressly agrees to do certain things. The court also states, however, that once the broker devotes time and energy to find a purchaser, he is acting in compliance with his *implied* promise to make such an effort. This language clearly suggests a bilateral contract in which one party makes an implied promise in return for the other party's express promise.

Whichever class of contracts one tries to classify the exclusive sales listing, difficulties are encountered if the listing becomes irrevocable once the broker makes efforts to perform. It is inconceivable that the listing can be classified as bilateral as there is no promise by the broker for the breach of which the owner can maintain an action. At the most, the broker only impliedly promises to make diligent and faithful efforts to procure a purchaser and does not actually promise to procure a purchaser. On the other hand, the owner promises only to pay a commission for the actual procurement of a purchaser and not for the efforts used by the broker in attempting to find a purchaser.

If one classifies the listing as unilateral, he is confronted with the general rule that an offer is revocable until accepted. Until the broker fully performs, it cannot be said that the owner's promise to pay a commission has been accepted, and as such, the offer may be revoked. In addition, difficulties are encountered if one tries to apply the part performance rule because the rule only applies where part of the consideration requested in the offer is given or tendered. The efforts that are expended by the broker do not constitute part of the consideration requested but only constitute *preparations* to accept the owner's offer. Although these preparations may be essential to accepting the offer and may be detrimental to the broker, they are not enough to invoke the part performance doctrine as applied to the acceptance of offers for unilateral contracts.

The court also considered a third possibility which avoids the bilateral and unilateral distinction. This theory provides that the broker's part performance in expending time, money, and effort furnishes acceptance and consideration for an implied subsidiary promise not to revoke the principal offer during the stated time. The collateral contract is, in effect, specifically enforced by holding that any attempt to revoke it is ineffectual so that the owner is bound according to the terms of the agreement from the time the broker begins to perform. This theory provides that the owner, at the time of the agreement, must reasonably contemplate that the broker will expend time and money in an attempt to carry out the offer, and once this expenditure is made, the offer becomes irrevocable. [While some courts have adopted the view with respect to an exclusive agency or sale listing that the broker's implied agreement to perform or the broker's performance furnishes consideration for the owner's promise not to revoke during a stated period of time, the courts have been less willing to adopt that view with respect to an open listing having a stated term. See e.g. Nily Realty Inc. v. Wood, 272 Md. 589, 325 A.2d 730 (1974).] The primary difficulty with this theory is reflected by the statement that the offer becomes irrevocable and the owner is bound according to the terms of the agreement. Though it is true that the owner may have sacrificed his *right* to revoke the offer, it is questionable that he gave up his *power* to do so. Thus, if the offer is revoked, the owner should be liable to the broker for damages and not for specific performance. In the *Garrett* case the owner informed the broker that the property was no longer for sale and that the broker's authority was revoked. The court * * * held that the owner was bound according to the original terms of the offer, and permitted the broker to disregard the owner's statement and to continue investing additional time and effort to procure a purchaser for land that was no longer for sale. By so holding, the decision appears to disregard the general rule that once a contract is breached, the party wronged is not entitled to compensation for harm that he could have reasonably avoided. Consequently, the owner who decides not to sell is put in an unfavorable position in that, although he may be willing to compensate the broker for services already rendered, he is not entitled to do so unless he can reach a collateral agreement with the broker. Otherwise, he must sit by idly and hope that the broker is unable to find a purchaser.

The decision also implies that even after the owner has attempted to withdraw the broker's authority, the only way in which the broker can recover compensation is by actually finding a purchaser. [See e.g. Dean Vincent, Inc. v. Krimm, 285 Or. 439, 591 P.2d 740 (1979).] Though this rule [possibly] produced fair results * * * in Garrett v. Richardson, situations may arise which would make it detrimental to the broker and to the prospective purchaser. The first problem confronting the broker attempting to arrange a sale of real property is the making of arrangements for the inspection of the property by prospects. Once the owner has decided not to sell, such arrangements will be difficult if not impossible to make. In Garrett v. Richardson, the broker was fortunate and did not have this problem because the prospect had inspected the property prior to the owners' withdrawal of authority. Furthermore, the broker is forced to misrepresent his position in the matter in order to persuade the prospect to enter into an agreement, which agreement the broker has reason to believe will not be honored. It is absurd to force the broker to such extremes for the sole purpose of recovering a commission for unwanted services.

It appears that the court went one step too far. Instead of allowing the broker to continue in his efforts after notice of revocation, the broker should be required to cease in his efforts and seek recovery in *quantum meruit* for damages resulting from the owner's revocation. The broker should be entitled to a reasonable recovery for the amount of effort, time and money expended before notice of the revocation, and if he is able to show that a purchaser would have been procured at no additional expense, the recovery should be equivalent to the commission.

A relevant issue which was not discussed by the court, is that the listing agreement did not expressly negate the owner's right to withdraw his property from the market. The listing expressly provided that in case of *any sale* during the listing period the broker would be entitled to a commission, but was silent as to a withdrawal. It is possible that the owner's privilege of withdrawal was denied by the term in which he granted the broker "the exclusive and irrevocable right to sell." This term, however, could also be construed to mean that the broker had an exclusive and irrevocable right only if the property remained for sale. Since the term is ambiguous, it should be given the latter interpretation, thus impliedly preserving the owner's right to withdraw his property from the market. If the parties desire to deprive the owner of such a right, they can incorporate it specifically in the terms of the listing. Such a requirement would be in accord with the requirement that the owner's right to sell the property himself without paying a commission must be expressly negated, and in the absence of such a clause, the owner's right to sell is impliedly preserved.

In view of the fact that both the exclusive sale and exclusive agency are exclusive listings and differ only in the respect that the latter reserves in the owner the privilege of procuring a purchaser through his own efforts, Garrett v. Richardson should further be applicable to the exclusive agency listing. There is additional support for this contention in that the court did not limit the discussion to exclusive sale listings but referred to "an exclusive, irrevocable listing for a fixed time." Such language can clearly include an exclusive agency listing.

Frequently the validity of a listing agreement is questioned if no definite time for performance by the real estate broker is stipulated. Though this problem does not arise with open listings because of their revocable character, the problem does arise with the exclusive agency and the exclusive right to sell listings. The failure of the parties to agree expressly to a definite time does not render the listing invalid, and a reasonable duration will be implied. A reasonable time is a question of fact determined by considering the nature of the listing, the particular circumstances under which it was entered into, the diligence used by the broker, and the reasons why it was not performed at an earlier date. * * *

Related Matters

If the listing is silent as to compensation or commission, the broker is entitled, upon performance of the requested services, to a reasonable reward determined by the ordinary and usual commissions charged by other brokers in the same general area.

* * *

It is important to recognize that actual consummation of a sale is not necessary for the broker to earn a commission under any of the aforementioned forms of listing contracts. The broker's duty in each situation is limited to the procurement of a purchaser ready, willing and able to buy on the terms set forth by the owner; once this is done, the owner cannot relieve himself of liability for the commission by a refusal to consummate the sale. Nor can the owner avoid paying a commission by a subsequent mutual agreement with the purchaser not to consummate the sale. If the broker's prospect is not willing to buy on the terms proposed by the owner, but the owner and prospect within a reasonable time agree to terms substantially equivalent to the originals, the broker is entitled to a commission. If the owner's terms in the listing agreement are not definite but are to be such as can be agreed upon by the owner and purchaser, the owner must make a good faith effort to reach an agreement with a broker's prospect who is willing to negotiate on any reasonable terms. However, the parties must come to a complete agreement on all terms of the proposed contract.

Though the broker's duties are completely performed with the procurement of a ready, willing and able purchaser, the commission for these services is not due and owing until the consummation of the sale or the defeat of the sale due to the refusal or neglect of the owner to consummate upon the terms imposed by the listing agreement [or those agreed upon by the owner and the purchaser]. This requirement protects the seller-owner from having to seek recovery of the commission paid to the broker if the prospective purchaser is not ready, willing or able to consummate the sale on the closing day. * * *

NOTE

1. In some jurisdictions a broker who has entered into an open or exclusive agency listing agreement with a seller must be notified by the seller of a sale of the property or a revocation of the agreement. When must the notification be given in order to be effective?

    a. For example, a seller has listed the same property with three brokers using an open listing agreement in all cases. While the seller is negotiating with a purchaser brought to him by the first broker, the second broker calls and informs the seller that he has a prospective purchaser. The seller tells the second broker to bring the prospect to see him, not mentioning his current negotiations. Prior to the arrival of the second broker and his prospect, the seller agrees to sell for a price less than that indicated in the listing agreement to the purchaser brought to him by the first broker. The second broker then arrives with his prospect who is ready, willing and able to buy the property on the terms and conditions specified in the listing agreement. A half an hour after the departure of the very upset second broker and his prospect, the third broker arrives with a signed purchase offer from yet a third prospective purchaser. The offer is on the terms and conditions specified in the listing agreement. Does the seller owe one, two or three commissions?

2. Is the exclusive agency or exclusive sales agreement compatible with a community multiple listing arrangement? If compatibility can be achieved, are there any apparent disadvantages to this combination?

    a. A multiple listing arrangement, at times, can lead to the setting of standard commissions for real estate brokerage services in a community. In *McLain v. Real Estate Board of New Orleans, Inc.,* 444 U.S. 232, 100 S.Ct. 502, 62 L.Ed.2d 441 (1980), the Supreme Court held that the activities of real estate brokers are so involved with the flow of interstate commerce that the practice of setting a standard commission for the sale of residential real estate in a community is subject to challenge under Section 1 of the Sherman Act. See Note, *Jurisdiction Under the Sherman Act: A Close Look at the Affects Test*, 60 Notre Dame L.Rev. 603 (1985).

3. To what extent can a real estate broker rely on the authority of an individual who claims to represent an entity with respect to the disposition of some of the entity's real estate? For example, can a broker rely on the authority of the president of a corporation or a general partner of a partnership to bind their respective entities to a listing agreement? Cf. *Southern Idaho Realty of Twin Falls, Inc.—Century 21 v. Larry J. Hellhake and Associates, Inc.*, 102 Idaho 613, 636 P.2d 168 (1981); *Spiers v. Seal*, 426 So.2d 631 (La.App.1982).

a. Does it make a difference if the property to be sold is all of the property of the entity or a small portion of the property owned by the entity?

b. If the seller is a corporation and the proposed sale is of all, or substantially all, of its real estate and out of the usual course of business of the corporation, is the broker entitled to a commission if 1) the president of the corporation was authorized by the board of directors of the corporation to sign the listing agreement, 2) the broker produced a ready, willing and able purchaser and 3) the sale was *not* approved by a majority of the shareholders of the corporation? See *Wishnow v. Kingsway Estates, Inc.*, 26 A.D.2d 61, 270 N.Y.S.2d 834 (1966), and compare with *Cushman & Wakefield, Inc. v. Dollar Land Corporation Ltd. (U.S.)*, 44 A.D.2d 445, 355 N.Y.S.2d 409 (1974), affirmed, 36 N.Y.2d 409, 330 N.E.2d 409, 369 N.Y.S.2d 394 (1975). Cf. *Acmer Corporation v. State Transport Co.*, 275 Or. 51, 549 P.2d 1114 (1976); *Garfield v. Tindall*, 98 Idaho 841, 573 P.2d 966 (1978).

c. If the president of the corporation controlled enough shares of stock that the voting of his shares in favor of the sale would be enough to approve the sale, would this make a difference? See e.g. *Julian James Stores, Inc. v. Bennett*, 250 Ark. 279, 465 S.W.2d 94 (1971); *Hauptman v. Edwards, Inc.*, 170 Mont. 310, 553 P.2d 975 (1976).

4. In the usual case the broker's duties are performed when he produces a ready, willing and able purchaser. In some states the broker's right to payment of the commission is not conditioned on the purchaser performing under the purchase agreement unless the listing agreement specifically so states. For example, in *Hecht v. Meller*, 23 N.Y.2d 301, 244 N.E.2d 77, 296 N.Y.S.2d 561 (1968), the improvements on the real estate were substantially damaged after the purchase agreement was signed. The purchaser rescinded because of the damage to the improvements. The court, however, awarded the broker his commission. Other states take the position that the broker is not due his commission until the closing or the defeat of the sale by seller's refusal to go through with the sale on the agreed-upon terms. See e.g. *Ellsworth Dobbs, Inc. v. Johnson*, 50 N.J. 528, 236 A.2d 843 (1967); *Brown v. Grimm*, 258 Or. 55, 481 P.2d 63 (1971); *Van Winkle & Liggett v. G.B.R. Fabrics, Inc.*, 103 N.J. 335, 511 A.2d 124 (1986); *Drake v. Hosley*, 713 P.2d 1203 (Alaska 1986). In some jurisdictions a broker, who has an exclusive agency agreement with the seller, is not entitled to a commission after producing a ready, willing and able purchaser if the seller, prior to signing a contract with the purchaser produced by the broker, locates a different purchaser and sells to that purchaser. See *Graff v. Billet*, 64 N.Y.2d 899, 477 N.E.2d 212, 487 N.Y.S.2d 733 (1984); *Capezzuto v. John Hancock Mut. Life Ins. Co.*, 394 Mass. 399, 476 N.E.2d 188

(1985); *Hunneman and Co., Ins. v. Lo Presti,* 394 Mass. 406, 476 N.E.2d 191 (1985). See Comment, *Right of a Broker to a Real Estate Commission,* 8 Willamette L.J. 85 (1972); Goldstein, *When Does a Real Estate Broker Earn His Commission?,* 27 # 5 Prac.Law. 43 (1981); Comment, *The Law of Real Estate Brokerage Contracts: The Broker's Commission,* 41 La.L.Rev. 857 (1981); Zeigler, *Brokers and Their Commissions,* 14 Real Est.L.J. 122 (1985).

   5. See generally Comment, *A Reexamination of the Real Estate Broker–Buyer–Seller Relationship,* 18 Wayne L.Rev. 1343 (1972); Barasch, *Negotiating Real Estate Brokerage Agreements,* 8 Real Est.L.J. 240 (1980); Harris, *Listing Agreements—The "Invisible" Real Estate Contracts,* 14 # 2 Real Est.Rev. 20 (1984); Ellis, *Preparing the Listing Agreement Between Owner and Broker,* 2 # 4 Prac.Real Est.Law. 51 (1986); Bergman, *How to Draft a Real Estate Brokerage Agreement (With Form),* 3 # 2 Prac.Real Est.Law. 45 (1987).

b. WHOM DOES THE BROKER REALLY REPRESENT?

No matter what type of agreement has been entered into by the vendor and broker, the broker's position is still quite unique. The broker's compensation usually depends on the sale of the real estate. Therefore, the primary objective of the broker is to secure a sale of the real estate. Frequently, this requires "bringing the vendee and vendor together." In the negotiations whom does the broker really represent? When bringing a vendee's counter-offer to the vendor, does the broker violate his responsibilities to the vendor by suggesting to the vendor that the counter-offer is acceptable?

THE REAL ESTATE BROKER—SCHIZOPHRENIA OR CONFLICT OF INTERESTS
Arthur Stambler and Jacob A. Stein
28 Journal of the Bar Association of the District of Columbia 16 (1961).
[footnotes omitted]

*   *   *

Perhaps the most problematic areas in realty brokerage law are the factual situations involving (1) the question of for whom the broker acts in the transaction, and (2) the precise outlines of his legal responsibilities to that principal. True, there is an ingrained general tenet that the broker "owes his principal the highest fidelity," * * *. This is, of course, transplanted from the law of agency that is generally held applicable to brokerage situations * * *. But while it is determinative and workable in clean-cut cases of gross breach of fiduciary duty * * *, it is of less help in resolving the ambiguous problems in the more conventional brokerage relationship. * * *

A hard, realistic view of these give-and-take brokerage transactions would seem in order. It makes clear that the broker acts as intermediary negotiator between the contracting parties, doing so for a contingent fee payable only and if the realty is actually sold. Moreover, since the broker is the active go-between, the basic direction and the intangible details of the evolving transaction are generally locked within his personal and private knowledge. With the buyer he offers and bargains; for the seller he interprets and recommends.

* * *

To illustrate the problem, let us now turn to the particular everyday situation where the broker returns to the vendor-principal with the counter-offer of the potential buyer who, in the ordinary course, has rejected the original asking price. [I]t is quite customary that the broker express a position respecting the negotiations. Indeed he is expected to. Otherwise he is no more than a messenger carrying price quotations between the parties. This aspect of negotiation raises the basic questions.

In [expressing his opinion], does the broker remain solely the vendor's agent; or is he now acting solely or partially for the buyer in perhaps urging a sale at the lower price; or is his status a jumbled hotchpot of all three interests? If the broker is to act in any dual capacity[,] can he be expected to segregate and properly serve such often-conflicting interests? Or, as a practical matter, can he pursue more than one interest only at cost to his fundamental duty to his principal, the vendor? In short, is he capable of conscious and controlled schizophrenia, or must his actions inevitably involve some conflict of interests?

Broker statutes, the reported cases, and the general texts are of limited assistance in finding appropriate answers. Thus, the *District of Columbia Code* (Section 45–1408) *inter alia* forbids realty brokers from acting for more than one party to the transaction without the knowledge of all. This principle is echoed by the courts and writers. (Keith v. Berry, 64 A.2d 300 (D.C.1949). See also Grossman v. Herman, 240 App.Div. 525, 270 N.Y.S. 669, aff.[,] 266 N.Y. 249, 194 N.E. 694 (N.Y.Ct. App.1935); * * *.) But these citations provide no solution. The very question at issue here is to determine the party or parties for whom the broker is acting and how he may do so. There are also decisions stating the proposition that the broker's fiduciary duties require his obtaining the highest price and best terms reasonably believed available for the principal. (Smith v. Fidelity & Columbia Trust Co., 227 Ky. 120, 12 S.W.2d 276 (App.1928)). He must inform his principal of the known availability of more advantageous terms than offered (Whiting v. Delozier, 82 Cal.App. 525, 255 P. 861 (1st Div., 1927)[;] Pederson v. Johnson, 169 Wis. 320, 172 N.W. 723 (1919)). Thus, the broker's concealment of a material fact is a breach of the fiduciary [obligation] of full disclosure * * *. (Rawlings v. Collins, 36 U.S.App.D.C. 72 (1910); Nat. Savings & Trust Co. v. Sands, 44 U.S.App.D.C. 20 (1915)). So is inducing the buyer to believe that the property may be available for less than asked (Haymes v. Rogers, 70 Ariz. 257, 219 P.2d 339, rev'd on rehearing[,] 70 Ariz. 408, 222 P.2d 789 (1950)). * * *

Yet[,] it must be clear that the indicated ordinary situation does not involve any of these prescribed activities. Rather, it entails the psychological inducement to the broker to find the transaction that will serve his self-interest (and simultaneously, or collaterally, the parties'), with this being done in ways so unconsciously subtle that no judge or jury—nor even a psychoanalyst—could recognize and deal with them. The ordinary buyer needs no inducement toward a lower price; that is his built-in goal. Similarly, the conventional transaction seldom involves the availability of pre-fixed better terms. The best price is, of course, that hammered out in the unhampered give-and-take of negotiation. It is just that which the principal may not get. But, by and large, there can be no proof of this; without proof, no remedy; and then ultimately, no effective legal right.

Some closer recognition of these practical circumstances is reflected in the holding that the broker does not become the buyer's agent merely by promising to obtain the best available price for him. (Carothers v. Caine, 38 Cal.App. 71, 175 P. 478 (1918)). Similarly, no * * * breach of duty was found where the broker after making the seller's offer conveys the buyer's answer or counter-offer back to [the seller]. (Meline v. Kleinberger, 108 Cal.App. 60, 290 P. 1042 (1930)).

* * * [T]he broker is at times carefully distinguished from a middleman who, not an agent, only brings the transacting parties together, and at other times from the agent who exclusively represents one party-principal, whereas the broker is in a sense the agent of both. (Moore v. Turner, 137 W.Va. 299, 71 S.E.2d 342 (West Va.Supr.Ct.App., 1952); Amer.Juris., Id., Sec. 167; C.J.S., Id., § 3). These authorities likewise uniformly assert the described limitations upon the broker acting for both parties. Yet they nonetheless also indicate that he may be a "common agent" for both parties, particularly so when acting as a middleman for them. (Harten v. Loffler, 31 U.S.App.D.C. 362 (1908); Pollatschek v. Goodwin, 17 Misc. 587, 40 N.Y.S. 682 (1921); Amer. Juris., Id., at p. 1083; C.J.S., Id., § 14).

* * * [I]t may be surmised that the difficult[ies] * * * result from the attempted forcing of general agency principles upon the uniquely special brokerage situation. * * * For the critical question is not whether the vendor[,] on his limited knowledge[, may] be satisfied with the sale. It is whether he might have been *more* satisfied had the broker acted otherwise in the *fullest* pursu[it] of his duties. In transactions such as these, it seems somewhat strange and artificial that the law has wholly refused to recognize the seemingly obvious fact that the broker may also be acting, in primary or integral part, for himself in the matter.

The final sale/purchase decisions are, of course, for the transacting parties. [T]he broker[, however,] brings a wide range of general and particular experience to bear on such decisional process. Included are his general background in the field, his evaluation of the potential buyer's status and attitude, and probably even his formal recommendations on the transaction. These undoubtedly have a major, if not often controlling, effect upon such ultimate decisions. The potential conflict in the broker's role is both fully understandable and socially acceptable if the law as well as the business world recognize it as a practical fact of life. In doing so [it] would [be taken] into consideration in all realty transactions. Its undesirability stems from the possibility that the law may continue to overlook it while voicing inoperative platitudes of duty and responsibility. And then the business world (i.e., the mass of individual sellers and buyers) may unfortunately follow suit, to its detriment. If this happens, our body of commercial law will be perpetuating [a] legal fiction that will prevent its coming fully to grips with the proper needs of the business world which, in the ultimate analysis, it is intended to guide and protect.

NOTE

1. In the exercise of this controlled (or uncontrolled) schizophrenia, just how schizophrenic can the broker be?

a. If a broker employed by a seller is advised in confidence by a prospective purchaser that the seller's property is the last in a series of five tracts that the purchaser is putting together for development purposes, must the broker disclose this to the seller in the course of negotiations?

1. If the broker discloses this information to the seller when he delivers the prospective purchaser's counter-offer to the seller, has he breached any duty to the purchaser which arose when he agreed to take the purchaser's counter-offer to the seller with knowledge of the prospective purchaser's situation? Cf. *Stortroen v. Beneficial Finance Co. of Colorado,* 736 P.2d 391 (Colo.1987); *Rohauer v. Little,* 736 P.2d 403 (Colo.1987).

b. A broker employed by a seller is advised in confidence by the purchaser of the names of the participants in the purchasing entity. If the seller asks, can the broker refuse to disclose the names to the seller? Is the broker obligated to disclose even if the seller does not ask? Cf. *White v. Boucher,* 322 N.W.2d 560 (Minn.1982); *First Nat. Bank v. Leonard,* 289 Ark. 357, 711 S.W.2d 798 (1986).

c. If the prospective purchaser indicates to the broker employed by the seller that the amount of the counter-offer might be increased if the seller refuses to accept it, must the broker disclose this statement to the seller if the seller is prepared to accept the counter-offer? If the seller rejects the counter-offer but indicates to the broker that something less than the amount of the initial offer might be accepted, can the broker disclose this statement to the prospective purchaser?

2. A broker also can be employed by a purchaser. For example, a developer may employ a broker to "put together" all of the real estate needed for a development.

a. What if one of the parcels which was needed for the development had been listed with the broker prior to his agreement with the developer, and the owner of that parcel wanted a price for the parcel which was more than the developer was willing to pay? Might the broker have some conflict of interest problems? Cf. *Cogan v. Kidder, Mathews & Segner, Inc.,* 97 Wash.2d 658, 648 P.2d 875 (1982); *Handy v. Garmaker,* 324 N.W.2d 168 (Minn.1982); *Smith v. Sullivan,* 419 So.2d 184 (Miss.1982). See generally Comment, *Dual Agency in Residential Real Estate Brokerage: Conflict of Interest and Interests in Conflict,* 12 Golden Gate U.L.Rev. 379 (1982).

3. Frequently, a prospective purchaser of real estate requests the assistance of a broker in locating appropriate real estate to purchase. Often the arrangement between the broker and the purchaser is, at best, oral and the obligations of the broker to the purchaser are not well defined. At a minimum, some courts have, on the basis of public interest, required the broker to act "honestly" with regard to the purchaser. See e.g. *Amato v. Latter & Blum, Inc.,* 227 La. 537, 79 So.2d 873 (1955). Cf. *Stevens v. Jayhawk Realty Co., Inc.,* 236 Kan. 90, 689 P.2d 786 (1984). See generally Note, *Real Estate Brokers' Duties to Prospective Purchasers,* 1976 B.Y.U.L.Rev. 513; Comment, *The Real Estate Broker–Purchaser Relationship: Louisiana and Common Law,* 52 Tul.L. Rev. 157 (1977); Comment, *A Real Estate Broker's Duty to His Purchaser: Washington State's Position and Some Projections for the Future,* 17 Gonz.L. Rev. 79 (1981); Adler, *Disclosure and the Buyer–Broker Relationship,* 11 # 4 Real Est.Rev. 94 (1982).

4. See generally Comment, *A Re-examination of the Real Estate Broker— Buyer–Seller Relationship,* 18 Wayne L.Rev. 1343 (1972); Herzfeld, *Quo Vadis, Broker? What's Your Role?,* 2 # 2 Real Est.Rev. (1972); Currier, *Finding the Broker's Place in the Typical Residential Real Estate Transaction,* 33 U.Fla.L. Rev. 655 (1981); Comment, *The Real Estate Broker's Fiduciary Duties: An Examination of Current Industry Standards and Practices,* 12 Pepperdine L.Rev. 145 (1984); Grohman, *A Reassessment of the Selling Real Estate Broker's Agency Relationship With The Purchaser,* 61 St. John's L.Rev. 560 (1987).

5. In addition to the broker's obligations and responsibilities to the seller and, at times, the purchaser, Section 6045 of the Internal Revenue Code requires the broker, in certain situations, to report to the Internal Revenue Service with respect to any real estate transaction in which the broker is involved. See Section 6045(e).

2. MEANS OF DISPOSITION OF THE REAL ESTATE

a. THE OPTION, THE CONTRACT OF PURCHASE, THE LAND CONTRACT, THE GROUND LEASE, FINANCING CONDITIONS, SUBORDINATION, AND THE USE OF THE NOMINEE OR STRAW MAN

The vendor's concerns with respect to the means of disposition of real estate have much in common with the concerns of the vendee with respect to the means of acquisition of real estate. For example, the vendor must consider whether to use an installment land contract or a land purchase agreement to dispose of the real estate. Should the vendor give the vendee an option to acquire the real estate? Should the vendor retain ownership of the real estate and lease the real estate to the vendee using a ground lease? The vendor also will be concerned with any financing conditions, subordination, and whether he should deal with a nominee in the event the vendee chooses to use a nominee.

b. SPECIFIC PERFORMANCE

In the usual case, if all of the preconditions provided for by the means of acquisition are performed and the vendor fails or refuses to convey the real estate, the vendee's remedy probably will be specific performance. The availability of this remedy to the vendee has been justified on the basis that "land is unique" or as a result of the concept of "equitable conversion." No matter how rationalized, however, specific performance is the usual remedy of the vendee upon default by the vendor. In the event of a default by the vendee, can the vendor obtain specific performance?

"SUBJECT TO FINANCING" CLAUSES IN INTERIM CONTRACTS FOR SALE OF REALTY
Ray J. Aiken
43 Marquette Law Review 265 (1960).
[footnotes omitted]

* * *

* * * [T]he acute lawyer, representing the seller[,] * * * [may] elect * * * specific performance. The sole drawback of this course, assuming a financially responsible buyer, is that the resale of the property is necessarily postponed pendente lite. That problem, however, may be present regardless of the form of action selected, assuming inability to negotiate settlement of the dispute, so that it constitutes no insuperable objection.

The most important practical advantage gained by proceeding in specific performance is that it enables seller to separate his proofs on the question of security-value from those on the question of fair market value, and effectively shifts the burden on the latter question. In addition, seller places himself in a position to recover the "demurrage" on the property (taxes, interest, insurance upkeep, heating, repairs etc.) over and above the basic contract debt.

The procedure is this: Seller commences suit praying that buyer be required specifically to perform by paying the balance of the purchase price, plus demurrage, and alleging that, upon such payment, seller will himself perform by conveyance. Buyer's most usual answering plea sets up the contingency.[1] This plea failing, judgment is entered for the full balance due on the contract, ordering payment within a reasonable period, and directing that, unless such amount is paid as ordered, the subject property (treated as equitably belonging to the buyer) be advertised and sold at equitable foreclosure sale to meet the judgment. To this point, the only question which has arisen respecting the value of the property is that respecting its security value, in connection with the availability of financing, and the seller's position is that such value was—at time of breach—adequate.

1. [Failure to secure financing necessary to go through with purchase.]

Subsequently, the foreclosure auction is held. Prominent among the bidders, and going as high as he must, is the seller-plaintiff. Following the auction, the matter comes back into court for confirmation—and determination of deficiency. If defendant-buyer intends now to defeat or lessen the impending deficiency, he has the burden of showing that the auction *did not* realize fair market value, against the presumption that it did. The inquiry now is not concerned with fair market at time of breach, but with fair market at time of sale; and opinion evidence offered on behalf of buyer is ranked against the fact of the open public auction sale.

The court's alternatives, even assuming its dissatisfaction with the bid, are limited: it may present plaintiff-seller with an option to reduce or waive his deficiency or submit to a resale; it may order resale, including an upset price; or it may simply order a resale. Meanwhile, the costs and demurrages continue to run against the buyer's account. Ultimately, he must either purchase or go bankrupt. If the necessary financing is in fact unavailable (regardless of the legal finding on the point), the buyer's only course is bankruptcy. The credit purchase which buyer originally contracted to make has been converted into a present cash liability.

* * * [T]he contract which is specifically enforced under the decree [may be] essentially unlike the one which the parties originally entered into. Buyer and seller [may have] both envisioned the necessity of third-party financing as the sine qua non of the transaction. It is inconceivable that buyer would have entered into the transaction at all had it been put to him as a cash proposition, with the money to come from his own assets. Even assuming that the buyer's failure to procure the financing and to complete the purchase was entirely deliberate, the hard fact of the matter is that equity cannot, after the event, restore the availability of\ such financing so that the purchase may proceed essentially as per contract. Its decree of specific performance, under such circumstances, amounts realistically to a hollow gesture, stripping the contract of its most vital provision.

The only apparent reason advanced for allowing the remedy to the seller is because, had seller defaulted, the same remedy would have been available to the buyer. This reasoning constitutes an affirmative application of the doctrine of mutuality of remedy—a doctrine which has never possessed any but the haziest logical support, and one which, at least in its affirmative applications, has been thoroughly discredited. In plain fact, the seller's action for specific performance is nothing but a debt-collection device; and no reason has even been suggested why the legal remedy is inadequate for those purposes. Indeed, once the specific performance decree has worked its tactical magic by dispensing the seller from proving his legal damage, all aspects of its equitable nature disappear, and the debt collection proceeds by ordinary legal processes.

Pursuing the mutuality concept a bit further, however, we find a common practice of attempting to block, by contract, even the buyer's well-established right of specific performance upon seller's attempted default. By insertion of the customary avoidance clause, the standard interim contract provides that should seller fail to make title as he undertakes to do, and buyer is unwilling to waive the default, the agreement shall be null and void. Not even a damage action is allowed buyer, to say nothing of specific performance. Under this common form of contract, therefore, not even the mutuality doctrine seems applicable to permit seller's action.

* * *

NOTE

1. Does the seller asking for specific performance make any sense when it is obvious to all concerned that the purchaser does not have the financial means necessary to pay the purchase price?

a. If so, in what situations does it make sense? If the property has appreciated since the execution of the contract? If it has depreciated?

b. If the purchaser defaults and the contract is recorded, what steps can the seller take to clear the cloud on title?

c. See generally Kronman, *Specific Performance,* 45 U.Chi.L.Rev. 351 (1978); Comment, *Missouri Stare Decisis: Specific Performance of Contracts for the Sale of Real Estate,* 43 UMKC L.Rev. 199 (1974); Note, *Specific Performance for the Seller of Real Estate—A North Caroline Remedy?,* 7 N.C.Cent.L.J. 94 (1975); Richards, *Mutuality of Remedy—A Call for Reform,* 13 Mem.St.U.L.Rev. 1 (1982).

d. Section 2–506 of the Uniform Land Transactions Act grants the seller the right to sue for the price of the property only when the property is not resaleable at a reasonable price with reasonable effort. The action for the price of the property, although substantially equivalent to an action for specific performance, is an action at law and not "in equity." See generally Balbach, *The Uniform Land Transactions Act: Articles 1 and 2,* 11 Real Prop., Prob. & Tr.J. 1 (1976); Maggs, *Remedies for Breach of Contract Under Article Two of the Uniform Land Transactions Act,* 11 Ga. L.Rev. 275 (1977).

2. In perhaps the first case to consider the issue, the court in *Centex Homes Corp. v. Boag,* 128 N.J.Super. 385, 320 A.2d 194 (Ch.1974), held that the vendor-sponsor of an apartment condominium project was not entitled to specific performance against a defaulting vendee of a unit. The court, after refusing to accept the vendor-sponsor's arguments based on mutuality of remedy and equitable conversion, held that the vendor-sponsor had an adequate remedy at law. The court stated:

"Here the subject matter of the real estate transaction—a condominium apartment unit—has no unique quality but is one of hundreds of virtually identical units being offered by a developer for sale to the public. The units are sold by means of sample, in this case model apartments, in much the same manner as items of personal property are sold in the market place. The sales prices for the units are fixed in accordance with [a] schedule filed by Centex as part of its offering plan, and the only variance as between apartments having the same floor plan (of which six plans are available) is the floor level or the building location within the project. In actuality, the condominium apartment units, regardless of their realty label, share the same characteristics as personal property.

"From the foregoing one must conclude that the damages sustained by a condominium sponsor resulting from the breach of the sales agreement are readily measurable and the damage remedy at law is wholly adequate. No compelling reasons have been shown by Centex for the granting of specific performance relief and its complaint is therefore dismissed as to the first count." 320 A.2d 198, 199.

If the "uniqueness" of real estate is the reason for granting specific performance, what result would the court have reached if it had been faced with the vendee of a condominium unit suing a defaulting vendor-sponsor for specific performance? Assuming that the vendee, upon completion of the purchase, would receive an undivided interest in the common elements in addition to the specific unit purchased, might the vendee, despite *Centex Homes Corp. v. Boag,* claim that a unit of an apartment condominium project is unique? See *Pruitt v. Graziano,* 215 N.J.Super. 330, 521 A.2d 1313 (1987). Did the court properly ignore this claim when approaching the question from the standpoint of the vendor-sponsor? See Note, *Equitable Relief Not Available Where Vendor–Sponsor of Multi–Unit Condominium Complex Was Unable to Make Clear Showing of Inadequacy of Remedy at Law,* 9 Suffolk U.L.Rev. 922 (1975).

3. If the vendor simply sues the vendee for damages for the breach of the contract, what problems does the vendor face in "proving-up" damages? See e.g. Comment, *Damages: The Illogical Differences in Measuring Breach of Contract Damages When The Contract Involves Land Rather Than Goods,* 26 Okla.L.Rev. 277 (1973).

The Uniform Land Transactions Act provides the generally accepted measure of damages for the seller in the event of the purchaser's default. The measure of damages is the difference between the contract price and the resale price (Section 2–504) or the fair market value of the property at the time for conveyance (Section 2–505). The Uniform Land Transactions Act also provides for the recovery of incidental and consequential damages (Section 2–507) and, in certain limited situations, it permits the seller to recover lost profits (Section 2–505(b)). See Balbach, *The Uniform Land Transactions Act: Articles 1 and 2,* 11 Real Prop., Prob. & Tr.J. 1 (1976); Maggs, *Remedies for Breach of Contract Under Article Two of the Uniform Land Transactions Act,* 11 Ga.L.Rev. 275 (1977).

c. LIQUIDATED DAMAGES

In many cases, specific performance will not be available to the vendor because (1) it is a futile act since there is no reason to believe that the vendee can consummate the sale or respond in damages, or (2) the court will not, as suggested by Professor Aiken, grant the specific performance remedy to a vendor. Therefore, the possibility of adding a liquidated damages provision to the agreement providing for the disposition of the real estate should be considered.

DRAFTING THE LIQUIDATED DAMAGE CLAUSE—WHEN AND HOW

Frank C. Dunbar, Jr.
20 Ohio State Law Journal 221 (1959).
[footnotes omitted]

* * *

Validity of Provision—Penalty?

Penalties Are Not Enforceable

* * *

The authorities generally distinguish between liquidated damages as being a genuine pre-estimate of damages, and a penalty as being a provision which operates in terrorem, by "penalizing for breach," "as punishment," or as a "deterrent." Absent infrequent statutory limitations, the courts rely upon the two basic tests of validity hereafter described, often additionally paying lip service to the "intention of the parties."

First Test—Reasonableness of Amount or Formula

* * * [T]he courts' first test of the validity of a covenant claimed to be for liquidated damages * * * [is whether] the amount thereby fixed * * * [is] a "reasonable forecast of just compensation for the harm that is caused by the breach. * * *" In enunciating this test, courts and writers use terms such as "honest" and "reasonable" estimates of damages or "attempts at pre-estimation." If an amount prescribed as purported liquidated damages, by the measure normally applicable, is obviously excessive, the courts will characterize it as a penalty and hold the provision invalid. * * *

Is the reasonableness of the amount or formula * * * judged in the light of the situation as viewed by the parties at the time they made their contract, or * * * in the light of conditions existing at the time of or after the breach? * * * [W]hen the question has been expressly considered it has nearly always been held that reasonableness is to be judged as of the time of the making of the contract.

Second Test—Difficulty of Ascertaining Damages

Fostered undoubtedly by the historical reluctance of courts to enforce liquidated-damages covenants, the rule has become firmly established that such a covenant is not enforceable unless "the harm that is caused by the breach is one that is incapable or very difficult of accurate estimation." * * *

Since the agreement liquidating damages must be reasonable, in the light of the rules of law for measuring damages, the draftsman of such an agreement cannot proceed with his drafting until he knows how the damages for a particular breach of a particular covenant would be measured in the jurisdiction whose law would control in the event of an action for recovery of damages.

To what extent is the element of foreseeability of harm from a specified breach of a particular covenant relevant to drafting an agreement liquidating damages for that breach? The answer is that it is probably no more relevant than in the case of a post-breach ascertainment of allowable damages. Hence, the careful draftsman will seek to anticipate whether the promisor might subsequently contend that the parties had not at the time of making their contract foreseen that particular consequences would flow from the promisor's breach. He can then incorporate a suitable recital in his contract to make it plain that the parties did, in fact, foresee particular consequences.

When shall the determination be made as to whether it will be difficult to ascertain the amount of damages? Since the answer may establish the validity of the stipulation as of the time of the making of the contract, that is the time as of which the determination should be made. * * *

Intention of Parties

The opinions of the courts dealing with the validity of covenants purportedly for liquidated damages are replete with discussions about the "intention of the parties." Time and again they are found to say that a covenant specifying a sum to be paid in the event of a breach will be deemed to be one for liquidated damages if the parties so intended; otherwise, a penalty. Rarely is there any doubt about what the parties intended. If the agreement is to the effect that if A fails to perform as promised he shall pay Y dollars to B, that is what they meant. What is there to construe? Contracting parties—businessmen, usually—do not contract in terms of legal doctrines. They have never heard of the proposition that "equity will relieve against a penalty." When they say that under specified circumstances one man shall pay another a sum of money, that is just what they intend.

The courts, however, * * * have proceeded, in terms of the example above given, first to determine whether Y dollars was a reasonable amount in relation to the harm done to B by A's failure to perform his promise. If they * * * conclude that it was reasonable, they * * * solemnly opine that it was the intention of the parties that Y dollars should be "liquidated damages." If they * * * determine that it was not reasonable, they [hold], often squarely in the face of an express declaration that Y dollars is fixed as "liquidated damages," that the parties intended that the payment of Y dollars should be a "penalty," serving as a club to compel performance by A.

The true rule surely is that the intention of the parties in this regard is irrelevant; that the law, as a matter of public policy, imposes a limitation upon the freedom of the power to contract, and that if a contractual provision is not within the limitation it is invalid.

Steuben—Cs.Real Est.Plan. 3d Ed. UCB—16　　* * *

Specific Sum Versus Formula

Will a contractual stipulation be valid if instead of specifying a definite single sum to be paid by the defaulting party it sets forth a formula or measure or basis to be used subsequent to the breach in computing the amount to be paid? Yes, even though an occasional aberrant decision may be found, such provisions are frequently used, and are often eminently satisfactory.

Relevant Statutes

Pertinent statutes applying to liquidated-damages covenants are a comparative rarity, but the draftsman should always verify their existence or nonexistence. For example, California and Oklahoma have provided that liquidated-damages agreements are void except in cases in which it is impracticable or extremely difficult to ascertain actual damages.

* * *

Consequences of Invalidity

If a provision specifying a payment by the promisee upon breach of his covenant is held to be invalid as constituting a penalty, the legal effect is as though it were expunged from the contract. The validity of the remainder of the contract is not impaired. In the event of breach the promisor may recover whatever damages he would be entitled to under the law if the provision had not been incorporated in the contract.

Characterizing Agreement as One for Liquidated Damages

* * * [S]hould the draftsman characterize his stipulated payment in such terms "as liquidated damages," or "as damages and not as a penalty"? The answer is yes. It can do no harm, and may possibly be helpful. One reason is that it may give a court which is already disposed to uphold the provision an additional peg upon which to hang its decision. * * * If a court construing the provision should be one that pays lip service to the "intention of the parties" test, the presence of an appropriate characterization may make it easier for it to render a favorable decision.

* * *

Interest on Liquidated Damages

In most jurisdictions interest on damages for breach of contract is allowed from the date when payment was due if the demand sued upon was liquidated. Conversely, it is ordinarily not allowed for the period prior to judgment upon claims for unliquidated damages. In the event of breach and necessity of suit to collect damages, will a covenant for liquidated damages enlarge the plaintiff's recovery by interest between date of breach or demand and judgment date? (With a lapse of sometimes several years between filing of suit and rendition of judgment, this could substantially increase the aggrieved party's recovery.) On principle, the answer should be yes. And it has been so held, although there is authority to the contrary.

Actual Damages Required?

Must a plaintiff suing on a covenant for liquidated damages prove not merely the breach but also that he has actually been damaged, in order to prevail? The majority rule appears to be that he need not prove actual damage. * * * Some states take the approach that there is a presumption of law that a breach results in damages, and that for a prima facie case the plaintiff need not prove either that he sustained actual damage, or that if he did the amount thereof was substantial and not merely nominal, but that if it is made affirmatively to appear that the plaintiff sustained no damages the provision for liquidated damages cannot be enforced.

Some courts not following the majority rule apparently do not even recognize the question in the terms above stated. If there be no actual damage sustained, the provision will be deemed one for a penalty, rather than liquidated damages.

* * *

Advantages of Liquidated Damages Provisions

We are now in a position to catalog some of the advantages which may accrue to one or both of the parties to a contract from the inclusion of stipulations for liquidated damages for one or more specified breaches.

(1) Often the determination of the amount of damages to be awarded for a breach of contract involves much expense and difficulty during the course of, and in preparation for, the litigation thereon. These are avoided or reduced substantially.

(2) In some jurisdictions, a stipulation may assure recovery when it would be difficult or impossible for the promisee to prove that he sustained actual damage or, if so proven, that the damage was substantial.

(3) In most of the cases and jurisdictions, inclusion will assure the plaintiff's right to recover interest from the date of breach or demand, rather than merely from the date of judgment.

(4) Other benefits may flow from the fact that the amount of the damages is liquidated earlier in point of time than the rendition of judgment. For example, in one case it made the claim for damages provable in bankruptcy, when otherwise it would not have been.

(5) From the standpoint of the party who promises to pay liquidated damages, while the provision may make it more certain that he will have to pay in the event of his breach, a valid provision establishes a firm maximum limit upon the amount of his obligation.

(6) The promisee under such a provision has some practical assurance, from the very fact of its incorporation in the contract, that the other party realizes that his default will be costly to him, thus having some of the deterrent effect of a penalty. This is especially likely to be the case if there have been substantial negotiations over the provision, for then the prospective defaulter will have the provision firmly in mind.

* * *

NOTE

1. Must the liquidated damages provision be reasonable when compared with the actual damages which might be recovered in the event of breach or may the provision take account of damages resulting from the breach which would not be recoverable in an action based on the breach? Cf. *Maxton Builders, Inc. v. Lo Galbo*, 68 N.Y.2d 373, 502 N.E.2d 184, 509 N.Y.S.2d 507 (1986).

a. A vendor is selling his home because he intends to move, for reasons of employment, to a different city. The vendor cannot move until he sells because he needs the proceeds of the sale to purchase a residence in the new city. A vendee enters into a contract to purchase the vendor's home with knowledge of the vendor's situation. If the vendee breaches, the vendor might assert as an element of damage an increase in the price of a residence in the new city. What of the "damages" incurred because the vendor's children are unable to enter the public schools in the new city at the beginning of the semester, and the damages incurred as a result of the vendor having to go to the new city to begin his employment without his wife and children since he cannot afford to acquire a residence?

b. Section 2–516 of the Uniform Land Transactions Act sets out the elements to be considered in determining the reasonableness of a liquidated damages clause. It also denies, subject to agreement to the contrary, to the party entitled to recover under a valid liquidated damages clause any other remedy for the breach to which the liquidated damages clause applies.

2. What are the consequences of the parties to a real estate purchase contract agreeing to waive all other remedies and look only to the liquidated damages provision, if the liquidated damages provision is held invalid?

a. Can the parties now obtain specific performance? Have they, by their acts, indicated that monetary relief is satisfactory?

3. See generally Comment, *Liquidated Damages as Prima Facie Evidence*, 51 Ind.L.J. 189 (1975); Goetz and Scott, *Liquidated Damages, Penalties and the Just Compensation Principle: Some Notes on an Enforcement Model and a Theory of Efficient Breach*, 77 Colum.L.Rev. 554 (1977); Comment, *A Critique of the Penalty Limitation on Liquidated Damages*, 50 S.Cal.L.Rev. 1055 (1977). Cf. Comment, *A New Standard for Liquidated Damage Provisions Under the Uniform Commercial Code?*, 38 Ohio St.L.J. 437 (1977). Division IV, pages 985 to 989 infra, further considers the liquidated damages concept.

d. RISK OF LOSS

An important consideration, when using an agreement for the sale of real estate, is whether the vendor or the vendee bears the risk of loss during the period from the date of the execution of the agreement to the date of the transfer of title to the real estate.

COMMENT:

UNIFORM VENDOR AND PURCHASER RISK ACT: EFFECT ON CALIFORNIA LAW

36 California Law Review 476 (1948).
[footnotes omitted]

Where a contract for the sale of real estate has been signed but prior to transfer of legal title the property is materially damaged by fire or other calamity without the fault of either party, the question arises as to who bears the loss. The cases are in conflict. As a consequence of the remedy of specific performance, one view regards the purchaser as the equitable owner from the date of the contract and places the risk of loss upon him. A number of jurisdictions place the risk of loss on the vendor, rejecting the doctrine of equitable conversion as contrary to the intent of the parties. Under this view the purchaser may refuse performance and recover any money already paid. A third rule, placing the risk of loss upon the party in possession when loss occurs, has been adopted in the Uniform Vendor and Purchaser Risk Act. This Act provides:

> Any contract hereafter made in this State for the purchase and sale of real property shall be interpreted as including an agreement that the parties shall have the following rights and duties, unless the contract expressly provides otherwise:
>
> (a) If, when neither the legal title nor the possession of the subject matter of the contract has been transferred, all or a material part thereof is destroyed without fault of the purchaser or is taken by eminent domain, the vendor cannot enforce the contract, and the purchaser is entitled to recover any portion of the price that he has paid;
>
> (b) If, when either the legal title or the possession of the subject matter of the contract has been transferred, all or any part thereof is destroyed without fault of the vendor or is taken by eminent domain, the purchaser is not thereby relieved from a duty to pay the price, nor is he entitled to recover any portion thereof that he has paid.
>
> * * *
>
> This section may be cited as the Uniform Vendor and Purchaser Risk Act.

* * *

* * * [If the contract contains a]n agreement by the vendee to insure the premises, the question arises whether such an agreement is an *express* provision in the contract precluding reference to the Act.

It is arguable that such an agreement does fix the rights and liabilities of the parties. Where neither title nor possession has been transferred, an agreement by the vendee to insure the premises against a specified risk may fairly be interpreted as an assumption of that risk by the purchaser. An agreement by the vendee to take out fire insurance, for example, seems tantamount to an agreement that "the purchaser assumes the risk of loss caused by fire."

At first glance it might seem immaterial what view as to risk of loss is adopted; that in any event the vendor is protected where the purchaser agrees to insure. If the purchaser has insured the premises, the vendor will receive the insurance money. If the purchaser has failed to insure the premises, it could be argued that he is liable either for the purchase price without deduction, having agreed to assume this risk, or for breach of contract, the measure of damages being the amount of the loss. The view adopted will, however, make a difference. Frequently the loss will exceed the insured value of the premises, in which case the vendor will not be rendered whole by receipt of the insurance money. Also, in every case where the destruction is "material," the right of the vendor to specific performance will depend upon which view is adopted. Certainly in the usual case the vendor will prefer performance of the contract to receipt of the insurance money even though the money fully compensates him for the value of the destroyed or damaged premises.

Where the contract requires the purchaser to insure the premises against loss by fire, and some other calamity such as flood or earthquake occurs, it would seem unquestionable that such an agreement could not be considered an *express* provision placing the risk of loss on the vendee. * * * Under the Uniform Act the vendor bears the loss unless the contract *expressly* provides otherwise. * * * Perhaps the parties merely failed to consider carefully the scope of the covenant to insure. At most it would seem that they *impliedly* provided that the purchaser should bear this risk; probably the implications are the other way. Placing the risk upon the vendee in this situation, even though the parties may have so intended, would not seem justifiable under the Uniform Act.

The problem is essentially one of draftsmanship, and parties entering into agreements for the sale of realty should *expressly* provide that the purchaser shall bear the risk of loss from any cause, if that is their intent. ·

The Materiality of the Destruction:

When neither title nor possession has been transferred, the Uniform Act provides that the risk falls on the vendor when "all or a material part" of the subject matter has been destroyed. In deciding whether or not loss in any particular instance is material, there will, of course, be many borderline cases. * * *

Effect of the Uniform Act on Remedies:

Where a material part of the subject matter is destroyed, the Act provides that the vendor "cannot enforce the contract, and the purchas-

er is entitled to recover any portion of the price that he has paid
* * *." It has been argued that this language deprives a vendor of
the action for breach of contract he might otherwise have. Suppose
property depreciates substantially in value between the signing of the
contract and the closing date, and the purchaser then refuses to carry
out the contract. A few days after the closing date a fire occurs.
Fearing that courts might construe this language as depriving the
vendor of his right of action against the purchaser for breach of
contract, New York, in adopting the Uniform Act, added a provision
expressly stating that neither the vendor nor vendee is deprived of a
right to recover for breach of contract. The Uniform Act should not,
even without such a provision, be construed as denying either the
vendor or vendee such rights. The Act clearly contemplates only
specific performance; the fact of destruction is irrelevant to an already
accrued cause of action for damages for breach of contract.

A further question arises, in the event of material damage before
transfer of possession or legal title, as to the right of a vendee to
specific performance with an abatement of the purchase price. Again,
the Uniform Act was not designed to settle this problem * * *.
Obviously the purchaser may, if he still desires to go through with the
transaction, tender the *full* purchase price and obtain the damaged
property. But a more difficult question arises when the vendee seeks
specific performance with an abatement of the price. * * *

It is generally accepted that the vendee has a right to a just
abatement of the purchase price for a slight deficiency in the quality of
an estate to compensate him for the vendor's failure to perform his
contract in full. Similarly an abatement is generally granted where
there has been a slight deficiency in the quantity of an estate. On
those principles a vendee should be entitled to specific performance
with an abatement of the purchase price where there has been immaterial damage to the subject matter of the contract.

Where the damage has been "material," a different problem is
presented. Although the vendor must bear the risk of loss in the sense
that the purchaser could not be forced to accept a conveyance of the
premises in a damaged state, it does not follow that the vendor should
be forced to convey property at half the contract price. A decree
requiring conveyance based on part payment only would be requiring
performance of a contract quite different from that contemplated by the
parties. Where * * * the vendor's loss is fully covered by insurance,
this is not true as to the vendor; no injustice results here from
enforcing the contract with an abatement. Where there is no insurance, however, this result seems unjust. Although it has been argued
that to refuse specific performance with abatement is to give to the
vendor an option which it is doubtful the parties intended, it would
seem preferable to regard the question as involving an impossibility of
performance, relieving both parties from the obligations of the contract.

Conclusions:

The adoption of the Uniform Act does not settle all the problems of risk of loss in sales of realty. It should be recognized that competent draftsmanship here can prevent litigation. Contracts for the sale of real property should be drafted with an awareness of the questions which remain unsettled by the Uniform Vendor and Purchaser Risk Act.

NOTE

1. If the improvements on real estate under contract are damaged by fire after the execution of the contract, there is no fire insurance on the improvements and the vendor is obligated to insure by the provisions of the contract, can the vendee obtain specific performance with abatement of the purchase price, even if the loss is material?

a. Certainly neither party is getting precisely what was bargained for, but when the vendee asks for this remedy he is indicating that he is satisfied with the results of the bargain.

b. Since the vendor breached the contract by failing to insure, can he now avoid conveying the property with an abatement by claiming impossibility of performance?

c. Does the Uniform Vendor and Purchaser Risk Act indicate how this problem should be resolved?

d. If the vendee is entitled to specific performance, should there be an abatement of the purchase price if the fair market value of the property after the fire is equal to, or greater than, the purchase price. Cf. *Ide v. Joe Miller & Company,* 703 P.2d 590 (Colo.App.1984).

2. If the vendor had insured but the insurance proceeds were inadequate to compensate for the loss through no fault of the vendor, can the vendee now obtain specific performance with an abatement of the purchase price?

a. If the contract required that the vendor "fully" insure against the risk of loss from any cause, would that affect the result?

1. If the contract provided that the vendor fully insure against loss from any cause but the vendor was unable to get earthquake insurance since no insurance company in the area would write such insurance, can the vendee now obtain specific performance plus an abatement of the purchase price equal to the loss caused by an earthquake?

a. Does the materiality of the loss make any difference?

3. As noted in the preceding excerpt, if a state follows the theory of equitable conversion, the vendee usually bears the risk of loss from the date of the execution of the contract. See Note, *Equitable Conversion And Its Effect on Risk of Loss in Executory Contracts For The Sale Of Real Property,* 22 Drake L.Rev. 626 (1973). With respect to when possession is deemed to have been transferred for the purposes of the Uniform Vendor and Purchaser Risk Act see Comment, *Possession to Satisfy the Uniform Vendor and Purchaser Risk Act,* 28 Okla.L.Rev. 455 (1975).

4. The Uniform Land Transactions Act adopts the same position as the Uniform Vendor and Purchaser Risk Act with respect to which party to a real estate purchase contract bears the risk of loss. In addition, Section 2–406 of

the U.L.T.A. sets out the buyer's remedies in the event of a loss when the seller bears the risk of loss. It permits the buyer to compel conveyance of the property with a reduction of the purchase price or the benefit of the seller's insurance proceeds in the event of a material or substantial loss. It also provides for the same result when the loss is immaterial or insubstantial. See Balbach, *The Uniform Land Transactions Act: Articles 1 and 2,* 11 Real Prop., Prob. & Tr.J. 1 (1976).

5. Aspects of fire, casualty, business interruption and use and occupancy insurance are discussed in Division IV, pages 1046 to 1071 infra.

e.　DEFECTS IN TITLE—THE QUIET TITLE SUIT

Frequently, the contract providing for the transfer of real estate requires that "marketable title" be conveyed and places the burden on the vendor to remove any defects which make the title unmarketable. Even if the burden is not expressly placed on the vendor to remove defects, as a result of the "marketable title" provision, defects will have to be removed by the vendor in order to consummate the transaction. In Division I, title insurance, registration and the Marketable Title Act were discussed, see pages 294 to 320 supra. In addition, a technique frequently employed to clear title defects is the suit to quiet title.

COMMENT:

ENHANCING THE MARKETABILITY OF LAND: THE SUIT TO QUIET TITLE

68 Yale Law Journal 1245 (1959).
[footnotes omitted]

* 　 * 　 *

The Suit to Quiet Title

The modern suit to quiet title is a statutorily authorized proceeding designed to establish a title's status by adjudicating the validity of adverse interests in real property. The suit may be in rem or quasi-in-rem; in either case, the court obtains jurisdiction to adjudicate all interests in the land at issue through its control of that land. When the suit is in rem, unknown parties served by publication may be bound by the decree. When the suit is quasi-in-rem, on the other hand, a decree can bind only those parties named by the petitioner's complaint and served process either actually or constructively.

* 　 * 　 *

Legislative Action and Judicial Reaction

* 　 * 　 *

* 　 * 　 * States with Rudimentary Legislation

[In a few states the] statutes provide an action similar to the ancient procedures of chancery. In * 　 * 　 * other jurisdictions, the scope and effect of the quiet-title decree has been somewhat enlarged by acts specifically permitting courts to adjudicate the rights of unknown persons who allegedly derive their adverse claims from known and named defendants.   Thus, unknown heirs, assignees and successors may be served by publication and ostensibly bound by the decree. Aside from these limited exceptions, though, [the] statutes [of all the states in this category] require an adversary, personal lawsuit.   Several of these acts do expand the availability of equitable remedies through the express removal or simple omission of technical prerequisites.   But, in general, these statutes are poor instruments for curing legally unmarketable titles and establishing functional marketability.

* * * Comparatively Advanced Enactments

In contrast, [a number of] states presently enable a petitioner to secure a relatively conclusive adjudication of the rights of all persons— known or unknown, living or dead—who either potentially or actually claim an adverse right, title or interest in property.   Of these, only [a few] provide a purely in rem action.   Though the others require a suit at least formally adversary, in that a defendant must be named, they authorize a decree which comprehends all possible claimants.   Thus, [the] legislatures [of the states in this category] have created elaborate remedial devices unknown to the courts of chancery, and have thereby sought to effectuate that certainty of land titles essential to free alienability.

Judicial hostility has largely nullified these legislative attempts to mold the suit to quiet title into a workable remedy for unmarketability. Many courts seemingly regard them as unwarranted and unwanted encroachments on the judicial domain.   Quiet-title statutes are remedial in nature and should be liberally construed, but they have been strictly interpreted, presumably on the ground that they are in derogation of the common law.   When an apparent conflict arises, it is ordinarily resolved in favor of traditional doctrines.   And an occasional diehard court, refusing to construe literally even the most pristine language, has stated that the legislature could not have intended to violate the state constitution by significantly expanding the equity jurisdiction which existed when that constitution went into effect.

Extreme instances of this sort to one side, the legislators themselves have invited the judiciary to mutilate their handiwork.   Many statutes are poorly drafted and their purpose obscure.   In particular, widely-used statements, such as "except as otherwise provided, the action is to be conducted according to established principles of equity," implicitly give the courts free rein to construe (or misconstrue) as they will.   Even those acts obviously designed to create an effective in rem proceeding often fail to specify that they are conferring a statutory jurisdiction unrelated to and independent of the ancient bills in equity. Public necessity does not clearly emerge as the touchstone of legislative action. Thus, largely left to its own devices, an antagonistic judiciary has been able to undercut the quiet-title enactments.

Judicial hostility has taken the form of direct or indirect restrictions on the availability of the suit to quiet title. [For example, some courts have] * * * adopt[ed] the singular view that a complaint naming no known adverse claimant does not present a justiciable issue. Petitioners have also occasionally been met with the aged technical prerequisites of possession and a sufficiently adverse claim. Most often, access to a forum is denied on the theory that "one seeking equity must do equity." For instance, a complainant seeking to remove an old unreleased mortgage as a cloud may be forced to tender payment of the underlying debt although it is otherwise barred by the statute of limitations. Legislation creating a purportedly conclusive in rem decree may encounter a more serious type of judicial subversion. Simply by finding that a petitioner has not conducted a reasonably diligent investigation into the identity and whereabouts of unnamed interest-holders, a court can open a decree to avoidance through direct or collateral attack. Under many statutes, the key issue of whether a court had jurisdiction to bind constructively-served individuals is determined in subsequent proceedings involving the prior decree. Though probably necessary to ensure compliance with the due-process clause of the Constitution, the requirement of reasonably diligent inquiry, as presently implemented, renders virtually all quiet-title decrees vulnerable.

Statutory and judicial extensions of the period available for direct attack may also prevent an in rem decree from becoming conclusive. Under prevailing doctrine, any person who was served constructively, who had no actual notice of a hearing, and who can present a meritorious defense may vacate a ruling within a stated period varying by jurisdiction from six months to five years. The quiet title statutes themselves often do not contain express provisions for reopening, but the courts then borrow such provisions from other enactments governing general civil litigation. And, sometimes, the judiciary applies laws creating a perpetual right of appeal irrespective of whether a quiet-title cut-off provision exists. Any party may then attempt to reopen a decree within, usually, one year after he obtains actual notice of adjudication, provided his nonappearance at trial was the result of inadvertence or excusable neglect. Though subject to judicial discretion, this kind of reopening is frequently allowed.

Direct-attack provisions also accord special rights to infants, incompetents and (occasionally) future-interest holders, and thereby eliminate any possibility of obtaining a conclusive decree. Generally, the provisions postpone the commencement of the reopening period until the legal disability of infancy or insanity is removed (in the latter case, an indefinite term). Moreover, these statutory safeguards have been substantially extended through judicial solicitude for the rights of the classes concerned. For example, an infant effectively represented by a guardian *ad litem* may still be allowed to relitigate an unfavorable decree upon reaching his majority. Judicial gloss of this sort has served to reduce the in rem quiet-title laws to impotence.

The facility with which in rem decrees can be directly or collaterally avoided has increased the danger that subsequent bona fide purchasers for value will be divested of their land. In the absence of express statutory provisions, the innocent buyer of a quieted title is accorded only the rights that the person who obtained the decree would have had were the decree contested. To protect purchasers investing in realty improvements, several state courts hold the decree ineffective to create a legally marketable title until the general direct-attack period has ended tranquilly. But, since the indeterminate time for attack accorded mental incompetents and future-interest holders leaves the decree indefinitely open to avoidance, this approach would appear to nullify quiet-title adjudications. While such an extreme result would probably be eschewed, even a period of temporary unmerchantability can irreparably harm a petitioner who expected to consummate a resale contract immediately after obtaining a favorable decree. Time may be of the essence, and the "successful" petitioner, unable to tender good title, may lose a beneficial bargain. In all events, the bona fide purchaser's title is perpetually susceptible to collateral attack by those parties over whom adequate jurisdiction was not obtained. The decree available in a suit to quiet title is thus an anomaly. Designed to overcome uncertainties stemming from recordation, it has substituted instead the threat of judicial avoidance. A sweeping re-evaluation is therefore indicated if the quiet-title suit is to fulfill its intended function of promoting the alienability of land.

* * *

NOTE

1.   If both registration of title (see Division I, pages 311 to 315 supra) and an "in rem" type of quiet title are available, are there situations in which quiet title rather than registration would be chosen to cure a defect? If so, when?

a.   If the only defect is a mortgage which was allegedly paid but not released on the record, how should this defect be cured?

1.   If the holder of the mortgage is deceased and tracing his heirs is difficult, if not impossible, do these facts change the choice?

2.   If the choice is between obtaining title insurance against a defect, for some additional premium, (insuring over the defect) or bringing a quiet title action to clear the defect, in what situations might insuring over be chosen and in what situations might a quiet title action be chosen? Title insurance is discussed in Division I, pages 294 to 311 supra and in this Division at pages 426 to 432 infra.

3.   TITLE INSURANCE FROM THE SELLER'S VIEWPOINT

Usually the vendor's title insurance policy will not only protect the vendor while he owns the real estate but also will protect him against certain defects discovered after transfer of the real estate if the defects existed on the date of the issuance of the vendor's policy and were not listed in the exceptions to the policy. The latter type of protection offered by a title insurance policy is found in a policy provision generally known as the "warrantor's" clause.

STEWART TITLE GUARANTY CO. v. LUNT LAND CORP.

Supreme Court of Texas, 1961.
162 Tex. 435, 347 S.W.2d 584.

NORVELL, Justice. The trial court granted defendant-petitioner's motion for summary judgment. This judgment was reversed by the Court of Civil Appeals, 342 S.W.2d 376. We reverse this order of the lower appellate court and affirm the trial court's action. The undisputed facts are as follows:

On March 10, 1954, L.D. Tuttle and wife, by warranty deed, conveyed 50.1 acres out of the Henry Gough Survey (Abstract No. 493) Dallas County, Texas, to D. Eldon Lunt for a consideration of $12,500. At that time, the tract was subject to an easement in favor of the Lone Star Gas Company executed by Tuttle in 1949 which gave the gas company the right to lay and maintain an underground high pressure gas transmission line across the premises. The easement contract provided that if the pipe line should interfere with any present or future permanent structure upon the property, the gas company would relocate the line so as to eliminate the interference. This easement was not excepted from the Tuttle warranty.

On May 1, 1957, D. Eldon Lunt and wife conveyed the property by warranty deed to Lunt Land Corporation, the plaintiff-respondent, for a recited consideration of $12,500. The warranty in this deed contained no exception as to the gas company easement.

On June 19, 1959, Lunt Land Corporation secured two policies of title insurance from petitioner, Stewart Title Company; one being a mortgagee's policy covering a $148,400 loan made to the land corporation by Hillcrest State Bank of University Park; the other being an owner's policy. Both policies covered five tracts of land in Dallas County, including the 50.1 acres out of the Henry Gough Survey (Abstract No. 493) which L.D. Tuttle had conveyed to D. Eldon Lunt. The face amount of this policy covering the five tracts was $175,000. The pertinent provisions of the policy were as follows:

> "Stewart Title Guaranty Company * * * does hereby guarantee to Party or Parties named below (Lunt Land Corporation) herein styled assured * * * that the assured has good and indefeasible title to the following described property subject to the following liens: (the Hillcrest Bank lien is then described followed by a description of the five tracts of land covered by the policy) * * *.

> "Said Company shall not be liable in a greater amount than the actual monetary loss of assured, and in no event shall said

Company be liable for more than One Hundred Seventy-five Thousand and No/100 Dollars, * * *.

"Upon the sale of the property covered hereby, this policy automatically thereupon shall become a warrantor's policy and the assured, heirs, executors and administrators, shall for a period of twenty-five years from date hereof remain fully protected according to the terms hereof, by reason of the payment of any loss he or they may sustain on account of any warranty contained in the deed executed by assured conveying said property. The Company to be liable under said warranty only by reason of defects, liens or encumbrances existing prior to or at the date hereof (and not excepted above) such liability not to exceed the amount above written."

This policy contained no exception relating to the Lone Star Gas Company easement.

In the first part of August, 1959, according to the testimony of D. Eldon Lunt, President of the land corporation (given in deposition form), he and his company for the first time gained knowledge of the gas company's easement.

On September 2, 1959, after he had obtained such knowledge, Lunt, acting for and on behalf of the corporation, entered into a valid contract of sale binding the corporation to convey the 50.1 acre tract out of the Henry Gough Survey (Abstract No. 493) to Bunker Hills, Inc. for a consideration of $1,875 per acre.

On September 11, 1959, nine days after * * * [the execution of the contract of sale of the property], Lunt, in behalf of his corporation, notified petitioner of its claim under the title insurance policy.

On September 17, 1959, Lunt Land Corporation conveyed the 50.1 acre tract by warranty deed to Mayflower Investment Company, the nominee of Bunker Hills, Inc. No exception was made in the warranty as to the Lone Star Gas Company's easement.

* * *

The nature of the easement itself is hardly common and seems to invite negotiation at some future time with reference to change in location or perhaps removal of the pipe line crossing the property.

Then there is the circumstance that in 1957, Lunt conveyed the property to the land corporation with full warranty of title. This was two years prior to the issuance of the Stewart title policy.

While photographs made a part of Lunt's deposition indicate that the gas line easement had been marked by a cindero and signs for some period of time, we accept his statement that he never gained knowledge of the easement until the early part of August, 1959. He did not, however, notify the title company of a prospective sale of the property so they could mitigate an impending loss under their policy by negotiating with the gas company for a removal of the pipe line or the purchase of its easement rights. On the contrary, he sold the property and even then did not notify the title company until nine days after the contract of sale was signed. The deed given by the Lunt Land Corporation in consummation of the contract of sale contained a clause binding it, its successors and assigns, "to warrant and forever defend, all and singular the said premises unto the said Mayflower Investment Company, its successors and assigns, against every person whomsoever lawfully claiming or to claim the same or any part thereof". This warranty covered the pipe line easement.

* * *

The language of the policy upon the particular point is clear and certain: "Upon the sale of the property covered hereby, this policy thereupon shall become a warrantor's policy * * *." It is hardly contemplated that the title guarantor would be liable to the same person for the same defect in title under both the "owner's policy" provisions and the "warrantor's title" provisions. The contract provides successive liabilities. This does not mean that liability having once accrued under the "owner's policy" will necessarily be extinguished by a sale of the property, but that the holder of the title policy, when he knows of the title defect, must give notice or take some appropriate action to prevent the automatic conversion of the contract from an owner's to a warrantor's policy. He cannot, having such knowledge, remain silent, sell the property, execute a full warranty deed thereto, and then contend that the policy remained in effect as an owner's policy despite the specific wording thereof.

The judgment of the Court of Civil Appeals is reversed and that of the trial court affirmed.

NOTE

1. What should Lunt Land Corporation have done to preserve its claim against the title insurance company?

    a. If it had notified the title insurance company in the early part of August when it first acquired knowledge of the defect, would the notification have preserved its claim?

    b. If it had notified the title insurance company and had executed the contract of sale on September 2 and conveyed the real estate on September 17th before the title insurance company had cleared the defect, might the title insurance company have taken the position that it was not liable under the owner's policy since the property had been conveyed and it was not liable under the warrantor's clause since the owner had knowledge of the defect prior to the conveyance?

        1. Is approximately one month a sufficient period of time to give the title insurance company to clear a defect?

            a. Should the period of time given the title insurance company to clear a defect make any difference with respect to its liability?

        2. If the title insurance company had been given notice of the defect and had managed to clear it prior to the sale of the real estate, would it have had no liability to the insured for either breach of

contract or for its negligence? See *Southern Title Guar. Co. v. Prendergast,* 478 S.W.2d 806 (Tex.Civ.App.1972), affirmed, 494 S.W.2d 154 (Tex. 1973), and Division I, pages 298 to 301 supra. Compare *Southern Title Guar. Co. v. Prendergast,* supra, with *Overholtzer v. Northern Counties Title Ins. Co.,* 116 Cal.App.2d 113, 253 P.2d 116 (1953) and *Hartman v. Shambaugh,* 96 N.M. 359, 630 P.2d 758 (1981). Cf. *Red Lobster Inns of America, Inc. v. Lawyers Title Insurance Corporation,* 656 F.2d 381 (8th Cir.1981).

c. Following the purchase of real estate, when is the most likely time for an owner to discover a title defect?

d. See generally Taub, *Rights and Remedies Under a Title Policy,* 15 Real Prop., Prob. & Tr.J. 422 (1980).

2. The agreement providing for the transfer of real estate frequently requires that the vendor obtain a title insurance policy insuring the vendee's fee. The title insurance company, at the vendor's request, issues a title report showing the state of the fee interest. This report is a "binder" or commitment by the title insurance company to issue an insurance policy containing the exceptions indicated in the report in addition to the standard exceptions. If a defect existing or arising during the vendor's ownership of the real estate is omitted from the title insurance policy and subsequently the vendee is reimbursed by the title insurance company for his loss resulting from the defect, can the title insurance company through subrogation sue the vendor for breach of the warranty or other provisions of the deed given to the vendee which failed to except the defect?

ZURICH GENERAL ACCIDENT & LIABILITY INS. CO. v. KLEIN

Superior Court of Pennsylvania, 1956.
181 Pa.Super. 48, 121 A.2d 893.

* * *

ERVIN, Judge.

* * *

[T]he defendants, appellants, sold certain real estate to a purchaser under general warranty deed, warranting that the property was free and clear of any incumbrances. The attorney who searched the title for the purchaser failed to discover the liens of certain unpaid taxes against the property for years prior to the date of purchase. Subsequently the purchaser, who was threatened with a tax sale, paid the delinquent taxes and claimed reimbursement from the attorney. Plaintiff, appellee, the insurer on the attorney's liability policy covering the title search, upon being notified of the claim by the attorney, paid the purchaser the amount of the delinquent taxes. Appellee, after demand for reimbursement, filed a complaint in equity claiming this amount from appellants * * *.

Appellants have appealed from the lower court's final decree entering a money judgment for appellee to reimburse it for the money paid to reimburse the purchaser.

* * *

Appellee paid a debt which was rightfully owed by appellants. * * * [A]ppellee was under a contractual duty to the attorney who searched the title. If his clients, the purchasers, had instituted an action against their title searcher and had recovered a judgment against him, * * * the appellee would have been obligated to pay the same to the purchasers. * * *

Appellants have been unjustly enriched because appellee has discharged an obligation owed by appellants under such circumstances that appellants would be unjustly enriched by the retention of the benefits thus conferred. Appellants had, by general warranty deed, conveyed the premises to the purchasers. A vendor by general warranty is obliged to deliver a deed that is free of liens for taxes and he covenants to defend the grantee's title against all mankind, the whole world. * * *

Appellants failed to deliver a deed free and clear of taxes and failed to pay the obligation rightfully owed by them. * * * It is our opinion that these facts require the application of the equitable doctrines of unjust enrichment and restitution in order to prevent a miscarriage of justice.

* * * Appellants argue that there was no privity of contract. Under the doctrines here considered there need be no privity of contract. * * * Equity for a long period of time has entertained jurisdiction of restitution actions for, inter alia, the reason that there was no privity of contract.

* * * A court of equity may give restitution to the plaintiff and prevent the unjust enrichment of the defendant, where the plaintiff's property has been used in discharging an obligation owed by the defendant or a lien upon the property of the defendant, by creating in the plaintiff rights similar to those which the obligee or lien-holder had before the obligation or lien was discharged. In such a case the procedure is called subrogation, and the plaintiff is said to be subrogated to the position of the obligee or lienholder.

* * * When appellee reimbursed the purchasers, it [was] entitled to be subrogated to the rights of the purchasers, one of which rights would have entitled purchasers to maintain an action against the appellants for the breach of their general warranty. Surely equity could and should take jurisdiction to * * * enable appellee to go directly against appellants.

* * *

Judgment affirmed at cost of appellants.

NOTE

1. In *Zurich General Accident & Liability Ins. Co. v. Klein* what obligation of Mr. and Mrs. Klein did the insurance company pay?

a. Was it the obligation to pay the real estate taxes assessed by the municipalities?

 1. Did the court find that all of the past due real estate taxes had been assessed and become liens during the period of the Kleins' ownership of the real estate?

 b. Or did the insurance company pay the damages which the Kleins were obligated to pay the purchaser as a result of the breach of their general warranty of title?

 2. A vendor's attorney does not examine title and relies on the title report (or a binder from the title insurance company) which the attorney on behalf of the vendor ordered for the benefit of the vendee and which indicates that there are no defects in title. The attorney, relying on the report, permits the vendor to give a general warranty deed with no exceptions. The title insurance company, however, failed to find a title defect. Is the vendor liable to the title insurance company under the principles developed in *Zurich General Accident & Liability Ins. Co. v. Klein* when the failure to find the defect was the title insurance company's? Might the title insurance company argue there is no privity of contract between it and the vendor? Cf. *Williams v. Polgar*, 391 Mich. 6, 215 N.W.2d 149 (1974); *First American Title Insurance Company, Inc. v. First Title Service Company of the Florida Keys Inc.*, 457 So.2d 467 (Fla.1984); Comment, *Attorney Negligence in Real Estate Title Examination and Will Drafting: Elimination of the Privity Requirement as a Bar to Recovery by Foreseeable Third Parties*, 17 New Eng.L.Rev. 955 (1982).

 3. If the vendors in *Zurich General Accident & Liability Ins. Co. v. Klein* had obtained a title insurance policy when they bought the real estate and the policy contained a warrantor's clause, would they have been able to recover against their title insurance company? Does the result depend on, among other things, when the lien for the unpaid taxes arose?

 4. Is the vendor, in a sale of real estate, safe in relying on the title report issued by the title insurance company insuring the vendee's fee? Does it make any difference if, as is the case in some areas of the country, the vendor paid the premium for the policy? If the vendor obtained a title insurance policy on his purchase of the real estate, can he safely rely on the warrantor's clause contained therein?

 a. If not, does the vendor's attorney at least have to examine title from the date of the vendor's policy to the date of sale in order to adequately protect the vendor? Are there other steps which the vendor's attorney should take to protect the vendor?

4. AUTHORIZATION OF THE DISPOSITION, AND POWER TO DISPOSE OF REAL ESTATE

a. THE POWER TO DISPOSE OF REAL ESTATE

 Subject to a provision to the contrary in the agreement forming the partnership, a partnership has the power to dispose of real estate. See Section 10 of the Uniform Partnership Act. There seems to be little doubt that a corporation also has the power to dispose of real estate. See Section 3.02(5) of the Revised Model Business Corporation Act. This power is subject to the caveat that there is nothing in the certificate of incorporation to the contrary. A trustee's power to dispose of real estate is governed by the state statutes regulating the operation of trusts and by the agreement governing the operation of the trust.

b. AUTHORIZATION OF THE DISPOSITION OF REAL ESTATE

Even though a partnership usually has the power to dispose of real estate, questions remain with respect to how the disposition is authorized and who can bind the partnership to a third party in respect of the disposition. Assume that a partnership's only asset is an office building. The disposition of the office building is proposed by one of the general partners. Under Section 10 of the Uniform Partnership Act, is a general partner's ability to bind the partnership with respect to the conveyance of the real estate determined under Section 9(1) or 9(2) of the Uniform Partnership Act?

ELLIS v. MIHELIS

Supreme Court of California, In Banc, 1963.
60 Cal.2d 206, 32 Cal.Rptr. 415, 384 P.2d 7.

GIBSON, Chief Justice. Herbert Ellis brought this action against Pericles Mihelis and Elias Mihelis to compel them to specifically perform a contract for the sale of real property and for damages resulting from their failure to convey the property to him. Defendants have appealed from the judgment decreeing specific performance and awarding damages. Plaintiff has cross-appealed on the issue of damages.

The principal contentions of defendants are * * * that the agreement [providing for the sale] can in no event be binding on Elias because he did not sign the contract and did not authorize Pericles in writing to enter into it on his behalf.

* * * [This] contention, if valid, would not, of course, be determinative of plaintiff's rights as against Pericles. We have concluded * * * that defendants are correct. * * *

Defendants, who are brothers, own two ranches, both operated in the usual manner as ranch or farming property, one by Pericles in Stanislaus County and the other by Elias in Santa Cruz County. In 1948, following the death of a third brother, a judicial decree was entered declaring that both ranches had been owned by the three brothers in joint tenancy with right of survivorship and that upon the death of the brother the title vested absolutely in Pericles and Elias. All income and expense of the two ranches were lumped together for income tax purposes, partnership tax returns were filed with respect to income from the ranches, and the income derived from the two operations was divided equally between the personal income tax returns of the two brothers.

In 1957 the brothers decided to sell the Stanislaus County ranch and agreed that Pericles should handle negotiations for the sale and submit any prospective deals to Elias. Pericles listed the property with a real estate broker in Stanislaus County, George Moreno, telling him that he was the owner.

About this time plaintiff became interested in purchasing a parcel of real property in Alameda County owned by the Ratto family, but the Rattos did not want to sell for cash because of the [income tax on the gain which they would recognize]. They were willing, however, to exchange their property for a ranch, and plaintiff orally authorized Antone L. Ratto, Jr., to act for him in locating and arranging for the purchase of a ranch to effect the exchange. An escrow was opened with an Oakland title company with respect to the Alameda County property, and plaintiff deposited $10,000 in that escrow. Ratto, learning that the Stanislaus ranch was for sale, contacted Moreno and told him of the arrangement between plaintiff and Ratto and of Ratto's interest in purchasing the ranch. Moreno, on the basis of what Pericles had said to him, told Ratto that Pericles was the owner. Ratto and Moreno thereafter informed Pericles of the trade arrangement and explained among other things that plaintiff, not Ratto, was to take title to the Stanislaus property initially.

On April 17, 1958, Pericles and Moreno with the assistance of Pericles' friend, the president of the Stanislaus County Title Company, prepared an instrument using a printed form denominated "Agent's Deposit Receipt." The instrument, bearing the above date, acknowledged receipt of $5,000 as a deposit on account of the purchase price of the described property and provided for a total purchase price of $165,000, the balance to be paid $30,000 within 30 days from date and $130,000 by note bearing interest at five per cent per annum, payable in specified installments, and secured by a deed of trust and crop mortgage. It also provided that "the amounts paid hereon" could be retained by the seller as consideration for execution of the agreement if the buyer failed to complete the purchase. On April 17 Pericles signed below a provision which recited, "I (or we) agree to sell and convey the above described property on the terms and conditions herein stated, * * *."

Moreno informed Ratto that the agreement had been signed by Pericles. Ratto notified plaintiff, who thereupon instructed him to sign plaintiff's name to the agreement. Pursuant to plaintiff's direction the Oakland title company made out a check in the sum of $5,000 payable to the Stanislaus title company "for the account of Herbert E. Ellis, Jr." On April 19 Ratto delivered the check to Moreno, and the blank space in the agreement for the signature of the buyer was signed by Ratto as follows: "Herbert E. Ellis Jr. By Antone L. Ratto, Jr." Moreno showed the agreement and the check to Pericles who said he was "very satisfied on the whole thing." Pericles asked if he could keep the money, and, when Moreno said that it would have to be deposited with the title company Pericles made no objection. The agreement and check were placed in escrow with the Stanislaus title company and the check was cashed by the title company. * * *

On May 2, 1958, Pericles, Elias, Ratto, and Moreno met at the ranch. Until then, neither Ratto nor Moreno knew that Elias had an interest in the property. Pericles stated that he had changed his mind and did not want to sell, that he was not "going through with the deal," that as a result of a frost occurring a few days earlier which had damaged some vineyards in the area but left his grapes unharmed his crop had become too valuable for him to sell the ranch, and that he could get the same price after the harvest. He also stated, "I will probably have to sell you my half, but my brother doesn't want to sell; Elias doesn't want to wait 10 years." Elias said that he did not want to sell and that he did not want to wait 10 years for his money.

On May 12 plaintiff ratified in writing Ratto's acts in connection with the purchase of the Stanislaus ranch and placed in the escrow the additional $30,000 called for by the agreement, the note for $130,000, the deed of trust, and the crop mortgage.

The trial court found among other things that Pericles and Elias operated the ranch as partners, that the ranch was an asset of the partnership, and that each orally authorized the other to sell the ranch, for the partnership. * * *

Although plaintiff may rely on the agreement, it does not follow that he may hold Elias, who did not sign it or authorize Pericles in writing to act as his agent. In seeking to overcome the requirement of the statute of frauds that an agreement for the sale of real property must be signed by the party to be charged or by an agent who has authority in writing, plaintiff contends that there is an overriding provision in the Uniform Partnership Act (Corp.Code, §§ 15001–15045) which is applicable to the facts of this case and which empowered Pericles to bind Elias in the absence of written authority. It may be helpful in this connection to keep in mind that there is no evidence that defendants were in the business of buying and selling real estate or that the sale of the ranch was in the usual course of the partnership business.

The Uniform Partnership Act makes it clear that, unless it is otherwise provided therein, the usual rules of law and equity, including the law of agency, apply. [U.P.A. Sections 4(3) and 5.] As a provision overriding the statute of frauds plaintiff relies on [U.P.A. Section 9] * * * which reads in part: "(1) Every partner is an agent of the partnership for the purpose of its business, and the act of every partner, including the execution in the partnership name of any instrument, for apparently carrying on in the usual way the business of the partnership of which he is a member binds the partnership, unless the partner so acting has in fact no authority to act for the partnership in the particular matter, and the person with whom he is dealing has knowledge of the fact that he has no such authority. (2) An act of a partner which is not apparently for carrying on of the business of the partnership in the usual way does not bind the partnership unless authorized by the other partners."

* * *

These provisions distinguish between acts of a partner which bind the partnership because of his status as a partner without any express authority being required and acts binding on the partnership only after express authorization by all partners. Under the express terms of subdivision (1) of the section all acts of a partner which are apparently within the usual course of the particular business bind the partnership. The effect of the provision is that the status of a partner, without more, serves as complete authority with respect to such acts, obviating the necessity of any express authority, either oral or written, from the other members of the firm. It necessarily follows that insofar as a partner limits his conduct to matters apparently within the partnership business, he can bind the other partners without obtaining their written consent. Subdivision (2), however, provides that there must be express authority for acts of a partner which do not appear to be in the usual course of the business. This subdivision does not concern the form of the required express authority, and, unlike the broad provision in subdivision (1), it contains no language which would justify a conclusion that written authority is not necessary in situations where the statute of frauds would ordinarily be applicable.

The distinction made by subdivisions (1) and (2) between acts which are apparently in the usual course of business and those which are not is in accord with the cases in other jurisdictions which have held, without mention of any statutory requirement for written authority of an agent, that a contract executed by one partner alone to sell partnership real estate is binding on the other partners provided the partnership is in the business of buying or selling real estate and the property covered by the contract is part of the stock held for sale. * * * The distinction is also followed in [U.P.A. Section 10] which provides that one partner may convey partnership realty or pass title to a partnership interest in realty depending, in some circumstances, upon whether the partner's act binds the partnership under subdivision (1) of [S]ection [9].

Since it does not appear that the sale of the ranch was in the usual course of the partnership business, a contract to sell it would come within subdivision (2) of [S]ection [9] not subdivision (1), even if the ranch were a partnership asset as found by the trial court. Accordingly, the statute of frauds would be applicable and Pericles could not bind Elias without authority in writing.

* * *

NOTE

1. Would the result in *Ellis v. Mihelis* have been different if there had been limited partners in the partnership and the partnership agreement, duly filed, had provided that the general partners could not take any of the acts specified in Section 9 of the Uniform Limited Partnership Act or subsection (b)

(6) of Section 303 of the Revised Uniform Limited Partnership Act without the affirmative vote of a majority of the limited partners and the general partners had attempted to sell the real estate without such a vote?

2.   Might the court in *Ellis v. Mihelis* have reached a different result if the agreement for the sale of the real estate had been signed by Pericles as follows: Mihelis Brothers, a partnership, by Pericles Mihelis, a general partner? If the court had found that the sale of the real estate was in the usual course of the partnership's business, would it have come to a different result? See *Owens v. Palos Verdes Monaco,* 142 Cal.App.3d 855, 191 Cal.Rptr. 381 (1983).

3.   If a sale or other disposition of the property of a corporation is contemplated, the parties, at times, must face substantially the same question discussed in *Ellis v. Mihelis,* that is, whether an officer of the corporation, without authorization, can bind the corporation to convey some or all of its property.

JEPPI v. BROCKMAN HOLDING COMPANY

Supreme Court of California, In Banc, 1949.
34 Cal.2d 11, 206 P.2d 847.

EDMONDS, Justice.   Frank Jeppi and W.B. Camp, Sr., are suing for damages assertedly sustained by them because of the refusal of Brockman Holding Company, Inc. and Mary C. Spalding, its president, to convey certain real property.   A decision of the appeal from the judgment which followed an order granting a nonsuit turns upon the authority of Mrs. Spalding to bind the corporation.

The evidence presented by the appellants, stated most favorably to them, may be summarized as follows: Brockman Holding Company, Inc. was organized in 1930 to manage and dispose of the estate of I.W. Brockman, deceased.   The corporation's principal place of business was at Pomona, where most of the directors lived.   Mrs. Spalding was a resident of Santa Cruz.   It was the custom to hold only one directors' meeting each year; during the interim matters were handled informally by the directors.

At the annual meeting held on May 1, 1944, the following resolution was adopted: "Motion was made by Bert Harvey, seconded by Spalding, that the property of Brockman Holding Company be sold in order to close up the company as soon as possible."   In May of the following year, at the conclusion of the stockholders' meeting, a majority of the directors, who controlled 29,000 shares of the 42,000 shares outstanding, held a meeting and, among other matters considered, informally discussed the sale of the land which is the subject of the present controversy.

This property, acreage in Kern County and a lot in Los Angeles County, constituted substantially all of the remaining assets of the corporation.   The minutes of the board meeting make no reference to the informal discussion. * * *

Three weeks after this meeting, Mrs. Spalding, * * * and Jeppi visited the property and Jeppi made an offer of $27,500 for it.   Mrs. Spalding said: "It suits me all right, and I will get in touch with my people in Pomona by phone and let you know." Jeppi replied: "All right, if your directors decide to sell * * * I will meet you at the abstract office * * *." The next day at the office of a title company, an escrow agreement was signed by Mrs. Spalding, as the president of the corporation, and Jeppi and he deposited his check for $27,500 in escrow. By the terms of this agreement, title was to be conveyed to Jeppi and W.B. Camp, Sr.

On the same day, the title company sent a letter to the corporation requesting that it forward deeds as called for by the escrow agreement concerning the sale of the land. A week later, the following telegram was received in reply: "Brockman Holding Company sale not approved by directors and better offer has been received. Directors meeting to consider all proposals will be held June 14th." Jeppi was advised that the corporation had received an offer of $30,000 for the property. Through his counsel, Jeppi gave notice that he intended to stand upon the agreement as stated in the escrow instructions but, to avoid a lawsuit, he would offer $30,100. On June 14th, Jeppi was notified that the property had been sold for $32,025, and the following day he withdrew his deposit from the title company.

At the conclusion of the appellants' presentation of this evidence, the court granted a motion for a nonsuit made on the grounds that there was no proof of a contract by Mrs. Spalding or by any authorized officer of the corporation. The appeal is from the judgment which followed that order.

Whether the ruling upon the motion was correct, primarily depends upon the narrow question as to the authority of Mrs. Spalding to execute the escrow instructions on behalf of the corporation. The appellants assert that the evidence shows such authority. She and the corporation take the position that (1) there was no evidence of any actual or implied authority to enter into a contract of sale; (2) as the escrow instructions included substantially all of the assets of the corporation, the approval of a majority of the stockholders was required; (3) the "equal dignity rule" requires that Mrs. Spalding's authority be in writing; (4) the record shows actual notice to Jeppi of her lack of authority; and (5) the appellants themselves canceled the alleged contract.

From the evidence in regard to the informal nature of the corporation's conduct of business, the general declaration of policy made by the directors in 1944 to sell the remaining property, the informal discussion immediately prior to Mrs. Spalding's trip to Kern County, and her execution of the escrow agreement after a delay in the negotiations for the express purpose of getting approval from her "people", it reasonably may be inferred that the board of directors had authorized her to enter into the contract and to bind the corporation. It is not material that the authorization was given at an informal meeting of the directors of which no minutes were kept. Brainard v. De La Montanya, 18 Cal.2d 502, 511, 116 P.2d 66.

The corporation relies upon section 343 of the Civil Code, now sec. 3901, Corporations Code, which reads: "No corporation shall sell * * * all or substantially all of its property and assets * * * unless under authority of a resolution of its board of directors and with the approval of the principal terms of the transaction and the nature and amount of the consideration by vote or written consent of [the] shareholders * * *." * * *

The testimony of the escrow agent who handled the transaction showed that the transaction concerned a sale of the sole remaining assets of the corporation. * * * "It is the rule at common law * * * that the directors of an ordinary business corporation have no power to dispose of all of its assets without the consent of all its stockholders. This rule has been modified * * * by statute, so that the corporation may dispose of all its assets and wind up its business when authorized by a majority vote of the outstanding stock * * *. The reason for this limitation is that a corporation is organized for the purpose of doing business of some nature, and, if so, its shareholders have the right to insist that the corporation continue for the purpose for which it was organized. A sale, therefore, of all its property, or so much thereof as would prevent it from continuing in such business, would constitute a violation of the corporate contract. * * * To this rule there are * * * exceptions. * * * If the conversion of all assets into cash * * * is in furtherance of the business for which the corporation was organized, the transaction is not ultra vires. For instance, if a corporation is organized for the purpose of buying, selling, and dealing in real estate, it would naturally have the power to sell all the real estate it owned at a particular time because that is the very object of its organization. The sale of its tangible assets under such circumstances furthers rather than hinders the carrying out of its contract with its stockholders. * * *" Thayer v. Valley Bank, 35 Ariz. 238, 276 P. 526, 527.

The provisions of the statute should not be applied solely upon the basis of the quantity of the property; the test which determines the question of the necessity for consent of the stockholder is, "whether the sale is in the regular course of the business of the corporation and in furtherance of the express objects of its existence, or something outside of the normal and regular course of the business. * * *"

The undisputed evidence in the present case is that the Brockman Holding Company was organized for the sole purpose of managing and disposing of the property of a decedent's estate. Further, at the 1944 meeting of the stockholders a motion was made that the remaining assets should be sold "in order to close up the company as soon as possible". The contract of sale, therefore, was made in the normal course of business and cannot be held subject to the restrictive provisions of former section 343 of the Civil Code.

Section 2309 of the Civil Code reads: "An oral authorization is sufficient for any purpose, except that an authority to enter into a contract required by law to be in writing can only be given by an instrument in writing." The language of the California decisions does not make entirely clear whether this statute, the so-called "equal dignity rule", is applicable to the acts of a corporation's executive officer. In Carrier v. Piggly Wiggly of San Francisco, 11 Cal.App.2d 180, 182, 53 P.2d 400, 401, the plaintiff was allowed to recover upon a contract, the court stating: "Corporations can act only through the agency of natural persons, and it has been held that the authority of an agent of a corporation need not be in writing, so far as the statute of frauds is concerned. McCartney v. Clover Valley Land & Stock Co. [8 Cir.] 232 F. 697, citing Boggs v. Lakeport Agricultural [Park] Ass'n, 111 Cal. 354, 43 P. 1106." Yet in Corporation of America v. Harris, 5 Cal. App.2d 452, 453, 43 P.2d 307, 310, after discussion of the cases, the court concluded: "The weight of authority, we believe, supports the view that the agent of a corporation, whether he be an executive officer or not, may not, merely because of his office, bind his principal upon a lease of real property for longer than a year, unless he has written authority from his principal so to do."

In discussing this conflict, the Court of Appeals of the Ninth Circuit said: "It should also be noted that McCartney v. Clover Valley Land & Stock Co., supra, cited and relied on in the *Piggly Wiggly* case, expressly limits the exception, there stated, to the executive officers of a corporation. * * * [I]n the case of an executive officer of a corporation an exception from the requirement of written authority finds at least plausible support in reason in that, as said in the *McCartney* case: 'The executive officer of a corporation is something more than an agent. He is the representative of the corporation itself.'" E.K. Wood Lumber Co. v. Moore Mill & Lumber Co., 97 F.2d 402, 408; * * *. This reasoning squares with sound principles and the necessities of modern business.

The language in Corporation of America v. Harris, supra, which does not recognize any exception to the rule, is, at most, dictum. The "crucial point" of the decision was not the extent of the agent's authority but, as the court stated it, whether the defendant "under all the facts and circumstances of the transaction, is in a position to avail itself of the statute of frauds as an avenue of escape from liability", there being grounds of estoppel present. So limited, the opinion is not authority for the position taken by the respondents in the present litigation, and the decision, insofar as it concerns the application of the statute to the act of an executive officer of a corporation, is disapproved.

* * *

The evidence of the appellants, with inferences which reasonably may be drawn therefrom, would amply support a finding that Mrs. Spalding was authorized to enter into the escrow agreement. Having that authority, she could of course bind the respondent corporation by her execution of the escrow agreement. Its motion for a nonsuit, therefore, should have been denied, and the same ruling made upon the motion by Mrs. Spalding. Although one is not liable personally on a contract executed by him as the officer of a corporation, he may, if he acted without authority, be held to account on a theory of breach of the implied warranty of authority, Civ.Code sec. 2342, or, if bad faith is found, as a principal, Civ.Code sec. 2343. The extent of Mrs. Spalding's liability, if any, depends upon the determination of questions of fact which cannot be made until the issue of her authority to act for the corporation is decided.

The judgment is reversed.

GIBSON, C.J., and CARTER and SPENCE, JJ., concur.

SHENK, Justice (dissenting). The judgment is reversed principally on the ground that the agreement to sell was merely an agreement to sell property in the ordinary course of business by a corporation whose only function was to sell the assets of the Brockman estate. There is thus projected an exception to the rule established by sec. 3901 of the Corporations Code which requires that a transfer of all corporate assets be authorized by resolution of the board and by written consent of shareholders.

It is undisputed that the purported agreement was intended to convey substantially all of the assets of the corporation. The statute makes no fine distinction between transfers of all the assets in the ordinary course of business and other transfers of the entire assets. On its face the statute would apply without exception wherever all assets are transferred. This was not an ordinary sale. It was an attempted complete disposal of the corporate property and required to be properly authorized. The evidence on which the opinion relies as showing that this was not a wind-up sale proves the opposite. On May 1, 1944, a resolution was adopted that "the property of Brockman Holding Company be sold in order to close up the company as soon as possible." Just a year later plaintiff and defendant's president entered into an agreement whereby all of the property of the corporation was to be transferred to the plaintiff.

The aim of the statute is "to give some protection to the shareholders by affording them a chance to have a vote in making a transfer." (Ballantine and Sterling, California Corporation Laws, [1949] 398.) More pointedly, the purpose of the statute is to prevent directors or officers from selling the corporation out from underneath the shareholders if they object to the terms of sale. Here the directors owned 29,000 of the 42,000 shares. All of the directors did not authorize Mrs. Spalding to sell the remaining property of the corporation. Only a majority of the directors, who for all that appears constituted less than a majority in stock ownership, orally sanctioned the sale. I am unable to conclude that this was not a case where the statutory protection was appropriate.

I would affirm the judgment in accordance with the opinion of the District Court of Appeal of the Fourth District, 191 P.2d 534.

TRAYNOR and SCHAUER, JJ., concur.

NOTE

1. Would the majority in *Jeppi v. Brockman Holding Co.* have been on firmer ground if the applicable statute had been worded the same as, or similar to, Section 12.02(a) of the Revised Model Business Corporation Act? See *Sutherland v. Kaonohi Ohana, Ltd.,* 776 F.2d 1425 (9th Cir.1985).

2. When considering the requirement of written authorization of a person selling real estate on behalf of another person, can the position be taken that a general partner is something more than an agent for the partnership, and therefore, written authorization is not needed when a general partner sells in the name of the partnership? Might this position gain further support if the selling general partner is also the "managing partner"?

3. If Mrs. Spalding listed the property with a real estate broker who produced Jeppi and Camp, would the broker be entitled to receive his commission?

    a. Does the answer depend on whether Mrs. Spalding had authority to sell? See *Spiers v. Seal,* 426 So.2d 631 (La.App.1982).

        1. Or is whether Mrs. Spalding can act on behalf of the corporation for the purpose of executing a listing agreement a somewhat different question? See *Wishnow v. Kingsway Estates, Inc.,* 26 A.D.2d 61, 270 N.Y.S.2d 834 (1966); *Cushman & Wakefield Inc. v. Dollar Land Corp. Ltd. (U.S.),* 44 A.D.2d 445, 355 N.Y.S.2d 409 (1974), affirmed, 36 N.Y.2d 490, 369 N.Y.S.2d 394, 330 N.E.2d 409 (1975). Cf. *Acmer Corp. v. State Transport Co.,* 275 Or. 51, 549 P.2d 1114 (1976); *Garfield v. Tindall,* 98 Idaho 841, 573 P.2d 966 (1978).

        2. Could a court find that Mrs. Spalding was not authorized to sell the real estate and, despite her lack of authority, that the corporation is liable for the broker's commission?

            a. If a court so found, could the corporation sue Mrs. Spalding for the amount of the commission? If the corporation could sue Mrs. Spalding, what would be the basis of its suit?

            b. If Mrs. Spalding did not have the authority to list the property with a real estate broker, might she personally be liable to the real estate broker for his commission or damages by reason of her acting without authority or in excess of her authority? See e.g. *Whitten v. Bob King's AMC/Jeep, Inc.,* 30 N.C.App. 161, 226 S.E.2d 530 (1976), reversed, 292 N.C. 84, 231 S.E.2d 891 (1977).

c. CORPORATE REQUIREMENTS

As discussed in the preceding case, there are certain steps which a corporation must take in order to authorize and carry out the sale or disposition of all or substantially all of its property if such sale or disposition is not in the ordinary course of business. Both the vendee and the vendor must be assured that the proper corporate actions have been taken.

WHEN CORPORATIONS DIVIDE: A STATUTORY AND FINANCIAL ANALYSIS

Stanley Siegel
79 Harvard Law Review 534 (1966).
[footnotes omitted]

*   *   *

A. Sale of Assets

It was generally held at common law that sale of all the assets of a corporation could be undertaken, except in rare circumstances, only upon unanimous vote of the shareholders, although a small body of law and informed commentary argued that only a majority vote was necessary. Today [almost] every state * * * has included in its corporation law a provision governing the sale of assets. * * *

*   *   *

1. "All or substantially all." Few cases have raised squarely the issue of what size or character of sale is covered by sale-of-assets statutes. The meaning of "all or substantially all" as used in the Model Act and a majority of state statutes remains unclear. Some guidance may be drawn from decisions under other statutes, which speak of sales of "all of its property and assets," "its property * * * or any part thereof," "any of its property * * * essential to the conduct of its corporate business and purposes," and several other formulations. * * *

[A] sale of "all assets" should be interpreted to include at least all the major assets held by the corporation. It seems clear that the size of a sale alone will not be determinative of whether the sale falls within the statute requiring shareholder approval. In all cases, the courts have engaged in a close examination of the facts surrounding the sale. The sale in In the Matter of Timmis [200 N.Y. 177, 93 N.E. 522 (1910)] of the calendar department of a printing company, together with the goodwill thereof, was held to be effectively "going out of business *pro tanto*," even though the assets of the division sold represented only one-thirteenth of the total assets of the corporation. In requiring stockholder approval, the court emphasized that the corporation was by virtue of the sale indefinitely barred from reentering the calendar business and that this amounted to a permanent contraction of the nature of the business. Such reasoning applied with equal force to the sale by a corporation of its newspaper plant, although the plant did not constitute its entire business. By contrast, the sale by a drugstore chain of one of its stores was held not substantially to contract either the size or the character of the corporate business.

In Klopot v. Northrup, [131 Conn. 14, 37 A.2d 700 (1944)] a corset manufacturer sold its surgical corset department, and dissenting stockholders failed in their attempt to bring the sale within the statute. The court noted that the surgical department was new and experimental, and that it did not constitute such an integral part of the assets as to be

essential to the corporate operations. Although factual distinctions
clarify some of the decisions, differences in the statutory terms have
often been determinative. In the *Klopot* case, some further explanation was necessary to demonstrate why a transaction strikingly similar
to that in *Timmis* led to an opposite result. The *Klopot* court rested
the distinction on the statutes involved:

> Our statute is not like that of New York, which authorizes a
> corporation, with the consent of two-thirds of its stock, to sell its
> property, rights, privileges and franchises "or any interest therein
> or any part thereof" * * * nor like the similar provision of the
> Maine statute * * * which applied to the sale of the franchises,
> entire property or any of the property of a corporation "essential to
> the conduct of its corporate businesses or purposes; " * * * nor
> even like the Ohio statute * * * which applied to the sale of "all
> or substantially all" the assets.

The Connecticut statute in *Klopot* was indeed different; at the time of
that decision it applied to sales by a corporation of "all its property and
assets, including its good will and franchises." While it may be argued
that the "all assets" language of the statute was intended to exclude
any sales of less than all assets, the *Klopot* court itself recognized the
possibility that sales of essential assets, or of assets without which
business could not be conducted, might fall within the statute. An
Illinois court, faced with a similar statute, has held that "all" means
"all or substantially all." But even with this modification, it is clear
that the statute in *Klopot* was less inclusive than the enactment in
Timmis and that this distinction was decisive.

These decisions suggest that * * * sales of all assets or essential
assets will fall within the ambit of virtually all statutes, whatever their
wording. * * * At one extreme, when language is presumptively
directed at all sales, as was the New York statute, the *Timmis* result
seems proper. At the other, when a statute appears limited to sales of
"all" or "essential" assets, the reasoning of *Klopot* may be expected to
prevail. Although the meaning of the "all or substantially all" test of
the Model Business Corporation Act has not been authoritatively resolved, it seems closer in import to the "all assets" criterion. Had the
drafters desired the *Timmis* result, they could have made the test "all
or a substantial part." It seems likely that the words "substantially
all" were inserted not to expand the class of sales covered, but rather to
prevent avoidance of the statute by retention of some minimal residue
of the original assets. The present Connecticut statute, which utilizes
the "all or substantially all" criterion, reinforces this interpretation
with the following paragraph:

> Any sale of assets made in the usual and regular course of business
> of the corporation, including a sale of all or substantially all assets,
> *and any sale of less than substantially all assets,* whether or not
> made in the usual and regular course of the business of the

corporation, may be made upon such terms and conditions and for such consideration as may be authorized by its board of directors.

2. *"Usual and regular course of business."* The Model Act and the statutes based on it require shareholder approval only for sales outside of the usual and regular course of business. Many statutes limit only the size of the sale and do not have this additional test. The statutes in both *Klopot* and *Timmis* were so drafted, but in *Timmis* the New York court judicially adopted the additional criterion: "Notwithstanding the broad language of [the sale of assets statute] * * * it is obvious that it was not addressed to ordinary sales by a corporation, nor even to those extraordinary in size but still in the regular line of its business * * *." Since the New York statute in *Timmis* covered the sale of corporate property "or any interest therein or any part thereof," the result of the decision was that any sale, however small, fell within the statute if it was outside the usual and regular course of business of the corporation. Under the *Timmis* rule, however, the sale of significant assets—as, for example, an entire store—would fall outside the statute if by virtue of its usual nature it were found to be within the ordinary course of business. The Model Act requires stockholder approval in fewer cases than does the *Timmis* rule, since the sales covered must be both outside the usual and regular course of business and dispositions of all or substantially all the assets of the corporation. However, since the Model Act's "all or substantially all" test remains open to varying interpretation, it is not unlikely that the nature of the sale—whether it is in the ordinary course of business—will be the major factor in determining whether the sale requires stockholder approval.

The courts have experienced some difficulty in defining a corporation's usual course of business: "The sale before us was not made in the ordinary course of the business of the corporation, for it was not organized to sell calendar departments, or any department that would involve going out of business *pro tanto*." Obviously the usual corporation is not organized to dispose of part of its business. Yet sales of major assets such as buildings or machinery in connection with replenishment programs are ordinarily within the powers specified or implied in the certificate of incorporation, although they may not be everyday occurrences. Corporate management would be hamstrung if every such transaction had to be submitted to a vote of shareholders. * * * Where is the line drawn? Sales of substantial assets by real estate corporations or by corporations organized to liquidate a business have been held within their usual course of business. Generally, a charter provision allowing sales of all assets without shareholder approval will also be held to render such sales usual. * * *

3. *Statutory Formalities.*

* * * [I]t is necessary to examine the statutory procedure for obtaining stockholder approval. The most detailed protection for stockholders is embodied in the statutes based on the Model Act. The initial steps are a resolution of the board of directors, followed by printed or

written notice to all stockholders of record announcing a meeting and stating that the sale or disposition will be considered. At the meeting [the shareholders] vote on the sale and its terms, * * *. [In general,] approval requires a [majority] vote [of the shares of the corporation entitled to vote thereon] * * *.

Local statutes will have to be carefully examined, since their requirements vary widely. The required vote may be anywhere from a majority to two-thirds, three-fourths, * * * four-fifths * * * [or even] a unanimous vote. The statutes, moreover, are about evenly split between requiring approval from the stated percentage of all outstanding shares or merely from the voting shares. Many states make no provision for class voting, but a substantial number * * * call for class voting when there are shares entitled to it, and a few make it mandatory whenever there are several classes of stock.

Nor does the statutory diversity end there. Although many of the statutes specifically require resolution, notice, and meeting, a substantial number merely provide for a special meeting without specifying details of the notice. Some statutes require only a vote, or a vote on the principal terms of the disposition. * * *

Directors[, however,] would be wise to seek the protection of full notice and a special meeting even when these are not required by the statute.

* * *

NOTE

1. If a corporation engaged in the development and operation of shopping plazas proposes to sell two of the three plazas it owns and operates, does the sale require shareholder approval under the Revised Model Business Corporation Act?

a. Is the determination whether shareholder approval is necessary affected by the corporation being obligated to give the purchaser of the plazas a covenant not to compete within a described area around each plaza sold? What does the phrase, "with or without the goodwill," in Section 12.02(a) of the Revised Model Business Corporation Act mean?

b. If the two plazas to be sold each contained eighteen stores and the plaza to be retained contained thirty, it is more or less likely that shareholder approval will be required?

c. Is the determination of the necessity of shareholder approval affected by the fact that the fair market value of the plaza retained is greater than the combined fair market value of the plazas to be sold?

d. If the corporation has a history of developing, operating and selling plazas, does this have a bearing on whether shareholder approval is necessary?

1. Would it be helpful to know how prior sales of plazas were authorized? See generally Reed, *Sale of Substantially All Corporate Assets,* 16 Colo.Law. 455 (1987).

2. A corporation is formed to develop an apartment complex. After purchasing thirty acres, it finds that twenty acres of the thirty are zoned for

single family residence and the zoning cannot be changed. Can the twenty acres be sold to a subdivision developer without shareholder approval?

   a. The corporation's certification of incorporation broadly defines its power and purposes to include buying, developing and selling real estate. Does this mean that a shareholder vote is not necessary?

   b. After completion of construction, the corporation receives an offer to purchase the apartment complex which is its only asset. Is shareholder approval of the sale necessary?

      1. Are any additional facts required in order to answer this question? Cf. *Schwadel v. Uchitel,* 455 So.2d 401 (Fla.App.1984).

5. RIGHTS OF CREDITORS AND DISSENTING PARTICIPANTS WITH RESPECT TO THE SALE OF ASSETS OF AN ENTITY AND ITS DISSOLUTION

a. SALE OF ASSETS

   An entity selling all or substantially all of its assets usually will have to comply with the bulk sales law of its state. Failure to comply may mean that the creditors of the selling entity will have the opportunity to upset the sale. The creditors also may gain certain rights against the transferee of the assets. The Uniform Commercial Code's bulk sales provisions provide, in subsection (3) of Section 6–102, that the enterprises subject to the bulk sales provisions are those whose principal business is the sale of merchandise from stock, including those who manufacture what they sell. In light of this provision, it is certainly arguable that an entity engaged in real estate development and operation is not subject to the bulk sales provisions since its principal business is certainly not the sale of merchandise from stock. This argument is reinforced by Section 6–102's definition of a bulk transfer as "any transfer in bulk * * * of a major part of the materials, supplies, merchandise, or other inventory * * * of an enterprise." If an entity is engaged in the development of a residential subdivision or if it is a "dealer" in commercial real estate, it might be said to have an inventory. To extend the bulk sales provisions of the Uniform Commercial Code any further than the real estate "dealer," however, would seem unwarranted on the basis of a literal reading of those provisions.

   The Uniform Commercial Code's commentators' notes also indicate that an entity engaged in real estate development and operation is not covered by the Uniform Commercial Code's bulk sales provisions. For example, in Comment # 2 under Section 6–102, the commentators state that the businesses covered by the bulk sales provisions do not include those whose principal business is the sale, not of merchandise, but of services. The comment further indicates that while some bulk sales risk exists in the excluded businesses they have in common the fact that unsecured credit is not commonly extended on the faith of a stock of merchandise. In the usual case, credit is not extended, on the faith of a stock of merchandise, to an entity engaged in real estate development and operation.

See generally Hawkland *Bulk Transfers According to Article 6,* 23 Prac.Law 47 (Jan.1977); Hawkland, *The Trouble With Article 6 of the UCC: Some Thoughts About Section 6–102,* 81 Com.L.J. 83 (1976); Dillsaver, *Notice in Bulk Sales,* 19 U.C.C.L.J. 353 (1987); Harris and Baker, *How the Proposed Revisions to UCC Article 6 (Bulk Transfers) Would Affect Creditors,* 92 Com.L.J. 123 (1987).

The bulk sales law in some states, however, extends to the sale of assets of any entity. Proposed revisions of Article 6 of the Uniform Commercial Code would extend its application to all entities except real estate businesses. In other states the judiciary has broadened the application of the bulk sales law. For example, based on the analysis set out above, it would appear that the sale of the assets of a restaurant is not covered by the bulk sales provisions of the Uniform Commercial Code, but see Zinni v. One Township Line Corp., 36 Pa.D. & C.2d 297, 53 Del.Co. 11 (1965), and compare with Kentucky Club, Inc. v. Fifth Third Bank, 590 S.W.2d 686 (Ky.1979).

Despite majority shareholder approval of the sale by a corporation of all or substantially all of its assets out of the usual course of business, some of the shareholders of the corporation may be unhappy with the terms of the sale or unwilling to have the corporation sell its assets. One must then consider the rights of the dissenting shareholders.

NOTE:

INTERPLAY OF RIGHTS OF STOCKHOLDERS DISSENTING FROM SALE OF CORPORATE ASSETS

58 Columbia Law Review 251 (1958).
[footnotes omitted]

* * *

[A number of states] have passed statutes authorizing directors to sell the assets, provided there was approval by a specified percentage of the stockholders and, in some instances, also of the directors. Such statutes, however, only reversed the opportunities for oppression. The minority stockholder was deprived of his ability to protect his equitable interests in the corporate property. In turn, the legislatures and courts have attempted to protect the minority stockholder from this abuse.

I. Appraisal Rights

A. Nature of Appraisal Statutes

[In many] states a dissenting stockholder has the right to demand appraisal of, and payment, for, his stock when a sale of assets is made.

This right is generally designed to arise whenever the sale is such that it would have been void at common law but has been validated by statute. The right to appraisal is absolute and is thus not defeated by an inability to prove the bad faith of the directors and majority stockholders. Since bad faith need not be proved, this remedy is more readily available than any other equitable relief.

Appraisal supposedly protects the stockholder from any monetary loss which he would sustain by submission to the dictates of the majority. There is, however, criticism of its efficacy, based on the realization that the appraised value of the stock is not always its real or full worth. Since it is probably impossible to derive any method which would always be accurate in arriving at a value fair to all, the availability of relief other than appraisal is often of utmost importance.

B. *Exclusivity of Appraisal Rights*

Some statutes specifically state that appraisal is the exclusive remedy of a dissenting stockholder. In other jurisdictions, notwithstanding a lack of express legislative direction, courts have come to the unnecessary conclusion that equitable relief is impliedly barred by the appraisal statute. These courts justified their position on the ground that a shareholder's right is merely the protection of his monetary interest in the corporation, that he has no right to continue in the business and can demand only that he be reimbursed for his investment. * * *

However, [some] courts have found [this] rule too strict, and have devised means of avoiding it, with the result that it probably has little remaining content. For example, if the transaction is ultra vires, illegal, or fraudulent, equitable jurisdiction is sustained. [See Section 13.02(b) of the Revised Model Business Corporation Act.] The theory is that the appraisal statute has no application, since the sale is void. The dissenter can also prevent the sale where it is part of a larger voidable transaction and obtain equitable relief where the appraisal statute is itself used to defraud him. Further, he can probably sue the directors for negligence in not accepting the best offer made for the assets, and, if the corporation is insolvent, the inadequacy of appraisal destroys its exclusivity. * * *

II. The Fiduciary Relationship Imposed by the Courts

A. *Analysis*

The need for a fiduciary relation arises because of the minority stockholder's inability to protect his equitable interest in the corporation's assets. Where appraisal rights are deemed exclusive, they are considered to be full protection for this interest, and the fiduciary analysis need not be employed.

Directors are, in actuality, representatives of the majority or controlling stockholders. Therefore, the courts do not restrict fiduciary responsibilities to directors, but are coming to insist that whenever anyone exercises control over the property of the minority stockholder, the fiduciary relation arises. If this control is exercised unfairly or in bad faith, the fiduciary obligation is breached.

There is disagreement as to what constitutes fraudulent conduct. Generally, the conduct must be such as to cause injury to the minority stockholder because of the fiduciary's disregard of his interests. Such disregard may be proved by a showing that the fiduciary would share in a benefit from the transaction while the *cestuis que trustent* would not, or that he had not obtained the best possible price for the assets sold. Since the courts will not interfere with an honest exercise of business discretion, mere poor judgment or inefficient management is not grounds for judicial relief.

B. Presumptions and the Burdens of Proof

Since the majority stockholders also stand to lose by receipt of inadequate consideration for the assets, courts presume that they do not deliberately accept an inadequate price. Directors are also presumed to be acting honestly. Thus, the breach of any fiduciary relation must be proved affirmatively by the plaintiff unless he can show that certain other factors are present, and, in large measure, plaintiff's success seems to depend on his ability to place the burden of proof on the defendant.

1. Proving inadequacy of consideration. In the usual case, the complainants protest an alleged inadequacy of consideration. However, the price received is, like other terms of the sale, within the discretionary powers of the directors. Thus, the plaintiff must prove that there was an abuse of this discretion. If the only fact demonstrated by the plaintiff is the alleged inadequacy of consideration, he will generally fail. * * *

Where there are two firm, cash, ready offers, the acceptance of the lower one is proof of fraud. However, this rule of thumb has little utility because it is rare to find two offers so identical in terms and circumstances that a director could not use honest judgment in choosing the lesser cash amount. Of course, it may well be a fraud on the minority for the fiduciary to fail to solicit any offer other than the one he himself has made. * * *

It seems, [the above] rationale only indicates the possibility of convincing courts that the insufficiency of consideration establishes the presence of other factors. These, in conjunction with the inadequacy of consideration, prove the fraud.

2. Proving benefit to the fiduciary. The presumption in favor of the fiduciary fails when, because of the relationship between him and the purchaser, his responsibilities to the corporation might be subordinated to his private interest in the sale. * * *

Where an interested director's vote or influence was necessary to authorize the sale, the mere protest of the stockholder generally renders the sale voidable by [the stockholder] unless there is stockholder approval. However, there are some cases permitting such sales if they are fair. There is also some authority that, regardless of fairness, all contracts between a corporation and a director are voidable, even if his vote was not required, on the theory that his influence is always present and might have affected the sale.

Where such sales are permitted, the fiduciary usually must show their fairness. He must prove that the stockholders and directors were aware of the relationship between the fiduciary and the purchaser at the time of approval of the sale and that his influence was not necessary to obtain such approval. Generally, where a disinterested majority of stockholders has ratified the sale, the burden of proving it unfair is once again placed upon the plaintiff. Barring a showing of waste, freeze-out, or fraud on the disinterested majority, the minority is bound by the ratification.

The precise relationships necessary to establish a conflict of interests in the fiduciary are often litigated. If he is a director, or a dominant, majority, controlling, or even substantial, stockholder of the purchaser, the conflict of interests is obvious and, accordingly, the burden of proof shifts to the fiduciary. Where a close relative, such as a wife or a son, is the purchaser, the interest is also clear. A more remote interest, however, may not suffice. * * *

As to the sort of benefit to be derived by the fiduciary, the courts have uniformly held that a mere employment contract with the purchaser, or payment to the fiduciary in exchange for his covenant not to compete with the purchaser, is insufficient to show a conflicting interest if the contract is supported independently by mutually sufficient consideration. However, where the purchaser promises the fiduciary benefits, such as a pension, without requiring a *quid pro quo,* the contract does establish fraud. In this case, the fiduciary has received a benefit which would otherwise have gone to the corporation, and both the conflict of interests and the fraud are proved.

There is no conflicting interest or fraud when the director obtains the purchaser's promise to pay all the corporation's debts due to the director, since the corporation would have to pay the debt in either case. Similarly, there is no fraud if the fiduciary purchases the corporation in order to prevent it from suing him, provided he pays a sufficient consideration to include settlement of the claim. The fact that the majority bought its stock on speculation and is trying to make a short-swing profit, or that it is trying to convert its entire holdings into cash does not of itself establish a conflict of interest. Likewise, it is not fraud for majority stockholders holding preferred stock to obtain terms which pay the amount due under the charter to the preferred shareholders, even if this results in leaving little for holders of the common. The personal motives of the fiduciaries are not necessarily inconsistent with the best interests of the corporation in this type of case. Though none of these factors even in combination establishes a conflict of interests, they may be probative of the unfairness of the price.

C. Effect of Statutory or Charter Provisions

Several jurisdictions have statutory provisions regarding contracts between directors and the corporation or between corporations with interlocking directorates. * * * [One] statute provided that contracts between directors and the corporation are not invalid per se, but the provision has been nullified by a decision holding it applicable only to cases where a disinterested majority of directors approve the sale. This is merely a return to the common law. * * * [Another statutory] provision permits the contract if a disinterested majority approve, if the stockholders ratify the contract, or if the sale is fair. [Compare this provision with Section 8.31 of the Revised Model Business Corporation Act.] In view of the provision expressly validating fair contracts, it would be difficult for the * * * courts to nullify the statute as [they] did the [first statute discussed above]. * * * [Other statutes] exclude the interested directors' votes, and essentially follow the majority of the common law jurisdictions. However, these statutes differ as to the requirements for a quorum and as to the permissibility of the interested directors' presence at the voting. * * *

Many corporations have attempted to take this problem in hand by inserting exculpatory clauses in the charter or by-laws permitting directors' contracts with the corporation. Where the issue has arisen, the contracts have been upheld, the cases holding that such a clause shifted the burden of proving unfairness to the plaintiff. In effect, since all the cases found for the defendant-directors, the cases uphold the validity of the contract by virtue of the exculpatory clause.

NOTE

1. In a jurisdiction which has adopted the Revised Model Business Corporation Act, when may a shareholder dissent from an act of a corporation and claim appraisal rights? See Section 13.02 of the Revised Model Business Corporation Act.

a. In the event of a sale of all of the corporation's assets out of the usual course of business, does shareholders' approval of the sale pursuant to Section 12.02 of the Revised Model Business Corporation Act deprive a dissenting shareholder of his appraisal rights?

b. If the sale is for cash and the corporation is to be dissolved and substantially all of the net proceeds of the sale distributed to the shareholders within one year after the date of sale, does a dissenting shareholder have appraisal rights? See Section 13.02(a)(3) of the Revised Model Business Corporation Act.

1. If the sale is approved on the terms described above, but in the eleventh month after approval and following the sale the directors and the shareholders who approved the sale properly rescind the resolu-

tions providing for the dissolution and distribution of the net proceeds of sale and authorize the corporation's investment of the proceeds of the sale in a new endeavor, what remedies are available to the shareholder who dissented when the sale was approved?

a. Can the dissenting shareholder now claim appraisal rights if he did not comply with the terms of Section 13.21 of the Revised Model Business Corporation Act upon the approval of the sale? Was the shareholder entitled to dissent at the time of the approval of the sale? See Section 13.02(a)(3) of the Revised Model Business Corporation Act.

c. If a sale of all of the assets of a corporation out of the usual course of business is for cash and notes of a purchaser, a AAA–1 credit, and the notes are fully secured by the assets purchased, does a shareholder, who does not approve of the sale, have the right to dissent and claim appraisal rights if the corporation is to be dissolved and the proceeds of the sale are to be distributed within twelve months after the date of the sale?

1. Does the fact that the notes are fully negotiable affect the answer?

2. If the resolution approving the sale directed the officers and directors of the corporation to sell the notes for cash immediately after the sale and to distribute the cash to shareholders, do these facts affect the result?

2. What position does the Revised Model Business Corporation Act take with respect to directors voting on matters in which they have or may have a conflict of interest? See Section 8.31 of the Revised Model Business Corporation Act. What result is reached under the Revised Model Business Corporation Act if an interested director does not make his interest known to the other directors and/or shareholders when they are voting on the matter?

3. A sale of all or substantially all of the assets of a partnership out of the ordinary course of business is properly authorized under the partnership agreement and governing state statutes and occurs prior to the date set in the partnership agreement for the dissolution of the partnership and the date on which a member can withdraw his interest. What are the rights of general and limited partners who do not approve of the sale?

a. Assuming that a partnership agreement can provide that a sale of all or substantially all of the partnership's assets out of the ordinary course of business can be made on the vote of less than all the partners, neither a general nor a limited partner who dissents from a sale has appraisal rights similar to those of a dissenting shareholder. In fact, subject to the terms of the partnership agreement or a finding that the sale terminated the "business" of the partnership, neither one has the right to withdraw from the partnership and obtain payment for his interest or cause the dissolution of the partnership (See Sections 31(1) of the U.P.A., 16(1), (2) and (4) of the U.L.P.A. and 602, 603 and 801 of the Revised U.L.P.A.), unless the circumstances render a dissolution equitable. See Sections 32(1)(f) of the U.P.A., 10(1)(c) of the U.L.P.A. and 802 of the Revised U.L.P.A.

1. Under Section 31(2) of the U.P.A., however, a general partner has the "power" to cause a dissolution of a partnership in contravention of the partnership agreement. In the event the other partners do not continue the business of the partnership, the partner causing the dissolution is entitled to have the partnership property applied to

discharge its liabilities, and the surplus applied to pay in cash the net amount owing to the respective partners subject to an action for damages for breach of the partnership agreement by the other partners against the partner who caused the dissolution. See Section 38(2) (c)(I) of the U.P.A. If the other partners decide to continue the business, the partner causing the dissolution is entitled to have the value of his interest in the partnership, less any damages caused to his co-partners by the dissolution, ascertained and paid to him in cash or in installment payments secured by bond approved by the court and to be released from all existing liabilities of the partnership. In determining the value of the interest of the partner who causes the dissolution, partnership goodwill is not included. See Section 38(2)(c) (II) of the U.P.A. A general partner in a limited partnership also has the "power" to withdraw, but if the withdrawal violates the partnership agreement, the withdrawing general partner is liable for the damages resulting from the breach of the partnership agreement. See e.g. Section 602 of the Revised U.L.P.A. Unless a limited partner can convince a court to decree dissolution of a limited partnership or the partnership agreement permits withdrawal or does not deal with withdrawal, a limited partner cannot withdraw or cause the dissolution of the partnership. See Sections 16 of the U.L.P.A. and 603 of the Revised U.L.P.A.

4.   The sale of all or substantially all of the assets of a partnership out of the ordinary course of business, in the case of a general partnership, may have to be authorized by all the partners. See Sections 9(2) and (3)(b) and (c) and 10(1) of the U.P.A. In the case of a limited partnership, however, it appears that the sale can be authorized by a vote of less than all of the general and limited partners if the limited partnership agreement so provides. See Sections 9 of U.L.P.A., and 302, 303, 403 and 405 of the Revised U.L.P.A. See generally pages 433 to 437 supra.

5.   General partners have a fiduciary relation to one another and to the limited partners of a limited partnership. See e.g. Section 21 of the U.P.A., 9(1) of the U.L.P.A., and Section 403 of the Revised U.L.P.A. In this context, much that was said in the preceding excerpt with respect to the fiduciary duties of directors and majority shareholders applies in the partnership form of doing business.

b.   DISSOLUTION AND LIQUIDATION

In many situations the sale of all or substantially all of the assets of an entity is followed by the dissolution and liquidation of the entity. Creditors and dissenting participants' rights upon the dissolution and liquidation of an entity are considered in this subpart.

DARCY v. BROOKLYN & N.Y. FERRY CO.

Court of Appeals of New York, 1909.
196 N.Y. 99, 89 N.E. 461.

WILLARD BARTLETT, J.   On November 15, 1900, the plaintiff duly recovered a judgment against the Brooklyn & New York Ferry Company upon a cause of action which had accrued on the 2d day of July, 1897. The execution upon this judgment was returned unsatisfied. The plaintiff found himself unable to enforce it because the defendant corporation on the 22d of August, 1898, had through its board of directors assumed to sell, assign, and transfer the entire corporate property to another corporation known as the Brooklyn Ferry Company of New York for $6,000,000. The present suit was instituted on the theory that the directors had violated their duties in making the transfer in the manner in which they made it and hence could be compelled to satisfy the plaintiff's claim. The consideration for the transfer did not pass from the purchasing corporation to the Brooklyn & New York Ferry Company or its directors, but was turned over directly to the stockholders of the selling corporation and distributed among them. The Brooklyn & New York Ferry Company thereupon immediately ceased doing business, having thus parted with all its franchises, although no proceedings were ever taken to effect a dissolution of the corporation according to law. No notice of the transfer was given to creditors nor was any property retained by the directors with which to meet the plaintiff's claim or any other indebtedness which might legally be established against the corporation. At the time of the transfer, however, the purchasing corporation did agree to assume all the then existing debts and liabilities of the selling corporation. This agreement was the sole provision made by the directors for the payment of the creditors of the corporation which they represented.

The narrative of the transaction leaves no doubt that what the directors of the Brooklyn & New York Ferry Company sought to bring about was a voluntary dissolution of the corporation and the distribution of its assets without taking the steps to that end which are prescribed by law. Notwithstanding their failure to proceed under the statute, they contend that a creditor of a corporation has no standing to compel them to pay a claim of which they were ignorant at the time of the transfer of the corporate property, in the absence of proof of actual fraud on their part. It is true that there is no allegation or finding of fraud; but there is evidence that the officers of the company had knowledge of the injury to the plaintiff which was the basis of his claim. The liability of the directors is predicated, not on the ground that their action in making the transfer was fraudulent, but upon the proposition that it is a violation of duty on the part of the directors of a corporation to divest it of all its property without affording a reasonable opportunity to its creditors to present and enforce their claims before the transfer shall become effective. This is the proposition involved in the judgment in this case which we are asked to reverse. We think it is sound in law, and should be upheld.

There is express statutory authority for the maintenance of an action by a creditor of a corporation against its directors to compel them to pay the value of any property which they have transferred to others by a violation of their duties. Code Civ.Proc. §§ 1781, 1782, substantially reenacted in 1909 as sections 90 and 91 of the general corporation law (Consol.Laws, c. 23). The assets of a corporation constitute a trust fund for the payment of its debts. Bartlett v. Drew,

57 N.Y. 587. A creditor cannot be deprived of his equitable lien thereon by an agreement between the corporation and a transferee of the property that the latter shall assume and pay all the corporate debts. The consent of the creditor to accept the substituted debtor is essential to make such an agreement valid as against him. Hence the fact that the Brooklyn Ferry Company of New York agreed with the Brooklyn & New York Ferry Company to assume all the debts of the latter did not justify the directors of the selling corporation in disposing of its assets without making some other provision for the payment of its creditors. The plaintiff was left in the position of the creditor so aptly described by Werner, J., in Hurd v. N.Y. & C. Steam Laundry Co., 167 N.Y. 89, 95, 60 N.E. 327, 328: "When he demands payment of his claim, he is referred to the empty shell which is all that is left of the live corporation whose tangible assets constituted a trust fund for the payment of his [claim] at the time of its creation." It is not necessary to determine precisely what the directors of a corporation must do in order to protect themselves against liability when they undertake to divest it of all its property and practically dissolve it without taking the proceedings for a voluntary dissolution which are prescribed by law. For the purposes of the present case, it is enough to say that they were bound to give some notice to creditors of the proposed transfer, and they gave none whatever. We think that their failure to do so was "a violation of their duties" under subdivision 2 of section 1781 of the Code of Civil Procedure, and rendered them liable to the plaintiff for the amount of the claim which he established against the corporation as having accrued before the transfer. The motives which induced the omission are immaterial. The entire assets could not lawfully be set over by the selling corporation to the purchasing corporation until some sort of opportunity had been given to the creditors of the [former] to present and enforce their claims. The neglect to afford this opportunity is what constituted a violation of the directors' duties, and it matters not that they may have supposed they were not required to do any more than they did for the protection of creditors. * * * Their omission to make adequate provision for the protection of the creditors was proof of their dereliction and good faith constitutes no defense. Indeed, business men have little cause for complaint when, as in this case, they find themselves in trouble because they have attempted to accomplish privately what the law contemplates shall only be accomplished publicly, namely, the voluntary dissolution of a corporation. The judgment enforces a sound lesson in business morals and should be affirmed, with costs.

Judgment affirmed.

NOTE

1. What was the "wrong" committed by the directors in *Darcy v. Brooklyn & N.Y. Ferry Co.*? Was it: (a) The failure to give creditors adequate notice of the transfer of the assets of the corporation to the purchaser; (b) The failure to obtain the creditors' consent to the assumption by the purchaser of the

liabilities of the corporation; (c) The failure to discharge or make provision for the discharge of the liabilities of the corporation prior to permitting the assets of the corporation to be given to its shareholders; or (d) The failure to give the creditors adequate notice of the dissolution and liquidation of the corporation?

a. If the directors had given notice of the transfer, dissolution and liquidation to the creditors, would Darcy have received notice?

b. In the event of the dissolution of a corporation, what steps must be taken, under the Revised Model Business Corporation Act, with respect to its creditors?

1. See Sections 14.05, 14.06 and 14.07 of the Revised Model Business Corporation Act.

2. The assets of a corporation are sold in dissolution and the purchaser is a AAA–1 credit and assumes all of the obligations of the dissolving corporation. Is this adequate "provision for the discharge of the liabilities of the corporation"?

a. If it is not, does anything less than payment in full amount to adequate provision for the discharge of the corporation's liabilities?

b. How can an unliquidated claim or a contingent claim be paid in full? See Sections 14.06 and 14.07 of the Revised Model Business Corporation Act.

3. What liabilities do the directors of a dissolving corporation incur if they fail to pay or make provision for the discharge of the liabilities of the corporation? See Section 8.33 of the Revised Model Business Corporation Act and *Hoover v. Galbraith,* 7 Cal.3d 519, 102 Cal.Rptr. 733, 498 P.2d 981 (1972), in which a corporation was dissolved and its assets distributed to its shareholders during the pendency of a creditor's action against the corporation on a claim which arose prior to dissolution. The court held the directors liable for failure to pay or provide for the payment of the claim even though judgment was rendered on the claim three years after dissolution and the judgment was affirmed five years after dissolution.

a. If the directors fail to pay or make provision for the discharge of a liability because they do not know of the existence of the liability, are they liable under Section 8.33? See Section 8.30. Has the corporation violated Section 14.05(a)(3)? See Section 14.07.

THE SHAREHOLDER'S APPRAISAL REMEDY: AN ESSAY FOR FRANK COKER

Bayless Manning
72 Yale Law Journal 223 (1962).
[footnotes omitted]

*   *   *

Dissolution

If it is serious surgery to change any part of the "corporation," it is much more serious to bring about its "death" by dissolution. By this logic, one might expect to find the appraisal remedy available to the shareholder dissenting from dissolution. In fact, however, no statute provides for it.

The main reason may have been that appraisal did not seem to be an appropriate or feasible remedy for the purpose. It was generally assumed that following upon dissolution of a corporation, all the corporate assets would promptly be turned into cash and distributed *pro rata* among the shareholders after the creditors were paid. According to this conception, all shareholders were about to be paid the "value" of their shares. Appraisal would be of no interest or use to anyone. In fact, of course, this analysis is erroneous in situations when the liquidation of the assets is spread out over many years, or where assets are not distributed in cash; or where the enterprise is broken-up after the dissolution, and it is found that the shareholders ultimately receive less than the amount they would have received as their *pro rata* share of the company's going concern value on the day dissolution was voted. In each of these cases, and perhaps others, it would be an advantage to the dissenting shareholder to be able to look to an appraisal remedy rather than wait around for his share of the liquidating distribution. But this is not the kind of analysis that was in vogue at the end of the last century.

On the other hand, the explanation just suggested may itself be biased off target by its twentieth century origins. It is not easy to think with the mind of others. Perhaps to the nineteenth century analyst, dissolution just did not seem as much a trauma as merger. Death was more "natural" than change; horses die more often than they change into cows. Perhaps the shareholder "assumed" the risk of dissolution and distribution, and that was the end of the thinking on the matter.

Whatever the mental processes involved, dissolution gives rise to the appraisal remedy under no statutes while merger yields the remedy under all statutes. It is worthwhile to look at these two propositions side by side for a moment.

If Corporation A merges into Corporation B, the enterprises are combined, A shareholders become B shareholders, and, under most statutes, shareholders of both A and B have the appraisal remedy open to them. [See, however, Section 13.02(a)(1) of the Revised Model Business Corporation Act.]

As has been suggested previously, it is hard to see why, even by nineteenth century reasoning, the shareholders of B should have this privilege; the only thing that happened to them was economic, and that doesn't count. On the other hand, the only conceptual thing that happened to Corporation A was that it went up in smoke. By force of the merger, Corporation A was dissolved. Yet it is agreed that in a dissolution shareholders are not entitled to the appraisal remedy. Then why should the A shareholders have the remedy in the merger with B?

The best answer available is pretty lame. One can say, if he wishes, that the difference is that in the merger the A shareholders received B stock. This answer keeps the player alive for only one more move. What if Corporation A *bought* the B stock, then dissolved and distributed the B stock to its shareholders? Here there is no appraisal remedy, either on the purchase or on the dissolution.

What emerges is that the rule on appraisal in mergers is "inconsistent" with the rule on appraisal in dissolutions. This is flagrantly apparent under the Connecticut and New York rule limiting the remedy in mergers to shareholders of the terminating company. [See Section 13.02(a)(1) of the Revised Model Business Corporation Act.]

It is even more profoundly true under the Delaware and majority rule giving the remedy to all shareholders involved, for now not only do the shareholders of A receive the remedy where they would not if their own corporation were dissolved, but the shareholders of B receive it where the only thing that happened was that some *other* corporation was dissolved.

* * *

NOTE

1. As pointed out by Professor Manning and as provided by the Revised Model Business Corporation Act, in general, shareholders do not have the appraisal remedy available upon dissolution of a corporation. When, however, the sale of all or substantially all of the corporation's assets occurs in dissolution, Section 13.02(a)(3) of the Revised Model Business Corporation Act grants appraisal rights with respect to a sale in dissolution, but excludes a sale for cash on terms requiring that substantially all of the net proceeds of the sale be distributed to the shareholders within one year after the date of the sale.

2. In the context of the exception to Section 13.02(a)(3) and a grant of appraisal rights when a sale of all or substantially all of the assets of a corporation is made out of the usual course of business in dissolution, what does the phrase "a sale for cash" mean?

a. For example, the assets of a corporation may be sold to more than one purchaser. If each sale is for cash and the cash is distributed to the shareholders within one year after the date of the first sale or if the sales are closed on the same day and the cash distributed immediately thereafter, does a shareholder who voted in the negative when the sales and dissolution were approved have appraisal rights?

b. Can appraisal rights be avoided, under Section 13.02(a)(3), if the purchaser of the assets of the corporation pays part of the purchase price in notes and part in cash?

1. If the notes are negotiable, the interest rate fair, the purchaser a AAA–1 credit and the notes fully secured, can it be said that the notes are a "cash equivalent"?

2. If the "a sale for cash" exception cannot be complied with in the above manner, is it complied with if the notes, immediately upon closing with the purchaser, are sold to a financial institution or another third party for cash and the proceeds of both sales immediate-

ly distributed to the shareholders? Does this approach comply with the "a sale for cash" exception?

    a. Is compliance with the "a sale for cash" exception more likely if the sale of the notes is part of a simultaneous closing including the sale of the assets?

3. The only act asked of shareholders is to approve a dissolution. See Section 14.02 of the Revised Model Business Corporation Act. The dissolution is approved by a majority vote. Can the directors now authorize the sale of all of the assets of the corporation for cash and notes of a purchaser without obtaining shareholder approval? See Section 14.05(a)(2) of the Revised Model Business Corporation Act. But see Section 13.02(a)(3).

    a. Does Section 14.05(a)(2) of the Revised Model Business Corporation Act authorize a dissolving corporation to dispose of all or substantially all of its assets without shareholder approval?

    b. Can it be argued that a sale of assets made by a corporation after its dissolution is approved by the shareholders is a sale in the usual course of business? See *Jeppi v. Brockman Holding Co.*, pages 437 to 442 supra. See also *Sutherland v. Kaonohi Ohana, Ltd.*, 776 F.2d 1425 (9th Cir.1985).

4. If a partnership agreement provides a definite date for dissolution of the partnership, a general or limited partner does not have the right to cause a dissolution or withdraw his interest prior to that date unless the partnership agreement so provides. See Sections 31(1) of the U.P.A., 16(1), (2) and (4) of the U.L.P.A. and Sections 602, 603 and 801 of the Rev.U.L.P.A. A member, however, might apply to a court for dissolution if another partner, or a general partner, wilfully commits a breach of the partnership agreement, such as selling all or substantially all the assets of the partnership without proper authorization. See Section 32(1) of the U.P.A., Section 10(1)(c) of the U.L.P.A. and Section 802 of the Rev.U.L.P.A.

    a. A general partner has the power to withdraw and to cause a dissolution of the partnership in contravention of the partnership agreement. See Sections 31(2) and 38(2)(c) of the U.P.A. and Sections 602, 603 and 801 of the Rev.U.L.P.A. The partners who have not wrongfully withdrawn or caused the dissolution may continue the business of the partnership in the same name paying to the partner who wrongfully withdrew and caused the dissolution the value of his interest, without considering the goodwill of the partnership, less any damages caused by the withdrawal and dissolution. In addition, the continuing partners can make the payment to the withdrawing partner in installments securing the payment by bond approved by the court and indemnifying the withdrawing partner against all present or future partnership liabilities. See Section 38(2)(b) of the U.P.A. Under the Rev.U.L.P.A. a general partner has the power to withdraw from a limited partnership at any time, but if the withdrawal violates the partnership agreement, the limited partnership may recover damages from the withdrawing partner. See Section 602 of the Rev.U.L.P.A.

    b. For a consideration of some of the problems involved in determining the amount to which a former partner is entitled when the business of the partnership is continued after dissolution see Note, *Settlement of Former Partner's Account When the Business is Continued After a Dissolution,* 39 Mo.L.Rev. 632 (1974).

5. Prior to the date set in the partnership agreement for dissolution or withdrawal of a member's interest, the partnership may be dissolved on, among other things, the express will of all the partners. See Section 31(1)(c) of the U.P.A. and Section 801 of the Rev.U.L.P.A. It appears, however, that the partnership agreement of a limited partnership can provide that the dissolution of the partnership will occur on the affirmative vote of less than all the partners. See e.g. Section 303(b)(6)(i) of the Rev.U.L.P.A. A partnership may be dissolved by decree of a court when, among other things, it is not reasonably practical to carry on the business of the partnership. See Section 32(1)(e) and (f) of the U.P.A. and Section 802 of the Rev.U.L.P.A.

a. A limited partnership interest may be withdrawn prior to the date set in the partnership agreement for dissolution or withdrawal of an interest on, among other things, the consent of *all* of the members of the limited partnership. See Section 16(1)(b) of the U.L.P.A. and Sections 603 and 801 of the Rev.U.L.P.A.

6. The U.P.A., the U.L.P.A. and the Rev.U.L.P.A. are very specific as to priorities with regard to the distribution of assets of a partnership on its termination (winding-up) after dissolution. The payment of the claims of creditors, who are not members of the partnership, is given first priority in Section 40 of the U.P.A. and Section 23 of the U.L.P.A. In Section 804 of the Rev.U.L.P.A., however, partners who are creditors share the creditors' priority.

7. See generally Hillman, *Misconduct as a Basis for Excluding or Expelling a Partner: Effecting Commercial Divorce and Securing Custody of the Business,* 78 Nw.U.L.Rev. 527 (1983); Hillman, *Private Ordering Within Partnerships,* 41 U.Miami L.Rev. 425 (1987).

8. The allocation of the purchase price among the assets acquired from a corporation or a partnership is usually of great importance to the purchaser and seller since, for income tax purposes, certain assets will be depreciable and other assets will not be. In addition, the gain on certain assets can be reported using the installment method and the gain on other assets must be reported at the time of the sale even though the consideration received for them is an installment obligation. Finally, certain assets will produce capital gain or capital loss while others will produce ordinary income or ordinary loss.

a. Section 1060 of the Internal Revenue Code requires that the purchaser and the seller of the assets of a going business and, in certain situations, of stock in a corporation and partnership interests in a partnership use the "residual" method to allocate the purchase price among the assets of the acquired business. Use of this method will result in the purchase price being allocated among the assets according to and to the extent of each asset's fair market value. If the purchase price exceeds the apparent aggregate fair market values of all the tangible and intangible assets, the excess is allocated to goodwill and going concern value. See Abrams and Cinnamon, *Purchase Price Allocations Restricted by Tax Reform Act of 1986,* 15 Tax'n Law. 210 (1987); Auster, *Allocation of Lump–Sum Purchase Price Upon the Transfer of Business Assets After Tax Reform,* 65 Taxes 545 (1987); Garland, *The Impact of New Sec. 1060 on Purchase Price Allocations,* 18 Tax Adviser 793 (1987).

b. The allocation of the purchase price among the assets other than goodwill and going concern value, if made within the fair market value range of each asset, in an arms-length transaction, and reflected in the agreement between the seller and the purchaser, is generally respected by the Internal Revenue Service since the interests of the purchaser and seller are somewhat divergent. Cf *KFOX Inc. v. United States*, 510 F.2d 1365 (Ct. Cl.1975), in which the taxpayer failed to convince the court that an allocation of the purchase price among the assets was made pursuant to the agreement between the parties to the sale of the assets. Should the failure of the taxpayer to convince the court result in the court's ignoring the allocation if, in fact, both the seller and the purchaser follow the allocation in reporting the income tax consequences of the sale? See generally Weiler and Erickson, *Purchase and Sale of Business Assets: Contract Failing to Allocate Purchase Price*, 56 Taxes 143 (1978); Bogdanski, *Contractural Allocation of Price in Sales of Businesses*, 15 J.Corp.Tax'n 99 (1988).

c. In *Moss American, Inc.*, 33 CCH Tax Ct.Mem. 1121 (1974), the acquiring corporation allocated the purchase price among the acquired assets in amounts equal to the acquiring corporation's determination of the fair market value of each of the assets. The Internal Revenue Service challenged the acquiring corporation's determination of the fair market value of certain assets and asserted a higher valuation of those assets generally based on a valuation report received by the parent corporation of the acquiring corporation. This assertion, if accepted by the court, would have had the effect of increasing the acquiring corporation's basis in the assets whose values were increased and lowering its basis in certain assets which were considered properly valued by the Internal Revenue Service. The proposed increase in the value of some of the assets, however, resulted in a value for all of the acquired assets in excess of the purchase price paid by the acquiring corporation. Approaching the matter in terms of aggregate fair market value, the Tax Court sustained the acquiring corporation's determination of the fair market value of the assets, holding that the purchase price was the best evidence of the aggregate fair market value of the assets.

9. A purchaser might acquire the stock rather than the assets of a corporation. While this approach might avoid some of the previously discussed problems involved in the purchase of assets, it is not without its particular concerns.

a. If the purchase price paid for the stock exceeds the aggregate adjusted bases of the assets, the purchaser will not realize a current or continuing tax benefit, such as depreciation, from the excess of the purchase price. Therefore, the purchaser will want the aggregate adjusted bases of the assets increased to reflect the purchase price of the stock. This increase can be achieved at some tax cost to the acquired corporation. See Section 338 of the Internal Revenue Code and pages 545 to 547 infra. See also Battle, *Section 338—Stock Purchases Treated as Asset Purchases for Tax Purposes*, 60 Taxes 980 (1982); Ginsburg, *Taxing Corporate Acquisitions*, 38 Tax L.Rev. 177 (1983); Heinkel, *Section 338—An Analysis and Proposals for Reform*, 59 Notre Dame L.Rev. 158 (1983); Amdur, *Federal Income Tax Treatment of Parties to a Taxable Stock Acquisition: The Impact of TEFRA*, 41 N.Y.U.Inst.Fed.Tax'n 51A–1 (1983); Hoops, *Acquiring the Stock of a Target—The Sec. 338 Election*, 15 Tax Adviser 138 (1984); Witt, *Practical Implications of Treating Stock Purchase as Asset Acquisition Under 338*, 61 J.Tax'n 8 (1984); Comment, *Section 338: The Result of the Legal Evolution of the Tax Treatment of Two–Step Asset Acquisitions*, 61 Tex.L.Rev. 1109 (1983); Silverman and Johnson, *New Tax Law Has Changed Many of the Ground Rules for Asset Acquisitions Under Section*

338, 62 J.Tax'n 40 (1985); Wexler and Welke, *Section 338—Consistency and Complexity*, 63 Taxes 916 (1985).

b. Rather than dealing with a single corporation, the purchaser, acquiring stock rather than assets, must, in many cases, deal with a number of shareholders and will have little or no assurance that the number of shares which the purchaser wants to acquire can, in fact, be acquired. A purchaser acquiring stock, however, can deal with the corporation to be acquired and can be relatively certain of the number of shares to be acquired if a compulsory share exchange is used. See Section 11.02 of the Revised Model Business Corporation Act. This approach raises some of the same considerations as a sale of assets. See Sections 11.03 and 13.02(a) (2) of the Revised Model Business Corporation Act.

c. If the stock to be acquired is stock of a close corporation, there may be restrictions on the transfer of the stock to outsiders. The validity of the restrictions and the ways in which the stock may be acquired in view of them or despite them is a matter of real concern to the purchaser. See O'Neal, *Restrictions on Transfer of Stock in Closely Held Corporations: Planning and Drafting*, 65 Harv.L.Rev. 773 (1952), and O'Neal, Close Corporations, chap. 7 (1971).

d. If stock is being acquired, the purchaser will require the sellers to give warranties of title to the stock. But what about title to the assets which are the real reason for the acquisition? How can this concern be satisfied?

1. If the fair market value of real estate and improvements owned by the corporation whose stock is being acquired exceeds its cost, can the purchaser of the stock obtain a new title insurance policy that reflects the present state of title and fair market value of the real estate and improvements?

e. Will a state's Blue Sky laws or the Federal Securities Acts apply to the purchase of stock? See Division III, pages 882 to 913 infra.

10. The participants in the partnership form of doing business also have the choice of selling partnership assets or the partners selling their partnership interests.

11. In Bravenec, *Disposition of the Partnership Continuing Business—A Problem of Creeping Confusion*, 26 Tax Law. 275 (1973), the author asserts that a disposition, even if carried out as a sale of partnership assets, should be treated as a sale of the partners' interests. He indicates, however, that the Internal Revenue Service may try to cast a disposition, no matter how carried out, as a disposition by the partnership of its assets. See Rev.Rul. 72–172, 1972–1 C.B. 265. But cf. Rev.Rul. 84–111, 1984–2 C.B. 88, in which the Internal Revenue Service takes the position that the method chosen by partners to incorporate a partnership will be respected.

12. If the partnership sells the assets, the purchaser will acquire an aggregate basis in the assets equal to the purchase price, under Section 1012. The result should be the same if the purchaser acquires the partnership interests of the partners. See Bravenec, *Disposition of the Partnership Continuing Business—A Problem of Creeping Confusion*, 26 Tax Law. 275, 277–278 (1973). If the purchaser acquires all of the partnership interests, the partnership will be treated as terminated under Section 708, and the purchaser will acquire an aggregate basis in the assets equal to the purchase price, under Section 732(b). If the purchaser acquires less than 50% of the interests in the

partnership, the basis of partnership assets may be adjusted for the benefit of the purchaser under Section 743 pursuant to a partnership election under Section 754.

13. Do any additional steps need to be taken to acquire the assets of a partnership if a single individual or corporation purchases the partnership interests of all the partners? Or, does the purchase itself terminate the existence of the partnership? For income tax purposes, the partnership will be considered terminated. See Section 708 and cf. *Austin v. United States*, 461 F.2d 733 (10th Cir.1972).

14. If less than all of the partnership interests are purchased and the partners whose interests are not purchased do not consent to the sale of the purchased partnership interests, what rights does the purchaser acquire? See Section 27 of the U.P.A., Section 19 of the U.L.P.A., and Sections 702 and 704 of the Rev.U.L.P.A. Can the purchaser of a general partnership interest petition a court for dissolution of the partnership? See Section 32(2) of the U.P.A. Can the purchaser of a limited partnership interest petition a court for dissolution of the partnership? Can the partners whose partnership interests were not purchased cause the dissolution and winding-up of the partnership, even if the time specified for dissolution of the partnership by the partnership agreement has not yet been reached? See Section 31(1)(c) of the U.P.A., and Sections 402 and 801(4) of the Rev.U.L.P.A. If so, can they require that the assets of the partnership be sold? See Section 38(1). If, however, the interest purchased is a limited partnership interest, the remaining limited and general partners do not have the ability to cause the dissolution of the partnership as a result of the purchase. Cf. Hillman, *The Dissatisfied Participant in the Solvent Business Venture: A Consideration of the Relative Permanence of Partnerships and Close Corporations,* 67 Minn.L.Rev. 1 (1982); Hillman, *Misconduct as a Basis for Excluding or Expelling a Partner: Effecting Commercial Divorce and Securing Custody of the Business,* 78 Nw.U.L.Rev. 527 (1983); Hillman, *Private Ordering Within Partnerships,* 41 U.Miami L.Rev. 425 (1987).

6. ORDINARY INCOME OR CAPITAL GAIN

While the concepts, methods and analyses which are used to distinguish capital gain from ordinary income and to determine whether a transaction produces capital gain or ordinary income are considered in this chapter, a number of related questions, situations and concerns are also examined. The following are examples of the related questions, situations and concerns which are considered in this chapter. (1) Since capital losses can be used in full against capital gains by corporations and other taxpayers and, in addition, other taxpayers can use capital losses only to the extent of $3,000 in any one year against ordinary income, it is important to determine whether a taxpayer has derived capital gain or loss or ordinary income or loss as the result of a transaction. See Section 1211. (2) Net capital gain is deductible in computing undistributed personal holding company income for the purpose of determining whether a corporation is subject to the penalty tax on personal holding companies. See Section 545(b)(5). (3) A taxpayer who is a dealer in real estate rather than an owner of rental real estate may not be subject to the limitations on the use of passive losses and credits, under Section 469. (4) In the ordinary case, a distribution of property by a partnership to a partner is a nontaxable event. If, however, Section 751 is applicable to the distribution, it may be treated as a taxable constructive sale. (5) If the "collapsible partnership" provision, Section 751(a), is applicable to the sale of a partnership interest, the selling partner may recognize ordinary income on the disposition of his interest in "Section 751 assets" and a capital loss on the disposition of the remainder of his partnership interest. If Section 751 is not applicable, the selling partner will only recognize capital gain or loss equal to the amount of ordinary income less the amount of capital loss. (6) Some of the gain realized on the sale of an asset in exchange for an installment obligation may have to be recognized at the point of sale, under Section 453(i), rather than when payments are received, because part of the gain represents depreciation recapture. (7) Part of the gain realized on the sale or redemption of a partnership interest in exchange for an installment obligation may have to be recognized on the date of the transaction, rather than when payments are received, because under Section 751, part of the transaction is treated as a sale of inventory, see Section 453(b)(2)(B), or as a disposition of installment obligations, see Section 453B, or as the recapture of depreciation, see Section 453(i). (8) The "collapsible corporation" provision, Section 341, may cause the gain from the sale of the stock of a corporation or its liquidation to be treated as ordinary income rather than capital gain thereby limiting the amount of capital loss which can be used to offset the gain.

a. INVESTOR OR DEALER

The treatment of the gain or loss realized by a vendor on the disposition of real estate depends on whether the real estate is a capital asset as defined in Section 1221 of the Internal Revenue Code or property subject to treatment under Section 1231 as property used in the trade or business. If the real estate is considered part of the vendor's stock in trade, inventory, or held by the vendor primarily for sale to customers in the ordinary course of business, the gain or loss will be treated as ordinary rather than as capital.

BIEDENHARN REALTY CO., INC. v. UNITED STATES

United States Court of Appeals, Fifth Circuit, 1976.
526 F.2d 409.
[some footnotes omitted]

GOLDBERG, Circuit Judge. The taxpayer-plaintiff, Biedenharn Realty Company, Inc. [Biedenharn], filed suit against the United States in May, 1971, claiming a refund for the tax years 1964, 1965, and 1966. In its original tax returns for the three years, Biedenharn listed profits of $254,409.47 from the sale of 38 residential lots. Taxpayer divided this gain, attributing 60% to ordinary income and 40% to capital gains. Later, having determined that the profits from these sales were entirely ordinary income, the Internal Revenue Service assessed and collected additional taxes and interest. In its present action, plaintiff asserts that the whole real estate profit represents gain from the sale of capital assets and consequently that the Government is indebted to taxpayer for $32,006.86 in overpaid taxes. Reviewing the facts of this case in the light of our previous holdings and the directions set forth in this opinion, we reject plaintiff's claim and in so doing reverse the opinion of the District Court.

I.

* * *

A. *The Realty Company.* Joseph Biedenharn organized the Biedenharn Realty Company in 1923 as a vehicle for holding and managing the Biedenharn family's numerous investments. The original stockholders were all family members. The investment company controls, among other interests, valuable commercial properties, a substantial stock portfolio, a motel, warehouses, a shopping center, residential real property, and farm property.

B. *Taxpayer's Real Property Sales—The Hardtimes Plantation.* Taxpayer's suit most directly involves its ownership and sale of lots from the 973 acre tract located near Monroe, Louisiana, known as the Hardtimes Plantation. The plaintiff purchased the [tract] in 1935 for $50,000.00. B.W. Biedenharn, the Realty Company's president, testified that taxpayer acquired Hardtimes as a "good buy" for the purpose of farming and as a future investment. The plaintiff farmed the land for several years. Thereafter, Biedenharn rented part of the acreage to a farmer who Mr. Biedenharn suggested may presently be engaged in farming operations.

1. *The Three Basic Subdivisions.* Between 1939 and 1966, taxpayer carved three basic subdivisions from Hardtimes—Biedenharn Estates, Bayou DeSiard Country Club Addition, and Oak Park Addition—covering approximately 185 acres. During these years, Biedenharn sold 208 subdivided Hardtimes lots in 158 sales, making a profit in excess of $800,000.00. These three basic subdivisions are the source of the contested 37 sales of 38 lots. Their development and disposition are more fully discussed below.

(a) Biedenharn Estates Unit 1, including 41.9 acres, was platted in 1938. Between 1939 and 1956, taxpayer apparently sold 21 lots in 9 sales. Unit 2, containing 8.91 acres, was sold in 9 transactions between 1960 and 1965 and involved 10 lots.

(b) Bayou DeSiard Country Club Addition, covering 61 acres, was subdivided in 1951, with remaining lots resubdivided in 1964. Approximately 73 lots were purchased in 64 sales from 1951 to 1966.

(c) Oak Park Units 1 and 2 encompassed 75 acres. After subdivision in 1955 and resubdivision in 1960, plaintiff sold approximately 104 lots in 76 sales.

2. *Additional Hardtimes Sales.* Plaintiff lists at least 12 additional Hardtimes sales other than lots vended from the three basic subdivi-

sions. The earliest of these dispositions occurred in November, 1935, thirteen days after the Plantation's purchase. Ultimately totaling approximately 275 acres, most, but not all, of these sales involved large parcels of nonsubdivided land.

C. *Taxpayer's Real Property Activity: Non–Hardtimes Sales.* The 208 lots marketed from the three Hardtimes subdivisions represent only part of Biedenharn's total real property sales activities. Although the record does not in every instance permit exactitude, plaintiff's own submissions make clear that the Biedenharn Realty Company effectuated numerous non–Hardtimes retail real estate transactions. From the Company's formation in 1923 through 1966, the last year for which taxes are contested, taxpayer sold 934 lots. Of this total, plaintiff disposed of 249 lots before 1935 when it acquired Hardtimes. Thus, in the years 1935 to 1966, taxpayer sold 477 lots apart from its efforts with respect to the basic Hardtimes subdivisions. * * *

Unfortunately, the record does not unambiguously reveal the number of *sales* as opposed to the number of *lots* involved in these dispositions. Although some doubt exists as to the actual *sales* totals, even the most conservative reading of the figures convinces us of the frequency and abundance of the non-Hardtimes sales. For example, from 1925 to 1958, Biedenharn consummated from its subdivided Owens tract a minimum of 125, but perhaps upwards of 300, sales (338 lots). Eighteen sales accounted for 20 lots sold between 1923 and 1958 from Biedenharn's Cornwall property. Taxpayer's disposition from 1927 to 1960 of its Corey and Cabeen property resulted in at least 50 sales. Plaintiff made 14 sales from its Thomas Street lots between 1937 and 1955. Moreover, Biedenharn has sold over 20 other properties, a few of them piecemeal, since 1923.

Each of these parcels has its own history. Joseph Biedenharn transferred much of the land to the Realty Company in 1923. The company acquired other property through purchases and various forms of foreclosure. Before sale, Biedenharn held some tracts for commercial or residential rental. Taxpayer originally had slated the Owens acreage for transfer in bulk to the Owens–Illinois Company. Also, the length of time between acquisition and disposition differed significantly among pieces of realty. However, these variations in the background of each plot and the length of time and original purpose for which each was obtained do not alter the fact that the Biedenharn Realty Company regularly sold substantial amounts of subdivided and improved real property, and further, that these sales were not confined to the basic Hardtimes subdivisions.

D. *Real Property Improvements.* Before selling the Hardtimes lots, Biedenharn improved the land, adding in most instances streets, drainage, water, sewerage, and electricity. The total cost of bettering the Plantation acreage exceeded $200,000 and included $9,519.17 for Biedenharn Estates Unit 2, $56,879.12 for Bayou DeSiard Country Club Addition, and $141,579.25 for the Oak Park Addition.

E. *Sale of the Hardtimes Subdivisions.* Bernard Biedenharn testified that at the time of the Hardtimes purchase, no one foresaw that the land would be sold as residential property in the future. Accordingly, the District Court found, and we do not disagree, that Biedenharn bought Hardtimes for investment. Later, as the City of Monroe expanded northward, the Plantation became valuable residential property. The Realty Company staked off the Bayou DeSiard subdivision so that prospective purchasers could see what the lots "looked like." As demand increased, taxpayer opened the Oak Park and Biedenharn Estates Unit 2 subdivisions and resubdivided the Bayou DeSiard section. Taxpayer handled all Biedenharn Estates and Bayou DeSiard sales. Independent realtors disposed of many of the Oak Park lots. * * * Of the 37 sales consummated between 1964 and 1966, Henry Biedenharn handled at least nine transactions (Biedenharn Estates (2) and Bayou DeSiard (7)) while "independent realtors" effected some, if not all, of the other 28 transactions (Oak Park Unit 2.). Taxpayer delegated significant responsibilities to these brokers. * * *

In contrast to these broker induced dispositions, plaintiff's non-brokered sales resulted after unsolicited individuals approached Realty Company employees with inquiries about prospective purchases. At no time did the plaintiff hire its own real estate salesmen or engage in formal advertising. Apparently, the lands' prime location and plaintiff's subdivision activities constituted sufficient notice to interested persons of the availability of Hardtimes lots. Henry Biedenharn testified:

> [O]nce we started improving and putting roads and streets in people would call us up and ask you about buying a lot and we would sell a lot if they wanted it.

The Realty Company does not maintain a separate place of business but instead offices at the Biedenharn family's Ouachita Coca–Cola bottling plant. A telephone, listed in plaintiff's name, rings at the Coca–Cola building. Biedenharn has four employees: a camp caretaker, a tenant farmer, a bookkeeper and a manager. The manager, Henry Biedenharn, Jr., devotes approximately 10% of his time to the Realty Company, mostly collecting rents and overseeing the maintenance of various properties. The bookkeeper also works only part-time for plaintiff. Having set out these facts, we now discuss the relevant legal standard for resolving this controversy.

II.

* * * In this case, we confront the question whether or not Biedenharn's real estate sales should be [treated as resulting in ordinary income] because they fall within the exception covering "property held by the taxpayer primarily for sale to customers in the ordinary course of his trade or business." 26 U.S.C. § 1221(1).[2]

2. Neither party contends, nor do we find, that Internal Revenue Code § 1237, guaranteeing capital gains treatment to subdividing taxpayers in certain instances, is applicable to the facts of this suit.

The problem we struggle with here is not novel. We have become accustomed to the frequency with which taxpayers litigate this troublesome question. Chief Judge Brown appropriately described the real estate capital gains-ordinary income issue as "old, familiar, recurring, vexing and ofttimes elusive." Thompson v. Commissioner of Internal Revenue, 5 Cir.1963, 322 F.2d 122, 123. The difficulty in large part stems from ad-hoc application of the numerous permissible criteria set forth in our multitudinous prior opinions. Over the past 40 years, this case by case approach with its concentration on the facts of each suit has resulted in a collection of decisions not always reconcilable. Recognizing the situation, we have warned that efforts to distinguish and thereby make consistent the Court's previous holdings must necessarily be "foreboding and unrewarding." *Thompson, supra* at 127. *See* Williams v. United States, 5 Cir.1964, 329 F.2d 430, 431. Litigants are cautioned that "each case must be decided on its own peculiar facts. * * * Specific factors, or combinations of them are not necessarily controlling." *Thompson, supra* at 127; Wood v. Commissioner of Internal Revenue, 5 Cir.1960, 276 F.2d 586, 590; Smith v. Commissioner of Internal Revenue, 5 Cir.1956, 232 F.2d 142, 144. Nor are these factors the equivalent of the philosopher's stone, separating "sellers garlanded with capital gains from those beflowered in the garden of ordinary income." United States v. Winthrop, 5 Cir.1969, 417 F.2d 905, 911.

Assuredly, we would much prefer one or two clearly defined, easily employed tests which lead to predictable, perhaps automatic, conclusions. However, the nature of the congressional "capital asset" definition and the myriad situations to which we must apply that standard make impossible any easy escape from the task before us. No one set of criteria is applicable to all economic structures. Moreover, within a collection of tests, individual factors have varying weights and magnitudes, depending on the facts of the case. The relationship among the factors and their mutual interaction is altered as each criteria increases or diminishes in strength, sometimes changing the controversy's outcome. As such, there can be no mathematical formula capable of finding the X of capital gains or ordinary income in this complicated field.

Yet our inability to proffer a panaceatic guide to the perplexed with respect to this subject does not preclude our setting forth some general, albeit inexact, guidelines for the resolution of many of the § 1221(1) cases we confront. This opinion does not purport to reconcile all past precedents or assure conflict-free future decisions. Nor do we hereby obviate the need for ad-hoc adjustments when confronted with close cases and changing factual circumstances. Instead, with the hope of clarifying a few of the area's mysteries, we more precisely define and suggest points of emphasis for the major *Winthrop* delineated factors [3] as they appear in the instant controversy. * * *

3. In *United States v. Winthrop*, 5 Cir. 1969, 417 F.2d 905, 910, the Court enumerated the following factors:

(1) the nature and purpose of the acquisition of the property and the duration of the ownership; (2) the extent and nature of the taxpayer's efforts to sell the property; (3) the number, extent, continuity and substantiality of the sales; (4) the extent of subdividing, developing, and advertising to increase sales; (5) the use of a business office for

III.

We begin our task by evaluating in the light of *Biedenharn*'s facts the main *Winthrop* factors—substantiality and frequency of sales, improvements, solicitation and advertising efforts, and brokers' activities—as well as a few miscellaneous contentions. A separate section follows discussing the keenly contested role of prior investment intent. Finally, we consider the significance of the Supreme Court's decision in Malat v. Riddell.[4]

A. *Frequency and Substantiality of Sales*

Scrutinizing closely the record and briefs, we find that plaintiff's real property sales activities compel an ordinary income conclusion. In arriving at this result, we examine first the most important of *Winthrop*'s factors—the frequency and substantiality of taxpayer's sales. Although frequency and substantiality of sales are not usually conclusive, they occupy the preeminent ground in our analysis. * * * [W]hen dispositions of subdivided property extend over a long period of time and are especially numerous, the likelihood of capital gains is very slight indeed. * * * Conversely, when sales are few and isolated, the taxpayer's claim to capital gain is accorded greater deference. * * *

On the present facts, taxpayer could not claim "isolated" sales or a passive and gradual liquidation. * * * Although only three years and 37 sales (38 lots) are in controversy here, taxpayer's pre–1964 sales from the Hardtimes acreage as well as similar dispositions from other properties are probative of the existence of sales "in the ordinary course of his trade or business." *See* Levin, *Capital Gains Or Income Tax on Real Estate Sales,* 37 B.U.L.Rev. 165, 170 & n. 29 (1957). * * * Biedenharn sold property, usually a substantial number of lots, in every year, save one, from 1923 to 1966. Biedenharn's long and steady history of improved lot sales at least equals that encountered in Thompson v. Commissioner of Internal Revenue, 5 Cir.1963, 322 F.2d 122, where also we noted the full history of real estate activity. Supra at 124–25. There taxpayer lost on a finding that he had sold 376½ lots over a 15 year span—this notwithstanding that overall the other sales indicia were more in taxpayer's favor than in the present case. Moreover, the contested tax years in that suit involved only ten sales (28 lots); yet we labeled that activity "substantial." Supra at 125.

The frequency and substantiality of Biedenharn's sales go not only to its holding purpose and the existence of a trade or business but also support our finding of the ordinariness with which the Realty Company

the sale of the property; (6) the character and degree of supervision or control exercised by the taxpayer over any representative selling the property; and (7) the time and effort the taxpayer habitually devoted to the sales.

The numbering indicates no hierarchy of importance.

4. 383 U.S. 569, 86 S.Ct. 1030, 16 L.Ed. 2d 102 (1966).

disposed of its lots. These sales easily meet the criteria of normalcy set forth in *Winthrop,* supra at 912.

Furthermore, in contrast with Goldberg v. Commissioner of Internal Revenue, 5 Cir.1955, 223 F.2d 709, 713, where taxpayer did not reinvest his sales proceeds, one could fairly infer that the income accruing to the Biedenharn Realty Company from its pre–1935 sales helped support the purchase of the Hardtimes Plantation. Even if taxpayer made no significant acquisitions after Hardtimes, the "purpose, system, and continuity" of Biedenharn's efforts easily constitute a business. * * * [T]he District Court sought to overcome this evidence of dealer-like real estate activities and property "primarily held for sale" by clinging to the notion that the taxpayer was merely liquidating a prior investment. We discuss later the role of former investment status and the possibility of taxpayer relief under that concept. Otherwise, the question of liquidation of an investment is simply the opposite side of the inquiry as to whether or not one is holding property primarily for sale in the ordinary course of his business. In other words, a taxpayer's claim that he is liquidating a prior investment does not really present a separate theory but rather restates the main question currently under scrutiny. * * * [W]e believe that the present case, with taxpayer's energetic subdivision activities and consummation of numerous retail property dispositions, is governed by our * * * recent decision in Thompson v. Commissioner of Internal Revenue, [322 F.2d 122 (5th Cir.1963)] at 127–28. There, the Court observed:

> The liquidation, if it really is that, may therefore be carried out with business efficiency. Smith v. Commissioner of Internal Revenue, 5 Cir.1956, 232 F.2d 142, 145. But what was once an investment, or what may start out as a liquidation of an investment, may become something else. The Tax Court was eminently justified in concluding that this took place here. It was a regular part of the trade or business of Taxpayer to sell these lots to any and all comers who would meet his price. From 1944 on when the sales commenced, there is no evidence that he thereafter held the lots for any purpose other than the sale to prospective purchasers. It is true that he testified in conclusory terms that he was trying to "liquidate" but on objective standards the Tax Court could equate held solely with "held primarily." And, of course, there can be no question at all that purchasers of these lots were "customers" and that whether we call Taxpayer a "dealer" or a "trader", a real estate man or otherwise, the continuous sales of these lots down to the point of exhaustion was a regular and ordinary (and profitable) part of his business activity.

* * *

B. *Improvements*

Although we place greatest emphasis on the frequency and substantiality of sales over an extended time period, our decision in this instance is aided by the presence of taxpayer activity—particularly improvements—in the other *Winthrop* areas. Biedenharn vigorously improved its subdivisions, generally adding streets, drainage, sewerage, and utilities. These alterations are comparable to those in *Winthrop,* supra at 906, except that in the latter case taxpayer built five houses. We do not think that the construction of five houses in the context of *Winthrop*'s 456 lot sales significantly distinguishes that taxpayer from Biedenharn. In Barrios Estate v. Commissioner of Internal Revenue, 5 Cir.1959, 265 F.2d 517, 520, heavily relied on by plaintiff, the Court reasoned that improvements constituted an integral part of the sale of subdivided realty and were therefore permissible in the context of a liquidating sale. As discussed above, Biedenharn's activities have removed it from any harbor of investment liquidation. Moreover, the additional sales flexibility permitted the *Barrios Estate* taxpayer might be predicated on the forced change of purpose examined in section IV. Finally, in *Thompson,* supra, the plaintiff's only activities were subdivision and improvement. Yet, not availing ourselves of the opportunity to rely on a *Barrios Estate* type "liquidation plus integrally related improvements theory," we found no escape from ordinary income.

C.   *Solicitation and Advertising Efforts*

Substantial, frequent sales and improvements such as we have encountered in this case will usually conclude the capital gains issue against taxpayer. See, e.g., *Thompson,* supra. Thus, on the basis of our analysis to this point, we would have little hesitation in finding that taxpayer held "primarily for sale" in the "ordinary course of [his] trade or business." "[T]he flexing of commercial muscles with frequency and continuity, design and effect" of which *Winthrop* spoke, supra at 911, is here a reality. This reality is further buttressed by Biedenharn's sales efforts, including those carried on through brokers. Minimizing the importance of its own sales activities, taxpayer points repeatedly to its steady avoidance of advertising or other solicitation of customers. Plaintiff directs our attention to stipulations detailing the population growth of Monroe and testimony outlining the economic forces which made Hardtimes Plantation attractive residential property and presumably eliminated the need for sales exertions. We have no quarrel with plaintiff's description of this familiar process of suburban expansion, but we cannot accept the legal inferences which taxpayer would have us draw.

The Circuit's recent decisions in *Thompson,* supra at 124–26, and *Winthrop,* supra at 912, implicitly recognize that even one inarguably in the real estate business need not engage in promotional exertions in the face of a favorable market. As such, we do not always require a showing of active solicitation where "business * * * [is] good, indeed brisk," *Thompson,* supra at 124, and where other *Winthrop* factors make obvious taxpayer's ordinary trade or business status. * * * Plainly, this represents a sensible approach. In cases such as *Biedenharn,* the sale of a few lots and the construction of the first homes, albeit not, as in *Winthrop,* by the taxpayer, as well as the building of roads, addition of utilities, and staking off of the other subdivided parcels constitute a highly visible form of advertising. Prospective home buyers drive by the advantageously located property, see the development activities, and are as surely put on notice of the availability of lots as if the owner had erected large signs announcing "residential property for sale." We do not by this evaluation automatically neutralize advertising or solicitation as a factor in our analysis. This form of inherent notice is not present in all land sales, especially where the property is not so valuably located, is not subdivided into small lots, and is not improved. Moreover, inherent notice represents only one band of the solicitation spectrum. Media utilization and personal initiatives remain material components of this criterion. When present, they call for greater Government oriented emphasis on *Winthrop*'s solicitation factor.

D. *Brokerage Activities*

In evaluating Biedenharn's solicitation activities, we need not confine ourselves to the *Thompson–Winthrop* theory of brisk sales without organizational efforts. Unlike in *Thompson* and *Winthrop* where no one undertook overt solicitation efforts, the Realty Company hired brokers who, using media and on site advertising, worked vigorously on taxpayer's behalf. We do not believe that the employment of brokers should shield plaintiff from ordinary income treatment. * * * Their activities should at least in discounted form be attributed to Biedenharn. To the contrary, taxpayer argues that "one who is not already in the trade or business of selling real estate does not enter such business when he employs a broker who acts as an independent contractor. Fahs v. Crawford, 161 F.2d 315 (5 Cir.1947); Smith v. Dunn, 224 F.2d 353 (5 Cir.1955)." Without presently entangling ourselves in a dispute as to the differences between an agent and an independent contractor, * * * we find the cases cited distinguishable from the instant circumstances. In both *Fahs* and *Smith,* the taxpayer turned the entire property over to brokers, who, having been granted total responsibility, made all decisions including the setting of sales prices. In comparison, Biedenharn determined original prices and general credit policy. Moreover, the Realty Company did not make all the sales in question through brokers as did taxpayers in *Fahs* and *Smith.* Biedenharn sold the Bayou DeSiard and Biedenharn Estates lots and may well have sold some of the Oak Park land. In other words, unlike *Fahs* and *Smith,* Biedenharn's brokers did not so completely take charge of the whole of the Hardtimes sales as to permit the Realty Company to wall itself off legally from their activities.

E. *Additional Taxpayer Contentions*

Plaintiff presents a number of other contentions and supporting facts for our consideration. Although we set out these arguments and briefly discuss them, their impact, in the face of those factors examined above, must be minimal. Taxpayer emphasizes that its profits from real estate sales averaged only 11.1% in each of the years in controversy, compared to 52.4% in *Winthrop*. Whatever the percentage, plaintiff would be hard pressed to deny the substantiality of its Hardtimes sales in absolute terms (the subdivided lots alone brought in over one million dollars) or, most importantly, to assert that its real estate business was too insignificant to constitute a separate trade or business.[5]

The relatively modest income share represented by Biedenharn's real property dispositions stems not from a failure to engage in real estate sales activities but rather from the comparatively large profit attributable to the Company's 1965 ($649,231.34) and 1966 ($688,840.82) stock sales. The fact of Biedenharn's holding, managing, and selling stock is not inconsistent with the existence of a separate realty business. If in the face of taxpayer's numerous real estate dealings this Court held otherwise, we would be sanctioning special treatment for those individuals and companies arranging their business activities so that the income accruing to real estate sales represents only a small fraction of the taxpaying entity's total gains.

Similarly, taxpayer observes that Biedenharn's manager devoted only 10% of his time to real estate dealings and then mostly to the company's rental properties. This fact does not negate the existence of sales activities. Taxpayer had a telephone listing, a shared business office, and a few part-time employees. Because, as discussed before, a strong seller's market existed, Biedenharn's sales required less than the usual solicitation efforts and therefore less than the usual time. Moreover, plaintiff, unlike taxpayers in *Winthrop,* supra and *Thompson,* supra, hired brokers to handle many aspects of the Hardtimes transactions—thus further reducing the activity and time required of Biedenharn's employees.

Finally, taxpayer argues that it is entitled to capital gains since its enormous profits (74% to 97%) demonstrate a return based principally on capital appreciation and not on taxpayer's "merchandising" efforts. We decline the opportunity to allocate plaintiff's gain between long-term market appreciation and improvement related activities. * * * Even if we undertook such an analysis and found the former element predominant, we would on the authority of *Winthrop,* supra at 907–908, reject plaintiff's contention * * *.[6]

5. This Court has repeatedly recognized that a taxpayer may have more than one trade or business for purposes of Internal Revenue Code § 1221(1). *See,* e.g., Ackerman v. United States, 5 Cir.1964, 335 F.2d 521, 524; Gamble v. Commissioner of Internal Revenue, 5 Cir.1957, 242 F.2d 586, 591; Fahs v. Crawford, 5 Cir.1947, 161 F.2d 315, 317.

6. In Galena Oaks Corp. v. Scofield, 5 Cir.1954, 218 F.2d 217, 220, the Court said:

"Congress intended to alleviate the burden on a taxpayer whose property has increased in value over a long period of time. When, however, such a taxpayer endeavors still further to increase his profits by engaging in a business separable from his investment, it is not unfair that his gain should be taxed as ordinary income."

IV.

The District Court found that "[t]axpayer is merely liquidating over a long period of time a substantial investment in the most advantageous method possible." 356 F.Supp. at 1336. In this view, the original investment intent is crucial, for it preserves the capital gains character of the transaction even in the face of normal real estate sales activities.

The Government asserts that Biedenharn Realty Company did not merely "liquidate" an investment but instead entered the real estate business in an effort to dispose of what was formerly investment property. Claiming that Biedenharn's activities would result in ordinary income if the Hardtimes Plantation had been purchased with the intent to divide and resell the property, and finding no reason why a different prior intent should influence this outcome,[7] the Government concludes that original investment purpose is irrelevant. Instead, the Government would have us focus exclusively on taxpayer's intent and the level of sales activity during the period commencing with subdivision and improvement and lasting through final sales. Under this theory, every individual who improves and frequently sells substantial numbers of land parcels would receive ordinary income.[8]

While the facts of this case dictate our agreement with the Internal Revenue Service's ultimate conclusion of taxpayer liability, they do not require our acquiescence in the Government's entreated total elimination of *Winthrop*'s first criterion, "the nature and purpose of the acquisition." Undoubtedly, in most subdivided-improvement situations, an investment purpose of antecedent origin will not survive into a present era of intense retail selling. The antiquated purpose, when overborne by later, but substantial and frequent selling activity, will not prevent ordinary income from being visited upon the taxpayer. * * * Generally, investment purpose has no built-in perpetuity nor a guarantee of capital gains forever more. Precedents, however, in certain circumstances have permitted landowners with earlier investment intent to sell subdivided property and remain subject to capital gains treatment. See, e.g., Cole v. Usry, 5 Cir.1961, 294 F.2d 426; Barrios Estate v. Commissioner of Internal Revenue, 5 Cir.1959, 265 F.2d 517; Smith v. Dunn, 5 Cir.1955, 224 F.2d 353.

The Government, attacking these precedents, argues that the line of cases decided principally in the 1950's represented by *Barrios Estate,* supra; Goldberg v. Commissioner of Internal Revenue, 5 Cir.1955, 223

---

7. The Government emphasizes the "unfairness" of two taxpayers engaging in equal sales efforts with respect to similar tracts of land but receiving different tax treatment because of divergent initial motives.

8. The Government suggests that taxpayer can avoid ordinary income treatment by selling the undivided, unimproved tract to a controlled corporation which would then develop the land. However, this approach would in many instances create attribution problems with the Government arguing that the controlled corporation's sales are actually those of the taxpayer. See, e.g., Ackerman v. United States, 5 Cir.1964, 335 F.2d 521, 527–528. Furthermore, we are not prepared to tell taxpayers that in all cases a single bulk sale provides the only road to capital gains.

F.2d 709; Ross v. Commissioner of Internal Revenue, 5 Cir.1955, 227 F.2d 265 and including United States v. Temple, 5 Cir.1966, 355 F.2d 67, are inconsistent with our earlier holdings in *Galena Oaks Corp.,* supra; White v. Commissioner of Internal Revenue, 5 Cir.1949, 172 F.2d 629, * * * and the trend of our most recent decisions * * *. Because of the ad-hoc nature of these previous decisions and the difficulty of determining in each instance the exact combination of factors which placed a case on one side or the other of the capital gains-ordinary income boundary, we are loath to overrule any of these past decisions. In a sense, we adhere to our own admonitions against efforts at reconciling and making consistent all that has gone before in the subdivided realty area. But in so avoiding a troublesome and probably unrewarding task, we are not foreclosed from the more important responsibility of giving future direction with respect to the much controverted role of prior investment intent, nor are we precluded from analyzing that factor's impact in the context of the present controversy.

We reject the Government's sweeping contention that prior investment intent is always irrelevant. There will be instances where an initial investment purpose endures in controlling fashion notwithstanding continuing sales activity. We doubt that this aperture, where an active subdivider and improver receives capital gains, is very wide; yet we believe it exists. We would most generally find such an opening where the change from investment holding to sales activity results from unanticipated, externally induced factors which make impossible the continued pre-existing use of the realty. *Barrios Estate,* supra, is such a case. There the taxpayer farmed the land until drainage problems created by the newly completed intercoastal canal rendered the property agriculturally unfit. The Court found that taxpayer was "dispossessed of the farming operation through no act of her own." Supra at 518. Similarly, Acts of God, condemnation of part of one's property, new and unfavorable zoning regulations, or other events forcing alteration of taxpayer's plans create situations making possible subdivision and improvement as a part of a capital gains disposition.[9]

* * * [When, however,] the changes ensued from taxpayers' purely *voluntary* responses to increased economic opportunity—albeit at times externally created—in order to enhance their gain through the subdivision, improvement, and sale of lots, * * * we gravitate toward the Government's view * * * and grant the taxpayer little, if any, benefit from *Winthrop*'s first criterion * * *.

9. A Boston University Law Review article canvassing factors inducing involuntary changes of purpose in subdivided realty cases enumerates among others the following: a pressing need for funds in general, illness or old age or both, the necessity for liquidating a partnership on the death of a partner, the threat of condemnation, and municipal zoning restrictions. Levin, *Capital Gains or Income Tax on Real Estate Sales,* 37 B.U.L.Rev.1965, 194–95 (1957). Although we might not accept all of these events as sufficient to cause an outcome favorable to taxpayer, they are suggestive of the sort of change of purpose provoking events delineated above as worthy of special consideration.

The distinction drawn above reflects our belief that Congress did not intend to automatically disqualify from capital gains bona fide investors forced to abandon prior purposes for reasons beyond their control. At times, the Code may be severe, and this Court may construe it strictly, but neither Code nor Court is so tyrannical as to mandate the absolute rule urged by the Government. However, we caution that although permitting a land owner substantial sales flexibility where there is a forced change from original investment purpose, we do not absolutely shield the constrained taxpayer from ordinary income. That taxpayer is not granted *carte blanche* to undertake intensely all aspects of a full blown real estate business. Instead, in cases of forced change of purpose, we will continue to utilize the *Winthrop* analysis discussed earlier but will place unusually strong taxpayer-favored emphasis on *Winthrop*'s first factor.

Clearly, under the facts in this case, the distinction just elaborated undermines Biedenharn's reliance on original investment purpose. Taxpayer's change of purpose was entirely voluntary and therefore does not fall within the protected area. Moreover, taxpayer's original investment intent, *even if* considered a factor sharply supporting capital gains treatment, is so overwhelmed by the other *Winthrop* factors discussed supra, that that element can have no decisive effect. However wide the capital gains passageway through which a subdivider with former investment intent could squeeze, the Biedenharn Realty Company will never fit.

V.

The District Court, citing Malat v. Riddell, 1966, 383 U.S. 569, 86 S.Ct. 1030, 16 L.Ed.2d 102, stated that "the lots were not held * * * primarily for sale as that phrase was interpreted * * * in *Malat* * * *." 356 F.Supp. at 1335. Finding that Biedenharn's primary purpose became holding for sale and consequently that *Malat* in no way alters our analysis here, we disagree with the District Court's conclusion. *Malat* was a brief per curiam in which the Supreme Court decided only that as used in Internal Revenue Code § 1221(1) the word "primarily" means "principally," "of first importance." The Supreme Court, remanding the case, did not analyze the facts or resolve the controversy which involved a real estate dealer who had purchased land and held it at the time of sale with the dual intention of developing it as rental property or selling it, depending on whichever proved to be the more profitable. Malat v. Riddell, 9 Cir.1965, 347 F.2d 23, 26. In contrast, having substantially abandoned its investment and farming [10] intent, Biedenharn was cloaked primarily in the garb of sales

---

10. The District Court found that Biedenharn "is still farming a large part of the land * * *." 356 F.Supp. at 1336. The record suggests neither that Biedenharn as opposed to a lessee currently farms on the Hardtimes Plantation nor that the magnitude of that lessee's farming operations is substantial. More importantly, the District Court did not find and the plaintiff does not assert that Biedenharn simultaneously held the subdivided land for sale and for farming either before or at the time of disposition. Taxpayer claims no dual purpose.

purpose when it disposed of the 38 lots here in controversy. With this change, the Realty Company lost the opportunity of coming within any dual purpose analysis.

We do not hereby condemn to ordinary income a taxpayer merely because, as is usually true, his principal intent at the exact moment of disposition is sales. Rather, we refuse capital gains treatment in those instances where over time there has been such a thoroughgoing change of purpose * * * as to make untenable a claim either of twin intent or continued primacy of investment purpose.[11]

VI.

Having surveyed the Hardtimes terrain, we find no escape from ordinary income. The frequency and substantiality of sales over an extended time, the significant improvement of the basic subdivisions, the acquisition of additional properties, the use of brokers, and other less important factors persuasively combine to doom taxpayer's cause. Applying *Winthrop*'s criteria, this case clearly falls within the ordinary income category delineated in that decision.[12] In so concluding, we note that *Winthrop* does not represent the most extreme application of the overriding principle that "the definition of a capital asset must be narrowly applied and its exclusions interpreted broadly." Corn Products Refining Co. v. Commissioner of Internal Revenue, 1955, 350 U.S. 46, 52, 76 S.Ct. 20, 24, 100 L.Ed. 29, 35. * * *

We cannot write black letter law for all realty subdividers and for all times, but we do caution in words of red that once an investment does not mean always an investment. A simon-pure investor forty years ago could by his subsequent activities become a seller in the ordinary course four decades later. The period of Biedenharn's passivity is in the distant past; and the taxpayer has since undertaken the role of real estate protagonist. The Hardtimes Plantation in its day

11. *Winthrop,* supra, although different from *Biedenharn* in respect to initial intent, is not contrary to our *Malat* analysis. In *Winthrop,* taxpayer inherited property, a method of acquisition which is necessarily neutral as to original purpose. We found that after receipt of his legacy, the *Winthrop* taxpayer at all times held the lots "primarily for sale." *Winthrop,* supra at 911. Although encountering original investment purpose instead of neutral intent in the present case, we conclude that Biedenharn dissipated that initial purpose by its later sales activities. This alteration resulted in Biedenharn, like Winthrop, holding retail lots over an extended period "primarily for sale to customers in the ordinary course of [his] trade or business." Thus, in both cases, taxpayers moved to and maintained a primary sales purpose over an extended period. In neither instance did they hold for dual purposes.

12. The greater percentage of realty sales income, the construction of five houses, the holding of a real estate license, the originally neutral acquisition purpose, and the slightly higher pitch of sales in the years immediately preceding suit all characteristic of *Winthrop* do not make that case significantly different from *Biedenharn* any more than the longer history of sales, additional acquisition of land, use of a business office, existence of a telephone listing, original investment purpose, or employment of brokers who advertised and actively solicited customers characteristic of *Biedenharn* materially distinguish the present suit from *Winthrop.* The cases are at bottom similar. One need not go beyond *Winthrop* in order to decide the present dispute.

may have been one thing, but as the plantation was developed and sold, Hardtimes became by the very fact of change and activity a different holding than it had been at its inception. No longer could resort to initial purpose preserve taxpayer's once upon a time opportunity for favored treatment. The opinion of the District Court is reversed.

* * *

NOTE

1. As is obvious from an examination of *Biedenharn Realty Co., Inc. v. United States*, the "dealer-investor" determination is made through a factual investigation focusing on a number of factors, the relative importance of which may vary from case to case depending on the circumstances present.

a. See generally Pennell, *Capital Gains in Real Estate Transactions*, 1959 Tul.Tax Inst. 23; Sills, *The "Dealer–Investor" Problem: Observations, Analysis, and Suggestions for Future Development*, II J.Real Est.Tax'n 51 (1974); Kirkpatrick, *Real Estate: How to Separate the Investors from the Dealers*, 23 Tul.Tax Inst. 407 (1974); Sills, *The "Dealer–Investor" Problem Revisited: Charting a Course to Avoid the Pitfalls*, 4 J.Real Est.Tax'n 24 (1976); Brown, *Individual Investment in Real Estate: Capital Gains vs. Ordinary Income; Attaining Non-dealer Status; Structuring Disposition of Investment; Dealer as Investor; Implications of Investor–Dealer Partnership*, 34 N.Y.U.Inst.Fed.Tax'n 189 (1976); Goggans and Englebrecht, *Tax Implications of Investor vs. Dealer Status in Real Estate*, 9 J.Real Est.Tax'n 169 (1982); Friedlander, *"To Customers": The Forgotten Element in the Characterization of Gains on Sales of Real Property*, 39 Tax'n L.Rev. 31 (1983); Iden, *The Dealer Problem: Capital Gains and the Real Estate Investor*, 13 Real Est.L.J. 99 (1984).

b. The factors considered in making the "dealer-investor" determination include:

1. Circumstances of acquisition and the taxpayer's intent at that time,

2. Motives in, and reasons for, selling,

3. The taxpayer's trade or business at the time of the sales,

4. The number, frequency and continuity of sales,

5. The holding period of the property,

6. The extent, nature and timing of the taxpayer's efforts to promote sales including improvement of the property,

7. The extent and continuity of the taxpayer's sales activities as compared with other income producing activities, and

8. The substantiality of sales income taken by itself and as compared with the taxpayer's income from other sources.

c. In some instances, despite a short holding period and frequent and substantial sales, the lack of any substantial marketing efforts on the part of a taxpayer has led the courts to conclude that the taxpayer is entitled to capital gain treatment. See *Byram v. United States*, 705 F.2d 1418 (5th Cir. 1983); *D.J. Williams v. United States*, 53 A.F.T.R.2d 84-884 (N.D.Tex.1984).

d. A recurring problem involving the "dealer-investor" determination is whether an investor who converts an apartment building into a condominium and sells the units can ever hope to have the gain, if any, treated as capital gain. While the Internal Revenue Service ruled in Rev.Rul. 80–216, 1980–2 C.B. 239 that Section 1237, which provides partial capital gain treatment when limited subdivision activities are undertaken, does not apply to a condominium conversion, it has indicated that this position will not preclude capital gain treatment under any applicable section of the Internal Revenue Code other than Section 1237. See Priv.Ltr.Rul. 8204031. One might draw the inference from this revenue ruling that capital gain may be available in certain situations. See *Robert Erfurth,* 53 CCH Tax Ct.Mem. 767 (1987); *Charles R. Gangi,* 54 CCH Tax Ct.Mem. 1048 (1987). See generally Miller, *Can a Straight Condominium Conversion Produce a Capital Gain? An Analysis,* 54 J.Tax'n 8 (1981); Guerin, *Condominium Conversions: An Analysis of Alternative Routes to Capital Gain Treatment,* 1 Tax L.J. 1 (1982); Boris, *Co-ops and Condominiums Capital Gain on Conversion and Other Problems,* 40 N.Y.U.Inst.Fed.Tax'n 22–1 (1982); Kedzierski and Reinhart, *How to Maximize Capital Gains Upon the Conversion of Rental Housing to Condominiums,* 14 Tax'n Law. 42 (1985).

e. Can one sale produce ordinary income rather than capital gain? See *S & H, Inc.,* 78 T.C. 234 (1982). See also Rentenbach and Sowell, *In the Trade or Business of an Isolated Sale of Real Estate,* 51 Tenn.L.Rev. 319 (1984); Dedon, *Dealer v. Investor: The Internal Revenue Service Chokes on the "One Bite" Rule,* 65 Taxes 293 (1987).

2. Would a provision similar to Section 1236 which enables a dealer in securities to obtain capital gain treatment on the sale of certain securities providing certain preconditions are met be appropriate or useful in the real estate area?

a. Might a real estate dealer urge its application by analogy?

3. The "dealer-investor" determination is usually made by examining the taxpayer's conduct with respect to real estate which he either owns or has sold.

a. The dealer or investor status of one or more shareholders becomes important when determining whether the exception to collapsible corporation treatment provided by Section 341(e) is available. See pages 496 to 511 infra.

1. When this determination is being made, however, the real estate is owned by the corporation, rather than the shareholders who are being tested.

2. Can the shareholder or shareholders in question, even though he or they hold similar real estate for sale to customers in the ordinary course of business, claim, for the purposes of Section 341(e), that he or they are not "dealers" since he or they hold the stock of the corporation as an investment and have complied with the provisions of Section 1236?

b. The "dealer-investor" determination is also important when determining whether a partnership owns "substantially appreciated inventory" and whether real estate owned by a partnership, if held by a partner selling his interest in, or receiving a distribution from, the partnership should be considered inventory for the purposes of the collapsible partnership provision, Section 751. See pages 486 to 496 infra.

4. Assume that the Biedenharn Realty Co., Inc. has $255,000 of passive losses which it has been unable to use. Is it now terribly unhappy with the

Fifth Circuit Court of Appeal's decision in Biedenharn Realty Co., Inc. v. United States? See Section 469(e)(2). In fact, if Biedenharn Realty Co., Inc. possessed the passive losses and was currently litigating the case, might the position taken by the taxpayer and the Internal Revenue Service be reversed?

b. DEPRECIATION RECAPTURE, INVESTMENT CREDIT RECAPTURE AND THE MINIMUM TAXES

Even if the gain from the sale of real estate would be treated as capital gain, Sections 1245 and 1250 of the Internal Revenue Code provide that in certain circumstances part or all of the gain, which represents the recovery of depreciation previously taken, must be treated as ordinary income. In addition, if the vendor previously had claimed investment credits on the acquisition or rehabilitation of the assets sold, in some circumstances part, or all, of the investment credits must be recaptured. Last, as a result of the taxpayer's ownership of the assets and their treatment for income tax purposes, the taxpayer may be subject to the alternative minimum tax.

Since the rules for computing depreciation recapture on the "disposition" of depreciable real property have gone through a number of formulations and reformulations since January 1, 1964, the following discussion describes the depreciation recapture rules applicable to the depreciation of depreciable real property taken during defined time periods and assumes that the owner of the depreciable real property has not yet disposed of it.

With respect to depreciation taken on depreciable real property prior to January 1, 1970, there will not be any depreciation recapture on a sale or other disposition of the property.

With respect to depreciation taken during the period after December 31, 1969 and prior to January 1, 1976, "(with the exception of those categories noted immediately below) * * *: all depreciation [actually taken in excess of straight line depreciation ('excess depreciation'), if any,] attributable to periods after [December 31,] 1969 [is] recaptured [to the extent it does not exceed the gain realized on the sale, exchange or involuntary conversion of the property, or the excess of the fair market value of the property over its adjusted basis on any other disposition of the property.]

"The exceptions to the depreciation recapture * * * generally applicable to post–1969 but pre–1976 depreciation [are] as follows: (1) * * * [I]f [residential rental property is] disposed of after 100 full months [of ownership], there [is] a one percent phase-out [of depreciation recapture] for each full month, so that there [is] no recapture if [the property is] held for 200 months (or sixteen years and eight months). (2) [There is no depreciation recapture on the sale or other disposition of a] qualified housing project * * *. The concept of 'qualified housing projects' applie[s] to [depreciable real] property constructed, etc., prior to December [31,] 1975, as to which the mortgage was insured under Section 221(d)(3) or Section 236 of National Housing

Act, or housing financed or assisted by direct loan or tax abatement under similar provisions (that is, a limited rate of return; Sections 221(d)(3) and 236 are limited to 6 percent on equity investment) of state or local laws, and with respect to which the owner was subject to the restrictions under Section 1039(b)(1)(B). (3) * * * [T]he recapture rules [for rehabilitation expenditures are] the same as for residential rental property, except that the recapture * * * appl[ies] to the excess of the depreciation taken under Section 167(k) over the depreciation which would have been allowed to the date of disposition based on the use of straight line depreciation over the useful life of the property.

"With respect to any post-[December 31,] 1975 [and pre-January 1, 1981] depreciation, * * * taken on the basis of any property (other than qualified housing projects) * * *, all post–1975 excess depreciation as to residential rental property and all post–1969 excess depreciation as to all other depreciable real property is recaptured, but such recapture [can]not exceed the amount realized on the sale, exchange, or involuntary conversion, or the fair market value of such property on any other disposition, over the adjusted basis of the property.

"[A]s to qualified housing projects, * * * if the property is held for more than twelve full months, but 100 full months or less, then all excess depreciation is recaptured; and * * * if the property is held for more than 100 full months, there is a one percent phase-out for each full month, so that there is no recapture if the property is held for 200 months (or sixteen years and eight months). 'Qualified housing projects' are * * * Section 221(d)(3) or Section 236 projects, or similar state or local projects; Section 8 leased housing; Section 167(k) rehabilitation expenditures; and projects financed under Title V of the 1949 Housing Act (Farmers Home Administration)." [13]

With respect to depreciation taken after December 31, 1980, if an accelerated method of depreciation is used, except for residential rental property and qualified housing projects, all depreciation, to the extent it does not exceed the gain realized on the sale, exchange or involuntary conversion of the property or the excess of the fair market value of the property over its adjusted basis, is recaptured. The depreciation on residential rental property and qualified housing projects is recaptured only to the extent of the excess of accelerated depreciation over straight-line, and the amount of recapture is limited to the gain realized on disposition of the property as described above. If the use of straight-line depreciation is elected, there is no recapture on disposition regardless of the nature of the real property.

Since the cost of real estate improvements placed in service after December 31, 1986 must be recovered using the straight-line method, such improvements will not be subject to depreciation recapture unless the improvements are subject to a tax credit, such as a rehabilitation

13. Tucker, *Real Estate Depreciation: A Fresh Examination of the Basic Rules,* 6 J.Real Est.Tax'n 101, 128–130 (1979).

credit, resulting in the basis of the improvement being reduced by 100% of the credit claimed. In this case the post-December 31, 1980 rules will apply.

* * *

NOTE

1. "A building or structure is considered residential rental property for a taxable year *only* if 80% or more of the gross rental income from such building or structure during such year is rental income from dwelling units. If a portion of the building is occupied by the taxpayer, Section 167(j)(2)(B) indicates that the rental value of the portion so occupied is included in the gross rental income from such building. (Note that the word 'occupied' has been used; this may be ambiguous, in that the terms 'occupy' and 'dwell' are not necessarily co-equal.)

"A 'dwelling unit' is defined by Section 167(k)(3)(C) as a house or an apartment used to provide living accommodations in a building or structure, but not including units in a hotel, motel, inn or other establishment more than half of the units in which are used on a transient basis.

"Even though the building or structure may not qualify under the residential rental property test for one year, the implication of Section 167(j)(2) is that it may qualify under such test for the following year. * * *

"Thus, it should be noted that the 80% test is determined on a year-by-year basis, rather than causing the taxpayer to be bound forever by what occurs during the first year. This certainly is not without its complexities for accountants. * * * Section 167(j)(2)(C) states that [any] change [in the computation of the allowance for] depreciation * * * because the 80% test method is met in one year and not the next (or vice versa) [shall] not be considered a change in a method of accounting." Tucker, *An Analysis of Real Estate Investment Strategies Under the New Tax Law,* 32 J.Tax'n 184 (1970).

2. The recapture rules for tangible personal property are simple when compared to the recapture rules for real estate. In general, all depreciation taken after December 31, 1961 is recaptured to the extent of the amount realized in the case of a sale, exchange or involuntary conversion, or to the extent the fair market value of the transferred property exceeds its adjusted basis in the case of any other "disposition."

3. The "disposition" of real estate and tangible personal property for the purpose of recapture includes much more than simply a sale. In fact, it includes some transactions which are not taxable, or with respect to which the tax can be deferred, under other sections of the Internal Revenue Code. See Sections 1245(b) and 1250(d). For example, if an office building, which was put into service prior to December 31, 1986 and has been depreciated using a method faster than straight-line, is traded for an apartment building in a like-kind exchange, under Section 1031, the depreciation recapture on the office building, to the extent of the gain realized on the exchange, will be recognized. See Section 1245(b)(4)(B). If the office building is sold for an installment obligation, the depreciation recapture will be recognized, to the extent of the gain realized, even though the seller does not receive any payments in the year of the sale and is otherwise entitled to use the installment method to account for the gain. See Section 453(i).

4. See generally Tucker, *Analyzing the Impact of the 1976 Tax Reform Act on Real Estate Investments,* 45 J.Tax'n 346 (1976); Schwartz and Livingston, *What Price Accelerated Depreciation?,* 6 J. Real Est.Tax'n 32 (1978); Kahn, *Accelerated Depreciation—Tax Expenditure or Proper Allowance for Measuring Net Income?,* 78 Mich.L.Rev. 1 (1979); Fowler, *ERTA Recapture Rules for Buildings Used for Both Residential and Nonresidential Purposes,* 13 J.Real Est.Tax'n 328 (1986).

5. If property with respect to which a low-income, investment or rehabilitation credit was claimed is disposed of prior to the expiration of the period described in Section 42(i)(1) and (j)(1) (15 years for low-income credit property) or Section 47(a)(5)(E)(ii) (3 or 5 years for investment credit property and 5 years for rehabilitation credit property) part or all of the credit taken must be recaptured. See Sections 42(j)(1) and (2) and 47(a)(5)(A) and (B).

   a. In general, a disposition of property with respect to which a low-income housing credit was taken occurs when, during the fifteen-year period for any reason other than a casualty loss, the number or amount of floor space of low-income units of the taxpayer at the close of any taxable year is less than the number or amount of floor space of low-income units at the close of the preceding taxable year. See Section 47(j)(1).

      1. It, therefore, appears that any transaction, whether taxable or not, in which low-income units are disposed of or, for that matter no longer held as low-income units, may result in the recapture of part or all of the credits taken.

   b. "Disposition" for the purpose of the recapture of investment or rehabilitation credits, is defined more broadly than disposition for the purpose of depreciation recapture and not quite as broadly as it is defined for the purpose of the recapture of low-income housing credits. See Section 47(b) and Reg.Sec. 1.47–3. For example, in *Charles Long v. United States,* 652 F.2d 675 (6th Cir.1981), the Sixth Circuit Court of Appeals held that tax credits are recaptured when an S corporation liquidates distributing all of its assets, including those for which the investment credits were claimed, pro rata, to its shareholders. The Tax Court in *Joe Alvin Sexton,* 42 CCH Tax Ct.Mem. 1030 (1981), reached the same result when the former shareholders of an S corporation continued the business in partnership form. Last, in *Siller Bros., Inc.,* 89 T.C. 256 (1987), the Tax Court held that all tax credits must be recaptured when a partnership liquidated despite the fact that one of the two partners continued using the assets in the same trade or business after the liquidation. In Priv.Ltr.Rul. 8722025, however, no recapture of investment credits was required when a partnership was incorporated and the former partners retained the same percentage interests in the corporation. See generally Kramer and Kramer, *Recapture of the ITC and the "Mere Change in the Form of Conducting a Trade or Business" Exception,* 14 Tax Adviser 648 (1983).

   c. The recapture of tax credits is treated as an addition to tax for the year during which the disposition occurs.

   d. See generally Madden, *Recapture in Corporate Liquidations,* 58 Taxes 425 (1980); Comment, *Investment Credit and Recapture in Partnership Transactions,* 59 Neb.L.Rev. 113 (1980); Dorr, *Working with the Investment Credit Recapture Rules: A Blend of the Old and New,* 56 J.Tax'n 354 (1982). The reduction of the basis of creditable property by 100% of the amount of the credit claimed, as required by Section 48(q)(3), can result in depreciation recapture on disposition of the property despite the use of the straight-line method to depreciate the property. See Pollack, *Claiming the Rehabilitation Credit Can Trigger 1245 and 1250 Recapture on Disposition,* 59 J.Tax'n 98 (1983).

6. The Alternative Minimum Tax applicable to taxpayers, other than corporations, is imposed on the taxpayer's alternative minimum taxable income. Alternative minimum taxable income is, roughly speaking, the taxpayer's adjusted gross income, increased by the tax preferences and adjustments described in Sections 56 and 57. For example, adjusted gross income is increased by the interest on tax exempt private activity bonds, the accelerated portion of depreciation, the amount by which the fair market value of a share of stock transferred pursuant to the exercise of an incentive stock option exceeds the option price and the amount by which a charitable deduction would be reduced if all "capital gain property" were taken into account at adjusted basis. The itemized deductions which can be deducted in computing alternative minimum taxable income include the allowances for casualty losses, charitable contributions, medical deductions subject to a 10% nondeductible floor, and "qualified interest" as defined in Section 56(e)(2), which, in general, limits the deduction of interest on amounts borrowed for other than certain residential purposes to the amount of investment income included in alternative minimum taxable income. In addition, Section 58 provides that passive activity losses in excess of passive activity income cannot be deducted in computing alternative minimum taxable income even though Section 469, which disallows certain passive activity losses, is phased in over five years with respect to investments held by a taxpayer on the date of the enactment of the Tax Reform Act of 1986 and at all times thereafter. Alternative minimum taxable income (computed as summarized above, but with certain other adjustments) is subject to an exemption of $40,000 (joint returns and surviving spouses), $30,000 (unmarried persons), or $20,000 (married persons filing separate returns, trusts and estates). The exemption amount is reduced by an amount equal to 25% of the amount by which the alternative minimum income of the taxpayer exceeds (A) $150,000, if the exemption amount is $40,000, (B) $112,500, if the exemption amount is $30,000 or (C) $75,000, if the exemption amount is $20,000. The Alternative Minimum Tax is 21 percent of the balance, payable if, but only if, it exceeds the taxpayer's regular tax. See generally Streer and Holland, *Working with the Revised Alternative Minimum Tax for Individuals,* 18 Tax Adviser 150 (1987); Zieser, *Alternative Minimum Tax Provisions Under the Tax Reform Act of 1986,* 16 Colo.Law. 615 (1987); Schlesinger, *Alternative Minimum Tax on Individuals Under TRA '86,* 59 N.Y.St.B.J. 46 (1987); Kern, *The Alternative Minimum Tax for Individuals Under the Tax Reform Act of 1986,* 65 Taxes 307 (1987); Middleton and Newcomb, *How the TRA of 1986 Alters the Scope of and Planning for the AMT,* 68 J.Tax'n 44 (1987); Comment, *The Alternative Minimum Tax for Individuals: Present Problems and Future Possibilities,* 63 Wash.L.Rev. 103 (1988).

7. The Alternative Minimum Tax applicable to a corporation is imposed on the corporation's alternative minimum taxable income at the rate of 20% and is coordinated with Section 291 which reduces the benefit to a corporation of certain tax preference items by 20% to 30%. A corporation's alternative minimum taxable income is, in general, its regular taxable income increased by certain adjustments and tax preferences, as provided in Sections 56 and 57, which include many of the same adjustments and preferences described above with respect to taxpayers, other than corporations, and, in general, further

adjusted by computing certain deductions in a manner that negates the acceleration of the deductions under the regular tax, as described in Section 56. The corporation's taxable income as increased and adjusted is then reduced by an exemption amount of $40,000 which is phased out at the rate of $.25 for every $1.00 by which the corporation's alternative minimum taxable income exceeds $150,000. A corporation is subject to a special adjustment, under Section 56(f), in computing alternative minimum taxable income. One-half of the amount by which the adjusted net "book income" of a corporation exceeds the corporation's alternative minimum taxable income, before any amount is added as a result of this adjustment, is included in a corporation's alternative minimum taxable income. "Book income" is, roughly speaking, the net income of the corporation as shown on its applicable financial statement. This adjustment is effective for the years 1987 through 1989. After 1989 the use of book income is replaced by the use of earnings and profits computed in a revenue-neutral manner. See Starr and Kindgren, *Corporate AMT: The Book Income Adjustment,* 18 Tax Adviser 621 (1987); Zimbler, *The Corporate Alternative Minimum Tax: Another Look,* 65 Taxes 846 (1987); Feinberg and Robinson, *The Corporate Alternative Minimum Tax: Working with BURP While Waiting for ACE,* 15 J.Corp.Tax'n 3 (1988); Brown and Massoglia, *Corporate Alternative Minimum Tax,* 45 N.Y.U.Inst.Fed.Tax'n 7-1 (1987); Degler, *The Corporate Minimum Tax and the Book Income Adjustment: Problems and a Possible Alternative,* 7 Va. Tax Rev. 753 (1988).

c. COLLAPSIBLE PARTNERSHIPS

Except in the rare case, a partnership interest is not considered stock in trade, inventory, or goods held for sale to customers in the ordinary course of business. It would initially appear, therefore, that a real estate "dealer" might obtain capital gains by having the real estate held by a partnership and selling his partnership interest. See Section 741. To solve this, and related problems, Congress enacted the collapsible partnership provision, Section 751 of the Internal Revenue Code. Division I, pages 35 to 36 supra, this Division, pages 548 to 550 infra, and Division IV, pages 1091 to 1100 infra consider the application of Section 751 in the context of the liquidation of a partner's interest in a partnership. Division IV, pages 1086 to 1100 infra considers its application in the context of a current distribution by a partnership to a partner. This Division, pages 490 to 492 supra briefly deals with its application to a sale by a partner of his partnership interest. For Section 751 to be applicable, there must be Section 751 property present. The following excerpt deals with how one determines which partnership assets constitute Section 751 property and the application of Section 751 to the sale or exchange of part or all of a partnership interest.

CUTTING A PATH THROUGH SECTION 751 PARTS ONE AND TWO

John J. Sexton
4 The Journal of Real Estate Taxation 72, 168 (1977).
[some footnotes omitted]

* * *

Section 751 will come into play where a partnership owns assets which fall into the category of "hot assets" (certain items described below containing potential ordinary income). If the partnership holds such hot assets, then Section 751 will affect the character of the gain or loss realized by a partner upon the sale or exchange of all or a portion of his partnership interest. Section 751 will also cause certain distributions from a partnership to a partner to constitute a constructive (but fully taxable) sale or exchange of partnership property between such partner and the partnership, notwithstanding the generally nontaxable nature of partnership distributions (other than money).

* * *

Hot Assets

Hot assets of a partnership fall in two categories: (1) unrealized receivables and (2) inventory items "which have appreciated substantially in value." The concept of inventory items which have appreciated substantially in value is the simpler of the two categories and will be addressed first.

Appreciated Inventory

"Inventory items" means primarily (1) property of the partnership which is inventory or property held primarily for sale to customers in the ordinary course of the partnership's trade or business; and (2) other property held by the partnership that, if held by the selling or distributee partner, would be considered such property.

For example, if a partnership acquired a tract of raw land and subdivided the land into undeveloped parcels for individual sale, the undeveloped parcels would be inventory in the hands of the partnership for purposes of Section 751.

The second concept in the definition of inventory noted above is rather interesting. Note that the frame of reference is the character of the property *in the hands of the selling or distributee partner* rather than the character of the property in the hands of the partnership. For example, assume a situation in which the partnership held several tracts of land for long-term investment rather than for sale in the ordinary course of its business. Suppose the partnership were to distribute [money] to one of its individual partners in liquidation of such partner's partnership interest. Suppose further that such individual partner is considered a dealer in real property due to prior transactions in the real estate area which he had undertaken in his own right.

Under such circumstances, the Service could argue that [tracts of land] constituted inventory, and accordingly bring the provisions of Section 751 into play.

Not all inventory of a partnership will be considered a hot asset. The inventory items must have appreciated substantially in value. For this purpose, an inventory item will be considered to have appreciated substantially in value if (1) the fair market value of such item exceeds 120 percent of the adjusted basis of the partnership of such property, *and* (2) the fair market value of the item exceeds 10 percent of the fair market value of all partnership property, other than money.

For example, assume that partnership *ABC* holds the following assets:

	Basis	**FMV**
Cash	$ 100,000	$ 100,000
Subdivided tracts of land held for sale	$ 100,000	$ 130,000
Office building held for investment and production of income	$ 800,000	$1,150,000
	$1,000,000	$1,380,000

The fair market value of the tracts of land is 130 percent of the partnership's basis in the asset. Accordingly, the first part of the test would be met. Similarly, the fair market value of the land ($130,000) exceeds 10 percent of the fair market value of all partnership property *other than money* ($1,150,000 + $130,000 = $1,280,000). Accordingly, the entire amount of the land would be viewed as substantially appreciated inventory. Now assume that the partnership * * * invest[s] $20,000 of its cash in government bonds or other securities. This would add $20,000 to the category of partnership assets "other than money." The new sum of the fair market value of all partnership assets other than money ($1,150,000 + $130,000 + $20,000 = $1,300,000) is exactly ten times the fair market value of the inventory ($130,000). Accordingly, the fair market value of the inventory does not *exceed* 10 percent of the fair market value of all partnership property other than money. Since this test has been failed, the inventory is not substantially appreciated in value (of course there can be variations in how the partnership and the Internal Revenue Service view the values).

Let us take a more creative approach. Assume that the office building was subject to a first mortgage of $600,000 with interest at 8 percent per annum. If the partnership used $96,000 to prepay two years' interest on the mortgage, this should convert the $96,000 into an asset other than money.[14] The fact that the Service may attack the deductibility of the prepayment as a matter of tax accounting should not preclude the $96,000 from constituting a prepaid expense item of the partnership which is arguably an asset "other than money" for purposes of Section 751.

14. See, e.g., G. Ralph Bartolme, 62 T.C. 821 (1974) (prepaid interest is partnership asset, amortizable by new partner).

Unrealized Receivables

The concept of "unrealized receivables" is more complicated. Unrealized receivables will include any rights (to the extent not previously includible in income) to payment for goods delivered or to be delivered (to the extent the proceeds therefrom would be treated as amounts received from the sale or exchange of property other than a capital asset) and rights to payment for services rendered or to be rendered. This portion of the definition is rather straightforward. [An example would be the receivables of a partnership using the cash method of accounting for income tax purposes.]

However, of more relevance to real estate, unrealized receivables also include the portion of depreciation recapture attributable to the partnership's assets pursuant to the provisions of, inter alia, Code Sections 1245 * * * and 1250 * * *.

For example, assume a partnership acquired an office building in [1981] and [used an accelerated] method of depreciation * * *. [The difference between the depreciation taken and the depreciation which could have been taken] under the straight line method * * * would constitute an unrealized receivable of the partnership for purposes of Section 751.

The term "unrealized receivables" thus includes depreciable and amortizable property to the extent of any gain which would be characterized as ordinary income if such property were sold at its fair market value at the time the sale of the partnership interest or distribution from the partnership takes place.

* * *

Hot Assets and Character of Amount Realized

Section 751(a) provides in general that the amount of any money, or the fair market value of any property, received by a partner in exchange for all or part of his interest in the partnership and which is attributable to unrealized receivables or substantially appreciated inventory shall be considered as an amount realized from the sale or exchange of property other than a capital asset. * * *

* * *

As a general matter, when a partner sells or exchanges all or any portion of his interest in a partnership, he must recognize gain or loss measured by the difference between his adjusted basis for his partnership interest and the amount he receives in exchange for such partnership interest. For purposes of determining the total amount received by the selling partner, the full amount of any underlying partnership liabilities allocable to the partnership interest being sold will be included as part of the consideration paid by the purchaser. Subchapter K specifically provides that in the case of a sale or exchange of an interest in a partnership, liabilities attributable to the partnership interest shall be treated in the same manner as liabilities in connection with the sale or exchange of property not associated with partnerships.[15]

15. I.R.C. § 752(c).

Subchapter K goes on to provide, as a general rule, that any gain or loss recognized in the transfer of a partnership interest shall be considered as gain or loss from the sale of a capital asset.[16]

An exception to this rule requires that the amount of any money, or the fair market value of any property, received by a transferor partner in exchange for all or a part of his interest in the partnership attributable to hot assets * * * shall be considered as an amount realized from the sale or exchange of property *other than* a capital asset and accordingly will serve to generate either ordinary gain or loss to the selling partner.

Earlier, we noted that the Section 751 provisions have often been referred to as the "collapsible partnership" provisions of Subchapter K. There are, however, interesting differences in approach between these rules and the collapsible corporation provisions of the Code. A primary distinction rests in the fact that the collapsible corporation provisions have an impact solely on the characterization of gain created pursuant to the sale of stock, while the collapsible partnership provisions can both "create" as well as characterize a gain in the sale of a partnership interest. This "creation" of a gain arises from the requirement of a separate determination of gain or loss attributable to the sale of the partner's allocable interest in hot assets and gain or loss attributable to the sale of the partner's allocable interest in all other partnership property. Surprising as it may seem, the application of the collapsible partnership provisions can result in situations where a taxpayer recognizes both ordinary income and a capital loss from the sale of a partnership interest.

For example, assume partnership XY with the following assets:

XY Partnership Assets

	Basis	Fair Market Value
Cash	$ 100,000	$ 100,000
Subdivided tracts of land held for sale	$ 100,000	$ 230,000
Office building held for investment and production of income	$ 800,000	$ 700,000
	$1,000,000	$1,030,000

Partnership Interest

	Basis	Fair Market Value
X	$ 500,000	$ 515,000
Y	$ 500,000	$ 515,000
	$1,000,000	$1,030,000

16. See I.R.C. § 741.

Next, assume that partner X sells his partnership interest to Z for $515,000. Since partner X's basis in his interest is $500,000 and the sales price is $515,000, one would expect that he would recognize a $15,000 gain on the sale of his partnership interest. Not so. Instead, Subchapter K requires that partner X recognize $65,000 in ordinary income and a $50,000 capital loss upon the sale of his interest! This result is mandated by the fractionalization of the sale of the partnership interest into a separate sale of X's allocable interest in partnership hot assets and his allocable interest in other partnership property.

In the above example, X's basis in partnership hot assets (the tracts of land) was $50,000 since the regulations provide that the portion of a partner's adjusted basis for his partnership interest to be allocated to hot assets shall be an amount equal to the basis such property would have had in the hands of such partner if the selling partner had received a share of such property in a current distribution made immediately before the sale.

The regulations also provide that the portion of the total amount realized which the seller must allocate to the hot assets to determine gain or loss will be the allocation which the seller and purchaser have agreed upon at arm's length. For purposes of the above example, we have presumed an allocation based upon the fair market value of 50 percent of $230,000 (or $115,000).

Accordingly, since partner X was not able to allocate more than $50,000 of his basis in his partnership interest to the $115,000 in value of hot assets sold, he must report a $65,000 ordinary gain with respect to such portion of the sale. The remaining $450,000 of partner X's basis can only be allocated to the $400,000 worth of partnership assets which do not constitute hot assets, thus resulting in a $50,000 capital loss.

The ability of the partners to agree upon the proper allocation of the purchase price may significantly change the tax consequences of the situation. * * * Not all inventory will constitute a hot asset to a partnership. Rather, [as discussed above,] the inventory must meet the substantial appreciation tests of Subchapter K in order to qualify as a hot asset. Negotiations between the parties can result in an allocation of a value to underlying partnership inventory which would take such property out of the classification of hot assets and accordingly remove the sale from the reach of the collapsible partnership rules.

For example, assume the following assets for partnership *AB*:

AB Partnership Assets

	Basis	Fair Market Value
Cash	$ 100,000	$ 100,000
Subdivided tracts of land held for sale	$ 100,000	$ 136,000
Office building held for investment and production of income	$1,000,000	$1,200,000
	$1,200,000	$1,436,000

Assume partner A has agreed to sell his partnership interest to C for $718,000. Since the fair market value of the land, as set forth above, exceeds 120 percent of the partnership's basis in the land and since the fair market value of the land also exceeds 10 percent of the fair market value of all partnership property other than money, the land will constitute a "hot asset." Accordingly, instead of recognizing a $118,000 capital gain on the sale of his partnership interest, A will recognize $18,000 in ordinary income and $100,000 in capital gain.

On the other hand, if C (the purchaser) were willing to agree to an allocation of less than $68,000 for A's share of the land, and agree to the allocation of additional amounts to the interest in the office building, A could shift his tax situation somewhat. If A and C were to agree to a fair market value of the land which was less than $120,000, the 120 percent test for substantial appreciation would not be met, and A could assert that the collapsible partnership rules had no application to the sale of his interest, thus permitting the entire $118,000 gain to be treated as capital gain.

The allocation of the purchase price away from the land is not in C's best interests since C would rather have a high basis in the partnership's ordinary income asset [and the asset which, in all likelihood, will be the first asset disposed of]. Accordingly, the adverse interests of the parties should cause their final allocation to be respected by the Internal Revenue Service, absent unusual circumstances.

In any event, this is an area where marginal adjustments can have interesting effects on the overall tax impact of a sale of a partnership interest.

NOTE

1. See generally Division I, pages 35 to 36 supra; this Division, pages 548 to 550 infra; Division IV, Pages 1086 to 1100 infra; Anderson and Bloom, *Collapsible Partnerships: The Complexities of Section 751*, 2 J. Real Est. Tax'n 425 (1975); Crumbley and Orbach, *Unraveling a Collapsible Partnership*, 9 Tax Adviser 47 (1978); Morgan and Larason, *Tax Effects of Partner's Departure Can Be Tailored to Meet Parties' Needs*, 12 Tax'n Law. 132 (1983); Hoeflich, *Transfers of Interests in Public Limited Partnerships and the Collapsible Partnership Rules: A Planning Pitfall*, 14 Tax Adviser 742 (1983); Grossman, *Choosing the Most Advantageous Method for Disposing of a Partnership Inter-*

est, 3 J. Ps. Tax'n 219 (1986); Wolff, *Planning a Partner's Withdrawal from a Partnership*, 33 # 3 Prac. Law. 55 (1987); Taylor and Kozub, *Real Estate Limited Partnerships: Is a Graceful Exit Possible?*, 14 J. Real Est. Tax'n 154 (1987); Moore and Patankar, *Secs. 736 and 741 for the Withdrawal of a Partner*, 19 Tax Adviser 307 (1988).

2. Even if a partnership is solely engaged in developing and operating commercial or residential rental real estate, Section 751 may be applicable to the sale of a partnership interest by a partner who is a "dealer" in the type of real estate owned by the partnership. The real estate owned by the partnership would be treated as inventory under Section 751(d) since it presumably would be inventory in the "dealer's" hands.

a. If the real estate is "substantially appreciated," but the partnership does not own any unrealized receivables, can the "dealer" safely avoid Section 751 problems by the partnership liquidating his interest under Section 736(b)? Or since the amount allocated to inventory is considered a distribution by the partnership, see Section 736(b)(1), will Section 751 apply as a result of Section 731(c)?

b. At times, Section 736(b) treats a payment with respect to a partner's share of goodwill as resulting in ordinary income to the recipient partner. Sections 741 and 751 always treat as a return of capital or capital gain the part of the purchase price of a partnership interest received for the selling partner's share of goodwill. How can this difference between Section 736(b) and Sections 741 and 751 be explained?

3. Generally, the leases held by a lessor partnership are not considered inventory. Can the rental due under a lease, however, be considered an unrealized receivable in the appropriate case?

a. If the term of the lease is from year to year does the answer depend on whether the partnership used the accrual or cash method of accounting for tax purposes?

b. If the term of the lease ran anywhere from two to twenty years and a partner sells his interest, receives an excess distribution or his partnership interest is liquidated in a transaction governed by Section 736(b), does the partner have any Section 751 or Section 736(b)(2) concerns?

1. Are the rentals provided for under the lease contract rights to payment for non-capital goods delivered or to be delivered or services rendered or to be rendered?

4. The inclusion of accounts receivable in inventory (as a non-capital asset), see Section 751(d)(2)(B), for the purpose of determining whether substantially appreciated inventory is present, may have a variety of effects.

a. If the partnership uses the cash method of accounting, including accounts receivable will increase the chances that the fair market value of the inventory will exceed 120% of its adjusted basis and 10% of the fair market value of all partnership property other than cash.

b. If the partnership uses the accrual method of accounting, including accounts receivable may reduce, or at least have no effect on, the chances that the fair market value of the inventory will exceed 120% of its adjusted basis, unless the partnership also uses the bad debt reserve method and the face amount less reserve of the receivables is less than their fair market value. Including accounts receivable, however, will increase the chances of the fair market value of the inventory exceeding 10% of the fair market value of all partnership property other than cash.

5. Consider the "investor" in a partnership controlled by a "dealer." If the investor sells his interest in the partnership, is the real estate owned by the partnership considered Section 751 inventory because the partnership is controlled by a dealer?

RIDDELL v. SCALES
United States Court of Appeals, Ninth Circuit, 1969.
406 F.2d 210.

HUFSTEDLER, Circuit Judge.   The taxpayers * * * obtained summary judgment in the District Court upholding their contentions that * * * gain derived from their profit interest in joint venture real estate was * * * [treated] as capital gain, not ordinary income.
* * *

* * * On April 9, 1953, Kearney Park Development Corp. ("Kearney Park") contracted to buy certain unimproved realty located near Miramar Naval Air Station in San Diego, California. As part of the purchase price Kearney Park gave one note for $80,000 and a second note for $553,750, each of which was secured by a deed of trust. At the time of the purchase, the land was subject to a prior improvement lien. By 1955 the notes were in default, and the improvement bond payments and the taxes were delinquent. During the same year news was released that the Navy might acquire the land to expand the Miramar flight pattern. In 1956 a real estate dealer, B.B. Margolis, and the taxpayers in this case bought the $80,000 note for $30,000 and the $553,750 note for $270,000 and placed the notes in two simple holding trusts. The trust declaration provided that the trustors, representing sixty per cent of the beneficial ownership, could instruct the trustee to dispose of the corpus or could enter into agreements with the owner of the security to participate in any gain realized from the sale of the property.

On June 15, 1956, Margolis and the taxpayers, acting through the trust, agreed with Kearney Park to postpone payment of the notes and to waive all past defaults and to pay the delinquent installments on the improvement bonds and the taxes. The parties further agreed that upon the sale or condemnation of the land, the proceeds would be disbursed in the following order: (1) to pay off the bonds and the taxes; (2) to pay principal and interest on the notes; (3) to reimburse the trusts for advancements; (4) to pay Kearney Park its original investment in the land; and (5) to divide the balance equally between Kearney Park and the trusts. The trusts' right to share in the gain on sale or other disposition of the land was secured by a further deed of trust.

In March 1958 Kearney Park and the trusts entered an agreement to sell a portion of the land to the Navy. In April 1958 Margolis sold his beneficial interest in the trusts to one of the taxpayers. The sale to the Navy was ultimately completed, and the proceeds were distributed to the taxpayers in accordance with their agreement. The assets distributed included the principal and interest collected on the notes, the trusts' share of the purchase price of the land, and an undivided interest in the unsold portion of the land.

In Margolis v. Commissioner of Internal Revenue (9 Cir.1964) 337 F.2d 1001, 1008–1009, modified (1964) 339 F.2d 537, this court considered the tax consequences to Margolis of these transactions. Margolis' beneficial interests in the trusts represented two distinct rights: (1) his right to payment of principal and interest due on the notes and (2) his right to share in any gain realized upon the sale or other disposition of the land. We held that * * * insofar as his sale of his beneficial interest in the trusts was attributable to his interest in the gain on sale of the land, the gain realized was ordinary income, rather than capital gain, because Margolis was individually in the business of buying and selling real estate.

* * *

The Government admits that the taxpayers' receipt through the trusts of a share of the gain realized upon the sale of the land by Kearney Park to the Navy was gain from the sale or exchange of property. It contends, however, that the taxpayers' interests in the land were not capital assets because the taxpayers held the land primarily for sale to customers in the ordinary course of business within the meaning of 26 U.S.C.A. § 1221(1). The Government's contention rests solely upon the taxpayers' association with Margolis, who was a real estate dealer, in a joint venture concerning the real property in issue. It is undisputed that the taxpayers were not otherwise engaged in the business of buying and selling land on their own account. We reject the Government's contentions.

Margolis' intent and purpose to hold his equitable interest in the land for sale in the ordinary course of his business cannot be imputed to the present taxpayers. "Not all participants in a joint venture need have the same intent and purpose. 'For some it may be just a step in carrying on their business; for others it may be merely a single opportune investment with a view of ultimate profit but unrelated to any business of the participant.'" (United States v. Rosebrook (9 Cir. 1963) 318 F.2d 316, 319.) The present taxpayers did not become real estate dealers solely because they were associated in a joint venture with a real estate dealer.

* * *

NOTE

1. The court in *Riddell v. Scales* does not appear to have treated the joint venture as a partnership for income tax purposes. Can its rationale, however, be applied to the income tax treatment of an investor partner who sells his partnership interest in a partnership controlled by a dealer partner? Cf. *Hyman Podell*, 55 T.C. 429 (1970).

a. Under Section 751, the property of the partnership is tested for its status as inventory at both the partnership level and the level of the partner receiving a distribution or selling an interest. Does the dealer status of the controlling general partner cause the property of the partnership to be considered inventory for Section 751 purposes on a sale of an interest by, or a distribution to, an investor partner, even though the dealer status does not "taint" the investor partner when the property is tested at his level?　See Reg.Sec. 1.751–1(d)(2).

b.　What is the income tax effect on investor partners when a capital, or Section 1231(b), asset in the hands of the partnership, which owns only capital and Section 1231(b) assets, is distributed to a partner who is a dealer in the type of asset distributed?　Assume that the distributed asset is substantially appreciated and the partnership's basis in each of its assets except money is below each asset's fair market value and the distributee is not a dealer in any of the assets retained by the partnership.　If Section 751(d)(2)(D) is followed literally, as a result of the distribution the investor partners will recognize ordinary income and the dealer partner will recognize capital gain.　Recognizing the impropriety of this result, the Regulations provide that Section 751(d)(2)(D) does not apply to assets actually distributed to a dealer partner.　See Reg.Sec. 1.751–1(d)(2)(iii).

2.　Under the exception to collapsible corporation treatment contained in Section 341(e), a 20% or more shareholder who is a dealer may "taint" the corporation and the remainder of the shareholders even if all of the remaining shareholders are investors.

d.　COLLAPSIBLE CORPORATIONS

As discussed above, the sale of a partnership interest is considered, in general, the sale of a capital asset.　See Section 741.　Similarly, the sale of shares of stock of a corporation or the receipt of a distribution in complete or partial liquidation of a corporation is, in general, considered a sale of a capital asset.　As a result, a dealer might hope to obtain capital gain rather than ordinary income treatment simply by having the real estate in which he deals owned by a corporation and selling the stock in the corporation.　Congress sought to close this and related loopholes by the collapsible corporation provision, Section 341.　Section 341 is a great deal more complex than the above simple illustration would indicate.

PLANNING OPPORTUNITIES FOR AVOIDING COLLAPSIBLE CORPORATION TREATMENT

Peter L. Faber
32 Journal of Taxation 76 (1970).

The First Question which the practitioner must concern himself with in the 341 area is whether the corporation has been formed or availed of principally for the manufacture, construction, or production of property of any kind under Section 341(b).

The distinction between "formed" and "availed of" is deliberate. The word "formed" applies to corporations organized for the purpose of acquiring property.　The words "availed of" cover, in addition, corporations *used* for the acquisition or production of property, even if not originally formed for such purpose.　In other words, the fact that a corporation has been engaged in the conduct of an active business for many years is no guarantee that it is not collapsible within the statutory definition.

The word "principally" refers to the acquisition or production of property and not to the collapse of the corporation or the disposition of its stock. Therefore, the existence of valid nontax business reasons for the use of the corporate form will not preclude the application of Section 341.

If a corporation is formed for the construction of property and the business is sold soon thereafter, a question may arise as to whether construction has begun. Although the statutory language is not entirely clear on this point, it is well established that the collapsible corporation provisions will not apply to a sale of stock prior to the commencement of construction. Section 341(b)(2)(A) provides that a corporation shall be deemed to have manufactured, constructed, or produced property if it engaged in such activity "to any extent" and the Service and the courts have interpreted this language broadly.

In Rev. Rul. 56–137, 1956–1 CB 178, the Service ruled that petitioning a zoning board for the rezoning of land from residential to commercial to enable the construction of a shopping center and litigating the propriety of the rezoning constituted construction even though, at the conclusion of the litigation, the plans for the shopping center were abandoned and actual physical construction never took place.

The Service noted that the zoning proceedings were "a step in the construction." Presumably, the Service's view is that construction begins with the first acts constituting part of a plan that contemplates actual physical construction. [The Tax Court, however, in Morris Cohen, 39 T.C. 886 (1963), nonacq. 1974–2 C.B. 5, held that construction had not begun even though water and sewer plans were developed, approval of water and sewer service was secured, contour maps and a first filing plat were prepared and a petition for rezoning was filed. See also Calvin A. Thomas, 42 CCH Tax Ct.Mem. 496 (1981).]

* * *

More extensive activities such as subdividing property, contracting for the installation of streets, and arranging for financing have been held to constitute construction,[17] as have hiring an architect, negotiating for a building permit, and obtaining tenants.[18]

Pinning down the date on which construction commences may also be a problem with older established corporations. Such corporations may have repaired or remodeled existing property and a determination must be made as to whether such activities involve construction within the meaning of Section 341(b).

* * * It would appear that the Service's approach [in determining whether a repair, remodeling, or alteration amounts to construction] is similar to that used in determining whether a given expenditure is a deductible repair or a capital improvement.

17.   Abbott, 258 F.2d 537 (C.A.–3, 1958).

18.   Sproul Realty Co., 38 T.C. 844 (1962).

The word "property" includes virtually all kinds of property. There is no exception for intangibles such as know-how and goodwill, although this would not seem to come within the intention of the statute and the Service has not tried to apply Section 341 to such assets.   Even if a corporation does not engage in the construction, manufacture, or production of property, Section 341(b)(2) provides that it will be deemed to have engaged in such activities if it acquires property other than by purchase from one who did so engage.   For example, if an individual manufactures property and transfers it to a corporation in a taxfree exchange under Section 351, the corporation will be deemed to have manufactured the property for purposes of Section 341.

Even if a corporation has not engaged in the manufacture, construction, or production of property, it may be collapsible if it purchases certain types of property.   Generally, this includes property that would produce ordinary income if sold by the corporation or which represents a right to receive ordinary income.   *   *   * The purchase of depreciable property or real property used in the conduct of the corporation's trade or business may also make the corporation collapsible.   There is a special exception for purchased property used in connection with the manufacture, construction, production or sale of property held primarily for sale to customers.   Another exception is made for purchased property held for three or more years.

If the corporation being sold has dealt with property as set forth in the statute, the next question that must be answered is whether the requisite "view" to the disposition of the stock or distribution to the shareholders prior to the realization by the corporation of a substantial part of the taxable income to be derived from the property existed.   It is not necessary to have a tax avoidance motive; the view has reference to objective events, the disposition of the corporation's stock or the distribution of property to the shareholders, and not to the reasons why such events occur.

Regulation 1.341–2(a)(2) takes an extremely broad approach to the question of what constitutes a "view."   The requisite view is deemed to be present if the distribution of property or disposition of stock is "contemplated, unconditionally, conditionally, or as a recognized possibility."   *   *   *

The object of the view is the "collapse" of the corporation prior to the realization of "a substantial part of the taxable income to be derived" from the property in question.   In determining the income to be derived from the property, it is assumed in the case of property held for sale that it will be disposed of at the same price as that prevailing on the date of the collapse, with expenses remaining the same.[19]   In the case of property held for rent or the production of other income, projections are made over the remaining useful life of the property.

19. E.g., Zongker, 39 T.C. 1046 (1963),
aff'd 334 F.2d 44 (C.A.10, 1964).

Overhead and general administrative expenses must be allocated to specific properties.

Substantial Realization Exception

* * *

[Section 341(b)(1)(A) provides that, if prior to the collapse of the corporation two-thirds of the taxable income to be derived from the manufactured, constructed, produced, and purchased property of the corporation has been realized, the corporation will avoid collapsible treatment.]

* * *

"View" to Disposition

Regulation 1.341–2(a)(3) provides that a corporation will be collapsible if the view exists at "any time" during the manufacture, construction, production, or purchase of the property. In other words, if a view to collapse is held while the property is being constructed but is later abandoned, Section 341 will still apply. Conversely, if the view does not arise until after the completion of construction, Section 341 will not apply, even if the collapse is done for the express purpose of saving taxes. * * *

Because the view must exist during construction, the question of when construction is completed may be of paramount importance. * * * The Tax Court approach seems to be that construction is complete when the property is ready to earn income. * * *

If a view to collapse the corporation * * * existed at the time that repairs were being made to its property, it must be determined whether the repairs were part of "construction." The Service has ruled that the remodeling of an office building is not part of construction if it does not change the character of the building, increase the area available for rentals, or increase the value of the building or its rental income potential.[20]

The burden of proving that the view to collapse the corporation did not arise until after the completion of manufacture or construction is a difficult one to meet since it involves showing the absence of a subjective state of mind. Generally, the burden can be met by showing that the sale of the business was prompted by unexpected circumstances arising after the completion of construction.

* * *

Reg[ulation] 1.341–2(a)(3)[, however,] states that a corporation will nevertheless be collapsible if the unexpected circumstances "reasonably can be anticipated" at the time of construction. There are few events that will not be "reasonably" subject to "anticipation" and the courts have not been as hard on taxpayers as this language would suggest. [But see Edward S. Zorn, 35 CCH Tax Ct.Mem. 1048 (1976); Peter G. Felix, 41 CCH Tax Ct.Mem. 1040 (1981).]

20. Rev.Rul. 63–114, 1963–1 CB 74.

Where a corporation has several shareholders, it will be important to determine who held the view to collapse. Reg[ulation] 1.341-2(a)(2) states that a corporation will be collapsible if the view is held by "those persons in a position to determine the policies of the corporation, whether by reason of their owning a majority of the voting stock of the corporation or otherwise." In other words, if only one of the shareholders sells his stock, it is not necessary for him to have contemplated the collapse of the corporation for the corporation to be collapsible with respect to his sale. * * *

Weighing the Collapsible Risk

It can be seen that the definition of "collapsible corporation" includes many uncertain elements; accordingly, there will frequently be doubt as to whether a given corporation meets the statutory tests. In advising a client with respect to the sale of a corporate business, the tax consultant must make a practical judgment with respect to the 341 exposure. * * *

If it is determined that there is a significant danger that the corporation will be held to be collapsible and if the possibility of ordinary income treatment is an unacceptable risk, the possible application of the exceptions to ordinary income treatment contained in Sections 341(d), (e), and (f) must be considered. The impact of these exceptions will vary, depending on [the type of transaction to be entered into]. * * *

If it is contemplated that the stock of the corporation is to be sold, the exceptions contained in Section[s] 341(d), [(e) and (f)] may be applicable, even though the corporation is collapsible by definition.

Section 341(d) Exceptions

Five per cent stock ownership. Section 341(d)(1) excepts from ordinary income treatment [the gain realized with respect to the] stock [of a corporation] by a person who, at no time after the commencement of manufacture, construction, production, or purchase of the property in question, owned more than 5% of the value of the corporation's stock.

* * * Section 341(d) contains rules of constructive ownership that are generally similar to those in the personal holding company provisions of the Code.

Normally, the 5% exception will not be much help in the sale of a business. Section 341 usually applies only to closely held corporations and the principal shareholders will invariably own more than 5% of the corporation's stock.

Thirty percent of gain rule. Section 341(d)(2) provides that the collapsible corporation provisions will not apply to the gain realized by a shareholder in a taxable year if the gain is 30% or more attributable to noncollapsible property, or property manufactured, constructed, produced, or purchased without a view to the collapse of the corporation.

If less than 30% of the gain is attributable to noncollapsible property, the entire gain will be ordinary income; conversely, if 30% or more of the gain is attributable to noncollapsible property, no part of the gain will be [treated as] ordinary income * * * under Section 341.

In applying the 30% rule, it is necessary to do more than simply determine the appreciation in the value of collapsible property. Reg[ulation] 1.341–4(c)(2) provides that, for purposes of Section 341(d)(2), the gain attributable to collapsible property is the excess of the total gain over that which would have been realized had the property not been produced or purchased. This includes the increased value of other property caused by the construction or purchase of the collapsible property. In other words, if the construction of a new building causes the value of an adjoining building owned by the corporation to increase, this increase is treated as attributable to the newly constructed building. In Rev. Rul. 68–476, [1968–2 Cum.Bull. 139], the Service ruled that a building and the underlying land are a single asset and that gain on the land is treated as part of the gain on the asset of which the building is a part even though part of the appreciation in the value of the land is due to general real estate conditions and not the construction of the building. The same reasoning would presumably apply to improvements on part of a building and it would be necessary to include general appreciation of the building along with the gain directly attributable to the improvements. [In addition, all inventory, stock-in-trade and property held primarily for sale to customers in the ordinary course of business is treated, to the extent provided in the regulations, as one item of property for the purpose of applying the seventy-thirty percent rule of Section 341(d)(2).]

If reliance is placed on Section 341(d)(2), the allocation of the sale price among the corporation's assets will be important because it will have a bearing on the gain attributable to particular properties. * * * An allocation of purchase price in a stock sale contract[, however, may] be given little weight by the courts since it is not an essential ingredient of the transaction and is usually not negotiated at arm's-length from conflicting positions. [Although, if the purchaser intends to make the election provided by Section 338, it will have a substantial interest in the allocation of the purchase price.]

Reg[ulation] 1.341–4(c) provides that gain from retained earnings produced by collapsible property is considered attributable to collapsible property for purposes of Section 341(d)(2). Such earnings have already been included in gross income and the validity of this provision is doubtful. If retained earnings from collapsible property are used to purchase vacant land that is held by the corporation for investment and is a capital asset in its hands, must subsequent appreciation in the value of the land be treated as attributable to the collapsible property? A literal reading of Reg. 1.341–4(c) would indicate an affirmative answer and this must be reckoned with in planning a transaction, yet such a result seems highly questionable. The application of the Regulation may involve formidable tracing problems, especially where part of the corporation's cash is attributable to collapsible property and part comes from other sources.

There is no authority with respect to the handling of liabilities in applying Section 341(d)(2). A logical approach would seem to be to allocate general liabilities over all assets in proportion to their gross (i.e., unencumbered) fair market values and to allocate liabilities attaching to specific assets to the assets to which they relate. [See generally Nicholson, *Avoiding Collapsibility on Partial Realization Tougher Due to Changes Flowing from DRA '84,* 64 J. Tax'n 2 (1986).]

Three-year rule. Section 341(d)(3) provides that Section 341 will not apply "to gain realized after the expiration of three years following the completion of such manufacture, construction, production, or purchase." Reg[ulation] 1.341–4(d) indicates that this exception applies on a property-by-property basis so that part of the gain can be protected if attributable to property completed more than three years previously even though other parts of the gain are not so protected.

Since the three-year period begins to run from the completion of the [construction,] production or acquisition of the property, the considerations discussed previously with respect to the completion of construction apply here as well. * * *

The Service has ruled that gain is "realized" for purposes of Section 341(d)(3) at the time of the sale, not when payments for the stock are received. Accordingly, setting up a transaction as an installment sale under Section 453 will not bring it within the protection of the three-year rule.[21]

Section 341(e) Exception

If the exceptions of 341(d) do not apply, or if their application is uncertain enough to preclude reliance on them in planning a transaction, relief may be available under Section 341(e). This subsection was added to the law in 1958 and is a codification of the principle that Section 341 should not apply to a gain unless a significant part of that gain is attributable to assets that would have produced ordinary income if sold by the corporation or a major shareholder. Otherwise, the tax avoidance at which Section 341 is aimed would presumably not be present. To a great extent, then advance planning for the possible use of Section 341(e) involves an investigation of the activities of the shareholders of the corporation in order to determine whether they are "dealers" in property similar to that held by the corporation.

The general approach of the statute is to make Section 341 inapplicable to [any sale or exchange of the stock of the corporation by a shareholder] if the unrealized increase in value of assets that would produce ordinary income if sold by the corporation or certain of its shareholders[' subsection (e) assets,] does not exceed 15% of the corporation's net worth. * * *

21. Rev.Rul. 60–68, 1960–1 CB 151.

"Net worth" is defined in Section 341(e)(7) as the excess of the fair market value of all a corporation's assets plus the amount of any previous distributions in complete liquidation over its liabilities. It can be seen that there is a direct correlation between the amount of a corporation's net worth and the ease with which it can qualify under 341(e). The Code provides that in determining a corporation's net worth, amounts received by it within the preceding year for stock or as contributions to capital or paid-in surplus are to be ignored if the transfer of such amounts to the corporation [was] not for a bona fide business purpose. It is questionable whether a contribution to a corporation's capital for the purpose of paying corporate debts before they normally would fall due will be treated as having been made for a bona fide business purpose unless the purchaser of the corporation's stock indicates that he does not want to assume the liabilities. It is not clear whether intangibles such as good will are counted as "assets" for purposes of Section 341(e)(7) but they would seem to fit within the literal meaning of the statute. Under certain circumstances, it may be possible to argue that loans from shareholders are really equity investments and, hence, do not constitute liabilities of the corporation. It would be imprudent to rely on this type of argument in planning a transaction in advance, although its use should not be ignored after the fact if the Service raises a 341 issue on audit.

The Regulations and cases are unclear as to how contingent claims and liabilities are to be treated. It may be impossible to value such items and prudent planning would indicate ascribing little or no value to contingent claims and a high value to contingent liabilities.

The valuation problem is not as great in the case of the sale of a business as it might otherwise be because the purchase price is presumably negotiated at arm's-length between the buyer and the seller. A problem may arise, however, with respect to the allocation of the total purchase price among the various assets of the corporation. This will be important if some but not all of the assets of the corporation are subsection (e) assets. * * *

The definition of subsection (e) assets is obviously of critical importance.

The term includes all property other than Section 1231(b) property that would produce ordinary income if sold at a gain by the corporation or any shareholder owning more than 20% in value of the corporation's outstanding stock. Reg[ulation] 1.341-6(b)(4) provides that if a 20% shareholder owns any property primarily for sale to customers in the normal course of his trade or business and the corporation owns similar property, such property will be a subsection (e) asset. The implication is that this will be so even if the shareholder also holds similar property for investment purposes. Arguably, the Regulation goes too far. Section 341(e)(5)(A)(i) refers to property which "would" produce ordinary income in the hands of a 20% shareholder and this suggests that if the property only "might" produce ordinary income if sold by a shareholder because the shareholder holds similar property for investment as well as for sale in his trade or business, such property would not be a subsection (e) asset. If a shareholder is in the real estate business but all the property held by him for sale to his customers in the ordinary course of his business is located in one tract of land and he owns many pieces of investment property, it would seem equitable not to treat him as a dealer for purposes of 341(e)(5). Still, for planning purposes, it must be assumed that the Regulation is valid. * * *

Reg[ulation] 1.341–6(b)(4) also provides that, even if a shareholder is not presently a dealer in property, it may be determined, based on his past activities, that if he held such property now it would be for sale to customers in the ordinary course of his trade or business. Presumably, if a shareholder had previously held property for sale to customers but now holds similar property only for investment, he would not be treated as a dealer.

Depreciable Business Property

A special set of rules applies to real property or depreciable property used in the trade or business of the corporation. If the unrealized depreciation on all such property exceeds the unrealized appreciation on all such property, all pieces of such property are subsection (e) assets. If the net unrealized appreciation on such property exceeds the unrealized depreciation on such property, then subsection (e) assets include only those pieces of such property as would produce ordinary income if sold by a person owning more than 20% in value of the corporation's stock. Presumably, the same considerations with respect to shareholders holding property for sale in a business and, in addition, for investment as were previously discussed, would apply here as well.

* * *

Section 341(e)(1) provides that gain realized on a sale of stock of a collapsible corporation will not be [treated as] ordinary income * * * to the selling shareholder if certain conditions are met. If the shareholder owns more than 20% in value of the corporation's stock, the sale must not be made to certain related persons. Appreciation in the value of certain types of assets cannot exceed 15% of the net worth of the corporation. These assets are broken down into three categories: (1) Subsection (e) assets of the corporation; (2) if the selling shareholder owns more than 5% in value of the corporation's stock, assets of the corporation which would, if sold by the particular selling shareholder, result in ordinary income to him by reason of his being a dealer in such property; (3) if the selling shareholder owns more than 20% in value of the corporation's stock, property which would produce ordinary income if sold by such shareholder if his status as a dealer was determined by reference not only to sales of similar property but also to sales of stock of certain corporations owning similar property.

Protection is not granted under Section 341(e)(1) to sales of stock to the corporation itself.

It is obvious that the application of Section 341(e)(1) to a given set of facts may be somewhat uncertain. Whether a 20% shareholder is a dealer in property is a question of fact and hundreds of court cases over the years attest to the difficulty of making such a determination. Similarly, there may be difficulties in determining whether property admittedly held by a shareholder for sale to customers is similar to property held by the corporation. [For an example of the successful use of Section 341(e)(1) to avoid collapsible treatment see Estate of C.A. Diecks, 65 T.C. 117 (1975), acq. 1978–1 Cum.Bull. 1. In this case, the court found that the only "subsection (e) assets" were certain "subscription agreements." The court then held that the value of the "subscription agreements" per se was zero since the cost of providing the service required by the agreements was greater than the income from the agreements. The value, if any, of the expectation of renewal of the agreements was in the nature of goodwill and therefore not a "subsection (e) asset." Considering that the corporation involved in this case provided cable television service, had a twenty year franchise in the area of its operation and was in its first two years of business, might there be some question raised as to the court's analysis of the "value" of the subscription agreements?]

Section 341(f) Exception

The exception to collapsible treatment contained in Section 341(f) offers the certainty that 341(e) does not. This provision was added to the law in 1964 and sets forth a procedure under which sales of stock in collapsible corporations can qualify [to be treated as] capital gains * * * if the corporation consents to have gain recognized by it on certain transactions that would normally be tax free.

Generally speaking, the effect of Section 341(f) is to [treat the gain as] capital gains * * * where the buyer of the stock and the remaining shareholders plan to continue the same business in the corporate form. In such cases, Congress felt that the corporate entity was not being abused and, hence, there was no reason to [treat the gain as] ordinary income * * *.

If a corporation files the required consent with the District Director pursuant to procedures set forth in Rev.Rul. 69–32, [1969–1 Cum.Bull. 100,] sales of stock by shareholders within the next six months will not be subject to Section 341.

By filing the consent, the corporation agrees to the recognition of gain on certain dispositions of property by it even though such dispositions would normally not be taxable events. * * * Gain is still not recognized in transfers to controlled corporations under Section 351 and pursuant to tax-free reorganizations.

The property referred to includes substantially all properties of the corporation other than personal property constituting a capital asset in the hands of the corporation. Normally, a business corporation will not hold personal property for investment purposes and, in most cases, the only property that will not be subject to the recognition of gain provisions of Section 341(f) will be securities and similar property. Only property that the corporation owns or has an option to acquire on the date of the sale of stock comes under the recognition of gain provisions.

As indicated, the big advantage of using the procedures set forth in 341(f) is that the certainty of result absent under Sections 341(d) and (e) is secured.

There are, however, certain disadvantages that must be considered by the sellers before deciding to use 341(f).

The corporate consent, once filed with the District Director, cannot be revoked. Moreover, the consent is not made ineffective by a subsequent showing that the corporation was not collapsible after all.

If there are minority shareholders, a conflict among the shareholders of the corporation may arise. If a majority shareholder wants to sell his stock, he can force the corporation to consent to the recognition of gain on future transactions. Arguably, such a consent is contrary to the interests of the corporation and is done solely for the personal convenience of the selling shareholder. It is conceivable that a dissenting minority shareholder might bring a lawsuit against the selling shareholder on behalf of the corporation for money damages. The consent might be attacked in advance as being ultra vires.

The filing of the corporate consent might affect the price that a * * * [buyer] would be willing to pay for the stock. The corporation, by so doing, incurs a potential liability that it otherwise would not have to face. It will be hard for the buyer to assess the significance of this potential liability unless he plans to dispose of the property of the corporation in the near future because the amount of gain and depreciation recapture will be uncertain. The prudent buyer should insist on a representation and warranty from the seller that a 341(f) consent has not and will not be filed by the corporation before the closing of the transaction. If the seller indicates a desire to utilize the provisions of 341(f), the buyer should consider this in the light of his plans for the corporation and, if a disposition of the corporation's property in [a nontaxable transaction which would be made taxable by Section 341(f)] is contemplated, he should consider negotiating for an adjustment in the purchase price.

Section 341(f) does not apply to sales of stock to the corporation itself. Therefore, it will not provide complete protection in "bootstrap" transactions in which the buyer acquires part of the selling shareholder's stock directly from the shareholder and the remainder is redeemed by the corporation with corporate property. The sale to the buyer will be protected by 341(f) but the redemption will not and [the gain, if any, on the redemption may be treated as] ordinary income under 341.

* * *

Planning Techniques

[G]eneral planning techniques are suggested as follows:

* * *

If the completion of construction of collapsible property occurred slightly more than two years previously, consideration should be given to deferring the sale until three years after the completion of construction in order to qualify for capital gains treatment under Section 341(d) (3). If there is an immediate need of cash, [the] sellers might borrow during the intervening period, pledging the corporation's * * * stock as collateral. The deferral of the transaction may be impractical if a specific sale is being considered and either the buyer is reluctant to wait or the seller does not want to let a good deal get away. A possible solution to this problem might be for the parties to enter into an executory contract of sale with the closing to be deferred until after the three year period has elapsed. The Service, in Rev. Rul. 67–100, 1967–1 C.B. 76, has ruled that the date of closing and not the date of the execution of the contract is the crucial date for purposes of 341(d)(3). It is possible, however, that the Service would disregard an unusually long deferral of closing that lacked a proper nontax business purpose.

If the buyer is willing and the seller would not object to the buyer's stock as consideration, the transaction might be changed to a tax-free reorganization that would be beyond the scope of the restrictive provisions of 341.

* * *

Impact on Real Estate Companies

The types of problems under Section 341 will vary from business to business.

Real estate sales and construction companies are particularly vulnerable to attack under Section 341 and it will usually be difficult to show that a corporation engaged in this business is not "collapsible" within the meaning of 341(b) unless the sale of the business is precipitated by a totally unforeseen event, such as the serious illness of a major shareholder.

Since the business of such a company consists of selling land or houses, substantially all of the assets of the corporation will be held for sale to customers in the course of its trade or business and, accordingly, will be subsection (e) assets. This means that the sellers of the business will probably not be able to qualify for capital gains treatment under Section 341(e).

If the corporation owns investment assets, it may be possible to qualify a sale of stock under Section 341(d)(2), although the presence of unrelated investment assets may make it difficult to sell the stock of the corporation.

Section 341(f) is a definite possibility in connection with the sale of a real estate sales business because, in the ordinary course of events, the buyer of the business will in turn sell the properties to customers and the corporation can then distribute the [cash] proceeds to the shareholders in liquidation without the payment of tax at the corporate level.

If the corporation has developed several tracts of land, a question may arise with respect to whether the tracts are separate properties for purposes of the 30% test of Section 341(d)(2). For example, if a substantial amount of income has been realized from one tract but not from another, the first tract, if a separate asset, will not be a collapsible asset while the second tract will. If 30% or more of the corporation's gain is attributable to the noncollapsible tract, the entire gain will be [treated as] capital gains * * *. If the two tracts are deemed to be the same property and a substantial amount of income remains to be realized from the two tracts taken together as a single asset, the transaction will not qualify under 341(d)(2) and [the gain will be treated as] ordinary income * * *. If two parcels of property are part of an "integrated project," they will be treated as one piece of property for purposes of the substantial realization and 30% rules.[22] Factors such as geographical proximity, similarity of use, and the time and manner of acquisition will be relevant in determining whether two parcels of property are part of an integrated project. If two tracts of land are contiguous and are developed in the same manner, they will probably be held to be one project.

Corporations holding rental real estate may be subject to collapsible corporation attack, especially if, as is often the case, they borrow more money than is needed for construction costs and operating expenses.

Ordinarily, a rental corporation will not have inventory or ordinary income property and, therefore, Section 341(e) may offer a way out if none of the shareholders is a dealer in the type of property held by the corporation. If a shareholder is a dealer in undeveloped land, it would seem reasonable that he should not be treated as a dealer in apartment houses, but the Regulations furnish no guidance in this regard and there is no case law in point.

In applying the substantial realization test to a real estate rental corporation, it is important to keep in mind that the test is applied with reference to taxable income, not gross income. Such a corporation may have very little taxable income in its early years despite a good cash flow because of depreciation deductions and, accordingly, it will usually be difficult for such a corporation to avoid collapsibility by showing that only an insubstantial part of the taxable income to be derived from the property has not been realized.

In a given case, it may be anticipated that the corporation will never realize taxable income from the property because of depreciation

22. Reg. 1.341–2(a)(4).

deductions. In these circumstances, it can be argued that the statute literally does not apply. Such a contention would be consistent with the statutory purpose because the collapse of the corporation would not convert what otherwise would have been ordinary income into capital gain.

* * *

NOTE

1. Do the foregoing excerpts present any considerations which should be taken into account when choosing the form of entity to be used for the development, operation, and possibly the sale of real estate?

    a. Even though the use of a corporation carries with it the collapsible corporation problems, are there other considerations which indicate the use of a corporation despite these problems?

    b. Can the collapsible problems be avoided by the use of a partnership?

        1. If not, is the provision of the Internal Revenue Code which produces similar results with respect to partnerships less of a danger, more of a danger, or about the same?

            a. Does this determination depend on the particular facts existing at the time of a proposed sale of the interests in the entity and the nature of the participants involved?

2. Can Section 341 problems be avoided by selling the assets of a corporation, closing the sale during the first month of the corporation's taxable year and having the corporation elect Subchapter S in the month prior to the month of the sale or in the month of the sale but prior to the sale?

    a. What is the tax cost of the transaction? Consider the effect of Section 1374. Cf. Marcus, *Using Sub S to Increase Shareholders' After–Tax Gains on Sales of Corporation's Realty,* 57 J.Tax'n 236 (1982).

    b. Does Section 341 apply to the gain recognized by shareholders on the liquidation of an S corporation?

        1. Should an S corporation sell less than all of its assets if it is going to be liquidated shortly after the sale?

        2. Should an S corporation take a substantial installment obligation in exchange for its assets if it is going to be liquidated shortly after the sale?

    c. If the S election is made and all of the assets of the corporation sold, after the sale has the corporation realized two-thirds of the taxable income to be derived from the assets?

    d. How soon after the sale of the assets can the S corporation be safely liquidated?

    e. See Division I, pages 101 to 116 supra.

3. The Internal Revenue Service in Rev.Rul. 63–114, 1963–1 C.B. 74, held that repairs, remodeling, and alterations are not construction for the purposes of Section 341 if they do not increase the area available for rental, change the character of the structure, appreciably increase the fair market value of the structure, or appreciably increase the net income that can be realized from the structure. The amount expended for alterations in this ruling was relatively

insignificant when compared with the cost of the structure. This raises the question whether the amount expended for alterations is, in any way, determinative of whether the alterations amount to construction. Revenue Ruling 72–422, 1972–2 C.B. 211, attempts to answer this question by stating that

> "＊ ＊ ＊ the amount expended for alterations in connection with an existing structure is not determinative of whether a taxpayer has engaged in 'construction' within the meaning of Section 341 of the Code, and is not relevant in making this determination except insofar as it advances the resolution of the four criteria enumerated in Revenue Ruling 63–114."

A significant expenditure, however, in all likelihood, would advance the resolution of the four criteria. For example, it would probably increase the fair market value of the structure. See Schwartz, *Can Building Alterations Make the Corporate Owner Collapsible?*, 2 # 4 Real Est.Rev. 117 (1973). In Rev.Rul. 77–306, 1977–2 C.B. 103, the Internal Revenue Service indicated that a lessor corporation which permits a lessee to build, at the lessee's expense, a structure with a useful life less than the maximum term of the lease, with the lessor having the right to approve the design, will not be considered as engaged in construction or production.

4. Can the specific ownership tests described in Section 341(d)(1) and in many places in Section 341(e) be relied on?

a. For example, assume that father, who is not a dealer, owns 97% of the stock of a collapsible real estate corporation and son, who is a dealer, owns 3%.

1. Can son sell his stock free of collapsible treatment pursuant to Section 341(d)(1)?

2. Can father sell his stock free of collapsible treatment under Section 341(e)(1) if the net unrealized appreciation in the corporation's assets is greater than 15% of its net worth?

3. Reconsider the questions asked in subparts 1 and 2 above after assuming the father owns 79% of the stock and is not a dealer, son owns 3% of the stock and is not a dealer, but participated with his friend, who owns 18% of the stock and is a dealer, in several real estate ventures.

4. See Sections 341(e)(1) and 341(d).

b. If the son referred to in subpart 3 above is a dealer, does the son and his friend being dealers prevent the father from escaping collapsible treatment, under Section 341(e)(1), of the gain he recognizes on the sale of his stock in the corporation if, prior to his sale, he purchases both the son's and friend's stock?

1. Will the son and friend be considered shareholders for the purposes of Section 341?

2. In Rev.Rul. 78–285, 1978–2 C.B. 137, the Internal Revenue Service approved of a sale of stock by a dealer shareholder in order to reduce his interest below 20% so that Section 341(e) could be used by the remaining shareholders.

5. If a sale of stock is contemplated, the obvious way out of Section 341 is the Section 341(f) consent. This procedure, however, is not without its attendant problems. See DeCastro and Rosenberg, *Shoring Up the Collapsible Corporation—The Section 341(f) Consent*, 48 L.A.Bar Bull. 204 (1973); Hall, *The*

Consenting Collapsible Corporation—Section 341(f) of the Internal Revenue Code of 1954, 12 U.C.L.A.L.Rev. 1365 (1965); Faber, *Collapsible Corporation Net Expands But Proposed Regs. on 341(f) Offer an Escape,* 48 J.Tax'n 84 (1978); Hammer, *Section 341(f): Interpretation and Comment,* 56 Taxes 541 (1978).

6. The Internal Revenue Service will rule on collapsible corporation status if (1) the corporation has been in existence for at least 20 years or has clearly demonstrated that it has realized two-thirds of the taxable income to be derived from the property defined in Section 341(b)(1)(A), (2) the aggregate change in shareholders' interests during the lesser of the 20 years or the period during which two-thirds of the income was realized was no greater than 10%, not counting intrafamily transfers and redemptions of stock to pay death taxes under Section 303, and (3) the corporation has conducted the same trade or business during the applicable period.

7. See generally Moses, *The Collapsible Corporation Provisions—A Look After Twenty-One Years,* 21 Tul.Tax Inst. 89 (1972); Holden, *The Collapsible Corporation: What, Why, How; Understanding the Creature as a Protection Against Unfortunate Tax Results,* 34 N.Y.U.Inst.Fed.Tax'n 11 (1976); Price, *Using "Collapsing" Corporations to Maximize Returns from Development Ventures,* 7 J.Real Est.Tax'n 260 (1980); Natbony, *The Onion or the Pearl? Peelings from Collapsibility and Dealership,* 11 J.Corp.Tax'n 91 (1984); Drucker and Segal, *Coping with Collapsible Corporations,* 10 Thurgood Marshall L.Rev. 27 (1984–85); Bittker, *Collapsible Corporations Under the Tax Reform Act of 1986,* 35 Clev.St.L.Rev. 1 (1986).

7. DEFERRAL OF INCOME TAX ON GAIN

If the payment of tax on a realized gain cannot be totally avoided, the next option, in most situations, is to defer the payment of tax as long as possible. At the minimum, the payment of tax should be deferred until the taxpayer has obtained enough money from the transaction which produced the gain to pay the tax.

a. LIKE–KIND EXCHANGES UNDER SECTION 1031(a)

One way to defer the tax on realized gain is the use of a like-kind exchange, under Section 1031. The theory underlying this section is that when a taxpayer trades property for similar property he has not liquidated his investment. Therefore, even though the property received has a fair market value greater than the adjusted basis of the property given up, the recognition of the gain is deferred until the disposition of the acquired property. The following excerpts examine the ways of structuring a transaction involving real estate in order to take advantage of the deferral provided by Section 1031.

PLANNING TAX–FREE LIKE–KIND EXCHANGES OF REAL ESTATE

Walter G. Van Dorn
5 The Journal of Real Estate Taxation 293 (1978).
[some footnotes omitted]

*   *   *

BASIC REQUIREMENTS FOR APPLICABILITY OF
SECTION 1031(a)

Attributes of Property Involved in the Exchange

Not all property is "property" for federal income tax purposes. Thus, rights to carved-out oil payments [treated] as ordinary income do not qualify as property for purposes of Section 1031. And a lessee's interest under a lease is not qualified property to the lessor so that the receipt of qualifying property from the lessee in exchange for the leasehold is a substitute for, and taxable as, rent. Similarly, a life estate carved out and transferred by the fee owner (in exchange for a remainder interest in other realty) results in the receipt of rent by the transferor. Although it is clear under the regulations that a leasehold with thirty years or more to run is "like" a fee interest, whereas a leasehold of under thirty years is not "like" a fee interest, it is not so clear that an under-thirty-year leasehold constitutes "property" which, for example will permit a tax-free exchange by a lessee of a ten-year leasehold in one property for a ten-year leasehold in another property. However, Revenue Ruling 76–301 [23] holds that an assignment by the lessee of a leasehold having twenty-seven and one-half years to run for a subleasehold in a portion of the same property for an identical term constitutes an exchange of like-kind property, thus precluding recognition of loss. Implicitly, the ruling holds that both leaseholds constitute property. * * *

Property of Like Kind

The regulations, past and present * * * and * * * cases and rulings, have established that virtually any kind of fee interest in real estate is "like" any other fee interest. Difficulties have arisen principally in the area of less-than-fee interests, such as undivided interests, leasehold interests, other limited interests such as mineral interests, and the historical dissimilarity of real and personal property.[24]

The Internal Revenue Service has consistently taken the position that real property and personal property are not of like kind. The

---

23. 1976–2 C.B. 241.

24. As to oil interests, see Rev.Rul. 68–331, 1968–1 C.B. 352; Rev.Rul. 68–186, 1968–1 C.B. 354. The inquiry is largely whether the interest constitutes real property under local law. Similarly as to water rights. Rev.Rul. 55–749, 1955–2 C.B. 295. As to a sale-leaseback (for more than thirty years constituting a tax-free exchange of like-kind properties resulting in denial of a loss deduction), see Rev.Rul. 60–43, 1960–1 C.B. 687, registering IRS disapproval of Jordan Marsh Co. v. Comm'r, 269 F.2d 453 (2d Cir.1959), and adherence to Century Elec. Co. v. Comm'r, 192 F.2d 155 (8th Cir. 1951). See also City Investing Co., 38 T.C. 1 (1962); Leslie Co. v. Comm'r, 539 F.2d 943 (3d Cir.1976), siding with *Jordan Marsh*, supra. In Rev.Rul. 78–72, 1978–1 C.B. 258, optional renewal periods were counted in computing the length of the term for this purpose, citing Century Electric, supra * * *.

Leasebacks of less than thirty years have uniformly been held not to be of like kind to a fee interest. Standard Envelope Mfg. Co., 15 T.C. 41 (1950); May Dep't Stores Co., 16 T.C. 547 (1951); Capri, Inc., 65 T.C. 162 (1975). In all these cases, loss was recognized. The exercise of a purchase option in a lease is also not an exchange of like-kind property. Vernon Molbreak, 61 T.C. 382 (1973), aff'd 509 F.2d 616 (7th Cir. 1975).

issue commonly arises under Section 1033(g)(1), allowing elective non-recognition of gain when involuntarily converted property held for investment or used in a trade or business is replaced by property of a like kind to be so held or used. The issue often is whether reinvestment of conversion proceeds in improvements on land already owned is a qualified reinvestment in like-kind property. The Service has consistently ruled that it is not, basically on the formalistic ground that the new improvements, by themselves, are unlike land—even though improved land is "like" unimproved land. This pushes to the extreme the historical distinction between real and personal property. The strain is evidenced in Davis v. United States,[25] which allowed nonrecognition for reinvestment in improvements to other land already owned and rejected the Service's position in favor of a liberal construction of the relief provision in question. * * *

In Revenue Ruling 68–394,[26] it was held that acquisition by a taxpayer-lessor of a forty-five-year outstanding leasehold on land owned by the taxpayer was a qualified "like kind" replacement for a condemned fee interest in other land.

Another facet of this issue, this time under Section 1031(a) and not Section 1033, is illustrated by Bloomington Coca–Cola Bottling Co. v. Comm'r,[27] where the taxpayer conveyed its old plant (land and buildings) to a contractor in partial payment for the construction of a new plant on land already owned by the taxpayer. It was unnecessary for the court to consider the like-kind issue at all, for it held that there was no "exchange," but only a "sale" of the old property since the contractor never "owned" the completed plant nor "had" like property, title to the land never having been in the contractor. Whether a complete building severed from the land would qualify as "like" real property seems never to have been decided.

Held for Productive Use

The taxpayer may not be a "dealer" with respect to the property given up in the exchange.

Property Received in the Exchange

[Section 1031(a) also requires] that the property received in the exchange * * * be * * * held [for productive use in trade or business or for investment], and is simply the application of the continuity-of-interest requirement. Virtually any type of early disposition of the received property will disqualify an otherwise qualifying exchange. It would not seem necessary for the taxpayer to be characterized as a "dealer" for this to happen. Assuming the taxpayer safely passes the dealer test and the continuity of interest requirement, it is clear that transferred property held either for (1) productive use in

---

25. 411 F.Supp. 964 (D.Hawaii 1976), aff'd 589 F.2d 446 (9th Cir.1979).

26. 1968–2 C.B. 338.

27. 189 F.2d 14 (7th Cir.1951).

trade or business, or (2) investment, may be exchanged for like-kind property to be held either for (1) productive use in trade or business, or (2) investment.

Investment Securities Exclusion

Language excluding exchanges of investment securities from tax-free treatment appeared in the 1924 Act and was first enacted in the 1923 amendments to the 1921 Act. [Section 1031(a)(2)(D) which excludes the exchange of partnership interests from treatment under Section 1031(a) was enacted in 1984 after several courts had concluded that, in certain situations, Section 1031(a) was applicable to the exchange of partnership interests.] * * *

Problem Areas

The Exchange Requirement

* * * Congress in enacting [what was to become Section 1031] in 1921 had in mind true barter exchanges or direct swaps of properties (apart from the question of boot) and not a distinct sale of property followed by reinvestment of the cash proceeds in new property, permitted by the elective nonrecognition provisions of Sections 1033 and 1034. * * *

Many of the difficulties and troublesome distinctions that have arisen in the multiparty exchange area are attributable to the need for an exchange as distinct from a separate sale and purchase. * * *

The overall consequence, which is of course not novel, is that the statute, as presently construed, places a premium on expert advice and planning from both a tax and conveyancing point of view, so that nonrecognition of gain can often be achieved even though the direct-exchange requirement need be observed only in form. In many situations, the shadowy distinction between a sale-purchase and an exchange causes the tax result to turn on seemingly insignificant factors. The vagaries that come into play can be illustrated by a series of examples.

Exchange for Property Already Owned

In *Bloomington Coca–Cola*,[28] taxpayer owned an old plant and a vacant lot. Its attempt to exchange the appreciated old plant tax-free to a builder as part consideration for the construction of a new plant on the lot was unsuccessful. If, however, taxpayer had wanted the new plant on a different lot that it did not already own, it could have exchanged the vacant lot or the old plant, or both, to the builder for the different lot, the builder having first bought that lot and erected the plant thereon.[29] Also, if Bloomington Coca–Cola happened to have had

---

28. Note [27] supra.

29. See Rev.Rul. 75–291, 1975–2 C.B. 332, wherein IRS acknowledges that "a taxable exchange is not deemed to arise merely because Y (the builder) acquired

the property specifically to complete the exchange, if the transaction otherwise qualifies. * * *" See also J.H. Baird Publishing Co., 39 T.C. 608 (1962), acq. 1963–2 C.B. 4; Coastal Terminals, Inc. v.

title to the vacant lot in a subsidiary or parent corporation instead of in its own name, the lot could have been sold to the builder by the affiliate (recognizing gain, if any), but Bloomington thereafter could have achieved its primary objective of trading the old plant tax-free to the builder for the new plant erected on the lot.[30] As an additional feature, Bloomington Coca-Cola could have loaned the builder all the funds needed to finance the purchase of the vacant lot in question. If, however, Bloomington Coca-Cola was wedded to the idea of using its existing lot as the site for the new plant, no satisfactory method of achieving the desired result occurs to the writer.

* * *

The Agency Problem

The basic requirement of an exchange has plagued both the Treasury and taxpayers over the years because of the nicety of the distinction between an exchange and a sale-purchase in certain cases. The earliest rulings [31] concern this point. If A trades one security then owned by A to B for another security then owned by B, there is a proper "exchange" (1921 Act). But, if B is really A's stockbroker who has been instructed to sell the first security and buy the second, there is no "exchange." The problem was intractable in the securities area because of the difficulty in determining whether B was acting as broker for A or as an independent dealer, in which latter capacity B was making an exchange with A. Even though tax-free securities exchanges of this kind were ended by the 1923 Act, the same "agent versus principal" problem in defining a qualified exchange persists in the real estate area.

This has led to the troublesome requirements sometimes enunciated or implied that (1) the reciprocal transfers constituting a proper exchange must necessarily be simultaneous, and (2) in the three-party situation (where, typically, A and B are the parties to the exchange, but B is acquiring from C the property that B is transferring to A), a direct conveyance from C to A necessarily disqualifies the exchange.

One of the most instructive cases in the Section 1031 area, J.H. Baird Publishing Co.,[32] focuses directly on the "agency" issue in connection with three-party exchanges involving newly constructed improvements. Publishing Co. operated a business which it did not wish to have interrupted. It agreed to transfer its appreciated old plant for a new plant to be constructed on another site. However, the transfer was actually arranged with an intermediary realty company which undertook to acquire the new site and erect the new plant thereon. The old plant was conveyed to Realty Co. and by Realty Co. to the third party

United States, 320 F.2d 333 (4th Cir.1963) (taxpayer already had options on new sites and assigned the options to a "builder" who exercised them).

30. Boise Cascade Corp., T.C.Memo. 1974–315.

31. I.T. 1377, I–2 C.B. 24; I.T. 1410, I–2 C.B. 25.

32. 39 T.C. 608 (1962), acq. 1963–2 C.B. 4.

who actually wanted it in October, 1956, subject to the rights of Publishing Co. to continue in occupancy until the new plant was ready. That did not occur until July 1, 1957, when Realty Co. conveyed the new plant to Publishing Co. and completed the exchange.

In holding that Publishing Co. made a qualifying exchange of the old plant, the Tax Court found that Realty Co.'s participation in the transaction was as principal and not as agent of Publishing Co. in arranging a sale of the old property and acquiring the new. The crucial factor may have been that Realty Co. had some risk of loss, and had some opportunity to profit, depending on the ultimate cost of the new plant, and generally bore the burdens of ownership during the construction period (which would not be so if it were merely the agent of Publishing Co.). Also, the cash funds paid to Realty Co. by the purchaser of the old plant were at all times held and controlled by Realty Co. and were not made available to or controlled by Publishing Co.

Another decision that merits attention in connection with transactions of the *Baird Publishing* type, where the "agency" aspect of the exchange issue arises, is Mercantile Trust Co. of Baltimore,[33] which dealt with a three-cornered exchange arranged through a title company as intermediary. It was there held that the title company was not acting as taxpayer's agent in arranging a separate sale and purchase, but that there was a qualifying exchange. Interestingly, the exchange agreement provided that the title company would pay taxpayer $300,000 cash for the taxpayer's property if the other property could not be acquired for the purpose of the exchange. However, the designated property was in fact acquired by the title company and conveyed to the taxpayer in the exchange, all simultaneously. In W.D. Haden Co. v. Comm'r[34] an intermediary realtor was held to have been acting as principal in acquiring property (desired by taxpayer) which was simultaneously exchanged for taxpayer's property in a qualifying exchange. The important feature of the *Haden* decision is the subsidiary holding that the exchange characterization was not upset by (1) the designated property being deeded directly to the taxpayer from the third party who owned it instead of being deeded to the realtor and then to taxpayer, or (2) taxpayer's property (which had been presold by the realtor) being conveyed by the taxpayer directly to the fourth party, the realtor's customer, instead of being conveyed to the realtor and then to the customer. It was clear that the conveyances were made at the realtor's direction in each case and thus were not inconsistent with the taxpayer's exchange with the realtor. *Haden* is practically important because it permits direct deeds (where appropriate) to save local transfer taxes on conveyances.

* * *

33. 32 B.T.A. 82 (1935), acq. XIV-1 C.B. 13.   **34.** 165 F.2d 588 (5th Cir.1948).

How not to close a three-party exchange is demonstrated by Carlton v. United States.[35] A third party, *P*, with whom Carlton was to carry out an exchange for property designated by Carlton, contracted to acquire the designated property from the seller *S*, but, at the closing, Carlton accepted an assignment of *P's rights to acquire the property and the cash funds* needed to go through with the purchase; and the property then acquired was deeded direct to Carlton. If, in truth, the only reason for this weird procedure was to secure a direct deed, it would have been simple for *P* to have continued to act as the purchaser of the designated property and to have directed *S* to name Carlton as the grantee in the deed, as was done in *Haden*.[36]

The opinion in Franklin B. Biggs [37] should be compared with the *Carlton* case. The *Biggs* case introduces what may prove to be a controversial new stage in the evolution of multiparty exchange analysis. Liberally applying step-transaction theory in the taxpayer's favor, the nub of the Court's holding is contained in the following statement:

> Having carefully reviewed the evidence in the case before us, we are convinced that the transfer of the Maryland property and receipt of the Virginia property were part of an integrated plan intended to effectuate an exchange of like kind properties, the substantive result of which was an exchange within the meaning of section 1031.[38]

This holding was expressed only after careful consideration of the following significant facts.

(1) The individual who initially agreed to acquire Biggs' Maryland property subsequently assigned his rights to a third party (who assigned such rights to a fourth party).

(2) Biggs' original "memorandum of intent" to sell his Maryland property did not refer to an exchange, and Biggs had not yet located suitable property to receive in exchange; however, Biggs, from the outset, clearly contemplated receiving other property as at least part of the consideration for his property.

(3) Thereafter, Biggs did locate suitable target property and arranged for its purchase in the name of a title company because the other party to the "exchange" was unwilling to take title. Biggs advanced all necessary funds for the cash portion of the purchase price and expenses, and he took back a bond secured by a deed of trust.

(4) The title company held title after closing the purchase of the target property for forty-eight days before agreeing to sell it to the individual to whom Biggs was conveying the Maryland property. Dur-

35. 385 F.2d 238 (5th Cir.1967).

36. The mechanics of carrying out a three-party exchange through escrow are tracked in Rev.Rul. 77–297, 1977–2 C.B. 304. The taxpayer party's inability to get at the escrowed cash put up by the other party to the exchange and lack of privity with the third party initially owning the designated property are emphasized.

37. 69 T.C. 905 (1978)[, aff'd, 632 F.2d 1171 (5th Cir.1980)].

38. Id. at 912.

ing this period, it was agreed by the title company and Biggs that the property would be conveyed to Biggs or his nominee at any time upon payment of the title company's costs and obligations relating to its acquisition and ownership of the property. Distinguishing the facts in the *Coupe* case,[39] the court observed that it did not find as a fact in the *Biggs* case that the title company was acting as agent for the party purchasing Biggs' property. Instead, the opinion states that in contracting to purchase the target property *Biggs was acting for the other individual,* and the title company took title "to facilitate an exchange."

(5) At the closings, which occurred two days apart, the target property was first conveyed to Biggs by deed executed by title company and by all the successive holders of the rights to purchase Biggs' property, although only the title company had legal title; and then Biggs' property was conveyed to the final assignee of the right to purchase Biggs' property by deed signed by Biggs and joined in by all prior holders of the purchaser's interest in the contract with Biggs, although only Biggs had legal title.[40] Previously, the purchaser of Biggs' property had assigned to Biggs all his right, title, and interest to the target property and the right to purchase it under the contract with the title company.

In response to the government's chief argument that Biggs had made a sale of his property and a separate purchase of the target property, the court held that the various steps were part of an integrated plan, the substance of which was an exchange.[41] The critical issue is whether nonrecognition exchange treatment should apply in circumstances where the taxpayer has assumed virtually all the risks in the acquisition of the target property and where the other party to the putative exchange has only nominally participated in the transfer of the target property to taxpayer.[42] Since, as is well known, the step-transaction doctrine is objective in nature and can be used against taxpayers as well as in their favor, the *Biggs* analysis may not be subject to the ultimate criticism that it improperly converts Section 1031 into an elective provision.

* * *

39. Leslie Q. Coupe, 52 T.C. 394 (1969), acq. 1970–2 C.B. xix.

40. Although reflective of a temperament untrammeled by the strictures of doctrinaire conveyancing precepts, the deeds served as evidence of the continuing plan to effect an exchange.

41. The court also distinguished the *Carlton* case, relying on *W.D. Haden Co.* Reliance was also placed on Redwing Carriers, Inc. v. Tomlinson, 399 F.2d 652 (5th Cir.1968), in which transactional analysis was applied to deny a loss on what was held to be a trade-in exchange of old trucks

for new trucks. The *Redwing* decision is unsatisfactory for its failure to explain its disregard of the corporate entities of parent and subsidiary. The *Biggs* decision enhances the risk that step-transaction analysis might be applied to deny recognition of loss on a sale which is tied in with a purchase of like property.

42. The degree of risk-taking with respect to the target property by the other party to the exchange presumably is an important factor in determining whether that party is acting independently or as the taxpayer's agent.

Designating the Property to be Received in the Exchange

It is now settled that in the typical three-party exchange, where *A* and *B* are the exchanging parties, and *A* desires the exchange to be tax-free, the agreement can provide that *B* will acquire specific property that *A* wants and convey it or cause it to be conveyed to *A* in exchange for *A*'s property.[43] In such a transaction, the target property is designated at the outset.[44]

* * * [In addition,] it is now settled that under a contract contemplating the designation of the exchange property prior to closing, if property is in fact located and is in fact acquired and exchanged "to" the taxpayer on the closing date, the exchange will not be treated as a taxable sale.[45]

It will be recalled that in *Baird Publishing Co.*, the conveyance of the old plant preceded the conveyance of the new plant to the taxpayer by several months (the entire construction period), but there was no question of the identity of the property ultimately to be conveyed in the exchange. But what if the party acquiring taxpayer's property desires to do so immediately or in any event before taxpayer succeeds in locating or designating any exchange property? Can taxpayer convey its property in return for the other party's surviving obligation to acquire and convey like property to taxpayer when and if taxpayer designates it? Should the agreement provide for the eventuality that taxpayer never designates any property prior to some outside date?

* * *

[The applicability of Section 1031 to a situation in which a taxpayer conveys property in return for the other party's obligation to subsequently acquire and convey like property when and if designated by the taxpayer is controlled by Section 1031(a)(3). Section 1031(a)(3) requires that, in order for Section 1031 to apply to a deferred like-kind exchange, the property to be received in the exchange must be identified within 45 days after the date on which the taxpayer transfers other property, and the property to be received must be received by the earlier of (i) 180 days after the transfer of the other property, or (ii) the due date of the tax return (determined with regard to extension) of the taxpayer for the year during which the taxpayer transferred the other property. It also appears that providing for a cash payment plus interest in the event that the taxpayer does not designate any exchange property by the end of the 45–day period will not prevent the transaction from qualifying under Section 1031 if Section 1031(a)(3) is complied

---

43. See Rev.Rul. 75–291, 1975–2 C.B. 332.

44. *B*'s exchange is not a qualifying exchange because *B* is acquiring the target property solely for the purpose of exchanging it to *A*, but this does not matter because *B* ordinarily realizes no gain.

45. IRS acknowledged this in Rev.Rul. 77–297, 1977–2 C.B. 304. Also, in the curi-

ous case of 124 Front St., Inc., 65 T.C. 6 (1975), nonacq. 1976–2 C.B. 3, the exchange property was designated by taxpayer subsequent to the original exchange agreement, pursuant to the right so to designate in the agreement.

with. The value of any property received in return for an interest obligation, however, will be treated as ordinary income to the taxpayer.[46]]

* * *

Receipt of Boot; Effect of Mortgages and Liens

Gain Aspects

Section 1031(b) provides that realized gain is recognized to the extent of money and the value of any nonqualifying property received in the exchange. In other words, there can be partial or total recognition of gain upon an otherwise qualifying Section 1031 exchange if "boot" is received in addition to the qualifying like-kind property.

The gain recognized as a result of the receipt of boot may be reported on the installment method.[47] * * *

The amount of a liability assumed or of mortgages to which the transferred property is subject is treated as money received by the taxpayer on the exchange, under the *Crane* doctrine. The following example is based on Regulations Section 1.1031(d)–2.

B owns property worth $800,000 (if unencumbered), subject to a $150,000 mortgage, so that the equity is worth $650,000. *B*'s basis is $500,000. *B* swaps the property, subject to the mortgage, with *C* for like property, which is unencumbered, worth $600,000, plus $50,000 cash. Each party has exchanged a total net value of $650,000. *B* *realizes* a gain of $300,000:

Value of like property received	$600,000
Cash received	50,000
Continuing mortgage on transferred property	150,000
Amount realized	$800,000
Less basis	500,000
Gain realized	$300,000

The amount of gain recognized (total boot) is $200,000, consisting of the $50,000 cash and $150,000 mortgage relief.[48]

Suppose *B*'s basis had been only $100,000, so that the mortgage exceeded it by $50,000. Although the gain realized would then be $700,000 (the above amount realized, $800,000, less the $100,000 basis), the amount recognized would seem to be the same $200,000 since the amount of boot is not changed. However, by analogy to the regulations

[46. See Starker v. United States, 75–1 U.S.T.C. ¶ 9943 (D.Or.1975); Starker v. United States, 77–2 U.S.T.C. ¶ 9512 (D.Or. 1977), reversed in part, affirmed in part, 602 F.2d 1341 (9th Cir.1979); Simmons, *Deferred Like–Kind Exchanges Under Section 1031(a)(3) After Starker*, 68 J.Tax'n 92 (1988).]

47. Rev.Rul. 65–155, 1965–1 C.B. 356. See also Franklin B. Biggs, 69 T.C. 905

(1978), [affirmed, 632 F.2d 1171 (5th Cir. 1980),] in which the gain recognized as a result of the receipt of boot was reported on the installment method. * * *

48. If *B* had sold the property for $650,000 cash, subject to the mortgage, *B* would have $300,000 of gain both realized and recognized.

under the installment-sale provisions,[49] the Service might contend that the $50,000 excess of mortgage over basis is *additional* boot, making the total recognized gain $250,000. The trouble with this contention is that it means counting that $50,000 of the mortgage twice, since the entire $150,000 mortgage already is treated as boot (subject to netting as explained below). Or, the Service might argue that the $50,000 excess of mortgage over basis is taxed as boot "off the top," not susceptible of reduction under the netting rules, leaving only the balance of $100,000 subject to netting against liens on the property received. More likely, Section 1031 provides one way to transfer property mortgaged in excess of basis without recognizing gain in the amount of the excess.

Regulations Section 1.1031(d)–2 *Example (2)* incorporates a rule, not contained in the Code, that boot deemed to be received in the form of liabilities assumed or mortgages on the transferred property (but not cash or other property received) is reduced or off-set by liabilities assumed in connection with, or mortgages remaining on, the property *received* in the exchange or by money or other property given in the exchange.

Thus, in the last example, suppose *C*'s property received by *B* in the exchange was worth $750,000, but was subject to a $150,000 mortgage, so that the equity was worth the same $600,000 as in the example and the economics of the exchange remained the same. Now, the $150,000 mortgage on *B*'s property is cancelled out by the $150,000 mortgage on the property received, so that *B*'s only boot is the $50,000 cash received. Is *B*'s recognized gain then only $50,000? If so, *B*'s basis in the property received is as follows:

Basis of property transferred:	$100,000
Plus mortgage on new property:	150,000
Total	$250,000
Less: cash received	(50,000)
mortgage on transferred property	(150,000)
Difference	50,000
Plus: gain recognized by *B* on the exchange	50,000
Basis of new property	$100,000

Thus, *B* has $150,000 less recognized gain when he receives a $750,000 property encumbered by a $150,000 mortgage than when he receives an unencumbered property worth $600,000.[50] It will be observed that on this hypothesis the $50,000 excess of mortgage over basis carries over into the new property.

49. Reg. § 1.453–4(c).

50. If *C*'s property were worth $800,000, if unencumbered, so that the equity was $650,000, then the cash boot would be eliminated and *B* would recognize no gain, still assuming the excess of mortgage over basis remains quiescent. In *Franklin B. Biggs*, note [87] supra the boot-netting rules were applied in the computation of the recognized gain. The gross boot received of $770,444.86 ($900,000.00 less $129,555.14) was reduced to a net of $627,900.00 by virtue of the $142,544.86 of mortgages on the qualifying property received.

Loss Aspects

Section 1031(c) provides that if an exchange would be tax-free under Section 1031(a) but for the receipt of boot, no loss will be recognized even if taxable boot is received. Thus, a tax-free exchange cannot be "busted" by the receipt of boot in order to deduct a realized loss. For example, Blackacre has a cost basis of $500,000 but is worth only $400,000, indicating a $100,000 loss. If it is exchanged for another property worth $399,999 plus one dollar, and all requirements of Section 1031(a) are met, no loss is recognized on the exchange. The basis of the received property is $499,999. Similarly, the exchange of property plus the payment of cash for like property does not permit recognition of loss on the property given up in the exchange.

* * *

Depreciation Recapture

Sections 1245(b)(4) and 1250(d)(4) provide limited exceptions to the recognition of depreciation recapture (ordinary income) in qualifying Section 1031 exchanges. Basically, the amount of recapture income that would be recognized on a taxable disposition is not taxed but is deferred and incorporated into the like property received so as to be taxable on an ultimate taxable disposition.

Gain recognized due to the receipt of boot will thus trigger potential recapture income. If the value of the like property received which is either Section 1245 or Section 1250 property is not sufficient to absorb the recapture potential, then the recapture income will be taxed. For example, if [an office building] with recapture potential is exchanged for land [or for an apartment building depreciated using the straight-line method] the entire recapture potential is taxed.

* * *

NOTE

1. How schizophrenic can a real estate broker be for income tax purposes? What does a broker do when he has a listing for a like-kind exchange and he finds a purchaser for the property who does not want to acquire like-kind property?

a. Can the broker, using the purchaser's money, acquire the like-kind property in the broker's name, exchange it for the seller's property and then convey that property to the purchaser?

1. If the broker is considered an independent third party, i.e., acting on his own account to earn his commission, is the requirement of a reciprocal exchange met?

2. The broker cannot be treated as an agent of the seller when he receives the purchaser's money. But, from whom does he collect his commission?

a. It would be helpful if the broker was considered to be the agent of the purchaser for the purpose of qualifying the transaction as a like-kind exchange. Can he serve two masters?

b.   Assume the broker formed a straw corporation to acquire the like-kind property as agent for an undisclosed principal (the purchaser) and then caused the corporation to exchange the property for the seller's property and to convey the seller's property to the purchaser.   What are the problems with this approach?

   1.   Can the broker simply have another member or employee of his real estate brokerage firm act "for" the purchaser?

2.   If a taxpayer desires like-kind exchange treatment, is there any reason for the taxpayer to sign a contract granting the purchaser the option to provide like-kind property or cash?

   a.   Does the answer depend on whether the option was for the benefit of the seller or purchaser?   See *Hubert Rutland*, 36 CCH Tax Ct.Mem. 40 (1977); *Hayden v. United States*, 50 A.F.T.R.2d 82–5570 (D.Wyo.1981).

3.   The exchange under Section 1031 must be of like-kind property.   Like-kind has a rather broad meaning since property held for investment or for use in trade or business can be exchanged for other property so held.   As a general matter, it is the nature or character of the property rather than its grade or quality which is determinative.   Therefore, an apartment house can be exchanged for a ranch and improved real estate for unimproved real estate.   See Reg.Sec. 1.1031(a)–1(b) and (c).   If an apartment house is received in exchange for a ranch which had been depreciated using a method faster than straight-line, the transferor of the ranch would have to recognize depreciation recapture.   See Section 1245(b)(4)(B); Dentino, *Recapture on the Exchange of Real Property after ERTA*, 11 J.Real Est.Tax'n 254 (1984).   See generally Scott, *Like Kind Replacement Property: Animal, Vegetable or Mineral?*, 23 San Diego L.Rev. 1067 (1986).

   a.   Section 1031 does not apply to an exchange of property for stock in a corporation owning like-kind property or to an exchange of stock in one corporation for stock in another corporation owning like-kind property. See Section 1031(a)(2)(B).   In the case of property for stock, the analysis is that it is not an exchange of like-kind property.   This type of exchange, however, may be tax free under other sections of the Internal Revenue Code such as Sections 351, 354, 355, 368 and 1032.   In Rev.Rul. 75–291, 1975–2 C.B. 332, the Internal Revenue Service ruled that a taxpayer which exchanged land and a manufacturing facility it owned and used for land and a manufacturing facility acquired and built by the transferee solely for the exchange is entitled to Section 1031 treatment.   See also Rev.Rul. 77–297, 1977–2 C.B. 304.   The transferee, however, is not entitled to Section 1031 treatment.   On the other hand, a taxpayer who entered into the exchange of admittedly like-kind property and, upon the receipt of the property, immediately conveyed it, under Section 351, to the taxpayer's newly created and wholly-owned corporation is not entitled to Section 1031 treatment.   A taxpayer who received property as a result of the liquidation of the taxpayer's wholly-owned corporation and, immediately after the liquidation, exchanged it for other like-kind property does not qualify for nonrecognition of gain or loss under Section 1031.   See Rev.Rul. 75–292, 1975–2 C.B. 333, and Rev.Rul. 77–337, 1977–2 C.B. 305.   But see *Joseph R. Bolker*, 81 T.C. 782 (1983), affirmed, 760 F.2d 1039 (9th Cir.1985), in which the taxpayer was held to be entitled to nonrecognition of gain on an exchange of like-kind real estate entered into shortly after he received the real estate which he exchanged as a result of the liquidation of his wholly owned corporation, and *Norman J. Magneson,* 81 T.C. 767 (1983), affirmed, 753 F.2d 1490 (9th Cir.1985), in which the taxpayers, immediately after receiving property in a like-kind exchange, transferred the property received to a partnership in return for a general partnership interest and were still afforded nonrecognition treatment. See also *Miles H. Mason,* 55 CCH Tax Ct.Mem. 1134 (1988). See generally Guttenberg, *Continuity of Investment is Key to Using 1031 in Combination with a Corporate Transaction,* 60 J.Tax'n 280 (1984); O'Connor, *Recent Court of Appeals Decision in* Magneson *Signals Wider Use of Like–Kind Exchanges of Real Estate,* 63 Taxes 431 (1985); Note, *The Holding Requirement of Section 1031— Magneson v. Commissioner,* 39 Sw.L.J. 943 (1985). Cf. Priv.Ltr.Ruls. 8443054 and 8445010; Spero, *When Can Exchange of Interest in Real Estate Partnership for Direct Interest be Tax–Free?,* 60 J.Tax'n 152 (1984); Burke and Friel, *To Hold or Not To Hold: Magneson, Bolker, and Continuity of Investment Under I.R.C. Section 1031,* 20 U.S.F.L.Rev. 177 (1986); Burke, *An Aggregate Approach to Indirect Exchanges of Partnership Interests: Reconciling Section 1031 and Subchapter K,* 6 Va.Tax Rev. 459 (1987). Finally, the exchange of undeveloped real estate for a long term lease of an apartment building was regarded as within Section 1031 in Rev.Rul. 78–72, 1978–1 C.B. 258, as was the exchange of undeveloped real estate for real estate subject to a 99–year lease in *Carl E. Koch,* 71 T.C. 54 (1978), acq. 1979–1 C.B. 1.

    1. In certain circumstances, Section 1033 permits nonrecognition when the proceeds from an involuntary conversion of property are invested in the stock of a corporation owning property similar or related in service or use to the converted property. See Section 1033(a)(2) and Division IV, pages 1065 to 1067 infra. Note, however, that the acquired property definition is more circumscribed than that of Section 1031.

    b. Section 1031 was amended in 1984 to make clear that the exchange of partnership interests between partners in different partnerships does not qualify for nonrecognition treatment. See Section 1031(a)(2)(D). To illustrate that there is more than one way to skin a cat, however, the Internal Revenue Service ruled in Rev.Rul. 84–115, 1984–2 C.B. 118, that Section 721 provides for the nonrecognition of gain and loss on the contribution to a partnership of a limited partnership interest in another partnership in exchange for a limited partnership interest in the former partnership, provided there is a business purpose for the exchange and it does not amount to an assignment of income. See generally Keating, *Congress Eliminated the Like–Kind Exchange of Partnership Interests—Or Did It?,* 64 Taxes 573 (1986); Burke, *An Aggregate Approach to Indirect Exchanges of Partnership Interests: Reconsidering Section 1031 and Subchapter K,* 6 Va.Tax Rev. 459 (1987).

    c. Related to the contribution of a partnership interest in one partnership for a partnership interest in a different partnership is the contribution of a general partnership interest in exchange for a limited partnership interest or the contribution of a limited interest in exchange for a general interest in the same partnership. It appears that both the contribution of a limited partnership interest for a general partnership interest and a general partnership interest for a limited partnership interest in the same partnership may be tax-free under Section 721. See Priv.Ltr.Rul. 7948063 and Rev.Rul. 84–52, 1984–1 C.B. 157. See generally Banoff, *New Opportunities Now Exist for General and Limited Partnership Conversions,* 52 J.Tax'n 130 (1980); Banoff, *Partnership Interest Conversions: Planning Possibilities,* 1 J.Ps.Tax'n 203 (1984); Banoff, *In New Revenue Ruling 84–52, the IRS Uses an "Exchange" Approach to Conversions,* 61 J.Tax'n 98 (1984).

4. The basis of property acquired in a like-kind exchange is equal to the adjusted basis of the property exchanged. The basis of the acquired property is increased by the amount of money paid to the other party, the amount of gain recognized on the exchange, and the liabilities assumed and to which the property received is subject. The basis of the acquired property is decreased by the amount of money received from the other party, the fair market value of non-like-kind property received from the other party, the amount of loss recognized on the exchange, the amount of liabilities assumed by the other party and the liabilities to which the property transferred to the other party is subject. See Section 1031(d) and Reg.Sec. 1.1031(d)–1 and 2. While one of the parties' assumption of, or the taking subject to, liabilities may result in boot to the other party in a like-kind exchange, liabilities assumed, or taken subject to, by both parties to an exchange can be netted-out. It now appears that other forms of boot, such as cash, also can be netted-out, in certain circumstances, against liabilities or other forms of boot. See *Earlene T. Barker,* 74 T.C. 555 (1980); Priv.Ltr.Rul. 8003004.

5. See generally Guerin, *A Proposed Test for Evaluating Multiparty Like Kind Exchanges,* 35 Tax L.Rev. 547 (1980); Goldstein and Lewis, *Tax Treatment of Like–Kind Exchanges of Property Used in a Trade or Business or for Investment,* 5 Rev.Tax'n Indiv. 195 (1981); Willis, *Of [Im]permissible Illogic and Section 1031,* 34 U.Fla.L.Rev. 72 (1981); Van Dorn, *How to Exchange Real Estate Investments, Both Directly and Indirectly, in Light of Current Developments Under IRC Section 1031,* 42 N.Y.U.Inst.Fed.Tax'n 20–1 (1984); Edwards and McIntosh, *Planning for Tax–Free Exchanges of Real Estate,* 1 Prob. & Prop. 36 (1987); Ruby, *Minimizing Taxes on Real Estate Dispositions Through Installment Sales and Tax–Free Exchanges,* 44 N.Y.U.Inst.Fed.Tax'n 19–1 (1986); Wasserman, *Mr. Mogul's Perpetual Search for Tax Deferral: Techniques and Questions Involving Section 1031 Like–Kind Exchanges in a World of Changing Tax Alternatives,* 65 Taxes 975 (1987).

b. INSTALLMENT AND DEFERRED PAYMENT SALES

When real estate is sold on a deferred payment basis, the Internal Revenue Code permits, in certain situations, the deferral of the recognition of some or all of the gain realized until receipt of the cash resulting from the sale. Installment sale treatment which is specifically authorized by the Code allows the vendor to defer recognition of some or all of the realized gain until receipt of the installments pursuant to the installment payment obligation. The vendor is taxed on that portion of the down payment, if any, and each installment which represents an allocable portion of the total gain realized on the transaction, plus the interest received. If the deferred payment method of accounting is used, assuming the vendor and the transaction qualify for such treatment, the gain realized on the sale is recognized when the installments received exceed the vendor's adjusted basis in the property sold.

INSTALLMENT SALES REVISION ACT OF 1980
John J. Mylan
17 Willamette Law Review 303 (1981)
[most footnotes omitted]

* * * [T]he installment reporting rules [are contained in] three distinct Code sections. Section 453 provides rules for sales of real property and * * * personal property under the installment method. Section 453A [provides special rules for certain installment sales of any property] and section 453B contains the rules governing all dispositions of installment obligations.

* * *

Basically, the rules * * * provide for the spreading of gain over the period during which the installment payments of the sale price are received. The gain reported in any taxable year under the installment method is that proportion of the installment payment received which the gross profit (realized or to be realized when payment is completed) bears to the total contract price.[51] The gross profit is the selling price less the seller's adjusted basis. In general, the contract price equals the selling price reduced by the portion of any indebtedness assumed or taken subject to by the buyer, which does not exceed the seller's basis in the property. Payments taken into account as being received in a taxable year do not include the purchaser's obligation to make future payments, unless the obligation is either payable on demand or has been issued by a government or a corporation and is readily tradable. [T]he installment sale provisions deal with the installment reporting of gain and do not affect the time for recognizing losses from the sale of property for deferred payments.

* * *

[F]or [nondealer] sales of real property and nondealer sales of personal property, [with the exception of stock and securities traded on an established securities market and other property of a kind regularly traded on an established market] the [Code] defines an installment sale, simply, as a disposition of property where at least one payment is to be received after the close of the taxable year in which the disposition occurs.

* * *

RECEIPT OF LIKE–KIND PROPERTY IN CONNECTION WITH INSTALLMENT SALES OF PROPERTY

* * *

[S]ection 453(f)(6)(C) provides that receipt of the like-kind property shall not be treated as a payment. The effect, for reporting purposes, is to postpone gain recognition until cash or nonlike-kind property is received. The total amount of gain to be reported is not affected. * * *

---

51. I.R.C. § 453(c). But see special rules for related party sales * * *.

[T]he like-kind property is eliminated from both the numerator and denominator of the profit ratio. The numerator or gross profit will be the amount of gain to be recognized solely from the face value of the installment obligation. The denominator or total contract price will consist of cash and the fair market value of nonlike-kind property received and the face amount of the installment obligation. * * *

The taxpayer's basis in the property transferred will first be allocated to the like-kind property received, up to its fair market value. Any remaining basis will reduce the taxpayer's gross profit.

* * *

TREATMENT OF THIRD PARTY GUARANTEE

In *J.K. Griffith,* the Tax Court held that a standby letter of credit used to secure future payment for the sale of a cotton crop constituted full payment in the year of sale, and therefore, the taxpayer could not report the transaction on the installment method.[52] The Tenth Circuit, however, * * * decided that a letter of credit used to secure payment for the sale of stock did not constitute a payment under the installment sales provisions.[53] Moreover, the letter of credit did not transform the buyer's promise to pay into a completed payment.[54] Section 453(f)(3) was enacted to resolve this controversy over the proper treatment of a standby letter of credit and other third party guarantees for installment sale purposes. It defines "payment" as not including a buyer's obligation even if payment of that obligation is guaranteed by another person. The statute does not directly address whether the third party guarantee will constitute a payment. The *Senate Report,* however, states clearly that, a "third party guarantee (including a standby letter of credit) used as security for a deferred payment sale should not be treated as a payment received on an installment obligation." [55] A third party evidence of indebtedness used by the purchaser is not a third party guarantee and * * * constitute[s] a payment.

[APPLICABILITY] OF INSTALLMENT REPORTING

* * * Installment reporting * * * appl[ies] automatically to a qualified sale unless the taxpayer elects not to have the provision apply. Providing * * * automatic application for a type of tax treatment that most qualified taxpayers would choose anyway * * * avoid[s] disqualification on technical grounds for failure to properly elect. * * * The election not to have installment method reporting applied to a deferred payment sale must be made on or before the due date (including extensions) for filing the income tax return for the year in which the sale occurs. * * * [R]eporting the entire gain in gross

52. 73 T.C. 933, 942 (1980). The court relied on J. Earl Oden, 56 T.C. 569 (1971) in which th[e] particular escrow arrangement was held to constitute a payment rather than a mere security for the performance of the purchaser.

53. Sprague v. United States, 627 F.2d 1044 (10th Cir.1980).

54. Id. at 1048.

55. S.Rep., [No. 1000, 96th Cong.2d Sess.] 18 [(1980)]. * * *

income for the taxable year in which the sale occurs will operate as an election. The section provides that an election not to have the installment method apply to any sale may be revoked only with the consent of the Service. * * * [A] revocation will not be permitted when one of its purposes is to avoid federal income taxes, or when the taxable year in which any payment was received is closed. * * * [A]llowing the taxpayer to forego installment reporting * * * represents a congressional decision not to require installment reporting treatment as the sole method of treating deferred payment sales.

SALES SUBJECT TO A CONTINGENCY

* * * [T]he installment sale method [applies] to sales in which all or a portion of the selling price cannot be readily ascertained.[56] Congress recognized that it could not prescribe specific rules for every conceivable transaction of this type. Therefore, the statutory provision merely states that the regulations under this section shall include regulations providing for ratable basis recovery in transactions in which the gross profit or the total contract price (or both) cannot be readily ascertained.[57] * * *

For sales under which a stated maximum selling price exists, * * * basis [is recovered] according to a gross profit ratio determined by reference to the stated maximum selling price. The maximum selling price is determined from the contract agreement as the largest price which could be paid to the taxpayer, assuming that all contingencies operate in the taxpayer's favor. Income from the sale would be reported on a pro rata basis from each installment payment, using the maximum selling price to determine the total contract price and the gross profit. * * *

The higher the maximum figure, the higher the profit ratio, and the higher the profit ratio, the lower the percentage of each payment treated as a taxfree recovery of basis. Therefore, taxpayers should be hesitant to set unrealistically high maximum dollar amounts.[58]

If it is subsequently determined that the contingency [will] not be satisfied in whole or in part, thus reducing the maximum selling price, the taxpayer's income from the sale [will] be recomputed. The taxpayer [will] then report reduced gain, as adjusted, from each installment payment received in the taxable year of adjustment and in subsequent taxable years.

If the taxpayer has reported more gain from installment payments received in previous taxable years than the total recomputed gain, a loss deduction [is] permitted in the adjustment year. * * *

56. I.R.C. § 453(i)(2). * * *   unless adequate interest is provided. * * *

57. I.R.C. § 453(i)(2).

58. The imputed interest rules of I.R.C. § 483 will be applicable in such situations

When the sales price is indefinite and no maximum selling price can be determined, and the obligation is payable over a fixed period of time, * * * the basis of the property sold [is] recovered ratably over that fixed period. * * *

If in any year the taxpayer receive[s] a payment which [is] less than the portion of his or her basis allocated to that year, a loss probably [is] not * * * allowed at that time. Any unrecovered basis would be carried forward to the succeeding year and a loss [can] be taken only in the year in which it [is] clearly determined that the entire basis in the property [will] not be recovered from the transaction.[59]

Finally, * * * in appropriate cases, basis recovery [is] permitted under an income forecast method. * * * [T]his method [is applicable to] sales of property qualifying for depreciation under the income forecast method, sales of mineral rights in which the selling price is based on production, and other cases in which [the] failure to take account of the nature or productivity of the property sold may be expected to result in a distortion of the taxpayer's income over time.

* * * [I]nstallment reporting [is clearly available in] situations in which the sale price [is] contingent. The installment method, however, requires ratable recovery of basis and ratable recognition of gain. A sales price that is indeterminate or contingent is often found to have no ascertainable fair market value, thereby entitling sellers to treat the transaction as "open."[60] In an open transaction, sellers are allowed to recover their entire basis before reporting any gain on the sale. Even though installment reporting is now available for such transactions, taxpayers may choose to elect out to seek the superior results available under the open transaction approach. The Service, however, has consistently maintained that it is only in "rare and extraordinary cases" that the fair market value of the purchaser's obligation cannot reasonably be ascertained. On occasion, the courts have agreed with the Service and denied open transaction treatment to the sale.[61] The result of closing the transaction is to require the seller to recognize gain in the year of sale, based on any cash payments received plus the fair market value of the promise to make future payments.[62] Since the

59. * * * If the agreement neither specifies a maximum selling price nor limits payments to a fixed period, the transaction will be closely scrutinized to determine whether in effect the payments received under the agreement are in the nature of rent or royalty income rather than sale proceeds. If it is determined that a sale has occurred, the taxpayer's basis shall be recovered in equal installments over a period of 15 years from the date of sale. Temp.Treas.Reg. § 15A.453-1(c)(4), 46 Fed.Reg. 10,715 (1981).

60. Burnet v. Logan, 283 U.S. 404 (1931).

61. See, e.g., Chamberlin v. Commissioner, 286 F.2d 850 (7th Cir.1960); Estate

of Abraham Goldstein, 33 T.C. 1032 (1960). *See* cases cited in Mylan, *Cost Recovery as a Method of Reporting Gain from Dispositions of Property*, 8 Willamette L.J. 1, 13–16 (1972).

62. Id. The fair market value of the obligation may be less than its face value, thus allowing for some deferral of gain until payments are received in excess of the value placed on the obligation. However, all cash payments in excess of the fair market value of the obligation are generally treated as ordinary income, since they are held not to relate to the original sale or exchange of property. Campagna v. United States, 290 F.2d 682 (2d Cir. 1961); Osenbach v. Commissioner, 198 F.2d

decision to elect out of installment reporting may be revoked only with the consent of the Service, taxpayers may choose ratable reporting of gain under the installment method to avoid the risk of having their open transaction argument denied and their gain from the transaction to the extent of the fair market value of the obligation taxed to them in the year of the sale.

[In fact, section 453(g)(1)(B)(ii), in dealing with a sale of depreciable property between related parties when the payments are contingent as to amount and with respect to which the fair market value cannot be reasonably ascertained, requires the seller to ratably recover basis and does not permit the purchaser to increase the basis of the property acquired in the sale by any amount until the seller includes such amount in income. This rule can be avoided if it is established that the transaction did not have as one of its principal purposes the avoidance of Federal income tax.]

* * * [A] cash basis taxpayer could argue that a sale for fixed future payments should be treated as an open transaction, on the ground that the promise to pay was not in a form which was the equivalent of cash.[63] Thus, the courts have ordinarily allowed open transaction treatment when the promise is unsecured and is represented by a nonnegotiable note or a mere contract right.[64] If the obligation is represented by a negotiable note or is secured, the transaction is usually treated as closed.[65] [In addition, the] courts have found some contractual promises to have a cash equivalent value, thus causing recognition of gain to the extent of that value in the year of sale.[66] The argument for open transaction treatment in the fixed purchase price cases always has been based on less secure ground.[67]

* * * The *Committee Reports,* * * * take the position that the * * * installment reporting rules eliminate any justification for treating transactions as open in fixed purchase price cases and reduce substantially the justification for treating contingent purchase price cases as open. The *Senate Report* states that:

> it is the Committee's intent that the cost recovery method not be available in the case of sales for a fixed price (whether the seller's obligation is evidenced by a note, contractual promise, or other-

---

235 (4th Cir.1952); Rev.Rul. 58–402 C.B. 1958–2, 15. Section 1232(a) states, however, that any payment in discharge of an obligation of a corporate or governmental obligor shall be treated as a sale or exchange.

63. Schlemmer v. United States, 94 F.2d 77 (2d Cir.1938); Estate of Coid Hurlburt, 25 T.C. 1286 (1956); Nina J. Ennis, 17 T.C. 465 (1951).

64. Id.

65. Alvin B. Lowe, 44 T.C. 363 (1965); Harry Leland Barnsley, 31 T.C. 1260 (1959); Walter I. Bones, 4 T.C. 415 (1944).

66. See, e.g., Jones v. Commissioner, 524 F.2d 788 (9th Cir.1975).

67. In Burnet v. Logan, 283 U.S. 404 (1931), a case involving an indeterminate purchase price, the Supreme Court expressed a constitutional concern about taxing capital if the promise to pay an indefinite sum was taxed in the year of sale. The fixed purchase price cases rest only on the argument that under the taxpayer's particular method of accounting (cash basis) he or she had not received the equivalent of cash.

wise), and that its use be limited to those rare and extraordinary cases involving sales for a contingent price where the fair market value of the purchaser's obligation cannot be reasonably ascertained.[68]

INSTALLMENT SALES TO RELATED PARTIES

The [Code] contains * * * rules governing installment sales between related parties. * * *

[A] number of tax advantages may be derived from an installment sale of appreciated property to a related party. The seller defers recognition of gain until installment payments are received from the related purchaser. If the related purchaser resells the property shortly after its acquisition, he or she usually will have to pay little or no tax. This is because the related purchaser's basis in the property is its full cost, including future payments due the seller. The related purchaser would have recognized gain only if the price obtained on resale exceeded that cost. Thus, the group consisting of the two related persons has cash proceeds equal to the value of the property, while deferring recognition of the gain which would have been immediately recognized if the initial sale had been for cash. * * *

When appreciated property is producing little or no income, an installment sale may provide the seller with a regular source of current income through principal and interest payments. When the property cannot be readily sold on the installment basis to an unrelated third party but the seller does not wish to make a cash sale, an installment sale to a related party, followed by that person's resale for cash may solve the problem.

An installment sale of property to a related party may achieve estate planning objectives since the value of the obligation will be fixed for estate tax purposes. Any subsequent appreciation in the value of the property sold will not be in the seller's gross estate. [But cf. section 2036(c).] The seller has been able to do this while keeping the property within the family group, if this is the desired result. Such a transaction may also provide a way to shift income from a high bracket to a low bracket member of a family group. This could be accomplished by an installment obligation that carries an interest rate which is lower than the rate of return the related buyer will receive from the property or from investment of the proceeds from a resale of the property.

[A]n installment sale of stock in a liquidating corporation to a related purchaser would avoid the hardship of the seller being required to recognize immediate gain on installment obligations distributed by the corporation in liquidation. * * * [N]ot all of these tax benefits can be properly characterized as abuses, and the [Code] does not attempt to curtail all of them.

68. S.Rep., supra note 55, at 24.

[Section 453] contains two main rules regarding sales to related parties.[69] The first of these rules, section 453(e), provides for an acceleration of gain being reported on the installment basis by the initial seller only if the related party purchaser resells the property within a specified period. The concern expressed by Congress over the judicial developments in this area was focused mainly on the fact that the resale of the property by the related party allows the related group to receive cash proceeds without the current payment of tax.[70] Thus, in situations other than those covered by section 453(g), Congress has decided not to enact a flat prohibition against an initial installment sale to a related party.

The amount treated as received by the initial seller in the year such a resale occurs is the total amount realized on the second disposition [71] or the total contract price for the first disposition, whichever is less, minus all payments received by the initial seller from the first sale before the close of the taxable year. Thus, the initial seller will face additional gain recognition only to the extent that the amount realized from the second disposition exceeds actual payments made under the installment sale. The seller's gross profit ratio would then be applied to the amount he or she is deemed to have received. Pursuant to section 453(e)(5), if any gain is recognized because of this resale rule, then future payments received under the initial sale will be recovered tax-free until they equal the amount treated as received from the resale.

* * *

For property other than marketable securities these rules are applicable only if the resale occurs not more than two years after the date of the first disposition.

The running of the two-year period is suspended with respect to any property for any period during which the related person's risk of loss with respect to the property is substantially diminished. This rule will apply with respect to the holding of a put or option to sell the property, the holding by another person of a right to acquire the property, a short sale, or any other transaction that has the effect of substantially diminishing the risk of loss.

The Act contains four exceptions to the rules on resale by a related person. The first exception applies to any nonliquidating installment sale of stock to the issuing corporation. Any such sale of stock is not treated as a first disposition and, therefore, the related person rules will not apply. * * *

---

69. I.R.C. § 453(e), (g). In addition, there are other sections of the Act which provide special treatment when related parties are concerned. *See* §§ 453(h)(1)(C), 453B(f)(2), 691(a)(5)(B), 1239(b).

70. S.Rep., supra note 55, at 14.

71. If the second disposition is not a sale or exchange, an amount equal to the fair market value of the property disposed of shall be substituted for the amount realized. I.R.C. § 453(e)(4).

* * *

Second, an involuntary conversion of property within the meaning of section 1033 and any transfer thereafter is not treated as a second disposition if the first sale occurred before the threat or imminence of the conversion.

Third, no acceleration of the recognition of gain would result from a second disposition which occurs after the death of either the installment seller or purchaser. * * *

Last, the resale rules would not apply to a second disposition if the taxpayer establishes to the satisfaction of the Service that neither the first nor the second disposition had as one of its principal purposes the avoidance of federal income tax. * * *

[C]ertain taxfree transfers which normally would not be treated as a second disposition, * * * include charitable transfers, like-kind exchanges, gift transfers, and transfers to a controlled corporation or partnership. * * * [A] second disposition will qualify under the nontax-avoidance exception when it is of an involuntary nature. For example, foreclosure upon the property by a judgment lien creditor of the related purchaser or bankruptcy of the related purchaser would qualify under this exception. In addition, the exception would apply in the case of a second disposition which is also an installment sale if the terms of payment under the installment resale are substantially equivalent to, or longer than, those for the first installment sale. The exception would not apply if the resale terms would permit significant deferral of recognition of gain from the initial sale when proceeds from the resale are being collected sooner.

For purposes of section 453(e), a related person is a person whose stock would be attributed under section 318(a) [or a person who bears a relationship described in section 267(b)] to the person first disposing of the property.[72] Thus, the term includes the taxpayer's spouse, children, grandchildren[,] parents [and] brothers [and] sisters. A related corporation would be one in which a person directly or indirectly owns 50 percent or more in value of the stock in the corporation * * *. The principles of section 318(a) [and the relationships described in section 267(b)] also will apply in determining the related party status of trusts, estates, [charitable and educational organizations, S corporations] and partnerships.

The second rule pertaining to related parties is contained in Code section 453(g). It provides that in the case of an installment sale of depreciable property between certain closely related parties, the installment method of reporting gain is unavailable. All payments to be received shall be deemed received in the year of sale; in effect, the accrual method of accounting is required. * * *

[T]he purpose of this rule is to deter transactions which are structured in such a way that the related purchaser is given the benefit of depreciation deductions measured by a stepped-up cost basis prior to

---

72. I.R.C. § 453(f)(1). Section 453(f)(1) provides, however, that the option rules of § 318(a)(4) do not apply for purposes of § 453(e).

the time the installment seller is required to report gain on the sale as income. [As noted earlier, a sale between related parties is excepted from this rule if the payments are contingent as to amount and with respect to which the fair market value cannot be reasonably ascertained.]

For purposes of section 453(g), the term related persons [includes the taxpayer and a corporation or a partnership if more than 50% of the value of the stock or capital interest or profits interest is owned directly or indirectly by or for the taxpayer, the taxpayer and any trust in which the taxpayer or his spouse is a beneficiary, other than a remote contingent beneficiary, the taxpayer and any entity which is a related person to the taxpayer under paragraphs (3), (10), (11), or (12) of section 267(b) and two or more partnerships in which the same persons own, directly or indirectly, more than 50% of the capital or profits interests.]

As with the first related party rule, the rule on sales of depreciable property between certain related parties will not apply if it is established to the satisfaction of the Service that the sale did not have as one of its principal purposes the avoidance of federal income tax. *   *   *

INSTALLMENT OBLIGATIONS DISTRIBUTED IN [CORPORATE] LIQUIDATIONS

*   *   *

Under prior law *   *   * shareholders [of a corporation] were not allowed to use installment reporting to defer gain on [installment obligations] distributed [in liquidation of the corporation] since the notes derived from a sale by another entity, the corporation.[73] Thus, an installment sale of assets by a corporation, followed by a distribution of the installment obligation to the shareholders in liquidation, required the shareholders to treat the current fair market value of the notes as having been received in full at the time of distribution.

To avoid this situation, a seller might urge that the transaction be structured as a sale of stock rather than a sale of assets when an installment sale is contemplated. In this way, the seller could make effective use of installment reporting. *   *   * Buyers are sometimes unwilling, however, to purchase stock due to concern over inheriting unknown or contingent liabilities. *   *   *

[Section 453(h), added to the Code by the Installment Sales Revision Act of 1980,] allows a shareholder to use installment reporting for an obligation distributed in liquidation and which arose from a corporate sale of assets *   *   *. [Section 453(h)(1) provides that a shareholder can use the installment method to account for the gain realized on receipt of an installment obligation in a section 331 liquidation of a corporation if the installment obligation was received by the corpora-

---

73. Rev.Rel. 73–500, 1973–2 C.B. 113; Mercedes Frances Freeman Trust v. Commissioner, 303 F.2d 580 (8th Cir.1962); West Shore Fuel, Inc. v. United States, 79–1 U.S.Tax Cas. ¶ 9357 (1979).

tion as a result of the sale or exchange of certain of its assets (including inventory, if sold to one buyer in one transaction) during the twelve-month period beginning on the date a plan of complete liquidation is adopted by the corporation and if the liquidation of the corporation is completed during the twelve-month period.]

* * *

[In enacting section 453(h)] Congress recognized that at the shareholder level the ability to use installment reporting should not depend on whether the installment obligation arose from a direct sale of assets at the corporate level or a sale of corporate stock by the shareholders. Congress also has recognized that prior law could cause a hardship when the shareholder incurred a large gain by receipt of the distributed installment obligation without the receipt of sufficient cash to pay the tax. * * *

The purpose of the legislation is to allow shareholder level installment reporting of distributed obligations that the corporation has received from liquidating sales of its assets * * *. Therefore, obligations generated by sales of property occurring before the adoption of [the] twelve-month plan of liquidation or from a sale of inventory other than a bulk sale, before or after adoption of a plan of liquidation, will not qualify for installment treatment by the shareholder.

Moreover, installment reporting of gain by the shareholder will be unavailable to the extent the obligation is attributed to a sale of depreciable property by the corporation if the installment purchaser is either the shareholder's spouse or [related to the shareholder within the meaning of section 1239(b)]. Rather, all payments to be received shall be deemed received in the year the obligation is distributed.

For the purposes of the related party resale rule of section 453(e), a disposition of property by the selling corporation also [is] treated as a disposition of such property by the shareholder. Thus, if the purchaser is a related person within the meaning of section 453(f)(1) and resells the property within the statutory time period, this second disposition will cause the shareholder to be taxed to the extent provided under section 453(e).[74]

DISPOSITION RULES

[Section 453B(a) generally provides that gain or loss is realized on the distribution, transmission, sale or other disposition of an installment obligation. The gain or loss is measured by the difference between the basis of the installment obligation and the amount realized in the case of a sale or exchange or the fair market value of the

---

74. This provision merely substitutes the shareholder for the liquidating corporation in applying the related party resale rules of § 453(e), and therefore, both the general provisions and the exceptions contained in § 453(e) would be applicable. The Senate Report states that the rule will apply only to related persons not covered by the special rule of § 453(h)(1)(C). S.Rep., supra note 55, at 22.

* * *

installment obligation in the case of a disposition other than a sale or exchange.]

A. Cancellation of an Installment Obligation

[T]he cancellation of an installment obligation is a disposition of the obligation at its fair market value at the time of the cancellation.[75] Moreover, when the obligor is a related party, within the meaning of section 453(f)(1), the fair market value of the obligation is not to be less than its face amount.[76] * * * [A]n installment obligation, which becomes unenforceable by cancellation or for some other reason, is governed by * * * section [453B(f)(1)] which taxes dispositions on the difference between the basis of the obligation and its fair market value * * *.

* * *

B. Bequest of Obligation to Obligor

Transmission of an installment obligation at death is not a disposition triggering unreported gain in the obligation.[77] Moreover, the receipt of the obligation by the estate or a person entitled to receive the obligation by reason of the death of the seller is not a taxable event.[78] Instead, the excess of the fair market value of the obligation over its basis in the hands of the decedent is treated as an item of gross income in respect of a decedent.[79] As such, the recipient of the obligation is taxed on the receipt of installment payments in the same manner as the seller would have been, had he or she lived to receive the payments.[80]

* * *

[A]ny previously unreported gain from an installment sale * * * will be recognized by the deceased seller's estate if the note is cancelled by the executor or is transferred to the obligor by bequest, devise, or inheritance.[81] If cancellation occurs at the death of the holder of the obligation, the cancellation is to be treated as a transfer by the estate of the decedent.[82] If the obligation is held by a person other than the decedent, before the decedent's death, the cancellation will be treated as a transfer immediately after the decedent's death by that other person.

75. I.R.C. § 453B(f)(1), (a)(2). * * *

76. I.R.C. § 453B(f)(2).

77. I.R.C. §§ 453B(c), 691(a)(2).

78. I.R.C. § 691(a)(2).

79. I.R.C. § 691(a)(4)(A).

80. I.R.C. § 691(a)(4)(B). I.R.C. § 691(c) allows a deduction for estate taxes attributable to the unreported gain on the installment obligation.

81. I.R.C. § 691(a)(5)[A](i), (ii). If the decedent and the obligor were related persons within the meaning of § 453(f)(1), the fair market value of the obligation will be treated as not less than its face amount for purposes of determining the amount of gain. I.R.C. § 691(a)(5)(B). * * *

82. I.R.C. § 691(a)(5)[(A)](iii). In the absence of some act which results in cancellation under the Uniform Commercial Code or other local law, the disposition will be considered to occur no later than the time the administration of the estate is concluded. S.Rep., supra note 55, at 27. An installment obligation which becomes unenforceable shall be treated as if it were cancelled. I.R.C. § 691(a)(5)(C).

C. *Transfer to Life Insurance Companies*

Transfers of installment obligations to a life insurance company [are] entitled to nonrecognition treatment to the same extent as transfers to other taxpayers.[83] * * * [Nonrecognition] treatment, however, will apply only if the life insurance company elects to report any remaining gain as investment income, under section 804(b), as payments are received.[84]

FORECLOSURE OF REAL PROPERTY SOLD ON THE INSTALLMENT METHOD BY A DECEASED TAXPAYER

Section 1038 provides that the amount of gain which results from an installment seller's repossession of real property is the amount by which the money and the fair market value of other property received by the seller prior to the reacquisition exceeds the amount of gain on the sale previously reported by the seller.[85] As a limitation on this amount, however, repossession gain cannot exceed the remaining unreported portion of the original gain.[86]

* * *

[S]ubsection [1038(g)] provides that the estate or other beneficiary inheriting * * * an installment obligation of a deceased seller will be entitled to the same limitation on recognition of gain upon a reacquisition of real property as the seller would have been. The basis of the real property acquired will be the same as if the property had been reacquired by the original seller. This basis will be increased by an amount equal to the section 691(c) deduction for federal estate taxes which would have been allowable had the repossession been taxable.[87]

* * *

SPECIAL RULES FOR CERTAIN INSTALLMENT SALES OF PROPERTY

[In general, the installment method is not available for sales by dealers. There are limited exceptions to this rule which are applicable to the sale of certain farm property, time shares and residential lots. With respect to the sale of time shares and residential lots, however, the tax imposed on the receipt by the dealer of any installment payment made on the purchaser's obligation is increased by an amount of interest determined by multiplying the amount of income tax de-

---

83. I.R.C. § 453B(e)(2). * * *

84. I.R.C. § 453B(e)(2). * * *

85. I.R.C. § 1038(b)(1). Under § 1038(b)(1) "other property" does not include obligations of the purchaser. I.R.C. § 1038(a) states that the section applies to sales of real property which gave rise to an indebtedness to the seller which was secured by the real property sold and where the seller reacquired the property in partial or full satisfaction of the indebtedness.

86. I.R.C. § 1038(b)(2) states that the remaining unreported gain is the amount

by which the original sale price exceeded the sum of the adjusted basis of such real property and the amount of gain reported by the seller in preacquisition periods. This latter amount is further reduced by any money and the fair market value of any property (other than the buyer's obligation received by the seller with respect to the sale), paid or transferred by the seller in connection with the reacquisition of such property. Essentially this means repossession costs. I.R.C. § 1038(b)(2)(B).

87. I.R.C. § 1038(g)(2).

ferred through the use of the installment method by the applicable Federal rate under section 1274. See section 453(*l*).

Section 453A applies to obligations that arise from the disposition of property by nondealers if the sales price of the property, combining all sales or exchanges which are part of the same transaction or a related series of transactions, exceeds $150,000. Section 453A is not applicable to installment obligations arising from the sale of personal use property, such as a residence, and property used or produced in the trade or business of farming. In addition, section 453A does not apply to any obligation which arises out of a sale of a residential lot or time share if the seller elects to pay interest on the amount of deferred tax attributable to the use of the installment method.

If section 453A is applicable to an installment obligation, the net proceeds of a loan with respect to which the obligation is pledged as security are treated as a payment received on the installment obligation. See section 453A(d)(1). In addition, interest, payable as an additional tax, must be paid on the deferred tax attributable to installment obligations to which section 453A is applicable to the extent the amount of deferred payments from sales made in part or in whole in return for installment obligations subject to section 453A during any year and which are outstanding at the end of the year exceed five million dollars. See section 453A(a)(1).]

NOTE

1. If a seller is entitled to use the installment method, the seller's sale of part of the installment obligation which he holds will not, in general, affect the validity of the use of the installment method for the part of the installment obligation retained. The seller, however, must report the gain present in the part of the installment obligation sold. How does he compute the gain? How does he determine his basis in the part of the installment obligation sold? See Section 453B.

    a. The Internal Revenue Service has ruled that the substitution of obligors or the assumption of an installment obligation by a new obligor does not constitute the disposition of the installment obligation so as to make the gain inherent in such obligation immediately taxable. See Rev. Rul. 75–457, 1975–2 C.B. 196; Rev.Rul. 82–122, 1982–1 C.B. 80.

    b. With respect to the treatment of the disposition of installment obligations and the analyses used to determine which transactions will, and which will not, be regarded as dispositions see generally Koltun, *The Tax Trap Inherent in the Disposition of Installment Sales Obligations Under the Installment Sales Revision Act of 1980*, 6 Rev. Tax'n Indiv. 227 (1982); Tinsey, *Accelerated Recognition of Gain Can Be Avoided for Some Dispositions of Installment Notes*, 14 Tax'n Law. 36 (1985); Roche, *Dispositions of Installment Obligations*, 41 Tax L.Rev. 1 (1985).

    c. The pledge of an installment obligation, to which Section 453A applies, as security for a loan results in the proceeds of the loan being treated as a payment on the installment obligation. See Section 453A(d).

2. If the cash down payment to be paid by the buyer is put into escrow by the buyer at closing and the seller leaves the cash in escrow until one day after

the close of the taxable year of the seller during which the sale occurred, will this procedure prevent the cash from being treated as a payment to the seller in the year of the sale? See *Everett Pozzi*, 49 T.C. 119 (1967), and compare with Rev.Rul. 68–246, 1968–1 C.B. 198; Rev.Rul. 73–451, 1973–2 C.B. 158 and *Preston R. Bassett*, 33 B.T.A. 182 (1935), affirmed, 90 F.2d 1004 (2d Cir.1937).

a. What else may be required for the seller to avoid treating the payment as received in the year of sale? Compare Rev.Rul. 77–294, 1977–2 C.B. 175; Rev.Rul. 79–91, 1979–1 C.B. 179; *Nannie Carr Harris*, 56 T.C. 1165 (1971), reversed, 477 F.2d 812 (4th Cir.1973), nonacq. 1978–2 C.B. 3; *Fred M. Wilmoth*, 38 CCH Tax Ct.Mem. 1216 (1979); *J.K. Griffith*, 73 T.C. 933 (1980); *Trivett, Jr. v. Comm'r*, 611 F.2d 655 (6th Cir.1979), with *Rebecca J. Murray*, 28 B.T.A. 624 (1933); *Fred M. Stiles*, 69 T.C. 558 (1978), acq. 1978–2 C.B. 83; *Estate of Sidney B. Bette*, 36 CCH Tax Ct.Mem. 1636 (1977); *C.J. Porterfield*, 73 T.C. 91 (1979); *Sprague v. United States*, 627 F.2d 1044 (10th Cir.1980); *Benjamin D. Hyman*, 53 CCH Tax Ct.Mem. 727 (1987). See *Reed v. Comm'r*, 723 F.2d 138 (1st Cir.1983), in which, at the seller's request, the agreement between the buyer and seller provided that, at closing, the buyer would put the purchase price in escrow with an independent agent. The period of escrow extended into the tax year following the year of sale and the seller could not obtain the proceeds from the escrow until the end of the escrow period. The First Circuit Court of Appeals held that the seller could be taxed on the gain present in the purchase price until the year the escrow ended.

b. A third party guarantee and a standby letter of credit can be used as security for the buyer's obligation, and their use will not prevent the seller's use of the installment method. See Temp.Reg.Secs. 15A.453–1(b)(3)(i) and (iii). A certificate of deposit or a deposit of cash by the purchaser, on the other hand, may prevent the seller's use of the installment method. See Temp.Reg.Sec. 15A.453–1(b)(3)(i). As described above, some courts have permitted the use of the installment method when the seller's access to the cash or certificate of deposit is subject to substantial restrictions, i.e., default by the buyer, and both the seller and the buyer intend the cash or certificate to be a form of security for the buyer's payment of the obligation. Temporary Reg.Sec. 15A.453–1(b)(5) Example (8), however, treats cash or a cash equivalent put into escrow to secure an installment obligation as a payment and does not distinguish between the seller having unconditional access to the escrow and the seller's access being subject to substantial restrictions. But see *Reed v. Comm'r*, 723 F.2d 138 (1st Cir. 1983), and cf. *Benjamin D. Hyman*, 53 CCH Tax Ct.Mem. 727 (1987).

c. See generally Comment, *Use of Escrow Arrangements in Installment Sales*, 27 Okla.L.Rev. 543 (1974); Wasserman, *Use of Escrow Agreements in Connection with Installment Sales in Light of Revenue Ruling 79–91*, 58 Taxes 63 (1980); Carlson, *Can the Installment Method Be Used When Payment on the Notes Has Been Secured?*, 53 J. Tax'n 104 (1980); Braubach and Wishaar, *Securing Installment Sales with Letters of Credit and Escrow Arrangements*, 9 J. Real Est. Tax'n 203 (1982); Ledlie, *Letters of Credit or Escrow Accounts Used as Security in Installment Sale Transactions*, 60 Taxes 130 (1982).

3. Section 453(f)(4) denies installment sale treatment when the obligations received from the purchaser are payable on demand and when issued by a corporation, government or political subdivision in a form designed to render them readily tradeable in an established securities market.

4. Pursuant to Section 453(i), depreciation recapture income is fully recognized in the year of an installment sale of property subject to recapture, regardless of the seller's eligibility to use, and use of, the installment method and regardless of the amount, if any, of payments received in the year of sale.

5. Can the seller of a partnership interest who receives an installment obligation from the purchaser use the installment method to account for the gain realized on the sale? Does the application of Section 751 to the amount received by the seller affect the determination whether the installment method can be used?

a. If the seller is treated, under Section 751, as selling his share of the depreciation recapture present in the partnership's assets, must the amount of the partner's gain attributable to his share of the depreciation recapture be recognized in the year of the installment sale regardless whether any payments are received during that year? See Section 453(i).

b. If the seller is treated, under Section 751, as selling his share of the partnership's unrealized receivables (cash method receivables or installment obligations accounted for using the installment method), might the gain derived from this part of the sale be treated as having been derived from the disposition of installment obligations, under Section 453B, and, as a result, the gain must be recognized in the year of the installment sale regardless whether any payments are received by the seller?

c. If the seller is treated, under Section 751, as having sold his interest in the partnership's substantially appreciated inventory, might the seller be treated as having disposed of personal property which is required to be included in inventory and, as a result, be ineligible to use the installment method to account for the gain from this portion of the sale? See Section 453(b)(2)(B).

1. Is the determination of the eligibility of the seller to use the installment method to report the portion of the gain attributable to the seller's share of the partnership's inventory affected by whether the inventory is substantially appreciated?

d. If the seller's share of the partnership's liabilities is greater than the seller's basis in his partnership interest and the purchaser assumes or takes subject to the seller's share of liabilities, is the difference between the seller's share of partnership liabilities and the seller's basis in his partnership interest treated as a payment received by the seller in the year of the installment sale? See Rev.Rul. 76–483, 1976–2 C.B. 131.

e. See generally James, *The Installment Sale of a Partnership Interest,* 43 Tenn.L.Rev. 307 (1976); Pitts, *The Sale of a Partnership Interest with a Section 453 Election,* 58 Taxes 481 (1980).

6. A seller has an adjusted basis of $10 in real estate he proposes to sell. The real estate has a fair market value of $50 and is encumbered by a first mortgage in the amount of $40. The purchaser proposes that he assume the first mortgage and give the seller a purchase money note and second mortgage for $10. If the seller accepts the purchaser's proposal, will he be able to spread the full $40 of gain he will realize over the term of the note and mortgage he will receive? If not, will the seller be able to defer recognition of the $40 of gain if the purchaser gives the seller a note and mortgage, or executes an installment land contract, in the amount of $50, and the seller remains personally liable for the $40 mortgage and agrees to apply the purchaser's payments under the $50 obligation to the amortization of the $40 mortgage

until it is paid? Is the seller in a better position if the holder of the $40 mortgage releases the real estate from the lien of the mortgage and takes a security interest in the purchaser's $50 note and mortgage or installment land contract as security for the $40 debt?

a. If the purchaser gives the seller a note and second mortgage of $10 and assumes the $40 first mortgage, the Internal Revenue Service will take the position that the "total contract price" is $40, $50 minus the first mortgage liability not in excess of the basis, of $10, and that the first mortgage liability in excess of the seller's basis, $30, must be treated as a payment made in the year of sale. Therefore, since the gross profit ratio is 100%, the "total contract price" is $40 and the total gain is $40, the entire $30 treated as paid in the year of sale must be reported as gain. The remaining $10 of gain can be reported by the seller, using the installment method, as the purchaser pays the $10 purchase money second mortgage. See Temp.Reg.Secs. 15A.453–1(b)(2) and (3). If the purchaser gives the seller the $50 wrap-around mortgage or installment land contract, the Internal Revenue Service may take the same position described above with the exception that the remaining $10 of gain can be reported by the seller, using the installment method and a "gross profit ratio" of one-fifth, as the purchaser makes the payments on the wrap-around mortgage. See Temp. Reg.Sec. 15A.453–1(b)(3)(ii). Cf. *Frank Hutchison,* 42 CCH Tax Ct.Mem. 1089 (1981); *William J. Goodman,* 74 T.C. 684 (1980). The Internal Revenue Service has met with a lack of success in persuading the courts that its position with respect to the wrap-around mortgage is correct. Initially, the Tax Court in *D.A. Hunt,* 80 T.C. 1126 (1983), while specifically reserving comment on Temp.Reg.Sec. 15A.453–1(b)(3)(ii), held that, under prior law, the excess of the wrapped mortgage over the seller's basis in the real estate sold was not a payment in the year of sale, the "total contract price" was not reduced by the principal amount of the wrapped mortgage, and the "gross profit ratio" was the amount of gain realized over the contract price. Subsequently, the Tax Court in *Professional Equities Inc.,* 89 T.C. 165 (1987), acq. 1988–37 I.R.B. 4, which involved a tax year to which Temp.Reg.Sec. 15A.453–1(b)(3)(ii) was applicable, followed its reasoning in *D.A. Hunt,* supra, and, as a result, held Temp.Reg.Sec. 15A.453–1(b)(3)(ii) invalid. See also *Vincent E. Webb,* 54 CCH Tax Ct.Mem. 443 (1987), in which the Tax Court followed its holding in *Professional Equities Inc.,* supra.

If the holder of the $40 first mortgage releases the real estate from the lien of the mortgage and takes a security interest in the $50 note and mortgage, or installment land contract, of the purchaser, the Internal Revenue Service and the seller will agree that the seller can report the $40 gain, using a four-fifths "gross profit ratio," as the purchaser pays the $50 note and mortgage, or installment land contract. But, is it realistic to assume that the holder of a first mortgage on real estate will release the real estate in return for a security interest in the purchaser's note and mortgage or installment land contract?

b. See generally Guerin, *A Tax Policy Analysis of Wrap–Around Financed Installment Sales,* 3 Va.Tax Rev. 41 (1983); Bronner, *The Wraparound Mortgage: Its Structure, Uses and Limitations,* 12 J.Real Est.Tax'n 315 (1985); Berkens, *Installment Method Treatment of Sale of Real Property With Mortgage in Excess of Basis: Will the Correct View Please Stand Up?,* 39 U.Miami L.Rev. 697 (1985); Kennedy, *Wraparound Mortgages*

Considered in the Context of the Commissioner's Temporary Installment Sale Regulations, 65 Taxes 530 (1987); Comment, *The Tax Consequences of Wraparound Mortgages,* 2 St. Johns J.Legal Commentary 166 (1987).

7.   See generally Kurn and Nutter, *The Installment Sales Revision Act of 1980: In the Name of Simplification Has a Measure of Complexity Been Added?,* 8 J.Real Est.Tax'n 195 (1981); Colleran and Rosenthal, *An Analysis of the Installment Sales Revision Act of 1980,* 12 Tax Adviser 4 (1981); Emory and Hjorth, *An Analysis of the Changes Made by the Installment Sales Revision Act of 1980—Part I,* 54 J.Tax'n 66 (1981); Emory and Hjorth, *Installment Sales Act, Part II: Cost Recovery, 337 Liquidations, Related Parties, Dispositions,* 54 J.Tax'n 130 (1981); Ginsburg, *Rethinking the Tax Law in the New Installment Sales World,* 59 Taxes 886 (1981); Mahoney and Knauf, *Installment Sales of Real Estate,* 43 N.Y.U.Inst.Fed.Tax'n 22–1 (1985); Schler, *The Sale of Property for a Fixed Payment Note: Remaining Uncertainties,* 41 Tax L.Rev. 209 (1986); Ruby, *Minimizing Taxes on Real Estate Dispositions Through Installment Sales and Tax–Free Exchanges,* 44 N.Y.U.Inst.Fed.Tax'n 19–1 (1986); Roche, *Installment Reporting After the Tax Reform Act of 1986,* 66 J.Tax'n 80 (1987); Robinson, *Installment Reporting for Real Estate: Complexification After the Tax Reform Act of 1986,* 14 J.Real Est.Tax'n 264 (1987); Childs and Strobel, *Seller–Financed Real Estate Transactions After the Tax Reform Act of 1986,* 14 J.Real Est.Tax'n 299 (1987); Note, *Fairness and Tax Avoidance in the Taxation of Installment Sales,* 100 Harv.L.Rev. 403 (1987); Cross, *The Continuing Evolution of the Installment Method of Tax Accounting,* 66 Taxes 421 (1988).

8.   Since the installment method is applicable to sales made for a contingent price, the use of the deferred, or open, method of accounting (all payments are treated as a recovery of capital until the seller recovers his basis in the property sold) is limited to those very rare instances in which the purchaser's obligation is contingent as to amount and the fair market value thereof cannot be reasonably ascertained.

a.   While a seller may be able to use the deferred or open method to account for the gain resulting from a sale if the purchaser's obligation is contingent as to amount and the fair market value of the purchaser's obligation cannot be reasonably ascertained, the purchaser, especially a related purchaser as defined by Section 1239(b), may not be able to increase the basis of the property acquired in the sale by any amount before the time when the seller includes such amount in income.   See Section 453(g) (1)(c);   Priv.Ltr.Rul. 8646055.

b.   See generally Goldberg, *Open Transaction Treatment for Deferred Payment Sales After the Installment Sales Act of 1980,* 34 Tax Law. 605 (1981); Friedman, *An Analysis of Contingent–Payment Sales Under the Installment Sale Regulations,* 57 J.Tax'n 24 (1982); Evetts and Keller, *Contingent Sales: How to Recoup Basis to Produce Best Tax Results,* 15 Tax'n Law. 174 (1986); Karjala, *Sales of Property Outside Section 453,* 64 Taxes 153 (1986).

8. INCOME TAX ASPECTS OF THE DISPOSITION OF THE ASSETS OF AN ENTITY

There are a variety of methods which can be used to dispose of the assets of an entity. For example, the entity might sell its assets to the purchaser and then distribute the consideration received to the participants in the entity. Or, the entity might distribute its assets to the participants in the entity and the participants in the entity would then sell the assets to the purchaser. Lastly, the participants in the entity might sell their interests in the entity to the purchaser.

Turning first to the corporate form, certain facts with respect to the assets to be disposed of and the purchase price to be paid must be assumed in order to examine the income tax effects of the various methods of disposing of the assets of a corporation. Assume that a corporation has cash in the amount of $20 and the following assets:

Asset A, which is machinery and equipment used in the trade or business with an adjusted basis of $10, a value of $35, and potential gain of $25 all of which is depreciation recapture;

Asset B, which is real estate used in the trade or business with an adjusted basis of $10, a value of $45, and potential gain of $35 none of which is depreciation recapture;

Asset C, which is furniture and fixtures used in the trade or business with an adjusted basis of $30, a value of $20, and a potential loss of $10; and

Asset D, which is goodwill with a basis of $0, a value of $20, and potential gain of $20.

Assume further that the total of the bases of the shareholders in the stock of the corporation is $50. Finally, assume that the purchaser has agreed to pay $120 for the assets. The $120 is to be paid $60 in cash and $60 in debt having a fair rate of return, a term of 10 years, payable in equal monthly installments of principal and interest and secured by the acquired assets.

The corporation could sell the assets to the purchaser and liquidate, distributing the consideration received to its shareholders. If this approach is chosen, the corporation will recognize gain or loss, at the corporate level, on the sale of the assets. The corporation will realize $25 of depreciation recapture with respect to Asset A, $35 of gain with respect to Asset B, $10 of loss with respect to Asset C, and $20 of capital gain with respect to Asset D. After setting off, for simplification purposes, the Section 1231 loss on Asset C against the Section 1231 gain on Asset B, the corporation will realize $70 of gain with respect to the sale. Since the corporation will receive an installment obligation as part of the consideration, it will recognize about $47.50 of gain at the time of the sale. This $47.50 of gain is made up of $35 of gain recognized with respect to the cash payment and $12.50 of depreciation recapture paid for by the debt but recognized immediately. See Section 453(i).

When the corporation distributes, in liquidation, the cash and debt to the shareholders, the corporation will recognize, under Section 336, the remaining $22.50 of realized but unrecognized gain in the debt distributed to the shareholders. The result to the corporation of the sale and distribution is that it recognizes a total of $70 of gain and is required to use approximately the $20 of cash it possessed before the sale to pay the income tax on the gain.

When the corporation liquidates it will distribute to the shareholders $60 of cash and the $60 secured debt of the purchaser. Under Section 331, the shareholders will realize $70 of gain which is the difference between the amount of cash and debt distributed and the total bases of the shareholders in the stock of the corporation. Assuming the corporation adopted a plan of liquidation prior to selling the assets and sold the assets and made the distribution in liquidation within 12 months of the adoption of the plan of liquidation, the shareholders recognize $35 of the $70 of realized gain on the receipt of the cash and debt and are able to spread the remaining $35 of gain over the installment payments on the purchaser's debt. See Section 453(h).

The result of the corporation's selling its assets and distributing to its shareholders, in liquidation, the consideration received is that the corporation recognizes $25 of ordinary income and $45 of capital gain and the shareholders realize $70 of capital gain, recognizing $35 of that gain on receipt of the distributions in liquidation and reporting the remaining $35 of that gain using the installment method.

If the corporation liquidates, distributing its assets to the shareholders who then sell the assets to the purchaser, the corporation will realize gain and loss on the distribution of its assets to the shareholders. The gain and loss recognized by the corporation is equal to the difference between the fair market value of, and the corporation's adjusted bases in, the distributed assets. See Section 336. Therefore, the corporation will recognize $25 of depreciation recapture with respect to Asset A, $35 of gain with respect to Asset B, $10 of loss with respect to Asset C, and $20 of gain with respect to Asset D. After setting off, for the purposes of simplification, the Section 1231 loss on Asset C against the Section 1231 gain on Asset B, the corporation will recognize, as a result of the distribution of its assets to the shareholders, $25 of ordinary income and $45 of capital gain and will be required to use approximately its $20 of cash to pay the income tax on the gain recognized.

The shareholders, under Section 331, will recognize gain on the distribution, in liquidation, of the assets by the corporation. The gain will be equal to the difference between the total of the bases of the shareholders in the stock of the corporation and the fair market value of the distributed assets. Therefore, $70 of gain will be recognized by the shareholders. None of this gain can be deferred since the shareholders do not, when this method of disposing of the assets is used, receive an installment obligation as part of the liquidating distribution. The shareholders, however, will receive a $120 basis in the distributed assets. See Section 334(a).

The shareholders will recognize no gain or loss when they sell the distributed assets to the purchaser since the purchase price is assumed to be $120, which is the fair market value of the assets, and the total of the shareholders' bases in the assets at the time of sale is also $120.

The result of this method of disposing of the assets of the corporation is that the corporation realizes and recognizes $25 of ordinary income and $45 of capital gain. The shareholders recognize $70 of gain and are unable to report any of the gain using the installment method.

Lastly, the purchaser might obtain control over the assets of the corporation by buying the shareholders' stock in the corporation. If the purchaser buys the stock of the corporation from the shareholders for the fair market value of the corporation's assets, the purchase price must be increased by $20 to reflect the $20 of cash possessed by the corporation. Therefore, the purchase price would be $140 and might be paid with $70 of cash and $70 of secured debt. As a result of the purchase of the stock, the purchaser will acquire a basis of $140 in the purchased stock and the total of the adjusted bases of the corporation in its assets will remain at $70 even though the purchaser has paid $140 to acquire control of the assets.

The shareholders will realize $90 of gain on the sale of their stock, the difference between the shareholders' total bases in the stock and the $140 purchase price paid for the stock. Unless Section 341 applies, the gain realized by the shareholders will be treated as capital gain. The shareholders will recognize, on the date of sale, $45 of gain and can use the installment method to spread the recognition of the other $45 of gain over the payments of the $70 in secured debt received from the purchaser.

"[T]he selling party almost always prefers a stock sale. A stock sale provides the seller with a clean break from the business and with a capital gain if the stock has been held for the requisite period under [S]ection 1222 * * *. [D]ue to the risk of successor liability for taxes and various contractual and tort obligations, [however,] the [purchaser] usually prefers an asset acquisition. * * *

"If[, however,] a stock purchase is acceptable to both parties or if the seller insists on a stock purchase, [a corporate purchaser] may obtain some of the advantages of an asset purchase, such as a stepped-up basis in assets, by making an election under [S]ection 338 to treat the stock purchase as an asset acquisition. The [purchaser] may make this election when 80 per cent of both the voting and nonvoting stock, except nonvoting stock that is limited and preferred as to dividends, is acquired within a 12–month period. The requisite 80 per cent can be acquired in a single purchase or in several purchases over the 12–month period. See [Section] 338(d)(3). Generally speaking, the election must be made no later than the fifteenth day of the ninth month after the 'acquisition date,' which is the first day on which the purchaser has acquired at least 80 per cent of the voting and nonvoting stock. See [Section] 338(g)(1), (h)(2).

"Pursuant to the election, the stock purchase is deemed to be an asset acquisition * * *. See [Section] 338(a). The acquired or 'target' corporation is treated as if it had sold all of its assets and liquidated on the acquisition date, and it will recognize depreciation recapture * * * and other items of income to the same extent that it would have under an actual * * * sale and liquidation. For purposes of determining gain and loss on the asset 'sale,' the target corporation is treated as having sold the assets at fair market value, which may be determined under a formula that takes into account liabilities, including recapture taxes, as prescribed in the Treasury Regulations. The target corporation need not actually be liquidated, but for tax purposes it is treated as a new corporation beginning the day after the acquisition. See [Section] 338(a)(2).

* * *

"Recapture items and other [gains] triggered by the 'sale' are reported on the 'final' return of the target corporation as of the acquisition date. Thus the 'new' corporation starts with a clean slate, and tax attributes of the 'old' corporation do not survive the acquisition. It should be remembered, however, that the target is treated as a 'new' corporation only for tax purposes, and liabilities for employee benefits and other contractual or tort liabilities will survive the acquisition as they would in any other stock sale.

"Typically, the assets are treated as purchased by the [purchaser] for an amount equal to the price paid for the target corporation's stock [plus the amount of the liabilities of the target corporation]. * * *

"Although treating the stock purchase as an asset purchase may seem simple in theory, in practice the application of [S]ection 338 can be exceedingly complex. Any transaction involving a [S]ection 338 election would require a careful review of the statute and regulations. Generally, the [purchaser] would want to make such an election where the step up in basis of the assets held by the 'target' corporation would yield deductions with a present value greater than the immediate cost of depreciation recapture and other tax liabilities triggered by the election. As in all stock purchases, the [purchaser] should negotiate a purchase price that reflects the burden of these recapture and other tax liabilities. Unlike a true asset purchase, the ultimate burden of recapture and other tax liabilities remains on the [purchaser] even though a [S]ection 338 election is made." [88]

If the purchaser in the hypothetical example is a corporation which elects Section 338, the recognized gain at the corporate level of the

88. Megaard, *Structuring Business Sales and Acquisitions*, 1 # 1 Prac. Tax Law. 43, 45, 60–62 (1986).

"target" corporation will be computed in the same manner it was in the example dealing with the actual sale of assets by the corporation and its liquidation. The "target" corporation will recognize $25 of ordinary income and $45 of capital gain resulting in approximately a $20 income tax liability. The purchaser should realize that this tax liability will be a cost which must be borne by it, since it will own the "target" corporation when the income tax is due. As a result, the purchaser should suggest reducing the purchase price by the approximately $20 of income tax liability. This might mean that the purchase price offered for the stock of the "target" corporation would be $60 in cash and a $60 secured debt.

If the purchaser reduces the purchase price of the stock, the stockholders will realize $70 of capital gain on the sale of the stock, recognizing $35 at the date of the sale and spreading the remaining $35 of gain, using the installment method, over the payments to be made on the $60 secured debt.

The income tax effects of the purchase of stock depend on whether the purchaser does or does not elect Section 338. If the purchaser does not elect Section 338, the shareholders will realize $90 of capital gain on the sale of the stock and can defer the recognition of $45 of that gain, using the installment method, until payments are made on the $70 secured debt given by the purchaser. The purchaser will acquire a basis of $140 in the stock of the "target" corporation and the "target" corporation's adjusted bases in its assets will not change. If the purchaser elects Section 338, the income tax effects, assuming the purchaser reduces the purchase price to take account of the "target" corporation's income tax liability, are the same as those encountered in an actual sale of assets by the corporation and its subsequent liquidation.

Participants in the partnership form of doing business also have the choice of the partnership selling its assets and distributing the proceeds to the partners, the partnership dissolving and distributing the assets to the partners who then individually sell the assets, or the partners selling their partnership interests. Since the partnership is, in an income tax context, regarded as a conduit—the partners rather than the partnership are subject to taxation—the income tax effect of the sale on the partners, in most cases, will be the same regardless of the method chosen to dispose of the assets.

Assume a partnership has $40 in fair market value of Section 751 property (unrealized receivables and substantially appreciated inventory), $60 in fair market value of assets which qualify for Section 1231 treatment, $30 of cash, and $10 of liabilities. The partnership has a zero basis in the Section 751 property and a $40 adjusted basis in the Section 1231 assets. There are four partners who each have a $17.50 adjusted basis in their partnership interests and share equally in profits and losses. None of the partners are dealers in any of the property or assets owned by the partnership. The partnership receives an offer for its property and assets, other than cash, in the amount of $100.

If the partnership sells the property and assets, pays the liabilities, dissolves and distributes the remaining cash on hand and the proceeds from the sale to each partner, each partner will receive $30. Of the $30, $10 is treated as ordinary income and $5 as capital gain. This result is derived from the application of Section 702 which requires that, in this situation, each partner treat as ordinary income his share of the gain on the sale of the Section 751 property and treat as capital gain his share of the gain on the sale of the Section 1231 assets. Each partner's adjusted basis in his partnership interest is increased by his share of the total amount of the gain, under Section 705(a)(1), and reduced by his share of the liabilities which are paid by the partnership. See Sections 752(b) and 733(1). Therefore, prior to the distribution of the proceeds of the sale and the partnership's cash left after payment of the liabilities, each partner has an adjusted basis in his partnership interest of $30 ($17.50 + $15 − $2.50). When the partnership distributes the proceeds and cash on hand, the partners will recognize no gain or loss since the adjusted basis in their partnership interests is equal to the amount of cash distributed. See Section 731(a).

If the partners sell their partnership interests for the fair market value of the partnership property and assets plus cash on hand less liabilities, each partner will receive $30 (fair market value of 751 property—$40, fair market value of 1231 assets—$60, cash—$30 less $10 in liabilities ÷ 4). The gain recognized on the sale of a partnership interest is considered gain from the sale or exchange of a capital asset except as provided in Section 751. See Section 741. Section 751(a) provides that the amount received by a partner in exchange for his interest in Section 751 property is considered as an amount realized from the sale of property which is not a capital asset. Ten dollars of the amount received by each partner is in exchange for his interest in Section 751 property.

$$\frac{\text{F.M.V. 751 Property} - \$40}{\text{Total Purchase Price} - \$120} = \frac{\frac{1}{3} \times \text{Each Partner's Share} -}{\$30 = \$10}$$

Since the partnership has no basis in the Section 751 property, none of the partner's adjusted basis in his partnership interest can be allocated to it. See Reg. Sec. 1.751–1(a)(2) and Section 732(a)(1). Therefore, each partner recognizes $10 of ordinary income. The partner then is treated as having received $22.50 for the remainder of his interest in the partnership. Twenty dollars is the remainder of the purchase price, and $2.50 is his share of partnership liabilities assumed by the purchaser. See Section 752(d). Subtracting the partner's adjusted basis in his partnership interest of $17.50, he recognizes a capital gain of $5 in addition to the ordinary income of $10. See Rev.Rul. 74–40, 1974–1 C.B. 159.

If the partnership pays the liabilities and dissolves, distributing the property, assets and remaining cash to the partners, and the partners individually sell the property and assets, each partner will receive a total of $30. When the partnership pays the liabilities, each partner's adjusted basis in his partnership interest is reduced by his share of the liabilities paid. See Sections 752(b) and 733(1). Therefore, each partner's basis, before distribution of the property, assets and remaining cash, is $15 ($17.50 — $2.50). On distribution of the property, assets and remaining cash, no gain is recognized except to the extent that money distributed exceeds the adjusted basis of a partner in his partnership interest and except as otherwise provided by Section 751. See Section 731(a) and (c). Since the cash distributed is less than each partner's adjusted basis and each partner receives his pro rata share of both Section 751 property and Section 1231 assets, see Section 751(b), no gain is recognized on the distribution. A partner's adjusted basis in the property and assets distributed is the partner's adjusted basis in his partnership interest reduced by the amount of money distributed. Therefore, each partner's basis, at this point in time, is $10 ($15 — $5). See Section 732(b). Upon the distribution, a partner's adjusted basis is first allocated to distributed Section 751 property in an amount equal to the adjusted basis of such property to the partnership. Since the partnership has a zero basis in the Section 751 property, no part of a partner's adjusted basis is allocated to it and all of a partner's adjusted basis in his partnership interest is allocated to the Section 1231 assets. See Section 732(c). Therefore, each partner has a zero basis in the Section 751 property which has a fair market value of $10, and a $10 basis in Section 1231 assets which have a fair market value of $15. When the property and assets are sold for their respective fair market values shortly after the distribution, the partners each recognize $10 of ordinary income on the sale of the Section 751 property, see Section 735(a)(1) and (2), and $5 of capital gain on the sale of the Section 1231 assets. See Section 735(b).

If the partners, since they are not dealers, do not sell the Section 751 property, which consists of inventory items, and hold such items for a period in excess of five years from the date of the distribution and then sell, they might convert some of the ordinary income into capital gain. See Section 735(a)(2).

Even though the above discussion indicates that no matter how the property and assets are sold, the income tax effect on the partners remains the same, if the fact situation was made more complex, such as defining the amount of substantially appreciated inventory included in Section 751 property or including inventory which was not substantially appreciated, different results might be achieved depending on the method of sale.

For example, if the inventory owned by the partnership was appreciated, but not substantially, the appreciation in the inventory would result in ordinary income if the inventory was sold by the partnership or by the partners after the inventory was distributed by the partnership. If, however, the partners sold their partnership interests, the appreciation in the interests caused by the appreciation in the inventory would be treated as capital gain. The partnership might make a non pro rata distribution of the property and assets, but a pro rata distribution of the value of partnership assets, to the partners followed by the partners individually selling the assets. In certain situations this procedure might produce income tax effects different than those produced by a sale by the partnership or a sale of partnership interests by the partners. See, however, Roger M. Dolese, 82 T.C. 830 (1984), affirmed, 811 F.2d 543 (10th Cir.1987), in which a non pro rata liquidating distribution of the assets of a partnership made to related partners was, in essence, treated by the Internal Revenue Service and the courts as a pro rata distribution coupled with an exchange of assets by the partners.

NOTE

1. As discussed above, Section 336 requires that a corporation recognize gain or loss on the distribution of its assets in complete liquidation. The gain or loss is measured by the difference between the fair market value of the assets distributed and the corporation's adjusted bases in the assets. If the assets distributed are subject to a liability or the recipient shareholders assume a liability in connection with the distribution, the fair market value of the distributed assets is treated as not less than the liability. See generally Dangoia and Goodman, *Tax Effects of Many Corporate Distributions Changed by Tax Reform Act of 1986*, 15 Tax'n Law. 152 (1986); Brode, *General Utilities Repeal: A Transactional Analysis*, 66 J. Tax'n 322 (1987); Battle, Filler and Schultz, *New Section 336: Selected Issues in the Taxation of Complete Liquidations*, 65 Taxes 775 (1987); Yin, *Taxing Corporate Liquidations (and Related Matters) After the Tax Reform Act of 1986*, 42 Tax L.Rev. 573 (1987).

The exceptions to the recognition of gain or loss on the distribution of the assets of a corporation in complete liquidation include the following. (1) Neither gain nor loss is recognized to the extent there is nonrecognition of gain or loss to the recipient under the tax-free reorganization provisions of the Code. (2) If the corporation being liquidated is a subsidiary of another corporation, the other corporation is at least an 80% shareholder of the liquidating corporation and Section 332 applies to the liquidation, the liquidating corporation will recognize neither gain nor loss with respect to the assets distributed to the corporate shareholder. (3) Certain losses may not be recognized if it appears that the taxpayers have attempted to take advantage of the recognition of gains and losses on liquidation of a corporation in order to recognize losses in inappropriate situations or to inflate the amount of losses actually sustained. See Section 336(d). (4) Prior to January 1, 1989, certain small corporations were not fully subject to the required recognition of gains and losses on distributions in liquidation. A small corporation for this purpose was a corporation all of whose stock had a total fair market value which did not exceed $10,000,000 and more than 50% of whose stock was held by 10 or fewer qualified persons. If the fair market value of the corporation's stock was less than $5,000,000, the general rule requiring recognition of gain or loss on distributions in liquidation did not apply. The corporation, however, had to recognize the ordinary gain or loss, the short-term capital gain or loss, and the gain from the disposition of installment obligations, if any, resulting from the liquidation. As the fair market value of the corporation increased from

$5,000,000 to $10,000,000, an increasing percentage of the remaining gain or loss realized as a result of the liquidation was recognized.

2. In the event a corporation sells its assets partially in return for an installment obligation of the purchaser and then liquidates, distributing the consideration received from the purchaser, including the installment obligation, to its shareholders, the shareholders can use the installment method to report their gain on the liquidation if the corporation had adopted a plan of liquidation and the sale and complete liquidation of the corporation both took place within 12 months after the adoption of the plan of liquidation. See Section 453(h).

a. Compliance with Section 453(h) may result in at least two problems. First, is there a way of assuring that the sale of the assets of a corporation will occur within 12 months after the corporation's adoption of a plan of liquidation? Second, in view of the possibility that a corporation may hold contingent and unliquidated claims and that there may be holders of contingent and unliquidated claims against the corporation, is there a way of assuring that the complete liquidation of the corporation will occur within 12 months after the adoption of a plan of liquidation?

b. In order to assure that the sale of the assets of a corporation occurs within the 12–month period following the adoption of the plan of liquidation, the adoption of the plan of liquidation might be deferred until it is certain that the sale of the assets will be closed. For example, the adoption of a plan of liquidation might be a condition precedent to the closing in the contract providing for the sale of assets. A day or two before, or possibly the morning before, the closing of the sale, the plan of liquidation would be adopted. This approach, however, might not be feasible if the selling corporation is publicly held. An alternative approach might be to have the corporation adopt a contingent plan of liquidation which would not become effective until, for example, a purchaser executed a contract providing for the sale of the corporation's assets. See Priv.Ltr.Rul. 8512017.

c. In order to be sure that the complete liquidation of the corporation occurs within the 12–month period following the adoption of the plan of liquidation in a situation in which the corporation holds contingent and unliquidated claims and third parties hold contingent and unliquidated claims against the corporation, perhaps all of the corporation's assets could be distributed to the shareholders who would then set up and fund an escrow account which would be used to pay contingent and unliquidated claims against the corporation and collect the corporation's claims, as the respective claims matured. One concern with this approach is whether the shareholders would be taxed on the amounts used to fund, and on the corporation's claims placed in, the escrow. Might this concern be minimized by having the shareholders organize and be the residual beneficiaries of a trust? The trust agreement would direct the independent trustee to pay all creditor's claims and collect all of the corporation's claims, as they mature and, after so paying and collecting the claims, to distribute any funds remaining in the trustee's hands to the beneficiaries. Upon liquidation, the corporation would distribute to the trustee amounts necessary to provide for creditors whose contingent or unliquidated claims were not paid prior to the liquidation of the corporation together with the contingent and unliquidated claims of the corporation. In Rev.Proc. 80–54, 1980–2 C.B. 848, amended by Rev.Proc. 81–51, 1981–2 C.B. 625, the Internal Revenue Service set out the conditions which must be met in order to obtain a ruling on the status of a liquidating trust, and in Rev.Rul. 80–150, 1980–1 C.B. 316, the Internal Revenue Service ruled on the status of a liquidating trust. See Dranginis, *Uses of Liquidating Trusts in Complete Liquidations,* 3 Corp.L.Rev. 238 (1980); Del Negro, *Liquidating Trusts— Their Nature and Uses,* 38 N.Y.U.Inst.Fed.Tax'n 23–1 (1980); Westin, *Shareholders' Liquidating Trusts After Revenue Procedure 80–54,* 9 J.Corp. Tax'n 63 (1982). For a description of the corporate procedures followed in the formation and funding of a liquidating trust see *Lone Star Industries, Inc. v. Redwine,* 757 F.2d 1544 (5th Cir.1985), reversing, 590 F.Supp. 547 (E.D.La.1984).

3. With respect to the requirements and operation of Section 338, see generally Hoops, *Acquiring the Stock of a Target—The Sec. 338 Election,* 15 Tax Adviser 138 (1984); Witt, *Practical Implications of Treating Stock Purchase as Asset Acquisition Under 338,* 61 J. Tax'n 8 (1984); Comment, *Section 338: The Result of the Legal Evolution of the Tax Treatment of Two–Step Asset Acquisitions,* 61 Tex.L.Rev. 1109 (1983); Wexler and Welke, *Section 338—Consistency and Complexity,* 63 Taxes 916 (1985); Indoe, *IRC Section 338,* 44 N.Y.U.Inst. Fed.Tax'n 26–1 (1986).

4. It appears that, with the exception of a sale of stock when the purchaser does not elect Section 338 and the other exceptions described in paragraph 1. above, the disposition of the assets of a corporation when the shareholders of the corporation directly or indirectly receive the consideration results in double taxation. Gain may be recognized at both the corporate and shareholder levels. Is this statement always true even when the assets disposed of were owned by an S corporation which had been an S corporation since its formation? If not, could a C corporation whose assets are to be disposed of elect S corporation status for the taxable year in which the sale occurs and, in this manner, avoid double taxation? See Section 1374.

5. With respect to the disposition of the assets of a partnership and the operation of Section 751, see generally Davis, *Disposition of Syndicate Realty,* 1 J. Real Est. Tax'n 172 (1974); Drucker and Segal, *Problems and Opportunities in Working with Collapsible Partnerships,* 61 Taxes 110 (1983); Grossman, *Choosing the Most Advantageous Method for Disposing of a Partnership Interest,* 3 J.Ps.Tax'n 219 (1986); Taylor and Kozub, *Real Estate Limited Partnerships: Is a Graceful Exit Possible?,* 14 J.Real Est.Tax'n 154 (1987). See also this Division, pages 486 to 493 supra; Division I, pages 35 to 36 supra; Division IV, pages 1086 to 1100 infra.

9. PERSONAL HOLDING COMPANIES

The existence and operation of a corporation might be continued in order to avoid the double taxation resulting from the disposition of a corporation's assets and its liquidation. The corporation would recognize gain or loss, to the extent required, on the sale of its assets, it would collect the payments on any installment obligations received as a result of the sale, and it would invest the proceeds of the sale. In the event the proceeds of the sale were not invested in a new "active" business, it is possible that the corporation, especially if it is closely held, would be subject to the personal holding company sections of the Internal Revenue Code.

When determining whether to continue or liquidate a corporation, a number of considerations must be taken into account. For example, the ways in which the application of the personal holding company sections can be avoided should be considered. In addition, assuming the application of the personal holding company sections, it should be determined whether the income tax effects resulting from their application are more or less desirable than the income tax effects resulting from the liquidation of the corporation.

PERSONAL HOLDING COMPANIES—YESTERDAY, TODAY AND TOMORROW

Donald C. Lubick
42 Taxes 855 (1964).
[footnotes omitted]

* * *

Rate of Tax

The personal holding company tax * * * is [applied to] the undistributed personal holding company income of a personal holding company. Personal holding companies are those companies which, with certain exceptions, meet two objective tests, one with respect to closely held stock ownership and the other with respect to a high percentage of income derived from passive investments or certain other activities where derivation of income in corporate form is indicative of [possible] tax avoidance.

* * *

Stock Ownership

In order to be a personal holding company, Section 542(a)(2) provides that:

> "At any time during the last half of the taxable year more than 50 per cent in value of its outstanding stock is owned, directly or indirectly, by or for not more than 5 individuals."

This has been the provision since the 1934 Act, except that since 1954 certain exempt organizations and charitable trusts have been treated as individuals to prevent avoidance of the stock ownership rules through a donor controlled foundation. Thus[,] if there are nine or fewer individual stockholders, more than 50 per cent of the stock will be owned by five or fewer individuals. If there are ten or more individuals owning stock or a stockholder is a corporation, trust, estate or partnership, the attribution rules of Section 544 must be applied. In addition, under that section certain convertible securities are treated as stock. * * *

Gross Income

Even if a corporation meets the stock ownership test, as most corporations do, it will not be a personal holding company unless at least 60 per cent of its adjusted ordinary gross income is personal holding company income. Personal holding company income is defined in detail and embraces various kinds of normally passive investment income and some special items of personal service income.

* * *

Use of Adjusted Ordinary Gross Income

The 60 per cent is applied to adjusted ordinary gross income. * * * [C]apital gains are eliminated entirely from both sides of the equation.

* * * [S]ince 1954 undistributed personal holding company income has been reduced by the excess of net long-term capital gain over net short-term capital loss so that capital gains are never subjected to the penalty tax even if not distributed.

* * * By excluding capital gains altogether from the gross income test[,] * * * capital gains from the sale of Section 1231 property on the installment method can no longer be used as part of the active income side of the ledger to shelter personal holding company income for many years following a sale; neither will a casual sale of stock or securities at a large capital gain be treated as personal holding company income to throw a corporation into personal holding company status.

* * *

* * * [T]he use of adjusted ordinary gross income * * * [requires] adjustments to both the over-all income to which the 60 per cent test applies and the items which are included as personal holding company income.

The adjustments apply to reduce gross income from rents, mineral income and, in limited situations, interest income. Gross rents are reduced by depreciation (with an exception designed to cover rentals from short-term leases of cars and other equipment), property taxes, interest paid allocable to the property leased and rent paid. Similarly mineral, oil and gas royalty gross income is reduced by deductions for depreciation and depletion, property and severance taxes, interest and rent. The same reductions apply to income from working interests in an oil or gas well even though such income is not personal holding company income in any case. There is eliminated from adjusted ordinary gross income and hence personal holding company income, interest received on a condemnation award, judgment or tax refund and certain interest received by dealers who make a primary market in United States Government Bonds.

The adjustments were intended to make the measurement of the percentage of personal holding company income as applied to total income a more accurate measure of the activity of the corporation—to determine whether in fact it was simply a shelter for investment type income or truly engaged in an active business enterprise.

* * * It was thought that an analogy to manufacturing or mercantile corporations would require reductions from gross income to be equivalent to the reduction from gross receipts by the cost of goods sold.

* * *

[D]epreciation in the case of a real estate corporation is the cost of the property sold to produce its gross receipts. The adjustments also prevent a corporation from avoiding personal holding company status through inflating its gross income to a point where gross rentals are more than 50 per cent of total gross income. Wash items, such as rent paid under a sublease arrangement whereby the holding company simply acts as an intervening lessee to inflate its gross rentals, are eliminated. Thus, a much greater proportion of rental activity to total income is required to meet the 50 percent test if rentals or royalties are to be treated as nonpersonal holding company income.[89]

It should be noted, however, that for a corporation which has less than 50 per cent of its income from rentals or royalties, the "adjusted ordinary gross income" concept makes it easier to meet the over-all 60 per cent test. A corporation which has some incidental rental income will be charged only with adjusted rentals as personal holding company income, and while the denominator of the fraction:

$$\frac{\text{personal holding company income}}{\text{adjusted ordinary gross income}}$$

is smaller, the equivalent decrease in the numerator more than offsets this.

* * *

The adjustments to interest can also constitute a liberalization. By and large they eliminate interest items not usually in the control of the recipient and hence have been eliminated from both parts of the fraction in measuring personal holding company status.

The Criteria Used to Classify Items as Personal Holding Company Income

In defining what is personal holding company income Congress has generally sought to classify those sorts of income which are not derived from the active conduct of a business and which do not involve risks requiring incorporation. * * * Hence dividends, interest, royalties (other than mineral, oil or gas royalties and copyright royalties), and annuities are clearly personal holding company income and have been since the 1934 Act.

Income from personal services of a taxpayer should not be insulated from personal taxation by purely formal corporate intervention. The same is true in cases where income is shunted to a corporation from its shareholder for use of corporate property, where there is

89. [As discussed at pages 559 to 560 infra, rent is not personal holding company income, if rental income is 50% or more of adjusted ordinary gross income and, gener- ally, other personal holding company in- come in excess of 10% of ordinary gross income is distributed.]

evidence that the arrangement is purely a shelter for portfolio investment.

Rentals from real property involve an area where there are legitimate reasons for incorporation to limit liability, yet this sort of income can in many cases be derived from investment requiring no operational talent and with no need to maintain a large portfolio for working capital. Hence, there are rules which permit accumulation in the [corporation] if the bulk of the income is from that activity and if the rentals are not used to shelter other passive income. Mineral, oil and gas royalties have been analogized to rentals with more dubious justification.

Finally some sorts of income are personal holding company income unless in addition to constituting the bulk of the corporate income, and not being used to shelter other passive income, there are sufficient expenses incurred to indicate activity, for example, copyright [and certain computer software] royalties.

*   *   *

Kinds of Personal Holding [Company] Income

Section 543(a) now lists the items of adjusted ordinary gross income which constitute personal holding company income. Those other than rentals may be briefly summarized.

Paragraph 1 specifies dividends, interest, royalties (other than mineral, oil or gas royalties or copyright royalties) as personal holding company income. Those corporations receiving interest as part of an active business such as banks and finance companies are excepted from classification as personal holding companies *   *   *. Certain special kinds of interest are excluded in determining adjusted ordinary gross income as well as personal holding company income, *   *   * as noted above.

Paragraph 2 deals with rents and deserves more extended treatment below.

Paragraph 3 includes mineral, oil and gas royalties. The 1937 Act added an exception to eliminate such royalties from personal holding company income if they constituted at least 50 per cent of gross income and if trade or business expenses under Section 23(a) of the 1939 Code (Section 162, [1986] Code) other than compensation for services of shareholders constituted at least 15 per cent of gross income.

The 1964 Act modifie[d] the tests to qualify as excepted mineral, oil and gas royalties. The 50 per cent test [is] applie[d] to the ratio of adjusted mineral, oil and gas royalties to adjusted ordinary gross income; [the] requirement that other personal holding company income including rents not exceed 10 per cent of ordinary gross income [was added]; and the Section 162 deductions usable in measuring the 15 per cent minimum business expenses to show activity are [defined as] those allowable only under Section 162 (thus excluding interest, taxes and depreciation).

* * * The 10 per cent test added in 1964 * * * helps insure that mineral, oil and gas royalties may not shelter an excessive amount of other passive income. The 10 per cent test applies absolutely to mineral, oil and gas royalties—if the other passive income exceeds the 10 per cent amount, all the mineral, oil and gas royalties become personal holding company income, even if the other passive income in excess of the 10 per cent is distributed. Such a distribution would avoid the personal holding company taint in the case of rents. There is, however, no particular need for an escape hatch in this area, since the need to maintain large portfolio reserves does not exist. In the rental area there is some need for reserves because of financing arrangements, requirements to maintain the property, etc.

Subparagraph 4 contains an exception to permit copyright royalties * * * to be classified as nonpersonal holding company income. As added in 1959[,] copyright royalties do not constitute personal holding company income if they are 50 per cent or more of gross income, the Section 162 deductions (other than compensation * * * paid to shareholders [and royalties paid or accrued]) constitute at least [25] per cent of [the amount by which the] gross income [exceeds the sum of the royalties paid or accrued and the depreciation deduction with respect to copyright royalties] and the sheltered income is not more than 10 per cent of gross income. This paragraph was slightly modified in the 1964 Act to perfect the tests originally designed.

The 1964 Act added a new category of personal holding company income—produced film rents where less than 50 per cent of ordinary gross income. Prior to 1964 all film rentals were classified along with ordinary rentals—not personal holding company income if total rentals were at least 50 per cent of gross income. The 1964 Act added a provision that purchased film rentals—amounts received from the distribution and exhibition of a film negative acquired after substantial completion—are to be treated as copyright royalties. Purchased film rentals are thus subjected to the more stringent tests limiting other sheltered personal holding company income to 10 per cent of ordinary gross and requiring substantial related business expense deductions. On the other hand, produced film rentals—where the interest in the film was acquired before substantial completion—[are] separated from ordinary rentals and left as nonpersonal holding company income if at least 50 per cent of ordinary gross income.

* * *

Paragraph 6 originated in the 1937 Act. It treats as personal holding company income amounts received for the use of property of a corporation from a 25 per cent or greater stockholder. The abuse was the incorporated yacht. A shareholder would incorporate his portfolio and along with it, his yacht or country residence and pay rental for the use of the yacht or residence to the corporation. The rental would thus shelter dividends and interest from the portfolio.

The statute applies whether the shareholder obtains the right to use the property directly or by sublease or other arrangement. This language has been construed to apply to all sorts of indirect use of the property. Thus[,] if a corporation leases property to another corporation and both are owned by the same shareholder, the shareholder has been held to be using the property through his lessee corporation and the rental would be personal holding company income to the lessor. The saving feature in the situation of the bona fide business lease between related corporations is provided by a 1954 amendment which prevents application of the paragraph unless the corporation has other nonrental personal holding company income in excess of 10 per cent of gross income (now "ordinary gross income"). Thus[,] if there is no sheltered income, Section 543(a)(6) will not be a problem. However, if there is dividend or interest income over 10 per cent of ordinary gross income, a distribution of the passive income alone will not help.

In addition, in determining undistributed personal holding company income, the base to which the personal holding company tax applies, business expenses and depreciation allocable to the operation of corporate property may not exceed the rental from the property unless the taxpayer establishes that the rent received was the highest available, that the property was held in the course of business carried on bona fide for profit and that either there was reasonable expectation that operation of the property would result in a profit or that the property was necessary to the conduct of the business. Thus excessive deductions cannot shelter dividend income from tax, even where the classification of the rental from property used by the shareholder as personal holding company income is not a serious hurdle to the corporation because the rentals do not produce net income.

Paragraph 7 was also added by the 1937 Act to deal with the incorporated talent device. If the corporation is to furnish personal services under a contract and if the services are required to be performed by a 25 per cent or more stockholder (directly or indirectly) either by the terms of the contract or by designation of someone other than the corporation furnishing the services, the payments are personal holding company income. The provision was originally aimed at actors, cartoonists and the like who incorporated their services * * *. It can also apply, however, to corporations performing services of all kinds, such as engineering and technical services,[90] where the party performing the services is designated by the purchaser. * * *

Paragraph 8 includes as personal holding company income amounts to be taken up as a corporate beneficiary of an estate or trust. It has been carried from the Revenue Act of 1937, where it was added to preclude the argument that gross income from a trust or estate was not personal holding company income. Sections 652(b) and 661(b) of the * * * Code would now preserve the character of income distribut-

---

90. [Consider the application of this section to the medical and legal professions. Can the sole practitioner incorporate? See Rev.Rul. 75–67, 1975–1 C.B. 169; Rev.Rul. 75–250, 1975–1 C.B. 172; Rev.Rul. 75–249, 1975–1 C.B. 171.]

ed to the beneficiary, although the trust instrument can allocate the classes of trust income among the beneficiaries. The instrument creating a trust with both individual and corporate beneficiaries and which has some operating income could still allocate the operating income to a corporate beneficiary, which in essence is the same as a passive investor receiving dividends. Hence[,] the provision is still necessary, and in fact ought to be expanded to include the similar situation of a *corporation which is a limited partner.* [Emphasis added.]

* * *

Rents

The original personal holding company provisions of the 1934 Act did not include rents as personal holding company income. Thus[,] by generating gross rents which constituted over 20 per cent of gross income, it was easy to avoid personal holding company status.

A rent roll is comparatively easy to acquire to avoid personal holding company status. Most taxpayers would hesitate to invest in an unfamiliar mercantile business simply to avoid personal holding company status. This is not true of real estate, since most business persons have some experience with it. In view of the availability of mortgage financing, a large investment is not needed. Also the owner can readily and safely employ agents to manage the property for him. This is not easy in the case of a mercantile operation. Thus[,] the most serious avoidance of personal holding company status has been through rentals.

The 1937 Act recognized this by classifying rentals as personal holding company income unless they constituted 50 per cent or more of gross income. The purpose of the 50 per cent rule was to permit a bona fide real estate operation to be conducted in corporate form. The 50 per cent rule, however, did not prevent the widespread use of gross rents to shelter portfolio income. * * *

* * *

The 1964 Act changed the 50 per cent test to require that the adjusted rents be at least 50 per cent of the adjusted ordinary gross income. As indicated above, this is helpful to the non-real estate corporation, but it requires a real estate corporation to use a more realistic measure to show a preponderance of real estate activity. Second, the 1964 Act added a new test, that the other personal holding company income (including for this purpose all copyright royalties and the adjusted income from mineral, oil and gas royalties, but not compensation from a shareholder for use of corporate property) in excess of 10 per cent of gross income be distributed. If both tests are met, the rentals are not personal holding company income and the corporation is not a personal holding company. If either is failed the rents become personal holding company income and if the cause of failure is the 10 per cent test, the combination of at least 50 per cent rentals and 10 per cent other personal holding company income will make the corporation a personal holding company. Thus[,] a real estate corporation cannot use rentals to shelter more than a modest amount of portfolio income; however, if rentals drop unexpectedly so that the portfolio income exceeds the 10 per cent, the corporation can purge itself by a distribution within two and one-half months after the close of its taxable year not of all its income, but only the amount necessary to meet the test. Thus[,] the required distribution, as long as the 50 per cent test has been met, will never be more than a portion of the nonrental personal holding company income.

The * * * rental provisions [are intended to] curb * * * the principal abuse in the personal holding company area, the real estate corporation sheltering portfolio income. At the same time the introduction of the pay-out concept to eliminate personal holding company status where a distribution of excessive portfolio income is made should avoid hardship to bona fide operating corporations.

* * *

NOTE

1. If a closely held corporation sells all of its assets and receives in return the purchaser's obligation which qualifies for installment treatment, under Section 453, and the corporation is not liquidated, can the personal holding company sections be avoided by the corporation's paying a yearly dividend equal to the interest in each installment payment received during the year?

a. If the corporation recognized some depreciation recapture as a result of the sale, might the recapture "insulate" some of the interest paid during the year of sale, i.e., the recapture would not be personal holding company income but would be included in adjusted ordinary gross income? See Section 543(b)(1)(B).

b. Might the double tax resulting from paying out the interest as dividends be avoided by paying an amount equal to the interest as salaries to the shareholders for managing the corporation?

c. See Kadens, *PHC Conversion—A Tax–Saving Way To Arrange the Sale of Many Closely–Held Corporate Businesses,* 5 Del.J.Corp.L. 40 (1980).

2. Is an S corporation subject to the personal holding company sections?

a. Can the double tax resulting from paying out the interest as dividends be avoided by having the corporation make an S election and having the installment obligation drafted so that the interest included in any installment never exceeds 25% of the gross receipts from that installment and the amount of interest received by the corporation each year is distributed to the shareholders?

b. Does this approach make economic sense when the amount of the installment obligation is large and the shareholders of the corporation are relatively young?

c. Are the gross receipts from each installment considered gross receipts for the purposes of Sections 1362(d)(3) and 1375, or do gross receipts for these purposes only include the portion of the installment representing gain and interest. Cf. Section 1362(d)(3)(C); *Alfred M. Sieh,* 56 T.C. 1386 (1971), affirmed, 31 A.F.T.R.2d ¶ 73–694 (8th Cir.1973); *Valley Loan Ass'n v. United States,* 258 F.Supp. 673 (D.Colo.1966). But cf. *I.J.*

Marshall, 60 T.C. 242 (1973), affirmed, *I.J. Marshall v. Comm'r,* 510 F.2d 259 (10th Cir.1975).

     1. Does the accounting method—cash, accrual or installment—employed by the corporation affect the result? Cf. *Alfred M. Sieh, supra.*

     d. Is the amount of interest included in an installment of any concern if the corporation possesses no earnings and profits accumulated during the years it was a C corporation or paid a dividend equal to the amount of such earnings when S corporation status was elected? See Sections 1362(d)(3)(A) and 1375.

     3. Even if double taxation cannot be totally avoided, might the overall tax cost be less in certain cases if the liquidation of the corporation is delayed until the demise of its current shareholders thereby avoiding the recognition of gain by the shareholders on the liquidation through the stepped-up basis of the shareholders' heirs, under Section 1014?

     4. The personal holding company sections are also of concern to a corporation engaged in the ownership and operation of commercial or residential rental property. If the corporation can maintain its adjusted income from rents at 50% or more of its adjusted ordinary gross income and its undistributed other personal holding company income at 10% or less of its ordinary gross income, it will not be subject to the personal holding company tax.

     a. Meeting the 10% and 50% tests may present some problems.

     1. Other personal holding company income, i.e., dividends or interest, may amount to more than 10% of ordinary gross income. An excess of other personal holding company income can be cured by paying out, as dividends, the amount of the other personal holding company income in excess of 10% of ordinary gross income. This approach, however, will result in the amounts paid as dividends by a C corporation being subject to tax at both the corporate and shareholder levels.

     2. Because of vacancies or a casualty such as a fire or a partial condemnation the adjusted income from rents may drop below 50% of adjusted ordinary gross income.

     a. For example, assume a corporation with $6 of adjusted income from rents, $3 of dividends and interest, $9 of adjusted ordinary gross income, and $15 of ordinary gross income. The corporation pays a dividend of $1.50 each year to avoid being treated as a personal holding company.

     b. A fire destroys some of the corporation's rental property resulting in the corporation's receiving $4 less in adjusted income from rents. The corporation, after the fire, receives $2 of adjusted income from rents, $3 of dividends and interest, $5 of adjusted ordinary gross income and, possibly, $7 of ordinary gross income.

     1. The rents are now personal holding company income since the adjusted income from rents is less than 50% of adjusted ordinary gross income. Therefore, the corporation is a personal holding company, if the stock ownership test is met, since 100% of adjusted ordinary gross income is personal holding company income.

c. Steps which might be taken to avoid classification as a personal holding company include:

1. Liquidating the investments which produce the interest and dividends in order to have available funds for reconstruction and repair; and

2. Requesting that remaining tenants prepay rent or requiring that tenants which propose to lease the renovated facilities prepay rent.

5. See generally Harris, *Recognizing Personal Holding Company Income: Sec. 543(a),* 54 Taxes 646 (1976); Ing, *Personal Holding Company Tax Provisions: Rental Income,* 64 A.B.A.J. 1167 (1978); Fuller, *Troubled Real Estate Leasing Companies Trapped Within the Personal Holding Company Income Tax Provisions,* 1978 B.Y.U.L.Rev. 980; Englebrecht and Wiggins, *How Corporations with Substantial Rents Can Avoid Personal Holding Co. Tax,* 8 Tax'n Law. 56 (1979).

Division III

FINANCING THE ACQUISITION AND DEVELOPMENT OF REAL ESTATE

1. REAL ESTATE FINANCING—IN GENERAL

Simplicity in the financing of the acquisition and development of real estate in many situations has gone the way of the horse and buggy. Increasing complexity has resulted from a number of considerations. Among these are tax considerations, demands that a high percentage of project costs be financed, and many innovated techniques for handling the special problems which often arise in the financing of industrial, commercial, and residential rental real estate developments.

CONTEMPORARY REAL ESTATE FINANCING TECHNIQUES: A DIALOGUE ON VANISHING SIMPLICITY

Francis P. Gunning and Frank E. Roegge
3 Real Property, Probate and Trust Journal 325 (1968).
[footnotes omitted]

* * *

I. Motivation Determining Type of Financing

A. On the Part of the Developer

Aside from baser motives, the developer may well have a real need, with which an institution can sympathize, for increasing the amount of the financing customarily available. This need may arise from unexpected and unusual costs for land, for the improvements or for fixtures to be incorporated therein. The increase in financing hopefully must be in lieu of secondary financing because of the additional costs. Leverage is the goal of all developers and this is achieved with a minimum cash equity, coupled with a high loan, which thereby results in the highest rate of return on this minimum equity. * * * [B]orrowers [also] are particularly sensitive of debt items on their annual statements and[, at times,] prefer an alternate financing which results only in rental obligations which, if shown at all, are carried merely as footnotes on the statements.

[A] frequent and significant consideration in structuring a modern financing arrangement is the income tax consequences to the developer. A resulting capital gain or increased ordinary income creates a corresponding need for * * * capital loss deductions and depreciation. Where an abundance of [losses, possibly passive losses, is present,] a financing to produce the greatest amount of * * * income[, possibly

563

passive income,] is indicated. In the case of depleted tax shelter, the classic example being that point in time when the amount of depreciation deduction equals the amount of amortization payable on the existing mortgage, a * * * refinancing [or possibly a disposition of the project] becomes [desirable].

The developer may desire to free an asset, upon which further financing has been frozen. An example would be a successful project producing an excess of spendable income, subject to existing but inadequate financing, without a privilege of prepayment or with a privilege requiring excessive prepayment penalty. The owner seeks supplemental financing but without the expense of the conventional secondary financing. Similarly handicapped is the developer who has gratuitously included in existing financing surplus properties which may now be developed. The corporate borrower will be compelled to explore unique financing arrangements where an earlier bond indenture has restricted further conventional debt financing. This same bond indenture may also contain an after-acquired property clause which thereby limits the financibility of the newly acquired property, so that some novel approach to financing must be found.

The unusual nature of the security offered in the financing may pose its own problems. A case in point is the extremely desirable location for which the developer is unable to acquire fee title but instead can obtain only a leasehold or a subleasehold therein. Even more exotic are the highly strategic locations above or below existing buildings, railroad tracks, public streets and even turnpikes to which the developer must obtain a legal estate susceptible of financing.

B. On the Part of the Institution

To the same extent, the peculiar self-interest of the institution will determine the nature of the financing which it is prepared to make available. These motivations are as equally diverse as with the developer.

The operation of the law of supply and demand in the present money market * * * [is reflected in] interest rates. * * * In addition, other factors * * * also influenc[e] rates, such as the degree of risk, the size of the desired financing and novelty of the project or security. A rate commensurate with the institution's evaluation of each of these factors is * * * demanded. Competing with the desire for the highest rate of return is the ogre of usury, so that the financing vehicle must be carefully assembled to avoid this fatal deficiency.

Historically, the institutional lender has always envied the large profits earned by developers with only minimal equity contributions. The situation was particularly aggravated in the cases of 100 per cent financing of developmental costs for which the lender received only a fixed and relatively modest rate of return. The institutions long nurtured a desire to occupy or obtain equity positions and thereby participate in the greater profits previously available only to the developers. ✳ ✳ ✳ This desire has become somewhat more urgent as they observe the entry into real estate equity positions of a large number of industrial corporations who are seeking outlets for their excess cash and capital accumulations as well as for tax shelter of one kind or another.

Life insurance companies as long term investors and also because of the extended terms of their insurance and annuity obligations are particularly susceptible to the vagaries of inflation. ✳ ✳ ✳ Equity participations are [among] the best possible sources of ✳ ✳ ✳ protection [against inflation].

Many institutions will endeavor to invest the largest permitted dollar amount in a high quality investment. Once satisfied as to quality, they would prefer that the investment continue nonamortizing or slow amortizing so that the greatest amount of return can be obtained. Such institutions, however, are limited[, at times,] by statute as to the size of certain of these investments. For mortgage investments there [may be] a loan-to-value ratio. For real estate investments there [may be] a single property dollar limitation. For all types of investments there are aggregate dollar limitations. The institutions[,] in the proper case, are therefore desirous of exploring alternate lawful means of avoiding the strictures of these limitations.

✳ ✳ ✳

To a lesser but still significant degree, tax considerations will determine the form of financing to be made available by an institution. ✳ ✳ ✳

Where an institution has provided the "seed" financing for a new project or venture[,] and there is the potential of future financing, ✳ ✳ ✳ quite naturally and reasonably [it] expect[s] to obtain the "harvest" financing as well. For this reason, [an institution] many times [will] incorporate in the particular financing arrangement an option of first refusal for all future financing. This occurs most frequently in the stage financing of an industrial park or of a large shopping center or apartment house complex.

II. Results of Motivation

Given the foregoing motivations, we must now see how, if at all, they can be realized.

The simple method, of course, is a high fixed interest rate. ✳ ✳ ✳ [T]his[, however,] cannot be the entire or even the principal answer. First, usury laws in many states clearly prevent a fixed rate high enough to satisfy the lender, even if the borrower [is] a corporation; second, the borrower does not want to be tied to high fixed rates which would have to be paid even though the project did not meet expectations; and, third, the lender is not satisfied with a higher rate that yields little in dollars when the loan is substantially paid down or is prepaid.

All these lead to a desire for some more contingent return which in effect will assure the lender of a participation in profits. This participatory interest can take many forms, as will be discussed, but to the business man it is considered "a piece of the action," a "kicker," the "icing on the cake," or some other indication that the lender gets some of the benefits [usually thought to accrue to] those in an equity position.

The borrower, under certain circumstances, is willing to give up "a piece of the action" to get his financing. The greater the lender's risk, the smaller the borrower's equity, the more marginal or novel the enterprise, the greater the willingness to let the lender in on hoped for profits. To accomplish his aims[,] the borrower wants a minimum of personal liability through use of subsidiaries, dummies, covenants not to seek deficiency judgments, general exculpation clauses and the like, with a maximum of financing by one or more lenders. * * *

III. Participation in Levering and Equity

A. Participation in Income

This added cost of financing * * * [is] in addition to the fixed interest under the loan, the fixed rental under the leaseback and the fixed payments under the installment sale.

The participation of the institution could be a percentage share either in all or in a defined part of the gross income received by the developer from the project or might be [a percentage share of the developer's] net income before taxes and depreciation, or, as is more prevalent, a participation in a defined net income under which certain items of expense are limited for the purpose of [the] computation.

B. Participation in Re–Finance or Re–Sale

If the participation in income relates to a mortgage loan, then the institution will permit prepayment, if at all, only after a fixed period in order to preserve the fruits of participation. Where prepayment is permitted, and in order to recognize the value to the institution of the participation, the premium for prepayment might very well be on the basis of a capitalization of the average amount of participation income previously paid or may take the form of a share in any re-financing in excess of the existing mortgage balance. The philosophy in each case is that the institution's contribution was something more than mere debt financing, [and the institution's interest] is akin to an equity [interest] and must be recompensed accordingly.

Where the financing is that of a sale and leaseback, it may incorporate a mandatory repurchase at an agreed price by the tenant, or more often it may provide only for an optional repurchase right. The purchase price would be a negotiated figure and a most interesting example of this was one where the repurchase price was equal to the original purchase price paid by the institution plus a capitalization of the average participation rental previously paid. In the case of a sale-

leaseback of land alone, a third element may be added to the repurchase price, namely an amount equal to some portion of the amortization paid on the leasehold mortgage which was obtained by the developer. This last element properly equates amortization with equity and
recognizes the institution's interest in such equity.

* * *

C.   Stock or Ownership

Another [form of] participation could be the additional privilege of
acquiring an interest by way of stock [or a partnership interest] in the
developer entity or an undivided interest in the property upon payment
of a nominal or negotiated consideration. The cautious and optimistic
developer might also provide for a privilege on his part to recapture the
outstanding purchase option upon payment of a premium above the
purchase option. Where the available financing is particularly troublesome, the consideration for the loan or other financing might be the
actual transfer of stock[, a partnership interest] or grant of an undivided ownership interest in the project.

D.   Limited Partnership or Joint Venture

In [certain situations] and for selected properties, we find institutions joining directly or by means of subsidiary corporations as [general
partners,] limited partners or as joint venturers with developers in real
estate developments.

E.   Pure Equity—Sole Venturer

The most original and dynamic arrangement to come to our attention is one which can only be described as pure equity. * * * [T]he
institution will, upon the application and recommendation of a developer, completely fund and acquire in the name of a corporation[,] owned
jointly by [the] institution and [the] developer[,] the land to be developed for the production of income. The institution will thereafter
provide all of the equity money required and the development will
proceed under the direction of the developer, with reasonable control by
the institution. Mortgage loan financing will be obtained from another
institution and the venturers will enjoy all the benefits of levered
income. Presumably, the extent of the developer's participation in
income will have been agreed upon in advance, although we are told
this may not be necessarily so. This would seem to be the Nirvana to
which all developers aspire, namely, an equity ownership without risk
or cash investment.

* * *

IV. Other Financing Devices

A. *Mortgage Financing*

The most normal, ordinary and ancient technique in financing real estate is the mortgage. Springing from the Roman hypotheca and the 15th century dead pledge, the 60–80 per cent mortgage has long been an accepted form of institutional lending on real estate. * * * But from this simple[,] low percentage[,] fee mortgage have come a host of new techniques.

* * * [T]he so-called 90 or 100 per cent high credit lease transaction [has been] * * * authorized [in a number of states]. The key to this type [of] transaction is 100 per cent financing based upon the assignment to the lender of a net lease to a single tenant who would qualify for an unsecured loan from the investor. In [some states] a mortgage is not required, but in view of the fact that the reversion recovered by the lessor upon lessee's default is considered in fixing damages to which the lender would be entitled by assignment upon termination, getting a mortgage seems highly desirable. Where a loan of less than 90 per cent of value is involved, [in some states] the lease need not be net and [more than one] lease can be involved and a * * * balloon [of around 10%] is permitted, whereas in the 100 per cent transaction[,] the rent from a single net lease must be sufficient to pay off the entire loan.

Further complications have arisen where (a) the tenant is willing to give a mortgagee the benefit of some covenants but not put them in the lease, (b) where a subleasehold estate is involved that is less than the ground leasehold estate and the tenant is restricted by other financing agreements from covenanting as to more than its subleasehold premises, and (c) where personal property as well as real property is to be financed, as in a department store. Frequently, (a) is solved by the use of side letter agreements; bringing in the high credit occupant as sublessor of the borrower with a covenant of quiet enjoyment is one solution to (b) and an attornment agreement with the fee owner is another. Furthermore, the assignment of lease must be air-tight. To a large extent[,] the owner must forego giving of consents, serving notices of default or doing anything with the lease without the consent of the lender. In case of fire or condemnation the tenant must make up deficiencies and under no circumstances can the tenant cancel the lease unless there are sufficient funds to pay or the tenant purchases the debt. Rent is usually paid directly to the lender or its trustee either by the lease assignment or by the lease terms. If rent exceeds debt service, prior to default[,] the rent may be split or the lender may refund the excess of each installment. * * *

In practice * * * the borrower [is] almost always * * * a subsidiary or affiliate corporation of the high credit tenant.

Mortgages in excess of the usual percentage limit may also be taken in many states under a so-called "leeway" or "basket clause."

[W]hile they are not subject to the legal requirements for assignment of high credit leases referred to above * * *[,] the lender going beyond 75 or 80 per cent may well want to look to strong leases from substantial tenants. * * *

Despite the complications of the high credit lease secured mortgage transaction, the fee mortgage is still a fairly simple thing and we suspect for that reason astute borrowers and lenders have taken to the leasehold mortgage. * * *

First, of course, the leasehold mortgage offers a chance to bring in the landlord in some capacity. Frequently[,] we hear that "his fee will be subordinated" meaning that the mortgage will encumber the fee. Perhaps the landlord has limited this to a loan of a certain size or a maximum rate, or perhaps it can only be done after a building is built. Perhaps the landlord will require that on foreclosure the lease be sold first. Even if the landlord does not require this, the court may require it under a theory of marshalling or sales in inverse order of alienation so as to subject the estate of the borrower to sale before that of the lessor as a sort of accommodation mortgagor. Many lenders, to avoid all this[,] require that the mortgaged estate be the fee, with the lessee signing to subordinate his lease and assume the mortgage covenants of which, in turn, the fee owner is relieved, except for the pure lien provisions.

Often a lessor is not willing to run the risk of losing his land, even to get a fine building and fine rents, but will do something for the mortgagee. He may, of course, accept complete[ly] prepaid rent to his probable tax disadvantage and the lessee's out-of-pocket disadvantage, or[,] more realistically[,] he may agree to subordinate his rent claim to the mortgage debt. This can be done by providing in the lease that in the event of a default on a certain mortgage loan the rent will abate in whole or in part until the mortgagee has been paid in full, not by taking title to the property, but from the rents, issues and profits of the property or payment by the borrower or a guarantor * * *. This, of course, makes the leasehold estate far more valuable and increases the maximum possible loan.

More normally, the fee owner does no such thing, of course, but he has still helped maximize the financing. In a state where banks and insurance companies are limited to 75 per cent loans, the fee owner's 100 per cent investment in land worth one-third the value of the building increases total financing to 100 per cent of one-quarter and 75 per cent of three-quarters or slightly over 81 per cent. * * *

In discussing 100 per cent financing, brief reference was made to a subleasehold mortgage. After some questioning as to whether a sublease is a "lease" under investment statutes, most lawyers eagerly accepted the greater possibility for complexity offered by use of this technique. The subleasehold mortgage combined with a ground leasehold mortgage * * * can increase [the] financing percentage. It, or even a combination of fee and leasehold mortgage, also increases legal problems. In one case, a university owns the fee and leases the ground at a certain rent to be reduced if the leasehold mortgage goes into default. The leasehold estate in the land and the title to the buildings are then mortgaged to Institution A. This mortgage is subordinate to a sublease[,] at a rent sufficient to cover debt service[,] to the true operator who mortgages his sublease to Institution B. Institution A, feeling that it can get to ultimate space rents if there is a default on the sublease and that if there [is] no default on the sublease it will always get debt service, values the center as though there were no sublease. Institution B views the problems as one of valuating its sublease and does so by capitalizing net income after deducting ground rent and rent to the mortgagor of Institution A. All rents are paid to a trustee who sees that mortgage payments are made. The deal was done [by] A and B, [although] each [was] limited to a 75 per cent loan[,] together invest[ing] 75 per cent plus 75 per cent of 25 per cent or over 93 per cent.

* * *

[T]here is, as previously stated, the problem of loss of the ground lease through default. If the estates are not physically coterminus[,] the right to perform the ground lessee's covenants is not pleasing to a subleasehold mortgagee who has no interest in the larger property outside [the] encumbered subleasehold estate. If the ground lease can be split by its terms into separate leases, much is gained. An offer of nondisturbance by the fee owner is helpful, but does not solve all problems. * * * [S]uppose the ground lessee goes into bankruptcy or reorganization and his trustee disaffirms the ground lease. How is the sublessee and the subleasehold mortgagee affected? Do they merely have damage claims against the bankrupt estate? If the ground lessor has agreed to give a new lease to sublessees on sublease terms, what effect if the ground lessor is also bankrupt? Unfortunately, case law is not extensive on these points.[1] There is even an absence of case law on the rights of a leasehold mortgagee opposed to disaffirmance against a lessee's trustee who desires disaffirmance. The moral seems to be that a few bankruptcies or reorganizations affecting properties subject to multi-leasehold financing could make some exciting law.

* * *

[U]p to now we have assumed a mortgage, fee or leasehold, covering one entire piece of real estate. However, buildings are being divided physically. A mortgage may encumber an air right estate included merely for zoning purposes, or it may be limited strictly to air rights. A railroad granting leases can limit the demised premises to areas above a certain level with support easements or[,] conversely[,] can reserve subsurface easements for itself for track purposes. Either accomplishes the same end, and neither is novel. What is new is a fee, or leasehold, mortgage on air space beginning high above the ground

---

1. [Under Section 365 of the Bankruptcy Code the sublessee appears to have the option to elect to remain in possession if the trustee of the ground lessee and, possibly, the trustee of the ground lessor disaffirm the ground lease.]

with support and other easements through space owned by another. Such split ownership will be discussed later and a mortgagee's problems are not too much greater than his mortgagor's. * * *

Another variant on straight mortgaging is the mortgage on an undivided interest in real estate. * * * [I]t poses the problems of joint ownership involved in participation in mortgage situations without the likelihood that the problem can be solved by advance documentation. An exception to this last statement is * * * the situation where the co-owner of the fee with the borrower is the lender.

* * *

The multi-participation mortgage, which does lend itself to advance documentation[,] can have some of the management problems involved in the mortgage on an undivided interest in real estate[,] plus foreclosure problems. The simplest participation transaction involves a senior and a junior participation—usually the latter—for a comparatively small share of the mortgage. This [form of participation] quite common[ly occurs] between [an] institutional lender and [a] mortgage banker. At times[,] it may accidentally be made necessary[,] when the mortgage banker correspondent has made a loan too large in relation to value to be a legal investment for the institutional lender who[,] nevertheless[,] will purchase a senior participation * * * in an amount which would be a legal first mortgage. The junior participant may also be a mortgage banker correspondent called upon to show its faith in a transaction in which it wishes the institutional investor to put its funds. In either event[,] the rights of the junior participant are short and the results are often brutal. There is [usually] no room for reinstating and carrying the senior as could be done in a first and second mortgage situation. Under usual documentation, upon default the junior participant can buy out the senior, bid at foreclosure or be wiped out. A well drafted document provides that [the junior participant] has no further interest. Theoretically this is so [even] if the senior participant bids in for the senior debt and immediately resells for a 100 per cent profit, though it is not clear that all courts would sustain such a result. To protect the junior's bid, however, in equity foreclosure states, the senior usually must agree to obtain a judgment equal to the total debt, rather than merely the senior share.

Far greater problems arise when the participation is *pari passu.* Here the ground rules should all be established in advance: who can call the loan for default, commence foreclosure, bid, and on behalf of whom, lease, evict tenants, make repairs or improvements and to what extent, sell at a profit, sell at a loss, take back a purchase money mortgage or participation therein, with the same rights all over again in case of the latter, who pays, who can bind the other to pay, and how is payment enforced? When one investor owns almost all the debt the answer is usually obvious. Where the two investors are of almost equal rank in size of investment the answer often may be neither acting alone. A useful technique is the consent or buy agreement[. Under this type of agreement if] one party * * * initiate[s] a transaction[,] the other must either consent or buy out the originator at cost or, in connection with a proposed sale, at the latter's share of the proposed price. The above questions merely scratch the surface ＊ ＊ ＊. [A] *pari passu* participation, unless one participant is absolutely dominant or one is obligated to buy out the [other's] interest, is a complicated, often legally untested device that does not lend itself to small transactions.

＊ ＊ ＊

Another example of a modern technique based on ancient devices— the first and second mortgage is the modern "wrap-around" mortgage. The modern wrap-around mortgage usually comes into being where there is an existing mortgage at a lower interest rate than the borrower is willing to pay for a larger loan. [The principal amount of the new loan includes the remaining principal balance of the old loan and the new lender disburses to the borrower the difference between the principal amount of the new loan and the remaining principal balance of the old loan.] The borrower pays a constant payment on the new loan and from this the new lender pays the installments due on the old loan. ＊ ＊ ＊ The new mortgagee ＊ ＊ ＊ has the advantage of the rate on the old loan and therefore can probably offer a lower rate than it would ask for on a totally separate new loan without the wrap-around feature. ＊ ＊ ＊ Sometimes a wrap-around is necessitated by the fact that the old mortgage cannot be prepaid except upon prohibitive terms.

Of course, there are some flies in the nectar. First is our old friend, usury. When the old loan is fairly large, compared to the new[,] resulting in a small advance and the difference in interest rate is great, the early yields [to the new lender] can be quite fantastic. [I]t is not clear whether yield to maturity or the rate in the early years [is] determinative for usury purposes, but where [the yield to the new lender] in the first year is at 25 or 30 per cent per annum, a court might be constrained to find usury though the overall yield is not in excess of the maximum rate [set by the usury statute]. Assuming self-denial can solve this problem, there is the further problem of title insurance and intervening liens. At least in theory the new loan is paid down with each monthly installment and then is increased by an advance. If this advance is obligatory, as the papers may provide, the advance should prime intervening liens in most states, but many lenders are unwilling to so completely obligate themselves in the face of known junior liens, nor do they want to rely on any doctrine of subrogation. Furthermore[,] there is the problem of a substantial advance to cover any balloon payment on the old loan, [which advance is, in the usual case,] at least partially voluntary by its terms.

＊ ＊ ＊

More complications arise by reason of statutory limits on lending. In [some] jurisdictions, institutional lenders, absent "basket" provisions, are limited to first mortgages. ＊ ＊ ＊ A wrap-around mortgage is on its face a second mortgage and thus should be limited to the basket. ＊ ＊ ＊ And, of course, there may be mortgage tax problems which could be avoided in the usual transaction by taking an assignment of the old mortgage.

* * *

Not content with innumerable and ingenious refinements which they have worked upon the lending techniques, the parties early turned their attention to the financing potential of the purchase and sale of real property. Once again, a commendable degree of imagination has been exercised and with comparable success.

B.   *Real Estate Financing by Purchase and Sale*

1.   Sale Leaseback—Improved Property

The financing technique of sale-leaseback is [subject to] innumerable variations [in its use] as well as [in] the types of properties to which it [is] applied. [I]t [is] utilized not only with fee estates, but [also] with leasehold estates, condominiums and air rights. The sale is for a price negotiated to serve the purposes of the buyer and seller, and the fixed rental payable under the lease will provide the agreed return to [the] purchaser on [the] purchase price. In addition, however, these leases many times provide for contingent rental [in order to provide the purchaser with] a participation in the income received from subtenants. * * * [T]he leaseback [also] may provide for mandatory or optional repurchase by [the] seller-tenant for a negotiated price, once again serving the purposes of both parties. * * *

Developer's [reason for engaging] in this type [of] financing is frequently the fact that his tax shelter has been depleted, the lines of depreciation and amortization have crossed, and he is now paying tax on the amortization payments he makes on an existing mortgage. [T]hrough this device [the developer] obtain[s] 100 per cent financing of his investment in the property. His investment and accrued profit in this particular property [is] freed up and is * * * available for investment elsewhere, while at the same time he retains the operational control and a continuing interest in * * * the project [by reason of his leasehold]. * * *

From the * * * standpoint [of the institutional lender], the purchase permits a 100 per cent investment in a seasoned quality property, with a fixed rate of return in excess of the mortgage rates and, in some cases, a participation in income. In addition, the institution has the benefit of depreciation and the fee estate is mortgageable thereby opening the possibility of further levering. The value to the institution of the residual value in the reversion upon expiration of lease or the premium payable upon exercise of a purchase option, if any, may also be [substantial].

2.   Sale–Leaseback of Land Only

This type of transaction originally involved the sale and leaseback of unimproved real property. The technique has been refined so that

*   *   * it is frequently used in the sale of improved land where the deed expressly excludes the building improvements followed by a lease-back of such land (excluding buildings). This latter transaction seeks to accomplish a legal severing of building improvements from the land. The net result in either case is a sale-leaseback of land only[,] with title to the building improvements vested in the tenant, subject to automatic transfer of such title in [the] buildings to the owner of the land upon expiration or sooner termination of the lease. This type [of] financing device is susceptible of use for a fee, a leasehold, a condominium or even air rights estates. The leaseback may also provide for repurchase options *   *   *.

[Similar to] the [sale and] leaseback of [the] entire property, the purchase price will be negotiated and will be determined by the particular objectives of the parties. The leaseback will provide for the fixed rentals based upon the negotiated return on the purchase price and [also] may *   *   * provide for a participation rental *   *   *.

The factors attracting a developer to this format *   *   * vary slightly from those involved in the [previously discussed] sale-leaseback situations. In this case, the developer may have a large capital invest-ment in expensive land which is now freed by means of this 100 per cent financing of the land. It is even more appealing since the land investment [is] nondepreciable. This device may be utilized for land banking purposes since the institution may be prepared to carry the land for an extended period until such time as the developer is pre-pared to proceed with the development. The developer [obtains] the benefit of rent as a deduction, but more [significantly the developer] has retained the benefit of the depreciation of improvements existing or [to be] erected. Of greatest importance to the developer is the fact that this type of leaseback is much more readily mortgageable since the tenant owns the improvements which are mortgaged together with the leasehold estate. The combined financing produces more proceeds than by mortgage financing alone.

Under this arrangement *   *   * the institution receives a higher fixed rate of return than by [a] mortgage and, in many cases as well, a participation rental. The institution is able to increase the amount of its investment in a quality property by furnishing 100 per cent financ-ing of the land and by furnishing, or receiving [the] right of first refusal to furnish[,] 75 per cent mortgage financing of the leasehold estate. The institution also has the residual value of the land or the proceeds of any repurchase option. If it so desires[,] the institution itself may mortgage the fee, thereby further levering its equity position.

3. Sale of Land and Improvements—Pregnant Leaseback

This contrivance will appeal to the developer of a project where development is in stages and extends over a considerable period of time. *   *   * This plan provides the developer with the benefits *   *   * of a sale-leaseback of the unimproved land and the improved portions of the project while [the developer] retain[s] the right and privilege to develop and separately finance[,] at a later date[,] the unimproved land included within the project. Under this program[,] the developer * * * sell[s] to the institution and lease[s] back the entire land and buildings, if any.

The leaseback will contain the usual provisions for a fixed rental and possibly a participation rental. In addition[,] * * * the developer [will] retain the right to improve the unimproved portions. To do so, however, he must first offer the additional financing to the landlord who, if it accept[s, will] advance the funds [as] a capital improvement [to the leased land] and the fixed rent [will] be increased in an amount to be agreed upon. * * * [I]f the parties cannot agree upon the financing, * * * for an agreed release price, the landlord [will] release the land to be improved from * * * the master lease and [will] separately lease it to the developer. * * * [T]his severed lease [will] be mortgageable and * * * provide for an agreed fixed rental, based upon the pro-rated original purchase price or an agreed formula and may include participation rental. The developer [will] then have the privilege of obtaining leasehold mortgage financing from the same or another institution.

* * *

4. Purchase and Installment Saleback

This * * * financing device is nothing more than a very clever adaptation of the familiar installment sales contract. Under this plan, [the] developer will sell improved real property to the institution for a purchase price equal to his actual cost. This purchase price usually represents 80 to 90 per cent of the then appraised value of the project and thereby provides the institution with a certain margin of security. The institution in turn agrees to re-sell the property to the developer under an installment sales contract for the original price plus carrying charges (interest). The fixed monthly payments [are] computed in the same way as the constant [payments are determined] in mortgage financing and * * * include both an interest component and a payment on principal.

The term of the contract generally runs ten years or more beyond the usual conventional mortgage term for similar property. The contract may * * * provide for a contingent payment representing a participation by the seller-institution in a defined [portion] of the [net] income being received by the buyer who continues in possession and operation of the property. The defined [portion of the] net [income] is customarily gross income less the fixed installment payments, taxes, insurance and permitted operating expenses.

For its own internal accounting and within the limits of the constant [payment] used, the institution can establish a minimum yield, with money back over some desired period of time less than the term of the contract. The contract also [will] provide for prepayment, after an initial closed period of perhaps fifteen years, at a price which [will] yield [to] the seller the same rate of return as if the contract had

continued to maturity. During that same minimum period, the institution * * * also [will] have * * * the benefit of the participation
payments. [One of t]he most important [aspects of this device] to the
developer * * * is the agreement by [the] seller to permit the purchaser to claim all depreciation deductions. The installment saleback
is available for use with fee properties, leaseholds, condominiums or
even air rights situations.

The advantages of this type financing are primarily for the developer. He receives 100 per cent financing and pays slightly higher than
mortgage interest, but with a longer term. He has an extended period
of tax shelter [through the] depreciation and interest deductions.
* * *

The advantages to the institution are somewhat more modest.
There is the attraction of a satisfactory fixed rate of return together
with the possibility of participation payments. A greater amount of
money may * * * be invested in a desirable project than through
mortgage financing and there is a greater amount of call protection
both by way of the closed prepayment period, as well as by the
premium payable on prepayment. * * *

C. *Combinations of Mortgage and Lease Financing*

Combinations of the techniques previously discussed, naturally
lend themselves to the greatest variety, complexity and often
financibility.

The leasehold mortgage and leaseback form a natural combination.
To the investor contemplating these two forms of investment in one
transaction, the important thing is that both be viable and legal as
separate investments. * * * [T]he lease must so be written that the
fee interest is reasonably protected while * * * [the lease also]
contains all the protection for a leasehold mortgagee that would be
expected where the fee owner is a stranger. Nevertheless, where the
leasehold estate is one that has existed for several years, * * * the
lessor [often] has an advantage [when seeking to provide] leasehold
financing over outsiders [since] lease amendments are frequently necessary.

The next logical step after being involved in fee ownership and
leasehold mortgage financing is for an institution to acquire an interest
in the leasehold estate subject to its own leasehold mortgage. This
alternative investment * * * takes many formats.

It * * * [might] be an interest held with other interests by a
trustee thus creating a legal entity distinct from the lender and
borrowers. * * * It could be a partnership or joint venture interest
* * *. Since a partnership or joint venture involves possible liability
to third parties, the investor may choose to set up a subsidiary to hold
its interest. * * *

Whether an interest in a joint venture or being a partner in a partnership owning real property is ownership of an interest in real property is an unresolved problem. Of course, a simpler device is to have the investor be a co-tenant in the leasehold estate. Here, as in the participation in mortgages, it is necessary to have an agreement as to management of the property, delineating the rights and duties of the participants. In such an agreement, as in [a] partnership or joint venture [agreement], it is necessary that the investor have at least a veto right over actions which might be inimicable to its best interests or which might involve it in actions it could not legally undertake.

* * *

Still dealing with a single use building, but using a combination of the techniques discussed above, it has been suggested that there can be at least twenty-five different financing positions. Actually the only limitation on this number is practical rather than legal. At some point the cost of arranging financing exceeds the amount of financing.

The tendency to multi-use buildings makes further complexity possible. Many buildings * * * have several uses [such] as store space on the ground floor, floors of garage space and[, possibly,] office and even apartment floors. Sometimes hotel use is included. This split in use suggests the possibility of separate ownership of different parts of the building. In states [which] have condominium laws this is easily done, but it can be done in most jurisdictions in the absence of such statutes. In some areas it is possible to get separate tax assessments. Where this is not possible unless the land is divided, it may be possible to get separate tax assessment[s] by [having] the owner of an upper portion of the building [hold a fee interest in] small areas [of the land] under elevator shafts and certain supports serving only the upper portion. Practical problems create the greatest difficulty for the draftsman. Who maintains common areas? Who decides upon repairs, upon alterations with respect to common facilities? How are contributions enforced? What easements are necessary for the upper interest and for the lower? What is the result of fire damage?

* * *

NOTE

1. One of the important reasons which leads a developer to finance a high percentage of the project costs is to increase the leverage and, consequently, the return on the equity investment. If the return on equity derived from the project is $5,000 per annum, it would be considered a good return if the developer had only invested $25,000 in the project, but a bad return if the developer's investment was $100,000.

    a. What are the dangers of attempting to maximize leverage?

        1. If 75% of project costs are financed, is the margin of error in under-estimating operating costs and over-estimating gross receipts more or less than when 90% of project costs are financed, assuming the same terms, other than the amount of each installment payment, for the financing?

2. One of the lender's responses to a request to finance a large percentage of project costs has been to ask for a participation in income. The lender's participation in income raises a number of problems.

a. How should the income in which the lender participates be defined?

1. A lender's participation in gross receipts probably is unacceptable to the developer. Is a participation in gross income any better?

a. If gross income is defined as gross receipts less the cost of goods sold, is it possible that the project could produce a negative cash flow and, despite the negative cash flow, the lender could be entitled to a payment with respect to its participation in addition to the interest on its loan?

2. Does a participation in net income before taxes and depreciation make sense in all cases?

b. Might the lender participate in cash flow or in the excess of cash flow over a certain minimum amount? What problems are presented by a participation defined in this manner? Does a participation in cash flow have any advantages over a gross or net income participation?

c. Might the lender participate in gross or net rentals over a certain minimum amount? What advantages does this method of participation have?

d. For a discussion of the above and other methods of defining the lender's participation, see pages 566 to 567 supra and pages 782 to 791 infra.

e. Is usury a problem when a lender is participating in income?

1. Since the participation is usually measured by a formula, the possibility exists that, in any one year, the return the lender receives from its participation in income plus the interest on the loan may exceed the usury limit. Is the loan usurious? See pages 788 to 795 infra. See Note, *Usury Implementation of Alternative Mortgage Instruments: The Uncertainty in Calculating Permissible Returns,* 1986 B.Y. U.L.Rev. 1105.

f. The lender also might participate in income by acquiring an equity interest in the project such as stock, a partnership interest or a limited partnership interest in the entity which owns the project, and/or direct ownership of a tenancy in common or a joint venture interest in the project. What problems can arise as a result of the lender acquiring an equity interest?

1. Even though the dollar limitations on the amount of a loan a lender can make probably do not apply to these types of investments, both federal and state laws and regulations governing most institutional lenders limit the amount and type of investments, other than loans, such institutions can make. See Committee Report, *Legal Restrictions on Equity Participation Financings,* 20 Real Prop., Prob. & Tr.J. 1139 (1985).

2. In the usual case a lender's participation in income ends with the repayment of the loan. The loan documents will contain suitable safeguards to prevent, or make very costly, prepayment of the loan. A partner's or a shareholder's participation does not end when his loan,

if any, to the partnership is paid back. What steps can the developer take to limit the amount and duration of the lender's participation if the participation is taken in the form of an equity interest?

3. In *Johns v. Jaeb,* 518 S.W.2d 857 (Tex.Civ.App.1974), the court ignored a limited partnership agreement which the "lender" and the developer had entered into, considered the substance of the transaction to be a loan, and held that the developer could recover the usury penalty because the loan was usurious. On the other hand, in *James B. Leahy,* 87 T.C. 56 (1986), the Tax Court, after considering the terms and conditions of a purported loan, held that the substance of the transaction was that the "lender" and "borrower" were joint venturers since the "lender" had a continuing interest in 75% of the net profits of the venture.

g. As described above, the Internal Revenue Service and the courts may treat a lender with participation rights as a joint venturer. See *James B. Leahy,* 87 T.C. 56 (1986). For example, a 40–year nonprepayable, nonrecourse loan to a partnership which, in addition to bearing fixed interest, provides for a participation in gross income and can be converted into a 50% partnership interest may be regarded as a capital contribution to the partnership rather than as a loan. Cf. G.C.M. 36702 (April 2, 1976) and G.C.M. 38133 (October 10, 1979). In Rev.Rul. 83–98, 1983–2 C.B. 40, the Internal Revenue Service held that subordinated, convertible notes on which the interest varied according to the amount of dividends paid on shares of the common stock of the issuer and which, under the most likely eventualities, would be converted into common stock, should be treated as equity rather than debt. It appears, however, that a payment to a lender measured by a share of the appreciation in the asset securing the loan will be treated as interest, at least when a personal residence is the asset securing the loan. See Rev.Rul. 83–51, 1983–1 C.B. 48; Rev.Proc. 83–31, 1983–1 C.B. 722; Milner, *Taxation of Residential and Commercial Shared Appreciation Mortgages After Revenue Ruling 83–51,* 62 Taxes 631 (1984); Comment, *Revenue Ruling 83–51: Tax Treatment of Shared Appreciation Mortgages,* 4 Va.Tax Rev. 409 (1985); Boyd and O'Dell, *Tax Consequences of Shared Appreciation Mortgages After Tax Reform,* 4 J.Ps. Tax'n 303 (1988). Lastly, in *Saviano v. Comm'r,* 765 F.2d 643 (7th Cir.1985), the court held that the "debtor" and "creditor" were, in substance, joint venturers when the debt was nonrecourse, provided for a participation in gross income in addition to fixed interest and was payable, both as to principal and interest (fixed and contingent), out of the proceeds of the mining venture which was financed with the proceeds of the purported loan.

1. Closely related to the question whether, for tax purposes, the relationship between a developer and a lender is that of debtor-creditor or members of a joint venture or partnership, is the question whether a loan from a general partner to the partnership of which he is a member should be treated as a loan or a capital contribution. In Rev. Rul. 72–135, 1972–1 C.B. 200, and in Priv.Ltr.Rul. 8140077, the Internal Revenue Service held that nonrecourse loans made by a general partner to a limited partnership were contributions to capital rather than loans. In *Dillingham v. United States,* 48 A.F.T.R.2d 81–5815 (D.Okla.1981), however, the court held that a loan from a general partner should be treated as a loan and not a contribution to capital. In Reg.Sec. 1.752–1T(d)(3)(B) the Internal Revenue Service changed its

position slightly by holding that a nonrecourse loan made by a partner to his partnership should be added to the creditor partner's basis in his partnership interest, under Section 752(a), since only the creditor partner bares the economic risk of loss with respect to the loan. Even if a nonrecourse loan made by a general partner is treated as a loan, the application of the at-risk rules of Section 465 of the Code will prevent a nonrecourse loan by a general partner from providing the limited partners with any additional at-risk amount for the purpose of using the losses of the venture. See the discussion of the at-risk rules in Division I, pages 150 to 153 supra.

h. See generally Feder, *Either a Partner or a Lender Be: Emerging Tax Issues in Real Estate Finance,* 36 Tax Law. 191 (1983); Lazzeri and Dean, *Shared Equity Arrangements—The Tax Consequences for the Lender and Borrower,* 14 Tax Adviser 34 (1983); Steuben, *The Convertible, Participating Mortgage: Federal Income Tax Considerations,* 54 U.Colo.L.Rev. 237 (1983); Strauss, *Tax Aspects of Equity Participation Financing,* 41 N.Y.U. Inst.Fed.Tax'n 21-1 (1983); Burnes, *The Shared Appreciation Mortgage—A Joint Venture, A Relationship Between Debtor and Creditor, Or Both?,* 12 J.Real Est.Tax'n 195 (1985); Platt and Long, *Equity Participation Real Estate Financing,* 3 B.U.J.Tax L. 1 (1985); Vargo, *Equity Participation by the Institutional Lender: The Security Status Issue,* 26 S.Tex.L.J. 225 (1985); Schneider, *Partner as Lender: Tax Consequences for Real Estate Partnerships,* 13 J.Real Est.Tax'n 3 (1985); Nasuti, *Unintentional Partnerships and How to Avoid them in Loan Joint Ventures,* 44 N.Y.U.Inst.Fed. Tax'n 23-1 (1986).

3. If two or more lenders are involved in providing the financing for a project, each lender could hold a separate mortgage with an agreed upon priority among the mortgages. Why would the lenders opt for participation in a single first mortgage?

a. If the total financing to value was within all of the lenders' limits, but the total amount of the financing was in excess of the amount which any one of the lenders could lend to a single borrower or invest in a single project, the participation would avoid any one of the lenders having to take other than a first mortgage.

b. Are the participants in a participated mortgage limited to traditional institutional investors?

c. Will a developer have to pay a greater rate of interest to a lender holding a second mortgage or a lender holding a junior participation in a first mortgage?

1. Should a developer expect that the term of a participated first mortgage will be longer than the term of a nonparticipated second mortgage?

a. Might a participation agreement provide that the junior participant is to be repaid over a shorter period of time than the senior participant while also providing that the borrower's installment payments are to be constant over the term of the mortgage?

d. The mechanics and drafting of a participation agreement are complex and require a great deal of care.

e. See pages 721 to 732 infra.

4. Some of the desirability of the sale and leaseback technique results from its income tax effects, i.e., avoiding the payment of tax on dollars used to amortize the principal of a mortgage, obtaining a current deduction (rent) for nondepreciable land, etc.

     a. As a result, it is important that the Internal Revenue Service regard the transaction as consisting of a sale and a lease. Yet, is the sale and the lease really a sale and a lease; certainly the lender is not the traditional purchaser and lessor?

         1. How should the transaction be handled and the documents drafted in order to be certain of the desired tax results? See pages 763 to 775 infra. See generally *Frank Lyon Co. v. United States*, 435 U.S. 561, 98 S.Ct. 1291, 55 L.Ed.2d 550 (1978); Kronovet, *Characterization of Real Estate Leases: An Analysis and Proposal*, 32 Tax Law. 757 (1979).

     b. The ultimate in tax and transactional planning for the developer comes about when the lender purchases the land thereby providing 100% financing of the land cost and a deductible payment (rent) for the developer, while the developer retains ownership of the improvements constructed and to be constructed thereby retaining the ability to deduct depreciation and the ability to grant a fee mortgage in the improvements.

         1. What are the practical and legal problems which must be solved if this technique is to be effectively used? How can the problems be solved? See pages 713 to 721 infra and pages 573 to 574 supra.

5. The purchase and installment sale-back offers some advantages to both the lender and the developer. But are the advantages offered any greater than, for example, the advantages offered by a sale and leaseback with the improvements severed—owned by the developer? Might a developer or a lender be reluctant to use a purchase and installment sale-back in view of the uncertain treatment of the installment land contract in some states? See pages 600 to 609 infra and pages 575 to 576 supra.

6. The possibilities in financing are many. As pointed out in the preceding excerpt, it has been suggested that there are as many as 25 different financing positions.

     a. Where is the line drawn? How much is enough? What factors should be considered? Is there a value in simplicity and traditional forms, besides being a little less costly?

     b. See generally Panel, *Real Estate Financing Techniques*, 9 Real Prop., Prob. & Tr.J. 617 (1974); Symposium, *Real Estate Financing Today and Tomorrow*, 13 Real Prop., Prob. & Tr.J. 1009 (1978); Heath, *New Developments in Real Estate Financing*, 12 St. Mary's L.J. 811 (1981); Lewis, *Creative Financing Techniques in Commercial Real Estate*, 72 A.B. A.J. 60 (1986); Ominsky, *A Lender's Primer on Pitfalls in Real Estate Loans*, 1 # 5 Prac.Real Est.Law 9 (1985); Malloy, *Creative Financing Exposes Lenders to Developers' Liabilities*, 15 # 2 Real Est.Rev. 60 (1985); Ling and Peiser, *Choosing Among Alternative Financing Structures: The Developer's Dilemma*, 17 # 2 Real Est.Rev. 39 (1987).

7. Mortgaging out is one possible result of the use of the variety of techniques of financing the development of real estate considered above. The proceeds of the financing, which generally is based on a percentage of the fair market value of the completed project, may be greater than the actual cost of the project and the developer's tax basis for the project. In this event, the

participants in the entity developing the project may be able to "pocket" the difference between the actual costs and the proceeds of the financing. Some of the significant considerations in mortgaging out are income tax concerns.

MORTGAGING OUT AND RELATED PROBLEMS

Ralph R. Neuhoff
1961 Washington Univ. Law Quarterly 132 (1961).
[most footnotes omitted]

*   *   *

Examples

The following examples are designed to show the consequences of excess or deficiency of market value with respect to the amount of mortgage which governs the equity and of excess or deficiency of market [value] with respect to basis which governs the potential for gain or loss: [2]

Case I

	Cost of land and building (basis)	$100,000
	Market	130,000
	Mortgage	100,000
	Equity	30,000
c	Excess of market over basis	30,000

Case II

	Cost of land and building (basis)	$100,000
	Market	130,000
a	Mortgage	115,000
	Equity	15,000
c	Excess of market over basis	30,000

Case III

	Cost of land and building (basis)	$100,000
	Market	130,000
a	Mortgage	130,000
	Equity	zero
c	Excess of market over basis	30,000

Case IV

	Cost of land and building (basis)	$100,000
	Market	100,000
a	Mortgage	115,000
b	Equity	*—15,000*
	Excess of market over basis	zero

*   *   *

2. In the following examples: c—Indicates market is higher than basis.
a—Indicates mortgaging out.
b—Indicates a negative equity.

Definitions

Mortgaging out will be used to indicate any case where the amount of the mortgage on property at the time it is made is greater than the basis of the property given as security, regardless * * * whether the market value justifies the amount of the mortgage.

Negative equity indicates that market value is less than the amount of [the] mortgage on the property at the time referred to.

Basis less than market indicates that the market value of the property given as security is greater than its basis. It might be called "potential for gain."

Basis means basis under the Internal Revenue Code which may initially be equivalent to cost.

Basic Principles

A. *First Principle*

Merely placing a mortgage on property, even though it is in excess of the cost of the property given as security, does not, without more, result in taxable income. Case II above is an example, the propriety of which would not be questioned. Case IV would apparently be improper where the negative equity existed at the time that the mortgage was placed on the property since the mortgagee obviously would not intend that such a situation should arise and one would suspect that he was induced to make the loan by misrepresentation of some sort.

The first principle applies even where there is no personal liability of the mortgagor. Where there is a positive equity such as in Case II above, there is no incentive for the owner to let the property go for the mortgage, even though he would have a clear profit over cost by simply taking the mortgage money and forgetting about the property. On the other hand, where there is no equity, as in Case IV, there will be, in many instances, a strong incentive to the owner to forget about the property. This is where mortgaging out probably got its bad name. Apparently the motive of the mortgagor is immaterial, and this is so even where the mortgagor intends to let the property go and, therefore, has, in his eyes, "sold" the property to the mortgagee.

* * * [A]n income tax should only be applied to an identifiable event. Normally, this implies that there has been a definite transaction which had a beginning and an ending. The courts apparently feel that the placing of the mortgage on the property is the *beginning* of a transaction and not the ending of another transaction which began when the land was bought and property was built. The rule could have been otherwise, apparently, in examples such as Case IV above, at least to the extent of putting the burden on the [mortgagor] to show that he did not intend to let the property go upon foreclosure at the time he placed the mortgage on the property.

* * *

One should distinguish instances involving compensation for personal service. A strong case could be made for taxing the economic gain where a taxpayer was in the business of building such houses and the increase in market value was merely the result of his efforts, skill and know-how which, in a different context, would earn compensation, as, for example, when he performed the same services for someone else for hire. Observe that pay for services rendered to others is taxable when received even if received in property other than money, but if one creates value in property by working for himself, this is not income until sold or exchanged.

* * *

B. Second Principle

A voluntary sale of property for a price in excess of basis will result in taxable income. An example would be Case I above if the property is sold for anything over basis. It would also apply in Case II above if it were sold for anything over basis. The mortgaging out which is present in Case II is irrelevant.

C. Third Principle

A foreclosure sale of property at a price in excess of basis plus expenses of sale results in taxable income. An example would be Case II if the bid is in excess of the basis. Here also mortgaging out is irrelevant.

D. Fourth Principle

Voluntary sale of the equity for something of value is deemed a sale for the mortgage plus the amount of the equity. [Cf. section 7701(g).] * * *

* * *

Related Problems

Where a taxpayer as an individual has mortgaged out and is in possession of funds upon which an income tax has not been paid, he cannot merely allow the property to be foreclosed if, as will normally be the case in such a situation, the foreclosure price will be in excess of the basis and will, under the Third Principle mentioned above, result in a closed transaction which may reflect income. We have also seen under the Fourth Principle that he cannot make a voluntary conveyance and part with the property prior to foreclosure in that manner because this also will reflect income. He might consider placing the property in a corporation of which he would own all of the stock.

If this could be done successfully, he would have no income as a result of the transfer to the corporation and the corporation could conceivably be formed with no other assets so that even though it was in receipt of taxable gain as a result of the subsequent foreclosure, it would have no assets with which to respond to the income tax imposed on that gain.

[T]he building contractor may have used the corporation which does the mortgaging out, and in this event he would like to have the corporation make a distribution of the excess cash resulting from mortgaging out prior to the foreclosure so that when the foreclosure took place, the corporation would be an empty shell and unable to pay the income tax levied on the constructive gain.

[T]he builder would not expect to receive the proceeds entirely tax free, but according to the Internal Revenue Code [and assuming that the corporation has no earnings and profits,] he would presumably apply the proceeds first against the basis for the stock of the corporation in his hands and the remainder would be [treated as] capital gains * * *. This would be a much lighter burden than accepting the proceeds of the mortgaging out [entirely] as ordinary income * * *.

[I]t [is] very difficult for the taxpayer who has mortgaged out, either with or without utilizing a corporation, to capture * * * the fruits of his achievement and not be deprived of them by subsequent events. We turn now to the special provisions of the Internal Revenue Code [governing these transactions].

Section 357(c)

Although under section 357(a) of the Internal Revenue Code a taxpayer is permitted to receive stock of a corporation under section 351 in an exchange for stock or securities and even have liabilities assumed [tax-free] if the purpose is not a prohibited one, this is specifically rendered inapplicable by section 357(c) in those cases where the sum of the liabilities assumed plus the liabilities to which property is subject, exceeds the total of the adjusted basis of the property transferred pursuant to the exchange. In such event the excess is considered a gain from sale or exchange of a capital asset or of property which is not a capital asset, as the case may be. But[,] where the property transferred is subject to the allowance for depreciation, then by section 1239 (applicable to sale from an individual to a controlled corporation) the gain from such a transfer is deemed to be a gain from sale or exchange of property which is neither a capital asset nor property described in section 1231. Section 1231 property is property used in a trade or business and held for more than [the required holding period for capital gain treatment]. The net result is to deprive the gain of capital asset treatment where the property transferred is subject to depreciation. [In addition, if section 357(c) applies, part or all of the depreciation recapture present in the transferred property will be recognized.]

[As a result] of section 357(c) a taxpayer is not able to convey to a corporation in a tax free exchange the property which has been mortgaged [assuming the total amount of mortgage liability exceeds the taxpayer's basis in the property]. If the taxpayer had been able to do so, * * * the corporation might have been substituted as the obligor (assuming that the taxpayer was not personally liable on the mortgage), so that when the foreclosure sale took place, the profit thereby reflected would be income to a corporation which might have no other assets and, therefore, not be in any position to pay the income tax thereby incurred. The net result of section 357(c) is that the transfer itself brings down the house of cards and the taxpayer [in] making the transfer to the corporation incurs a gain * * * by that very transfer.

Section 312(i)

Whe[n] a corporation mortgages out and the loan is guaranteed by the United States [or any agency or instrumentality thereof], a distribution by the corporation [of the excess proceeds of the loan] is ordinary income [to the stockholders]. Section 312(i) [produces this result]. [Section 312(i)] applies regardless of the percentage of the loan guaranteed and it applies to guarantees of FHA loans. It also applies to guarantees of any other federal agency. It should be noted, however, that by section 312(i), the basis [of the mortgaged property] for this purpose only is [determined without] regard [to any adjustment produced] by depreciation. This remedy may not go far enough. For example, it does not apply to loans not insured by the United States Government, but by others, although the public policy involved would seem to be the same. * * * It has been suggested[, however,] that under section 341, the distribution of proceeds of mortgaging out would be held to be made by a collapsible corporation.

[S]ection 312(i) is directed to a different kind of tax reduction device. Here the corporation does the mortgaging out and the problem is to have a distribution by the corporation to the stockholders which will not be subject to taxation as an ordinary dividend. * * *

[Since] a distribution can be taxed as a dividend to the stockholders only if the corporation possesses earnings and profits, section 312(i) creates earnings and profits even though the corporation has not realized any gain. Immediately prior to the distribution, earnings and profits are considered to be increased by the amount of the excess mortgage funds, and immediately after the distribution, earnings and profits so credited are reduced by the amount of the [excess mortgage funds].

[T]his section places a substantial obstacle in the way of the builder since he must either allow the windfall profits arising out of mortgaging out to remain in the corporation, or must accept them as an ordinary dividend, neither of which is very palatable.

Even without section 312(i), it might * * * be * * * that the provisions of the Internal Revenue Code with respect to collapsible corporations would tax the amount of the excess of the distribution over the stockholders' basis as if it were a dividend.

Section 311[(b)(2)]

The corporation which has succeeded in obtaining a windfall by mortgaging out might contemplate distributing all of the property to the stockholders. [I]f it does so, under section 311[(b)(2)], a gain will be recognized [by] the distributing corporation in an amount equal to the excess which the liability on the property exceeds the adjusted basis of such property. * * * This is, of course, a different question from recognizing gain or loss to the stockholders [which will depend on whether the corporation has any earnings and profits and on the stockholders' bases in their stock].

Conclusion

From the foregoing it * * * appear[s] that: (1) Mortgaging out without more does not result in taxable income. (2) However, if one mortgages out property and then places it in a corporation, he is not permitted to do this tax free even though he obtains eighty percent or more of the stock. (3) A voluntary sale of property for a price in excess of cost or basis will result in income and in this connection the selling price of mortgaged property where the mortgage remains on the property is the sum of the mortgage plus the amount paid for the equity. (4) The same thing happens at a foreclosure sale, that is, the selling price or amount bid for the property is compared with the basis and if it is higher than the basis, it may result in taxable income to the owner, who at that time is *losing his property.*

NOTE

1. "Negative equity" may be present on the purchase of improved real estate—the amount of the purchase money mortgage may exceed the fair market value of the real estate. Since the amount of the purchase money mortgage is included in the purchaser's cost basis for the purpose of depreciation, see Greenbaum, *The Basis of Property Shall be the Cost of Such Property: How is Cost Defined?,* supra pages 368 to 373, the purchaser may be willing to pay more than fair market value to obtain the depreciation deductions especially if the purchaser is not personally obligated to pay the mortgage. The purchase money mortgage usually will be a long term mortgage with small equal installments, and/or possibly have a large balloon payment at the end of the term of the mortgage.

a. It is unlikely that the purchaser can be taxed on the difference between the amount of the mortgage and the fair market value of the property since the purchaser has not "realized" anything. Is a more appropriate result to reduce the purchaser's basis to the fair market value of the property or not even take account of the purchase money mortgage in determining basis until the purchaser paid the mortgage? Cf. *Manuel D. Mayerson,* 47 T.C. 340 (1966), acq., 1969–1 C.B. 21; *David F. Bolger,* 59 T.C. 760 (1973), acq., 1976–1 C.B. 1 and Rev.Rul. 69–77, 1969–1 C.B. 59. But see *Edna Morris,* 59 T.C. 21 (1972), acq., 1973–2 C.B. 3. In this case the shareholders of a corporation acquired notes which were secured by first and second mortgages on certain real estate. The corporation, for a minimal amount of cash, then acquired the real estate subject to the mortgages securing the notes. The corporation claimed a basis in the real estate equal to the cash paid plus the principal amounts remaining unpaid on the notes secured by the mortgages. The Tax Court found that the fair market value of the real estate was equal to the unpaid principal amount of the notes secured by the first mortgage. It limited the corporation's basis in the real estate to this amount plus the cash paid, stating:

> "Where worthless debt is acquired without consideration, as a part of an overall plan to transfer the property to a corporation to be owned and controlled by the holder of the debt, such debt becomes solely a device to inflate the true cost of the property for tax purposes. Neither the *Crane* case, [331 U.S. 1, 67 S.Ct. 1047, 91 L.Ed. 1301 (1947),] nor any decision which followed, warrants the inclusion of such worthless paper as a part of the taxpayers' cost or basis for depreciation. See *Burr Oaks Corp. v. Commissioner,* 365 F.2d 24 (7th Cir.1966)."

Edna Morris, supra at 34.

Anytime a mortgage debt exceeds the value of the real estate subject to the mortgage, if the maker is not personally liable for payment of the debt, it can be said that, at the time of the execution of the note and mortgage, the amount of the note in excess of the value of the real estate is worthless. Yet, through the operation of the real estate subject to the mortgage, the note may be paid in future years. Was the court in the *Edna Morris* case, supra, influenced by the fact that the shareholders of the corporation which acquired the real estate were also the holders of the notes? If the value of the real estate was less than the amount of the principal remaining unpaid on the notes secured by the first mortgage, would the court have reduced the corporation's basis by the difference? Should it?

b. Can the analysis described above be carried one step further and applied in the case in which a developer creates a "negative equity" by placing a mortgage on the developer's real estate in an amount greater than the fair market value of the real estate? If the developer is not personally liable for the mortgage debt, can the developer be said to have recognized gain equal to the difference between the amount of the mortgage and the fair market value of the property? Cf. *Leonard Marcus,* 30 CCH Tax Ct.Mem. 1263 (1971), affirmed 493 F.2d 1401 (3d Cir.1974) (Court Order). If the mortgage incurred on the purchase of real estate is in excess of the value of the real estate and the purchaser is not liable for the mortgage debt, it might be argued that, in substance, no purchase had occurred. See *Estate of Franklin v. Comm'r,* 544 F.2d 1045 (9th Cir.1976); Rev.Rul. 77–110, 1977–1 C.B. 58. Cf. Rev.Rul. 77–125, 1977–1 C.B. 130. Generally, however, when the value of acquired real estate is substantially less than the mortgage debt incurred on its purchase, or the taxpayer is not able to prove that the value is at least equal to the mortgage, or it appears that the value plus the income stream generated by the property will not be sufficient to pay the debt plus interest when due, the Internal Revenue Service has argued, and some courts have agreed, especially when the purchaser is not personally liable for the mortgage debt, that the mortgage debt cannot be included in the basis of the acquired real estate. See e.g. *John C. Beck,* 74 T.C. 1534 (1980), affirmed, 678 F.2d 818 (9th Cir.1982); *David L. Narver, Jr.,* 75 T.C. 53 (1980), affirmed, 670 F.2d 855 (9th Cir. 1982); *Carol W. Hilton,* 74 T.C. 305 (1980), affirmed, 671 F.2d 316 (9th Cir. 1982); *E.A. Brannen,* 78 T.C. 471 (1982), affirmed, 722 F.2d 695 (11th Cir.

1984); *Fortune Odend'hal,* 80 T.C. 588 (1983), affirmed, 748 F.2d 908 (4th Cir.1984); *John M. Elliott,* 84 T.C. 227 (1985), affirmed, 782 F.2d 1027 (3d Cir.1986). See generally Guns, *Re–Examining the Sham Doctrine: When Should An Overpayment Be Reflected in Basis?,* 30 Buffalo L.Rev. 95 (1981); Avent and Grimes, *Inflated Purchase Money Indebtedness in Real Estate and Other Investments,* 11 J.Real Est.Tax'n 99 (1984). In addition, the mortgage debt may be nonrecourse and its repayment so contingent that characterization as a liability of the borrower in order to be included in the basis of the borrower may be denied by the Internal Revenue Service and the courts. See *Werner Graf,* 80 T.C. 944 (1983); *Ernest J. Saviano,* 80 T.C. 955 (1983), affirmed, 765 F.2d 643 (7th Cir.1985); *Stuart I. Fox,* 80 T.C. 972 (1983), affirmed sub nom., 731 F.2d 230 (4th Cir.1984). Cf. *Brountas v. Comm'r,* 692 F.2d 152 (1st Cir.1982). Finally, while a contingent debt, in certain circumstances, may be treated as a liability for income tax purposes, the Internal Revenue Service may take the position, if the debt was incurred to acquire property, that the purchaser-debtor can only reflect the debt in the basis of the acquired property as the debt is paid. See Priv.Ltr. Rul. 8646005. Cf. Section 453(g)(1)(c).

c. If the amount of the mortgage liability incurred for development of a parcel of real estate exceeds the cost of development, does the developer's basis include the amount of the mortgage liability or only the actual cost of development?

d. When property subject to a liability is acquired by a partnership, the liability, in addition to increasing the basis of the property to the partnership, may have the effect of increasing the bases of the partners in their partnership interests. See Section 752(a) and pages 74 to 87 supra and pages 709 to 713 infra. The increase in the bases of the partners in their partnership interests, however may be limited to the fair market value of the property, if the liability exceeds the fair market value. See Section 752(c). Section 752(c) provides that a liability to which property is subject is a liability of the owner of the property to the extent of the fair market value thereof. Therefore, under Section 752(a) it might be said that the liability of the partnership (the owner of the property) is limited to the fair market value of the property. But see *Comm'r v. Tufts,* 461 U.S. 300, 103 S.Ct. 1826, 75 L.Ed.2d 863 (1983), in which the Supreme Court held that Section 752(c) did not apply to limit the amount of gain on the sale of a partnership interest. For the purpose of computing the amount of gain recognized by a partner on the sale of his partnership interest, the full amount of a nonrecourse liability was included despite the fact that it exceeded the fair market value of the property subject to the liability. In the opinion of the Supreme Court, Section 752(c) does not limit the "amount realized" to the fair market value of the property since Section 752(c) only applies to transactions between the partners and the partnership. See Miller, *The Supreme Court Does It Again in Tufts—Right Answer, Wrong Reason,* 11 J.Real Est.Tax'n 3 (1983); Sanders, *Sup.Ct. Ending Crane Controversy, Says Nonrecourse Debt Is Always Part of Sales Price,* 59 J.Tax'n 2 (1983); Bertha, *Tufts and Tax Shelters,* 62 Taxes 28 (1984); Blackburn, *Important Common Law Developments for Nonrecourse Notes: Tufting It Out,* 18 Ga.L.Rev. 1 (1983); Comment, *Nonrecourse Liabilities as Tax Shelter Devices After Tufts: Elimination of Fair Market Value and Contingent Liability Defenses,* 35 U.Fla.L.Rev. 904 (1983); Zimmerman, *Crane and Tufts: Resolved and Unresolved Issues,* 12 Pepperdine

L.Rev. 631 (1985). Section 7701(g) appears to confirm the result in *Tufts,* supra, by providing that, in determining gain or loss with respect to property, the fair market value of the property shall be treated as being not less than the amount of any nonrecourse indebtedness to which the property is subject. Can the rule for determining basis be different than the rule for determining gain? Cf. Section 1274(b)(3).

e. Section 465 sets further limits on the effect of mortgage liabilities. For example, under Section 465, a partner, for the purpose of determining the amount of the partner's share of the losses of a partnership which the partner can personally use, cannot include in the partner's at-risk amount any portion of any partnership liability with respect to which the partner has no personal liability unless, under Section 465(b)(6)(A), the partner is considered at-risk with respect to "qualified nonrecourse financing" secured by the real property used in this activity of the partnership. Qualified nonrecourse financing is defined in Section 465(b)(6)(B) and, in general, means financing (other than in the form of convertible debt) provided by (or guaranteed by) a federal, state, or local government, or provided by a person actively and regularly engaged in the business of lending money provided that person is not (a) the person who sold the real property to the partnership (or a person related to the seller), or (b) a person who received a fee with respect to the investment in the real property (or a person related to such person). The lender can have an interest in the partnership (be a person related to the borrower) if the terms of the loan are commercially reasonable and on substantially the same terms as loans involving unrelated persons. See generally Division I, pages 150 to 153 supra.

f. See generally Lurie, *Bolger's Building: The Tax Shelter that Wore No Clothes,* 28 Tax L.Rev. 355 (1973); Wangard, *Use of Nonrecourse Loans in Tax Planning: The Possibilities and the Pitfalls,* 39 J.Tax'n 286 (1973); Caruthers, *True Debt: Leveraging in Real Estate Limited Partnership Tax Shelters,* 4 J.Real Est.Tax'n 5 (1976); Weidner, *Realty Shelters: Nonrecourse Financing, Tax Reform, and Profit Purpose,* 32 Sw.L.J. 711 (1978); Bittker, *Tax Shelters, Nonrecourse Debt, and the Crane Case,* 33 Tax Law Rev. 277 (1978); Halpern, *Liabilities and Cost Basis: Some Fundamental Considerations,* 7 J.Real Est.Tax'n 334 (1980); Goggans, *Leverage—A Strategy for Real Estate Investments,* 58 Taxes 89 (1980); Comment, *Federal Income Tax Treatment of Nonrecourse Debt,* 82 Colum.L.Rev. 1498 (1982).

2. Assume that a developer's adjusted basis in improved real estate is $90,000. The fair market value of the improved real estate is $140,000 and the developer secures a 90% mortgage. Three years later, because of a change in the surrounding area, the fair market value of the improved real estate drops to $100,000. The principal amount of the mortgage at this point in time is $115,000. The lender forecloses and sells the improved real estate for fair market value. The developer is liable for any deficiency. What financial and tax results occur?

a. The above hypothetical illustrates a couple of the dangers of overfinancing. Do the results change if the developer is not personally liable for the mortgage debt?

b. The greater the percentage of the fair market value of real estate represented by a mortgage debt, the greater the impetus for an "in rem," nonrecourse or no personal liability mortgage.

3. Assume a developer personally owns some improved real estate having an adjusted basis of $50,000 and a fair market value of $120,000. The developer decides to put the real estate into a wholly-owned corporation in return for common stock in the corporation. Prior to exchanging the real estate for the stock of the corporation, the developer borrows $100,000 securing the debt by a mortgage on the real estate. The developer then conveys the real estate to the corporation which assumes the mortgage. The developer retains the proceeds of the loan. Is the developer taxed on $50,000, see Section 357(c), or $70,000, see Section 357(b)?

4. See generally Sherman and Lewis, *Transfers of Negative Basis Property,* 115 Tr. & Est. 159 (1976); Fuller, *Transferring Liabilities: Tax Effects,* 12 Ga.L. Rev. 33 (1977); Popkin, *The Taxation of Borrowing,* 56 Ind.L.J. 43 (1980).

5. Upon the disposition of improved real estate the recapture of depreciation may be required. Is the granting of a mortgage on real estate a disposition of the real estate? See Reg.Secs. 1.1250–1(a)(2) and 1.1245–1(a)(3).

     a. Assume a partnership owns improved real estate having a cost of $100,000, an adjusted basis of $30,000, and a fair market value of $80,000. What will be the tax effects on the partners if the real estate is mortgaged for $64,000 and the proceeds of the mortgage are distributed to the partners?

         1. See Section 731(a) and pages 709 to 713 infra. Will the tax effects change if the mortgage is nonrecourse or the distribution is made to limited partners? See pages 28 to 29 and 70 to 71 supra. The limitation on the inclusion of a partner's share of a nonrecourse liability in the at-risk amount of the partner, as provided by Section 465, only applies in determining the partner's personal use of the partner's share of losses of the partnership. It does not apply in determining the gain, if any, resulting from a distribution by the partnership to a partner. Section 465, however, does provide for the recapture of losses previously taken if the at-risk amount of a partner drops below zero as a result of a distribution. See Section 465(e). As mentioned above, Section 465 does not apply if the nonrecourse liability is qualified nonrecourse financing. See Section 465(b)(6)(A).

     b. Assume the same facts as above with the exception that the entity mortgaging the real estate and making the distribution is a corporation which has no current or accumulated earnings and profits. It is possible for a corporation to declare and pay a dividend even though the corporation has no current or accumulated earned surplus. See Division IV pages 1100 to 1108 and Comment, *Appreciated Property as a Source of Dividends: Its Use and Effects in Mississippi,* 48 Miss.L.J. 309 (1977). What is the income tax effect of the distribution on the shareholders of the corporation?

         1. Consider the implications of Section 312(i). What are the implications of Section 312(k) if the corporation had been using an accelerated method of depreciation?

         2. Assuming that Section 312(i) does not apply and the corporation has no earnings and profits even considering Section 312(k), the excess of the distribution over the shareholders' bases in their stock normally would be treated as capital gains. But, what about the possible application of Section 341 (the collapsible corporations provision)?

BENEDEK v. COMMISSIONER

United States Court of Appeals, Second Circuit, 1970.
429 F.2d 41, cert. denied, 400 U.S. 992, 91 S.Ct. 455, 27 L.Ed.2d 439 (1971).

HAYES, Circuit Judge.   *   *   *

Appellants, together with one other person not involved in the present litigation, owned all the stock of Newstrand Realty Corporation. In 1947 Newstrand bought an unimproved tract of land in Brooklyn at a price of $1,764,238.66.

     *   *   *

In 1949 the stockholders of Newstrand organized five corporations, called Farragut Gardens Nos. 1 to 5, for the purpose of leasing the land owned by Newstrand and constructing housing projects on this land. The Farragut corporations were to finance the projects through mortgages insured by the Federal Housing Administration.

The leases from Newstrand to the Farragut corporations, executed in 1949, were in the form prescribed by the FHA and were for a term of 99 years, renewable at the option of the lessees for an additional 99 years. The leases provided that should the mortgagee or the FHA acquire title to the leaseholds by reason of a default by the mortgagors, the mortgagee or the FHA could acquire the lessor's fee upon payment of a recapture price totaling $1,924,000.

Mortgages were negotiated in the total amount of $21,719,300 and were insured by the FHA. Under FHA policy the amount of the insured mortgages was equal to 90 percent of estimated replacement cost of the property. Thus the value of the leaseholds was not considered in computing the amount of the mortgages.

The Farragut corporations constructed 59 apartment buildings on the leased property at a total cost of $18,118,987.

In 1949, 1950 and 1951 the Farragut corporations distributed a total of $3,158,000 to the stockholders. At the time the distributions were made the Farragut corporations had no accumulated earnings. Indeed the corporations sustained operating losses at least through 1954. They were engaged in no activity other than the construction and operation of the apartment buildings.

The leaseholds for which the Farragut corporations had paid Newstrand "little or nothing" (apparently nothing) were found by the Tax Court to have a fair market value of $1,517,333 at the time of the distributions to stockholders. No part of this market value was attributable to the construction of the apartment buildings on the leaseholds. The leaseholds, the Tax Court found, would have had the designated market value if the land had remained unimproved.

The taxpayers reported the amounts received from the cash distributions of the Farragut corporations as capital gains. The Commissioner ruled that the distributions [should be treated] as ordinary income. The Commissioner was upheld by the Tax Court *   *   *.

The taxpayers concede that the Farragut corporations were "collapsible corporations" as defined by Section [341], which provides that distributions by collapsible corporations shall be treated as ordinary income. Taxpayers contend, however, that the distributions they received come within the limitation provision of Section [341(d)(2)] which provides that the general rule of Section [341(a)] "shall not apply to the gain recognized during a taxable year unless more than 70 percent of such gain is attributable to the [collapsible property, in this case, the apartment buildings]." The taxpayers claim that of the total cash distribution of $3,158,000, almost 50% ($1,517,333) is "attributable" to [the] increase in the value of the leaseholds and not to the collapsible property.

There appears to us to be no special mystery about the word "attributable" as it is used in the statute. The question to be answered is "where did the money come from?" The answer will ordinarily be the source to which the gain is "attributable." Here it is perfectly clear that the money came from the FHA insured loans.[3] The distributions were made from the excess of the loans over the cost of building the apartments. The corporations had no other source of cash, since their operation of the apartment projects had resulted in a loss and they were engaged in no other business. Considered conversely the corporations' cash distributions could not have represented the value of the leaseholds because the profit on the leaseholds was not realized before or during the period of the distributions. Accepting, as we do, the findings of the Tax Court, the corporations had a valuable asset in the leaseholds and at some future time they might have realized on that asset, presumably by selling the buildings together with the leaseholds. If they did so[,] they might have additional cash to distribute to the stockholders and the tax treatment of such a distribution would constitute a quite different question from that now before us.

As the court said in Payne v. C.I.R., 268 F.2d 617, 621 (5th Cir. 1959):

> "The funds which provided [the distributions] were [derived from] a loan secured by the improved property. The only basis for the making of F.H.A. loans was the construction of rental property. Without the buildings there would have been no loan. Without the loan there would have been no redemption of the stock. We think the gain was 'attributable' to the property constructed. The same conclusion was reached in Glickman v. C.I.R., 2 Cir., 256 F.2d 108 where it was said on page 111:

> 'The petitioners further contend that the gains recognized on the cash distribution and the sale of stock are not within § [341(a)] because at least 30% of those gains was attributable to appreciation of the land "apart from building construction." This is far too narrow an interpretation of the statute to be accepted. As to the

---

3. Income arising from government insured loans is given special treatment un- der § 312(i) of the Internal Revenue Code * * *.

cash distribution the Tax Court correctly held that all of it was directly attributable to the constructed property, since it was paid out of the funds advanced * * * on the F.H.A. mortgage.' "

See also Mintz v. C.I.R., 284 F.2d 554, 559–60 (2d Cir.1960); Short v. C.I.R., 302 F.2d 120, 124–25 (4th Cir.1962).

Appellants seek to rely for support for their position on Treas.Reg. [1.341–4(c)(2)] which provides in pertinent part:

> "For the purpose of this limitation, the gain attributable to the property referred to in section [341(b)(1)] is the excess of the recognized gain of the shareholder during the taxable year upon his stock in the collapsible corporation over the recognized gain which the shareholder would have if the property had not been * * * constructed."

The answer to the contention based on this sentence from the Regulations is that, since without the construction there would have been no mortgage money to distribute, there was *no* "recognized gain which the shareholder would have if the property had not been * * * constructed."

The decision of the Tax Court is affirmed.

NOTE

1. The effective date of Section 312(i) was June 22, 1954. The section only applies to distributions made after that date.

    a. If Section 312(i) had been in effect in 1949, 1950, and 1951 when the distributions in the *Benedek* case were made, could the Commissioner have used the section to achieve the same result which was reached in *Benedek* using Section 341?

        1. Does Section 312(i) apply to a distribution which qualifies as a redemption, under Section 302(b)? Will it change the nature of the gain from capital gain to ordinary income?

            a. Does Section 341 apply to a redemption which qualifies as an exchange, under Section 302(b)?

        2. The corporations making the distributions in *Benedek* sustained operating losses each year from 1949 through 1954. If Section 312(i) was applicable and had the effect of increasing the earnings and profits of the corporations by the excess of the proceeds of the loans over the adjusted basis of the real estate improvements, might the deficit in earnings and profits caused by the losses of the corporations have been greater than the increase in earnings and profits pursuant to Section 312(i)? Might this have been the case even if earnings and profits were computed on a yearly basis? If so, the treatment of the distributions to the shareholders would still have been governed by Section 301(c)(3)(A). The distribution would have been treated as a return of capital to the extent of the shareholders' bases in their stock of the corporation and then the excess would have been treated as capital gains, unless Section 341 applied to the excess.

    3. See *Edward Zorn*, 35 CCH Tax Ct.Mem. 1048 (1976).

2. Did the court in *Benedek* stop one step short in its analysis?

a. The court attributed all of the gain to the construction of the buildings, "since without the construction there would have been no mortgage money to distribute." Without the leaseholds, however, there would have been no property on which to construct the buildings.

1. If the appreciation in the value of the leaseholds resulted from the construction, this appreciation would have been included in the gain attributable to the collapsible property for the purpose of applying the 70% test. See Reg.Sec. 1.341–4(c)(3).

2. See Division II pages 496 to 511 supra for a general discussion of the collapsible corporations provision.

2. FINANCING THE INITIAL LAND ACQUISITION

a. THE PURCHASE MONEY MORTGAGE

One of the most common ways of financing the initial land acquisition is using a purchase money mortgage. When attempting to use a purchase money mortgage there are many questions which must be considered by the vendor and vendee. For example, what is a purchase money mortgage, what is its priority, and how does it relate to other security interests taken or to be taken in the real estate.

NOTE:

PRIORITY OF PURCHASE–MONEY MORTGAGES
29 Virginia Law Review 491 (1943).
[footnotes omitted]

* * *

What Is a Purchase–Money Mortgage?

A purchase-money mortgage is just what its name implies, a mortgage given by a vendee to secure a purchase price or an unpaid balance: its distinction lies in the fact that the sale and the mortgage are both part of one continuous transaction. A few lines quoted from a leading case will point out the essential theory behind a purchase-money mortgage:

> "A purchase-money mortgage * * * is predicated on the theory that upon the simultaneous execution of the deed and mortgage the title to the land does not for a single moment rest in the purchaser, but merely passes through his hands and, without stopping, rests in the mortgagee. It follows, therefore, that no lien of any character can attach to the title of the mortgagee."

It becomes clear, then, why a purchase-money mortgage should take precedence over any prior lien against the property arising through or against the purchaser. Where there is one continuous transaction, prior liens do not have time to attach until after the purchase-money mortgage has been executed, and the incumbrance may be considered, as being on the land when the vendee acquires it. Consequently, as to the land in question, the mortgage is prior to any lien arising through the purchaser.

As for the concept of one continuous transaction, the courts seem to have resolved difficulties on this point by applying a subjective, rather than an objective, test. In other words, if the parties intend that the deed and the mortgage be part of the same transaction, the courts will consider them as simultaneous even though some time elapses between their execution. * * *

The subjective intent of the two parties being the determining factor, the fact that the two instruments were executed on the same day, though of strong evidential value, is not conclusive proof of contemporaneous transactions without some showing of intent. On the other hand, if the time elapsed is of unreasonable length, the presumption of simultaneousness will be seriously weakened, if not lost. Accordingly, in order to protect the vendor the purchase-money mortgage should be denominated as such and executed concurrently with the sale. This will make clear the intent of the parties and will leave no doubt as to the continuity of the transaction.

In granting priority to purchase money mortgages the courts have in some cases considered the vendee as taking the land with the incumbrance already on it, while in other cases have held that the transaction involves an instantaneous seisin. Resort to such fictions undoubtedly attains proper results, but care must be taken not to carry the fictions too far. Consider this situation: A property owner has given first and second mortgages. The first mortgage becomes due and is unpaid, and at the subsequent foreclosure sale the owner of the property buys it in, giving a purchase-money mortgage to a third person. Now the issue arises as to the priority of the second mortgage or the new purchase-money mortgage. * * * [Priority can be given to] the purchase-money mortgagee, [reasoning] that the junior lienor [is] no worse off than before and that there [is] no equitable ground for promoting him to first place.

It is interesting to note at this point that it is not necessary that the vendor of the land be the purchase-money mortgagee. If a vendee of land borrows the purchase money from a third person and gives him a mortgage for it, it will be accorded the same priority as a mortgage between the vendor and the vendee, provided, of course, that it meets the other requirements. And, as a necessary part of a tri-partite transaction, the money must always be loaned for the express purpose of buying the land. But where a debt for the purchase of land has already been incurred and the vendee later borrows money from a third party to pay off the [debt] and gives a mortgage therefor, the mortgage will not be accorded the priority of a purchase-money mortgage.

Purchase–Money Mortgage v. Other Liens

Most of the instances in which the courts are called upon to consider purchase-money mortgages arise from controversies as to whether a certain mortgage is really a purchase-money mortgage. But there are occasions where a purchase-money mortgage will come into conflict with various other liens. * * *

Judgments against Purchaser

It seems to be uniformly held that the lien of a purchase-money mortgage is superior to that of a judgment against the mortgagor, even though the judgment against such mortgagor is rendered before the purchase of the property. The fiction most often used is, again that of instantaneous seisin, it being said that the purchaser is not seized of the land long enough for the judgment lien to attach. It is unnecessary here to criticize this reasoning, since the result is obviously sound. Suffice it to say that, if, for instance, a day were to elapse between the deed and the mortgage, it would be difficult logically to understand how a thing so adhesive as a judgment could fail to become firmly attached.

* * *

Other Mortgages Executed by Purchaser

An interesting situation, and one in which the dividing line is much more tenuous, arises when a vendee of land borrows part of the purchase money from a third person, giving him a mortgage on the land for the loan, and also gives a purchase-money mortgage to the vendor for the unpaid balance of the purchase money. Technically, if it is so intended, both could be regarded as purchase-money mortgages. But when the two come into conflict, one must prevail, or they must share equally. The courts, as a rule, have seen fit to give precedence to the vendor of the land. This, of course, is unquestionably sound where the vendor has no knowledge of the other mortgage, and it seems the better view even where the vendor has constructive notice by recordation * * *. A similar conflict may arise where a prospective buyer approaches a third party, tells him of his intended purchase and asks him to lend part of the purchase price. The third party agrees and takes a purchase-money mortgage and records it—this even before the vendor has made any conveyance to the buyer. Then the buyer takes the money to the unsuspecting vendor and executes a purchase-money mortgage to him. Certainly a vendor of land should not be compelled to search the record to discover an encumbrance which was placed on property while it was still his own. Moreover, the third party made his loan relying only on the intention of the purchaser to buy the land. If instead he had taken the money and absconded[,] the third person would have had no security at all, for the legal title to the land in question would still be in the hands of the vendor. But on the other hand, the vendor had the land to start with, and he took a mortgage on it as part of a continuous transaction. He, certainly, is entitled to priority. However, if the vendor has actual notice of the prior mortgage and of its recordation and says nothing about it, it would appear that he is acquiescing in favor of such mortgage and is agreeing to take second place. But where he has contracted to make the sale before learning of the other mortgage, no suit for specific performance will lie against him if he refuses to execute a deed unless he is given first place. And, finally, any bona fide agreement between the vendor, the vendee and the third party should be given effect; if the vendor wishes to give up his rights in favor of a third party, he is entitled to do so.

Another situation which should be considered here is where a purchase-money mortgage comes into conflict with an after-acquired property clause in a prior general mortgage. Although in one state the after-acquired property clause is allowed to prevail, the great majority of the courts follow the general trend in regard to purchase-money mortgages and hold that they constitute a prior lien.

Mechanics' Liens

The general rule is that a mechanics' lien for labor or materials furnished to a vendee of land is subordinate to a purchase-money mortgage later executed by him on acquiring title. * * *

In view of what has already been said about purchase-money mortgages the above is far from surprising. A purchaser does not have title to land until a sale is completed, and, when he does take title in a transaction which involves a purchase-money mortgage, his ownership is subordinate to the rights of the grantor-mortgagee. Therefore, a mechanics' lien, which attaches through him, could never rise above the rights secured by the purchase-money mortgage.

It may happen that the vendor and vendee, in making a contract to sell land, will include therein a clause providing for work to be done before the actual conveyance. The courts seem to be at variance as to the effect of such a clause, but these differences may, in part at least, be due to differences in statutory provisions. A large group of courts hold that a purchase-money mortgage will prevail over a mechanics' lien even where the contract of sale provides for the vendee to have work done on the premises. The reasoning seems to be based on strict compliance with the long-established notion that a lien can attach only to what equity or interest a purchaser has. But other courts, in the same situation, allow the mechanics' lien to prevail. They seem to feel that, when a vendor makes provision in the executory contract of sale for work to be done on the premises, he is subjecting his interest to any liens which may arise therefrom. But such would not be the case if, between the parties, the provision was no more than a permission to enter and to begin to make improvements in preparation for taking possession under the forthcoming deed. Most "work provisions" seem to partake of this latter, permissive tenor, and in fairness to all, the best rule would be to give the mortgage priority as to the land and the mechanics' lien priority as to the work done if its worth can be estimated separately. If it cannot be given a separate value, the mortgage should prevail. It would seem that the rule should be the same where the work is authorized by the vendor or done with his knowledge or consent, but many courts, by statute or by prior decision, are forced to hold otherwise in such cases. Perhaps the fairest kind of statute is that which allows a vendor to retain his priority if he files a notice of dissent within a specified time after learning of the work in progress, for if he fails to file such notice, it is clear that he intends his rights to be subordinate to the mechanics' lien.

NOTE

1. Conceptually, "instantaneous seisin," title passing through the hands of the purchaser and coming to rest in the hands of the mortgagee, appears to work well to rationalize the priority of a purchase money mortgage in a title theory state. But what rationalization can be used in a lien theory state?

   a. Might the rationalization in a lien theory state be that the purchaser takes the real estate with the mortgage already on it?

   b. In a conflict over priority between the holder of a purchase money mortgage and another lien holder might this difference in rationale lead to a difference in result? If so, in what type of situation?

2. Frequently, a purchase money mortgage is given to a lender which provides funds to the purchaser to enable the purchaser to buy the real estate.

   a. As pointed out in the foregoing excerpt, in the "pure" case the lender will be accorded the priority of a purchase money mortgage.

      1. Will the lender be accorded the priority of a purchase money mortgage if the purchaser acquires the real estate with funds other than those made available to the purchaser by the lender?

         a. What steps can be taken from the standpoint of the lender to prevent this question arising?

   b. In a large transaction both the vendor and a lender may take a mortgage for part of the purchase price of the real estate. If nothing is said about priority and the deed and mortgages are executed at the same time, in the same room, with the vendor and lender both having knowledge of the other's mortgage, who has priority, the vendor or the lender? Cf. *Pulse v. North American Land Title Co. of Montana*, 218 Mont. 275, 707 P.2d 1105 (1985).

      1. Does the result depend on who records first?

      2. Can this problem be avoided? How?

   c. When a lender, providing part of the purchase price of real estate, desires the priority of a purchase money mortgage, is the simultaneous execution of the deed and mortgage or the simultaneous recording of the deed and mortgage the important operative fact?

      1. For example, if the deed and mortgage are executed at the same time, the deed recorded, a judgment lien against the purchaser properly filed and then the mortgage is recorded, who has priority, the judgment lienholder or the lender?

a. Is the lender in a better or worse position if the deed is executed, a judgment lien against the purchaser properly filed, then the mortgage is executed and both the deed and mortgage recorded?

3. A contract of sale permits the purchaser, prior to closing, to enter the premises and make improvements. A third party lender provides the purchaser with part of the funds necessary to purchase the real estate and desires the priority of a purchase money mortgage.

a. If a mechanics' lien arising from the improvements is filed against the property, prior to the execution and recording of the deed and mortgage, does it have priority over the mortgage given to the lender?

1. Is the position of the lender better or worse if the improvements were not only permitted to be done by the contract of sale but the contract contemplated and specifically authorized the improvements to be done prior to closing?

a. Might it be difficult to determine whether a contract of sale merely permits improvements prior to closing or specifically authorizes them? Can the same words have different meanings?

b. In the above situation does the lender's actual knowledge of the making of the improvements, and/or whether the state had adopted the equitable conversion theory, make any difference in determining who has priority?

c. What steps can the lender take to avoid the above problem?

1. Is it possible for a lender to obtain title insurance which insures that a mortgage it receives has the priority of a purchase money mortgage?

a. Even if it is possible to obtain such insurance, does the standard title insurance policy cover mechanics' liens? See pages 305 to 307 supra.

4. Since a nonrecourse purchase money mortgage given to the seller of real estate cannot be treated as qualified nonrecourse financing, under Section 465, such a nonrecourse mortgage, generally, will not provide the purchaser with any at-risk amount for the purpose of using the losses produced by the activity in which the acquired real estate is used.

5. See generally Bell, *Negotiating the Purchase–Money Mortgage*, 7 # 1 Real Est.Rev. 51 (1977); Bergman, *When the Seller Gives a Purchase Money Mortgage—A Lawyer's Primer on Advising the Client*, 59 N.Y.St.B.J. 46 (1987).

b.   INSTALLMENT LAND CONTRACT

In Divisions I and II the installment land contract was examined as a means of acquisition and disposition of real estate. The installment land contract also can be considered a security device—a means of financing the initial land acquisition. The following excerpts, although written with particular reference to California law, deal with many of the problems which may be encountered when the installment land contract is used as a security device.

THE CALIFORNIA LAND CONTRACT
John R. Hetland
48 California Law Review 729 (1960).
[footnotes omitted]

*   *   *

The Security Contract
*   *   *

The only meaningful inquiry *   *   * relat[es] the advantages the installment contract offers the vendor[, or the lender,] over the power of sale mortgage or deed of trust. Since the installment contract's justification is that in theory its quick, inexpensive enforceability permits closer financing, there remains no purpose for it if it is no longer summarily enforceable and is, in fact, often more cumbersome than the mortgage or deed of trust. Its usefulness to the vendor depends, in part, upon the vendee's rights—his equity of redemption, his right to compel judicial sale, his statutory right of redemption, his deficiency judgment protection and his right to restitution. *   *   *

A. *Vendee's Equity of Redemption*

Before the willfully defaulting vendee was given the right to refuse restitution and insist instead that the vendor perform the contract that the vendee had breached, the possibility of an equity of redemption was not particularly discouraging to the installment vendor. The fact that the vendee could not with impunity repudiate to harass or to try to force acceleration of the nonaccelerable instrument left the occasional redemption possibilities unimportant. Thus, *   *   * [a] significant change lies in *   *   * [the possible] extension of the right to specific performance, viz., the equity of redemption, to the willfully defaulting vendee. If *   *   * [this extension of the right of specific performance is not accepted by the courts], the land contract remains at least an acceptable *   *   * security [device]. *   *   * If it is, the contract is obsolete as a security device.

To appreciate the significance of *   *   * [the case purporting to extend the equity of redemption to a willfully defaulting vendee [4]], it is necessary to consider, individually, all three of the changes *   *   * [the case] would make in California Law. *   *   * [The case] assumed that in the vendor's action to quiet title the willfully defaulting vendee would be entitled to an interlocutory decree affording him an opportunity to perform before the vendor's title could be quieted. It then held that the willfully defaulting vendee could by his own action compel such redemption and refuse the vendor's proferred restitution without, incidentally, proving that a forfeiture in the technical sense would otherwise result. Finally *   *   * [it] suggested that the vendee, by a

4. [Ward v. Union Bond & Trust Co.,
243 F.2d 476 (9th Cir.1957).]

proper showing, could force a judicial sale followed by a statutory period of redemption.

Not even * * * [the] first assumption may be considered as settled * * *. It may be, or it may become, the law that the willfully defaulting vendee can insist upon a period within which to redeem before the vendor's title is quieted * * *.

Again a little history may help resolve the question. For years a nonwillful defaulter has had an equity of redemption in the sense that the court would not enforce the forfeiture. While it was true that the vendor, if the title were not clouded and if the vendee voluntarily relinquished possession, could retain the excess paid over actual damage as a part of his private enforcement, it was also true that the vendor could not quiet his title or regain possession without the court affording the nonwillfully defaulting vendee some opportunity to perform. This does not mean, of course, that the land contract could not be strictly foreclosed; it could be, but only in the sense that a judicial sale was not required. Before the final order quieting the vendor's title, however, the innocent defaulting vendee would be given a limited opportunity to perform and thus avoid any forfeiture. In 1949 the nonwillful defaulter's rights were expanded to afford him his own action for redemption, i.e., to reinstate the contract, whether or not the vendor sought any affirmative action.

In the absence of close analysis, the rights of the willful defaulter seem to have stopped short of the first step, viz., he apparently was denied even the interlocutory decree designed to give a period to redeem before the quieting of title * * *. It is arguable that this apparent denial is based upon "clean hands". * * * Civil Code section 3369 prohibits specific or preventive relief to enforce a penalty or forfeiture in any case; fault is irrelevant. While Civil Code section 3275 compels consideration of fault and provides for affirmative relief to the nonwillful defaulter in his own action, it is irrelevant with respect to the forfeiture problem in the vendor's action. Only section 3369 is relevant in deciding whether or not the court may enforce a forfeiture at the request of the vendor, i.e., whether it may quiet his title without giving the vendee a limited opportunity to perform. * * * [T]here are now cases where the California courts have given the willful defaulter the benefit of the interlocutory decree even though none have specifically considered its propriety.

This * * * does not lead inevitably to the right of the willful defaulter to refuse restitution and insist, instead, upon an opportunity to perform even under Section 3369. A forfeiture, after all, is avoided by restitution too. But the * * * [California courts have] said that reinstatement is preferable to restitution because of the vendee's difficult burden of proof, and * * * even the willfully defaulting vendee is to be protected from forfeiture. If reinstatement is the nonwillful defaulter's preferred remedy to avoid a forfeiture, presumably reinstatement is also preferable for the willful defaulter. And as limited to the section 3369 area, i.e., to the avoidance of forfeiture in the vendor's action, the California Supreme Court seems to have assumed that fault is irrelevant regardless of remedy. * * *

Whether or not * * * [the] next step [is correct], * * * predicting that * * * the willfully defaulting vendee can compel reinstatement by his own action (viz., in predicting that every vendee has a clear equity of redemption) is simply unanswerable. The * * * reasoning [and results of some cases decided by the California Supreme Court] * * * supports it. There is authority both ways in the intermediate courts, but probably the trend is in favor [of it] * * *. The most decisive single factor, however, seems to be the tendency of the California courts to equate the installment land contract with the mortgage or deed of trust.

While the ultimate answer lies in the philosophy of the court— either it does or it does not believe there are reasons for preserving the installment contract as a separate security device—it seems to be necessary to separate the marketing and security contracts in arguing either side of the issue. * * * A good argument against * * * is that * * * [it] allows the vendee to speculate on value before choosing between reinstatement or restitution. But this realistically argues only against * * * [its] application to the marketing instrument; an application which for this and other reasons seems unlikely when the contracts are separated by purpose. The installment vendee can also speculate to a limited extent. But unlike the marketing vendee, his liability is based upon (i.e., his refund is reduced by) rental value or difference value, whichever is greater. So speculation, for him, is not particularly attractive—it is, at least, speculation and not a sure thing.

It remains true that * * * unrestricted equity of redemption allows the vendee to harass the vendor by consecutive defaults. But he has no greater opportunity for harassment under [this analysis] * * * than he would have under the other security devices; in all cases he has an equity of redemption regardless of fault and the statutory penalties under the other two instruments are no more discouraging than the contractual penalties found in practically all contracts. So again the effectiveness of the argument depends upon whether the court wants to equate the land contract to the other devices or whether it wants to leave some remedial advantages to it.

Similarly, whether * * * [the] reinstatement of the contract contemplates specific performance of the entire instrument including the acceleration clause, or whether it means the contract is to be continued without acceleration in the absence of a judicial sale, depends upon the extent to which the court is inclined to carry the mortgage analogy. Under a mortgage or deed of trust, the debtor may reinstate without acceleration for a period of three months following notice of default if the security is to be sold under the power, or at any time prior to the foreclosure judgment if the creditor chooses judicial en-

forcement. Under the installment contract, there are indications that
the result * * * [could] be the same. * * *

Whether or not * * * [the willful defaulter's] total equity of
redemption is California law cannot be answered until the California
Supreme Court has had an opportunity to consider it. The answer
could go either way consistently with California precedent—it is a
question solely of the court's underlying approach to the installment
contract as a security device. * * * In any event, a vendor choosing
between the deed of trust or installment contract as a security device
should make the choice upon the assumption * * * [that the willful
defaulter will be given an opportunity to perform and the right to
refuse restitution].

There remains, however, * * * [the] third step * * * that the
vendee by proper showing could force a judicial sale followed by a
statutory right of redemption.

1. Statutory Right of Redemption

Traditionally the trial court has had the power to order a judicial
sale of the property. But because of the availability of strict foreclosure and because of the applicability of the anti-deficiency legislation,
foreclosure by sale was rare. Had the choice of remedy following his
own breach been the vendee's undoubtedly the judicial sale would have
been the paramount remedy—the vendee in any event would be im-
mune from a personal judgment and, assuming a year for redemption,
would have had an additional year's possession together with an additional year's look at values. But the choice was not that of the
breaching vendee. Granting that he always had a limited opportunity
to complete the contract before the vendor could quiet title, granting
that * * * the nonwillful defaulter could reinstate the contract on his
own initiative, * * * [and] that the willful defaulter could get restitution in his own action, and even * * * that the willful defaulter
* * * [might be able] to refuse restitution and reinstate, never have
the California courts said that he can so name the vendor's remedy that
he can * * * compel a judicial sale.

[The case purporting to extend the equity of redemption to the
willful defaulter, however,] suggested that to further protect the vendee
the trial court could order a judicial sale, thus giving the vendee a
statutory year of redemption. In context, the court's suggestion means
that the vendee's showing of possible inability to redeem during an
interlocutory period is itself a sufficient basis for the trial court to order
the sale notwithstanding the vendor's objection. Neither the vendor's
offer of restitution nor his acquiescence in the interlocutory redemption
period would be sufficient to prevent the willfully defaulting vendee
from insisting upon and getting a judicial sale. * * * Again, the
ultimate California determination of the issue is unanswerable. But
again, if California chooses to carry the mortgage-land contract analogy
the whole way, * * * [the case] may be right.

The next step is easy. If there is a judicial sale, there will be a statutory year of redemption. * * * In selecting a security device, * * * the seller should assume that the vendee's choice of the vendor's remedies includes restitution, reinstatement, or judicial sale with redemption but without a deficiency judgment. And in choosing his security device, the creditor should compare the contract's possible judicial sale and year of redemption with the power of sale available under the other security devices. * * *

2. Restitution

Never will the vendor be forced to make restitution; he can avoid it by insisting upon a judicial sale, but here again he is struggling to approach the advantages he would have had under the deed of trust or mortgage. * * *

In any event, it is in the restitution area alone that the measure of the installment vendor's damages is important.   The anti-deficiency legislation moots the damages question for all purposes other than deciding how much the vendor must return, a question upon which the defaulting vendee has the theoretical burden of proof. Although there is considerable loose authority to the effect that the measure of damage under the installment contract is difference value, the measure probably is rental value unless it is converted to a forced difference value by judicial sale.   In addition to rental value, the vendor is entitled to expenses incurred in enforcing the security to the extent reserved by contract; but under a clear security instrument, the expenses of sale and increase or decrease in value are irrelevant.

To round out the picture, perhaps a quick look at what remains of the vendor's affirmative remedies will demonstrate that it is nonsense to continue to call the land contract the California vendor's preferred security device, as some still do.

B. *Vendor's Affirmative Remedies*

1. Effect of Anti-Deficiency Legislation

Because Code of Civil Procedure section 580b prohibits a deficiency judgment under the installment land contract, the existence of any meaningful remedy for the vendor depends upon his somehow avoiding it.   Several avoidance possibilities have been suggested; none of them will work. * * *

Given a security instrument, section 580b applies.

2. Cancellation; Private Enforcement

Private enforcement of the contract by cancellation and forfeiture is generally considered to be the vendor's best remedy. If it still worked, it would be. It is true, of course, that the vendee may acquiesce—he may move off, he may not cloud the title, he may execute a quitclaim, he may not sue for restitution, he may just give up on the whole thing—but this does not mean the vendor can count on the remedy by acquiescence. It is equally true that a mortgagor or trustor by later contract may give up his equity of redemption, but certainly no one seriously argues that this possibility makes private strict foreclosure a good remedy for the mortgagee or beneficiary. The point is that the vendee no longer can be compelled to acquiesce and thus private strict foreclosure is no longer one of the vendor's remedies. Consider some of the difficulties he might expect with private enforcement.

First, he must regain possession. Perhaps he can coerce the vendee into giving it to him. Perhaps the trial court will enforce the fairly common contract provision changing the contract into a lease upon default and make unlawful detainer available. But judging by the reported cases in California, the vendor runs a substantial risk of having to resort to major litigation to eject the vendee and considering expense and calendar delay, there really is little to choose between this remedy and the inexpensive "repossession" offered by the power of sale under the other security devices.

After he has regained possession, the vendor still has problems. The vendee, even if his breach was willful, has the right to have the contract reinstated or specifically enforced. So he may start an action, file a notice of *lis pendens* and effectively * * * [prevent] a resale. Or he may simply cloud the title. Again the choice between a quiet title action and the power of sale procedure is obvious.

Even if the vendor has both possession and a quiet title, the burden of making restitution remains. Actually, restitution will most commonly be necessary as a prerequisite to the vendor's relief in a quiet title or ejectment action. But overlooking this, the vendee may bring an action for restitution on his own whether or not his breach was willful. This can be a serious risk to the vendor. * * * [For example, the vendor may have resold the property providing close to 100% financing and will not have the cash with which to make restitution.] * * * Again, he could have avoided the problem by a sale under the power—he would then either have taken out his interest in cash or bid in for the amount of his lien, avoiding under the latter alternative any question of restitution while still being in a position to offer for sale a quiet title within three and one-half months of the default.

3. Damages, Action for the Price, Specific Performance

* * * [Despite some recent cases arguably indicating a possibly contrary result,] it seems that any vendee inclined to raise section 580b has a complete defense to any action for damages based upon his default. Collateral damages, those based upon fraud, for example, are possible of course, but they have no relation to the deficiency problem that arises when the vendor seeks damages on the contract.

The anti-deficiency section also prevents a meaningful action for specific performance. While specific performance is available, the result of the action would be an alternative decree under which the property would be sold by judicial sale if the vendee were unwilling or unable to pay the price. There can be, of course, no deficiency judgment following the judicial sale. Thus, it seems highly unlikely that a vendor would choose specific performance in preference to a quiet title action followed by a more profitable nonjudicial resale. Forcing the vendor to this choice, however, deprives him of specific performance as a remedy by indirection.

C. Present Status of the Installment Contract as a Security Device

*   *   *

A short summary of the position of the land contract today is that it offers far more disadvantages than advantages to both buyer and seller. Its disadvantages to one are not offset by commensurate advantages to the other.

Limiting the choice to a power of sale mortgage or a deed of trust on the one hand and an installment land contract on the other, the disadvantages of the contract to the vendor include the time and expense of quieting title and of regaining possession by action and the possibility of having to make restitution, an additional investment in possibly overencumbered property. The quick, certain and relatively inexpensive solution of these problems by a sale under the power leaves little to recommend the contract. The contract, moreover, offers no deficiency judgment advantage over the purchase money mortgage or deed of trust—the judgment is not proper under any instrument.

The disadvantages to the buyer are equally discouraging. The transfer of his interest frequently is restricted by covenants against assignment. Obsolete, or perhaps overly conservative, opinion among lenders that his interest is subject to more rapid termination upon default makes his interest poor collateral if he needs security to raise additional money. Upon completion of his payments under an installment contract, a purchaser faces the possibility of receiving either a defective title or no title whatever. And if the vendor is adjudicated bankrupt, if title has passed to the vendor's heirs or if the vendor is under a legal disability, the purchaser can look forward to frustrating litigation before obtaining his deed upon completion of his payments.

Despite all of this, it would be naive to assume that the contract is not still the preferable device to some. Thus, abstract comparison of the advantages and disadvantages of the contract overlooks, again, people. Undeniably the land contract remains attractive to several of the large developers because the low (in comparison to rental value) installment payments make it unlikely that the defaulting purchaser will do anything other than leave the property, with sufficient prodding, thus making it again available for sale without litigation or even an extrajudicial sale. In other words, the risk of an occasional clouded title or of an occasional ejectment action is more than offset by the advantages of old-fashioned private enforcement which, while theoretically barred, remains an excellent remedy against an uninformed purchaser. And undoubtedly the land contract offers far greater opportunity for unconscionable manipulation by those so inclined. *   *   *

NOTE

1. Professor Hetland states that the installment land contract might be an acceptable security device if a willful defaulter does not have the right to assert a complete equity of redemption after default. In 1971, the Supreme Court of California in *MacFadden v. Walker,* 5 Cal.3d 809, 97 Cal.Rptr. 537, 488 P.2d 1353 (1971), held that a willfully defaulting vendee who had made certain improvements to the land and had paid approximately one-half of the contract price was, upon payment of the unpaid balance of the contract price plus interest and certain taxes, entitled to specific performance of the contract in the vendor's action to quiet title. See also *Petersen v. Hartell,* 40 Cal.3d 102, 219 Cal.Rptr. 170, 707 P.2d 232 (1985).

 a. Although a complete equity of redemption may be available to the willful defaulter in California, such is not the case in all states. See e.g. *Borchert v. Hecla Mining Co.,* 109 Idaho 482, 708 P.2d 887 (1985); *Grombone v. Krekel,* 754 P.2d 777 (Colo.App.1988).

  1. In some states, however, the nonwillful defaulter has rights at least akin to a complete equity of redemption. In those states, the rights of the vendee, after default, depend on whether the vendee is a willful defaulter.

  2. Is a vendee who fails to make a payment when due a willful defaulter?

   a. Does the answer to this question turn, at least in part, on the vendee's reason for not making the payment? For example, the vendee prepared the check, put it in a stamped, properly addressed envelope, put the envelope in his pocket, forgot to mail it, then remembering, mailed it one day late. Or, not having sufficient funds to make the payment when due, the vendee waited two weeks until the receipt of his next pay check and then immediately made the payment. In *MacFadden v. Walker,* supra, the vendee who was approximately 83 years old discovered that timber had been cut and taken from the property under contract. As a result, the vendee stopped making payments under the contract. The vendee did not make any payments for a two year period until the vendor instituted a quiet title action. The vendee mistakenly believed that she was entitled to a credit against her payments for the value of the timber taken. The California Supreme Court held that under these circumstances the vendee had willfully defaulted.

   b. Might a court in a state retaining the distinction in available remedies between the willful and nonwillful defaulter feel constrained to severely limit the definition of a willful defaulter?

 b. See generally Cunningham and Tischler, *Disguised Real Estate Security Transactions as Mortgages in Substance,* 26 Rutgers L.Rev. 1 (1972); Nelson and Whitman, *The Installment Land Contract—A National Viewpoint,* 1977 B.Y.U.L.Rev. 541; Comment, *Remedying the Inequities of*

Forfeiture in Land Installment Contracts, 64 Iowa L.Rev. 158 (1978); Jones, *Drafting the Installment Contract,* 62 Chi.B.Rec. 97 (1980); Cathey, *The Real Estate Installment Sale Contract: Its Drafting, Use, Enforcement and Consequences,* 5 U.Ark. Little Rock L.J. 229 (1982); Nelson and Whitman, *Installment Land Contracts—The National Scene Revisited,* 1985 B.Y.U.L. Rev. 1.

2. If a state has adopted a position with respect to the installment land contract, when used as a security device, similar to California's, does it make any difference if the contract is recorded?

    a. If the contract is recorded, the vendor's remedy, if the vendee breaches, is a quiet title action. If the contract is not recorded, the vendor's remedy probably is ejectment. Does the form of remedy make any substantial difference? If not, why record?

3. Professor Hetland's analysis of the advantages and disadvantages of the installment land contract primarily focuses on the vendor-vendee relationship. Might an evaluation of the usefulness of the installment land contract differ somewhat if the relationship considered is that of lender-borrower?

    a. An institutional lender usually is subject to various restrictions on the amount of a mortgage loan it can make to a borrower. These restrictions may include the amount of the loan not exceeding a certain percentage of the value of the real estate and improvements which secure the loan or the cost of the improvements constructed using the proceeds of the loan, or a maximum amount which can be lent to one borrower or for one project.

        1. If, under federal and state laws and regulations, the lending institution or a subsidiary thereof can own real estate other than for its offices or to realize on loans it has made, the position may be taken that a sale of real estate using an installment land contract is a sale and not a mortgage loan. As a result, the transaction would not be subject to the monetary limitations on mortgage loans.

        2. Does the distinction made above between an installment sale and a mortgage loan make sense? If certain courts treat an installment land contract as a mortgage, why should not bank examiners and superintendents of insurance?

4. Can an installment land contract be rejected by the trustee in bankruptcy of a bankrupt vendee? See Countryman, *Executory Contracts in Bankruptcy: Part I,* 57 Minn.L.Rev. 439 (1973); Lacy, *Land Sale Contracts in Bankruptcy,* 21 UCLA L.Rev. 477 (1973). But see Weintraub and Resnick, *What is an Executory Contract? A Challenge to the Countryman Test,* 15 U.C. C.L.J. 273 (1983). If the vendor's trustee in bankruptcy rejects an installment land contract, the vendee, if in possession, has the option, under Section 365 of the Bankruptcy Code, to remain in possession and receive a deed to the real estate upon completion of the payments called for by the contract. See generally Shanker, *The Treatment of Executory Contracts and Leases in the 1978 Bankruptcy Code,* 25 # 7 Prac.Law. 11 (1979); Fogel, *Executory Contracts and Unexpired Leases in The Bankruptcy Code,* 64 Minn.L.Rev. 341 (1980); Epling, *Treatment of Land Sales Contracts Under the New Bankruptcy Code,* 56 Am.Bankr.L.J. 55 (1982); Nimmer, *Executory Contracts in Bankruptcy: Protecting The Fundamental Terms of the Bargain,* 54 U.Colo.L.Rev. 507 (1983); Comment, *Installment Land Contracts and Section 365 of the Bankruptcy*

Reform Act, 49 Mo.L.Rev. 337 (1984); Andrew, *Real Property Transactions and the 1984 Bankruptcy Code Amendments,* 20 Real Prop., Prob. & Tr.J. 47 (1985).

c. THE GROUND LEASE

The use of a ground lease as a means of acquisition of real estate was discussed in Division I. When using a ground lease as a means of acquisition of real estate and/or as a financing device for initial land acquisition, the developer must be sure that the ground lease is a mortgageable lease. In the usual case, the developer will require development financing and the suppliers of this financing, at the minimum, will request a security interest in the developer's leasehold.

DRAFTING A LEASE WHICH IS MORTGAGEABLE

Alan Wayte
42 Los Angeles Bar Bulletin 62 (1966).
[footnotes omitted]

* * *

Basically, a mortgage lender will be concerned with:

(1) the lessee's ability to mortgage its interest;

(2) the marketability of the leasehold estate in the event foreclosure of the leasehold mortgage is necessary;

(3) adequate protection from defaults, terminations and modifications of the lease;

(4) adequate protection from termination of the lease by the foreclosure of a fee mortgage;

(5) obtaining assurance from the lessor, from time to time, regarding the status of the lease;

(6) adequate protection in the event of the exercise of the power of eminent domain or the occurrence of a casualty, and

(7) assurance that subleases will remain in effect notwithstanding foreclosure of the leasehold mortgage and that the lessee-sublessor cannot take action to modify the terms of subleases.

Mortgageability and Marketability

Although the ability of the lessee to mortgage the leasehold estate and the marketability of the leasehold estate are separate problems, they are both affected by any clause restricting assignments and subleases which is conditioned on first securing the lessor's written consent. Thus the leasehold mortgagee will prefer a lease which clearly states that the lessee has the right to mortgage its interest under the lease and contains no restrictions upon the free marketability of the lessee's interest. If this is not possible because of the lessor's attitude towards assignments and subletting, the customary provisions restricting assignment and subletting must at least be qualified to (i) eliminate any implication of a restriction upon hypothecation of the lessee's interest, and (ii) provide that any restrictions upon assignment shall not apply to transfers made to the leasehold mortgagee or to third parties by reason of the default of the lessee under the leasehold mortgage.

The foregoing suggestion for a compromise should not be interpreted to suggest that one may pass lightly over the question of free assignability. The lessee's interest must be marketable in the event the lender finds it necessary to acquire the interest by foreclosure and, even if assignments are permitted at the foreclosure sale, a clause restricting or limiting future assignments restricts acceptability of the leasehold interest upon a sale. Very few mortgage lenders will wish to risk the marketability of the lessee's interest upon the willingness of the lessor to grant consent to an assignment, even if the lessor has agreed to be reasonable.

Often a provision is included in a lease which requires assignees of the lessee's interest to assume the obligations of the lessee under the lease. If such a clause is included, it should be stated clearly that any leasehold mortgagee, in the event that it becomes lessee under the lease, shall be released from any such obligation[s] upon a subsequent assignment by it to a third party.

* * *

Protection from Defaults, Terminations and Modifications

* * * [A] properly drawn lease should provide that the lease cannot be terminated or amended without first securing the prior written consent of any leasehold mortgagee and that before the lessor can terminate the lessee's estate because of a default, notice of the default must be given to the leasehold mortgagee. * * *

But acquiring knowledge of a default is not enough. The leasehold mortgagee must be able to cure any default or otherwise be able to protect itself by remedial action to prevent the termination of the leasehold estate and the destruction of its security. * * *

If a leasehold mortgage is in effect, the leasehold mortgagee should (a) have the power to correct any curable default, (b) be given sufficient rights of entry to allow it to do so and (c) be given an appropriate extended period of time in which to perform after receiving notice of the default.

Many mortgage lenders will not lend upon the security of a lease which includes provisions giving the lessor the right to terminate the lease upon the occurrence of non-curable defaults, such as the bankruptcy of the lessee,[5] but others will permit such clauses if the lease gives the leasehold mortgagee adequate protection. If the lessor insists upon such clauses, the lease should at least provide that the lessee's interest may not be terminated by the lessor until a leasehold mortga-

---

5. [A provision of a lease providing for automatic termination in event of the lessee's bankruptcy may be invalidated under Section 365 of the Bankruptcy Code. Under Section 365, such a provision will not cause the termination of the lease unless the lessee's trustee in bankruptcy elects to reject the lease.]

gee has been given sufficient time to proceed diligently to foreclose its mortgage or otherwise acquire or sell the interest of the lessee under the lease. In the event that the lessor [will] not agree * * * to postpone a termination of the lease for a foreclosure period, * * * it can be provided as an alternative that upon the occurrence of a non-curable default, and the termination of the lease, the lessor shall enter into a new lease with the leasehold mortgagee upon the same terms and conditions set forth in the original lease.

Merger Protection

* * * [T]he lease should provide that neither the conveyance of the lessor's interest to the lessee nor the conveyance of the lessee's interest to the lessor shall result in any merger so as to affect the rights of a leasehold mortgagee.

Protection from the Fee Mortgage

Many long-term leases include standard provisions that the lease shall be subordinate to any existing or future mortgage affecting the fee interest of the lessor. Most lenders considering a leasehold mortgage will, of course, strenuously object to such a clause, since foreclosure of the fee mortgage will automatically terminate the lease and no provision of the lease or the leasehold mortgage can protect the leasehold mortgagee from the elimination of its security. * * *

If circumstances require that the lease be subordinated to a fee mortgage, leasehold mortgagees will usually require the inclusion of either (a) a non-disturbance clause pursuant to which any fee mortgagee agrees that upon foreclosure of the fee mortgage it must enter into a new lease with the lessee upon the same terms and conditions set forth in the terminated lease or permit the purchaser of the fee at the foreclosure sale to do so, or (b) a clause permitting the lessee or the leasehold mortgagee to make payments to discharge the fee mortgage in lieu of rent in the event that a default occurs under the fee mortgage. In the latter instance the required payments under any such fee mortgage should be limited to an amount which is equal to or less than the rent payable under the lease. In either event, the leasehold mortgagee should be assured of receiving all notices of default given by the fee mortgagee pursuant to the fee mortgage.

Estoppel Certificates

* * * A specific provision should be included requiring the lessor, on request, to give a certificate stating the date to which rent has been paid and whether or not there are any existing defaults under the lease.

Insurance and Eminent Domain Awards

* * * The leasehold mortgagee must be a named insured on all hazard insurance policies pursuant to a standard mortgagee clause and

should have all losses otherwise payable to the lessee payable to it. Preferably, the leasehold mortgagee should have the option to apply the insurance proceeds to the mortgage debt or to the restoration of the premises, but since this would usually be unacceptable to the lessor (and even the lessee), lenders will often be satisfied if adequate language is included in the lease which requires that the loss proceeds will be used to restore the premises. The leasehold mortgagee should also have the right to participate in the adjustment of losses.

Similar provisions should be included in the eminent domain clause allowing the lessee and the mortgagee to participate in the proceedings. In addition, the leasehold mortgagee should be entitled to receive the award payable to the lessee, and the lessee must receive an adequate payment for the value of the leasehold estate. If the lease is not terminated by a partial taking, the award should be applied to the restoration of the premises, through payments from a trustee or otherwise, as in the provisions relating to the use of proceeds of hazard insurance.

Options

In the event that the lessee is given the option to extend the term of the lease, an option to purchase the lessor's interest, or an option of first refusal if the lessor desires to sell its interest, then it should be clearly stated in the lease that a leasehold mortgagee has the right to exercise any such option. In the case of an option to renew, if the initial term of the lease expires prior to the maturity date of the indebtedness secured by the mortgage, the leasehold mortgagee cannot allow the lease to terminate in the event that the lessee fails to exercise its option. The right of the mortgagee to exercise the option should be exercisable on behalf of the lessee as attorney-in-fact for the lessee. Since most lenders are reluctant to rely on such an option to renew, it is preferable to provide that any such renewal option can be exercised at any time during the initial term, so that a leasehold mortgagee can be protected by requiring that the renewal option be exercised prior to consummation of the loan.

Renegotiation and Arbitration

It is the policy of most leasehold mortgagees that the lease should not contain any provisions for renegotiation of rent or other material terms. If any matters must necessarily be left to later agreement between the parties, or if any matters are to be referred to arbitration, a leasehold mortgagee should be included as a necessary party to the renegotiations and the appointment of arbitrators.

Fixtures and Improvements

* * * Since the improvements on the property may be a valuable part of the security given to the leasehold mortgagee, the lessee should have the right to remove appropriate improvements and the lessor should have no lien or reversionary interest therein except upon the occurrence of carefully phrased conditions which would give the lessee and any leasehold mortgagee the right to remove the property before its loss to the lessor.

Subleases

* * * [A]dequate provision must be included in the lease which will assure the leasehold mortgagee that future subleases will be granted on satisfactory credit arrangements and that the lessee-subles-sor will not amend the terms of subleases, reduce the rent thereunder, or accept prepayments of rent or surrenders without the consent of the leasehold mortgagee. * * * It would also be appropriate to require the lessee to include in all subleases adequate provisions insuring the acceptability of a transfer of the lessee-sublessor's estate in the event of foreclosure. The lease should, therefore, contain a covenant requiring that all subleases must contain an agreement by the subtenant to attorn to the leasehold mortgagee if it becomes the holder of a new master lease. Satisfactory protection for the subtenant can be provided by a reciprocal clause to the effect that the leasehold mortgagee will accept the attornment and recognize the continued existence of the sublease. * * *

NOTE

1. A developer proposes to acquire real estate from the owner through the use of a long term ground lease. The developer plans to construct improvements on the real estate using the funds made available to it by a leasehold mortgagee. See generally Underberg, *Ground Leasing Makes Dollars and Sense for Developers,* 1 # 2 Real Est.Rev. 38 (1971).

    a. If the lessor is willing to subordinate the fee, or sever the improvements from the fee, or defer collection of rent, or have the rent abate if the leasehold mortgage is in default, see pages 252 to 256 supra and pages 637 to 649 infra, are many of the problems which Mr. Wayte considers in the above excerpts present in the drafting of the ground lease?

       1. In addition, if the lender is permitted by law and regulation to own real estate, the lessor and the leasehold mortgagee could be one and the same party. See pages 569 to 571 supra.

    b. See generally Bovell, *The Subordinated Ground Lease,* 23 # 6 Prac. Law. 41 (1977); Halper, *People and Property: Introducing the Ground Lease,* 15 # 3 Real Est.Rev. 24 (1985); Halper, *Mortgageability of Unsubordinated Ground Leases, Part II,* 16 # 1 Real Est.Rev. 48 (1986); *Part III,* 16 # 2 Real Est.Rev. 72 (1986); *Part IV,* 16 # 3 Real Est.Rev. 64 (1986); *Part V,* 16 # 4 Real Est.Rev. 60 (1987).

2. Both the lessee and the leasehold mortgagee desire free assignability of the lessee's interest. The lessor, however, may have based its decision to lease on the particular attributes of the lessee, for example, its management, credit rating, etc., and may be unwilling to permit free assignability of the lease.

a.   How can this conflict be resolved?

1.   At the minimum, the terms of the lease must permit assignment of the lessee's interest to the leasehold mortgagee on foreclosure of the mortgage.

2.   The leasehold mortgagee, however, probably does not want, or have the ability, to operate commercial, industrial, or residential rental real estate, and the lessee wants some ability, albeit limited, to transfer its interest other than in foreclosure.

a.   Is a provision of the lease permitting assignment or sale to a third party with a credit rating equal to or better than the present lessee an acceptable compromise?

1.   Are there any problems with this solution from the lessor's or leasehold mortgagee's standpoint?

b.   Would it be acceptable to the lessee and the leasehold mortgagee if the terms of the lease required the consent of the lessor to the assignment or sale of the lessee's interest and provided that the lessor's consent would not be unreasonably withheld? See Todres and Lerner, *Assignment and Subletting of Leased Premises: The Unreasonable Withholding of Consent,* 5 Fordham Urb.L.J. 195 (1977).

1.   In a minority of states, when the lessor's consent to an assignment or sale of a lease is required, the lessor cannot unreasonably withhold consent even though the terms of the lease do not require that the lessor give any reason for the refusal to consent. See e.g. *Kendall v. Ernest Pestana, Inc.,* 40 Cal.3d 488, 220 Cal.Rptr. 818, 709 P.2d 837 (1985); *Tucson Medical Center v. Zoslow,* 147 Ariz. 612, 712 P.2d 459 (App.1985).

c.   Even if the terms of the lease prohibit assignment or sale of the lessee's interest, the lessee may have available alternative courses of action which would produce a similar result. For example, if assignment or sale by a corporate lessee was prohibited and the lease was the only asset of lessee, the shareholders of the lessee could sell their stock in the lessee to a third party who wanted the lease. See *Richardson v. La Rancherita La Jolla, Inc.,* 98 Cal.App.3d 73, 159 Cal.Rptr. 285 (1979).

3.   If a ground lease covers the entire parcel of real estate owned by the lessor and has a term of thirty years or more, does the lessor gain anything by reserving the right to mortgage the fee?

a.   If the lessor has the right to assign or pledge his interest in the lease and/or the rents, is his position equivalent to having the right to mortgage the fee?

1.   Might there be a question whether an institutional lender can take the lease or rents as security for a loan?

a.   If the lessee's interest in a lease is subject to a leasehold mortgage, might it be said that the lender who takes the lessor's interest in the lease or rents as security for a loan has taken the equivalent of a second mortgage?

b.   If a ground lease subject to a leasehold mortgage is prior to a fee mortgage, is the fee mortgage equivalent to a second mortgage? If the leasehold mortgagee forecloses, can it cut off the fee mortgage? If the fee mortgagee forecloses, can it cut off the leasehold mortgage?

4. Section 365 of the Bankruptcy Code defines the respective rights of the lessor, lessee and the trustee in bankruptcy upon the bankruptcy of either the lessor or lessee. A lessee has the option of remaining in possession of the leased premises despite rejection of the lease by the lessor's trustee in bankruptcy. The lessee's trustee in bankruptcy can assign the leasehold interest, despite a provision in the lease prohibiting assignment, upon giving the lessor adequate assurance of the assignee's performance of the lessee's obligations under the lease. See Division I, pages 243 to 245; Shanker, *The Treatment of Executory Contracts and Leases in the 1978 Bankruptcy Code,* 25 # 7 Prac.Law. 11 (1979); Halper, *Bankruptcy Cancellation Clauses Under the Bankruptcy Reform Act,* 9 # 3 Real Est.Rev. 75 (1979); Fogel, *Executory Contracts and Unexpired Leases in The Bankruptcy Code,* 64 Minn.L.Rev. 341 (1980); Simpson, *Leases and the Bankruptcy Code: The Protean Concept of Adequate Assurance of Future Performance,* 56 Am.Bankr.L.J. 233 (1982); Simpson, *Leases and the Bankruptcy Code: Tempering the Rigors of Strict Performance,* 38 Bus.Law. 61 (1982); Ehrlich, *The Assumption and Rejection of Unexpired Real Property Leases Under the Bankruptcy Code—A New Look,* 32 Buffalo L.Rev. 1 (1983); Comment, *Landlord's Bankruptcy: An Analysis of the Tenant's Rights and Remedies Under Bankruptcy Code Section 365(h),* 35 Rutgers L.Rev. 631 (1983); Andrew, *Real Property Transactions and the 1984 Bankruptcy Code Amendments,* 20 Real Prop., Prob. & Tr.J., 47 (1985).

5. What is the position of the leasehold mortgagee when the lessee has defaulted on its obligations under the lease but not under the mortgage? One absolute in drafting the ground lease and the leasehold mortgage is that an event of default under one should be an event of default under the other.

(i) INCOME TAX CONSIDERATIONS

When an acquiring entity uses sophisticated techniques such as a ground lease in the acquisition and financing of a real estate development, the income tax considerations become more complex. The following excerpts examine the income tax effects of leasing transactions.

TAX CONSEQUENCES OF LEASING TRANSACTIONS
Ralph E. Davis
1962 University of Illinois Law Forum 56 (1962).
[footnotes omitted]

* * *

Lease versus Sale

* * *

The [Code] provisions for * * * depreciation, of course, do not apply where the asset involved is land—an undepreciable asset. Thus the only way a user of land can obtain a tax deduction for the cost of such use is to lease the land and deduct the rent.

* * *

Section 162(a)(3) of the Code grants a deduction for rents paid as a condition to the continued use or possession, for purposes of a trade or business, of property to which the taxpayer has not taken or is not taking title or in which he has no equity. In other words, the lessee must not be purchasing the property. The question of whether a lessee is acquiring an equity is difficult of determination and has given rise to much litigation.

The courts have held that a lease which provides for fixed rentals with title passing to the lessee upon the payment of little or no purchase price is to be treated as a sale, regardless of the form of the instrument or the nomenclature used. In other words, if the option price is low in relation to the value of the property so that the lessee cannot reasonably be expected to let the option lapse, it will be treated as a sale[, or as the equivalent of a mortgage]. * * *

Difficult cases arise where the lease contains an option to purchase at a substantial price and where the rentals paid are fair, i.e., where there is a true element of election as to whether the option will be exercised. In such circumstances the payments may turn out to be only rent or they may turn out to be partial payments of the purchase price.

Since 1948 the Tax Court and the courts of appeals have sought the answer to the question of whether a so-called lessee is acquiring an equity by different approaches. Prior to 1948 the Tax Court used the "intent" test. Since that time, however, the Tax Court has used the so-called "economic factors" test, inquiring whether the option price is less than the value of the property and whether the rental paid represents the fair rental value of the property. In other words, the Tax Court attempts to determine whether the lessee, by payment of rents, has acquired something more than the use of the property so that he is compelled by economic necessity to exercise the option. Furthermore, the Tax Court examines the economic factors in the light of the facts as of the time of the determination.

On the other hand, the courts of appeals [generally] have used the "intent" test, whereby the essential question is what the lessor and lessee intended at the time the lease was entered into. Under this test, economic factors are considered along with other evidences of intent to determine whether the lessee is acquiring an equity.[6]

The Commissioner has chosen to side with the Tax Court. [The] rulings * * * issued * * * on this point * * * state that the intent of the parties is controlling. However, they then set forth strictly economic tests for making the determination. Actually, the rulings are not too helpful, since they [deal with] relatively clear cases, i.e., where portions of the rental payments are applied to the purchase price; where the lessee will acquire title to the property upon payment of the rents or a nominal purchase price; where rents to be paid over a short period of time are unusually large compared to the amount to be paid by the lessee to obtain title; where rents are substantially higher

6. [The Supreme Court has chosen, for the most part, to use an "economic factors" test. In Frank Lyon Co. v. United States, 435 U.S. 561, 98 S.Ct. 1291, 55 L.Ed.2d 550 (1978), the Court stated that the relevant test is whether "the lessor retains significant and genuine attributes of the traditional lessor's status." 435 U.S. at 584.]

than the fair rental value; or where a portion of the rent is designated as, or clearly is, interest.

If any of the foregoing factors is present, the rulings state that a so-called lease will be treated as a sale. This goes far beyond the case law, which in most instances has held a lease to be a sale only where there was a combination of a number of these factors.

In addition, [some of] the rulings state that a lease may be treated as a sale for tax purposes, even though it specifically prevents the acquisition of title by the lessee. * * * In most instances it is absurd, of course, to treat a lease as a sale where the lessee never exercises the option or where the lessee never acquires title. * * *

If a lease is treated as a lease for tax purposes, the lessor is taxed on the rent as ordinary income and the lessee is entitled to a deduction for the payment. * * *

If the lease is treated as a sale for tax purposes, the rental payments are treated as installment payments of the purchase price, and, if gain results from the sale, it may be reported on the installment basis. * * * The lessee is not entitled to a deduction for the so-called "rental" payments but * * * [the "interest" element in the payments is deductible by the lessee and income to the lessor].

* * *

The Commissioner continues to compare the option price with the value of the property at the end of the lease or at the date of the determination rather than at the date the lease was made. This would appear erroneous, as his 20/20 hindsight is substituted for the judgment and foresight of the lessor and lessee at the time the lease was entered into.[7]

* * *

From the foregoing, it is obvious that caution must be exercised if it is important that a lease be treated as a lease and not as a sale [or a mortgage]. If possible, it is wise to avoid leases with options to purchase. If this is not possible, make sure that the rents are fair; that no portion of the rents is applied to the purchase price; and that the option price represents the best estimate of what the fair market value of the property will be at the end of the lease. Also the acts of lessor and lessee should be consistent with a lease, i.e., the lessee should claim a deduction for rent; the lessor should report the income as rent; and the lessor should carry the leased property on his books * * *.

* * *

Improvements by Lessee

* * *

7. [It appears that the "traditional status" test adopted by the Supreme Court in Frank Lyon Co. v. Comm., 435 U.S. 561, 98 S.Ct. 1291, 55 L.Ed.2d 550 (1978), looks at the significant rights and attributes of the parties at the time the lease is entered into.]

Section 109 of the * * * Code provides that improvements by a lessee on a lessor's property do not give rise to taxable income to the lessor on termination of the lease unless the improvements constitute rent. * * *

Section 109 leaves the door open for the Commissioner to argue that lessee improvements were intended as "rent." * * * Whether a particular improvement constitutes rent depends upon the intent of the parties as disclosed by the lease and the surrounding circumstances. * * * In determining the intent of the parties, * * * the language of the lease, the surrounding circumstances, the nature of the benefits derived or to be derived by the lessor and by the lessee from the agreement to improve, whether the lessee treated the obligation to improve as rental expense on its books or whether it was capitalized as a leasehold improvement, the fairness or unfairness of the rent provided in the lease, whether comparable rents were being paid for similar properties, and whether the rent more fairly reflected the fair rental value of the property if the obligation to improve was or was not considered as rent [are among the factors to be considered]. * * *

If the lessor is taxed on the value of improvements, he may increase his basis in the property by an amount equal to the taxable income so realized. However, if the value of such improvements is excluded from the lessor's income under section 109, the amount so excluded is not taken into account in determining his basis.

In spite of section 109, careful preparation of a lease is required to avoid realization of income by the lessor when the lessee improves the leased property. The lease period should not be substantially shorter than the useful life of the improvement. The rights of the lessee in and to the improvements should be superior to those of the lessor. Where possible, give the lessor an option to buy the improvements on termination of the lease or give the lessee an option to remove the improvements on termination. The cost of the improvements should not be credited against rental payments and should not be stated to be in lieu of rent. Generally, improvements required under leases providing for rent without recoupment by the lessee for the cost thereof are not rental income to the lessor unless the rent is substantially below a fair rental.

Depreciation and Amortization by Lessee

Amounts expended by a lessee for improvements to leased property are capital expenditures to be [recovered] over the life of[, or recovery period for,] the improvement * * *. This is true even though the lessee has no title to the improvement, since depreciation is not predicated on ownership of property but rather on investment in property. * * * [Upon the termination or cancellation of the lease, the lessee determines gain or loss by reference to the lessee's adjusted basis in the improvement at that time.]

* * *

Where the lessor is considered to have received income as a result of a lessee improvement, the cost thereof is probably not deductible by the lessee but should be amortized and deducted only in the year *for which* paid. This is on the theory that the costs are in the nature of advance rental payments and such treatment would be consistent with the rules concerning deductibility of advance payments. [Cf. Code section 467.]

* * *

The cost of acquiring a lease may be amortized by the lessee if the lease is for property used in a trade or business. Section 178 * * * establishes rules for the amortization of these costs. Such costs may be amortized over the term of the lease exclusive of renewal periods if * * * seventy-five per cent [or more] of the cost is attributable to the unexpired lease term. If this percentage test is not met, the cost must be amortized over the lease term plus renewal periods * * *.

Expenditures by Lessee

Leases often provide that the lessee shall pay certain obligations of the lessor, such as loans, taxes, or interest. Such payments give rise to income to the lessor, and are deductible by lessee as rent. Thus payment by the lessee of interest owed by the lessor is taxable to the lessor and deductible by him as interest paid. Real estate taxes paid by the lessee for the lessor are taxable to the lessor as rental income and deductible by the lessor as taxes paid. * * *

Likewise, it has been held that the lessor realizes taxable income if the lessee pays the lessor's income taxes. [T]his leads to a pyramiding of payments by the lessee, for he must then pay the tax on the initial tax payment made by him, the tax on the tax, *ad infinitum.* * * * In 1952 the Commissioner ruled that all income taxes of the lessor paid by the lessee were taxable income of the lessor, including tax upon the tax upon the tax, *ad infinitum.* In 1956, however, the Court of Claims held that the tax paid on a tax by a lessee for a lessor was not taxable income to the lessor. The current status of the law would, therefore, appear to be that only the initial tax payment by the lessee will be treated as taxable income to the lessor.

Section 110 of the Internal Revenue Code * * * provides some slight relief from the taxability to the lessor of income taxes of the lessor paid by the lessee. It provides that if a corporate lessee pays the federal income tax of a corporate lessor on the rentals derived under a lease entered into before January 1, 1954, such payment is not taxable income to the lessor nor is a deduction allowed to the lessee. A lease is considered as having been entered into before January 1, 1954 if it is a renewal or continuance of a lease entered into prior to that date and if such renewal or continuance was made in accordance with an option contained in the lease prior to that date.

Leases often require the lessee to replace, repair, or maintain leased furnishings and equipment. The cost thereof to the lessee has been held to be a deductible business expense if the items replaced have short useful lives or if similar expenditures can be expected regularly over the term of the lease. On the other hand the courts have not permitted the deduction as a business expense where the assets replaced have a useful life substantially in excess of one year and are not the type requiring regular replacement during the lease term. In such cases the expenditure must be capitalized by the lessee and amortized over * * * the useful life of[, or recovery period for,] the asset * * *.

Advance Payments by Lessee

Advance payments by a lessee to a lessor may be classified either as advance rentals or as security deposits.

Advance rental is taxable income to the lessor in the year of receipt regardless of the accounting method employed by the lessor, even though the payment is for rent to accrue in later years. Even though taxed to the lessor in the year of receipt, the payment by the lessee is treated as a capital expenditure and must be deducted by him ratably over the remaining term of the lease.

A security deposit, i.e., an amount paid to protect the lessor against defaults of the lessee and which will be returned to the lessee if he performs the covenants of the lease, is not taxable income to the lessor until the conditions occur which make the deposit the property of the lessor. Obviously, the lessee is not entitled to a deduction for a security deposit until it becomes the property of the lessor.

The classification of payments either as advance rentals or as security deposits is not always easy. The language of the lease is extremely important in making the classification. * * *

One other word of warning should be given: do not provide for the payment to serve a dual purpose, i.e., as a security deposit and as a rent payment. In all likelihood such a payment will be taxed as an advance rental. It has also been suggested that a security deposit result can be strengthened by requiring the lessor to pay the lessee interest on the deposit.

In drafting leases, if a security deposit result is desired, (1) the payment should not be applied against rent; (2) it should be referred to as a "security payment" and not as "advance rental"; (3) the funds should not be used by the lessor; (4) provision should be made for return of the funds to the lessee if he is not in default; (5) they should be set aside in a restricted fund; and (6) they should secure substantial covenants of the lessee.

Depreciation and Amortization by Lessor

The general rule is that improvements erected by a lessor during the term of the lease are depreciable over the useful life of the asset without regard to the term of the lease. However, the lessor is entitled to depreciation only where he has sustained a loss through the exhaustion, wear and tear, or obsolescence of an improvement.

The provisions of the lease determine whether the lessor is entitled to the deduction for depreciation in a particular case. Where the lessee covenants to return the leased property to the lessor in the same condition or of the same value as when leased, the lessor is not permitted a deduction for depreciation. The theory is that the lessor will have his property returned to him in the same condition and will suffer no loss. To the extent that the lessee makes expenditures for capital replacements pursuant to such a covenant, he is entitled to depreciation deductions. On the other hand, where the lessee merely covenants to maintain and repair, the lessor is entitled to the depreciation deduction. * * *

When a lease is cancelled or expire[s] by its terms, unamortized leasehold [acquisition] costs may be written off by the lessor. However, if a new lease is entered into, the unamortized costs may have to be written off over the life of the new lease * * *, on the theory that the unamortized costs are part of the cost of acquisition of the new lease.

* * *

Lease Cancellation or Modification

* * *

The tax treatment of a bonus paid by a lessor to secure the cancellation of a lease depends upon the lessor's reasons for desiring the cancellation. If the lessor cancels to rent to a new tenant, the bonus is treated as payment for the old leasehold interest and must be amortized over the remaining term of the old lease. [Some courts, however, have held that the cancellation payment is an acquisition cost of the new lease and must be amortized over the term of the new lease.]

If the lessor seeks to cancel the lease in order to erect a new building on the property, the cost of cancellation is added to the cost of the new building and amortized over its useful life. If the lessor obtains a cancellation in order to sell the property, the cost of cancellation is added to the cost of the property.

As a general rule, amounts paid by the lessee for cancellation of a lease are deductible in the year in which paid. It has also been held that an accrual-basis lessee may deduct such amounts in the year the lease is cancelled, even though the payments are to be made over a number of years. In addition, the lessee may, in the year of cancellation, deduct the unamortized costs of acquiring the lease * * *.

Section 1241 of the Internal Revenue Code provides that amounts received by a lessee for cancellation of a lease are to be considered as received in exchange for the lease. Thus the lessee is treated as selling a capital asset and realizes a capital gain on the cancellation. The Commissioner has ruled, however, that an amount received by a lessee for the cancellation of a sublease is ordinary income on the theory that it is in lieu of the rentals from the [sublessee].

Amounts received by a lessor for cancellation, modification, extension, or renewal of a lease are taxable as ordinary income * * *.

Payments by a lessee to obtain a modification, extension, or renewal of a lease are treated the same as an advance rental and must be capitalized and amortized over the remaining term of the lease. Payments made [by a lessee] to obtain cancellation of an old lease in order to acquire a new lease, together with the unamortized cost of the old lease, are treated as costs of acquiring the new lease. The lessor must report the cancellation payments as ordinary income in the year received.

* * *

Purchase of Fee by Lessee

Occasionally, a lessee will purchase the fee to leased land on which he has constructed valuable improvements which would pass to the lessor at the end of the lease. If the lessee pays a price in excess of the value of the unimproved land * * * the excess * * * [may be] treated as additional cost of the improvement[s] to be depreciated [by the lessee] over the remaining useful life of the improvement[s].

* * *

If[, however,] the remaining useful life of the improvement[s] at the time of the purchase of the fee by the lessee is less than the remaining term of the lease, * * * the lessor would have no right to the improvements and, therefore, the lessee would not be purchasing such right when he acquires the fee. After acquisition, the lessee would be entitled to depreciate his unamortized cost of the improvement[s] over [their] remaining useful life.

* * *

NOTE

1. If a lessee constructs improvements on leased premises, Section 168(i)(8) requires that the cost of the improvements be recovered by the lessee pursuant to the cost recovery rules generally applicable to the improvements made regardless of the term of the lease, unless the improvements are reasonably expected to have no residual value at the end of the lease term. In the usual case, the lessee will treat the expiration or termination of the lease as a disposition of the improvements and compute gain or loss at that time.

2. If the ground lessee uses the accrual method of accounting and the ground lessor uses the cash method, how should the parties account for the rent which was deferred during the first two years of the lease, while the lessee completed construction of the improvements, and was then actually paid by the lessee, in addition to the current rent, over the next two years of the lease? See Section 467. See also Hamilton and Comi, *The Time Value of Money: Section 467 Rental Agreements Under the Tax Reform Act of 1984*, 63 Taxes 155 (1985); Shenkman, *Impact of the Deferred Rent Provisions of TRA '84 on Real Estate Leasing*, 13 J.Real Est.Tax'n 51 (1985); Whitesman, *Section 467: Tax Planning for Deferred–Payment Leases*, 5 Va.Tax Rev. 345 (1985); Reeves, *Section 467: Its Application to and Effect on Leases Containing Stepped or Deferred Rents*, 13 J.Real Est.Tax'n 346 (1986).

3. A ground lease of real estate will be treated as a passive activity, under Section 469. Therefore, unless the ground lease is excepted from treatment as the holding of property for rent, under Reg.Sec. 1.469–1T(e)(5), or the lessor actively participates, both of which seem unlikely in a typical ground lease situation, any losses realized by the lessor from the ground lease will be treated as passive losses. The lessor's net income derived from the ground lease, however, will be treated as portfolio income if less than 30% of the unadjusted basis of the real estate subject to the ground lease is depreciable property. See Reg.Sec. 1.469–2T(f)(3).

4. The owner of certain real estate is willing to sell the real estate for 10% down and take back a 30 year note and mortgage for the balance bearing an interest rate of 12% per annum, or lease the real estate for 30 years at an annual rental which will yield the owner an effective 12% per annum return on the present fair market value of the real estate.

a. Apart from the income tax treatment, what are the economic differences between the sale and lease transactions?

1. Is there a significant possibility that a lessee or a purchaser will sell its interest within the 30 year period, especially after the development reaches the "cross-over" point, the point at which the annual amortization of the principal of a mortgage exceeds the annual depreciation deduction?

2. Are there less economic differences if the term of the note and mortgage and the lease is 90 years and, at the longest, the useful life of the improvements constructed by the lessee is 45 years?

b. A possible significant income tax distinction between the acquisition of a ground lease and the acquisition of a fee interest is that the taxpayer who acquires a ground lease may not be regarded, in certain circumstances, as engaged in the activity of holding real property so as to be eligible to treat "qualified nonrecourse financing" as an amount at risk. See Section 465(b)(6).

1. If the term of a ground lease exceeds 30 years, the lessee will be considered as engaged in the activity of holding real property. Cf. *Century Electric Co. v. Comm'r*, 192 F.2d 155 (8th Cir.1951); Rev.Rul. 60–43, 1960–1 C.B. 687.

2. If the term of a ground lease is less than 30 years, the lessee may not be considered as engaged in the activity of holding real property. Cf. *May Dept. Stores Co.*, 16 T.C. 547 (1951); *Capri, Inc.*, 65 T.C. 162 (1975).

a. If, however, the improvements constructed by the lessee are severed from the land, the lessee, with respect to the improvements, may be considered as being engaged in the activity of holding real property. Or, if the improvements are severed, is the lessee engaged in the activity of building and holding tangible personal property?

5. If the term of a ground lease is longer than the useful life or recovery period, for income tax purposes, of improvements constructed by the lessee, is there any danger of the cost or value of the improvements being considered rent to the lessor?

a.   Might the cost or value of the improvements be considered rent to the lessor, if the ground rent was less than the fair market rent for the land?

    1.   Why would a lessor find such a transaction in its interest?

        a.   Might such a transaction result in the establishment of the location as a good site for commercial development?   If so, is that currently taxable?

        b.   What is the relationship between useful life or recovery period for income tax purposes and the actual life of an improvement?

    2.   If the lessee was not required by the lease to construct improvements, could the cost or value of improvements constructed by the lessee be treated as rent to the lessor?

6.   As part of a ground lease transaction, improvements are severed from the land and title to the improvements is vested in the lessee.   The ground lease provides that the lessee will pay all real estate taxes assessed against the land and improvements.   The land and improvements are separately assessed.

a.   Is there any advantage to the lessee or the lessor in having the real estate taxes paid with respect to the improvements and the land deductible by the lessee and lessor as real estate taxes rather than, for example, as rents?

    1.   Are there times in the life of a real estate development when real estate taxes are deductible and rents are not?   In addition, consider Section 216 which permits the tenant stockholders of a cooperative housing corporation to deduct their proportionate share of real estate taxes.

7.   The foregoing excerpts generally consider the income tax consequences to the lessee and lessor of a payment made by either the lessee to the lessor or the lessor to the lessee in respect of the cancellation or modification of the lease.

a.   What are the income tax consequences to the lessor of a payment by the lessee to the lessor in consideration of the modification of a covenant in the lease which obligates the lessee to return the real estate plus improvements in the same condition or the same value as when leased to a covenant obligating the lessee to maintain and repair?   Compare *Sirbo Holdings, Inc.,* 57 T.C. 530 (1972), vacated and remanded, 476 F.2d 981 (2d Cir.1973), with *Boston Fish Market Corp.,* 57 T.C. 884 (1972).   For the treatment of the lessee see Rev.Rul. 73–176, 1973–1 C.B. 146.

    1.   On remand, the Tax Court in *Sirbo Holdings, Inc.,* 61 T.C. 723 (1974), adhered to its prior holding that the payment by the lessee was taxable as ordinary income to the lessor.   The Second Circuit Court of Appeals affirmed the decision of the Tax Court.   See *Sirbo Holdings, Inc. v. Comm'r,* 509 F.2d 1220 (2d Cir.1975).   The affirmance by the Court of Appeals, however, was based, at least in part, on the failure of Sirbo Holdings, Inc. to demonstrate how the payment it received from the lessee was allocated between the part of the covenant which obligated the lessee to pay for the removal of, or damage to, the leased property and the part which obligated the lessee to remove its own property from the leased premises.   The Court of Appeals intimated that had the allocation been made the part of the payment made by

the lessee in return for its release from the first part of the covenant described above could have been treated by the lessor as capital gains. See generally Salter and McGowan, *Tax Treatment of Payment to Lessor in Lieu of Restoration: What Sirbo Holdings, Inc. Will Decide,* 2 J.Real Est.Tax'n 145 (1975); Note, *Capital Gains Treatment of Restoration Payments,* 7 Conn.L.Rev. 775 (1975).

8. Whether the lease is treated as a lease or recharacterized as an installment sale is of real concern to the parties. The determination is not hard to make in the extreme cases. But, what about the close cases? How is the "traditional status" or "economic factors" test employed? One commentator suggests the following.

"The difficulty with [most] commentators' analyses is that they either do not reach a conclusion, or, if they do, the conclusion is too vague to be helpful in tax planning or predictability.

"Similarly, the language of the courts provides little guidance. The factors, criteria and tests enunciated are not truly helpful even in terms of the perceived problem, much less in terms of the unperceived problem.

"What, then, can be gleaned from all the writing in this area? Although it is not possible to evolve a definitive set of standards from the present authorities, some conclusions can be drawn.

"We are dealing with an all or nothing approach. An investor is an owner, lessee or lender. There is no in-between.

"It is also clear that current tax law gives the parties the first shot at characterizing themselves by assigning status labels. There is an excellent chance that such characterization, as determined by the parties, will be recognized for tax purposes unless the parties engage in a clear tax avoidance scheme or attempt outrageous repurchase options.

"The lesson of [Frank Lyon Co. v. U.S., 435 U.S. 561, 98 S.Ct. 1291, 55 L.Ed. 2d 550 (1978),] is not in what was said but in what was done. * * * The Court based its decision primarily on the evidence pertaining to the single most significant item running through all the cases, i.e., ownership of the 'residuals.' In *Lyon,* the Supreme Court was not certain that [the lessee] would exercise its purchase options. Also, * * * the Court could not find that Lyon could only recoup its investment plus an agreed-upon yield. * * * Thus, the Court could not conclude that [the lessee] owned the residuals.

"In this regard, the decision in *Lyon* differed little from the Fourth Circuit's decision in American Realty Trust [v. United States, 498 F.2d 1194 (4th Cir.1974)]. That court also concluded it was not readily apparent that the lessee would exercise its purchase options. On the other hand, in *Sun Oil Co. v. Comm.*[, 562 F.2d 258 (3d Cir.1977)], the Third Circuit rejected the status labels of the parties when it was clear that the lessee 'owned' the full residuals to the property. * * *

"[N]o court has yet recharacterized a transaction in which there were no bargain purchase rights by the lessee and, of course, no court has recharacterized a transaction in which there were no repurchase rights by the lessee. These factors relate solely to the ownership of the residuals.

* * *

"Accordingly, the lesson of the cases seems to be that the most critical item, and perhaps the *only* critical item, to be considered by the courts at the present time, is the right to the residual values of the property. To the extent that 'tradition' has any meaning, the landlord always owned the residuals.

"The difficulty encountered by each of the courts in the *Lyon* case was that ownership of the residuals was neither simple nor clear. [The lessee] would ultimately own all the residuals at the end of seventy-five years because it remained the fee owner of the land. Nevertheless, Lyon was the tenant for the full seventy-five years and [the lessee's] sublease [of the land and lease of the improvements] ran only for the first sixty-five years. Thus, since Lyon owned a ten year 'shirttail' in the residuals after the [lessee's] sublease terminated, the ownership of the residuals was in doubt.

"Although the cases indicate that the residuals are critical, examining the economics of the residuals reveals that these same residuals are relatively worthless. For example, the present discounted value of Lyon's ten year shirttail as of the date of the lease transaction was less than one percent of its future value. Similarly, the present discounted value of [the lessee's] ultimate residuals was less than one half of one percent of such future value.

"In light of the actual values at the beginning of the lease term in *Lyon*, e.g., 7,600,000 dollars for the building alone, the residuals could have no real significance to either party on any rational, economic basis. Nevertheless, under present law, to avoid a serious tax challenge to a lease relationship, all residuals should reside in the party designated as 'owner.' If the lessee requires protection (usually psychological protection only), a long-term lease should be enough. A 100 year lease, or its equivalent in terms of original term and renewal options, should be adequate to protect all the legitimate interests of the tenant. So far, no case has held that the tenant under such lease is the 'owner.'

"This conclusion leads to the question of the appropriate rent to be charged the tenant during the later or renewal periods of a long-term lease. If the tenant has, in fact, paid off the mortgage[, incurred by the lessor to construct the improvements,] during the initial term of the lease, is it not appropriate to provide for reduced rentals thereafter?

"It would appear that there is some flexibility in this area. Although low renewal rental terms have been discussed as a factor in some of the cases and have also been discussed by commentators, there is no case yet that has recharacterized a lease because of such renewal rentals in the absence of a shift of the residuals from the landlord to the tenant.

"This is not to say that the next development of the law may not be in this area. Perhaps there is no logic in having the tax decision depend on the ownership of the residuals. But it is no less logical to fragment ownership among different time periods based on the relationship of renewal rentals to fair market rentals. As of this date, however, no court or commentator has gone so far.

"In evaluating the significance of low renewal rentals, the present value tables may show that the value of the future rent bargain sought may be so small that it will not justify jeopardizing tax status." Kronovet, *Characterization of Real Estate Leases: An Analysis and Proposal*, 32 Tax Law. 757, 770–773 (1979). See generally Burstein, *Distinguishing True Leases From Conditional Sales and Financing Arrangements*, 63 Taxes 395 (1985); Simonson, *Determining Tax Ownership of Leased Property*, 38 Tax Law. 1 (1984); Lucas, *The Lyon Dethroned: Federal Income Taxation Characterization of Leases and Leasebacks*, 15 Cumb.L.Rev. 431 (1984–85). See also *Oesterreich v. Comm'r*, 226

F.2d 798 (9th Cir.1955), in which a ground lease was recharacterized as a purchase money mortgage.

  a. Even if a lease is treated as a lease for income tax purposes, it may be treated as an installment sale or a mortgage loan for accounting purposes. See Financial Accounting Standards Board, Statement of Financial Accounting Standards No. 13—Accounting for Leases (Nov. 1976).

  9. See generally Morris, *Taxation of Leases: Profits and Pitfalls*, 30 Sw. L.J. 435 (1976); Bartlett, *Tax Treatment of Replacements of Leased Property and of Leasehold Improvements Made by a Lessee*, 30 Tax Law. 105 (1976); Thompson, *Some Tax Problems on Mid–Stream Modifications and Terminations of Leases*, 4 J.Real Est.Tax'n 214 (1977); Stern, *The Tax Impact on The Lessor of The Lessee's Improvements to Real Estate*, 8 J.Real Est.Tax'n 99 (1981); Levin, *Lease Terminations: Tax Treatment to Landlord and Tenant; Tenant Improvements; Landlord and Tenant Payments for Lease Terminations*, 41 N.Y.U.Inst.Fed.Tax'n 19–1 (1983); Pinner and Kelley, *Planning Opportunities in Structuring Leases of Commercial Real Property*, 64 J.Tax'n 88 (1986).

d. TRANSFER OF ENCUMBERED PROPERTY

  Another means of financing the initial land acquisition, in a situation in which the land to be acquired is subject to a mortgage which has a remaining principal balance which represents a high percentage of land value, is for the vendor to convey the land to the vendee subject to the mortgage or for the vendee to assume the mortgage as part of the consideration for the land. In either case, a transaction which involves the transfer of encumbered property is not without concerns to the vendee, the vendor, and the mortgagee.

SOME ASPECTS OF THE RIGHTS AND LIABILITIES OF MORTGAGEE, MORTGAGOR AND GRANTEE
J. Louis Warm
10 Temple Law Quarterly 116 (1936).
[footnotes omitted]

* * *

Conveyance "Subject" to Mortgage

  * * * [A] conveyance "subject" to a mortgage does not affect the obligation of the mortgagor to the mortgagee, nor does it, without anything more, create a personal liability on the part of the grantee either to the mortgagor or to the mortgagee. The grantee who takes "subject" to a mortgage is merely purchasing the equity of redemption from the mortgagor and the purchase price is, therefore, based upon the value of the property over and above the mortgage indebtedness upon it. The grantee acquires, of course, the privilege of removing the incumbrance by meeting the indebtedness when it comes due. If he fails to exercise this privilege either the mortgagee or the mortgagor may apply the property to the indebtedness. * * *

  [A]s between the mortgagor and his grantee, the mortgagor assumes a position analogous to that of a surety and the grantee becomes the principal debtor to the extent of the property conveyed. This quasi-suretyship relation carries with it an implied agreement under which the grantee must indemnify his grantor to the extent of the value of the property conveyed.

* * * The mortgagor cannot require the mortgagee to exhaust the incumbered premises before compelling payment from him of the debt. * * * On the other hand, the grantee cannot prevent the mortgagee from first exhausting the mortgaged premises in payment of the incumbrance, should the mortgagee desire to adopt that method of procedure. It may also be noted that the purchaser of the equity of redemption in incumbered property cannot discharge the indebtedness and then hold his grantor, the mortgagor, liable for the amount paid because a purchaser who is willing to buy the equity of redemption, which is the primary fund for the payment of the debt, cannot with good grace contend against the mortgagor that the land is not worth the amount of the debt.

* * *

There is a considerable number of cases which, on the surface, appear to be conveyances subject to the mortgage but which have been treated by a number of courts as cases in which the grantee has actually assumed and agreed to pay the mortgage debt. These cases fall into two general fact situations. The first of these is the situation in which the deed of conveyance is drawn "subject" to the mortgage but the purchase price agreed upon includes the value of the equity of redemption and the amount of the mortgage indebtedness. Actually, however, the grantee has paid only the amount of the value of equity of redemption. The second situation arises when the parties have, by a written or oral agreement in connection with the conveyance, agreed that the grantee shall assume and pay the mortgage indebtedness but for one reason or another have failed to include the agreement in the deed of conveyance with the result that the deed, on its face, conveys the property only "subject" to the mortgage.

* * *

Conveyance "Subject" to Mortgage But Assumption of Debt by Grantee in Exterior Agreement

* * * The question * * * [is] whether parol or other evidence may be introduced to show what the agreement was.

It has been held that in an action in which a stranger to the contract is involved, parol evidence may be admitted even if it tends to vary or modify the contract, and there is no longer any doubt that it may be introduced even as between the parties to the contract where its purpose is merely to explain an ambiguity. Evidence, parol or otherwise, may always be introduced to explain the terms of a receipt. Thus, where the consideration set forth in a deed is not contractual in nature but rather in the form of a receipt or recital only, as for example "One dollar and other good and valuable considerations", evidence may be given to explain what the consideration was, that is, to show the true consideration for the conveyance. As a corollary to this view, it is generally held that previous written or oral contracts and negotiations of the parties are not merged in the deed of conveyance so as to prevent the introduction of proof that the grantee had agreed to assume and pay the mortgage debt. The great weight of authority supports the view that this is not a violation of either the parol evidence rule or of the statute of frauds in those cases where the assumption was by an oral agreement. The proof, however, must be clear, convincing and satisfactory.

* * *

Assumption of Personal Liability by Mortgagor's Grantee

* * *

In the usual case the deed of conveyance from the mortgagor contains a covenant that the grantee, for one consideration or another, expressly assumes and agrees to pay the mortgage indebtedness on the premises conveyed. * * * Such a transaction does not result in a discharge of the mortgagor from his obligation on the indebtedness for the reason that the rights of the mortgagee cannot be changed, by any arrangement between the mortgagor and his assuming grantee, without his consent. * * *

Furthermore, the mortgagee cannot prevent the conveyance even if he knows it is being contemplated and were he to object it would be of no avail. As a matter of fact, in the usual case he does not know anything about the transaction until after it is completed. Hence the courts hold unanimously that the mortgagee need not take any cognizance of the mortgagor's grantee and may proceed directly against the mortgagor upon default or, if he desires, he may treat both the mortgagor and his assuming grantee as principal debtors and enforce the liability against both or against the assuming grantee alone.

The Assuming Grantee's Liability to the Mortgagee

* * * [U]pon the assumption of the mortgage by the mortgagor's grantee, as between a grantor who is personally liable for the debt, and his assuming grantee, a relationship in the nature of a suretyship arises, the grantor becoming surety and the assuming grantee principal for the debt. Though it is not strictly a suretyship situation, all the principles of suretyship are applied by the courts in working out the various rights and liabilities of the parties concerned. While it is held that the mortgagee need not take any cognizance of the mortgagor's assuming grantee, yet he is bound to respect the rights of the surety in subsequent dealings with the mortgagor or his assuming grantee after he has received notice of the agreement or promise to assume. * * *

We come then to a discussion of the basis upon which the liability of the mortgagor's grantee, who has assumed and agreed to pay the incumbrance, is founded, and the basis for the enforcement of that liability. The important question is: Is the grantee's liability founded on the doctrine of equitable subrogation or does it rest upon a contract? Can the mortgagee maintain a personal action against the mortgagor's assuming grantee directly at law without impleading the mortgagor and without foreclosing the mortgage, or must he proceed in equity by way of foreclosure and the determination of a deficiency judgment against the assuming grantee?

There are two parallel lines of analysis, one of which leads to an action in equity, the other to an action at law. In the course of this discussion we will find that the action is in equity in those jurisdictions in which the promise on the part of the grantee to assume and pay the incumbrance is considered a collateral security of the grantor to which the mortgagee, as a creditor, is entitled to be subrogated. The action may be at law in those jurisdictions in which the liability of the grantee is based upon contract.

The starting point of both of these remedies is the common law rule that no action can be maintained upon a contract except by the person who is either a party to the contract or from whom the consideration actually moved, that is, there must be privity of contract between the plaintiff and the defendant in order to render the defendant liable to an action by the plaintiff on the contract. As a result, the early cases held unanimously that the mortgagee, who is certainly not privy to the contract between the mortgagor and his assuming grantee, must maintain his action against the assuming grantee in equity, if at all.

* * *

Action at Law—The Third Party Beneficiary Theory

To the common law doctrine that one not a privy to a contract cannot maintain an action upon it, there have developed several exceptions. Among these exceptions is the now almost universally accepted proposition that a contract made between two for the primary, direct, sole, or express benefit of a third party may be enforced by that third party. The action thus permitted is obviously an action on the contract and is at law. Thus, an action in a court of law is permitted to a party who heretofore has had no recourse except in equity, if at all.

Based upon a misconception of the third party beneficiary doctrine, a number of courts have gone completely awry and have allowed a direct personal action at law by the mortgagee against the mortgagor's grantee, who has assumed and agreed to pay the mortgage, without requiring the impleading of the mortgagor and without foreclosure. * * * The great weight of authority supports the position that an incidental benefit to the third party is not sufficient to base an action at law by the third party against the promisor. The parties to the contract must have contracted with an intention to primarily benefit the third party before that third party can obtain the benefit of an action at law by virtue of the third party beneficiary doctrine. The question, therefore, immediately arises, is the agreement between the

mortgagor and his grantee[,] by which the grantee assumes and promises to pay the mortgage, made by the parties for the primary benefit of
the mortgagee or is its benefit to him incidental only? * * * The
imagination requires considerable prodding before it can be said that in
the usual case of this kind the mortgagor and his assuming grantee are
contracting with the benefit of the mortgagee either primarily, directly,
solely or expressly in mind. True, the mortgagee will obtain an
incidental or indirect benefit as a result of the carrying out of the
contract, but, as we have seen, an incidental beneift is not enough to
sustain a direct action at law upon the third party beneficiary theory.
The better reasoning appears to be on the side of those jurisdictions
which allow the action by the mortgagee against the mortgagor's
assuming grantee in equity only.

* * *

There is considerable difference of opinion as to the end result in
the situation in which there is a break in the chain of assumptions.
Obviously, the chain must be unbroken in those jurisdictions which
permit an action by the mortgagee against a remote assuming grantee
in equity only. The promise of the assuming grantee being to indemnify the grantor in case he has to pay the debt, it follows that if the
grantor is not liable he has no reason to be indemnified. Since the
action of the mortgagee is based upon an equitable subrogation to the
rights of the grantor against the assuming grantee, then, as the grantor
possesses no such rights, the mortgagee possesses none. But [some]
courts permit an action at law by the mortgagee against a grantee who
has assumed and agreed to pay the mortgage indebtedness where that
grantee's grantor, or some previous grantee, did not assume and is not,
therefore, personally liable to the mortgagee. They permit the action
at law on the ground that here, if ever, is a case in which the promisee
contracted with reference to the primary or sole benefit of a third party
and, therefore, the action may be properly brought at law. * * *
[T]he only person who can be benefited by the agreement to assume in
such a case is the mortgagee. The primary benefit is to him and it is
reasonable to suppose that the promisee must have so intended.
* * *

In the usual donee beneficiary case, it is generally quite clear that
the promisee intends the benefit to be solely to the third party. But in
the case of a conveyance of mortgaged premises there are other considerations which complicate the situation and it is not so easy to come to
the conclusion that the parties, or to be more specific, the promisee,
intended any benefit to anyone except himself.

* * * Generally, deeds of conveyance are drawn by lawyers who
are, by training and experience if not by nature, conservative. Further, these deeds are in the normal course of events usually drawn by
the attorney representing the grantor. Though he may be aware that
his client is not personally liable for the indebtedness, yet he is also
aware that there is a mortgage on the property and in order to fully
protect his client so that if by any chance or for any reason of which he

may not be apprized, his client may be liable for the debt, he may place in the deed an assumption covenant. The client is usually concerned with only one thing and that is to consummate the transaction as quickly as possible. Then again the assumption clause, if not deliberately placed in the deed by counsel for the grantor, may have been placed there by mistake either on the part of counsel or of the grantor who may think himself personally liable for the mortgage debt, when actually he is not, but will insist upon its being included in order to minimize any chance of his failing to obtain as much protection as possible. Certainly under none of the circumstances referred to is it possible to contend that the parties, or either of them, desire to primarily benefit the mortgagee. Anyone who has dealt to any considerable extent in real estate transactions will find it difficult to show more than a rare case in which the parties intend primarily or expressly to benefit the third party mortgagee either in the type of situation now under consideration or in the situation in which there is no break in the chain of assumption. To contend otherwise is to ignore realities and to draw intentions from the acts of the parties to the contract which are not within their contemplation.

However, in those instances in which a court is convinced that there was no mistake and that the promisee, not being personally liable for the mortgage indebtedness, did intend, as a gesture of friendliness to the mortgagee [or to obtain the mortgagee's consent to the sale pursuant to a due-on-sale clause contained in the mortgage], to see that the mortgagee was paid, it may treat this situation as a true donee beneficiary contract and allow an action at law by the mortgagee against the assuming grantee without being considered inconsistent when it refuses to allow an action at law in the case where the defendant is the assuming grantee of property on which there is an unbroken chain of assumptions.

* * *

Effect of Agreements Between Mortgagee and Mortgagor's Grantee

Another type of situation which deserves attention is one that arises when the mortgagee for a consideration enters into a valid contract with the mortgagor's assuming grantee who has assumed and agreed to pay the mortgage for an extension of time of payment of the mortgage indebtedness. What effect does such an agreement have upon the mortgagor's personal liability—upon the incumbrance? Generally, * * * the courts have held that such a contract, if valid, releases the mortgagor from all personal liability for the mortgage indebtedness if the mortgagor is able to prove that the mortgagee knew at the time of the making of the extension agreement that the grantee had assumed the indebtedness. * * *

The reasoning which results in the conclusion that the mortgagor's personal liability is totally discharged would logically result from the same kind of interference with any suretyship relation by a third party.

One of the valuable rights which a mortgagor possesses[,] after he has conveyed to a grantee who has assumed and agreed to pay the mortgage, is to be immediately subrogated to the position of the mortgagee if he pays the incumbrance upon its maturity. This right is rendered ineffective if the mortgagee has entered into a valid and binding agreement with the assuming grantee for an extension, because the maturity date of the debt has been extended and even though the mortgagor pays the debt to the mortgagee at the original maturity date, the mortgagor cannot immediately recoup from his grantee by reason of the extension. Thus, his right of subrogation is emasculated and of no value. The creditor must always be in such a position that when the surety comes to be substituted in his place by paying the debt, he may have an immediate right of action against the principal. Whether or not the mortgagor is actually damaged by the extension is of no consequence and is not open to inquiry since the loss of the right, or the injury, occurs at the time the extension agreement is made and not at the expiration of it—the injury to the mortgagor is presumed.

The result is somewhat different where the extension agreement occurs when the mortgagor's grantee is not personally liable for the incumbrance. In this case the relationship of surety and principal, as between the grantor and grantee, does not materialize except, as it has sometimes been said, to the extent of the value of property conveyed, the land itself being the primary fund out of which indemnity to the surety is to be made. Thus should the mortgagee enter into a binding arrangement with the mortgagor's grantee for an extension of the time of payment of the mortgage, without the mortgagor's consent, the mortgagor is discharged from personal liability on the mortgage only to the extent of the value of the property at the time of the execution of the agreement to extend the time of payment. The reason for this is that the mortgagor in this instance possesses only the right to be substituted to the right of the mortgagee against the nonassuming grantee upon payment of the debt and that is to apply the land to the payment of the debt. Therefore, if the land depreciates in value between the time of the execution of the extension agreement and its expiration, the mortgagee suffers the loss.

It is important to note that a mere delay on the part of the mortgagee in taking action to collect the debt does not discharge the mortgagor from any personal liability. There is nothing in the agreement between the mortgagee and the mortgagor which requires the mortgagee to take prompt action upon the maturity of the mortgage debt. However, the mortgagor may request the mortgagee to proceed to take appropriate action necessary to collect the debt, and if he fails to do so, the mortgagor is discharged from personal liability to the extent of the value of the property at that time. The mortgagee may not increase the damage to the mortgagor once he has been notified to proceed.

* * *

Release of Grantee by Mortgagor

* * * The release is usually accomplished by a conveyance of the premises back to the mortgagor and an assumption of the mortgage by the mortgagor as part of the consideration. Generally, in such a case where there has been a valid and sufficient consideration paid and it has been accomplished before the mortgagee either assents to or acts with reference to the original assumption, the mortgagee cannot object. His right is purely derivative—whatever rights he acquires come through the mortgagor. Since, at the time the mortgagee desires to proceed against the mortgagor's grantee, the mortgagor does not possess any right of action against his grantee, neither does the mortgagee.

The holding is reversed in some jurisdictions in a case where the grantor is not personally liable for the debt but his grantee agrees to assume and pay it and then, before the mortgagee has either assented or acted with reference to the assumption, the parties to the contract rescind it. In this case the argument is that the mortgagee is in the position of a donee beneficiary and, therefore, the contract between the grantor and grantee by which the grantee agreed to assume and pay the mortgage, is a gift to the mortgagee and is deemed to be for his pure benefit and his assent is presumed unless he expressly dissents. The contention seems unwarranted. The argument of these courts is by analogy to the ordinary situation in which the promisee is not indebted to the third party. The difficulty with this analogy is that though there are many situations in which a gift or benefit is intended where the promisee is not a debtor of the third party, this is not generally the case where the promisee is a grantor of property who is not personally liable and the third party is the mortgagee.

* * *

NOTE

1. In general terms, a purchaser who takes subject to a mortgage is not personally liable for the amount of the obligation secured by the mortgage and impliedly agrees to indemnify the mortgagor against the obligation to the extent of the value of the real estate acquired. On the other hand, a purchaser who assumes a mortgage is liable for the obligation secured by the mortgage.

    a. A purchaser buys real estate with a fair market value of $110,000 by assuming a mortgage on the real estate of $90,000 and paying the seller $20,000 in cash. The seller held the real estate subject to the mortgage. What is the amount of the purchaser's liability in the event of a default in the payment of the obligation secured by the mortgage if at the time of the default the real estate is worth only $70,000 and the mortgage liability is $80,000? See *Somers v. Avant,* 149 Ga.App. 515, 254 S.E.2d 722 (1979), reversed, 244 Ga. 460, 261 S.E.2d 334 (1979).

        1. In the situation described above, did either the purchaser or the seller gain anything by the purchaser assuming the mortgage?

2. The above excerpts indicate that a mortgagee's objection to a purchaser's acquisition of real estate and assumption of a mortgage is of no avail.

a. Does this make sense? Most lenders, even when lending on the security of real estate, look to more than simply whether on foreclosure they can obtain repayment of the loan. For example, a lender may look to the credit rating, management, performance, etc. of the mortgagor.

    1. If the mortgagee included a provision in the note and mortgage that they can not be assumed without consent of the mortgagee, would this solve the problem?

    2. What if the conveyance of the real estate to the purchaser is subject to the mortgage?

    3. How can the concerns of the mortgagee be satisfied without unduly limiting the mortgagor's ability to sell the real estate? See pages 706 to 709 infra.

b. If a mortgagee desires the ability to commence an action directly against an assuming purchaser, what steps can the mortgagee take in a jurisdiction which does not allow an action at law against an assuming purchaser?

c. Is it conceivable, in a state which permits a mortgagee to bring a direct action against an assuming purchaser, that the assuming purchaser, after being sued by the mortgagee, might bring an action against the original mortgagor using subrogation? If so, when?

3. A purchaser acquires real estate subject to a mortgage. The seller is personally liable for the mortgage. The purchaser is unable to make the installment payments called for by the mortgage and the purchaser and mortgagee execute a modification of the mortgage extending the term and reducing the payments. What is the liability of the seller to the mortgagee if two years after the modification was executed there is another default in payment of the mortgage at a time when the value of the real estate is $60,000 and the mortgage liability is $72,000?

a. If the mortgagee, for good business reasons, wanted to extend the mortgage but also wanted the seller to remain fully liable for the obligation secured by the mortgage, how could the mortgagee's desire be accomplished?

b. Would the result of the actions of the mortgagee described in 3. above differ if, instead of extending the term of the mortgage, the mortgagee had simply reduced the interest rate?

    1. Would the result differ if the modification was to increase the interest rate?

        a. A number of lenders are writing mortgages with variable interest rates. For example, the interest rate charged for the loan may be 1% greater than the prime rate. If the prime rate increases after a purchaser acquires the real estate subject to a variable rate mortgage, does this affect the seller's liability to the mortgagee?

4. The basis of real estate for income tax purposes generally includes a purchase money mortgage given by the purchaser. See pages 368 to 370 supra. Does basis also generally include a mortgage liability assumed or taken subject to? See Bluhm, *Tax Considerations in Financing Real Estate Transactions,* 47 Taxes 844 (1969); Fuller, *Transferring Liabilities: Tax Effects,* 12 Ga.L.Rev. 33 (1977).

5.   The purchaser who acquires real estate subject to a mortgage is said to impliedly agree to indemnify the seller against the mortgage liability to the extent of the value of the real estate acquired.

a.   Is the purchaser's agreement to indemnify the seller considered a personal liability of the purchaser for income tax purposes?

1.   If so, what effect does a mortgage liability on real estate acquired, subject to the mortgage, by a partnership have on the bases of the limited partners in their partnership interests?

a.   See pages 75 to 87 supra and Bluhm, *Tax Considerations in Financing Real Estate Transactions,* infra pages 710–712.

6.   If acquiring property subject to a mortgage has the effect of permitting the purchaser to increase its basis in the property in an amount equal to the unpaid principal amount of the mortgage, should the same result follow if the unpaid principal amount of the mortgage exceeds the fair market value of the property?   Or, should the increase in basis be limited to the fair market value of the property if the fair market value is less than the unpaid principal amount of the mortgage?   See pages 371 to 373 supra and *Edna Morris,* 59 T.C. 21 (1972), acq., 1973–2 C.B. 3.

a.   If a partnership is the purchaser of property subject to a mortgage, should the partners be able to increase their bases in their partnership interests in a total amount equal to the mortgage liability or should the increase be limited to the fair market value of the property if less than the amount of the mortgage liability?   See Section 752(c); pages 75 to 87 supra. Cf. Epstein, *The Application of the Crane Doctrine to Limited Partnerships,* 45 S.Cal.L.Rev. 100 (1972); Fuller, *Transferring Liabilities: Tax Effects,* 12 Ga.L.Rev. 33 (1977).

b.   Section 465 may prevent a purchaser from adding the amount of a mortgage liability on real estate acquired subject to the mortgage to the purchaser's at-risk amount for the purpose of using the losses derived from the operation of the real estate.   Section 465(b)(6)(A), however, excepts "qualified nonrecourse financing" from this prohibition.   Might a mortgage liability on real estate acquired subject to the mortgage qualify as "qualified nonrecourse financing"?   See Section 465(b)(6)(B) and pages 150 to 153 supra.

e.   SUBORDINATION OF THE INTEREST SECURING THE FINANCING OF THE INITIAL LAND ACQUISITION

The subordination of interests in real estate was discussed in connection with the consideration of the acquisition of real estate.   See pages 252 to 256 supra.   In most situations it is the development of the land rather than the acquisition of the land which requires substantial financing.   Generally, the development financier will require a first lien on the real estate to secure the development financing.   This requirement imposes on the developer the burden to plan for, and affect, the subordination of other interests in the real estate to the lien of the development financier.

COMMENT:

SUBORDINATION OF PURCHASE—MONEY SECURITY

52 California Law Review 157 (1964).
[footnotes omitted]

Typically, when an individual purchases a large amount of raw acreage * * * he has neither the entire purchase price nor the capital for [development of the land]. Therefore the buyer will usually operate on long term credit. This credit often takes the form of purchase-money security in favor of the seller, and a construction loan secured by a deed of trust on the property in favor of a third party lender, normally an institutional lender.

A problem arises because the commercial lender [may be] required by statute[, or its lending policies,] to hold the first deed of trust on the property. However, the purchase money security is usually the senior lien. Therefore it is necessary, in order to obtain the construction loan from the institutional lender, that the buyer obtain the promise of the seller to waive his statutory priority and accept the junior lien on the property. This waiver is [one form of] "subordination."

There are several reasons why the seller is willing to subordinate. He doubtless receives additional consideration, usually in the form of a higher purchase price. Further, it is assumed that the actual value of the construction lien will increase only as the property under development enjoys a corresponding increase in value, due to the accompanying progress in the construction. This assumption is not always correct. The risk nevertheless is a significant one.

* * * This risk has been the cause of a number of challenges to the validity of particular agreements to subordinate. The challenges have occurred at two points in the transaction.

The most frequent has involved the seller's attempt, evidently upon reassessment of the wisdom of his agreement, to disclaim the enforceability of the subordination promise. The disclaimer occurs prior to the execution of the construction loan, when the agreement to subordinate is still executory. The context has been a suit by the buyer for specific performance.

The second challenge occurs at the executed stage, when the construction loan has been issued to the buyer. The seller seeks a declaration that the subordination was not effective and that he holds the senior lien on the property. The direct cause of the second challenge has been foreclosure proceedings by the construction lender.

* * *

I

Enforcement of the Executory Agreement

* * *

[A] critical problem for the courts is to determine the requisite specificity for enforcement. The majority of opinions have required that the subordinating loan be described with great detail. Failure to do so has meant that the entire contract was unenforceable. Clearly, failure to specify the maximum amount of the loan is significant. Enforcement has also been denied for failure to state the interest rate, mode of repayment, and amount of monthly payments. Identity of the construction lender has not appeared critical.

The strict judicial attitude has suppressed the use of the automatic subordination clause. * * * The degree of certainty required should insure that the seller does not assume a substantially greater risk than that originally anticipated. The buyer should be restricted to terms of the loan which would limit the amount borrowed to the difference between the estimated value of the land with improvements, and the amount of the seller's lien. Further, the principal and interest should not fall due prior to the anticipated return of the investment. An agreement with substantially less certainty than those held unenforceable would provide these safeguards, and the transaction would not be unduly complicated. This leads to the conclusion that the inherent unfairness of the particular transactions concerned the courts more than the single question of certainty of the subordination agreement. * * *

When the seller subordinates to other purchase money security, he receives the principal of the subordinating loan as a cash payment on the purchase price. The lender therefore has presumptively loaned for less than the market value of the property, and the sum of the two liens should not exceed the purchase price. Barring deflation in value of the land, the seller's junior security will not be exhausted by the senior's foreclosure and sale. Conversely, in the construction loan situation, until the value of the improvements has substantially increased the market value, the property is overencumbered. The substantially smaller risk in the purchase-money situation justifies a less complete subordination agreement. * * *

[In determining the validity of the subordination a court should first] * * * make an express finding of reasonableness. Only if the agreement is just is the court to determine whether the fundamental terms are present. If so, it is to fill in the details in conformity with present business practices.

The question remains: What are the fundamental terms? * * * [A] partial answer * * * [is that the subordination agreement must] provide that the construction loan may not exceed a maximum amount, nor that interest exceed a maximum rate. Payment should not be made over a period in excess of thirty years, and the loan is to be from an institutional lender. ＊ ＊ ＊

This [answer] is ＊ ＊ ＊ unsatisfactory. First, the seller is equally, if not more, concerned with establishing a *minimum* period than a maximum for repayment. If the loan is subject to call within a short period, it is likely that the buyer will not have realized the return on his investment, and will be unable to meet the payment schedule. The longer the period over which payments are amortized, the less likely is the probability of default. Further, if the payments on the construction loan do not fall due prior to the return on the investment, it is more likely that at least part of the initial profits will be applied to the purchase money lien.

Another criticism is that [it provides] ＊ ＊ ＊ no limitation on the amount of the lender's fees. These fees may [constitute] a substantial part of the payment in excess of the principal, and may be greater than the interest rates. Unless a restriction on fees is included, the lender may circumvent the interest restriction by complying with that restriction and charging correspondingly higher fees.

Provision for the nature of the lender should not be a *sine qua non* for enforcement. The seller may wish to restrict the automatic subordination to a loan from an institutional lender. Otherwise there is no statutory requirement that the lender hold the first lien, and the necessity of subordination is [lessened]. The consequences of the selection of a private lender are not significantly disadvantageous to the seller. The private lender may be more prone to foreclose at the first evidence of default. This possibility is weighed against the usury limitation applicable to the private lender from which the institutional lender [may be] exempt. The nature of the lender is not of such consequence that it should be characterized as a fundamental term.

In conclusion, the duty of protection to the seller that the courts have assumed should be fulfilled when the agreement specifies the maximum amount of the loan, maximum interest, including fees, and the minimum period for repayment.

II

Enforcement of the Executed Agreement

In addition to the limitations on the terms of the loan, it is common to include in the subordination agreement a limitation on the use of the funds. Typically it is specified that the money is to be used only for construction purposes, or is not to be used for "off-site" improvements. What is the effect upon priorities (1) if the buyer obtains a loan that does not conform to the specified terms, or (2) if the buyer uses the funds for purposes other than those designated in the agreement?

＊ ＊ ＊ [An answer] is that the specified terms are conditions of subordination, and subordination occurs only upon fulfillment. Is this also true of the use requirement? Perhaps the use requirement is a promise between the seller and buyer, the breach of which has no effect on the lender's rights. * * *

A. Non-compliance With the Specified Loan Terms

What if the buyer obtains a loan that does not conform with the specified terms? Non-compliance * * * results in retention of priority by the seller. * * *

It is not conceptually difficult to require that the construction loan be consistent with the specified terms of the agreement, at the risk that the lender will in fact hold a junior lien. The seller has expressly specified a lien to which he will subordinate. The lender should be aware of the restrictions, and will have obtained title insurance on his priority. The burden on the seller would be disproportionate to the burden on the lender if the subordination is effective without compliance.

* * *

B. Non-compliance With Use Requirements

The conclusion was reached in the previous section that if the terms of the construction loan deviate substantially from those prescribed by the seller, the subordination will not occur. Does the same result follow when the loan money is not applied to the purpose designated in the construction loan?

* * * If priority is dependent on proper use, the construction lender should hold seniority as to the amount correctly used for construction purposes; the amounts advanced should be considered severable. The priority of the construction loan lien vests at the time the funds are applied to the construction purpose. Therefore, if the seller is to recover the entire amount of his purchase money lien from the construction lender, * * * the misappropriated funds must exceed the balance due on the purchase price.

* * * Assuming that the lender is unaware of the intended misuse, the question is one of allocation of risk: if the buyer intends to defraud the parties, between the seller and the lender who should suffer the loss? Three considerations are important: (1) who can best afford the loss; (2) who is in the best position to prevent the misuse; and (3) what will be the effect on subsequent transactions.

Financially, the lender is likely to be in the best position to absorb the loss. He may provide for such a contingency by his profit and loss estimate. * * *

If the seller does retain his priority, and the lender purchases at the seller's foreclosure, the lender is in the position of owning the property for a price presumably less than the market value; the proceeds paid on the loan are at least partially recouped through the improvements made, if any.

* * *

Another consideration is that the lender is in the best position to prevent the contingency from occurring. Cash payments on the loan should be made only upon presentation of evidence, in the form of receipts and on-site inspections, that the expenses have been incurred. In theory this prevents misuse. While it is a greater burden on the lender to impose this duty of supervision, this is balanced against the position of the seller; it is impossible for him to control the use.

The conclusion is that the lender's greater ability to absorb the loss, the probability that his loss will be substantially less, and his position of relative control over the use of the funds should place the risk of misappropriation on him. He holds the senior lien only to the extent the disbursed funds are applied to the designated purpose.

The allocation of loss for misuse to the lender should be significant only to the extent that it will force the parties to provide for the relevant contingencies by contract. A major cause of the manifold problems which have arisen has been poor draftsmanship of the subordination agreements. Consequently the courts have been confronted with agreements which inadequately define the parties' rights. * * *

But this law is only suppletive. There is no bar to contractual allocation of responsibility for the misappropriation; the relative rights should be set forth with specificity. A procedure has developed whereby at the time of execution of the construction loan, an agreement is signed by the three parties concerned, defining the loans and setting forth the priorities. Provision for this agreement may be made in the "automatic" clause. This procedure should be expanded to include provision for the contingencies which might arise after subordination. * * *

NOTE

1. There are at least two methods of providing for subordination. The instrument granting the subordinating party its interest in the land can provide for the subordination. For example, the purchase money mortgage given to the seller can provide that it is subordinate to the mortgage to be given to the development financier. Or, the developer and the subordinating party can execute an agreement which obligates the subordinating party to subordinate its interest to that of the development financier when the development financing is consummated.

   a. Which of the methods of providing for subordination is the best choice from the standpoint of the developer, the subordinating party, the development financier?

   1. If the subordinating party is the lessor in a ground lease transaction, the method of providing for subordination will be an agreement which obligates the subordinating party to subordinate.

   b. See generally Bell, *Negotiating the Purchase–Money Mortgage*, 7 # 1 Real Est.Rev. 51 (1977); Bovell, *The Subordinated Ground Lease*, 23 # 6 Prac.Law. 41 (1977); McNamara, *Subordination Agreements as Viewed by Sellers, Purchasers, Construction Lenders and Title Companies*, 12 Real Est.L.J. 347 (1984).

2. Regardless of the method used to provide for subordination, its enforceability is going to depend on compliance with at least two requirements: (1) Its "fairness," and (2) The certainty and specificity of the description of the "fundamental" terms of the subordinating loan. See generally *Stenehjem v. Kyn Jin Cho,* 631 P.2d 482 (Alaska 1981).

a. The fundamental terms of the subordinating loan include the maximum amount of the loan, the maximum interest rate, the maximum amount of lender's fees, both the minimum and maximum term of the loan and, possibly, the use of the proceeds of the loan and the requirement that the lender be an institutional lender.

1. Could, or should, the maximum yearly amortization of the loan be included in this list?

b. In determining whether the subordination complies with the "fairness" requirement, the percentage which the subordinating loan bears to the value of the land and improvements is considered and, possibly, the limitation on the use of the proceeds of the subordinating loan.

1. The reasoning underlying the "fairness" requirement is that it is not fair to destroy the value of the subordinating party's interest through subordination, at least if the subordinating party, with full knowledge, does not agree. See *Handy v. Gordon,* 65 Cal.2d 578, 55 Cal.Rptr. 769, 422 P.2d 329 (1967) and Division I, pages 252 to 256 supra.

2. If the subordinating party's interest is only subordinate to a loan which constitutes a percentage of the value of the improvements constructed with the proceeds of the subordinating loan, why, in addition, should the use of the proceeds of the subordinating loan be limited to the purposes of construction?

a. If the anticipated value of the improvements is realized, the value of the subordinating party's interest is protected, and there are certain advantages to the developer in mortgaging-out. See pages 582 to 591 supra.

b. Is the reason for the limitation on the use of the construction proceeds that, if the value of the improvements and the amount of the subordinating loan exceed the cost of improvements, the excess proceeds "in fairness" should be applied against the obligations of the developer to the subordinating party?

c. Or, is the reason that, as the construction loan is disbursed during the course of construction, one cannot be certain that the value of the improvements when constructed will be equal to or greater than the amount of the subordinating loan so that the limitation on the use of the proceeds of the subordinating loan provides some protection to the subordinating party during the construction period? Cf. *Kennedy v. Betts,* 33 Md.App. 258, 364 A.2d 74 (1976); *G. Credit Company v. Mid–West Land Development, Inc.,* 207 Kan. 325, 485 P.2d 205 (1971); *Dugan v. First National Bank in Wichita,* 227 Kan. 201, 606 P.2d 1009 (1980); *Peoples Bank & Trust Co. v. L & T Developers, Inc.,* 434 So.2d 699 (Miss.1983); Note, *Landowner's Subordination of Deed of Trust is Effective Only to Extent That Lender Uses Reasonable Diligence to Ensure Loan Proceeds Are Applied to Project,* 53 Miss.L.J. 691 (1983).

3.   Regardless of how the limitation on the use of the proceeds of the subordinating loan is analyzed, if such a limitation is present, how should a breach of this limitation be treated?   See Note, *Purchase Money Subordination Agreements in California: An Analysis of Conditional Subordination,* 45 S.Cal. L.Rev. 1109 (1972); Korngold, *Construction Loan Advances and the Subordinated Purchase Money Mortgagee: An Appraisal, A Suggested Approach, and the ULTA Perspective,* 50 Fordham L.Rev. 313 (1981).

a.   Is a workable answer having the subordination agreement provide that the subordinating party will not be subordinate to any amount of the subordinating loan diverted from the prescribed use?

1.   Does this solution create problems for the development financier and the title insurance company insuring the priority of the development financier's interest?   How can these problems be solved?   See pages 668 to 671 infra.   Cf. *National Mortgage Corporation v. American Title Insurance Company,* 299 N.C. 369, 261 S.E.2d 844 (1980).

b.   If the solution suggested in a. above is desired, how should it be implemented?   In considering the implementation of the solution, assume a $100,000 purchase money mortgage, a $500,000 construction mortgage and a diversion of $50,000 of the construction loan proceeds.

1.   If the rationale is that the diverted proceeds should have been applied to construction or paid to the purchase money mortgagee, it can be provided that the purchase money mortgagee receives priority to the extent of the diverted proceeds.   The resulting priorities would be:

1st $50,000 Purchase Money Mortgage;

2nd $500,000 Construction Mortgage;

3rd $50,000 Purchase Money Mortgage.

2.   If the rationale is that the limitation on the use of proceeds protects the subordinating party during the construction period, it provides some assurance that the value of the improvements will be equal to or greater than the construction loan, it can be provided that the construction mortgage loses its priority as to any diverted proceeds. The resulting priorities would be:

1st $450,000 Construction Mortgage;

2nd $100,000 Purchase Money Mortgage;

3rd $50,000 Construction Mortgage.

See e.g. *Miller v. Citizens Savings & Loan Ass'n,* 248 Cal.App.2d 655, 56 Cal.Rptr. 844 (1967); *United States Bldg. & Loan Ass'n v. Salisbury,* 217 Cal. 35, 17 P.2d 140 (1932).

3.   If the rationale is a combination of the reasons suggested in 1. and 2. above, the priorities can be determined by providing for an allocation of the amount of diverted proceeds using the ratio between the purchase money mortgage and the construction mortgage.   The resulting priorities would be:

1st $10,000 Purchase Money Mortgage;

2nd $450,000 Construction Mortgage;

3rd $90,000 Purchase Money Mortgage;

4th $50,000 Construction Mortgage.

Are there any other possibilities? If so, what are they?

c. A subordinating party has agreed to subordinate to a loan which is no greater than 70% of the value of the improvements constructed and to be constructed using the proceeds of the subordinating loan. The development financier, pursuant to the subordinating party's request, informs the subordinating party that the subordinating loan complies. The subordinating party then subordinates its interest. The subordinating party later finds out that the development financier was wrong and that the subordinating loan is 95% of the value of the improvements. Can the subordination be rescinded?

FIFTY ASSOCIATES v. THE PRUDENTIAL INS. CO. OF AMERICA

United States Court of Appeals, Ninth Circuit, 1971.
450 F.2d 1007.

WILLIAM M. BYRNE, District Judge: * * * [T]he district court granted a * * * motion for summary judgment and entered a judgment of foreclosure in favor of Prudential. Fifty has appealed.

As part of a lease agreement executed in 1959 in which Fifty let certain real property located in Phoenix, Arizona, to Mayer–Central Building Company (Mayer) for a term of ninety-nine years, Fifty was required to subject its fee interest to a loan of $2,500,000 for construction of an eight story office building on the leased premises. In 1960, Mayer, in return for its promissory note, obtained the required loan of $2,500,000 from Prudential. Pursuant to the terms of the lease agreement, Fifty's fee interest was subjected to a mortgage executed by Fifty and Mayer for $2,500,000. Thereafter, the office building was erected.

Another feature of this lease agreement required Fifty to subject its fee interest to a subsequent mortgage if the mortgage loan did not exceed seventy percent (70%) of the appraised value of the property and improvements.

In early 1962, Mayer applied to Prudential for a loan of $5,400,000 on the property. Of this total, $3,400,000 was to be secured by Fifty's fee interest in the property.[8] Pursuant to this application, Prudential conducted a so-called "three draw" appraisal: (1) appraisal of the existing property; (2) appraisal of the property upon completion of a portion of proposed improvements; and (3) appraisal of the entire complex as proposed including adjoining property owned by Mayer.

Following its appraisal of the property, Prudential notified Mayer that its loan application had been approved. Thereafter, Mayer pre-

---

8. The balance of this loan was not disbursed and is not in issue on appeal.

sented the new mortgage to Fifty which balked at signing unless it was first provided with an independent written appraisal of the property.

In response to Fifty's recalcitrance, Mayer solicited A.G. Oaks, Prudential's officer in charge of this loan, to issue a statement that the loan ratio was less than 70% of the property's appraised value. Acting thereupon, Oaks wrote two letters to Mayer who forwarded copies thereof as well as the mortgage documents to Fifty. Oaks' second letter contained the following statement: "It is not possible for us to disclose a precise valuation of a property. We can state that upon the disbursement of $3,000,000 now and $400,000 later, the loan amount will be approximately 70% of valuation." Following its receipt of these copies, Fifty executed the mortgage.

Beginning with the installment due February, 1965, and continuing thereafter, Mayer defaulted on its payments. Although it avoided a specific reference to Mayer's nonpayment, Fifty, in June, 1965, requested that Prudential notify it of any default prior to acceleration of the loan or commencement of any foreclosure action. On July 9, 1965, Prudential complied with this request by notifying Fifty that Mayer was in default and that Prudential was accelerating the debt and that its intention was to foreclose the mortgage after expiration of a ten day period during which Fifty could reinstate the loan.

On July 15, 1965, Mayer filed a petition for reorganization under * * * the Bankruptcy Act. The district court entered a stay order prohibiting any interference with the possession or control of the property. Almost two years later, May 24, 1967, Fifty notified Prudential by letter that it did "not recognize the validity of that mortgage as against our interest in the property." The next day, May 25, 1967, but prior to its receipt of Fifty's letter of May 24, Prudential wrote to Fifty and reiterated its intention to institute a foreclosure action unless the default was cured within ten days after receipt of the letter. On May 29, 1967, two events occurred: (1) the Bankruptcy Court entered an order terminating Fifty's lease with Mayer and directing that the property be returned to Fifty subject to the rights of Prudential; (2) following receipt of Fifty's letter repudiating the mortgage, Prudential commenced the foreclosure action which has become the subject of this appeal.

We first address ourselves to Fifty's assertion that the district court acted without propriety when it granted Prudential's motion for summary judgment. In essence, Fifty maintains that Prudential's denials of the allegations [9] that it misrepresented the property's value to Fifty and that Fifty relied upon this misrepresentation have raised the spectre of genuine questions of fact.

With this conclusion we cannot agree, for in reality Fifty has wrongly assumed that denying an allegation, *ipso facto,* creates a genuine issue of fact. Such an assumption is clearly contrary to the

---

9. In response to Prudential's complaint, Fifty set forth separate defenses and a counterclaim which included the denoted allegations.

law. Minnesota Mining & Manufacturing Co. v. United States Rubber Co., 279 F.2d 409 (4th Cir.1960); Piantadosi v. Loew's, Inc., 137 F.2d 534 (9th Cir.1943). Fifty's misplaced assumption avoids the thrust of Prudential's denials, i.e., the nature of the "representation" was such as to deny Fifty a defense to the foreclosure action as well as to an independent cause of action. In short, Prudential's denials have placed in dispute the *legal* consequences of its "representation" and not the factual matters relating to accurate statements of value or to actual reliance upon said statements. Under these circumstances, we are satisfied that there is no merit to the contention that a motion for summary judgment was improper. Greyhound Corp. v. Excess Insurance Company of America, 233 F.2d 630 (5th Cir.1956); General Accident Fire and Life Assurance Co. v. Prosser, 239 F.Supp. 735 (D.Alaska, 1965).

As already indicated, the Prudential officer in charge of the loan to Mayer, acting in response to the latter's prodding, wrote to Mayer that it was "not possible to disclose a precise valuation" of the property but that upon disbursement of $3,400,000 "the loan amount (would) be approximately 70% of valuation." Following receipt of a copy of this letter, Fifty agreed to the terms of the new mortgage. On appeal, Fifty repeats its "concession" made below that "Prudential is entitled to a lien against the property in some amount," but renews the contention that its execution of the mortgage was induced by Prudential's "misrepresentation." Arguing that this "misrepresentation" is grounds for rescission, Fifty has set forth multiple reasons for negating the second mortgage. In our view, none of the approaches advanced by Fifty is persuasive.

Fifty's initial claim that the statement of value constituted a representation of fact glosses over the reality that land values cannot be calculated pursuant to a precise formula. Long ago, the Supreme Court recognized this fact of commercial life:

> " * * * True, in large cities, where articles of personal property are subject to frequent sales, and where market quotations are daily published, the value of such personal property can ordinarily be determined with accuracy; but even there, where real estate in lots is frequently sold, where prices are generally known, where the possibility of rental and other circumstances affecting values are readily ascertainable, common experience discloses that witnesses the most competent often widely differ as to the value of any particular lot; and there is no fixed or certain standard by which the real value can be ascertained."

Montana Railway Co. v. Warren, 137 U.S. 348, 11 S.Ct. 96, 34 L.Ed. 681 (1890). This court has echoed this view by acknowledging that the question of land value "is generally a matter of opinion only." Sacramento Suburban Fruit Lands Co. v. Melin, 36 F.2d 907, 910 (9th Cir. 1929), cert. denied Suburban Fruit Lands Co. v. Lindquist, 282 U.S. 853, 51 S.Ct. 31, 75 L.Ed. 756 (1930). * * *

In the context of this case, it is clear that Prudential's assessment of the property's value amounted to no more than the proverbial "educated guess." * * * [I]t is true this "education" was costly, Prudential having received $27,000.

Our "appraisal" of the law as it applies to the facts of this case, has been held intact despite Fifty's accurate restatement of the law that an expression of opinion can be treated as a representation of fact when it is propounded by an expert. See Eastern States Petroleum Co. v. Universal Oil Products Co., 24 Del.Ch. 11, 3 A.2d 768 (1939); Restatement of the Law, Contracts § 474.

We are of the persuasion that this general principle of law is without applicability to this dispute. As indicated in the record, Fifty is an enterprise which has been engaged in business for over 140 years. Its principal concern is in the field of real estate. By contrast, Prudential is a leading insurance company which invests premium income in real property mortgages. It engages in the appraising of land to aid in the evaluation of loan applications, not to conduct a personal service for others whose business concern is real estate investment. In the instant case, Prudential's appraisal was the product of this business practice. Accordingly, we cannot agree that Prudential acted as an "expert" when its appraisal was knowingly conveyed to a business that had specialized in real estate for almost a century and a half.

Under the circumstances of this case, we cannot agree with Fifty's position that it is entitled to rescission because it justifiably relied upon the statement of value made by Prudential's loan officer. As we see it, the expressed caveat that Prudential's appraisal was only an "approximation" served to make suspect this statement of value. Fifty's blind faith acquiescence to so suspicious an estimation raises serious questions as to the validity of its claim that it has been victimized by deception. Indeed, as noted by Prudential, under the agreement entered into by Mayer and Fifty, the latter was entitled to appraisals made by three certified appraisers in the event the property's value was in dispute. In such a context, it borders on the incredible to ask this court to negate the execution of a valid mortgage on the ground, in effect, that the executing party disregarded, inadvertent as it may be, a contractual proviso, and incurred unsatisfactory consequences as a result.

* * *

Affirmed.

NOTE

1. If Fifty Associates had not attempted to rescind the entire subordination but only had attempted to limit the amount it was subordinated to, would it have been more successful?

    a. At the minimum, it would have had to demonstrate the value of the real estate and improvements at the time of the subordination. What effect would the "opinion" of Prudential have had in this context?

2. Did Fifty Associates' failure to get three certified appraisals influence the court? Should it have?

    a. Fifty Associates was given this right only in the event of a dispute as to the value of the property. Was there any dispute after Prudential's appraisal was given to Fifty Associates?

    b. If there was no dispute with respect to value at the time of subordination, should Fifty Associates be allowed to later contest the value?

        1. Might the answer to the question raised in b. above be different if the absence of a dispute was a result of a misrepresentation by Prudential?

            a. Can the giving of an opinion ever amount to a misrepresentation?

            b. If Prudential knew its valuation of the real estate was high when the valuation was given to Fifty Associates, might this be considered a misrepresentation?

3. Could Fifty Associates have sued Prudential for damages caused it as a result of Prudential's erroneous valuation?

    a. Would Fifty Associates' chances of winning the law suit be better if it had specifically employed Prudential to provide it with a valuation of the real estate and Prudential was not the lender involved? See generally Malloy, *Lender Liability for Negligent Real Estate Appraisals*, 1984 U.Ill.L. Rev. 53.

4. Did Fifty Associates' experience and expertise affect the result? Would the result have been different if the subordinating party was a farmer with no prior experience in real estate development? If so, why?

3. INTERIM AND CONSTRUCTION FINANCING

---

a. INTERIM FINANCING

A developer usually needs an extended period of time during which to repay development financing. This means, in many cases, that the developer will have to have interim or construction financing during the construction period and replace this financing with long term financing when construction is complete. Construction financing and other forms of interim financing are very specialized. Many sources of long term financing do not have the expertise necessary to provide interim or construction financing. In general, lenders who provide interim or construction financing do not make a practice of providing long term financing.

SHORT–TERM FUNDS THROUGH INTERIM FINANCING
Blumberg
National Real Estate Investor, February 1965.

* *。*

Too many constructive real estate projects are deferred or abandoned each year due to the inability to qualify for conventional financing or to generate the funds internally. This decision to defer or abandon constructive projects becomes even more regretful in view of the fact that, in many cases, the real estate executive could have generated the necessary funds through interim financing.

Interim financing is a flexible financing concept that differs from other financing methods in the following areas.

Funds are extended only when they are unavailable from conventional sources such as banks, insurance companies and other institutional lenders. Interim financing firms, * * * do not compete with these sources but work closely with them in providing additional financing to fill gaps in the real estate credit structure. * * *

It is evident that the growth in the scale and scope of real estate projects now being undertaken has caused a substantial gap between the capital funds needed and the cash available either internally or through conventional financing. The alternatives, in this case, are to dilute the equity by taking in additional investors; abandon the project; or to utilize interim financing.

Interim financing has become increasingly recognized as a prudent and economic method of enabling constructive programs to be moved forward—without dilution of the equity.

* * * [For example, interim financing] enables owners to borrow against existing equities to finance new ventures * * *, to borrow against the values partially created in growing enterprises during the period in which the properties are acquiring the seasoning required for optimum permanent financing * * * [and] to borrow against assets which may not be recognized adequately, or may not be recognized at all, by conventional lending institutions.

The interim lender is governed by economic considerations and is not subject to rigid lending procedures as a result of statute or administrative regulation or perhaps, if you will, a confining sense of style that one encounters on occasion in institutional financing agencies. * * * [The interim lenders] are flexible in providing the financing indicated by the economic values even though the problem may be unusual and the solution unorthodox.

In addition to direct loans, [the interim lenders] are in a position to utilize the financing technique of a take-out commitment in association with banks and other conventional lending sources. It is a technique that has significant merit to the real estate and banking communities since it enables both to carry out their plans without impairing or otherwise reducing their existing banking relationships.

An excellent example of the take-out commitment is its application to construction lending. To secure a construction loan from his bank, a builder needs a commitment for the permanent financing. Many times, however, a maximum mortgage cannot be secured until the building is substantially leased. Rather than accept less favorable permanent first mortgage terms on the project in its formative stage, the builder may well decide to defer his permanent financing. He can still obtain his construction financing by having the interim financing agency issue a first mortgage take-out commitment to the construction lender, conditioned upon completion of the building in accordance with approved plans and specifications. In this way, the builder can realize a substantial saving through the use of a take-out commitment rather than accepting a less favorable first mortgage on the project in its formative stage. In many such cases, the take-out is never utilized because the builder realized adequate rentals and obtained favorable long-term institutional financing before the take-out expired.

[The] fee for the take-out commitment is a price well-paid for the significant improvement in the terms of the permanent mortgage.

Where the permanent first mortgage provides for an escalation clause based upon leasing, the interim financing agency, in proper cases, can enable builders to anticipate the escalation and to obtain construction funds in the full amount of the first mortgage, long before leasing has triggered the increase in the permanent first mortgage.

A recently completed 50–story office building on Park Avenue serves as an example of escalation anticipation. * * * [T]he mechanism of a second mortgage take-out, in the amount of the escalation clause in the permanent mortgage, * * * enabled the construction lender to advance the full amount of the permanent mortgage. * * * [I]nterest rates [of] interim financing lenders reflect the degree of risk and the fact that [they] are meeting a financing need which has already been rejected by conventional sources. * * * [T]he cost is not excessive for the benefits purchased. The interest cost is only a minor portion * * * of the total capital cost of getting a constructive real estate project into operation.

NOTE

1. The interim lender usually is not an institutional lender such as a bank or insurance company, although, in the appropriate case, such lenders may make loans for similar purposes in their commercial lending operations. The interim lender is more likely to be found among commercial finance companies.

2. What "gaps" does the interim lender fill?

     a. Assume a developer recently completed the development of an apartment complex in which the developer invested most of its liquid assets. The opportunity to develop a new apartment complex presents itself. The institutional lenders consulted are willing to provide only 75% of the costs of land and construction. If the developer has sufficient equity in the first apartment complex, this may be a situation appropriate for an interim lender.

     b. Assume that the value of a completed development will greatly exceed its costs. The institutional lenders are unwilling to commit to a loan any greater than 75% of costs prior to completion of the development. Yet, the institutional lenders will loan 75% of value with respect to a completed and fully rented development. If 75% of value is close or equal to costs, can an interim lender be used to maintain the developer's liquidity?

3. Interim financing is what the name denotes. It is short term lending which the parties anticipate will be replaced by longer term financing or will be repaid in a fairly short period of time. In this context, construction lending is a form of interim financing.

b. CONSTRUCTION FINANCING

Construction financing is a sophisticated "art." For this reason many real estate lenders who make long term loans do not engage in construction financing. They have neither the personnel nor the expertise to successfully pursue this type of an investment. On the other hand, many construction lenders prefer the (hopefully) short term nature of construction lending and do not want to provide the long term financing which is necessary to make a major real estate development a viable economic endeavor. As a result, construction lenders look to permanent lenders to provide the funds to repay the construction loan on completion of construction.

The construction lender must be concerned with a myriad of details and, since the lender is concerned, the developer and the contractor also must be concerned. Care and forethought are the watchwords of the construction lender. As opposed to many real estate lenders, and without regard to the permanent lender's take-out commitment, the dollars being lent, for the most part, are to be used to create the security for the loan. Obviously, construction lending is not without risk. The construction lender must minimize the risks while attempting to fulfill the legitimate expectations of the developer, the contractor and the permanent lender.

THE NEGOTIATION OF CONSTRUCTION AND PERMANENT LOAN COMMITMENTS (PARTS 1 AND 2)
Marvin Garfinkel
25 The Practical Lawyer 13 (March, 1979), 27 (April, 1979).

To understand a construction loan transaction, it is necessary to consider the identity and objectives of each of the parties to the transaction, the character of the particular project, the applicable law, and the documentation that will be needed.

* * *

Objectives of the Parties

A construction lender, whether a bank, savings institution, or mortgage company, is interested in securing a high rate of return consistent with a reasonably assured repayment of principal within a relatively short period of time, usually one to [two] years. The net return on the loan to the construction lender is dependent not only upon the interest charged on the monthly outstanding principal balance, but also upon various fees payable to it, such as a service fee for the administration of the loan, a placement fee or other front end points, and possibly a standby fee based on the undisbursed portion of the loan.

These fees and interest on the outstanding balances are customarily paid from the construction loan itself to the extent that funds are available. Typically, upon the closing of the construction loan and as construction advances, the lender is credited with the fees and interest by way of disbursements of principal. Upon the completion of construction, the outstanding principal balance of the construction loan thus consists not only of the sums actually advanced by the construction lender but also of a sum equal to the fees and interest that the construction lender credited to itself during the term of the loan and charged against principal.

In the case of an investment type project [owned and operated by the developer, such as a shopping plaza], the construction loan balance is usually paid to the construction lender by the permanent lender when the latter acquires the loan upon the completion of construction and the satisfaction of other appropriate conditions. Under these circumstances, the permanent loan is the intended repayment source and may be viewed practically as the primary security for the construction loan. Other security is intended to satisfy the permanent lender's requirements as they are set forth in the commitment for the permanent loan, thus constituting an integral part of the loan package to be acquired by the permanent lender. This security is, of course, also available for liquidation by the construction lender if the borrower defaults and the permanent loan does not close.

Although the construction lender views the permanent lender's commitment as the source for the repayment of the construction loan, the commitment itself would not qualify as the sole security. Good banking practice would generally condemn a loan on the basis of security that would be inadequate without the permanent lender's commitment. In other words, a banker should be satisfied that if, for any reason, the intended permanent lender fails to honor its commitment, the project to be constructed will, if liquidated, fetch proceeds sufficient to satisfy the entire anticipated advance.

A primary concern of the construction lender is that the project be completed; hence, with a reasonable margin for safety and contingencies, the cost of completion should at no time exceed the available undisbursed balance of the construction loan. In the language of the industry, the loan at all times must "remain in balance."

To this end, the construction lender will require at the construction loan settlement evidence of the anticipated cost of the completion of construction and proof that any amount—"gap"—by which the anticipated construction costs—including all professional fees, interest, taxes, and other builder's reserve items—exceed the construction loan will be available. It is not unusual for the construction lender to require that

cash equal to the gap be deposited in escrow with it prior to commencement of construction, and that this gap money be disbursed prior to any
loan proceeds. * * *

The construction lender is also interested in insuring that any
conditions precedent to the obligation of the permanent lender to pay
off the construction loan be either reasonably within the construction
lender's control or be satisfied prior to the disbursement of any construction loan funds. In the case of a for-sale type project [such as a
residential subdivision], the construction lender seeks, prior to making
its first advance, to assure itself that upon completion of the individual
housing units, a market will exist for them.

The Permanent Lender

In the case of an investment type project, the long term or permanent lender—the so called "take-out lender"—seeks a completed facility
capable of producing a long term income stream adequate to service the
permanent loan, with a reasonable margin for safety. To this end, in
its commitment, it will specify in detail the physical character of the
improvements to be constructed. This is usually done either by a
general description or, more often, by reference to an approved set of
plans and specifications. The manner in which it seeks to insure that
the project will yield the anticipated income stream needed to pay
operating expenses and service the permanent indebtedness with a
margin for safety will vary according to the character of the project.

Conditions precedent to the closing of the permanent loan on an
investment type project often involve a specific number of executed
leases in a form approved by the permanent lender. The tenant
achievement requirements will, of course, vary with the nature of the
project. * * * Other conditions precedent imposed by the permanent
lender may relate to the availability of utilities and public services,
approval by governmental units, and highway access.

* * *

The function of the long term lender in the case of a for-sale
residential development project is significantly different from its role in
the investment type development project. This is especially true with
the * * * advent of various secondary markets that will commit
themselves to acquire standardized residential mortgages in the future.
The for-sale residential permanent mortgage commitment assures the
construction lender only that if the dwelling unit is completed within a
specified period of time and if, within that time period, the unit is sold
and delivered to a qualified purchaser, the permanent lender will
finance the purchase of the unit on specified terms. These terms will
include either a designated rate of interest or the market rate at the
time of delivery.

The Borrower–Developer

The borrower-developer is seeking to construct one or more buildings or other real estate improvements with a minimum, if any, investment of its own capital. It is important to the developer that, as the project progresses, sufficient funds become available to finance construction and construction-related costs such as interest, overhead expenses, taxes, insurance premiums, professional fees, and marketing expenses. A developer may also try to limit its exposure in terms of liability in excess of its investment in the project.

The developer of a for-sale project ∗ ∗ ∗ markets its project to users who will themselves probably borrow from a permanent lender a significant portion, if not substantially all, of the funds to be paid to the developer. Upon completion of the construction and sale of a housing unit, the developer, in turn, uses a portion of the funds it receives from the purchaser of the unit to pay off the construction loan and pockets any balance to offset any funds it had previously invested in the project and, if the project is successful, as profit.

The investor-developer, on the other hand, is concerned that the project be completed on time in accordance with the approved plans and specifications, and that all the conditions precedent to the funding of the permanent loan are satisfied in time for the loan to be delivered to the permanent lender in accordance with the permanent loan commitment. To the developer, all of the conditions of the permanent and construction loans must be satisfied so that the permanent lender is not provided with a basis for refusing to acquire the loan.

The General Contractor

If a general contractor not related to the developer is employed to build the project, the general contractor will want, as a minimum, to be paid promptly for work in place as construction proceeds, and to be paid all retainage within a reasonable period after substantial completion of construction. Ideally, the general contractor would like to be certain that so long as it performs its obligations under the general contract, the owner-developer will likewise perform its obligations. This requires an owner who has substantial financial resources other than the construction loan and the project that is being developed—a circumstance all too often unattainable.

The general contractor's investment in the project at any point in time prior to the disbursement of the full retainage is equal to the amount by which the sums it has expended or incurred for labor, material, and overhead and paid to subcontractors exceeds the sum drawn against the construction loan or otherwise paid by the owner to the general contractor. To these out-of-pocket and accrued expenses must be added the liability of the general contractor under equipment and material purchase orders and to subcontractors for work to be performed at later stages of construction.

To reduce its investment and perhaps even to anticipate profits, the general contractor, and, in turn, its various subcontractors, may seek to "front-end load" the job—that is, structure the payment schedule so that the amount paid during the early part of the job exceeds the actual value, less retainage, of the work done. This attempt tends to defeat the objective of the construction lender—and the developer, if other than the general contractor—that at all times the undisbursed balance of the construction loan must exceed the sum that would probably be required to complete the work. An alternative to front-end loading of the payment schedule is to overestimate the value of work already performed. The owner and construction lender will, however, seek to avoid this by diligent inspection and evaluation of the rate of progress of the job and by exercising corresponding control of the payment vouchers approved during the course of construction.

Risk Shifting

The construction lender, developer, general contractor, and permanent lender are all concerned with the completion of the project in conformity with the permanent commitment or marketing program, satisfaction of all conditions precedent to finalizing the permanent loan commitment or the sale of units, and the funding of the project as construction proceeds. Absent unforeseen circumstances or a miscalculation on the part of one or more of these parties, these objectives should all be realized and the expectations of each of the parties satisfied. Often, even in the best economic climate, this does not happen. * * *

The attorney representing each of the parties to a construction loan transaction seeks to shift the risk of the unexpected from his client.

* * *

The Construction Loan

* * *

A construction lender will often ask for items of security in excess of those demanded by the permanent lender in order to better protect itself during the high risk construction period. It will seek security that is ample to satisfy any loan balance which might remain if the permanent loan closes but fails to produce sufficient funds to repay the entire loan balance. This might occur, for instance, if, as a result of construction delays or a dramatic increase in interest rates, the interest reserve initially established fails to cover actual interest accruing prior to the closing of the permanent loan. Under those circumstances, if the borrower is unable to cover the gap from its own resources, the construction lender may be forced to increase the loan amount to prevent a default. The need to enlarge the loan amount may become particularly significant when a condition of funding the permanent loan is that the construction loan not be in default, not an unusual requirement when it is anticipated that the permanent loan will be closed by the assignment of the construction loan mortgage to the permanent lender.

* * * Personal guarantees by the individual principals of the developer are usually required by the construction lender to provide a most significant inducement for them to complete the job and deliver the loan to the permanent lender. * * *

It is unusual for a construction lender not to require some form of personal guarantee unless the actual construction is to be performed by a bonded general contractor. When that happens, the construction lender depends upon the obligation under the performance bond coupled with an adequate holdback as reasonable assurance of completion. Since a performance bond only guarantees performance of the general contractor's obligations under the construction contract, it is most important for a construction lender who is relying upon a performance bond to be sure that, to the greatest extent possible, the general contract actually requires the delivery of a completed building by the contractor for a specified maximum sum without any conditions that are not reasonably within the control of the construction lender.

Even at its best, a performance bond is not security in the true sense of the term. It is a safe document for a loan officer to require in order to complete his file and evidence his due diligence. As a practical matter, a lender seeking to collect under such a bond has a rough row to hoe.

The ability of a contractor to deliver a bond does, at least, qualify him as being considered an appropriate bonding risk by a bonding company. Since a contractor's ability to secure bonds may be his life blood, there is some possibility that he will protect his bonding line of credit by fully performing his contractual obligations under bonded contracts. A corporate contractor's individual principals will often provide security in the form of personal guarantees to their bonding company that go far beyond what an owner would require of a general contractor.

The Construction Loan Commitment

* * *

A developer of an investment type project will primarily concern itself with satisfying the permanent lender's prerequisites once it has received a construction lender's agreement in principal to advance funds for a particular project. A final construction loan commitment can generally be fashioned only after the details of the permanent loan and an arrangement with the general contractor, if other than the developer, have been established. Before the construction loan can be concluded, the commitment for permanent financing must be acceptable to the construction lender, the general contract arrangement basically completed, and the costs of construction through subcontracts must be settled. Specified lease achievement is often a precondition to funding by the permanent lender of projects such as * * * shopping centers, warehouses, industrial parks, and office buildings; in that case, the necessary leases must be secured.

* * *

As previously noted, in the case of an * * * investment type project, the construction lender is depending primarily on the permanent loan commitment as its source of repayment; while with * * * townhouse, single family residence, condominium, and other for-sale type projects, the loan, including interest and fees, is intended to be repaid out of sales proceeds. Thus, in a for-sale project, the construction lender is depending upon the ability of the developer to sell the housing units being constructed, rather than upon the satisfaction of the conditions of a specific permanent loan commitment. The ability to sell housing units is dependent upon the completion of the unit, including all offsite improvements, in a proper manner, the ability of the developer to transfer good title to a purchaser, the existence of a market for the product being built, and adequate financing for the ultimate purchaser.

As a result, in the case of the * * * investment type property, the market analysis is performed basically by the permanent lender and is not a major concern of the construction lender so long as it has a secure permanent commitment for the repayment of the construction loan. On the other hand, in the case of for-sale housing, a market analysis is all important to the construction lender.

The Terms

The actual construction loan commitment, if one is used, will concern itself in more or less detail with such matters as the loan amount, interest rate, service charges and loan fees, term, and security. It will also establish various conditions precedent to closing on the construction loan, including an acceptable permanent loan commitment, the quality of the title to be provided, a specification of fire, liability, rent loss, and workmen's compensation insurance requirements, and possibly a personal guaranty requirement. The commitment should specify generally the provisions to be contained in the construction loan agreement itself, including a requirement that construction be completed in accordance with certain plans and specifications for a maximum specified sum. If the interest rate is based on a prime rate, the method of determining the applicable prime rate should be stated. The construction loan commitment should also describe the manner in which the difference between the loan amount and the total project cost will be provided by the developer.

Commercial banks and mortgage brokers and other mortgage intermediaries that customarily borrow funds from commercial banks will often relate the interest rate to a prime rate. Although the practice varies throughout the country, the interest rate on loans by insurance companies, savings banks, and savings and loan associations will often be based on the market rates in effect at the time the commitment is issued. * * *

The dangers inherent in a variable interest loan pegged to a prime rate are obvious. Predictability of total project cost is, from the point of view of both the construction lender and the developer, the keynote of a successful project. A variable rate without a limit injects an unknown factor of possible catastrophic magnitude. The interest is typically paid from the construction loan advances. It is doubtful whether a construction lender would ever proceed with a project if any other cost item were so uncertain. As a rule of thumb, approximately half of the full loan amount will be outstanding for the full term of actual construction. * * *

* * * The conditions precedent to settlement on the construction loan that are found in a construction loan agreement provide a good summary of the various items that must be handled by the developer's counsel in preparation for the construction loan settlement.

Construction Related Conditions

The paramount concern of the construction lender is the completion of the facility upon which the loan is predicated. To the construction lender, the facility consists not only of a building such as a single family house, a phase of a condominium project, an apartment house, or a warehouse, but it also includes all onsite and offsite improvements required before the building can be sold or produce its full projected income. The construction lender will seek to assure that the completed for-sale facilities conform with the descriptions of the market survey and the appraisals. Conformity is particularly important to a regulated lender, like a bank, saving and loan association, or insurance company, as the appraisal constitutes the basis on which to establish the required loan to value ratio upon which the loan was based. There is a significant possibility that the loan may experience serious problems if the physical improvements constructed differ significantly from those contemplated by the loan commitment.

Drawings and Specifications

Since the construction lender is looking to a take-out permanent lender to acquire the loan upon the completion of construction, it is essential to the construction lender that the facility be constructed strictly in conformity with the requirements of the permanent loan commitment. The optimum approach is for the construction and permanent loan commitments to describe the improvements to be constructed by reference to the same set of working drawings and specifications approved by all interested parties. As a practical matter, this is often not feasible due to the unavailability at this stage of a full set of working drawings and specifications.

If a complete set of working drawings and specifications is available, the physical description of the project will be given in the loan commitments by reference to these plans and specifications. Otherwise the project will be described in a less detailed manner, usually by reference to the then available preliminary plans, with the proviso that the final plans and specifications must be approved by the permanent lender. In accepting such a commitment by the permanent lender and substantially changing position in reliance upon it, a developer is ever sensitive to the possibility that should the permanent lender become less enthusiastic about the loan, the conditions for approval of final construction documents may become significantly more stringent than anticipated. It is imperative to be ever conscious of a basic fact of life— the developer's bargaining position significantly changes once a permanent commitment has been accepted and a fee paid. It is always best to leave as few items as possible open and subject to later approval.

In contract negotiations, an often used escape for parties that do not wish to face directly the problem of establishing objective standards for later approvals is to provide that the approvals shall "not be unreasonably withheld." Most lenders will strenuously resist any attempt to condition approval in this manner. * * *

Developers will generally seek to postpone incurring the substantial cost of working drawings and complete specifications until they are reasonably certain they have a project—until after a permanent loan commitment has been secured on the basis of site plans, schematic drawings, outline specifications, and perhaps a market survey. Such a commitment naturally will be conditional upon the permanent lender's approval of final working construction documents. The final set of working drawings for a high rise structure may not be completed until after construction has actually commenced. Time pressures arising from such ever present factors as escalating costs and the need of the developer to complete the improvements prior to the lapse of the permanent loan commitment often lead to an early start of construction before all the variables have been finalized—an approach that greatly increases the risk inherent in what is, at best, a very risky business.

* * *

Mechanics' Liens

The commencement of construction prior to the execution of all construction documents presents major problems in those states in which the priority of the lien of the construction mortgage is based upon the "obligatory advance doctrine." Under this doctrine, the lien of a mortgage is established upon each advance of funds as to such advance, not upon the recording of the mortgage, unless the mortgagee is obligated to advance the funds on the basis of the occurrence of circumstances over which it has no independent control. Most obligatory advance states also generally adhere to the "relation back doctrine," pursuant to which a mechanic's lien dates from the commencement of construction on the project even by a contractor or subcontractor other than the one claiming the lien. In those states that apply both doctrines, the lien of the construction mortgagee as to funds advanced after the commencement of construction will have priority over a mechanic's lien only if the construction loan mortgage is recorded prior to the commencement of construction *and* the construction lender is obligated at that time to advance the loan proceeds on the basis of objective criteria that are not subject to his control.

* * *

Progress Payments

The schedule of progress payments may be based upon either designated stages of construction or the percentage of completion by the various construction trades. Under the stages of completion approach, which is the simplest to arrange and is common for smaller or for single family house projects, a specified number of dollars are disbursed at each visible stage of construction.

* * *

Under the percentage completion by trades approach, the general contractor or developer submits a schedule to the construction lender that allocates the entire contemplated hard construction cost—the so-called "brick and mortar costs"—among the various construction trades, such as carpenters, masons, excavators, electricians, plumbers, plasterers, and painters. As construction proceeds, progress payments are disbursed on the basis of the estimated percentage completion of each trade. This approach is customarily employed on larger projects, and its use raises the front-end load problem.

It is vital to the construction lender and, if an unrelated general contractor is used, also to the owner, that the progress payments as construction proceeds do not exceed a predetermined percentage—usually 90 per cent—of the actual cost of construction to that point in time. * * * [T]he undisbursed balance of the retainage, less any "punch-list" reserve, is generally distributed only upon substantial completion.

The construction documents generally provide that a project is substantially complete when the owner can "occupy or utilize the project" or a designated portion thereof "for the use for which it is intended." A variation of this definition which perhaps better protects the owner requires that to be classified as being "substantially completed," a phase of construction or the entire project must be capable of being occupied or utilized for its intended use without substantial diminution in its utility to the occupant. Warranty and guarantee periods generally commence to run from substantial completion.

A building is typically considered to be substantially complete although there are a number of punch-list items to be completed by the contractor. The punch-list consists of items to be completed or corrected after substantial completion. This list is usually prepared by the general contractor and submitted to the architect for approval. Typical punch-list items might include touch-up painting, the installation of some missing door hardware, and the balancing of mechanical systems.

An owner or contractor will often seek to front-end load the trade payment breakdown by allocating a disproportionate part of the cost of completion of the project to the trades that are on construction phases which are completed earlier in the project. The front-end trades include excavators, rough graders, and framers of structures, whether this be rough carpentry in the case of a wood-framed structure, or concrete, structural steel, and, perhaps, masonry, in the case of the multistory high or midrise building. A front-end loaded trade payment breakdown will favor these start-up trades at the expense of the finishing trades, such as painters, plasterers, and installers of hardware, fixtures, and appliances.

One method that construction lenders use against front-end loading is to review the subcontracts covering the major trades and compare the contract price for each subcontract with the trade payment breakdown. Adjustments are often necessary, since a particular construction lender's trade payment schedule will often not parallel the work allocation among the subcontractors on the basis of the subcontracts that were actually written. * * *

The provisions of the construction loan commitment relating to the physical process of construction will vary according to whether the developer will also function as its own general contractor or whether there will be a financially responsible and possibly bonded general contractor who will build the project under a legally binding contract with the developer. If an unrelated general contractor is involved, the construction lender will often require that the general contract itself be assigned to the construction lender, and if a performance bond is required, that the construction lender be made a joint obligee under the bond. The construction loan commitment will provide for the approval by the construction lender of the general contract and, possibly, also of the prime subcontracts, as well as [the construction lender's] acceptance of the performance and payment bonds issued thereunder.

Assignment of Interests

The construction lender will seek to assure that, in the event of a default, either it or, more practically, its nominee will be in a position to step into the shoes of the borrower-developer in order to complete the construction * * *. The construction lender will [obtain] a contractual right in the event of default to succeed to the developer's various project-related rights and assets—including the architectural contract, purchase orders, subcontracts, the building permit, sewer and utility connection authorizations, and leases. * * * Nevertheless, the experience of most construction lenders has been that it is far better under default circumstances to work with the defaulting developer in attempting to complete the project * * * than for the lender to take over the physical construction.

A construction lender providing funds for an investment-type project will invariably require that the permanent loan commitment be assignable to it and actually be so assigned. Many lenders will seek to buttress the assignment with undertakings by the permanent lender running directly to the construction lender. At a minimum, the direct undertakings will acknowledge the validity of the assignment, obligate the permanent lender to provide the construction lender with copies of all notices sent by the permanent lender to the developer, and afford the construction lender an opportunity to cure specified defaults by the developer that might impair the ability of the construction lender to enforce the permanent commitment.

The Buy–Sell Agreement

Under a buy-sell agreement—on occasion referred to as a "tripartite agreement"—the permanent lender agrees that if all conditions precedent to acquisition of the loan are satisfied by a specified date, it will buy the loan from the construction lender at par or at a specified discount. In turn, the construction lender generally agrees that it will not accept prepayment of the loan obligation nor sell the loan to any other permanent lender, and that it will deliver the loan to the permanent lender if all conditions precedent not waived by the permanent lender are satisfied.

* * *

[A] common form of tripartite agreement requires that the construction loan be made in conformity with the construction loan agreement. A breach of that provision might constitute a ground for the permanent lender to refuse to honor its permanent commitment, to the detriment of both the construction lender and the developer. Nevertheless, that provision, in modified form, might perhaps be appropriate in a relation back-obligatory advance mechanics' lien state. In such a jurisdiction, the provision would be intended to protect the permanent lender from the possibility of a mechanics' lien acquiring priority over the mortgage on the basis that the construction lender's advances have been voluntary.

Typically, tripartite agreements will prohibit construction lenders from releasing any part of the security for the loan, accepting prepayment, accelerating maturity, or otherwise assigning or transferring the loan other than to the permanent lender, unless the developer should be in default. * * *

The developer, being the third party to the arrangement, agrees on its part that it will not prepay the obligation, that it will seek to satisfy all the conditions precedent to the sale of the loan by the construction lender to the permanent lender, and that it will execute those documents—in particular, the affidavit of no set-off—which are critical to the assignment of the loan. * * *

The Permanent Loan Commitment

* * *

The Significance of Postsettlement Terms

Although the construction lender is most concerned with the terms of the permanent commitment, once it delivers the loan to the permanent lender, the permanent commitment has served its function. On first impression, therefore, the construction lender should not be concerned with the postsettlement terms of a permanent loan commitment—whether, for instance, the rate of interest the developer will pay the permanent lender is substantially in excess of the market rate, or whether the permanent loan becomes due and payable on demand or within a relatively short time thereafter.

* * * [A]ny knowledgeable construction lender has reason to be concerned with postsettlement terms, for, if the terms of a permanent commitment are too onerous, the developer may, if pushed to the wall, prefer to prevent the assignment of the construction loan to the permanent lender, who would immediately assert its default remedies. A developer will often have reason to believe that it is preferable to be in default to a local bank than to an institution located possibly halfway across the continent.

On the other hand, if there is some form of personal guarantee of the construction loan and no personal liability on the permanent mortgage, the motivation for the developer to complete the assignment of the construction loan and thus be relieved of any personal obligation is obvious. The problem then is that the onerous terms of the permanent loan commitment are symptomatic of the lack of any desire by the permanent lender to acquire the loan. It may seek to avoid honoring the permanent loan commitment on some basis or other. Hence, another reason a construction lender will seek personal guarantees from a developer is to encourage the developer to satisfy the permanent lender's delivery conditions, however harsh they may be.

The Standby Commitment

Permanent loan commitments might be roughly classified as "standby commitments" or "funding commitments." Funding commitments are issued by insurance companies and other institutional lenders that desire to acquire the loan upon the completion of construction. Standby commitments are more traditionally issued by mortgage brokers * * * that do not really want the loan. For a fee, a standby lender provides the construction lender with a commitment that if alternative permanent funding is not secured by a specified date, the standby lender will acquire the loan upon the satisfaction of specific conditions precedent. * * * [M]any construction lenders will not advance construction funds on the basis of standby commitments.

* * *

Gap Standby Commitments

Standby commitments might be characterized either as gap standby commitments or full-value standby commitments. A gap standby commitment is often intended to cover the contingent portion of the permanent commitment—that amount by which the maximum sum to be advanced by the permanent lender in the event of maximum rental achievement exceeds the sum to be advanced without regard to rental achievement. The minimum sum to be paid under the most disadvantageous rental experience is referred to as "the floor" of a permanent commitment, while the spread between the minimum and maximum amount of the commitment is referred to as the "gap."

The conventional practice is for the gap to be covered by the developer's cash deposit with the construction lender. An exceptionally credit-worthy developer might be permitted to cover the gap with a personal guarantee. Other developers may supply a letter of credit from a bank or deposit securities or other collateral with the construction lender. A marginal developer with neither cash, credit, or securities to cover the gap may resort to a commitment from a standby lender to provide a second mortgage for the amount of the differential.

Dependence upon a gap standby commitment is, at best, a dangerous approach for the developer, for it may face a catastrophic exposure in the event projected rental or sales are not achieved. A knowledgeable construction lender will be leery of any standby commitment so onerous as to indicate that the standby lender does not contemplate funding the commitment or that the developer will seek to prevent the construction lender from assigning the loan to a standby lender who may immediately call the loan.

Holdbacks

Commitments for investment type projects often involve holdbacks of all or a portion of the loan proceeds pending satisfaction of completion, occupancy, or rental achievement requirements. On occasion, holdback requirements are absolute in nature, as when the full funding of the permanent commitment is conditioned upon meeting specific conditions. More often, a period of time after the delivery of the loan will be allowed for the satisfaction of the holdback requirements. * * * Since the construction lender is looking to the permanent commitment as its principal payment source, it will generally not disburse funds equal in amount to the contingent portion of the permanent commitment until it is satisfied that all * * * [holdback requirements] have been met.

As with all commitment conditions, a construction lender feels most secure when the permanent lender acknowledges prior to the commencement of construction that a commitment condition has either been satisfied or waived. Thus, a construction lender will seek at the time of the construction loan closing to have the permanent lender waive a condition based on a lease that is already in existence. There is, of course, the possibility that circumstances occurring after the construction loan settlement and prior to permanent loan closing may invalidate or terminate the lease. At issue is whether the construction lender or the permanent lender should bear the risk of changed circumstances, such as the bankruptcy of a major tenant prior to the permanent loan closing or the failure of the developer to satisfy all of the conditions of a major lease. Usually it is the construction lender who assumes substantially all the risks of events prior to the permanent loan closing.

Thus, the manner in which the permanent lender acknowledges the satisfaction of conditions precedent can be quite vital to the construction lender in the event of unanticipated problems arising after the construction loan settlement and before settlement on the permanent loan. The construction lender would prefer that the permanent lender waive conditions rather than acknowledge that certain circumstances constitute a satisfaction of the conditions. The permanent lender, on the other hand, normally feels that the risk of intervening adverse events should be the construction lender's.

* * *

Transfer of Permanent Commitment

A permanent commitment normally will be issued on the basis not only of the facility being built but also the developer who is responsible. On occasion, a permanent commitment will even stipulate that the developer must manage the project for a specified period of time, often for 5 years after the permanent loan closing. Thus, the assignment of the permanent commitment is usually prohibited and often a specified entity is required to own the project at the time of settlement on the permanent commitment.

A construction lender will be [concerned about] any limitations in the permanent commitment upon the transferability of the commitment, the underlying real estate, or the owning entities, since it seeks to fund the commitment with the permanent loan even if it or its nominee takes over the project following a default by the developer. The construction lender will therefore require that the commitment be assignable to it. It will also generally require that[,] in the event of a default, it be permitted to reassign the commitment to any party to whom the real estate is transfer[red]. The permanent lender will generally resist any such right and, in fact, will seek to include "no adverse change" clauses and condition its obligation to close on the permanent loan upon the absence of default on the construction loan.

If the assignment clause permits an assignment to the construction lender but not a reassignment by the construction lender, * * * in the event the developer fails to complete construction, the construction lender will be forced to complete the project itself so as to be able to transfer its loan to the permanent lender. Its decision may be academic since, in the event of a developer default, the time required for the construction lender to exercise its remedies and complete the project will usually exceed the period within which the permanent commitment must be delivered. In most construction-phase project workouts, the developer remains involved in some manner, while the construction lender controls all expenditures and advances the funds to complete the project. As a practical matter, in default situations the construction lender often has to renegotiate the permanent commitment—if it is fortunate enough to have a prospective permanent lender who continues to be interested in the project.

* * *

Default Problems

Construction lenders are becoming increasingly sensitive to the possible use by developers[,] and others with a conflicting interest[,] of the debtor rehabilitation provisions of the Bankruptcy [Code]. So-called "chapter proceedings" are often initiated to prevent a construction lender seeking to limit its losses from taking control of a defaulting project. The developer will often threaten to utilize these procedures in order to extract from the construction lender concessions in the form of releases from personal liability, cash payments for equity positions of little value, or agreements not to proceed against posted collateral security or under or against performance bonds or third party guarantees. To reduce their exposure to demands in the event of trouble, construction lenders will often require assignments absolute on their face of all the various rights held by the developer.

A developer is much more likely to subject a corporation he controls to a debtor rehabilitation proceeding than to subject himself. If the lender can foreclose against the stock of the corporation, the developer has little motivation to seek relief on behalf of the corporation. The only relief that would be of value would be a stay of execution against the assets of the developer—i.e., the stock of the corporation—and such a stay would generally be available in the context of a chapter proceeding only if the holder of the stock, and not the corporation itself, were subject to the protection of the bankruptcy court.

Lenders will on occasion require hypothecation of the stock or other evidence of ownership of the entity owning the real estate so as to avoid the necessity of real estate foreclosure proceedings. It is usually more expeditious to proceed under the Uniform Commercial Code against personalty such as stock than to foreclose against real estate. In subjecting the stock to a lien in its favor, the construction lender should be sure that the corporation is more than a mere nominee titleholder, with the real ownership in the developer or some other entity such as a limited partnership. The construction lender will also secure an assignment of all development rights, like building permits and authorizations by governmental authorities, franchises, in the case of hotels and restaurants, leases, and all construction related documents, such as architectural and engineering agreements, the general contract purchase orders, and subcontracts.

Furthermore, many construction lenders require that all subcontractors agree that in the event of a default by the developer under the construction loan, they will complete the work for the unpaid balance due in the subcontracts if requested by the construction lender, and that these undertakings be assignable, subject only to the obligation of the construction lender to pay for work done and materials supplied *after* it takes over the project.

Th[e] provision that third parties acknowledge rights in the construction lender may lead to negotiations between the construction lender and the third parties. The general contractor, for instance, often has no choice but to look to the construction loan as its sole source of payment. Hence, it may seek some assurances from the construction lender that in the event the construction lender * * * take[s] over the job in a default situation, the construction lender will make all payments to which the general contractor is entitled. Most construction lenders will resist such an obligation. A possible alternative for the construction lender is to agree that if it avails itself of the general contractor after taking over the project, it will pay both for work prior to, as well as following, its assumption of the project. * * *

[If] the general contractor [knows] that the owner has no significant resources other than the funds from the construction loan, the general contractor often will enter into a contract only if the construction lender agrees that in the event the lender takes over the project and proceeds to complete construction, the general contractor will be employed by the construction lender to finish the work. * * *

NOTE

1. Why is the construction lender concerned about changes during construction in the approved plans and specifications? Might the construction lender be faced with serious problems if the following occurred?

a. The subordination agreement, executed by the party providing the land acquisition financing, limits the use of the proceeds of the subordinating loan to construction in accordance with the approved plans and specifications, see pages 637 to 645 supra, and the subordinating party does not consent to a change.

b. The take-out commitment is conditioned on completion of the development in accordance with the approved plans and specifications and the permanent lender does not consent to a change.

c. A change in the approved plans and specifications leads to an increase in costs not covered by the amount of the permanent take-out plus the amount of the developer's investment. In this situation can the construction lender be required, as a practical matter, to make an illegal loan—a second or third mortgage—for the amount of the increase in costs?

d. See generally Wilner, *The Engineer's Role on the Construction Loan Team,* 4 # 4 Real Est.Rev. 109 (1975).

2. Why does the construction lender want the developer and permanent lender to agree on the form of the permanent lender's note and mortgage prior to closing the construction loan?

a. If the construction lender's note and mortgage are in a form acceptable to the permanent lender, the take-out by the permanent lender is simplified, see pages 682 to 689 infra.

b. If the take-out commitment is a tripartite buy-sell agreement, the note and mortgage which the permanent lender buys from the construction lender must be acceptable to the permanent lender and the borrower as well as to the construction lender.

3. Is a construction lender unreasonable in insisting on its own policy of title insurance and on its own inspection of construction progress?

a. There is the possibility that the construction lender might end up with the long term financing or the title to the development if something goes wrong.

1. Is the cost of title insurance increased if the title insurance company issues a binder to the construction lender, increases the amount of the binder on each draw under the construction loan, the binder and policy are in a form acceptable to the permanent lender, and the binder is assigned to the permanent lender at the time of take-out? The actual policy is then issued to the permanent lender.

b. Problems with respect to a subordination or take-out commitment can be caused by a deviation from the approved plans and specifications which is not consented to, or a diversion of loan proceeds from the purposes of construction.

1. Trusting your borrower is one thing, being foolhardy is another.

c. See generally Urban, *Future Advances and Title Insurance Coverage,* 15 Wake Forest L.Rev. 329 (1979); Maller, *The Priority Problem in Mortgages for Future Advances,* 14 Real Est.L.J. 360 (1986).

4. If the borrower is a limited partnership, is it important that no partner bear the economic risk of loss for the construction loan in order that the limited partners can each add a share, based on each one's share of profits, of the construction loan to each limited partner's basis in his or her partnership interest? See Reg.Sec. 1.752–1T(e).

a. Since there is usually no cash flow available for distribution to the partners during construction, the increase in basis might be desired so that the limited partners can personally deduct losses, incurred during the construction period, in excess of the actual cost of their partnership interests.

b. If a construction loan is nonrecourse but the general partner has guaranteed completion of the construction, is there an absence of economic risk of loss on the part of all partners, so that the provisions of Reg.Sec. 1.752–1T(e) can be relied on?

c. If the permanent loan is a nonrecourse loan, is there any income tax need for the construction loan to also be nonrecourse?

1. Considering the required capitalization and amortization of prepaid interest and points, preopening expenses, and construction period interest and taxes, is there a significant chance that the limited

partners' shares of the construction period losses of the partnership will exceed the actual costs of their partnership interests? See Sections 461(g), 195, and 263A.

5. With respect to the considerations involved in drafting a loan commitment, see Debusk, *Some Considerations in Drafting Mortgage Loan Commitments,* 8 Law Notes 15 (Oct.1971), published by the American Bar Association Sections of General Practice and Young Lawyers. See generally Albright, *Processing the Construction Mortgage,* 3 # 3 Real Est.Rev. 72 (1973); Ridloff, *A Sample Construction Loan Commitment,* 10 # 4 Real Est.Rev. 87 (1981).

6. Why is a construction loan agreement needed in addition to the construction loan commitment and the mortgage? Cannot the matters covered in the loan agreement be adequately covered in the commitment and/or the mortgage? See generally Nellis, *A Construction Loan Agreement,* 1 # 4 Prac. Real Est.Law. 65 (1985).

7. What is the meaning of the provision in the commitment and loan agreement that the construction loan will be opened only after the building is "under roof"?

   a. Does it mean that no advance of the proceeds of the construction loan will be made until the roof is on the building? That may be a long time in a twenty floor office building.

8. If a construction loan is made at the maximum permitted interest rate under a state's usury law, will charging interest on the total amount of the loan, rather than just amounts advanced, make the loan usurious? See pages 795 to 803 infra.

9. If the subordination agreement executed by the party providing the financing for the land acquisition limits the use of the proceeds of the subordinating loan to construction in accordance with the approved plans and specifications, can the construction lender pay the interest, service charges, title expense, costs of credit reports, taxes and insurance premiums out of the construction loan proceeds?

   a. Even if the lender can avoid problems with subordinating parties, is the payment of commitment and service fees, interest, etc., out of the construction loan proceeds a good idea for income tax purposes?

      1. Might the Internal Revenue Service take the position that this procedure is the equivalent of the construction lender making a discounted loan, and even if the item or items paid would have been currently deductible if paid or accrued by the borrower, the borrower must amortize or ratably deduct the amount of the item over the term of the permanent loan, assuming a buy-sell agreement, since that is when the borrower actually pays the construction loan interest, etc. See e.g. Rev.Rul. 75–12, 1975–1 C.B. 62; *Sanford Campbell,* 29 CCH Tax Ct.Mem. 539 (1970); *Kenneth A. Cathcart,* 36 CCH Tax Ct.Mem. 1321 (1977); *John B. Howard,* 36 CCH Tax Ct.Mem. 1140 (1977); *G. Douglas Burck,* 63 T.C. 556 (1975), affirmed, 533 F.2d 768 (2d Cir.1976); *Alan A. Rubnitz,* 67 T.C. 621 (1977); page 870 infra.

      2. On the other hand, is the borrower really giving up that much in current deductions? To the extent the items are regarded as costs of acquiring the construction loan, for example, service fees, credit reports and title insurance premiums, they would have to be amortized over the term of the construction loan and, if the permanent lender

acquired the construction loan, possibly over the term of the permanent loan, even if the borrower paid these expenses from other funds. In addition, Section 263A requires that a borrower capitalize the construction period interest and taxes into the basis of the improvements constructed and recover these expenses through depreciating the improvements. Lastly, if the expenses amounted to preopening costs, Section 195 requires their capitalization and amortization. The period of amortization, however, is five years from the commencement of trade or business and the permanent loan will certainly have a term longer than five years.

    3.   The choice between having these costs paid out of the proceeds of the construction loan or using other funds to pay them probably will turn on the value to the borrower of any current deductions which might be taken or shorter amortization periods as opposed to the value of not having to use other funds to pay these items.

    10.   Considering the control which the construction lender usually exercises over the payments to contractors, subcontractors, etc., should it be concerned if a contractor or a subcontractor, to its knowledge, is not paying social security taxes on, or is using for other purposes the income taxes and social security taxes withheld from, the wages of the contractor's or subcontractor's employees? See Section 3505 of the Internal Revenue Code. Can the construction lender be considered a "person" required to collect and pay over the taxes and, as a result, be subject to the 100% penalty provisions of Sections 6671 and 6672 of the Internal Revenue Code? Cf. *United States v. Park Cities Bank & Trust Co.,* 30 A.F.T.R.2d 72–5370 (D.Tex.1972), affirmed in part, reversed in part, 481 F.2d 738 (5th Cir.1973); *United States v. First National Bank of Circle,* 37 A.F.T.R.2d 76–974 (D.Mont.1976), reversed mem., 556 F.2d 589 (9th Cir.1977), on remand, 44 A.F.T.R.2d 79–5860 (D.Mont.1979), reversed and remanded, 652 F.2d 882 (9th Cir.1981); *United States v. Coconut Grove Bank,* 545 F.2d 502 (5th Cir.1977); *Fidelity Bank N.A. v. United States,* 616 F.2d 1181 (10th Cir.1980); *Commonwealth National Bank of Dallas v. United States,* 665 F.2d 743 (5th Cir.1982); *Jersey Shore State Bank v. United States,* 479 U.S. 442, 107 S.Ct. 782, 93 L.Ed.2d 800 (1987). See generally Thannhauser, Riemer, and Friedman, *Lender's Liability for Unpaid Withholding Taxes of Borrower—Employer—I.R.C. Sections 3505 and 6672,* 80 Com.L.J. 137 (1975); Weinstein, *Incurring Tax Liability by Lending Money,* 92 Banking L.J. 763 (1975); Note, *Exercise of Only "Significant" Control over Debtor's Operations Subjects Lender to 100 Percent Withholding Tax Penalty,* 43 Fordham L.Rev. 898 (1975); Note, *Lender Liability Under I.R.C. § 3505(a),* 39 Okla.L.Rev. 348 (1986); Cozort, *Lender Liability for Borrower's Withholding Tax,* 20 U.C.C.L.J. 354 (1988).

    11.   See generally Jensen, *The Perils of Construction Lending: The Investor's Risk,* 1977 F. Nat'l Mort. Ass'n Gen. Counsel's Conf. 95; Tockarshewsky, *Reducing The Risks in Construction Lending,* 7 # 1 Real Est.Rev. 59 (1977); Hall, *How to Build Lender Protection Into Construction Loan Agreements,* 6 Real Est. L.J. 21 (1977); Ridloff, *Smoothing Out The Mechanics of Construction Loan Advances,* 10 # 1 Real Est.Rev. 83 (1980); Ridloff, *A Checklist for the Construction Lender's Attorney,* 11 # 4 Real Est.Rev. 103 (1982); Reitz, *Construction Lenders' Liability to Contractors, Subcontractors, and Materialmen,* 130 U.Pa.L.Rev. 416 (1981); Hoops, *Tax Problems of Development and Construction,* 44 N.Y.U. Inst.Fed.Tax'n 18–1 (1986).

    12.   Much of the emphasis in construction lending is focused in two areas. First, there is concern with avoiding liens which may arise during the construc-

tion period and achieve priority over the lien of the construction lender or attach to the undisbursed proceeds of the construction loan, such as mechanics' liens. Second, the construction lender must make sure that the terms of the permanent lender's take-out commitment are complied with.

(i) CONSTRUCTION LENDING AND THE MECHANICS' LIEN

One of the primary concerns of a construction lender is that the lien of the construction mortgage have first priority with respect to the mortgaged real estate. In addition, the construction lender anticipates using the undisbursed proceeds of the construction loan for construction. As a result, a construction lender wants to avoid liens arising during the course of construction which will have priority over the construction lender's lien or attach to undisbursed loan proceeds.

AN OVERVIEW OF MECHANICS' LIENS AND FUTURE ADVANCE MORTGAGES

Harold E. Leidner
3 # 3 Practical Real Estate Lawyer 39 (May 1987)

* * *

WHAT IS A MECHANICS' LIEN?

Every person who does work or labor on, or furnishes machinery, material or fuel for, construction or improvements by virtue of a contract—oral or written—with the owner, part owner or lessee of real property has a right to a lien on the property so improved to the extent of the interest of the owner, part owner, or lessee in the property.

Every person who as a subcontractor, laborer, or materialman performs any labor or furnishes machinery, material, or fuel to a contractor, or any subcontractor, in carrying forward, performing or completing such contract has a right to a lien on the property so improved to the extent of the interest of the owner, part owner, or lessee in the property.

Defining Terms

Before reviewing the operation and intricacies of mechanics' liens, some basic terms should be defined.

Owner

In most jurisdictions "owner," "part owner," or "lessee" normally include all legal or equitable interests that such a person may have in the real estate on which the improvements are made, and include interests held under contracts of purchase (such as land contracts or purchase agreements), whether written or otherwise.

* * *

Contractor

The contractor is one who undertakes to construct, alter, erect, improve, repair, remove, dig, or drill any part of any structures or improvements under a contract directly with the owner. Mechanics' lien statutes seldom make reference to a "general contractor," but may use the term "original contractor" or just "contractor."   *   *   *

Subcontractor

A subcontractor is one who undertakes to construct, alter, erect, improve, repair, remove, dig or drill any part of any structures or improvements under a contract with any person other than the owner.

Materialman

A materialman is a person who furnishes any machinery, materials, or fuel in (or for) any construction, erection, alteration, repair, or removal of improvements to property. However, one who installs materials in addition to furnishing them is not usually deemed a materialman, but will be deemed a subcontractor.

Laborer

A mechanic, workman, artisan, or laborer who is neither a contractor or subcontractor, but who is employed in or about the improvement work is a laborer.

Mortgagee

A mortgagee is any person who enters into an agreement to provide financing for improvements to the property. The financing is secured by a mortgage on the real estate upon which the improvements are contemplated by the contract between the owner and contractor(s) *   *   *. The mortgagee also makes direct disbursements under an instrument of security with the owner for the financing to the owner or a contractor.

Preferences and Priorities

The statutes and cases in most jurisdictions provide that all mechanics' liens relating to any particular project are effective from the date the first labor is performed by any contractor under his contract with the owner, and continue as to each claimant for a specified period following the time each claimant files his lien affidavit or claim with the appropriate public recorder or authority.

Usually if several mechanics' liens are obtained by several persons upon the same project, they have no priority among themselves so that all mechanics' liens arising from the same project will have equal priority as against each other, regardless of:

When the lien claims are filed;

When the work is started or completed; or

Whether they arise under one or several contracts.

All of the mechanics' liens usually have preference over all other titles, mortgages, judgment liens, or other encumbrances that may attach after the date that any single item of labor or material has been furnished to a project by any party, regardless of when a person may perfect his lien by filing his lien claim.

Mechanics' liens, however, usually do not override or have priority over valid liens, mortgages and other encumbrances already in existence or perfected at the time of the accrual of the mechanics' liens.

ISSUES OF PRIORITY

Assume the following general factual setting. A mortgagee has agreed to pay out loan proceeds to an owner for construction of improvements to a property as the various stages of construction are reached. The mortgage is recorded [and the construction loan agreement filed] prior to the commencement of any construction of improvements to the property. Funds advanced under the mortgage are in fact used to construct the improvements. Then, liens of unpaid contractors, subcontractors, and materialmen are perfected against the property subsequent to the recording of the mortgage but prior to the time when all advances to be made under the mortgage have actually been paid. Who prevails?

General Principles

Mortgagees are often given broad priority protections over mechanics' liens by statutes or case decisions when all or a part of the consideration will be advanced by the mortgagee at one time or at times subsequent to the execution and recording of the mortgage. These mortgages are usually referred to as "future advance mortgages," "construction mortgages," "installment mortgages," or "open-end mortgages."

While statutes and case law in different jurisdictions may set up varying requirements with respect to the formalities of future advance mortgages, the general rule applied in most jurisdictions in determining priority relates to the issue of optional versus obligatory advances by a mortgagee. This rule and its corollaries essentially are as follows:

When a mortgagee is under a legal obligation to make further or future advances by reason of his agreement with his mortgagor, such advances are entitled to priority over intervening mechanics' liens if the mortgage is recorded [and, in many states, the construction loan agreement filed] before the mechanics' liens attach, despite the fact that the lien attaches to the property prior to the making of future advances by the mortgagee.

When a mortgagee is under no legal duty to make subsequent advances, a mechanics' lien attaching to the property after the recording of the mortgage will have priority over the amounts of any subsequent advances made under the mortgage.

Recovery under the mortgage will in all events be limited to the amounts actually advanced and not to the total sum secured by the mortgage.

Are Advances Optional or Obligatory?

Although the issue of what constitutes an obligatory as opposed to an optional advance is far from clear, certain patterns can be found in various cases indicating the conditions that will cause advances under the mortgage to be deemed obligatory and not optional:

Advancement of funds conditioned upon the owner reaching various predetermined stages of construction;

Advancement of funds conditioned upon the owner complying with formal statutory requirements;

Advancement of funds conditioned upon the owner complying with building codes;

Advancement of funds conditioned upon the owner complying with covenants in the loan agreement and mortgage;

Advancement of funds conditioned upon the owner using advances solely for constructing improvements; and

Advancement of funds conditioned upon the owner securing and delivering paid receipts and affidavits from contractors.

Similarly the following conditions have caused courts to find advances under the mortgage to be optional and not obligatory:

Advancement of funds conditioned upon mortgagee's subjective satisfaction as to the progress of constructing the improvements;

Advancement of funds by the mortgagee to complete construction of improvements after the mortgagor has abandoned work on the improvements;

Advancement of funds by the mortgagee for purposes other than construction of improvements.

In most jurisdictions, absent special statutory treatment, * * * all mechanics' liens will be given priority over all advances made under [a] mortgage [recorded subsequent to the commencement of construction]. This is commonly referred to as the "early start" situation. Since the mechanics' lien laws of most jurisdictions state that all liens relate back to the first work done by any contractor, all liens will be deemed to have priority over the mortgage and all advances made pursuant to the mortgage.

Statutes and case law vary widely among jurisdictions with respect to advances made by a mortgagee after notice to the mortgagee of the filing of a mechanics' lien. In most jurisdictions the knowledge or notice is immaterial provided that the mortgage has been recorded prior to the commencement of construction and provided that the mortgagee is obligated to make future advances, although differentiations may be made between actual and constructive notice to the mortgagee.

In some jurisdictions statutes will set forth procedures and requirements to be followed by a mortgagee to retain his priority, such as payment of or segregation of funds—to be held in a form of trust or otherwise—necessary to satisfy such intervening liens. In other jurisdictions case law has held that if, under the mortgagee's agreement with the owner, it is optional with the mortgagee as to whether a further advance is to be made after the attachment of a mechanics' lien, and the mortgagee nevertheless makes additional advances, the mechanics' lien will have priority over the mortgage to the extent of the later advance.

Common Law Rule

The basic common law rule in most jurisdictions in the absence of governing statutes. * * * is [that] "if the advance is obligatory, it takes its priority from the date of the original mortgage, and the subsequent creditor is junior to it. However, if the advance is optional, and if the mortgagee has notice when the advance is made that a subsequent creditor has acquired an interest in the land, then the advance loses its priority with respect to that creditor." [Osborne, Nelson and Whitman, *Real Estate Finance Law* (1979), at 759.]

STATUTORY TREATMENT OF PRIORITY RULES

A significant number of jurisdictions have enacted statutes that simply provide for the priority of "future advances" under a mortgage over intervening liens. * * * [Some states' statutes] treat optional advances the same as obligatory advances. [A number of states' statutes] provide that an intervening lien will have priority over optional future advances by a mortgagee if the mortgagee has *actual* notice of the lien.

[A few states' statutes] provide that an intervening lien will have priority over optional future advances if the mortgagee has *constructive* notice of the lien.

Furthermore, most statutes require the mortgage document to impose formal requirements necessary to create protection for future advances, the most common of which are:

Special captions or headings for the mortgage;

Special language within the mortgage permitting future advances;

Time limitations within which secured future advances can be made; and

Maximum amounts to be secured by the mortgage.

In any event, prior to granting a future advance loan and mortgage, a mortgagee should determine the statutory and case law requirements of the particular jurisdiction where the property is located with respect to the following:

Is protection of priority of future advances afforded to a mortgagee under statute or case law?

Is protection afforded only to obligatory advances or to optional advances as well?

If protection is afforded only to obligatory advances, how have statutes or cases defined what is an obligatory or optional advance?

Will actual or constructive notice of an intervening lien cause a loss of priority with respect to advances made after receipt of the notice?

Does the mortgage instrument meet all formality requirements to secure the afforded priority protections?

TITLE INSURANCE CONSIDERATIONS * * *

Most title companies will offer endorsements * * * affirmatively insuring the validity, enforceability, and priority of the insured mortgage as security for future advances. Exceptions to coverage will be taken for:

Future advances made after the filing of bankruptcy by the mortgagor;

Assessments, taxes, or federal tax liens;

Divestment of title in the mortgagor to the insured premises;

A default under the terms of the insured mortgage; and

Loss of priority of future advance made after the mortgagee has actual or, as appropriate, constructive knowledge of the existence of liens, encumbrances, or other matters affecting the insured premises intervening between the date of the policy and that future advance.

Furthermore, coverage will be modified depending on the applicable law of the jurisdiction with respect to the obligatory or optional nature of the future advance and the treatment of priorities.

Seldom will a title company insure the priority of the mortgage over any mechanics' liens if work has commenced on improvements prior to the recording of the mortgage, unless elaborate escrow procedures are set up with the title company to handle payments to the contractors and to monitor closely any lien filings.

Title companies may still insist on "taking down" and "continuing" title to the property to the date of each future advance to insure that no liens have intervened, especially when the statutes or other laws of the jurisdiction protect priority only when the mortgagee is obligated to make future advances.

MORTGAGEE'S DUTIES

With respect to future advance mortgages, the following * * * should be required[:] * * *

An accurate survey;

Approval by the mortgagee of plans and specifications of the project; * * *

Approval by the mortgagee of all contracts that * * * contain the scope of contractor's work; schedules of completion; the agreed payment for work, change orders and values assigned to changes; requirements of and standards for proper performance by contractor; supervisory authority over the contractor; insurance and payment and performance bond requirements; rights of the contractor to employ subcontractors; approval of subcontractors and subcontracts by the owner; remedies upon breach; rights of parties to terminate and rights and obligations upon termination; draw procedures, progress payments and holdbacks; and agreements and obligations of contractor with respect to mechanics' liens[; and]

[D]raw procedures should be established so that no progress payments will be made to the contractor unless the work to date has been performed properly and all necessary lien certificates, waivers, and releases provided for under applicable lien statutes have been delivered to the owner and mortgagee with the periodic draw request. The draw procedures should also include:

Formal and timely requests to be made on specified forms;

Inspection and certification of work by the architect;

Provision of updated survey if deemed necessary; and

Update of title through the draw period.

DEFENSES AGAINST MECHANICS' LIENS

The requirements for perfecting a mechanics' lien vary considerably by jurisdiction. The statutes of some jurisdictions require little documentation to perfect a mechanics' lien while other jurisdictions require extensive documentation and strict compliance by a lien claimant with the statutory requirements. With such a wide variety of requirements, appropriate defenses depend on the jurisdiction.

If a lien has obtained priority over a mortgage, numerous defenses may yet be available to the mortgagor and the mortgagee to defeat the lien. The rights to mechanics' liens are given by statute and are in derogation of the common law. As such, strict compliance by the lien claimant with all statutory prerequisites is usually required, although many statutes mandate only a substantial compliance. The following are examples of certain defense categories.

Defects

* * *

Time Limit

All statutes set a time limit within which a lien affidavit or other form of claim must be filed. If the time limit is not complied with, the lien may be declared invalid.

Form of Lien Affidavit

Most jurisdictions require strict compliance with formal statutory requirements relating to content and completeness of the lien affidavit or claim form and/or supporting affidavits, certificates and ancillary documents, service of proper parties, attestation, signing, and recording. Many jurisdictions have varying requirements for contractors, subcontractors, materialmen and laborers with respect to lien perfection requirements. Therefore, understanding the "category" of each claimant can become significant in any defense. A defect with respect to one or more of the elements usually cannot be amended or revised at a later time, and the lien may be declared invalid by reason of any defect.

Improper Performance

If standards were established by contract with which the lien claimant was required to comply and these standards were not met, the lien may totally fail or at least the claimant may be entitled to less money than claimed.

* * *

Insufficient Interest of Contracting Party

A construction contract for leasehold improvements with a tenant in most states will not give rise to a lien on the fee interest of the owner. The same principle prohibits a lien on the owner's fee interest when the contracting party is the vendee under a land contract. The lien usually may attach only to the interest of the party entering into the contract with the general contractor, although some jurisdictions may permit a lien on the owner's fee interest under a theory of unjust enrichment. If the mortgage is on the owner's fee interest, it would be unaffected by a mechanics' lien on a lesser estate, absent a merger of estates.

* * *

NOTE

1. At times, when it is clear that the mortgage of the construction lender has priority over mechanics' liens, "the materialmen's only hope for payment is the construction money still held by the lender.

"Priority to these funds is awarded [in some states under a] stop notice statute to an unpaid materialman, if he has filed a bonded stop notice with the holder of the construction fund to enjoin further disbursements. But materialmen probably for lack of knowledge have been slow to avail themselves of this right. They have, instead, petitioned the ＊ ＊ ＊ courts for priority to undisbursed funds, and the courts have granted them an equitable lien.

"The courts' rationale for the use of the equitable lien doctrine could be that construction lenders are at fault when construction money is misspent, or at least that they are more culpable than materialmen. ＊ ＊ ＊

"It is also possible that the ＊ ＊ ＊ courts are employing a better, if more subtle, rationale for their equitable lien doctrine awarding the undisbursed funds ＊ ＊ ＊ to the materialmen. They may be using an 'allocation of resources' concept. ＊ ＊ ＊

"Efficiency ＊ ＊ ＊ requires that liability be placed on the party best able to assess costs and prevent or insure against loss. The 'allocation of resources' rationale is therefore appropriate when one of the litigants is demonstrably superior to the other at assessing, insuring, or preventing. The more equal the parties become in these respects the less appropriate the rationale.

＊ ＊ ＊

[Lastly, the courts have used the doctrine of equitable estoppel based on the materialmen's reliance on the funds available under the construction loan to award materialmen an equitable lien on undisbursed construction funds.]

＊ ＊ ＊

"The doctrine ＊ ＊ ＊ is founded, ＊ ＊ ＊ on two assumptions about construction lending: first, speculative construction should be policed; second, construction lenders have reasonable means at hand to prevent the defalcations which sometimes result. ＊ ＊ ＊ "

Lefcoe and Schaffer, *Construction Lending and the Equitable Lien,* 40 S.Cal.L.Rev. 439, 441–446 (1967).

2. It has been suggested that construction lenders could use bonding or a voucher system to protect themselves from mechanics' liens and equitable liens on undisbursed construction loan proceeds.

    a. "*Bonding.* Lenders could require of the borrower or general contractor a bonded guarantee for the amount of the construction loan which assures performance (a structure completed according to plans and specifications), or a bond assuring payment of all materialmen and mechanics. ＊ ＊ ＊ " Lefcoe and Schaffer, supra, at 449.

    b. "*Vouchers.* The second preventive technique is the voucher system, under which payment is due only after receipt of a bill for services rendered. Its administration demands more bookkeeping and inspection than the progress payment method. While the typical progress payment arrangement calls for payments to be made at five stages requiring five on-site inspections, lenders using a voucher system inspect weekly to avoid paying on vouchers except for completed work." Lefcoe and Schaffer, supra, at 451.

＊ ＊ ＊

3. From the construction lender's standpoint, does bonding, if possible, provide an answer to the problems presented by mechanics' liens?

    a. A performance bond may assure completion, but does it assure that subcontractors, materialmen, and laborers will be paid? See pages 989 to 990 infra.

    b. A labor and material bond may assure payment. If, however, the mechanics and materialmen are entitled to a prior lien on land and improvements and, possibly, an equitable lien on undisbursed construction loan proceeds, cannot the bonding company, when it makes payment, claim that it can enforce the rights of the payees through subrogation?

c. See Comment, *Mechanics Liens and Surety Bonds in the Building Trades,* 68 Yale L.J. 138 (1958); Dwyer, *New Protection for Construction Lenders,* 3 # 3 Real Est.Rev. 76 (1973); Milana, *The Performance Bond and the Underlying Contract: The Bond Obligations Do Not Include All of the Contract Obligations,* 12 Forum 187 (1976).

4. Using a voucher system will reduce the risk to the construction lender, but unless the lender pays directly to the subcontractors, the materialmen, and even the laborers, there is still some risk present.

a. How far should the lender go? When do the costs of processing a construction loan make the loan or, for that matter, the entire development uneconomic? At what point is the risk of loss less than the cost to prevent it?

1. Is there a substitute for honesty?

5. In many states, the lien of the construction lender is prior to mechanics' liens if the construction mortgage is recorded and the loan agreement filed prior to the start of construction. In general, obligatory subsequent advances pursuant to the construction mortgage and loan agreement, even if made after a mechanics' lien has attached to the property, have the priority of the construction mortgage since the advances relate back to the recording of the mortgage. In many states, however, if one mechanic's lien gains priority over the construction mortgage, all mechanics' liens are given that priority. See e.g. *Valley Fed. Sav. & Loan Ass'n v. T–Bird Home Centers, Inc.,* 106 N.M. 223, 741 P.2d 826 (1987).

In the typical situation, the construction loan agreement and/or the mortgage will contain provisions permitting the lender to withhold advances in certain events such as the failure of the borrower to perform an obligation imposed on the borrower by the construction loan documents. Even in the event of a default by the borrower, the lender, in some situations, may deem it in its best interest to have the borrower complete construction. If a default by the borrower which gives the construction lender the right to withhold future advances is followed by the attachment of mechanics' liens and a determination by the lender to have the borrower complete construction, is the amount of the advances made by the construction lender after the borrower's default entitled to priority over the mechanics' liens? See Kratovil and Werner, *Mortgages for Construction and the Lien Priorities Problem—the "Unobligatory" Advance,* 41 Tenn.L.Rev. 311 (1974); Skipworth, *Should Construction Lenders Lose Out on Voluntary Advances If a Loan Turns Sour?,* 5 Real Est. L.J. 221 (1977). The Uniform Land Transactions Act provides that sums advanced by a construction lender to complete a structure which is part of the lender's security are secured by the real estate even if such advances, when added to other advances, exceed the maximum amount stated in the mortgage. See Section 3–205(e). In addition, a construction mortgage takes priority as of the date of its recording as to advances by the lender to enable completion of the agreed improvement, whether or not the advances exceed the maximum amount stated in the mortgage or the construction lender has knowledge of an intervening interest. See Section 3–301(b). Consider, however, whether the priority granted the construction lender by Section 3–301(b) applies when the intervening lien is a mechanic's lien. See Section 3–104(3), which provides that Article 3 does not apply to nonconsensual liens such as mechanics' liens. See generally Kuklin,

Uniform Land Transactions Act: Article 3, 11 Real Prop., Prob. & Tr. J. 12 (1976); Comment, *Future Advances Under the ULTA and USLTA: The Construction Lender Receives a New Status,* 34 Wash. & Lee L. Rev. 1027 (1977).

6. See generally Quinlan, *Mechanics' Liens,* 5 # 3 Real Est. Rev. 20 (1975); Smith and Cobbe, *Questions of Priority Between Mechanics' Lienors and Construction Loan Mortgagees,* 38 Ohio St. L.J. 3 (1977); Urban and Miles, *Mechanics' Liens for the Improvement of Real Property: Recent Developments in Perfection, Enforcement, and Priority,* 12 Wake Forest L. Rev. 283 (1976); Comment, *Mechanic's Liens—Priority Over Mortgages and Deeds of Trust,* 42 Mo.L.Rev. 53 (1977); Elkins, *Rights of Subcontractors, Laborers, and Materialmen to Contract Balances,* 18 Forum 695 (1983); Jones and Messall, *Mechanic's Lien Title Insurance Coverage for Construction Projects: Lenders and Insurers Beware,* 16 Real Est. L.J. 291 (1988).

(ii) THE TAKE–OUT COMMITMENT

In the usual situation the construction lender does not intend to become the long-term or "permanent" financier of a project. Therefore, the availability and enforceability of the take-out commitment from the permanent lender is a matter of substantial concern to the construction lender. If the construction lender is not prepared to lend without an available and enforceable take-out commitment, construction may be delayed until such a commitment is obtained by the developer.

PROCEDURES, FORMS AND SAFEGUARDS IN CONSTRUCTION LENDING WITH A PERMANENT TAKEOUT

Robert H. Haggerty
85 Banking Journal 1035 (1968).
[footnotes omitted]

What is a takeout? When a savings bank or other long-term lending institution (hereinafter collectively termed the "permanent") gives a commitment for a long-term mortgage loan, that commitment, in the view of the commercial banks which will finance the construction, is the takeout—the source of repayment of the [construction] loan.

* * *

Although it falls short of the assurance of security in its true sense, the takeout is, nevertheless, a significant feature of the construction lending process. * * * If nothing else, [the takeout] serves as some confirmation of the validity of the borrower's conception of his project, some endorsement of the supposed justification for the loan. However, since it does not behave like security, there is no justification for abridging normal loan underwriting procedures just because there is a takeout. The construction lender can never permit the existence of a takeout to be a substitute for the independent exercise of his own lending judgment.

In addition to the significance of the takeout to the borrower as giving him greater practical leverage in procuring his construction loan, the takeout, depending on its terms, may give the construction lender, which is a national bank[,] * * * some flexibility [with respect to the loan].

The [regulations of the Comptroller of the Currency issued under the] section of the Federal Reserve Act which permits national banks to make real estate loans provide that loans made to finance the construction of [a building or] buildings and which mature in [not more than 60] months are not considered real estate loans if there is a "valid and binding agreement" from a "financially responsible lender" to pay off the loan *"upon completion of the buildings."* [12 C.F.R. Sec. 34.3(f)].

* * *

How "binding" must the takeout commitment be? What conditions on the enforceability of the takeout would be regarded as so restrictive that a construction loan would no longer be outside the real estate loan limits? * * *

It is believed that * * * conditions, which are usually found in takeout commitments, would probably not disqualify them for the purposes of the [regulatory] exemption. This is because these conditions pose no greater risk than the condition of completion which the [regulations] explicitly contemplate. * * *

The first step in any program designed to protect the takeout is to analyze the conditions of the takeout. For this purpose the conditions of the takeout should be divided into two categories: (i) those which can be satisfied at the time of the construction loan closing, or, whether or not they can be satisfied at the time, are nevertheless subject to the control of the construction lender and its team; (ii) those which are completely beyond the control of the construction lender. * * *

Counsel must * * * bear in mind that the permanent should be one which is authorized to make the loan in the state in which the property is located, and it is authorized to make the loan in the form proposed. * * *

One other word of caution: you must be sure that the person or entity to whom you are making the [construction] loan is one which is entitled to the permanent mortgage. A takeout addressed to an individual can only be satisfied by loan documents executed by that individual, yet real estate transactions are commonly consummated by special purpose corporations.

Although it is the second category of conditions which are a construction lender's major source of concern, * * * the matter of title and survey [should be briefly mentioned]. * * * [T]he mailing frank of a mid-western title company [appropriately] says, "title is vital." Obviously, all easements and restrictive covenants must be carefully scrutinized. * * *

In the event that the construction being financed is a part of a larger project, it is essential that there be in existence cross-easement agreements which will assure that the project will always be maintained as an integrated unit, and that a mortgage[e] in possession or a purchaser at foreclosure of a part of the project will not, in any way, be able to operate his part of the property in a manner prejudicial to the portion [being] financed. * * *

This analysis is not only applicable to shopping centers but to commercial building projects as well. The question of cross-easement agreements arises in cases where existing buildings are being expanded, and the permanent mortgagee has a first lien on the new construction. In the Madison Square Garden complex, which consists of an office building and a sports arena, both built on 99–year leasehold interests, the air-conditioning equipment for both buildings is located in the office structure. Provision had to be made for servicing of both buildings with air conditioning in the event, at some future time, they came under separate ownership. * * *

The approval of the plans and specifications by major tenants, which is generally required by their leases, is more critical than approval of these items by the permanent lender, since the ultimate security for [the] loan is the leases. For that reason, [construction loan] advances should not be commenced prior to such approval. Moreover, since the permanent mortgagee's security is the same as the construction lender's, [the permanent mortgagee] will be hard put to reject consummation of [the permanent] loan for failure to approve the completed improvement if the major tenants have accepted their space.

The completion date in [construction] loan documents should be consistent with the completion dates set forth in the leases and in the permanent commitment. All major leases should, if possible, have been approved by the permanent lender before the making of [the] first advance [pursuant to the construction loan]. However, this is not an inflexible rule, and where [the construction lender has] had dealings with a particular borrower over a period of time and know[s] of his experiences with the tenants in question, this requirement may be waived.

If [there is] a clause in the takeout permitting the borrower to substitute tenants of similar quality for those named, it may alleviate any qualms [about] making a particular advance prior to the execution of a specified lease.

The conditions beyond [the] control [of the construction lender] will require either the amendment of the permanent commitment or the assumption by [the construction lender] of a calculated business risk. One such condition is a requirement that there be an appraisal of the building on completion. The ordinary appraisal requirement can be satisfied prior to the first building loan advance, but if, for example, the permanent requires a certification by the appraiser that "there has been no material adverse change in the appraisal," the construction lender is subject to the exposure of potential changes. That particular clause could be changed to read that "the appraiser shall certify to the lender that he has inspected the property following completion of construction thereof and has found that the same represents improvements of the same type, size and quality as envisioned by him in his original appraisal." Even this is a compromise, since it should have been enough that the improvements were completed substantially in accordance with the plans and specifications which had been approved by the permanent and upon the basis of which the original appraisal was made.

[The construction lender] is presented with a comparable problem if the permanent requires a certificate of a third party that completion has been effected in accordance with the plans and specifications. When we are confronted with this condition, we always endeavor to have the permanent accept the certificate of the independent architects or engineers which our client retains for supervision of construction and approval of construction advances. * * *

We will, of course, also want the permanent to accept the supervising architects' approval of changes in the plans and specifications.

Leasing requirements are beyond [the construction lender's] control, but are subject to [its] judgment, and if key leases or letters of intent with respect thereto are in hand at the time of initial closing, the fact that they are not met is a business risk which can reasonably be taken.

We sometimes see a requirement that "the property be undamaged" at the time of closing. This kind of condition gives the permanent a "second look" even if the damage is relatively insignificant. We suggest a stipulation as to the scope of damage which will excuse the permanent's performance, with the understanding, of course, that it would have been an insured loss. * * *

If the permanent wants an opinion on doing business dated the date of the closing, * * * its local counsel [should] render the opinion as of the date of [the construction loan] closing, recognizing that it could change.

A requirement for an estoppel certificate from all lessees can be difficult, even if the leases stipulate that one must be given. Some qualification of that kind of a requirement is desirable.

Any requirement which is couched in terms of some state of facts being "satisfactory" to the takeout is troublesome. For example, the simple question of satisfactory title. It should be enough if [the construction lender is] able to deliver a mortgage which is insured by a responsible title insurer to be a first lien. Title questions which do not affect the permanent's security, should not excuse performance. In any such case, and in any case where the "approval" of the permanent is required, it would be desirable to state an objective test for meeting that approval, so that * * * the question of what such approval is to consist of [does not have to be litigated]. * * *

If [the construction lender has] managed, after reviewing the commitment, to secure amendments to the takeout which substantially reduce or eliminate the number of conditions which are beyond [its] control to satisfy, [the construction lender] will then want to be sure that [it], or [its] nominee, can enforce the commitment, so [the construction lender] will have [the commitment] assigned to [it] with the permanent's consent if that is required. More frequently than not, the permanent will want * * * to [enter into] what is called a "buy-sell" agreement" which, some cynics say, means that the construction lender must, if all goes well, sell the mortgage to the permanent. * * *

One of the customary accompanying requirements of the buy-sell is that the interim lender use the permanent lender's documentation. This can be a processing burden to construction lenders, since it means that the construction lender may find itself using as many mortgage forms as there are permanent mortgagees, and that in every such case, the drafting of the mortgage to include the necessary features relating to construction and those which may be in the permanent's but not in the construction lender's form can involve, in relation to the results achieved (which is simply the merger of two fairly standard forms) an extraordinarily time-consuming process. It seems to us that this can be bypassed by what amounts to an automatic modification provision, which means that we simply attach the permanent's form to the construction mortgage form and provide that, when [the permanent] becomes the owner of the mortgage, the terms of the permanent mortgage supersede the terms of the construction mortgage. * * *

In the case of the fee-purchase leaseback-leasehold mortgage takeout, we cannot, of course, use this arrangement. In that situation, where it seems indicated, we have required, either as a condition of the initial closing or as a condition of the interim advances, that the documents necessary to effect the consummation of that form of takeout be executed by the parties and placed in escrow. It is comforting to know that when the loan is advanced and the building completed there is nothing further to do but trigger the escrow. If the title company should prove unwilling to give unqualified assurance that it will issue the necessary policies upon the release of the escrow, on the theory that a rescission of corporate authority may somehow be effected, * * * the escrow procedure [can be supplemented] with a voting trust agreement, so that [the construction lender can] step into control of the borrowing corporation (the lessee-mortgagor) and the selling corporation and maintain the authority. * * *

NOTE

1. The regulations of the Comptroller of the Currency issued under the Federal Reserve Act except a construction loan made by a national bank from treatment as a real estate loan, if the loan matures in not more than 60 months and there is a valid and binding agreement from a financially responsible lender to pay off the loan upon completion of the building.

   a. If a strike delays completion of a building beyond the 60–month period, does a national bank have to treat a construction loan as a real estate loan? Can the term of a construction loan be extended, if the permanent agrees?

b. If it is known at the time of the making of the construction loan that completion will take more than 60 months, is there any way of taking advantage of the regulatory exception of construction loans from treatment as real estate loans?

1. Can the loan have a term of 60 months with an agreement by the construction lender to extend if the building is not completed within the 60 months? Some state statutes regulating state banks provide a period much shorter than 60 months.

2. What is the effect of a violation of lending restrictions? See page 875 infra.

2. Frequently, the entity borrowing the money from the permanent or the entity holding title during construction will be different than the entity which eventually holds title to and operates the real estate. See pages 114 to 115 supra. What provisions should the construction lender require be placed in the take-out commitment in order to solve this problem?

3. The take-out commitment could provide for prior approval by the permanent of any change in or to, or any deviation from, the plans and specifications which had been approved by the permanent or the take-out commitment could provide, as a condition precedent to the permanent's performance under the take-out commitment, that the permanent receive a certificate from a third party that the building was completed substantially in accordance with the plans and specifications.

a. As a matter of fact, the take-out commitment could contain both provisions. But, if the construction lender has its choice, which should it prefer?

1. The former may be an administrative headache and the latter imposes a condition outside of the control of the construction lender.

4. A requirement that certain key leases must be executed as a condition precedent to the permanent's performance under the take-out commitment is subject to the control of the construction lender. If, however, the condition to the performance of the permanent under the take-out commitment is that the terms, conditions, and obligations of certain key leases must be met and in force at the time of the closing of the permanent loan, the condition is outside of control of the construction lender.

a. What is the construction lender's recourse if a key tenant, after signing a lease, backs out at the last minute?

1. Can the construction lender sue the tenant for the damage caused it? Is there any privity of contract?

b. This condition requires that the construction lender use its business judgment. The better the credit and responsibility of the key tenants, the less the risk.

5. If a take-out commitment contains a provision which requires that the borrower be eligible to do business within the state at the time of the closing of the permanent loan, might it make sense to supplement the opinion of the borrower's counsel, delivered at the time of the closing of the construction loan, with respect to the borrower's qualification to do business in the state with an agreement by the borrower that it will take or suffer no act directly or

indirectly, intentionally or inadvertently to cause it not to qualify to carry on business in the state at the time of the closing of the permanent loan?

6. When any state of facts is subject to the approval of the permanent at the time of the closing of the permanent loan, at a minimum, should not the approval provision provide that approval will not be unreasonably withheld?

   a. Better yet, the criteria to be used in determining whether to approve should be objective criteria.

7. What are the construction lender's and the borrower's remedies if, at completion of construction in accordance with the terms and conditions of the take-out commitment, the permanent refuses to go through with the take-out?

   a. Can they sue for specific performance? If the developer can arrange for another permanent loan, it appears that in most cases a damages remedy is adequate. See Restatement of Contracts 2d, Sec. 359(1) (1981); A. Corbin, 5A Corbin On Contracts, Sec. 1152 (1964).

   One of the situations in which damages might not be an adequate remedy is when, even though there is money available in the market and the developer has sufficient time to do so, the developer is unable to arrange for new permanent financing. See Restatement of Contracts 2d, Sec. 360(b) (1981); A. Corbin, 5 Corbin On Contracts, Sec. 1078 at 447 (1964); *Higgins v. Arizona Savings and Loan Ass'n,* 85 Ariz. 6, 330 P.2d 504 (1958); *Leben v. Nassau Savings and Loan Ass'n,* 40 A.D.2d 830, 337 N.Y.S. 2d 310 (1972); *Selective Builders, Inc. v. Hudson City Savings Bank,* 137 N.J.Super. 500, 349 A.2d 564 (1975); *First National State Bank of New Jersey v. Commonwealth Federal Savings and Loan Association of Norristown,* 610 F.2d 164 (3d Cir.1979). In *Southampton Wholesale Food Terminal, Inc. v. Providence Produce Warehouse Co.,* 129 F.Supp. 663 (D.Mass. 1955), specific performance of the defendant's commitment to make a construction loan secured by a mortgage on plaintiff's real estate was ordered by the court. The court distinguished between a contract to lend money and a contract to advance money on the security of a mortgage on real estate. 5A Corbin On Contracts, Sec. 1152, supra, recognizes that specific performance may be the appropriate remedy in exceptional circumstances such as where the developer has materially changed his position, made new contracts, and transferred the real estate to the lender as security for the promised loan. See generally Groot, *Specific Performance of Contracts to Provide Permanent Financing,* 60 Cornell L.Rev. 718 (1975); Mehr and Kilgore, *Enforcement of the Real Estate Loan Commitment: Improvement of the Borrower's Remedies,* 24 Wayne L.Rev. 1011 (1978); Brannon, *Enforceability of Mortgage Loan Commitments,* 18 Real Prop., Prob. & Tr.J. 724 (1983).

   Can the construction lender obtain specific performance? The answer to this question depends on whether the construction lender is an intended or incidental beneficiary, a party to the take-out commitment, or whether the commitment has been assigned to it. See Restatement of Contracts 2d, Sec. 302 (1981). In most cases the permanent lender knows the identity of the construction lender and that most or all proceeds of its loan will be used to repay the construction loan. Even if the construction lender is an intended beneficiary, it cannot obtain specific performance if the specific performance remedy is not available under Sec. 359(1) of the Restatement. See Restatement of Contracts 2d, Sec. 307 (1981). If, however, the construction lender is an intended beneficiary, can it achieve substantially the same result as might be gained through specific performance by recovering the "value of the promised performance" under Sec. 347(a) of the Restatement? See Restatement of Contracts 2d, Sec. 347(a) (1981).

b.   What is the measure of damages if the developer and construction lender sue for damages? See Restatement of Contracts 2d, Sec. 346, supra; 5 Corbin On Contracts, Sec. 1078, supra. But see *Higgins v. Arizona Savings & Loan Ass'n*, supra; *United California Bank v. Prudential Insurance Company of America*, 140 Ariz. 238, 681 P.2d 390 (1983). If the construction lender is an intended beneficiary, might a nominal damages recovery under Sec. 346(2) be avoided by bringing the action within Restatement of Contracts 2d, Sec. 347(a), supra? The foreseeability of the damages by the lender, as suggested by Corbin, may also, in some states, avoid a nominal damages result. See 5 Corbin On Contracts, Sec. 1078, supra; *Pipkin v. Thomas & Hill, Inc.*, 33 N.C.App. 710, 236 S.E.2d 725 (1977); *Coastland Corporation v. Third National Mortgage Company*, 611 F.2d 969 (4th Cir.1979).

c.   Are there techniques which might be used to avoid this problem ever arising, or techniques which will insure that the developer and construction lender both have a remedy?

d.   If, rather than the permanent refusing to go through with the take-out commitment, the borrower finds a source of permanent financing more to its liking and it refuses to honor the commitment, does the permanent have any remedy? See Draper, *The Broken Commitment: A Modern View of the Mortgage Lender's Remedy*, 59 Cornell L.Rev. 418 (1974); Groot, *Specific Performance of Contracts to Provide Permanent Financing*, 60 Cornell L.Rev. 718 (1975); Zinman, *Mortgage Loan and Joint Venture Commitments: The Institutional Investor's Remedies*, 18 Real Prop., Prob. & Tr.J. 750 (1983). See also *Lincoln National Life Ins. Co. v. NCR Corp.*, 772 F.2d 315 (7th Cir.1985). Can the lender at least retain the commitment fee paid by the borrower? See *Weiner v. Salem Five Cents Savings Bank*, 371 Mass. 897, 360 N.E.2d 306 (1977).

8.   See generally Davis, *The Permanent Lender's Role in the Construction Process*, 3 # 1 Real Est.Rev. 70 (1973); Draper, *Tight Money and Possible Substantive Defenses to Enforcement of Future Mortgage Commitments*, 50 Notre Dame Law. 603 (1975); Fingersh, *The Long–Term Mortgage Commitment—A Borrower's Perspective*, 3 J. Real Est.Tax'n 269 (1976); Smith and Lubell, *The Buy–Sell Agreement*, 9 # 1 Real Est.Rev. 13 (1979); Ridloff, *A Construction Lender Looks at Permanent Loan Commitments*, 10 # 2 Real Est. Rev. 60 (1980); Fisher, *How to Draft Loan Commitments*, 3 # 5 Prac.Real Est. Law. 9 (1987).

4.   LONG TERM FINANCING

a.   THE NEGOTIATIONS FOR PERMANENT FINANCING

In most situations, the success or failure of a real estate development project will depend on whether satisfactory long term financing can be obtained. The negotiation of long term financing is quite complex. A myriad of details and factors must be considered. Although the following excerpts deal with the negotiation of the financing for a shopping center, the considerations involved in negotiating financing for other types of real estate development are not dissimilar.

ON SUBMITTING MORTGAGE APPLICATIONS
Francis P. Gunning
International Council of Shopping Centers
Shopping Report No. 20 (1967).

* * *

Preliminary Decisions

Considerably in advance of his research for a financial helpmate, our developer must necessarily have made a great many preliminary decisions in respect to the proposed shopping center, e.g.:

(a) *Physical Details:* * * *

(b) *Amount of Loan Desired:* * * * He is not unaware of the fact that most institutional loans are on the basis of 75% of appraised value which, on average, will provide him with 80% to 90% of his actual costs. The excess of appraised value above actual costs is a recognized and legitimate increment of equity and is in the nature of profit.

(c) *Income Stream:* The developer will also have made a generally optimistic, albeit mystical, projection of anticipated net income and found that it relates quite favorably to the modest amount of loan desired. After deducting from this net income an amount representing a reasonable return upon his own equity investment, if he then divides the modest amount of desired loan into the remaining net income, the result is a rough estimate of the constant debt service which the project will support.

* * *

(d) *Method of Financing:* Possibly because of his special or unusual circumstances, the developer may well have considered, in addition to conventional mortgage financing, any one of a number of other financing techniques currently available. * * *

(e) *Interim Financing:* The developer is reasonably certain, once he has acquired his permanent loan financing, that construction financing will be readily available.

Selecting the Lender

(a) *Sources:* There are within the United States in excess of 1,700 insurance companies. * * *

In addition, there are countless local thrift and savings and loan associations. * * * Commercial banks with their growing trust accounts as well as the private pension funds are also * * * important sources of long-term mortgage money. * * *

A new and relatively untapped source of financing both of the equity and loan types, may now be found with a growing number of large industrial corporations * * *.

For a fee, however, the most expeditious service in uncovering available money sources is performed by your friendly mortgage broker. * * * It is also sometimes fruitful to examine the local land records to determine which institutions are then currently active in the area.

(b) *Particular Considerations:* In some bachelor circles, the size of the possible dowry is an intriguing speculation. It is an equally relevant inquiry also in the selection of a financing partner since there must be some relationship between the modest amount of loan desired and lender's capacity to provide it. Most institutional lenders are limited as to the amount of loan which may be made on the security of any one property.

For example, * * * a loan of as much as 75% of the appraised value can be made but, at the same time, cannot exceed 2% of the * * * [lender's] total [uncommitted] assets.

* * * [T]he developer must determine whether the lender can be approached directly or whether entree can only be had by way of a local correspondent or loan agent. Other companies maintain regional offices which accept mortgage applications within the geographic area. This information can only be obtained by inquiry.

Most companies, especially in a high interest market, will require a commitment fee to accompany any loan application. [T]his fee [may be] * * * refundable but the size of the required fee and conditions of refund should be explored beforehand. Some companies require that prior to the application, a required dollar amount of rental under *signed* leases and in a prescribed ratio between national and local tenants have been achieved. Others require such leasing together with occupancy only prior to actual disbursement. The foregoing factors may likewise scratch a number of entries.

General Market Study

(a) *Scope:* The scope of any survey of [market] area should always be directly proportional to the size of the center itself and to the mix of tenants represented. * * *

(b) *Objective[s] of Lender:* * * * He desires assurance first and foremost of the existence and expected continuance of a healthy economic climate within the [market] area together with the reasonable promise of future growth. Geographically, the proposed site should be easily accessible to the largest segments of population within the market area and the site should be free of, or equipped to contend with, any present or then known future competition. * * *

(c) *Economy of the Market:* In all cases, there must be submitted a so-called economic feasibility study. In order to be most effective and credible, any such study is best prepared by professionals skilled in assembling such data. * * * All remotely relevant factors affecting economic growth should be presented. There should be every expectation that much of the same data which so influenced the developer and his principal tenants will have no less an effect, if not love at first *site*, upon the investor.

(d) *Geography of the Market:* The trading area is defined by its accessibility to the shopping center [or, for that matter, to the office building or apartment complex]. For this reason, extensive maps and charting of the road networks servicing the area must be presented. All major future highways, in particular the interstate routes, should be determined and their access to the site plotted. The sole objective is easy and timely accessibility to all desirable pockets of population. To achieve this, the area must be free from geographic and topographic obstacles. * * *

(e) *Competition:* The lender will insist upon full disclosure and detailed information on the location and character of existing and potential competition. The developer's evaluation of how he can contend with this competition must be fully discussed. * * *

All available unimproved or under-improved land within a competitive radius and which, under any circumstances, could have the potential for future [competitive use] must be surveyed. * * *

We must assume that the ardor of the developer's suit and the glitter of his trinkets have completely mesmerized the lender, who now pleads to be romanced with further details of the project itself.

Project Analysis

(a) *Objectives of Lender:* Although now smitten, the lender will nevertheless insist upon getting to know the developer better, for which purpose biographical data will be furnished. Prior experience * * * is highly desirable. Real infatuation blossoms, however, when a favorable economic analysis of the project itself can be demonstrated. Lenders also display a keen interest in the tenant composition and the amenities provided in the center [or in the office building] * * *.

(b) *Developer:* Lenders now attach a premium for prior successful experience. * * * [O]f course, the general good reputation and integrity of the developer is essential as well as evidence of financial responsibility. The importance of this personal factor is increasingly evidenced by the requirement of many lenders that the original developer remain in management * * * for a minimum period during the loan.

(c) *Economics:* In the final analysis, it is the [e]conomics of the project itself which eventually determines financing approval or rejection. It is the vital ingredient. Sufficient income from satisfactory leases overshadows all considerations.

The amount of any loan represents a capitalization by the lender of net income and the capitalization rate utilized reflects his evaluation of the quality of the income source. In order to appraise the income, the investor must be furnished a detailed pro-forma statement setting forth the proposed tenant roster, both actual and potential, a pro-forma rent roll and the resulting projected income and expenses. All items so presented will be carefully weighed by the lender in the formulation of his own estimate of income and expenses. The figures more readily accepted are those which have been better justified and documented.

Income

The projected income will consist of minimum annual rental from all occupancies including stores, offices, kiosks, advertising space and coin machines. Percentage rent, however, is speculative and therefore not usually appropriate for initial underwriting although it may properly be included, on the basis of actual experience, in a refinancing. The one exception, however, is in the case of particular tenants under no-minimum leases where some lenders are prepared to estimate sales and resulting percentage rents on the basis of satisfactory previous regional and local sales data for this tenant. Tax stops, using the earliest lease year as a base, are an absolutely essential requirement. The effect of these tax stops is then reflected not as income but as a set-off against expenses. * * *

The source of the income determines its quality and all investors insist upon a large proportion of national tenants, although most are willing to consider [including] strong locals. * * *

The terms of the leases with the larger major tenants [should be] reasonably co-extensive with the desired loan term. Developers now recognize that the more longer leases submitted the more readily a longer loan term can be obtained and with it a lower constant of debt service. * * *

Operating Expenses

The first lovers' spat may well occur at this point, for it is here that the parties have their most serious disagreements. Lenders are generally uncompromising about the reasonableness of expense estimates because they are convinced it is here that sponsors of distress centers [or office buildings or apartment complexes] made their initial miscalculation. The burden of justifying all of the expense figures is with the developer and he must come prepared to discharge this responsibility. * * *

Investors are particularly chary on the subject of taxes and assessments. Their concern is alleviated in the main where satisfactory tax stop provisions are contained in all of the leases. Where there is any possibility of tax exposure, considerable justification must be furnished for the tax estimate used in the pro-forma statement. * * *

The irreducible exposure, however, even with a tax stop which uses the earliest lease year as a base is the accuracy of the tax estimates for the period prior to and including the base year. The most ingenious solution for this problem which has come to the attention of this writer is a tax stop which uses a specific base *rate* per square foot rather than a base *year*. This base rate can then be used, with complete impunity, by both borrower and lender as their maximum tax expense under all circumstances. This rate presumably will vary for different areas.

* * *

Underwriting Formulas

For purposes *only* of general information and with strong reservations as to their validity on a case basis, there follows a number of underwriting formulas used from time to time by investors. As with any averaging, these are merely rules of thumb subject to wide variation and [are] not consistently adhered to by all lenders nor [are they] consistent with each other. These figures vary with market conditions and with the type and quality of the project. * * *

Value:

Overall Capitalization Rate—8% to 9% [10]

(i.e., a rate determined from comparison sales data in the real estate market place and which represent[s] a return on land and building investment and a recapture of building investment)

Loan Amount:

Loan per G.L.A.[11]—$12 to $27

Loan as a multiple of gross income—5× to 7×

Loan as a multiple of net income—8× to 9×

As a percentage of Value—70% to 75%

Major Leases and Rents:

As a percentage of occupancy—70% to 80%

As a percentage of gross rent—65% to 75%

As a percentage of operating costs and debt service—90% or more

Major rent plus minor rental estimate (at $1.00 [12] per square foot) = operating cost and debt service

Major minimum rents—$1.30 to $1.65 [12] per G.L.A.

Minor Rent Coverage:

(After satisfying major rental requirement)

With no vacancies—minor rent can decline 30% to 40% from initial underwriting

10. [This means multiplying a representative annual "net income" figure agreed on by the developer and lender by a factor of 12.5 to 11 to arrive at the value of the development.]

11. [Gross Leasable Area.]

12. [These amounts are probably somewhat low in terms of today's market.]

With 10% minor vacancy—minor rent can decline 25% to 35% from initial underwriting

Minor minimum rents—$2 to $4 [12] per G.L.A.

Income Coverage:

Net income as a multiple of debt service—$1\frac{1}{4}\times$ to $1\frac{1}{2}\times$ [13]

Gross income as a multiple of debt service—$1\frac{1}{2}\times$ to $1\frac{3}{4}\times$

Operating expenses (fixed and variable) as a percentage of gross income—30%

Debt service and operating expenses as a percentage of gross income—75% or less

Major rent less operating expenses = 8% or more return on the loan [14]

Good Percentage Rent Experience:

Percentage rent = 9.5% to 10% of minimum rent

Total Charges:

Debt service and operating expenses per G.L.A.—$1.75 to $2.15 [14]

Major Tenant: A Dun and Bradstreet rating of AAA1 which indicates net assets of over one million dollars and a high composite credit appraisal. Most financial institutions, such as banks and savings and loans, as well as governmental agencies, however, are generally considered as major [tenants].

Tenant Composition: Desired apportionment of major and minor occupancy both on the basis of area and rent are reflected in the foregoing formulas. These figures will, of course, vary with different lenders and with the circumstances of particular centers [or other real estate developments]. The tenant roster should reflect a satisfactory mix not only as to lines of merchandise and services but, as well, quality and price range within such lines. There must be an economic compatibility of the identity of tenants, types of merchandise and price lines with the per capita income and purchasing habits of [the market] area.

Amenities: The underlying philosophy on layout should be discussed.

* * *

If available, the preliminary plans and specifications can be submitted, together with the proposed form of lease and all then executed leases. Where relevant and where the project involves a leasehold, an executed copy of the ground lease should be submitted. If the center utilizes reciprocal parking on adjoining land, then the parking declara-

12. [These amounts are probably somewhat low in terms of today's market.]

13. [The representative annual net income figure should exceed the total annual payments with respect to the loan by 25% to 50%.]

14. [See footnote 12 on page 694]

tion or easement agreement must be included.   In the case where one or more separately owned department stores are to be integrated into the center, then an overall operating agreement will have been prepared and should be submitted.   *   *   *

NOTE

1.   If a developer has established a good relationship with a local commercial bank, a senior loan officer can be an invaluable aid in locating sources of financing.   Insurance companies, pension trusts, etc., frequently use correspondent commercial banks as loan origination sources.

2.   A professionally-prepared economic feasibility study generally is a costly endeavor.   Obviously, the larger the development the more justification exists to incur this cost.

    a.   There is a point, however, at which the size of the development compared with the cost of the study does not justify a professionally-prepared study.   In this case, the developer will have to prepare the study.

        1.   What sources are available to the developer and its advisers to obtain the information needed for the study?

3.   There is a reluctance on the part of lenders, when projecting the income of a development, to include estimates of the rent to be received under percentage leases.

    a.   If the tenants having percentage leases are triple A–1 national or regional tenants with experience in the market area, is there a reasonable basis for including their estimates of percentage rent?

    b.   In a time of rising real estate taxes, "tax stops"—real estate taxes over a defined amount allocated to the tenant's portion of the development and payable as additional rent by the tenant to the developer—are an important ingredient in firming up projections of income.

4.   Capitalized earnings have long been used to determine the value of a business.

    a.   The early years of a real estate development, in most cases, will show, as a result of the large amount of depreciation and interest being deducted, a loss or relatively low net income while quite possibly showing a substantial cash flow.   In this context, attempting to derive a representative net income figure from among the first four to five years of operation for use as the earnings component in determining the value of the development on a capitalized earnings basis, will result in a low and quite possibly unrepresentative value for the development.   There are several ways of handling this problem.

        1.   The income statement of a development might be projected to a year at, or near, the "cross-over" point.   A representative net income figure could be derived from an analysis of the years preceding and following the "cross-over" point.   Although this method might produce an accurate valuation, its speculative nature is obvious.

        2.   In the early years of a development net income is not the only return to the developer.   The cash flow in excess of net income also can be considered part of the developer's return.   This concept can be employed in valuing the development when using the first four or five years of operation.   Typically, a developer might expect a 2–3% return

of the cash flow in excess of net income and a 6–7% return of net income. The first four or five years can be analyzed to derive a representative figure for the excess of cash flow over net income and for net income. A multiple of 33–50 might be applied to the excess cash flow figure and a multiple of 14–17 might be applied to the net income figure. The results are combined to produce a value for the development.

b. The use of a representative net income figure derived through an analysis of the early years of a development can result in some distortions when used to determine income coverage with respect to the debt service on a loan. There are other, possibly more accurate, ways of making this determination, assuming that the term of the loan or loans is equal to, or less than, the useful life of the depreciable real estate improvements.

1. "Net operating income" or "net spendable income" can be used in the place of net income. Net operating income is the income of a development prior to the deduction of depreciation and principal payments on the loan or loans. Net spendable income is the cash flow less income taxes, if any.

2. In some cases, net operating income or net spendable income can be substituted for net income in determining the loan amount as a multiple of net income when using the early years of the development.

c. See generally Blazar, *Valuing Real Estate: The Puzzle of Meaningful Disclosure,* 7 # 4 Real Est.Rev. 72 (1978); Valachi, *Determining the Value of a Real Estate Investment,* 7 # 4 Real Est.Rev. 64 (1978); Siegelaub and Meistrich, *How the Professional Shopping Center Developer Obtains a Mortgage,* 9 # 1 Real Est.Rev. 50 (1979); Committee on State and Local Taxation, *Realistic Appraisal Techniques of Large Income–Producing Properties,* 18 Real Prop., Prob. & Tr.J. 20 (1983). For the application of appraisal techniques to income-producing property see *County Dollar Corp. v. City of Yonkers,* 97 A.D.2d 469, 467 N.Y.S.2d 666 (1983); *Matter of AMFAC, Inc.,* 65 Hawaii 499, 654 P.2d 363 (1982); *Jim Paws, Inc. v. Equalization Board of Garland County,* 289 Ark. 113, 710 S.W.2d 197 (1986).

5. A means of assuring the permanent lender, at least in a commercial setting, of the continuity of the rent flow is lease guarantee insurance. An insurance company, writing this type of insurance, will guarantee the monthly rent, or a percentage thereof, called for in the leases entered into by the tenants and the borrower. The minimum policy period is five years, the maximum is twenty years or the term of the lease, whichever is less.

b.   THE LONG TERM MORTGAGE

After the application for long term financing is approved and the commitment made, the next step which must be taken by the long term lender and the developer is the preparation of the note, mortgage, and other instruments providing for the security for the note, if that is the way in which the financing is to be provided. Most of the value of a residential or commercial rental real estate project is determined by the leasing of space to tenants. A beautiful office building is worth little if the space in the building cannot be leased. Therefore, one of the primary concerns in the preparation of a long term mortgage and other instruments providing for the security for the note, from both the financier's and developer's standpoint, is the treatment of the leases and rental income of the mortgagor.

MORTGAGES—PROBLEMS IN POSSESSION, RENTS AND MORTGAGEE LIABILITY

Robert Kratovil
11 DePaul Law Review 1 (1961).
[footnotes omitted]

* * * In general, the title states regard the mortgage as retaining some of its early character, that is, they view it as a sort of conveyance of the land, so that *immediately on the signing of the mortgage,* the mortgagee has the right to take possession of the property and collect the rents thereof. On the other hand, the lien states regard the mortgage as merely creating *the right to acquire the land through foreclosure of the mortgage,* so that the mortgagor remains the full owner of the land with the right to possession and rents until the statutory redemption period has expired and the foreclosure deed has issued. * * * *In title states, therefore, rents are an important part of the mortgagee's security. In lien states, rents are not part of the mortgagee's security.* * * *

1. In a number of title theory states (Alabama, Maryland and Tennessee, for example) the mortgagee immediately upon execution of the mortgage has the right to take possession and collect the rents of the mortgaged property. This right exists even though the mortgage is silent on this point. There are two exceptions: (1) In recent times laws have been passed in some title states giving the mortgagor the right of possession until default occurs. In effect, these laws convert such states into intermediate states. (2) Many mortgage forms used in title states give the mortgagor the right of possession until default.

2. In intermediate states (Illinois, North Carolina, New Jersey and Ohio, for example) the mortgagor has the right of possession until his first default, but after default the mortgagee has the right to take possession. In other respects these states follow title theory.

3. In lien theory states, in the absence of a provision in the mortgage to the contrary, the mortgagor is entitled to possession and rents at least until the foreclosure sale.

4. In some lien states the mortgagor may, either by express provision in the mortgage or by a separate assignment of rents signed at the time the mortgage is signed, give the mortgagee the right to take possession and collect rents as soon as a default occurs, and such provisions are valid.

5. In other lien states provisions such as those described in paragraph four above are considered void as against public policy.

6. In all states, if the mortgagor, *after defaulting in his mortgage payments,* voluntarily turns over possession to the mortgagee, the mortgagee has the legal right to remain in possession. Notice that in

paragraph five it is the clause *in the mortgage* binding the mortgagor to give up possession at some future time when default occurs that is held void. The same agreement made after default is valid. The mortgagee is then called a *mortgagee in possession.*

7. Whenever a mortgagee takes possession before he has acquired ownership of the property by foreclosure, the rents he collects must be applied in reduction of the mortgage debt. A mortgagee *does not* become the owner of the property by taking possession. Foreclosure is necessary today in all states for the mortgagee to acquire ownership of the land.

8. Whenever a mortgagee has the right to possession, if he fails to exercise that right and allows the mortgagor to remain in possession collecting rents, it is the universal rule that the rents so collected belong to the mortgagor.

* * *

Leases Prior to Mortgage

* * *

1. Such a lease, since it is prior and superior to the mortgage, cannot be extinguished by foreclosure of the mortgage.

2. If such a lease contains an option to purchase the property, the option must be subordinated to the mortgage. Otherwise there is danger that exercise of the option would extinguish the mortgage.

3. Complete subordination of a prior lease to a subsequent mortgage is legally possible. * * *

4. In title and intermediate states, on default in the mortgage payments, the mortgagee has the right to serve a demand on a senior lessee (one whose lease antedates the mortgage) and the lessee must thereafter pay rent to the mortgagee. The lessee has no right to move out, as is true of junior lessees, as hereinafter explained. This rule stems from the notion in title and intermediate states that the mortgage is a transfer of some sort of title to the mortgagee, a notion previously referred to herein. Because of this mysterious transfer of title, there is created between the lessee and the subsequent mortgagee an equally mysterious link called "privity of estate." It is this privity of estate that makes the lessee liable to a subsequent mortgagee for rents. * * *

In lien theory states, the mortgagee ordinarily is not entitled to make such a demand on the tenant. This follows from the fact that in these states a mortgage conveys no title; hence privity of estate is lacking.

Leases Junior to the Mortgage

* * *

1. Such a lease can be extinguished by foreclosure of the mortgage.

2.   Occasionally a mortgagee will wish to foreclose his mortgage without extinguishing the lease. In some states this is possible and in others not. In states where it is legally impossible to preserve a junior lease when a mortgage is foreclosed, a mortgagee must be wary of placing reliance on such leases.

3.   In title and intermediate states the mortgagee has the right to evict junior lessees as soon as default occurs in the mortgage payments. This is also true in lien states where a clause is inserted in the mortgage giving the mortgagee the right to possession on default and the state is one that recognizes the validity of such a provision. Alternatively the mortgagee may serve a demand which gives the tenant a choice as between moving out or paying rent to the mortgagee. However, the mortgagee cannot compel the tenant to remain and pay rent to him. * * *

4.   If the mortgagee enters under his mortgage, as stated in paragraph three, and the tenant chooses to remain and pay rent, in many states the result is to terminate the lease and create a month-to-month or year-to-year tenancy. * * *

Assignment of Rents

At the time the mortgage is signed, the mortgagee should require the mortgagor to sign a *separate* assignment of leases and rents. * * * [This] assignment [should be] recorded. * * *

1.   In most lien states an assignment of rents enables the mortgagee to reach the rents accruing prior to foreclosure sale and treat them as part of the security for his debt. * * * In one or two lien states an assignment of rents, like the mortgage clause giving the right to take possession on default, is held invalid as being opposed to public policy. Also in a few lien states an assignment signed contemporaneously with the mortgage is given only limited recognition. * * * [R]ents collected by the mortgagee can be applied only to maintain the property or to pay taxes or insurance. They cannot be applied in reduction of the mortgage debt.

2.   Since the assignment does not contemplate that the mortgagee will begin collecting rents immediately upon the signing of the assignment, but only after a default occurs, the assignment is inoperative until it is "activated" by some action of the mortgagee. Rents collected by the mortgagor before the assignment is activated belong to the mortgagor, or they may become the property of a junior mortgagee who exercises greater diligence. * * *

Even specific language that the assignment will operate automatically on default has been held insufficient to activate the assignment. * * *

3.   Everywhere the assignment is properly activated if the mortgagor consents to collection of the rent after default and pursuant to the assignment, and the tenants begin paying rent to the mortgagee.

4. In title and intermediate states the assignment is activated on default by the mortgagee's serving notice on the tenants to pay rent to the mortgagee. The mortgagor's consent is unnecessary.

5. In some lien states the assignment can be activated in the same manner as in title states.

6. In other lien states the assignment can be activated only by the mortgagee's filing a foreclosure suit and applying for the appointment of a receiver. * * *

7. In one or two lien states an assignment can only be activated by the mortgagor voluntarily turning over possession to the mortgagee or allowing the mortgagee to collect rents.

8. Rents collected by the mortgagee under an activated assignment must be applied to taxes, repairs, insurance and, in most states, the mortgage debt.

9. Whenever a mortgagee acts under an activated assignment, he does not destroy existing leases, as sometimes occurs when a mortgagee takes possession under his mortgage. An assignment preserves valuable leases.

* * *

Rent Reductions, Lease Cancellations and Advance Payments of Rent

* * *

1. In title and intermediate theory states, when the lease is [entered into after execution and recording of] the mortgage, the mortgagee is not bound by any advance rent payments made by the tenant to the mortgagor, and on appointment of a receiver or on the mortgagee's taking possession of the land, the tenant will nevertheless have to pay rent thereafter to such receiver or mortgagee, even though he has already paid his rent in advance to the mortgagor. * * *

2. In title and intermediate states, if the lease antedates the mortgage, recording of the mortgage does not give the tenant notice of the mortgagee's rights, for recording of the mortgage gives notice only to those persons who acquire rights in the property *after* recording of the document. The question therefore arises, if the tenant, acting in good faith and in ignorance of the mortgage, prepays his rent to the mortgagor, and the mortgagor thereafter defaults, is this prepayment binding on the mortgagee, or must the tenant pay his rent again to the mortgagee? Some cases hold for the mortgagee and some hold for the tenant. The mortgagee can protect himself by procuring, at the time the mortgage is signed, an assignment of all existing leases, and by giving tenants notice at that time of his rights under such assignment.

3. In many lien theory states, the mortgagee is bound by advance payments of rents made in good faith by the tenant to the mortgagor.

* * *

4. But even in lien theory states * * * if the mortgagee, at the time the mortgage is made, obtains from the mortgagor an assignment of rents and leases and notifies the tenants thereof * * * the mortgagee will not be bound by any advance payments of rent made by the tenant to the mortgagor. Also no rent reduction granted by the mortgagor after the tenant has notice of this assignment will be effective.

5. Where the mortgagor, at the time of making the mortgage, by a separate instrument, assigns an existing lease to the mortgagee, and the lessee is notified of the assignment, the tenant and mortgagor thereafter cannot cancel the lease, or reduce the rent, so far as the mortgagee is concerned. On the mortgagee's taking possession, or on the appointment of a receiver, the tenant can be held to his lease. If there is no assignment of [the lease] and the lease is prior to the mortgage, a cancellation of the lease made by the mortgagor and lessee may be valid.

* * *

Restrictive Covenants

If there are any recorded restrictive covenants binding the premises, a mortgagee who takes possession whether by virtue of his mortgage, an assignment of rents, or through foreclosure of the mortgage will naturally be enjoined from violating the restrictions * * *.

Covenant Liability

Suppose a lease contains some covenant that places a heavy burden on the landlord, such as a covenant on the part of the landlord to rebuild buildings on the leased premises in the event of their destruction by fire or other casualty. If the leased property is thereafter mortgaged, and the mortgage is later foreclosed, subject, of course, to the lease, and the lease survives the foreclosure, and after the mortgagee has become the owner of the property by foreclosure there is a failure to rebuild, the mortgagee in all states would be liable. He has taken over all the privileges and burdens of being a landlord. Questions arise, however, as to the mortgagee's liability arising *before* foreclosure has been completed. Unfortunately the cases on these questions are so meager that few conclusions can safely be drawn.

* * *

Covenant Liability in Title and Intermediate States

* * * Whenever the mortgagee is allowed to step into the landlord's shoes for the purpose of reaping benefits as against the lessee he must also stand in the landlord's shoes for the purpose of carrying some of the landlord's liabilities. It would therefore appear to follow that in title and intermediate states, where the lease antedates the mortgage, there is danger that the mortgagee will be held liable to the tenant for breach of any lease covenants that "run with the land." * * * In

some states, however, and this includes some title, intermediate and lien states the courts have refused to hold the mortgagee liable * * * unless he takes possession of the property.

* * *

Of course, where the mortgage antedates the lease we have said that the mortgagee cannot compel the tenant to remain in possession and pay rent, since privity of estate is lacking. This lack of privity of estate should insulate the mortgagee from covenant liability, prior to completion of his mortgage foreclosure.

Covenant Liability in Lien States

* * * [W]here a lease antedates a mortgage in a lien state, the mortgage will not create any privity of estate and therefore the mortgagee will have no liability on the landlord's covenants contained in the lease, * * * absent any valid assignment of [leases] or any valid provision in the mortgage conferring on the mortgagee the right to possession or rents. * * * Unfortunately this solution, while logical, may not be universally accepted by the courts. * * *

Of course, where the mortgage antedates the lease, in lien states as in title states there is a total absence of privity of estate; hence the mortgagee cannot be held liable on any covenants running with the land prior to the completion of the foreclosure. With the completion of the foreclosure, ownership of the land passes to the mortgagee, assuming he is the successful bidder at the foreclosure sale, and with this ownership liability on lease covenants will attach, since privity of estate will then be present.

Covenant Liability Under an Assignment of Rents

Suppose that in a title or intermediate state A leases to B. Thereafter A mortgages to C and assigns the lease to C. When default occurs under the mortgage, C chooses to collect rent *not under the mortgage but under the assignment.* There is authority for the view that such an assignment is not a transfer of the reversion, and C is entitled to rents without the creation of the privity of estate on which liability depends. If this is true, it should follow that C would not be liable to the tenant for breach of the lease covenants. It cannot be stated flatly that this solution will command universal acceptance. Courts might understandably be reluctant to allow C the benefits under the lease without bearing the burdens. * * *

It is possible that the answer to this question may rest in part on the form of the assignment. If the assignment purports to be an assignment of the *lease* as well as an assignment of the *rents,* it is arguable that an assignment in this form creates some sort of privity of estate and liability would therefore ensue on covenants that run with the land. * * *

For this reason, some mortgagees deliberately omit any assignment of the lease in the assignment of rents form. They argue that, while an assignment of the lease is automatically an assignment of rents accruing thereunder, an assignment of rents is not automatically an assignment of the lease and the covenants therein. As against this, one must weigh the fact that it is the assignment of the lease to the mortgagee that appears significant to the courts in protecting the mortgagee against lease cancellations and advance payment of rents to the mortgagor. * * *

In lien states the danger of covenant liability, even where the mortgage is accompanied by an assignment of leases and rents, should always be less than in a title or intermediate state. There is less likelihood that a court might find privity of estate to be present.

* * *

NOTE

1. In a lien theory state which permits it, the mortgagor assigns the rents to the mortgagee—the assignment to be effective in the event of a default by the mortgagor.

    a. Where should the assignment be recorded? Should it be recorded in the office where the mortgage is recorded, or should a financing statement be recorded in the office or offices specified under the state's enactment of the Uniform Commercial Code?

    1. Is an assignment of rents the assignment of an interest in real property? Can rents be considered the accounts receivable of a real estate developer? Does the position taken in the regulations issued by the Comptroller of the Currency classifying loans secured by an assignment of rents under a lease as commercial loans rather than real estate loans affect whether the lender taking such an assignment must file under the Uniform Commercial Code? See 12 C.F.R. § 34.3(c).

    2. Is an assignment of leases—the lessor's interest in the leases—the assignment of an interest in real property? See *In re Bristol Associates, Inc.*, 505 F.2d 1056 (3d Cir.1974), reversing, 369 F.Supp. 1 (E.D.Pa.1973); *Western Savings and Loan Assoc. v. CFS Portales Ethanol I, Ltd.*, 107 N.M. 143, 754 P.2d 520 (1988). Cf. *In re LeSueur's Fiesta Store, Inc.*, 40 B.R. 160 (Bankr.D.Ariz.1984). *In re Bristol Associates, Inc.*, supra, may also have some bearing on whether the Uniform Commercial Code applies to an assignment of only rents. The assignment of the lease in *In re Bristol Associates, Inc.*, supra, provided that none of the lessor's duties under the lease were assigned to the lender. See 369 F.Supp. 1 at page 2. See generally Comment, *An Article Nine Scope Problem—Mortgages, Leases, and Rents as Collateral*, 47 U.Colo.L.Rev. 449 (1976); Bowmar, *Real Estate Interests as Security Under the UCC: The Scope of Article Nine*, 12 U.C.C.L.J. 99 (1979); Comment, *Security Interests in Notes and Mortgages: Determining the Applicable Law*, 79 Colum.L.Rev. 1414 (1979). Cf. *In re Equitable Development Corp.*, 20 UCC Rept.Serv. 1349 (S.D.Fla.1976); *In re Maryville Savings & Loan Corporation*, 743 F.2d 413 (6th Cir.1984); *In re Shuster*, 47 B.R. 920 (Bankr.D.Minn.1985), reversed, 784 F.2d 883 (8th Cir.1986); *In re Preston*, 52 B.R. 296 (Bankr.M.D.Tenn.1985); *Jackson County Fed. Sav. & Loan Ass'n v. Maduff Mortgage Corp.*, 608

F.Supp. 588 (D.Colo.1985); *Security Bank v. Chiapuzio,* 304 Or. 438, 747 P.2d 335 (1987).

b. Consistent with the Uniform Land Transactions Act's rejection of existing title and lien theories, the Act provides that a security interest in real estate attaches to rents from the real estate only if the security agreement so provides. With respect to the priority of such a security interest, the Act provides that recording as to the real estate is not recording as to the profits and proceeds of the real estate which, as original collateral, would not be covered by such recording. See Section 3–210(a) and (c). Therefore, if it is determined that an assignment of rents or leases is subject to recording under the Uniform Commercial Code, the assignment is treated as an unrecorded security interest in determining its priority even though such an assignment is contained in a recorded mortgage, or was itself recorded in the real estate records.

2. Why should an assignment of rents and/or leases be accomplished by an instrument separate from a mortgage given by the assignor? Cf. *Taylor v. Brennan,* 621 S.W.2d 592 (Tex.1981).

    a. If the assignment is made in a lien theory state, does the assignee want it consented to and agreed to by the lessees?

    b. Under the Uniform Land Transactions Act, a creditor which holds a security interest in rents, without taking possession of the real estate, may notify the lessees, after the debtor's default, to make rental payments to the creditor. See Section 3–504(a).

3. Does a mortgagee want the mortgage senior or junior to the leases of the mortgaged real estate? Does the answer depend on the type of state in which the mortgaged real estate is located?

    a. Are any advantages gained by the mortgagee if the leases are senior to the mortgage?

        1. What are the disadvantages of this approach? Cf. *Silverstein v. Schak,* 107 Ill.App.3d 641, 63 Ill.Dec. 370, 437 N.E.2d 1292 (1982).

    b. If an assignment of rents and/or leases is effective and valid in a state, are there any advantages in the leases being senior to a mortgage?

        1. If there are some advantages, are they outweighed by the disadvantages?

    c. The Uniform Land Transactions Act gives the mortgagee the right to take possession of the real estate on the mortgagor's default and before foreclosure. The possession of the mortgagee, however, is subject to the terms of any lease executed by the mortgagor before the mortgagee took possession, with certain limited exceptions. See Section 3–502(a) and (e). In addition, a mortgagee in possession may notify lessees to make rental payments to the mortgagee even though the mortgagee holds no assignment of rents and the debtor has assigned future rents to another. The mortgagee, however, receives the rents subject to the payment of any claim to such rents having priority over the mortgagee's interest in them. See Section 3–504(a) and (h).

4. Assume that a mortgagee can be put in a position in which it can collect the rents after default by the mortgagor or, at worst, after foreclosure, and can hold the tenants to their leases.

    a. What steps can be taken to avoid the mortgagee being obligated to perform the lessor's covenants under the leases?

1. In the event that this potential liability cannot be totally avoided, can it be minimized? How?

2. What are the advantages and disadvantages of the steps which can be taken to avoid or minimize the mortgagee's liability?

b. Section 3–504 of the Uniform Land Transactions Act provides for the rights and obligations of a mortgagee in possession after default by a mortgagor.

c. See generally with respect to the Uniform Land Transactions Act's impact on mortgage transactions Comment, *Secured Transactions Under Article 3 of the Uniform Land Transactions Act,* 1976 Wis.L.Rev. 899; Kuklin, *The Uniform Land Transactions Act: Article 3,* 11 Real Prop., Prob. & Tr.J. 12 (1976); Bruce, *Mortgage Law Reform Under the Uniform Land Transactions Act,* 64 Geo.L.J. 1245 (1976).

5. See generally Draper, *The Mortgage Triangle: Protecting the Mortgagee's Reliance on High Credit Tenants,* 13 Real Prop., Prob. & Tr.J. 419 (1978); Randolph, *The Mortgagee's Interest in Rents: Some Policy Considerations and Proposals,* 29 U.Kan.L.Rev. 1 (1980); Report of Committee on Real Estate Financing, Real Property Division, *Disposition of Rents After Mortgage Default,* 16 Real Prop., Prob. & Tr.J. 835 (1981); Weg, *The Secured Creditor's Rights to Rents from Real Property,* 17 Real Est.L.J. 29 (1988).

6. A mortgagee also is concerned about a possible sale of the mortgaged property coupled with an assumption of, or a taking subject to, the mortgage. In addition, a mortgagee prefers that a mortgagor not be able to create additional liens against the mortgaged property.

a. Is a covenant in the mortgage prohibiting the mortgagor from taking such actions effective? What is the measure of the mortgagee's damages if the covenant is breached?

b. Is the mortgagee better protected if the mortgage provides that the entire balance of the loan is due upon the sale of the mortgaged property or upon the creation of a lien against it, if the mortgagee has not consented to the sale or the creation of the lien?

1. Might this or a similar provision be held void as an unreasonable restraint on alienation?

a. The current trend in judicial decisions is that such a clause, or a similar clause, is not void as an unreasonable restraint on alienation. See e.g. *Coast Bank v. Minderhout,* 61 Cal.2d 311, 38 Cal.Rptr. 505, 392 P.2d 265 (1964); *Baltimore Life Ins. Co. v. Harn,* 15 Ariz.App. 78, 486 P.2d 190 (1971); *Gunther v. White,* 489 S.W.2d 529 (Tenn.1973); *Malouff v. Midland Fed. Sav. & Loan Ass'n,* 509 P.2d 1240 (Colo.1973); *Tucker v. Pulaski Federal Sav. & Loan Ass'n,* 252 Ark. 849, 481 S.W.2d 725 (1972). As stated by the court in *Tucker v. Pulaski Federal Sav. & Loan Ass'n,* supra, at pages 728–729:

"The acceleration clause in this case is clearly a restraint on the mortgagors' ability to dispose of their property. We believe that so long as an acceleration clause does not purport to restrict absolutely the mortgagors' ability to dispose of their property there is not the type of restraint on alienation that would render the clause void. It follows that the invocation of the clause must be based on grounds that are reasonable on their face.

"Of course, we can certainly see why a mortgagee would object to some transfers; a mortgagor, if permitted, could sell his equity in property and transfer the indebtedness to a person who had been convicted of operating a bawdy house, operating a gambling house, or illegally selling whiskey or drugs, and naturally a mortgagee would not desire to accept such a person, realizing that the property could be used by that person for a similar purpose. The same might be true of an individual who persistently had failed to pay his obligations, who was without a job, or who had a record of permitting property to deteriorate.

"On the other hand, and this frequently happens, a mortgagor could be transferred from his job to another location and, if persons to whom he desired to sell the property could be arbitrarily disapproved by the loan company, he could be in the position of being forced to sell to someone at great sacrifice. This could well be true even though a loan might be three-fourths paid. The validity of such a requirement would leave a mortgagor much at the mercy of the mortgagee. Accordingly, * * * there must be legitimate grounds for refusal to accept a transfer to a particular individual or concern."

b. The Uniform Land Transactions Act permits the conveyance by a mortgagor of the mortgaged property and the creation of additional liens against it notwithstanding a provision in the mortgage which prohibits such acts. The Act, however, recognizes the validity of a due on sale without the consent of the mortgagee clause, subject to the general unconscionability provision. See Sections 1–311 and 3–208(a). The Act indicates that a legitimate purpose of a due on sale clause is to restrict the power of the mortgagor to sell the mortgagor's favorable interest rate. Therefore, within reasonable limits, the mortgagee can condition its consent to sale on the payment, after the sale, of a higher rate of interest. Some authorities have reached the same result without reliance on the Act. See e.g. *Mutual Federal S & L Ass'n v. Wisconsin Wire Works,* 58 Wis.2d 99, 205 N.W.2d 762 (1973); *Crockett v. First Federal S. & L. Ass'n,* 289 N.C. 620, 224 S.E.2d 580 (1976); *Century Fed. Savings & Loan Ass'n v. Van Glahn,* 144 N.J. Super. 48, 364 A.2d 558 (1976); *Tierce, II v. APS Company,* 382 So. 2d 485 (Ala.1979); *Siegel v. Empire Savings Bank,* 304 N.W.2d 335 (Minn.1981); *Martin v. Peoples Mutual Savings and Loan Association,* 319 N.W.2d 220 (Iowa 1982); Finch, *Due–On–Sale Clauses in Debt Instruments: Reconciling Legal Doctrine and Market Realities,* 98 Banking L.J. 300 (1981); Crocker, *The "Due–On–Sale" Mortgage Clause as a Method of Reconciling the Competing Interests of Lender and Borrower,* 84 W.Va.L.Rev. 301 (1982); Kratovil, *Epilogue: Wellenkamp v. Bank of America,* 15 J.Marshall L.Rev. 435 (1982); Kinzler, *Due–On–Sale Clauses: The Economic and Legal Issues,* 43 U.Pitt.L.Rev. 441 (1982); Epstein, *Due-on-Sale Clauses: An Argument for Adopting the Majority Approach,* 26 Wash.U.J.Urb. & Contemp.L. 71 (1984). But see e.g. *Nichols v. Ann Arbor Federal S. & L. Ass'n,* 73 Mich.App. 163, 250 N.W.2d 804 (1977); *Wellenkamp v. Bank of America,* 21 Cal.3d 943, 148 Cal.Rptr. 379, 582 P.2d 970 (1978); *Fogel v. S.S.R. Realty Associ-*

ates, 183 N.J.Super. 303, 443 A.2d 1093 (1981), affirmed, 190 N.J. Super. 47, 461 A.2d 1190 (1985); *Perry v. Island Sav. & Loan Ass'n,* 101 Wash.2d 795, 684 P.2d 1281 (1984); *Boyes v. Valley Bank of Nevada,* 101 Nev. 287, 701 P.2d 1008 (1985); Wein, *Due on Sale in New York,* 49 N.Y.St.B.J. 203 (1977); Note, *Mortgages—Due-on-Sale Clause: Restraint on Alienation—Enforceability,* 28 Case W.Res.L.Rev. 493 (1978); Jennings, *The "Due-on-Sale" Bail-out for Mortgage Lenders: An Analysis of Its Economic and Legal Soundness,* 30 St.Louis U.L.J. 1151 (1986).

c. The Federal Home Loan Bank Board which regulates federal savings and loan associations has issued regulations authorizing the use by associations subject to its regulatory authority of due-on-sale clauses and, specifically, their use to secure a higher rate of interest. See 12 C.F.R. § 545.8–3(f) (1981). The Comptroller of the Currency has issued similar regulations applicable to national banks. These regulations preempt contrary state law. See 46 Fed.Reg. 46964 (1981). Section 341(b) of the Garn–St. Germain Depository Institutions Act of 1982, Pub.L. 97–320, authorizes the use of due-on-sale clauses by lenders and preempts any state laws to the contrary. It does not, however, extend to the use of a due-on-mortgage clause to prevent an encumbrance subordinate to the lender's security if the encumbrance does not relate to a transfer of rights of occupancy in the property which constitutes the security. See Section 341(d)(1) of the Garn–St. Germain Depository Institutions Act. The Supreme Court in *Fidelity Federal Savings and Loan Association v. de la Cuesta,* 458 U.S. 141, 102 S.Ct. 3014, 73 L.Ed.2d 664 (1982), held that the regulations of the Federal Home Loan Bank Board preempted California law in the case of a federal savings and loan association. See also *Washington Savings and Loan Assn. of Florida v. Concepcion Del Portillo,* 419 So.2d 805 (Fla.App.1982). See generally Henkel and Dilworth, *Federal Pre-emption of State Due-on-Sale Clause Restrictions: Jurisdictional Considerations,* 47 Mo.L.Rev. 225 (1982); Barad and Layden, *Due-on-Sale Law as Preempted by the Garn–St. Germain Act,* 12 Real Est.L.J. 138 (1983); Coleman, *Federal Preemption of State Law Prohibitions on the Exercise of Due–On–Sale Clauses,* 100 Banking L.J. 772 (1983); McGuire, *The Due–On–Sale Controversy: Restraints on Alienation and Federal Regulation of Real Estate Mortgages after de la Cuesta and the Garn–St. Germain Act,* 1982 S.Ill.U.L.J. 487; Nelson and Whitman, *Congressional Preemption of Mortgage Due-on-Sale Law: An Analysis of the Garn–St. Germain Act,* 35 Hastings L.J. 241 (1983); Schmelzer, *The Preemptions for Alternative Mortgage Transactions and Due–On–Sale Clauses in the Garn–St. Germain Act,* 102 Banking L.J. 256 (1985).

d. If a mortgagor, rather than not wanting to pay off a mortgage on the transfer of the underlying real estate, wants to prepay the mortgage, and the note and mortgage do not prohibit prepayment, can the note and mortgage be prepaid. See *Mahoney v. Furches,* 503 Pa. 60, 468 A.2d 458 (1983).

c. See generally Jennings and McGuire, *Due-on-Sale Clauses: What's Due? Plenty!,* 11 Real Est.L.J. 291 (1983); Segreti, *The Borrower as Servant to the Lender: Enforcement of Mortgage Due-on-Sale Clauses,* 51 U.Cin.L.

Rev. 779 (1982); Roszkowski, *Drafting Around Mortgage Due–On–Sale Clauses: The Dangers of Playing Hide–And–Seek,* 21 Real Prop., Prob. & Tr.J. 23 (1986).

One of the reasons for a mortgagee's use of a due-on-sale clause is to enable the mortgagee to increase the interest rate if the interest rate provided in the mortgage is below the current rate at the time of the sale of the real estate subject to the mortgage. Is the use of a variable interest rate in the note and mortgage an acceptable alternative? See Stansell and Millar, *How Variable–Rate Mortgages Would Affect Lenders,* 5 # 4 Real Est.Rev. 116 (1976); Eplay, *Can Variable–Rate and Fixed–Rate Mortgages Coexist?,* 5 # 4 Real Est.Rev. 119 (1976); Werner, *Usury and the Variable–Rate Mortgage,* 5 Real Est.L.J. 155 (1976); Lusht, *A New Twist to the Variable Payment Mortgage,* 7 # 2 Real Est.Rev. 72 (1977); Jeka, *Variable Rate Mortgages: The Transition Phase,* 61 Marq.L.Rev. 140 (1977); Boykin and Philips, *The New Challenger: The Variable–Rate Mortgage,* 8 # 2 Real Est.Rev. 83 (1978); Kanner, *Renegotiable Rate Mortgages,* 9 Real Est.L.J. 55 (1980); Draper, *Alternative Mortgage Instruments,* 11 # 3 Real Est.Rev. 32 (1981). The Housing and Community Development Act of 1977, Pub.L. 95–128, Oct. 12, 1977 authorized the making and insuring of certain graduated and variable payment mortgages and provided, in general, that such mortgages are not subject to state usury laws. The Garn–St. Germain Depository Institutions Act of 1982, Pub.L. 97–320, authorized the use by all "housing creditors" of "alternative mortgage transactions" such as variable and adjustable rate mortgages. See Title VII—Alternative Mortgage Transactions—Garn–St. Germain Depository Institutions Act of 1982.

7. In general, with respect to the considerations affecting the permanent lender see Simmons, *Representing the Permanent Lender,* 8 Forum 454 (1973); Smith and Lubell, *The Promissory Note: Forgotten Document,* 8 # 1 Real Est. Rev. 15 (1978); Halper, *Mortgage Exculpation Clauses,* 8 # 2 Real Est.Rev. 35 (1978); Nelson, *The Impact of Mortgagor Bankruptcy on the Real Estate Mortgagee: Current Problems and Some Suggested Solutions,* 50 Mo.L.Rev. 217 (1985).

(i) INCOME TAX CONSIDERATIONS

The effect of a long term mortgage on the basis of a developer in acquired and improved real estate has been previously discussed. See pages 368 to 373 supra. In addition to the effect of a long term mortgage on a developer's basis in the real estate, if the developer is a partnership, the long term mortgage may affect the partners' bases in their partnership interests.

TAX CONSIDERATIONS IN FINANCING REAL ESTATE TRANSACTIONS

Neil G. Bluhm
22 Annual Tax Conference of the Univ. of Chicago
Reprinted in 47 Taxes 844 (1969).
[footnotes omitted]

* * *

Partnership Mortgages

* * * [I]n the case of a partnership, the existence of a mortgage has additional significance in determining the partner's basis for his partnership interest. The partner's basis for his interest in a partnership is particularly important in view of Section 704(d) which limits the amount of a partner's share of the partnership loss to the adjusted basis of such partner's interest in the partnership at the end of the partnership year in which such loss occurred. [In addition, a partner will recognize gain to the extent cash distributions paid to him by the partnership exceed his basis in his partnership interest. See Section 731(a)(1).]

Generally, the initial basis of a partner's interest in a partnership acquired by a contribution to the partnership is an amount equal to the amount of money and the basis of any property contributed. The basis of an interest in a partnership acquired other than by contribution to the partnership is cost. The partner's basis in his partnership interest is increased by an amount equal to the increase in the partner's share of the liabilities of the partnership and the increase in the partner's individual liabilities by reason of the assumption by such partner of a partnership liability. For this purpose a liability to which property is subject is, to the extent of the fair market value of such property, considered as a liability of the owner of the property.

* * *

[I]f the partnership[, however, is] a limited partnership, * * * each partner's basis in his partnership interest * * * depend[s] upon whether the mortgage [is recourse or nonrecourse]. * * * [I]n the case of a limited partnership, * * * where none of the partners has any [economic risk of loss] with respect to a partnership liability (as in the case of a mortgage, no part of which is assumed by the partnership or any of the partners), then all of the partners, including limited partners, are considered as sharing the liability in the same proportion as they share profits. * * * [Therefore, if the partners can avoid personal liability for the mortgage debt, the limited partners can, under Section 752(a), add their shares, determined in accordance with the ratio for sharing profits under the partnership agreement, of the mortgage debt to their respective bases in their partnership interests. The at-risk rules of Section 465, however, may prevent the limited partners from adding their shares of the nonrecourse mortgage debt to their at-risk amounts for the purpose of personally making use of the losses of the partnership, unless the mortgage debt qualifies as "qualified nonrecourse financing" as defined in Section 465(b)(6)(B). See pages 150 to 153 supra, for a discussion of the at-risk concept.]

     * * * One way to [avoid personal liability for the mortgage debt] is to place the property in a land trust and have the land trustee execute the mortgage and loan agreement solely in his capacity as trustee. If a land trust is not used, both the mortgage and loan agreement should make it absolutely clear that there is no personal liability. The mere provision that the partnership shall not be responsible for any deficiency judgment may not be sufficient, because if the mortgagee elected not to foreclose, but instead to sue for each installment on the note, it is arguable that some personal liability still exists.

     What can the limited partners do if the mortgagee insists that [there be personal liability for] the debt? Will it be helpful if the mortgage[e] were willing to have [personal liability for] only a portion of the debt? * * * [The Internal Revenue Service has indicated that limited partners can add their shares of the nonrecourse portion of a partially recourse-partially non-recourse liability to their bases in their partnership interests. See Reg.Sec. 1.752–1T(j)(2); Rev.Rul. 84–118, 1984–2 C.B. 120.]

     [P]erhaps the limited partners can [also] get * * * increased bas[e]s if two separate loans are made, one secured by a first mortgage which is [a recourse loan] and another secured by a second mortgage which is not [a recourse loan]. This arrangement is economically different than if a single mortgage is partially [recourse] because the general partner's obligation is limited to the prior first mortgage debt instead of a part of the entire debt. Therefore, even though the first and second mortgagee is the same party, a good argument can be made for permitting the limited partners to increase the bas[e]s of their partnership interests by their allocable share of the second mortgage debt.

     If the mortgagee insists on * * * full [personal liability for the] mortgage debt it might be advisable to have the partnership agreement provide that the limited partners are obligated to make an additional contribution to the limited partnership of a specified amount. Such amount could be an estimate of the amount by which the tax losses are expected to exceed the capital contributions of the limited partners, reduced by any distributions to the limited partners. * * * [The agreement to contribute might have the effect of permitting the limited partners to increase their bases, in the amount of their additional contributions, in their partnership interests for purposes of Section 704(d).]

* * *

     If none of the above approaches is feasible, it should be remembered that if a limited partner's loss is disallowed under Section 704(d), such disallowed loss can, in a limited way, be carried forward against future partnership profits. Any loss disallowed under Section 704(d) is allowed as a deduction at the end of any succeeding taxable year of the partnership to the extent that the partner's adjusted basis for his partnership interest at the end of such year exceeds zero. [The same type of carryover is permitted for any loss disallowed under Section 465. The loss may be deducted at the end of any subsequent taxable year to the extent that a partner's at-risk amount exceeds zero.] In any succeeding year in which the partnership recognizes taxable income, the adjusted basis of each partner's interest in the partnership [and the partner's at-risk amount] will be increased by the allocable share of such taxable income. If partnership distributions during such year do not otherwise reduce each partner's adjusted basis [and at-risk amount], the previously disallowed losses can be used to offset such taxable income. However, in order for the loss to be carried forward in this manner, it is essential that the partnership be continued for tax purposes and the limited partner remain as a partner.

* * *

NOTE

1. Another method of avoiding personal liability for a mortgage debt is for a partnership to cause a corporation to be formed to execute the note and the mortgage. The corporation then conveys the real estate subject to the mortgage to the partnership.

    a. This approach is not without concerns. See pages 264 to 279 supra.

    b. An alternative approach, the use of the nonrecourse or in rem mortgage, also may present some problems. To have the effect of increasing the bases of the limited partners in their partnership interests, the mortgage truly must be in rem or nonrecourse and not just contain a waiver of any deficiency judgment. If the mortgage is in rem or nonrecourse, however, is it enforceable in a lien theory state? See pages 776 to 782 infra.

2. In order for limited partners to be able to add their shares of nonrecourse financing to their at-risk amounts for the purpose of personally using the losses of the partnership, the financing must be "qualified nonrecourse financing" as defined in Section 465(b)(6)(B). If the financing does not meet the definition of "qualified nonrecourse financing," the limited partners must find another way to be considered at-risk for at least each one's share of the partnership financing, in addition to being entitled to add a share of the financing to the basis of each one's partnership interest, under Section 752.

    a. An obligation to make additional contributions, the assumption or guarantee of partnership liabilities and the giving to the partnership of notes secured by letters of credit as separate ways of increasing the basis and the at-risk amount of a limited partner are subject to question. See Reg.Secs. 1.752–1T through 4T; Priv.Ltr.Rul. 8504005; Rev.Rul. 83–151, 1983–2 C.B. 105; *Hugh M. Brand,* 81 T.C. 821 (1983); *Richard C. Brown,* 40 CCH Tax Ct.Mem. 725 (1980); *Danoff v. United States,* 499 F.Supp. 20 (M.D.Penn.1979); Volet and Millman, *Liability Assumption Under Section 752: An Analysis of the Underlying Theory,* 60 J.Tax'n 374 (1984); Madere and Weitz, *Recent IRS Rulings Take a Restrictive View of Limited Partnership Basis Rules,* 61 J.Tax'n 90 (1984); Note, *The Tax Treatment of a Partner's Contingent Liability,* 6 Va.Tax Rev. 221 (1986).

    b. On the other hand, a limited partner is entitled to increase the basis in his partnership interest and his at-risk amount by assuming or guaranteeing part, or all, of a nonrecourse liability of the partnership. See Reg.Sec. 1.752–1T(f)(2)(ii); *George F. Smith,* 84 T.C. 889 (1985); *Edwin D.*

Abramson, 86 T.C. 360 (1986). In addition, if a limited partner combines a guarantee or assumption of the limited partner's share of partnership recourse liabilities with a release of the general partner(s) and a commitment to make a capital contribution to the partnership equal to the limited partner's share of the liabilities, the limited partner can add the share of liabilities to basis and at-risk amount. See Reg.Sec. 1.752–1T(d); Priv.Ltr. Ruls. 8636003, 8636004 and 8702006; *Sidney J. Gefen,* 87 T.C. 1471 (1986); *Marcus W. Melvin,* 88 T.C. 63 (1987); *Pritchett v. Comm'r,* 827 F.2d 644 (9th Cir.1987); Bobrow and Boyle, *Section 752 and Limited Partners: The "Ultimate Liability" Doctrine as Applied to Partnership Recourse Indebtedness,* 4 J.Ps.Tax'n 172 (1987).

3. See generally Seago and Horvitz, *What is a Partnership Liability and How is a Partner's Share Determined?,* 11 Tax Adviser 18 (1980); Levine, *Structuring Real Estate Loans to Preserve Investors' Tax Benefits, (Part I),* 1 # 5 Prac.Real Est.Law. 55 (1985); *(Part II),* 1 # 6 Prac.Real Est.Law. 75 (1985); Coven, *Limiting Losses Attributable to Nonrecourse Debt: A Defense of the Traditional System Against the At–Risk Concept,* 74 Calif.L.Rev. 41 (1986); Eisenstadt and Giroux, *Real Estate Now Subject to At–Risk Rules; Rehab Credit Reduced by Tax Reform Act,* 15 Tax'n Law. 242 (1987); Maples, *Limited Partner Obligations and At–Risk Amounts: The Tax Court Speaks But Not Too Clearly,* 18 Tax Adviser 117 (1987); Hirsh, *Extension of At–Risk Rules to Real Estate Leaves Many Issues Unclear,* 4 J.Ps.Tax'n 226 (1987); Division I, Pages 74 to 87 and 150 to 153; this Division, pages 589 to 590.

c. MORTGAGING THE GROUND LEASE

If a developer, instead of acquiring a fee interest in the land to be used for the development, acquires a leasehold interest, the use of that interest as security for the long term financing presents a host of problems to be solved by the financier and the developer. Earlier in this Division the problems involved in acquiring a mortgageable lease were examined. See pages 610 to 616 supra. The following materials consider the problems involved in mortgaging that lease.

GROUND LEASES AND THEIR FINANCING

4 Real Property, Probate and Trust Journal 437 (1969).
[footnotes omitted]

* * *

[Fee Subordinated to Mortgage]

* * *

Recording Requirements

The lease or a memorandum thereof, if permitted under applicable state law, should be recorded upon execution. In the case of an unsubordinated lease, it has been suggested that it is good practice always to record the entire lease. This then brings up the further question of whether or not under the Uniform Commercial Code the filing of a financing statement is necessary or proper because the mortgage is not only a lien on the land and buildings, but also in certain cases a portion of the building which would be considered "fixtures" under the UCC. * * *

Manner of Subordination; Examples of Each

Once the landlord has agreed to subordinate, the question arises as to the type of clause or documentation necessary to effect such subordination. Obviously the joinder by the landlord in the execution of the note and mortgage is the simplest and most effective. Needless to say, the joinder by the landlord in any note and mortgage should * * * be limited to the mortgaging of his fee and eliminating any personal liability on his part for any deficiency and for any violations of the mortgage causing a default. One way of handling the problem is for the landlord to execute a separate agreement in recordable form, subordinating his fee to the mortgage. Another manner of effecting the subordination is by means of a power of attorney granted to the tenant by the landlord, giving [the tenant] the authority and power to execute a mortgage on the fee. This method requires exact compliance with the local formalities for the valid execution of a power of attorney and serious questions can still be raised as to whether or not such a power is valid in the event of the death, disability, bankruptcy, etc., of the landlord between the time of the execution of the power and the execution of the mortgage. * * *

Provisions of Mortgage

1. DESCRIPTION OF MORTGAGED ESTATE

The lender will insist that the mortgage describe both estates, the leasehold and fee estates; and that it be entitled to foreclose either estate. The mortgagee will want freedom of action in this respect. It will want to be able to conduct separate foreclosure sales of the fee and leasehold. One estate or the other may be uneconomical to the mortgagee. * * *

2. RESTRICTION OF LEASE MODIFICATIONS

The mortgagee will require that there be no material changes or modifications to the lease without its consent; and that the tenant waive any subrogation rights unless such rights are subordinate to the rights of the mortgagee.

3. MORTGAGE TO CONFORM TO LEASE

Since the lease is the first document that is customarily drawn, and is the one that must be followed, * * * the mortgage [must] conform with the lease and * * * not contain provisions that are in conflict or inconsistent with it. The problems usually arise in regard to condemnation and fire insurance proceeds. Another matter of concern is the question of whether or not there is a provision in the lease calling for an abatement of rent in the event of damage or destruction and, if not, whether the tenant is financially able to meet his rental obligation despite the loss of the income from the subtenants.

4. DAMAGE OR DESTRUCTION TO PREMISES

* * * The landlord and the tenant are both interested in seeing that the proceeds of the fire insurance be available for use for reconstruction of the damaged or destroyed improvements. It is not to their best interests to permit the proceeds to be applied on the mortgage indebtedness. The mortgagee generally is agreeable to the application of the proceeds to the reconstruction, provided it is assured this will be done. * * *

5. CONDEMNATION

* * * If there is a total condemnation, provision should be made for the mortgage to be paid and then the adjustments made on the division of the award between the landlord and tenant, as provided in the lease. This division problem can also be difficult as the relative positions of the landlord and tenant change with the passage of time and the remaining term of the lease decreases. The mortgagee must concern itself * * * with [whether] the division of proceeds between landlord and tenant provided for, either under state law or in the [lease and] mortgage, is of such a nature that it is adequately protected. The mortgage should contain an assignment to the mortgagee of the tenant's right to the condemnation award in the amount of the debt in the event of a total taking.

The bigger problem, however, arises in the event of a partial taking. In such case, the lease * * * [generally] is not terminated, and the usefulness of the project is impaired to varying degrees, depending upon the amount of taking and the damage to the tenant and probably to the subtenants. The latters' rent obligation[s] may be abated in part, resulting in less money being available for debt service and payment of rent on the lease.

If there is a partial taking, the award for the building or improvements [will] probably be used to restore or replace the building and improvements if possible and practical. The mortgagee [will] be interested in receiving that part of the proceeds awarded to the tenant if they are [to be] utilized for something other than the replacement of the building and improvements. The tenant's share of any money not used for restoration should probably be applied to the mortgage without, of course, any penalty for prepayment.

6. WAIVER OF RIGHT TO DEFICIENCY JUDGMENT AGAINST LANDLORD

If the landlord has agreed to, and does, join in the execution of the mortgage, the mortgage should, of course, contain a provision relieving him of any personal liability under the mortgage [regardless] whether * * * the same is done for the tenant.

7. NONDISTURBANCE AND ATTORNMENT

The mortgage should also contain an agreement by the mortgagee that it will agree to any reasonable nondisturbance or attornment agreement required by any acceptable high credit subtenant. * * *

8. NOTICE OF DEFAULT TO LANDLORD

The landlord, of course, is interested and should require an agreement in the mortgage that notice of any default in the mortgage will be given to him and that an opportunity will be given to him to cure it. This goes hand in hand with the mortgagee's requirements that the lease contain a provision that the landlord notify [it] of any default in the lease and that it be afforded the opportunity to cure it if possible.

9. WAIVER OF RIGHT TO REQUIRE MARSHALLING OF ASSETS OR FIRST PROCEED AGAINST TENANT

* * * [I]nasmuch as the landlord may show that he is no more than a surety of the tenant, he can, unless the right is waived, require the mortgagee to proceed against the leasehold estate first. * * *

Partial Subordination

* * * [T]he landlord, instead of subordinating the fee as such, subordinates his rent claim to the mortgage debt. This is done by having a provision in the lease that in the event of default under the mortgage, the rent will abate in whole or in part until the mortgagee has been paid in full by taking possession of the property and collecting the rents. This makes the mortgaged leasehold much more valuable, although not as valuable as the unencumbered fee. * * *

Leasehold Mortgage

A. *Nature of Leasehold Mortgage*

A lender whose security is a leasehold mortgage, that is a security interest in the interest of the tenant under a lease, has the same concerns as any lender secured by a fee or any other mortgagee would have, plus certain special concerns which are peculiar to the fact that the security is a leasehold mortgage. * * *

The principal special consideration of a lender secured by a leasehold mortgage is that the security of the lender is a defeasible estate under circumstances where the lender cannot cure all defaults. Therefore, the leasehold mortgagee must be in a position to control all contingencies which could terminate the tenant's leasehold estate and thus wipe out the lender's security. He should have notice of defaults and an opportunity to cure them.

The leasehold mortgagee is in effect a third party to the principal lease, a tenant once removed. The leasehold mortgagee must have at least all of the rights which the tenant has. * * *

B. *What is Security?*

The lender's security is the tenant's leasehold estate, which is essentially the right to possession of the leased premises for a stated term provided that the tenant performs the covenants and satisfies the conditions of the lease.

Prior to closing a leasehold mortgage, the leasehold mortgagee should be sure the tenant is not in default, that the lease is in full force and effect, that all conditions for effectiveness of the lease are satisfied, that the leasehold mortgagee knows what the entire lease contains, including all amendments, and that tenant's estate is not primed by prior encumbrances which are unsatisfactory to the leasehold mortgagee either because they violate statutory requirements or because they pose undue business risks. Therefore, a title search by the mortgagee and warranties by the tenant are required. In addition, the best protection for the leasehold mortgagee is to obtain an estoppel certificate from the landlord.

C. *Provisions of Lease*

* * *

To be financible, a leasehold must be acceptable to the proposed mortgagee and comply with the legal investment or insurance or banking laws of the domicile of the mortgagee. In general, this means that there must be no way in which the leasehold can be cut off or terminated without a right in the mortgagee to preserve its security.

* * *

Statutory limitations on leasehold mortgages must be considered. In addition to the statutory rules in many jurisdictions limiting the principal amount of a loan to a certain percentage of the value of the security, there are special limitations in many jurisdictions on leasehold mortgages, and requirements that the lease have a minimum term which is longer than the term of the loan. In this connection, the leasehold mortgagee should pay particular attention to clauses giving the landlord the right to terminate the lease * * * in the event of destruction of improvements. Any such right must be limited so that the basic statutory requirement [with respect to the] term [of the lease] is not infringed. Even if there is no statutory rule on length of the term, the leasehold mortgagee would want to have a lease term longer than the life of the loan and no right in the landlord to terminate the lease by reason of destruction of improvements.

If the lease is subordinated to the fee mortgage, but the fee mortgagee executes a nondisturbance agreement, the tenant[, nevertheless,] may * * * find that he cannot mortgage his leasehold interest. The laws of some states and the policies of [certain] mortgagees require that the leasehold be on the "unencumbered fee." A bare nondisturbance agreement will not protect the leasehold mortgagee in case of fire or condemnation. * * *

The landlord should have little objection to placing the lease first. The true security is the improvement and investment to be made by the tenant. So long as the tenant will erect improvements upon the premises, the landlord will have substantial security. After putting the lease first, the landlord normally retains the right to mortgage his reversion and [assign] the rent payable under the lease. If the tenant is a so-called "high credit tenant," the landlord [should] be [able] to obtain a substantial mortgage loan.

* * *

Multiple Encumbrances—Individual Leases

Occasionally, a tenant will enter into a lease involving land area sufficient in size to accommodate the construction of several buildings, it is usually the intention of the tenant to develop the entire tract as an integrated whole, similar to shopping center developments, apartment house complexes and the like. He may desire to sublease the entire tract to one or more high-credit subtenants or he may enter into the lease with the intention of developing and subleasing the tract by sections. In either such situation, he may find it necessary to finance improvements with several lenders, each of whom will demand a first claim on the leasehold interest of the tenant with respect to a portion of the tract, as well as on his interest in the high-credit sublease. In order to protect this priority in the mortgagee, as well as the integrity of the sublease, not only must all existing mortgages of the fee be subordinated to the later ground lease and the leasehold mortgage made inferior to the high-credit sublease, but there will need to be an agreement with the landlord to the effect that the landlord will recognize the continued validity of the sublease in the event of termination of the [ground] lease through default of the tenant.

Where substantially the entire tract is under sublease to one or more high-credit subtenants, the problem of multiple lenders can be simplified through the use of an open-end trust mortgage. * * * This arrangement * * * permit[s] the issue of equally secured notes to any number of lenders. Financing of additions to existing improvements * * * also [are] made feasible through the issue of equally secured improvement notes under supplemental trust mortgages. Clauses in the trust mortgage [will] limit the amount of improvement notes to the cost and expense attributable to the new construction, limit the maturity of the notes to the maturity date of the original notes or the term of the high-credit subtenant, provide for an increased rental by [requiring] amendment of the sublease in order to fund the additional indebtedness, and give the existing lenders a pro rata right of first refusal to purchase the improvement notes. When such improvement notes are issued, the sublease amendment should contain a clause making it clear that the sublease amendment is superior to the trust mortgage as supplemented. It * * * also [is] desirable to include a clause in the supplemental trust mortgage to the effect that the supplemental mortgage is subordinate to the sublease as amended.

Problems regarding subordination of interests * * * seem to be of greater incidence where a tenant enters into a lease with the intention of developing the area on a piece-meal basis and of obtaining separate mortgage financing as such development proceeds. As a starting point, the original lease [must] contain a clause requiring the landlord to execute individual ground leases of particular areas to the tenant, upon surrender of part or all of the original lease. No mortgagee of a leasehold estate wants to be placed in [a] position [in which] it will have to pay the rent on the entire premises in order to cure defaults under the lease, where its mortgage encumbers only a portion of the premises. Each individual lease [of an area] together with a high-credit sublease of the same area, [will constitute the security for the financing of the improvement of the area].

A clause in each individual lease could provide that upon satisfaction of all mortgage loans affecting the entire development, the original lease of the entire tract will * * * be reinstated upon surrender of all individual leases to the landlord. There also [must] be a clause in the original lease showing how rent is to be allocated in each individual lease (possibly on the basis of square feet of leased area) and prohibiting the landlord from imposing a condition in each individual lease that a default therein will constitute a default in all individual leases, since this would have the effect of severely restricting the tenant's ability to secure financing. Except as changed by circumstances of time and facts surrounding each individual lease, provisions in the original lease, in each individual lease and in the reinstated lease should be substantially the same.

Where areas are developed and financed by sections or where areas are to become a part of adjacent commercial areas which are under other ownership, problems will arise involving reciprocal easements for parking of automobiles, party walls, utilities, ingress and egress and the like. * * *

In summary, the following would seem to be of importance where cross-easements are involved in development of an area on a piece-meal basis or where there are to be cross-easements involving adjacent areas:

1. The landlord should agree in each lease to recognize and be bound by all declarations of easements creating servitudes on the leased estate entered into by the tenant as permitted by the master lease.

2. Mortgages of the servient estate, including the fee and the leasehold interest, should be inferior to all such easement dedications.

3. Each sublease should give the right to a tenant-sublessor to dedicate or grant easements creating servitudes on the leased premises if such servitudes do not materially interfere with the sublessee's business and if the sublessee is entitled to the benefits of all nonexclusive easements granted in other areas of the development.

4. Each leasehold mortgage should give the right to the tenant-mortgagor to grant easements creating servitudes on the mortgaged premises if such servitudes do not materially impair the value of the

mortgage security, including the assigned sublease, and if all easements granted in other areas of the development are to become a part of the mortgage security.

5. Where a dominant or servient estate is to be mortgaged or subleased, all easements attaching to the dominant estate should be described in the mortgage [and] in the sublease and all servitudes should be excepted from the description in the mortgage [and] sublease.

NOTE

1. How should any doubt as to the execution and filing under the Uniform Commercial Code of a financing statement applicable to fixtures be resolved by a mortgagee financing the improvement of leased premises? See Note, *Fixtures and Personal Property in Mortgage Transactions Under UCC,* 9 Real Prop., Prob. & Tr.J. 653 (1974); Berry, *Priority Conflicts Between Fixture Secured Creditors and Real Estate Claimants,* 7 Mem.St.U.L.Rev. 209 (1977).

2. Any time the subordination of the fee to the development financier's mortgage is desired, the validity and enforceability of the subordination agreement between the lessor and lessee must be considered. See Division I, pages 252 to 256 and this Division, pages 637 to 649.

3. Even though a mortgagee may be willing to have the insurance proceeds received as a result of damage to the improvements applied to the reconstruction of the improvements, what steps should be taken, and what provisions should be included in the mortgage and lease, to assure the mortgagee that the proceeds will be so applied?

　　a. If the amount of the insurance proceeds is less than the cost of reconstruction, what conditions might the mortgagee place on its consent to the use of the proceeds for reconstruction?

4. If the fee is only partially subordinated—the lessor agrees that the rent under the ground lease will abate in whole or in part or be deferred until the mortgagee has been paid in full by taking possession of the real estate and collecting the rent from subtenants or disposing of the real estate—might the loan by the mortgagee be considered an illegal loan under state laws and regulations governing loans made by institutional lenders which require that the lender's mortgage have first priority?

　　a. If the ground lessor can mortgage the fee interest and does so, does this act have any bearing on whether the institutional lender's loan is considered an illegal loan? Does the answer to this question depend on whether the lease is senior to the fee mortgage?

　　b. Might the ground lessor be permitted to mortgage the fee, without the illegal loan possibilities, if the lease is senior to any fee mortgage and the improvements constructed and to be constructed are severed from the land—title to the improvements is conveyed to the lessee? The lessee can grant a first mortgage on the leasehold and the improvements to the mortgagee, and since the ground lease is prior to any mortgage of the fee interest, the foreclosure of a fee mortgage will not terminate the lease.

　　　　1. Are there any problems with this approach from the standpoint of the leasehold and improvements mortgagee and the ground lessor?

a. If the leasehold and improvements mortgagee foreclosed its mortgage, and the ground lessor terminated the lease, because of the lessee's default, how does the mortgagee or the purchaser on foreclosure get across the lessor's land to the improvements?

b. Should one party have ownership of the improvements and the land after the termination of the lease? If so, how should this result be provided for at the inception of the ground lease?

c. If the ground lessee defaults on the leasehold and improvements mortgage during the last year of the term of the lease and the leasehold and improvements mortgage is not fully paid at the end of the term of the lease, does the mortgagee have any interest which can be sold in foreclosure in order to generate enough funds to pay the remaining principal balance of the mortgage?

5. A mortgagee which makes a loan secured by a leasehold mortgage also is concerned about its rights upon the bankruptcy of the mortgagor-lessee or the lessor. See generally Orr and Klee, *Secured Creditors Under the New Bankruptcy Code,* 11 U.C.C.L.J. 312, 338 (1979); Shanker, *The Treatment of Executory Contracts and Leases in the 1978 Bankruptcy Reform Act,* 25 Prac. Law. 11 (Oct.1979); Halper, *Bankruptcy Cancellation Clauses Under the Bankruptcy Reform Act,* 9 # 3 Real Est.Rev. 75 (1979). See also Division I, pages 243 to 245 and this Division, page 616.

6. See generally Smith and Lubell, *Mortgaging The Leasehold,* 7 # 3 Real Est.Rev. 13 (1977); Levitan, *Leasehold Mortgage Financing: Reliance on The "New Lease" Provisions,* 15 Real Prop., Prob. & Tr.J. 413 (1980); Report, *Model Leasehold Encumbrance Provisions,* 15 Real Prop., Prob. & Tr.J. 395 (1980); York, *The Ground Lease and the Leasehold Mortgagee,* 99 Banking L.J. 709 (1982); Halper, *Introducing the Ground Lease,* 15 # 3 Real Est.Rev. 24 (1985); Halper, *Mortgageability of the Unsubordinated Ground Lease, Part II,* 16 # 1 Real Est.Rev. 48 (1986); *Part III,* 16 # 2 Real Est.Rev. 73 (1986); *Part IV,* 16 # 3 Real Est.Rev. 64 (1986); *Part V,* 16 # 4 Real Est.Rev. 60 (1986).

d. PARTICIPATION

At times, one lender, either because of federal, state or self-imposed lending limits or because of the large amount of financing required for the development under consideration, cannot by itself satisfy the financing needs. The solution to this problem often is a participation in the financing by two or more lenders.

WHAT EXACTLY IS A LOAN PARTICIPATION?
Jeffrey D. Hutchins
9 Rutgers Camden Law Journal 447 (1978).
[some footnotes omitted]

* * *

Practice in Loan Participations

In a typical bank loan participation there is a "lead" bank and one or more participants. The lead usually originates the loan and sells participations at the time the loan is closed. Normally the lead will retain a portion of the loan for its own account, although this is not always the case. In some instances participations will be sold long after the lead has disbursed the entire amount of the loan from its own funds. The lead normally holds all the loan documents in its own name and handles all dealings with the borrower.

Participations are sold for various reasons. Banks may wish to share the risk on a particularly large loan. A loan may exceed the legal lending limit of a small bank were it to make the loan without selling participations. Mortgage bankers may sell participations in loans that they originate since they do not have the capital available to finance all of their mortgages. Banks may also join in participations with finance companies, insurance companies, pension funds, and governmental agencies such as the Small Business Administration * * *.

A participation agreement is often used to embody the terms of a participation transaction with certificates of participation issued evidencing the amount contributed by each participant. These may, however, be combined in one document. Since the relationship between lead and participant is contractual, it may take on a variety of special characteristics. For instance, participations are sometimes labeled "senior" and "junior," with the senior participant given first priority in payments made on the loan. Participations have also been structured to meet the demands of mortgage lending. Since construction loans usually require future advances, the participants may be required to fund their pro rata share of each advance as it is made to the borrower. Under this method of operation, upon each advance the lead will issue a new participation certificate to each participant, evidencing the total amount contributed by that participant to date and superseding all previous certificates.

A participation agreement usually specifies that the participant is purchasing an "undivided interest," a "participating interest," a "fractional interest" or some similar interest in the loan. The interest rate payable to the participant is often the same as the rate paid to the lead, but this may be varied. The lead may retain certain fees or a fraction of the interest to cover servicing of the loan, or the lead may subsidize additional interest in order to attract a participant. A lead may even guarantee the loan as added inducement to a participant, although this does not appear to be standard practice.

* * *

While defining the legal relationship between a lead and a participant can have significant practical consequences, it is not an easy task. The terms of the participation agreement will, of course, govern the participation relationship, but when the participation agreement contains very little detail or is ambiguous, then the agreement must be supplemented by the growing body of case law on the subject of loan participations. As will be seen, however, the cases fail to provide a uniform interpretation of the participation relationship.

Debtor–Creditor Relationship

* * *

[A]t least two early cases held that participation certificates sold in mortgage pools created a debtor-creditor relationship between issuer and participant.[15]　The effect of this holding in People v. Title and Mortgage Guarantee Co.[16] was to determine that the certificate holders had no ownership rights warranting due process protection.　In Prudential Insurance Co. v. Liberdar Holding Corp., the effect was to prevent the certificate holders from acquiring rights in an individual property after there had been a partial foreclosure.　On the other hand, subsequent cases dealing with participations in single mortgages explicitly rejected the debt theory.[17]　Although there is some support for treating a guaranteed assignment of a chose in action as a loan rather than a sale, thus subjecting the transaction to the usury laws, this approach seems to have been limited to assignments of accounts receivable.

The largest single consequence of finding a loan relationship between participant and lead occurs when the lead goes into bankruptcy. If the participant is viewed as a secured creditor, its preferred position must be secured by perfecting its security interest in the underlying note.　If it failed to do so, the participant would be relegated to the status of an unsecured creditor of the lead. * * *

If there is any doubt whether a particular loan participation may be classified as a loan or as an assignment, the participant should take steps to perfect its interest.　When the underlying obligation is an unsecured note or a note secured by a mortgage on real estate, the proper method for perfecting a security interest in such a note is to take delivery of the note.　This would be impossible in a case involving several participants.　Also, the lead may be unwilling to give up the note when the participation is for substantially less than the face amount of the note.　The lead, as debtor, would not be allowed to retain possession as agent of the participant, thereby perfecting the participant's interest through constructive possession.　Perhaps in such a case perfection would have to be made by delivery of the note to a third party to hold it as agent for the participants.

Several factors should be present to warrant finding a loan relationship between participant and lead lender.　These include a guaranty by the lead; substantially different payment arrangements between the original borrower and the lead on the one hand, and the lead and participant on the other; a participation that lasts for a shorter or longer term than the underlying obligation;　and a large discrepancy

---

15.　72 F.2d 395 (2d Cir.1934); 264 N.Y. 69, 190 N.E. 153 (1934).

16.　264 N.Y. 69, 190 N.E. 153 (1934).

17.　In re Westover, Inc., 82 F.2d 177, 181 (2d Cir.1936).

between the interest rate due on the underlying note and the interest rate specified in the participation agreement.

* * *

Assignment

Participation agreements frequently state that the participant is "purchasing" an "undivided interest" or a "fractional interest" in the loan. Given this language, it is logical to assume that the participant is getting a partial assignment. Some early New York guaranteed mortgage cases support this interpretation. In re Westover, Inc.[18] the certificate holders were found not to be creditors of the issuer, but rather creditors of the underlying borrower, and thereby were entitled to participate in the borrower's bankruptcy proceeding as creditors. Likewise, in In re Prudence Co.[19] the certificate holders were deemed the "real owners" of the mortgage.

The major advantage to the participant in having a partial assignment relationship with the lead is that the participant need not perfect a security interest against the lead for protection in the event of bankruptcy. Other benefits are that the participants may become entitled to interest at the rate called for in the mortgage, instead of at the lower rate called for in the certificates, if the lead defaults on any of its obligations. If the assignment creates a tenancy in common, the participants may be entitled to the remedy of partition when a mortgage is foreclosed and differences develop with the lead or other participants. An assignment relationship, however, carries adverse consequences as well. For example, should a mortgage loan go into foreclosure, the participants, as co-owners of the mortgage, could be required to share expenses on the property, such as taxes.

In 1960, the United States Supreme Court confronted the problem of defining a participant's interest in a loan. Small Business Administration v. McClellan[20] concerned a bank loan in which the SBA was a seventy-five percent participant. As phrased by the Court, the issue was "whether, when the Administration has joined a private bank in a loan and the borrower becomes bankrupt, the Administration's interest in the unpaid balance of the loan is entitled to the priority provided for 'debts due to the United States.' "[21] Obviously, if the SBA were considered a creditor of the lead, it would be one step removed from the borrower and would not be able to claim a priority in the borrower's assets. The Court held, however, that "beneficial ownership" of seventy-five percent of the debt belonged to the SBA from the inception of its participation, even though formal assignment of the note for collection by the SBA did not take place until a later date.[22] Implicit in the Court's holding is that the sale of the participation, allowing the

---

18. 82 F.2d 177 (2d Cir.1936).

19. 89 F.2d 689 (2d Cir.1937).

20. 364 U.S. 446 (1960).

21. Id. at 447.

22. Id. at 450.

participant to assert a claim directly against the borrower, conveyed a partial assignment of ownership of the note.

* * *

Under the heading of assignment, one other theory remains to be considered. It has been suggested that a participation is in reality an assignment of the proceeds of a loan and does not convey an interest in the note itself. There is dicta to this effect in In re Erie Forge & Steel Corp.,[23] wherein the court stated that the participant in a loan "acquired no ownership right in the note from [the lead], but only the right of participation in the proceeds."[24] The argument was also advanced in Wittner v. Metzger[25] in which the participants claimed that they had purchased only a participation in the collections made by the lead. The court, however, found that a joint venture had been created.

The argument that participating banks are real parties in interest in a loan participation was rejected in Midland Nat. Bank v. Cousins Properties, Inc.[26] In that case the lead bank sued the borrower for fraud and the borrower claimed that the nine participating banks were required to be joined for just adjudication under Rule 19 of the Federal Rules of Civil Procedure. The lead bank argued that each participant purchased only "a par value portion of the proceeds of a note" and that the "note and the participation are entirely distinct agreements" giving the participants recourse only against the lead.[27] Although the court appeared to agree with the lead bank's assertions, it stated in dicta that "there is little question that the participating banks have an 'interest' in the notes in question."[28] The court, however, was silent about the nature of that interest. The court's finding that the participants were not required to be joined was based on the following: (1) the gravamen of the action was not for recovery on the notes; (2) the participants would have recourse against the lead under their participation certificates; and (3) the defendant would not be subjected to multiple liability since the fraud alleged was only between defendant and the lead.

* * *

participants (as assigns) have recourse against a lead

Tenancy in Common

Closely related to the concept of assignment is the notion that participants in a loan become tenants in common or cotenants of the loan and security. The use of the phrase "undivided interest" in participation agreements indicates this type of relationship because tenants in common of property are said to own an undivided interest in

---

23. 456 F.2d 801 (3d Cir.1972).

24. Id. at 806. The court made this statement despite the fact that the participation agreement stated that one bank *shall purchase* for cash from the other Bank receiving payment at a lesser rate *an interest or interests in the Note or Notes* payable to such other Bank in such amounts as shall result in equal pro rata participation by both Banks in the principal amount of the Notes then outstanding.

Id. at 803 n. 2 (emphasis supplied).

25. 72 N.J.Super. 438, 178 A.2d 671 (App.Div.), certif. denied, 37 N.J. 228, 181 A.2d 12 (1962).

26. 68 F.R.D. 427 (N.D.Ga.1975).

27. Id. at 429.

28. Id. at 430.

that property. Both federal cases [29] and some of the early New York guaranteed mortgage cases [30] classified the participants as tenants in common of the mortgage. In one case this classification enabled the certificate holders to claim interest at the rate stated in the mortgage rather than at the rate stated in the certificate.[31]

Classification of participants as tenants in common would probably have its greatest impact in a typical mortgage loan after foreclosure. If a falling out among the lead and participants about how to administer the property occurred, a participant could possibly sue for partition. This is a right that equity grants to tenants in common and may be defeated only if the partition would be unduly prejudicial.

* * *

Joint Venture

When would a loan participation cross the line to become a joint venture? What are the consequences of such a classification? A list of joint venture characteristics compiled by Williston is frequently cited:

(A) A contribution by the parties of money, property, effort, knowledge, skill or other asset to a common undertaking;

(B) A joint property interest in the subject matter of the venture;

(C) A right of mutual control or management of the enterprise;

(D) Expectation of profit, or the presence of "adventure," as it is sometimes called;

(E) A right to participate in the profits;

(F) Most usually, limitation of the objective to a single undertaking or *ad hoc* enterprise.[32]

One other element that should be added to this list is an agreement between the parties to share losses.[33]

It would not be too difficult to find all of these elements present in a routine loan participation. The only two characteristics that might be lacking are (A) and (C); (A) because the lead may "undertake" the loan on its own and sell participations only at a later date and (C) because the participants may have no say in the management of the loan. Some cases, however, hold that management of a joint venture may be entrusted to one of the joint venturers.[34] Furthermore, the administration of a loan does not usually require a great deal of active

---

29. See e.g. In re Westover, Inc., 82 F.2d 177 (2d Cir.1936) and Delatour v. Prudence Realization Corp., 167 F.2d 621 (2d Cir. 1948).

30. See Metropolitan Inv. Serv. v. Manhattan Co., 292 N.Y. 463, 466, 55 N.E.2d 738, 739 (1944); Title Guarantee & Trust Co. v. Mortgage Comm'n, 273 N.Y. 415, 422–23, 7 N.E.2d 841, 844 (1937).

31. Delatour v. Prudence Realization Corp., 167 F.2d 621 (2d Cir.1948).

32. 2 S. Williston, Contracts § 318A (3d ed. 1959).

33. See Jaeger, Joint Ventures: Origin, Nature and Development, 9 Am.U.L.Rev. 1, 12, 21 (1960).

34. See Britton v. Green, 325 F.2d 377, 383 (10th Cir.1963); Wittner v. Metzger, 72 N.J.Super. 438, 448, 178 A.2d 671, 676 (App.Div.), certif. denied, 37 N.J. 228, 181 A.2d 12 (1962).

management and if a major problem arises, participants would probably be asked for their advice.

There are at least three consequences of some importance that derive from a finding of a joint venture. First, a fiduciary relationship is implied among the joint venturers. Thus a lead may be held to a higher standard of care in a joint venture. Second, an agreement to share losses will be implied when a joint venture is found, even though such a clause is not expressly stated. Third, in some jurisdictions an agency power is granted to the joint venturer to bind his associates.[35]

In In re Alda Commercial Corp.[36] a participant claimed that he was a joint venturer with the lead rather than a secured creditor of the lead. This was rejected by the referee, who found that

> petitioner was not to share in the profits of the bankrupt's business except to the extent that he would receive interest on his investment; that petitioner played no part in the bankrupt's initial determination to lend money to [the borrowers]; that petitioner did not manage the accounts or have any say as to how the bankrupt would attain security or arrange for collections.[37]

In an earlier case a joint venture was found to have been created by the sale of a participation. In Wittner v. Metzger [38] the court was confronted with the issue of whether the participant was required to share a loss that had occurred in the lead's factoring operations. The court found a joint venture and held the participant liable. Since the agreement expressly stated that the participant would bear his pro rata share of any loss, the result of the case should have been the same without the finding of a joint venture.[39]

* * *

Agency

* * *

In some recent loan participation cases there is language to the effect that after an assignment or partial assignment of a note the assignor (lead bank) automatically became the agent for collection of the loan.[40] In Midland Nat. Bank v. Cousins Properties, Inc.[41] one of

---

35. [Might a fourth consequence resulting from a finding of joint venture be the obligation to file a partnership return and be governed by Subchapter K of the Internal Revenue Code? Might the participants elect to avoid this consequence by electing not to be treated as a partnership? See Section 761(a)(1).]

36. 327 F.Supp. 1315 (S.D.N.Y.1971).

37. Id. at 1317.

38. 72 N.J.Super. 438, 178 A.2d 671 (App.Div.), certif. denied, 37 N.J. 228, 181 A.2d 12 (1962).

39. Participation agreements often call for sharing losses. See State of Pennsylvania v. Curtis Nat. Bank, 427 F.2d 395 (5th Cir.1970), in which the agreement stated that the participant would "pay the [lead] on demand its pro rata share of any expenses or liability incurred by the [lead] in connection with the loan * * *." Id. at 400. Surprisingly, the court held the participant liable for its share of an expense (extra interest payments) caused by the lead's mismanagement. Id. at 401.

40. See FDIC v. Mademoiselle of Cal., 379 F.2d 660, 665 (9th Cir.1967); Heights v. Citizens Nat'l Bank, 463 Pa. 48, 63, 342 A.2d 738, 745 (1975).

41. 68 F.R.D. 427 (N.D.Ga.1975).

the alternative theories of the lead bank was that under the participation certificates it was designated "agent for collection of principal and interest," and that, as such, it was the real party in interest in its suit against the borrower.[42] Although the court held that the participating banks were not required to be joined, it is unclear whether this was one of the grounds of the decision.

In two other loan participation cases it was argued that there was a principal-agent relationship between participant and lead going beyond a mere agency for collection. In the *Alda* case the participant advanced the theory that it was the lead's principal, rather than a secured creditor that had failed to perfect. The court thought otherwise, holding that the participant did not exercise any control over the lead, as would be necessary for an agency relationship to exist.[43]

In Slaughter v. Philadelphia Nat. Bank [44] the borrower, in an attempt to hold the participant liable for certain acts of the lead, argued that an agency relationship existed between participant and lead. The question was submitted to the jury, which returned a special verdict stating that the participant did not exercise control, nor did it have the right to exercise control, over the stock that the lead had wrongfully retained.[45] *Slaughter* and *Alda* indicate that the finding of an agency relationship will be by case-by-case determination.

Trust

The presence of a trust between a lead and a participant can have at least two major consequences. First, the lead will obviously be held to a higher standard of conduct in administering the loan if a trust relationship is found. Second, under a trust relationship the participant will not have to worry about being subordinated to the lead's trustee in bankruptcy should the lead become insolvent. Any collections the lead made on the loan would be held in trust for the participant, giving the participant a preference therein.[46]

* * *

The leading case on the existence of a trust under a participation agreement is Stratford Financial Corp. v. Finex Corp.[47] Although *Stratford* was a very close case on its facts, the court arrived at the more equitable decision in finding a trust relationship.[48] The court

---

42. Id. at 429–30.

43. 327 F.Supp. at 1318.

44. 417 F.2d 21 (3d Cir.1969).

45. Id. at 25. Cf. Citizens Bank v. American Ins. Co., 289 F.Supp. 211 (D.Ore. 1968) (one bank assigned a note to plaintiff bank, but kept in its own possession the bonds securing the note. The court held, as one of its alternative grounds, that the first bank was the agent of plaintiff and held the bonds for plaintiff's benefit. This allowed plaintiff to recover a loss under its banker's blanket bond).

46. One other ramification of a trust relationship would be the possibility that a participant would be entitled to priority over the lead in the proceeds of a loan, even in the absence of a guaranty by the lead. See Title Guarantee & Trust Co. v. Mortgage Comm'n, 273 N.Y. 415, 428, 7 N.E.2d 841, 846–47 (1937).

47. 367 F.2d 569 (2d Cir.1966).

48. Cf. In re Alda Commercial Corp., 327 F.Supp. 1315 (S.D.N.Y.1971).

listed several factors pointing to the creation of a trust: the parties used the words "in trust"; no lawyers were used in drafting the agreement, rather, it was prepared by the lead and the participant relied upon the lead's greater experience in such transactions; the commingling of certain funds was very brief and without the participant's knowledge; there was an oral promise to keep the notes in question separate; most of the proceeds were delivered directly to the participant without commingling, even though the lead was pressed for funds at the time; and there was no promissory note from lead to participant.

     * * * In Jefferson Savings and Loan Ass'n v. Lifetime Savings and Loan Ass'n [49] the Ninth Circuit readily found a trust between Lifetime, the lead, and Jefferson, the participant, when Lifetime foreclosed on certain mortgages covered by the participation agreement. The court stated: "Lifetime, which held the whole of the properties in its name, was a trustee for Jefferson. As a trustee, Lifetime had no right to place itself in a position where its interests were, or might be, antagonistic to the interests of the beneficiary of the trust." [50] Since Lifetime had sold property in violation of this trust, Jefferson had the right to pursue the trustee for either the proceeds of the sale or damages.[51]

Analysis and Recommendations

     It has been the purpose of this Article to discuss the various legal relationships that might characterize a loan participation. Clearly these legal categories are not all mutually exclusive. For instance, a partial assignment may be accompanied by the finding of a trust or an agency. For the past several years the courts have been building a definition of loan participations without really looking beyond the particular case. A more unified theory of loan participations would bring to the field a degree of predictability that has so far been lacking. The following proposals are offered as one possible model for achieving this unity.

     First, the theory that a participation creates a debt from the lead to the participant should be restricted to those rare cases in which the lead has guaranteed payment to the participant and the terms of the participation differ significantly from the terms of the loan made by the lead. This would comport with the language of most participation agreements, but would allow for the finding of a loan when this was clearly the substance of the transaction.

---

49.   396 F.2d 21 (9th Cir.1968).

50.   Id. at 24.

51.   Id. But see Prudential Ins. Co. v. Liberdar Holding Corp., 72 F.2d 395, 397 (2d Cir.1934) in which the Second Circuit held that when the guaranty company foreclosed on a mortgage, it did not thereafter hold title in trust for the certificate holders. The cases are not readily distinguishable since both involved foreclosures on certain mortgages contained in mortgage pools. However, the *Prudential* court used the theory that a participation certificate created a debt from the issuer to the holder.

Second, a participation should not be viewed as an assignment of proceeds only, unless the participation agreement specifically so states. This would seem to be more in keeping with the intention of the parties when the agreement refers to the sale of an "undivided interest" in the note and any obligations securing the note.

* * *

* * * [I]f a participation is classified as a partial assignment this would free the participant from the problem of perfection of a security interest against the lead, and would at the same time remove any need for revising Article 9 of the Uniform Commercial Code to exempt participation agreements from its provisions.

Third, courts should not hastily reject arguments that a loan participation constitutes a joint venture. The joint venture theory seems especially appropriate when a participation agreement is entered into prior to or at the time of the making of the loan and when the participant has at least a small voice in decisions concerning the loan.

Lastly, a uniform approach viewing loan participations as partial assignments would forestall any need for legislation to define the rights of the parties under a participation agreement, since these rights could be drawn from the body of case law on assignments. This would free loan participations from their present position as a halfway house between a loan and a sale and dispense with the necessity for strained rules of judicial construction to make the working of the participation agreement fit into the pattern.

* * *

NOTE

1. The documentation of a typical participated loan usually is prepared in only the name of the lead. In a participated real estate loan the note and mortgage of the borrower name only the lead as creditor and mortgagee.

   a. If there are three participants in the loan, the documents could name all three as creditors and mortgagees. What are the advantages of a typical participation when compared with naming all the participants as creditors and mortgagees? Cf. *State ex rel. Drum v. District Ct.,* 169 Mont. 494, 548 P.2d 1377 (1976); *Northern Trust Co. v. F.D.I.C.,* 619 F.Supp. 1340 (W.D.Okl.1985).

      1. What are the disadvantages of a typical participation?

2. A participation agreement can be analyzed as a "sale" or "assignment" by the lead to the participant of an undivided interest in the borrower's note and mortgage, at least if the note and mortgage are assignable in whole or in part. On the other hand, it also can be analyzed as a loan to the lead secured by an undivided interest in the borrower's note and mortgage.

   a. Are there any differences in consequences between these two possible means of analysis? Cf. *Interfirst Bank Abilene, N.A. v. F.D.I.C.,* 590 F.Supp. 1196 (W.D.Tex.1984), affirmed, 727 F.2d 1092 (5th Cir.1985); *Savings Bank of Rockland County v. F.D.I.C.,* 668 F.Supp. 799 (S.D.N.Y. 1987).

b. Either analysis is possible and the choice between them probably is dictated by the terms of the note, mortgage and participation agreement.

c. If the participation is treated as a sale or assignment of an undivided interest in the borrower's note and mortgage, where should the participant record its interest in the mortgage? Should the participant record its interest in the office or offices specified by the state's enactment of the Uniform Commercial Code or the office or offices where the mortgage was recorded? Does the participant's interest in the mortgage have to be recorded? Does the participant have to record its interest in the borrower's note?

d. If the participation is treated as a loan, albeit an in rem one, to the lead secured by the borrower's note and mortgage, where should the participant record its security interest? Against whom should the participant record?

e. What steps should be taken and provisions included when drafting the note, mortgage and participation agreement to clarify whether the participation is a sale, assignment or a loan?

3. A participation can be on a senior-junior basis. In the event of the borrower's default, the lead, if the lead is the senior participant, is entitled to recover its share of the loan in full before any payments are made to the other participants. A participation also can provide that the term of some participants' pay-outs is shorter than the pay-outs of other participants. For example, assuming equal participation by the lead and a participant, the agreement could provide that two thirds of every payment made by the borrower will be paid to the participant until the participant's investment plus interest is paid in full.

a. Are these variations of a participation consistent with treating a participation as a sale or assignment by the lead?

4. Drafting the documents so that it is clear whether the participation is a sale, assignment or a loan accomplishes only a part of the required undertaking.

a. If the participation is treated as a loan, in rem or otherwise, to the lead, the relationship between the lead and the participant is that of debtor-creditor. The further questions to be answered include whether the loan is in rem or nonrecourse and what constitutes the security for the loan.

b. If the participation is treated as a sale or assignment, the first question is whether it is a sale or assignment of an undivided interest in the borrower's note and mortgage or only an undivided interest in the proceeds thereof. Assuming that the participation is treated as a sale or assignment of an undivided interest in the note and mortgage, the second question is what is the relationship between the lead and participant. Are they tenants in common or joint venturers? Or, is the lead the agent of, or trustee for, the participant? A carefully drafted agreement will clarify the relationship and provide answers to the other questions raised above.

5. See generally Armstrong, *The Developing Law of Participation Agreements*, 23 Bus.Law. 689 (1968); Stroup, *A Model Participation Agreement*, 95 Banking L.J. 74 (1978); Drake and Weems, *Mortgage Loan Participations: The Trustee's Attack*, 52 Am.Bankr.L.J. 23 (1978); Tompsett, *Interbank Relations in Loan Participation Agreements: From Structure to Workout*, 101 Banking L.J.

31 (1984); Ledwidge, *Loan Participations Among Commercial Banks,* 51 Tenn.L.
Rev. 519 (1984); Kiefer, *Participating Mortgages: The Risk for Lenders,* 14 Real
Est.L.J. 218 (1986); Weiner, *Rights of a Participant Bank Against a Lead Bank
in a Participation Loan Agreement,* 104 Banking L.J. 529 (1987); Hansford and
Sowell, *Loan Participation and the UCC,* 106 Banking L.J. 62 (1989).

6. The Securities and Exchange Commission Staff has taken the position
that, under certain circumstances, a participation in a loan can be considered a
security for the purposes of the Securities Acts. See *National Association of
Securities Dealers, Inc.,* CCH Fed.Sec.L.Rep. ¶ 80,187 ('74–'75 Tr. Bin.). Is the
determination whether a participation constitutes a security affected by whether the participation takes the form of a loan or a sale? If the participation is a
sale, is the determination affected by the relations among the participants and
the lead? In the typical case, even if the participation is considered a security,
the offering and sale may be exempt from registration as a private offering.
Does exemption as a private offering mean, however, that the participating
financial institution must comply with Rule 144 if they want to dispose of their
interests? See e.g. *United American Bank of Nashville v. Gunter,* 620 F.2d
1108 (5th Cir.1980); *American Fletcher Mortgage Company, Inc. v. United States
Steel Credit Corporation,* 635 F.2d 1247 (7th Cir.1980); *Elson v. Geiger,* 506
F.Supp. 238 (E.D.Mich.1980), affirmed, 701 F.2d 176 (6th Cir.1982); *Union
Planters National Bank of Memphis v. Commercial Credit Business Loans, Inc.,*
651 F.2d 1174 (6th Cir.1981); *Union National Bank of Little Rock v. Farmers
Bank, Hamburg, Arkansas,* 786 F.2d 881 (8th Cir.1986); Pollock, *Notes Issued in
Syndicated Loans—A New Test To Define Securities,* 32 Bus.Law. 537 (1977);
Comment, *Bank Loan Participations as Securities: Notes, Investment Contracts,
and the Commercial/Investment Dichotomy,* 15 Duq.L.Rev. 261 (1977); Com-
ment, *Liabilities of Lead Banks in Syndicated Loans Under the Securities Acts,*
58 B.U.L.Rev. 45 (1978); Scholl and Weaver, *Loan Participations: Are They
Securities?,* 10 Fla.St.U.L.Rev. 215 (1982); Comment, *Loan Participation Agreements as Securities: Judicial Interpretations of the Securities Act of 1933 and
the Securities Exchange Act of 1934,* 24 Wm. & Mary L.Rev. 295 (1983); Knight,
Loan Participation Agreements: Catching Up with Contract Law, 1987 Colum.
Bus.L.Rev. 587; and pages 905 to 906 infra.

e.   SECONDARY FINANCING AND THE WRAP-AROUND MORTGAGE

As an alternative to, or in conjunction with, a participated loan in
which the participants generally share on pro rata basis, secondary
financing may be used to satisfy the financing requirements of a
developer when one institutional lender, or several lenders participating in a first mortgage loan cannot fully satisfy those requirements.
While the lenders' participation in a participated loan can be on a
senior-junior basis, the situation considered in the following pages is
that in which a lender secures its loan by a subordinate lien on real
estate and improvements. The following discussion deals with the
rights, obligations, and concerns of the secondary lender.

A BANKER'S TOUR THROUGH THE SECOND MORTGAGE MARKET

Julius Spellman
148 # 2 Bankers Magazine 19 (1965).

* * *

* * * With roughly half of our material wealth represented by real estate, even the vast amount of institutional first mortgage lending activity in this country leaves a great deal of capital still to be raised to finance commercial, industrial and residential realty. Significant sums of junior capital are needed, which—in contrast to conventional corporate demands for funds—are not generally available through routine investment banking channels.

Much junior capital for real estate purposes is furnished by means of the second mortgage device. Both institutional lenders and individuals make such loans. * * *

Commercial banks enter the second mortgage picture indirectly, but in a number of ways. * * * [B]anks have real estate customers and therefore must develop an awareness and knowledge of the second mortgage market. * * * Because banks lend at wholesale to finance companies, they must be familiar with the fields in * * * which their borrowers are [doing business]. In addition, bankers must be *au courant* on the availability of second mortgage money, to be able to refer their own customers to secondary lenders when their requirements for such additional funds arise. Frequently, the bank can fulfill its customer's needs in cooperation with a secondary lender. * * *

Willing Lenders

The secondary mortgage market is made up of a variety of lenders wishing to obtain a high yield on relatively short-term paper. These include:

Commercial financing companies. * * *

Real estate finance companies * * * having a capital structure similar to commercial financing companies, but oriented to real estate lending.

Industrial corporations * * * which seek to invest their excess cash.

Small Business Investment Companies which seek medium-term loans convertible into real estate equities.

Other specialized lenders such as * * * private pension funds, and many individual funds.

Foreign investors seeking dollar obligations at near-equity returns without the inconvenience of ownership.

Private individuals and syndicates of private individuals.

In addition, Governmental agencies, notably the Small Business Administration, * * * have available second mortgage funds at low rates as part of their program to provide small business with working capital, particularly in areas of high unemployment. [Certain] state and local agencies [also] make long-term, low rate second mortgages to encourage local industrial development.

* * *

Safe Seconds

A second mortgage may sometimes be safer than a first mortgage on the same property, for the very reason that the second mortgage is for a shorter term. The idea of a junior position being safer than a senior position appears to be self-contradictory, but the term is the key. Consider a new office building fully rented. The tenants are substantial companies who have executed five-year leases for rentals which are comparable to the rentals for similar properties. The rental is sufficient to pay all taxes, expenses and debt service on the first mortgage (which is [a] 20–year self-liquidating institutional mortgage) plus an additional cash flow of X dollars. A second mortgage is granted for 5 times X dollars, less interest over the period and a margin of safety. Assuming that all of the tenants pay their rent, the second mortgagee's position will be liquidated in five years, while 90% of the original first mortgage will still be unpaid at the end of this period. In a sense the first mortgagee has, in exchange for his preferred position, underwritten the potential of the building for the remaining 15 years; for no one can guarantee that the leases will be renewed at comparable rentals or that economic conditions will be such that the space can be re-rented at that time, not to mention the fact that the first mortgagee [may be] committed to a fixed interest rate for the entire term of its loan.

On the other hand, many second mortgages carry with them a considerable amount of risk. Where the economic success of the property is based largely upon the character and success of a business being conducted at the premises, the lender is not dealing with space as a commodity, but rather with management skill as an investment. So-called "specialty" properties, such as bowling enterprises, restaurants, nightclubs and, to a lesser extent, hotels, motels and nursing homes, are considered to fall into this category. The pattern of financing for these properties shows that the first mortgage is typically for a very low ratio to appraised value—generally 30% to 50%—to compensate for the added risk.

Many second mortgage loans are also made for the purpose of adding to, improving or renovating an existing property. The term "mezzanine" financing has been coined by some secondary lenders for these situations, it being felt that the first mortgagee has the "ground floor" financing. The improved income after the addition or renovation is then applied to liquidate the second mortgage.

* * *

Terms

[Interest rates on] second mortgage[s] generally [exceed the rates charged on institutional first mortgages]. The term of [a second mortgage] loan depends in part on the lender's financial structure. Finance companies whose permitted borrowing ratios presuppose a short-term portfolio prefer maturities of up to three years and rarely exceed five years, while SBIC's operating under governmental regulations make relatively long-term loans, since they are not permitted to make loans for less than five years. Many loans are written on a discount basis, so that the mortgage itself will appear on record to bear a conventional rate of interest * * *[,] the true yield to the lender being undisclosed. In addition, the borrower will pay, as is customary, recording taxes and fees, stamp taxes, title insurance fees and premiums, legal and appraisal fees, and brokerage charges.

* * *

Legal Matters

The documentation of a second mortgage transaction necessarily contains the same features as a first mortgage and the closing requirements are usually similar with certain covenants customarily added:

1. A default on the first mortgage is an event of default under the second mortgage.

2. The borrower will not amend the terms of the first mortgage, or of any lease, or cancel any lease, or accept any advance rentals except as contemplated by the leases, or grant any rent concessions not set forth in the leases.

3. The borrower will pay the first mortgage payments and all taxes, insurance, water rents, sewer charges and similar items and upon failure to do so, the second mortgagee may pay them and add them to the second mortgage debt.

4. The borrower shall, at the second mortgagee's request, enter into an escrow arrangement to provide for the first mortgage payments, and (if not previously escrowed by the first mortgagee) taxes, insurance and similar items.

5. The second mortgagee may accelerate the loan if the property is sold or there is a change of management.

6. The borrower will insure the property for an amount sufficient to cover the first and second mortgages and will also provide rent insurance or business interruption insurance where required.

* * *

The first mortgage should be examined for special provisions which may affect the second mortgagee's security. Since the second mortgagee will invariably find the property more easily marketable with existing first mortgage financing intact, an effort should be made to correct unusual default or acceleration provisions in the first mortgage. An "open end" clause in the first mortgage which may subsequently increase the first mortgage lien to the disadvantage of the second mortgagee should be similarly dealt with. Wherever possible, a certificate of reduction of mortgage, lienor's estoppel certificate, or similar certification by the first mortgagee should be obtained, fixing the mortgage amount and certifying that, to the knowledge of the first mortgagee, no default exists under its loan.

Servicing

A second mortgage is serviced in the same manner as a first mortgage, except that the second mortgagee must at all times be vigilant as to the first mortgage covenants. [One] technique involves creating an escrow for [the] purpose [of making the payments on the first mortgage]; an alternate is to have properly spaced payment dates, requiring the borrower to exhibit timely proof that the first mortgage payment has been made. A third is to have the borrower forward the first mortgage payments to the second mortgagee for transmittal prior to the due date of the payment.

Many second mortgagees also notify the first mortgagee of their interest, requesting that copies of notice[s] of default be forwarded to them. Although first mortgagees are reluctant to enter into agreements obligating themselves to provide such notice[s], the reputable institutions will usually note their records and cooperate with the second mortgagee, especially since it is invariably in their interest to do so, as the second mortgagee may intervene and cure a first mortgage default.

Existing insurance may be adequate to protect the first mortgagee but not the second, and should be reviewed. The possibility of an inadequate amount of insurance is not remote in situations where the property has appreciated in value since the time the first mortgage was placed, and the old insurance may very well be inadequate. Where the second mortgagee is relying upon income from lease rentals, the need for rent insurance in addition to the usual fire and extended coverage should be considered.

* * *

NOTE

1. In recent years institutional lenders holding first mortgages have frequently required that mortgagors pay variable interest rates. If the mortgagor must pay a variable interest rate to the first mortgagee, what risks does this present to the second mortgagee?

2. The lenders in the secondary market rarely write mortgages over three to five years in length. Why is such a short term mortgage of interest to a real estate developer?

a. Does a short term mortgage permit the developer to achieve the leverage and liquidity resulting from high loan to value financing? What does the developer anticipate when entering into a short term second mortgage?

3. The second mortgagee of certain real estate would like the first mortgagee of the real estate to agree that the second mortgagee is entitled to receive notices of any default under the first mortgage, and that the second mortgagee can cure any default and can make the payments required by the first mortgage in lieu of the mortgagor.

a. Will the first mortgagee agree to giving the second mortgagee these rights? What advantages and disadvantages does giving the second mortgagee these rights afford to the first mortgagee?

1. Many first mortgagees prohibit the acquisition of secondary financing by their mortgagors.

a. Since the first mortgagee has a prior lien, what objections does it have to secondary financing? See Ominsky, *Why a Mortgagee Should Hesitate to Permit Junior Financing,* 1 # 2 Prac.Real Est.Law. 83 (1985).

b. If one of the purposes of the prohibition is to make sure the mortgagor maintains an interest in the development by having some of its own money at stake, does not the possibility of a deficiency, where permitted, do the same thing?

b. If the first mortgagee agrees to secondary financing, should it have any objections to giving the second mortgagee notice of defaults, the right to cure defaults and the right to make payments required by the first mortgage?

4. The wrap-around mortgage, a form of secondary financing, has grown in use in the United States during recent years. It has been in common use in Canada for more than forty years. " * * * This * * * financing arrangement takes various forms, shaped primarily by the purpose it is to serve. * * * [W]e [shall] first consider the particular circumstances when each can best be utilized.

"*The Borrower's Objectives*

"A borrower will have a real incentive to consider WA [wrap-around] financing in the following situations:

"(1) When additional financing is desired but the present mortgage holder is unwilling or unreasonable in his demands, and the mortgage permits no prepayment, or prepayment only with an exorbitant penalty; at the same time, conventional secondary financing is too costly in rate and too heavy in debt service.

"(2) When the existing first mortgage rate is very low and terms are otherwise quite favorable, but the borrower desires additional financing which the first mortgagee will not advance at a favorable rate. Conventional secondary financing would not meet these requirements.

"(3) When the existing first mortgage is satisfactory in amount but borrower desires to obtain debt-service relief to improve his return on equity.

"(4) When a commitment for permanent financing is inadequate, although the lender has agreed to lend its statutory maximum, so that additional financing is required but conventional secondary financing would be too expensive and burdensome.

"In situations (1) and (2) described above, WA financing is available in the form which herein we call the additional-funds WA mortgage. Another WA financing form is likewise available for situation (3), to be known as the extended-term WA mortgage. Situation (4) is remedied with a financing form we call the simultaneous WA mortgage. * * *

"The Lender's Objectives

"The WA lender's motivation in each of these situations is quite simple and consistent: He expects to obtain the best possible effective yield, with the least amount of cash investment, yet to have the widest coverage (geographic and property type) with his limited available investment funds.

"The WA Form Generally

"The WA mortgage is a second mortgage subordinate in all cases to an existing first mortgage which remains outstanding and unsatisfied. It differs from the conventional second mortgage in that the face amount overstates the actual indebtedness, and also in that it incorporates a special agreement between the parties for payment of the debt service on the first mortgage. The loan is otherwise evidenced and secured by the usual form of promissory note and second mortgage.

"The face amount of the mortgage is the sum of the outstanding balance under the first mortgage plus the amount of additional funds, if any, to be disbursed by the WA mortgagee, with an annual debt service computed on this face amount. The WA mortgage interest rate is always higher than the interest rate on the first mortgage. This contract rate inevitably is equal to, or slightly less than, the then market rate for conventional first mortgage loans. The WA mortgage is, therefore, generally effective only in a high-interest period, and is seldom used in a declining interest rate market. The WA loan term and amortization, relative to the maturity of the first mortgage, will vary according to the purpose of the financing.

"It is immediately obvious that, if the *contract* rate is computed on the sum of the first mortgage and any new money advanced, a much higher *effective* rate of interest on the new money will result. This provides the leverage incentive for the WA lender.

"Its most distinctive feature, however, is the agreement by the WA lender, upon receipt of debt service on the WA mortgage, to deduct therefrom and remit directly to the first mortgagee the required debt service on the first mortgage. In the extended-term type, there may be a deficit in such debt service which is made up by the WA lender, who then remits the full debt service on the first mortgage. The borrower in all cases expressly agrees not to make any further payments to the first mortgagee on account of the first mortgage.

"In some documents the exuberance of the parties has produced language tantamount to an assumption of the first mortgage by the WA lender. The legal effect of assumption, however, is almost always dispelled by conditioning this obligation upon *actual* receipt of the debt service on the WA mortgage. If the WA lender does not receive the debt service on the WA mortgage, there is no obligation to remit the debt service on the first mortgage. Failure to pay debt service on a WA mortgage, of course, constitutes a default under that mortgage.

"The WA mortgage will otherwise contain covenants by the borrower identical with those in the first mortgage, including the escrow of taxes and insurance premiums which, upon receipt by the WA lender, will be remitted to the first mortgagee. Of course, the first mortgage cannot contain covenants personal to the borrower and covenants that cannot be cured or complied with by the WA mortgagee.

"The WA borrower further agrees to comply with all nonmoney covenants in the first mortgage and, as in any other second mortgage, a default in the first mortgage constitutes a default in the WA mortgage.

"The borrower will notify the first mortgagee that the payments of debt service, as well as any prepayment or payment after acceleration, are to be received from the WA lender, on behalf of the borrower. He also authorizes the first mortgagee to accept such payments and where possible, directs the due delivery to the WA lender of all notices, of default or otherwise, required to be given by the lender under the first mortgage.

"Highly desirable, from the WA lender's viewpoint, is an agreement, where obtainable, by the first mortgagee to give the WA lender notice of[,] and opportunity to cure all[,] defaults on the part of the borrower under the first mortgage.

"A first mortgagee might consider the possibility of cure by the WA lender to be additional security for his loan. On the other hand, the opposite reaction may result where the WA financing has the effect of locking in a first mortgagee to an unsatisfactory low-interest loan for which he would rather receive prepayment.

"As an added measure of security, it is also desirable that the first mortgage, in fact, be prepayable, even with penalty. In a distress situation, the WA lender's inevitable remedy is to satisfy the prior lien as quickly as possible and regardless of the penalty. As to any such prepayment penalty, the WA lender might consider taking a deposit or a separate and personal undertaking of payment by the borrower. This separate arrangement is recommended, since the amount of the penalty is not included in the mathematics of the WA transaction.

"In the additional-funds WA mortgage and the simultaneous WA mortgage, the face amount in excess of the first mortgage balance is disbursed at the time of closing. This is the only actual advance of funds made by the WA lender unless there is a balloon in the first mortgage, and except also in a distress situation where advances are made to cure defaults of the borrower, including possibly the payoff of the first mortgage. The payments remitted monthly on the first mortgage are not actually additional disbursements by the WA lender since he simply remits all or part of the debt service received from the borrower. For this purpose, he merely acts as a conduit for the payment of the debt service to the first mortgagee.

"As a matter of fact, there are two account ledgers maintained for the WA mortgage. One ledger conforms with the regular amortization schedule for a loan in the face amount of the WA mortgage, with interest at the contract rate and for the stated maturity. This particular accounting has no basis in reality and is used simply in the mathematical process. The second ledger is the true picture of the indebtedness and records the actual investment of the WA lender in the property. This latter figure we shall hereinafter call the net investment.

This net investment, at any point in time, is simply the difference in amount between the unamortized balance of the WA mortgage and the unamortized balance of the first mortgage, using in each case their regular amortization schedules.

"In the case of the additional-funds and simultaneous WA mortgages, the net investment will consist of the loan proceeds actually advanced out-of-pocket by the WA lender, plus that part of the interest thereon which is earned but not currently paid (i.e., deferred) until the first mortgage has been satisfied or the WA mortgage prepaid. The total interest earned, for any period, on the net investment is equal to the contract interest on the unamortized face amount of the WA mortgage less the interest payable on the first mortgage.

"The same amount is obtained by adding contract interest on the net investment plus interest at the differential in rates (between the two mortgages) on the balance outstanding under the first mortgage.

"The extent to which earned interest is deferred is determined by the difference in debt service between the WA mortgage and the first mortgage. If the difference in debt service is less than the amount of interest earned, then such excess of earned interest is deferred. The difference in debt service which is retained by the WA lender is the only way in which he receives a return *currently* on his advance, while the first mortgage remains outstanding. The interest earned but deferred will thereafter be recouped either upon prepayment of the net investment or during the payout (according to the amortization schedule) of the WA mortgage following the pay-off of the first mortgage.

*   *   *

"In the additional-funds and extended-term WA mortgages, the net investment of the lender generally increases until the first mortgage is paid off; thereafter it commences to amortize. However, in the simultaneous WA mortgage, the net investment of the WA lender is amortizing during the term of the first mortgage. This occurs because the differential in debt service between the WA mortgage and the first mortgage exceeds the amount of earned interest and the excess represents amortization of the net investment." Gunning, *The Wrap–Around Mortgage Friend or U.F.O.?*, 2 # 2 Real Est.Rev. 35–38 (1972).

    a. Because of its nature, the wrap-around mortgage raises a number of incidental concerns.

      1. Since it is a second mortgage it is not considered a "legal" real estate loan for many institutional lenders. Where the governing statute or regulations, however, have a "basket" or leeway exception, see e.g. Section 1404(b) of the New York Insurance Law (McKinney Supp.1988), the institutional investor can carry the loan in the basket. The amount at which the loan must be carried remains subject to some debate.

      2. In addition, the usury, title insurance and income tax concerns attendant to a wrap-around mortgage must be considered.

        a. In order to illustrate the concerns involved, assume that a seller has real estate worth $200,000 with an adjusted basis of $60,000. The real estate is subject to a mortgage with a remaining principal balance of $100,000, having an interest rate of 9% and a remaining term of 20 years. The seller proposes to sell the property for $40,000 in cash and a wrap-around purchase money mortgage in the principal amount of $160,000, bearing interest at

21% and having a term of 20 years. The maximum interest rate permitted in the seller's state is 21%.

1. While the purchaser does not pay interest on the principal amount of the wrap-around mortgage in excess of the permitted interest rate, the seller's return on his $60,000 "investment" is substantially above the permitted interest rate. See *Mitchell v. Trustees of United States Mutual Real Estate Investment Trust,* 144 Mich.App. 302, 375 N.W.2d 424 (1985).

2. If the seller requests mortgagee title insurance, what is the face amount of the policy? Does the seller have an insurable interest in excess of $60,000?

3. How should the seller report the gain on the sale if he uses the installment method provided by Section 453? If the purchaser had assumed, or taken the property subject to, the $100,000 mortgage, given the seller a second mortgage of $60,000 and $40,000 in cash, the seller's profit ratio would have been 100% and he would have been treated as having received a payment of $80,000 on the date of sale. The seller might argue, however, that when the wrap-around purchase money mortgage is used the purchaser has not assumed the $100,000 mortgage nor has the purchaser taken subject to it since the purchaser is paying the seller the full value of the real estate and the seller remains liable on the mortgage. If the seller's argument is accepted, his profit ratio will be 70% and he will be treated as having received a payment of $40,000 on the date of sale. Cf. *Stonecrest Corp.,* 24 T.C. 659 (1955), nonacq. 1956–1 C.B. 6; *Estate of Lamberth,* 31 T.C. 302 (1958), nonacq. 1959–1 C.B. 6; *United Pacific Corp.,* 39 T.C. 721 (1963); *D.A. Hunt,* 80 T.C. 1126 (1983). But see *Frank Hutchison,* 42 CCH Tax Ct.Mem. 1089 (1981); *Republic Petroleum Corporation v. United States,* 613 F.2d 518 (5th Cir.1980). The Internal Revenue Service did not accept this position when it issued the temporary regulations under Section 453. The Internal Revenue Service treated the transaction in a manner similar to the way it would have been treated if the purchaser had assumed or taken subject to the existing mortgage. See Temp.Reg.Sec. 15A.453–1(b)(3)(ii). The Tax Court, however, has agreed with this position in two recent cases. See *Professional Equities, Inc.,* 89 T.C. 165 (1987), and *Vincent E. Webb,* 54 CCH Tax Ct.Mem. 443 (1987).

See Davies and Zumpano, *The IRS Approach to the Wrap Around Mortgage: A Contradiction of Tax Fundamentals,* 12 Tax Adviser 260 (1981); Levingston, *Wrap–Around Mortgages Revisited: Temp.Regs.Sec. 15A.453–1(b)(3)(ii),* 12 Tax Adviser 452 (1981); Cuff, *Avoiding the Tax Impact of the Temporary Installment Sale Regs. on Wraparound Debt,* 55 J.Tax'n 144 (1981); Levine, *Wraps—The "Hunt" for an Escape of Mortgage over Basis,"* 62 Taxes 271 (1984); Dickens and Orbach, *Installment Reporting: Wraparound Mortgages After the IRS's Temporary Regulations and Hunt,* 12 J.Real Est.Tax'n 137 (1985); Kennedy, *Wraparound Mortgages Considered in the Context of the Commissioner's Temporary Installment Sale Regulations,* 65 Taxes 530 (1987); Comment, *The Tax Consequences of Wraparound Mortgages,* 2 St. Johns J. Legal Commentary 166 (1987).

4. Assume that, rather than selling the property, the taxpayer refinances by means of an "additional-funds" wrap-around mortgage in the amount of $160,000, bearing interest at 21% and having a term of 20 years. The existing mortgage, with a remaining principal balance of $100,000, has only 10 years remaining of the original 30 year term. If both mortgages provide for level payments, part of the interest received by the wrap-around mortgagee will be applied to the payment of the remaining principal balance on the $100,000 mortgage until the mortgage is paid. Is the mortgagor permitted to treat as interest paid, under Section 163, that part of the interest paid on the wrap-around mortgage which is applied to the payment of the remaining principal balance of the $100,000 mortgage? Cf. *Barton Beek,* 80 T.C. 1024 (1983), affirmed, 754 F.2d 1442 (9th Cir.1985). Must the wrap-around mortgagee treat as interest income the portion of the interest on the wrap-around mortgage applied to the payment of the remaining principal balance of the $100,000 mortgage?

b. See generally Galowitz, *How to Use Wraparound Financing,* 5 Real Est.L.J. 107 (1976); Levinton, *Use of Wrap–Around Mortgages Can Expand Installment Sales Despite IRS Opposition,* 51 J.Tax'n 166 (1979); Kraus, *Tax Advantages of Wraparound Mortgages,* 8 J.Real Est.Tax'n 264 (1981); Guerin, *A Tax Policy Analysis of Wrap–Around Financed Installment Sales,* 3 Va.Tax Rev. 41 (1983); Bronner, *The Wraparound Mortgage: Its Structure, Uses and Limitations,* 12 J.Real Est.Tax'n 315 (1985); Messinger, *Wrap–Around Mortgages: Valuations and Interest Accruals,* 42 N.Y.U.Inst. Fed.Tax'n 22–1 (1984).

f. SALE AND LEASEBACK

A form of long term financing known as the sale and leaseback, in appropriate situations, presents an attractive alternative to the more typical borrowing transaction involving a note and mortgage. A sale and leaseback has both advantages and disadvantages when compared with long-term borrowing. The following excerpts consider both the advantages and disadvantages of this form of financing and deal with the many concerns inherent in its use.

SALE AND LEASEBACK TRANSACTIONS
Frank C. Bernard and Sidney M. Perlstadt
1955 Univ. of Ill.Law Forum 635 (1955).
[footnotes omitted]

* * *

Comparison of Sale and Leaseback with Long–Term Borrowing

[From the standpoint of the Developer]

Advantages. Typical insurance code provisions limit mortgage loans made by life insurance companies to a stated percentage of the value of the security.[52] These limitations do not apply to real estate purchases, hence the seller normally receives the entire cost of the

---

52. [As do some state statutes and regulations applicable to banking institutions.]

property, including all improvements, or its full fair market value. This means that the party seeking financing can obtain a greater amount of cash through a leaseback than through conventional mortgage borrowing. * * *

If the transaction is properly conceived, the rental payments under the lease, representing an amortization of both land and building, will be fully deductible as expense for income tax purposes.

From an accounting standpoint, future installments of rent are not regarded as liabilities to be reflected as such in the company's balance sheet.[53] This result is claimed, by some, to present a more favorable financial statement and raise the company's credit standing over that which would occur had borrowing been resorted to. Others contend that this reasoning is self-delusion and that it * * * can result in disaster.

* * *

Disadvantages. The interest factor upon which the rental will be based will normally be slightly higher than prevailing rates for funds borrowed on a long-term basis. In most instances, this is regarded as a small penalty to pay for the advantageous features of the device.

* * * [I]t is usually unwise to grant the lessee an option to repurchase. Without an option to repurchase, the lessee has nothing comparable to a call or prepayment privilege which is common in the case of a long-term loan. Furthermore, when the primary term and all extension options have expired, the lessee, as in the case of any other expired lease, has nothing, since the lessor then comes into the enjoyment of its reversion.

The lease may contain restrictions on the lessee's power of alienation of the leasehold estate. Even if it does not, and particularly as time goes by, the chances of the lessee to realize upon the value of the leasehold estate, if the lease should become burdensome, are materially less than in the case of fee ownership. In the latter case, not only does the owner have a readily marketable asset, but a prospective purchaser has relative freedom in arranging the financing of the purchase.

Another distinct disadvantage of having only a leasehold interest is that it is extremely difficult, and in many instances impossible, for the tenant to finance the construction of additions * * * once the lease has been made.

* * *

[From the standpoint of the Investor]

Advantages

As previously pointed out, the rental under the lease will be predicated upon the complete amortization of the purchase price over

---

53. [The future installments of rent may be treated as a liability and reflected on the company's balance sheet, depending on the nature and terms of the transaction. See Financial Accounting Standards Board, Statement of Financial Accounting Standards. No. 13–Accounting for Leases, Nov. 1976.]

the primary term of the lease, which is normally twenty to thirty years. If the lessee exercises one or more options to extend the term of the lease, even at a substantially lower rate of rental, the investor will have had its investment completely amortized at a higher rate of interest than in the case of borrowed funds and will derive additional return during the option period, (normally twenty or twenty-five years after the expiration of the primary term.)

Whether or not the lessee renews the lease, the investor has a reversionary interest in the land and in such of the improvements as may remain. Furthermore, as previously pointed out, there is usually no feature tantamount to the call privilege conferred upon a borrower under a long-term loan.

* * *

As previously mentioned, the interest rate upon which the lease rental is predicated is ordinarily slightly higher than prevailing rates for borrowed funds. While a slight differential in the rate of interest is ordinarily of little consequence to the borrower who employs its funds as working capital, this differential looms very large in the eyes of the investor. An increase in terms of a fraction of one per cent of net yield on investments is regarded as an achievement by the investment department of an insurance company.

Thus a sale and leaseback transaction with its higher ratio of investment to value and higher rate of return for funds invested, and with its *permanency* is, in many instances, a highly tempting form of investment * * *.

Disadvantages

* * *

We have previously [mentioned] that the rental under the lease is not carried on the lessee's balance sheet as a liability.[54] In the case of a loan, a *debt* immediately arises and, in case of a default, the creditor may accelerate the debt and immediately resort to the security or avail itself of its remedies against the debtor for the full amount unpaid. In case of a bankruptcy or reorganization, the creditor has an immediate liquidated claim for the full amount of the unpaid balance of the debt.

Normally, a claim for future rent is not regarded as a debt. Various devices have been used by draftsmen of leases in an effort to create a provable debt, at least after the occurrence of a default. One such device is to specify the rental for the entire term of the lease as a lump sum payable in installments. Another is to provide that in case of default the lessor may accelerate all of the unpaid rent. The problems which face the landlord in an attempt to collect future rent or damages for an anticipatory breach of the lease are not peculiar to sale and leaseback transactions. For the purpose of this article, it is

54. See footnote 53 and pages 748 to 750 infra.

sufficient to point out that there is no clear-cut right of action for the full amount of the unpaid rent.   *   *   *

The purchase price being usually the full value of the property, the investor runs more risk of loss, in case of default and depreciation in the value of the asset, than in the case of a loan, the amount of which is less than the full value of the security.

*   *   *

The Sale

*   *   * [A] sale and leaseback is really two transactions wrapped into one. All of the ordinary problems involved in a sale of real estate and all of the ordinary problems involved in the preparation and execution of a long-term lease are encountered. The discussion here will relate only to those phases of the transaction which are peculiar to deals of this type.

Since the leasing back of the property is to occur at the instant of the transfer of title, and is one of the prime requisites of the purchaser's obligation to pay the purchase price, it necessarily follows that neither party can be firmly bound to the deal until the form of lease, [and] all of its details, [have] been agreed upon. A second requisite is that the parties shall have agreed on the form of the evidence of title and the matters to which the title is to be subject. Consequently, though a formal contract of sale may be desirable, it is impossible for the parties to enter into a definitive contract until the form of lease has been agreed upon and until the purchaser has examined an abstract or guarantee policy and expressed its approval of the state of the title.

*   *   *

In those cases where the purchase price is to be based upon the actual cost of improvements being constructed or upon an appraisal to be made of the property, the final preparation and execution of the lease must be deferred to the time of closing. While the form of lease may be agreed upon in advance, the date of commencement of the term and of rental payments, the effective dates for exercise of options and matters of like kind must hinge upon the date of completion of construction. If the purchase price is to be based upon the seller's cost, it is impossible to specify the amount of rent in advance of the determination of the construction cost, unless it is specified in the lease as a percentage of the purchase price. Since the lease is for a long term, it is preferable to [defer] the actual execution of the lease until these dates and amounts have been determined so that they can be set forth specifically in the lease instead of being determined extraneously.

Accordingly, following the pattern of mortgage loan transactions, it is customary for the [lender] or a loan correspondent to issue a commitment setting forth the terms of the purchase and outlining the terms of the lease. If a formal contract is not used, then, by successive stages, agreements are made regarding the form which the lease is to take and the condition of title which the purchaser will accept. If new construction is involved, agreements will also be made, probably informally between the attorneys, as to such matters as security against mechanic's lien claims, whether the transaction is to be closed by means of an escrow, how rental for a fraction of a month is to be adjusted, and matters of like kind. Also, in the case of new construction, some arrangement will be made for final inspection and approval of the improvements by the purchaser, means of insuring final completion, appraisal or reappraisal, and final determination of the purchase price.

One peculiar feature of these transactions is that there are normally no proratings since the prorations made in connection with the sale are usually offset by the prorations which would be made under the lease.

*   *   *

The Lease

*   *   *

In general, the form of lease will have most of the characteristics of a long-term lease. It will differ from a ground lease to the extent that the lessor, having paid for the improvements in purchasing the property, will have a vital interest in seeing that the value of the improvements is not impaired during the term of the lease.

Furthermore, while the transaction is not a loan, it has many of the attributes of a loan, particularly in the eyes of [an officer of an institutional lender] whose thinking has been solidified by the established practices which have grown up over the years in making mortgage loans.

The underlying intent being that the full management and control of the property shall be vested in the lessee and that the lessor shall be assured of a net yield, the lease is a so-called "net lease." The lessee agrees to pay all taxes and assessments, including those accrued at the commencement of the term of the lease, and, usually, also to pay any taxes against the income to be derived by the lessor under the lease if a levy of such taxes should be made as a substitute for real estate taxes. The lessee is usually given the right to contest taxes.

*   *   *

In order to conserve the lessor's security, some provision must be included regarding substantial alterations or rebuilding. In some instances, the lessor's consent is required, perhaps with a provision that it be not unreasonably withheld. In other instances, the lessee is given wide latitude in making alterations or in rebuilding, subject only to the requirement that upon completion the value of the improvements be not less than the value immediately prior to the commencement of the work.

*   *   *

Since the lessor's title will have been derived directly from the lessee, presumably by means of a warranty deed, the ordinary covenant of quiet enjoyment is not applicable and, indeed, would probably give rise to circuity of action. Accordingly, this covenant should be limited to the acts of the lessor or of persons claiming by, through, or under the lessor. In some cases, a provision is included relieving the lessor of its covenants upon assignment of the reversion so that only the owner of the fee for the time being is liable on the lessor's covenants.

* * *

The attitude of the lessor, generally, is that it is making a conservative and well-secured investment and that the purchase price and interest thereon will be fully amortized by the regular payment of rental under the lease and, meanwhile, will be secured by the land and all of the improvements. Furthermore, it must be assumed that the lessee is deriving the claimed advantages of this type of transaction, else the lessee would have borrowed funds instead of selling its property and leasing it back.

Accordingly, the so-called contingency clauses are more favorable to the lessor than in the case of most long-term leases. They are usually designed to assure the lessor the return of its initial investment and interest thereon and to maintain the lessor's security until this occurs. Generally, the lessee is required to carry fire insurance with extended coverage for the full insurable value of the improvements. Sometimes the lessee is also required to carry rent insurance to cover the payment of rentals during rebuilding in case of damage or destruction.

The lessee is usually obligated, at its own expense, to restore or rebuild regardless of the extent of damage even if the destruction is total. Sometimes the lessee is permitted to terminate the lease, where there is total destruction or serious damage near the end of the term, upon the payment to the lessor of its unamortized cost, plus a premium, applying the insurance proceeds to the payment thus required.

Perhaps the most variation occurs in the condemnation clause. If there is a taking of the whole or substantially all of the premises, the lessor normally requires assurance that it will receive at least its unamortized cost out of the award before the lessee participates in any portion. In some cases the lease provides for payment of the whole award to the lessor.

Where there is a partial taking, provision is generally made to require the lessee to restore the premises, using the proceeds of the award for that purpose and, thereafter, to adjust the rent. This clause should include provision as to the retention by one of the parties or a division between them of any surplus that may remain after use of the award for rebuilding and should spell out a formula upon which the rental is to be adjusted. The alternatives for such adjustment would include: (a) an appraisal or some form of arbitration; (b) retention by the lessor of any surplus in the award to apply on its unamortized cost and a corresponding reduction in the rental; (c) adjustment of the rental on the basis of reduction, if any, in the rentable area remaining;

or (d) retention by the lessee of the surplus in the award, leaving the rental unaffected.

* * *

Because the purchase price will normally be based either upon an appraisal or upon the seller's cost, a question sometimes arises as to the extent to which fixtures are to be included in the purchase. Whatever fixtures are paid for by the lessor (by inclusion in the appraisal or in the item of "cost") should be clearly stated either in the deed of conveyance or by means of a separate declaration to constitute part of the real estate and appropriate provision should then be incorporated in the lease so that these fixtures will be leased as a part of the premises and the provisions of the lease regarding maintenance, replacement, surrender, etc., made applicable to [the fixtures].

Normally, the lease will contain one or more options [permitting] the lessee to extend the term of the lease at[, possibly,] a reduced rate of rental. * * * [T]he granting of an option to the lessee to repurchase the property can nullify all of the tax advantages which the lessee anticipates in entering into the transaction.

Apart from the tax consequences, there is another danger in granting an option to the lessee to repurchase the property. Unless extreme care is used in granting such an option, the lessee might, in the future, contend that the conveyance, though absolute on its face, is intended as a mortgage and claim a right of redemption if the lease were terminated by the lessor, or if an attempt were made to do so, by reason of the lessee's default. This hazard is acute in view of the strictness with which the courts scrutinize a transaction where a deed is claimed to constitute a mortgage and in view of the expense and complications attendant upon foreclosure of a mortgage.

* * *

NOTE

1. One of the advantages to the lender of the sale-leaseback transaction is that it avoids the problems of foreclosure on default. This conclusion assumes that the transaction is not considered, in substance, a borrowing transaction and the lease is not considered the equivalent of a mortgage. How can the lender insure that a court will not treat the lease as, in substance, a mortgage?

a. One of the advantages to the seller-lessee is sometimes said to be the ability to keep the obligation for future installments of rent off its financial statements. Statement of Financial Accounting Standards No. 13—Accounting for Leases sets out the views of the Financial Accounting Standards Board of the American Institute of Certified Public Accountants with respect to when, for accounting purposes, a sale and leaseback should be treated by the parties as a "purchase and an operating lease," in which case the transaction is treated, for the most part, as a true sale and true lease, and when it should be treated as a "capital lease" by the lessee and a "purchase and direct financing lease" by the lessor, in which case the transaction is treated, for the most part, as the equivalent of mortgage financing.

The Financial Standards Accounting Board takes the position that if the lease meets one of the following criteria the seller-lessee must account for the lease as a capital lease; otherwise, as an operating lease.

1. The lease transfers ownership of the property to the lessee by the end of the lease term.

2. The lease contains a bargain purchase option.

3. The lease term is equal to 75 percent or more of the estimated economic life of the leased property. If, however, the beginning of the lease term falls within the last 25 percent of the total estimated economic life of the leased property, including earlier years of use, this criterion is not used for purposes of classifying the lease.

4. The present value at the beginning of the lease term of the minimum lease payments, excluding that portion of the payments representing executory costs such as insurance, maintenance, and taxes to be paid by the lessor, including any profit thereon, equals or exceeds 90 percent of the excess of the fair value of the leased property to the lessor at the inception of the lease over any related investment tax credit retained by the lessor and expected to be realized by him. If, however, the beginning of the lease term falls within the last 25 percent of the total estimated economic life of the leased property, including earlier years of use, this criterion is not used for purposes of classifying the lease. A lessor must compute the present value of the minimum lease payments using the interest rate implicit in the lease. A lessee must compute the present value of the minimum lease payments using his incremental borrowing rate, unless (i) it is practicable for him to learn the implicit rate used by the lessor and (ii) the implicit rate used by the lessor is less than the lessee's incremental borrowing rate. If both of those conditions are met, the lessee must use the implicit rate.

In general, if the lease is treated as a capital lease, any profit or loss on the sale is deferred and amortized in proportion to the amortization of the leased asset, or if the leased asset is land only the amortization is taken on a straight-line basis over the lease term. If the lease is treated as an operating lease then any profit or loss on the sale is also deferred and amortized in proportion to rental payments over the period of time the asset is expected to be used. When, however, the fair value of the property at the time of the transaction is less than its undepreciated cost, a loss shall be recognized immediately up to the amount of the difference between undepreciated cost and fair value.

If the lease meets one of the above listed criteria and both of the following criteria, the purchaser-lessor must treat the transaction as a purchase and a direct financing lease; otherwise, he must treat the transaction as a purchase and an operating lease.

1. Collectibility of the minimum lease payments is reasonably predictable.

2. No important uncertainties surround the amount of unrebursable costs yet to be incurred by the lessor under the lease. Important uncertainties might include commitments by the lessor to guarantee performance of the leased property in a manner more extensive than the typical product warranty or to effectively protect the lessee from obsolescence of the leased property. The necessity, however, of esti-

mating executory costs such as insurance, maintenance, and taxes to be paid by the lessor does not by itself constitute an important uncertainty.

Even if a lease is treated as an "operating lease" under the Statement of Financial Accounting Standards No. 13—Accounting for Leases, the liability for future installments of rent is not completely eliminated from the lessee's financial statements. The following must be disclosed in the lessee's financial statements.

"a. For capital leases:

"i. The gross amount of assets recorded under capital leases as of the date of each balance sheet presented by major classes according to nature or function. This information may be combined with the comparable information for owned assets.

"ii. Future minimum lease payments as of the date of the latest balance sheet presented, in the aggregate and for each of the five succeeding fiscal years, with separate deductions from the total for the amount representing executory costs, including any profit thereon, included in the minimum lease payments and for the amount of the imputed interest necessary to reduce the net minimum lease payments to present value * * *.

"iii. The total of minimum sublease rentals to be received in the future under noncancelable subleases as of the date of the latest balance sheet presented.

"iv. Total contingent rentals (rentals on which the amounts are dependent on some factor other than the passage of time) actually incurred for each period for which an income statement is presented.

"b. For operating leases having initial or remaining noncancelable lease terms in excess of one year:

"i. Future minimum rental payments required as of the date of the latest balance sheet presented, in the aggregate and for each of the five succeeding fiscal years.

"ii. The total of minimum rentals to be received in the future under noncancelable subleases as of the date of the latest balance sheet presented.

"c. For all operating leases, rental expense for each period for which an income statement is presented, with separate amounts for minimum rentals, contingent rentals, and sublease rentals. Rental payments under leases with terms of a month or less that were not renewed need not be included.

"d. A general description of the lessee's leasing arrangements including, but not limited to, the following:

"i. The basis on which contingent rental payments are determined.

"ii. The existence and terms of renewal or purchase options and escalation clauses.

"iii. Restrictions imposed by lease agreements, such as those concerning dividends, additional debt, and further leasing." Financial Accounting Standards Board, Statement of Financial Accounting Standards No. 13—Accounting for Leases, November 1976, at pages 15 and 16.

The Securities and Exchange Commission, Release No. 33–5812, CCH Fed. Sec.L.Rep. ¶ 80,988 ('76–'77 Tr.Bin.), the Comptroller of Currency, P–H Fed. Control Banking ¶ 9680, and the Federal Reserve Board, P–H Fed.Control Banking ¶ 9686, require financial reports filed with them, or prepared by entities under their supervision or control, to be prepared in accordance with Statement of Financial Accounting Standards No. 13—Accounting for Leases. See generally Schiffman, *Accounting for Leases: How to Work with the Complex Rules of FASB 13,* 13 Prac.Acct. 57 (July 1980).

2. When carrying out the sale portion of the sale and leaseback transaction, should any state of title which is acceptable to the seller-lessee be acceptable to the purchaser-lessor? Why not?

a. Is an action by the seller-lessee against the purchaser-lessor resulting from a title defect which impairs the lessee's quiet enjoyment of the premises of any real concern to the purchaser-lessor if the defect arose during the lessee's period of fee ownership?

1. How can this problem be avoided by the purchaser-lessor?

3. If the take-out commitment given by the permanent financier provides that the permanent financing will take the form of a sale and leaseback of the land and improvements constructed on the land, should the construction lender permit the preparation of the contract of sale and the lease to await the time of take-out? If not, how can (a) the amount of the rent and purchase price (assuming these are based on fair market value or costs), (b) the commencement date of the lease and (c) the exercise date of any option, be provided for in the contract of sale and the lease?

a. A separate agreement between the seller-lessee and purchaser-lessor setting forth the agreed-upon method of determining these items is not as acceptable as specifically providing for them in the contract of sale and the lease. Is there a way in which the separate agreement and the contract of sale and the separate agreement and the lease can be combined?

4. Even if the lessor has a "vital interest" in making sure that the value of the improvements is not impaired during the term of the lease, is it wise to have a clause obligating the lessee to return leased property to the lessor in the same condition or of the same value?

a. Can the lessor depreciate the "cost" of the improvements if such a clause is included? See pages 621 to 622 supra.

5. In the event of the destruction or taking of a substantial part of the leased premises the lessor usually receives its unamortized cost out of the proceeds or award prior to the lessee receiving anything. What then happens to the remaining proceeds or award and the property? The disposition of the remainder of the proceeds or award, if any, should be provided for in the lease. The disposition of the remainder of the property presents a difficult problem. If the form of financing had been a note and mortgage, the mortgagor would own the remainder of the property.

a. In a sale and leaseback transaction should the lease give the lessee an option to reacquire the fee after the destruction or taking of a substantial portion of the leased property? If so, how should the option price be determined? Should it be the amount of return, discounted to the present, the lessor would have received if the lease had run its term, the present value of the remaining real estate, or?

6. See generally Strum, *Sale–Leasebacks: Protection for Depreciation Deduction and Clear Title,* 7 Real Prop., Prob. & Tr.J. 785 (1972); Davis, *Real Estate Leasebacks From the Lessee's Point of View: An Economic and Tax Analysis,* 3 J.Real Est.Tax'n 454 (1976); Egan, *Sale–Leasebacks: Protecting the Institutional Investor Against New Risks,* 6 Real Est.L.J. 199 (1978); Note, *The Financing Lease as a Security Agreement,* 56 Neb.L.Rev. 354 (1977); Claxton, *Lease or Security Interest: A Classic Problem of Commercial Law,* 28 Mercer L.Rev. 599 (1977); Segal, *Structuring a Sale–Leaseback of Commercial Property,* 2 # 3 Prac.Real Est.Law 21 (1986); Maller, *Structuring a Sale–Leaseback Transaction,* 15 Real Est.L.J. 291 (1987).

(i) INCOME TAX CONSIDERATIONS

An important consideration in the sale and leaseback transaction is the income tax effect on the parties to the transaction.

TAX ASPECTS OF SALES AND LEASEBACKS AS PRACTICAL DEVICES FOR TRANSFER AND OPERATION OF REAL PROPERTY

Herbert M. Mandell
18 N.Y.U. Institute on Federal Taxation 17 (1960).
[footnotes omitted]

*   *   *

Tax Considerations for Seller

*   *   *

Treatment of Gain or Loss on Sale

Where the property is sold to an unrelated party at its fair market value, the seller will be able to obtain tax advantages and still retain the use of the property [as a result of] the leaseback. If the property has been held for more than [the prescribed holding period,] the gain will be treated as [capital] gain *   *   *. If there is a loss on the sale, the loss [in most cases] would be deductible as an ordinary loss.[55] The benefits to the seller are apparent where the tax basis of the asset is higher than its fair market value. The deduction of the loss may reduce the income tax liability or in some situations permit a refund of prior years' taxes. This reduction or refund of taxes will add to the funds available from the proceeds of the sale. Where the selling price of the property is greater than its tax basis [the excess will be treated as capital gain.]

[C]apital gain and ordinary loss treatment, with the continued use of the property as a result of the leaseback, may not be available under

---

55. [A loss on the sale would be deductible as an ordinary loss if the property sold was property held by the taxpayer for sale to customers in the ordinary course of business or was property qualified for ordinary loss treatment under the terms of Section 1231, for example, real property used in the taxpayer's trade or business. In the latter case, however, the loss must first be "netted-out" against the gain received by the taxpayer on the sale of any other "1231" property.]

various situations. Special problems may arise in the following circumstances: * * *

  1. Leaseback is for a period of thirty years or more.

  2. Sale is to related parties.

  3. Selling price is less than full value of property.

  4. Lessee has option to repurchase property.

  5. Sale-leaseback is not a bona fide transaction.

Rental Payments vs. Depreciation and Interest Deductions

* * *

The rental payments, which are fully deductible, * * * include interest and a return of capital to the purchaser-lessor. By comparison, the property owner may deduct only the interest portion of the cost of carrying a mortgage, not the amounts paid for amortization. However, he is allowed a deduction for depreciation of the property. Where the depreciation is less than the amortization, a fee owner will be paying out funds without comparable tax benefits. By the use of the sale-leaseback, all of the rental payments become deductible.

Low Depreciation

Rental payments under a leaseback should indicate tax savings when compared to the low depreciation allowances available to a fee owner under certain circumstances. For example, where assets are almost fully depreciated, obviously there is little cost basis to depreciate in future years.

Where the ratio of land value to building value is high, depreciation will be relatively limited, as the land is not depreciable. On the other hand, rental payments are [determined by] the entire value of the property, including the land. Thus by utilizing the sale-leaseback, the vendor-lessee obtains a deduction for the cost of using the land as well as the building.

Where the tax basis of real property is substantially less than its fair market value, a fee owner does not have the advantage of a depreciation allowance based on actual values. By disposing of the property, he not only realizes cash equal to the value of the property, but also obtains, on the leaseback, a deduction for rental payments related to the full value of the property.

Accelerated Depreciation

It may be advisable, in some cases, to purchase property and utilize * * * the * * * depreciation [deduction]. After maximum advantage has been taken of the depreciation deduction, consideration might then be given to the sale and leaseback of the property. [Assuming the depreciation deduction has been computed using the straight-line method,] the selling price at full value would result in capital gain and

rental payments based upon full value would be substituted for the
* * * depreciation [deduction.]

* * *

"Group Accounting" for Depreciation

It may often be possible to obtain higher depreciation in the early
years by the use of group accounting for [land improvements and
personal] property [used in conjunction with the building]. Under this
method, assets similar in kind with approximately the same useful lives
may be grouped together and depreciated separately from the building.
For example, in depreciating real property it may be advisable to
segregate assets with shorter lives such as asphalt parking areas, air
conditioning, elevators or other equipment. This group account
method ordinarily results in a greater allowance for depreciation in the
earlier years than the composite account method. Under the latter
method, depreciation is computed annually on the average useful life of
the entire building without segregating the assets which have shorter
lives.

The use of the group account method * * * may result in * * *
substantial depreciation allowances in the early years following acquisition or construction of the property. After [the lives of the separately
depreciated land improvements and personal property] have been exhausted, consideration might be given to a sale and leaseback of the
property. [The group accounting method, however, is not available for
real estate assets eligible for treatment under Section 168.]

Interest on Mortgage

* * *

This becomes significant in view of the fact that most mortgages
provide for constant payments as a result of which the interest deduction is greatest in the early years. As the mortgage balance declines
the interest portion decreases and the amortization [of principal] increases.

Therefore, after property has been held for a number of years, the
sale-leaseback offers even greater advantages because at that time the
deductions for both depreciation and interest are substantially less than
in the earlier years.

Types of Rental Payments

While depreciation allowances are spelled out in the tax law and
regulations and interest deductions are measured by the terms of the
mortgage, it may be possible to formulate various types of rental
arrangements in a leaseback that will provide substantial tax benefits
to the lessee.

The normal arrangement is one under which rent is paid equally
over the period of the lease. However, it is possible to arrange a lease
where the payments are larger in the early years and smaller in later

years. Where the rental is reasonable in amount and the lease does not contain a clause permitting the lessee to repurchase the property, the rental payments should be deductible when paid.

However, if the payments are unreasonably high in the early years of the lease and drop sharply thereafter, a portion of the early rental, if considered to be excessive, might be regarded as the cost of acquiring a leasehold. If these payments were so treated, they would have to be capitalized and amortized over the life of the lease.

Another type of lease which may be attractive to a lessee is one [in which the rent is a percentage of] its sales or profits. This will permit rental payments [determined by] income and allow greater deductions in years in which the lessee is in higher tax brackets.

Tax Considerations for Buyers

* * *

The tax advantages of real estate investments lie in the fact that part of the return may be partially tax [free]. [T]he depreciation allowance [may] be greater than the mortgage amortization. • This will result in an annual cash return greater than the income subject to tax.

* * *

Deductibility of Loss on Sale

Where property is irrevocably conveyed to an independent purchaser in a bona fide arm's length sale and as a part of the sales agreement the seller retains the right to lease back the property for a period of less than 30 years upon payment of a reasonable rental, the loss on the sale is deductible. Inasmuch as the real property subject to the sale-leaseback is ordinarily used in the trade or business of the seller, the loss on the sale would be deductible against ordinary income.

Leasebacks for 30 Years or More

The Regulations provide that no loss is recognized where a taxpayer exchanges property used in his trade or business, together with cash, for other property of like kind for the same use. It is further stated that for this purpose "a leasehold of a fee with 30 years or more to run" and "real estate" are property of like kind. Therefore, according to the Regulations, if real estate is sold for less than its basis and as part of the same transaction leased back for a period of 30 years or more, the leasehold is an asset of "like kind," received by the seller, so that the loss on the sale is not recognized.

* * *

However, where property is sold [at fair market value] to an unrelated party in an arm's length negotiated transaction and leased back [at a fair rental] for a term of 30 years or more, there is apparently a conflict [among] the courts [as to whether to follow the Regulations] * * *.

Treatment of Unrecognized Loss

If the loss is not recognized because the transaction is treated as an exchange of "like kind" property, the loss should be capitalized and amortized over the life of the lease. * * *

Effect of Renewal Options on 30 Year Rule

What is the effect of renewal options on leases with initial terms of less than 30 years which, if exercised, will bring the total life to more than 30 years? Under these circumstances, unless the lease has been renewed or the facts indicate with reasonable certainty that the lease will be renewed, the renewal periods should not be taken into account in determining whether the lease is for a term of 30 years or more. It is usually difficult to determine, at the time the property is sold and leased back, that the lease will be renewed * * * at the expiration of a long term lease such as 25 years. However, an example of such a situation might be a lease with an initial term of 25 years, with a renewal option for five years or more at greatly reduced rentals. This type of renewal clause might indicate that the tenant intended with reasonable certainty to renew the lease, thereby bringing the entire term of the lease to at least 30 years.

* * *

Loss on Bargain Sale

As previously noted if property is sold to an independent purchaser in an arm's length transaction the loss will be recognized, providing there is no 30 year leaseback issue involved. If the selling price is less than the fair market value, will the loss be recognized? Where the seller does not have any option to repurchase the property, the sale is a completed transaction and the loss should therefore be deductible. However, where the property is sold for an amount which is substantially less than its full value and the seller may repossess the property either during the lease term or at the expiration of the lease, there may not be a bona fide sale. Under these circumstances, the loss would not be deductible.

* * *

Treatment of Gain on Sale
* * *

Gain on Sales with Long Term Leasebacks

In today's real estate market, long term leases often have a definite market value. This is especially true where the purchaser pays less than full value for the property and the rents payable under the lease are less than prevailing rates for leasing of similar property. Although the seller has disposed of the tangible real property, he has received in return a valuable intangible asset in the leasehold. Therefore, gain to the seller might be measured not only by the cash received, but the consideration for the sale of the property would include the value of the leasehold. This leasehold value would then be amortized over the term of the lease.

The effect of this taxwise is that the seller would report an immediate capital gain[, and possibly some ordinary income under Sections 1245 and 1250] on the value of the leasehold even though he did not receive its equivalent in cash at the time of sale. This, however, [might] be offset by the savings of reduced rentals in future years. Thus, over the full term of the lease, the seller would be substituting deductions of leasehold amortization and low rentals for the higher rentals he would have paid had the rentals been at full value.

* * *

Gains on Sales of Depreciable Property between Certain Related Parties

Where depreciable property is the subject of a sale and leaseback between certain related parties, any gain on the sale is taxable as ordinary income under Section 1239 of the Code. Sales between the following parties are [included]: * * * a corporation and an individual, where the individual, his [parents, brothers and sisters,] spouse [or] minor children * * *, own [more than 50]% [in value] of the stock of the corporation; [two corporations, where more than 50% in value of the stock of each corporation is owned directly or indirectly by or for the same individual;] a partnership and [a more than 50]% partner; [and a] partnership [and a corporation,] controlled by persons owning [more than 50]% of both [the partnership and the corporation].

* * *

NOTE

1. Considering the tax on the capital gains and possible recapture of depreciation if the selling price of a development is in excess of its adjusted basis, in what situations does a sale and leaseback of a "mature" development present a desirable method of refinancing?

    a. The direct income tax cost of this technique will be less when it is used as an initial means of long term financing since the purchase price usually is equal to or not substantially in excess of the cost of land and improvements.

    b. If, however, the sale and leaseback is used as a means of providing the initial long term financing of a development, the developer must give up both the depreciation and interest deductions, which combined may be substantially in excess of the rental deduction, at least during the early years of operation of the development.

2. The value of the leasehold, especially if the rents are less than fair market rents, may be included in the purchase price for the purpose of measuring the seller's gain. This may present a significant concern to a developer contemplating the use of the sale and leaseback as a method of

financing or refinancing since the receipt of the leasehold does not provide any cash with which the developer can pay the income tax imposed on the gain recognized on the sale.

3. The above excerpts indicate that the possibility exists that a sale and leaseback, when the lease has an initial term of more than thirty years, may be treated as a like-kind exchange by the Internal Revenue Service in order to prevent the seller's recognition of a loss on the transaction.

LESLIE CO. v. COMMISSIONER

64 T.C. 247 (1975), nonacq. 1978–2 C.B. 3.
[footnotes omitted]

IRWIN, Judge: * * *

The [issue] presented for our determination [is] whether the sale and leaseback of property by petitioner in 1968 constituted an exchange of property of a like kind within the meaning of section 1031(a) * * *.

* * *

Findings of Fact

* * *

Petitioner Leslie Co. (hereinafter referred to as Leslie or petitioner) is a New Jersey corporation primarily engaged in the design, manufacture, and industrial distribution of pressure and temperature regulators and automatic instantaneous water heaters.

* * *

For many years prior to 1966 Leslie operated its entire business, plant, and office in Lyndhurst, N.J. In 1966 Leslie determined that the Lyndhurst plant would be inadequate for future use and decided to construct a new facility in Parsippany. Upon completion of the new plant the Lyndhurst property was to be sold. Pursuant to the decision to move, Leslie acquired land in Parsippany in March 1967.

On October 30, 1967, after having explored other financing possibilities without success, Leslie agreed to a sale and leaseback of the land with improvements to the Prudential Insurance Co. of America (hereinafter referred to as Prudential). The agreement provided that Prudential would enter into a contract for the purchase and leaseback of the Parsippany property, subject, inter alia, to the following requirements and conditions:

1. The sale price shall not exceed $2,400,000 or the actual cost of land, building and other improvements erected thereon, whichever is the lower. * * *

2. Leslie Co. shall have erected and completed on the above premises a one story, 100% sprinklered, masonry and steel industrial building containing approximately 185,000 square feet * * *. The building is to be constructed and improvements made according to detailed plans and specifications which have been approved by The Prudential. Any changes to the plans * * * must be approved by Prudential prior to commencement of construction.

* * *

4. Prudential will be furnished with the following prior to closing:

(a) A lease with Leslie Co. satisfactory in form and substance to Prudential and Leslie Co. for a term of 30 years at an absolute net rental of $190,560, or 7.94% of purchase price if less than $2,400,000, to be paid monthly, in advance, in equal monthly installments. The lease shall include two (2) renewal options of 10 years each with an absolute net annual rental of $72,000, or 3% of purchase price if less than $2,400,000. The lease shall further include a rejectable offer to purchase at the end of the fifteenth, twentieth, twenty-fifth or thirtieth year based on the following schedule:

at the end of the 15th year	$1,798,000
at the end of the 20th year	$1,592,000
at the end of the 25th year	$1,386,000
at the end of the 30th year	$1,180,000

On December 16, 1968, after completion of the plant as approved by Prudential, Leslie delivered the deed to the Parsippany property to Prudential for $2.4 million. The fair market value of the property at the time of sale was in the neighborhood of $2.4 million. Contemporaneously with the transfer of title to Prudential, Leslie and Prudential entered into the lease as specified in the above agreement. The annual net rental of $190,560 was comparable to the fair rental value of similar types of property in the northern New Jersey area. The lease also provided that all condemnation proceeds, net of any damages suffered by Leslie with respect to its trade fixtures and certain structural improvements, would become the property of Prudential without deduction for the leasehold interest of petitioner.

Leslie's total cost in purchasing the land and constructing the plant was $3.187 million, consisting of the following:

Land	$ 255,000
Building	2,410,000
Paving and landscaping	72,000
Boiler (including special features)	140,000
Special electrical wiring	138,000
Miscellaneous personal property (including certain special items)	140,000
Interim finance costs	20,000
Selling costs	12,000
Total cost	3,187,000

Leslie would not have entered into the sales part of the transaction without the guarantee of the leaseback.

The Parsippany plant was not in operation on December 16, 1968, the date of closing, and did not become fully operational until mid-January 1969. The useful life of the new plant was stipulated to be 30 years. Leslie sold the Lyndhurst plant for $600,000 when it moved into the Parsippany facilities.

Leslie is not a dealer in real estate.

On its 1968 corporate income tax return Leslie reported the disposition of the Parsippany property as a sale with a gross sale price of $2.4 million and a cost of $3,187,414 with a loss thereon of $787,414. The claimed loss resulted in a net operating loss of $366,907, which was carried back to 1965. * * * Respondent [disallowed] the claimed loss * * *. Respondent would allow the loss as a cost of obtaining the 30–year lease and permit it to be amortized over the period of the lease.

Leslie treated the claimed loss as an unrecovered cost of plant construction on its books to be amortized over 30 years.

Prudential treated the rental receipts as rental income and depreciated the property on its corporate income tax returns.

Opinion

Respondent, relying upon section 1.1031(a)–1(c), Income Tax Regs., and Century Electric Co., 15 T.C. 581 (1950), affd. 192 F.2d 155 (8th Cir. 1951), cert. denied 342 U.S. 954 (1952), submits that the sale and leaseback between petitioner and Prudential falls within the nonrecognition provisions of section 1031, and that, therefore, petitioner's claimed loss is not allowable. In the same breath, respondent would allow the claimed loss as a "cost" of acquiring the leasehold and amortize it over the 30–year term. Petitioner, on the other hand, submits that there was no "exchange" within the meaning of section 1031, and that, therefore, the claimed loss must be recognized. We agree with petitioner that section 1031 is inapplicable and that the loss must be recognized. The amount is not in dispute.

As an exception to the general rule requiring the recognition of all gains and losses, section 1031 must be strictly construed. See sec. 1002 and the regulations thereunder, particularly sec. 1.1002–1(b), Income Tax Regs. In order for this nonrecognition provision to come into play it must first be established that an exchange occurred. An exchange is defined in the regulations as a transaction involving the reciprocal transfer of property, as distinguished from a transfer of property for a money consideration. Sec. 1.1002–1(d), Income Tax Regs. See also Vernon Molbreak, 61 T.C. 382, 390–392 (1973), affd. per curiam 509 F.2d 616 (7th Cir.1975).

In the instant situation petitioner executed a sale and leaseback agreement with respect to the Parsippany property. It is clear that the sale and leaseback were merely successive steps of a single integrated transaction. It is also equally clear that petitioner, unable to obtain financing to construct a new plant, employed the sale and leaseback mechanism to obtain the needed new facilities. These factors, however, do not dispose of the issue.

While the leaseback arrangement was a necessary condition to the sale, we are of the opinion that, based on the record before us, the leasehold herein did not have any separate capital value which could be properly viewed as a portion of the consideration paid or exchanged. Petitioner received $2.4 million on the sale of the property. The sale and leaseback agreement, executed prior to construction of the new facility, provided that the sale price was to be actual cost to petitioner or $2.4 million, whichever was less. This was based on Prudential's appraisal of the worth of the property after improvements. As it turned out, the actual cost to construct the new facilities (including purchase of the land) totaled $3.187 million. Although we are troubled by the disparity between $2.4 million and $3.187 million, the only evidence in the record (and this presented by respondent) indicated that the fair market value of the property as improved at the date of sale was in the neighborhood of $2.4 million, not $3.187 million. Respondent has also not objected to petitioner's proposed finding of fact that the property as improved had a fair market value of $2.4 million at the date of sale. We also note that the evidence presented indicated that this valuation was comparable to the fair market value of similar types of property in the area. The annual net rental was also comparable to the fair rental value of similar types of property in the area. Based on the record before us, we have no choice but to find that the fair market value of the property was within the $2.4 million range. In our judgment, therefore, the sole consideration paid for the property was the $2.4 million in cash. The leasehold, while integral to the transaction, had no separate capital value and was not a part of the consideration. See City Investing Co., 38 T.C. 1, 9 (1962). In support of our finding that the leasehold had no capital value in and of itself at the time of the sale, we also note that in addition to the fact of the sale price and net rentals being for fair value, the condemnation clause in the lease agreement provided (with certain exceptions not material herein) that in the event of condemnation all proceeds would be paid to Prudential without deduction for the leasehold interest. This clause, while clearly not conclusive on the issue, is further evidence of a lack of capital value.

Respondent, however, in the body of his reply brief, argues that since petitioner's cost exceeded the contract price, the difference must be equal to the capital value of the lease. We find this unsupported by the evidence presented. In essence, it would appear that respondent is arguing that although the leasehold had no capital value, it had a premium value to petitioner. The excess expenditures over $2.4 million would not be a loss as such to petitioner since it would be able to utilize the improvements as lessee and thus would be willing to spend more than $2.4 million. Although this argument seems to comport to economic realities, it does not give the leasehold value. The difference between $2.4 million and $3.187 million is clearly attributable to the cost of building the plant (including the purchase of land); it is not attributable to the leasehold. While it may be true that it was only because of the leasehold that petitioner was willing to spend $3.187 million, it does not follow that the leasehold had a value equal to the difference between $2.4 million and $3.187 million. To reach such a result, it must be shown that the fair market value of the improved property was $3.187 million, not $2.4 million. This was not done.

From an accounting standpoint it is true that the loss, being an extraordinary item, may cause a distortion of income. That is probably why petitioner amortized the unrecovered costs over the 30–year term in its financial statements. Petitioner's treatment of the item on the books, however, is not dispositive of the issue for tax purposes. It is not at all uncommon to find that the book and tax treatment of a given transaction differ. Although losses may be amortized for book purposes, nothing in the Code permits such amortization for tax purposes.

When all the cards are on the table, the fact remains that petitioner had a cost basis of $3.187 million in the improved property and realized $2.4 million on the sale. The bonafideness of the sale was not questioned by respondent. As stated previously, since the evidence indicates that petitioner would be paying a net rent comparable to the fair rental value, the leasehold could have no value at the time of sale, and thus could not be a part of the consideration paid. It was merely a condition precedent to the sale; no more and no less. The fact that petitioner was willing to sell the property "only with some kind of leaseback arrangement included does not of itself detract from the reality of the sale." Cf. City Investing Co., supra.

We, therefore, conclude that there was a bona fide sale of the property and not an "exchange" within the meaning of section 1031. See Jordan Marsh Co. v. Commissioner, 269 F.2d 453 (2d Cir.1959), nonacq. Rev.Rul. 60–43, 1960–1 C.B. 687, revg. a Memorandum Opinion of this Court.

We need not consider Century Electric Co., supra, and its possible conflict with Jordan Marsh Co., since we have found that there was no "exchange" within the meaning of section 1031. We do note, though, that if an "exchange" had been found, then, assuming "like kind" property, the fair market value of such property would appear not to be relevant.

Since the nonrecognition provisions of section 1031 are not applicable, the general rule of recognition under 1002 applies.

* * *

Reviewed by the Court.

Decision will be entered for the petitioner.

NOTE

1. While six of the Tax Court judges dissented from the opinion in *Leslie Co.,* none of the six reached the conclusion that Section 1031 applied to the transaction. The dissenting judges concluded that the difference between the cost of the plant and the purchase price paid by Prudential should be amortized over the term of the lease rather than currently deducted. They reasoned that the difference between the cost and the purchase price was similar to a bonus paid for the lease and the renewal and purchase options provided by the lease, generally a cost of the entire transaction. The decision of the Tax Court was

affirmed in *Leslie Co. v. Comm'r*, 539 F.2d 943 (3d Cir.1976). It is noted in *Conveyance of Property for Fair Market Value in Cash with Concurrent Lease-back is a Sale on Which Loss is Recognized in the Year of Transaction,* 22 Wayne L.Rev. 953 (1976), and *Sale of Property at its Fair Market Value Conditioned Upon Long–Term Leaseback for Fair Market Rentals Constitutes a Sale Solely for Cash Consideration and Not a Like Kind Exchange,* 21 Vill.L. Rev. 332 (1976). See also Massey, *Sale–Leaseback Transactions: Loss Realization—The Neglected Issue,* 6 J. Real Est. Tax'n 308 (1979); Harmelink and Shurtz, *Nontaxable Exchange Treatment in the Sale–Leaseback of Real Estate,* 8 Real Est.L.J. 307 (1980); Comment, *Loss Recognition Upon Sale and Leaseback: The Like Kind Exchange Controversy,* 28 Loy.L.Rev. 1146 (1982).

2. Why did the Commissioner argue in *Leslie Co.* that Section 1031 applied to the transaction rather than that the transaction should be considered in substance as a loan, secured by a mortgage, made by Prudential? Could it be that since the purchase price was at fair market value, the rent was at fair market value, Prudential had the right to substantially all of the condemnation proceeds in the event of condemnation and there was no assurance that the lessee would exercise the purchase options and, even if it did, there was no assurance that the lessor would accept the lessee's offer, the lease looked like a lease and not a borrowing transaction? If the criteria for classifying leases set out in the Financial Accounting Standards Board's Statement of Financial Accounting Standards No. 13, discussed at pages 748 to 750, are applied to the transaction in *Leslie Co.,* how should the lease and the excess of cost over purchase price be accounted for on the books of the seller-lessee?

3. The Internal Revenue Service, at times, has asserted that a sale and leaseback should be treated, for income tax purposes, as, in substance, a borrowing transaction or simply ignored.

FRANK LYON CO. v. UNITED STATES

Supreme Court of the United States, 1978.
435 U.S. 561, 98 S.Ct. 1291, 55 L.Ed.2d 550.
[footnotes omitted]

* * *

Mr. Justice BLACKMUN delivered the opinion of the Court.

This case concerns the federal income tax consequences of a sale-and-leaseback in which petitioner Frank Lyon Company (Lyon) took title to a building under construction by Worthen Bank & Trust Company (Worthen) of Little Rock, Ark., and simultaneously leased the building back to Worthen for long-term use as its headquarters and principal banking facility.

I

* * *

A

Lyon is a closely held Arkansas corporation engaged in the distribution of home furnishings * * *. Worthen in 1965 was an Arkansas-chartered bank and a member of the Federal Reserve System. Frank Lyon was Lyon's majority shareholder and board chairman; he also served on Worthen's board. Worthen at that time began to plan the construction of a multistory bank and office building to replace its existing facility in Little Rock. * * *

Worthen initially hoped to finance, to build, and to own the proposed facility at a total cost of $9 million for the site, building, and adjoining parking deck. This was to be accomplished by selling $4 million in debentures and using the proceeds in the acquisition of the capital stock of a wholly owned real estate subsidiary. This subsidiary would have formal title and would raise the remaining $5 million by a conventional mortgage loan on the new premises. Worthen's plan, however, had to be abandoned for two significant reasons:

1. As a bank chartered under Arkansas law, Worthen legally could not pay more interest on any debentures it might issue than that then specified by Arkansas law. But the proposed obligations would not be marketable at that rate.

2. Applicable statutes or regulations of the Arkansas State Bank Department and the Federal Reserve System required Worthen, as a state bank subject to their supervision, to obtain prior permission for the investment in banking premises of any amount (including that placed in a real estate subsidiary) in excess of the bank's capital stock or of 40% of its capital stock and surplus. * * * Worthen, accordingly, was advised by staff employees of the Federal Reserve System that they would not recommend approval of the plan by the System's Board of Governors.

Worthen therefore was forced to seek an alternative solution that would provide it with the use of the building, satisfy the state and federal regulators, and attract the necessary capital. In September 1967 it proposed a sale-and-leaseback arrangement. The State Bank Department and the Federal Reserve System approved this approach, but the Department required that Worthen possess an option to purchase the leased property at the end of the 15th year of the lease at a set price, and the federal regulator required that the building be owned by an independent third party.

Detailed negotiations ensued with investors that had indicated interest, namely, Goldman, Sachs & Company; White, Weld & Co.; Eastman Dillon, Union Securities & Company; and Stephens, Inc. Certain of these firms made specific proposals.

Worthen then obtained a commitment from New York Life Insurance Company to provide $7,140,000 in permanent mortgage financing on the building, conditioned upon its approval of the titleholder. At this point Lyon entered the negotiations and it, too, made a proposal.

Worthen submitted a counterproposal that incorporated the best features, from its point of view, of the several offers. Lyon accepted the counterproposal * * *. Worthen selected Lyon as the investor. * * * Lyon in November 1967 was approved as an acceptable borrower by First National City Bank for the construction financing, and by

New York Life, as the permanent lender. In April 1968 the approvals of the state and federal regulators were received.

In the meantime, on September 15, before Lyon was selected, Worthen itself began construction.

B

In May 1968 Worthen, Lyon, City Bank, and New York Life executed complementary and interlocking agreements under which the building was sold by Worthen to Lyon as it was constructed, and Worthen leased the completed building back from Lyon.

1. Agreements between Worthen and Lyon. Worthen and Lyon executed a ground lease, a sales agreement, and a building lease.

Under the ground lease dated May 1, 1968 Worthen leased the site to Lyon for 76 years and 7 months through November 30, 2044. The first 19 months were the estimated construction period. The ground rents payable by Lyon to Worthen were $50 for the first 26 years and 7 months and thereafter in quarterly payments:

12/1/94 through 11/30/99	(5 years)—$100,000 annually
12/1/99 through 11/30/04	(5 years)—$150,000 annually
12/1/04 through 11/30/09	(5 years)—$200,000 annually
12/1/09 through 11/30/34	(25 years)—$250,000 annually
12/1/34 through 11/30/44	(10 years)—$ 10,000 annually

Under the sales agreement dated May 19, 1968, Worthen agreed to sell the building to Lyon, and Lyon agreed to buy it, piece by piece as it was constructed, for a total price not to exceed $7,640,000, in reimbursements to Worthen for its expenditures for the construction of the building.

Under the building lease dated May 1, 1968, Lyon leased the building back to Worthen for a primary term of 25 years from December 1, 1969, with options in Worthen to extend the lease for eight additional 5–year terms, a total of 65 years. During the period between the expiration of the building lease (at the latest, November 30, 2034, if fully extended) and the end of the ground lease on November 30, 2044, full ownership, use, and control of the building were Lyon's, unless, of course, the building had been repurchased by Worthen. Worthen was not obligated to pay rent under the building lease until completion of the building. For the first 11 years of the lease, that is, until November 30, 1980, the stated quarterly rent was $145,581.03 ($582,324.12 for the year). For the next 14 years, the quarterly rent was $153,289.32 ($613,157.28 for the year), and for the option periods the rent was $300,000 a year, payable quarterly. The total rent for the building over the 25–year primary term of the lease thus was $14,989,767.24. That rent equaled the principal and interest payments that would amortize the $7,140,000 New York Life mortgage loan over the same period. When the mortgage was paid off at the end of the primary term, the annual building rent, if Worthen extended the lease, came down to the stated $300,000. Lyon's net rentals from the building would be further reduced by the increase in ground rent Worthen would receive from Lyon during the extension.

The building lease was a "net lease," under which Worthen was responsible for all expenses usually associated with the maintenance of an office building, including repairs, taxes, utility charges, and insurance, and was to keep the premises in good condition, excluding, however, reasonable wear and tear.

Finally, under the lease, Worthen had the option to repurchase the building at the following times and prices:

11/30/80 (after 11 years)—$6,325,169.85
11/30/84 (after 15 years)—$5,432,607.32
11/30/89 (after 20 years)—$4,187,328.04
11/30/94 (after 25 years)—$2,145,935.00

These repurchase option prices were the sum of the unpaid balance of the New York Life mortgage, Lyon's $500,000 investment, and 6% interest compounded on that investment.

2. Construction financing agreement. By agreement dated May 14, 1968, City Bank agreed to lend Lyon $7,000,000 for the construction of the building. This loan was secured by a mortgage on the building and the parking deck, executed by Worthen as well as by Lyon, and an assignment by Lyon of its interests in the building lease and in the ground lease.

3. Permanent financing agreement. By Note Purchase Agreement dated May 1, 1968, New York Life agreed to purchase Lyon's $7,140,000 6¾% 25-year secured note to be issued upon completion of the building. Under this agreement Lyon warranted that it would lease the building to Worthen for a noncancelable term of at least 25 years under a net lease at a rent at least equal to the mortgage payments on the note. Lyon agreed to make quarterly payments of principal and interest equal to the rentals payable by Worthen during the corresponding primary term of the lease. The security for the note were a first deed of trust and Lyon's assignment of its interests in the building lease and in the ground lease. Worthen joined in the deed of trust as the owner of the fee and the parking deck.

In December 1969 the building was completed and Worthen took possession. At that time Lyon received the permanent loan from New York Life, and it discharged the interim loan from City Bank. The actual cost of constructing the office building and parking complex (excluding the cost of the land) exceeded $10,000,000.

* * *

On audit of Lyon's 1969 return, the Commissioner of Internal Revenue determined that Lyon was "not the owner for tax purposes of any portion of the Worthen Building," and ruled that "the income and expenses related to this building are not allowable * * * for Federal income tax purposes." He also added $2,298.15 to Lyon's 1969 income as "accrued interest income." This was the computed 1969 portion of a gain, considered the equivalent of interest income, the realization of which was based on the assumption that Worthen would exercise its option to buy the building after 11 years, on November 30, 1980, at the price stated in the lease, and on the additional determination that Lyon had "loaned" $500,000 to Worthen. In other words, the Commissioner determined that the sale-and-leaseback arrangement was a financing transaction in which Lyon loaned Worthen $500,000 and acted as a conduit for the transmission of principal and interest from Worthen to New York Life.

* * *

II

This Court, almost 50 years ago, observed that "taxation is not so much concerned with the refinements of title as it is with actual command over the property taxed—the actual benefit for which the tax is paid." Corliss v. Bowers, 281 U.S. 376, 378, 50 S.Ct. 336, 74 L.Ed. 916 (1930). In a number of cases, the Court has refused to permit the transfer of formal legal title to shift the incidence of taxation attributable to ownership of property where the transferor continues to retain significant control over the property transferred. E.g., Commissioner v. Sunnen, 333 U.S. 591, 68 S.Ct. 715, 92 L.Ed. 898 (1948); Helvering v. Clifford, 309 U.S. 331 (1940). In applying this doctrine of substance over form, the Court has looked to the objective economic realities of a transaction rather than to the particular form the parties employed. The Court has never regarded "the simple expedient of drawing up papers," Commissioner v. Tower, 327 U.S. 280, 291, 66 S.Ct. 532, 538, 90 L.Ed. 670 (1946), as controlling for tax purposes when the objective economic realities are to the contrary. "In the field of taxation, administrators of the laws, and the courts, are concerned with substance and realities, and formal written documents are not rigidly binding." Helvering v. Lazarus & Co., 308 U.S., at 255, 60 S.Ct. at 210, 84 L.Ed. 226 (1939). See also Commissioner v. P.G. Lake, Inc., 356 U.S. 260, 266–267, 78 S.Ct. 691, 2 L.Ed.2d 743 (1958); Commissioner v. Court Holding Co., 324 U.S. 331, 334, 65 S.Ct. 707, 89 L.Ed. 981 (1945). Nor is the parties' desire to achieve a particular tax result necessarily relevant. Commissioner v. Duberstein, 363 U.S. 278, 286, 80 S.Ct. 1190, 4 L.Ed.2d 1218 (1960).

In the light of these general and established principles, the Government takes the position that the Worthen–Lyon transaction in its entirety should be regarded as a sham. The agreement as a whole, it is said, was only an elaborate financing scheme designed to provide economic benefits to Worthen and a guaranteed return to Lyon. The latter was but a conduit used to forward the mortgage payments, made under the guise of rent paid by Worthen to Lyon, on to New York Life as mortgagee. This, the Government claims, is the true substance of the transaction as viewed under the microscope of the tax laws. Although the arrangement was cast in sale-and-leaseback form, in substance it was only a financing transaction, and the terms of the repurchase options and lease renewals so indicate. It is said that Worthen could reacquire the building simply by satisfying the mortgage debt and paying Lyon its $500,000 advance plus interest, regardless of the fair market value of the building at the time; similarly, when the mortgage was paid off, Worthen could extend the lease at drastically reduced bargain rentals that likewise bore no relation to fair rental value but were simply calculated to pay Lyon its $500,000 plus interest over the extended term. Lyon's return on the arrangement in no event could exceed 6% compound interest * * *. Furthermore, the favorable option and lease renewal terms made it highly unlikely that Worthen would abandon the building after it in effect had "paid off" the mortgage. The Government implies that the arrangement was one of convenience which, if accepted on its face, would enable Worthen to deduct its payments to Lyon as rent and would allow Lyon to claim a deduction for depreciation, based on the cost of construction ultimately borne by Worthen, which Lyon could offset against other income, and to deduct mortgage interest that roughly would offset the inclusion of Worthen's rental payments in Lyon's income. If, however, the Government argues, the arrangement was only a financing transaction under which Worthen was the owner of the building, Worthen's payments would be deductible only to the extent that they represented mortgage interest, and Worthen would be entitled to claim depreciation; Lyon would not be entitled to deductions for either mortgage interest or depreciation and it would not have to include Worthen's "rent" payments in its income because its function with respect to those payments was that of a conduit between Worthen and New York Life.

The Government places great reliance on Helvering v. Lazarus & Co., supra, and claims it to be precedent that controls this case. The taxpayer there was a department store. The legal title of its three buildings was in a bank as trustee for land-trust certificate holders. When the transfer to the trustee was made, the trustee at the same time leased the buildings back to the taxpayer for 99 years, with option to renew and purchase. The Commissioner, in stark contrast to his posture in the present case, took the position that the statutory right to depreciation followed legal title. The Board of Tax Appeals, however, concluded that the transaction between the taxpayer and the bank in reality was a mortgage loan and allowed the taxpayer depreciation on the buildings. This Court, as had the Court of Appeals, agreed with that conclusion and affirmed. It regarded the "rent" stipulated in the leaseback as a promise to pay interest on the loan, and a "depreciation fund" required by the lease as an amortization fund designed to pay off the loan in the stated period. Thus, said the Court, the Board justifiably concluded that the transaction, although in written form a transfer of ownership with a leaseback, was actually a loan secured by the property involved.

The Lazarus case, we feel, is to be distinguished from the present one and is not controlling here. Its transaction was one involving only two (and not multiple) parties, the taxpayer-department store and the trustee-bank. The Court looked closely at the substance of the agreement between those two parties and rightly concluded that depreciation was deductible by the taxpayer despite the nomenclature of the instrument of conveyance and the leaseback. See also Sun Oil Co. v. Commissioner, 562 F.2d 258 (3d Cir.1977) (a two-party case with the added feature that the second party was a tax-exempt pension trust).

The present case, in contrast, involves three parties, Worthen, Lyon, and the finance agency. The usual simple two-party arrangement was legally unavailable to Worthen. Independent investors were interested in participating in the alternative available to Worthen, and Lyon itself (also independent from Worthen) won the privilege. Despite Frank Lyon's presence on Worthen's board of directors, the transaction, as it ultimately developed, was not a familial one arranged by Worthen, but one compelled by the realities of the restrictions imposed upon the bank. Had Lyon not appeared, another interested investor would have been selected. The ultimate solution would have been essentially the same. Thus, the presence of the third party, in our view, significantly distinguishes this case from Lazarus and removes the latter as controlling authority.

III

It is true, of course, that the transaction took shape according to Worthen's needs. As the Government points out, Worthen throughout the negotiations regarded the respective proposals of the independent investors in terms of its own cost of funds. It is also true that both Worthen and the prospective investors compared the various proposals in terms of the return anticipated on the investor's equity. But all this is natural for parties contemplating entering into a transaction of this kind. Worthen needed a building for its banking operations and other purposes and necessarily had to know what its cost would be. The investors were in business to employ their funds in the most remunerative way possible. And, as the Court has said in the past, a transaction must be given its effect in accord with what actually occurred and not in accord with what might have occurred. Commissioner v. National Alfalfa Dehydrating & Milling Co., 417 U.S. 134, 148–149, 94 S.Ct. 2129, 40 L.Ed.2d 717 (1974); Central Tablet Mfg. Co. v. United States, 417 U.S. 673, 690, 94 S.Ct. 2516, 41 L.Ed.2d 398 (1974).

There is no simple device available to peel away the form of this transaction and to reveal its substance. The effects of the transaction on all the parties were obviously different from those that would have resulted had Worthen been able simply to make a mortgage agreement with New York Life and to receive a $500,000 loan from Lyon. Then *Lazarus* would apply. Here, however, and most significantly, it was Lyon alone, and not Worthen, who was liable on the notes, first to City Bank, and then to New York Life. Despite the facts that Worthen had agreed to pay rent and that this rent equaled the amounts due from

Lyon to New York Life, should anything go awry in the later years of the lease, Lyon was primarily liable. No matter how the transaction could have been devised otherwise, it remains a fact that as the agreements were placed in final form, the obligation on the notes fell squarely on Lyon. Lyon, an on-going enterprise, exposed its very business well-being to this real and substantial risk.

The effect of this liability on Lyon is not just the abstract possibility that something will go wrong and that Worthen will not be able to make its payments. Lyon has disclosed this liability on its balance sheet for all the world to see. Its financial position was affected substantially by the presence of this long-term debt, despite the offsetting presence of the building as an asset. To the extent that Lyon has used its capital in this transaction, it is less able to obtain financing for other business needs.

* * * Worthen was not allowed to enter into the type of transaction which the Government now urges to be the true substance of the arrangement. Lyon and Worthen cannot be said to have entered into the transaction intending that the interests involved were allocated in a way other than that associated with a sale-and-lease-back.

Other factors also reveal that the transaction cannot be viewed as a mortgage agreement between Worthen and New York Life and a loan from Lyon to Worthen. There is no legal obligation between Lyon and Worthen representing the $500,000 "loan" extended under the Government's theory. And the assumed 6% return on this putative loan—required by the audit to be recognized in the taxable year in question—will be realized only when and if Worthen exercises its options.

* * * The rents alone, due after the primary term of the lease and after the mortgage has been paid, do not provide the simple 6% return which, the Government urges, Lyon is guaranteed, * * *. Thus, if Worthen chooses not to exercise its options, Lyon is gambling that the rental value of the building during the last 10 years of the ground lease, during which the ground rent is minimal, will be sufficient to recoup its investment before it must negotiate again with Worthen regarding the ground lease. There are simply too many contingencies, including variations in the value of real estate, in the cost of money, and in the capital structure of Worthen, to permit the conclusion that the parties intended to enter into the transaction * * * according to which the Government now urges they be taxed.

It is not inappropriate to note that the Government is likely to lose little revenue, if any, as a result of the shape given the transaction by the parties. No deduction was created that is not either matched by an item of income or that would not have been available to one of the parties if the transaction had been arranged differently. While it is true that Worthen paid Lyon less to induce it to enter into the transaction because Lyon anticipated the benefit of the depreciation deductions it would have as the owner of the building, those deductions would have been equally available to Worthen had it retained title to the building. * * * The fact that favorable tax consequences were taken into account by Lyon on entering into the transaction is no reason for disallowing those consequences. We cannot ignore the reality that the tax laws affect the shape of nearly every business transaction. See Commissioner v. Brown, 380 U.S. 563, 579–580, 85 S.Ct. 1162, 14 L.Ed.2d 75 (1965) (Harlan, J., concurring). Lyon is not a corporation with no purpose other than to hold title to the bank building. It was not created by Worthen or even financed to any degree by Worthen.

The conclusion that the transaction is not a simple sham to be ignored does not, of course, automatically compel the further conclusion that Lyon is entitled to the items claimed as deductions. Nevertheless, on the facts, this readily follows. As has been noted, the obligations on which Lyon paid interest were its obligations alone, and it is entitled to claim deductions therefor under § 163(a) of the * * * Code, 26 U.S. C.A. § 163(a).

As is clear from the facts, none of the parties to this sale-and-leaseback was the owner of the building in any simple sense. But it is equally clear that the facts focus upon Lyon as the one whose capital was committed to the building and as the party, therefore, that was entitled to claim depreciation for the consumption of that capital. The Government has based its contention that Worthen should be treated as the owner on the assumption that throughout the term of the lease Worthen was acquiring an equity in the property. In order to establish the presence of that growing equity, however, the Government is forced to speculate that one of the options will be exercised and that, if it is not, this is only because the rentals for the extended term are a bargain. We cannot indulge in such speculation in view of the District Court's clear finding to the contrary. We therefore conclude that it is Lyon's capital that is invested in the building according to the agreement of the parties, and it is Lyon that is entitled to depreciation deductions * * *. Cf. United States v. Chicago B. & Q. R. Co., 412 U.S. 401, 93 S.Ct. 2169, 37 L.Ed.2d 30 (1973).

IV

We recognize that the Government's position * * * is not without superficial appeal. One, indeed, may theorize that Frank Lyon's presence on the Worthen board of directors; Lyon's departure from its principal corporate activity into this unusual venture; the parallel between the payments under the building lease and the amounts due from Lyon on the New York Life mortgage; the provisions relating to condemnation or destruction of the property; the nature and presence of the several options available to Worthen; and the tax benefits * * * that accrue to Lyon during the initial years of the arrangement, form the basis of an argument that Worthen should be regarded as the owner of the building and as the recipient of nothing more from Lyon than a $500,000 loan.

We, however, ＊ ＊ ＊ find this theorizing incompatible with the substance and economic realities of the transaction: ＊ ＊ ＊ Worthen's undercapitalization; Worthen's consequent inability, as a matter of legal restraint, to carry its building plans into effect by a conventional mortgage and other borrowing; the additional barriers imposed by the state and federal regulators; the suggestion, forthcoming from the state regulator, that Worthen possess an option to purchase; the requirement, from the federal regulator, that the building be owned by an independent third party; the presence of several finance organizations seriously interested in participating in the transaction and in the resolution of Worthen's problem; the submission of formal proposals by several of those organizations; the bargaining process and period that ensued; the competitiveness of the bidding; the bona fide character of the negotiations; the three-party aspect of the transaction; Lyon's substantiality and its independence from Worthen; the fact that diversification was Lyon's principal motivation; Lyon's being liable alone on the successive notes to City Bank and New York Life; the reasonableness, as the District Court found, of the rentals and of the option prices; the substantiality of the purchase prices; Lyon's not being engaged generally in the business of financing; the presence of all building depreciation risks on Lyon; the risk, borne by Lyon, that Worthen might default or fail, as other banks have failed; the facts that Worthen could "walk away" from the relationship at the end of the 25–year primary term, and probably would do so if the option price were more than the then-current worth of the building to Worthen; the inescapable fact that if the building lease were not extended, Lyon would be the full owner of the building, free to do with it as it chose; Lyon's liability for the substantial ground rent if Worthen decides not to exercise any of its options to extend; the absence of any understanding between Lyon and Worthen that Worthen would exercise any of the purchase options; the nonfamily and nonprivate nature of the entire transaction; and the absence of any differential in tax rates and of special tax circumstances for one of the parties—all convince us that Lyon has far the better of the case.

In so concluding, we emphasize that we are not condoning manipulation by a taxpayer through arbitrary labels and dealings that have no economic significance. Such, however, has not happened in this case.

In short, we hold that where, as here, there is a genuine multiple-party transaction with economic substance which is compelled or encouraged by business or regulatory realities, is imbued with tax-independent considerations, and is not shaped solely by tax-avoidance features that have meaningless labels attached, the Government should honor the allocation of rights and duties effectuated by the parties. Expressed another way, so long as the lessor retains significant and genuine attributes of the traditional lessor status, the form of the transaction adopted by the parties governs for tax purposes. What those attributes are in any particular case will necessarily depend upon its facts. It suffices to say that, as here, a sale-and-lease-back, in and of itself, does not necessarily operate to deny a taxpayer's claim for deductions.

The judgment of the Court of Appeals, accordingly, is reversed.

It is so ordered.

NOTE

1. The test used by the Supreme Court in *Frank Lyon Co.* to determine whether the sale-leaseback should be treated as such or as a financing device was whether the lessor, and possibly the lessee, had "significant and genuine attributes of the traditional status." The Court listed more than thirty factors which led to its conclusion that significant and genuine attributes of the traditional status were present.

    a. Which of these factors are significant, apart from the specific facts of *Frank Lyon Co.,* so as to be of assistance in planning a sale and leaseback transaction? The following factors have been suggested.

    1. The transaction involving three parties.

    2. The lessee being unable to directly own the real estate.

    3. The "downside" risk undertaken by Lyon in being personally liable on the loans and having no assurance that Worthen would exercise the purchase or renewal options.

    4. The "upside" possibility that Lyon might recognize some of the appreciation in the building. Lyon's lease of the ground had a term of approximately 75 years while Worthen's lease of the building had a term of approximately 65 years.

    5. Equating the payments to be made by Worthen to Lyon to payments to be made in repayment of a loan required substantial speculation with respect to events which would or might occur in the future.

    6. Overall tax revenues were not substantially affected by the form of the transaction.

    7. The renewal rentals and option prices had been found reasonable by the district court.

    8. The option price at the end of the primary term was substantial.

    b. The Court concluded that Lyon had a risk of loss and a possibility of gain that was more consistent with the "traditional status" of a lessor than the "traditional status" of a lender. In addition, Lyon had an interest in "residuals," the ten-year difference between the ground lease and the lease of the improvements, which could be only explained in terms of traditional lessor status.

    c. See Krovenet, *Characterization of Real Estate Leases: An Analysis and Proposal,* 32 Tax Law. 757 (1979); Zarrow and Gordon, *Supreme Court's Sale–Leaseback Decision in Lyon Lists Multiple Criteria,* 49 J.Tax'n 42 (1978); Kaster, *Another View of the Implications of the Supreme Court Decision in Lyon,* 49 J.Tax'n 44 (1978); Fuller, *Sales and Leasebacks and the Frank Lyon Case,* 48 Geo.Wash.L.Rev. 60 (1979); Robbins, *Sale and Leaseback of Real Property after Frank Lyon Co.,* 11 Tax Adviser 476 (1980); Wolfman, *The Supreme Court in the Lyon's Den: A Failure of Judicial*

Process, 66 Cornell L.Rev. 1075 (1981); Comment, *Sale–Leaseback v. Mere Financing: Lyon's Roar and the Aftermath,* 1982 Ill.L.Rev. 1075; Lucas, *The Lyon Dethroned: Federal Income Taxation Classification of Leases and Leasebacks,* 15 Cumb.L.Rev. 431 (1984–85).

2. See and compare *American Realty Trust v. United States,* 498 F.2d 1194 (4th Cir.1974); *Cal–Maine Foods, Inc.,* 36 CCH Tax Ct.Mem. 383 (1977); *T. Wayne Davis,* 37 CCH Tax Ct.Mem. 1441 (1978); *Belz Investment Co., Inc.,* 72 T.C. 1209 (1979), affirmed, 661 F.2d 76 (6th Cir.1981), acq. 1980–1 C.B. 1; *Paul D. Dunlap,* 74 T.C. 1377 (1980), reversed, 670 F.2d 785 (8th Cir.1982); *William N. West,* 48 CCH Tax Ct.Mem. 796 (1984) (sale and leaseback treated as such) with *Sun Oil Co. v. Comm'r,* 562 F.2d 258 (3d Cir.1977); *Otis B. Miller,* 68 T.C. 767 (1977); *Carol W. Hilton,* 74 T.C. 305 (1980), affirmed, 671 F.2d 316 (9th Cir. 1982); *Cynthia Schaefer,* 41 CCH Tax Ct.Mem. 100 (1980) (sale and leaseback treated as a financing device).

    a. See generally Comment, *Taxation of Sale and Leaseback Transactions—A General Review,* 32 Vand.L.Rev. 945 (1979); Shurtz, *A Decision Model for Lease Parties in Sale–Leasebacks of Real Estate,* 23 Wm. & Mary L.Rev. 385 (1982); Del Cotto, *Sale and Leaseback: A Hollow Sound When Tapped?,* 37 Tax L.Rev. 1 (1981); Harmelink and Shurtz, *Sale–Leaseback Transactions Involving Real Estate: A Proposal for Defined Tax Rules,* 55 S.Cal.L.Rev. 833 (1982); Rubinstein and London, *Sales and Leasebacks: Some Valuation Problems,* 37 Tax Law. 481 (1984); Simonson, *Determining Tax Ownership of Leased Property,* 38 Tax Law. 1 (1984); Steele, *Sham in Substance: The Tax Court's Emerging Standard for Testing Sale–Leasebacks,* 14 J.Real Est.Tax'n 5 (1986); Comment, *Sale–Leasebacks: A Search for Economic Substance,* 61 Ind.L.J. 721 (1986).

3. In addition to treating the sale and leaseback as a like-kind exchange or as a financing device, in appropriate cases, the Internal Revenue Service has asserted and the courts have held that the transaction should be treated as a sham when the purchaser-lessor has few, if any, of the benefits, risks and burdens of ownership and bears little economic risk, especially when compared with the income tax benefits received. See, e.g., *Milbrew Inc. v. Comm'r,* 710 F.2d 1302 (7th Cir.1983). A sale-leaseback was treated as an option to purchase by the purported lessor-purchaser when the lessor-purchaser did not demonstrate that the fair market value of the property equaled or exceeded the purchase price, the rental payments were about the same amounts as the required amortization of the mortgage given to the seller-lessee and the mortgage was nonrecourse and provided for a substantial "balloon" payment. See *Estate of Franklin v. Comm'r,* 544 F.2d 1045 (9th Cir.1976), affirming, 64 T.C. 752 (1975).

    4. See generally Davis, *Real Estate Leasebacks From the Lessee's Point of View: An Economic and Tax Analysis,* 3 J.Real Est.Tax'n 454 (1976); Morris, *Sale–Leaseback Transactions of Real Property—A Proposal—,* 30 Tax Law. 701 (1977); Avent and Grimes, *Inflated Purchase Money Indebtedness in Real Estate and Other Investments,* 11 J.Real Est.Tax'n 99 (1984); Tucker, *The Sale and Leaseback as a Financing Tool,* 124 # 10 Tr. & Est. 27 (1985).

    5. In a related area, the Internal Revenue Service has imposed strict guidelines as preconditions to its ruling whether a "leveraged lease" will be considered a lease for income tax purposes. See Rev.Proc. 75–21, 1975–1 C.B. 715, modified by Rev.Proc. 76–30, 1976–2 C.B. 647, and Rev.Proc. 75–28, 1975–1 C.B. 752. These guidelines have produced a great deal of commentary. See e.g.

Javaras and Nelson, *The New Leveraged Lease Guidelines,* 53 Taxes 388 (1975); Mann and Schmidt, *The New Leveraged Lease Guidelines,* 6 Tax Adviser 390 (1975); Berlin, *Leveraged Leasing Transactions: An Analysis of the Service's Two Rulings,* 43 J.Tax'n 26 (1975); Weinstein, *Safe Harbor Rules for Leveraged Leases,* 92 Banking L.J. 631 (1975). In addition, if a lease, including a lease which is part of a sale and leaseback transaction, provides for a deferral of rent, the provisions of Section 467 may be applicable. In fact, a leaseback, in some ways, is specially treated under Section 467. See Sec. 467(b)(3) and (4) and (c) (1). See Rosenberg, *Deferred Rent Transactions and Leveraged Sale–Leasebacks under TRA 84,* 15 # 1 Real Est.Rev. 26 (1985); Hamilton and Comi, *The Time Value of Money: Section 467 Rental Agreements Under the Tax Reform Act of 1984,* 63 Taxes 155 (1985).

g. GOVERNMENT ASSISTANCE

Although a complete discussion of the various forms of governmental assistance in the financing of the development of commercial, industrial and residential real estate is beyond the scope of these materials, a discussion of long term financing would be incomplete without its mention. At the present time, the principal real estate incentives contained in the Internal Revenue Code of 1986 are the following. Tax credits are available for the acquisition, construction and renovation of low-income housing units. See Section 42 and Division I, pages 389 to 390 supra. In addition, certain tax credits are available for the rehabilitation of certified historic buildings and for the rehabilitation of nonresidential buildings which are over fifty years old. See Section 48(g) and Division I, pages 388 to 389 supra. A 27½ year recovery period can be used to recover the cost of residential rental real estate as opposed to a 31½ year recovery period which can be used to recover the cost of nonresidential real estate. See Section 168(c) and Division I, pages 385 to 386 supra. Lastly, the nonrecognition concept applicable to like-kind exchanges, see Section 1031 and Division II, pages 511 to 525 supra, has been broadened to permit a taxpayer to receive cash or its equivalent on the disposition of certain qualified low-income housing if the disposition is an approved disposition, see Section 1039(b)(2), and within the reinvestment period, see Section 1039(b)(3), the taxpayer constructs, reconstructs or acquires another qualified housing project.

Direct governmental assistance is available in a variety of forms. At the federal level assistance may include an outright grant, a low interest long-term mortgage loan, the insurance of a mortgage loan made by a private lender, the payment of the difference between a set rate of interest and the interest rate charged by a private lender and rent supplements. This type of assistance, while commonly associated with residential development, at times and in some forms may be available to commercial and industrial developments such as industrial parks, shopping plazas, nursing homes, etc. pursuant to programs administered by agencies such as the Small Business Administration, the Economic Development Administration and the Department of

Health and Human Services. A compilation of the various types of assistance available at the federal level may be found in Stevenson, Handbook of Federal Assistance (Warren, Gorham & Lamont, Inc.). In addition, many states and localities have enacted statutes and ordinances providing for similar types of assistance to qualified real estate developments.

The concerns of a developer who receives governmental assistance, beside the red tape involved, are the same, in many cases, as those of a developer who is not receiving governmental assistance. For example, the developer receiving governmental assistance must consider what type of entity to use, how the initial land acquisition can be accomplished, how the long term financing can be accomplished and what are the income tax effects of the transaction. See generally Bourdeaux, *Representing the Subsidized Housing Sponsor,* 42 Miss.L.J. 346 (1971); Comment, *The HUD Interest Subsidy Programs: Some Economic Realities Affecting Project Feasibility and Investor Participation,* 41 UMKCL.Rev. 37 (1972); McDonough, *The Sponsoring of Low– and Moderate–Income Housing Through Local Limited Partnerships Having Nonprofit Corporate General Partners,* 13 B.C.Ind. & Com.L.Rev. 910 (1972); Hopfl, *Financing Land Development Under Title X,* 5 # 3 Real Est.Rev. 118 (1975).

5. LIMITATION OF PERSONAL LIABILITY

Often, the participants in the acquiring entity or the acquiring entity itself prefer to avoid personal liability to the financier. In simple terms, both the participants and the acquiring entity want the lender's recourse, in the event of default, to be limited to the real estate development which the lender financed. One way of obtaining this result is the use of a nominee or straw man (preferably a straw corporation) for the purpose of borrowing the necessary financing from the lender.

a. USE OF THE NOMINEE OR STRAW MAN

Division I, pages 256 to 279 supra, contains a discussion of the concerns and problems which must be dealt with when a nominee, straw man or straw corporation is used.

b. THE IN REM MORTGAGE

Personal liability also can be avoided if the lender can be persuaded to use an "in rem" or nonrecourse mortgage when providing the financing for a real estate development. This type of limitation of personal liability can take a number of forms, but the effect generally is to limit the lender's rights on default solely to the real estate for which the lender provided the financing. Before this technique is used in a jurisdiction, it must be determined whether a mortgage is valid when there is no personal liability for it to secure. This question can be a substantial concern in a civil law jurisdiction and the answer is not entirely free from doubt in many common law jurisdictions. The following excerpts deal with the validity of an "in rem" or nonrecourse mortgage under Louisiana law. Much of the analysis used to support the validity of the "in rem" or nonrecourse mortgage, however, is applicable to common law, particularly lien theory, states.

THE "IN REM" MORTGAGE
Max Nathan, Jr.
44 Tulane Law Review 497 (1970).
[footnotes omitted]

* * *

* * * [T]here have been more and more requests for "in rem" mortgages in recent years, and the ingenuity of the bar has manifested itself in the numerous ways in which such mortgages have been attempted.

As an example of such ingenuity, the following provision is typical of the kind of drafting used to accomplish the dual purpose of limiting personal liability while at the same time preserving the validity of the mortgage:

> Payment of this note and the payment of every obligation contained in the mortgage with which this note is identified and by which this note is secured shall be enforced solely from the property mortgaged as security for this note and no deficiency, after applying the net proceeds of any foreclosure or other judicial sale of such mortgaged property, or any part or parcel thereof, shall ever be asserted against the maker(s) of this note, any partner thereof, his (their) successors, heirs, legal representatives and assigns, or in any other manner realized upon their personal liability to pay this note. These provisions are not intended as any release or discharge of the indebtedness represented by this note and secured by the mortgage with which it is identified or of any portion thereof but are intended only as a covenant not to sue, the indebtedness represented by this note to remain in full force and effect as fully as though these provisions were not contained in this note or in the mortgage with which this note is identified and by which this note is secured. The maker(s) of this note expressly recognizes and acknowledges that the holder and every future holder or holders of this note have expressly reserved all other legal rights and remedies, including, but without limitation on the generality of the foregoing, in the event of default in the payment of this note or any other part hereof, or in the event of default under any of the covenants or conditions of this note and of the mortgage with which this note is identified and by which this note is secured, to foreclose said mortgage by a sale of the mortgaged property; to receive the proceeds of loss under any insurance policy maintained or carried as provided in said mortgage; and to receive the proceeds of any condemnation or eminent domain proceedings

as provided in said mortgage; and to receive the proceeds resulting from the collateral assignment of leases and rents of even date herewith, executed by the maker(s) of this Mortgage Note as further security for this Mortgage Note. * * *

Another example of drafting ingenuity * * * is as follows:

Mortgagee does specially covenant and agree, for itself, its successors and assigns, that it shall enforce payment of any obligation contained in this mortgage or in the note secured hereby solely from the property mortgaged herein and hereby and that no deficiency, after applying the net proceeds of any foreclosure or other judicial sale of the mortgaged properties, or any part or parcel thereof, shall ever be asserted against Mortgagor, its successors, heirs, legal representatives and assigns, or in any other manner realized upon the personal liability of Mortgagor to pay the note secured hereby. It is hereby expressly understood and agreed that this covenant is not intended as any release or discharge of the indebtedness secured by this mortgage, or any portion thereof, but as a covenant not to sue and that such indebtedness shall remain in full force and effect as fully as though this covenant not to sue had not been given; provided, however, that the Mortgagee expressly reserves all other legal rights and remedies, including, but without limitation on the generality of the foregoing, the right, in the event of default in the payment of such indebtedness, or any part thereof, or any of the covenants or conditions of this mortgage, or of the note secured hereby, to foreclose this mortgage by a sale of the properties hereon and hereby mortgaged and to collect and receive the rents and profits, either before or during the period of any such foreclosure proceedings; and to receive the proceeds of loss under any insurance policy maintained or carried as provided in this mortgage; and to receive the proceeds of any condemnation or eminent domain proceedings as hereinabove provided.

Obviously, the phraseology may be different in common law states, and may vary widely depending on stylistic preferences of the attorney-scrivener. Whether couched in language of a covenant not to sue, a waiver of deficiency judgment rights, an express waiver of rights against the mortgagor personally, or a statement that the mortgagor expressly binds only his property and does not bind and obligate himself personally, or any combination of these, the thrust of these clauses is to limit the mortgagee's recourse to foreclosure on the land and buildings. * * *

The important point for consideration * * * is the core problem of validity of a mortgage on which the mortgagor is not personally liable.

* * *

The ordinary conventional mortgage in Louisiana is *not* an independent obligation, but an accessory obligation only, by which a creditor obtains a special kind of security for the debt owed to him, namely certain rights over specific property of the debtor. In particular, in default of payment of the principal debt, the mortgage gives the creditor the power to have the mortgaged property seized and sold and the proceeds of the sale applied to satisfy the debt with preference and priority over other creditors, including unsecured creditors and secured creditors holding inferior encumbrances.[56] * * * [U]nlike many common law jurisdictions, and despite the historical developments of the common law mortgage, the civil law mortgage, and particularly the Louisiana mortgage, has never followed a "title" theory, whereby the mortgagor transfers title to the mortgagee or to a trustee, who holds in trust for the mortgagee. On the contrary, Louisiana has properly and consistently followed a "lien" theory, by which the mortgagee merely acquires a security right on the property, while ownership remains in the mortgagor.

* * * [T]he basic conceptual problem with the "in rem" mortgage is the question of whether there can be rights *in rem* where there are no rights *in personam,* since in theory the mortgage is only an accessory obligation. An accessory obligation does not stand on its own two feet. By definition, it is accessory to some other "principal" obligation, and stands or falls with that other obligation.

* * * A basic argument against validity of the "in rem" mortgage, then, is that in the absence of a personal obligation on the part of the mortgagor, there is no "principal debt" for the mortgage to secure, and therefore there can be no "accessory obligation" of mortgage. * * *

Since the mortgage as such has no independent existence and cannot stand alone, the focal point is the principal obligation which supports the mortgage. The "in rem" mortgage starts out with no personal liability on the part of the mortgagor, but theoretically it should make no difference in determining invalidity of a mortgage whether the principal obligation *never* came into existence, or came into existence and expired. In either event, at the operative time for consideration, the mortgage is invalid, either because it was invalid *ab initio* or because it has been extinguished. The key in either case is the principal obligation. * * *

* * * It seems tenuous to argue that the act of the mortgagee in consenting to the inclusion of a clause *in the mortgage* denying personal liability amounts to a renunciation of the mortgage, when the very purpose of the document containing the clause is to create a mortgage. It makes little sense that the same instrument that creates the mortgage would also renounce and extinguish it. But it can be argued that since a mortgage is only a security right and not an independent obligation, and since it can only exist where authorized by law, the acquiescence in a condition which destroys the right to proceed against

---

56. [The same general statement could be made with respect to a mortgage given in a lien theory state.]

the principal obligor extinguishes the primary obligation that is required to support the mortgage and therefore the mortgage is never
effective.

While the argument might have some appearance of merit, it can
easily be reduced to both conceptual and practical absurdity. By
stipulation of the parties, there is no personal liability on the part of
the mortgagor. Thus, the loss of the mortgage could not revive or give
rise to a personal obligation of the mortgagor to repay the funds
advanced. And if there is no *in rem* liability because of the conceptual
problem discussed, and no *in personam* liability because of the express
stipulation of the parties, then there is no liability to repay the funds.
The net result of that conclusion is that no one is obligated to repay the
funds, the creditor has no recourse to recover the money he has
advanced, the mortgagor is unjustifiably enriched and the mortgagee
unjustifiably impoverished. The only escape hatch from this *reductio
ad absurdum* would be to grant the creditor an action in quasi-contract,
on the theory of unjust enrichment, but this of course would clash with
the express stipulation of no personal liability. * * *

If C loans D $25,000, which is repayable only out of specified assets,
there is a "duty" to repay the $25,000 even though not all of D's estate
is obligated to repay it. Whether the correlative aspect of C's right to
be repaid the $25,000 which he has advanced is called a "duty" or an
"obligation" or a "debt" [of D], it seems perfectly apparent that C *is*
entitled to be repaid. And it appears naive to contend that the
correlative aspects of that right are not in the nature of a debt or
obligation. * * * In other words, unless C intends the $25,000 as a
gift to D, there is a duty to repay. That duty to repay should suffice as
a principal obligation and ought to be sufficient to support an accessorial obligation.

* * * [O]n balance, the "in rem" mortgage should be held valid.
* * * The "in rem" mortgage is commercially reasonable, being
desirable in many instances from both the creditor's and debtor's
viewpoints. To uphold it would clearly do no violence to the public
welfare or morals, and it affects no basic fundamental of public policy
such as contracts *contra bonos mores*. If one rejects the over-literal
view and regards the accessorial principal of [a] mortgage as requiring
merely an *indebtedness* rather than a personal debt, there is no problem rationalizing the limitation of personal liability. Under general
obligation law, such a condition is simply a modification suggested by
the will of the parties and should be upheld unless expressly forbidden
by law. Thus[,] while not expressly authorized by law, the "in rem"
mortgage is not expressly forbidden by law. Nor is there a problem of
failure of consideration, as funds are advanced by the creditor in
reliance on the security. Nor is the debtor imposing upon himself a
greater penalty than the law permits,[57] * * * but rather is stipulating

57. [What if the interest rate charged is
above the usury limit?]

a provision for his greater benefit. Viewed liberally, from the backdrop of commercial and practical desirability, the "in rem" mortgage can easily be upheld on the basis that there is a principal "indebtedness," satisfying the accessory obligation principle, and the mortgage is specifically contracted for, satisfying the *stricti juris* principle. The opposite result would be over-literal, unnecessary and commercially unreasonable. In addition, the principal obligation, the duty to repay, can be analogized to a natural obligation, so that it is considered binding on the obligor, but not actionable on the part of the obligee. Thus it may be argued that the mortgagor who stipulates to limit his personal liability nevertheless contracts a natural obligation to repay the loan and that this is sufficient to sustain an accessory obligation. * * *

NOTE

1. The modern position in common law states, although not entirely free from doubt, is to uphold the validity of the "in rem" or nonrecourse mortgage at least when used in financing the development of commercial, industrial or residential rental real estate. See Nelson and Whitman, Real Estate Finance Law, 2d ed., Sections 2.1 and 2.2 (1985).

2. If the developer is a limited partnership, an "in rem" or nonrecourse mortgage is desirable since the limited partners can add their shares of the mortgage to their bases in their limited partnership interests, and if the mortgage constitutes "qualified nonrecourse financing," the limited partners can add their shares to their at-risk amounts. See Division I, pages 75 to 77 supra.

    a. How should the covenant in the note and mortgage providing for the "in rem" or nonrecourse nature of the instruments be drafted so as to avoid any possibility that, for income tax purposes, any one or more of the partners could be said to bear an economic risk of loss with respect to the mortgage liability? Should the covenant be a covenant by the mortgagee not to sue, a waiver of any deficiency, a waiver of rights against the mortgagor and its partners personally, a statement that the mortgagor binds only its property and not itself or its partners personally, a combination of these or some other form?

        1. As the absence of any personal liability is made more clear, the concern with preserving the validity of the mortgage becomes greater.

    b. Can a "duty to repay the debt out of certain assets" be said to amount to personal liability for income tax purposes?

        1. If a nominee corporation is used to execute a note and mortgage on certain real estate and the real estate is thereafter conveyed to a limited partnership subject to the mortgage, the limited partnership does not owe any duty to the mortgagee. The limited partnership, however, may be said to have a duty to indemnify the mortgagor corporation against the mortgage debt to the extent of the value of the real estate.

           a. Can the duty to indemnify be said to amount to personal liability for income tax purposes?

3.   In some jurisdictions the statutes and/or regulations governing certain institutional lenders, prohibit lenders from taking "in rem" or nonrecourse mortgages.

a.   Can this prohibition be avoided by a nominee corporation executing a note and mortgage which impose personal liability on the corporation and then conveying the real estate subject to the mortgage to the developer? If the developer is an individual or a partnership and the state's usury law applies to loans to both but does not apply to corporate borrowers, the lending institution may be able to receive a rate of interest in excess of usury limits by using this technique.

4.   It can be argued that a state's usury law does not apply to the interest charged on an "in rem" or nonrecourse mortgage, even if the mortgagor is an individual, since there is no "personal obligation" to repay the loan and the interest thereon. What effect does the acceptance of this analysis, with respect to the application of the state's usury law, have on the concern about the validity of an "in rem" or nonrecourse mortgage in a "lien theory" state?

5.   For an analysis of some of the income tax consequences of using an "in rem" or nonrecourse mortgage see Division I, pages 70 to 71 and pages 74 to 77 and this Division, pages 709 to 713.

6. THE LENDER'S RETURN

---

a. IN GENERAL

USURY AND "NEW LOOK" IN REAL ESTATE FINANCING
Mendes Hershman
4 Real Property, Probate and Trust Journal 315 (1969).
[footnotes omitted]

* * *

Mortgagee's Participation in Income—Contingent Interest

Participation by the mortgagee in income from the mortgaged property above fixed interest on the loan takes several forms, namely, percentage of gross income, percentage of gross income in excess of a specified dollar amount (representing 100 per cent or lesser percentage of current anticipated gross), percentage of overages, percentage of net income before taxes and depreciation or before depreciation and a percentage of a defined net income under which certain items of expense are limited for the purpose of the computation. Taking a percentage of gross in excess of a specified dollar amount is of value where there are short term leases with anticipated increases in gross income if the project is successful. Taking a percentage of overages is applicable primarily to shopping center loans with store tenants on leases providing for overage payments.

Participations in income as a form of additional compensation raise serious usury questions where the fixed interest is close to the statutory maximum and certainly where the fixed interest is at the statutory maximum, and the loan does not fall within statutory exemptions from usury restrictions such as the corporate exception, the exception for business purpose and the exception [for] loans over a specified amount. While it has been held that contingent interest is not usurious, the general rule would appear to be to the contrary if the contingent interest raises the return to the lender substantially in excess of the statutory maximum and the fixed interest is close to the ceiling.

While the contingent interest may, when added to the fixed interest, exceed the maximum in a particular year, this does not necessarily mean a violation of the usury law so long as over the term of the loan as contracted for, the contingent interest, when added to the fixed interest, does not exceed the statutory maximum. * * *

This conclusion is based on analogy to discounts and other add-ons which the courts normally apportion over the contract term of the loan. The reason is the general rule that in testing a contract for usury "the entire period of the loan must be taken into consideration." * * *

Mortgagee's Participation in Proceeds of Refinancing or Resale

* * * For example, [a] mortgage could provide that as a price for the exercise of the prepayment privilege, the mortgagor would pay a premium based on a capitalization of the average amount of participation income (contingent interest) previously paid or based on a percentage of the proceeds of refinancing in excess of the existing mortgage balance.

Inasmuch as the premium is payable only on the happening of a contingency, which is in the control of the borrower, it should not be deemed interest so as to render the loan usurious if added to the fixed interest. There might be some doubt if by reason of the exercise of the prepayment privilege more than the total of all interest at the highest rate for the entire term of the loan would be payable.

Mortgagee's Participation by Receipt of Ownership Interest as Inducement for Making Loan

* * * Such * * * [interests] may take the form of ownership of stock in the developer corporation, a tenancy in common, an interest in a joint venture or a partnership or a beneficial interest in a land trust and without payment therefor by the mortgagee. Such equity positions are frequently taken by the mortgage lender through a wholly owned subsidiary rather than directly. All of these devices have usurious implications where exceptions to the usury law are not applicable.

There is a horrendous possibility that the court would evaluate the additional consideration for the loan and add it to the interest payable during the first year. This is not likely. The court would either spread the consideration over the term of the loan or regard the income from the additional consideration as the interest to be added to the fixed interest. The reason is, as previously suggested, that the court looks at the loan over the entire original term of the loan to determine whether the fixed interest plus what the lender is likely to get as contingent or additional compensation substantially exceeds the interest ceiling of the usury statute. * * *

The root question is whether the transaction was intended as a means of avoiding the usury restriction and is therefore an issue of fact to be tried. * * *

The serious usury question in taking an equity position as a bonus does, however, discourage lenders from entering into such transactions unless, of course, the nature of the lender, * * * the nature of the borrower, * * * or the size of the loan under the applicable statute obviates the question of usury. Lenders do not like buying into lawsuits, particularly in view of the often dire results of a holding of usury in a goodly number of states.

The Sale Leaseback

A. *Land and Building* * * *

For the developer who has taken so much depreciation that to hold on to the property would mean he was paying taxes on the [principal] amortization payments he is making on his mortgage, it [may be] preferable to [recognize] his * * * gain and get 100 per cent financing of his investment in the property while retaining operational control through the leaseback with the possibility of continued profitable return and tax deductions for the lease payments. For the investor there is a 100 per cent investment in a property which he knows is earning enough to pay the fixed return plus possibly a contingent return by way of participation which he could not get as a mortgagee, with the further possibility of leverage by mortgaging the fee.

B. *Land Alone—Unimproved or with Improvement Severed*

* * * While the ground rent plus debt service on the leasehold mortgage (in the case of improved property with the building severed and retained by the lessee) will exceed the debt service on a straight mortgage of land and building, the difference would normally be more than offset by the substantial reduction in the equity requirement by sale of the land and the increase in tax shelter; hence, a considerable increase in cash flow by utilizing the sale leaseback plus leasehold mortgage rather than the straight mortgage of the fee in land and building. Is there a usury problem in either case of sale leaseback of land and improvements or of land alone?

Inasmuch as rent is not interest on a debt, the additional "interest" required by the investor would be achieved in the rental terms for the land. The rate of interest on the leasehold mortgage held by the investor would not exceed the statutory usury limit. This would seem to solve the usury problem. It does not, at least not necessarily. If the lease contains an obligation on the part of the lessee to repurchase, it is quite possible that a court would regard the transaction as in reality a loan. A requirement to repurchase is rarely encountered but options to purchase are frequently given. Do these also present a danger that a court may regard the entire transaction as a loan? * * *

If the sales price [paid by the purchaser-lessor] is substantially less than the market value, it would seem that the title was conveyed as security and the deed would be regarded as a mortgage. If there was a comparatively short term lease with no option to renew but only an option to repurchase at a time when not to repurchase would involve a substantial loss of investment, it would obviously make no sense for the lessee not to exercise the option to repurchase, i.e., the economic realities would dictate exercise of the option. This would influence the court to hold the transaction a loan. On the other hand, if there were several options to extend, perhaps beyond the economic life of the structure, at a fair rental based on then appraised value of the property, the economic realities would not dictate exercise of the option to repurchase and the transaction takes on the appearance of a genuine sale and leaseback. * * *

The "Sale–Buy Back"

The "sale-buy back" technique of financing real estate involves the purchase of the property by the investor at a mutually agreed upon sales price—usually between 80 per cent and 90 per cent of economic value and 100 per cent of audited cost of land and improvements to the developer—and immediate resale by the investor at the same price to the developer on a long term installment sale contract. The term of the contract of sale is usually about ten years longer than [the term of a mortgage], but the installment contract payments are geared to liquidate the investment over the normal mortgage period at somewhat below the current mortgage rate. * * *

The contract of sale usually provides for a closed period of about 15 years after which the developer has the option of terminating the contract and taking legal title by paying the balance due on the contract. * * * In addition, in the usual "sale-buy back" transaction, the investor may be given a contingent yield by way of a percentage of the net income less the contract payments.

For the developer, the income stream is largely tax sheltered. By reason of his equitable ownership of a wasting asset, he is permitted a deduction for depreciation, * * * [based on] his cost basis for the improvements. In addition, he can deduct the interest portion of his contract payment. * * *

Inasmuch as this is a financing technique, the question is whether the deed in the hands of the investor will be deemed a mortgage and the "interest" portion of the contract payment "interest" within the meaning of the usury statutes. * * *

The general test as to whether the transaction is a sale or loan is the hazard of loss. In other words, if the property is considerably more valuable than the amount paid at the time of the transaction, the court is more likely to consider that it was given as security for a loan. This is not true of the modern "sale-buy back." In addition, in a number of states * * * the installment sale contract is a recognized sale device and hence less likely to be deemed a secured loan transaction than the leaseback with option. Finally, there are sound business reasons for the form of the transaction having nothing to do with evasion of the usury statutes—for the developer, tax shelter, complete leverage and a constant installment payment program; for the investor, equity participation and frequently more expeditious means of enforcing remedies on default. Hence, at least in states where the installment sales contract is a customary sale device, there is very little chance of the transaction running afoul of the usury statutes [unless a usury statute applies to interest paid on the deferred portion of a sale price]. * * *

While the Internal Revenue Service will regard the installment sale contract as a transfer of an equitable ownership or interest sufficient to permit the developer to take the depreciation deduction, particularly if the parties so agree, it will nevertheless impute an interest factor for the deferral of payments of the purchase price if none is stated or if a fair rate of interest on unpaid balances is stated, accept that as the interest, includible as taxable income to the investor. The [payment of the purchase price] is return of capital to the investor and not, of course, taxable to the investor. The transaction from an income tax point of view is therefore treated substantially like a mortgage rather than a leaseback where the entire installment payment (of rent) is treated as income to the investor but the investor takes the depreciation deduction.

It is noteworthy that while this type of transaction will be treated as a mortgage from the income tax point of view, actually it is more favorable to the investor. In the usual mortgage situation the interest portion of the installment payment starts out at its highest point so that in the early years the mortgagee gets the largest share of interest, which is, of course, includible in his taxable income and then as soon as the lock-in period ends, the mortgagor refinances. Under the "sale-buy back," since the interest portion of each installment payment remains constant during the closed period, the investor does not get more interest in the early years. Hence there is less income tax for the investor in the "sale-buy back" than in the mortgage.

The "Wrap–Around" Mortgage

A "wrap-around" mortgage usually involves an existing property where the present financing either cannot be readily prepaid or where the interest rate on the present financing is so low as to make prepayment impractical. However, because of additions, improved leasing and/or increased property value, there is justification for a much larger loan. In this instance, the investor makes a new mortgage based on the current value of the property, advances to the owner the difference between the principal amount of this loan and the existing first mortgage and assumes [58] the existing financing. Since the original mortgage is not paid off and discharged, the new mortgage becomes a secondary lien. The "wrap-around" mortgagee need not assume the existing mortgage but merely agree to meet the debt service out of the payments received on the "wrap-around" mortgage.

The interest rate on the new loan is usually below the market for a more normal conventional loan, but because of the leverage provided by the very low rate on the original mortgage, the return on the funds invested to the holder of this second mortgage is usually very high. The risk is greatest at the outset but the return at that time is also at its peak. Both the risk and the return decrease as the first mortgage is amortized.

* * * [T]he lien [of the wrap-around mortgage] is not in a primary position and [in many jurisdictions] the investment must be carried in the "basket" until the first mortgage is repaid or prepaid since the "wrap-around" mortgage is a junior lien until the first mortgage has been repaid * * *. Parenthetically, the "basket" for the institutional investor is the limited proportion of its assets which may be invested in otherwise ineligible investments.

There are serious legal problems other than usury problems involved in these "wrap-around" mortgages, particularly title and eligibility for investment questions because they are second mortgages. The usury problem is complicated because it is not clear whether yields through maturity or the rates in the early years are determinative for usury purposes. It is more likely in view of analogous situations that the courts would test the usury question against the original life of the loan. Assuming over the original life of the loan that the rate earned on the mortgage exceeds the usury rate, a court is still likely to hold that no usury is involved because the determination of the usury is not what the lender receives but what is charged by the lender against the borrower. The borrower, whether it be on the first lien or the second lien, does not pay more than the law allows. The high interest rate is received by the lender by reason of the leverage between the low rate of the existing first mortgage and the high rate on the additional money.

"Front Money" Deals

This * * * technique normally calls for the investor to put up or arrange to have put up 100 per cent of the required cash investment in a project. The developer contributes his time and entrepreneurship to the undertaking. Sometimes he is the owner or has an option on the land to be developed and the deal involves sale of one-half of it to the

---

58. [The lender may not personally assume liability for the existing financing.]

investor for a price which gives the developer the cash to contribute his part to the undertaking.

The investor and the developer enter into a joint venture or partnership, or form a corporation in which the two share in the stock. The division of ownership and profits is negotiated and, in many instances, where the investor is putting up all of the cash, there is provision for the investor getting all of his money out first with an appropriate return on the investment before any split of the net income takes place. The investor may also provide the mortgage financing or at least provide a back-up "umbrella" commitment to enable the development corporation or partnership to secure interim and even permanent financing to prepare the site and construct the improvements. Inasmuch as the investor is risking loss of his investment in the joint venture and there is no obligation on the developer's part to repay the investment, with or without interest, there is obviously no usury question involved. * * *

NOTE

1. Even though the payment of contingent interest probably will not violate the usury laws if, over the term of the loan, the contingent interest when added to the fixed interest does not exceed the statutory maximum, how can the lender insure, when drafting the documents for the lending transaction, that the total of the contingent interest and the fixed interest will not exceed the statutory maximum? See *Imperial Corp. of America v. Frenchman's Creek Corp.*, 453 F.2d 1338 (5th Cir.1972), for a consideration of the effect of a "saving clause." See also Comment, *Lender Participation in Borrower's Venture: A Scheme to Receive Usurious Interest*, 8 Hous.L.Rev. 546 (1971); Barton and Morrison, *Equity Participation Arrangements Between Institutional Lenders and Real Estate Developers*, 12 St. Mary's L.J. 929 (1981); Kellsy, *Advantages of Participating Mortgages*, 17 # 1 Real Est.Rev. 54 (1987).

2. Is refinancing or sale really a contingency within the control of the borrower if the payment required to take advantage of the prepayment privilege is large enough to discourage prepayment? Of course, if the borrower never prepays, the usury issue, in this context, will not arise.

3. Earlier in these materials the undesirable income tax consequences and the serious problems on default which will arise if the form of a ground lease or a sale and leaseback is disregarded and the transaction treated as the equivalent of a mortgage were discussed. See pages 763 to 774 supra. As the above excerpts indicate, the possibility of violation of the usury laws can be added to those concerns.

   a. How can a ground lease or sale and leaseback be structured so as to avoid these problems and yet fulfill the desires of the parties to the transaction. See Comment, *Lender Participation in Borrower's Venture: A Scheme to Receive Usurious Interest*, supra; Podell, *The Application of Usury Laws to Modern Real Estate Transactions*, 1 Real Est.L.J. 136 (1972). See also Division I, page 243 and this Division pages 616 to 618 and 626 to 628.

4. If a wrap-around mortgage is used by a lender, would the lender's assumption of the first mortgage be of assistance in avoiding a violation of the

usury law? Or, can the lender merely agree with the borrower that it will make the payments on the first mortgage if, and so long as, the borrower makes the payments on the wrap-around mortgage?

　　a. For example, assume that the maximum permitted rate of interest is 20%. A borrower's real estate is worth $100,000 and is subject to an existing first mortgage of $30,000 at 9%. A lender lends the borrower an additional $60,000, using a wrap-around mortgage of $90,000 at 20%. If the remaining term of the first mortgage is about the same as the term of the wrap-around mortgage, the return to the holder of the wrap-around mortgage is in excess of 20%.

　　b. Some courts have taken the position that as long as the interest rate stated in the wrap-around note and mortgage does not violate the usury limit, the loan is not usurious regardless of the return to the lender. See *Grossman v. Sirianni* (Cal.App. filed Jan. 27, 1974). But see *Mitchell v. Trustees of United States Mut. Real Estate Inv. Trust,* 144 Mich.App. 302, 375 N.W.2d 424 (1985), in which a wrap-around note and mortgage was held to be usurious since interest, at or slightly below the usury limit, was calculated on the entire face amount while a much smaller amount was actually advanced. Cf. *Mindlin v. Davis,* 74 So.2d 789 (Fla.1954); Note, *Wrap–Around Financing: A Technique for Skirting The Usury Laws?,* 1972 Duke L.J. 785; Gunning, *The Wrap–Around Mortgage ＊ ＊ ＊ Friend or U.F.O.?,* 2 # 2 Real Est.Rev. 35 (1972); Comment, *The Wrap–Around Mortgage: A Critical Inquiry,* 21 UCLA L.Rev. 1529 (1974). Consider the implications of Rev.Rul. 75–99, 1975–1 C.B. 197, with respect to the determination whether a wrap-around loan is usurious. Revenue Ruling 75–99 holds that for the purpose of determining the interest income of a real estate investment trust, the indebtedness giving rise to an obligation to pay interest is not the total amount of a wrap-around loan but only the amount actually advanced by the wrap-around lender and, therefore, only the interest on the actual advance is included in the real estate investment trust's gross income. But cf. *Barton Beek,* 80 T.C. 1024 (1983), affirmed, 754 F.2d 1442 (9th Cir.1985). The position taken by the drafters of the Uniform Land Transactions Act appears to be that the rate of interest paid by the borrower rather than the rate of return to the lender determines whether there is a violation of the usury limit. See Sections 3–401(1) and 3–403(d) of the Uniform Land Transactions Act.

　　5. Another technique, used by banking institutions, is to require the borrower, as a condition of the loan, to maintain a compensating balance with the bank. For example, a bank might agree to make a $300,000 mortgage loan at the maximum permitted interest rate on condition that the borrower maintain $30,000 on deposit with the bank at all times while the loan is outstanding. The deposit might be in a checking account, certificate of deposit, etc. The bank has use of the $30,000 during the term of the loan. The use of this technique may raise a number of concerns. See Austin and Solomon, *The Antitrust Implications of Compensating Balances,* 58 Va.L.Rev. 1 (1972). The Securities and Exchange Commission, in an informal memorandum dated Nov. 24, 1972, CCH Fed.Sec.L.Rep. ¶ 79,131 ('72–'73 Tr.Bin.), issued proposed guidelines on the disclosure of compensating balances in financial statements subject to Regulation S–X. The Commission's position is that compensating balances "＊ ＊ ＊ are a factor in measuring the effective cost of financing ＊ ＊ ＊ [and are] ＊ ＊ ＊ in effect (if not legally) [a] limit [on] the usage of reported cash ＊ ＊ ＊." In appropriate situations, requiring the maintenance of a compensat-

ing balance may result in a violation of the usury laws, especially if the compensating balance is placed in a non-interest bearing account and is funded with the proceeds of the loan for which the maintenance of the compensating balance is required. Cf. *Grundel v. Bank of Craig,* 515 S.W.2d 177 (Mo.App. 1974); *Phalen Park State Bank v. Reeves,* 312 Minn. 194, 251 N.W.2d 135 (1977).

6. Frequently, a lender, when committing to make a substantial loan, will charge a commitment fee of some percent of the principal amount of the loan. This fee is in addition to the interest on the loan. At times, the commitment fee is partially or fully applied toward service charges when the loan is "taken down" by the borrower. At other times, the fee is consideration for the lender making the commitment and keeping the funds available to loan to the borrower. Cf. Rev.Rul. 56–136, 1956–1 C.B. 92; Rev.Rul. 70–540, 1970–2 C.B. 101, amplified by Rev.Rul. 74–607, 1974–2 C.B. 149; Rev.Rul. 74–258, 1974–1 C.B. 168. But see Rev.Rul. 81–160, 1981–1 C.B. 312 and Rev.Rul. 81–161, 1981–1 C.B. 313.

a. Can the receipt of a commitment fee result in usury problems for a lender? See *Imperial Corporation of America v. Frenchman's Creek Corporation,* supra page 788; *Gonzales County Savings and Loan Association v. Freeman,* 534 S.W.2d 903 (Tex.1976); *People v. Central Fed. Sav. & Loan Ass'n of Nassau County,* 46 N.Y.2d 41, 412 N.Y.S.2d 815, 385 N.E.2d 555 (1978); *Stedman v. Georgetown Savings and Loan Association,* 595 S.W.2d 486 (Tex.1979); Podell, *The Application of Usury Laws to Modern Real Estate Transactions,* supra page 788; Note, *Savings and Loan Associations May Not Charge Premiums in Addition to Maximum Legal Interest, But Lenders May Charge Bona Fide Commitment Fees in Addition to Maximum Legal Interest,* 54 Tex.L.Rev. 1487 (1976); Note, *Loan Fees: Additional Interest or "Reasonable Expenses"?,* 13 Hous.L.Rev. 773 (1976); Note, *A "Commitment Fee" or "Service Charge" Disbursed From Principal After Closing is Interest,* 32 Ark.L.Rev. 608 (1978).

The Uniform Land Transactions Act includes within the definition of "finance charge" (the equivalent of interest) any amount payable under a point, discount, or other system of charges, however denominated. See Section 3–401(3)(i). The Act, however, distinguishes a "finance charge" from "additional charges" for other benefits conferred on the debtor if the benefits are of value to him and the charges are reasonable in relation to the benefits and are of a type which is not for credit. See Sections 3–401(3), 3–403(b) and 3–404(a)(4). Is a commitment fee a "finance charge" or an "additional charge"? Does this determination turn on why the commitment fee was paid?

b. Assuming that the amount of a commitment fee is not so large that it would be considered unconscionable or a forfeiture if the fee was retained by the lender, is the lender entitled to retain the commitment fee if the borrower does not comply with the commitment? See *White Lakes Shopping Center, Inc. v. Jefferson Standard Life Ins. Co.,* 208 Kan. 121, 490 P.2d 609 (1971); *Boston Road Shopping Center, Inc. v. T.I.A.A.,* 11 N.Y.2d 831, 227 N.Y.S.2d 444, 182 N.E.2d 116 (1962); *Hawkins v. First Federal Savings and Loan Association,* 291 Ala. 257, 280 So.2d 93 (1973); *Weiner v. Salem Five Cents Savings Bank,* 371 Mass. 897, 360 N.E.2d 306 (1977).

c. The method of computing the amount of interest paid by the borrower, for the purpose of determining whether there is a violation of the usury laws, raises some interesting problems at times. See *Band Realty*

Co. v. North Brewster, Inc., 37 N.Y.2d 460, 373 N.Y.S.2d 97, 335 N.E.2d 316 (1975); Comment, *Usury Implications of Front–End Interest and Interest in Advance*, 29 Sw.L.J. 748 (1975); Comment, *Usury: Issues in Calculation*, 34 Ark.L.Rev. 442 (1980); Ridloff, *Calculation of Interest—Lenders Beware!*, 9 # 4 Real Est.Rev. 91 (1980). The Uniform Land Transactions Act sets out the method to be used under the Act to compute the interest paid by a borrower. See Section 3–401(1).

7. Rather than charging a high interest rate, a lender may attempt to protect itself from inflation by indexing the principal repayment. Is there a violation of the usury laws when an increase in principal resulting from indexing plus the interest payments result in the borrower paying more for the use of money than permitted by the usury laws? See *Aztec Properties, Inc. v. Union Planters Nat. Bank of Memphis*, 530 S.W.2d 756 (Tenn.1975); Note, *Indexed Principal is Interest, and Violative Per Se of Federal Law*, 7 Mem.St. U.L.Rev. 145 (1976); Note, *Purchasing—Power Adjusted Loans*, 45 UMKC L.Rev. 140 (1976); Note, *Indexed Principal: A Way Around the Usury Laws?*, 31 Ark.L.Rev. 141 (1977). Cf. Note, *New Tests for Variable Interest Loans*, 30 Hastings L.J. 1843 (1979); Comment, *The New Mortgages: A Functional Legal Analysis*, 10 Fla.St.U.L.Rev. 95 (1982); Comment, *Alternative Mortgage Instruments: Authorizing and Implementing Price Level Adjusted Mortgages*, 16 U.Mich.J.L.Ref. 115 (1982); Comment, *Adjustable Rate Mortgages: A Proposed Statutory Reform*, 26 Santa Clara L.Rev. 253 (1986); Comment, *Usury Implications of Alternative Mortgage Instruments: The Uncertainty in Calculating Permissible Returns*, 1986 B.Y.U.L.Rev. 1105. Title VIII—Alternative Mortgage Transactions—of the Garn–St. Germain Depository Institutions Act of 1982 authorized the use by "housing creditors" of "alternative mortgage transactions" which include adjustable, variable rate and, shared appreciation mortgages.

8. Is an equity bonus given by a borrower to a lender taken into account when determining whether usury restrictions have been violated, and, if it is, how is it taken into account?

KESSING v. NATIONAL MORTGAGE CORP.

Supreme Court of North Carolina, 1971.
278 N.C. 523, 180 S.E.2d 823.

* * *

[O]n 14 May 1969 Mortgage Corporation notified Kessing Company that its application for a loan in the amount of $250,000 had been approved and that "funding will take place, in the increments previously agreed upon, as soon as the formal loan agreement is completed and executed by all parties." No [formal] loan agreement was entered into by the parties, but all the terms and conditions concerning the loan were agreed upon by the parties prior to 30 June 1969. The loan was closed on 9 July 1969. On that date Kessing Company executed and delivered to Mortgage Corporation a note payable to Mortgage Corporation in the principal sum of $250,000, payable in monthly installments of $500 commencing on 1 May 1970, and with interest at the rate of 8% per annum, payable monthly commencing on 1 August 1969, the monthly payments of principal and interest to continue until 1 June 1974 at which time any unpaid balance of principal [and] accrued

interest became due and payable. The note was endorsed by Kessing and his wife and was secured by a first deed of trust on a leasehold interest in a lot located in Chapel Hill and a second deed of trust on five acres of land in Chapel Hill on which were located 42 garden apartments known as Castillian Apartments. As an additional requirement and condition for making the loan, Mortgage Corporation required that Kessing and Mortgage Corporation enter in a partnership agreement by the terms of which Kessing was the sole general partner and one of the two limited partners, and Mortgage Corporation was the other limited partner. This partnership agreement provided that Mortgage Corporation [was the owner of] a 25% interest in the Partnership [and] 25% of the profits of the Partnership[, in return for a contribution of $25,] but [that Mortgage Corporation's] liability would be limited to its capital contribution of $25. Kessing Company was required to convey to the Partnership the same properties as described in the deed of trust securing [the] loan. The partnership agreement and the deed from Kessing Company to the Partnership were all executed on 9 July 1969 and defendant's check for $250,000 was delivered and disbursed that day. Kessing Company has made all payments on the principal and the interest at 8% in accordance with the note and is not in arrears. No earnings from the Partnership have been paid to defendant.
* * *

After hearing the motions of plaintiffs and defendant and the testimony offered by Kessing and Mortgage Corporation, Judge Canaday made findings of fact and entered judgment in plaintiffs' favor on the motion for summary judgment and adjudged (1) that plaintiff recover $50,000 as twice the amount of usurious interest paid, (2) that all further interest be forfeited, (3) that the partnership agreement between the parties be voided and the deeds of conveyance to the Partnership be cancelled, and (4) the counterclaims of defendant be dismissed.

From this judgment defendant appealed.

* * *

MOORE, Justice. * * * In an action for usury plaintiff must show (1) that there was a loan, (2) that there was an understanding that the money lent would be returned, (3) that for the loan a greater rate of interest than allowed by law was paid, and (4) that there was corrupt intent to take more than the legal rate for the use of money. * * * The corrupt intent required to constitute usury is simpl[y] the intentional charging of more for money lent than the law allows. Associated Stores, Inc. v. Industrial Loan & Invest. Co., 202 F.Supp. 251 (E.D.N.C. 1962). Where the lender intentionally charges the borrower a greater rate of interest than the law allows and his purpose is clearly revealed on the face of the instrument, a corrupt intent to violate the usury law on the part of the lender is shown. * * * And where there is no dispute as to the facts, the court may declare a transaction usurious as a matter of law. * * *

Under G.S. § 24–8 [the usury statute] prior to the 1969 amendment, the legal interest allowed on the loan in question was 8%. The president of defendant corporation testified that the loan of $250,000 was secured by a deed of trust which had full warranty, and the loan was repayable to defendant under any circumstances. Defendant's president further testified that defendant would not have made this loan at the simple rate of 8% but that the added equity participation provided for by the creation of the Partnership and the conveyances to it were considerations for the making of the loan; that from the 25% of the profits to be realized by the Partnership the defendant had an expected or "hoped for" yield of between 16% and 20%—certainly over 8%. Our courts do not hesitate to look beneath the forms of the transactions alleged to be usurious in order to determine whether or not such transactions are in truth and reality usurious. Pratt v. American Bond and Mortgage Co., 196 N.C. 294, 145 S.E. 396; * * * Comment, Usury Law in North Carolina, 47 N.C.L.Rev. 761, 776 (1969). Under G.S. § 24–8 before the 2 July 1969 amendment, this agreement would have been usurious, for as is said in Ripple v. Mortgage and Acceptance Corp., 193 N.C. 422, 137 S.E. 156:

> " * * * Where a transaction is in reality a loan of money, whatever may be its form, and the lender charges for the use of his money a sum in excess of interest at the legal rate, by whatever name the charge may be called, the transaction will be held to be usurious. The law considers the substance and not the mere form or outward appearance of the transaction in order to determine what it in reality is. If this were not so, the usury laws of the State would easily be evaded by lenders of money who would exact from borrowers with impunity compensation for money loaned in excess of interest at the legal rate."

G.S. § 24–8 as amended [in 1969] specifically prohibited the very type equity participation created by the Partnership formed in connection with this loan by providing "No lender shall * * * require * * * any borrower, directly or indirectly, to * * * transfer or convey * * * for the benefit of the lender * * * any sum of money, thing of value or other consideration other than that which is pledged as security * * *." A 25% interest in the Partnership (which owned the realty conveyed to it by Kessing Company) was a "thing of value." This made the partnership agreement unlawful. Under the statute, the loan was usurious.

The penalty for charging a greater rate of interest than permitted by law, either before or after the interest accrues when knowingly done, shall be a forfeiture of the entire interest which the note o[r] other evidence of debt carries with it. In the event a greater rate of interest has been paid than allowed by law, the person or corporation which has paid such usurious interest may recover twice the amount of interest paid. G.S. § 24–2; * * * Sloan v. Piedmont Fire Ins. Co., 189 N.C. 690, 128 S.E. 2; Waters v. Garris, 188 N.C. 305, 124 S.E. 334 * * *. In the present case a greater rate of interest than allowed by law was charged by means of the partnership agreement required, but no profit has yet inured to the defendant under this agreement. The only interest actually paid by Kessing Company was the 8% provided for in the note. This in itself was a legal rate. No usurious interest has been paid, and Kessing Company is not entitled to recover double the amount of the interest. Clark v. Hood System Industrial Bank of Reidsville, 200 N.C. 635, 158 S.E. 96; Briggs v. Industrial Bank of Richmond, 197 N.C. 120, 147 S.E. 815; * * * 45 Am.Jur.2d, Interest and Usury § 316 (1969). The statutory penalty for *charging* usury is the forfeiture of *all* interest on the loan. The charging of usurious interest as provided for by the partnership agreement in this case is sufficient to cause a forfeiture of all the interest charged. The charging of such usurious interest strips the debt of all interest. It becomes simply a loan which in law bears no interest. Any payments of interest which have been made at a legal rate are by law applied to the only legal indebtedness—the principal sum. Williams v. First National Bank, 161 N.C. 49, 76 S.E. 531; Ervin v. First National Bank, 161 N.C. 42, 76 S.E. 529 * * *. In the instant case Kessing Company has paid $25,000. Since all interest has been forfeited, the payments made should be credited on the principal amount of the loan.

We hold, therefore, that the plaintiffs are not entitled to recover double the amount of the interest paid on this loan and that the trial court erred in so holding. We further hold that all interest on the loan is forfeited and that the payments made should be credited on the principal amount of the loan. * * *

NOTE

1. If National Mortgage Corporation, prior to making the loan, had required the plaintiffs to organize and convey the real estate to the partnership, had paid full value for its limited partnership interest and, after purchasing its partnership interest, had loaned the partnership the remainder of the $250,000 at 8% per annum, would the loan have been usurious?

a. Would structuring the transaction in this manner have been acceptable to National Mortgage Corporation?

b. Might the transaction, structured as described in 1 above, be usurious if National Mortgage Corporation gave Kessing and/or the partnership the right to buy its partnership interest, at any time after the loan was repaid, at the partnership interest's then value, but in no case could the purchase price be less than an amount equal to the amount paid for the partnership interest plus interest at 8% per annum from the date of National Mortgage Corporation's purchase of the interest?

1. Would there be less risk of violation of the usury law if the "floor" price for National Mortgage Corporation's partnership interest was reduced by the amount of any partnership distributions made to it as a partner prior to the date of the sale of the partnership interest?

2. Would limiting the type of distribution which reduced the amount of the "floor" to an income or a capital distribution increase the risk of violation of the usury law?

     3. If Kessing's and/or the partnership's right to purchase National Mortgage Corporation's partnership interest was coupled with National Mortgage Corporation having the right to "put" its partnership interest to Kessing or the partnership—requiring Kessing and/or the partnership to buy National Mortgage Corporation's partnership interest—at the "floor" price, would this increase the risk of violation of the usury law?

     c. See Note, *Usury—Kessing v. National Mortgage Corporation—Is Participation Dead?*, 8 Wake Forest L.Rev. 304 (1972)

     2. See generally Oeltjen, *Usury: Utilitarian or Useless?*, 3 Fla.St.U.L.Rev. 169 (1975); Smith and Lubell, *A Lender Looks at Usury,* 6 # 1 Real Est.Rev. 14 (1976); Comment, *Equity Participation in Real Estate Finance,* 7 N.C.Cent.L.J. 387 (1976); Barton and Morrison, *Equity Participation Arrangements Between Institutional Lenders and Real Estate Developers,* 12 St. Mary's L.J. 929 (1981); Comment, *Usury's Intent Requirement: Should There Be a Good Faith Defense?,* 1985 B.Y.U.L.Rev. 789.

b. USURY AND OTHER LIMITATIONS ON THE LENDER'S RETURN

MONEY, MORTGAGES, AND MIGRAINE—THE USURY HEADACHE

Marion Benfield
19 Case Western Reserve Law Review 819 (1968).
[footnotes omitted]

*   *   *

Factors Involved in Determining the Price of Money

     Before discussing the theory and *   *   * effect of usury laws, the factors which are involved in fixing the interest rate at which a loan will be made will be briefly examined. There are four components involved in determining the free market rate at which a particular loan will be made: (1) the cost of money; (2) the cost of administering the loan; (3) the amount of risk that the loan will not be repaid; and (4) the competition confronting the particular lender.

     (1) The Cost of Money.—The basic factor affecting interest rate levels is the amount which borrowers are willing to pay and lenders are willing to accept for the use of money in those instances where the risk is for all practical purposes nonexistent and costs of making and administering the loan are an insignificant proportion of the total return. *   *   *

     In addition to the factor of supply of money, as against demand for credit at a particular time, the duration for which the loan is requested is also a factor in setting the market rate. The longer the term of the loan, the less liquid the position of the lender and the less ability he has to react to changes in the money market. Because of this loss in liquidity, in most economic circumstances rates are higher for long term loans than for short term loans.

However, it is probably correct to assume that the principal factor in setting prime interest rates is the relationship between total money supply and total borrowing demand. The sources which make up the total *supply* of funds for investment may be placed in several classes. First, there are funds from private sources which would have been available in the market no matter what interest rates were being paid, but which are more or less sensitive to interest rates and will seek the highest possible return. Many individual savings accounts are in this class, and good institutional examples of such funds are pension funds and assets of life insurance companies. * * *

The second classification of savings is that which is induced only by attractive interest rates. Some indeterminate amount of money saved and made available for lending falls in this category. Some savers who would forego present consumption at a 5 percent return would not forego present consumption if the rate of return were only 3 percent. * * *

The present money market in the major industrialized nations of the world has a peculiar source of lendable funds in a third category, the demand deposits of commercial banks. * * *

The prime interest rate is substantially affected by the discount rate at which the Federal Reserve Board will loan money to banks and by the fiscal policies of the Federal Reserve Board. The Board, through various devices, can substantially reverse trends toward inflation or recession by increasing or decreasing the amount of money available for lending.

The other side of the market prime interest rate-fixing mechanism is the demand for funds. Borrowers who seek funds are of two types, those who seek the funds for productive purposes, that is, to enhance their earning capacity, and those who seek the funds for consumptive purposes, that is, to anticipate their future income. The strength of the demand for productive loans depends on the spread between the interest rates on money and the general profit levels of business. If the spread is great, the demand will be high, and if it is narrow, the demand will be smaller. Of course, the forces of the market tend to narrow the gap between interest rates and profit. The forces as to consumptive borrowing are not subject to factors as objective as the spread between profits and interest, for the rate which a consumer-borrower is willing to pay depends substantially on his subjective feeling as to the desirability of anticipating future income. * * *

(2) Cost of Administering the Loan.—* * * This cost becomes particularly significant in smaller loans, especially installment loans, where substantial time is spent in evaluating the loan request and in handling the disbursement and bookkeeping expenses included in the loan. * * * [A]s the loan gets bigger the ratio of cost to loan goes down * * *.

(3) Risk That the Loan Will Not Be Repaid.—* * * Since this factor is always a characteristic of the particular borrower, rather than

the particular lender, loans are not at all interchangeable as to rate. * * * In each case some judgment must be made as to the risk that all or some of the loan will not be paid and the amount which is to be charged for taking this risk must be determined.

* * *

(4) Competition to the Lender.—* * * If money markets were monopoly markets then usury statutes would have the same justification as regulation of telephone company or electric power company rates. However, this writer does not believe that the present money supply system can be characterized as a monopoly. Borrowers, large and small, generally have access to a number of different lenders who are not, by any means, acting in concert. However, competitive forces can be made to operate more efficiently by allowing lenders free access to the credit market and by requiring disclosure of the rates charged on comparable terms by all lenders if the borrower is not otherwise likely to understand rate differences.[59]

* * *

Usury Laws and Their Effects

Usury laws in the United States * * * present a mixture of motives. [S]tatutes [which set a maximum rate close to actual money rates] perhaps come close to being price-fixing statutes * * *. [Maximum] rates of [20 to 40] percent, however, do not attempt to fix the market price of money, but only set limits on the kinds of money contracts which can be made.

* * *

Present General Usury Statutes and Their Exceptions and Exemptions.

Existing State legislation regulating maximum interest rates is typically a jumble of statutes fixing a basic usury rate and then exempting from the basic rate small loans, installment loans, loans by industrial banks, and perhaps totally exempting banks, savings and loan associations, or other particular types of lenders. * * *

The impact of these usury laws depends very substantially on the penalty for violation. * * * Generally, the lower the interest ceiling, the smaller the penalty imposed for a violation, though there are notable exceptions. [The penalties may include loss of excess interest, uncollectibility of the entire debt, double the excess interest, a misdemeanor or a felony in extreme cases.]

* * *

Exemptions for Loans to Corporations.—* * * The basis for the legislative exemptions would seem to be that corporations do not need the protection of usury statutes. A corporate borrower will nearly

---

59. [Both the federal Truth–In–Lending Act and the Uniform Consumer Credit Code take some significant steps in this direction, at least in the "consumer" credit field.]

always be fully aware of the rate it is paying. It will, also, have looked carefully for the best possible terms and, if it ends up paying a very high rate, it will almost always be because its credit position does not justify a loan at a lower rate. Though some corporations may ultimately fail because of a high interest burden, others will survive on borrowed money which they could not have secured at usury limit rates. On balance, it would seem that in the corporate area it is better to let the parties make their own bargains.

*   *   *

The corporate exception statutes fix differing qualifications for the exemption. Many of them provide blanket corporate exemptions, but in some States there are special limitations. [F]or example, the exemption [may] not apply to a corporation whose principal asset is a one- or two-family dwelling if it was organized within 6 months prior to the execution of any notes or security instruments issued in connection with the loan. [Or] a corporate borrower [may be] subject to the usury law on [its] obligations [with respect to] which an individual is also liable.

There has been a split of authority as to whether the exemption statutes apply to a corporation organized specially for the purpose of taking advantage of them. *   *   *

The effect of the corporate usury exemption, in spite of the cases holding that it cannot be used for the sole purpose of avoiding the usury statutes and in spite of exclusions from the corporation exceptions [such as those described above], is to provide a vehicle by which borrowers for a business purpose can escape the general usury laws. Incorporation may be inconvenient and may increase the total cost of the loan, but the incorporation method can be and is used to provide financing which would not otherwise be available.

Exemption of Banks and Savings and Loan Associations or Savings Banks.—A number of States exempt banks and savings and loan associations from usury laws. *   *   *

The reason for the exclusion presumably is that these are public investment institutions under governmental supervision and under a fiduciary duty to depositors which makes it very unlikely that any rate which they might charge would be unreasonable.

Other Exemptions.—In addition to the various exemptions covered above, there are a variety of miscellaneous exemptions or special higher rates which may be found scattered through the States. *   *   * [F]or example, *   *   * [in some states there is] no statutory maximum on any business loan, nor on loans of $5,000 or more secured by warehouse receipts, or negotiable instruments or securities [nor] *   *   * [on] loans of $5,000 or more secured by "bona fide" mortgages of real property. Some States exempt Federal Housing Authority (FHA) insured home improvement loans and *   *   * FHA-insured home mortgage loans. There are, no doubt, other exemptions scattered through the statute books of the 50 States and the District of Columbia which could be forced to the surface by a skindiver willing to spend weeks poking about in the murky waters of the State laws.

*   *   *

Some Significant Effects of Usury Laws

*   *   *

Business Loans and Usury Statutes.—While the corporate, bank, and installment loan exemptions to the usury statutes detailed above remove much of the sting from, and pressure upon, usury laws in relationship to business loans, cases still occur, even in States which are most liberal in rates and exemptions, involving loans which are in areas subject to usury laws but in which the risk factor is so great that loans cannot reasonably be made within the statutory limit.

*   *   *

A common banking practice used to secure a return higher than that allowed by usury statutes is the requirement of "compensating balances."   *   *   *

*   *   *

[A]mong other schemes which have been used are (1) the tie-in sale, a sale of goods at a very high price as a condition to making the loan; (2) the sale of credit, which requires two lender parties, one to make the loan at the highest legal rate and the other to guarantee the loan for an additional payment from the borrower; and (3) making the loan payable only upon the nonoccurrence of a contingency like the total destruction of Manhattan Island (this has sometimes been considered to make payments above the usury statute nonusurious because they are merely compensation for the increased risk).

*   *   *

The Uniform Consumer Credit Code

*   *   *

Consumer Real Estate Loans and the Consumer Code.—The *Consumer Code* *   *   * maximum interest rate also applies to home mortgage loans. This maximum is intended to set the outside limit for conscionable transactions, but is not otherwise intended to affect the free operation of the real estate mortgage market. This writer believes that the *Consumer Code* scheme is the proper way of dealing with real estate mortgage rate limitations. It has already been pointed out that mortgage rates are responsive to general money market conditions and stay near the prime interest rate even where there are no statutory ceilings. It has also been pointed out that, when market interest rates reach or go above the general usury rates applicable to real estate transactions, lenders either use subterfuges to secure the return justified by market conditions or they withdraw from the mortgage market.

*   *   * [T]he only statutory maximums which are justified are those which attempt solely to reach the occasional individual unconscionably high rate. This is what the [*Consumer Code* maximum interest rate] does.   *   *   * It may be objected that an ordinary first

mortgage at [the *Consumer Code* maximum interest rate] would be unconscionable. But whether that would be so as to any particular loan depends upon the credit worthiness of the borrower, the size and repayment terms of the loan, and the ratio of the loan to security. The [*Consumer Code* maximum interest rate] is a compromise figure which may be too low, and which will itself no doubt force some legitimate loans out of the market. On the other hand, under developing unconscionability concepts, even interest rates under [the *Consumer Code* maximum interest rate] may be struck down or reduced by a court as unconscionable if the rate is not, as a matter of fact, reasonably justified on the facts. * * *

* * *

Small Individual Business Loans and the Consumer Code.—The *Consumer Code* drafters were convinced that large business operations should be able to borrow at whatever rates they can negotiate free of arbitrary statutory restrictions. * * * On the other hand, the very small businessman is really in many respects indistinguishable from the consumer. * * * Therefore, a distinction between types of businesses is made by the *Consumer Code* which, while it preserves part of the corporate exemption idea, is somewhat more sophisticated. The *Consumer Code* establishes a category of small business credit transactions (those under [a specific dollar amount such as] $25,000) which is subject to [the *Consumer Code* interest rate] ceiling but which is not subject to the special disclosure and limitation of remedy rules which apply to consumer transactions. This category includes loans or credit sales for nonconsumer purposes to individuals or to an organization if the loan is secured primarily by a one- or two-family dwelling occupied by a person related to the organization. However, the parties may by contract provide that the loan shall be treated as a consumer transaction, in which event the higher rates for under $1,000 amounts apply as do all the limitation of remedy and disclosure provisions applicable to consumer transactions.

Other Loans and the Consumer Code.—The *Consumer Code* provides outside rate protection for smaller individual business borrowers under the provisions just discussed, but, similar to the law already in effect in a few States, it imposes no statutory ceiling at all on business loans or credit sales of amounts of more than [a specific dollar amount such as] $25,000. Also, there is no statutory ceiling rate on any loan or credit sale to a corporation, except for the "incorporated house" situation noted above.

In the business debt area, the only difference between the *Consumer Code* rules and the present law of the many States which exempt corporations from the usury laws is that *noncorporate* business borrowers of amounts above [a specific dollar amount such as] $25,000 may also deal free of rate regulation. There are noncorporate business situations in which rigid statutory ceilings are unrealistic. The legislature cannot determine, in advance, rates which are proper for a particular transaction and there does not seem to be any reason why business borrowers should not be able to go into the market and pay whatever is necessary to obtain money. Here, the *Consumer Code* continues the judgment presently made by most States that major business deals should not be limited by an arbitrary statute interest rate * * *. Of course, this is not to say that there will be absolutely no control upon oppressive and overreaching lenders. It is most likely that courts will apply unconscionability concepts to set aside or scale down interest payments in the unusual case in which the lender has unjustifiably overcharged. However, courts should, and no doubt will, move very cautiously because of a realization that rates which on first glance appear to be excessive may, on closer examination, appear to have been entirely justified on the facts. * * *

NOTE

1. It may be true, as a general rule, that the ratio of the cost of servicing a loan to the amount of the loan decreases as the amount of the loan increases. On the other hand, as the amount of the loan increases so may the complexity, thereby increasing the cost of servicing.

    a. Lending institutions can remove some or all of the cost of administering a loan from the interest computation by the use of commitment fees, service charges and requiring the borrower to pay all closing costs, including attorney's fees, associated with a loan.

2. Have sound assumptions been made in exempting banks, savings and loan associations and other institutional lenders from the operation of the usury laws?

    a. Do the fiduciary duties owed depositors include concern about the "welfare" of borrowers? What is the nature and purpose of federal and state regulation of institutional lenders? If the regulation is to assure good business practices and management, how does this regulation protect a borrower?

3. What assumptions are made in exempting corporate borrowing from the operation of the usury statutes? Are these assumptions entirely sound? Does it make sense for a loan made to a partnership with a million dollar net worth and engaged in commercial real estate development to be subject to the usury laws while a $1,000 loan to a corporation running a corner grocery store is not?

    a. The solution presented by the Uniform Consumer Credit Code may be somewhat more rational, drawing the line between loans subject to the usury limits and those not, at, with some exceptions, small business loans under $25,000. On the other hand, why totally exempt corporations, except for the "incorporated house" situation?

        1. The exemption of the "business loan" over $25,000 results in fewer lending transactions being subject to usury limits under the U.C. C.C. than under many states' usury statutes.

4. Congress, in enacting the federal Truth–In–Lending Act, made about the same assumption that the drafters of the U.C.C.C. did when they exempted business loans over $25,000. The assumption was that business borrowers can take care of themselves. Is that true?

a. The Truth–In–Lending Act does not apply to credit transactions involving "credit for business or commercial purposes * * *." Section 104(1).

5. Since "business loans" are exempt from the requirements imposed by both the Uniform Consumer Credit Code and the federal Truth–In–Lending Act, a lender's return on a loan to a real estate developer, in most cases, will not be limited by these acts. What is meant by the phrase a business loan?

a. For example, does the Truth–In–Lending Act apply to a loan made to and secured by a mortgage on the residence of a homeowner who is employed full-time as a salesman, if the purpose of the loan is to construct an apartment house and the borrower intends eventually to reside in one of the apartments? See *Sapenter v. Dreyco, Inc.,* 326 F.Supp. 871 (E.D.La. 1971), affirmed without opinion, 450 F.2d 941 (5th Cir.1971), cert. denied, 406 U.S. 920, 92 S.Ct. 1775, 32 L.Ed.2d 120 (1972). Does the U.C.C.C. apply to the loan? In what circumstances might the U.C.C.C. apply?

b. The "business loan" exemption does not mean that a lender who lends to a real estate developer and the developer can ignore the U.C.C.C., where adopted, and the Truth–In–Lending Act. For example, in a "for sale" development such as a condominium, at the primary stage, the money will be lent to the developer for development purposes and the transaction should qualify under the business loan exception. At the secondary stage, the sale of the condominium units, the financing of these purchases by either the assumption of part of the developer's existing financing or the lender or developer making a new loan to the purchaser, in most cases, will be subject to the provisions of the Truth–In–Lending Act and the U.C.C.C. See generally Rickert, *Some Real Estate Aspects of Truth–In–Lending,* 42 N.Y.St.B.J. 219 (1970); Meyers, *Real Estate Transactions, Rates, and the Uniform Consumer Credit Code,* 23 Okla.L.Rev. 263 (1970); Comment, *The Uniform Consumer Credit Code and Real Estate Financing—A Square Peg in a Round Hole,* 28 U.Kan.L.Rev. 601 (1980); Shevin, *Truth–In–Lending Simplification and Reform Act Analysis,* 86 Com.L.J. 504 (1981); Woocher and Geltzer, *Legislative Background to Truth in Lending Simplification and Reform Act,* 54 N.Y.St.B.J. 506 (1982).

c. The only type of credit subject to a maximum finance charge under the Uniform Land Transactions Act is that extended to a "protected party." See Section 3–403(b). In general, this applies to financing extended for, or assumed or taken subject to, upon the purchase or refinancing of improved or to be improved real estate containing not more than 3 acres, not more than 4 dwelling units, and no nonresidential uses with respect to which the recipient of the financing or a related party is the lessor, and the recipient of the financing or a related party occupies or intends to occupy all or a part of the real estate as a residence. See Section 1–203. With respect to all other types of financing secured by real estate, the parties may contract for and receive any finance charge and additional finance charge agreed upon. See Section 3–403. This broad grant of freedom of contract, however, is subject to the general unconscionability provision, Section 1–311 of the Uniform Land Transactions Act.

6. The variable rate mortgage is a relatively recent financing device. Through its use a lender, especially a long term lender, attempts to assure itself of a return equal to the "going rate" of interest throughout the term of the loan. It benefits the borrower by allowing the borrower to take advantage of

future lower rates of interest without refinancing. In its simplest form the interest rate to be paid by the borrower is determined by the prime rate of the lender or of another named institutional lender. If the prime rate goes up or down so does the interest rate on the mortgage. The use of a variable rate mortgage is far from free of problems. See New York State Bar Association Real Property Law Section: Committee on Mortgages, *Report on the Variable Rate Mortgage*, 45 N.Y.St.B.J. 112 (1973); Werner, *Usury and the Variable-Rate Mortgage*, 5 Real Est.L.J. 155 (1976); Jeka, *Variable Rate Mortgages: The Transitional Phase*, 61 Marq.L.Rev. 140 (1977); Note, *New Tests for Variable Interest Loans*, 30 Hastings L.J. 1843 (1979); Comment, *Adjustable Rate Mortgages: A Proposed Statutory Reform*, 26 Santa Clara L.Rev. 253 (1986). Indexing the principal amount of a mortgage loan is another means of dealing with the problems of inflation used by some long term lenders. See Note, *Indexing the Principal: The Usury Laws Hang Tough*, 37 U.Pitt.L.Rev. 755 (1976); Note, *Inflation and Indexing—Usury in Commercial Loans*, 11 Tulsa L.J. 450 (1976); Comment, *The New Mortgages: A Functional Legal Analysis*, 10 Fla.St.U.L.Rev. 95 (1982); Comment, *Alternative Mortgage Instruments: Authorizing and Implementing Price Level Adjusted Mortgages*, 16 U.Mich.J.L.Ref. 115 (1982). Title VIII of the Garn–St. Germain Depository Institutions Act of 1982 authorizes the use of alternative mortgage transactions by "housing creditors."

7. A National Bank can charge interest at the maximum rate permitted by state law to any competing state-chartered or licensed lending institution and, if state law permits a higher interest rate on a specified class of loans, a National Bank may make such loans at the higher rate. For example, if a state limits state commercial banks to an 11% interest rate and permits state savings and loans to charge a 13% interest rate, a National Bank can charge 13% on its loans, if such loans can be made by a state savings and loan. See 12 U.S.C.A. § 85; *Northway Lanes v. Hackley Union Nat'l Bank & Trust Co.*, 334 F.Supp. 723 (W.D.Mich.1971). Alternatively, a National Bank can charge interest at a rate of 1% in excess of the discount rate on ninety day commercial paper in effect at the Federal reserve bank in the Federal reserve district where the National Bank is located. See 12 U.S.C.A. § 85; Comptroller of the Currency Inter. Ltd. # 101, P.H.Fed. Control Banking ¶ 3948.

A National Bank can take as consideration for a loan, a share in the profit, income or earnings of a business enterprise of a borrower. Such a share may be in addition to or in lieu of interest. Comptroller's Interpretative Ruling 7.7312, 36 Fed.Reg. 17,015 (Aug. 26, 1971).

8. For more on monetary policy, economics and interest rates see Proceedings of A Symposium on Money, Interest Rates and Economic Activity (The American Bankers Association, 1967); Wallace, *The Uses of Usury: Low Rate Ceilings Reexamined*, 56 B.U.L.Rev. 451 (1976); Giles, *The Effect of Usury Law on the Credit Marketplace*, 95 Banking L.J. 527 (1978); Higgs, *Rate Limitations, Interest and Usury*, 33 Bus.Law. 1043 (1978); Comment, *Usury Legislation—Its Effects on the Economy and a Proposal for Reform*, 33 Vand.L.Rev. 199 (1980); Long, *Trends in Usury Legislation—Current Interest Overdue*, 34 U.Miami L.Rev. 325 (1980); Nosari and Lewis, *How Usury Laws Affect Real Estate Development*, 9 Real Est.L.J. 30 (1980); Ackerman, *Interest Rates and the Law: A History of Usury*, 1981 Ariz.St.L.J. 61.

(i) THE CORPORATE BORROWER EXCEPTION

As previously discussed, a corporate borrower is often excepted from the limits imposed by usury statutes. At times, a lender may require the formation of a corporation by a borrower, which is an individual or a partnership engaged in business, in order to take advantage of the corporate borrower exception to a usury statute. Consider whether the nominee corporation formed by the borrower qualifies for the corporate borrower exception.

LEADER v. DINKLER MANAGEMENT CORP.

Court of Appeals of New York, 1967.
20 N.Y.2d 393, 283 N.Y.S.2d 281, 230 N.E.2d 120.

* * *

KEATING, J. The plaintiff in this action, I. Theodore Leader, and the defendant Joseph Durst were the promoters and controlling stockholders of the Leader–Durst Corporation. The corporation was organized in December, 1961. Shortly thereafter the Leader–Durst Corporation made a public offering of a large block of its Class A stock at a price of $5.00 per share. In order to insure compliance with the registration statement filed with the Securities and Exchange Commission, Leader and Durst found it necessary to acquire personally 80,000 shares of the corporation's Class A stock. Finding themselves without the necessary funds with which to make the purchase, Leader and Durst sought to borrow $400,000 from the Dinkler Management Corporation (herein called Dinkler).

An agreement to this effect was negotiated by the defendant Durst and Dinkler. Dinkler agreed to the loan, but only if it were made to a corporation, and, for this purpose, Leader and Durst formed the Leatex Investing Corporation on May 8, 1962. The authorized capital of Leatex consisted of 200 shares of common stock, of which 50 shares were issued to Leader and Durst respectively. The remaining shares were not issued. Durst was elected president and Leader vice-president of the corporation. Leatex opened a bank account at the Manufacturers Hanover Trust Company.

On May 9, 1962, Dinkler agreed to lend Leatex the sum of $400,000. The agreement provided that the loan would be closed the following day. On May 10, 1962, Dinkler delivered a check for $400,000 payable to Leatex. In return Dinkler received a note from Leatex for $480,000 payable on November 10, 1962. Both Leader and Durst were listed as guarantors of the note. Some 160,000 shares of the Leader–Durst Corporation's Class A stock were pledged as security for the loan. Of these 80,000 were pledged by Leatex and 80,000 by Leader and Durst. Leatex had purchased its 80,000 shares with the proceeds of the loan agreement.

The execution of the loan agreement was approved and ratified at a special meeting of the shareholders of Leatex. At the closing of the deal there was delivered to Dinkler a certified copy of the resolutions of approval, along with an opinion letter from counsel for Leatex and the two shareholders, stating that the corporation had the authority to borrow the $400,000 and that the note and collateral security given to secure the loan were valid and legally binding.

In addition to the afore-mentioned agreements, Leader and Durst agreed to grant Dinkler an irrevocable option exercisable on or before December 31, 1964 to purchase 16,000 shares of Class B (voting) stock of the Leader–Durst Corporation at 25 cents per share.

The loan was repaid in several installments. In the course of the payments, the lender agreed to a reduction in the interest charged from $80,000 to $55,000, and, therefore, the total sum repaid was $455,000. After the loan was repaid, Dinkler gave notice of its intention to exercise its option under the loan agreement to purchase 16,000 shares of the Class B (voting) stock.

The plaintiff, concerned that the exercise of the stock option might result in the seizure of control of the corporation by Dinkler and Durst, entered into negotiations with Dinkler. These negotiations resulted in an agreement by which Dinkler agreed to give up its option to purchase the Class B stock in return for 6,667 shares of Class A stock valued at $4.00 per share and a general release of all claims including the one based upon usury.

Six months later Leader commenced an action * * * for the return of interest paid in excess of 6% and for a return of the 6,667 shares of Class A stock. The plaintiff claimed that the release was entered into as a result of "economic duress" and was, therefore, not enforcible.

* * *

Setting aside for a moment the question of the enforcibility of the release, the first question to be considered is the contention that "[t]he loan was made by respondent to appellant and defendant Durst, individually, though in form to a corporation in order to hide the fact that respondent exacted an illegal rate of interest". It is urged by the plaintiff that triable issues exist which bar the [trial court's] grant of summary judgment [for the respondent].

After reviewing the affidavits and applicable law in this area and accepting as true the allegations contained in the plaintiff's complaint, affidavits and testimony before trial, we reach the conclusion that there were no triable issues and that summary judgment was properly granted.

The appellant asserts that the purpose of the loan was to further the individual interest of the appellant and defendant Durst—the individual shareholders; that the loan was made to a corporation whose certificate was filed on the day preceding the loan agreement and which was organized for the specific purpose of avoiding the usury laws; and that Leatex was simply a shell corporation that had neither assets nor business of any kind. In addition, it appears from allegations in the complaint that some $130,000 of the $455,000 was paid directly to Dinkler by the individual shareholders. Although the remainder appears to have been paid by Leatex, there is little question that the funds for the repayment came from the individual shareholders.

One of the early and significant cases in this area is Jenkins v. Moyse (254 N.Y. 319, 172 N.E. 521). The case involved an action to cancel and discharge of record a mortgage given by a corporation on real property transferred to it by the plaintiff, the ultimate borrower. The plaintiff sought the relief on the ground that the mortgage was executed for a sum greatly in excess of the amount actually borrowed by the corporation.

In holding that the plaintiff could not succeed in its action and in sustaining the defense that the loan was a corporate obligation and, therefore, not subject to the usury laws, Judge Lehman wrote (254 N.Y., supra, pp. 324–325, 172 N.E., pp. 522–523): "The test of whether this loan is usurious is whether it was in fact made to the plaintiff. Doubtless at times loans are made in fact to an individual though in form they are made to a corporation to hide the fact that the lender has exacted an illegal rate of interest from the real borrower. We do not now deal with such a situation. Here the corporation was formed and the loan made to it, rather than to the individual who owned the corporate stock, because the parties sought to avail themselves of the rights the law accords to those who do business in corporate form under a franchise from the State. The fact that the sole owner of the stock of the corporation is an individual does not change those rights. He did not in his individual capacity borrow any money or agree to repay any money. The defendants have obtained a judgment against the corporation enforceable against property owned by the corporation at the time the action was brought. That judgment is based upon a valid contract."

Thus it is clear from *Jenkins* that a loan will not be struck down as usurious merely because the purpose of creating the corporation was to avoid the usury laws. Moreover, we have in subsequent cases gone even further in sustaining such loan transactions and have held that a shareholder who binds himself as guarantor or indorser of a corporate obligation will likewise not be permitted to raise the defense of usury nor will that circumstance have the effect of avoiding the transaction on the ground of usury. This rule has prevailed even where the corporation was a mere shell having no assets other than pledged security and where it transacted no business other than serving as a conduit for the transmission of the funds from the lender to the borrower. (Werger v. Haines Corp., 302 N.Y. 930, 100 N.E.2d 189, affg. 277 App.Div. 1108, 101 N.Y.S.2d 361; General Phoenix Corp. v. Cabot, 300 N.Y. 87, 89 N.E.2d 238; New York Credit Men's Ass'n v. Manufacturer's Discount Corp., 298 N.Y. 512, 80 N.E.2d 660.)

The real basis of these decisions has not been judicial blindness to reality but rather a response to it—a response which has in fact been impliedly sanctioned by the Legislature. Almost all of the cases in which we have sustained these loan agreements against charges of usury are cases in which the loans, though made to "dummy" corporations, were being used to further business ventures of the individuals who ultimately benefited from the transactions. Moreover, they involved circumstances, such as those present in our case, where it was, for some reason, inconvenient to merge the business venture with the corporation to whom the loan was made. Though in form the business venture and the "dummy" corporations were separate, in fact they were both part of the same enterprise, and the situation was similar to those in which a loan was made to a corporation actually transacting business. The results reached clearly conformed to the legislative policy of refusing to permit corporations—even though they be close corporations—to avoid obligations on which they had become bound.

Viewed in this light, the case of 418 Trading Corp. v. Oconefsky (37 Misc.2d 745, 234 N.Y.S.2d 747, aff'd 19 A.D.2d 593, 240 N.Y.S.2d 956, aff'd 14 N.Y.2d 676, 249 N.Y.S.2d 876, 198 N.E.2d 907), heavily relied upon by the plaintiff, does not conflict with any of the earlier decisions nor does it lend support to the plaintiff's position. *Oconefsky* involved a loan made to finance the purchase of a one-family residence with title taken in the name of the corporation and the loan secured by a mortgage on the dwelling. The interest rate exceeded the legal rate, and the individual shareholder was permitted to attack the loan as usurious even though the corporation had been in existence for more than six months. (Cf. General Obligations Law, § 5–521.)

The case not only involved an area in which the Legislature had demonstrated particular concern, but the facts revealed that the lender had paid the money directly to the individual shareholder who, in turn, paid the seller of the house. The loan was made directly to the individual and never in fact passed through the corporation.

In the case at bar the loan was made by a check payable to the corporation. The money was deposited in the corporate account. The corporation purchased the shares of the Leader–Durst Corporation and pledged them as security. Under these circumstances, the additional fact the guarantors repaid directly to the lender a portion of the loan would not and should not suffice to render this a loan subject to attack as usurious. (See Werger v. Haines Corp., supra.)

We have examined on the merits the plaintiff's contentions with regard to the unenforcibility of the release and find them to be without substance.

The order of the Appellate Division should be affirmed, with costs.

Judges VAN VOORHIS, BURKE, SCILEPPI, BERGAN and BREITEL concur with Judge KEATING; Chief Judge FULD taking no part.

Order affirmed.

NOTE

1. The New York courts have been among the most liberal in construing the corporate exception. For example, in *Leader v. Dinkler Management Corp.,* supra, there was no business reason for the existence of Leatex Investing Corp. other than to borrow money from Dinkler Management Corp.

  a. The usury limit in New York at the time Leatex Investing Corp. borrowed the money was 6%. The initial interest rate charged for the loan was 20%. It was later reduced to 13.5%.

  b. The court indicated it would have held that the corporate exception applied even if Dinkler Management Corp. had been suing the individual guarantors for payment of the principal and interest of the loan. Does this make sense when the borrower corporation has no assets and the sole reason for its organization is to avoid the usury limits?

    1. In similar situations, other states, either through judicial decision or legislation, have reached the opposite result.

2. Is the court in *Leader v. Dinkler Management Corp.,* supra, combining a business loan exception with a corporate exception? The court points out that the loan was used to further the business venture of the individuals, it was inconvenient to merge the venture with the borrowing corporation, and the borrowing corporation and business venture were, in fact, both part of the same enterprise.

  a. Would the court have reached a different result if the venture was carried on individually or as a partnership? See *First Nat. Bank in Albuquerque v. Danek,* 89 N.M. 623, 556 P.2d 31 (1976); *National Equipment Rental Ltd. v. Hendrix,* 565 F.2d 255 (2d Cir.1977).

  b. If the loan proceeds had not passed through the borrowing corporation or had not been repaid by it, would the result reached by the court have been different? Cf. *Schneider v. Phelps,* 41 N.Y.2d 283, 391 N.Y.S.2d 568, 359 N.E.2d 1361 (1977).

  c. Some courts have required that there be a business purpose for the loan or that the proceeds of the loan be used in a business venture in order to find that the corporate exception applies. See e.g. *Monmouth Capital Corp. v. Holmdel Village Shops, Inc.,* 92 N.J.Super. 480, 224 A.2d 35 (Ch. Div.1966). Cf. Note, *Incorporation for the Purpose of Borrowing at an Otherwise Usurious Rate of Interest,* 29 Sw.L.J. 959 (1975).

3. In what capacities were Leader and Durst acting when they granted Dinkler Management Corporation the options to acquire the shares of Class B voting stock of Leader–Durst Corporation at $.25 a share? Since the Class A stock was offered to the public at $5.00 a share, it can be assumed that the value of the Class B voting stock might have exceeded $.25 a share. Cf. *First Nat'l Bank in Albuquerque v. Danek,* 89 N.M. 623, 556 P.2d 31 (1976).

  a. If the value of the Class B stock greatly exceeded $.25 a share could the difference have been considered part of Dinkler Management Corporation's "usurious" return with respect to its loan? See *Kessing v. National Mortgage Corp.,* 278 N.C. 523, 180 S.E.2d 823 (1971), supra, pages 791 to 795. Is there any way to avoid the application of the corporate borrower exception with respect to this aspect of the lending transaction? Does the answer depend on whether the option was to acquire the Class B stock directly from the individuals, or to acquire it from Leader–Durst Corporation?

4. The New York courts do have some "heart."

RANHAND v. SINOWITZ

Court of Appeals of New York, 1970.
26 N.Y.2d 232, 309 N.Y.S.2d 323, 257 N.E.2d 877.

BURKE, Judge. Between February, 1961 and February, 1963 the plaintiff made various loans to the defendant in return for which the defendant executed and delivered promissory notes in series to the plaintiff. The defendant signed the notes in his individual name. Defendant made the scheduled payments on the notes for a period of time but then defaulted on further payments and plaintiff brought an action to recover the amounts due under them. Plaintiff made use of the "motion-action" provided for by CPLR 3213, serving on the defendant a summons and a notice of motion for summary judgment upon instruments for the payment of money only. Defendant's answering papers opposed plaintiff's motion for summary judgment and cross-moved for summary judgment dismissing the action and declaring the promissory notes sued upon to be void for usury and directing that such notes be surrendered and canceled pursuant to section 5–511 of the General Obligations Law, Consol.Laws c. 24–A. By means of exhibits, defendant demonstrated that the notes were in fact usurious, absent exempting facts, since they called for the payment of interest at the rate of 15% per annum. In his reply affidavit, the plaintiff alleged that the defendant "owned" about five restaurant corporations and that defendant told him that they were "in financial difficulty." He further alleged that the defendant suggested that the plaintiff loan him money to be used for these corporations in return for "half the moneys" defendant would save by settling with some of his creditors for 50% of his debts to them. Plaintiff refused such an arrangement and defendant then asked that plaintiff loan him money at 15%; when plaintiff inquired which of the corporations was to receive the loan, defendant answered that, although the money would be used to take care of obligations of his corporations, "he needed fluidity in controlling and managing the funds [and] so preferred that a single transaction with him be made instead of separate transactions with the various corporations."

* * * At best, plaintiff's allegations, taken as true, demonstrate that the loans were made to the defendant personally to be used for the benefit of the corporate enterprises "owned" by the defendant. However, it is clear that the obligations represented by the promissory notes sued upon were those of the defendant individually and there is no indication whatever of any corporate obligation. The mere fact that the borrowed funds were expected to be or were intended to be used for corporate purposes cannot transform an individual obligation into a corporate obligation. Indeed there is an anomaly in the plaintiff's position to the extent that, for purposes of avoiding the impact of

defendant's usury defense, plaintiff contends that the loans were in fact made to the corporations whereas, for the purpose of recovering the amounts due on the notes, the plaintiff is proceeding against the defendant individually.   Manifestly, either the notes are corporate obligations of the various corporations "owned" by the defendant (and plaintiff has not specified which loans went to which corporation and in what amounts) and are, therefore, not subject to the usury defense (General Obligations Law, § 5–521) or they are the personal obligations of the defendant and are subject to that defense.   Even assuming *arguendo,* that there are sufficiently raised by these papers triable issues as to whether the corporations or the defendant borrowed the funds, defendant's unambiguous status as maker of the notes necessitates the conclusion that he would be a primary obligor (see Uniform Commercial Code, §§ 3–401, 3–413) and, as such, entitled to the usury defense even if the corporate obligor were not (Matter of Waldman's Estate, 32 A.D.2d 780, 302 N.Y.S.2d 233, aff'd 25 N.Y.2d 677, 306 N.Y.S.2d 679, 254 N.E.2d 909; Schwartz v. Fifty Greenwich St. Realty Corp, 265 N.Y. 443, 193 N.E. 263).

* * *

NOTE

1.   If the plaintiff in *Ranhand v. Sinowitz,* supra, had required the defendant to organize a corporation solely to borrow the money and use it for the benefit of the defendant's operating corporations, would the court have reached a different result?

a.   Is there a reason why the defendant would have been unwilling to cast the transaction in that form?   Does the reason have anything to do with income tax consequences?

2.   Is not *Ranhand v. Sinowitz,* supra, a better case for the application of the "business venture" analysis than *Leader v. Dinkler Management Corp.,* supra, pages 804 to 807?   In *Ranhand v. Sinowitz,* supra, the loan was clearly for the benefit of various business corporations.   It was inconvenient for the loan to be made to only one of the operating corporations and the purpose of the loan was to further the business ventures in corporate form of the individual who received the proceeds of the loan.

a.   Is the distinction between *Ranhand v. Sinowitz,* supra, and *Leader v. Dinkler Management Corp.,* supra, that in *Ranhand v. Sinowitz,* supra, the proceeds of the loan were paid directly to the individual and were to be repaid by him, whereas in *Leader v. Dinkler Management Corp.,* supra, the proceeds of the loan were paid to the corporation and the loan was repaid, for the most part, by it, albeit the loan was personally guaranteed by the individuals?

1.   If the corporation in *Leader v. Dinkler Management Corp.,* supra, had no assets other than the notes of Leader and Durst, it reloaned the money to Leader and Durst and they individually acquired the stock of Leader–Durst Corporation, would the above-described distinction between the two cases be more than ephemeral?

b.   Cf. *First Nat'l Bank in Albuquerque v. Danek,* 89 N.M. 623, 556 P.2d 31 (1976); *National Equipment Rental Ltd. v. Hendrix,* 565 F.2d 255

(2d Cir.1977); *Selman v. Manor Mortgage Company,* 551 F.Supp. 345 (E.D. Mich.1982).

c.　An April 3, 1975 Opinion of the Attorney General of Texas, No. H–589 holds that a loan to a partnership comprised solely of two corporations is considered a loan to a partnership and the maximum rate applicable to the loan is 10% rather than the 18% rate applicable to corporate loans. On the other hand, in *Wild, Inc. v. Citizens Mortgage Investment Trust,* 95 Wis.2d 430, 290 N.W.2d 567 (1980), the court held that the corporate exception to the usury statute applied to loans made to a limited partnership in which the general partners were a corporation and its sole shareholder. A number of individuals were limited partners.

3.　In some states, the courts have limited the corporate borrower exception by insisting that the corporation must be more than a shell to cloak a loan to an individual. See e.g. *Gilbert v. Doris R. Corp.,* 111 So.2d 682 (Fla.App. 1959). In other states the courts have held that the question whether the borrower is an individual or a corporation is a question of fact. See e.g. *Gelber v. Kugel's Tavern,* 10 N.J. 191, 89 A.2d 654 (1952). In situations in which individuals have guaranteed the note of the corporation some courts require that the transaction be examined in order to determine which is the true obligor, the corporation or the individuals. See e.g. *Walnut Discount Co. v. Weiss,* 205 Pa.Super. 161, 208 A.2d 26 (1965). See generally Note, *Incorporation to Avoid the Usury Laws,* 68 Colum.L.Rev. 1390 (1968); Comment, *Washington's Corporate Exemption from Usury,* 12 Gonz.L.Rev. 312 (1977).

4.　The use of a corporation to avoid usury problems may result in income tax problems. For example, an individual taxpayer may form a corporation in order to borrow money at an interest rate higher than that permitted to be charged to an individual under state law. It may be held that the corporation must be recognized, and not treated as an agent of the taxpayer, for income tax purposes, thereby denying the individual taxpayer the deduction for the interest paid on the borrowed money. See generally Comment, *Using a "Dummy" Corporate Borrower Creates Usury and Tax Difficulties,* 28 Sw.L.J. 437 (1974).

a.　In Priv.Ltr.Ruls. 8105040 and 8106017 the Internal Revenue Service set out in detail its reasons for finding that the corporations involved were neither nominees nor agents for the limited partnerships which had directly or indirectly caused their formation. Among the reasons given by the Internal Revenue Service for its conclusion was that the corporations were formed to avoid usury laws and it would be incongruous to allow the partnerships to deduct the interest on loans that could not be obtained by the partnerships because of the usury laws. The partnerships might have been entitled to the deductions if the real estate subject to the loans had been transferred by the corporations to the partnerships immediately after the loans were closed. See *Schlosberg v. United States,* 47 A.F.T.R.2d 81–1208, (E.D.Va.1981); Note, *Schlosberg v. United States: Straw Corporations and the Interest Deduction,* 2 Va.Tax Rev. 131 (1982). But see Priv.Ltr.Rul. 7950003. Might, however, the transfer of the real estate by the corporations to the partnerships be regarded, for income tax purposes, as the liquidation of the corporations?

b.　A taxpayer finally convinced the Tax Court that a corporation formed to avoid usury limits should be treated as an agent of the partnership which operated the real estate. The decision of the Tax Court, however, was reversed by the Fifth Circuit Court of Appeals. See *Joseph*

A. Roccaforte, 77 T.C. 263 (1981), reversed, 708 F.2d 986 (5th Cir.1983). The Tax Court was not persuaded by the reasoning of the Fifth Circuit Court of Appeals in *Roccaforte,* and, on facts similar to those present in *Roccaforte,* the court found in favor of the taxpayer in *Florenz R. Ourisman,* 82 T.C. 171 (1984). This decision of the Tax Court was subsequently reversed by the Fourth Circuit Court of Appeals in *Ourisman v. Comm'r,* 760 F.2d 541 (4th Cir.1985). Meanwhile, the Fifth Circuit Court of Appeals, the Claims Court, and the Federal Circuit Court of Appeals all found appropriate fact situations in respect to which they could hold that a corporation, formed to avoid usury limits, was an agent of the taxpayer. See *Moncrief v. United States,* 730 F.2d 276 (5th Cir.1984), and *Raphan v. United States,* 3 Cl.Ct. 457 (1983), affirmed on this issue, 759 F.2d 879 (F.Cir.1985), cert. denied, 474 U.S. 843, 106 S.Ct. 129, 88 L.Ed.2d 106 (1985). Subsequently, the Tax Court, in a case in which the corporation was not owned by the partnership or all of its partners, and in a case which would be appealed to the Sixth Circuit Court of Appeals, found that the corporations should be treated as agents. See *Gary R. Frink,* 49 CCH Tax Ct.Mem. 386 (1984), and *Jesse C. Bollinger,* 48 CCH Tax Ct.Mem. 1443 (1984). The Fourth Circuit reversed the decision of the Tax Court in *Gary R. Frink.* See *Frink v. Comm'r,* 798 F.2d 106 (4th Cir.1986). The Sixth Circuit Court of Appeals, however, affirmed the Tax Court's decision in *Jesse C. Bollinger.* See *Jesse C. Bollinger v. Comm'r,* 807 F.2d 65 (6th Cir.1986). The Supreme Court granted certiorari in *Jesse C. Bollinger v. Comm'r,* supra, and affirmed the decision of the Sixth Circuit Court of Appeals. See *Comm'r v. Bollinger,* ___ U.S. ___, 108 S.Ct. 1173, 99 L.Ed.2d 357 (1988). The Supreme Court subsequently vacated and remanded the Fourth Circuit Court of Appeals' decision in *Frink v. Comm'r,* supra. See *Frink v. Comm'r,* ___ U.S. ___, 108 S.Ct. 1264, 99 L.Ed.2d 476 (1988). As a result of the decisions of the Supreme Court, it appears that the Tax Court's initial opinion in *Joseph A. Roccaforte,* 77 T.C. 263 (1981), is an accurate expression of the law in this area. This means that if the proper steps are taken in organizing the corporation and defining its relationship to the partnership, which is the actual operating entity, the corporation will be treated, for income tax purposes, as an agent of the partnership. See the discussion of this issue in Division I, at pages 264 to 279. See also Payne, *Playing a Shell Game with Usury Statutes,* 10 Real Est.L.J. 337 (1982); Comment, *Corporate Agents and the Flow–Through of Tax Advantages,* 12 Seton Hall L.Rev. 798 (1982); Comment, *The Use of Corporations in Real Estate Transactions: Judicial Acceptance of the Agency Theory,* 8 J.Corp.L. 361 (1983); Note, *"Nominee" Corporation May Be Treated as True Agent of Taxpayers Rather Than Separate Taxable Entity,* 11 Mem.St.U.L.Rev. 631 (1981); Riese, *Supreme Court Provides Safe Harbor for Use of Straw Corporations,* 16 J.Real Est.Tax'n 99 (1988).

(ii) THE PURCHASE MONEY EXCEPTION

Usury statutes are frequently limited in their application to transactions involving "loans or forbearance of any money." If a usury statute is worded in this manner, there is some doubt whether a vendee's purchase money note and mortgage given to the vendor of real estate constitutes a transaction to which the usury statute applies. This transaction may be said to be subject to the fairly common "time-price" exception to usury statutes—that the interest paid with respect to the purchase price of property sold on time is not subject to the provisions of the usury statutes since it is not "interest" but merely a means of formulating a higher price for the goods, when payment in full is deferred for a period of time.

MANDELINO v. FRIBOURG

Court of Appeals of New York, 1968.
23 N.Y.2d 145, 295 N.Y.S.2d 654, 242 N.E.2d 823.

BERGAN, J. Plaintiff, a real estate broker, purchased from defendants a building in Flatbush Avenue, Brooklyn, for $15,500. He paid $1,000 in cash and executed a purchase-money mortgage for $14,500. The purchase-money mortgage in terms required the payment of 7% interest. This was in January, 1964. The statute on usury then in effect (General Business Law, former §§ 370, 371) prescribed the rate of interest "upon the loan or forbearance of any money, goods, or things, in action" should be 6%. * * *

The basic question, then, is whether a purchase-money mortgage is to be regarded in law as a loan. A fairly well definable line of decisional law suggests it is not a loan. There never seems to have been a case in this court, however, where, as part of the expression of a sale of property made and entirely performable by a noncorporate individual within the State, a rate of interest has been stated baldly and explicitly on the face of the paper in excess of the statutory rate.

* * *

If it be held that the weight of authority of the decided cases in New York has in the past been not to treat a true purchase-money mortgage as a loan, the further question for the court is whether, as a matter of policy, this apparent exception to the interdiction of the usury statute should be continued in contemporary law.

* * *

From an analysis of cases stemming from the Statute of Anne in 1713, on which most American usury statutes are modeled, Williston reaches the conclusion that where property is sold "the parties may agree that the price, if paid after a certain time, shall be a sum greater by more than legal interest than the price payable at an earlier day" (6 Williston, Contracts [rev. ed.], § 1685, p. 4766). This is so, he notes, even though "stated in the form of interest" greater than the legal rate. A leading English case on the usury statute of that country, consistent with Williston's view, is Beete v. Bidgood (7 B. & C. 453, 108 Eng.Rep. 792).

The general American rule is drawn together in the statement: "An owner of property may sell it at such a price and on such terms as he may see fit, and such a sale, if bona fide, is not usurious, but a usurious loan in the form of a sale will not be permitted" (C.J.S. Usury, § 18, subd. a, p. 588).

The earliest case in this court (Dry Dock Bank v. American Life Ins. & Trust Co., 3 N.Y. 344 [1850]) treated Van Schaick v. Edwards (2 Johns.Cas. 355) as authority for the general statement that where a contract is, in form, one of sale or exchange, "if the court in looking at the whole transaction can see, that the value secured to the vendor, was in good faith but the price of the thing sold, or exchanged by him, there can be no usury, whatever the price may be, or the mode in which it may be reserved" (Gardiner, J., p. 359).

It was held that an exchange of notes or other obligations for a premium greater than the legal rate of interest where the transaction is not a mere disguise for usury is not prohibited by the statute.

In Cutler v. Wright (22 N.Y. 472 [1860]), a note had been executed, probably in New York but payable in Florida, for a sale of lands in the latter State. It called for interest at 8% which would have been permissible in Florida. Judge Davies assumed that even if executed in New York, it would be governed by the law of Florida (p. 474); but Judge Selden, concurring, felt that even if made and performable in New York and thus governed by New York law "the defence of usury cannot prevail * * * to constitute usury, there must be either a present loan or a forbearance in respect to some debt previously existing; in such a case as this, there is neither", since he had noted earlier that the note "was not given for a loan of money or of goods, or for a pre-existing debt of any kind, but upon a sale of lands" (p. 482).

A similar result was reached by the General Term, First Department, in Frank v. Davis (53 Hun 636, opn. in 6 N.Y.S. 144), where Willard Bartlett, J., writing for the court, was of opinion that on an agreement to sell real estate the payment of interest to begin some months before the date of the instrument was not usurious. "No usury can be predicated", he noted (p. 145), "on an agreement to sell real estate and receive in payment therefor a purchase-money mortgage bearing the legal rate of interest, to be calculated from a date prior to the agreement". Such an arrangement "is simply the means of increasing the purchase price". The decision was affirmed here at 127 N.Y. 673.

A synthesis of the rule in quite classic terms was made by Proskaufer, J., in McAnsh v. Blauner (222 App.Div. 381, 382, aff'd 248 N.Y. 537, 162 N.E. 515): "There was in fact no usury. A contract which provides for a rate of interest greater than the legal rate upon a deferred payment, which constitutes the consideration for a sale, is not usurious."

This principle seems to have been regularly followed at the Appellate Division. "There is no usury in the normal purchase-money transaction where a seller demands a higher price because the consideration is not all in cash" (Butts v. Samuel, 5 A.D.2d 1008, 174 N.Y.S.2d 325 [2d Dept.]). To the same effect and in almost the same language see Bennis v. Thomas, 14 A.D.2d 895, 221 N.Y.S.2d 350 [2d Dept.]. An instrument which appears on its face to be a purchase-money mortgage may in truth be a cloak for an actual loan at excessive interest and in this situation it may be deemed usurious (cf. Del Rubio v. Duchesne, 284 App.Div. 89, 130 N.Y.S.2d 572). But that is not this case. There is no doubt at all here that the instrument is what it purports to be: a purchase-money mortgage. And there is no subterfuge about it. The 7% is spelled out on its face. Thus it is either good or bad according to its express terms.

* * *

Upon settled authority, then, the purchase-money mortgage here in issue is not void for usury. * * *

Chief Judge FULD and Judges BURKE, SCILEPPI, KEATING, BREITEL and JASEN concur.

Order reversed, etc.

NOTE

1. A third party lender can obtain the status of a purchase money mortgagee if it provides part or all of the purchase price of real estate. See pages 596 and 599 supra. Can the third party lender also claim that the transaction is exempt from the usury laws?

2. If the purchase money mortgage Fribourg received from Mandelino had a 7% interest rate and Fribourg immediately sold it to a bank at a 1% discount so that the bank received an effective return in excess of 7%, when the bank sues Mandelino to collect the loan can he successfully interpose the usury defense? Cf. Note, *Commercial Law—Usury and the Time–Price Differential,* 1975 Wis.L.Rev. 246; Note, *Usury and Time Price Differentials in Tennessee,* 8 Mem.St.U.L.Rev. 91 (1977); Allen and Staaf, *The Nexus Between Usury, "Time Price" and Unconscionability in Installment Sales,* 14 U.C.C.L.J. 219 (1982); Comment, *Application of the Time–Price Doctrine in the Credit Sales of Real Property,* 40 Baylor L.Rev. 573 (1988).

3. If an institutional lender purchased the property from Fribourg and sold it to Mandelino taking back a purchase money mortgage bearing interest at 7%, would the transaction involve a violation of the usury law?

   a. If the institutional lender sold the property to Mandelino by means of an installment land contract which provided for an effective 7% return, does the transaction involve a violation of the usury law?

4. If Fribourg wanted to refinance rather than sell and an institutional lender had provided the financing using a sale-installment buy back and realized a return greater than 7%, has a violation of the usury law occurred? See pages 785 to 786 supra.

5. The Uniform Land Transactions Act treats the term "finance charge" as including a time-price differential. See Section 3–401(3)(ii). Since a finance charge is subject to a maximum rate, see Section 3–403(b), it appears that there is no purchase money exception under the Uniform Land Transactions Act.

c. THE INTEREST DEDUCTION

THE INTEREST DEDUCTION
Michael Asimow
24 University of California Los Angeles Law Review 749 (1977).
[some footnotes omitted]

*   *   *

The Definition and Identification of Interest

The Definition of Interest

Interest has been defined as the amount which one contracts to pay for the use of borrowed money, or, somewhat more broadly, as "compensation for the use or forbearance of money." [60] These straightforward definitions conceal a fundamental issue: whether interest should be identified by using economic analysis or by referring to the perception of the ordinary person. In its early decisions, the Supreme Court chose the common-man approach. Ever since, the courts have struggled to substitute a more sophisticated, economic analysis.

*   *   *

On many occasions *   *   * the courts have contented themselves with superficial reliance on dictionary definitions of interest or on assumptions about whether the common man might identify the item as interest.[61] This approach is unsatisfactory; it relies exclusively on the labels which the parties have chosen and on the external form of the transaction as opposed to its substance. Regardless of what the parties call the transaction or what an ordinary person might think of it, the underlying issue is whether the item is, in an economic sense, compensation for the use of money. The prevailing view, therefore, rejects this sterile approach and analyzes the issue in economic terms.

*   *   *

[For example] the *   *   * cases are surely correct in treating an original issue discount as interest. In practical terms, it matters little whether the borrower receives $900 and must repay $1000 (an original issue discount transaction) or whether the borrower receives $900 and must repay $900 plus $100 interest. *   *   *

Other items which serve the economic function of payment for borrowed capital have also been treated as interest, even though they have other names or are not conventionally structured as a percentage of the unpaid balance. Thus "points," which are lump sum payments made by the borrower to the lender at the outset of the loan, are considered interest.[62] Similarly, if the borrower is obligated to reimburse the lender for a state tax on bond interest, the borrower can treat

---

60. Deputy v. DuPont, 308 U.S. 488, 498 (1940). The broader definition makes it clear that interest frequently arises from transactions which involve no contracts, such as tax liabilities or judgments.

61. E.g., Elverson Corp., 40 B.T.A. 615, 644 (1939), aff'd, 122 F.2d 295 (2d Cir.1941).

62. Lewis v. Commissioner, 65 T.C. 625 (1975); Rev.Ruls. 69–188, 1969–1 C.B. 54;

the reimbursement as interest.[63]   Also, payments computed by reference to a percentage of the borrower's profits or his net income, rather than as a fixed percentage of the loan, can constitute interest.[64]

Usurious interest presents a significant problem which has not been clearly resolved.   Generally, in order to support an interest deduction, an enforceable obligation must exist; merely discretionary payments are not deductible.[65]   Since state law typically protects the debtor against liability for the payment of usurious interest, there is a substantial argument that because the obligation is unenforceable, any interest paid is not deductible.[66]   This result is unjustified.   If the debtor actually pays the usurious interest together with the principal of the loan, despite a legal right to resist payment, what purpose is served by denying a deduction?   The interest is, in economic terms, compensation for the use of money and usually cannot be recharacterized.[67]

69–290, 1969–1 C.B. 55; 74–395, 1974–2 C.B. 45 (origination fee).   Points have been explicitly recognized as interest in I.R.C. § 461(g)(2). * * * Although the immediate deduction of prepaid interest is not allowed, I.R.C. § 461(g) permits immediate deduction of points incurred in connection with the purchase of a taxpayer's principal residence if such payments represent established business practice in the area and the amount of the payment does not exceed the amount generally charged.

* * *

63.   Warner Co., 11 T.C. 419 (1948), aff'd, 181 F.2d 599 (3d Cir.1950).

64.   Dorzback v. Collison, 195 F.2d 69 (3d Cir.1952); Stevens Bros. & Miller–Hutchinson Co., 24 T.C. 953 (1955), acq. 1956–2 C.B. 8; Kena, Inc., 44 B.T.A. 217 (1941); Rev.Rul. 72–2, 1972–1 C.B. 19 (tuition postponement plan in which graduates must pay a percentage of their income). But see Pacific Northwest Fin. Corp., 3 T.C. 498 (1944), nonacq. 1944 C.B. 46 (personal holding company case casting doubt on whether payments of two percent of income can be interest).   Debts which require the payment of a percentage of profits invite reclassification as equity.   This occurs most frequently in the corporate area, in which purported debt held by stockholders is reclassified as equity, but can occur in connection with other relationships.   See Farley Realty Corp. v. Commissioner, 279 F.2d 701 (2d Cir.1960), noted in 74 Harv.L.Rev. 1224 (1961).

65.   See Equitable Life Assurance Soc'y v. Commissioner, 321 U.S. 560 (1944), denying a deduction for interest payments which were discretionary.   There seems to be little reason to deny a deduction of interest on an otherwise binding indebtedness, simply because the payment is discretionary, so long as the payment cannot be

characterized as something other than interest.   Cf. Howell Turpentine Co., 6 T.C. 364 (1946), rev'd on other grounds, 162 F.2d 319 (5th Cir.1947), in which a nonobligatory interest payment could be characterized as a purchase of stock or as a sham. Hypotheek Land Co. v. Commissioner, 200 F.2d 390 (9th Cir.1952), is a good example of the allowance of a deduction of a probably nonmandatory interest payment under highly sympathetic circumstances.

66.   Fahs v. Martin, 224 F.2d 387 (5th Cir.1955), seems to assume that usurious interest is not deductible but avoids the problem by holding that the interest was not usurious.   Several cases allow deductions of interest where the transactions were structured to avoid state law usury limitations.   Arthur R. Jones Syndicate v. Commissioner, 23 F.2d 833 (7th Cir.1927); Jules R. Green, T.C.Memo. 1965–272, aff'd, 367 F.2d 823 (7th Cir.1966).   It is not clear in those cases whether state law would have respected the arrangements or would have branded them as usurious.   See also Guantanamo & W.R.R., 31 T.C. 842 (1959), acq. 1959–2 C.B. 4, allowing an interest deduction in spite of a Cuban debt moratorium.   However, the taxpayer might have been liable for the interest in American courts notwithstanding the moratorium.

* * *

67.   See note [65] supra.   If the debtor has made only partial payments of principal and interest, and the interest payments are recharacterized under state law as payments of principal, see note [66] supra, there is no justification for treating any of the payments as interest for tax purposes. If the debtor pays both interest and principal, despite having a defense under state law, his interest payments should be deductible for tax purposes.

Furthermore, denial of the deduction punishes the wrong party—the borrower, who was obliged to enter into the transactions because of his need for funds and his weak bargaining position.

Distinguishing Interest from Other Payments

Even though the economic approach to defining interest is reasonably well accepted, many problems remain in distinguishing interest from other items. Payments which might be interest are frequently susceptible to other characterizations which would produce sharply different tax consequences. This section considers the problems of distinguishing interest from such payments as principal payments, the seller's profit on the sale of goods and services, the purchase of property, penalties, service charges, carrying charges, and damages.

Distinguishing Interest Payments from Principal Payments

A recurring problem is to distinguish the interest element of a payment from the principal element. This delineation concerns both the borrower and the lender. The lender seeks to avoid interest income * * * by characterizing such receipts as principal. The borrower, on the other hand, seeks an interest deduction. As in other areas of tax law where the same dollar amount can realistically be characterized in several ways, considerable latitude is given the parties in allocating payments between principal and interest. Thus, the parties generally are free to arrange their affairs so that * * * the interest is paid before the principal or the principal before the interest. The parties also have free rein to decide whether a payment on a delinquent debt should be allocated to principal or interest.

It seems justifiable to allow the parties to characterize the payments so as to resolve their conflicting interests. They presumably will bargain over the allocation and reach a result which corresponds to both parties' desires. Moreover, there is usually no obvious economic model to which the payments should conform. Thus, the practicalities of administration counsel that a contractual allocation usually be dispositive. Nevertheless, particularly arbitrary allocations can always be questioned by the Service on the ground that the substance of the event is different from its form. The Service is also warranted in holding the parties to their written agreement, even though one or both of them seek to depart from the agreement in order to avoid taxes. Strong proof should be required before the trier of fact may conclude that the written agreement should be abandoned because it does not describe the reality of the transaction.

When the parties have not clearly characterized a payment, state law will determine the allocation. State law is sufficiently uniform for a number of general rules to have crystallized: The debtor is allowed to signify at the time he makes a payment whether it is to be applied to delinquent principal or interest; in the absence of such a designation, the debtor may be bound by an allocation made by the creditor. Where neither party has designated how a voluntary, partial payment should be applied, it is generally applied to delinquent interest in preference to principal and to older debts before newer ones. On the other hand, if the payment is a lump sum which discharges the entire amount of principal and interest, it is applied to principal first. Similarly, when the security for the loan is foreclosed upon, the proceeds from the sale are applied to principal rather than interest, at least where the debtor is insolvent. * * * Where state law is silent, a pro rata allocation between interest and principal has been approved. All these rules relating to the characterization of payments made without an agreement of the parties assume that they are consistent with state law; a showing that state law requires a different allocation might require the court to follow the state law rather than the precedents in tax cases.

Distinguishing Interest from the Purchase Price of Property

Sometimes an item might plausibly be described either as interest or as part of the purchase price of property. For example, the seller of goods or services may increase the sale price to compensate for expected delay in payment. Although such an increase usually can be deducted as interest, the facts may be such that the buyer cannot establish the interest element with sufficient clarity.[68]

A situation in which an amount might be characterized as either interest or purchase price arises when a borrower is compelled to purchase property in order to obtain a loan. If he must pay more than the market value of the property, the excess would seem to be interest. * * *

As a general rule, the taxpayer is not permitted to add to the basis of his property an amount in excess of its value at the time it was acquired.[69] Therefore, taxpayers should be allowed to establish that overpayments for property which they are required to purchase in order to obtain a loan are in fact interest payments.

The problem of distinguishing interest from a portion of the purchase price is similar to that of distinguishing interest from principal. The realities of administration suggest that the written agreement usually should be controlling. Upon a showing of strong proof, however, either party should be permitted to establish that the written agreement does not reflect the parties' actual intentions.

68. See, e.g., Arthur C. Erwin, 4 T.C.M. (CCH) 398 (1945) (deduction disallowed). Cf. M.C. Parrish & Co., 3 T.C. 119 (1944), aff'd, 147 F.2d 284 (5th Cir.1945), involving warrants issued to sellers of goods to the state of Texas. The sellers added an amount to their bid prices to reflect the delay they would encounter before the warrants could be paid (or the discount they would incur in selling the warrants). It was held that the additional amounts added to the bid prices were not exempt state bond interest in the hands of purchasers of the warrants since the sellers had simply added some unproven amount to their lump sum bid price.

69. Majestic Securities Corp. v. Commissioner, 120 F.2d 12 (8th Cir.1941).

Distinguishing Interest from Penalties

Many penalties [70] imposed on debtors are appropriately treated as interest since they represent the cost of borrowing money. For example, prepayment penalties and bond call premiums have been treated as a form of interest. These charges represent the additional cost to the borrower of shorter, rather than longer, term debt. * * * The Service has appropriately ruled that a five percent "late-charge" by a utility company for late payment of bills is interest, even though it is assessed only once and does not vary with the length of time of nonpayment. [71]

Nevertheless, considerable confusion remains about the characterization of penalties imposed on borrowers. A number of decisions have indicated that penalties for defaults and for obtaining extensions of time are not "interest" under the personal holding company tax or under the exclusion for state and local bond interest. These cases may be wrongly decided; it is also conceivable that they would not be followed under section 163, although there is no reason to believe that the term "interest" has different meanings in different sections of the Code.

* * * Payments from debtor to creditor which are designed to obtain extensions of a loan, or which provide extra compensation to the creditor upon default, clearly are forms of compensation for borrowed money.

Penalties paid by a debtor to a *governmental* creditor present different issues. If such a penalty is designed to *punish* the debtor, rather than to compensate the creditor, it cannot be deducted as a business expense because the allowance of such deductions would lessen the sting of punishment. Even if they are called penalties, however, such payments are deductible as business expenses if they are intended to encourage prompt compliance with filing or other requirements and are more in the nature of interest than punishment.

It is not yet settled whether penalties paid to the government and intended to punish can be deducted as interest, as opposed to being deducted as business expenses. An example of such a penalty is the "addition to the tax" * * * for failure to pay the tax shown on a return. This penalty, which deters the filing of a return without payment of the tax, resembles interest very closely. [72] If the creditor were not the government, it presumably would be deductible as interest. Allowing the deduction as interest of such penalties, however, collided with the rule precluding deductions which would frustrate

---

70. A penalty is a charge imposed upon the borrower because a specific event has occurred.

71. Rev.Rul. 74–187, 1974–1 C.B. 48.

72. The penalty resembles interest because it is triggered by non-payment of a debt, it is computed as a percentage of the debt and it increases with the length of time the debt is delinquent.

sharply defined public policies. Although most of the cases enunciating this rule involve business expenses, there is authority supporting its application to other deductions as well.[73] There seems to be no logical reason why the public policy rule should not be applicable to all deductions, including interest.

There is a strong counterargument, however, that the 1969 amendments to section 162 relating to business expenses[74] foreclose any application of the public policy rule to the interest deduction. These amendments codify the public policy rules as they apply to business expenses. The legislative history states that the statutory provisions are intended to be "all-inclusive," suggesting that the courts are precluded from disallowing deductions except as set forth in the statute. Thus far, however, the Tax Court has continued to apply the pre–1969 public policy rules to deductions other than business expenses.[75] The Tax Court is probably correct, because it is unlikely that Congress wished to remove the public policy rules for deductions other than business expenses without substituting anything in their place. Thus it seems probable that penalties paid to the government, and intended to punish the taxpayer, will remain nondeductible as interest.

Distinguishing Interest from Service Charges

Frequently, lenders charge borrowers fees for specific services relating to loans. Such service charges may be levied for appraising the assets and investigating the credit of the borrower, for preparing the loan documents, and for similar services beneficial to the lender. Issuance costs charged by third parties, such as commissions or printing costs, may also be borne by the borrower. The Service refuses to permit interest deductions for service charges and issuance costs.

* * * If the borrower uses the loan for business or investment purposes, the service charges must be capitalized and deducted by amortization over the period of the loan. If the intended use of the loan is personal, the charges are not deductible at all. The charges could not even be added to the basis of the purchased property since they are considered part of the cost of the loan, not of the property.

* * *

73. Luther M. Richey, Jr., 33 T.C. 272 (1959) (loss deductions under I.R.C. § 165). Although there is authority for the proposition that penalties cannot be deducted as interest, it seems to be based upon the supposition that penalties cannot be interest. Kossar & Co., 16 B.T.A. 952 (1929); Rev.Rul. 55–65, 1955–1 C.B. 277 (relying on Kossar). See also Rev.Ruls. 60–127, 1960–1 C.B. 84 (modifying Rev.Rul. 55–65); 60–128, 1960–1 C.B. 85. A number of cases preclude deductions of interest-like penalties as business expenses under section

162, both before and after its amendment in 1969. See May v. Commissioner, 65 T.C. 1114 (1976) (dictum); John Reuter, Jr., 37 T.C. 599 (1961); Benjamin T. Smith, 34 T.C. 1100 (1960), aff'd per curiam, 294 F.2d 957 (5th Cir.1961); Rev.Rul. 61–210, 1961–2 C.B. 31. But see Keystone Metal Co. v. Commissioner, 264 F.2d 561 (3d Cir.1959).

74. I.R.C. § 162(c), (e), (f), (g).

75. Mazzei v. Commissioner, 61 T.C. 497 (1974).

Distinguishing Interest from Carrying Charges

Closely related to the problem of differentiating between interest and service charges is the issue presented by carrying charges.[76] Prior to the adoption of the 1954 Code, the Service took the position that carrying charges were not deductible as interest. Taxpayers who troubled to litigate the point, usually over trifling amounts, were successful; the Tax Court consistently held that carrying charges on installment purchases were interest.[77] Nevertheless, it is likely that many taxpayers lost interest deductions by reason of the IRS's position on carrying charges.

To deal with the problem, Congress added section 163(b) to the 1954 Code. This section provides that carrying charges can be treated as interest and deducted to the extent of six percent per year on purchases of personal property. The section was later extended to cover installment purchases of educational services.

Although section 163(b) was intended to expand the amounts deductible by taxpayers, it appears to have had the opposite effect.[78] The section disallows as deductions payments in excess of six percent. Absent section 163(b), it seems likely that the entire amount of carrying charge payments would be deductible. The restriction in section 163(b) of the amount deductible has been alleviated by * * * IRS rulings which permit the entire amount of "finance charges" on credit card and installment purchases to be deducted as interest.[79] These rulings are based on the fact that the entire charge represents interest, rather than a mixture of interest and other costs.[80] Section 163(b) also is inapplicable to loans of money, regardless of what the proceeds are used for, and to loans which finance either the purchase of services (other than educational services) or the purchase of real property. Finally, the limitation is inapplicable if the amount of carrying charges is not stated separately from the purchase price of the goods or services.

* * *

76. Carrying charges are the amount a credit purchaser is charged in excess of the cash price of an item. Normally these charges increase the periodic payments due the creditor.

77. O.G. Russell, T.C. Memo. 1953–357; Oliver W. Bryant, T.C. Memo. 1952–129; Arthur S. McKenzie, T.C. Memo. 1952–126; Carl E. Noe, T.C. Memo. 1952–124.

78. See Gilmore v. Commissioner, T.C. Memo. 1974–41.

79. Rev.Ruls. 73–137, 1973–1 C.B. 68; 73–136, 1973–1 C.B. 68; 72–315, 1972–1 C.B. 49; 71–98, 1971–1 C.B. 57. It seems that the Truth in Lending Act, 15 U.S.C.

§§ 1601 et seq. (1970), with its required statement of annual percentage rate of interest, id. § 1631, has, as a practical matter, superseded § 163(b). Apparently the Service is prepared to concede the deductibility of the entire amount of the annual percentage rate. See especially Rev.Rul. 73–137, supra; Bedell, *The Interest Deduction: Its Current Status*, N.Y.U. 32d Inst. on Fed Tax. 1117, 1120–23 (1974).

80. Section 163(b) is applicable only if the "interest charge cannot be ascertained." I.R.C. § 163(b)(1)(B); Rubin v. Commissioner, T.C. Memo. 1974–216.

Distinguishing Interest from Damages

Judgments for damages often include an element of interest, both for periods prior to and after judgment. There is some authority for the proposition that the element of interest before judgment is part of the underlying damages. Thus it would not be considered interest income, nor would an interest deduction be appropriate. Although not squarely overruled, this line of authority has been thoroughly discredited.

* * *

* * * In each case, the plaintiff suffered from a particular wrong on a particular date. If the plaintiff had sued immediately, he would have recovered compensation for that loss. Since suit was brought later, the court awarded an additional sum as compensation for the additional loss resulting from the delay, during which time the defendant had the plaintiff's money. This compensation is interest, whether the test utilized is that of the common man or the economist.

The Definition and Identification of "Indebtedness"

The preceding section of this Article explored the definition of interest and the problems of distinguishing it from other payments. Section 163(a) also requires the existence of an indebtedness in order to deduct interest.

The Definition of "Indebtedness"

The meaning of indebtedness is a product of years of judicial interpretation. In order to support an interest deduction, there must be a present obligation to repay a money debt, which is not a sham or a disguise for some other relationship. The obligation to repay the debt cannot be conditioned on an event which has not yet occurred.[81] The debt must also be enforceable,[82] although personal liability is not

---

81. This is true whether the taxpayer uses the cash or accrual method of accounting. See, e.g., Estate of Franklin v. Commissioner, 544 F.2d 1045 (9th Cir.1976) (property worth less than loan; repayment unlikely); Guardian Inv. Corp. v. Phinney, 253 F.2d 326 (5th Cir.1958) (second mortgage on which no payments had to be made unless and until a first mortgage was paid); United States v. Virgin, 230 F.2d 880 (5th Cir.1956) (repayment not required until borrower decides that his economic security would not be jeopardized); Gilman v. Commissioner, 53 F.2d 47 (8th Cir.1931) (alternate ground). Where a debt may become unenforceable upon the occurrence of a condition subsequent, interest is deductible until the condition occurs. See Mountain States Steel Foundries, Inc. v. Commissioner, 284 F.2d 737 (4th Cir.1960) (debt for stock redemption may become unen-

forceable if corporation lacks surplus at time payments are due).

82. See, e.g., George T. Williams, 47 T.C. 689 (1967), aff'd, 409 F.2d 1361 (6th Cir.1968), cert. denied, 394 U.S. 997 (1969) (deductions disallowed for interest payments on an unenforceable expired insurance policy loan). For a particularly lenient application of the rule requiring enforceability, see First Nat'l Co. v. Commissioner, 289 F.2d 861 (6th Cir.1961), in which the court allowed deduction of interest on a debt which had been ignored for years and which was barred by the statute of limitations. Sometimes it is stated that the debt must have a fixed maturity date, Farley Realty Corp. v. Commissioner, 279 F.2d 701 (2d Cir.1960); it seems likely that this would not be required if all of the other indicia of enforceability were pres-

required. Many purchase money obligations, for example, impose no personal liability on the debtor; they are secured exclusively by the property purchased. Yet the interest on such loans is deductible. However, where personal liability is lacking, the taxpayer must prove that the purchased property is worth at least the amount of the debt.[83]

* * *

The enforceability requirement has often been fatal to the deductibility of interest on debts incurred as gifts. Transactions involving gratuitous debts have been cast in various imaginative forms [84] but the courts have consistently refused to allow a deduction, * * *. A more difficult problem is whether interest on gratuitously incurred debts should be deductible if the debt is legally enforceable. The cases have allowed interest to be deducted in such circumstances despite a lack of consideration for the debt. * * *

* * *

Distinguishing Indebtedness from Other Relationships

As with the definition of interest, the definition of indebtedness is largely a product of judicial interpretation. As is also true of interest, what may be viewed as indebtedness can often be characterized differently. * * * [For example the courts have been called upon to distinguish debt from equity, see Division IV, pages 1121 to 1139, debt from a sale of assets, see the discussion of the sale-repurchase transaction in this Division, pages 785 to 786, and debt from lease, see particularly the discussion of the sale-leaseback transaction in this Division, pages 763 to 775.]

* * *

The Underlying Debt Must Be the Taxpayer's Obligation

Interest is not deductible unless the underlying debt is owed by the taxpayer rather than by someone else. There are many circumstances in which a taxpayer pays interest on the debt of another. For example, the taxpayer might be making a gift, or he might be paying the interest to protect his own financial position.[85] In such cases, the person who

---

ent. See Wynnefield Heights, Inc., T.C. Memo. 1966–185.

83. Estate of Franklin v. Commissioner, 544 F.2d 1045 (9th Cir.1976)[; John M. Elliot, 84 T.C. 227 (1985), affirmed, 782 F.2d 1027 (3d Cir.1986).]

84. For example, in Gilman v. Commissioner, 53 F.2d 47 (8th Cir.1931), the taxpayer first made a gift of property to his wife and then repurchased it with a promissory note. Viewing the transactions together, the court held that the taxpayer had simply promised to make a gift at the time the note was due.

85. For example, a second mortgagee might pay delinquent interest on a first mortgage, in order to forestall foreclosure of the first. The interest is not deductible, but must be added to the basis of the debt. Estate of Broadhead, T.C.Memo. 1966–26, aff'd 391 F.2d 841 (5th Cir.1968). Similarly, payments of interest by a guarantor of the underlying debt are not deductible. William H. Simon, 36 B.T.A. 184 (1937). [See also George F. Smith, Jr., 84 T.C. 889 (1985), in which the Tax Court denied an interest deduction to the taxpayer with regard to interest paid by him on a nonre-

pays the interest cannot deduct it, but the underlying debtor probably is entitled to the deduction.[86]

The rule that the underlying debt must be the taxpayer's has frequently been invoked to deny a property owner's deductions for both interest and depreciation when he is found not to be the true debtor. Although in form the taxpayer appears to own property subject to a mortgage, in reality a different party is the debtor. The approach taken by the courts in these cases is to analyze the facts of the transaction to determine whether the taxpayer assumed the risks and benefits of an owner of property.

The general rule that the debt must be the taxpayer's has a corollary: The taxpayer may deduct the interest only for the period during which he is the obligor. Interest attributable to prior or subsequent periods is not deductible. For example, even after a guarantor becomes primarily liable on a debt, he cannot deduct the interest which accrued during the period when he was only secondarily liable.[87] Once the taxpayer becomes the primary obligor, interest accruing from that time on is deductible by him. This principle can be illustrated by considering transferees of corporate assets who are subject to the debts of the predecessor corporation. Interest on such debts accruing after the transfer is deductible by the transferee; interest accruing prior to the transfer is not deductible.

The taxpayer is entitled to deduct interest payments on an obligation, however, even though he is only one of several joint obligors or joint owners of the property subject to the obligation. The theory is that the taxpayer is liable to repay the entire principal; consequently,

course indebtedness which he "assumed" but which was secured by property owned by a corporation. The court reasoned that the obligation, if any, to pay the indebtedness remained with the corporation despite the taxpayer's purported assumption.]

86. Leward Cotton Mills v. Commissioner, 245 F.2d 314 (4th Cir.1957); Central Elec. & Gas Co. v. United States, 159 F.Supp. 353 (Ct.Cl.1958); Andrew Jergens, 17 T.C. 806 (1951), acq. 1952–1 C.B. 2; Norman Cooledge, 40 B.T.A. 1325 (1939); George Overbeck, T.C. Memo. 1955–243; Rev.Rul. 76–75, 1976–1 C.B. 14. But see Robbins Tire & Rubber Co., 53 T.C. 275 (1969), acq. 1973–2 C.B. 3, denying the debtor a deduction if he has no obligation to reimburse the person who paid the interest, and gave no consideration to the payor for the payment. See also Hanna Furnace Corp. v. Kavanagh, 50–2 U.S.Tax Cas. ¶ 9443 (E.D.Mich.1950). The *Robbins* rule is too narrow. If, for example, a father pays interest on a debt owed by his child, the child should receive an interest deduction; the transaction should be treated as if the father made a gift to the child who then used the money to pay the interest. Treas.Reg. § 1.163–1(d), T.D. 7408, 1976–1 C.B. 48, also denies an interest deduction to the borrower when the interest is paid by the government in the form of a subsidy. Apparently, the Service takes the anomalous view that the taxpayer cannot deduct interest when he has received the wherewithal to do so in the form of welfare. It does not seem to matter in this situation whether the government pays the interest directly to the lender or to the taxpayer, who then passes it on to the lender.

87. Nelson v. Commissioner, 281 F.2d 1 (5th Cir.1960); Rushing v. Commissioner, 58 T.C. 996 (1972), acq. 1973–2 C.B. 3; Rev. Rul. 74–592, 1974–2 C.B. 47. Assuming that the amounts expended by the guarantor are not recoverable from the original debtor, the entire amount is deductible as a bad debt. See Putnam v. Commissioner, 352 U.S. 82 (1956).

he should be able to deduct all interest which he actually pays.[88] These cases are somewhat anomalous; presumably the person who pays more than his pro rata share of interest on a debt is entitled to be reimbursed by the other obligors or co-owners who have been benefited by the payment. This right of reimbursement should preclude a deduction for the portion of the interest which the taxpayer has a right to recover.[89] Moreover, the rule allowing one joint owner to deduct the entire amount of interest is inconsistent with the rules which allocate both income and net operating loss from the property equally between the joint owners.[90]

Once the property which represents the security for a debt is transferred to others, the taxpayer usually is no longer primarily liable for the interest on the underlying debt. Thus if he becomes the guarantor, rather than the primary debtor, or if he is no longer liable for the debt at all, or if he was never personally liable, he can no longer deduct interest on the obligation, even if he pays it.[91] If the taxpayer retains personal and primary liability for the debt after the security is transferred, he can continue to deduct interest on the debt.[92]

* * *

88. Lewis v. Commissioner, 65 T.C. 625 (1975); Elma M. Williams, 3 T.C. 200 (1944), acq. 1944 C.B. 30; Rose B. Larson, 44 B.T.A. 1094 (1941), acq. on this ground 1942–1 C.B. 10, aff'd on other grounds, 131 F.2d 85 (9th Cir.1942); Rev.Rul. 71–179, 1971–1 C.B. 58. If the payment is made with funds furnished by one joint owner to the other, the person furnishing the funds is entitled to the deduction. Edward C. Kohlsaat, 40 B.T.A. 528 (1939), acq. 1939–2 C.B. 21; Finney v. Commissioner, T.C. Memo. 1976–329. See Brock v. Commissioner, 59 T.C. 732 (1973), acq. 1973–2 C.B. 1, in which the owners of property were entitled to the entire deduction for interest even though the seller reserved an interest of 10% in the proceeds from resale of the property.

89. See, e.g., Estate of Elmer B. Boyd, 28 T.C. 564 (1957), in which a tenant in common paid repair costs on the property and sought to deduct them. He was permitted to deduct only half of the costs since he was entitled to reimbursement of the other half from his cotenant. See also Rev.Rul. 62–39, 1962–1 C.B. 17, in which the husband was obligated to pay alimony to the wife who was required to use a portion of the payment to pay interest on property owned by them as tenants in common. The Service held that half of the interest should be treated as alimony and half of it should be treated as a payment of interest by the husband. See also Cothran v. Commissioner, 57 T.C. 296 (1971). Rev. Rul. 62–39 emphasizes the distinction between tenancy in common and joint ownership. If the property was held jointly, rather than in common, the husband could deduct the entire payment as interest. See Rev.Rul. 62–38, 1962–1 C.B. 15 (property tax deductions on property held as tenants by the entirety allowed to husband who pays them as earmarked alimony to the wife).

90. See Oren C. White, 18 T.C. 385 (1952). *White* held that a net operating loss carryover from a farm owned as tenants by the entirety had to be equally divided between husband and wife, even though the husband had paid all of the expenditures from separate property. The court held that the rules relating to allocation of loss carryovers should be consistent with the rules requiring an even division of income from jointly held property. Noting the inconsistency of its result with cases which allow the entire interest and property tax deductions to the person who pays them, the court simply stated that the husband had failed to prove how much of the loss carryover was made up of interest and taxes.

91. Maher v. Commissioner, 55 T.C. 441, 459 (1970), supp. op. 56 T.C. 763 (1971), rev'd on other grounds, 469 F.2d 225 (8th Cir.1972); J. Simpson Dean, 35 T.C. 1083 (1961).

92. Walther v. Commissioner, 316 F.2d 708 (7th Cir.1963); Edward C. Kohlsaat, 40 B.T.A. 528 (1939), acq. 1939–2 C.B. 21.

Finally, there is an ill-defined category of cases in which the courts have allowed an interest deduction even though the taxpayer was not the primary obligor on the loan.[93] Typically, in these situations the taxpayer, rather than the obligor, has received the benefits of the loan, and the obligations of the actual obligor seem more formal than real.

* * *

NOTE

1. There is not complete correlation between what is interest for usury purposes and what is interest for income tax purposes.

> a. For example, the interest paid on a purchase money mortgage or installment land contract may not be interest for usury purposes, see pages 812 to 815 supra, but is interest for income tax purposes. Cf. Barton Beek, 80 T.C. 1024 (1983), affirmed, 754 F.2d 1442 (9th Cir.1985). On the other hand, a commitment fee may be interest for usury purposes, see pages 790 to 791 supra, but not for income tax purposes.

> b. Requiring a borrower to maintain a compensating balance with the lender may result in a violation of the usury laws in certain circumstances, see pages 789 to 790 supra, but the borrower will not be entitled to an interest deduction since no interest has been paid or accrued.

2. Can a grantee who purchases real estate subject to a mortgage deduct the interest paid or accrued on the mortgage after the grantee receives title to the real estate?

> a. A grantor is personally liable for a mortgage obligation and the mortgagee does not release the grantor upon conveyance to the grantee. The grantee, who acquired the real estate "subject to," defaults on the mortgage. The mortgagee sues the grantor and collects the remaining principal balance and interest due on the mortgage. The value of the real estate is less than the remaining principal balance of the mortgage. Can the grantor deduct the interest paid to the mortgagee?

3. A wrap-around mortgagee usually does not assume the mortgagor's obligations under the wrapped-around mortgage. Instead, the wrap-around mortgagee who advances new funds usually will make the payments called for by the wrapped-around mortgage if and when payments are made on the wrap-around mortgage. See pages 788 to 789 supra. Can the wrap-around mortgagee deduct the interest payments made on the wrapped-around mortgage?

> a. If part of the interest payment made by a wrap-around mortgagor is used by the mortgagee to make a principal payment on the wrapped-around mortgage, can the mortgagor deduct that part of the interest payment? Cf. *Barton Beek,* 80 T.C. 1024 (1983), affirmed, 754 F.2d 1442 (9th Cir.1985).

---

93. A statutory exception to the rule that the debt must be the taxpayer's is found in I.R.C. § 691(b), relating to deductions in respect to a decedent. Under § 691(b), deductions not allowable to the decedent can be taken by the estate. If the estate is not required to discharge the obli- gation, the person who acquires property subject to the obligation receives the deduction. See Estate of Pat E. Hooks, 22 T.C. 502 (1954), acq. 1955–1 C.B. 5 (beneficiary deducts interest on insurance policy loan).

    1. Is the answer to the above question affected by whether the wrap-around mortgage was incurred in a refinancing or as a result of a sale of the real estate?

    4. The Internal Revenue Service has taken the position that, in general, interest cannot be computed under a method such as the Rule of 78's which tends to artificially distort the amount of interest paid in the early years of a long-term loan. See Rev.Rul. 83–84, 1983–1 C.B. 97. In addition, the Internal Revenue Service will not allow the deduction of accrued but unpaid interest (not payable until the end of the term of the loan or the sale of the real estate securing the loan) when the loan upon which the interest accrues is nonrecourse and the value of the real estate securing the loan is less than the sum of the principal amount of the loan and the accrued but unpaid interest. See Rev. Rul. 84–5, 1984–1 C.B. 32. In fact, is the current deduction of interest which accrues but is unpaid until the end of a long-term loan a proper application of the accrual method of accounting even if there is personal liability for the payment of the loan and accrued interest? In order to avoid accrual method taxpayers borrowing from related parties who use the cash method and then taking a deduction for accrued but unpaid interest while the related party does not recognize any income until the interest is actually paid, Section 267(a)(2), in effect, puts both parties on the cash method of accounting. See generally Smith, *Accrued But Unpaid Interest—A Hot Tax Shelter Technique Under Fire*, 14 # 2 Real Est.Rev. 24 (1984); Cliff and Levine, *Interest Accrual and the Time Value of Money*, 34 Am.U.L.Rev. 107 (1984); Messinger, *Wrap–Around Mortgages; Valuations; and Interest Accruals*, 42 N.Y.U.Inst.Fed.Tax'n 22–1 (1984).

    5. Whether, and the extent to which, interest is deductible depends in large measure on the use the borrower-taxpayer makes of the borrowed funds. There are essentially five categories of expenditures which must be considered. First, the borrowed funds might be used in a trade or business which is not a passive activity. If they are so used, the interest is fully deductible. Second, the funds may be used in, or treated as having been used in, a passive activity or former passive activity. If so, the deduction of the interest is subject to the limits provided by Section 469. Third, the proceeds of the loan may be used with respect to property held for investment or to acquire or produce portfolio income. If so, in general, the deduction of the interest is limited, under Section 163(d), to the amount of net investment or portfolio income of the borrower-taxpayer. Fourth, the interest may be classified as "qualified residence" interest, as defined by Section 163(h)(3), in which case it is fully deductible. Fifth, in general, any interest which does not fall into the four prior categories is treated as personal interest and is not deductible by a borrower-taxpayer, other than a corporation, pursuant to Section 163(h)(1).

    Regulations which govern the allocation of interest expense among the categories described above have been issued by the Internal Revenue Service. See Reg.Sec. 1.163–8T. In general, the regulations provide that interest expense is to be allocated among the above categories by tracing the disbursement of the borrowed funds to specific expenditures. See Reg.Sec. 1.163–8T(a)(3). The regulations also contain rules resolving certain problem areas. For example, if funds borrowed and not borrowed are commingled in the same account, the borrowed funds are treated as expended prior to funds which were not borrowed. Or, if the proceeds of two or more loans are deposited in the same account, the proceeds are treated as expended in the order in which they were deposited. See Reg.Sec. 1.163–8T(c)(4)(i) and (ii). The regulations also contain rules for determining what portions of a loan have been repaid when the proceeds of the loan have been expended in more than one category. Finally, the regulations allocate interest incurred to acquire an interest in a pass-through entity, such as a partnership, among the assets of the entity, and interest incurred by a pass-through entity in order to make a distribution is allocated among the expenditures of the distributed proceeds. See Reg.Sec. 1.163–8T(d)(1). See Finer, *The Allocation of Interest Expense Regulations: An Overview,* 17 Colo.Law. 441 (1988).

6. See generally Berger, *Simple Interest and Complex Taxes,* 81 Colum.L. Rev. 217 (1981); McIntyre, *An Inquiry into the Special Status of Interest Payments,* 1981 Duke L.J. 765; Canellos and Kleinbard, *The Miracle of Compound Interest: Interest Deferral and Discount After 1982,* 38 Tax L.Rev. 565 (1983); Sackett, *Interest Expense Deductions Under the Tax Reform Act of 1986,* 1 # 2 Prac.Tax Law. 17 (1987); Johnson, *Is an Interest Deduction Inevitable?,* 6 Va.Tax Rev. 123 (1986); Bandy, *Of Interest,* 66 Taxes 493 (1988).

(i) INVESTMENT AND PREPAID INTEREST

The Investment Interest Limitation Under the Tax Reform Act of 1986

Paul E. Smith
16 Colorado Lawyer 39 (1987).
[footnotes omitted]

* * *

The Tax Reform Act made two primary changes to § 163(d) [the limitation on the deduction of investment interest]. First, the deduction for investment interest is limited to net investment income. Under prior law, the taxpayer was permitted to deduct the following: investment interest in an amount equal to the sum of net investment income, $10,000 (or $5,000 for married individuals filing separately) and excess expenditures attributable to net leases. Second, the concept of investment property and the definitions used to calculate net investment income [have been] refined. These definitional changes are largely designed to eliminate the overlap between § 163(d) and the new provisions concerning passive losses, qualified residence interest and personal interest. The changes also account for most of the complexity and uncertainty under the new rules.

As under prior law, excess investment interest can be carried to the next year and treated as investment interest paid or accrued in that year.

Definition of "Investment Property"

In applying § 163(d), the first task is to determine which of a taxpayer's assets constitute "property held for investment." This determination governs both whether interest expenditures are investment interest and whether income is investment income. The term "property held for investment" is defined in large part by reference to the passive loss rules under new Code § 469. It generally includes property that (1) is held other than in the ordinary course of business and (2) produces interest, dividends, annuities or royalties. Thus, the new investment interest limitations apply to interest on debt attributable to "portfolio assets," but not to interest on debt attributable to passive activities or used in a trade or business. * * *

Definition of "Investment Interest"

Subject to certain exclusions described below, the term "investment interest" is defined to include amounts that constitute "interest" otherwise allowable as a deduction [which is] "paid or accrued on indebtedness incurred or continued to purchase or carry property held for investment."

*   *   *

[I]nvestment interest does not include interest that is taken into account under the passive loss rules. The Conference Report states that interest on debt incurred to acquire an interest in a passive activity is investment interest to the extent the activity generates portfolio income. * * *

[T]he definition of investment interest assumes that indebtedness can be attributed to specific uses. * * *

Definition of "Net Investment Income"

The term "net investment income" is defined as the excess of investment income over investment expenses. Investment income is the sum of gross income from investment property plus any net gain attributable to the disposition of such property, but only to the extent such amounts are not derived from the conduct of a trade or business. Income from passive activities is excluded. * * *

The new definition of investment income makes two changes which are related to the passive loss rules. First, rental income under certain net leases, now subject to the passive loss limitations, is excluded from the definition of investment income. Second, for years 1987 through 1990, investment income is reduced by the amount of any passive losses that are deductible under the passive loss phase-in rules but that would not otherwise be allowable.

The term "investment expenses," [is] defined as deductions (other than interest) that are otherwise allowable and are directly connected with the production of investment income * * *. Expenses relating to passive activities under * * * Code § 469 are not taken into account. Also, the Conference Report indicates that investment expenses will be taken into account only to the extent they exceed the new 2 percent floor.

*   *   *

[A]ctual depletion (whether cost or percentage) and depreciation deductions are used [to calculate a taxpayer's investment expense].

Effective Date and Phase–In

The amended investment interest rules generally apply to taxable years beginning after December 31, 1986. * * * [T]he elimination of the $10,000 exclusion (or $5,000 exclusion as the case may be) is phased [in]. For taxable years beginning in calendar years 1987 through 1990, only a percentage of the deduction that would be disallowed by reason of losing the exclusion is actually disallowed. That percentage is 35 percent in 1987, 60 percent in 1988, 80 percent in 1989 and 90 percent in 1990.

* * *

NOTE

1. Section 163(d) is applicable to all taxpayers, other than corporations, and includes the shareholders of an S corporation.

2. Section 163(d) may apply to some investments in real estate.

a. It will apply to the interest paid or accrued on indebtedness incurred to acquire undeveloped real estate for speculation or investment purposes.

1. Can a taxpayer avoid the application of Section 163(d) in this instance, by electing to capitalize the interest expense under Section 266?

b. It will apply to the interest paid or accrued on indebtedness incurred to acquire or carry unimproved real estate subject to a ground lease from which the lessor is receiving income. See Reg.Sec. 1.469–2T(f) (3).

3. If a partner or an S corporation shareholder does not materially participate in the trade or business of the partnership or S corporation (or own 10% or more and actively participate if the entity is in the trade or business of operating rental real estate), the interest paid or accrued on funds the partner or S corporation shareholder borrowed to purchase an interest in the entity will be treated as part of the partner's or shareholder's passive activity loss rather than being treated as investment interest, except to the extent the entity generates net investment or portfolio income. See Falk and Dougherty, *Interest Paid or Accrued to Purchase or Carry an S Corporation or Partnership Interest: A Senate–IRS Conflict*, 65 Taxes 52 (1987).

4. As discussed in the above excerpt, subject to the five-year phase-in, investment interest is only deductible to the extent of net investment income. The excess, however, can be carried over indefinitely. Investment interest is generally defined as interest paid or accrued on indebtedness incurred or continued to purchase or carry property held for investment and specifically does not include "qualified residence" interest and interest from activities subject to the passive loss rules. See Section 163(d)(3)(A) and (B). Investment income is gross income from property held for investment and any net gain from this type of property. See Section 163(d)(4)(B). Property held for investment includes property which produces interest, dividends, annuities, or royalties not derived in the ordinary course of business and any interest in an activity involving the conduct of a trade or business which is not a passive activity and with respect to which the taxpayer does not materially participate. See Section 163(d)(5).

5. Another limitation on the deductibility of investment interest is found in Section 56(b)(1)(C). In computing an individual's alternative minimum taxable income, for the purpose of determining the applicability of the 21% tax on alternative minimum taxable income under Section 55, investment interest

is deductible only to the extent of the net investment income included in alternative minimum taxable income. Investment interest and net investment income are defined in substantially the same manner as in Section 163(d). There is, however, no phase-in with respect to the limitation on the deductibility of investment interest for the purpose of determining alternative minimum taxable income.

6. See generally Bierman and Stechel, *New Investment—Interest Rules Restrict Deductions and Pose Definitional Problems*, 46 J.Tax'n 242 (1977); Hasselback, *Tax Planning Under the Excess Investment Interest Limitation*, 6 J.Real Est.Tax'n 234 (1979); Fink, *Tax Planning for Avoiding The Limitation on Investment Interest Expense*, 59 Taxes 727 (1981); Marx, *Limitation on Investment Interest Expense*, 13 Tax Adviser 160 (1982); Bernard and Duncan, *Planning Strategies in View of the Limit on the Excess Investment Interest Carryover*, 59 J.Tax'n 152 (1983); Ludtke, Vitek and Witt, *Tax Aspects of the Formation and Initial Operation of a Real Estate Limited Partnership*, 39 Tax Law. 195 (1986).

7. Following the publication of Rev.Rul. 68–643, 1968–2 C.B. 76, which, in essence, held that prepaid interest was not deductible if its deduction would result in a material distortion of income, the Internal Revenue Service began to contest the deduction of prepaid interest.

a. Despite the Tax Court's assertion in *G. Douglas Burck*, 63 T.C. 556, (1975), affirmed, 533 F.2d 768 (2d Cir.1976) that Rev.Rul. 68–643 is only advisory and does not carry the force of law, and therefore, does not bind the court in the slightest degree, the Internal Revenue Service had great success in denying the current deduction of prepaid interest by the use of material distortion of income analysis. See e.g., *Andrew A. Sander*, 62 T.C. 469 (1974), affirmed, 536 F.2d 874 (9th Cir.1976); *Kenneth D. La Croix*, 61 T.C. 471 (1974); *James V. Cole*, 64 T.C. 1091 (1975), affirmed, 586 F.2d 747 (9th Cir.1979); *Bernard Resnik*, 66 T.C. 74 (1976), affirmed, 555 F.2d 634 (7th Cir.1977); *John N. Baird*, 68 T.C. 115 (1977).

b. In *S. Rex Lewis*, 65 T.C. 625 (1975), and *Jackson B. Howard*, 35 CCH Tax Ct.Mem. 14 (1976), the Tax Court used the "deposit" analysis and permitted the deduction of prepaid interest to the extent of the prepayment penalty. Cf. *Kenneth D. La Croix*, 61 T.C. 471 (1974); *Irwin Holtzman*, 35 CCH Tax Ct.Mem. 1088 (1976); *Alan A. Rubnitz*, 67 T.C. 621 (1977); Note, *Material Distortion of Income: A New Approach?*, 55 Neb.L.Rev. 491 (1976).

c. See generally McGuire, *What Will be the Effect of the Decisions in La Croix and Sandor on Tax Shelters?*, 42 J.Tax'n 118 (1975); Zarrow and Gordon, *Tax Court's Burck Decision: Where Does It Leave Us on the Issue of Prepaid Interest?*, 42 J.Tax'n 326 (1975); Schapiro, *Prepayments and Distortion of Income Under Cash Basis Tax Accounting*, 30 Tax L.Rev. 117 (1975); Comment, *The Prepaid Interest Deduction Viewed from the Perspective of Real Estate Transactions*, 29 Sw.L.J. 412 (1975); Weary and Wilbert, *How Does Tax Court's Retreat on Prepaid Interest Deduction Affect Taxpayers?*, 44 J.Tax'n 258 (1976).

d. The Tax Court in *S. Rex Lewis*, 65 T.C. 625 (1975), felt that the question whether the prepayment of interest constituted a material distortion of income should be determined at the partner level. The deduction of prepaid interest clearly had a substantial effect at the partnership level. The partnership's 1969 loss was $1,974.17. The partnership's 1970 loss, taking into account the prepaid interest, was $81,549.95.

In *Bernard Resnik,* 66 T.C. 74 (1976), affirmed, 555 F.2d 634 (7th Cir. 1977), when it was arguable whether the partner's share of the loss resulting from the prepayment of interest materially distorted his income, the Tax Court held that material distortion, at least initially, should be tested at the partnership level. The court found that since the partnership had earned no income and had neither paid nor incurred any other deductible expenses, the prepayment was more than a distortion of income; it was "a distortion of nonincome." Id. at 81. Once the court determined that the partnership's income was distorted, the court saw no necessity to go further and determine whether the partners' income was distorted. See *Benderson Development Co., Inc.,* 38 CCH Tax Ct.Mem. 540 (1979).

1. See Note, *The Material Distortion of Income Test as Applied to Prepaid Interest and Points Paid by Partnerships,* 1973 Duke L.J. 1318, in regard to whether such payments should be tested at the partnership or partner level. Apparently, the position of the Internal Revenue Service, relying on Reg.Sec. 1.702–1(a)(8)(ii), is that the material distortion of income test should be applied at the partnership level unless it is shown that the prepayment results in a material distortion of the income of one partner. If it does, the material distortion of income test should be applied at the partner level rather than the partnership level. Cf. Rev.Rul. 77–304, 1977–2 C.B. 59. But cf. *Bernard Resnik,* 66 T.C. 74 (1976). See Lowenstein, *Prepaid Interest— Should the Material Distortion of Income Test be Applied at the Partnership or Partner Level?,* 1 J.Real Est.Tax'n 398 (1974).

e. While the courts, in general, have limited the deductibility of prepaid interest, the Ninth Circuit Court of Appeals permitted the deduction by a cash method taxpayer of a twelve-month prepayment of rent. See *Zaninovich v. Comm'r,* 616 F.2d 429 (9th Cir.1980). See also Section 467.

8. The adoption of Section 461(g) laid to rest most of the problems with respect to the current deductibility of prepaid interest.

SENATE REPORT NO. 94–938

94th Cong.2d Sess.
101–105.
[footnotes omitted]

Interest

a. Treatment of Prepaid Interest (sec. 205(a) of the bill and sec. 461(g) of the Code)

Present law

Under the present law, a taxpayer may claim deductions in the year which is proper under the method of accounting which he uses in computing his taxable income (sec. 461). A taxpayer using the cash receipts and disbursements method of accounting may generally claim a deduction for interest paid within his taxable year (sec. 163(a)). However, if the taxpayer's method of accounting does not clearly reflect income, the Internal Revenue Service may recompute the income using the method which the Service believes clearly reflects income (sec.

446(b)). The income tax regulations also provide that, even under the cash method of accounting, an expense which results in the creation of an asset having a useful life which extends substantially beyond the close of the taxable year may be deducted only in part in the year in which payment is made.

No specific statutory provision expressly permits prepaid interest to be deducted in full when paid by a cash method taxpayer. The authority for deducting prepaid interest rests on court cases and on administrative rulings by the Service. Until the late 1960's tax-oriented investors were able to prepay as much as five years' interest with apparent approval by the courts and the Service.

In 1968, however, the Service published a revenue ruling holding that an interest prepayment by a cash-basis taxpayer for a period extending for more than 12 months beyond the end of the current taxable year will be deemed to create a material distortion of income. In such a case the interest will be allocated over the taxable years involved. Deductions for interest paid in advance for a period not in excess of 12 months after the last day of the taxable year of payment will be considered on a case-by-case basis to determine whether a material distortion of income has resulted. Recent Tax Court cases have disallowed prepaid interest deductions of taxpayers in situations where the Internal Revenue Service has relied on this ruling as authority to disallow the deduction. The Tax Court has indicated, however, that it might not be willing to disallow prepaid interest in all cases where the prepayment relates to periods extending more than 12 months beyond the end of the current taxable year.

The tax treatment of a loan requiring prepaid interest or points contrasts with the tax treatment of a discount loan under present law, although in many situations the economic substance of both transactions is similar. In a discount loan, the lender delivers to the borrower an amount which is smaller than the face amount of the loan. The difference between the face amount and the amount delivered to the borrower is the charge for his use of the borrowed funds. Under present law, a borrower on the cash method cannot deduct the entire interest element in the year in which he receives the loan proceeds. He can deduct the interest element only when and as he actually repays the face amount of the loan.

Reasons for change

Prepaid interest has been extensively used in many types of tax shelters to defer tax on income * * *. The deduction for prepaid interest has become highly important to investors seeking year-end tax losses who acquire their interests in a property (such as land, an apartment building, cattle, computers, motion pictures and the like), or in a partnership which will own the property, toward the end of the calendar year. In such cases, the investors will not be able to operate the property long enough in that taxable year to generate either income or a large amount of ordinary and necessary business expenses. Therefore, deductions arising from prepaying as much of the financing costs as possible have been central to the creation of year-end tax losses. If the investors have income from other sources, the interest deductions can be used to offset this other income (rather than offsetting income from the property itself, which will be realized in a later year). Prepaid interest thus gives a taxpayer the time value of deferring taxes on his other sources of income.

* * *

In many cases a deduction for prepaid interest can be generated without adverse cash flow consequences by borrowing more money than is needed and promptly repaying the excess as "prepaid interest."

A * * * technique used to justify larger amounts of prepaid interest within the Service's present guidelines than can be obtained under conventional financing is the "wraparound" mortgage (sometimes referred to as an all-inclusive deed of trust). Often, a farm, shopping center or other property which investors are purchasing is encumbered by an existing first mortgage. The investors execute to the seller a new purchase money obligation whose face amount includes both the unpaid balance of the first mortgage and the new financing supplied by the seller (which would ordinarily take the form of a second mortgage). The buyers agree to pay (and to prepay) interest on the face amount of the "wraparound" note, while the seller agrees to continue paying the interest on the first mortgage out of the interest payments which he receives from the buyers. Since a wraparound mortgage usually bears a higher rate of interest than the first mortgage (and in some cases the additional prepaid interest which the buyers claim on the note is negotiated as a substitute for a larger down payment), this type of arrangement has been widely used to increase the amount of interest which can be prepaid in the initial year of a purchase of property and claimed as a deduction for one year's prepaid interest within the Service's present guidelines.

The committee believes that the creation of a tax shelter with prepaid interest cannot be justified even under the cash method of accounting. The policies underlying the cash method, namely, simplicity and avoidance of complex recordkeeping or computations, do not apply to prepaid interest, which can be allocated over the term of a loan.

Under present law there is considerable uncertainty as to the deductibility of prepaid interest. Under the Tax Court's holdings, the deductibility of prepaid interest depends on a case-by-case determination. Even under the Internal Revenue Service position, a case-by-case determination must be made in all cases where interest is prepaid for a period which does not extend more than 12 months beyond the taxable year in which the prepayment is made. Consequently, a deduction of prepaid interest by the same taxpayer might be allowed in one year and perhaps not in another year. Also, prepaid interest might be deductible by one taxpayer who has a large amount of income in a given year after the deduction (so that the deduction arguably does not "distort" his income) but possibly not be deductible by another taxpayer who has little or no taxable income after taking the deduction. In the case of prepaid interest, the clear reflection of income test (under present law) should focus less on comparing the interest deduction with the taxpayer's general income stream from year to year than on matching interest and other costs of carrying a particular property against its income or loss over the term of the loan.

Explanation of provision

The committee has adopted a rule which permits a cash method taxpayer to deduct prepaid interest only in the taxable year in which (and to the extent that) the interest represents a charge for the use or forbearance of borrowed money during that period.

Under this provision of the committee amendment, if a taxpayer uses the cash receipts and disbursements method to compute his taxable income, interest which he pays and which is properly allocable to any later taxable year must be charged to capital account and treated as paid by him in the periods in which (and to the extent that) the interest represents a charge for the use or forbearance of borrowed money during each such taxable year. In determining whether an interest prepayment is properly allocable to one or more taxable years after the year of payment, the committee intends that the allocation be made to the period or periods in which the interest represents a cost of using the borrowed money in that period, regardless of whether allowing prepaid interest to be deducted when paid would materially distort the taxpayer's income in the year of payment (or the income of a partnership of which the taxpayer may be a member).

This rule applies to all taxpayers, including individuals, corporations, estates and trusts and covers interest paid for personal, business or investment purposes.

The new statutory rule relates to interest prepayments by a cash method taxpayer. It is intended to conform the tax deductibility of prepaid interest by cash method taxpayers to the rule which the committee understands to be proper under present law for interest prepayments by an accrual method taxpayer.

* * *

In adopting the new rule, the committee does not intend to change present law with regard to defining "interest." Before this provision can apply, an interest payment must be otherwise deductible as interest under present law.

In certain cases, the Treasury is authorized to treat interest payments under a variable interest rate as consisting partly of interest computed under an average level effective rate of interest and partly of an interest prepayment allocable to later years of the loan.

The amendment does not contemplate that interest will be treated as paid in level payments over the term of every loan. Thus, interest paid as part of a level constant payment (including principal and interest) will not be subject to this provision merely because the payments consist of a larger interest portion in the earlier years of the loan than in the later years.

Prepaid interest on an indebtedness secured by a "wraparound mortgage" will be subject to the general rule of this provision.

The committee does not intend the new rule to change the treatment of a discount loan under present law by a cash method taxpayer. Nor does the new rule prevent the Treasury from treating interest as paid under the terms of a discount loan rather than under a conventional loan as prepaid interest.

Points are additional interest charges which are usually paid when a loan is closed and which are generally imposed by the lender in lieu of a higher interest rate. Where points are paid as compensation for the use of borrowed money (and thus qualify as interest for tax purposes) rather than as payment for the lender's services, the points substitute for a higher stated annual interest rate. As such, points are similar to a prepayment of interest and, under the committee amendment, are to be treated as paid over the term of the loan. This rule also applies to charges similar to points, whether called a loan-processing fee or a premium charge.

The committee amendment permits points paid by a cash method taxpayer on an indebtedness incurred in connection with the purchase or improvement of (and secured by) his principal residence to be treated as paid in the taxable year of actual payment. A loan will not qualify under this exception, however, if the loan proceeds are used for purposes other than purchasing or improving the taxpayer's principal residence, or if loan proceeds secured by property other than his principal residence are used to purchase or improve his residence. The exception applies only to points on a home mortgage, and not to other interest costs on such a mortgage. A further limitation is that in order to qualify under this exception, the charging of points must reflect an established business practice in the geographical area where the loan is made, and also the deduction allowed under this exception may not exceed the number of points generally charged in the area for this type of transaction.

*   *   *

NOTE

1. Is a commitment fee subject to the provisions of Section 461(g)?

   a. Does the answer to the above question depend on the purpose of, and reasons for, the commitment fee? See *Vernon J. Cristina*, 38 CCH Tax Ct.Mem. 1093 (1979); Note, *Loan Fees: Additional Interest or "Reasonable Expenses"?*, 13 Hous.L.Rev. 773 (1976).

b. If the commitment fee is paid by the borrower in consideration of the lender's agreement to make the loan and to hold funds available to make the loan, is the fee currently deductible? See Rev.Rul. 56–136, 1956–1 C.B. 92; *John N. Baird,* 68 T.C. 115 (1977); *Duffy v. United States,* 690 F.2d 889 (Cl.Ct.1982). Cf. *Blitzer v. United States,* 684 F.2d 874 (Cl.Ct.1982). But see *Lyndell E. Lay,* 69 T.C. 421 (1977); *H.K. Francis,* 36 CCH Tax Ct. Mem. 704 (1977); *Ulysses G. Trivett, Jr.,* 36 CCH Tax Ct.Mem. 675 (1977); *Billy J. Gaines,* 45 CCH Tax Ct.Mem. 363 (1982); *Delford G. Williams,* 42 CCH Tax Ct.Mem. 1616 (1981); *Karl G. Von Muff,* 46 CCH Tax.Ct.Mem. 1185 (1983); *Martin H. Fishman,* 51 CCH Tax Ct.Mem. 738 (1986); and *Dennis H. Wetterholm,* 51 CCH Tax Ct.Mem. 988 (1986).

Revenue Rul. 81–160, 1981–1 C.B. 312 revoked Rev.Rul. 56–136 and required the ratable deduction of a commitment fee over the term of the loan for which it was paid. Revenue Rul. 81–161, 1981–1 C.B. 313 provided that a commitment fee for a permanent loan must be capitalized and amortized over the term of the permanent loan. See Neuman and Elfman, *The Tax Treatment of Loan Commitment Fees After Rev.Ruls. 81–160 and 81–161,* 60 Taxes 394 (1982). In addition, even if a commitment fee is held not to be an expense incurred to acquire an asset, the loan, it is usually incurred and paid prior to, or during, construction and since the developer has not yet put the assets to be, or being, constructed to use in producing income, the Internal Revenue Service will deny a current deduction for the commitment fee using the preopening expense concept, Section 195, since the developer was not engaged in a trade or business at the time the fee was incurred and paid. See *Richard C. Goodwin,* 75 T.C. 424 (1980).

2. Does Section 461(g) apply if the terms of a loan provide for no amortization of principal for the first five years and the payment of interest during that period at the rate of 10% per annum, and then, for the remaining twenty years of the loan, constant amortization of principal and interest is provided for and interest will be paid at the rate of 9% per annum during this period?

3. Senate Report No. 938 refers to a wrap-around mortgage in the part of the Report setting out the reasons for the adoption of Section 461(g). Certainly, if a wrap-around mortgagor prepays the interest on a wrap-around mortgage, Section 461(g) applies. Does Senate Report No. 938 go beyond this simple assertion?

a. A taxpayer who owns real estate valued at $250,000 which is subject to a mortgage with a remaining principal balance of $100,000, a remaining term of 10 years, an interest rate of 8% and which provides for equal installment payments of principal and interest, refinances using a wrap-around mortgage of $200,000 with a term of 30 years, an interest rate of 13% and which also provides for equal installment payments. During the early years of the wrap-around mortgage some of the interest paid by the mortgagor will be used by the mortgagee to pay part of the principal on the underlying mortgage. The interest so used is usually considered as earned but deferred by the wrap-around mortgagee and will be recovered by the wrap-around mortgagee out of later installment payments made on the wrap-around mortgage. Is the mortgagor subject to Section 461(g) with respect to that part of the interest paid on the wrap-around mortgage which is considered as earned but deferred by the wrap-around mortgagee?

4. If lenders in a geographic area did not, prior to the enactment of Section 461(g), charge points with respect to home mortgages, will points

charged after the adoption of Section 461(g) be deductible if all of the lenders in the area now get together and decide to charge points? Is such an agreement by all of the lenders in a geographic area a violation of the antitrust laws?

5. See generally Sexton, *Elimination of the Prepaid Interest Deduction by the TRA 1976 Analyzed*, 46 J.Tax'n 146 (1977); Note, *The Deductibility of Commitment Fees, Financing Fees, and "Points"*, 31 Tax Law. 888 (1978).

6. Section 461(i), in a manner similar to Section 461(g), prevents a "tax shelter" from deducting any item earlier than the point in time at which economic performance occurs with respect to that item. In general, a tax shelter cannot deduct any prepaid expenses and cannot use the cash method of accounting. See Sections 448(a)(3) and 461(i).

(ii) COMMITMENT FEES, POINTS AND OTHER MISCELLANEOUS CHARGES

Many lenders in today's market charge borrowers points, commitment fees, service fees and other types of miscellaneous "front-end" charges. These charges are frequently imposed in order to increase the lender's return from the loan. The treatment of these charges for income tax purposes is of concern to both the borrower and lender.

REVENUE RULING 69–188
1969–1 Cum.Bull. 54.

*   *   *

A taxpayer on the cash receipts and disbursements method of accounting who wished to purchase a building, arranged with a lender to finance the transaction. A conventional mortgage loan of $1,000x$ dollars was negotiated, secured by a deed of trust on the building, and repayable in monthly installments over a ten-year period at a stated annual interest rate of 7.2 percent. In addition to the annual interest rate the parties agreed that the borrower would pay a "loan processing fee" of $70x$ dollars (sometimes referred to as "points") prior to receipt of the loan proceeds. The borrower established that this fee was not paid for any specific services that the lender had performed or had agreed to perform in connection with the borrower's account under the loan contract. The loan agreement provided for separate charges for these services. *   *   *

In determining the amount of this "loan processing fee" the lender considered the economic factors that usually dictate an acceptable rate of interest. That is, he considered the general availability of money, the character of the property offered as security, the degree of success that the borrower had enjoyed in his prior business activities, and the outcome of previous transactions between the borrower and his creditors.

The taxpayer tendered a check for $70x$ dollars drawn on a bank account owned by him, which contained a sufficient balance, in payment of the fee. The monies in this account were not originally obtained from the lender.

Section 163(a) of the * * * Code * * * provides that there shall be allowed as a deduction all interest paid or accrued within the taxable year on indebtedness.

Section 446(a) of the Code provides that taxable income shall be computed under the method of accounting on the basis of which the taxpayer regularly computes his income in keeping his books. Section 446(b) of the Code provides, in part, that if the method used does not clearly reflect income, the computation of taxable income shall be made under such method as, in the opinion of the Secretary of the Treasury or his delegate, does clearly reflect income.

For tax purposes, interest has been defined by the Supreme Court of the United States as the amount one has contracted to pay for the use of borrowed money, and as the compensation paid for the use or forbearance of money. * * * A negotiated bonus or premium paid by a borrower to a lender in order to obtain a loan has been held to be interest for Federal income tax purposes. L–R Heat Treating Co. v. Commissioner, 28 T.C. 894 (1957).

The payment or accrual of interest for tax purposes must be incidental to an unconditional and legally enforceable obligation of the taxpayer claiming the deduction. Paul Aulenreith v. Commissioner, 115 F.2d 856 (1940). There need not, however, be a legally enforceable indebtedness already in existence when the payment of interest is made. It is sufficient that the payment be a "prerequisite to obtaining borrowed capital." *L–R Heat Treating Co.* The fee of 70x dollars in the instant case was paid prior to the receipt of the borrowed funds; however, this does not preclude the payment from being classified as interest.

It is not necessary that the parties to a transaction label a payment made for the use of money as interest for it to be so treated. See *L–R Heat Treating Co.* The mere fact that the parties in the instant case agreed to call the 70x dollars a "loan processing fee" does not in itself preclude this payment from being interest under section 163(a) of the Code. Further, this conclusion would not be affected by the fact that this payment is sometimes referred to as "points." * * *

The method of computation also does not control its deductibility, so long as the amount in question is an ascertainable sum contracted for the use of borrowed money. See Kena, Inc. v. Commissioner, 44 B.T.A. 217 (1941). The fact that the amount paid in the instant case is a flat sum paid in addition to a stated annual interest rate does not preclude a deduction under section 163 of the Code.

To qualify as interest for tax purposes, the payment, by whatever name called, must be compensation for the use or forbearance of money per se and not a payment for specific services which the lender performs in connection with the borrower's account. For example, interest would not include separate charges made for investigating the prospective borrower and his security, closing costs of the loan and papers drawn in connection therewith, or fees paid to a third party for servicing and collecting that particular loan. See Workingmen's Loan Ass'n v. United States, 142 F.2d 359 (1944); Rev.Rul. 57–541, C.B. 1957–2, 319. Compare Revenue Ruling 57–540, C.B. 1957–2, 318, relating to the classification as interest of the fees imposed on borrowers by a mortgage finance company. Also, even where service charges are not stated separately on the borrower's account, interest would not include amounts attributable to such services. See Rev.Rul. 67–297; compare Norman L. Noteman, et al., Trustees v. Welch, 108 F.2d 206 (1939) relating to the classification as interest of the charges paid by borrowers to a personal finance company.

Accordingly, in the instant case, because the taxpayer was able to establish that the fee of 70x dollars was paid as compensation to the lender solely for the use or forbearance of money, and because he did not initially obtain the funds to pay this fee from the lender, the 70x dollars is considered to be interest.

NOTE

1. Loan processing fees paid by a borrower, according to Rev.Rul. 69–188, supra, can be considered interest when the lender, in determining the amount of the fees, considers the economic factors that usually dictate an acceptable rate of interest.

a. Under Section 461(g), the loan processing fees will be treated as prepaid interest or points and must be capitalized and amortized over the term of the loan or the period of the loan to which they are applicable.

b. Might the analysis used in Rev.Rul. 69–188, supra, apply in some situations to a "commitment fee"—a fee charged the borrower by the lender at the time of the lender's agreement to make the requested loan to the borrower? Does the answer to the above question depend on how the borrower and lender view the purpose of the fee?

1. Many times, the lender and the borrower regard the fee as the consideration for the lender's agreement to make the loan, and a charge by the lender for keeping the funds available to loan to the borrower.

In this situation, since the amount of the fee is not determined by considering the economic factors which usually dictate an acceptable rate of interest, the fee is not interest but consideration for the lender's commitment. As consideration for the lender's commitment it might be asserted that the fee is an ordinary and necessary business expense currently deductible under Section 162. See e.g. Rev.Rul. 56–136, 1956–1 C.B. 92; Rev.Rul. 70–540, 1970–2 C.B. 101, as amplified by Rev. Rul. 74–607, 1974–2 C.B. 149; Rev.Rul. 74–258, 1974–1 C.B. 168; Priv. Ltr.Ruls. 7809011 and 7924002; *John N. Baird,* 68 T.C. 115 (1977); *Donald Wilkerson,* 70 T.C. 240 (1978), reversed, 655 F.2d 980 (9th Cir. 1986). But cf. *Vernon J. Cristina,* 38 CCH Tax Ct.Mem. 1093 (1979).

2. The Internal Revenue Service, however, currently takes the position that a commitment fee, in the situation described above, is a cost of acquiring the loan committed for and must be amortized over the term of the loan. See Rev.Rul. 81–160, 1981–1 C.B. 312, revoking Rev.Rul. 56–136; Rev.Rul. 81–161, 1981–1 C.B. 313; Priv.Ltr.Rul.

8138092; *Delford G. Williams,* 42 CCH Tax Ct.Mem. 1616 (1981); *Billy J. Gaines,* 45 CCH Tax Ct.Mem. 363 (1982); *Karl G. Von Muff,* 46 CCH Tax Ct.Mem. 1185 (1983); *Martin H. Fishman,* 51 CCH Tax Ct.Mem. 738 (1986); *Dennis H. Wetterholm,* 51 CCH Tax Ct.Mem. 988 (1986). The Claims Court, in a few cases, has permitted the current deduction of commitment fees. See *Duffy v. United States,* 231 Ct.Cl. 679, 690 F.2d 889 (1982); *Blitzer v. United States,* 231 Ct.Cl. 236, 684 F.2d 874 (1982).

On the other hand, it might be asserted that a commitment fee, in the situation described above, should be capitalized and amortized over the term of the commitment, as a cost of acquiring the commitment. See *Julia Lovejoy,* 18 B.T.A. 1179 (1930); *Parks v. United States,* 434 F.Supp. 206 (N.D.Tex.1977); *Ulysses G. Trivett, Jr.,* 36 CCH Tax Ct. Mem. 675 (1977). In *Lyndell E. Lay,* 69 T.C. 421 (1977), the taxpayer allowed the commitment, for which the fee was paid, to expire, but the Tax Court required the fee to be capitalized and amortized over the term of the loans which were eventually obtained by the taxpayer.

3. Even if a commitment fee, in the situation described above, is regarded as an ordinary and necessary expense, it is usually paid prior to the start of construction. When the fee is paid, is the borrower taxpayer engaged in trade or business so that the fee may be deducted under Section 162 or must the fee be capitalized and amortized, under Section 195, as a preopening expense? See Priv.Ltr.Rul. 7842007; *H.K. Francis,* 36 CCH Tax Ct.Mem. 704 (1977). While the Internal Revenue Service has persuaded the Tax Court to apply the preopening expense concept to commitment fees, see *Richard C. Goodwin,* 75 T.C. 424 (1980), affirmed, 691 F.2d 490 (3d Cir.1982), it has had less success in the federal court system. See *Duffy v. United States,* 231 Ct.Cl. 679, 690 F.2d 889 (1982); *Blitzer v. United States,* 231 Ct.Cl. 236, 684 F.2d 874 (1982). Since, however, Section 195(c)(2)(A) provides that the determination of when active trade or business begins is to be made in accordance with the regulations, the Internal Revenue Service will eventually prevail on this issue.

a. If the current deduction of a commitment fee is disallowed because it is a preopening expense, the amount of the fee can be amortized over 60 months from the start of business, under Section 195. If, however, the deduction is disallowed because the fee is a cost of acquiring a loan, the fee must be amortized over the term of the loan.

4. If a commitment fee, in the situation described above, must be capitalized and amortized over the term of the acquired loan, should a commitment fee for a construction loan be amortized over the term of the construction loan or over the combined terms of the construction loan and the permanent loan? Does the answer to the above question depend on whether the same lender made both loans or, if the loans are made by different lenders, whether the permanent lender purchased the construction loan? See *Aboussie v. United States,* 779 F.2d 424 (8th Cir.1985).

a. If the commitment fee for a construction loan is amortized over the term of the construction loan, must the amount amortized each year be capitalized and amortized pursuant to Section 195 since no trade or business is conducted during the construction period?

　　b.　Can a commitment fee for a construction loan be treated as an indirect cost of construction and, if Section 263A is otherwise applicable, be capitalized pursuant to Section 263A?

　　c.　If part, or all, of a loan processing fee or commitment fee is used to pay the lender's closing costs, how should the fee be treated for income tax purposes? See e.g. *John R. Parks v. United States,* 434 F.Supp. 206 (N.D. Tex.1977); *Lyndell E. Lay,* 69 T.C. 421 (1977); *Planned Communities, Inc.,* 41 CCH Tax Ct.Mem. 552 (1980).

　　d.　If, in addition to a loan processing fee and/or commitment fee, the borrower is obligated to and pays all of the lender's closing costs, is the amount of the closing costs currently deductible by the borrower? See Rev. Rul. 70–360, 1970–2 C.B. 103; Rev.Rul. 75–172, 1975–1 C.B. 145. Cf. *Doehring v. Comm'r,* 527 F.2d 945 (8th Cir.1975), reversing, 33 CCH Tax Ct. Mem. 1035 (1974).

　　1.　Is not the payment of the lender's closing costs clearly a cost of acquiring the loan?

　　2.　If a lessor required, as a condition to entering into a lease of certain real estate, that the lessee assume an existing mortgage on the real estate, can the lessee treat the remaining principal balance of the mortgage as a cost of acquiring the leasehold and amortize the remaining principal balance over the term of the lease? Will the remaining principal balance of the mortgage be considered income to the lessor? If so, when will it be considered income to the lessor and will it be considered rental or some other type of income? Do the answers to the above questions change if the lease is subordinate to the mortgage and the lessee does not assume the mortgage? As a practical matter, if the lessor does not pay the mortgage, the lessee, in order to preserve the leasehold, may be required to.

　　2.　Does it make any difference if a loan processing fee, commitment fee or service charge to pay the lender's closing costs is withheld by the lender from the loan proceeds and the borrower only receives the net proceeds of the loan? See Rev.Rul. 70–360, 1970–2 C.B. 103; Rev.Rul. 75–12, 1975–1 C.B. 62; *Kenneth A. Cathcart,* 36 CCH Tax Ct.Mem. 1321 (1977); *Herbert W. Dustin,* 36 CCH Tax Ct.Mem. 1654 (1977); *Parks v. United States,* 434 F.Supp. 206 (N.D.Tex.1977).

　　3.　See generally Note, *Loan Fees: Additional Interest or "Reasonable Expense",* 13 Hous.L.Rev. 773 (1976); Note, *The Deductibility of Commitment Fees, Financing Fees, and "Points",* 31 Tax'n Law. 888 (1978); Jarchow, *Deducting Front–End Loan Costs,* 9 # 3 Real Est.Rev. 56 (1979); Malloy and Hayes, *Deductibility of "Commitment Fees": Are They for Services or for the Use of Money?,* 51 J.Tax'n 278 (1979); Feder, *Financing Real Estate Construction: The IRS Challenge to Construction Period Deductions,* 8 J.Real Est.Tax'n 3 (1980); Neuman and Elfman, *The Tax Treatment of Loan Commitment Fees After Rev. Ruls. 81–160 and 81–161,* 60 Taxes 394 (1982); Lane, *Pre–Opening Expenditures; Organizational and Syndication Costs, Construction Period Interest and Taxes, and Loan Acquisition Costs,* 42 N.Y.U.Inst.Fed.Tax'n 21–1 (1984); Hoops, *Tax Problems of Development and Construction,* 44 N.Y.U.Inst.Fed.Tax'n 18–1 (1986).

(iii) CONSTRUCTION PERIOD INTEREST

Another form of interest which receives special treatment under the Internal Revenue Code is construction period interest. Section 189, which was added to the Internal Revenue Code by the Tax Reform Act of 1976, provided for the capitalization and amortization, over a ten-year period, of most of construction period interest. Section 189 was repealed by the Tax Reform Act of 1986 and the treatment of construction period interest was made part of Section 263A, which the Tax Reform Act of 1986 added to the Internal Revenue Code.

GENERAL EXPLANATION OF THE TAX REFORM ACT OF 1986

Joint Committee on Taxation.
Comm. Print 1987 501–512.
[some footnotes omitted]

* * *

Prior Law

In general

Under both present and prior law, producers of property generally may not deduct currently the costs incurred in producing the property. Rather, such costs must be capitalized and recovered through an offset to sales price if the property is produced for sale, or through depreciation or amortization if the property is produced for the taxpayer's own use in a business or investment activity. * * *

Interest and taxes incurred during construction

Under prior law, interest and taxes incurred by a taxpayer during construction or improvement of real property (other than low-income housing) to be used or held for sale in a trade or business or used in an activity for profit generally were required to be capitalized and amortized over 10 years (sec. 189). The construction period commenced with the date on which construction of the building or other improvement began and ended on the date it was ready to be placed in service or held for sale.

The legislative history of amendments to section 189 indicated Congress' intention that the Treasury Department issue regulations allocating interest to expenditures for real property during construction consistent with the method prescribed by Financial Accounting Standards Board Statement Number 34 (FAS 34). Under FAS 34, the amount of interest to be capitalized is the portion of the total interest expense incurred during the construction period that could have been avoided if funds had not been expended for construction. Interest expense that could have been avoided included interest costs incurred by reason of additional borrowings to finance construction, and interest costs incurred by reason of borrowings that could have been repaid with funds expended for construction.

* * *

Reasons for Change

The Congress believed that the rules of prior law regarding the capitalization of costs incurred in producing property were deficient in two respects. First, those rules allowed costs that were in reality costs of producing, acquiring, or carrying property to be deducted currently, rather than capitalized into the basis of the property and recovered when the property was sold or as it was used by the taxpayer. This treatment produced a mismatching of expenses and the related income and an unwarranted deferral of Federal income taxes. Second, different capitalization rules could apply depending on the nature of the property and its intended use. The Congress was concerned that these differences could create distortions in the allocation of economic resources and the manner in which certain economic activity was organized.

The Congress believed that, in order to more accurately reflect income and make the income tax system more neutral, a single, comprehensive set of rules should govern the capitalization of costs of producing, acquiring, and holding property, including interest expense, subject to appropriate exceptions where application of the rules might be unduly burdensome.

Explanation of Provisions

Overview

In general, the Act applies a single set of capitalization rules (the "uniform capitalization rules") to all costs incurred in manufacturing or constructing tangible property. * * * Interest costs are subject to capitalization only where the interest is allocable to construction of real property or to production of personal property that is long-lived property or requires an extended period to produce.

* * *

Uniform capitalization rules

In general

Under the Act, uniform capitalization rules to be prescribed by the Treasury Department govern the inclusion in inventory or capital accounts of all costs which are (1) incurred in manufacturing, construction, and other types of activities involving the production of real or tangible personal property, or (2) incurred in acquiring or holding property (whether tangible or intangible) for resale. Thus, the rules apply to assets or improvements to assets constructed by a taxpayer for its own use in a trade or business or in an activity engaged in for profit and to assets, whether manufactured or purchased, to be held by a taxpayer in inventory or for sale to customers in the ordinary course of business.

* * *

Interest expense

Under the Act, interest paid or incurred during the production period of certain types of property that is allocable to the production of the property must be capitalized.[94] Property subject to the interest capitalization requirement includes property produced by the taxpayer for use in its trade or business or in an activity for profit, but only if it (1) is real property, (2) has an estimated production period exceeding two years (one year if the cost of the property exceeds $1 million), or (3) has a class life of 20 years or more under Code section 168 as amended by the Act.[95] The production period of property for this purpose begins when construction or production is commenced and ends when the property is ready to be placed in service or is ready to be held for sale. * * * Activities such as planning or design generally do not cause the production period to begin.

The determination of whether interest is allocable to the production of property is made under rules similar to the "avoided cost" principles applicable under section 189 of prior law.[96] Under those rules, any interest expense that the taxpayer would have avoided if production expenditures had been used to repay debt of the taxpayer is treated as allocable to production of property. Accordingly, under the Act, any debt that can be specifically traced to production expenditures is first allocated to production and interest on such debt is capitalized. If production expenditures exceed the amount of the specifically traceable debt, interest on other debt of the taxpayer must be capitalized to the extent of the excess. For this purpose, the assumed interest rate is an average of the rates on the taxpayer's outstanding debt, excluding debt specifically traceable to production or construction.

The term "production expenditures" for purposes of the interest allocation rule means cumulative production costs required to be capitalized, including interest required to be capitalized as a production cost

---

94. Section 189 of prior law also required capitalization of real property taxes. Under the Act, taxes that are properly allocable to such property (for example, income taxes) are subject to capitalization (or inclusion in inventory) to the same extent as other types of costs. Capitalization of interest is not required in the case of property acquired for resale (i.e., inventory held by a dealer).

95. Where property is constructed by another for a taxpayer under a contract, interest could be subject to capitalization by the taxpayer under the rule that treats the taxpayer as the producer of the property.

96. The avoided cost method of determining the amount of interest allocable to

production was intended to apply irrespective of whether application of such method (or a similar method) is required, authorized, or considered appropriate under financial or regulatory accounting principles applicable to the taxpayer. Thus, for example, a regulated utility company must apply the avoided cost method of determining capitalized interest even though a different method is authorized or required by Financial Accounting Standards Board Statement 34 or the regulatory authority having jurisdiction over the utility. No inference was intended that the avoided cost method was not required in such circumstances under section 189 of prior law.

for prior periods. Where an asset is used in the production of property, interest on the entire cost of that asset must be capitalized as part of the production costs of that property whether or not the entire cost of the asset previously has been reflected in the property account.

The interest allocable to that cost is to be determined under the general rules for allocating debt (i.e., the "specific tracing allocation method" on debt directly allocable to the asset and the "avoided cost allocation method" on other debt). Where an asset is used for other purposes in addition to the production of property, only an allocable portion of the allocable interest costs must be capitalized as part of the production costs of the property.

In the case of partnerships or other flow-through entities, the allocation rules are applied first at the entity level and then (to the extent the entity has insufficient debt to support the full amount of the production expenditures) at the partner or beneficiary level.[97]

The Treasury Department is authorized to issue regulations to prevent the avoidance of these rules through the use of related parties, pass-through entities, or intermediaries. For example, such regulations could provide that where a subsidiary corporation is owned by two 50–percent parent corporations, and the subsidiary is engaged in constructing long-lived property for its own use, but has no outstanding debt, each 50–percent parent is required to capitalize interest expense as if each had directly incurred one-half of the construction expenditures incurred by the subsidiary.

If a taxpayer has property produced for it by another under a contract, the taxpayer is treated as producing the property for purposes of the uniform capitalization rules, including the interest capitalization rule. Thus, the portion of the taxpayer's interest expense allocable to costs required to be capitalized (including progress payments, advances to the contractor, and an allocable portion of the general and administrative expenses of the taxpayer) must be charged to a capital account.

The Act exempts from the interest capitalization rule interest that is qualified residence interest within the meaning of section 163(h), as amended by the Act.

* * *

NOTE

1. Construction period interest must be added to the basis (capitalized) of the real estate improvements constructed. It is then recovered by the taxpayer according to the cost recovery method applicable to the improvements constructed. Section 263A is applicable to all taxpayers.

2. Interest costs paid or incurred during the construction period which are allocable to the improvements constructed must be capitalized. See Section 263A(f)(1). It, therefore, becomes important to determine when the construc-

---

97. Interest of the partner (beneficiary) that must be capitalized under this rule may be recovered by the partner (beneficiary), under regulations issued by the Secretary of the Treasury, at the same time and to the same extent as if the interest had been paid or incurred directly by the partnership.

tion period begins. The latest point at which the period could begin is when actual construction of the real estate improvement is undertaken. The Internal Revenue Service, however, has not been as charitable in defining the beginning of construction for the purposes of Section 341. See Rev.Rul. 56–137, 1956–1 C.B. 178, in which filing an application for rezoning and litigating the propriety of the rezoning constituted construction. See generally Cook, *Determining "When Construction Period Begins" Key to Realty Deductions Under 189*, 47 J.Tax'n 8 (1977). The regulations issued under Section 263A indicate that, as a general rule, planning and design activities are incurred before the construction period commences. See Reg.Sec. 1.263A–1T(b)(2)(iv)(B). Notice 88–99, 1988–36 I.R.B. 29 indicates that, for the purposes of Section 263A, construction begins when physical activity is first performed on the real estate. For example, grading of the real estate in anticipation of the construction of a building on the real estate may mark the beginning of the construction period.

3. After the beginning of the construction period has been ascertained, the end of the construction period must be determined. Section 263A(f)(4)(B)(ii) provides that the period ends when the "property is ready to be placed in service or is ready to be held for sale."

a. In many situations, the receipt of the certificate of occupancy for the improvements constructed should mark the end of the construction period. In other situations, however, construction may continue on part of an improvement or project while another part is put into service. For example, on many occasions an office building will be used by the tenants while interior construction is still going on with respect to the restaurant on the top floor or the parking area in the basement, or some units in an apartment complex may be occupied by the tenants while other units are still under construction, or stores at one location in a shopping plaza may be occupied while construction is still being carried on with respect to the interior of other stores or the parking lot or with regard to the landscaping.

4. What constitutes construction in order for there to be a construction period and construction period interest under Section 263A?

a. Construction includes reconstruction and at least certain types of renovation. See Rev.Rul. 63–114, 1963–1 C.B. 74 and Rev.Rul. 72–422, 1972–2 C.B. 211.

b. Construction, for the purposes of Section 263A, does not include repair. Where, however, is the line drawn between construction and repair? Current maintenance falls on the repair side, but what if the work undertaken is somewhat more than just maintenance? See *Moss v. Comm'r*, 831 F.2d 833 (9th Cir.1987). Cf. Rev.Rul. 63–114, 1963–1 C.B. 74 and Rev.Rul. 72–422, 1972–2 C.B. 211.

5. When computing the earnings and profits of a corporation for income tax purposes, construction period interest is not deductible and must be capitalized into the basis of the property constructed. See Section 312(n)(1). In addition, depreciation of real property improvements is limited to the use of the straight-line method over a term of 40 years. See Section 312(k).

6. See generally Comment, *The Deductibility of Real Estate Acquisition and Construction Expenses*, 11 Cumb.L.Rev. 689 (1980); Jones and Cole, *Construction Period Taxes and Interest*, 12 Tax Adviser 532 (1981); Lane, *Pre-Opening Expenditures; Organizational and Syndication Costs, Construction Period Interest and Taxes, and Loan Acquisition Costs*, 42 N.Y.U.Inst.Fed.Tax'n

21-1 (1984); Hoops, *Tax Problems of Development and Construction*, 44 N.Y.U. Inst.Fed.Tax'n 18-1 (1986).

(iv) ORIGINAL ISSUE DISCOUNT AND UNSTATED INTEREST

The owner of real estate, when selling the real estate in part for a deferred payment obligation of the purchaser, may choose to have a low interest rate stated in the deferred payment obligation and increase the principal amount of the obligation somewhat to make up for the low interest rate.

The hoped for results of this approach are to decrease the amount which the seller of the real estate must treat as interest income and increase the amount treated as received by the seller for the real estate. Correspondingly, the purchaser must reduce the amount treated as an interest expense and increase the amount of the basis of the real estate. These adjustments take place while the amount of dollars passing from the purchaser to seller stays about the same. Congress has found unacceptable the ability of taxpayers to cause these adjustments to be made without any significant change in the amount of dollars paid by the purchaser to the seller.

Original issue discount can also arise in a lending transaction. For example, a lending institution charges a borrower five points to make the borrower a $500,000 loan. Instead of requiring the borrower to pay $25,000 to the lender on disbursement of the proceeds of the $500,000 loan, the lender disburses $475,000 to the borrower in return for the borrower's note of $500,000. In this way the borrower hopes to obtain a current deduction for the $25,000 and the lender, using the cash method, hopes to avoid treating the $25,000 as income until the loan is paid. In order to deal with the simple examples illustrated above and their more sophisticated siblings and cousins, Congress enacted the original issue discount and imputed interest rules.

The Time Value of Money Rules

Lawrence Lokken
42 Tax Law Review 1 (1986).
[most footnotes omitted]

* * *

Original Issue Discount

Introductory

A debt instrument bears original issue discount (OID) if the face amount of the instrument (the stated redemption price at maturity) exceeds the price paid on original issue (the issue price). Section 1272 requires that the holder of an obligation issued at a discount report OID as gross income as it accrues over the instrument's term. Section 163(e) allows the issuer to deduct OID accruals, subject to the usual limitations on the interest deduction.

This matching of the recognition of OID by issuer (borrower) and holder (lender) is an important aspect of the present regime. * * *

Another fundamental aspect of the present rules is that OID accruals are computed on a constant interest basis. That is, the OID accrual in each period is computed so that the holder's investment return (consisting of OID and any stated interest) is an unchanging percentage of unpaid principal. For this purpose, unpaid principal includes both the original issue price and accrued but unpaid OID. On a constant interest basis, OID thus usually accrues in ever increasing amounts to reflect the gradual build-up of principal.

* * *

The rules apply both to instruments issued for cash and to many obligations issued in sales and exchanges of property. * * *

Debt Instrument

Sections 163(e) and 1271 through 1275 apply to debt instruments. The statute defines the term "debt instrument" to include any "bond, debenture, note, or certificate or other evidence of indebtedness." [98] * * *

Issue Price

The term "original issue discount" refers to an excess of the "stated redemption price at maturity" over the "issue price." [99] If a $100 bond is issued for $90, for example, OID is $10. The stated redemption price at maturity usually consists of the principal amount stated in the instrument. The issue price * * * is generally the amount received by the issuer when the instrument is issued. * * *

Instruments Issued for Cash

If an instrument issued for cash is "not publicly offered," the issue price is "the price paid by the first buyer." [100] * * * This rule * * * applies to instruments that are not usually thought of as securities, including notes given and received in ordinary lending transactions.

Points and other cash payments from borrower to lender on the origination of a loan, for example, are often treated as OID. * * *

If a seller of property pays points to the buyer's mortgage lender, the rules are applied by treating the payment as made by the buyer-borrower. * * *

---

98. I.R.C. § 1275(a)(1)(A). See also I.R.C. § 163(e)(2)(A).

99. I.R.C. § 1273(a)(1).

100. I.R.C. § 1273(b)(2). The term "price paid by the first buyer" includes "the aggregate payments made by the purchaser under the purchase agreement, including modifications thereof." I.R.C. § 1273(c)(1).

* * *

Instruments Issued in Sales and Exchanges of Property

If a debt instrument is issued in a sale or exchange of property and neither the instrument nor the property received in exchange is traded on an established securities market, one of [the following] regimes applies to the instrument.

Section 1274 applies to such an instrument if (1) any payment under the instrument is due more than six months after the instrument is issued, (2) the total of the payments under the instrument is at least $250,000, and (3) none of several exceptions applies. Section 1274 is an elaborate mechanism for determining the issue price. If it applies, the issue price fixed by that provision is used in computing OID, and the OID, if any, is reported by the parties under the general rules for OID.

*   *   *

If section 1274 does not apply, the instrument might be governed by section 483. Section 483 provides an independent set of imputed interest rules for instruments within its orbit. It applies to most obligations received in sales and exchanges of property that are not governed by section 1274. Section 483, like the OID rules, requires that imputed interest be allocated over an instrument's term by compounding on a constant interest basis. The principal difference between section 483 and the OID rules is that imputed interest is recognized under section 483 only as payments are received, whereas OID is recognized as it accrues even if no payments are made. *   *   *

Original Issue Discount (OID)

Once an instrument's "stated redemption price at maturity" and "issue price" have been established, computation of total OID on the instrument is usually easy. OID is simply the excess of stated redemption price at maturity over the issue price.[101] If the stated redemption price is $1,000 and the issue price is $900, for example, OID is $100.

*   *   *

Under section 1272(a)(1), a holder of a debt instrument issued at a discount after July 1, 1982 is taxed annually on OID. More specifically, the holder must include in gross income "the sum of the daily portions of the original issue discount for each day during the taxable year on which such holder held such debt instrument."[102] Section 163(e)(1) allows the issuer of such an instrument an annual deduction for "the aggregate daily portions of the original issue discount for days during such taxable year."

The rules defining "daily portions" are the heart of the system requiring the accrual of OID on a constant interest basis. They require that an interest rate be computed representing the yield on the instrument from the date of issue to maturity. This yield includes both stated interest and OID. The yield rate is applied periodically to an increasing principal amount consisting of the sum of the original issue

---

101. I.R.C. § 1273(a)(1).   **102.** I.R.C. § 1272(a)(1).

price and accrued but unpaid OID. The amount so computed for a particular period, reduced by the stated interest payable during the period, is the accrual of OID for the period.

* * *

Sections 483 and 1274

Introductory

Sections 483 and 1274 establish two alternative interest imputation schemes for debt instruments issued in sales and exchanges of property.[103] Section 1274 is the general rule; it applies to a note issued in a sale or exchange unless the note is excepted from its application. Section 483 applies to most notes excepted from section 1274. The exceptions are numerous, but the two most general are exceptions for (1) a note issued in a transaction where the sum of all of the payments does not exceed $250,000 and (2) a note for $2 million or less where the parties elect to have section 483 apply instead of section 1274.

When section 1274 applies, * * * OID is imputed unless the instrument bears interest at least equal to a market measure of interest called the applicable Federal rate (AFR). When OID is imputed, its amount is calculated so that the instrument's yield, including stated interest and OID, equals the AFR.

Secton 483 differs in terminology, but yields a similar result. When it applies, an interest equivalent called unstated interest is imputed unless the instrument bears interest at an annual rate at least equal to a test rate. Most commonly, the test rate is the lesser of the AFR or 9%. When a note subject to sections 483 bears no interest or bears interest at a rate less than the test rate, unstated interest is imputed in an amount sufficient to raise the yield to the test rate.

The principal difference between sections 483 and 1274 is that the former operates on a cash basis, while the latter is an accrual regime. When section 1274 applies, both parties report OID year by year as it accrues, even in years in which the accruals exceed the payments.

* * *

Unstated interest under section 483, in contrast, is gross income to the seller (the holder of the note) and is deductible by the buyer (the obligor) only as payments are made. Interest accruals are computed in essentially the same way as they are under section 1274, but are not reported by the parties until payment occurs. Generally, each payment is interest to the extent of the accruals since the last payment. * * *

Section 1274

Under section 1274, if an obligation issued in a sale or exchange of property does not bear adequate stated interest, a portion of the stated principal of the obligation is recharacterized as original issue discount

---

103. Neither § 483 nor § 1274 applies if the debt instrument or the property bought and sold in the transaction in which it is issued is a stock or security that is traded on an established securities exchange. * * *

(OID), and both parties to the instrument must recognize this OID as interest as it accrues on a constant interest basis over the life of the instrument. Also, where an obligation issued in a sale or exchange of property bears adequate stated interest, but the interest either is not computed at a fixed, unconditional rate or is not payable at least annually, section 1274 requires that the stated interest be recognized as it accrues on a constant interest basis, rather than as it is paid.

The adequacy of stated interest is tested and interest is imputed under section 1274 by the AFR. Stated interest is inadequate unless it at least equals the AFR. If stated interest is inadequate, additional interest is imputed so that the combination of stated and imputed interest equals the AFR. There are three AFRs, for short-term, mid-term, and long-term obligations, respectively. Each of the AFRs is an average of the original yields of recent federal borrowings of comparable terms.

When section 1274 applies because stated interest is inadequate, the following steps are followed: An imputed principal amount is computed. This amount is usually the present value of all payments under the instrument, determined with a discount rate equal to the AFR. In other words, the imputed principal amount is the amount that, if invested at a compound interest rate equal to the AFR, would grow to an amount just sufficient to make all payments under the note when due. If the obligation is issued in a transaction having potential for tax avoidance, however, the imputed principal amount is instead the fair market value of the property sold, less the down payment given by the buyer.

The imputed principal amount becomes the issue price of the instrument for purposes of the OID rules. The excess of the stated redemption price at maturity over the issue price is OID. As it accrues on a constant interest basis, the seller-holder includes the OID in gross income, and the buyer-obligor is allowed an interest deduction, subject to the many limitations on interest deductions.

* * *

Section 1274 also applies when stated interest is adequate, but is not unconditionally payable at a fixed rate at least annually. In this case, the stated principal amount of the obligation becomes the issue price for purposes of the OID rules. The stated redemption price payable at maturity, however, includes both the stated principal amount and the amounts designated as interest in the instrument. The excess of the stated redemption price over the issue price is OID. This excess typically equals the interest provided by the instrument. The OID is reported by the parties as it accrues on a constant interest basis.

* * *

Section 1274 is riddled with exceptions. It does not apply, for example, to notes issued in (1) a sale where the total of all payments is less than $250,000, (2) a sale of the seller's principal residence, (3) a sale of a farm by an individual or small business entity for less than $1 million, or (4) a sale of a patent for a price contingent on usage. The parties to an instrument are also allowed to elect out of section 1274 when the stated principal amount does not exceed $2 million and various other requirements are met.

Section 483

Many cases covered by exceptions to section 1274 are subject to the alternative interest imputation scheme of section 483. If the total of all payments in a sale is less than $250,000, for example, any debt issued in the sale is excepted from section 1274, but section 483 typically applies instead. Also, section 483 applies if the parties are eligible to and do elect out of section 1274.

Section 483 is essentially a cash method adaptation of the accrual scheme of section 1274. The total of the imputed interest recognized over an instrument's term is computed similarly under sections 1274 and 483. The standard by which the adequacy of stated interest is judged is usually the lower of the AFR or 9%. If stated interest is at least equal to this test rate, it is deemed adequate, and section 483 does not apply, whether interest is paid more or less as it accrues or is deferred to maturity. * * *

If, in a case within the orbit of section 483, stated interest is not adequate, the note bears unstated interest. The unstated interest is the excess of the deferred payments of sales price (principal) over the present value of these payments and any stated interest. The present value figure is determined by discounting the principal and interest payments at the imputed interest rate, typically the lesser of the AFR or 9%. The effect of this is that the note's yield, consisting of unstated and perhaps stated interest, equals the imputed interest rate.

Unstated interest is allocated over the note's term by a constant interest computation that is substantially the same as the mechanism for accruing OID when section 1274 applies. The interest accruals, however, are reported by the parties only as payments occur. Each payment is deemed to include interest (stated and unstated) equal to the interest accrued to the date of the payment, reduced by the interest portions of prior payments. In addition, a payment is deemed to include a prepayment of interest if the portion labeled interest in the contract exceeds accrued interest. An interest prepayment is gross income to the seller-holder when the payment occurs, but is deductible by the buyer-obligor only as the interest accrues. Any portion of a payment that is not considered to be a payment of accrued interest or an interest prepayment is treated as principal.

The cash method rules of section 483 frequently defer the recognition of accrued interest. The deferral is usually beneficial to the holder of the instrument (the seller) because it delays the recognition of income. For the buyer-obligor, the consequence—deferral of deductions—is usually not desired.

Applicable Federal Rule (AFR)

Generally

The concept of AFR is used in applying sections 1274 and 483 * * *. Section 1274(d) requires that three federal rates be computed monthly. The Federal short-term rate is the AFR for debt instruments whose terms are three years or less. The Federal mid-term rate applies to instruments whose terms exceed three years but are no greater than nine years, and a Federal long-term rate is provided for obligations with terms longer than nine years.

* * *

Choosing AFR From Among Various Federal Rates

The AFR that applies to a particular note is the Federal short-term, mid-term, or long-term rate, depending on the term of the instrument, for the month in which there is "a binding contract in writing" for the sale or exchange or, if lower, the appropriate rate for the preceding month or the second preceding month. * * *

Testing for Applicability of Section 1274

In General

Section 1274 applies to a debt instrument only if (1) the instrument is "given in consideration for the sale or exchange of property," (2) at least one payment is due under the instrument more than six months after the sale or exchange, and (3) stated interest either is not adequate or is not unconditionally payable at a fixed rate at least annually.[104]

[F]or purposes of the first of these requirements, (1) the term "sale or exchange" includes "any transaction treated as a sale or exchange for tax purposes," and (2) "property" includes "debt instruments and investment units, but does not include money, services, or the right to use property." * * * These exclusions have the effect of largely exempting notes issued in payment for services or rent from the OID rules. * * *

Testing for Adequacy of Stated Interest

If a note issued in a sale or exchange of property calls for at least one payment more than six months after the sale or exchange, section 1274 applies unless the payments characterized by the note as interest (the stated interest) are adequate. Very generally, to be adequate, stated interest must equal or exceed AFR, compounded semiannually.

* * *

A rate other than the AFR is the basis of the test rate for only three types of notes: (1) notes to which section 1274A(a) applies, (2) notes issued in sale-leaseback transactions, and (3) notes issued in sales and exchanges occurring between January 1 and June 30 of 1985. * * *

---

104. I.R.C. § 1274(c)(1).

When Section 1274A(a) Applies

Section 1274A(a) places a 9% cap on the test rate for a "qualified debt instrument."[105]   A note is a qualified debt instrument if two requirements are met. First, it must be issued in a sale or exchange of property that is not new section 38 property.[106] That is, the property cannot be of a type that prior to the repeal of the investment credit in 1986, would have qualified the purchaser for the credit. Second, the stated principal amount of the note cannot exceed a "qualified amount," which is $2.8 million for 1989 and earlier years and will be adjusted for inflation for subsequent years.[107] To prevent evasion of the dollar limit, all notes issued in a sale or exchange, or a group of related sales or exchanges, are aggregated.[108]

When section 1274A(a) applies to a note, stated interest is adequate if provided at a rate no less than the lower of the AFR or 9%, compounded semiannually in either case. * * *

Notes Issued in Sale–Leaseback Transactions

The test rate for a note issued in a sale-leaseback transaction is based on 110% of the AFR, rather than the usual 100%.[109] The term "sale-leaseback" is defined as a sale or exchange of property where, "pursuant to a plan, the transferor or any related person leases a portion of such property after such sale or exchange."[110]

* * *

Application of Test in Potentially Abusive Situations

If a note is issued in a "potentially abusive situation," the following procedure is used to test the adequacy of stated interest. A testing amount is determined. This amount equals the fair market value of the property sold or exchanged in the transaction in which the note is issued, reduced by the buyer's down payment and any consideration given by the buyer other than the note and cash down payment. The note is subject to section 1274 if the stated principal amount exceeds the testing amount.

* * *

A transaction is considered a "potentially abusive situation" for this purpose if it (1) involves a "tax shelter," or (2) is a "type" of transaction that is identified by regulation as "having potential for tax avoidance."[111] The term "tax shelter" is defined to include any entity, plan, or arrangement "the principal purpose" of which is "the avoidance or evasion of Federal income tax."[112] The statute suggests the

---

105. I.R.C. § 1274A(a).

106. I.R.C. § 1274A(b).

107. I.R.C. § 1274A(b) * * *.

108. Specifically, "all sales or exchanges which are part of the same transaction (or a series of related transactions) shall be treated as 1 sale or exchange." I.R.C. § 1274A(d)(1)(A). Also, "all debt instruments arising from the same transac-

tion (or series of related transactions) shall be treated as 1 debt instrument." I.R.C. § 1274A(d)(1)(B). * * *

109. I.R.C. § 1274(e)(1). * * *

110. I.R.C. § 1274(e)(3).

111. I.R.C. § 1274(b)(3)(B).

112. I.R.C. §§ 1274(b)(3)(i), 6661(b)(2)(C)(ii).

following as factors that might be taken into account under regulations in determining whether a transaction has potential for tax avoidance: "recent sales transactions," "nonrecourse financing," "financing with a term in excess of the economic life of the property," and "other circumstances."[113]

*　*　*

Testing for Applicability of Section 1274 When Stated Interest Is Adequate

A note issued in a sale or exchange of nonpublicly traded property that bears adequate stated interest is nevertheless subject to section 1274 if the stated interest is not computed at a fixed rate, is not unconditional, or is not payable at regular intervals of one year or less over the note's term.

The statute says that a note with adequate stated interest is subject to section 1274 if (1) it is issued in a sale or exchange of property, (2) at least one payment under the note is due more than six months after the sale, and (3) the stated redemption price at maturity exceeds the stated principal amount.[114] The stated redemption price includes the stated principal amount plus interest that is not "based on a fixed rate" or is not "payable unconditionally at fixed periodic intervals of 1 year or less during the entire term of the debt instrument."[115] A note with adequate stated interest thus can be subject to section 1274 only if the stated interest fails one or more of the tests established by the words quoted in the preceding sentence.

*　*　*

Application of Section 1274: Determining Issue Price, Basis, and Amount Realized

Generally

Literally, the only function of section 1274 is to define the issue price of instruments within its jurisdiction. It contains two definitions of the issue price for the two categories of notes which it covers.

First, if an instrument does not bear adequate stated interest, the issue price is the imputed principal amount. The imputed principal amount is usually the present value of all payments under the instrument, determined with a discount rate equal to the AFR (adjusted for the length of the compounding period). If the note is issued in a potentially abusive situation, however, the imputed principal amount is the fair market value of the property sold or exchanged, reduced by the buyer's down payment.

This issue price is used in applying the usual definition of OID—the excess of the stated redemption price at maturity over the issue price. The stated redemption price usually consists of amounts identified as principal in the note, but also includes payments characterized by the

113. I.R.C. § 1274(b)(3)(B)(ii).

114. I.R.C. § 1274(c)(1).

115. I.R.C. 1273(a)(2). *　*　*

instrument as interest if this interest is not unconditionally payable at a fixed rate at least annually. When the present value definition of imputed principal amount applies and the stated redemption price includes only the stated principal amount, OID under this rule is the excess of the stated principal amount over the present value of all payments under the note, discounted at the AFR.

Section 1274 applies to an instrument that bears adequate stated interest only if the stated redemption price at maturity includes amounts characterized by the instrument as interest—that is, only if stated interest is not unconditionally payable at a fixed rate at least annually. When this is so, the issue price equals the stated principal amount, and the OID (the excess of stated redemption price over issue price) equals the nonperiodic or conditional interest. In this case, the usual effect of the rules is to require that interest not payable at least annually be reported as it accrues on a constant interest basis.

* * *

Imputed Principal Amount in Nonabusive Situations

If a note is issued in a sale or exchange of nonpublicly traded property and the transaction is not a potentially abusive situation, the imputed principal amount is the present value of all payments of principal and interest under the note, determined with a discount rate equal to the test rate used in testing the adequacy of stated interest. The test rate is usually determined and applied for this purpose using the rules for testing the adequacy of stated interest. The imputed principal amount thus usually equals the testing amount computed under the testing rules.

* * *

Imputed Principal Amount for Installment Obligations in Nonabusive Situations

With one added wrinkle, the foregoing rules also apply to installment obligations. If stated interest under an installment obligation is inadequate under all testing rules, the imputed principal amount is determined with the AFR appropriate for the last principal payment under the note, excluding nominal principal payments that are tacked on to take advantage of a lower long-term rate.

* * *

Imputed Principal Amount in Potentially Abusive Situations

In a potentially abusive situation, the imputed principal amount is the fair market value of the property sold or exchanged, reduced by the buyer's cash down payment and the fair market value of any property other than cash and notes that is given by the buyer. This amount equals the testing amount used in testing for the adequacy of stated interest.

Basis and Amount Realized

The issue price, plus any consideration other than the note given by the buyer, becomes the sales price in the sale or exchange. The sales price, in turn, is the amount realized by the seller in the transaction and the buyer's cost basis for the property.

* * *

Section 483

Section 483 applies to two types of debt issued in sales and exchanges of property: (1) debt instruments falling within exceptions to section 1274, and (2) instruments that would be subject to section 1274, but for the parties' election under section 1274A(c) to proceed under section 483, rather than under section 1274. * * *

Section 1274A(c) Election

When section 1274 applies to a transaction, original issue discount (OID) is recognized by both parties to the note as it accrues, regardless of their accounting methods. Section 1274A(c), however, provides an election to use the cash method scheme of section 483 for notes that would otherwise be subject to section 1274 if the stated principal amount of the note does not exceed $2 million and various other requirements are met. An obligation with respect to which an election has validly been made under section 1274A(c) is referred to as a "cash method debt instrument."[116]

a. Requirements for Election

An election under section 1274A(c) is allowed only if all of the requirements described below are satisfied.

First, an instrument is a cash method debt instrument only if "section 1274 would have applied to such instrument but for [the] election."[117] That is, the note must have been issued in a sale or exchange of property, the note must call for at least one payment due more than six months after the sale or exchange, none of the exceptions to section 1274 can be applicable, and stated interest under the note must either be inadequate or not be unconditionally payable at a fixed rate at least annually.

Second, the property sold or exchanged in the transaction in which the note is issued must not be new property of a type that would have qualified the purchaser for the investment credit had the property been purchased before the credit's repeal in 1986.[118] * * *

Third, the seller-holder (the person who will have interest income from the note) must not use the accrual method as his general method of accounting.[119] * * *

Fourth, the seller-holder cannot be a "dealer with respect to the property sold or exchanged."[120] * * *

Fifth, the transaction in which the note is issued cannot be a sale-leaseback transaction.

116. I.R.C. § 1274A(c)(2).
117. I.R.C. § 1274A(c)(2)(C).
118. I.R.C. § 1274A(b), (c)(2).

119. I.R.C. § 1274A(c)(2)(B).

120. Id.

Sixth, the stated principal amount of the note cannot exceed the "cash method amount."[121]   The cash method amount is $2 million for notes issued in 1989 and earlier years.   For 1990 and succeeding years, the amount is $2 million, adjusted for inflation.[122]   To prevent evasion of this limitation, the statute requires that "all sales or exchanges which are part of the same transaction (or a series of related transactions) shall be treated as 1 sale or exchange."[123]   Also, "all debt instruments arising from the same transaction (or a series of related transactions) shall be treated as 1 debt instrument."[124]

Finally, the election under this provision must be "jointly made" by the seller-holder and buyer-obligor.[125]   The election, once made, is irrevocable, and generally applies to successors to the original parties to the note.[126]   *   *   * A transfer of the note, however, ends the election if the transferee uses the accrual method of accounting.[127]

Consequences of Election

If the cash method election is validly made, section 1274 does not apply, and both parties to the note instead report all interest, including both stated and unstated interest, on the cash method of accounting.[128] [T]his means that section 483 applies.

2.   Payments to Which Section 483 Applies

Section 483 applies to some or all of the payments under a contract if the following conditions are met: [129]   First, the payment must be required by a contract, the contract must be one for sale or exchange, and the subject of the sale or exchange must be property.   Second, at least one payment under the contract must be due more than one year after the sale or exchange.   Third, there must be total unstated interest.   These requirements are always met when a cash method election has validly been made under section 1274A(c).[130]   They are not necessarily satisfied in other cases within the ambit of section 483.

---

121. I.R.C. § 1274A(c)(2)(A) *   *   *.

122. The figure used for notes issued in sales and exchanges during a particular calendar year after 1989 will be $2 million multiplied by a fraction whose numerator is the consumer price index for the 12 months ending with September 30 of the preceding year and whose denominator is the consumer index for the 12 months ending September 30, 1988. I.R.C. § 1274A(d) (2). The Service will publish the figure for each year in a revenue ruling. *   *   *

123. I.R.C. § 1274A(d)(1)(A). Assume a seller of land sells an undivided one-half interest in the land by one contract and sells the other one-half interest to the same buyer by another contract. Under the aggregation rule, a fee interest in the land is deemed sold by a single transaction. *   *   *

124. I.R.C. § 1274A(d)(1)(B). If two or more sales or exchanges are aggregated, all notes issued in the aggregated transactions are treated as a single note. *   *   *

125. I.R.C. § 1274A(c)(2)(D). *   *   *

126. I.R.C. § 1274A(c)(3)(A).

127. I.R.C. § 1274A(c)(3)(B). The effect of the termination of the election is that the OID accrual rules of § 1272 thereafter apply. *   *   *

128. I.R.C. § 1274A(c)(1). *   *   *

129. I.R.C. § 483(c)(1).

130. This is so because (1) a cash method election can be made only with respect to an instrument to which § 1274 would otherwise apply *   *   *, and (2) § 1274 does not apply when any of these requirements is not met *   *   *.

When these requirements are met, section 483 applies to each payment under the contract that (1) is a part of the sales price and (2) is due more than six months after the date of the sale or exchange. The consequence of section 483 is that some portion of each payment to which it applies is recharacterized as unstated interest.

*   *   *

Unstated Interest

Generally

Section 483 applies only if * * * a contract for the sale or exchange of property * * * does not provide for "adequate stated interest." * * *

Testing Adequacy of Stated Interest

[T]wo tests of the adequacy of stated interest [are provided], a test for simple cases and an alternative test applied whenever the test for simple cases is not met.

Test for Simple Cases

Stated interest is adequate under the test for simple cases if all of the following requirements are satisfied. First, the contract must provide for stated interest on the outstanding balance at a fixed rate. Second, the fixed rate must be no lower than the test rate. Generally, the test rate is the lesser of the AFR, or 9%. Third, stated interest must be paid or compounded at the end of [regular intervals of a year or less if payments are due under the contract on less than an annual basis,] throughout the term of the contract. Fourth, if the obligation is a cash method debt instrument with respect to which an election has been made under section 1274A(c), the transaction must not be a potentially abusive situation. If all of these requirements are met, section 483 does not apply. If one or more of the requirements is not satisfied, the alternative test * * * determines whether section 483 applies.

*   *   *

Alternative Test for Obligations Not Meeting Test for Simple Cases

If an obligation does not pass the test for simple cases, stated interest is adequate only if the sum of the deferred payments of principal is no greater than the present value of these payments and all stated interest.[131] For this purpose, only payments due more than six months after the sale are counted as deferred payments.[132] Present value is determined using the test rate as the discount rate.

*   *   *

---

131. I.R.C. § 483(b) * * *.

132. I.R.C. § 483(c)(1). All interest, including interest on principal payable with-

in six months, is included in the present value calculation. * * *

Determining Unstated Interest Where Stated Interest Is Inadequate

Section 483(b) defines total unstated interest as the excess of (1) the sum of the payments to which section 483 applies over (2) the sum of the present value of these payments and the present value of all stated interest under the contract. [A] special rule [is provided] for cash method debt instruments (that is, any obligation subject to section 483 because of an election under section 1274A(c)) that are issued in potentially abusive situations; unstated interest under such a note is the excess of (1) the sum of the deferred payments of sales price over (2) the fair market value of the property sold in the transaction, reduced by any cash down payment or other consideration given by the buyer.

When the general rule of section 483(b) applies, the present value figure is determined by discounting each deferred payment of principal and interest "from the time it becomes due to the date of the sale or exchange at the imputed rate of interest applicable to the contract." The imputed rate of interest is usually the lower of the AFR, or 9%.

* * *

Test and Imputation Rates

Generally

For each contract of sale, there is an interest rate that serves both as the test rate used in determining whether stated interest is adequate and, if stated interest is inadequate, as the imputed rate used in computing total unstated interest.

The rate used as the test and imputed rates of interest for a contract is usually the lower of the AFR or 9%. Both of these rates, however, are appropriate only when an instrument provides for semiannual payments or interest compoundings. When the interval between payments or compoundings is shorter or longer than six months, an adjustment in the AFR or 9% rate is necessary. In the Service's monthly publication of AFR's, each AFR is given as a semiannual rate and as adjusted for monthly, quarterly, and annual compounding periods. The 9% rate is adjusted to 8.84%, 8.9%, and 9.2% for monthly, quarterly, and annual compounding periods. * * *

Rates Potentially Higher Than 9%

The test and imputed interest rates applied to various types of contracts can be higher than 9%.

First, the rate is 110% of the AFR if the sale or exchange is part of a sale-leaseback transaction.[133] A sale-leaseback transaction is a sale or exchange of property "all or a portion of which, pursuant to a plan, is leased by the transferor of the property or a person related to the transferor . . . after the sale or exchange."[134]

133. I.R.C. § 1274(e). * * *

134. Prop.Reg. § 1.483–4(b)(1)(ii). The definition of relatedness found in § 168(e) (4)(D) is used here. * * *

Second, the rate is the AFR, whether higher or lower than 9%, if the transaction is not a sale-leaseback transaction, but the property sold or exchanged by the contract is * * * new tangible personal property of a type that, prior to the repeal of the investment credit in 1986, qualified the purchaser for the investment credit.[135]

Third, the rate is the AFR if the property sold or exchanged is the seller's personal residence and the stated principal amount of the deferred payments exceeds $2.8 million.

* * *

Six Percent Rate for Sales of Land to Related Persons

The test and imputed rates are limited to 6% in a "qualified sale."[136] A qualified sale is a sale or exchange of land made by an individual to another individual who is a member of the seller's "family."[137] The term "family" is defined to mean an individual's spouse, siblings, ancestors, and lineal descendants.

If the selling price in a qualified sale exceeds $500,000 or if the parties make more than one qualified sale in a single calendar year and the aggregate of the prices in those sales exceeds $500,000, the special rule for qualified sales only applies to $500,000 of the selling price or prices.[138]

Also, the special rule is wholly inapplicable if either seller or buyer is a nonresident alien.[139]

Accounting for Stated and Unstated Interest

Proposed regulations under section 446 provide detailed rules for allocating stated and unstated interest over the life of a deferred payment obligation. These rules apply to stated and unstated interest on obligations subject to section 483. They also apply to stated interest on obligations that would be subject to section 483 but for the fact that stated interest is adequate and unstated interest is thus zero.

The fundamental concept of the rules is that all interest, stated and unstated, accrues over the life of the instrument at a constant rate of interest. The basic steps in the application of the method are as follows: The term of the obligation is divided into a series of accrual periods. If payments under the obligation are due at regular intervals of one year or less, an accrual period ends with the due date of each payment. A yield to maturity is computed. The yield is the interest rate that, when applied throughout the obligation's term (with payment or compounding at the end of each accrual period), produces total interest equal to the sum of stated and unstated interest. The accrual for each period is the product of the outstanding principal balance and

---

135. * * * I.R.C. § 1274A(b).

136. I.R.C. § 483(e)(1). * * *

137. I.R.C. § 483(e)(2). * * *

138. I.R.C. § 483(e)(3). * * *

139. I.R.C. § 483(e)(4).

the yield. Each payment is usually considered interest in an amount equal to the sum of the accruals since the last payment.

* * *

Allocation of Interest to Payments

Generally

Unstated interest is recognized by the parties to a contract subject to section 483 as payments are made and received or fall due. Also, a seller-holder or buyer-obligor recognizes stated interest as payments are made or received if his regular method of accounting is the cash method. Generally, each payment under an obligation subject to these rules consists of interest (stated and unstated) to the extent of the interest accruals since the last payment. The instrument's characterization of the payment is usually ignored.

* * * First, a payment is considered interest in an amount equal to the "accrued and unpaid interest . . . as of the date the payment becomes due."[140] The accrued and unpaid interest is (1) the sum of the accruals of stated and unstated interest from the date of the sale or exchange to the date the payment falls due, reduced by (2) the sum of the interest portions of all prior payments.

Second, if the amount characterized by the contract as interest exceeds interest accruals, the excess is treated as prepaid interest. * * * An interest prepayment is included in the gross income of the seller-holder when it is received. The buyer-obligor's deduction for the prepayment is deferred until the interest accrues.

Third, any excess of the payment over the amounts characterized by the first two rules is principal.

* * *

Special Rules for Some Small Transactions

In two cases, the allocation of payments between stated interest and principal provided by the parties' contract is followed for tax purposes in lieu of the rules just described. The first of these cases is where (1) section 483 does not apply because stated interest is adequate and (2) the total of the deferred payments of principal and interest does not exceed $250,000. * * *

Treatment of Unstated Interest

Unstated interest is treated as interest for all federal tax purposes. It must, for example, be reported by the seller (the holder of the obligation) as interest income, and is usually allowed as a deduction to the buyer-obligor.

A buyer-obligor's deductions for unstated interest, however, are subject to all of the limitations on the interest deduction. * * *

---

140. Prop.Reg. § 1.446–2(d)(1)(i).

Also, unstated interest is not included in the seller's amount realized or the buyer's cost basis for the property. * * *

Exceptions and Rules for Interrelating Sections 1274 and 483

The respective jurisdictions of sections 1274 and 483 are defined as follows: Section 1274 is the basic interest imputation rule for deferred payment sales; any debt instrument subject to section 1274 is exempted from the application of 483. Obligations issued in several kinds of transactions are excepted from section 1274, however, and most of these transactions are covered by section 483.

Debt issued in a few types of sales and exchanges of property is exempted from both section 1274 and section 483. * * *

Transactions Normally Covered by Section 483 Rather Than Section 1274

Sale for $250,000 or Less

A note is excepted from section 1274 if it is issued in a sale or exchange where the total consideration given by the buyer is no greater than $250,000.[141] The exception applies only if the sum of the following is $250,000 or less: (1) the aggregate of all payments of principal and interest under the note and all other notes given by the buyer in the sale or exchange, (2) the buyer's cash down payment, (3) any liability that the buyer assumes or takes subject to, and (4) the fair market value of all property other than cash and notes given by the buyer. Also, the consideration received in "all sales and exchanges which are part of the same transaction (or a series of related transactions)" are lumped together in determining whether the $250,000 limit is exceeded.[142]

If section 1274 would apply to a note but for this exception, unstated interest is usually imputed to the note under section 483.

Sale of a Farm for Less Than $1 Million

A debt instrument issued in a sale of property is excepted from section 1274 if (1) the property is a farm, (2) the seller falls within one of several categories of eligible sellers, and (3) the sale price is less than $1 million. Although the qualification criteria refer only to the seller, this exception, if applicable, applies to both parties to the obligation. An obligation excepted from section 1274 by this rule usually falls within the jurisdiction of section 483.

For purposes of the exception, the term "farm" is defined to include "stock, dairy, poultry, fruit, fur-bearing animal, and truck farms, plantations, ranches, nurseries, ranges, greenhouses or other similar structures used primarily for the raising of agricultural or horticultural commodities, and orchards."[143]

---

141. I.R.C. § 1274(c)(3)(C). * * *   **143.** I.R.C. §§ 1274(c)(3)(A)(i), 6420(c)(2).

142. I.R.C. § 1274(c)(3)(C)(iii). * * *

Eligible sellers include all individuals, estates, and testamentary trusts.[144] A domestic corporation is an eligible seller if the total of the amounts it has received on the issuance of stock and as contributions to capital is no greater than $1 million.[145] A domestic partnership is an eligible seller if the sum of the capital contributions it has received from its partners is $1 million or less.[146]

The third requirement of this exception—that the selling price not exceed $1 million—is met "only if it can be determined at the time of the sale or exchange that the sales price cannot exceed $1,000,000." [147]

Sales of Land Between Related Persons

Section 483(e) provides that, for purposes of section 483, the discount rate used in measuring imputed interest on a note received in a sale or exchange of property is 6% if the property is land, the sale or exchange is between related persons, and various other requirements are met. A note qualifying for this special treatment is excepted from section 1274.[148]

Sale of a Principal Residence

A note issued in a sale or exchange of property is excepted from section 1274 if, prior to the transaction, the seller used the property as his principal residence.[149] When this exception applies, neither the seller (the holder of the note) nor the buyer (the issuer-obligor) is subject to any of the OID rules, but the note may bear unstated interest under section 483.

If the buyer of real property uses it as a personal residence, the exception described below for purchases of personal use property makes both sections 1274 and 483 inapplicable to the buyer. None of the exceptions from section 483 can apply to the seller in such a sale, however. Section 483 thus imputes unstated interest to the seller's receipt of deferred payments in a sale of her residence unless (1) all payments in the sale are due within one year of the sale or (2) the payments bear adequate stated interest.

* * *

Transactions Exempted From Sections 483 and 1274

Purchases of Personal Use Property

* * *

If a note is given in a purchase of "personal use property," neither section 1274 nor section 483 applies to the buyer-obligor.[150] The term "personal use property" is defined to include any property "substantially all of the use of which" by the buyer is not "in connection with" a

---

144. I.R.C. § 1274(c)(3)(A)(i)(I).

145. I.R.C. §§ 1274(c)(3)(A)(i)(II), 1244(c) (3). * * *

146. I.R.C. § 1274(c) (3) (A) (i) (III). * * *

147. I.R.C. § 1274(c)(3)(A)(ii). * * *

148. I.R.C. § 1274(c)(3)(F). * * *

149. I.R.C. § 1274(c)(3)(B). The statute says the term "principal residence" has the same meaning here as it does for purposes of § 1034. * * *

150. I.R.C. § 1275(b)(1). * * *

trade or business or the production or collection of income.[151] The consequence of this rule is that the buyer-obligor treats all payments as they are characterized by the instrument. Interest deductions are allowed only for stated interest, and payments characterized as principal are usually nondeductible, but are includable in the adjusted basis of the property.[152]

* * *

A special rule is also provided for debt not covered by the foregoing exception that is "incurred in connection with the acquisition or carrying of personal use property." [153] The full panoply of the OID rules apply to such an obligation, with one exception: If the obligor uses the cash method of accounting, OID is deductible "only when paid," not under the normal accrual scheme for OID. This rule applies to debt incurred on a purchase of personal use property if the lender is someone other than the seller, and probably applies to most subsequently incurred debt that is secured by personal use property.

* * *

Sales for $3,000 or Less

Section 483 does not apply to any payment in a sale or an exchange of property if, when the sale or exchange occurs, it is certain that the sales price will not exceed $3,000.[154] All transactions so exempted from section 483 are also exempted from section 1274 by the rule described above for sales where the total of all payments is $250,000 or less.

* * *

Rules and Concepts Common to Sections 483 and 1274

Prepayment and Other Options

Special rules are provided for cases where the buyer or seller has an option to prepay or require prepayment of a note subject to section 483 or 1274 or an option to extend the term of the note. If the buyer (the obligor on the note) has an option to prepay or extend, section 483 or 1274 is applied as though this option will be exercised (that is, as though the prepayment or extended maturity date were the maturity date and as though the amount payable on this date were the stated principal amount) if the effect is to (1) cause section 483 or 1274 to apply or (2) increase the unstated interest or OID under section 483 or 1274.[155] If the seller (the holder of the note) has the right to require the buyer-obligor to prepay or has the right to extend the note's term,

---

151. I.R.C. § 1275(b)(3). The determination of whether property is personal use property is made when the note is issued.

* * *

152. This exception does not apply to a seller-holder. Unless some other exception applies, § 1274 or § 483 is applied to the seller-holder to require that implicit interest be reported as gross income as it accrues. The exception thus typically benefits no one, and operates as a penalty against buyers who fail to express interest implicit in their consumer purchase arrangements as stated interest.

153. I.R.C. § 1275(b)(2).

154. I.R.C. § 483(d)(2). * * *

155. Prop.Reg. §§ 1.483–4(e), 1.1274–6(f) (1), (3). A buyer-obligor presumably has an option to prepay only if he can prepay without payment of any interest accruing after the prepayment or any other penalty.

section 483 or 1274 is applied as though the option will be exercised if the effect is to (1) make section 483 or 1274 inapplicable or (2) reduce unstated interest or OID.[156] * * *

Modifications

If a debt instrument is modified "materially either in kind or in extent," the modification is treated as an exchange of the unmodified instrument for the modified instrument * * *. The modified instrument is deemed issued in an exchange of property to which section 483 or 1274 can apply. The application of section 483 or 1274 to the modified instrument is independent of the circumstances of the issuance of the unmodified instrument. Section 483 or 1274 thus can apply to the modified instrument even if it did not apply to the unmodified instrument.

* * *

Assumptions

If the buyer in a sale or exchange of property assumes a debt or takes the property subject to a debt, the assumption or taking subject to is usually not taken into account in applying sections 483 and 1274.[157] That is, the debt instrument assumed or taken subject to is not treated as an instrument issued in the sale or exchange, payments under the instrument are not considered payments under the contract of sale, and the assumption or taking subject to is generally treated as consideration given at the time of the sale or exchange, not as an agreement to make deferred payments.

* * *

Section 483 or 1274, however, can be relevant in various situations involving the assumption of and taking property subject to liabilities. First, if a debt instrument assumed or taken subject to in a sale or exchange of property was originally issued at a discount or in a prior sale or exchange subject to section 1274, the OID, as computed when the instrument was issued, continues to be recognized.[158] In computing the seller's amount realized and the buyer's basis for the property, the debt is taken into account at the original issue price, increased by all OID recognized up to the date of the sale.[159] The holder and the buyer-obligor (the substitute issuer) recognize further accruals of OID for periods after the sale.

* * *

156. Prop.Reg. § 1.1274–6(f)(1), (2).

157. I.R.C. § 1274(c)(4) * * *.

158. * * * Similarly, if § 483 applies to payments under a contract of sale and the buyer resells the property to a second buyer who assumes or takes subject to the debt under the original contract, the seller continues to report unstated interest (determined under the schedule established at the time of the original sale) as payments are received from the second buyer, and the second buyer steps into the original buyer's shoes with respect to deductions for unstated interest. * * *

159. If § 483 applies, the amount of the debt at the time of the sale is (1) the sum of the as yet unpaid payments, less (2) the unstated interest allocable to these payments.

NOTE

1.　Obviously, the "safe" procedure in most cases, with respect to Sections 483 and 1274, is to provide for an interest rate at least equal to the applicable federal rate or 9%, whichever applies, and provide for regular, at least annual, payments of interest or principal and interest with respect to any deferred payment obligation received on the sale or exchange of real estate.

　　a.　Might Sections 483 and 1274 be avoided, if, instead of purchasing 100 acres for $500,000 with a $50,000 down payment and an obligation to pay the remaining $450,000 over the following nine years, the grantor and grantee agree that the grantee will purchase and the grantor will sell 10 acres each year for 10 years at a price of $50,000 an acre? The grantor will retain title to and possession of the real estate which has not been purchased by the grantee until the actual closing for each 10 acre parcel. Cf. Rev.Rul. 69–93, 1969–1 C.B. 139. But cf. Rev.Rul. 75–563, 1975–2 C.B. 199, in which the Internal Revenue Service concluded that Section 483 applied when the grantee received possession and use of the real estate subject to the agreement and assumed payment of taxes assessed against the real estate.

　　b.　Should the means through which the grantee, described above, received possession and use of the real estate subject to the agreement make any difference with respect to whether Section 483 or 1274 applied to the transaction? Is there a difference between the agreement, providing for the purchase of the real estate, giving the grantee the right to possession and use of all the real estate so long as the grantee is not in breach of the agreement and the grantor leasing to the grantee at a fair rental the real estate which the grantee had not yet purchased?

　　c.　Is the fair rental mentioned above more or less than a fair interest rate on the $500,000 purchase price? If it is about the same, what have the grantor and grantee accomplished by selling and purchasing 10 acres a year rather than the grantee immediately purchasing 100 acres for a $50,000 down payment and a $450,000 deferred payment obligation?

2.　Instruments subject to the original issue discount rules of Sections 1271 to 1275 are not subject to Section 483. As a general matter, this limits the applicability of Section 483 to instruments resulting from a sale of property involving total consideration, including the debt instrument, of no more than $250,000. See Section 1274(c). As a practical matter, however, most instruments which will be subject to Section 483 in the future probably will be "qualified debt instruments," as defined in Section 1274A(b).

3.　Since, for the most part, the "safe harbor" and "imputed" rates under Section 483 are the same rates as used under Section 1274, see Section 483(b), why are debt instruments arising from sales of property involving total consideration of $250,000 or less excepted from Section 1274 and brought under Section 483? See Sections 1274(c)(3)(C) and 483(d)(1).

　　a.　Is the "interest" component computed in the same manner under both Section 483 and the original issue discount rules?

　　b.　Under Section 483, is any unstated interest treated as paid and received in a year in which no payments of principal or interest are made, or required to be made, under the deferred payment obligation? Is a

similar result available under the original issue discount rules?   See
Section 1274A(c).

4.   As discussed above, in many situations if a lender withholds interest
or other charges, which the borrower owes the lender, from the proceeds of a
loan, the loan will be treated as a discounted loan and the borrower will not
be able to deduct the withheld charges, if deductible, until, and as, the loan is
paid.   Can this result be avoided by a lender making available the entire
proceeds of the loan to a cash method borrower and then loaning the
borrower an amount equal to the charges which the borrower owes the
lender?   See *G. Douglas Burck,* 63 T.C. 556 (1975), affirmed, 533 F.2d 768 (2d
Cir.1976);   *Alan A. Rubnitz,* 67 T.C. 621 (1977);   *Charles Jay Brown,* 37 CCH
Tax Ct.Mem. 571 (1978);   *Richard S. Heyman,* 70 T.C. 482 (1978), affirmed,
652 F.2d 598 (6th Cir.1980).   But see *Battelstein v. Internal Revenue Service,*
611 F.2d 1033 (5th Cir.1980), cert. denied, 451 U.S. 938, 68 L.Ed.2d 325, 101
S.Ct. 2018 (1981), in which the Fifth Circuit Court of Appeals treated a
transaction in which the taxpayer and the lending institution swapped checks
in the amount of the interest due as a discounted loan.   In *Donald L.
Wilkerson,* 70 T.C. 240 (1978), nonacq., 1982–2 C.B. 3, a current deduction was
allowed when the full amount of the loan proceeds was delivered to the
borrower and placed in the borrower's bank account which contained a small
amount of other funds of the borrower and the charges owed the lender were
paid immediately thereafter by the borrower's check drawn on this account.
The decision in *Donald L. Wilkerson,* supra, was reversed by the Ninth
Circuit Court of Appeals in *Wilkerson v. Comm'r,* 655 F.2d 980 (9th Cir.1981).
See also *H.C. Franklin,* 77 T.C. 173 (1981), reversed, 683 F.2d 125 (5th Cir.
1982);   *Blitzer v. United States,* 231 Ct.Cl. 236, 684 F.2d 874 (1982);   *John B.
Noble,* 79 T.C. 751 (1982);   *Norman W. Menz,* 80 T.C. 1174 (1983);   *Robert S.
Coit,* 54 CCH Tax Ct.Mem. 816 (1987).   In I.R. 83–93, 1983 CCH Standard Fed.
Tax Rep. ¶ 6638, the Internal Revenue Service announced that, if the interest
owed a lender was borrowed from the lender by a cash method taxpayer and
then paid to the lender by the taxpayer, the interest would not be deductible
until, and as, the debt incurred as a result of borrowing the interest was paid.
See *William M. Roberts,* 53 CCH Tax Ct.Mem. 787 (1987).   See generally
Freeman, *Interest, Contingent Interest and Original Issue Discount: Some
Emerging Tax Strategies in Corporate and Real Estate Financings,* 59 Taxes
942 (1981);   Comment, *Deductibility of Interest Payments Financed by Additional Loans from the Same Lender,* 35 Tax Law. 275 (1981).

5.   See generally Cliff and Levine, *Interest Accrual and the Time Value
of Money,* 34 Am.U.L.Rev. 107 (1984);   Fisher and Norris, *The Ins and Outs of
the New OID/Imputed Interest System as Applied to Sales of Real Estate: Is
the Partnership an Alternative?,* 63 Taxes 877 (1985);   Halperin, *Interest in
Disguise: Taxing the "Time Value of Money,"* 95 Yale L.J. 506 (1986);   Schler,
The Sale of Property for a Fixed Payment Note: Remaining Uncertainties, 41
Tax L.Rev. 209 (1986);   Mankoff, *The Application of Original Issue Discount to
Real Estate Transactions,* 1 Real Est.Fin.L.J. 132 (1985);   Moore, *Analyzing
the Complex New Proposed Regs. on Imputed Interest and Original Issue
Discount,* 65 J.Tax'n 14 (1986);   Geis and Christner, *Seller–Financed Transac-
tions: The New Imputed Interest Rules,* 17 Tax Adviser 728 (1986);   Slagle,
*Accounting for Interest: An Analysis of Original Issue Discount in the Sale of
Property,* 32 S.D.L.Rev. 1 (1987);   Davis, *Buying· and Selling Property: The
Determination and Treatment of Imputed Interest,* 44 N.Y.U.Inst.Fed.Tax'n
33–1 (1986).

7. POWER AND AUTHORITY TO BORROW AND TO LEND

a. THE UNAUTHORIZED LOAN

Most institutional lenders are limited by applicable federal and state statutes and regulations in the type, amount and kind of loan and investment they can make. What are the consequences when a loan made, or to be made, violates these limitations?

HIGGINS v. ARIZONA SAVINGS & LOAN ASS'N
Supreme Court of Arizona, 1958.
85 Ariz. 6, 330 P.2d 504.

JOHNSON, Justice. This is an appeal from a judgment entered in an action filed by appellants, Fred Higgins and wife, against the Arizona Savings and Loan Association, to recover damages for the breach of an alleged contract to lend the appellants money on the security of a mortgage. The ultimate question presented is: did the trial court properly direct a verdict in favor of appellee?

The appellants made a written application to the appellee, Arizona Savings and Loan Association, an Arizona corporation, hereinafter referred to as the Association, for a loan of $100,000 to be secured by a first mortgage on certain real estate owned by appellants, which loan was to refinance two first mortgages, one second mortgage, and pay a tax lien on said real property. The Association's head loan officer, Jerome J. Smrt, arranged for an appraisal to be made of appellants' real property, and later informed appellants that an appraisal had been made by a Mr. Archer, a qualified paid appraiser, and that he had filed a signed report, dated October 21, 1954, finding the reasonable value of the real estate of appellants to be the sum of $158,250, and as the Association under the statute could only loan sixty per cent of the appraised value that the loan application of appellants was changed to the sum of $94,800.

Thereafter, appellants were advised that Mr. Smrt had taken a leave of absence and that Mr. Dick, Vice President from the Tucson office of the Association, would handle the loan application; arrangements were made for him to inspect the real estate and complete the application in the absence of the Association's regular loan officer. Mr. Dick, in the company of appellants, inspected the property and ascertained that the present values were as shown by Mr. Archer's appraisal, and advised appellants that he was approving the loan and that an escrow would be set up at the Phoenix Title and Trust Company. The title report showed certain requirements to be met by the appellants before the escrow could be completed and the money disbursed to [the appellants].

Through the efforts of appellants all of the requirements of the title report were eventually met although it took some time because the property was subject to a federal tax lien which had to be cleared.

On March 21, 1955, a document of the Association entitled "Loan Settlement Statement" was signed by an official of the Association notifying the appellants that their application for a loan had been granted in the sum of $94,800, and that after deducting the expenses incurred in making the loan the sum of $89,937.85 was available for escrow at the Phoenix Title and Trust Company, and that a check for that amount was deposited with the title company along with escrow instructions.

The Association on March 30, 1955 sent the appellants a "Loan Passbook" advising that their first monthly payment on the loan would be due on May 1, 1955, in the amount of $625.93.

Mr. Smrt testified that when appellants made application for a loan and the property was inspected he informed appellants that he would try to make the loan if the property across the street were cleared of trees, old shacks and a junk yard, and that appellants promised to have this done. That upon his return from his vacation he again inspected the property, and when he found that the objectionable debris had not been removed he went to the title company on May 19, 1955, and withdrew from escrow the check for $89,937.85, which had been deposited by the Association during his absence, and cancelled the escrow. The appellants were not formally notified that the escrow had been cancelled until August 25, 1955, when the Association wrote appellants that it was unable to approve and make the loan, stating as a reason the following:

> "While the property offered as security is good property, certain surrounding circumstances, location, street conditions, and the ratio of the desired loan, to reasonable marketable value, as determined by alternate appraisals make it impossible for our favorable consideration of this loan."

The appellants proved that as a result of the Association failing to make the loan upon which they had relied they lost their real property by foreclosure of two of the mortgages and sustained damages in an amount equal to their equity in the property.

The Association for the first time on February 25, 1957, one day before trial, interposed the defense that the Association was unable to obtain a report in writing of two appraisers giving the conservative market value of the real property of appellants in an amount sufficient to authorize the loan applied for by appellants.

At the conclusion of appellants' evidence the Association made a motion for a directed verdict, which was granted, upon the ground that the provisions of A.R.S. § 6–410 had not been complied with. That section provides that a building and loan association may make loans:

"1. Upon notes secured by first mortgages on improved real property, or on real property to be improved under contract with the association. Unless the federal housing administrator has insured or made a commitment to insure the property, the loan shall not exceed sixty percent of the conservative market value of the improved real property mortgaged. * * * *No loans shall be made except upon the report in writing of two appraisers giving the conservative market value of the property to be mortgaged.*"

* * *

We believe that the only question for this court to pass upon is whether, assuming that the Association did not fully comply with the provisions of A.R.S. § 6–410, the purported contract with appellant was illegal and incapable of enforcement, or was it a question of fact for the jury as to whether the Association, on the record presented, was estopped to deny its compliance with said section?

There is a definite distinction between an act of an association which is merely without authority and one which is illegal. The association may not be allowed to defeat an ultra vires contract because of failure to comply with certain formalities but an ultra vires contract which is beyond the power of association to make cannot be enforced; in other words, acts or contracts wholly beyond the corporate powers are void. C.J.S. Corporations § 965.

In the instant case the Association had the power to enter into the contract with appellants to loan them money, and such contract was neither illegal nor against public policy, but was in fact the primary purpose of its organization. A.R.S. § 6–401.

Where the contract is within the scope of the charter of the association and the statutory law of the state, and the defect relied upon depends upon some extrinsic fact peculiarly within the knowledge of the officers and agents of the association, and the person dealing with the association is without notice of the nonperformance of any formality prescribed by statute as a condition precedent to the association's authority to act, such person will be entitled to assume that the formalities and all matters of internal management have been duly complied with. In such cases the association could, if the facts warranted, be estopped from showing that [it] could not enter into the contract by reason of a failure to comply with the prescribed conditions. C.J.S. Corporations § 968; 13 Am.Jur., Corporations § 758.

The evidence discloses that at all times until the letter of August 25, 1955, the officials of the Association led the appellants to believe that the contract would be carried out and the appellants in good faith, while relying upon the promises that the loan would be made, changed their position and as a result suffered damage.

Certainly the contract in question was within the scope of the power of the Association to make and the appellants, in good faith dealing with it, were under no obligation to examine the minutes and records of the Association (assuming the Association would permit it) to see if the provisions of A.R.S. § 6–410 had been complied with, but the appellants had a right to assume that the necessary steps would be taken by the officials to comply with all formalities required by statute, and under such circumstances the Association would be estopped to deny that it did contract in the manner provided by statute.

It appears to us that the ends of justice require that an association which has not followed the required formalities in the exercising of its powers should be estopped by its own acts from asserting, in defense of its assumed obligations, that they were ultra vires. To apply the principle of estoppel is not to enlarge the powers of the association; nor does it give warrant to the association to disregard or violate the restrictions which have been expressly imposed upon it.

The statement of this court in Leon v. Citizens' Building & Loan Ass'n, 14 Ariz. 294, 127 P. 721, 722, is particularly applicable to the facts in the instant case, wherein we said:

> "* * * The principles of common honesty and fair dealing are appropriate alike to measure the conduct of individuals as well as corporations. The doctrine of ultra vires, when invoked, should not be allowed where it would not advance justice, but, on the contrary, would accomplish a legal wrong * * *."

The trial court erred in directing a verdict in favor of the defendant since it appears there were sufficient facts under the record warranting submission of the matter to the jury.

Judgment reversed and new trial ordered.

UDALL, C.J., and WINDES, PHELPS and STRUCKMEYER, JJ., concur.

NOTE

1. Why did Mr. and Mrs. Higgins, the appellants in the above case, sue for damages rather than specific performance of the contract to make a mortgage loan?

    a. Did the court hold, in the above case, that more than nominal damages can be recovered for breach of a contract to lend money? If the court so held, is the holding consistent with Restatement of Contracts (Second) Sec. 346 (1981), or A. Corbin, 5 Corbin on Contracts Sec. 1078 at 447 (1964)? Is there another way in which the holding can be explained? See Brannon, *Enforceability of Mortgage Loan Commitments,* 18 Real Prop., Prob. & Tr. J. 724 (1983); Groot, *Specific Performance of Contracts to Provide Permanent Financing,* 60 Cornell L.Rev. 718 (1975); Draper, *Tight Money and Possible Substantive Defenses to Enforcement of Future Mortgage Commitments,* 50 Notre Dame Law. 603 (1975). For an examination of the remedies of the lender upon the borrower's default in performing the borrower's obligations under a mortgage loan commitment see Zinman, *Mortgage Loan and Joint Venture Commitments: The Institutional Investor's Remedies,* 18 Real Prop., Prob. & Tr.J. 750 (1983); Draper, *The Broken Commitment: A Modern View of the Mortgage Lender's Remedy,* 59 Cornell L.Rev. 418 (1974).

2. Assume that Mr. and Mrs. Higgins had requested, in the above case, an $80,000 mortgage loan and were aware that two appraisals secured by the lender gave the real estate a "conservative market value" of $100,000 and despite the appraisals the lender committed to make the $80,000 mortgage loan. If the lender later refused to make the loan, would Mr. and Mrs. Higgins have been able to recover more than nominal damages in an action for damages against the lender? See *Powder River County Bank v. Arness-McGriffin Coal Co.,* 732 P.2d 1326 (1987).

    a. Should a borrower or potential borrower be held to have constructive notice of the statutory and regulatory restrictions and limitations imposed on a lender?

3. If a lender made a mortgage loan which was in violation of statutory lending limitations, the borrower failed to make the required payments and the lender is attempting to foreclose the mortgage, can the borrower plead the illegality of the loan as a defense in the foreclosure action? Are the statutory and regulatory restrictions and limitations on loans and investments intended to be for the benefit of borrowers?

    a. See e.g. *Washington Heights Fed. Savings & Loan Ass'n v. Brooklyn Fur Storage Corp.,* 5 Misc.2d 997, 161 N.Y.S.2d 674 (Sup.Ct.1957); *Century Fed.Sav. & Loan Ass'n v. Sullivan,* 116 N.Y.S.2d 323 (Sup.1952), modified, 281 App.Div. 830, 118 N.Y.S.2d 479 (1953).

4. The sanctions which may be imposed by a supervisory body on an institutional lender for making an illegal loan include a cease and desist order, an order directing the lender to dispose of the illegal loan, the suspension or revocation of the lender's charter or authority and, in extreme cases, the appointment of a conservator or receiver for the liquidation of the lender. In addition, the directors and officers of a bank responsible for an illegal loan may be liable to the bank in damages. See *Larimore v. Conover,* 775 F.2d 890 (7th Cir.1985), reversed, 789 F.2d 1244 (7th Cir.1986); Note, *Larimore v. Comptroller of the Currency: Agency-Ordered Liability of Bank Directors and Officers Under 12 U.S.C.A. § 1818(b)(1),* 71 Minn.L.Rev. 1035 (1987).

    a. The knowing violation of lending restrictions or limitations by a National Bank may result in the forfeiture of its franchise. See 12 U.S.C.A. § 93 (West 1988). In addition, every director who participated in, or assented to, the violation is liable in a personal and individual capacity for all damages which the bank, its shareholders or any other person may have sustained as a result of the violation. See 12 U.S.C.A. § 93 (West 1988). Apparently, if a bank sues a director under 12 U.S.C.A. § 93 (West 1988), the measure of damages is the total amount of the illegal loan. See *Corsicana Nat. Bank v. Johnson,* 251 U.S. 68, 40 S.Ct. 82, 64 L.Ed. 141 (1919). If the violation, however, resulted from a series of transactions, only those transactions which actually result in the violation constitute the measure of damages. See *First Nat. Bank of Lincolnwood v. Keller,* 318 F.Supp. 339 (N.D.Ill.1970). A director who is sued by a bank for authorizing, or participating in the authorization of, an illegal loan has a right of contribution from the other directors and officers who participated in the making of the illegal loan. See *Cache National Bank v. Hinman,* 626 F.Supp. 1341 (D.Colo.1986).

5. How is the choice of governing law made when determining whether a loan is, or is not, illegal? Assume that an insurance company makes a loan in

a state other than the state of its incorporation and head office. The lending limits of the state in which the loan is made are lower than those of the state of the insurance company's incorporation and head office. Which lending limits govern?

    a. Does the situation described above involve the internal or external operations of the insurance company?

    b. Would it affect the choice of governing law if the insurance company was not qualified to write insurance in the state in which it made the loan?

    c. Can the insurance company and the borrower determine which state's law governs by specifying the governing law in the lending documents? Are the various states' supervisory agencies bound by the specification?

    d. See Restatement (Second) of Conflicts Sections 187 and 188, at 561–586 (1971); cf. *M/S Bremen v. Zapata Off-Shore Co.,* 407 U.S. 1, 92 S.Ct. 1907, 32 L.Ed.2d 513 (1972); Comptroller of the Currency, Interpretive Ltr. # 116, P.H.Fed. Control of Banking ¶ 3963; Comment, *The Regulation of Insurance Company Investments—A Theory for Uniform Legislation,* 1978 Utah L.Rev. 271; Comment, *The Policies Behind Lending Limits: An Argument for a Uniform Country Exposure Ceiling,* 99 Harv.L.Rev. 430 (1985).

6. Section 403 of the Garn–St. Germain Depository Institutions Act of 1982 simplified and broadened the real estate lending authority of a National Bank. A real estate loan made by a National Bank is subject to such terms, conditions and limitations as may be prescribed by the Comptroller of the Currency. See 12 U.S.C.A. § 371. Interpretive Rulings issued by the Comptroller of the Currency prior to the Garn–St. Germain Depository Institutions Act of 1982 which dealt with the real estate lending limits of National Banks were withdrawn effective September 9, 1983. See 48 Fed.Reg. 40,698 (Sept. 9, 1983).

b. POWER AND AUTHORITY TO BORROW

(i) THE PARTNERSHIP

    A general partner of a real estate development partnership, in many situations, can borrow in the partnership name and mortgage the real estate of the partnership to secure such borrowing. See Sections 9(1) and 10(1) of the Uniform Partnership Act. A partnership agreement, however, can deny such authority to a partner.

    The authority of a partner to borrow money on behalf of a partnership and mortgage partnership real estate to secure such borrowing is derived from the wording in Section 9(1) of the Uniform Partnership Act, " * * * including the execution in the partnership name of any instrument." A note and mortgage should be encompassed in the phrase "any instrument." Section 10(1) refers to Section 9(1) in providing for a partner's ability to convey partnership real estate.

The authority granted by Section 9(1) of the Uniform Partnership Act, however, is limited by the phrase "carrying on in the usual way the business of the partnership." Therefore whether a general partner has the authority to borrow for and mortgage the real estate of the partnership, is determined by whether the transactions are for the purpose of "carrying on in the usual way the business of the partnership."

LEE v. FIRST NAT. BANK OF FT. SCOTT

Supreme Court of Kansas, 1890.
45 Kan. 8, 25 P. 196.

* * *

SIMPSON, C. Suit was brought by the First National Bank of Ft. Scott against Golden and Lee on [a] promissory note: " * * * [of] G.S. Golden & Co." Golden made no defense, but Lee pleaded a denial of the partnership, and that he had never executed the note, nor was it executed for him by any one acting by his authority, or under his direction, and that said note was not his obligation. There was a trial by the court at which these facts were developed: Golden and Lee formed a partnership some time in August, 1887, to carry on the real-estate, loan, and insurance business on commission at Ft. Scott. Lee did not know of the existence or execution of this note until after its maturity. The bank at the time of the making of the note did not know who composed the firm of G.S. Golden & Co., and required Golden to make a statement as to whom composed the firm, and this he did in writing on the back of the note. It is claimed on this state of facts that this was merely a partnership of occupation or employment, and not a commercial or trading one, and that there was no authority, actual or implied, for the making of commercial paper in the firm name by one member thereof. The bank introduced the evidence of several real-estate agents at Ft. Scott, to show that it was customary for those in that business at Ft. Scott to borrow money from the banks. The primary question is whether or not the execution of this note was within the scope of the partnership. The test of the character of the partnership is buying and selling. If it buys and sells, it is commercial or trading. If it does not buy or sell, it is one of employment or occupation. Winship v. Bank, 5 Pet. 529; Kimbro v. Bullitt, 22 How. 256; 1 Bates, Partn. § 327.

In partnerships of occupation, when one member executes a note in the firm name, the holder must show express or implied authority from the firm to make the note, before a recovery can be had. Smith v. Sloan, 37 Wis. 285; Judge v. Braswell, 13 Bush. 67; Horn v. Bank, 32 Kan. 518, 4 Pac.Rep. 1022. In commercial partnerships a note executed by one member in the firm name is *prima facie* the obligation of the firm, and if one of the parties seeks to avoid its payment, the burden of proof lies upon him to show that the note was given in a matter not relating to the partnership business, and that also with the knowledge of the holder of the note. Deitz v. Regnier, 27 Kan. 94. In Bays v.

Conner, 105 Ind. 415, 5 N.E.Rep. 18, and in Smith v. Sloan, 37 Wis. 285, it is held that notwithstanding the fact that the proceeds of the note were applied to the payment of the debts of the firm, one member of a non-trading partnership cannot bind the other by the execution of a note in the firm name. This, for the reason that there is a want of power, and the application of the proceeds is not controlling or decisive of the question of authority.   *   *   * It is also agreed in the articles of copartnership that neither of the said partners shall subscribe a bond, sign or indorse any note of hand, accept or indorse any draft or bill of exchange, or assume any other liability in the name of the firm, without the written consent of the other. These conditions embodied in the articles make it clear beyond all dispute that this was a partnership of occupation and employment, and not a trading or commercial one. It is said, however, on behalf of the bank, that it could not be bound by these unpublished restrictions; but, if we are right in the determination of the character of this partnership, then the plain duty of the bank, when one of the partners applied to it for a loan in the firm name, was to investigate his authority, and if investigation had taken place, knowledge of the restrictions would have followed. It is recommended that the judgment be reversed.

PER CURIAM. It is so ordered; all the justices concurring.

NOTE

1. The distinction between the trading and non-trading partnership, as described in the above case, is not specifically contained in the Uniform Partnership Act. In fact, the specific distinction is not even mentioned. On the other hand, the distinction between Sections 9(1) and 9(2) is embodied in the words "apparently for the carrying on of the business of the partnership." If a partner's act is apparently for the carrying on of the business of the partnership, he can bind the partnership pursuant to Section 9(1). Under Section 9(2), if his act is not apparently for the carrying on of business, he cannot bind the partnership. A court, in construing the language of Sections 9(1) and 9(2), might read in the trading, non-trading distinction discussed in the *Lee* case.

2. Is, however, the trading—non-trading distinction cutting with too broad a sword?

    a. Can a note and mortgage executed by one of the partners of a real estate development partnership (which would probably be classified as trading) ever be out of the usual course of business of the partnership? If so, in what circumstances?

3. What steps can counsel to an institutional lender take to insure that the authority problem considered in the above case and this note will not arise?

4. Under the Uniform Limited Partnership Act, a general partner has the authority to borrow and mortgage the real estate of the partnership in the ordinary course of business, unless the partnership agreement denies the authority. See U.L.P.A. Section 9(1). The partnership agreement might give the limited partners the right to approve borrowing and the mortgaging of partnership real estate particularly outside of the ordinary course of business. See Section 9(1)(a). Under the Revised Uniform Limited Partnership Act, the limited partners can be given the right to approve the mortgage of all or

substantially all of the assets of the partnership and borrowing by the partnership other than in the ordinary course of business. See Rev.U.L.P.A. Section 303(b)(6)(ii) and (iii).

(ii) THE CORPORATION

A corporation has the power to borrow money and to secure the loan by a mortgage of its real estate. (See Revised Model Business Corporation Act Sections 3.02(5) and (7) and 12.01(a)(2).) Section 12.01(a)(2) provides that a mortgage of a corporation's property can be authorized by its board of directors, and unless the articles of incorporation require it, no approval by shareholders is required. Cf. Carroll v. Wyoming Production Credit Association, 755 P.2d 869 (Wyo.1988). Can, however, the executive officer of a corporation borrow money on behalf of the corporation and mortgage its assets to secure the loan without the authorization of the board of directors?

MONTROSE LAND AND INVESTMENT CO. v. GREELEY NAT'L BANK

Supreme Court of Colorado, 1925.
78 Colo. 240, 241 P. 527.

* * *

Mr. Justice DENISON delivered the opinion of the court. * * *

The note in question was signed by the Montrose [Land and Investment Co.] by Hoffman, its president, and attested by Riley, its secretary, dated June 1, 1921, and payable on demand. Its only consideration was a previous note from the Montrose [Land and Investment Co.] to the Greeley Loan Company, a corporation under the control and management of Hoffman, signed in the same way, dated March 1, 1921, and due June 1st, and discounted by the bank through Neill, its cashier, April 11, 1921; this note was cancelled and surrendered when the note in suit was delivered.

* * *

The stock [of Montrose Land and Investment Co.] except two or three shares, was equally divided between the [Holly] Sugar Company, Neill, Hoffman and Moynihan. The corporation was organized accordingly in December, 1919. At the times in question Hoffman, Moynihan, Neill, Riley and one Armstrong, who lived in Illinois, were the directors. The Sugar Company paid for its own stock in cash and for Neill's and Hoffman's and Moynihan's. They gave their notes [to the Sugar Company] for the price of theirs and secured them by the stock which was issued to them. The Sugar Company * * * [made] advances [to Montrose Land and Investment Co., hereinafter referred to as the Montrose Company] for some time and it is not shown that it ever refused to do so. Hoffman was president and made the note to the Loan Company, which we have mentioned. April 11th the bank discounted it. The ostensible consideration was advances by the Loan Company. * * * June 11, 1920, Hoffman gave the note in suit.

Upon the first issue: Was the note executed? The answer depends (1) on whether Hoffman had authority to execute it, and (2) whether its execution was ratified by the company.

Had Hoffman authority? [T]hat is, is there evidence to justify the court in so finding? Under the by-laws it was his duty to sign "all * * * contracts and other instruments in writing authorized by the board of directors to be executed." There was no such authorization. His authority, then, must be sought outside the by-laws. To borrow money or execute a promissory note are not powers incident to the office of the president of an ordinary corporation. The bank, however, claims that the Montrose Company, by permitting Hoffman to manage and completely control its affairs, has held him out as its agent with power to give negotiable paper. The conduct of the Montrose Company without doubt made Hoffman its general manager, but not ipso facto, with power to borrow money or make notes. McClellan v. Morris, 71 Colo. 304, 310, 206 P. 575, 578; Schramm v. Liebenberg, 42 Colo. 516, 94 P. 345. A general agent to carry on business, has not, ipso facto, power to borrow money or issue paper. Sanford Cattle Co. v. Williams, 18 Colo.App. 378, 381, 71 P. 889, 890; Schramm v. Liebenberg, supra; Ruedy v. Alamosa Nat. Bank, 77 Colo. 112, 235 P. 350; Rizzuto v. R.W. English Lumber Co., 44 Colo. 413, 98 P. 728, unless such action is a necessary incident to the business of the principal. The land and investment business carries no such incident. Every lawyer knows that corporations in such business act by their board of directors in such matters; the by-laws of this company had so provided, the financing of the company had all been provided for through the Holly Sugar Company and Hoffman had never, so far as the record shows, executed any promissory notes without the board's authority except these two. The conduct of a principal tacitly conceding powers to an agent works in two ways, as evidence tending to show actual authority and by way of estoppel, i.e., by misleading some one to believe that there is actual authority. In the present case the evidence shows that there was no actual authority and the bank was not misled because the cashier Neill, a director and one of the original organizers of the Montrose Company, knew of the arrangement that had been made for supplying that company with funds, and that it stood in no need of money, and had no reason to believe that Hoffman had authority. The bank knew only through Neill, so it was not misled.

Was there ratification? The answer must be, "No". The bank claims ratification by silence and failure to repudiate after knowledge. Ratification requires knowledge by the principal of all the circumstances of the transaction. The Montrose Company, except Hoffman and Riley, who made the notes, and Neill, who was acting for the bank, knew nothing of the first note until after it had been taken up by the second, and nothing of the second until after Hoffman's death which was in December, 1921, and on the 29th of that month [it] repudiated the notes by letter to the bank. The evidence is that all that the company knew, up to the 28th of October, 1921, was that there had been a note to the Loan Company, that it had been renewed, which was untrue, and that the Loan Company claimed it was given to cover advances. At that time it knew nothing of the transactions with the bank, and there is no evidence that it knew of them till in December. Here was no ratification by silence. We must then say that the execution of the note is not supported by the evidence. It follows that the issues as to consideration and notice are immaterial.

* * *

The judgment is reversed with directions to enter judgment for the defendant.

Mr. Chief Justice ALLEN and Mr. Justice WHITFORD concur.

NOTE

1. Is the court correct when it states, in the above case, that the borrowing of money is not a necessary incident to the business of a land and investment corporation? Did the court make this statement as a matter of law or fact?

2. Would the result in the above case have been different if the bank cashier had not been on the board of directors of the borrower and did not know that its financial needs usually were supplied by Holly Sugar Company?

3. On the other hand, if the cashier's knowledge of the business operations of the borrower can be imputed to the bank on the authority issue, why is not the cashier's knowledge of the loan to the corporation imputed to the corporation on the ratification issue? Three of the five directors knew of the loan at least six months before the borrower repudiated it.

4. Whether the president of a corporation can bind it to a note and mortgage given by him without authorization by the board of directors may turn on: (a) Whether the president had actual authority to execute the agreements—the by-laws gave him the authority and the grant of authority was permitted by the state's corporate statute; (b) Whether the authority to execute the agreements was implied or inherent in his position when acting in the usual course of business of the corporation, for example, the president of a real estate development corporation; (c) Whether the president's position and duties in the operation of the corporation were the equivalent of those of a "general manager"—a person who has the supervision and control of the entire corporation or a distinct unit thereof, and the agreements were made in the usual course of business; and (d) Whether the corporation ratified or adopted the agreements which might be done in the appropriate case by silence or accepting their benefits. See *Farmers State Bank of Victor v. Johnson,* 188 Mont. 55, 610 P.2d 1172 (1980). See generally Kempin, *The Corporate Officer and the Law of Agency,* 44 Va.L.Rev. 1273 (1958).

5. As asked before, what steps might counsel for an institutional lender take to insure that the problems discussed above do not arise?

(iii) THE TRUST

Suffice it to say that the power of a trust to borrow money and mortgage its real estate and the authority of the trustee to borrow and execute a mortgage on behalf of the trust are controlled in most states by statutory provisions and the trust agreement. Therefore, to determine whether the power and the authority to borrow and to mortgage exist, the statutory provisions in effect in the state regulating the conduct of trusts and the trust agreement pertaining to the specific trust in question must be examined.

8. PUBLIC FINANCING

This Division, prior to this point, has dealt with the considerations and problems involved in obtaining from a limited number of institutional and other private lenders and investors the financing necessary to acquire land and construct a project. It is also possible that a developer might meet some, or all, of its financial needs by offering "interests" in the developer or the project to the public or a segment thereof.

If a developer decides to offer interests to the public, carrying out the decision may require registration of the offering under the Securities Act of 1933 unless the interests offered are not securities or the offering is exempt from the provisions of the Act. Registration under the "Blue Sky" laws of the state or states in which the interests are offered may also be required. In addition, even if the interests offered are not securities—the developer plans to sell undeveloped lots or condominium units to be used as principal residences—the interests may be subject to federal regulation through the Interstate Land Sales Full Disclosure Act and/or various state's regulatory schemes. See e.g. Comment, *Legal Protection for Florida Condominium and Cooperative Buyers and Owners*, 27 U.Miami L.Rev. 451 (1973); Minahan, *State and Federal Regulation of Condominiums*, 58 Marq.L.Rev. 55 (1975); Pohoryles, *Condo Regulation on the Local Level*, 5 # 2 Real Est.Rev. 18 (1975); Comment, *Condominium Regulation: Beyond Disclosure*, 123 U.Pa.L.Rev. 639 (1975); Malloy, *The Interstate Land Sales Full Disclosure Act: Its Requirements, Consequences, and Implications for Persons Participating in Real Estate Development*, 24 B.C.L.Rev. 1187 (1983); Chasnow and Lirot, *The Federal Interstate Land Sales Act: An Overview*, 2 Prob. & Prop. 59 (1988).

a. THE SECURITIES ACT OF 1933

THE WHY AND HOW OF REAL ESTATE SYNDICATIONS REGULATION ASPECTS

Milton P. Kroll
5 # 3 Practical Lawyer 70 (March, 1959).
[footnotes omitted]

* * *

On the federal level, securities regulation is governed primarily by the Securities Act of 1933. However, when the Securities Act was passed, Congress took pains to specifically preserve the right of the individual states to also regulate securities transactions within their borders. Thus, this is an area in which there is dual regulation, and both sets of laws must be kept in mind. * * *

The Securities Act of 1933

This law, in general, requires that before a security can be offered or sold by any use of the mails, or by any interstate means, it must be registered with the SEC in Washington. [In addition,] every offeree or purchaser of a registered security must be furnished an official prospectus designed to set forth all of the pertinent information necessary in order that the investor may exercise an informed judgment as to whether or not he wishes to make the investment.

* * *

"Securities"

Do the interests offered in connection with real estate syndications constitute "securities" within the meaning of this law? * * *

Certainly, the usual syndicate interest—whether it be an interest in a limited partnership or in a joint venture—does not fall within the common concept of a "security." Usually, one thinks of stocks, bonds or debentures when asked to define a "security." However, the definition of that term in the Securities Act goes far beyond this common concept.

After defining the term to include the commonly known documents, the definition goes on to include certain catch-all phrases such as "investment contract" or "certificate of interest or participation in any profit sharing agreement."

The courts and the administrative agencies have put a substantial gloss on these catch-all phrases. They have come to include any arrangement whereby a person invests his money in a common enterprise with the expectation of deriving profits from the efforts of the promoter or some third party.

* * * [T]he federal courts * * * have held * * * [that] types of limited partnerships involve "securities" under the law, and the cases are certainly broad enough to cover any other type of real estate syndicate.

Although the direct conveyance of title to real property, without more, is clearly outside the scope of the Securities Act, such sales are held to involve investment contracts when there is a profit-sharing aspect or arrangement. * * * [It has been] held that "securities" were involved in a real estate syndication, notwithstanding that the investors received deeds to undivided fractional interests in the real estate itself.

* * *

Exemptions

What then, are the exemptive possibilities? The Act contains a number of specific exemptions from the registration requirements. Only [four] of these exemptions have any application to real estate syndications.

The [four exemptions] are the exemption for intrastate offerings found in section 3(a)(11), the exemption for transactions not involving any public offering, provided for in section 4[(2), the small offering exemption found in section 3(b), and the exemption of limited offerings to accredited investors, under section 4(6). In addition to the exemptions contained in the Act, two regulations issued by the Securities and Exchange Commission are of interest to the real estate syndicator. Regulation A contains the rules under which an issuer may qualify for the small offering exemption of section 3(b), and Regulation D sets out standards which, if complied with, will qualify the issuer for exemption under sections 4(2) and 4(6).]

Local Enterprise

The section 3(a)(11) exemption is designed to cover purely local enterprises. It applies only where the entire issue is offered and sold exclusively to residents of the state in which the issuer is organized and does business.

* * *

The entire issue must be offered and sold only to residents. Even a single offer or sale to one who in fact is a non-resident destroys the exemption for the whole issue—even as regards the sales made to residents. What is more, the issuer must be assured that such resident purchasers are not buying with a view to subsequent resale to non-residents. As the SEC puts it, "The securities must be in the hands of residents at the time of completion of the distribution."

The underlying partnership must be organized and doing business in that same state. In cases where the property is located in another state, the SEC takes the position that the exemption is not applicable, notwithstanding that the property is operated by a third person under a net lease, and the partnership does no more than collect rent. * * * As can be seen[,] this is a rather dangerous exemption to rely upon, and the burden of proving that any exemption is available is upon the claimant. It is especially risky where the amount of the syndication is large and solicitors are employed. * * *

No Public Offering

[S]ection 4[(2)] [exempts] "transactions not involving any public offering." The Act does not define this concept of public offering. It is far easier to say what is a public offering than to say what is not one, and the latter is the important question.

The determination must be made on a balance of several factors. As early as 1935, the SEC stated that the following are the significant ones:

Number of offerees:—To how many persons is the offering addressed? The important thing here is the number to whom the offer is made, as distinguished from the number of persons who actually purchase.

The type of offeree:—Are they sophisticated persons who can fend for themselves? Do they have access to the sort of information that would be provided in a registration statement? Have they participated in previous deals? Are they relatives or clients? All these factors are important on the issue of public offering.

The number of units and their denomination:—Obviously, where a large number of small units is offered, the arrangement is more likely to be public than where a small number of large units is offered.

Manner of offering:—Is the offer to be made on a personal basis, or is it to be advertised or sold through solicitors?

*　*　*

[Small Offering

Section 3(b) of the Securities Act permits the Securities and Exchange Commission by its rules and regulations to exempt an issue of securities if it finds that registration of the securities is not necessary in the public interest and for the protection of investors by reason of the small amount involved or the limited character of the offering. The aggregate amount at which an issue exempt under this section is offered to the public can not exceed $5,000,000. Regulation A, issued by the Commission under Section 3(b), however, presently limits the amount of the offering to $1,500,000.

Limited Offering to Accredited Investors

Offers and sales to accredited investors are exempt under section 4(6) of the Securities Act if the aggregate offering price of the issue of securities offered in reliance on section 4(6) does not exceed the amount allowed under section 3(b), there is no advertising or public solicitation in connection with the offering and the issuer files a notice with the Securities and Exchange Commission.

Accredited investors, as defined by section 2(15) of the Securities Act and regulations issued by the Securities and Exchange Commission, include institutional investors (such as banks, savings and loans, insurance companies, etc.), insiders (such as directors, executive officers and general partners of the issuer), individuals having a substantial income or net worth and trusts having substantial assets and a sophisticated person making investment decisions.]

[Regulation A]

Where the syndication does not involve more than [$1,500,000], the SEC's Regulation A [which implements the exemption contained in section 3(b) of the Securities Act] should * * * be considered. This [regulation provides] an exemption from registration * * * in cases where the aggregate offering in any 12–month period does not exceed [$1,500,000]. To obtain this exemption, the issuer must file certain information with the applicable Regional Office of the SEC and must [in most cases] provide investors with an offering [statement] that is rather less detailed than the prospectus required in the case of a registered offering. * * * [T]his procedure is less complex, less time-consuming and less costly than registration * * *.

[Regulation D

Regulation D provides certain standards which, if complied with, qualify an offering for the exemptions contained in either section 4(2) or 4(6) of the Securities Act. Three types of offerings are covered by Regulation D. These offerings are described in rules 506, 505 and 504 of the regulation.

Rule 506 provides, generally, that an offer, sale and delivery after sale of securities will be exempt from registration if the issuer complies with the following: (1) offers the securities without general advertising or solicitation; (2) offers and sells the securities to an unlimited number of accredited investors (or to persons whom the issuer reasonably believes are accredited investors) and not to more than 35 nonaccredited but sophisticated investors; (3) furnishes requisite information if nonaccredited investors are involved; (4) sells restricted securities (securities must be acquired for the investors' own accounts and not with a view toward disposition thereof); and (5) files a timely notice of sale in Washington, D.C.

Rule 505 is available to an issuer who: (1) is not an investment company nor disqualified under Regulation A; (2) offers securities not in excess of $5,000,000; (3) sells securities to no more than 35 nonaccredited investors and an unlimited number of accredited investors without any consideration as to the sophistication of the 35 nonaccredited purchasers; (4) sells restricted securities without general advertising or solicitation; (5) supplies requisite information to nonaccredited investors; and (6) timely files the appropriate notice of sale with the Commission.

Rule 504 is available to all issuers, other than reporting companies and investment companies, for offers and sales of securities (a) of up to $1,000,000 during any 12–month period as long as no more than $500,000 worth of securities are offered and sold without registration under states' securities laws, (b) accomplished without general advertising or solicitation, (c) to an unlimited number of persons, (d) which are restricted securities, and (e) with respect to which a timely notice of sale is filed with the SEC.]

Registration

If no exemption is available and the interests must be registered, just what is entailed? Before the interests can be offered, a registration statement must be filed with the SEC in Washington. The SEC is very sensitive to pre-filing publicity about an offering, and it should be avoided. No sales can be made until the registration statement is declared effective by the SEC. During the interim between filing and effectiveness, oral offers can be made, and written offers also can be made in a limited way, primarily by means of a so-called "red herring" or preliminary prospectus. But, no binding commitments can be made until the registration is effective, and the purchaser is provided with a statutory prospectus.

Prospectus

Registration consists of filing with the SEC a registration statement that includes the prospectus that is to be furnished to investors. The prospectus is meant to include all of the information that an investor needs to exercise an independent and informed judgment.

*   *   *

Financial Statements

The registration statement must include financial statements, including a certified balance sheet for the [issuer] and five-year operating statements for the property (three years of which must be certified to by an independent accountant). Pertinent documents must be filed as exhibits, and the entire statement is open to public inspection at the SEC offices.

SEC Comments

*   *   *

The items most generally stressed in a realty syndication registration relate to whether the earnings history of the property supports the stated yearly cash distributions that the syndicators propose to pay. Another essential relates to the profits that the organizers of the syndicate will obtain from the transactions. Then, there are matters such as [income tax considerations,] the physical condition of the property, facts about occupancy and competition, rights and possible obligations of participants and the terms of any net lease of the premises. Finally, the SEC requires a breakdown showing the proportion of the proposed cash distribution that will represent a return of capital, as distinguished from the part that will constitute income to the investor. Of course, the facts peculiar to a given syndication may result in emphasis being placed on other disclosures.

NOTE

1. The Securities Act of 1933 prohibits the offering of securities to the public without registration and a preceding or accompanying prospectus and imposes both civil and criminal liabilities for violation of this prohibition and for fraudulent, false or misleading registration statements and/or prospectuses. See Sections 5, 11, 12, 17 and 24 of the Securities Act of 1933. The Securities Act also contains a general anti-fraud provision that applies to fraudulent practices in the sale of securities through the means of interstate commerce whether or not registered, or required to be registered, under the Act. See Section 17 of the Securities Act. See generally Note, *Real Estate Limited Partnerships and Allocational Efficiency: The Incentive to Sue for Securities Fraud,* 63 Va.L.Rev. 669 (1977). There is substantial disagreement with respect to whether Section 17 may be used as the basis for civil liability. See e.g. *Landry v. All American Assurance Company,* 688 F.2d 381 (5th Cir.1982); *Deviries v. Prudential–Bache Securities, Inc.,* 805 F.2d 326 (8th Cir.1986); *Puchall v. Houghton, Cluck, Coughlin & Riley,* 823 F.2d 1349 (9th Cir.1987), for the view that Section 17 may not be used as a basis for private right of action. See e.g. *Newman v. Prior,* 518 F.2d 97 (4th Cir.1975), for the view that a private right of action can be based on Section 17. See generally Scholl and Perkowski, *An Implied Right of Action under Section 17(a): The Supreme Court Has Said "No," But Is Anybody Listening?,* 36 U.Miami L.Rev. 41 (1981); Comment, *Section 17(a) of the Securities Act of 1933: Implication of a Private Right of Action,* 29 UCLA L.Rev. 244 (1981); Note, *The Existence of Implied Private Rights of Action Under Section 17(a) of the 1933 Securities Act,* 39 Wash. & Lee L.Rev. 1149 (1982); Schneider, *Implying Private Rights and Remedies Under the Federal Securities Acts,* 62 N.C.L.Rev. 853 (1984); Daniels, *The Existence, Necessity, Recognition and Contradiction of an Implied Right of Action Under Section 17(a) of the 1933 Securities Act,* 28 Santa Clara L.Rev. 43 (1988); Note, *What Did Congress Really Want?: An Implied Private Right of Action Under Section 17(a) of the 1933 Securities Act,* 63 Ind.L.J. 623 (1988).

a. Section 12(2) of the Securities Act is a general liability section and applies even when the securities offered or sold are exempt from registration. The issuer and/or its controlling parties are liable to the immediate purchaser of the securities, under Section 12(2), if the issuer offers or sells the securities by an instrument of interstate commerce and makes a material misrepresentation by omission or commission with respect to the securities.

1. A life insurance company, making a long term mortgage loan on a development, may have an action for rescission or money damages under Section 12(2) if, during negotiations for the loan, the developer, through the use of the mails or telephone, made a material misrepresentation. The life insurance company's use of Section 12(2) depends on whether the note and mortgage amount to a "security." See pages 906 to 913 infra.

2. The Securities Act of 1933 only requires full and fair disclosure. The Securities and Exchange Commission does not pass on the merits of an offering being registered. Many of the states' regulatory schemes, however, incorporate an evaluation of the merits of an offering as a condition to the states' registration of the securities. In addition, the national stock exchanges, the National Association of Securities Dealers, the North American Securities Administrators, the Central States Administrator's Council and the Midwest

Securities Commissioner's Association have regulations, particularly with respect to interests in real estate syndications, which incorporate evaluation of these offerings in terms of the "suitability for investment" of the interest offered. Merit evaluation is also involved in some states', such as New York, California and Arizona, regulatory schemes for supervising the sale of land and interests in land such as condominiums, unimproved lots, interests in cooperatives and other interests in real estate. See generally Mosburg, *Regulation of Tax Shelter Investment*, 25 Okla.L.Rev. 207 (1972); Comment, *Legal Protection for Florida Condominium and Cooperative Buyers and Owners*, 27 U.Miami L.Rev. 451 (1973); Comment, *Investor Suitability Standards in Real Estate Syndication: California's Procrustean Bed Approach*, 63 Calif.L.Rev. 471 (1975); Comment, *Condominium Regulation: Beyond Disclosure*, 123 U.Pa.L.Rev. 639 (1975); Minahan, *State and Federal Regulation of Condominiums*, 58 Marq.L. Rev. 55 (1975); Goodkind, *Blue Sky Law: Is There Merit in the Merit Requirements?*, 1976 Wis.L.Rev. 79.

a. The type of matters which must be disclosed and are regulated include: 1. minimum income and net worth levels for investors, 2. net worth and experience levels of general partners and sponsors, 3. compensation of syndicators and general partners, 4. the "track record" of the sponsor and the income tax consequences of the investment, and 5. the rights of the limited partners.

b. The Report of the Real Estate Advisory Committee of the Securities and Exchange Commission submitted October 12, 1972 recommended that separate disclosure guidelines for preparation of registration statements and prospectuses with respect to real estate securities be prepared by the Securities and Exchange Commission's staff. The Securities and Exchange Commission adopted disclosure guidelines in 1976. See *Guide 60, "Preparation of Registration Statements Relating to Interests in Real Estate Limited Partnerships," of the Guides for Preparation and Filing of Registration Statements*, Release No. 33–5465, March 1, 1974, CCH Fed.Sec. L.Rep. ¶ 79,683 ('73–'74 Tr.Bin.), and Release No. 33–5692, March 17, 1976, CCH Fed.Sec.L.Rep. ¶ 80405 ('75–'76 Tr.Bin.). In Release No. 33–6384, March 3, 1982, CCH Fed.Sec.L.Rep. ¶ 3760, the Securities and Exchange Commission redesignated Guide 60 as Securities Act Industry Guide 5. The guidelines require disclosure of a number of factors including: 1. suitability standards used, including those established by the registrant, self-regulatory organizations or state agencies regulating securities offerings, 2. compensation and fees which the general partner and affiliates may receive, 3. transactions which may result in a conflict between the interests of the investors and those of the general partner and affiliates, 4. risks inherent in the program proposed, 5. track record of the general partner and affiliates, 6. investment objectives and policies, 7. federal income tax status of the entity and federal, state and local tax consequences of the program, and 8. summary of the limited partnership agreement. See CCH Fed.Sec.L.Rep. ¶ 3820. Guide 60 was supplemented by Release No. 33–5745, September 27, 1976, CCH Fed.Sec.L.Rep. ¶ 80,727 ('76–'77 Tr.Bin), which added to the Guide 60 requirements that registrants undertake to furnish to investors the financial statements required by Form 10–K for one full year of operation of the registrant after the effective date of the registration statement. Release No. 33–6405, June 3, 1982, CCH Fed.Sec.L. Rep. ¶ 3761, made certain revisions in Guide 60, redesignated as Guide 5, which included simplifying and standardizing the disclosures to be made of the sponsor's track record.

3. After the Securities and Exchange Commission, in Guide 5, required disclosure of federal income tax matters, the Internal Revenue Service, in proposed amendments to Circular 230 dealing with practice before the Internal Revenue Service, attempted to regulate the conduct of those attorneys who prepare opinions on federal income tax matters pertaining to tax shelter offerings—those offerings in which the claimed tax benefits are likely to be perceived as the principal reason for participation. The amendments required, in general, that the attorney preparing the opinion exercise due diligence to assure that (1) all facts which bear significantly on the important federal tax aspects are disclosed, (2) each important federal tax aspect is fully and fairly described and, unless inappropriate, a conclusion is stated as to the likely legal outcome, and (3) the opinion is accurately and clearly described in any discussion of federal tax aspects appearing elsewhere in the offering materials. In addition, the opinion could only be provided if the drafter of the opinion concluded that it was more likely than not that the bulk of the federal tax benefits, on the basis of which the tax shelter was promoted, were allowable under the tax law. See Goldfein and Weiss, *An Analysis of the Proposed Changes Under Circular 230 Affecting Tax Shelter Opinions,* 53 J.Tax'n 340 (1980); Sax, *Lawyer Responsibility in Tax Shelter Opinions,* 34 Tax Law. 5 (1980); A.B.A.Sec.Tax'n, *Statement on Proposed Rule Amending Circular 230 with Respect to Tax Shelter Opinions,* 34 Tax Law. 745 (1981).

a. In response to the proposed amendments to Circular 230, the American Bar Association issued Ethics Rule 346 and subsequently revised it. Revised Ethics Rule 346, 68 A.B.A.J. 471 (1982), requires any attorney issuing an opinion (which includes the preparation of the "tax risks" and "tax aspects" parts of the offering materials) in a "tax shelter" offering to:

1. Require from the client a full disclosure of the structure and intended operations of the venture and complete access to all relevant information,

(a) The attorney may rely on the facts given to him by the client and those ascertained by review of relevant documents if, under the facts and circumstances, such reliance is reasonable;

2. Exercise due diligence in order to be satisfied that all material facts are accurately and completely stated in the offering materials and that the representations as to intended future activities are clearly identified, reasonable and complete;

3. Relate the law to the actual facts to the extent ascertainable, and when addressing issues based on future activities, clearly identify what facts are assumed;

4. Make inquiries to ascertain that a good faith effort has been made to address legal issues other than those addressed in the tax opinion;

5. Take reasonable steps to assure that all material income and excise tax issues have been considered and all of those issues which involve the reasonable possibility of a challenge by the Internal Revenue Service have been fully and fairly addressed in the offering materials;

6. When possible, provide an opinion as to the likely outcome on the merits of the material tax issues addressed in the offering materials;

7. Where possible, provide an overall evaluation of the extent to which the tax benefits in the aggregate are likely to be realized; and

8. Assure that the offering materials correctly represent the nature and extent of the tax shelter opinion.

For the purposes of Revised Rule 346, the following definitions are used.

1. "Tax Shelter" means an investment which has as a significant feature for income or excise tax purposes either or both of the following attributes:

(a) Deductions in excess of income in any year which may be used to reduce income from other sources;

(b) Credits in excess of tax attributable to income from the investment which is available to offset tax on income from other sources.

2. "Material Tax Issue" is any income or excise tax issue relating to the tax shelter that would have a significant effect in sheltering from federal taxes income from other sources by providing deductions in excess of income in any year or tax credits which will offset tax liabilities in excess of the tax attributable to the investment in any year.

b. While not overjoyed about an opinion which advises investors that the tax benefits described in the offering materials are not likely to be realized, the Internal Revenue Service revised Circular 230 so that it was consistent with Revised Ethics Rule 346. See 31 C.F.R. §§ 10.7(c), 10.33, 10.51(j) and 10.76. See generally Marsan, *Tax Shelter Opinions: Ethical Responsibilities of the Tax Attorney,* 9 Ohio N.U.L.Rev. 237 (1982); Schlenger and Watkins, *Exploring the Myths of Circular 230,* 62 Taxes 283 (1984); Falik, *Standards for Professionals Providing Tax Opinions in Tax Shelter Offerings—an Analysis of the Treasury's Final Circular 230 Regulations and a Comparison to ABA Formal Opinion 346,* 37 Tax Law. 701 (1984); Goldfein and Cohn, *Final Circular 230 Amendments Prescribe Disciplinary Standards for Shelter Opinions,* 60 J.Tax'n 330 (1984); Herzog, *Tax Shelter Opinions After TEFRA, Circular 230, and ABA Formal Opinion 346: Who Will Want to Sign Them?,* 14 Cumb.L.Rev. 493 (1983–1984); Holden, *New Professional Standards in the Tax Marketplace: Opinions 314, 346 and Circular 230,* 4 Va.Tax Rev. 209 (1985); Note, *Redefining the Attorney's Role in Abusive Tax Shelters,* 37 Stan.L.Rev. 889 (1985). In addition to setting standards for tax shelter opinions, the Internal Revenue Service takes the position, and the courts have agreed, that the costs of such opinions are syndication costs and therefore, are neither deductible nor amortizable. See Rev.Rul. 88–4, 1988–3 I.R.B. 8; *Arthur B. Surloff,* 81 T.C. 210 (1983); *John K. Johnsen,* 83 T.C. 103 (1984), reversed, 794 F.2d 1157 (6th Cir.1986). Cf. Winston, *Partnership Syndication Costs—The Problem That Will Not Go Away,* 63 Taxes 742 (1985); Comment, *Internal Revenue Code Section 709: To Deduct, Amortize or Capitalize, That is the Question,* 65 Neb.L.Rev. 385 (1986).

c. With respect to an attorney's liability exposure in issuing a tax shelter opinion, see *Morgan v. Prudential Group, Inc.,* 527 F.Supp. 957 (S.D.

N.Y.1981), affirmed, 729 F.2d 1443 (2d Cir.1983), which used the "reckless-ness" standard to determine if the attorneys acted with scienter since it was forseeable that their opinion would be relied on by investors. See also *Securities and Exchange Commission v. Martin,* CCH Fed.Sec.L.Rep. ¶ 99,509 (1983–1984 Tr.Bin.) (D.D.C.1983); *Lubin v. Sybedon Corporation,* 688 F.Supp. 1425 (S.D.Cal.1988); Apke, *Professional Liability for Tax Shelter Opinions,* 13 # 4 Real Est.Rev. 73 (1984); Gimenez, *Tax Shelter Opinions—Securities and Tax Liabilities After TEFRA,* 35 Baylor L.Rev. 25 (1983); Ellis, *TEFRA and Circular 230 Further Define the Legal Malprac-tice Standard of Care of the Tax Opinion Writer Toward the Client and the Non–Client Tax Shelter Investor,* 4 B.U.J.Tax L. 157 (1986); Delsack, *The Lawyer's Professional Responsibility in Rendering Tax Shelter Opinions,* 33 # 4 Prac.Law. 63 (1987).

d.   In a related area, the American Bar Association in Formal Opinion 85–352 reconsidered the minimum basis which would have to exist in order for an attorney to advise a client to take a position with respect to a tax issue. For a number of years the standard had been whether there was a reasonable basis for the position taken. See Formal Opinion 314. In Formal Opinion 85–352 the American Bar Association attempted to tight-en, and to some extent raise, the standard. The standard adopted by Formal Opinion 85–352 is that the position taken must have a realistic possibility of success if the tax issue in question is litigated. See *Formal Opinion 85–352,* 39 Tax Law. 631 (1986); Sax, *Report of the Special Task Force on Formal Opinion 85–352,* 39 Tax Law. 635 (1986); Falk, *Tax Ethics, Legal Ethics, and Real Ethics: A Critique of ABA Formal Opinion 85–352,* 39 Tax Law. 643 (1986).

e.   In recent years Congress has taken steps to eliminate abuses in the tax shelter area. Among the steps taken is the enactment of civil penalties for (1) overvaluation and undervaluation of assets and services, (2) promot-ing abusive tax shelters, (3) substantial understatement of tax liability, and (4) aiding and abetting the understatement of tax liability. In addition, the Internal Revenue Code has been amended to permit an action for injunc-tive relief against promoters of abusive tax shelters, to require registration with the Internal Revenue Service of tax shelter offerings and to charge a higher interest rate on deficiencies resulting from tax-motivated items. See generally Roth, *New Penalty Provisions and Their Effect on Aggressive Tax Planning,* 61 Taxes 52 (1983); Khoury, *TEFRA's Compliance Provi-sions: Impact on Tax Shelter Investments,* 7 Rev.Tax'n Indiv. 195 (1983).

4.   In determining whether to register under the Securities Act of 1933 at least three questions must be answered. First, are the interests being offered "securities"? If the interests being offered are securities, the following ques-tions must be answered. Is the offering exempt as a private offering under Section 4(2) or as a limited offering to accredited investors under Section 4(6) and can Regulation D be complied with? Are the securities exempt since they are only offered and sold to residents of a single state—the intrastate exemp-tion under Section 3(a)(11)?

a.   In addition, the amount of the securities offered may qualify the offering for a small issue exemption under Section 3(b). A Regulation A offering, registration, in a somewhat shorter form, is accomplished at a regional Securities and Exchange Commission office rather than in Wash-ington. If Regulation A is not available, Form S–18, a short and simplified registration form, may be available for use by certain issuers offering securities for an aggregate offering price of up to seven million five hundred thousand dollars.

b.   Because of the nature of some of the entities which invest in real estate syndications, a question may arise with respect to whether a sale of an interest to one entity which qualifies for the intrastate, private offering or sale to an accredited investor exemption, may amount to an offer or sale to the participants in the purchasing entity and therefore, be subject to registration.

5.   In evaluating the general application of the Federal securities laws to real estate syndications, one should consider whether the sponsors of a real estate syndication can be classified as brokers or investment advisers and whether the Investment Company Act of 1940 applies. See generally Wertheimer and Mark, *Special Problems of Unregistered Real Estate Securities,* 22 UCLA L.Rev. 1219 (1975); Cohen and Hacker, *Applicability of the Investment Company Act of 1940 to Real Estate Syndications,* 36 Ohio St.L.J. 482 (1975); Hacker and Rotunda, *Sponsors of Real Estate Partnerships as Brokers and Investment Advisers,* 23 UCLA L.Rev. 322 (1975).

(i) THE MEANING OF "SECURITIES"

The usual interests purchased by investors in a real estate syndication probably are securities as that word is used in the Securities Act of 1933. How broadly, however, is the word "securities" defined? A direct conveyance of the title to real estate without any additional understandings or agreements is clearly outside the scope of the Securities Act. Is a conveyance of title to a condominium unit always outside the scope of the Securities Act?

SECURITIES ACT RELEASE NO. 5347
January 4, 1972.
[footnotes omitted]

The Securities and Exchange Commission today called attention to the applicability of the federal securities laws to the offer and sale of condominium units, or other units in a real estate development, coupled with an offer or agreement to perform or arrange certain rental or other services for the purchaser. The Commission noted that such offerings may involve the offering of a security in the form of an investment contract or a participation in a profit sharing arrangement within the meaning of the Securities Act of 1933 and the Securities Exchange Act of 1934. Where this is the case any offering of any such securities must comply with the registration and prospectus delivery requirements of the Securities Act, unless an exemption therefrom is available, and must comply with the anti-fraud provisions of the Securities Act and the Securities Exchange Act and the regulations thereunder. In addition, persons engaged in the business of buying or selling investment contracts or participations in profit sharing agreements of this type as agents for others, or as principal for their own account, may be brokers or dealers within the meaning of the Securities Exchange Act, and therefore may be required to be registered as such with the Commission under the provisions of Section 15 of that Act.

The Commission is aware that there is uncertainty about when offerings of condominiums and other types of similar units may be considered to be offerings of securities that should be registered pursuant to the Securities Act. The purpose of this release is to alert persons engaged in the business of building and selling condominiums and similar types of real estate developments to their responsibilities under the Securities Act and to provide guidelines for a determination of when an offering of condominiums or other units may be viewed as an offering of securities. Resort condominiums are one of the more common interests in real estate the offer of which may involve an offering of securities. However, other types of units that are part of a development or project present analogous questions under the federal securities laws. Although this release speaks in terms of condominiums, it applies to offerings of all types of units in real estate developments which have characteristics similar to those described herein.

The offer of real estate as such, without any collateral arrangements with the seller or others, does not involve the offer of a security. When the real estate is offered in conjunction with certain services, a security, in the form of an investment contract, may be present. The Supreme Court in Securities and Exchange Commission v. W.J. Howey Co., 328 U.S. 293, 66 S.Ct. 1100, 90 L.Ed. 1244 (1946) set forth what has become a generally accepted definition of an investment contract:

> "a contract, transaction or scheme whereby a person invests his money in a common enterprise and is led to expect profits solely from the efforts of the promoter or a third party, it being immaterial whether the shares in the enterprise are evidenced by formal certificates or by nominal interests in the physical assets employed in the enterprise." (298)

The *Howey* case involved the sale and operation of orange groves. The reasoning, however, is applicable to condominiums.

As the Court noted in *Howey,* substance should not be disregarded for form, and the fundamental statutory policy of affording broad protection to investors should be heeded. Recent interpretations have indicated that the expected return need not be *solely* from the efforts of others, as the holding in *Howey* appears to indicate. For this reason, an investment contract may be present in situations where an investor is not wholly inactive, but even participates to a limited degree in the operations of the business. The "profits" that the purchaser is led to expect may consist of revenues received from rental of the unit; these revenues and any tax benefits resulting from rental of the unit are the economic inducements held out to the purchaser.

The existence of various kinds of collateral arrangements may cause an offering of condominium units to involve an offering of investment contracts or interests in a profit sharing agreement. The presence of such arrangements indicates that the offeror is offering an opportunity through which the purchaser may earn a return on his investment through the managerial efforts of the promoters or a third party in their operation of the enterprise.

For example, some public offerings of condominium units involve rental pool arrangements. Typically, the rental pool is a device whereby the promoter or a third party undertakes to rent the unit on behalf of the actual owner during that period of time when the unit is not in use by the owner. The rents received and the expenses attributable to rental of all the units in the project are combined and the individual owner receives a ratable share of the rental proceeds regardless of whether his individual unit was actually rented. The offer of the unit together with the offer of an opportunity to participate in such a rental pool involves the offer of investment contracts which must be registered unless an exemption is available.

Also, the condominium units may be offered with a contract or agreement that places restrictions, such as required use of an exclusive rental agent or limitations on the period of time the owner may occupy the unit, on the purchaser's occupancy or rental of the property purchased. Such restrictions suggest that the purchaser is in fact investing in a business enterprise, the return from which will be substantially dependent on the success of the managerial efforts of other persons. In such cases, registration of the resulting investment contract would be required.

In any situation where collateral arrangements are coupled with the offering of condominiums, whether or not specifically of the types discussed, above, the manner of offering and economic inducements held out to the prospective purchaser play an important role in determining whether the offerings involve securities. In this connection, see Securities and Exchange Commission v. C.M. Joiner Leasing Corp., 320 U.S. 344, 64 S.Ct. 120, 88 L.Ed. 88 (1943). In *Joiner,* the Supreme Court also noted that:

> "In enforcement of [the Securities Act], it is not inappropriate that promoters' offerings be judged as being what they were represented to be." (353)

In other words, condominiums, coupled with a rental arrangement, will be deemed to be securities if they are offered and sold through advertising, sales literature, promotional schemes or oral representations which emphasize the economic benefits to the purchaser to be derived from the managerial efforts of the promoter, or a third party designated or arranged for by the promoter, in renting the units.

In summary, the offering of condominium units in conjunction with any one of the following will cause the offering to be viewed as an offering of securities in the form of investment contracts:

1. The condominiums, with any rental arrangement or other similar service, are offered and sold with emphasis on the economic benefits to the purchaser to be derived from the managerial efforts of

the promoter, or a third party designated or arranged for by the promoter, from rental of the units.

2.   The offering of participation in a rental pool arrangement; and

3.   The offering of a rental or similar arrangement whereby the purchaser must hold his unit available for rental for any part of the year, must use an exclusive rental agent or is otherwise materially restricted in his occupancy or rental of his unit.

In all of the above situations, investor protection requires the application of the federal securities laws.

If the condominiums are not offered and sold with emphasis on the economic benefits to the purchaser to be derived from the managerial efforts of others, and assuming that no plan to avoid the registration requirements of the Securities Act is involved, an owner of a condominium unit may, after purchasing his unit, enter into a non-pooled rental arrangement with an agent not designated or required to be used as a condition to the purchase, whether or not such agent is affiliated with the offeror, without causing a sale of a security to be involved in the sale of the unit.   Further a continuing affiliation between the developers or promoters of a project and the project by reason of maintenance arrangements does not make the unit a security.

In situations where commercial facilities are a part of the common elements of a residential project, no registration would be required under the investment contract theory where (a) the income from such facilities is used only to offset common area expenses and (b) the operation of such facilities is incidental to the project as a whole and are not established as a primary income source for the individual owners of a condominium or cooperative unit.

* * * It is difficult * * * to anticipate the variety of arrangements that may accompany the offering of condominium projects.   The Commission, therefore, would like to remind those engaged in the offering of condominiums or other interests in real estate with similar features that there may be situations, not referred to in this release, in which the offering of the interests constitutes an offering of securities. Whether an offering of securities is involved necessarily depends on the facts and circumstances of each particular case.   * * *

NOTE

1.   The concepts discussed in the above excerpt, in many states, are used to determine whether the offer and sale of "interests" by a real estate developer are regulated by the state's "Blue Sky" law.   If the offer and sale of interests are not regulated by the "Blue Sky" law, however, a state may have other statutory provisions governing the sale of interests in land.

2.   The test applied in the above Release to determine whether the conveyance of a condominium unit is the purchase of an "investment contract," which is defined as a security under Section 2 of the Securities Act of 1933, is whether the purchase results in the purchaser acquiring an interest in a "common enterprise," the results of which are "dependent on the efforts of one

other than the purchaser." See e.g. *Cameron v. Outdoor Resorts of America, Inc.,* 608 F.2d 187 (5th Cir.1979), modified, 611 F.2d 105 (5th Cir.1980); *Hocking v. Dubois,* 839 F.2d 560 (9th Cir.1988). See generally Minahan, *State and Federal Regulation of Condominiums,* 58 Marq.L.Rev. 55 (1974); Byrne, *Securities Regulation of the Time–Sharing Resort Condominiums,* 7 Real Est.L.J. 3 (1978); Ellsworth and Prendergast, *Securities Maze Awaits Resort Time–Share Offerings,* 10 # 1 Real Est.Rev. 59 (1980).

a. Is a limited partnership interest an investment contract? Is a general partnership interest an investment contract when the partnership agreement provides that all decisions with respect to the conduct of the business of the partnership are to be made by the "managing partners" and the general partnership interest being considered is not that of a managing partner?

The courts generally treat a limited partnership interest as an investment contract. See e.g. *McGreghar Land Company v. Meguiar,* 521 F.2d 822 (9th Cir.1975); *Frazier v. Manson,* 651 F.2d 1078 (5th Cir.1981); *Mayer v. Oil Field Systems Corporation,* 721 F.2d 59 (2d Cir.1983); *Siebel v. Scott,* 725 F.2d 995 (5th Cir.1984), cert. denied, 467 U.S. 1242, 104 S.Ct. 351, 82 L.Ed.2d 823 (1984); *Rodeo v. Gillman,* 787 F.2d 1175 (7th Cir.1986). But see *Bank of America Nat. Trust and Sav. Ass'n v. Hotel Rittenhouse Associates,* 595 F.Supp. 800 (E.D.Pa.1984), reversed on other grounds, 800 F.2d 339 (3d Cir.1986), and *Bamco 18 v. Reeves,* 675 F.Supp. 826 (S.D.N.Y. 1987), in which limited partnership interests, the terms of which had been negotiated between the limited and the general partners, and which gave the limited partners a right to participate in a number of aspects of management were held not to be securities. The courts have been reluctant to treat a general partnership interest as a security. See e.g. *Frazier v. Manson,* 651 F.2d 1078 (5th Cir.1981); *Odom v. Slavik,* 703 F.2d 212 (6th Cir.1983); *Goodwin v. Elkins & Co.,* 558 F.Supp. 1375 (E.D.Pa.1983), affirmed, 730 F.2d 99 (3d Cir.1984), cert. denied, 469 U.S. 831, 105 S.Ct. 118, 83 L.Ed.2d 61 (1984); *Deutsch Energy Co. v. Mazur,* 813 F.2d 1567 (9th Cir. 1987); *Rivanna Trawlers Unlimited v. Thompson Trawlers, Inc.,* 840 F.2d 236 (4th Cir.1988); *Matek v. Murat,* 862 F.2d 720 (9th Cir.1988). The courts, however, may treat a general partnership interest as a security when the holder of the interest's participation in the management of the partnership is limited by the partnership agreement and/or by the abilities, experience and knowledge of the holder and/or by the unique managerial ability of the managing partner. See e.g. *Williamson v. Tucker,* 645 F.2d 404 (5th Cir.1981), cert. denied, 454 U.S. 897, 102 S.Ct. 396, 70 L.Ed.2d 212 (1981); *Gordon v. Terry,* 684 F.2d 736 (11th Cir.1982), cert. denied, 459 U.S. 1203, 1035 S.Ct. 1188, 75 L.Ed.2d 434 (1983); *Securities and Exchange Commission v. Professional Associates,* 731 F.2d 349 (6th Cir.1984); *McGill v. American Land and Exploration Co.,* 776 F.2d 923 (10th Cir.1985); *Less v. Lurie,* 789 F.2d 624 (8th Cir.1986).

See generally Long, *Partnership, Limited Partnership, and Joint Venture Interests as Securities,* 37 Mo.L.Rev. 581 (1972); Dahlk, *Real Estate Partnerships and the Securities Laws: A Primer* 12 Creighton L.Rev. 781 (1978); Morgenstern, *Real Estate Joint Venture Interests as Securities: The Implications of Williamson v. Tucker,* 59 Wash.U.L.Q. 1231 (1982); Levinson, *General Partnership Interests and the Securities Act of 1933: Recent Judicial Developments,* 10 Ohio N.U.L.Rev. 463 (1983); Comment, *General*

Partnership Interests as Securities Under the Federal Securities Laws: Substance Over Form, 54 Fordham L.Rev. 303 (1985).

b.   Is an interest in a cooperative housing corporation a security? See *Silverman v. Alcoa Plaza Associates*, 37 A.D.2d 166, 323 N.Y.S.2d 39 (1971), discussing this issue in the context of the Uniform Commercial Code. It is a stock interest and, therefore, within the literal wording of Section 2(1) of the Securities Act. Does this mean that, when arranging for the sale of interests in a cooperative housing corporation, the developer must register under the Securities Act? Consider Section 3(a) of the Act which exempts certain classes of securities. Apart from treating the interest in a cooperative housing corporation as a security, certain states, for example New York, have comprehensive regulatory schemes dealing with the sale of interests in cooperative housing corporations. In addition, if F.H.A. and/or H.U.D. assists in the financing of the project, they too will regulate aspects of the acquisition of an interest in the cooperative.

UNITED HOUSING FOUNDATION, INC. v. FORMAN

Supreme Court of the United States, 1975.
421 U.S. 837, 44 L.Ed.2d 621, 95 S.Ct. 2051.
(footnotes omitted)

Mr. Justice POWELL delivered the opinion of the Court.

The issue in this case is whether shares of stock entitling a purchaser to lease an apartment in Co–Op City, a state subsidized and supervised nonprofit housing cooperative, are "securities" within the purview of the Securities Act of 1933 and the Securities Exchange Act of 1934.

I

Co–Op City is a massive housing cooperative in New York City. Built between 1965 and 1971, it presently houses approximately 50,000 people on a 200–acre site containing 35 high rise buildings and 236 town houses. The project was organized, financed, and constructed under the New York State Private Housing Finance Law, commonly known as the Mitchell–Lama Act, enacted to ameliorate a perceived crisis in the availability of decent low-income urban housing. In order to encourage private developers to build low-cost cooperative housing, New York provides them with large long-term, low-interest mortgage loans and substantial tax exemptions. Receipt of such benefits is conditioned on a willingness to have the State review virtually every step in the development of the cooperative. See N.Y. Private Housing Finance Law §§ 11–37, as amended, (McKinney's Consol.Laws, c. 44B, Supp.1974–1975). The developer also must agree to operate the facility "on a nonprofit basis," id., at § 11–a(2a), and he may lease apartments only to people whose incomes fall below a certain level and who have been approved by the State.

The United Housing Foundation (UHF), a nonprofit membership corporation established for the purpose of "aiding and encouraging" the creation of "adequate, safe and sanitary housing accommodations for wage earners and other persons of low and moderate income," Appendix, at 95a, was responsible for initiating and sponsoring the development of Co–Op City. Acting under the Mitchell–Lama Act, UHF organized the Riverbay Corporation (Riverbay) to own and operate the land and buildings constituting Co–Op City. Riverbay, a nonprofit cooperative housing corporation, issued the stock that is the subject of this litigation. UHF also contracted with Community Services, Inc. (CSI), its wholly owned subsidiary, to serve as the general contractor and sales agent for the project. As required by the Mitchell–Lama Act, these decisions were approved by the State Housing Commissioner.

To acquire an apartment in Co–Op City an eligible prospective purchaser must buy 18 shares of stock in Riverbay for each room desired. The cost per share is $25, making the total cost $450 per room, or $1,800 for a four-room apartment. The sole purpose of acquiring these shares is to enable the purchaser to occupy an apartment in Co–Op City; in effect, their purchase is a recoverable deposit on an apartment. The shares are explicitly tied to the apartment: they cannot be transferred to a nontenant; nor can they be pledged or encumbered; and they descend, along with the apartment, only to a surviving spouse. No voting rights attach to the shares as such: participation in the affairs of the cooperative appertains to the apartment, with the residents of each apartment being entitled to one vote irrespective of the number of shares owned.

Any tenant who wants to terminate his occupancy, or who is forced to move out, must offer his stock to Riverbay at its initial selling price of $25 per share. In the extremely unlikely event that Riverbay declines to repurchase the stock, the tenant cannot sell it for more than the initial purchase price plus a fraction of the portion of the mortgage that he has paid off, and then only to a prospective tenant satisfying the statutory income eligibility requirements. See N.Y. Private Housing Finance Law § 31–a (McKinney Supp.1974–1975).

* * *

* * * The heart of respondents' claim was that the 1965 Co–Op City Information Bulletin falsely represented that CSI would bear all subsequent cost increases due to factors such as inflation. Respondents further alleged that they were misled in their purchases of shares since the Information Bulletin failed to disclose several critical facts. On these bases, respondents asserted two claims under the fraud provisions of the federal Securities Acts of 1933 and 1934, 15 U.S.C.A. § 77q(a); 15 U.S.C.A. § 78j(b), and 17 CFR § 240.10b–5. They also presented a claim against the State Financing Agency under the Civil Rights Act, 42 U.S.C.A. § 1983, and 10 pendent state law claims.

Petitioners, while denying the substance of these allegations, moved to dismiss the complaint on the ground that federal jurisdiction was lacking. They maintained that shares of stock in Riverbay were not "securities" within the definitional sections of the federal Securities

Acts.   In addition, the state parties moved to dismiss on sovereign immunity grounds.

*   *   *

In view of the importance of the issues presented we granted certiorari.   United Housing Foundation, Inc., v. Forman, 419 U.S. 1120, 95 S.Ct. 801, 42 L.Ed.2d 819 (1975).   As we conclude that the disputed transactions are not purchases of securities within the contemplation of the federal statutes, we reverse.

II

*   *   *

A

We reject at the outset any suggestion that the present transaction, evidenced by the sale of shares called "stock," must be considered a security transaction simply because the statutory definition of a security includes the words "any * * * stock."   Rather, we adhere to the basic principle that has guided all of the Court's decisions in this area:

> "[I]n searching for the meaning and scope of the word 'security' in the Act[s], form should be disregarded for substance and the emphasis should be on economic reality."   Tcherepnin v. Knight, 389 U.S. 332, 336, 88 S.Ct. 548, 553, 19 L.Ed.2d 564 (1967).   See also [Securities & Exchange Commission v. W.J. Howey Co., 328 U.S. 293, 298, 66 S.Ct. 1100, 1102, 90 L.Ed. 1244 (1946)].

The primary purpose of the Securities Acts of 1933 and 1934 was to eliminate serious abuses in a largely unregulated securities market. The focus of the Acts is on the capital market of the enterprise system: the sale of securities to raise capital for profit-making purposes, the exchanges on which securities are traded, and the need for regulation to prevent fraud and to protect the interest of investors.   Because securities transactions are economic in character Congress intended the application of these statutes to turn on the economic realities underlying a transaction, and not on the name appended thereto.   Thus, in construing these Acts against the background of their purpose, we are guided by a traditional canon of statutory construction:

> "[A] thing may be within the letter of the statute and yet not within the statute, because not within its spirit, nor within the intention of its makers."   Church of the Holy Trinity v. United States, 143 U.S. 457, 459, 12 S.Ct. 511, 512, 36 L.Ed. 226 (1892). See also United States v. American Trucking Assns., Inc., 310 U.S. 534, 543, 60 S.Ct. 1059, 1063, 84 L.Ed. 1345 (1940).

*   *   *

In holding that the name given to an instrument is not dispositive, we do not suggest that the name is wholly irrelevant to the decision whether it is a security.   There may be occasions when the use of a traditional name such as "stocks" or "bonds" will lead a purchaser justifiably to assume that the federal securities laws apply.   This would clearly be the case when the underlying transaction embodies some of the significant characteristics typically associated with the named instrument.

In the present case respondents do not contend, nor could they, that they were misled by use of the word "stock" into believing that the federal securities laws governed their purchase. Common sense suggests that people who intend to acquire only a residential apartment in a state-subsidized cooperative, for their personal use, are not likely to believe that in reality they are purchasing investment securities simply because the transaction is evidenced by something called a share of stock. These shares have none of the characteristics "that in our commercial world fall within the ordinary concept of a security." H.R. Rep. No. 85, at 11. Despite their name, they lack what the Court in *Tcherepnin* deemed the most common feature of stock: the right to receive "dividends contingent upon an apportionment of profits." 389 U.S. at 339, 88 S.Ct. at 555. Nor do they possess the other characteristics traditionally associated with stock: they are not negotiable; they cannot be pledged or hypothecated; they confer no voting rights in proportion to the number of shares owned; and they cannot appreciate in value. In short, the inducement to purchase was solely to acquire subsidized low-cost living space; it was not to invest for profit.

B

The Court of Appeals, as an alternative ground for its decision, concluded that a share in Riverbay was also an "investment contract" as defined by the Securities Acts. Respondents further argue that in any event what they agreed to purchase is "commonly known as a 'security'" within the meaning of these laws. In considering these claims we again must examine the substance—the economic realities of the transaction—rather than the names that may have been employed by the parties. We perceive no distinction, for present purposes, between an "investment contract" and an "instrument commonly known as a security." In either case, the basic test for distinguishing the transaction from other commercial dealings is

> "whether the scheme involves an investment of money in a common enterprise with profits to come solely from the efforts of others." *Howey,* supra, 328 U.S., at 301, 66 S.Ct., at 1104.

This test, in shorthand form, embodies the essential attributes that run through all of the Court's decisions defining a security. The touchstone is the presence of an investment in a common venture premised on a reasonable expectation of profits to be derived from the entrepreneurial or managerial efforts of others. By profits, the Court has meant either capital appreciation resulting from the development of the initial investment, as in [Securities & Exchange Commission v. C.M. Joiner Leasing Corp., 320 U.S. 344, 64 S.Ct. 120, 88 L.Ed. 88 (1943)] (sale of oil leases conditioned on promoters' agreement to drill exploratory well), or a participation in earnings resulting from the use of investors' funds, as in Tcherepnin v. Knight, supra (dividends on the investment based on savings and loan association's profits). In such cases the investor is "attracted solely by the prospects of a return" on his investment. *Howey,* supra, 328 U.S., at 300, 66 S.Ct., at 1103. By contrast, when a purchaser is motivated by a desire to use or consume the item purchased—"to occupy the land or to develop it themselves," as the *Howey* Court put it, 328 U.S., at 300, 66 S.Ct., at 1103—the securities laws do not apply. See also [Securities & Exchange Commission v. C.M. Joiner Leasing Corp., supra].

In the present case there can be no doubt that investors were attracted solely by the prospect of acquiring a place to live, and not by financial returns on their investments. The Information Bulletin distributed to prospective residents emphasized the fundamental nature and purpose of the undertaking:

> "A cooperative is a nonprofit enterprise owned and controlled democratically by its members—the people who are using its services. * * *

> "People find living in a cooperative community enjoyable for more than one reason. Most people join, however, for the simple reason that it is a way to obtain decent housing at a reasonable price. However, there are other advantages. The purpose of a cooperative is to provide home ownership, not just apartments to rent. The community is designed to provide a favorable environment for family and community living. * * *

> "The common bond of collective ownership which you share makes living in a cooperative different. It is a community of neighbors. Home ownership, common interests and the community atmosphere make living in a cooperative like living in a small town. As a rule there is very little turnover in a cooperative." Appendix, at 162a–166a.

Nowhere does the Bulletin seek to attract investors by the prospect of profits resulting from the efforts of the promoters or third parties. On the contrary, the Bulletin repeatedly emphasizes the "nonprofit" nature of the endeavor. It explains that if rental charges exceed expenses the difference will be returned as a rebate, not invested for profit. It also informs purchasers that they will be unable to resell their apartments at a profit since the apartment must first be offered back to Riverbay "at the price * * * paid for it." Id., at 162a. In short, neither of the kinds of profits traditionally associated with securities were offered to respondents.

The Court of Appeals recognized that there must be an expectation of profits for these shares to be securities, and conceded that there is "no possible profit on a resale of [this] stock." 500 F.2d, at 1254. The court correctly noted, however, that profit may be derived from the income yielded by an investment as well as from capital appreciation, and then proceeded to find "an expectation of 'income' in at least three ways." Ibid. Two of these supposed sources of income or profits may be disposed of summarily. We turn first to the Court of Appeals' reliance on the deductibility for tax purposes of the portion of the monthly rental charge applied to interest on the mortgage. We know of no basis in law for the view that the payment of interest, with its consequent deductibility for tax purposes, constitutes income or profits. These tax benefits are nothing more than that which is available to any homeowner who pays interest on his mortgage. See Internal Revenue Code, 26 U.S.C.A. § 216; Eckstein v. United States, 452 F.2d 1036, 196 Ct.Cl. 644 (1971).

The Court of Appeals also found support for its concept of profits in the fact that Co–Op City offered space at a cost substantially below the going rental charges for comparable housing. Again, this is an inappropriate theory of "profits" that we cannot accept. The low rent derives from the substantial financial subsidies provided by the State of New York. This benefit cannot be liquidated into cash; nor does it result from the managerial efforts of others. In a real sense, it no more embodies the attributes of income or profits than do welfare benefits, food stamps or other government subsidies.

The final source of profit relied on by the Court of Appeals was the possibility of net income derived from the leasing by Co–Op City of commercial facilities, professional offices and parking spaces, and its operation of community washing machines. The income, if any, from these conveniences, all located within the common areas of the housing project, is to be used to reduce tenant rental costs. Conceptually, one might readily agree that net income from the leasing of commercial and professional facilities is the kind of profit traditionally associated with a security investment. See Tcherepnin v. Knight, supra. But in the present case this income—if indeed there is any is far too speculative and insubstantial to bring the entire transaction within the Securities Acts.

Initially we note that the prospect of such income as a means of offsetting rental costs is never mentioned in the Information Bulletin. Thus it is clear that investors were not attracted to Co–Op City by the offer of these potential rental reductions. See *Joiner,* supra, 320 U.S., at 353, 64 S.Ct., at 124. Moreover, nothing in the record suggests that the facilities in fact return a profit in the sense that the leasing fees are greater than the actual cost to Co–Op City of the space rented. The short of the matter is that the stores and services in question were established not as a means of returning profits to tenants, but for the purpose of making essential services available for the residents of this enormous complex. By statute these facilities can only be "incidental and appurtenant" to the housing project. N.Y. Private Housing Law § 12(5) (McKinney Supp. 1974–1975). Undoubtedly they make Co–Op City a more attractive housing opportunity, but the possibility of some rental reduction is not an "expectation of profit" in the sense found necessary in *Howey.*

There is no doubt that purchasers in this housing cooperative sought to obtain a decent home at an attractive price. But that type of economic interest characterizes every form of commercial dealing. What distinguishes a security transaction—and what is absent here—is an investment where one parts with his money in the hope of receiving profits from the efforts of others, and not where he purchases a commodity for personal consumption or living quarters for personal use.

III

In holding that there is no federal jurisdiction, we do not address the merits of respondents' allegations of fraud. Nor do we indicate any view as to whether the type of claims here involved should be protected by federal regulation. We decide only that the type of transaction before us, in which the purchasers were interested in acquiring housing rather than making an investment for profit, is not within the scope of the federal securities laws.

Since respondents' claims are not cognizable in federal court, the District Court properly dismissed their complaint. The judgment below is therefore reversed.

Reversed.

Mr. Justice BRENNAN, with whom Mr. Justice DOUGLAS and Mr. Justice WHITE join, dissenting.

[Dissenting opinion omitted.]

NOTE

1. Is the holding of *United Housing Foundation, Inc. v. Forman* that interests in a cooperative housing corporation are not securities under the Securities Act of 1933, or is the holding more limited?

a. Would the Supreme Court have reached the same result in *United Housing Foundation, Inc. v. Forman* if the interests in the cooperative could have been sold or assigned at a profit by the tenants? The Federal District Court for the Southern District of New York held that this factor distinguished the interests considered in *United Housing Foundation, Inc. v. Forman* from those considered in *1050 Tenant's Corp. v. Jakobson*, 365 F.Supp. 1171 (S.D.N.Y.1973), affirmed, 503 F.2d 1375 (2d Cir.1974), and the District Court concluded that the interests in the latter case were securities. After the Supreme Court's decision in *United Housing Foundation, Inc. v. Forman*, the District Court for the Southern District of New York again faced a situation in which the interests in a cooperative could be sold or assigned at a profit. It followed its decision in *1050 Tenant's Corp. v. Jakobson*, supra. See *Grenader v. Spitz*, 390 F.Supp. 1112 (S.D.N.Y.1975), reversed, 537 F.2d 612 (2d Cir.1976), cert. denied, 429 U.S. 1009, 97 S.Ct. 541, 50 L.Ed.2d 619 (1976). Can one sell his or her home at a profit? See *Grenader v. Spitz*, 537 F.2d 612 (2d Cir.1976). The purchase of a home rarely involves the purchase of a security. Cf. *Davis v. Rio Rancho Estates, Inc.*, 401 F.Supp. 1045 (S.D.N.Y.1975); *Happy Investment Group v.*

Lakeworld Properties, Inc., 396 F.Supp. 175 (N.D.Cal.1975); *Northbridge Park Cooperative Offering*, CCH Fed.Sec.L. Rep. ¶ 76,330 (1980 Tr.Bin.).

    b. Might the interests in a cooperative be considered securities if the units in the cooperative do not have to be used as the residences of the purchasers of the interests in the cooperative, the units can be subleased when the purchasers are not in residence, and the units must be put into a rental pool managed by the cooperative corporation? Cf. Securities Act Release No. 5347 at page 893 to 896.

    c. If the purchasers of interests in the cooperative have voting rights in the cooperative corporation according to the number of units of interest purchased rather than one vote per one apartment, might an interest in the cooperative be considered a security? See *Grenader v. Spitz*, 390 F.Supp. 1112 (S.D.N.Y.1975), reversed, 537 F.2d 612 (2d Cir.1976), cert. denied, 429 U.S. 1009, 97 S.Ct. 541, 50 L.Ed.2d 619 (1976).

    d. If the cooperative includes space which is leased to commercial and retail tenants, is the amount of rental income derived from the commercial space relevant to whether an interest in the cooperative is a security or, in determining security status, is whether the commercial and retail space is frequented by the general public of greater concern? Might both be relevant in determining whether the interests in the cooperative are securities? Cf. Securities Act Release No. 5347 at pages 893 to 896.

    2. Does the status of the sponsor of the cooperative as a profit-oriented developer or a nonprofit or governmental entity make any difference in determining whether interests in the cooperative are securities? Cf. *Wheatbelt Merchandising Group, Inc.*, CCH Fed.Sec.L.Rep. ¶ 76,446 (1980 Tr.Bin.).

    3. See generally Note, *United Housing Foundation v. Forman: Shares of Stock in Nonprofit Housing Cooperative are Not "Securities"*, 29 Sw.L.J. 987 (1975); Comment, *Cooperative Housing Shares: A Security or Substantively Secure?*, 12 Urb.L.Ann. 277 (1976); Note, *Shares in Privately Financed Cooperative Apartment Corporations and the Federal Securities Law After Grenader v. Spitz*, 30 Rutgers L.Rev. 432 (1977).

    4. There are other types of real property interests which may be held, in appropriate circumstances, to amount to securities. For example, interests in notes and mortgages, see e.g. *Los Angeles Trust Deed and Mortgage Exchange v. S.E.C.*, 285 F.2d 162 (9th Cir.1960), cert. denied, 366 U.S. 919, 81 S.Ct. 1095, 6 L.Ed.2d 241 (1961); *Walter Musa, Jr.*, CCH Fed.Sec.L.Rep. ¶ 80,973 ('76–'77 Tr. Bin); *S.E.C. v. Garfinkle*, CCH Fed.Sec.L.Rep. ¶ 96,465 (1978 Tr.Bin) (S.D.N.Y. 1978), and interests in installment sale contracts, see e.g. *Jenne v. Amrep Corp.*, CCH Fed.Sec.L.Rep. ¶ 96,343 (1978 Tr.Bin) (D.N.J.1978); *Cornwall Company*, CCH Fed.Sec.L.Rep. ¶ 78,129 ('85–'86 Tr.Bin), have been held to be securities under the Securities Act of 1933. The sale of participations in loans, see e.g. *National Association of Securities Dealers, Inc.*, CCH Fed.Sec.L.Rep. ¶ 80,187 ('74–'75 Tr.Bin); *Bank of America National Trust and Savings Ass'n*, CCH Fed. Sec.L.Rep. ¶ 81,193 ('77–'78 Tr.Bin); *Commercial Discount Corp. v. Lincoln First Commercial Corp.*, 445 F.Supp. 1263 (S.D.N.Y.1978), and the sale of a "cotenancy" in real estate coupled with a management contract and power of attorney, see *Cook v. Farrell*, CCH Fed.Sec.L.Rep. ¶ 95,337 ('75–'76 Tr.Bin.) (N.D.Ga.1975), have been held to involve the sale of securities. There is, however, a limited exemption from registration for the sale of participations in notes secured by a first lien on a single parcel of real estate on which there is a residential or commercial structure. See Section 4(5) of the Securities Act of 1933 and

Mason–McDuffie Investment Co., CCH Fed.Sec.L.Rep. ¶ 81,336 ('77–'78 Tr.Bin). In certain contexts, participations in loans have been held not to amount to securities. See e.g. *United American Bank of Nashville v. Gunter,* 620 F.2d 1108 (5th Cir.1980); *American Fletcher Mortgage Company, Inc. v. United States Steel Credit Corporation,* 635 F.2d 1247 (7th Cir.1980), cert. denied, 451 U.S. 911, 101 S.Ct. 1982, 68 L.Ed.2d 300 (1981); *Union Planters National Bank of Memphis v. Commercial Credit Business Loans, Inc.,* 651 F.2d 1174 (6th Cir. 1981), cert. denied, 454 U.S. 1124, 102 S.Ct. 972, 71 L.Ed.2d 111 (1981); *Elson v. Geiger,* 506 F.Supp. 238 (E.D.Mich.1980), affirmed, 701 F.2d 176 (6th Cir.1982); *Union National Bank of Little Rock v. Farmers Bank,* 786 F.2d 881 (8th Cir. 1986). The sale of an apartment development coupled with an agreement granting the seller management rights, which agreement could be terminated on thirty days notice, was held not to involve the sale of a security. See *Fargo Partners v. Dain Corp.,* 405 F.Supp. 739 (D.N.D.1975), affirmed, 540 F.2d 912 (8th Cir.1976). See also *Schultz v. Dain Corp.,* 568 F.2d 612 (8th Cir.1978); *Perry v. Gammon,* 583 F.Supp. 1230 (N.D.Ga.1984); *Kaplan v. Shapiro,* 655 F.Supp. 336 (S.D.N.Y.1987). The sale of vacant land coupled with a promise by the seller to provide certain facilities and amenities has been considered the sale of a security. See e.g. *Timmreck v. Munn,* 433 F.Supp. 396 (N.D.Ill.1977); *Fogel v. Sellamerica, Ltd.,* 445 F.Supp. 1269 (S.D.N.Y.1978); *Anderson v. Grand Bahama Dev. Co. Ltd.,* 67 Ill.App.3d 687, 24 Ill.Dec. 114, 384 N.E.2d 981 (1978); *Aldrich v. McCulloch Properties, Inc.,* 627 F.2d 1036 (10th Cir.1980). But see e.g. *Commander's Palace Park Associates v. Girard & Pastel Corp.,* 572 F.2d 1084 (5th Cir.1978); *Woodward v. Terracor,* 574 F.2d 1023 (10th Cir.1978); *De Luz Ranchos Investment, Ltd. v. Coldwell Banker & Company,* 608 F.2d 1297 (9th Cir.1979); *Westchester Corporation v. Peat, Marwick, Mitchell & Company,* 626 F.2d 1212 (5th Cir.1980).

See generally Hart, *Securities Regulation of Real Estate Developments— Financing Arrangements Considered as an Extension of Credit,* 35 Ohio St.L.J. 300 (1974); Note, *Bank Loan Participations: The Affirmative Duty to Disclose Under SEC Rule 10b–5,* 27 Syracuse L.Rev. 807 (1976); Pollack, *Notes Issued in Syndicated Loans—A New Test to Define Securities,* 32 Bus.Law. 537 (1977); Comment, *Bank Loan Participations as Securities: Notes, Investment Contracts, and the Commercial/Investment Dichotomy,* 15 Duq.L.Rev. 261 (1977); Comment, *Recreational Land Subdivisions as Investment Contracts,* 13 Hous.L.Rev. 153 (1975); Note, *Real Estate as Securities: Sales of Residential Subdivision Lots,* 1979 Wash.U.L.Q. 965 (1979); Scholl and Weaver, *Loan Participations: Are They Securities?,* 10 Fla.St.U.L.Rev. 215 (1982); Note, *When is a Security Not a Security? Promissory Notes, Loan Participations, and Stock in Close Corporations,* 39 Wash. & Lee L.Rev. 1123 (1982); Note, *Loan Participation Agreements as Securities: Judicial Interpretations of the Securities Act of 1933 and the Securities Exchange Act of 1934,* 24 Wm. & Mary L.Rev. 295 (1983); Fields, *Real Estate Interests as Investment Contracts: An Update and a New Application—The Shared–Equity Program,* 12 Real Est.L.J. 307 (1984); Vargo, *Real Estate Transactions: The Existence of a Federal Security,* 14 Cumb.L.Rev. 301 (1984).

5. The Federal Securities Acts specifically exempt a note which has a maturity date not exceeding nine months at the time of issuance. See the Securities Act of 1933, Sections 2(1) and 3(a)(3) and the Securities and Exchange Act of 1934, Section 3(a)(10). While it might be assumed as a result of these provisions that all other notes and forms of indebtedness will be classified as

securities, the courts have attempted to distinguish between notes and other forms of indebtedness which are securities and those which are not securities.

SECURITIES AND EXCHANGE COMM. v. DIVERSIFIED INDUSTRIES, INC.

United States District Court, District of Columbia, 1979.
465 F.Supp. 104.
[footnotes omitted]

RICHEY, District Judge: * * *

Counts IV through VI relate to a fraudulent real estate transaction. Count IV charges the defendants Castle, Aronoff, Penn–Dixie and the JDL Trust with violations of section 10(b) of the Securities Exchange Act of 1934 (hereinafter, "The Act"), 15 U.S.C.A. § 78j(b) and Rule 10b–5, 17 C.F.R. 240.10b–5 (1978). The Commission alleges that Aronoff conspired with Castle, then President and Chairman of the Board of Penn–Dixie, to arrange for the purchase of undrainable Florida swampland by Penn–Dixie for over five million dollars from the JDL Trust, a trust set up by Aronoff for the benefit of his parents and children. According to the complaint, the defendants conspired to defraud the shareholders of Penn–Dixie by fraudulently inducing a public corporation to issue a security, the mortgage for the land, in connection with the acquisition of this investment property.

Counts V and VI of the complaint allege violations of the reporting provisions of the federal securities laws. Count V charges that Castle, Penn–Dixie, and Aronoff violated section 13(a) of the Act, 15 U.S.C.A. § 78m(a) and Rules 12b–20 and 13a–1, 17 C.F.R. 240.12b–20 and 240.13a–1 (1978) by filing false and misleading Annual Reports which failed to disclose the allegedly fraudulent activities surrounding the purchase by Penn–Dixie of the Florida real estate. Count VI charges Castle and Penn–Dixie with violations of section 14(a) of the Act, 15 U.S.C.A. § 78n(a) and Rule 14a–9, 17 C.F.R. 240.14a–9 (1978) for filing false and misleading proxy statements which also failed to disclose the alleged swampland fraud.

* * *

On December 21, 1976, Aronoff filed a motion to dismiss and other relief and an alternative motion for severance and transfer. On January 11, 1977, the JDL Trust filed a similar motion for dismissal and other relief and an alternative motion for severance. Oral argument on these motions was held on June 15, 1977 before Judge Waddy. On October 6, 1977, Castle filed a motion to dismiss, for summary judgment, and to strike the complaint as sham. This case is currently before the Court on these motions.

The Purchase Money Mortgage Penn–Dixie Issued to the JDL Trust is a "Security" Within the Meaning of the Federal Securities Law

The defendants in their papers in support of their motion to dismiss and in their oral argument before Judge Waddy have tried to characterize this case as an attempt by the Commission to convert the securities laws into a general remedy for real estate fraud. The defendants contend that if the Court finds that the securities laws apply in this case every homeowner who sells his or her home would be subject to the anti-fraud provisions of the 1934 Securities Exchange Act. The Commission distinguishes this situation from the average home-owner's case by pointing to three factors: (1) the note was issued for the acquisition of an investment asset, (2) the note was issued by a public company, and (3) the note was not initially issued to a bank or other party in the business of making loans.

To render the Securities Exchange Acts of 1933 or 1934 applicable to a transaction, a "security" must be exchanged. The Commission relies on the ten-year purchase money mortgage note Penn–Dixie issued to the JDL Trust as part payment for the Florida real estate to satisfy this requirement.

Although there are slight differences in wording between the 1933 and 1934 Acts, the definitions of "security" in the two acts have been treated as functionally equivalent. See Tcherepnin v. Knight, 389 U.S. 332, 335–336 (1967), 88 S.Ct. 548, 19 L.Ed.2d 564; * * *.

The definitional section of the Securities Exchange Act of 1934, 15 U.S.C.A. § 78c(a)(10) (1976), provides that, "unless the context otherwise requires—* * * (10) the term 'security' means any note * * * but shall not include * * * any note * * * which has a maturity date at the time of issuance of not exceeding nine months. * * *" The definitional section of the 1933 Act has a similar definition of "security" with the exception of the nine-month limitation. 15 U.S. C.A. § 77b(1) (1976). Although the statutes on their faces are readily discernible, judicial interpretation has clouded their clarity. In the words of a recent commentator:

> The courts have recently made it clear that despite the apparently contrary language of (the definitional statutes), (1) not all notes of more than 9 months' duration are "securities" and not all notes of less than such duration are not "securities," (2) the decisive factor in the determination of whether notes fall within the 1933 or 1934 Act is the type of note, and not its duration, and (3) this decisive factor is itself not readily determinable.

Kaplan, Promissory Notes as Securities Under § 2(1) of Securities Act of 1933 (15 U.S.C.A. § 77b(1)), and § 3(a)(10), of Securities Exchange Act of 1934, 39 A.L.R.Fed. 357, 365 (1978).

Unfortunately, the U.S. Circuit Courts of Appeals that have confronted this issue have devised somewhat different tests to determine whether a note constitutes a "security," and the judges of this circuit court have yet to address this problem. Accordingly, the Court must examine the varying approaches taken by the different circuits to the problem before the Court.

A. The Commercial/Investment Dichotomy Test of the Third, Fifth, Seventh, and Tenth Circuits

The "investment/commercial dichotomy test," which has been followed in the Third, Fifth, Seventh, and Tenth Circuits, is premised on the view that Congress' concern in enacting the securities laws was with practices associated with investment transactions and that the securities laws were not designed to regulate commercial transactions. See C.N.S. Enterprises, Inc. v. G. & G. Enterprises, Inc., 508 F.2d 1354, 1359 (7th Cir.) cert. denied 423 U.S. 825, 96 S.Ct. 38, 46 L.Ed.2d 40 (1975). The decision of the U.S. Court of Appeals for the Seventh Circuit in *C.N.S. Enterprises, Inc.* contains a helpful description of the investment/commercial test:

> The ultimate question is whether the plaintiffs are simply borrowers in a commercial transaction who are not protected by the 1934 Act or investors in a securities transaction who are protected.
>
> In one sense every lender of money is an investor since he places his money at risk in anticipation of a profit in the form of interest. Also in a broad sense every investor lends his money to a borrower who uses it for a price and is expected to return it one day.
>
> On the other hand, the polarized extremes are conceptually identifiable: buying shares of common stock of a publicly-held corporation, where the impetus for the transaction comes from the person with the money, is an investment; borrowing money from a bank to finance the purchase of an automobile, where the impetus for the transaction comes from the person who needs the money, is a loan. In between is a grey area which, in the absence of further congressional indication of intent or Supreme Court construction, has been and must be in the future subjected to case-by-case treatment. Id. at 1359 (citations omitted).

Although a case-by-case approach has been adopted under the commercial/investment dichotomy approach, courts have focused on certain factors to guide the application of the test. Despite the defendants' contentions to the contrary, one of the factors the courts have focused on in applying the test is the nature of the assets acquired in exchange for the notes. The defendants are correct in pointing out that every time an investment asset is acquired, the notes have not been determined to be securities under this test. See Lino v. City Investing Co., 487 F.2d 689 (3d Cir.1973) (franchise); C.N.S. Enterprises, Inc. v. G. & G. Enterprises, Inc., 508 F.2d 1354 (7th Cir.), cert. denied, 423 U.S. 825, 96 S.Ct. 38, 46 L.Ed.2d 40 (1975) (dry cleaning business); Bellah v.

First National Bank, 495 F.2d 1109 (5th Cir.1974) (cattle business). Nevertheless, the asset acquired has been recognized to be an important, and often determinative, factor in the court's determination. In McClure v. First National Bank, 497 F.2d 490 (5th Cir.1974), cert. denied, 420 U.S. 930, 95 S.Ct. 1132, 43 L.Ed.2d 402 (1975), Judge Roney analyzed prior federal decisions and concluded:

> [W]here notes have been deemed securities within the meaning of the securities laws, either of two factors * * * usually indicated the investment overtones of the underlying transaction. * * * [The] notes were [either] offered to some class of investors, [or] were * * * acquired * * * for speculation or investment. * * * Second, * * * the borrower [obtained] investment assets, directly or indirectly, in exchange for its notes. Id. at 493–94. (Citation omitted). * * *

The Court finds that the note issued by Penn–Dixie in part payment for the real estate would qualify as a security under the investment/commercial test. First the land was not acquired to provide housing for a family or to build a new corporate headquarters, but was acquired for purely investment purposes. Second, the note was issued by a publicly held corporation, Penn–Dixie, to a trust not normally in the business of making loans, the JDL Trust. See Lino v. City Investing Co., 487 F.2d 689, 696 (3d Cir.1973). Third, the duration of the note, ten years, signifies a long-term stake in the progress of the investment, since the collateral for the loan, the land itself, would fluctuate in value with the success of the venture. Therefore, the Court finds that in the "complete context of [this] transaction," id. at 696 n. 15, the note was a security under the investment/commercial dichotomy test of the Third, Fifth, Seventh, and Tenth Circuits.

B. The Risk Capital Test of the Ninth Circuit

The U.S. Court of Appeals for the Ninth Circuit applies a risk capital test in determining whether a note is a security. See Amfac Mortgage Corp. v. Arizona Mall, Inc., Case No. 76–1495 (9th Cir. October 3, 1978). Under this test, the ultimate inquiry is whether the lender has contributed risk capital subject to the entrepreneurial or managerial efforts of others. United California Bank v. THC Financial Corp., 557 F.2d 1351, 1358 (9th Cir.1977); Great Western Bank & Trust v. Kotz, 532 F.2d 1252, 1257 (9th Cir.1976). Six factors have been considered in *Amfac Mortgage, Great Western,* and *United California Bank* to determine if the lender has contributed risk capital. The factors focused on are: (1) time, (2) collateralization, (3) form of the obligation, (4) circumstances of issue, (5) relationship between the amount borrowed and the size of the borrower's business, and (6) the contemplated use of the funds. In this case, the mortgage was for an extended period (ten years). The collateralization was intertwined with the success or failure of the venture. The obligation took the form of the seller providing the loan to facilitate the sale. The circumstances of issuance were such that one not normally in the business of making loans made the loan to a publicly held corporation. The amount borrowed was a significant portion of the value of the venture. Finally, the funds were used to obtain an investment asset. The Court finds that in combination these factors demonstrate that the lender, the JDL Trust, has contributed risk capital subject to the entrepreneurial and managerial efforts of Penn–Dixie. Therefore, the purchase money note is a security under the risk capital test of the Ninth Circuit.

C. The Literal Approach of the Second Circuit

The broadest approach to determining whether a note constitutes a security under the federal securities laws has been taken by the U.S. Court of Appeals for the Second Circuit. In Exchange National Bank v. Touche Ross & Co., 544 F.2d 1126 (2d Cir.1976), Judge Friendly, writing for the court, held that a party asserting that a note with a maturity longer than nine months is not a security within the 1934 Act, has the burden of proving that the "context" requires that result. In the course of his opinion, Judge Friendly offered some guidance for future cases:

> One can readily think of many cases where (the context otherwise requires)—the note delivered in consumer financing, the note secured by a mortgage on a home, the short-term note secured by a lien on a small business or some of its assets, the note evidencing a "character" loan to a bank customer, short-term notes secured by an assignment of accounts receivable, or a note which simply formalizes an open-account debt incurred in the ordinary course of business (particularly if, as in the case of the customer of a broker, it is collateralized). When a note does not bear a strong family resemblance to these examples and has a maturity date exceeding nine months, § 10(b) of the 1934 Act should generally apply. Id. at 1138 (citation omitted).

Since the mortgage in this case is on land held for investment purposes, instead of a home, as in Judge Friendly's example, the note would plainly constitute a security under the Second Circuit's test.

The Court feels that the Second Circuit's approach is most consistent with the language of the statute and Congressional intent and is by far the easiest test to apply. The defendants in this case urge the Court to reject this test because of its inconsistency with the Supreme Court's decision in United States Housing Foundation, Inc. v. Forman, 421 U.S. 837, 95 S.Ct. 2051, 44 L.Ed.2d 621 (1975).

In *Forman* the Court reversed a decision by the Second Circuit for taking an excessively literal approach to the problem of defining securities. The approach taken by the Second Circuit in *Forman*, although termed literal, bears little resemblance to the approach taken by Judge Friendly in *Exchange National Bank*. In *Forman*, the tenants of Co-op City, a low-income cooperative in the Bronx, brought suit alleging violations of the federal securities laws. To lease an apartment in Co-op City, a prospective tenant has to purchase shares of what is termed "stock." The Court rejected the extremely literal approach of the court of appeals in favor of one in which form would be disregarded in favor of substance, and the emphasis would be on economic realities. Id. at 848. And, applying that test in *Forman,* the Court ruled that the tenants were buying a place to live, not investing their money; therefore, the "stock" was not a security.

In the course of its opinion, in language the defendants heavily rely upon in this case, the Court observed:

> The touchstone is the presence of an investment in a common venture premised on a reasonable expectation of profits to be derived from the entrepreneurial or managerial efforts of others. * * * By contrast, when a purchaser is motivated by a desire to use or consume the item purchased—"to occupy the land or to develop it themselves," * * *—the securities laws do not apply.

Id. at 852–53 (citations omitted). The holder of the note in this case, the JDL Trust, has attributes that satisfy the holding of the Court in *Forman.* In this case, the "purchaser" of the security (the recipient of the note) is the JDL Trust, and plainly the holder of the note did not plan to occupy or develop the land, but relied on the skills of Penn–Dixie to reap the benefits of the investment. In cases in which the note is acquired for investment purposes, the *Forman* test is satisfied. Therefore, the decision of Judge Friendly in *Exchange National Bank* is consistent with the Court's decision in *Forman* and the result in this case.

Accordingly, the Court finds that the purchase money note issued by Penn–Dixie to the JDL Trust as part payment for the Florida real estate is a security within the meaning of the federal securities laws as construed by all of the available standards.

* * *

NOTE

1. In the traditional relationship between a real estate developer, especially one developing commercial or residential rental property, and its long term lender, a loan is almost always made to enable the developer to acquire "investment" assets. The loan, in the usual case, has a twenty to thirty-five year term. Often the developer is a publicly-held entity. The lender is usually an institutional lender, such as a bank or an insurance company, in the business of making loans. The loan, at least at the time of its inception, is usually adequately secured so that, in the event of the failure of the developer's enterprise, the lender is able to recover the amount of the loan out of assets pledged as security. The business of the debtor is the development of real estate. A loan made to assist the developer in carrying on such business bears some "family resemblance" to a loan made to a manufacturer of aluminum products to enable it to acquire the assets needed to conduct its business.

2. The determination whether a loan made to a real estate developer involves a security under the Federal Security Acts is made on a case by case basis and may vary, at least at the present time, depending on the jurisdiction

in which the question arises. In certain situations and jurisdictions it may involve a security. See e.g. *The Exchange National Bank of Chicago v. Touche Ross & Co.,* 544 F.2d 1126 (2d Cir.1976), modified, *Chemical Bank v. Arthur Andersen & Co.,* 726 F.2d 930 (2d Cir.1984), cert. denied, 469 U.S. 884, 105 S.Ct. 253, 83 L.Ed.2d 190 (1984); *Peoples Bank of LaGrange v. North Carolina National Bank,* 139 Ga.App. 405, 228 S.E.2d 334 (1976); *Hunssinger v. Rockford Business Credits, Inc.,* 745 F.2d 484 (7th Cir.1984); *Underhill v. Royal,* 769 F.2d 1426 (9th Cir.1985). While, in other situations and jurisdictions, it may not involve a security. See e.g. *McClure v. First National Bank of Lubbock, Texas,* 497 F.2d 490 (5th Cir.1974), cert. denied, 420 U.S. 930, 95 S.Ct. 1132, 43 L.Ed.2d 402 (1975); *C.N.S. Enterprises, Inc. v. G. & G. Enterprises, Inc.,* 508 F.2d 1354 (7th Cir.1975), cert. denied, 423 U.S. 825, 96 S.Ct. 38, 46 L.Ed.2d 40 (1975); *Emisco Industries, Inc. v. Pro's Inc.,* 543 F.2d 38 (7th Cir.1976); *Great Western Bank & Trust v. Kotz,* 532 F.2d 1252 (9th Cir.1976); *National Bank of Commerce of Dallas v. All American Assur. Co.,* 583 F.2d 1295 (5th Cir.1978); *United Sportfishers v. Buffo,* 597 F.2d 658 (9th Cir.1978); *Lincoln National Bank v. Herber,* 604 F.2d 1038 (7th Cir.1979); *American Bank & Trust Company v. Wallace,* 529 F.Supp. 258 (E.D.Ky.1981), affirmed, 702 F.2d 93 (6th Cir.1983); *Futura Development Corporation v. Centex Corporation,* 761 F.2d 33 (1st Cir. 1985), cert. denied, 474 U.S. 850, 106 S.Ct. 147, 88 L.Ed.2d 121 (1985); *South Carolina National Bank v. Darmstadter,* 622 F.Supp. 226 (D.S.C.1985), affirmed, 813 F.2d 403 (4th Cir.1986); *Smith International, Inc. v. Texas Commerce Bank,* 844 F.2d 1193 (5th Cir.1988); *Danner v. Himmelfarb,* 858 F.2d 515 (9th Cir.1988). Might the determination whether a mortgage loan involves a security turn in part on whether, in addition to interest, the lender received some sort of "kicker" in connection with the lending transaction? There exists a limited exemption from registration for the offer, sale and resale of notes, or the sale of participations in notes, originated by a banking institution or "approved mortgagee" secured by a first lien on a single parcel of real estate on which there is a residential or commercial structure. See Securities Act of 1933, Section 4(5).

    3. See generally Lipton and Katz, *"Notes" are not Always Securities,* 30 Bus.Law. 763 (1975); Comment, *The Status of the Promissory Note Under the Federal Securities Laws,* 1975 Ariz.St.L.J. 175; Schweitzer, *Commercial Paper and the Securities Act of 1933: A Role for Registration,* 63 Geo.L.J. 1245 (1975); Carter, *Bank Loans and Bank Credit Agreements: Federal Securities Laws Status,* 93 Banking L.J. 1020 (1976); Comment, *The Status of Promissory Notes Under the Securities Act of 1933 and the Securities Exchange Act of 1934,* 52 St. John's L.Rev. 92 (1977); Comment, *An Overview of Promissory Notes Under the Federal Securities Laws,* 6 Fordham Urb.L.J. 529 (1978); Lizzul, *The Evolution of Bank Term Lending and the Status of Term Notes Under the Federal Securities Laws,* 31 Syracuse L.Rev. 959 (1980); Note, *The Economic Realities of Defining Notes as Securities Under the Securities Act of 1933 and the Securities Exchange Act of 1934,* 34 U.Fla.L.Rev. 400 (1982); Vargo, *Equity Participation by the Institutional Lender: The Security Status Issue,* 26 S.Tex.L.J. 225 (1985).

(ii) EXEMPTIONS FROM THE SECURITIES ACT

(a) SMALL AND LIMITED OFFERINGS

Section 3(b) of the Securities Act of 1933 permits the Securities and Exchange Commission to exempt from registration, by its rules and regulations, certain small offerings of securities. No issue of securities, however, may be exempted under this section if the aggregate amount at which the issue is offered to the public exceeds $5,000,000. The Commission issued Regulation A pursuant to Section 3(b).

Regulation A, in substance, provides for a simplified means of registration. The securities to be offered pursuant to Regulation A are registered through the Regional Office of the Securities and Exchange Commission for the region in which the issuer's principal business operations are conducted or proposed to be conducted. A simplified registration form (offering statement) is used, and, in most cases, an offer or sale of the securities must be preceded or accompanied by the offering statement. The offering statement cannot be false or misleading in the light of the circumstances existing at the time of its use. A revised offering statement must be filed and used if the offering is not completed within nine months following the date of the original offering statement. In addition, all "sales material" must be filed with the Regional Office prior to its use. Finally, a report of the sale of securities made under Regulation A must be filed with the Regional Office within 30 days after the end of each six month period following the date of the original offering statement.

The aggregate amount of the securities of an issuer presently exempted under Regulation A is $1,500,000 during any 12 month period. Lesser amounts are provided if the securities are offered on behalf of any person other than the issuer or the estate of a decedent. In determining the aggregate amount of securities offered, all securities issued in return for assets or services prior to the filing of the offering statement and all securities issued or proposed to be issued pursuant to options will be included unless such securities are escrowed, or subject to a similar arrangement which assures that none of such securities will be reoffered to the public within one year after the commencement of the offering under Regulation A.

The aggregate offering price of securities with a determinable market value is the greater of (a) the market value on a specified date within 15 days prior to the date the offering statement is filed, or (b) the offering price to the public. The aggregate gross proceeds received from the public, however, cannot exceed $1,500,000. The aggregate offering price of securities without a determinable market value exchanged for property, services or other securities is determined using: (a) the cash offering price of securities of the same class or, if there is no cash offering, (b) the value of the property, services or other securities received based on bona fide sales of such within a reasonable period or, if there are no such sales, (c) the value of the property, services or other securities determined by an acceptable standard.

Regulation A is available to most entities incorporated or organized under the laws of any State of the United States or province of Canada which have, or propose to have, their principal business operations in the United States or Canada and most individuals who are residents of, and have or propose to have their principal business operations in, any State or province. Regulation A, however, is not available to any issuer which is, for example, subject to a stop order or suspension by the Securities and Exchange Commission or which has been convicted of a crime or offense involving the purchase or sale of securities or which has any similarly situated director, officer, principal stockholder, promoter or underwriter, or partner, director or officer of any such underwriter.

Offers and sales to accredited investors are exempt, under Section 4(6) of the Securities Act of 1933, if the aggregate offering price of the issue of securities offered in reliance on Section 4(6) does not exceed the amount allowed under Section 3(b), there is no advertising or public solicitation in connection with the offering and if the issuer files a notice of the offering with the Securities and Exchange Commission. The amount presently allowed under Section 3(b) is $5,000,000.

Accredited investors, as defined by Section 2(15) of the Securities Act of 1933 and by regulation issued by the Securities and Exchange Commission, include institutional investors (such as banks, savings and loan associations, insurance companies, etc.), insiders (such as directors, executive officers and general partners of the issuer), individuals having a substantial income or net worth (a net worth of $1,000,000, income of $200,000 individually or $300,000 jointly with the individual's spouse in each of the last two years and the reasonable expectation of the same or greater income in the current year) and trusts having substantial assets ($5,000,000 in total assets) and a sophisticated person making investment decisions.

NOTE

1. *Restaurant Investors Ltd.*, CCH Fed.Sec.L.Rep. ¶ 80,687 ('76–'77 Tr. Bin.), contains an interesting discussion of some of the problems involved in a limited partnership, which engages in real estate development, qualifying for the small offering exemption under Regulation A.

2. As a result of the maximum dollar limit on the aggregate amount of securities exempt under Regulation A, it is the position of the Securities and Exchange Commission that Regulation A cannot be utilized in the context of a "spin-off" distribution of securities since there would be considerable uncertainty in ascertaining the value of the securities issued and the aftermarket price is probably unascertainable. See *Entron, Inc.*, CCH Fed.Sec.L.Rep. ¶ 80,430 ('75–'76 Tr. Bin.).

3. See generally Green and Brecher, *When Making a Small Public Offering Under Reg. A*, 26 # 2 Prac.Law. 25 (1980), 26 # 3 Prac.Law. 41 (1980).

(b) THE PRIVATE OFFERING

Another exemption from registration requirements under the Securities Act of 1933 is the private offering exemption contained in Section 4(2). The exemption is a transactional exemption. Registration is not required if the transaction qualifies as a private offering. The securities, however, are not themselves exempt, and therefore, their subsequent disposition is limited. This exemption, in most cases, is available for the financing of the initial land acquisition through the seller or an institutional lender. It also is available for the construction financing and permanent financing by an institutional lender. The question is when may this exemption be relied on beyond the limited transactions mentioned above. While there is some latitude, it cannot be taken too far as the following release of the Securities & Exchange Commission indicates.

SECURITIES ACT RELEASE NO. 4552
November 6, 1962.
[footnotes omitted]

Non–public Offering Exemption

＊　＊　＊ Traditionally, the second clause of Section 4([(2)]) has been regarded as providing an exemption from registration for bank loans, private placements of securities with institutions, and the promotion of a business venture by a few closely related persons. However, an increasing tendency to rely upon the exemption for offerings of speculative issues to unrelated and uninformed persons prompts this statement to point out the limitations on its availability.

Whether a transaction is one not involving any public offering is essentially a question of fact and necessitates a consideration of all surrounding circumstances, including such factors as the relationship between the offerees and the issuer, the nature, scope, size, type and manner of the offering.

(Number of Offerees)

The Supreme Court in S.E.C. v. Ralston Purina Co., 346 U.S. 119, 124, 125, 73 S.Ct. 981, 97 L.Ed. 1494 (1953), noted that the exemption must be interpreted in the light of the statutory purpose to "protect investors by promoting full disclosure of information thought necessary to informed investment decisions" and held that "the applicability of Section 4([(2)]) should turn on whether the particular class of persons affected need the protection of the Act." The Court stated that the number of offerees is not conclusive as to the availability of the exemption, since the statute seems to apply to an offering, "whether to few or many." However, the Court indicated that "nothing prevents the Commission, in enforcing the statute, from using some kind of numerical test in deciding when to investigate particular exemption claims." It should be emphasized, therefore, that the number of persons to whom the offering is extended is relevant only to the question whether they have the requisite association with and knowledge of the issuer which make the exemption available.

(Identity of Offerees)

Consideration must be given not only to the identity of the actual purchasers but also to the offerees. Negotiations or conversations with or general solicitations of an unrestricted and unrelated group of prospective purchasers for the purpose of ascertaining who would be willing to accept an offer of securities is inconsistent with a claim that the transaction does not involve a public offering even though ultimately there may only be a few knowledgeable purchasers.

(Offering to Employees)

A question frequently arises in the context of an offering to an issuer's employees. Limitation of an offering to certain employees designated as key employees may not be a sufficient showing to qualify for the exemption. As the Supreme Court stated in the *Ralston Purina* case: "The exemption as we construe it, does not deprive corporate employees, as a class, of the safeguards of the Act. We agree that some employee offerings may come within Section 4([(2)]), e.g., one made to executive personnel who because of their position have access to the same kind of information that the Act would make available in the form of a registration statement. Absent such a showing of special circumstances, employees are just as much members of the investing 'public' as any of their neighbors in the community." The Court's concept is that the exemption is necessarily narrow. The exemption does not become available simply because offerees are voluntarily *furnished* information about the issuer. Such a construction would give each issuer the choice of registering or making its own voluntary disclosures without regard to the standards and sanctions of the Act.

(Sale to Promoters)

The sale of stock to promoters who take the initiative in founding or organizing the business would come within the exemption. On the other hand, the transaction tends to become public when the promoters begin to bring in a diverse group of uninformed friends, neighbors, and associates.

(Size of Offering)

The size of the offering may also raise a question as to the probability that the offering will be completed within the strict confines of the exemption. An offering of millions of dollars to non-institutional and non-affiliated investors, or one divided, or convertible into many units would suggest that a public offering may be involved.

(Facilities Used in Public Offering)

When the services of an investment banker, or other facility through which public distributions are normally effected, are used to place the securities, special care must be taken to avoid a public offering. If the investment banker places the securities with discretionary accounts and other customers without regard to the ability of such customers to meet the tests implicit in the *Ralston Purina* case, the exemption may be lost. Public advertising of the offering would, of course, be incompatible with a claim of a private offering. Similarly, the use of the facilities of a securities exchange to place the securities necessarily involves an offering to the public.

(Acquisitions for Investment)

An important factor to be considered is whether the securities offered have come to rest in the hands of the initial informed group or whether the purchasers are merely conduits for a wider distribution. Persons who act in this capacity, whether or not engaged in the securities business, are deemed to be "underwriters" within the meaning of Section 2(11) of the Act. If the purchasers do in fact acquire the securities with a view to public distribution, the seller assumes the risk of possible violation of the registration requirements of the Act and consequent civil liabilities. This has led to the practice whereby the issuer secures from the initial purchasers representations that they have acquired the securities for investment. Sometimes a legend to this effect is placed on the stock certificates and stop-transfer instructions issued to the transfer agent. However, a statement by the initial purchaser, at the time of his acquisition, that the securities are taken for investment and not for distribution is necessarily self-serving and not conclusive as to his actual intent. Mere acceptance at face value of such assurances will not provide a basis for reliance on the exemption when inquiry would suggest to a reasonable person that these assurances are formal rather than real. The additional precautions of placing a legend on the security and issuing stop-transfer orders have proved in many cases to be an effective means of preventing illegal distributions. Nevertheless, these are only precautions and are not to be regarded as a basis for exemption from registration. The nature of the purchaser's past investment and trading practices or the character and scope of his business may be inconsistent with the purchase of large blocks of securities for investment. In particular, purchases by persons engaged in the business of buying and selling securities require careful scrutiny for the purpose of determining whether such person may be acting as an underwriter for the issuer.

(Period of Retention)

The view is occasionally expressed that, solely by reason of continued holding of a security for the * * * capital-gain period specified in the income-tax laws, or for a year from the date of purchase, the security may be sold without registration. There is no statutory basis for such assumption. Of course, the longer the period of retention, the more persuasive would be the argument that the resale is not at variance with original investment intent, but the length of time between acquisition and resale is merely one evidentiary fact to be considered. The weight to be accorded this evidentiary fact must, of necessity, vary with the circumstances of each case. Further, a limitation upon resale for a stated period of time or under certain circumstances would tend to raise a question as to original intent even though such limitation might otherwise recommend itself as a policing device. There is no legal justification for the assumption that holding a security in an "investment account" rather than a "trading account," holding for a deferred sale, for a market rise, for sale if the market does not rise, or for a statutory escrow period, without more, establishes a valid basis for an exemption from registration under the Securities Act.

(Change of Circumstances)

An unforeseen change of circumstances since the date of purchase may be a basis for an opinion that the proposed resale is not inconsistent with an investment representation. However, such claim must be considered in the light of all of the relevant facts. Thus, an advance or decline in market price or a change in the issuer's operating results are normal investment risks and do not usually provide an acceptable basis for such claim of changed circumstances. Possible inability of the purchaser to pay off loans incurred in connection with the purchase of the stock would ordinarily not be deemed an unforeseeable change of circumstances. Further, in the case of securities pledged for a loan, the pledgee should not assume that he is free to distribute without registration. The Congressional mandate of disclosure to investors is not to be avoided to permit a public distribution of unregistered securities because the pledgee took the securities from a purchaser, subsequently delinquent.

(Institutional Investors)

The view is sometimes expressed that investment companies and other institutional investors are not subject to any restrictions regarding disposition of securities stated to be taken for investment and that any securities so acquired may be sold by them whenever the investment decision to sell is made, no matter how brief the holding period. Institutional investors are, however, subject to the same restrictions on sale of securities acquired from an issuer or a person in a control relationship with an issuer insofar as compliance with the registration requirements of the Securities Act is concerned.

(Integration of Offerings)

A determination whether an offering is public or private would also include a consideration of the question whether it should be regarded as a part of a larger offering made or to be made. The following factors are relevant to such question of integration: whether (1) the different offerings are part of a single plan of financing, (2) the offerings involve issuance of the same class of security, (3) the offerings are made at or about the same time, (4) the same type of consideration is to be received, (5) the offerings are made for the same general purpose.

(Related Series of Offerings)

What may appear to be a separate offering to a properly limited group will not be so considered if it is one of a related series of offerings. A person may not separate parts of a series of related transactions, the sum total of which is really one offering, and claim that a particular part is a non-public transaction. Thus, in the case of offerings of fractional undivided interests in separate oil or gas properties where the promoters must constantly find new participants for each new venture, it would appear to be appropriate to consider the entire series of offerings to determine the scope of this solicitation.

(Strict Construction)

As has been emphasized in other releases discussing exemptions from the registration and prospectus requirements of the Securities Act, the terms of an exemption are to be strictly construed against the claimant who also has the burden of proving its availability. Moreover, persons receiving advice from the staff of the Commission that no action will be recommended if they proceed without registration in reliance upon the exemption should do so only with full realization that the test so applied may not be proof against claims by purchasers of the security that registration should have been effected. Finally, Sections 12(2) and 17 of the Act, which provide civil liabilities and criminal sanctions for fraud in the sale of a security, are applicable to the transactions notwithstanding the availability of an exemption from registration.

NOTE

1. As the above release makes clear, in determining whether the private offering exemption is available it is the offerees who count, not just the eventual purchasers.

2. The private offering exemption applies to the issuance of securities to the promoters of the venture. How is a promoter distinguished from other offerees?

    a. What does the phrase "who take the initiative in founding or organizing the business" mean?

b. Can securities be offered under the private offering exemption to a few knowledgeable and sophisticated friends of the promoters, if the promoters make available to the friends all of the information about the venture which would be disclosed if the securities were registered?

1. Does the answer to the above question change, if the friends are only clients of the promoters? If the offerees have no relationship to the promoters, but they are sophisticated and few in number, is the private offering exemption available?

a. The purpose of the private offering exemption is not to give the issuer the option of voluntary disclosure, as opposed to registration.

2. If there are any doubts whether the transaction qualifies for the private offering exemption, what steps can be taken to resolve those doubts?

a. What is the effect of a no action letter from the staff of the Securities and Exchange Commission?

1. Does a no action letter provide the issuer with an absolute defense to a suit by a purchaser of the securities for violation of Section 5 of the Act?

3. An issue cannot be fractionalized. A private offering exemption cannot be claimed for part of an issue. A small offering exemption cannot be claimed for another part, and an intrastate offering exemption claimed for a third part.

a. If promoters' securities are issued under a valid exemption, however, Rule 253(c) provides that the securities will not be integrated with those issued under the small offering exemption (a Regulation A registration) in determining the maximum amount of securities permitted to be issued under Regulation A, if the securities issued to the promoters are escrowed to keep the securities off the market.

b. The traditional integration tests used to determine what offers, sales, etc. are part of the same offering are described in Securities Act Release No. 4552 set out above at pages 916 to 920. With respect to the factors used to determine when, and if, offerings must be integrated, compare *Martin Exploration Co.,* CCH Fed.Sec.L.Rep. ¶ 80,794 ('76–'77 Tr. Bin.), in which the SEC Division of Corporation Finance indicated that no integration is required of offerings of limited partnership interests by two limited partnerships with the same general partner, both engaging in drilling for oil and gas in the same state, when each partnership had different specific prospects, in all other respects were completely separate, and the investments in each were subject to different risks, with *J I C Drilling Companies,* CCH Fed.Sec.L.Rep. ¶ 80,765 ('76–'77 Tr.Bin.), in which integration was required under essentially the same facts as *Martin Exploration Co.,* but with the following differences, each of the two partnerships was to drill in a different state, no specific prospects had been assigned to either partnership, all of the prospects were owned by a third party with which each partnership would form a joint venture, and the investments in each partnership were subject to about the same risks. See *Westminster Co.,* CCH Fed.Sec.L.Rep. ¶ 80,791 ('76–'77 Tr.Bin.), in which concepts similar to those discussed above are employed with particular reference to the possible integration of securities issued by limited partnerships engaged in real estate development. See also *Metropolitan Capital Corp.,* CCH Fed. Sec.L.Rep. ¶ 80,485 ('75–'76 Tr.Bin.); *Midstate Telephone Co.,* CCH Fed.Sec.

L.Rep. ¶ 80,800 ('76–'77 Tr.Bin.); *Tell–Tower, Inc.,* CCH Fed.Sec.L.Rep. ¶ 81,540 (1978 Tr.Bin.); *Thomas A. Latta,* CCH Fed.Sec.L.Rep. ¶ 81,590 (1978 Tr.Bin.), in which integration was not required because of substantial differences in the terms of the securities issued. See generally Deaktor, *Integration of Securities Offerings,* 31 U.Fla.L.Rev. 465 (1979).

4. See generally Note, *Reforming the Initial Sale Requirements of the Private Placement Exemption,* 86 Harv.L.Rev. 403 (1972); McDermott, *The Private Offering Exemption,* 59 Iowa L.Rev. 525 (1974); Hrusoff, *Securities Aspects of Real Estate Partnerships,* 11 Cal.W.L.Rev. 425 (1975); Note, *The Defective Private Offering: A Comparison of Purchaser's Remedies,* 62 Iowa L.Rev. 236 (1976); Kessler, *The Effect of the Securities Laws upon the Small Business,* 28 # 6 Prac.Law. 11 (1982).

5. Purchasers must buy for investment and not for resale in order for the private offering exemption to apply. Beyond requiring each purchaser to deliver an "investment letter," how can the issuer make sure that a purchaser does not sell in a manner which calls into question the purchaser's investment intent?

a. If a legend restricting the transfer of the stock is not found on the face of a stock certificate, does a purchaser of the stock from the owner receive good title under the Uniform Commercial Code even if transfer of the stock was in fact restricted? See generally Hoblin and Kelly, *Registration of Transfer of Restricted Securities Under the Uniform Commercial Code: A Conflict of Law With the Securities Act of 1933,* 25 Mercer L.Rev. 581 (1974).

b. Release No. 4552 indicated that the purchaser of securities issued under a private offering exemption can sell the securities if circumstances change, without the purchaser being considered a statutory underwriter. In 1972, the rules changed with the adoption of Rule 144 by the Securities and Exchange Commission.

SECURITIES ACT RELEASE NO. 5223

January 11, 1972.
[footnotes omitted]

NOTICE OF ADOPTION OF RULE 144 RELATING TO THE DEFINITION OF THE TERMS "UNDERWRITER" IN SECTIONS 4(1) AND 2(11) AND "BROKERS' TRANSACTIONS" IN SECTION 4(4) OF THE SECURITIES ACT OF 1933, ADOPTION OF FORM 144, AND RESCISSION OF RULES 154 AND 155 UNDER THAT ACT

* * *

Rule 144 will become effective on and after April 15, 1972.

In brief, the rule provides that any affiliate or other person who sells restricted securities of an issuer for his own account, or any person who sells restricted or any other securities for the account of an affiliate of the issuer, is not deemed to be engaged in a distribution of the securities, and therefore is not an underwriter as defined in Section 2(11) of the Act, if the securities are sold in accordance with all the terms and conditions of the rule. The rule requires, among other things, that the restricted securities must have been beneficially owned for a period of at least two years by the person for whose account they are sold; that the amount sold shall not exceed one percent of the class outstanding, or if traded on an exchange, the lesser of that amount or the average weekly volume on all such exchanges during the four weeks preceding the sale; and that the securities must be sold in brokers' transactions. In addition, there must be adequate information available to the public in regard to the issuer of the securities and notice of the sale (Form 144) must be filed with the Commission concurrently with the sale.

A number of persons have commented that it is not clear whether the rule, as proposed, was intended to be the exclusive means for selling restricted securities without registration under the Securities Act. In this connection, certain commentators asserted that the Commission does not have the statutory authority to adopt such an exclusive rule while others stated that the Commission had such power and urged it to adopt an exclusive rule. The Commission does not believe it is necessary to reach these questions relating to its statutory authority at this time, since the rule as adopted is not exclusive. However, persons who offer or sell restricted securities without complying with Rule 144 are hereby put on notice by the Commission that in view of the broad remedial purposes of the Act and of public policy which strongly supports registration, they will have a substantial burden of proof in establishing that an exemption from registration is available for such offers or sales and that such persons and the brokers and other persons who participate in the transactions do so at their risk.

Moreover, with respect to restricted securities acquired after the effective date of the rule, the staff will not issue "no-action" letters relating to resales of such securities. Further, in connection with such resales, the Commission hereby puts all persons including brokers and attorneys on notice that the "change in circumstances" concept should no longer be considered as one of the factors in determining whether a person is an underwriter. The Commission recognizes that this concept has been in existence in one form or another for a long period of time. However, administrative agencies as well as courts from time to time change their interpretation of statutory provisions in the light of new considerations and changing conditions which indicate that earlier interpretations of such provisions are no longer in keeping with the statutory objectives. Thus, the "change in circumstances" concept in the Commission's opinion fails to meet the objectives of the Act, since the circumstances of the seller are unrelated to the need of investors for the protections afforded by the registration and other provisions of the Act.

Further, with respect to restricted securities acquired after the effective date of the rule but not sold pursuant to the provisions of the rule, the Commission hereby gives notice that in deciding whether a person is an underwriter, the length of time the securities have been held will be considered but the fact that securities have been held for a particular period of time does not by itself establish the availability of an exemption from registration.

* * *

Background and Purpose

* * *

Resales of securities acquired in private placements are frequently made under claims of an exemption pursuant to Section 4(1) of the Act, that is, a transaction by a person other than an issuer, underwriter, or dealer. This Section was intended to exempt only trading transactions between individual investors with respect to securities already issued and not to exempt distributions by issuers or acts of other individuals who engage in steps necessary to such distributions.

Generally, the majority of questions arising under this Section have dealt with whether the seller is an "underwriter." The term underwriter is broadly defined in Section 2(11) of the Act to mean any person who has purchased from an issuer with a view to, or offers or sells for an issuer in connection with, the distribution of any security, or participates or has a direct or indirect participation in any such undertaking, or participates or has a participation in the direct or indirect underwriting of any such undertaking. The interpretation of this definition has traditionally focused on the words "with a view to" in the phrase "purchased from an issuer with a view to * * * distribution." Thus, an investment banking firm which arranges with an issuer for the public sale of its securities is clearly an "underwriter" under that Section. Not so well understood is the fact that individual investors who are not professionals in the securities business may be "underwriters" within the meaning of that term as used in the Act if they act as links in a chain of transactions through which securities move from an issuer to the public. It is difficult to ascertain the mental state of the purchaser at the time of his acquisition, and the staff has looked to subsequent acts and circumstances to determine whether such person took with a view to distribution at the time of his acquisition. Emphasis has been placed on factors such as the length of time the person has held the securities ("holding period") and whether there has been an unforeseeable change in circumstances of the holder. Experience has shown, however, that reliance upon such factors as the above has not assured adequate protection of investors through the maintenance of informed trading markets and has led to uncertainty in the application of the registration provision of the Act.

Moreover, the Commission hereby emphasizes and draws attention to the fact that the statutory language of Section 2(11) is in the disjunctive. Thus, it is insufficient to conclude that a person is not an underwriter solely because he did not purchase securities from an issuer with a view to their distribution. It must also be established that the person is not offering or selling for an issuer in connection with the distribution of the securities and that the person does not participate or have a participation in any such undertaking, and does not participate or have a participation in any such underwriting of such an undertaking.

* * *

Explanation and Analysis of the Rule

In view of the legislative history, statutory language and judicial interpretations of Sections 2(11), 4(1), and 4(2) of the Act, and in light of the many helpful suggestions and comments received on the proposed "160 Series" of rules and thereafter on proposed Rule 144, the Commission is of the view that "distribution" is the significant concept in interpreting the statutory term "underwriter." In determining when a person is deemed not to be engaged in a distribution several factors must be considered.

First, the purpose and underlying policy of the Act to protect investors requires, in the Commission's opinion, that there be adequate current information concerning the issuer, whether the resales of securities by persons result in a distribution or are effected in trading transactions. Accordingly, the availability of the rule is conditioned on the existence of adequate current public information.

Secondly, a holding period prior to resale is essential, among other reasons, to assure that those persons who buy under a claim of a Section 4(2) exemption have assumed the economic risks of investment, and therefore, are not acting as conduits for sale to the public of unregistered securities, directly or indirectly, on behalf of an issuer. It should be noted that there is nothing in Section 2(11) which places a time limit on a person's status as an underwriter. The public has the same need for protection afforded by registration whether the securities are distributed shortly after their purchase or after a considerable length of time.

A third factor, which must be considered in determining what is deemed not to constitute a "distribution," is the impact of the particular transaction or transactions on the trading markets. It is consistent with the rationale of the Act that Section 4(1) be interpreted to permit only routine trading transactions as distinguished from distributions. Therefore, a person reselling securities under Section 4(1) of the Act must sell the securities in such limited quantities and in such a manner so as not to disrupt the trading markets. The larger the amount of securities involved, the more likely it is that such resales may involve methods of offering and amounts of compensation usually associated with a distribution rather than routine trading transactions. Thus, solicitation of buy orders or the payment of extra compensation are not permitted by the rule.

In summary, if the sale in question is made in accordance with all the provisions of the rule, as outlined below, any person who sells restricted securities shall be deemed not to be engaged in a distribution of such securities and therefore not an underwriter thereof. The rule also provides that any person who sells restricted or other securities on behalf of a person in a control relationship with the issuer shall be deemed not to be engaged in a distribution of such securities and therefore not to be an underwriter thereof, if the sale is made in accordance with all the conditions of the rule.

* * *

Related Rules and Other Amendments

Rule 237

The Commission recognized that noncontrolling persons owning restricted securities of issuers which do not satisfy all of the conditions of Rule 144 might have difficulty in selling those securities due to circumstances beyond their control. Accordingly, in order to avoid unduly restricting the liquidity of such investments, the Commission has adopted Rule 237 under Section 3(b) of the Act. Under that rule any person satisfying the conditions of the rule will be permitted to sell an amount of securities not exceeding the lesser of the gross proceeds from the sale of one percent of the securities of the class outstanding or $50,000 during any twelve month period, reduced by the amount of any other sales pursuant to an exemption under Section 3(b) of the Act or Rule 144 during the period. Those conditions are:

1. The person is not an issuer, an affiliate of the issuer or a broker or dealer;

2. The person has owned and fully paid for the securities for five or more years;

3. The issuer is a domestic organization which has been actively engaged in business as a going concern for at least the last five years;

4. The securities are sold in negotiated transactions otherwise than through a broker or dealer; and

5. The person files the required notice with the appropriate regional office of the Commission at least 10 days before the sale, indicating, among other things, his name, the name of the issuer, the amount of securities to be sold and the amount sold within the past 12 months.

Regulation A

The Commission has adopted amendments to Regulation A so that an offering not to exceed $100,000 can be made by non-controlling persons, or an aggregate of $300,000 by all such persons, during any one year without offsetting such amounts against the amount available to the issuer under a Regulation A offering. This broadening of the availability of Regulation A will provide a means by which noncontrolling investors in small businesses may resell their restricted securities.

* * *

Use of Legends and Stop–Transfer Instructions

Precautions by issuers are essential to assure that a public offering does not result from resale of securities initially purchased in transactions claimed to be exempt under Section 4(2) of the Act. (Attention is directed to Securities Act Release No. 5121 which discusses the use of legends and stop-transfer instructions as evidence of a non-public offering.) Although such assurance cannot be obtained merely by the use of an appropriate legend on stock certificates or other evidences of ownership, or by appropriate instructions to transfer agents, these devices serve a useful policing function, and the use of such devices is strongly suggested by the Commissioner and will be considered a factor in determining whether in fact there has been a private placement.

Contractual Registration or Other Rights for Resale of Restricted Securities

Issuers, brokers, dealers, private placees and other holders of restricted securities are hereby put on notice that the Commission deems it appropriate that such persons when acquiring such securities, should consider contracting for registration or other rights, so that, if they desire to distribute their securities rather than resell in trading transactions pursuant to the rule, they can do so in a manner consistent with the provisions of the Act, i.e., by filing a registration statement or a notification under Regulation A. If the issuer does not file reports pursuant to Sections 13 or 15(d) of the Exchange Act, such persons should consider obtaining an agreement by the issuer to register voluntarily under that Act so that Rule 144 may be available.

*   *   *

NOTE

1. Although directed at the sale of securities purchased under a private offering exemption, can the rationale of Rule 144 be applied to the sale of securities purchased under an intrastate exemption or under the limited offering exemption contained in Section 4(6)?

    a. It is the position of the staff of the Securities and Exchange Commission that the provisions of Rule 144 do not apply to the resale of securities acquired under the intrastate exemption, Section 3(a)(11). See *John F. Davis*, CCH Fed.Sec.L.Rep. ¶ 79,240 ('72–'73 Tr.Bin.). Does Rule 144 apply to the resale of securities acquired in a transaction which qualifies under both the private offering exemption, Section 4(2), and the intrastate exemption?

    b. Rule 144 is applied to the resale of certain securities purchased under Regulation D which is considered at pages 928 to 933 infra. See Release No. 33–6389, March 8, 1982, CCH Fed.Sec. L. Rep. ¶ 83,106 ('81–'82 Tr.Bin.), and Release 33–6758, March 3, 1988, CCH Fed.Sec.L.Rep. ¶ 84,221 ('87–'88 Tr.Bin.).

2. Should a purchaser of securities, under a private offering exemption, obtain any commitments on the part of the issuer in order to be able to sell the securities if "circumstances change"?

    a. Does asking for those commitments at the time of purchase "call into question" the purchaser's "investment intent"?

3. The holding period requirement of Rule 144 generally can be met by an "at-risk" holding period of two years. After the two year period, the owner of

the securities may sell, during any six month period, the lesser of, 1% of the class of securities outstanding or the average weekly reported volume of trading in such securities during the four weeks preceding the sale. The sale, however, can be made only through a broker's transaction which, in general, means that the broker cannot solicit offers to buy. In most situations, there must be available, at the time of sale, current public information concerning the issuer. This requirement is met if the issuer is, or becomes, a reporting company under the Securities Exchange Act of 1934 and files the reports required by Section 13 or 15(d). If the issuer is not a reporting company, it must currently make available to the public the information required by clauses (1) to (14) and (16) of paragraph (a)(4) of Rule 15c2–11 under the Securities Act of 1934.

4. The Securities and Exchange Commission has eliminated the requirements of Rule 144 with respect to the amount limitation, notice, manner of sale and the availability to the public of current information about the issuer for certain nonaffiliated persons who have held their securities for three years. As a result, nonaffiliated persons may sell unregistered securities in compliance with Rule 144 by simply meeting a three-year holding period. See Securities Act Release No. 33–6286, Feb. 6, 1981, CCH Fed.Sec.L.Rep. ¶ 82,821 (1981 Tr. Bin.); Securities Act Release No. 6488, September 23, 1983, CCH Fed.Sec.L.Rep. ¶ 83,428 ('83–'84 Tr.Bin.); Barron, *Major Liberalization of Rule 144—The Rule 144(k) Shareholder,* 9 Sec.Reg.L.J. 281 (1981).

5. See Bloomenthal, *Rule 144, The SEC, and Restricted Securities,* 49 Den. L.J. 301 (1973); Linden, *The Resale of Restricted and Control Securities Under SEC Rule 144: The First Five Years,* 8 Seton Hall L.Rev. 157 (1977).

(c) REGULATION D

On March 8, 1982, the Securities and Exchange Commission adopted Regulation D. Regulation D became effective April 15, 1982. See Release No. 33–6389, CCH Fed.Sec.L.Rep. ¶ 83,106 ('81–'82 Tr.Bin.). Regulation D was subsequently revised. See Release No. 33–6758, March 3, 1988, CCH Fed.Sec.L.Rep. ¶ 84,221 ('87–'88 Tr.Bin.). Regulation D, as revised, provides certain rules with respect to limited and private offerings of securities. As revised, Regulation D expands and defines the availability of the limited offering and private placement exemptions. There are three rules in Regulation D which provide for exemptions: Rule 504 (which covers offerings of up to $1,000,000); Rule 505 (which covers offerings of up to $5,000,000); and Rule 506 (which covers offerings in an unlimited amount).

General Concepts of Regulation D

Certain concepts applicable to all aspects of Regulation D are contained in Rules 501, 502 and 503. Regulation D is available to all forms of legal entity, including partnerships. A notice of sale must be filed for all offerings claimed to be exempt under the Regulation.

Regulation D further defines the "accredited investor" concept set out in Section 2(15) of the Securities Act of 1933. An accredited investor is any person who comes within any of the following categories or who the issuer reasonably believes comes within these categories. (a) *Institutional Investors.* This category includes banks, saving and loan associations and similar institutions such as credit unions, insurance companies, registered investment companies, business development companies, small business investment companies licensed by the SBA, employee benefit plans subject to the provisions of ERISA, nonprofit organizations (with total assets of $5,000,000) and corporations, partnerships and business trusts (with total assets of $5,000,000). (b) *Insiders.* Directors, executive officers, and general partners of the issuer of the securities being offered for sale are included in this category. If the general partner of the issuer is a corporation or partnership, directors, executive officers or general partners of that entity are also included. (c) *Individuals Having a Substantial Net Worth and Certain Trusts.* Individuals having a net worth in excess of $1,000,000 (net worth derived from all sources, including the net worth of a spouse may be taken into account) and trusts if they have $5,000,000 in total assets and their investment decisions are made by a sophisticated person can be treated as accredited investors. (d) *Individuals Having a Substantial Income.* Individuals who had net income in excess of $200,000 individually or $300,000 jointly with their spouses in each of the last two years and who reasonably expect to have net income in excess of $200,000 individually or $300,000 jointly with their spouses in the current year are included in this category. In addition, certain entities composed solely of persons who are in any of the foregoing categories, other than (c), can be treated as accredited investors.

The general principles of integration will determine when sales of securities must be aggregated to determine compliance with dollar limitation ceilings. The concept, however, of "predecessor of an issuer," which would have included sales by partnerships with the same or an affiliated general partner is not applicable to Regulation D. Under Regulation D, the Securities and Exchange Commission has established a safe harbor rule. All securities offered or sold pursuant to an exemption provided by Section 3 or Section 4(2) of the Securities Act of 1933 or pursuant to a Registration Statement more than six months prior to or more than six months subsequent to a transaction exempt from registration pursuant to Regulation D will not be integrated with that transaction, provided that there have been no other offers or sales of securities of the same class of securities by or for the issuer during either of the two six-month periods. If there have been offers or sales during these periods, the traditional principles of integration will apply not only to the offers and sales inside the six month periods, but also to offers or sales outside the periods.

The antifraud and civil liability provisions of the Federal securities laws are applicable, even if the transaction is exempt. Likewise, the state blue sky and general antifraud rules are applicable. Reliance on an exemption provided by Regulation D is not an election, and even if a notice of sale is filed under Regulation D the issuer also may claim the availability of any other exemption. Regulation D is available solely to an issuer of securities. The regulation, however, is not available to an issuer who, although in technical compliance with the regulation, sells securities as part of a plan or scheme to avoid registration.

Rule 506.

Rule 506 provides, in general, that an offer, sale and delivery after sale of securities will be deemed to qualify as a private offering and thus be exempt from the registration requirements of Section 5 of the Securities Act of 1933 if the issuer complies with the following: (1) offers the securities without general advertising or solicitation; (2) to an unlimited number of accredited investors (or to persons whom the issuer reasonably believes are accredited investors) and to not more than 35 nonaccredited but sophisticated investors; (3) furnishes requisite information if nonaccredited investors are involved; (4) sells restricted securities; and (5) files a timely notice of sale in Washington, D.C.

1. *Manner of Offering.* No general advertising or general solicitation may be made. The Securities and Exchange Commission indicated in Release No. 33–6389, supra, that when a very large number of purchasers participate in an offering, a violation of the prohibitions against general solicitation and general advertising may have occurred. It appears that meetings and seminars may be held as long as no general solicitation or general advertising takes place.

2. *Number of Investors.* Under Rule 506, as throughout Regulation D, the focus is on the number and nature of investors. It may be implicit, however, in the prohibition of general advertising that the number of offerees is important—at least as an evidentiary matter. Under Rule 506, the securities may be sold to an unlimited number of persons who are accredited investors or whom the issuer reasonably believes are accredited investors. If the issuer sells to nonaccredited investors, the issuer must reasonably believe, prior to making a sale, that the nonaccredited investors (either alone or with their "purchaser representatives") understand the merits and risks of the offering.

3. *Furnishing Information.* If the securities are offered solely to accredited investors, information about the issuer need not be supplied. If nonaccredited investors are involved, the issuer must provide "the same kind of" information that would be required in a registration statement to the extent that such information is material to an understanding of the issuer and the securities being offered. For offerings not in excess of $2,000,000, the information required in Regulation A offerings will satisfy the information requirements of Regulation D if the issuer provides the investors with a certified balance sheet dated within 120 days of the commencement of the offering.

4. *Limitations on Dispositions and Advice with Respect Thereto.* The issuer must exercise reasonable care to assure that purchasers are acquiring securities for investment, i.e., for their own accounts and not with a view toward distribution. The issuer must also advise the offerees in writing of the restricted nature of the securities and that

purchasers may be required to bear the risk of the investment indefinitely. Rule 144 applies to the disposition of securities purchased under Regulation D.

5. *Report of Offering.* As indicated above, under all provisions of Regulation D it is necessary to make a timely report of the offering in Washington, D.C.

6. *Purchaser Representatives.* A purchaser, under Regulation D, need not be sophisticated if the purchaser and his purchaser representative together are capable of evaluating the investment. A person may not be a purchaser representative if (with certain exceptions) he is an affiliate, director, officer, employee or beneficial owner of 10% or more of the issuer. In addition, the purchaser representative must: (i) have such knowledge and experience in financial and business matters that he, either alone or together with other purchaser representatives or the purchaser, is capable of evaluating the investment; (ii) be acknowledged in writing by the purchaser as the purchaser's purchaser representative in connection with the specific investment; and (iii) disclose to the purchaser in writing, prior to the purchaser's acknowledgement, any material relationship between the purchaser representative or his affiliates, and the issuer or its affiliates. The issuer and any person acting on its behalf must, after inquiry, believe and have reasonable grounds to believe that the purchaser representative meets the above conditions.

Rule 505.

Rule 505 is similar to Rule 506 except that: (a) it is not available for offers in excess of $5,000,000; and (b) it is not available to an investment company or an issuer disqualified under Regulation A. The principal advantage of Rule 505, as compared to Rule 506, is that if Rule 505 is available and if the offer is made to nonaccredited investors, the nonaccredited investors are not required to be sophisticated or have a purchaser representative.

Rule 505 is available to an issuer who (1) is not an investment company nor disqualified under Regulation A, (2) offers securities not in excess of $5,000,000, (3) sells securities to no more than 35 nonaccredited investors and an unlimited number of accredited investors (subject to the manner of offering requirement), the sophistication of the 35 nonaccredited purchasers not being required, (4) sells restricted securities without general advertising or solicitation, (5) supplies requisite information to nonaccredited investors, and (6) timely files the appropriate notice of sale with the Securities and Exchange Commission.

All sales of securities within the previous 12 months which were sold in reliance on any exemption under Section 3(b) of the Securities Act of 1933 (which includes securities sold in reliance on Rules 505 and 504) or in violation of Section 5 of the Act (securities sold in violation of the registration provisions) must be included in the $5,000,000 limitation. Securities sold pursuant to 4(2), 4(6) or Rule 506, unless otherwise required to be integrated, are not included in computing the ceiling.

Rule 504.

Rule 504 applies to offerings of up to $1,000,000 as long as no more than $500,000 worth of securities are offered and sold without registration under states' securities laws. In summary, the Rule is available to all issuers, other than reporting companies and investment companies, for offers and sales of securities (a) of up to $1,000,000 during any 12–month period as long as no more than $500,000 worth of securities are offered and sold without registration under states' securities laws, (b) accomplished without general advertising or solicitation, (c) to an unlimited number of persons, (d) which are restricted securities, and if a timely notice of sale is filed with the Securities and Exchange Commission. If the offering is conducted in states in which the securities are registered and a disclosure document is delivered under the securities laws of those states, general solicitation is permitted, the securities are not treated as restricted and up to $500,000 worth of securities can be offered and sold in states which have no registration procedures or which do not provide for registration and delivery of disclosure documents prior to sale.

NOTE

1. See generally Parnall, Kohl and Huff, *Private and Limited Offerings After a Decade of Experimentation: The Evolution of Regulation D,* 12 N.M.L. Rev. 633 (1982); Donahue, *New Exemptions from the Registration Requirements of the Securities Act of 1933: Regulation D,* 10 Sec.Reg.L.J. 235 (1982); Kessler, *The Effect of the Securities Laws upon the Small Business,* 28 # 6 Prac.Law. 11 (1982); Note, *Regulation D: Coherent Exemptions for Small Business Under the Securities Act of 1933,* 24 Wm. & Mary L.Rev. 121 (1982); Simonson, *Regulation D and Real Estate Limited Partnerships,* 13 # 3 Real Est.Rev. 55 (1983).

2. In Release No. 33–6663, October 2, 1986, CCH Fed.Sec.L.Rep. ¶ 84,032 ('86–'87 Tr.Bin.), the Securities and Exchange Commission provided a uniform notification form for Regulation D offerings. This form can be filed with the Securities and Exchange Commission and with appropriate state regulatory bodies. In addition, in Release No. 33–6825, March 14, 1989, CCH Fed.Sec.L.Rep. ¶ 84,404, the Securities and Exchange Commission amended Regulation D. The amendments broaden the category of accredited investor by including states, municipalities, public colleges and universities, and pension plans for state, municipal and public college and university employees if the plans have either a bank, savings and loan, insurance company or registered investment advisor as plan fiduciary and the plan imposes requirements governing fiduciary responsibility similar to those established by ERISA. The amendments add Rule 508 which provides that minor and isolated failures to comply with the mandates of Regulation D will not necessarily cause the loss of the exemption. In addition, the amendments require the issuer to demonstrate that reasonable care has been taken to guard against an inappropriate distribution of restricted securities and to make certain that investors appreciate the restricted nature of the securities. The taking of the actions presently

listed in Rule 502(d) will be a satisfactory demonstration of reasonable care. Lastly, the amendments eliminate the filing of the Form D notification as a condition of the Regulation D exemptions and adopt new Rule 507 which disqualifies an issuer from the use of the Regulation D exemptions if the notification was not filed, the Securities and Exchange Commission has the authority to waive the disqualification if the issuer shows good cause that the Regulation D exemption should not be denied.

(d) INTRASTATE EXEMPTION

Section 3(a)(11) provides the intrastate exemption from the registration under the Securities Act of 1933. This exemption is also strictly interpreted by the Securities and Exchange Commission.

SECURITIES ACT RELEASE NO. 4434

December 6, 1961.
[footnotes omitted]

* * *

"Issue" Concept

A basic condition of the exemption is that the *entire issue* of securities be offered and sold exclusively to residents of the state in question. Consequently, an offer to a non-resident which is considered a part of the intrastate issue will render the exemption unavailable to the entire offering.

Whether an offering is "a part of an issue", that is, whether it is an integrated part of an offering previously made or proposed to be made, is a question of fact and depends essentially upon whether the offerings are * * * related part[s] of a plan or program. * * * Thus, the exemption should not be relied upon in combination with another exemption for the different parts of a single issue where a part is offered or sold to non-residents.

The determination of what constitutes an "issue" is not governed by state law. * * * Any one or more of the following factors may be determinative of the question of integration: (1) are the offerings part of a single plan of financing; (2) do the offerings involve issuance of the same class of security; (3) are the offerings made at or about the same time; (4) is the same type of consideration to be received; and (5) are the offerings made for the same general purpose.

Moreover, since the exemption is designed to cover only those security distributions, which as a whole, are essentially local in character, it is clear that the phrase "sold only to persons resident" as used in Section 3(a)(11) cannot refer merely to the initial sales by the issuing corporation to its underwriters, or even the subsequent resales by the underwriters to distributing dealers. To give effect to the fundamental purpose of the exemption, it is necessary that the entire issue of securities shall be offered and sold to, and come to rest only in the hands of residents within the state. If any part of the issue is offered or sold to a non-resident, the exemption is unavailable not only for the securities so sold, but for all securities forming a part of the issue, including those sold to residents. * * * It is incumbent upon the issuer, underwriter, dealers and other persons connected with the offering to make sure that it does not become an interstate distribution through resales. It is understood to be customary for such persons to obtain assurances that purchases are not made with a view to resale to non-residents.

Doing Business Within the State

In view of the local character of the Section 3(a)(11) exemption, the requirement that the issuer be doing business in the state can only be satisfied by the performance of substantial operational activities in the state of incorporation. The doing business requirement is not met by functions in the particular state such as bookkeeping, stock record and similar activities or by offering securities in the State. * * *

If the proceeds of the offering are to be used primarily for the purpose of a new business conducted outside of the state of incorporation and unrelated to some incidental business locally conducted, the exemption should not be relied upon. * * * So also, a Section 3(a)(11) exemption should not be relied upon for each of a series of corporations organized in different states where there is in fact and purpose a single business enterprise or financial venture whether or not it is planned to merge or consolidate the various corporations at a later date. * * *

Residence Within the State

Section 3(a)(11) requires that the entire issue be confined to a single state in which the issuer, the offerees and the purchasers are residents. Mere presence in the state is not sufficient to constitute residence * * *. The mere obtaining of formal representations of residence and agreements not to resell to non-residents or agreements that sales are void if the purchaser is a non-resident should not be relied upon without more as establishing the availability of the exemption.

An offering may be so large that its success as a local offering appears doubtful from the outset. Also, reliance should not be placed on the exemption for an issue which includes warrants for the purchase of another security unless there can be assurance that the warrants will be exercised only by residents. * * *

Resales

From these general principles it follows that if during the course of distribution any underwriter, any distributing dealer (whether or not a member of the formal selling or distributing group), or any dealer or other person purchasing securities from a distributing dealer for resale were to offer or sell such securities to a non-resident, the exemption would be defeated. In other words, Section 3(a)(11) contemplates that the exemption is applicable only if the entire issue is distributed pursuant to the statutory conditions. Consequently, any offers or sales to a non-resident in connection with the distribution of the issue would destroy the exemption as to all securities which are a part of that issue, including those sold to residents regardless of whether such sales are made directly to non-residents or indirectly through residents who as part of the distribution thereafter sell to non-residents. It would furthermore be immaterial that sales to non-residents are made without use of the mails or instruments of interstate commerce. Any such sales of part of the issue to non-residents, however few, would not be in compliance with the conditions of Section 3(a)(11), and would render the exemption unavailable for the entire offering including the sales to residents. * * *

This is not to suggest, however, that securities which have actually come to rest in the hands of resident investors, such as persons purchasing without a view to further distribution or resale to non-residents, may not in due course be resold by such persons, whether directly or through dealers or brokers, to non-residents without in any way affecting the exemption. The relevance of any such resales consists only of the evidentiary light which they might cast upon the factual question whether the securities had in fact come to rest in the hands of resident investors. * * * It may be noted that the non-residence of the underwriter or dealer is not pertinent so long as the ultimate distribution is solely to residents of the state.

Use of the Mails and Facilities of Interstate Commerce

The intrastate exemption is not dependent upon non-use of the mails or instruments of interstate commerce in the distribution. Securities issued in a transaction properly exempt under this provision may be offered and sold without registration through the mails or by use of any instruments of transportation or communication in interstate commerce, may be made the subject of general newspaper advertisement (provided the advertisement is appropriately limited to indicate that offers to purchase are solicited only from, and sales will be made only to, residents of the particular state involved), and may even be delivered by means of transportation and communication used in interstate commerce, to the purchasers. Similarly, securities issued in a transaction exempt under Section 3(a)(11) may be offered without compliance with the formal prospectus requirements applicable to registered securities. Exemption under Section 3(a)(11), if in fact available, removes the distribution from the operation of the registration and prospectus requirements of Section 5 of the Act. It should be emphasized, however, that the civil liability and anti-fraud provisions of Sections 12(2) and 17 of the Act nevertheless apply and may give rise to civil liabilities and to other sanctions applicable to violations of the statute.

Conclusion

In conclusion, the fact should be stressed that Section 3(a)(11) is designed to apply only to distributions genuinely local in character. From a practical point of view, the provisions of that section can exempt only issues which in reality represent local financing by local industries, carried out through local investment. * * *

NOTE

1. The Securities and Exchange Commission, in Securities Act Release No. 5450, January 7, 1974, CCH Fed.Sec.L.Rep. ¶ 79,617 ('73–'74 Tr.Bin.), announced the adoption of Rule 147 which provides guidelines with respect to qualification for the intrastate exemption.

a. Rule 147 recognizes that the intrastate exemption is a transaction exemption rather than a securities exemption.

b. For the purposes of Rule 147 all securities of the issuer offered, offered for sale, or sold pursuant to the exemptions provided by Section 3 and Section 4(2) of the Securities Act of 1933 or registered pursuant thereto, prior to, or subsequent to, the six month period immediately preceding, or subsequent to, any offer, offer for sale, or sale pursuant to Rule 147 will be deemed not to be part of the Rule 147 offering provided, that there are no offers, offers to sell, or sales of securities of the same or similar class to those offered in the Rule 147 offering by or for the issuer during either of the six month periods.

c. Rule 147 provides objective standards for determining whether the "residency" and "doing business" requirements of the intrastate exemption have been met.

1. In order to be considered a resident issuer, a corporation, limited partnership, trust or other form of business organization must be incorporated, organized or established pursuant to the laws of the state in which residency is claimed. A general partnership or other form of business entity which is not formed under a specific state law must have its principal office within the state of claimed residency. An individual issuer is a resident of the state in which his principal residence is located.

a. Nonresident limited partners will not affect the residency of a limited partnership. If, however, the limited partnership consisted of one resident general partner and 200 nonresident limited partners who owned substantially all of the financial interests in the partnership, the residency of the limited partnership might be subject to some question. Cf. *Grenader v. Spitz*, 390 F.Supp. 1112 (S.D.N.Y.1975), reversed on another issue, 537 F.2d 612 (2d Cir.1976), cert. denied, 429 U.S. 1009, 97 S.Ct. 541, 50 L.Ed. 2d 619 (1976); *R. Edmund McMullan*, CCH Fed.Sec.L.Rep. ¶ 80,799 ('76–'77 Tr.Bin.); *Eugene T. Ichinose, Jr.*, CCH Fed.Sec.L.Rep. ¶ 82,148 (1979 Tr.Bin.). What is the residency of a corporation which was incorporated as a matter of convenience in one state, but which is qualified to do business and has all of its assets, its principal place of business and earns all of its income in another state?

b. In *North American Investments,* CCH Fed.Sec.L.Rep. ¶ 76,366 (1980 Tr.Bin.), the Division of Corporate Finance concluded that, for the purposes of Rule 147, a corporation which had its sales offices in California and conducted all of its business in California can be considered a California resident despite the fact that its directors and shareholders were Canadian citizens.

2. For the purpose of determining the residency of offerees and purchasers, a corporation, partnership, trust or other form of business entity is considered a resident of the state in which its principal office is located. If, however, the entity was organized for the specific purpose of acquiring part or all of an issue offered pursuant to Rule 147, it is not considered a resident of the state unless all of the beneficial owners of the entity are residents of the state. An individual, in order to be considered a resident, must have his principal residence in the state. An individual's principal residence is determined, for the purposes of Rule 147, without regard to the individual's intention to move. See *Minnesota Cablesystems—Southwest,* CCH Fed. Sec.L.Rep. ¶ 76,845 (1981 Tr.Bin.). In addition, when a trustee is solely and purely a custodian it is the principal residence of the beneficiary that is determinative. See *Fair Valley Properties No. 2,* CCH Fed.Sec. L.Rep. ¶ 77,003 ('81–'82 Tr.Bin.).

d. In order to be considered to be "doing business" within a state an issuer must: 1) derive 80% of its gross revenues on a consolidated basis during its most recent fiscal year from the operation of a business or property located in, or the rendering of services within, the state; 2) prior to the first offer of any part of an issue, have 80% of its assets on a consolidated basis as at the end of its most recent fiscal semi-annual period located within the state; 3) intend to use and use in the state in connection with the operation of a business or property or the rendering of services not less than 80% of the net proceeds from the sale of securities pursuant to Rule 147; and 4) have its principal office located in the state.

1. Eighty percent is an absolute floor for the purposes of Rule 147. In *Berkeley and Co., Inc.,* CCH Fed.Sec.L.Rep. ¶ 80,356 ('75–'76 Tr. Bin.), the Division of Corporation Finance held that the rounding off of 79.8% of assets to 80% in order to meet the requirements of Rule 147 was inappropriate. In addition, the Division of Corporation Finance did not believe that the 80% standard should be measured against assets valued at fair market value since this method of valuation would not be in accordance with generally accepted accounting principles in this instance.

2. The 80% of gross revenues requirement has proved troublesome for issuers who sell or distribute their products in a number of states in addition to the state in which the issuer is organized, where substantially all of its assets are located and where the proceeds of the proposed offering will be used. Compare *Medix of Wisconsin Inc.,* CCH Fed.Sec.L.Rep. ¶ 80,638 ('76–'77 Tr.Bin.); *American Computer Communications Co., Inc.,* CCH Fed.Sec.L.Rep. ¶ 80,686 ('76–'77 Tr.Bin.); and *David S. Cook,* CCH Fed.Sec.L.Rep. ¶ 80,792 ('76–'77 Tr.Bin.), with *Midco Pipe and Tube, Inc.,* CCH Fed.Sec.L.Rep. ¶ 80,416 ('75–'76 Tr. Bin); *Worldwide Motor Club, Inc.,* CCH Fed.Sec.L.Rep. ¶ 80,716 ('76–'77 Tr.Bin.); and *Perimeter Movie Associates,* CCH Fed.Sec.L.Rep. ¶ 80,744 ('76–'77 Tr.Bin.).

3. An issuer's principal office is located where its accountant, lawyer, buyers and officers are located, even if so located simply as a matter of convenience. See *Alaska Commercial Company,* CCH Fed. Sec.L.Rep. ¶ 76,820 (1981 Tr.Bin.).

e. Rule 147 also provides certain limitations on reoffers and resales and precautions against interstate distributions. The rule is a nonexclusive rule, but offers a "safe harbor" to those who comply with its requirements.

1. Rule 147 limits the resale of securities offered and sold under the rule, during the period in which the securities are being offered and sold by the issuer and for a period of nine months from the date of the last sale by the issuer of the securities, to offers and sales to persons resident in the state in which the offering is made. After the nine-month period, the securities can be resold to nonresidents. The nine-month period is a safe harbor, and securities issued relying on the intrastate exemption can be resold to a nonresident at any time after the offering has "come to rest" without invalidating the exemption. See *Busch v. Carpenter,* 598 F.Supp. 519 (D.Ut.1984), affirmed in part, reversed in part, 827 F.2d 653 (10th Cir.1987).

2. For an analysis of Rule 147 and the developments under the intrastate exemption, see Hicks, *Intrastate Offerings Under Rule 147,* 72 Mich.L.Rev. 463 (1974); Cummings, *The Intrastate Exemption and the Shallow Harbor of Rule 147,* 69 Nw.U.L.Rev. 167 (1974); Gardiner, *Intrastate Offering Exemption: Rule 147—Progress or Stalemate?,* 35 Ohio St.L.J. 340 (1974); Comment, *SEC Rule 147—Distilling Substance from the Spirit of the Intrastate Exemption,* 79 Dick. L.Rev. 18 (1974); Long, *A Lawyer's Guide to the Intrastate Exemption and Rule 147,* 24 Drake L.Rev. 471 (1975); Carney, *Exemptions From Securities Registration for Small Issuers: Shifting From Full Disclosure—Part II: The Intrastate Offering Exemption and Rule 147,* 11 Land & Water L.Rev. 161 (1976); Comment, *Securities Regulation: SEC Rule 147: Ten Years of SEC Interpretation,* 38 Okla.L.Rev. 507 (1985).

(iii) THE "SPIN–OFF" DISTRIBUTION OF SECURITIES

Generally, in order for the Securities Act of 1933 to apply there must be a "sale" of, or an "offer to sell," securities. In some circumstances, there is a question whether a sale of, or an "offer to sell," securities has in fact occurred. For example, a publicly held corporation buys a minority interest in a closely held corporation claiming that the transaction is exempt as a private offering. The intent of the purchaser, known and agreed to by the seller, is to distribute the stock of the seller to the shareholders of the purchaser by means of a stock dividend. After the sale and distribution, the original shareholders of the closely held corporation now own a majority interest in a publicly held corporation. Have they succeeded in going public without registration?

SECURITIES REGULATION: CORPORATE SPIN–OFFS AS A DEVICE FOR PUBLIC DISTRIBUTION WITHOUT REGISTRATION

Comment
42 University of Colorado Law Review 111 (1970).
[footnotes omitted]

*   *   *

The SEC's Answer

In a July 2, 1969, release the SEC announced a rationale for subjecting spin-off securities to registration under the '33 Act. The spin-off release treats the problem in the following manner: When the public corporation *   *   * acquires the stock of the closely held corporation, a sale takes place. The acquiring corporation is a statutory underwriter within the meaning of section 2(11) because it purchased from an issuer with a "view to *   *   * the distribution of any security" or as one who "[h]ad a direct or indirect participation in any such undertaking." The release acknowledges that there is no sale involved in the issuance of shares as a stock dividend. However, the SEC attempts to circumvent the traditional view that a distribution must include a sale by announcing that a distribution includes subsequent sales by the recipients of the stock dividends to the general public. Therefore, there is a distribution, and the shares must be registered under section 5 because a statutory underwriter is involved.

The validity of the commission's interpretation is open to doubt. There is no evidence either in the language of the Act or its legislative history that a distribution is incomplete when it reaches the investing public, but rather includes the redistribution by the initial distributees. While it is true that the SEC had defined distribution broadly in prior cases and opinions, it would appear that this interpretation has the effect of conflicting with the intent of Congress to exempt stock dividends from the definition of sale. It can, of course, be argued, as the SEC did in the release, that the spin-off situation is distinguishable from the ordinary stock dividend, and that, therefore, different rules can logically be applied. Nonetheless, the SEC's interpretation seems artificial and overly complicated, although the result it reaches is one which promotes the purpose of the Securities Act. It is suggested that the same goal could be reached using a theory quite different from the one on which the SEC now relies.

Third–Party Beneficiary Contract Theory

Section 2(3) of the '33 Act provides in part that "[t]he term 'sale' or 'sell' shall include every *contract of sale* or disposition of a security or interest in a security, for value." *   *   * [A] conventional stock dividend is not a sale within section 2(3), because it is not a "disposition for value." It is clear, however, that the stock dividends in the above example are not conventional, and were not of the kind contemplated by Congress when it expressed its intention to exclude stock dividends. It is suggested, therefore, that the transaction can be brought within the literal language of the statute by defining sale broadly enough to include the transfer of an enforceable contract right. Applying the rules of third-party beneficiary contract theory to the spin-off situation, the shareholders of the public corporation are the donee beneficiaries of a contract entered into between the publicly held corporation and the closely held corporation. Since the donee beneficiaries can enforce the contract to issue the stock dividend, there is a "contract of sale or disposition of a security" under section 2(3) and it is "for value" given by the close corporation. There is nothing in section 2(3) which requires that the recipients of the securities must be the ones who furnish the value.

It might be argued, however, that the third-party beneficiary argument is not valid because [the public corporation's] [share]holders are not donee beneficiaries but rather they are merely incidental beneficiaries. The universal rule is that the beneficiary has a right to enforce the contract if the parties to the contract have intended a benefit to flow to him. A mere incidental benefit which might accrue to a third person if the contract is performed is not enough to give the third person a right to sue on the contract. There is, however, an important distinction between the *intent* of the contracting parties and their *motive*. If by the terms of the contract the promisor must necessarily confer a benefit upon a third person, then the parties intend to benefit that person. On this basis the third person should be able to enforce the contract even if the parties to the contract were also benefited and their motives were purely selfish ones. Since the spin-off scheme depends on the issuance of the stock dividend to the [share]holders of the public corporation, there is clearly an intent to benefit the shareholders. * * *

The third-party beneficiary contract theory is not without weaknesses. Perhaps the major weakness is that it is conceptualistic. It is also possible that a judge would disregard the theory on the ground that securities law is *sui generis* and that therefore the transplantation of common law contract theory is inappropriate. Notwithstanding these problems, the theory does promote the purpose of the '33 Act, and it could not be construed to require registration of the conventional stock dividends which Congress intended to exclude from the registration requirements. Furthermore, the language of the sale section indicates an intention on the part of Congress to permit further definition of the term, at least where to do so would promote the purposes of the Act.

Of course, the third-party beneficiary contract theory does not dispense with the requirement of finding an underwriter, which means that there must be a distribution within the meaning of section 2(11). The SEC tried to solve this problem by declaring that, even though the issuance of a stock dividend is not in itself a distribution, the anticipated later sales by the recipients of the dividend qualify the prior transaction as a distribution. Using the third-party beneficiary concept, the corporation which purchased securities under an agreement to issue them to its shareholders would be engaged in a distribution and thus would be an underwriter because the shareholders would have an enforceable right to receive the securities.

* * *

Distribution Without a Sale

[T]he term distribution is not defined in the '33 Act. A common interpretation is that distribution is synonymous with "public offering" and thus includes a sale. However, no court has ever considered a case of a distribution without a sale, and the term could logically include the entire process by which shares reach the public, without a sale requirement. Thus, a public corporation which purchased shares with a view to distribution of them to its shareholders would be a statutory underwriter. While this would make the issuance of conventional stock dividends (shares of the distributing corporation) distributions, the shares would not have to be registered because there would be no underwriter in the usual stock dividend transaction.

The primary difficulty with this theory is that it depends on judicial acceptance of a broadened definition of distribution. However, the suggested redefinition would seem to be consistent with a common sense interpretation of the term.

* * *

NOTE

1. Does it make any difference under the Securities and Exchange Commission's analysis and the distribution without a sale analysis if the original issuer does not benefit from, or even desire, the subsequent distribution by the purchaser to its shareholders?

     a. If the purpose of the analysis is to avoid a closely-held corporation's going public without registration, should whether the closely-held corporation desired that result make a difference?

         1. On the other hand, is the purpose of the analysis to keep unregistered securities out of the hands of the public, regardless of the reasons for the transaction?

2. Do the desires of the closely-held corporation affect the result under the third party beneficiary contract analysis?

     a. If the subsequent distribution of the stock does not enter into the negotiations for the initial sale, it is difficult to say that the distributees are any more than incidental beneficiaries.

     b. If, however, the purchaser informs the seller that it may distribute the interest purchased to its shareholders and, to accommodate the purchaser's wishes, the interest to be purchased is divided into units suitable for distribution, are the eventual distributees now third party beneficiaries?

3. See generally *S.E.C. v. Harwyn Industries Corp.*, 326 F.Supp. 943 (S.D. N.Y.1971); Note, *Securities Regulation—Section 5 of the Securities Act of*

1933—Registration of Spin–Off Distributions of Subsidiary's Stock Required, 25
Vand.L.Rev. 454 (1972); Orlanski, *Going Public Through the Backdoor and the
Shell Game,* 58 Va.L.Rev. 1451 (1972); Long, *Control of the Spin–Off Device
Under the Securities Act of 1933,* 25 Okla.L.Rev. 317 (1972); Comment, *Registration of Stock Spin–Offs Under the Securities Act of 1933,* 1980 Duke L.J. 965.

b.   STATE REGULATION OF SECURITIES—THE BLUE–SKY CONCEPT

In addition to federal regulation, the offering and sale of securities
within a state is, in most cases, regulated by state legislation.   Therefore, a developer, seeking to sell securities, to raise part, or all, of its
financial needs, must comply with not only the federal statutes regulating the offer and sale of securities but also the applicable state statutes
in the state or states in which the securities are offered and sold.

A PRIMER ON STATE SECURITIES REGULATION
State Legislation Committee of the
Investment Bankers Association of America.
July 1, 1969 edition.

* * *

Types of State Regulation

* * *

There are three principal types of state regulation:

(a) Antifraud provisions. * * *

(b) Requirements for registration of dealers and salesmen. * * *

(c) Requirements for registration of nonexempt securities. * * *

Registration of Dealers and Salesmen

Dealers and salesmen are required to register * * * by filing
applications or statements with the state Securities Administrator.
*The fact that a dealer is registered under the federal Securities Exchange Act of 1934 does not exempt him from the state registration
requirement.*

Surety Bonds and Net Capital Requirements: Some state laws
require or authorize the Administrator to require registration applicants to post a surety bond.   Other states require a bond unless a
registrant's net worth exceeds a designated amount.   A few states
require or authorize the Administrator to require dealers to have a
minimum capital or net worth.   The Uniform [Securities] Act authorizes the Administrator to require that a broker-dealer supply a surety
bond in an amount up to $10,000, except that no such bond may be
required of any registrant whose net capital exceeds $25,000. * * *

Examinations: In [a majority of] states applicants for registration
are required to pass an examination to prove their knowledge of the
securities business.   Many of these states accept passing of the NASD

examination to meet the requirement for a general securities examination. * * *

Records and Reports: The laws of most states authorize the Administrator to require that registered dealers keep certain records and file certain reports. Here, again, the case for uniformity in state securities laws is very much in evidence. Much of the required information is identical with—or, at least, similar to—the data stipulated by the SEC, various stock exchanges, and other regulatory agencies. * * *

Revocation and Suspension: Registration of a dealer or salesman may be denied or revoked on grounds specified in the state acts. The most common grounds for such action are (a) violation of the act, and (b) fraudulent activities in the sale of securities. The registration of a dealer or salesman may be suspended for less serious violations.

Requirements for the Registration of Securities

Exemptions: In all states which require registration of securities, certain classes are exempt. Others are exempt when sold in certain transactions. *But the fact that securities are registered under the federal Securities Act does not exempt them from state registration.*

U.S. Government and municipal bonds are exempt in all states. Most state laws exempt securities listed on specified stock exchanges. Securities issued by public utilities are exempt in some states if the issuer is supervised as to the issuance of its securities by a federal or state commission, and are exempt in other states if the issuer is supervised as to its rates and charges by a state commission. There are numerous other classes of exempt securities and exempt transactions, varying from state to state.

Manual Exemption: In the past there has been confusion over the necessity of dealers registering securities for trading in the secondary market, if such securities had not previously been registered in the state. In recent years, many states have adopted an exemption—familiarly known as the Manual Exemption—for sales by registered dealers in the secondary market of securities about which specified information is published in a recognized securities manual. * * *

Types of Registration of Securities: It is very important to distinguish between the different types of "registration" of securities.

Registration under the federal Securities Act of 1933 is based on "full disclosure", requiring principally (a) the filing of a registration statement containing detailed information; and (b) the delivery to each purchaser of a prospectus containing specified information. The administrative agency (SEC) has no authority to deny registration of securities if the required disclosure is made.

The foregoing must not be confused with registration under the various state acts (and under both Uniform Acts), where the state Administrator is authorized to deny registration of securities on specified grounds, even though full disclosure as required under the federal act has been made. Thus, an issue might be registered under the federal act with the required full disclosure, but registration might still be, and often is, denied under state acts on one of the grounds specified.

(a) Registration by Notification: In most states (and both Uniform Acts), a simplified procedure known as "registration by notification" is provided for securities which meet certain standards (*i.e.*, the issuer has been in business for a specified number of years, and has had average earnings above a specified minimum). This registration becomes effective automatically after a certain period of time, unless the Administrator acts to deny registration on one of the specified grounds.

Under provisions of the old Uniform Act, which are presently in effect in some states, registration by notification becomes effective "when filed"; but under both the new Uniform Act and the Modified Uniform Act such registration becomes effective at 3 p.m. EST, on the second full business day after filing the registration statement (or the last amendment), or at such earlier time as the Administrator determines.

* * *

(b) Registration by Coordination originated in the new Uniform Act and it is also a part of the Modified Act. It is designed to coordinate state registration of securities which are also being registered under the federal Securities Act of 1933. It permits the filing of copies of the federal prospectus and amendments thereto, with a few additional items of information as the state registration statement. If that statement has been on file with the Administrator for at least 10 days, and specified price information has been on file for two full business days (unless the Administrator waives these conditions), state registration by coordination becomes effective simultaneously with federal registration (unless the Administrator denies state registration on grounds specified in the state act).

* * *

(c) Registration by Qualification: All nonexempt securities not eligible for registration by some other procedure must be registered by a procedure known as "qualification." Registration by qualification does not become effective until the Administrator takes affirmative action to grant the registration.

It should be emphasized again that no state securities act bases registration of securities upon the "full disclosure" philosophy of the federal act, and in every state where registration of securities is required the Administrator has authority to deny registration on specified grounds.

For a long time, only one state act (Colorado) required delivery of a prospectus to purchasers. But in recent years several states have authorized the Administrator to require delivery of a prospectus.

Grounds for Denial of Registration: There are wide variations in different states in the Administrator's authority to deny registration of securities. Under provisions of the old Uniform Act, his broadest powers were found in the authority to register securities if he finds that their sale "would not work or tend to work a fraud upon the purchaser, and that the enterprise or business of the issuer is not based upon unsound business principles." Any finding to the contrary was sufficient grounds for denial of registration.

The old Uniform Act also authorized the Administrator, with respect to securities registered by qualification, to "fix the maximum amount of commission or other form of remuneration to be paid in cash or otherwise, directly or indirectly for or in connection with the sale or offering for sale of such securities in this state."

*   *   *

Under the new Uniform Act, the two broadest authorizations for the Administrator to deny registration are findings that the offering "has worked or tended to work a fraud upon the purchasers or would so operate," and:

> "the offering has been or would be made with unreasonable amounts of underwriters' and sellers' discounts, commissions, or other compensations or promoters' profit, or participation, or unreasonable amounts or kinds of options."

The Modified Uniform Act has omitted this provision regarding unreasonable commissions or compensation because such a provision, in effect, permits the Administrator to fix the amount of underwriters' commissions or compensation on each issue, and there is no real statutory standard as to what constitutes "unreasonable" commissions or compensation.

*   *   *

The laws of several states authorize the Administrator to deny registration of securities if he finds that the proposed plan of business of the issuer would be "unfair, unjust or inequitable." This authority has been widely criticized on the ground that it provides no statutory standard and permits the Administrator to deny registration of any issue that he personally dislikes, regardless of its actual investment merit.

In a few states the acts provide a specific percentage limitation on the amount of underwriting remuneration permitted, or on total marketing expenses [and on promoter's profits, participation, options, etc.]

*   *   *

In several states the Administrator is authorized to impose "such conditions, limitations and restrictions" on any registration as he believes necessary to carry out the purposes of the act.

*   *   *

NOTE

1. A securities offering exempt under the Securities Act of 1933 will not necessarily be exempt under a state's Blue Sky Law. The Uniform Securities Act, however, provides for certain exemptions similar in purpose to the private offering exemption.

a.   Section 402(b) of the Uniform Securities Act exempts from registration the following transactions: (1) Any isolated non-issuer transaction; (2) Any transaction pursuant to an offer directed by the offeror to not more than ten persons in the state within any period of twelve consecutive months, if the offeror believes all buyers are purchasing for investment and no commissions are paid for soliciting buyers; and (3) Any offer or sale of a preorganization certificate or subscription on the same conditions, with the exception of the 12 month period, as described in (2) above.

1.   A state administrator can withdraw or further condition the exemption described in (2) above or increase or decrease the number of offerees permitted.

2.   A number of states have adopted an approach toward exemption from registration similar to that contained in Regulation D of the Securities and Exchange Commission.   The Securities and Exchange Commission has made Form D, the notification form for transactions claimed to be exempt under Regulation D, a uniform notification form for both federal and state purposes.   See Release No. 33–6683, January 16, 1987, CCH Fed.Sec.L.Rep. ¶ 84,054 ('86–'87 Tr.Bin.).

3.   See Royalty and Jones, *The Private Placement Exemption and The Blue Sky Laws—Shoals in the Safe Harbor,* 33 Wash. & Lee L.Rev. 877 (1976); Maynard, *The Uniform Limited Offering Exemptions: How "Uniform" is "Uniform"?,* 36 Emory L.J. 357 (1987).

b.   See generally Tompkins, *The Uniform Securities Act—A Step Forward in State Regulation,* 77 West Va.L.Rev. 15 (1974); Shapiro and Sachs, *Blue Sky Law and Practice: An Overview,* 4 U.Balt.L.Rev. 1 (1974); Goodkind, *Blue Sky Law: Is There Merit in the Merit Requirements?,* 1976 Wis. L.Rev. 79; Comment, *State Securities Regulation of Interstate Land Sales,* 10 Urb.L.Ann. 271 (1975); Mofsky and Tollison, *Demerit in Merit Regulation,* 60 Marq.L.Rev. 367 (1977); Note, *State Securities Regulation: Investor Protection Versus Freedom of the Marketplace,* 29 U.Fla.L.Rev. 947 (1977); Hillard and Ricciardelli, *Investment Contracts Under the Colorado and Uniform Securities Acts,* 49 U.Colo.L.Rev. 391 (1978).

2.   The type of conditions, limitations and restrictions a state administrator might impose on a securities offering under a state's Blue Sky law include: a) impounding the proceeds of the sale of securities until a certain percentage or all of the amount proposed to be raised by the offering has been achieved; and b) escrowing, for a period of time, the securities issued to the promoters.

a.   For a discussion of state securities regulation of real estate investments see Van Camp, *Securities Regulation of Real Estate Investments: The California Model,* 35 Ohio St.L.J. 309 (1974); Hrusoff, *Securities Aspects of Real Estate Partnerships,* 11 Cal.W.L.Rev. 425 (1975); Report, *Regulation of Real Estate Securities, Including the Applicability of Federal Rule 146 and Its Use in State Blue Sky Laws,* 13 Real Prop., Prob. & Tr.J. 841 (1978).

Division IV

DEVELOPMENT AND OPERATION OF REAL ESTATE

---

1. IMPROVING THE REAL ESTATE

---

a. THE ARCHITECT

The employment of an architect is usually one of the first steps in the development of real estate. In order to obtain commitments for the financing of the development, the developer will need plans and specifications. In addition, the architect's prediction of construction costs will be used to determine the amount of financing needed and to do the financial projections with respect to the development. The prediction of construction costs plays a significant part in determining the amount of the loan described in a subject to financing clause, subordination agreement, construction loan commitment and permanent take-out. As a result, serious problems may occur if the architect's prediction is wrong.

ARCHITECTURAL COST PREDICTIONS: A LEGAL AND INSTITUTIONAL ANALYSIS

Justin Sweet and Lesly Sweet.
56 California Law Review 996 (1968)
[footnotes omitted]

* * *

Once the client decides to retain a particular architect, the architect's function is to develop a design solution which will achieve the client's goals. To accomplish this, it is necessary for the architect and client to work together. The architect's function is to take the general needs and wants of the client and convert them to a design solution expressed in the plans and specifications. To do this, he prepares schematic designs, which represent a skeletal design solution, and then the design development, a more detailed design solution. These two phases of the architect's performance have been known in the past as and still are sometimes called the preliminary studies.

After the design development or preliminary studies are approved by the client, the architect proceeds to draft the construction documents, or working drawings. These are more detailed and technical in nature. Their primary function is to provide prospective bidders with bidding information upon which they can base their proposals. They

947

will comprise a major part of the successful bidder's contractual obligation.

* * *

After approval of the construction documents, invited contractors are given copies of them to use in making their construction bids. The crisis usually arises when the lowest bid substantially exceeds anticipated costs.

* * *

The Law

A. *Judicial Lawmaking: A Look at the Decisions*

1. Promises and Conditions

An architect may promise the client that the contractors' bids will be within a cost figure set by the client. If this event—the bids being within the figure—does not occur, the architect may be liable for any damages suffered by the client because of delay or rising costs during redesign.

* * *

Cost problems usually involve a determination of the exact nature of the architect's promise with regard to costs and of the exact nature of the event which must occur or be excused before the client is obligated to pay a fee. The exact nature of the architect's promise first depends on what assurance he has given the client, orally or in writing. Next, it will depend on the nature of the promises that are implied, rather than expressed. Promises may be implied from surrounding circumstances, custom, trade usage, and implied by law. The architect may have promised: (1) To use due care; (2) to be accurate; and (3) that the project cost would not exceed a particular amount. If the architect has promised to be accurate, normally the reason for inaccuracy is not relevant. In effect, he has guaranteed the accuracy of his estimate. If he is not correct, he has breached and is liable for any foreseeable damage caused by the breach.

The exact nature of the event that conditions the client's obligation to pay the fee depends upon the agreement, surrounding facts and circumstances, and the application of the legal doctrine of conditions. The event might be: (1) Use of due care in preparing architectural cost estimates; (2) the project cost not exceeding a specified amount or the final cost estimate; (3) the client being satisfied with the bids (or bidders); (4) the availability of adequate funds; and (5) the project being built.

A promise can be, and often is, a condition. The architect might promise to use due care, and the exercise of due care could also condition the client's obligation to pay the fee. The architect might promise to be accurate, as well as condition his fee upon the accuracy of his cost estimate. In the latter case, the architect's inaccuracy would cost him his fee and he could also be liable for damages for breach.

The promise and the condition need not be identical. The architect might promise to use due care, and yet, by agreement, his fee could be conditioned upon the accuracy of his estimate, the bids being acceptable, or the project being built. He might promise to be accurate, but the agreement might condition his right to receive his fee upon the use of due care. In the latter case, his inaccuracy would not cost him his fee if he used due care, but he would be liable for damages.

2. Agreement on Costs

* * * The two principal legal issues relevant to the resolution of the question of whether a cost condition has been created are:

1. Does the execution of a written agreement that does not contain a cost condition preclude the client from testifying about the asserted agreement?

2. What factors are relevant in the determination of whether such an agreement took place?

* * *

Prediction concerning the admissibility of testimony about an alleged prior or contemporaneous oral agreement on costs is hazardous because of the differing attitudes toward the rule from state to state, and even within a given state. Nevertheless, certain generalizations can be extrapolated from a reading of the many decisions which have involved architect-client contracts.

If the agreement is silent on the question of costs or fixed cost limitations, it is likely that the client will be permitted to testify on the alleged agreement. There have been a few cases to the contrary, usually where the contract has mentioned cost estimates in some way. However, most courts assume that costs are discussed by the parties in every case. If the writing makes no mention of any understanding on costs, these courts assume that the writing is not complete.

Prediction on admissibility of evidence of prior oral agreements relating to costs is more difficult if there is language in the writing which deals in one way or another with this question. Prior to 1961, the standard AIA contract stated that the architect did not guarantee estimates. * * *

If the agreement is signed before completion of preliminaries, the pre–1961 disclaimer will not be of much use in avoiding testimony by the client about an alleged prior oral agreement on costs. Subsequent AIA contracts are more complete and are reasonably well drafted. They may do better in the courts than did their predecessors even though subjected to a test of completeness based upon when the contract is executed.

Nevertheless, there is always a risk that, when the client's expectations differ from the contract, the courts will interpret the clause narrowly. Even well-drawn clauses can be attacked by assertion of fraud or mistake, by a request that the writing be reformed because it did not correctly express the true understanding of the parties, or by a claim that the agreement was made after formation of the contract and thus not affected by the parol evidence rule. The oral agreement is used to interpret the writing if the contract does not explicitly state that the client need not pay if the costs are too high. No contractual provision, however well drawn, will ensure that the client will not be able to bring his contention before the judge and jury.

The courts have looked at factors other than the written or asserted oral agreement in resolving the question of the creation of the cost condition. Even if the client's testimony is received into evidence, the question of determining whether the agreement did take place as alleged must be resolved by the court or jury. Courts have admitted evidence of custom in the profession. Architects have been permitted to introduce evidence that customarily architects do not assume the risk of the accuracy of their cost predictions. Also, courts have been more favorably disposed toward holding for the architect if the project in question has involved remodeling rather than new construction, because estimating costs in remodeling is extremely difficult. The same result should follow if the type of construction involves experimental techniques or materials.

Courts sometimes distinguish between cases and justify varying results on the basis of the amount of detail given to the architect by the client in advance. Generally, the greater the detail, the easier it should be for the architect to predict accurately. However, it is much more difficult for the architect to fulfill the desires of the client within a specified cost figure if the client retains a great deal of control over details, especially if these controls are exercised throughout the architect's performance. For this reason, some courts have held that a cost condition is not created where the architect is not given much flexibility in designs or materials.

Some courts have looked at the stage of the architect's performance in which the cost condition was created. If it is created at an early state, it is more difficult for the architect to be accurate in his cost predictions. Generally, the later the cost limit is imposed in good faith, the more likely it is to be a cost condition. But courts should recognize that if it is imposed later, creation—or, more realistically, imposition—may be an unfair attempt by the client to deprive the architect of his fee.

*   *   *

Courts have sometimes cited provisions for interim payments as an indication that the architect is not assuming the risk of losing his fees on the accuracy of his cost estimates. However, standard printed clauses buried in a contract are not always an accurate reflection of the understanding of the party not familiar with the customs or the forms. If payments have actually been made during the architect's performance, this is a clear indication that the client is not laboring under the belief that he will not have to pay any fee if the low bid substantially exceeds the final cost estimate. A few cases have looked for good faith on the part of the client. For example, if the client has offered some payment to the architect for his services, this may impress a court as a show of fairness and good faith.

*   *   *

3. Interpretation

If it is established that a cost condition has been created, the next issue is that of interpretation. What is necessary to satisfy the cost condition? The architect is permitted some margin of error. Courts have adopted a test which employs a type of substantial performance. Many architects suggest, and often contracts permit, a deviation of ten percent.

The cost figure which determines the occurrence of the condition is usually the construction bid submitted by the contractor. Normally cost of acquiring the land, consultants' fees, and fees of the architect are not considered costs for this purpose.

Sometimes ultimate costs exceed the low bid because of extra work or because unforeseen circumstances develop in performance which lead to the contractor being given an increase in the contract price. The cost of extra work should not bear upon the cost condition unless the extra work is needed to compensate for design errors of the architect. An illustration of unforeseen circumstances would be the discovery of unexpected subsoil conditions, which could lead to a price increase. This should have no bearing upon the cost condition.

To sum up, in the normal situation, the condition has occurred if a low, enforceable bid is received which is reasonably close to the cost-condition figure.

satisfaction of cond

4. Implication of Terms—Redesign

In addition to determining what the parties have expressly agreed to, courts are often called upon to fill in contractual gaps which either were not considered by the parties or were terms which they believed to be so obvious that contractual expression was unnecessary. As a rule, courts are hesitant to imply terms. They will do so if firmly convinced that: (1) Had the question been called to the attention of the parties at the time the contract was made, the parties would have agreed to this interpretation; or (2) without implication, the object of one or both of the contracting parties would be drastically frustrated; or (3) implication is needed to make a binding contract when the parties intended to be bound; or (4) in extreme cases, an implication of terms is demanded by basic notions of fairness and good sense.

Implication of terms is important in relation to the problems of redesign by the architect and cooperation by the client in reducing costs. If all the bids are too high, does the architect have a right to redesign in order to meet the cost condition? The first consideration must be that of the contract terms. However, even if there is no contractual provision providing for a right to redesign, the architect should be given this opportunity. The arrangement between architect and client is a professional relationship, where both parties should do their utmost to accomplish the goals of both. Frequently, redesign can avoid forfeiture of the architect's fee.

Cooperation by the architect should also be required. The client should not be expected to agree to a material change of the design solution agreed to earlier by architect and client. The client should not have to go farther than agreeing to cheapening of the work. The basic design should continue, but the changes should relate to reducing the cost without affecting the utility and purpose of the project.

* * *

There are limits to the right to redesign. If the delay inherent in redesign would work a material hardship on the client, the architect should not be given the opportunity to redesign. Also, if the variance between the low bid and the cost condition is so extreme that it appears unlikely that redesign will be successful, then the architect should not have the right to redesign.

Should the law imply a promise by the architect that he will redesign if the client so wishes? If a cost condition is created, and the architect does not want to redesign, he should not be required to do so. He has already lost his fee, and it would be unfair to require him to try to bring the project within the cost condition if he does not think it feasible. The implication of such a promise would be a type of compulsion hardly suitable to the architect-client professional relationship. Even if there is no cost condition, it is unlikely that the law would or should require redesign. Usually, the architect does not promise to bring the project in at a specified cost.

5. Condition Excused

The duty to perform a promise does not arise until events which condition performance either occur or are excused. Excuse can be divided into a number of related, but analytically different, concepts.

* * *

(a) Prevention, Hindrance, or Lack of Cooperation.—If the client unjustifiably prevents the cost condition from occurring, hinders the occurrence of the condition, or fails to take reasonable, positive action which would cause the condition to occur, the condition is excused and the promise matures. The client should not be permitted to set up the failure of the condition to occur as a defense under these circumstances.

* * *

Even if there is prevention, hindrance, or lack of cooperation, the condition analytically should not be excused unless the architect can show, with reasonable certainty, that the cost condition would have occurred had it not been prevented or hindered, or had there been cooperation. When courts want to overlook this requirement, they often use waiver. This, as will be seen, does not require a showing that the condition would have occurred. In any case, judicial inquiry into probability of occurrence is likely to be perfunctory if the conduct, or failure to act, by the client seems motivated by bad faith.

(b) Estoppel.—* * *

In the architect-client context, estoppel would result if the client, either by words or acts, led the architect to believe the cost condition would not be enforced by the client, and the architect failed to take steps which he could have taken to bring the costs within the amount established by the cost condition. To illustrate, estoppel might result if the client tells the architect he is so pleased with the design that he does not care about the cost. If the architect then proceeded with the design, when he could have changed the design and caused the condition to occur, the client would be estopped from asserting the condition, and the condition would be excused.

* * * [If] the architect [is] reasonably * * * led to believe that the client no longer intends to enforce the original cost condition, [and] * * * has relied on this as reason for not redesigning, the condition should be excused.

Estoppel could also arise if the client used the plans, despite knowledge of the excessive cost. Here, the client's knowledge is usually easy to establish, since the use usually occurs after the bids are in. If the client let the contract rather than permitting the architect to redesign, and if this was due to inadequate time for redesign, the question of estoppel would depend upon the reason for the time pressure. If the fault was that of the architect, it is probable that he has no right to redesign, and the cost condition would not be excused. Recovery in such a case would have to be based on quasi-contract or unjust enrichment.

Since quasi-contract is based upon unjust enrichment, the measure of recovery will be the benefit conferred on the client by the use of the plans. This might be measured by the reasonable value of the architect's services, a measure not too different from that of the contract remedies available to the architect had there been no cost condition. If the architect did not estimate very accurately, he would be likely to find that a court would hold that the benefit conferred was of a lesser value than what the architect would have received under the contract.

Note that estoppel is not based upon an actual intention on the part of the client to dispense with the cost condition. It is based upon words or acts which lead the architect so to believe, followed by detrimental reliance.

(c) Waiver.—Waiver is related to estoppel, but there is an analytical distinction not always drawn by courts. Estoppel is based upon detrimental reliance, upon the concept that, but for the act constituting the estoppel, the architect would have caused the cost condition to occur. To create a waiver, there need be no showing of reliance, or that the condition would have occurred. All that is required is evidence that the client has communicated an intention to pay the fee, despite the failure of the cost condition to occur. The condition was for his

benefit. If he manifested an intention to give up this benefit, he should be held to his communicated intention, and the cost condition should be excused.

* * *

The most difficult aspect of this seemingly simple formula for excusing conditions is in determining what acts manifest waiver, other than express statements. Often, waiver is predicated upon acts that have been discussed—approval of plans, excessive changes, payments, or use of plans. Acts such as these can often have ambiguous meanings. Do they manifest an intention on the part of the client to dispense with the condition? An important element in deciding on the legal effect of these acts is awareness by the client, when the acts are performed, that costs are likely to exceed the amount of the cost condition. The architect can hardly assume that these acts manifest the requisite intent of waiver on the part of the client if the client is not aware of the likelihood of excessive costs. * * *

If acts such as payment, changes, approval of plans, or use of plans occur, but the client makes it quite clear that he is not giving up the condition, there is no waiver. Estoppel will be difficult to find, because the statement of the client's intention to stand on the condition should make any reliance by not redesigning unjustifiable. In such a case, the condition is still in effect. If the client has used the plans, the recovery should be predicated upon quasi-contract.

(d) Impossibility.—Architects sometimes assert that performance of the cost condition became impossible because of circumstances over which they have no control. A condition of a minor or technical nature may be excused if its occurrence has become impossible, and if the risk of impossibility has not been assumed by the promisee (in this case, the architect). Without going into the difficult question of whether a cost condition is minor or technical, the creation of a cost condition means the architect assumes the risk of most prediction factors. This includes a steep rise in wage and material costs, or volatility of the construction market, factors which help to make cost prediction difficult. This is one of the primary reasons for avoiding the creation of a cost condition by a clear understanding with the client and by use of an appropriate disclaimer clause in the contract.

A cataclysmic event, such as a war or great natural catastrophe, might cause a different result. If costs become excessive for these reasons, normally use of the plans will constitute a waiver, and the cost condition will be excused. If the plans are not used, the architect should recover if the contract provided that he would be paid if the project was abandoned for any reason. Even without such an "abandonment" clause, the condition should be excused. The architect created the design requested by the client but not at the price limit set because of extraordinary reasons beyond his control. Creation of a cost condition places most risks upon the architect, but not every conceivable risk.

* * *

6. Measure of Recovery

(a) By Architect.—If the court finds that no cost condition was created, or that if one was created, it was excused, what is the measure of the architect's recovery? This discussion assumes that the client does not permit the project to be continued.

Under normal contract principles, the architect should be put in the position he would have been in had the contract been fully performed. This would be a protection of his expectation interest. Under this test, he would be entitled to his entire fee, based on full performance (determined by the contract rate times the estimated cost) less interim fee payments received and less the expense saved by him in not having to perform further. In addition, he would be entitled to any additional damages caused by the breach which were foreseeable at the time the contract was made.

*   *   *

Other possible recoverable items would be losses incurred due to the need for a sudden reduction in the architect's staff or the diminished productivity of personnel especially hired for the project who could not be immediately released. The architect would have to show causation and foreseeability to recover for these losses, however, and both are usually difficult to prove.

As an alternative to expectancy, the architect might be able to recover his reliance, or out-of-pocket expenses. This would normally be the reasonable value of the architectural services performed, without regard to future services. As a rule, like most professionals, this is all the architect will try to recover.

Generally, AIA contracts permit the architect to recover the reasonable value for his services performed to date of termination plus "terminal expenses" if the project is abandoned. This clause might be held to preclude his right to recover expectation damages, if it were found that the contractual measure of recovery was exclusive. No cases have discussed this question. If the architect wishes to preserve his right to expectancy damages, this clause, if used, should be amended to state that it is not the exclusive remedy.

*   *   *

(b) By Client.—*   *   *

Normally, both architect and client assume that the architect will use due care in the performance of his work. Whether the architect has used due care depends upon the customary methods of measuring professional competence. He is held to the standard of care of others of his profession with his experience, judged by the standards of the community in which he practices.

Whatever effect disclaimers have upon the architect's right to collect his fee, disclaimers should certainly preclude any action against the architect for inaccuracy. However, disclaimer clauses should have no effect where the architect is negligent.

If the architect has breached, and the project is abandoned, the architect will not be able to collect for his services, since performance of his promise also conditions the client's promise to pay. Also, the client can recover any intcrim fee payments that have been made, as well as any reasonably foreseeable reliance expenses made valueless or less valuable due to abandonment of the project.

If the client proceeds with the project as designed, complications develop. Presumably, the client has not been damaged, since he has a project which is worth what it cost him. A court might use the diminished economic value of the project as a measure for the client's recovery, if this can be established.

*   *   *

If the project is completed by the client, a problem arises under the rule of avoidable consequences. Normally, damages which could have been reasonably avoided by the nonbreaching party (here the client) are not recoverable. Proceeding with the project should not constitute enhancing damages, unless the principal motive was to enlarge the architect's liability. Use of the plans by the client, by itself should not constitute waiver of any cause of action the client may have for damages.

While use of the plans should not waive the client's right to recover for damages, use does affect the architect's right to be paid for his work. If the use of the plans is accompanied by evidence manifesting a waiver of the cost condition, the architect would be entitled to be paid under the contract. The measure of the architect's recovery in such a case would be the rate of commission times the cost of the project. If the use is not held to constitute waiver of the condition, the architect's measure of recovery would be based on quasi-contract, or benefit conferred. The architect's breach is likely to cause the court to place a low value on the benefit conferred on the client by the use of the plans.

Any recovery for the use of the plans, whether based on contract or quasi-contract, will be diminished or canceled out by any damages recoverable because of a breach by the architect. This discussion assumes a breach which has not been waived and for which damages are recoverable by the client.

*   *   *

B. Mass Private Lawmaking: A Study of AIA Standard Contracts

While courts are the visible lawmaking institution, many more transactions are governed by standardized provisions in printed form contracts created by the American Institute of Architects. Where such forms are used, they usually provide a method for resolving a cost dispute. If one party refuses to comply with the provision, litigation is the usual result. Where there is litigation such a printed form, while not always given literal effect, often controls the judicial determination of the dispute. The drafters of such mass contracts are probably the most important lawmakers.

* * *

[T]he AIA [has] issued a * * * form [architect-owner] contract. There were no essential changes in the obligation of the architect to give statements of probable construction costs.[1] However, there were major changes * * * dealing with nonnegligent, erroneous estimates of probable construction costs.

In article 3, section 3.4, the * * * form states:

Statements of Probable Construction Costs and Detailed Cost Estimates prepared by the Architect represent his best judgment as a design professional familiar with the construction industry. It is recognized, however, that neither the Architect nor the Owner has any control over the cost of labor, materials or equipment, over the contractors' methods of determining bid prices, or over competitive bidding or market conditions. Accordingly, the Architect cannot and does not guarantee that bids will not vary from any Statement of Probable Cost or other cost estimate prepared by him.

Section 3.4 eliminates the professional cost estimator and gives a more detailed and well written recital on why there may be unpleasant surprises when the bids are opened. The clause obligates the architect to make his cost predictions with due care, but does not require that he be accurate.

Section 3.5 states:

When a fixed limit of Construction Cost is * * * established, the Architect shall be permitted to determine what materials, equipment, component systems and types of construction are to be included in the Contract Documents, and to make reasonable adjustments in the scope of the Project to bring it within the fixed limit. The Architect may also include in the Construction Documents alternate bids to adjust the Construction Cost to the fixed limit.

In the * * * form * * * the owner must cooperate in cutting down the quality and must make reasonable adjustments in quantity. Again, such an allocation would be fair if the owner were warned in advance. If such a clause were pointed out in advance, and if the owner had the usual superiority of bargaining power, such a clause might be deleted. If the owner objects to the clause, the architect might assure him that despite the clause control over design details would remain with the owner. But note that this protection only applies where there is a fixed cost limitation. Such provisions are an attempt on the part of the AIA either to discour-

1. [The Owner is entitled to receive statements of probable construction costs at various stages of the architect's performance.]

age the use of fixed cost limitations or to give the architect complete protection in the event a dispute arises over this question.

In addition to requiring the owner * * * to cooperate in reducing quantity and quality, section 3.5.1 requires the owner to "authorize rebidding the Project within a reasonable time." It would seem superfluous to both give the architect control over details and require the client to cooperate in revising the scope. Perhaps client control of the scope is so ingrained in custom that section 3.5.1 was needed to legitimate the power of the architect under section 3.5 to control quantity and quality when a fixed limit is chosen. More important, section 3.5.1 states that in case the project is revised:

> [T]he Architect, without additional charge, shall modify the Drawings and Specifications as necessary to bring the Construction Cost within the fixed limit. The providing of this service shall be the limit of the Architect's responsibility in this regard and having done so, the Architect shall be entitled to his fees in accordance with this Agreement.

Section 3.5.1 directly deals with the right to redesign. This is a private law codification of a practice among architects. It should be noted that redesign is a very expensive operation for the architect. Also, section 3.5.1 for the first time directly confronts the fee problem. Instead of a vague nonguarantee of estimates or a backdoor use of the abandonment clause, there is a direct handling of the fee problem. The architect takes the risk he will have to redesign, but does not risk his fee. This, if made clear to the owner, is a marked improvement.

Note that all of these protective provisions apply only if there is a fixed cost limitation. Earlier forms stated that such a limitation must be "stated herein." This phrase [has been] dropped in [recent forms]. Instead article 12 states:

> This Agreement represents the entire and integrated agreement between the Owner and the Architect and supersedes all prior negotiations, representations or agreements, either written or oral. This Agreement may be amended only by written instrument signed by both Owner and Architect.

This integration clause is designed to protect against assertions made by the owner that there had been an agreement for the creation of a fixed cost limitation and a fee contingency, as well as other oral conditions. Whether this clause will accomplish this purpose is questionable. Perhaps the oral condition "exception" will be used, though here performance has commenced. It may take some nimbleness, such as the use of mistake, reformation, fraud or sham to avoid the clause. But if it appears the oral agreement was made, many courts will find a way to consider the evidence of agreement.

The protective provisions apply if there is a fixed cost limitation. If there are cost budgets suggested by the owner, or there are statements of probable costs given by the architect during the course of his performance, these protective provisions will not be needed to give the architect his fee.

* * *

Some Suggestions to the Legal Profession

A. *Planning*

* * *

1. Bringing Cost Problems into the Open

The parties must confront the possibility of a substantial variation between anticipated costs and construction bids, with the hope that they can come to a mutually agreeable understanding on how such a problem should be handled. At the very least there should be agreement on the following issues: (1) Will the cost figure used be a cost budget or a fixed cost limitation? (2) If there is a fixed cost limitation, what kind of control will the architect have over quantity and quality and what must the client do if bids are too high? (3) Must the client permit the architect to redesign if there is a fixed cost limitation? (4) Is the architect to be paid for his work if the project is given up because the low bid exceeds a nonnegligent cost prediction?

If these basic questions can be answered to the mutual satisfaction of the parties, the common understanding should be clearly and completely expressed in a written contract. The written contract need not be a long and detailed form contract. It can be encompassed within the parameters of an informal letter agreement which covers the basic architectural services, extra services, client obligations, computations, payment of the basic fee, and what expenses are reimbursable.

* * * [C]ases which are relatively easy to resolve are those where the parties make a conscious risk allocation one way or the other. On the one hand, the architect will not be paid unless he is accurate, where he has expressly assumed this risk. On the other hand, if a cost budget has been agreed upon, the client must pay because he has assumed the risk by contract. However, the fact that the parties have assented to a form contract should not invariably mean that they have allocated the risk by contract. If the assent is to a standardized form contract and it is relatively clear that the client did not have crucial provisions pointed out to him and explained, the contract should not allocate the risk. Conversely, the undisclosed intention or "understanding" of the client that he would not have to pay should not be determinative.

* * *

NOTE

1. Can a developer wait until after bids are in to finalize the subject to financing clauses in the agreement providing for the acquisition of the land, the subordination agreements, the construction lender's commitment and the permanent take-out?

2. Among the consequences of a failure to have a bid come in at the architect's estimate are the following: (a) The architect may lose his fee—the accuracy of the estimate is a condition precedent to the architect receiving his fee; (b) The architect may be liable for damages—the accuracy of the estimate is a promise by the architect. Both or neither of these results may be present in the agreement between the architect and the owner.

    a. Which of these consequences provides the greatest protection for the developer?

    b. What are the foreseeable damages resulting from an architect's breach of a promise that the estimate is accurate?

    c. A condition or a promise may require only that the architect use due care in the preparation of the estimate.

        1. Does it make sense to condition the architect's fee on due care in the preparation of the estimate and have the architect promise that the estimate is accurate?

3. The above excerpt indicates that a cost condition might be read into a contract by a court. Should a court as freely read in a cost promise?

    a. Is the effect of the trade custom of architects not to assume the risk of the accuracy of an estimate equally applicable to both a condition and a promise?

    b. What factors should a court consider in determining whether a cost condition or promise exists? Are the factors different, or given different weight depending on whether a condition or promise is at issue?

        1. Should the fact that interim payments were made to the architect have any bearing on whether a promise exists?

    c. While redesign may be employed to avoid forfeiture of the architect's fee, should an architect be able to use this technique to avoid liability for damages for breach of a promise?

        1. For example, should the architect, by redesigning, be able to avoid liability for damages resulting from the delay caused by the redesign?

    d. If a developer accepts a high bid because of a belief that redesign will not bring the costs within the estimate, has the developer, by this action, waived both a cost condition and promise, or is the developer estopped from asserting them?

        1. If a developer accepts a high bid for other reasons, for example the option on the real estate is about to expire, the time for take-down of the construction loan is close at hand, the date of the closing of the contract of purchase of the real estate is imminent, has the developer waived or is the developer estopped from asserting a cost condition and a promise?

        2. If the developer has not waived and is not estopped, does the architect receive nothing for the work? If the architect might still receive something for the work, to what is the architect entitled?

        3. Are the same tests used by courts to determine the existence of waiver and estoppel, regardless whether a condition or promise is at issue?

4. If neither a condition nor a promise is contained in the developer-architect agreement and the bids come in over estimate so that financing is not

available and the project is dropped, what is the measure of the architect's recovery if the developer refuses to pay the architect? Should the architect receive the entire fee? See *Vrla v. Western Mortgage Co.,* 263 Or. 421, 502 P.2d 593 (1972), in which the architect was awarded the reasonable value of his services despite the fact that a construction loan could not be obtained.

a. If an architect is negligent in estimating the costs, should he still receive his fee or reliance damages if the developer-architect agreement contains neither a cost condition or promise? Does the developer, possibly, have a cause of action against the architect?

1. Should an architect be able to disclaim his own negligence?

b. A developer, however, can condition the payment of the architect's fee on the obtaining of necessary financing. See *Parsons v. Bristol Development Co.,* 62 Cal.2d 861, 44 Cal.Rptr. 767, 402 P.2d 839 (1965).

5. Many of the above questions and problems can be avoided by careful drafting of the agreement between the architect and the developer.

a. Section 3.4 of the A.I.A. form contract discussed in the above excerpt, which is similar to the 1987 Edition of the forms contract, imposes a general due care standard with regard to cost estimates, and Section 3.5, when the accuracy of the estimate is guaranteed, gives a great deal of control to the architect.

1. Which provision would a developer prefer? Are there situations in which a developer might be willing to agree to the due care standard?

a. If a developer opts for the "fixed cost" provision, will the developer be willing to give the architect the degree of control it calls for? Will the architect agree to less?

b. If the architect redesigns, under Section 3.5.1, and the redesign does not bring the project within the cost limitation, can the developer sue the architect for breach of the guarantee of the accuracy of the cost estimate?

b. Cost conditions and promises are not the only matters which are of concern to the developer in the agreement with the architect. For example, the agreement should describe the services which the architect will perform, the manner of payment for the services, if and when the agreement terminates, the ownership of the plans and the responsibilities of the architect and the developer. See Fisher, *Agreements With Architects and Contractors: The Developer's View,* 2 # 4 Real Est.Rev. 54 (1973); McCormick, *Representing the Owner in Contracting With the Architect and Contractor,* 8 Forum 434 (1973); Aubrecht, *The Owner–Architect Agreement: A Mutual Understanding,* 5 # 3 Real Est.Rev. 105 (1975); Kaskell, *How Architects and Engineers, in Their Contractual Arrangements, Can Anticipate and Avoid Exposure to Liability,* 48 Ins.Couns.J. 650 (1981); Halper, *Negotiating Architectural Contracts—Part I,* 17 # 2 Real Est.Rev. 65 (1987), *Part II,* 17 # 3 Real Est.Rev. 50 (1987), Ellis, *The Agreement Between Owner and Architect: The Perspective of an Owner's Lawyer,* 15 Real Est.L.J. 99 (1986); Sherman, *Owner Design of Owner/Architect Agreements,* 3 # 6 Prac.Real Est.Law. 43 (1987).

c. The A.I.A. form contract has been revised since the form described in the above excerpt. The revised contract contains a rather elaborate group of provisions dealing with cost estimates which are similar to the provisions discussed in the above excerpt. Not surprisingly, the provisions are quite protective of the architect.

6. The cost of construction may also exceed the cost estimate as a result of "extras" ordered during construction. Might the construction cost exceeding the cost estimate as a result of extras be considered a breach by the architect in some circumstances?

7. If a project is bid at a cost equal to, or reasonably close to, the architect's estimate, construction, in all likelihood, will begin. The architect serves in this phase of development in the capacity of a construction supervisor on behalf of the developer. Not only are the developer, architect and contractor involved at this stage, but the construction lender will have entered the picture and the enforceability of a subordination agreement and take-out commitment can be affected by the actions of the parties.

OWNER–ARCHITECT–CONTRACTOR: ANOTHER ETERNAL TRIANGLE

Justin Sweet
47 California Law Review 645 (1959).
[footnotes omitted]

*   *   *

I

Power of Architect to Bind Owner Contractually

A. *Source of Architect's Authority*

The owner, architect, and contractor typically set forth their rights and duties with respect to each other in two separate agreements. Owner and architect have a contract, often oral, which generally provides that the architect will furnish plans and specifications and will exercise general supervision over the work to insure that the contractor performs in accordance with the contract. The contract between owner and contractor is more detailed and specifically limits the authority of the architect. This second contract, in the absence of other acts by the owner creating apparent authority beyond the terms of the agreement, is usually the source of the architect's authority. However, this instrument may not always control.

*   *   *

B. *Scope of Architect's Authority*

Authority to Enter Into or Modify Existing Contracts

Unless he has specific authority to do so, the architect, by reason of his position, has no authority to enter into a contract on behalf of the owner. This result conforms to custom and usage of the industry. A more difficult problem arises when the issue is the architect's authority to modify an existing contract.

The statement is often made that in the absence of specific authority to do so, the architect, as agent or judge of performance, has no authority to modify a contract. While this general rule is unquestioned, contract modification problems may arise in analytically distinct situations.

* * *

A modification situation may * * * arise when the owner refuses to pay the balance due under the contract, claiming the building does not conform to the plans and specifications. The contractor may assert that the architect either ordered or accepted the variation. If the architect has authority to make such changes, the owner must pay. If no such authority exists, the contractor's right to compensation for the work depends upon whether he has substantially performed under the original contract. Cases involving this issue have reached different results. Some courts have held the architect did have authority to modify while other decisions faced with the same issue have held no such authority existed. The apparently contradictory holdings can be resolved by a consideration of the nature of the variance accepted or ordered by the architect. The greater the variance, the less likely the court will find authority in the architect. A more orderly analysis would be effected if the courts considered the ordering or accepting of the work by the architect as evidence tending to prove substantial performance, rather than regarding his act as the operative fact upon which liability turned. * * *

* * * [T]he contractor should not suffer because the owner had hired an incompetent architect. Certainly if the contractor can sue the owner for damages caused by the errors of the architect, a point which will be developed in detail later, he ought to be able to use these errors as an excuse for his non-performance. Authority to modify should not be considered as the issue in this situation.

Authority to modify, usually called waiver by the courts, may arise in another context. As a rule, construction contracts require that certain notices be given in writing by the contractor and that certain orders by the architect be in writing. Also, the contract may require the contractor to furnish proof that he has paid his subcontractors and materialmen. These provisions are inserted to protect the owner [and the construction lender]. With the exception of an occasional dictum, the courts have held firmly that the architect cannot eliminate these requirements.

* * *

The preceding discussion has assumed that the sole source of the architect's power to affect the owner has stemmed from the owner-contractor contract. The result may be different when subsequent acts of the owner are relied on. In such a case, the contractor may claim the owner is estopped from denying the architect's authority, that the owner has ratified the architect's unauthorized act, or that apparent authority in the architect has been created by the owner. * * *

Authority to Receive Mechanics' Lien Notices and Notices of Assignments

Mechanics' Lien laws often require that a notice of lien be served upon the owner or his agent by the lien claimant. The contractor may serve the architect and the question is whether such service complies with the statute. In deciding this, the courts must face the question of scope of authority. The cases have held that the architect, unless his authority extends to paying out money, has no authority to receive lien notices even if he makes out estimates and certificates upon which payments are made. A few States have modified this rule by statute. Also, if an assignee gives notice of his assignment to the architect, this notice does not protect the assignee if the owner, without knowledge of the assignment, pays the assignor.

*   *   *

Authority to Order Extra Work and to Excuse the Condition Precedent of a Written Order for the Extra Work

*   *   *

Building contracts customarily contain a clause which provides that no claim will be allowed for extra work unless it is ordered in writing by the owner, the architect, or both. [In addition, building contracts usually] provide that if the contractor receives an instruction, by drawing or otherwise, which he believes will be extra work, he must give the architect written notice within a reasonable time after receipt of the instruction or before the work is done if he is to collect for it. There is an exception for work which is necessary in emergency situations endangering life or property.

*   *   * The writing requirement has four purposes:

(1) To keep the owner informed as to his costs.

(2) To protect the owner from having to pay for work he does not want.

(3) To insure that the work has been ordered.

(4) To constitute evidence that the work is, in fact, extra.

*   *   * [W]ork which is ordered may fall into three categories: (1) It may be required under the contract and not be an extra; (2) it may not be required under the contract, but be sufficiently related to the subject matter of the basic contract to be governed by the extras provision; (3) it may be so unrelated in subject matter to the basic contract or be so extensive in scope that it is not controlled by the extras provision. *   *   *

Prior to analyzing the writing requirement, there must be an order for the extras by the owner or someone who has authority to order extras, whether orally or in writing. As pointed out earlier, the architect has no inherent authority to contract on behalf of the owner or to modify an existing contract. Therefore, where he has no specific authority, or where the contract requires the authorization of the architect *and* someone else, the courts have not held the owner [liable], in the absence of conduct of the owner which would create apparent authority, constitute a waiver or estop the owner from raising the writing requirement as a defense.

Where the owner-contractor agreement authorizes the architect to order extras but limits this authority by requiring that the order be in writing, an oral order by the architect or comparable official will not bind the owner. The courts have so held in cases where the contractor has been able to make out a persuasive case on the equities. It has even been held that performance without a written order is a waiver of a claim for payment. Also, the owner will not be bound if the architect fails to demand written estimates relating to the extra work if such estimates are required by the contract. Even establishing custom and usage of the industry will not cure a failure to comply with the express terms of the contract.

Despite the formidable barrier imposed by the writing requirement, there have been a number of cases where the contractor has recovered for oral orders of the architect. Since the oral order itself is not enough, these cases have involved additional facts which gave the court a peg upon which to hang its holding for the contractor.

* * *

(1) Order given by someone with more authority than that usually possessed by an architect.

(a) Corporate officers, manager, or other employee of owner or

(b) Relative of owner.

(2) Owner present when work ordered orally.

(3) Owner's course of conduct in

(a) Disregarding contract requirements for writing, or being aware that the architect was doing so or

(b) Paying for previous extra work ordered orally.

(4) Owner having paid for part of the work ordered orally.

(5) Owner accepting and retaining benefits of extra work.

(6) Situations requiring speedy action consisting of

(a) An emergency, or

(b) Objections to work made by building inspector.

(7) Impracticality of giving written order.

(8) Extra work caused by error of the architect.

(9) Architect's refusal to issue written order based upon belief that the work is not extra.

(10) Written order not executed until work was completed with the delay due to architect.

* * *

The majority of the issues in these "extras" cases will be submitted to the jury unless there is a written integrated contract clearly setting forth the architect's authority, or the waiver is predicated entirely upon the acts of the architect without any conduct of the owner which would (1) enlarge the architect's authority, (2) create apparent authority, (3) ratify the unauthorized acts of the architect, or (4) estop the owner from setting up the clause as a defense. Unless the contractor can tie in the owner somehow, he runs the risk of a directed verdict for the owner and may never get a chance at a usually sympathetic jury.

* * *

II

Liability of Owner for Conduct of Architect which Results in Added Expense to the Contractor

A. Owner–Contractor Agreement as Basis for Recovery

* * *

If the architect fails to exercise due care in the performance of [his] duties, the contractor may incur added expense. In many such cases, the contractor will seek to reimburse himself from the owner. * * *

In cases involving both public (which often have a private architect) and private contracts, the courts have held the owner liable where the errors of the architect have caused the contractor additional expense in doing the job. Some cases look at the contract between the owner and the contractor. Where that contract imposes certain duties on the architect, his failure to perform them properly is charged to the owner. Even where the contract between the owner and the contractor has not placed expressly certain duties upon the architect, the courts have filled in the gaps by implying promises by the owner not to hinder, interfere or delay, to keep the work in such a state of forwardness that the contractor may do the work in the most economical manner, and to coordinate the work with the other contractors. Using these techniques, the courts have held the owner impliedly promises that the contractor shall have access to the work and that the work will be laid out in an orderly fashion. When the owner is found to have this duty, the courts usually call the architect the agent of the owner and decide that the failure of the architect to perform the act with due care places liability upon the owner. Another approach found in some of the cases is to hold without a discussion of the status of the architect that nonperformance is simply a breach by the owner. The owner's procurement of a promise by the architect to perform does not enable the owner to shed ultimate responsibility for the failure of the *promised* performance to occur. In effect, the owner promises expressly or impliedly that the architect will perform.

* * * In private contracts, the court struggled indecisively for a time with the question of whether a provision for an extension of time impliedly denied the contractor a right to sue for damages. The * * * majority of the cases permit the contractor to sue for damages despite the presence of the extension clause.

Some mention should be made of the independent contractor rule. That venerable rule, or what is left of it, absolves the employer from liability for torts committed by the independent contractor unless one of the many exceptions to the rule is available. For many purposes the architect is considered an independent contractor. The owner, indeed, may feel that he should not have to pay for the errors of a licensed, professional person whom he selected with care and with whom he did not interfere. But these actions by the contractor against the owner are in contract. Even though the breach may have been caused by the negligence of the architect, the rights and duties were established expressly or impliedly by the owner-contractor agreement. Without it there could be no action.

B. Courses Open to the Owner if Sued

* * * [T]he owner has a cause of action against the architect only if the latter has breached his contract with the owner. The owner must not lose sight of the fact that the duty which the contractor claims was owed him was created by the contract between owner and contractor. The claim against the architect must be based upon the contract between owner and architect. Unless the owner can find that the architect undertook to perform these duties under the owner-architect contract, the owner may find himself in the unhappy position of losing both ways.

* * *

If the architect is financially responsible and the statutes permit the assertion of the claim in the same action, the owner should do so. All the issues will be decided in one lawsuit. If the owner loses to the contractor, he will also take a collectible judgment against the architect, provided only the owner can show the architect has breached the owner-architect contract.

It is possible that the owner's action against the architect will be brought separately. The owner must be aware of certain dangers and take steps to avoid them in the event of a separate action.

These cases are often very close on the issues of negligence and the extent of damages. It is not inconceivable that a jury in the first case might find the architect negligent while a second jury might come to a contrary result. Also, the second jury might find lower damages even if they found the architect negligent. Juries often favor contractors in these actions, especially if the contractor is local. Also, the second suit may very well be in the architect's home area and the plaintiff owner may be an outsider.

* * * There is one step the owner may take to attempt to avoid this dilemma. The principal, if sued as a result of the acts of his agent, can notify the agent to defend the action. If the agent does defend, the issues decided in the first action will be res judicata in the action by the principal against the agent. If the agent does not defend after notice, and the principal loses after a good faith defense, the principal can sue

for legal expenses and the issues decided in the first action are res judicata between principal and agent. The only questions to be decided in the second action will be whether the legal expenses in the first case were reasonable and who was responsible as between owner and architect. This would mean a determination of whether the architect has breached his contract with the owner.

C. Methods by Which the Owner Can Minimize His Risk

* * *

First, the owner must not engage his architect by a casual oral arrangement. The supervisory duties of the architect as set forth in the owner-contractor agreement should be compared with the promises made by the architect in his contract with the owner. There should be no areas where the owner-contractor agreement requires acts of the architect which are not clearly covered in the owner-architect agreement. The duties of the architect are very vague in the latter type contract. If it is desired to keep the agreement short, incorporation by reference may be used.

Second, the owner should be certain that the claim over will be collectible. He should require the architect to carry and maintain insurance for the duration of the job and a reasonable time thereafter. The insurance should be paid for in advance for this period in order to avoid any possibility that the policy will not be in force for failure to pay premiums. Since these policies usually can be cancelled for a failure to give notice, the owner should make certain that notice is given if a claim is made. If the architect has the duty of coordinating separate contractors, the owner should consider retaining until completion of the building a [substantial] percentage of the architect's fee * * *, especially if the architect is a nonresident. If a claim is made against the owner based upon acts of the architect, the owner should not release any fee due the architect, especially if the owner is going to assert a claim over. However, he should not retain an unreasonable amount in light of the amount of the claim.

Third, the owner must be certain he will be able to obtain personal service on the architect if he uses a nonresident architect. The statutes on constructive service should be checked to see if they are broad enough and the "doing-business" cases must be analyzed. If there is any doubt, the owner should require the architect to appoint an agent for service of process.

Fourth, the owner should extract an express promise on the part of the architect to appear and defend any action upon notification by the owner that the contractor is suing the owner based upon the acts of the architect. While this is restating the common law, an express provision would refute any argument by the architect that the common law does not apply.

* * *

NOTE

1.   A modification of or change in the construction plans and specifications can have an effect on parties other than the developer and the contractor. Consider the effect on: (1) A party subordinating its interest to the development financing, see pages 637 to 649 supra; 2) The amount available for construction financing, see pages 652 to 672 supra; and (3) The enforceability of the permanent take-out, see pages 682 to 689 supra.   See generally McNamara, *Subordination Agreements as Viewed by Sellers, Purchasers, Construction Lenders, and Title Companies,* 12 Real Est.L.J. 347 (1984).

   a.   If an architect authorized a modification which increased costs and the architect did not have the authority to do so, is the architect liable to the developer?   If so, what is the developer's measure of damages?

   1.   Is the architect liable to the construction lender?

   2.   If the architect had actual, apparent or implied authority to order a modification, the contractor can recover from the developer.   If the change was not approved by a subordinating party, the construction lender or the permanent lender, does a developer have concerns beyond its liability to the contractor?

   a.   If a modification is necessary because of the architect's defective design, is the architect liable to the developer, if the developer had initially approved the plans and specifications?

2.   The above excerpt lists four reasons for the strict writing requirement in the case of extras.   In view of the financing considerations discussed in Division III can a few more reasons be added to the list?   A contractor, however, can, in certain circumstances, recover for an extra without a writing. What financing concerns does this present to the developer?

3.   What are the rights of all parties involved in the construction and financing of a development if work ordered by the architect is: (a) Required under the contract; (b) Not required but so related to the subject matter of the contract to be considered subject to the extra provisions of the contract; or (c) Unrelated to the subject matter or so extensive that the work is not subject to the extra provisions?

4.   If a developer is sued by a contractor for damages caused the contractor by the failure of the architect to do his job properly and the contractor recovers, does the developer have a cause of action against the architect?

   a.   Does the answer to the above question depend on the contract between the owner and the architect?

   1.   Can two juries differ as to whether the same acts constitute negligence?

   2.   Can these problems be avoided?   How?

5.   See generally Note, *Supervisory Duties of An Architect,* 3 Mem.St.U.L. Rev. 139 (1972); Comment, *The Roles of Architect and Contractor In Construction Management,* 6 U.Mich.J.L.Ref. 447 (1973); Hoeveler, *Building Failure and the Respective Liabilities of The Architect and The Engineer,* 8 Forum 480 (1973); Note, *Liability of Design Professionals—The Necessity of Fault,* 58 Iowa L.Rev. 1221 (1973); Sweet, *Your First Construction Contract,* 21 # 2 Prac.Law. 27 (1975); Comment, *Architectural Malpractice: A Contract–Based Approach,* 92 Harv.L.Rev. 1075 (1979); Ricchini, *The Authority and Responsibility of the*

Architect as Administrator of the Contract, 23 St. Louis U.L.J. 370 (1979); Sweet, *Site Architects and Construction Workers: Brothers and Keepers or Strangers?,* 28 Emory L.J. 291 (1979); Espel, *Liability and Loss Allocation for Economic Losses in Construction Litigation Involving Design Professionals,* 13 Wm. Mitchell L.Rev. 81 (1987); Hever, *Dealing with Change Orders During Construction: The AIA System,* 2 # 3 Prob. & Prop. 41 (1988).

b. THE CONTRACTOR

(i) CONTRACTOR'S REMEDIES AS A RESULT OF ARCHITECT'S ERRORS, ORDERS, CHANGES AND MODIFICATIONS

The duties of the architect as supervisor of construction were considered above. The following materials examine the problems which may arise during construction, the contractor's remedies and the steps that must be taken in the event that the architect, as supervisor of construction, makes an error, orders an extra or makes a change in the plans and specifications.

POWERS OF DIRECTION AND DETERMINATION UNDER CONSTRUCTION CONTRACTS

Edgar A.B. Spencer
41 Virginia Law Review 343 (1955).
[footnotes omitted]

*   *   *

I

Basic Principles

*   *   *

Misconstruction of Contract

Many construction contracts contain a provision to the effect that the architect shall determine the true construction and meaning of the drawings and specifications. It has been held that such a clause is not applicable to the construction of the contract itself, and that the decision of the architect relative thereto is not controlling if it misconstrues the contract. *   *   *

Refusal to Issue Certificate

It is generally true that:

Where a certificate of an architect, surveyor or engineer is a condition precedent to a duty of immediate payment for work, the condition is excused if the architect, surveyor or engineer

(a) dies or becomes incapacitated, or

(b) refuses to give a certificate because of collusion with the promisor, or

(c) refuses to give a certificate after making examination of the work and finding it adequate, or

(d) fails to make proper examination of the work, or

(e) fails to exercise an honest judgment, or

(f) makes a gross mistake with reference to facts on which a refusal to give a certificate is based.

* * *

Undercertification of Amounts Earned by the Contractor

An architect's refusal to issue a certificate to a contractor in the correct amount is, for all practical purposes, equivalent to an unreasonable refusal to issue any certificate at all for the items omitted.

* * *

Orders of the Architect, Engineer, or Department Head Making the Contractor's Performance More Expensive Than It Would Have Been Under the Terms and Conditions of the Contract

While contract work is proceeding, the contractor frequently receives revised plans, specifications, or orders which make the performance of the contract more onerous and expensive to him than it would have been under the terms of the original contract, plans, and specifications. Architects are interested in having the work completed as they want it, and they frequently give little or no thought to the effect that the issuance of revised plans, specifications, or orders may have upon the contractor's cost of performance; they may not even realize that extra costs to the contractor may result therefrom. Though such revisions do not necessarily constitute final orders or determinations by the architect, this situation can create many difficulties for the contractor.

It is imperative under these circumstances for the contractor carefully to review the revised plan, specification, or order. If extra costs of contract performance are entailed, that fact should be called to the attention of the architect. If the revision or order is insisted upon, then, and probably not before, there exists a final order or determination and an exercise of the powers delegated to the architect.

When the revision or order is [outside of] the general scope of the contract and causes the contractor extra and additional losses, costs, damages, and expenses, its issuance is considered a breach of the contract. The contractor then has the following alternatives: he may elect to refuse to obey the order, stop work under the contract, and recover on a *quantum meruit* for the work already done; or he may elect to continue work under protest and recover the value of the extra cost imposed upon him.[2]

To refuse to obey the order would have some very practical disadvantages. The courts might hold that the architect was correct and the contractor incorrect. Therefore, in refusing to proceed with the contract, the contractor may himself breach the contract and be held liable for damages. * * *

1. The protest. Upon receiving an order or determination by the architect which involves extra and additional costs of completion, the contractor must, unless he intends to stop work, protest the order and proceed thereafter to carry on the work under protest. If he does not do so and complies with the order, he acquiesces therein and cannot recover his extra expenses.

The form of the protest does not appear to be important, so long as it is in fact a protest and contains a statement that a claim will be made for the extra cost involved. * * *

To whom the protest is made could be an important question. As a matter of precaution, * * * always protest to both the owner and the architect. * * * [W]here a breach of contract is to be claimed, the owner is entitled to knowledge thereof so that he can examine his own position and avoid the breach if one would result from the action of his architect. * * *

2. Damages recoverable. The recovery by the contractor is on the theory of breach of contract. * * *

While the principle that the contractor may recover damages in cases like these has been well established, the measure of his damages has not. * * *

By way of example, the following items have been specifically allowed as damages:

(1) All *Quantum meruit* items;

(2) All out-of-pocket expenses;

(3) Extra insurance;

(4) Increased wages;

(5) Extra labor;

(6) Extra material;

(7) Extra overhead expenses;

(8) Profit on extra costs;

2. [If the order is within the general scope of the contract and constitutes an extra under the provisions of the contract dealing with extras, the issuance of the order will, in general, not constitute a breach of the contract. If, however, the architect refuses to authorize payment to the contractor for the necessary additional costs, damages and expenses entailed in complying with the order and the owner refuses to pay, the refusal is considered a breach of the contract. Upon this occurrence, the contractor has the various alternatives described in the text.]

(9) Extra cost of excavating, pipe-laying, pumping, machinery-moving, etc.

Before taking any action, however, the contractor should remember that, under some circumstances, the issuance of revised plans and specifications may constitute orders for extra work, even if the contract provides that such orders must be in writing. This is important, since under some circumstances it is simpler and easier to prove a claim for extra work than to prove a claim for damages for breach of contract. If the additional work specified by the architect is clearly outside the terms of the contract, and the contractor nevertheless performs it, even a timely protest will not enable him subsequently to recover damages.

* * *

II

Enforcement of the Contractor's Rights

What steps the contractor should take to enforce his rights will, of course, depend upon the provisions of the particular contract. * * *

Contracts Containing Compulsory Arbitration Clauses

A commonly used contract form of this type is the form issued by the American Institute of Architects. This form provides as follows with respect to engineers' powers:

Art. 39. Architect's Decisions.—The Architect shall, within a reasonable time, make decisions on all claims of the Owner or Contractor and on all other matters relating to the execution and progress of the work or the interpretation of the Contract Documents.

The Architect's decisions, in matters relating to artistic effect, shall be final, if within the terms of the Contract Documents.

Except as above or as otherwise expressly provided in the Contract Documents, all the Architect's decisions are subject to arbitration.

If, however, the Architect fails to render a decision within ten days after the parties have presented their evidence, either party may then demand arbitration. If the Architect renders a decision after arbitration proceedings have been initiated, such decision may be entered as evidence but shall not disturb or interrupt such proceedings except where such decision is acceptable to the parties concerned.

Arbitration clauses vary widely. In the event of a disagreement, it is important that the arbitration clause be carefully examined to see whether the dispute in question must be arbitrated. If arbitration is required, the contractor should give all notices and do all those things which he would do were he planning to bring suit, but the decision will be made by the arbitrator.

* * *

Contracts Which Appear To Give the Architect Final and Complete Power of Disposition

The following clause taken from a * * * New York City subway contract is a good example of this type of contract provision:

ARTICLE XXIV. *Engineer's Determination Final.* To prevent disputes and litigations, the Engineer shall in all cases determine the classification, amount, quality, acceptability and fitness of the several kinds of work and materials which are to be paid for under this contract, shall determine every question in relation to the Works and the construction thereof and shall determine every question which may arise relative to the fulfillment of this contract on the part of the Contractor. His determination and estimate shall be final and conclusive upon the Contractor, and in case any question touching this contract shall arise between the parties hereto, such determination and estimate shall be a condition precedent to the right of the Contractor to receive any money under this contract.

It is this type of provision which leads to most of the litigation concerning claimed abuses of authority by an architect. * * *

NOTES

1. An architect may refuse to certify payment for part of the work done on a phase of a project, because the architect is not satisfied with the quality of the work.

   a. What steps should the contractor take if the contractor disagrees with the architect and claims that the work has been substantially performed?

   1. Should the contractor accept payment for the work completed to the architect's satisfaction? If the contractor, like so many, is using the money from this project to cover operating costs on another project, the contractor may not have a choice.

   a. If the contractor accepts the part payment, what steps can be taken in order to preserve a claim for the rest? Can the contractor file a lien against the development?

2. The standard A.I.A. construction contract provides that the architect makes the initial decisions on all claims of the owner and contractor. His decisions in matters relating to artistic effect are final, all others are subject to arbitration.

   a. A construction contract provides for a certain type of facing for an office building. The contractor obtains, from a nearby supplier, facing which has the required composition. The architect, however, does not like the grain of the facing obtained by the contractor and orders the contractor to put on facing which can be obtained only from a supplier 300 miles away. The price of the facing which the architect wants put on the building is the same as the facing obtained by the contractor, but the transportation costs are doubled for the architect's facing. The architect determines, when the contractor asks for an extra for the increased transportation costs, that the facing which the architect ordered the contractor to obtain was required under the contract. Is the architect's decision subject to arbitration?

b. If a construction contract provides that all decisions of the architect are final, does the contractor have any recourse from an adverse decision by the architect?

c. A contractor's claim against an owner may result from an error or omission on the part of the architect. In this instance is the contractor required initially to obtain the architect's decision?

1. "For example, a contractor's claim may be based on allegations of defective plans and specifications prepared by the architect or the delay or failure of the architect to issue certain necessary directives or drawings. * * *

"It is true that even if the architect renders a decision on a matter involving allegations of his own fault, [generally] the decision may nevertheless be appealed to an arbitrator for a de novo evaluation of the claim or dispute. It is also true that the architect's decision in such instance is impeachable on the grounds that it has the obvious appearance of bias. However, there lurks the possibility that an arbitrator, consciously or subconsciously, may still give some weight to such a decision. For this reason, sound professional judgment may well dictate that an architect faced with this type of claim or dispute should refrain from rendering any decision thereon. In that event, the AIA General Conditions would permit the parties to bring the matter directly before an arbitrator. This would avoid the possibility of a costly and time-consuming initial presentation of the dispute to an architect whose ultimate decision would be immediately challengeable as biased.

"The thesis that an architect should not render a decision on matters involving allegations of his own fault or negligence in the performance of his duties is based on elementary concepts of fairness as well as prevailing law. * * *

"The architect may be faced with a further dilemma in view of a provision in his contract with the owner which requires the architect to make decisions on all claims of the owner or contractor. * * * However, where there are allegations of architect fault, the principles discussed above clearly would apply with equal force to such provision.

"In view of the foregoing, it is plain that, in all propriety, and under the clear mandate of judicial decisions, an architect should not render a decision on any claims or disputes which are premised, in whole or in part, upon allegations of the architect's errors, omissions, acts or failure to act in regard to the performance of his duties." Kent, *The Architect's Duty: Owner–Contractor Disputes Involving Allegations of Architect's Fault,* 46 Ins.Couns.J. 31, 32, 33 (1979).

d. See generally Kaskell, *Possible Avenues of Liability of the Architect and Engineer to Contractors and Subcontractors. Or How Claimants Will Try to Anticipate and Overcome the A/E's Favorite Defenses,* 47 Ins.Couns.J. 353 (1980); Note, *Architects' Liability to Third Party Contractors for Economic Loss Resulting from Faulty Plans and Specifications,* 27 Ariz.L. Rev. 139 (1985).

3.   An architect may revise the plans or order new work to be done during the course of construction. The revision or new work may result in increased costs to the contractor. The revision or new work might be construed to be part of the original contract, an extra, or outside of the scope of the original contract, see pages 962 to 969 supra.

a.   If the contractor refuses to go ahead and the revision or the new work ordered is considered part of the original contract or an extra, the contractor will have breached the contract. What steps should the contractor take to preserve his rights and, yet, not breach the contract?

CITIZENS NATIONAL BANK OF MERIDIAN v. L.L. GLASCOCK, INC.

Supreme Court of Mississippi, 1971.
243 So.2d 67.

PATTERSON, Justice. * * * In 1964 the appellant, hereinafter owner, and appellee, hereinafter contractor, entered into a written contract for the demolition and removal of the owner's existing bank building in the city of Meridian and for the construction of a new bank building upon the same site. Subsequent to the removal of the old building the contractor, in testing the site for placing of concrete piling for the foundation of the new building, encountered the existing foundations of the old building. These foundations were about five feet below the surface of the basement level of the old building. Although the presence of these old foundations was anticipated, their precise location and size were unknown to the parties until disclosed by testing operations. Their location obstructed the placing of the new piling, necessitating that they either be bored through or removed.

Thereafter, the contractor contacted the structural engineer, an employee of the architect, and asked if some of the old foundations could be used as foundation for the new structure. Upon being advised that this was not feasible, the contractor removed the foundations which entailed much labor and expense, but which was nevertheless less expensive than boring through the existing foundations. A conflict of evidence arose between the engineer and the contractor as to whether the removal was directed by the engineer. The engineer testified that he advised the contractor that it would be necessary for him to remove only that portion of the existing foundation as would give room for the new piling. The testimony of the contractor's witnesses was that he directed that the old foundations be completely removed.

During the time the removal of the foundations was under way the contractor advised the owner's architect that he considered this labor to be supplementary to the contract for which payment in excess of the contract price would be expected. Accordingly when the work was completed in May 1965, the architect was presented a bill for this work.

The architect testified that he never directed the removal of the old foundations and that he was unaware the contractor expected additional pay for the labor performed until shortly before the bill was presented. Subsequently, they discussed the matter on several occasions. It is apparent that the architect initially thought the contractor was entitled to be paid over the contract price for the work performed. He informed the contractor that he would aid him in obtaining this payment. However, upon reexamining the contract, he concluded that the work was not extra and was within the contract price. He, therefore, declined to certify to the owner that the contractor was due reimbursement for extra work.

* * *

The relevant portions of the contract are:

2–F Concrete Piling

(a) Scope: *Furnish labor and materials to complete bored, cast in place concrete pilings* as indicated, specified herein or both.

* * *

(4) Equipment: Use drilling equipment generally used in standard pile boring practice, as approved.

(5) If obstructions such as maconry (sic) *old foundations,* etc., are encountered, bore thru as directed.

(6) Payment:

a. Except as herein provided, *no separate payment will be made for specified work; include all costs in connection therewith in Stipulated Sum for entire work under contract.* (Emphasis added.)

* * *

Attached to the contract and made a part thereof is a pamphlet prepared by the American Institute of Architects entitled "General Conditions." Article 15 thereof is as follows:

CHANGES IN THE WORK

The Owner, without invalidating the Contract, may order extra work or make changes by altering, adding to or deducting from the work, the Contract Sum being adjusted accordingly. All such work shall be executed under the conditions of the original Contract except that any claim for extension of time caused thereby shall be adjusted at the time of ordering such change.

In giving instructions, *the Architect shall have authority to make minor changes in the work, not involving extra cost,* and not inconsistent with the purposes of the building, *but otherwise,* except in an emergency endangering life or property, *no extra work or change shall be made unless in pursuance of a written order from the Owner,* signed or countersigned by the Architect, or a written order from the Architect stating that the Owner has authorized the extra work or charge, *and no claim for an addition to the Contract Sum shall be valid unless so ordered.*

* * *

Should conditions encountered below the surface of the ground be at variance with the conditions indicated by the Drawings and Specifications the Contract Sum shall be equitably adjusted upon claim by either party made within a reasonable time after the first observance of the conditions. (Emphasis added.)

Article 16 of the bulletin relating to claims for extra cost states:

If the Contractor claims that any instructions by drawings or otherwise involve extra cost under the Contract, he shall give the Architect written notice thereof within a reasonable time after the receipt of such instructions, and in any event before proceeding to execute the work, except in emergency endangering life or property, and *the procedure shall then be as provided for changes in the work. No such claim shall be valid unless so made.* (Emphasis added.)

The architect's status and authority are related in Article 38 which is set forth in part below:

ARCHITECT'S STATUS; ARCHITECT'S SUPERVISION

The Architect shall be the Owner's representative during the construction period. * * * He *shall have authority to act on behalf of the Owner only to the extent expressly provided in the Contract Documents or otherwise in writing,* which shall be shown to the Contractor. * * * (Emphasis added.)

The contractor's primary contention is that he was entitled to additional pay for supplemental work not within the terms of the contract since it is customary within the trade for a contractor to comply with the request of the owner's representative, who in this instance was the structural engineer, an employee of the owner's architect. The owner maintains that the very purpose of the contract was to assure it the building desired at the contract price of $679,560. No argument is advanced by either of the parties that they were unfamiliar with the terms of the contract.

* * *

We are of the opinion that the written contract expresses the agreement of the parties and that it prevails over custom. Courts do not have the power to make contracts where none exist, nor to modify, add to, or subtract from the terms of one in existence. Kalavros v. Deposit Guaranty Bank & Trust Co., 248 Miss. 107, 158 So.2d 740 (1963), and Phenix Insurance Co. v. Dorsey, 102 Miss. 81, 58 So. 778 (1912).

With the above premise in mind and the contract before us, there remains the question of whether the terms of the contract between the parties permit an award on a quantum basis. We note initially that such an award, if proper, would require a finding by the court that the labor was not anticipated by the contract, and also that there were no provisions of the contract by which payment could be made for unanticipated labor. In the recent case of Delta Construction Company of Jackson v. City of Jackson, 198 So.2d 592, 600 (Miss.1967), though relating to a public contract, nevertheless, expresses a principle of law we think equally applicable to private contracts. We there stated:

> The contract in the instant case requiring a supplemental agreement for extra work over minor changes is essential, because municipalities and other governmental agencies obtain funds with which to build public improvements from bond issues based upon estimates furnished to them, and municipalities must reserve the right to stop a project if they determine the extra work will exceed the amount of money allocated to any given phase of a project. Mallett v. City of Brookhaven, 217 Miss. 491, 64 So.2d 641 (1953). Furthermore, it has been generally held that no recovery can be had on an implied contract, or quasi contract, or upon quantum meruit for extra work where the claim is based upon an expressed contract. * * *

The old foundations were anticipated since Section 2–F of the contract refers to them with provision for method of procedure upon their being encountered and with the further provision that no separate payment would be made for this labor. Article 15 sets forth the method of payment for extra work, notable of which is that, "no extra work or change shall be made unless in pursuance of a written order from the owner," and Article 16 provides that in any event no claim for extra work shall be valid unless the contractor gives the architect written notice of his claim "before proceeding to execute the work. * * *" Finally, Article 38 limits the architect's authority on behalf of the owner to the express terms of the contract, or otherwise in writing.

We can only conclude in comparing these plain terms to the vague assumption of the contractor that custom of the trade would implement the written document in his behalf, that the former prevails. The written contract anticipated every contingency upon which this suit was based. Its very purpose was to forestall imposition of vague claims derivative of custom within the trade with which laymen are often unfamiliar. The owner, being desirous of limiting its financial obligation, should not have its pocketbook exposed to the custom of architects and contractors unless it agrees thereto. In this instance the owner agreed to pay for extra work only if it was authorized in writing prior to its execution. Having contracted directly upon the point, there was no leeway for an award on a quantum meruit basis.

Reversed and rendered.

GILLESPIE, P.J., and INZER, SMITH, and ROBERTSON, JJ., concur.

NOTE

1. Could the contractor in the above case have taken any steps which would have improved its position in litigation?

a. If the contractor, in writing, requested an extra, the architect refused to certify the costs to the owner since in his opinion the work was required under the original contract and the contractor protested and then proceeded with the work, would the contractor have been in a better position in the above case?

b. See McCormick, *Contract Changes and the Extras Clauses, Their Validity and Binding Effect,* 10 Forum 5 (1974); Petro, *Contract Changes and Extras Clause Improperly Applied—Contractor's Refusal to Perform,* 10 Forum 29 (1974); Halper, *Avoiding Construction Extras,* 10 # 2 Real Est. Rev. 53 (1980); Heuer, *Dealing with Changes During Construction: The AIA System,* 2 # 3 Prob. & Prop. 45 (1988); Houghton and Heuer, *A Practical Introduction to Change Orders,* 3 # 4 Prac.Real Est.Law. 17 (1987).

2. If the developer breaches the construction contract, what is the contractor's measure of damages?

a. If the breach results from a failure to make all, or part, of a progress payment and the contractor continues on the job, the contractor should be able to recover the payment. If the contractor was depending on the receipt of the payment to pay certain costs it had incurred on another job and the failure to receive the payment caused it to default in its performance of the latter job, can this result of the developer's failure to make a progress payment be taken into account in computing the contractor's damages? The developer will claim that any damages resulting from the contractor's default on the latter job were not reasonably foreseeable and, therefore, should not be considered. See A. Corbin, 5 Corbin on Contracts, Sec. 1007–1011 (1964). Might a different result be reached if the developer knew that, as a general rule, during the construction season contractors stretch their working capital to the limit and frequently use progress payments from one job to finance their performance on others? If the developer knew this about the specific contractor in question, could the contractor recover the damages resulting from its default on other jobs from the defaulting developer? Cf. A. Corbin, 5 Corbin on Contracts, Sec. 1014 (1964); *Christensen v. Slawter,* 173 Cal.App.2d 325, 343 P.2d 341 (1959); *United States Fidelity & Guar. Co. v. Peterson,* 91 Nev. 617, 540 P.2d 1070 (1975). See generally Hart, *The Ripple Effect: Proving Contractors' Losses,* 3 Litigation 12 (1976).

b. If the developer's breach is substantial and the contractor refuses to continue, the usual measure of damages is the full amount of the contract price promised, diminished by the amount which is saved by the contractor since it does not have to complete the construction. A. Corbin, 5 Corbin on Contracts, Sec. 1094, p. 510 (1964).

3. See generally Goldberg, *The Owner's Duty to Coordinate Multi–Prime Construction Contractors, A Condition of Cooperation,* 28 Emory L.J. 377 (1979); Halper, *Controlling Construction Contractors,* 10 # 1 Real Est.Rev. 74 (1980); Goldenhersh, *Essentials of Building Construction Contracts,* 13 Colo.Law. 1 (1984); Halper, *Negotiating Construction Contracts, Part I,* 17 # 4 Real Est.Rev. 73 (1987); *Part II,* 18 # 1 Real Est.Rev. 28 (1988); *Part III,* 18 # 2 Real Est. Rev. 45 (1988).

(ii) FAILURE OF THE CONTRACTOR TO PERFORM

(a) MEASURE OF DAMAGES

A contractor may fail to complete a project or may complete the project but not in conformity with the plans and specifications. In either of these situations, the developer may sustain damages as a result of the contractor's failure to perform. What is the measure of the developer's damages?

NOTE: APPLICATION OF THE COST AND VALUE THEORIES IN MEASURING CONTRACTOR'S LIABILITY

48 Kentucky Law Journal 432 (1960).
[footnotes omitted]

* * *

The difficulties involved in deciding when to use the cost rule (cost of completing the contract) as opposed to the value rule (difference in the market value of the contractor's actual performance and the value of full performance) must be considered in order to realize the full scope of the problems. In the ordinary case, the cost rule is the generally accepted mode of determining the damages, but the value rule has proven useful in situations where economic waste is a potential threat if the cost rule is applied without sound discretion. * * *

There are several ways of stating when the value rule may be used instead of the cost rule. Basically, however, these statements may be placed in two broad categories, the distinguishing factor being the weight placed on good faith. * * *

Williston, after pointing out that where the contractor fails to keep his agreement the measure of the damages should be the sum which will put the employer in as good a position as if the contract had been performed, goes on to say:

> If the defect is remediable from a practical standpoint, recovery generally will be based on the market price of completing or correcting the performance, and this will generally be shown by the cost of getting work done or completed by another person. If the defect is not thus remediable, damages are based on the difference between the value of the defective structure and that of the structure if properly completed.

It is significant that in this statement of the rule for measuring damages no mention is made of good faith or lack of wilfulness.
* * *

The rule for measuring damages as formulated in the *Restatement of Contracts* emphasizes the need for avoiding economic waste whenever possible. Section 346 provides that the measure of damages for defective or unfinished construction work shall be either:

(i) the reasonable cost of construction and completion in accordance with the contract, if this is possible and does not involve unreasonable economic waste; or

(ii) the difference between the value that the product contracted for would have had and the value of the performance that has been received by the plaintiff, if construction and completion in accordance with the contract would involve unreasonable economic waste.[3]

The comments to this section point out that the purpose of allowing recovery is to put the injured party in a position comparable to that for which he bargained. But this does not mean that he is to be placed in the "same specific physical position." The injured party is allowed either a "sum of money sufficient to produce the physical product contracted for" or "the exchange value that that product would have had if it had been constructed." The two may at times be equal, but where they are not, consideration must be given to whether it would be "imprudent and unreasonable" to tear down and reconstruct the structure in question. If it is unreasonable, then "[t]he law does not require damages to be measured by a method requiring such economic waste."

* * *

A third formulation of the rule for measuring damages which also omits any reference to good faith is that provided by Corbin. The similarity between his formulation of the rule and that contained in the *Restatement* can be easily detected. He says:

For breach of defective construction, whether it is partial or total, and for a total breach by refusal and failure to complete the work, the injured party can get a judgment for damages measured by the reasonable cost of reconstruction and completion in accordance with the contract, if this is possible and does not involve unreasonable economic waste.

In the following section Corbin adds:

If it is made to appear that physical reconstruction and completion in accordance with the contract will involve unreasonable economic waste by destruction of usable property or otherwise, the damages awarded for the contractor's breach will be measured by the difference between the market value that the structure contracted for would have had and that of the imperfect structure received by the plaintiff.

3. [The Restatement (Second) of Contracts, Section 348 (1981), takes a similar position, while emphasizing recovery based on loss of value. Section 348(2) provides that "[i]f a breach results in defective or unfinished construction and the loss in value to the injured party is not proved with sufficient certainty, he may recover damages based on

(a) the diminution in the market price of the property caused by the breach, or

(b) the reasonable cost of completing performance or of remedying the defects if that cost is not clearly disproportionate to the probable loss in value to him."]

The application of this rule, just as with the rules set forth by Williston and the *Restatement,* will not guarantee that the injured party will obtain a completed structure meeting the exact specifications of the contract, but his pecuniary position will be as good.

The remaining authority, *American Jurisprudence,* is specific in requiring lack of wilfulness as a prerequisite to use of the value rule. First it states as a general rule one is entitled to have what he contracts for or its equivalent and that a majority of jurisdictions apply the cost rule where the defects are such as can be remedied without unreasonable reconstruction so as to make the work conform to the contract. This authority then goes on to say:

> But where, in order to conform the work to the contract requirements, a substantial part of what has been done must be undone, *and the contractor has acted in good faith,* or the owner has taken possession, the latter is not permitted to recover the cost of making the change, but may recover the difference in value. [Emphasis added.]

Such a rule as this can give rise to a rather harsh result. It can be interpreted so as to invoke the cost rule even though correction of defects would involve "unreasonable economic waste" and even though the result is to award damages which are greater than the difference in value between the work as done and as it ought to have been done. * * *

At first glance it may be thought that there is little practical difference among the aforementioned rules. No doubt this is true of the first three which omit any reference to good faith. Perhaps in the ordinary case they could be used interchangeably, and the results would be the same. But this would not hold true with reference to the fourth rule.

* * * [Under the fourth rule] [w]hen the [contractor is] found to have intentionally deviated from the contract, and * * * such deviation * * * constituted a wilful deviation, then [the contractor] * * * [can]not successfully invoke the value theory under a rule which requires as a prerequisite lack of wilfulness.

It is submitted the position * * * that "intentional" conduct constitutes "wilfulness" is questionable. At least one authority, Corbin, disagrees with the * * * conclusion that substantial performance cannot exist when any part of the variance from the contract specifications is "intentional." * * *

* * * Corbin submits that anything less than full performance is a breach, but he concedes that breaches are not all the same size or of the same degree of importance. He concludes that a "trivial" breach should not prevent substantial performance, thereby causing use of the [value] rule, even if the breach is "intentional," for too often actual completion would cause unreasonable economic waste. * * *

There is much to be said against placing too much significance on the terms "wilful" and "intentional." * * * Professor Corbin points out that such words are "epithets characterizing the quality of the conduct of one guilty of a breach of contract and expressing the mental attitude of the court." These words ought to be used with discretion, and it should always be kept in mind that the rules surrounding them are flexible. The operation of these terms should be such that "punishments are not 'cruel and unusual,' so that 'the penalty may fit the crime.' Not even a 'wilful' wrongdoer is an outlaw; and the enrichment of even an injured man may become unjust." Corbin takes a realistic view with regard to the interpretation of these terms, and consequently makes one realize that there is always room for leniency.

In support of this plea for leniency, it is interesting to note that there is an extremely liberal variant rule which provides that a defendant contractor is entitled to either the cost rule or the value rule, whichever proves to be the less costly of the two. This doctrine is admittedly a minority view, but the fact that it does exist lends support to the idea that courts do use discretion in determining what damages to apply. * * *

NOTE

1. Assume that a contractor places the footings for the foundation of a building two feet shallower than called for in the plans and specifications or digs the foundation four feet shallower. Neither of these errors affect the integrity or stability of the building, and by the time the architect discovers the error the contractor has the first three floors in place.

 a. Should the contractor have to tear down the building to correct the error?

2. Assume the architect refuses to certify part of the payment for the foundation phase of the development because of the deviation from the plans and specifications described above. Since the deviation does not affect the stability or integrity of the building, there may be no difference in value. If the construction contract is a cost plus contract, the contractor has not gained anything by the deviation and the developer has not been significantly damaged. If, however, it is a lump sum contract, the contractor may have increased profits by deviating from plans and specifications. In addition, the construction and permanent lender may have something to say about the deviation.

 a. If the contractor properly protests the architect's decision, completes the rest of the building and the value of the completed building is the same as the value of a building completed in strict accordance with the plans and specifications, should the contractor recover the part of the progress payment which was not certified?

 b. What should the developer do if, as a result of the above described dispute, the contractor files a lien against the development thus getting the construction lender upset? See Division III pages 672 to 682 supra. In addition, the permanent lender may not be too happy with this state of affairs.

  1. Does a surety company take a significant risk if it promises to pay on behalf of the developer the amount the contractor claims if and

when it is eventually determined that the money is owed to the contractor? If the surety does promise to pay the contractor, its promise is substituted for the lien and construction continues. This is what is known as "bonding-off" a lien.

3. See generally Leslie, *When Trouble Comes—Contractor Default—Representing The Owner,* 8 Forum 492 (1973); Bergman, *When the Subcontractor Fails to Perform—The Notice Problem,* 21 # 3 Prac.Law. 85 (1975); Beck, *The Doctrine of Substantial Performance: Conditions and Conditions Precedent,* 38 Mod.L.Rev. 413 (1975).

(b) LIQUIDATED DAMAGES

One means, at least when dealing with delay in completion, of avoiding the problems involved in proving damages is to provide for liquidated damages in the construction contract. The damages resulting from delay are frequently quite difficult to prove and may be quite substantial. The liquidated damages solution is, however, not without its pitfalls.

LIQUIDATED DAMAGE PROBLEMS IN CONSTRUCTION CONTRACTS

Newton E. Anderson
5 # 2 Practical Lawyer 72 (1959).
[footnotes omitted]

* * *

Owner's Delay

* * *

As an elementary proposition, a builder who has bound himself to a time limit will not be assessed for a breach of it if his delinquency is caused by the other party. This is not to say that the builder may not remain responsible for the diligent performance of his contract. * * * He may still be held liable for unreasonable delay on his own part. It is an open question whether or not he will be held liable for his delay under conventional rules or under a stipulated liquidated damages clause.

Delay Due to Alterations and Additions

In the case of a prolongation of the work caused by alterations or additions done at the instance of the owner, the builder is not responsible for the delay caused even though he acquiesces in the increased or changed undertaking. Beattie Mfg. Co. v. Heinz, 120 Mo.App. 465 (1906); Williams v. Rosenbaum, 57 Wash. 94 (1910).

* * *

Delay Caused by Both Parties

* * * The courts feel where delays are occasioned by the mutual fault of the parties that it is difficult or impractical to determine the responsibility of each and, therefore, generally refuse to apportion the delay. United States v. United Engineering & Contracting Co., 234 U.S. 236, 34 S.Ct. 843, 58 L.Ed. 1294 (1914); Gogo v. Los Angeles County Flood Control Dist., 45 Cal.App.2d 334, 114 P.2d 65 (1941).

Apportionment

There are a few jurisdictions that permit apportionment. They hold that where the fault for a delay rests with both the builder and the owner, this does not necessarily prevent the owner from recovering liquidated damages, but only entitles the builder to credit, against his period of default, of such number of days as is proved to be attributable to the owner's delay. Wallis v. Wenham, 204 Mass. 83, 90 N.E. 396 (1910); Bedford–Carthage Stone Co. v. Ramey, 34 S.W.2d 387 (Tex.Civ. App.1930).

* * *

Where a construction contract expressly permits the owner to require extras—and most standard forms of contracts do—then it can be strenuously argued upon substantial authority that delays caused by the extras are to be taken as only postponing the completion date. Small v. Burke, 92 App.Div. 338, 86 N.Y.S. 1066 (1st Dep't 1904). As a practical matter, this very often circumvents an apportionment problem.

Occasionally, a contract expressly provides that delays should be apportioned or allowed for at a designated rate. In this situation it is unquestioned that the delay attributable to the owner will be determined, and the builder will be held for liquidated damages at the daily or weekly rate for the length of his delay less that caused by the owner.

* * *

Notice of Claim for Delay

Standard forms of construction contracts often require as a condition to any right on the part of the builder to be absolved from the time limit that, in case of any claim for delay on the part of the owner, the [builder] shall give notice of the delay, or make application for an extension of time, either when the cause occurs or within a stated period thereafter. Such clauses are usually intended for the benefit of the builder in obtaining grace from the architect or engineer for delays occasioned by "extras." They are also often intended to protect the owner against a claim of release from the contractual time limit, a defense available to builders in most jurisdictions when the owner has caused some of the delay. The courts generally interpret such a provision as a condition precedent to any right of the builder to assert he has been excused by a mutual delay. United States v. Cunningham, 125 F.2d 28 (D.C.Cir.1941); Trauts Realty Corp. v. Casualty Co. of America, 166 N.Y.S. 807 (1st Dep't 1917).

* * *

Abandonment

A question that has produced extensive litigation in recent years is whether a builder is liable for delay under a liquidated damage clause where he abandons the work after the scheduled date of completion.

The courts are irreconcilably divided on the point, and the liability of the builder will depend on the law of the jurisdiction by which the contract is to be interpreted.

Some courts permit the owner to recover liquidated damages under circumstances that actually involve double delay—the delay represented by the period between the agreed completion date, and the abandonment date, and the delay represented by the period between the abandonment date and the actual completion date. Southern Pacific Co. v. Globe Indemnity Co., 21 F.2d 288 (2d Cir.1927); Bankers' Surety Co. v. Elkhorn River Drainage Dist., 214 F. 342 (8th Cir.1914); Austin–Griffith, Inc. v. Goldberg, 224 S.C. 372, 79 S.E.2d 447 (1953).

* * *

There is likewise authority that the builder is not liable for liquidated damages in case of a failure to complete the work specified where subsequent to the completion date he abandoned the work. The cases following this course apparently reason that to enforce the liquidated damage clause would lead to abuse by owners who, as the work neared completion, would tend to delay because of the additional damages accruing in their favor. Six Companies of California v. Joint Highway Dist., 311 U.S. 180, 61 S.Ct. 186, 85 L.Ed. 114 (1940); Canton v. Globe Indemnity Co., 201 App.Div. 820, 195 N.Y.S. 445 (3d Dep't 1922); Clark v. Fleischmann Vehicle Co., 187 N.Y.S. 807 (Sp.Ct., N.Y. Co. 1921).

* * *

It is recognized, however, that the parties may contractually provide that the right to liquidated damages shall survive in the event the builder defaults and the owner completes the work. Kidd v. McCormick, 83 N.Y. 391 (1881); Morrell v. Irving Fire Ins. Co., 33 N.Y. 429 (1865); M'Kegney v. Illinois Surety Co., 180 App.Div. 507, 167 N.Y.S. 843 (1st Dep't 1917); Comey v. United Surety Co., 160 App.Div. 698, 145 N.Y.S. 674 (1st Dep't 1914). * * *

NOTE

1. The tests typically used to determine whether a liquidated damages provision is an unenforceable penalty are also employed in analyzing a liquidated damages clause in a construction contract. Do the parties intend, as determined by the full scope of their agreement or agreements, a penalty? Is the amount of actual damage, in the event of default, extremely difficult or impossible to measure at the time the parties enter into the agreement? Is the stipulated sum or formula a just and reasonable approximation of actual damage as determined at the time of formation of the agreement? See pages 413 to 418 supra for a discussion of these considerations in the context of a liquidated damages provision in a contract for the sale of real estate. See also

Section 2–516(a) of the Uniform Land Transactions Act. Rather than providing for liquidated damages in the event of delay, in some situations the parties might provide that there will be no damages recoverable in the event of delay. See Counert, *The Enforceability of "No Damage for Delay" Clauses in Construction Contracts,* 28 Loy.L.Rev. 129 (1982).

2. The majority of courts will not apportion a delay caused by both parties. Can this result be avoided by providing in the construction contract that, in the event of delay caused by both parties, the contractor can credit against his period of default the number of days of delay caused by the owner? Can the architect make this determination, or is it beyond the scope of the architect's authority?

   a. Since extras are considered within the scope of the original contract, should the additional time required, if any, to accomplish extras be taken into account in determining whether there has been a delay? Should the contractor, when he files his written claim for an extra, include a request for an extension of the completion date if performance of the extra will cause a delay?

   1. If the architect allows the claim for the extra, but refuses the requested extension of the completion date, how can the contractor preserve his rights?

   b. Generally, the damages for delay are computed on a per diem or a weekly basis or formula.

3. What should the construction contract provide with respect to abandonment after the completion date? Should the liquidated damages continue to accrue until the eventual completion or only to the date of abandonment?

   a. If completion is achieved with dispatch by the owner, it is the contractor's fault the delay occurred?

   b. If the liquidated damages accrue to eventual completion, might the liquidated damages be considered a penalty?

   c. See generally Plotnick, *Understanding and Proving Construction Delay Claims,* 2 # 4 Prac.Real Est.Law. 67 (1986).

4. If the contractor wishes to abandon, can the owner compel the contractor or the contractor's bonding company to complete the project? See Note, *Specific Performance of Construction Contracts—Archaic Principles Preclude Necessary Reform,* 47 Notre Dame L.Rev. 1025 (1972); Axelrod, *Judicial Attitudes Toward Specific Performance of Construction Contracts,* 7 U.Dayton L.Rev. 33 (1981).

   a. If a liquidated damages provision is included in the construction contract, can the owner still obtain specific performance? Cf. Section 2–516(b) of the Uniform Land Transactions Act.

   b. If the contractor has a performance bond, the bonding company may voluntarily step in and complete the project.

5. One interesting suggestion which avoids some of the problems raised by the general contractor approach to construction is to hire for a fee a construction manager and have the manager direct the work of a variety of specialized contractors. See Tishman, *The Construction Manager Bids to Replace the G.C.,* 2 # 1 Real Est.Rev. 30 (1972). See generally Comment, *The Roles of Architect and Contractor In Construction Management,* 6 U.Mich.J.L.Ref. 447 (1973); Powers, *Representing the Subcontractor,* 8 Forum 472 (1973); Lambert, *The*

Legal Profile of the Construction Manager, 4 # 4 Real Est.Rev. 84 (1975); Simpkin and Nielsen, *The Rise of Project/Construction Management,* 6 # 4 Real Est.Rev. 47 (1977).

(iii) BONDING

An important concern of a developer is whether, if the contractor fails in any way to perform, the contractor can respond in damages. Frequently, a contractor cannot, or at least he does not possess sufficient liquid assets to permit him to respond in damages. In most situations, this problem can be solved by "bonding the job." The surety will be responsible to the developer in the event the contractor fails to perform. The surety's obligation may be discharged by the payment of damages or by completion of the project. This obligation on the part of the surety is called a Performance Bond. See Webster, *The Surety's Decision on What to Do,* 17 Forum 1168 (1982); Thompson, *Completion Options Available to a Performance Bond Surety Other than Financing Its Principal,* 17 Forum 1215 (1982).

In addition, a contractor may fail to pay the subcontractors, materialmen or laborers for work done or material purchased. One or more of the foregoing may file a lien against the development, or claim a lien against the undisbursed construction loan proceeds. This type of problem can be avoided, to some extent, by a Labor and Material or Payment Bond. This type of bonding occurs less frequently than performance bonding. See generally Comment, *Mechanics' Liens and Surety Bonds in the Building Trades,* 68 Yale L.J. 138 (1958).

Bonding is not limited to the general or prime contractor. In theory, there is no reason why an electrical subcontractor, for example, cannot be bonded. Some substantial, credit-worthy contractors obtain a commitment from a bonding company that the company will bond them on any projects they undertake, up to a certain amount in total liability. This is known as a "bonding-line" and is of as much importance to the construction contractor as, for example, the contractor's line of credit from a bank. When the contractor is the successful bidder on a project the bonding company issues a bond or bonds for the project, charging the contractor the appropriate premiums.

The less substantial or credit-worthy contractor may have to apply for bonding on a project-by-project basis. When the contractor is going to bid on a contract it informs the bonding company. The bonding company then reviews the risks, the credit and the other attributes of the contractor and determines whether it will bond the contract if the contractor is the successful bidder. Frequently, in the case of smaller contractors, the bonding company will require the principals of the contractor to individually guarantee the contractor's performance.

While contractors on local, state or federal projects are generally required to be bonded, see, for example, the Miller Act, 40 U.S.C.A. § 270, bonding is not required, as a matter of course, in private real estate development. With respect to larger real estate projects, however, both payment and performance bonds may be required. The absence of a universal bonding requirement stems, in part, from the inability of some contractors to obtain bonding, and the additional costs of construction added by bond premiums.

Since developers and construction lenders are most concerned with the timely completion of the development, the most frequent type of bond written is the performance bond. This type of bond guarantees the faithful performance of the contract. The bonding company promises the obligee (the developer and, possibly, the construction lender) that the work undertaken by the principal (the contractor) will be done pursuant to the contract bonded.

In addition, the developer and the construction lender may be concerned about payment by the contractor to subcontractors, materialmen and laborers. This problem can be dealt with, at least partially, by procuring a payment bond. This type of bond guarantees to the obligee (the developer and, possibly, the construction lender and the permanent lender) that all labor and material bills incurred by the principal (the contractor) will be paid. Salzman, *What You Can Do to Get Contractors and Suppliers Paid,* 3 # 1 Prac.Real Est.Law. 27 (1987).

Bonding companies are reluctant to "get stuck holding the sack." If the developer and construction lender are not careful, after the bonding company pays the subcontractors, materialmen and laborers, it may claim, through subrogation, the liens and rights the payees were entitled to. What steps can the developer and construction lender take to avoid this result? See generally Dauer, *Government Contractors, Commercial Banks, and Miller Act Bond Sureties—A Question of Priorities,* 14 B.C.Ind. & Com.L.Rev. 943 (1973); Spriggs, *Repayment of Performance and Payment Bond Losses: State Government and Private Contracts,* 11 Forum 600 (1976); Atkins, *Repayment of Performance and Payment Bond Losses: State Government and Private Contracts,* 11 Forum 615 (1976); Milana, *The Performance Bond and the Underlying Contract: The Bond Obligations do not Include All of the Contract Obligations,* 12 Forum 187 (1976); Geva, *Bonded Construction Contracts: What are the Surety's Rights to Withheld Funds?,* 3 Corp.L.Rev. 50 (1980).

See generally Dwyer, *New Protection for Construction Lenders,* 3 # 3 Real Est.Rev. 76 (1973); Hart and Kane, *What Every Real Estate Lawyer Should Know About Payment and Performance Bonds,* 17 Real Prop., Prob. & Tr.J. 674 (1982). The 1970 and 1984 Editions of the AIA Performance and Payment Bonds are set out in Sweet, Legal Aspects of Architecture, Engineering, and the Construction Process, 3d ed. (1985) at pages 937–948.

c. INCOME TAX TREATMENT OF LAND DEVELOPMENT AND DEMOLITION COSTS

The development of real estate frequently requires demolition of existing structures and land preparation and improvement. The developer, in many instances, would prefer to expense these costs. If that alternative is not open, and generally it is not, the developer's preference would be to capitalize the costs into the asset acquired, the lease with a new tenant or the depreciable improvement constructed. Since land is a nondepreciable asset, the preference of the developer is to allocate as many of the land development and improvement costs as possible to depreciable assets.

AURORA VILLAGE SHOPPING CENTER, INC. v. COMMISSIONER

29 CCH Tax Ct.Mem. 126 (1970).

FAY, Judge: * * * Several issues were settled by the parties. The issues remaining to be decided are: (1) whether certain earthmoving expenses incurred in preparing a shopping center site are attributable to the nondepreciable land or to the depreciable buildings erected thereon, and (2) whether petitioner is entitled to a loss deduction arising from the demolition of four residences acquired by purchase. If petitioner is entitled to a loss deduction, we must determine the correct amount of said loss.

* * *

During its taxable years 1959 through 1961 while petitioner was engaged in the construction of Aurora Village Shopping Center, petitioner incurred expenditures for earth moving and land improvements totaling $86,472.81. Petitioner allocated such expenditures as follows:

Items charged to land account—

1959–1960	Howard S. Wright & Co.—Rock wall, etc.	$ 7,842.13
5/5/59	Morford & Mowry—Survey	385.00
6/2/60	Holland Nurseries—Grading, soil preparation and planting shrubbery	1,239.99
10/10/60	Fred Wall—Moving top soil	1,248.00
1961	John H. Sellen Construction Co.— Excavating and grading, etc.	13,289.62
3/13/61–12/8/61	Malmo Nurseries and others re shrubs, landscaping, etc.	9,772.47
Re 1960	Share of $52,695.60 (see following schedule)	10,539.12
	Total	$44,316.33

Charged to building accounts—(see following schedule) ... $42,156.48

Total $86,472.81

Summary of Work Performed and Charges by All–City Excavating Co. during the Period November 17, 1959 to July 7, 1960

11/17/59	I.	Pittsburgh Testing—Soil Testing .... $	50.00
	II.	Soil Testing:	
	A.	(22) Field Density Tests 7/3/59 through 7/8/59 at $10 each .... $ 220.00	
	B.	(2) Graph Reports 7/1/59 through 7/4/59 at $50 each 100.00	
	C.	Soil Compaction Labor (Field Density Reports), 8/6/59 through 8/31/59, 8¼ days at $50 a day 412.50	
	D.	Laboratory Moisture–Density Relationship (Proctor Test) 8/27/59 50.00	
	E.	Soil Compaction Labor (Field Density Reports) 9/1/59 through 9/14/59, 3½ days at $50 a day 175.00	957.50
12/10/59	III.	Contract:	
	A.	Clearing and Grabbing $ 2,135.00	
	B.	Stockpiling Top Soil—1300 cu. yd. at $0.30 cu. yd. 390.00	
	C.	Relocating Ditch—1,750 lin. ft. at $0.25 lin. ft. 437.50	
		Sales Tax 118.50	3,081.00
12/10/59	IV.	Change Order # 1 to above Contract:	
	A.	Extra Excavating for Former Service Station Area .... $ 1,100.00	
		Sales Tax 44.00	1,144.00
1/22/60	V.	Common Excavating Work:	
	A.	Excavating—148,000 cubic yards—90% × 148,000 cu. yds. times $0.27 cu. yds. .. $35,964.00	
		Sales Tax 1,438.56	37,402.56

7/07/60   VI.   Contract:
              A.   Excavating—14,800 cu.
                     yds. at $0.27 cu. yd. .. $ 3,996.00
              B.   Relocating Ditch—950
                     lin. ft. at $0.25 lin. ft.   237.50
                        Sales Tax 169.34   4,402.84

7/07/60   VII. Change Order # 2 to above
                   Contract:
              A.   Extra Excavating and
                     Grading for Spillane
                     Property (Dispose of all
                     buildings, breakup ma-
                     sonry and concrete and
                     dispose of it. Burn un-
                     salvageable materials
                     on site.) .... $ 680.00
              B.   Excavating—17,630 cubic
                     yards at $0.27 cu. yd.   4,760.10
                        Sales Tax ....   217.60 $ 5,657.70

            Total $52,695.60
Deduct—Portion to land account at 12/31/60 ....   10,539.12
            Balance $42,156.48

The entire amount of $52,695.60 * * * was paid to All–City
Excavating Company. The expenditures of $33,777.21 allocated to
petitioner's land account were paid to others.

The $42,156.48 allocated to its buildings accounts was further
allocated by petitioner to the four buildings, and depreciation was
computed thereon, as follows:

1960 Big Bear Store $10,840.54
1960 Pay N' Save Store 6,970.57
1960 Small Stores 3,267.13

                                                         $21,078.24
1961 Phase II Stores 21,078.24
                                                         $42,156.48

On April 27, 1959, petitioner had entered into a contract with John
Graham and Company ("Graham") for architectural services for the
design of the shopping center. Graham recommended that the level of
the land be raised because the present level was below the street.
Raising the level of the land would make the buildings to be constructed thereon more conspicuous to passing traffic. Graham further recommended leveling of the land to less than a three percent grade. Any
steeper grade would cause discomfort to women walking in the parking
lot. Pursuant to the recommendations of Graham, petitioner hired
All–City to perform the above-described work.

During 1961 and 1962, petitioner acquired residential property located on the perimeter of the shopping center. Petitioner allocated the purchase prices between land and buildings as follows:

Seller and Address	Date	Land	Building
Myers—Parcel # 12 (20019 Wallingford Ave. N.)	8/28/61	$8,462.00	$11,538.00
Young—Parcel # 14 (1307 N. 200th)	7/21/62	3,714.10	9,285.90
Kropp—Parcel # 15 (1147 N. 200th) (Exchanged for land at May 15, 1964 Hanson—1301 N. 200th)	8/01/62	2,105.15	9,261.74
Thomas—Parcel # 16 (1620 N. 200th)	9/01/62	1,386.11	5,975.08

Apportionment of the purchase price as between land and building, for each parcel, was made on the basis of percentages of assessed valuations.

Depreciation on the buildings was computed on a straight-line five-year life.

Parcels 12, 14, and 16 were rented during the years in question at the following monthly rates:

Parcel 12—$70; Parcel 14—$60; Parcel 16—$60.

Petitioner exchanged parcel 15 (Kropp) in 1964 for unimproved land known as parcel 17. Petitioner had rented the house on parcel 15 prior to the exchange.

The houses on the aforesaid parcels varied between 800 and 1,000 square feet and each house had one or two bedrooms.

Petitioner purchased the aforesaid parcels to protect the perimeter of the shopping center. When petitioner acquired the parcels it took into consideration that the rentals from the houses were sufficient to cover the installment payments on the purchase contract. The residences on parcels 12, 14, and 16 were still in existence and rented as of December 31, 1968.

In the statement attached to his notice of deficiency, respondent attributed to land costs an additional $21,078.24, a portion of the amount paid by petitioner to All–City. Since petitioner had included this amount in the cost of its buildings, respondent's allocation reduced the amount of depreciation allowed to petitioner for taxable years 1962 through 1966.

Respondent also reduced the amount of depreciation allowed on the rental dwellings on the premise that the bases of such improvements should be limited to the estimated gross rental to be received for a period of five years.

Opinion

* * *

[R]espondent has issued a revenue ruling stating that grading costs "directly associated with the construction of buildings and the paved roadways, are not inextricably associated with the land itself." Under the facts presented in that ruling it was held that "the costs attributable to excavation, grading and removing soil necessary for the proper setting of the buildings and paving of the roadways are part of the cost of those assets and should be included in the depreciable base for the buildings and roadways." Rev.Rul. 65–265, 1965–2 C.B. 52, clarified by Rev.Rul. 68–193, 1968–1 C.B. 79. The clarification in the latter ruling related only to the costs of grading for roadways.

Petitioner has allocated to building costs $42,156.48 of a total $52,695 paid to All–City. Relying on Rev.Rul. 65–265, supra, petitioner contends that such expenditures were "directly associated with the construction of buildings" because they were incurred for raising the level of the building site and reducing the grade of the parking area. On the other hand, respondent contends that only $21,078 of such expenditures were properly allocable to buildings. Thus, the sole task of the Court is to determine which party's allocation should be upheld.

In resolving this dispute, we have considered closely the testimony of Manson Backus, an officer of petitioner, and the only witness to testify. He stated that one of the purposes of the earth moving was to clear and level the land located in the southeastern area of the shopping center site, for not all of the site had been cleared prior to Graham's architectural study. Later during the trial Manson Backus also testified that the earth moving was needed to move the high places into the low places.

We believe that the earth-moving expenditures required for the purposes described in the preceding paragraph are properly attributable to land costs. The record, however, provides us no basis to make even an approximate estimate of such costs. Although Manson Backus stated that he relied upon his accountant's advice, the accountant did not testify. * * * Furthermore, a topographical survey was made after petitioner engaged Graham to do an architectural study. Neither Graham's report nor the survey were introduced into evidence. These items would have aided the Court in allocating the earth-moving expenses between building and land accounts.

On the basis of this record we have no alternative but to uphold respondent's determination since petitioner has failed to satisfy its burden of proof. Therefore, of the $52,695 paid to All–City, approximately $31,617 is allocable to land costs. This total amount represents the sum of approximately $10,539 which petitioner itself allocated to land and the adjustment of $21,078 made by respondent.

The other issue remaining for our decision is whether petitioner acquired four residential properties with the intent of demolishing them.

Respondent has disallowed a substantial amount of the depreciation claimed on such residences. Relying on section 1.165–3(a)(2) of his regulations, respondent contends that the depreciable bases of the residences can not exceed the present value of petitioner's right to receive rentals from the buildings over the period of their intended use.

The foregoing provision of respondent's regulations applies only where a taxpayer acquires buildings with an intent to demolish formed at the time of purchase.

We disagree with respondent's interpretation of petitioner's motivations for purchasing the residences. Instead, we believe the testimony of Manson Backus that the residences were acquired to protect the perimeter of the shopping center from encroachment by undesired business interests. We view as strong evidence on petitioner's behalf that the residences were still being rented in 1968, six years after their acquisition.

* * *

Since we do not think that petitioner's bases in the four residences should be limited by the formula prescribed in section 1.165–3 of respondent's regulations, we must consider whether the method in fact adopted by petitioner was proper. Petitioner determined the bases of the residences by allocating the purchase prices between land and improvements according to the ratios of assessed values. Respondent has not questioned the accuracy of petitioner's figures. Accordingly, we uphold petitioner's method of determining the bases of such residences. 2554–58 Creston Corp., 40 T.C. 932, 940 (1963).

* * *

NOTE

1. In the above case, the court accepted the Commissioner's allocation of land development costs between land and buildings since the taxpayer did not meet its burden of proof. The court agreed that some of the land development costs could be allocated to buildings.

a. What steps should the taxpayer have taken to improve its chances in litigation or to avoid litigation entirely? What land development costs can be legitimately allocated to buildings? See Rev.Rul. 80–93, 1980–1 C.B. 50, which distinguishes between land preparation costs which must be added to the basis of the land and land preparation costs which can be added to the basis of the building constructed and, as a result, depreciated.

In appropriate circumstances, it may be possible to depreciate certain landscaping costs over the life of the constructed buildings. See Rev.Rul. 74–265, 1974–1 C.B. 56, and cf. *Tunnell v. United States*, 512 F.2d 1192 (3d Cir.1975), cert. denied, 423 U.S. 893, 96 S.Ct. 190, 46 L.Ed.2d 124 (1975). Land improvements such as sidewalks, roads, fences, landscaping, sewers, drainage facilities and bridges, however, should be depreciated over their own lives rather than the constructed buildings' lives if their own lives are shorter than the buildings' lives. In addition, estimated future costs can be presently added to basis in certain limited circumstances. See Rev.Proc. 75–25, 1975–1 C.B. 720; Rev.Rul. 76–247, 1976–1 C.B. 217; *Robert F. Haynsworth,* 68 T.C. 703 (1977). In order to add estimated future costs to basis, however, the taxpayer must be legally obligated to incur the costs. The intention of the taxpayer to incur the costs or the necessity of incurring the costs will not be enough to permit the present addition to basis of the estimated future costs. See *Bryce's Mountain Resort, Inc.,* 50 CCH Tax Ct.Mem. 164 (1985).

b. See generally *Trailmont Park, Inc. v. Commissioner,* 30 CCH Tax Ct.Mem. 871 (1971); Henderson, *Land Cost Expenditures: Recent Trend Shows Many Such Costs Are Now Depreciable,* 38 J. Tax'n 78 (1973); Sandison and Waters, *Tax Planning For the Land Developer: Cost Allocations of Land and Improvements,* 37 J. Tax'n 80 (1972). Revenue Rul. 75–524, 1975–2 C.B. 342, indicates that the beginning of the holding period of a building under construction occurs progressively as construction of the building is completed. Depreciation, however, cannot be taken until the building is placed in service. The current deduction of a developer's costs of a park area or an open space easement conveyed to a municipality as a charitable or ordinary business deduction has frequently led to litigation. Compare *Allen v. United States,* 541 F.2d 786 (9th Cir.1976), with *W. Lawrence Oliver,* 35 CCH Tax Ct.Mem. 656 (1976), affirmed per curiam, 553 F.2d 560 (8th Cir.1977). See also *William H. Eggert,* 36 CCH Tax Ct.Mem. 1071 (1977); *James E. Forkan,* 36 CCH Tax Ct.Mcm. 798 (1977); *John C. Dockery,* 37 CCH Tax Ct.Mem. 317 (1978); *Richard H. Foster,* 80 T.C. 34 (1983), affirmed on this issue, 756 F.2d 1430 (9th Cir.1985), cert. denied, 424 U.S. 1055, 106 S.Ct. 793, 88 L.Ed.2d 770 (1986); *Ottawa Silica Company v. United States,* 699 F.2d 1124 (F.Cir.1983); *Robert P. Osborne,* 87 T.C. 575 (1986); *Johnie V. Elrod,* 87 T.C. 1046 (1986); *William G. McConnell,* 55 CCH Tax Ct.Mem. 1284 (1988).

2. In *Aurora Village Shopping Center, Inc.* the Internal Revenue Service attempted to deny part of the taxpayer's depreciation deductions with respect to four houses which the taxpayer acquired on the perimeter of the shopping center. The Internal Revenue Service alleged that the taxpayer acquired the houses with the intent to demolish them, and thus the amount of the purchase price of the land and buildings which could be allocated to the buildings and form their bases for depreciation purposes was limited, under Reg.Sec. 1.165–3. The taxpayer convinced the court that the houses were not acquired with the intent to demolish, and therefore, the amount of the purchase price which could be allocated to the houses was not limited by Reg.Sec. 1.165–3.

a. If a purchaser acquires improved real estate and subsequently demolishes the improvements, is any of the purchase price of the real estate allocated to the improvements?

1. Regulation Sec. 1.165–3 considers the intent of the purchaser at the time of acquisition the key factor.

a. If the intent to demolish, immediately or subsequently, is present at the time of acquisition, the amount of the purchase price which normally would be allocated to structures is treated as a land cost. See Reg.Sec. 1.165–3(a)(1).

b. If, however, the improvements are used for trade or business or the production of income prior to demolition, a portion of the purchase price can be allocated to the improvements but it cannot exceed the present value of the right to receive rentals from the improvements over the period of their intended use. This amount may be depreciated. See Reg.Sec. 1.165–3(a)(2). Cf. *Nash v. Comm'n,* 60 T.C. 503 (1973), acq. 1974–2 C.B. 3; *William I. Nash,* 39 CCH Tax Ct.Mem. 1105 (1980).

      c. Whether real estate and improvements have been acquired with the intent to demolish is a question of fact, and Reg.Sec. 1.165–3(c) suggests certain factors which may be taken into account when answering this question. Cf. *Robert W. Lawver,* 41 CCH Tax Ct.Mem. 1306 (1981).

    3. Even if a taxpayer has a basis in a real estate improvement at the time of its demolition, the taxpayer cannot currently deduct the basis of the demolished improvement and the costs of demolition as a demolition loss. Section 280B prohibits the deduction by the owner or lessee of demolished improvements of any demolition expense or loss and requires the capitalization of any such expense or loss into the basis of the land on which the demolished structure was located.

2.   THE LEASING TRANSACTION

    The leasing transaction is at the heart of the development and operation of industrial, commercial and residential rental real estate. The negotiation and drafting of leases between the developer and tenants constitute a major part of the activities of the developer and its advisors. The following materials describe many of the considerations involved in negotiating and drafting a lease of space in a commercial rental real estate development.

PROBLEMS OF THE DEVELOPER
Norman M. Kranzdorf
1965 University of Illinois Law Forum 173 (1965).
[footnotes omitted]

*   *   *

Parties to the Lease

    It is important that each lease contain the accurate name of the landlord and the tenant. Usually that of the landlord is no problem; it will be either a corporation or an individual owning title to the land or the leasehold interest upon which the project is to be built. In the case of individual parties, it is most important that a husband and wife both execute the lease and that they be named as jointly and severally liable. In certain states it is necessary for a wife not only to sign the lease but also to execute a separate disclaimer of dower. In any case where a corporation is used as either landlord or tenant, it should be a duly existing and qualified corporation. Care should be taken not to execute a lease before a corporation is formally formed and qualified.

Definition of Demised Premises and Shopping Center

The two most common terms used throughout the shopping center form lease are "shopping center" and "demised premises." The "shopping center" should be defined as and limited to the entire area upon which the shopping center project is to be constructed. This can be accomplished by either annexing a plot plan to the lease as a schedule or a legal description. In all events, care should be taken so that the shopping center description does not contain more land than is actually needed for the present shopping center project. * * *

The "demised premises" is the actual store demised or leased to the tenant. For obvious reasons the demised premises should be spelled out as an area limited in nature. A typical provision reads: "said Demised Premises having approximate dimensions of 20' × 100' without basement (but shall in no event extend beyond the rear wall or window of the proposed store nor beyond the actual store front thereof)." The reason for this exact terminology is that many architects and designers have a habit of designing slanted or indented store fronts. If such irregular premises are defined as a rectangular area of 20 feet by 100 feet, then that would include areas outside of the store proper. The tenant would then have the right to use this exterior sidewalk space as a business area. Most shopping center developers frown on this practice and do not allow outside displays or selling practices. Limiting the demised premises to the actual building helps control this practice.

Use Provisions

The provision of the lease most susceptible to error and least susceptible to a "boiler plate" form is the use clause. The use clause defines what business or practice may be conducted within the demised premises. In the modern day composition of the shopping center, it is important to have well co-ordinated and integrated merchants * * *. It is equally important to be sure that there is not undue competition within the shopping center and among neighboring tenants. Before drafting a use clause the attorney should be careful to understand the type of business involved, as it is difficult to draft a proper clause if there is no experience with such type of business. This is especially true in cases where there are two or more stores of a similar nature except for a differential of price or style. For example, a ladies ready-to-wear store encompasses no less than three separate and distinct types of business which should be separated within a shopping center. One such business would be "a ladies popular priced ready-to-wear store featuring blouses, skirts, separates, and sportswear." This, naturally, is different from a "ladies ready-to-wear store featuring higher priced dresses, suits, coats, and evening wear." Both of these stores are different from a "ladies specialty store featuring lingerie, foundation garments and accessories."

* * *

Term of Lease

The lease will have a term usually set forth as a specific number of years. This part is easy. However, most shopping center leases are drawn for buildings not yet completed. Therefore, a commencement date of a lease cannot be established at the time the lease is drawn. If you cannot establish the commencement date, you cannot establish the expiration date. Accordingly, provision must be made that the lease will commence at some time in the future and expire a given number of months or years thereafter. Typical language of this type of provision would be:

> "The term shall commence on the expiration of thirty (30) days after notice to Tenant that the Demised Premises are ready for occupancy by Tenant or the date when Tenant commences business operations, whichever is sooner, and the term shall expire on the last day of the month ten (10) years after the aforementioned Commencement Date."

In the last several years some concern has arisen about this type of provision, but it now appears that the entire matter has been settled by both interpretation and legislation. In any event, the concern can be obviated by inserting language in the lease which then takes the same out of the purview of the rule against perpetuities. Such typical language would be:

> "In the event the Commencement Date of this Lease shall not have in fact occurred within four (4) years of the date hereof, this Lease thereupon shall be automatically null and void and of no force and effect."

Guaranteed Minimum Rent

* * * The minimum rent is the annual amount which the tenant pays as the basic cost for the lease. * * * Rental payments should be specified as being payable in equal monthly installments in advance without setoff or deduction. It is important that the tenant not be allowed any setoff or deductions against the minimum rent; a mortgage lender will require that all rent be paid without question, as this is the security for [its] mortgage loan.

Repairs

* * * The ordinary language is to the effect that the landlord takes care of all exterior and structural repairs while the tenant repairs all interior and nonstructural items. This dichotomy is so vague as to leave nothing but doubt. In the writer's viewpoint, the tenant should take care of all repairs and replacements in and about the demised premises, and it should be further provided:

> "The Landlord will keep in repair the structural exterior of the Demised Premises only (except any doors, moldings, trim, window

frames, door frames, closure devices, door hardware, door hinges and/or windows) * * * provided that the damage thereto shall not have been caused by the negligence or the act of Tenant, in which event Tenant shall be responsible therefor. Landlord's obligation with respect to repairs to the Demised Premises shall be only as expressly set forth in this paragraph." * * *

It should be noted that there is a difference between a repair and a replacement. The tenant should be responsible for both, and the lease should tend to give a tenant all of the indicia of ownership except for title. Repair provisions often contain obligations on the part of the tenant to use the premises in a neat and orderly manner, and to comply with all ordinances, notices, and regulations which may be issued at any time by any authority, including the Board of Fire Underwriters. The tenant should also have the burden of notifying the landlord as soon as possible of any damage that may occur on the demised premises. This is important for insurance policy reporting.

Increased Fire Insurance Rates

* * * [T]he standard lease should contain a provision whereby the tenant will take such steps as are necessary to cause the rate of insurance to remain at the minimum rate obtainable. Also, the tenant should not do any act on the demised premises which will contravene the insurance policy or policies. * * *

Assignment

One of the most argued-over clauses in a lease is that pertaining to the right of assignment. Naturally, the perfect landlord lease contains an absolute prohibition against an assignment or subletting of the demised premises by the tenant. Since the right to assign is such a coveted item, the tenants have become increasingly canny in their circumvention of this provision. Accordingly, assignment clauses must now be written to cover the known subterfuges. A tenant should be prohibited from assigning, mortgaging, encumbering, or subletting the premises. A prohibition should also be [contained] in * * * the lease against permitting the demised premises to be used by others through concessions or licenses. In the event the tenant is a corporation, it should be spelled out that any transfer, sale, pledge, or other disposition of the corporate stock or voting securities by the tenant shall be deemed an assignment. Undoubtedly there are other ways to circumvent the assignment provision. However, the corporate aspect is covered by the above and this is the most common in use today.

During the course of negotiations, the most prevalent compromise language is that "the Landlord shall not unreasonably withhold its consent." While this language may seem to solve the immediate problem of negotiations, it does little to solve the future problem of what is "reasonable." Accordingly, * * * [include] a proviso that "in no event shall the Landlord be responsible in monetary damages for such withholding of consent." * * *

Continued Business Operations

* * *

The clause itself should require the tenant to continuously use the demised premises for the exact purposes stated in the lease. It can then be embellished by adding provisions to the effect that the tenant will adequately stock the premises, employ sufficient labor, and take such other steps as are reasonably required to promote business activities therein. Guidelines should be established for such matters as the days and hours of operation in the premises. * * *

Since the continued business operation provision is so eagerly sought by landlords, it can be anticipated that the provision is equally rejected by chain tenants who do not want to be restricted or obligated in this sense. Many chain stores find it more profitable to close a low-volume store and pay the rent rather than sustain an operating loss. Accordingly, they universally reject such provisions when possible. Many landlords find that an adequate compromise is for the tenant to agree to remain open for the first five years of the lease, with the landlord having the option to cancel the lease and resume possession or allow the tenant to remain closed and pay rent if the tenant attempts to close thereafter.

It should not go without comment that in the event the landlord enters into a straight percentage lease, this operations clause is essential and cannot be omitted from the lease.

Bankruptcy

* * * One of the most vital (and least included) provisions of this sort is a reference to the fact that any such bankruptcy or insolvency proceedings on behalf or against any guarantor, assignor, and/or assignee of the lease shall be deemed the same as that of the tenant. The reason for this inclusion is the fact that many leases are executed by subsidiary companies and guaranteed by the parent corporation or are assigned from a financially strong tenant to a weaker subtenant. If bankruptcy by a party not actually a signatory to the lease depletes the actual security, the landlord should have the right to take any actions available to it under the lease itself.[4]

4. [Section 365 of the Bankruptcy Code prevents the "automatic" termination of a lease upon the bankruptcy of the lessee despite a provision in the lease providing for such. This does not mean, however, that the comments made in the text are no longer pertinent. It may be that, while the lessee is not in bankruptcy, the bankruptcy of a guarantor, assignor, assignee or possibly even a sublessee will so deplete the "security" of the lessor as to make the termination of the lease desirable. Whether Section 365 of the Bankruptcy Code will prevent the termination of a lease with a lessee-sublessor, which is not bankrupt, upon the bankruptcy of a sublessee is presently an open question. An argument could be made, however, that Section 365 does prevent termination in such an instance. See generally Division I, pages 243 to 245; Halper, *Bankruptcy Cancellation Clauses Under The Bankruptcy Reform*

Litigation

* * * A lease should contain provisions whereby the landlord is either kept out of or adequately protected against third party claims. Being the owner of the premises, a landlord is the first one sued under a mechanic's lien proceeding. Appropriate protections should be included so that the tenant will promptly remove the landlord from all such litigation.

* * *

It should also be noted that many states have statutes whereby after a default and abandonment, a tenant has the right to redeem the lease and re-enter the premises within a given amount of time. This right should be waived so that the landlord can be free to relet or otherwise deal with the premises once the original tenant is gone.

* * *

Utilities

* * *

In this connection, the tenant should be liable for all utilities consumed on the demised premises and these should include such items as water, gas, electricity, heat, sewer rental and related charges and any other utility charges. There should also be a provision that in the event the landlord elects to supply these utilities, the tenant will agree to purchase the same from the landlord. When this latter provision is included in the lease, most tenants' attorneys will immediately ask that the rates to be paid for such utilities not exceed the applicable rates charged by local utility companies. In most cases this provision should be acceptable to a landlord. However, there are cases whereby there are no applicable utility rates because of the remoteness of the premises. In such cases a tenant should pay its proportionate share of such charges without regard to comparable utility rates.

* * *

Common Area Maintenance

* * * This common area maintenance charge is usually borne on a pro rata share by the tenants, based on a formula of the total floor area of the demised premises as to the total floor area of the shopping center. * * *

Some astute draftsmen draft this formula so that the tenant pays a percentage based on his demised premises over the floor area "then rented or occupied." This wording gives the landlord the advantage of not bearing the burden of the vacant premises in the shopping center. Most of the chain stores throughout the country will agree to some contribution. However, they will insist upon a maximum charge for which they may be liable. * * *

Act, 9 # 3 Real Est.Rev. 75 (1979); Shanker, *The Treatment of Executory Con-* *tracts and Leases in The 1978 Bankruptcy Code,* 25 # 7 Prac.Law. 11 (1979).]

Interior and Exterior Store Appearance

* * * Nearly all shopping center form leases contain provisions whereby the tenants are limited in their right to display window signs and garish merchandise displays. The tenant should be obligated to maintain its show windows in a neat and clean condition, with the landlord having the right to set the requirements for window signs, pictures and advertisements. * * *

In addition, the tenant should be denied the right to alter the interior of the demised premises without the prior written consent of the landlord. The landlord originally constructed a building for a given retail purpose and he is vitally interested in seeing that his investment is not depreciated. * * *

Fire Clause

Another one of the more actively negotiated clauses in the standard form lease pertains to fire and casualty. Splits in theory between the landlord and the tenant are simple. The tenant wants the landlord to assume the obligation of repairing the demises premises to the condition as they existed prior to the casualty so that he can resume business as soon as possible. On the other hand, the landlord wants an option whereby he can either repair the premises or cancel the lease and deal with the property as he sees fit. Somewhere between these two interests a clause must be drafted.

* * *

In all events, the landlord should not have any obligation to repair or rebuild during the last two or three years of the term. The landlord should not be put to the burden of repairing the building unless he is sure he is going to have a tenant when he is finished. This can be approached in two methods. If a tenant has an option under the lease, he should be forced to exercise the same before the landlord decides whether or not to rebuild. Otherwise the landlord should have the option to require the tenant to extend its present lease for an additional term before rebuilding. In any case where the landlord is either under an obligation to rebuild or has the option to rebuild, the obligation should be limited to the basic building and any interior work which was originally installed at landlord's expense. * * *

Tenant Parking Rights

* * *

Naturally, the landlord should be prohibited from destroying the concept of the parking area as being open and available to all customers and invitees. * * * [T]he tenant's right to use such parking area [should be] on a nonexclusive basis and * * * be termed a "revocable license." Perhaps the best way to satisfy both parties is for the landlord to agree that throughout the term of the lease it shall maintain a paved parking area to accommodate a sufficient and specified number of standard sized automobiles and which gives the tenant the guarantee of available adequate parking. * * *

Tenant and Landlord Liability

* * * The landlord should not be under any responsibility or liability for the quantity, quality, or impairment of any services supplied to the shopping center, as these are usually items beyond its control. The same is true for liability for damage to the property of the tenant or others located on the demised premises. * * * It should be spelled out that all personal property kept or stored in the demised premises shall be at the sole liability of the tenant. [T]he lease [should make clear] that there is no subrogation claim against the landlord by any insurance carrier of the tenant.

On the other hand, since the tenant has assumed possession and control of the demised premises, it should be responsible for damage to the property of the landlord and any act done within the demised premises. The tenant should be responsible for liability claims occurring within the demised premises. In any case, the tenant should carry adequate public liability and property damage insurance and furnish the landlord with a certificate showing such insurance to be in full force and effect, with the landlord covered as an additional insured. * * *

Percentage Rent

As mentioned earlier, rent for most shopping center stores is divided between minimum rent and percentage rent. The percentage rent is calculated on the annual gross sales volume in each respective store. Ordinarily this percentage rent is due and payable only in excess of the guaranteed minimum rent. In other words, the percentage rent is a sum equal to the amount by which the minimum rent is less than a certain percentage of gross sales. * * *

There are as many different forms of percentage rent clauses as there are landlords' attorneys. None is probably any better than another so long as it contains the necessary elements of protection. Among these protections are such items as monthly gross sales reports by the tenant, a CPA statement of gross sales once a year, and the right to audit the books of the tenant and those of its affiliated operations to verify that the proper allocations have been made between stores.

A proper definition of gross sales is essential. Gross sales should include the entire amount of the actual sales price, whether wholly or partly for cash or on credit. It should include services as well as merchandise and all other receipts of business conducted, such as telephone sales, deposits not refunded, and sales by any sublessee, concessionaire or licensee. Normal exclusions from gross sales are made for returns, interstore transfers and sales taxes. * * *

Subordination

* * * The more prevalent view today seems to be that those leases for tenants with a high credit rating should be superior to the mortgage and those tenants of a "local" character should be subordinated. The theory behind this logic is that there should be no superior lien to the leases which form the basic security for the loan. If the mortgagee forecloses, he wants to foreclose subject to the lease so that the tenant thereafter becomes the tenant of the mortgagee. The same logic dictates that the mortgagee wants to be able to control the space occupied by local, noncredit-rated tenants. In the event of a foreclosure, the mortgagee can force the vacation of this "local" space to use for any purpose it sees fit.

* * *

A subordination clause which refers only to the ultimate permanent financing of the shopping center is one half of a subordination clause. The clause should contain provision whereby the subordination is effective as to all present and future mortgages as well as advances made or thereafter to be made upon the security. A well-drafted provision will go even one step further and provide for subordination to ground leases or other methods of financing which may be employed by the developer. This sort of subordination will be effective for "sale—lease back" transactions and ground leases. The clause should also provide that the tenant is to execute further instruments of subordination if requested and that upon its failure to do so the tenant is deemed to have appointed the landlord as its attorney-in-fact to execute such instruments.

The present tendency among developers and mortgagees is to allow "nondisturbance" clauses to be incorporated into the subordination provision. Such a nondisturbance provision will honor the legal technicalities of subordination, while providing for the continued and uninterrupted occupancy of the tenant. * * *

Exclusive Operations

* * * [A] lease provision * * * frequently requested by tenants, and least found in landlords' printed form leases is that regarding exclusive protection for a tenant's business operation. Such provisions prohibit the landlord from leasing other space in the shopping center to any similar or competing type business [to] that of the tenant. * * * [Such] provisions naturally take away all of the flexibility which a landlord should have for the successful operation of a well-rounded shopping center. Partial exclusives usually are to the effect that the landlord will not lease to a similar type operation except for certain named * * * tenants or to competing tenants having a specified store area and operation. * * *

Naturally, exclusives granted to one tenant amount to restrictions on the balance of the tenants in the shopping center. If one tenant is granted an exclusive for the operation of a shoe store, it automatically means that every other tenant is restricted from operating a shoe store. Since many tenants will not accept any restrictions, including restrictions on use, the attorney must be careful originally to draft the lease provisions so that this type of tenant is not included in the restriction.

*   *   *

Default Clauses and Remedies of Landlord

*   *   * While it is not possible to review the statutes of all fifty states in this article, some of the actions which should constitute a default under a typical shopping center lease can be pointed out. These include: (1) default in the payment of rent or other sums due; (2) failure to take occupancy of the demised premises when tendered; (3) default in the event there is a levy attempted upon the demised premises or an execution of attachment; (4) default in the event this tenant defaults with respect to any other lease between it and the landlord or any affiliate of the landlord; (5) desertion, vacation, or abandonment of the premises or suspension of business operations.

After the defaults have been enumerated, the remedies should be listed. These remedies are classed as either those for the recovery of monoy or those for the recovery of possession. All remedies should be nonexclusive and the exercise of one should not preclude the exercise of any other. Some of the leases written for selected shopping center tenants call for rent to be paid only on a percentage basis. In other words, no guaranteed minimum rent is established and the tenant is obligated only for a certain percentage of its gross sales. In such event it would be extremely difficult to establish the monetary loss to the landlord after a default by the tenant, as no minimum rent is set and the percentage rent would be an unliquidated sum. In such cases a basis of collection or judgment upon default should be set forth in the lease. *   *   * In all events, the clause should provide that the sums payable under the lease by the tenant are deemed to be "additional rent," and the landlord should have the same rights to collect such additional rent as for minimum rent. Such sums might include percentage rent, parking area maintenance charges, excess taxes, attorneys fees, court costs, and utility bills. The reason for the necessity for such provision is that some specific state statutes provide for summary proceedings by the landlord for the nonpayment of rent or additional rent. Such swift proceedings are not available for money due for items other than rent. Also, in many states the right to distrain is available only for the nonpayment of rent or additional rent.

Somewhat related to a default provision is the question of the rights of the parties in and to the fixtures in the demised premises after a default. If the default occurs by the tenant vacating and abandoning the premises, it can be assumed that he has abandoned all of the contents of the demised premises. Appropriate language should be inserted into the lease whereby such action on the part of the tenant constitutes abandonment of the property, with it vesting as the property of the landlord. * * *

Security

* * * The security provision should provide that the sum held is without interest and that it is to be returned thirty days after the day set forth for the expiration of the lease if the tenant has fully and faithfully complied with the lease.[5]

It is unwise to allow a tenant to "work off" the security at the end of the lease by not paying rent and applying the security to the last month's rent. When this is allowed, the landlord has no security for the restoration of the demised premises or for damages caused by the tenant. * * * [T]he lease should contain a provision that the security is transferable to successive landlords and that upon a transfer of the security the present landlord shall be considered released from liability for the return of such security.

The tenant should not have the right to mortgage, assign, or encumber the security without the written consent of the landlord. An equally essential provision is one which relieves and releases any mortgagees of the landlord from any obligation to return such security in the event the mortgagee comes into possession by reason of foreclosure or other proceedings in lieu thereof. If such a provision is not included in the lease, many mortgagees will insist that the security be deposited with it or that an equal amount be deducted from the mortgage proceeds. * * *

In any event, a lease provision should state that in the event of bankruptcy or similar proceedings, the security held shall be deemed to have been applied to rent and other charges first due to the landlord for all periods prior to the filing of such proceedings.

Excess Taxes

* * * [I]t is the custom to require the tenant to pay those real estate taxes assessed against the demised premises which are in excess of the assessment first levied on the demised premises. Simply speaking, a tenant is responsible for the increase in taxes over the original sum payable by the landlord as applicable to the demised premises.

The calculation of such payments is on a formula similar to that used in the common area maintenance provision discussed earlier. Most of what has been said in that provision concerning proration and maximum payments is equally applicable to excess tax provisions. When calculating the excess tax proportion due, it is necessary to establish a base year which will set the original sum to be paid by the landlord. The base lease year easiest to define and calculate is that lease year in which the demised premises are delivered to the tenant. Most well-versed tenants' attorneys will insist that the base year be the

---

5.   [If permitted by applicable state law.]

year in which the premises are first existing as a fully completed shopping center. In this way the tenant will receive credit for the higher base figure and will not be faced with the problem of paying all of the taxes over those calculated on an "in process" condition.

* * *

[T]he lease should provide that * * * the tenant will be responsible for the entire tax upon the personal property of the tenant. Similarly, it should be carefully spelled out that in the event a [tax] is [imposed] on the value of the improvements made by the tenant and on machinery, fixtures, inventory, and other assets of the tenant, then the tenant should pay the entire tax bill on such items.

* * *

Condemnation

* * * The tenant is interested in protecting his possession of the demised premises and obtaining as great a portion of the award as possible. Conversely, the landlord is desirous of retaining the entire award and [the] flexibility of cancellation of the lease in the event of such condemnation.

First, in regard to the award, the landlord should reserve to itself all damages that may be covered under a condemnation proceeding against the shopping center and the demised premises. The landlord should attribute to the tenant those damages payable for trade fixtures installed by the tenant at its own cost and expense and any moving expenses which are attributable to the tenant in the case of a cancelled lease.

Secondly, the condemnation clause should allow the landlord the election to terminate the lease if 10 per cent or more of the demised premises or 15 per cent or more of the shopping center is condemned. The same arguments apply in this case as were applicable to the fire clause. The landlord wants the option to restore the premises or deal with it as he sees fit. After a partial condemnation the project may lose economic feasibility as a shopping center while not losing its feasibility to a given type tenant. Naturally, a landlord needs the flexibility to arrive at an economically justified investment. Without the right to cancel leases in the event of a condemnation, the landlord will be seriously handicapped. In the event of partial condemnation which does not destroy the feasibility of the project, the landlord will want to repair and restore the premises to an integrated shopping center unit. In such case, the landlord should repair and rebuild what remains of the demised premises for the occupancy of the tenant and a proportion of the minimum rent should be abated to the extent of the damages. In all events, the landlord should not be required to spend more in the repair of the building than it received or to restore other than the basic building which it first supplied to the tenant.

* * *

NOTE

1. If a lessor is leasing space in an office building, how are the demised premises described? If the space to be leased is only part of the fourteenth floor, how can these demised premises be described?

2. Do concerns with respect to restricting a lessee's use of the demised premises arise in the office building context? If the first five floors of the building are devoted to retail use, will the lessor want a lessee on the eighth floor engaging in a retail business? How many cafeterias can an office building support? If a restaurant leases the top floor and also provides cafeteria service, should the commercial and retail lessees be allowed to have their own dining rooms or luncheonettes? Can a lessee bank have an executive dining room for the bank officers? How will the food be provided for the partners' meeting of the lessee law firm or accounting firm?

3. In the above excerpt, Mr. Kranzdorf suggests a possible solution to the problems involved in executing a lease before its commencement date is known. It is desirable, however, to have a definite date for commencement, exercise of options, etc. contained in the lease.

   a. Can the clause Mr. Kranzdorf suggests, together with similar clauses describing other dates and other factors, be incorporated in a separate agreement with the understanding that the specific dates and factors will be inserted in the presently executed lease, attached to the agreement, at the commencement of the lease? Are there any problems with this approach?

   b. Frequently, a lease is drafted and executed before construction begins. This will raise problems, in addition to those mentioned above, such as the design and location of the demised premises, occupant mix, premature entrance of the lessee to do fixturing, satisfactory completion of the demised premises and the development, commencement and completion of construction, etc. See Williams, *Before the Shopping Center Opens: A Survival Manual for Developer and Tenant,* 2 # 2 Real Est. Rev. 15 (1972).

4. Is it really "fair" to make the lessee responsible for all repairs and replacements within the demised premises? See Halper, *Can You Find a Fair Lease?,* 14 Real Est. L.J. 99 (1985).

   a. If a leak in the roof of the building, which is the lessor's responsibility to repair or replace, causes the plaster on the ceiling of the demised premises to crack or the paint to peel, should the lessee be obligated to repair the ceiling? See generally Halper, *Repair Clauses in Store Leases,* 8 # 1 Real Est.Rev. 65 (1978).

   b. In addition to placing the responsibility for repairs and replacements within the demised premises on the lessee, the lease may provide that the lessee must pay for all utilities it uses, its proportionate share of the maintenance costs for common areas, and either all of the real estate taxes assessed against its portion of the development or, at minimum, a "tax-stop"—all real estate taxes over a described amount. The purpose of these provisions is to make the rental return to the lessor as "net" as possible. See Howard and Howard, *Suggestions for Negotiating a Net Lease,* 28 # 5 Prac. Law. 39 (1982); Cohen, *What to Look for When You Negotiate Net Leases,* 4 #5 Prac. Real Est. Law 22 (1988).

1. The more "fixed" the net income from a development, the better chance of obtaining suitable long term financing. See pages 689 to 697 supra.

2. See generally Goldstein, *Drafting a Tax Escalation Clause in a Lease*, 25 # 1 Prac. Law. 63 (1979).

c. See generally Fisher, *Insurance and Restoration Provisions in Commercial Leases*, 3 # 3 Prac. Real Est. Law. 73 (1987).

5. Why is a lessor concerned about a lessee's ability to assign the lessee's interest in the lease?

a. Does a provision permitting assignment to a third party with a credit rating equal to, or better than, the lessee, the third party being in the same business as the lessee, answer some of the lessor's concerns? The lease also could provide that, in other cases, the lessor would not unreasonably withhold consent.

1. What are the problems with this solution from the lessor's and lessee's standpoints?

2. If a lessor unreasonably withholds consent to a lessee's assignment of a lease, can the lessee terminate the lease rather than compel the lessor to consent or sue the lessor for damages suffered as a result of the lessor's action? See *Ringwood Associates, Ltd. v. Jack's of Route 23, Inc.*, 153 N.J.Super. 294, 379 A.2d 508 (1977), affirmed, 166 N.J. Super. 36, 398 A.2d 1315 (1979). But cf. *Carisi v. Wax*, 192 N.J.Super. 536, 471 A.2d 439 (1983).

3. In a minority of states, when the lessor's consent to an assignment of a lease is required, the lessor must have a good reason to refuse to consent to the assignment even though the lease does not provide that the lessor will not unreasonably withhold consent. See e.g., *Kendall v. Pestana, Inc.*, 40 Cal.3d 448, 709 P.2d 837, 220 Cal.Rptr. 818 (1985); *Campbell v. Westdahl*, 148 Ariz. 432, 715 P.2d 288 (1985); *Tucson Medical Center v. Zoslow*, 147 Ariz. 612, 712 P.2d 459 (App. 1985); *Newman v. Hinky Dinky Omaha-Lincoln, Inc.*, 229 Neb. 382, 427 N.W.2d 50 (1988).

b. See generally Todres and Lerner, *Assignment and Subletting of Leased Premises: The Unreasonable Withholding of Consent*, 5 Fordham Urb.L.J. 195 (1977); Kehr, *The Changing Law of Lease Assignments*, 11 # 2 Real Est. Rev. 54 (1981); Levin, *Withholding Consent to Assignment: The Changing Rights of the Commercial Landlord*, 30 De Paul L.Rev. 109 (1980); Pundeff, *The Anti–Assignment Clause and the Landlord's Legitimate Interests*, 11 Real Est. L.J. 146 (1982); Comment, *The Approval Clause in a Lease: Toward a Standard of Reasonableness*, 17 U.S.F.L.Rev. 681 (1983); Berkman, *Negotiable Issues in Commercial Subleasing*, 13 Real Est. L.J. 28 (1984); Kane, *Dealing With Assignment, Use, and Operating Covenant Lease Clauses*, 2 # 3 Prac. Real Est. Law. 45 (1986); Di Scivelo, *The Kendall Case: Momentum for a Reasonableness Standard in Lease Transfer Cases*, 1 Prob. & Prop. 32 (1987); Note, *Kendall v. Ernest Pestana: Standard of Reasonableness Applied to Commercial Assignment Clauses*, 18 Pac. L.J. 327 (1986).

c. If the lease prohibits assignment by the lessee and the lessee is a corporation whose only asset is the lease, can the prohibition against assignment be avoided by selling the stock of the lessee to the third party who wants to acquire the leasehold? See *Richardson v. La Rancherita La Jolla, Inc.,* 98 Cal.App.3d 73, 159 Cal.Rptr. 285 (1979). Cf. *Heflin v. Stiles,* 663 S.W.2d 131 (Tex.App.1983), in which the succession of one of two partners to the leasehold interest of the dissolved lessee partnership was held to violate the lease provision prohibiting assignment without the consent of the lessor.

6. Frequently, an office or apartment building will have a limited supply of underground parking. In this instance, the lease may provide the lessee with a certain number of designated spaces.

7. If the lessor supplies utilities—the lessor operates a generating plant for electricity for the development or a waste disposal facility or a central air conditioning facility—should the lessor be responsible for the quality, quantity and improvement of such services? If not the lessor, who is responsible? Cf. Note, *Landlord–Tenant: Should a Warranty of Fitness Be Implied in Commercial Leases?,* 13 Rutgers L.J. 91 (1981).

8. Must percentage rent be computed using gross sales? See Division III pages 782 to 783 supra. Would a lessee who operated a restaurant choose to use gross sales? If the lessee is a high-volume low-profit-margin retailer, is the use of gross sales appropriate? Both of the above-mentioned lessees might agree to a low percentage of gross sales and a high guaranteed minimum. The use of a base other than gross sales, however, might be more appropriate. See pages 1016 to 1019 infra.

9. The position taken in the above excerpt with respect to when a lease should be subordinated to a mortgage is that the "prime" leases should not be subordinate and the "local" leases should. The leases which are subordinate, however, contain a nondisturbance clause.

     a. Is a nondisturbance clause, which the mortgagee agrees to, consistent with the lease being subordinate to the mortgage? If the mortgagee forecloses and attempts to evict the lessee, what are the lessee's rights?

10. The bankruptcy of the lessee, sublessee or any guarantor, assignor or assignee of the lease should be an event of default under the lease and give the lessor the right to terminate the lease. Should a lessee agree to a clause providing that the institution of bankruptcy proceedings is an event of default? See *W.F.M. Restaurant, Inc. v. Austern,* 35 N.Y.2d 610, 364 N.Y.S.2d 500, 324 N.E.2d 149 (1974).

     a. Section 365 of the Bankruptcy Code prevents the automatic termination of a lease on the bankruptcy of the lessee despite the presence in the lease of a bankruptcy termination clause. Section 365, however, may not prevent the termination of the lease upon the bankruptcy of a guarantor, assignor, assignee or a sublessee. In addition, a bankruptcy termination clause may prevent the lessee from continuing in possession of the leased premises if the lessee's trustee in bankruptcy rejects the lease. See Halper, *Bankruptcy Cancellation Clauses Under the Bankruptcy Reform Act,* 9 # 2 Real Est.Rev. 75 (1979); Shanker, *The Treatment of Executory Contracts and Leases in the 1978 Bankruptcy Code,* 25 # 7 Prac.Law. 11 (1979); Fogel, *Executory Contracts and Unexpired Leases in the Bankruptcy Code,* 64 Minn.L.Rev. 341 (1980); Ehrlich, *The Assumption and Rejection of Unexpired Real Property Leases Under the Bankruptcy Code—A New Look,* 32 Buffalo L.Rev. 1 (1983); Leta and Jones, *Selected Bankruptcy Considerations in Drafting Real Estate Documents,* 1984 Utah L.Rev. 227; Chervin and Bindler, *What Rights Does the Commercial Landlord Have When the Tenant Goes Bankrupt?*, 2 # 2 Prac. Real Est. Law. 51 (1986).

11. See generally Anderson, *Negotiating and Drafting Leases for the Landlord*, 25 U. Miami L.Rev. 361 (1971); Smith and Lubell, *What Lenders Want In Leases*, 6 # 4 Real Est.Rev. 11 (1977); Kemph, *Drafting Commercial Leases*, 10 Real Est.L.J. 99 (1981); Olschwang, *Negotiating a Commercial Lease*, 12 # 4 Real Est.Rev. 74 (1983); Switzer, *Changing Lender Requirements for Commercial Leases*, 13 # 4 Real Est.Rev. 48 (1984); Halper, *People and Property: Insurance Clauses Revisited—Part II*, 14 # 3 Real Est.Rev. 76 (1984); Goldberg, *Reviewing Leases for a Small Shopping Center*, 57 N.Y.St.B.J. 28 (1985); McAndrews, *A Practical Guide to Reviewing a Commercial Lease*, 19 Real Prop., Prob. & Tr. J. 891 (1984); Auerbach, *A Transactional Approach to Lease Analysis*, 13 Hofstra L.Rev. 309 (1985); Davidson, *Leasing Commercial Real Estate: Issues and Negotiating*, 18 # 1 Real Est.Rev. 69 (1988); Saltz, *The Treatment of Insurable Risks in Commercial Leases*, 18 #4 Real Est. Rev. 56 (1989).

12. The leasing transaction between the developer and tenant is of great concern to the developer's financier. The financier regards the leases as the means of securing a return sufficient to pay the loan or loans the financier has made to the developer. As a result, the developer, in negotiating and drafting the leases, must keep in mind the financier's desires.

    a. The concerns of the mortgagee have been described as follows.

"The first question to which the mortgagee's attorney must obtain an answer is whether his client is making a so-called brick and mortar mortgage, in which the land improvements alone warrant the mortgage, or whether the consideration primarily motivating the lender is the credit rating of a strong tenant who has entered into a long-term lease, assuring a steady stream of rental checks the flow of which must be preserved at all costs. In the former case the mortgagee's attorney need only be sure that the lease contains no covenants detrimental to his client should it be forced to foreclose or should the mortgage lien be transferred to insurance proceeds, condemnation award, or some other fund. In the latter case he must also determine if the lessee is afforded any means of terminating the contract and escaping the rent obligation.

"The importance of distinguishing between the two types of loans is illustrated by the different treatments accorded condemnation clauses. Many leases provide that the lessee may terminate in the event of a taking of the demised premises 'in whole or in part.' Under such a clause any taking except possibly one so insignificant as to come under under the 'de minimis' rule will entitle the lessee to break his lease. When the lease contains no condemnation clause a partial taking neither terminates the lease nor, under the majority rule, operates to abate the rents. In a short-term lease to the neighborhood barber, grocer, or druggist a termination covenant will not trouble the mortgagee. On the other hand, if the mortgage is on a supermarket in an outlying section where the loan would not be made except for a long-term lease to a tenant with impeccable credit standing, the mortgagee will probably reject the loan unless the lease is amended so that it can be canceled only upon a taking that will substantially destroy the usefulness of the property to the tenant. Objection to this clause may be withdrawn, even when the credit of the lessee is of paramount importance, if the location and nature of the demised premises are such that the risk of condemnation is virtually nonexistent." * * * Anderson, *The Mortgagee Looks at the Commercial Lease,* 10 U. of Fla.L. Rev. 484 at 485–486 (1957).

   1. Should a mortgagee ever rely on foreclosure to repay its loan? Should the mortgagee's primary concern, in all cases, be to assure an income stream sufficient to repay its loan in normal course?

b. What does the mortgagee desire in insurance and condemnation clauses? How should the insurance proceeds and condemnation awards be allocated?

c. Are the provisions of a lease which govern the withholding or prepayment of rent and the assignment of the lessee's interest of any interest to the mortgagee? What would a mortgagee like to see in these provisions?

d. If the lease contains a promise by the lessor to make further improvements or additions at the request of the lessee, what are the concerns of the mortgagee?

"Some leases require the lessor to erect an addition on demand of the lessee or if the volume of sales exceeds an agreed-upon figure. They usually provide that a fixed or minimum guaranteed rent be increased and that the term be extended. To be acceptable such clauses should also provide that the lessee will pay any cost of the improvement in excess of a fixed figure when the increased rent is not based upon a percentage of cost, since no one can accurately predict future construction costs. Even then, unless the lessee is highly solvent and the mortgagee will commit itself to advance the additional construction money when needed, the lessor may find it impossible to obtain a satisfactory mortgage. Although the mortgagee may not covenant to finance the improvement, it may be compelled as a practical matter to do so. A suggested solution is for the lessee either to waive its right to the addition in the event that the lessor cannot obtain added financing on terms predetermined by the lease or for the lessee to agree to put up the cost itself, the money to be secured by a junior mortgage.

"Even with the tenant's agreement to lend the cost of the improvement, mortgagees may still object to the covenant to erect improvements unless the covenant terminates upon foreclosure, their position being that if they purchase at foreclosure they will not consent to mortgage the property for the cost of the improvements and will therefore still be required to advance the construction costs. Although they may sometimes relent for national chain stores and other preferred tenants, a lessor is foolish indeed who does not ascertain before he executes the lease whether such a clause will be acceptable to the proposed mortgagee.

"A lease providing that the tenant's right to demand an improvement will not survive foreclosure should not cause the tenant undue concern. He should merely include in the lease the right to cure defaults under the first mortgage. If carrying costs are less than rent, he can always prevent foreclosure at no cost to himself.

"Sometimes when shopping centers are contemplated the initial tenant will require that his landlord covenant to erect other buildings on neighboring land within a limited period of time. Such a provision is almost certain to prevent financing of the first building unless the others are constructed contemporaneously with it. Frequently this is impractical.

Nevertheless the tenant is not willing to pay the lease rental without the benefit of adjoining stores. In several instances this problem has been solved by inserting in the lease a covenant limiting the remedy for failure to erect other stores to a suit for damages against the original promoter and requiring him to post a performance bond or other adequate security, which may take the form of a second mortgage on the demised store and appurtenant parking areas." Anderson, *The Mortgagee Looks at the Commercial Lease,* supra at 492–493.

1. Does a mortgagee have any concerns with a lease that gives the lessee the right to remodel, replace, demolish or improve? If the lessee required such rights, how can the mortgagee's interest be protected?

e. At times, a lease will grant the lessee the right of exclusive operation. "Normally [exclusive operation clauses] present no very great hazard when the mortgage covers the entire area in which the restriction applies, since it will be no more to the lessor-mortgagor's interest to lose his tenant than to the mortgagee's. When the restriction includes property not encumbered by the mortgagee, as is frequently the case, there is always the danger that the unmortgaged property may fall into the hands of someone other than the owner of the demised premises, who may find it to his interest to lease to a competitor. A reasonably effective solution is to place of record a restriction senior to all mortgages, prohibiting the forbidden use. It is desirable, although not always essential, that the lessee's remedies be limited to injunctive relief and damages against the violator because of the possibility that a breach of the covenant may occur as the result of another tenant's act in violation of his covenant with the lessor. Frequently, however, no-competition clauses that go to unreasonable lengths are encountered. The following is an extreme example:

During the term of this lease and any extension thereof the Landlord shall not use or permit to be used any other part of the shopping center or any other property directly or indirectly owned or controlled by the Landlord within a radius of five thousand feet of the shopping center for the sale of food for consumption off premises. If this covenant be violated the Tenant without liability of forfeiture of its term, may withhold payment of any or all installments of rent accruing during such violation. The total amount of such rents thus withheld shall be deemed to be liquidated damages for such breach of covenant and not as a penalty therefor. In addition to this remedy[,] the Tenant shall be entitled to injunctive or other appropriate relief upon a breach of this covenant.

"Another one, though not so unreasonable, is a constant irritation to lenders:

The Lessor agrees that he will not lease, rent, or permit to be occupied for such operation or business as Super Market, Grocery Store, Meat Market, Poultry Market, Fish Market, Fruit Market, Vegetable Market, Produce Market, or any combination or portion thereof, any store or building on any land owned or acquired by Lessor or any in which he is interested within 500–ft. of any part of the land covered by or set forth in this lease during the term of this lease and any extensions thereof.

"There is no justification for either of these covenants. The tenant is injured just as much by a competitor on someone else's land as his landlord's, if it is within the forbidden area. The inclusion of the first covenant makes it impossible to obtain an institutional mortgage without an amendment to the lease, and many mortgagees will not go along with the second. The lessee will receive ample protection and the lessor can finance the building if the no-competition clause applies only to specific property owned by the lessor, and if the lease requires that a restrictive covenant be recorded and limits the remedy to injunctive relief. An action for damages is permissible if it is expressly made inapplicable to those claiming by, through, or under the mortgage. * * *" Anderson, *The Mortgagee Looks at the Commercial Lease,* supra at 496–498.

f. A fairly recent innovation which helps to give a mortgagee assurance of a continuing rent flow is lease guarantee insurance. An insurance company offering this type of insurance, for a premium based on a percentage of the aggregate rent to be guaranteed, will issue to the lessor a noncancelable policy having a minimum term of five years and a maximum of the term of the lease or twenty years whichever is less. The policy usually will guarantee all or a percentage of the monthly rent called for in a lease.

a. THE PERCENTAGE LEASE

Frequently, a lease will define the rent which the tenant is obligated to pay as a fixed minimum rent and an additional amount equal to the amount by which a percentage of the tenant's gross receipts, income, net income, taxable income or some other base amount exceeds the minimum rent. The computation of the amount payable under a percentage rent clause can become a matter of controversy between the tenant and the developer if the method of computing the percentage rent is not clearly set out. A percentage rent clause with low or no minimum rent raises the concern that a tenant might decide to terminate business on the leased premises since without the operation of a business the percentage rent clause is meaningless.

RIVER VIEW ASSOCIATES v. SHERATON CORP. OF AMERICA

Court of Appeals of New York, 1970.
27 N.Y.2d 718, 314 N.Y.S.2d 181, 262 N.E.2d 416.

* * * Plaintiff was the fee owner of the Sheraton Motor Inn, located at 12th Avenue and 42nd Street in the City of New York, and, on July 29, 1964, had executed a net lease of said motor inn to Inverurie Corporation, which had thereupon assigned said lease to Hudson Sheraton Corporation (tenant), a wholly-owned subsidiary of defendant. It sought to recover upon a guarantee executed by defendant, which guaranteed the performance of the tenant's obligations for the first 12 years of the initial 21–year term of the lease, alleging that the tenant had, during the first year of the lease, made a net profit in excess of $1,030,000 and, accordingly, owed it overage rent under a

provision in the lease for an annual fixed rent of $670,000 plus a sum equal to 27½% of the tenant's net profit during the lease year in excess of $1,030,000. Defendant alleged that the tenant's net profit for the year involved was less than $1,030,000. The disagreement between the parties arose out of the manner in which each construed provisions in the lease relating to the meaning and method of ascertaining the tenant's net profit. The Appellate Division found that in calculating its net profit, the tenant had improperly deducted an item consisting of interest paid by it on a leasehold mortgage and a loan made to it by defendant in connection with its purchase of the leasehold and an item consisting of promotional expenses, but had properly deducted an item consisting of the cost to it of utility services and insurance and an item consisting of taxes and license fees, and that, with the deduction of the latter items, the net profit realized by it for the year involved, as said term was used in the lease, was less than the minimum which would give rise to a claim by plaintiff for overage or additional rent.

* * *

Order affirmed, with costs.

Concur: Chief Judge FULD and Judges BURKE, BERGAN and GIBSON, Judge SCILEPPI dissents and votes to reverse in the following opinion in which Judges BREITEL and JASEN concur.

SCILEPPI, J. (dissenting). * * * The relevant sections with respect to this "overage rent" provision are 10.01 and 13.02. They provide in relevant part:

"Section 13.01. If the net profit of Tenant in the operation of the leased premises shall exceed $1,030,000 in any lease year in the initial term * * * Tenant shall pay to Landlord, as additional rent ('Overage Rent') for that lease year, 27½% of such excess.

"Section 13.02. The words 'net profit,' as used in this Article, shall mean the net profit in a given lease year derived from the operation by Tenant of the leased premises, as ascertained through the use of standard accounting practices, as hereinafter defined, but (a) before deducting (i) the fixed net rent and *additional rent reserved in this lease* for that lease year" (emphasis added).

The entire controversy herein revolves about the phrase "additional rent reserved in this lease".

The landlord argues, and the trial court found, that the "net profit" statement submitted by the defendant indicating $745,000 as the net profit, was more than $725,000 understated by virtue of improper deductions made by the defendant. Accordingly, the trial court found: "Based upon the foregoing, Hudson's net profit is computed to be $1,470,422.37; and the overage rent due, on the basis of 27½% of said net profit above $1,030,000, amounts to $121,116.15, for which judgment is hereby given to the plaintiff."

As the trial court stated, its conclusion was reached by "a simple application of a comparatively few sections of the lease". Section 1.01

(subd. [A], par. [iv]) defines additional rent as: "All other sums and charges required to be paid by Tenant under the terms of this lease, which shall constitute, and are sometimes hereinafter referred to as 'additional rent.'" Thus, the trial court, accepting the landlord's construction of the lease, found that the sums and charges required to be paid by the tenant under the terms of the lease [6] were items of "additional rent reserved in this lease" and, therefore, could not be deducted in computing the tenant's "net profit".

The defendant argues, however, that the term "additional rent" was never intended to include such charges, for to do so would change "net profit" to "gross revenue" as the base in computing the percentage rent due. The defendant contends, and a majority of the Appellate Division agreed, that the phrase in section 13.02 as to the non-deductability of "additional rent reserved in this lease" was only a provision precluding deduction of "overage rent" in arriving at the amount of overage rent due, i.e., the tenant could not determine its overage rent in the first instance, then deduct that sum from net profit to arrive at a lower base for overage rent purposes.[7]

Although the defendant has argued persuasively that to disallow the many deductions herein would render the phrase "net profit" meaningless, we are unable to accept defendant's position, for to allow those deductions under the unambiguous terms of this lease would be tantamount to making a new agreement for the parties. As we stated in Black v. General Wiper Supply Co. (305 N.Y. 386, 394, 113 N.E.2d 528): "It may be that, if the parties were to contract today, they might agree [otherwise.] * * * We may not, however, make a new bargain for them. Our function is limited to construction of the agreement that the parties actually made".

It is of singular importance that section 13.02 provides that, standard accounting practices notwithstanding, net profit is to be computed "before deducting (i) the fixed net rent and additional rent reserved *in this lease*" (emphasis added). Of course, if the parties had used the phrase "additional rent" or "additional rent reserved *in this article*" then by looking to the intention of the parties, it would be possible to accept the defendant's construction of equating additional rent with the phrase "Overage Rent" found in section 13.01. However, by using "additional rent reserved in this lease", only one reasonable construction arises—"All * * * sums and charges required to be paid by Tenant under the terms of this lease * * * shall constitute * * *

---

6. These charges included real estate taxes ($282,395.35), gross receipts taxes ($9,313.13), water taxes ($6,365.84), insurance ($27,892.55), utility charges ($213,787.63) and licenses ($4,999.30).

7. The majority of the Appellate Division found, however, that the net profit statement submitted by the defendant was understated by almost $180,000 due to the improper deductions of interest on a leasehold mortgage, a loan from the parent company and certain promotional expenses. When adding these items to net profit, however, the resulting figure is still far less than the $1,030,000 overage base and thus defendant has not cross-appealed from the Appellate Division's determinations as to these items.

'additional rent' " (§ 1.01, subd. [A], par. [iv]), and thus, under section 13.02, are not to be deducted in computing net profit.

Accordingly, the order of the Appellate Division should be reversed and the judgment of the Supreme Court, New York County, reinstated.

* * *

NOTE

1. Despite the reasoning of the minority in the above case, the majority held that the phrase "additional rent reserved in this lease," for the purpose of computing the percentage rent, did not include the utility charges, insurance premiums, real estate and gross receipts taxes and license fees, and therefore, these items could be deducted from the lessee's gross receipts in arriving at net profit.

a. Is this result consistent with the terms of the lease? The percentage rent clauses prohibited the deduction of "additional rent reserved in this lease," and the lease defined the above listed expenses as items of additional rent.

1. If the parties to the lease, at the time of its drafting and execution, had intended the reference to additional rent in the clause defining net profit to mean only the overage rent, they could have specifically said so.

b. Why does the majority in the above case include only the overage rent as additional rent when computing the overage rent?

1. Are there any ambiguities in the description of the computation of overage rent contained in the lease?

a. If the lessee cannot deduct the expenses at issue when computing the percentage rent, the base for computing the percentage rent is other than net profit.

1. The base for computing the percentage rent, however, is other than net profit if the fixed net rent is not deducted, and the majority, minority and the lessee all agree that it cannot be deducted.

b. Why did the lease provide that the lessee's obligation to pay the various expenses listed above is an obligation to pay additional rent? See pages 1007 to 1008 supra.

c. If the minority's determination of net profit for the purpose of computing the percentage rent is correct, is the percentage rent then based on gross revenues as the defendant asserted?

1. What can the lessee deduct from gross receipts under the minority interpretation?

2. How should the lessor have drafted provisions 13.01 and 13.02 to make clear the result which it desired? Should the lessor have used the term net profit in 13.01?

A GUIDE TO PROBLEMS IN SHOPPING CENTER LEASES

Frank E. Colbourn
29 Brooklyn Law Review 56 (1962).
[footnotes omitted]

* * *

Rent

* * *

The primary reason for the spreading use of "percentage" leases is lessor's uncertainty regarding the future buying power of money. If there is inflation, a lessor who ties up his property for a long term at a fixed dollar rent will have declining income in terms of real buying power. Such a landlord would be better advised to negotiate leases for short terms only, in anticipation of renewals at rentals which would increase as the real value of money fell. However, because of the heavy costs of setting up and commencing operation in a large new shopping center location (often as much or more than the cost of landlord's building) lessees will not undertake a new location unless assured of a term adequate to reasonably write-off lessee's investment. Percentage leases are attractive to lessees as well as to lessors; a lessee thereby gains low fixed charges if business declines or during deflation. If business is good the average lessee anticipates he can afford to pay increased rent, if the rental market justifies it also.

* * *

Because the lessor's return will, to some extent, depend on the lessee's energy in using the demised premises, some courts have implied covenants to occupy and use the property; or to [use] reasonable diligence to operate the business in a manner reasonably calculated to produce profits or receipts. * * *

Therefore, in percentage rent leases, the lessee's right to assign or sublet or vacate should be clearly spelled out or the courts may infer a covenant against assignment or against subletting the leasehold without the consent of the lessor.

Because of the indefiniteness of a percentage rent based on lessee's "profits", the typical lease of this type is geared to the lessee's "gross sales" or "receipts from sales" and "services" in the demised premises and, perhaps, in other premises, too. All items to be included should be set out at least in a general way for the lessor's protection, and all items to be excluded should be set out at least in a general way for the lessee's protection. Commonly excluded items, on which no percentage rent is paid, include:

1. Receipts by customers' special service units such as pay toilets, pay phones, lockers, weighing machines, stamp machines, where they are not always an integral profit-making part of lessee's business but are mere conveniences to draw customers for the lessee's real business.

2. Limited areas sub-let to licensees or to concessionaires which enhance the draw or flow of customers to the main operation of the lessee. Substantial lessees are reluctant to be responsible for certifying to any lessor as accurate the sales reported to the lessee by subtenants.

3. Sales made outside of the demised premises.

4. Taxes on gross receipts whether or not called sales taxes.

5. Merchandise exchanged, refunds.

6. Merchandise transferred to other stores of the lessee or to lessee's warehouse.

The "key" to successful percentage rent article operation is to take considerable care in defining the terms used in it when it is drafted.

Commonly all sales whether cash or credit are included in the bases for computation of percentage rent. Conversely, often a cafeteria operated in leased premises for the sole use of the lessee's employees may be excluded from the base on the grounds it is nonprofit making; or, if profit making, that it is merely incidental to the lessee's main business from which lessee and lessor each must expect to obtain their real return.

Reliable figures are essential to the functioning of a percentage rent arrangement; these are usually obtained by:

1. Lessee's periodic reports to the lessor (e.g., monthly or yearly) certified as correct by a C.P.A., lessee's accountant, or an officer of the lessee, depending on the character of the lessee.

2. Lessor's right to inspect the lessee's records during stated times at places where the lessee is obligated in the lease to produce his sales and related records. This right is obviously important to obtain, although rarely used in practice. Undoubtedly, some types of fraud or unfair advantages taken by unscrupulous lessees under percentage rent leases can only be detected through long and systematic independent examination of the lessee's books and records.

Percentage leases sometimes provide for continuous operation of the demised premises for the lessee's retail business in order that there may be sales on which percentage rent may be computed. However, a lessee will usually insist that there be no duty to operate, especially if their business becomes unprofitable or whenever they are forced out of business for conditions beyond their control. Lessees often are willing to agree to cancel their lease and surrender the premises to the lessor if they discontinue business in the demised premises, or open another store within a certain distance, etc. * * *

The higher the minimum rent stated in a given lease, the less justification or need is there for the lessor attempting to exact a covenant to operate.

The cases appear to support the rule which now seems well settled, that where a real or substantial minimum rent is payable by the lessee, in the absence of a specific covenant to operate a business in the leased premises, the courts will not [imply a] covenant to operate against the lessee or in the lessor's behalf.

 * * * [I]mplied covenants are not favored in the law; * * * if a covenant is to be implied, the implication must arise:

a. From the language used by the parties; or

b. Be indispensable to effectuate the intention of the parties;

c. Be so clearly within the contemplation of the parties that they deemed it unnecessary to express it;

d. Where it can be rightfully assumed that it would have been made if attention had been called to it;

e. Where the subject has not been completely covered by the contract; and

f. Where it is justified by legal necessity. * * *

Where no minimum, or a nominal minimum, rent is required by a lease, several courts have readily * * * implied [a] promise by the lessee to operate the premises and have imposed such a duty.

 * * *

Often where a lessee under a percentage lease expends its own funds to enhance the demised premises in an agreed way, the lessor and lessee agree that the lessee may withhold any percentage rent otherwise due the lessor until the lessee's costs of such improvement have been recovered. If the lease provides for any extension periods, it is desirable for the lessee's protection to spell out that this right to withhold percentage rent applies to percentage rent during any optional period if full recovery has not been had during the basic term of the lease. * * *

Where a percentage rent lease permits the lessee to sublet the demised premises, it is common practice to provide that in addition to the minimum rent, if any, payable to the lessor, a further sum in lieu of percentage rent will be paid to the lessor. This further sum is often $\frac{1}{3}$ of the percentage rent payments made during the prior three years or $\frac{1}{5}$ of such payments made during the prior five years, or some similarly ascertained figure. * * *

Unless care is taken in drafting what elements will be included in the sales on which percentage rent is paid, a tenant who sublets may be obligated to pay more rent than he anticipated or more than he paid while doing business himself. * * *

Wherever a lessee under a percentage lease having a minimum rent must pay any other sums to the lessor as additional rent (e.g. fees for parking area maintenance, or for air-conditioning or heating, etc.), it is to the lessee's advantage that all such sums be identified in the lease as a component of the "minimum rent," because where the percentage rent is worded in the common fashion "Should ___% of tenants' gross sales as herein defined exceed the minimum rent payable hereunder for the same period" the lessee gets full allowance for all sums paid and the sales volume at which he must commence paying percentage rent is correspondingly higher and less likely to be reached.

* * *

Percentage rents are usually computed on gross sales. It is obvious, due to disputes regarding what income and expense items are to be included, that a percentage of "net profits" or "net income" before or after taxes has built-in pitfalls making it rarely advisable.

* * *

NOTE

1. Gross sales do not usually include merchandise transferred by the lessee to its other stores and back to its warehouse. How can the lessor be protected against the lessee reducing its sales by directing its customers to its other store locations and then transferring the desired merchandise to other locations? Can any sales which originate with the lessee be included in gross sales? How does the lessor know what sales originate with the lessee?

2. If a percentage lease is being drafted, should the lessor rely on a court to imply a business operation provision rather than making it expressly part of the lease? See *Mercury Inv. Co. v. F.W. Woolworth Co.,* 706 P.2d 523 (Okla. 1985).

   a. A business operation provision is often a source of conflict between the lessor and lessee in the drafting and negotiation of a lease. The lessee does not want to be obligated to operate at an unprofitable location. It probably would prefer to pay a fixed rent and leave the location vacant rather than compound its losses by the overhead involved in operating its business.

   1. Is a minimum term of operation coupled with an option in the lessor to terminate the lease in the event the lessee ceases business operations after the minimum term a satisfactory compromise?

   b. See generally Thigpen, *Good Faith Performance Under Percentage Leases,* 51 Miss.L.J. 315 (1981); Comment, *Implied Covenants of Continuous Operation in Commercial Lease Settings,* 25 Ariz.L.Rev. 792 (1983); Kane, *Dealing With Assignment, Use, and Operating Covenant Lease Clauses,* 2 # 3 Prac. Real Est. Law. 45 (1986); Fishman, *What Counsel Must Know About Continuous Use Covenants,* 3 # 2 Prac. Real Est. Law. 35 (1987).

3. If a lessee is obligated to improve the leased premises, it may request a provision in the lease allowing it to "recapture" the cost of the improvements it makes out of the percentage rent. Simply stated, the lessee would like to deduct the cost of the improvements from the percentage rent which it is obligated to pay under the lease.

   a. Will the cost of the improvements be considered income to the lessor, if the lessor permits the lessee to recapture the cost out of the percentage rent? See pages 618 to 619 supra, and page 1039 infra; Section 109 of the Internal Revenue Code and Reg. Sec. 1.109–1(a).

   b. During the period in which the lessee recaptures the cost of the improvements out of the percentage rent, who depreciates the improvements for income tax purposes?

   c. Does a provision which allows the lessee to reduce the base amount for the computation of the percentage rent by an amount equal to the depreciation of the improvements for the period for which the percentage rent is being computed, cause the lessor and lessee any less problems?

1.   If depreciation for these purposes is computed using the 200% declining balance method and a fairly short useful life, is the lessee's position much worse than if it simply recaptured the cost of the improvements out of the percentage rent it owed?

d.   Can this problem be solved more simply by obligating the lessor to buy the leasehold improvements from the lessee at the termination of the lease for a price equal to the improvements' cost less the depreciation taken by the lessee prior to the termination of the lease? If this method is used, will the lessee recover all of its cost for the improvements?

e.   See generally Dalessio and Shenkman, *Improvements to Leased Property: Maximizing the Tax Benefits Regardless of Who Makes Them,* 13 Tax'n Law. 246 (1985).

4.   If the lease allows the lessee to sublet portions of the leased premises, how should a sublease be taken account of in the percentage rent provisions?

a.   The sales of sublessees or the rent received from sublessees by the lessee could be included in the base, or the lessor could extract, for the privilege of subletting, a payment by the lessee of a percentage of the total percentage rent paid by the lessee during a defined period prior to the date of the sublease, or a combination of the foregoing.

1.   What are the advantages and disadvantages of the above suggestions from the standpoint of the lessee and lessor?

5.   See generally Blair, *Are Percentage Rents Unfair to Tenants?,* 7 # 4 Real Est.Rev. 42 (1978); Schloss, *Inflation–Proofing Retail Investments With Percentage Leases,* 7 # 4 Real Est.Rev. 36 (1978).

b.   RESTRICTIVE COVENANTS

At times, both the developer and the tenants want the development to contain complementary rather than competitive tenants. This desire is often fulfilled by restrictive covenants in the tenants' leases. Restrictive covenants usually prohibit the developer's leasing to competitive tenants and limit the tenant's activities to those which do not compete with other tenants. A number of problems are involved in drafting restrictive covenants. The problems include: what area is covered; what type of businesses are prohibited; what businesses may the tenant engage in; what constitutes a violation of the provisions; and what are the remedies in the event a violation occurs. Lastly, on a more general level there is a question whether a restrictive covenant constitutes an unreasonable restraint of trade or is unenforceable for a variety of other similar reasons.

NOTE:

LESSOR'S COVENANTS RESTRICTING COMPETITION: DRAFTING PROBLEMS

63 Harvard Law Review 1400 (1950).
[footnotes omitted]

*   *   *

The problems involved in drafting such a covenant can, perhaps, best be illustrated by considering a hypothetical situation. Suppose a client tells his attorney that he wishes to lease for five years a store in a new development called Sunshine Brook, that he is willing to use the lessor's form lease, but, in view of the considerable risk which this new venture involves, is anxious to include an ironclad clause—to which the lessor is amenable—giving him the exclusive right to carry on a "modern drug store" in the sixteen square blocks of the development. In response to questions by his attorney, the client reveals that he has agreed to increase the monthly rent of $150 by $75 in return for the exclusive right, and that a large part of his business consists not only of medicines, but also of fountain drinks, ice cream, cosmetics and other articles. The attorney investigates, finds that the lessor owns most of the property in the development and all of the property between D and E streets on either side of Sunshine Avenue, in the center of the suburb (the only area presently zoned for business use in the development), and prepares the following draft:

Section 23. (a) Lessor covenants that no other property owned by lessor in "Sunshine Brook Business Block" between D and E Streets on both sides of Sunshine Avenue, shall be used, or leased, or allowed to be used, during the term of this lease, or any renewal thereof, for the sale of any one or more of the following items: fountain drinks, ice cream, candy, salted nuts, light lunches, medicines, patent medicines, drugs, bandages, cigars, cigarettes, pipe tobacco, pipes, cigarette lighters, cosmetics, soap and other soap products, greeting cards, stationery and stationery supplies, ink, fountain pens, school supplies, toothpaste, toothpowder, toothbrushes, men's shaving soaps, talcum powder, razors, razorblades, electric razors, combs, hair brushes, and other men's toilet goods.

(b) In the event of a breach of the covenant specified in paragraph (a), lessee is entitled (i) to terminate this lease; (ii) to enforce the covenant specifically; (iii) to recover as liquidated damages $90 per month for every month such breach continues.

(c) It is the intention of the parties hereto that the covenant specified in paragraph (a) of this Section 23 is to inure to the benefit of lessee, his heirs, executors, administrators, assigns and sublessees, and to bind lessor, his heirs, executors, administrators, assigns and grantees.

The covenant prepared for the new druggist in the Sunshine Brook Development is in many ways imperfect; it is the purpose of this Note to examine in detail the problems that may arise under any covenant restricting competition, and to illustrate these problems by showing the difficulties that could have been avoided in this particular case by more careful drafting.

Validity.—Although the validity of these restrictive covenants is seldom discussed in the cases, * * * courts should and probably would apply the same rules as those applied to other contracts in restraint of trade. Thus, the covenant probably cannot be a "naked" restraint of trade, but must be a beneficial part of some other relationship between the parties which is substantial enough to be worthy of judicial protection—usually, the lease.

* * *

A second and more difficult requirement imposed by the common law is that the covenant must be reasonable, as to area covered, businesses prohibited, and duration. * * * Duration usually presents no serious problem, since the restriction is tied to a lease which ordinarily will continue only for a short, definite period. The five-year period in our hypothetical case is clearly not too long.

* * *

Area Covered.—In determining whether the geographical area encompassed by the restriction is "reasonable" the courts have looked to both the protection required by the lessee in view of his trading area and the harm to the public which might result from an over-extended restriction. A court should measure harm to the public not only by the square mileage of the restriction but also by the utility of the activity involved, and the amount and location of restricted property presently owned by the lessor. * * *

It is clear that the Sunshine Brook covenant as now written (covering one block) would be upheld. But the cases also indicate that the attorney could have secured greater protection for his client by adding a clause that would cover the entire development—which would normally be his trading area—even though most of the property in that development is owned by the lessor. For example, insert at line 3 after "Avenue":

or any property owned by lessor in Sunshine Brook Development if it is hereafter zoned or used for business purposes.

The use of this new clause would involve the slight additional risk that the entire restriction might be struck down. A court could hardly avoid this problem by narrow construction, but it might be willing, if the clause was not so broadly phrased as to have an *in terrorem* effect on the lessor, to apply the so-called blue-pencil rule—literally striking out those descriptive portions of the area which are invalid—particularly if the parties' intention to allow severance was clearly expressed. In view of the possibility that an area on the fringe of the development might be zoned for business purposes, and that a court might then consider the restriction unreasonable, the following clause might be added at line 21 after "grantees":

The parties hereto agree that if any part of this covenant is for any reason declared void and of no effect, the rest of the covenant specified in this Section 23 shall continue in force; but nothing contained in the last clause shall be construed to excuse any breach of the covenant on the part of lessor.

Judicial hostility to restraints of trade has also led to narrow construction of the words used to define the area of the restraint. For example, "adjoining" has been held in England to mean only that property physically touching the demised premises, and the phrase "on the other corners" has been held by an American court not to include a building next door, which was not on the corner. These difficulties could be avoided in the hypothetical case by specifically referring to the plat of Sunshine Brook, and by marking on it the exact area presently restricted. Furthermore, the clause as presently worded would probably be construed as not including any property—even though in the development—which the lessor acquired after the execution of the lease. This could be met by adding the phrase, "now or hereafter" at line 1 after "property" and at the appropriate place (after "property") in the clause extending the restriction to the entire development.

* * *

Businesses Prohibited.—In determining whether the businesses specified in the covenant are reasonably prohibited, the courts seem to have looked solely to their competitive effect on the lessee's trade and have enforced covenants operating in sweeping categories. No case has been found in which a court struck down an entire restrictive covenant on the ground that the prohibition was too broad; but a New Jersey court has indicated that it would refuse to protect those items which constitute only a small percentage of the covenantee's business. In view of the lack of precedents and the general policy against any undue restraint of trade, it may well be that further judicial restrictions would be imposed were the case to present itself. Thus, an overelaborated list, which included unimportant items, might create some risk of invalidating the whole covenant. The severability clause already inserted supplies some protection. But a court might also react to such a list by narrowly defining the area in which the covenant may be effective, or by construing the list as all-inclusive, or as typifying the articles prohibited, regardless of words to the contrary. The list also presents serious practical difficulties: in view of the broad coverage attempted, it could breed disputes and eventually lead to unwelcome litigation; the numerous exclusive rights purportedly granted the druggist might engender ill will among the residents of Sunshine Brook.

* * *

One way of handling this problem would be to incorporate in the covenant the percentage test of the New Jersey court. Thus, the draftsman could provide that the restriction would apply only if the druggist's sales of the particular article during a fixed period equalled a certain percentage of his total gross sales. If the percentage were fixed high enough, it might avoid ill will. But it would be difficult to draft such a clause in terms which would provide exactly for all business contingencies. Unless the druggist kept detailed records, proof could be expensive. Moreover, the scope of such a restriction would vary with the druggist's business, and the people affected by it would seldom know where they stood.

A second way of handling the businesses prohibited would be to drop the list entirely and refer to "a modern drug store" instead. But this ambiguous term would create constructional difficulties. * * *

The better solution for our druggist might be to combine a specific list and a generic term. The restriction should be clearly worded so as to avoid constructional difficulties; it should be carefully limited so as to avoid constructional temptations. A way of doing this would be to protect the druggist against any other modern drug stores, against stores selling the same lines of goods as modern drug stores, and against competition by anyone in the three or four major items which are vital to his business. Delete from "for" at line 4 to "goods" at line 12, and substitute the following:

for any of the following retail trades or businesses: (1) a modern drug store; or, without intending to limit or define (a)(1), (2) any store substantially competitive therewith (whether or not designated "drug store"); or, without intending to limit or define (a)(1) or (a)(2), (3) any retail store selling or dealing in any one or more of the following articles (regardless of whether the sale of such articles by such store is incidental to that store's business or not: (i) medicines, including, but not limited to, the compounding and/or commercial sale thereof according to the prescriptions of physicians, drugs, patent medicines, and medical and pharmaceutical supplies; (ii) ice cream and fountain drinks (consumed on the premises) including, but not limited to, ice cream and milk drinks, charged water and drinks made of charged water, and fruit drinks; (iii) cosmetics, including, but not limited to, skin lotions and salves, hair oil and dressings, lipsticks, facial powder and other beauty aids, and other powders, salves, lotions, and polishes classified as cosmetics in the trade.

What Constitutes Violation by the Original Covenantor.—Two formulae are utilized to define the lessor's obligation, one a statement that the lessee has an "exclusive right," the other, and apparently more commonly used one, a promise by the lessor. The result of these two formulae would be the same, provided that the lessor's promise, in terms, refers to using and allowing to be used as well as mere letting, as is the case in our hypothetical covenant (line 3). If letting was all that was specified in the covenant, some American courts have followed the English rules, under which the lessor—and any successor to him—may compete himself, and is not liable if a subsequent tenant of burdened land competes, unless the lessor has expressly consented to such competition. Other American courts have taken the view that the lessor is liable if a subsequent tenant competes but that the lessor—and any successor to his title—may compete himself. Finally, in recent years, an increasing number of American courts have held that a prohibition simply against letting would have the same effect as one expressly prohibiting "using" or "allowing to be used" as well; thus, the landlord would be liable when he himself competes, when he knowingly fails to take action against a tenant who competes, and when he has previously disabled himself from taking such action.

A second difficulty is, however, not dealt with by the covenant as now drawn. Some cases have held that the mere omission of a restrictive covenant from the subsequent lease does not constitute a prohibited letting by the lessor and that the covenantee must wait for competition in breach of that part of his covenant covering user. There seems to be no reason why a court would not enforce a clause requiring restrictive covenants to be included in subsequent leases; in any event, a prudent lessor would ordinarily include such restrictions so that the second lessee would be required to indemnify the lessor in the event of a breach of the first covenant.

The Sunshine Brook covenant as now drawn also fails to take possible advantage of restrictive covenants in prior leases which might benefit the druggist. Of course, the lease will not affect the estates of prior lessees—which may seriously reduce the protection for which the druggist is bargaining—but, even without a specific provision in the restrictive agreement, the lessor might be required to enforce earlier covenants.

These two omissions might be cured by adding the following clause at line 13 after "(b)":

Lessor covenants that he will expressly include in any subsequent lease, or deed, a covenant binding subsequent lessees, or purchasers, their heirs, executors, administrators and assigns, in the same manner and to the same extent that lessor is bound by the covenant contained in this Section 23 of the lease; and a failure to include such a restrictive covenant in such deed or lease hereafter executed by lessor shall constitute a breach of the covenant contained in this Section 23 of the lease. Lessor further covenants that he will enforce any and all restrictions (in leases heretofore or hereafter made by him) on any one or more of the stores or businesses specified in paragraph (a) of this Section 23.

The Running of the Burden and Benefit.—Most courts have held—over the opposition of some theorists—that a lessor's covenant restricting competitive use of his other land, if it benefits the business of the covenantee but does not "physically" improve the covenantee's leasehold, is not a real covenant running with the land because it does not "touch and concern" the leasehold. * * * [H]owever, an agreement which only improved the value of the business could run as an equitable servitude if it was intended to. It is safer, as in the Sunshine Brook Covenant, not to rely on the presumption that such servitudes are intended to run. (Lines 17–21 of the draft covenant.)

* * *

The servitude can run in favor of any taker, regardless of "privity of estate," but a jurisdiction which views the servitudes as a contract protected in equity rather than as an equitable interest in land ("equitable easement") might require that the taker have notice of the servitude at the time of the taking. * * *

The servitude will also burden any subsequent taker of that property, affected by the covenant, which the lessor owns at the time of the letting, but only if the taker had notice of the restriction. Recordation of the lease, or perhaps of only the covenant itself, might assure constructive notice; it would probably be necessary to record separately under each piece of burdened property. It might not be possible, however, to enforce the covenant against a subsequent taker of after-acquired property if the jurisdiction adopts the text writers' view that an equitable servitude is an equitable easement which must be created at the time of the lease. * * *

Some of the difficulties caused by the equitable servitude theory may be cured by the new clause requiring the lessor to insert a restrictive covenant in any subsequent lease or deed. Such a covenant, if inserted, would serve as notice to the subsequent taker. Furthermore, the original covenantee may be able to enforce the second covenant as a third party beneficiary, particularly where, as here, the second covenant was inserted to satisfy the lessor's obligation to the original covenantee.

* * *

Remedies.—Assuming that there has been a violation of the restrictive covenant, the covenantee may have several remedies available. He can treat the lease as terminated by giving notice and vacating, * * * or can continue to pay rent under the lease, expressly retaining, in either event, whatever right to damages he may have. * * * The covenantee may also be able to sue a subsequent vendee or lessee for damages, either on the theory that the covenantee is a third party beneficiary where a restrictive covenant included in a subsequent deed or lease has been violated, or, conceivably, on a tort theory where the third party has knowingly induced the covenantor to break his contract. Finally, the covenantee can obtain an injunction, or a declaratory judgment, to prevent the lessor from letting or selling without the agreed restrictive covenant, or from competing himself. He can also obtain injunctive relief against subsequent lessees and purchasers with notice of the restriction. In addition to an injunction against the prohibited act, the covenantee can obtain damages from the lessor for the period of the breach.

The main difficulty is that American courts are not in agreement as to a proper measure of damages, in the absence of a provision for liquidated damages. * * *

In the Sunshine Brook covenant an attempt has been made to avoid the need for proving damages by including a liquidated damages clause. As now drafted the clause fails to reserve the lessee's alternate remedies; under analogous clauses, older courts have denied equitable relief on the ground that the contract granted the promisor an option to perform or pay damages. Furthermore, the clause might be invalidated as a penalty because for some breaches the $90.00 would be unreasonable. A limitation on liquidated damages, like the limitation on businesses prohibited, would also help avoid the danger that, as a result of the numerous extensions of the covenant, a court would strike down the combination as invalid even though the parts, taken separately, would be upheld. Delete from "to recover" at line 15 to "continues" at line 16, and substitute the following:

To recover $90.00 per month (but no more than $90.00 in any month without regard to the number of breaches or persons liable) for every month of such breach as liquidated damages unless lessor can show that ten (10) percent of the gross sales of the prohibited article or articles by competitor is less than $90.00, in which event such ten (10) percent shall be the liquidated damages; but nothing herein contained shall be construed to deprive lessee of any other remedy available to him at law or in equity.

As now drafted the covenant is adapted to a particular fact situation, and is not intended to be a model or standard. Since it was drawn exclusively from the lessee's point of view, few lessors would agree to all the burdens which it now imposes. The covenant might, for example, hinder the later financing of other property in the development.

* * *

NOTE

1. Will a mortgagee of the lessor accept a restrictive covenant which gives the lessee the remedy of terminating the lease in the event the covenant is breached? See pages 1015 to 1016 supra.

   a. Does the lessee need the remedy of terminating the lease? Can the purpose of the restrictive covenant be met by giving the lessee the ability to enjoin the lessor, any other lessee and any assignee? What must be done in order for the lessee to be able to enjoin breaches of the restrictive covenant?

2. How should the area covered by the restrictive covenant be described in a lease of a store in a shopping plaza, in a lease of an office in an office building, or in a lease of retail space in an apartment complex?

   a. What are the competing concerns of the lessor and lessee? How can they be resolved? The area covered by the restrictive covenant must be limited to that area which is reasonable in the context of the relationship between the lessor and lessee, and in the interest of the public.

   b. In *Jacobs Pharmacy Co., Inc. v. Richard & Associates, Inc.*, 229 Ga. 156, 189 S.E.2d 853 (1972), Jacobs Pharmacy leased space for a drug store from Richard & Associates. The lease prohibited the lessor from leasing any store for use as a drug store "in the shopping center" in which the leased premises were located. The shopping center, as then constituted, was described on a plat attached to the lease. Subsequently, the lessor acquired adjoining premises and Gibson Products Co., a lessee of a store in those premises proposed adding a drug department. "It [was] contended by the appellant that the property on which the Gibson store is located is an extension of the shopping center in which the appellant's store is located, and that it has become so integrated with the original shopping center as to become a part of it. The appellant introduced evidence showing that one vehicular driveway furnishes the only access to the rear of any of the stores; that there is a single paved parking area serving the stores in the original shopping center and the Gibson store; that pedestrians and vehicles move freely back and forth between the area in front of the Gibson store and the area in front of the other stores; that only a service driveway separates the two areas; and that people commonly refer to the entire area, including the Gibson store, either as the Greenville Street Shopping Center or the Newnan Shopping Center." Id. 189 S.E.2d at 855. The appellate court affirmed the lower court's denial of an injunction, stating "under the terms of the lease contract between Richards and Jacobs, the restrictive covenant applies only to a plainly delineated shopping center. There is no language in the lease which would extend the restrictive covenant to later acquired adjoining property, and there is no ambiguity in the description of the property composing the shopping center. The fact that the public may use the original shopping center and the property later acquired by Richards as one shopping center, and consider the whole shopping area as one center, is not determinative of the intention of the parties at the time the lease was entered into concerning the limits of the shopping center in which the restrictive covenant applies." Id.

3. With respect to defining the businesses prohibited, the drug store example used in the above excerpt is relatively simple. See *Belvidere South Towne Center, Inc. v. One Stop Pacemaker, Inc.*, 54 Ill.App.3d 958, 12 Ill.Dec. 626, 370 N.E.2d 249 (1977). The vitality and feasibility of a shopping plaza may depend on leasing space to a national chain department store or stores and a regional or national chain supermarket. With these requirements in mind, how should the description of the businesses prohibited be drafted in the leases with the department stores and supermarket.

a. Does one department store necessarily compete with another? What distinguishes competitive department stores from non-competitive department stores? Even if the department stores do compete, there may be a substantial difference in the lines of merchandise they carry and having this variety available to the public may be in the interest of the lessor and the lessees. How can this consideration be taken into account in drafting a restrictive covenant?

b. If a department store or supermarket in a local shopping plaza desires a restrictive covenant, can a covenant be drafted which gives the department store and the supermarket appropriate protection but permits the presence in the plaza of local specialty shops such as a shoe store, men's clothing shop, sporting goods store, gift shop, ice cream parlor, delicatessen, etc.? If competition in certain articles of merchandise is prohibited, the lessor cannot lease to specialty shops selling those articles of merchandise. Is the desire of a department store or supermarket to prevent competition in the articles it sells or in the scope and the variety of articles it sells?

1. A full-line department store, however, presents a competitive threat to a specialty shop. Can the restrictive covenant for a specialty shop be drafted so that a future lease with a department store will not violate the covenant and yet, still protect the specialty shop from undue competition by the department store?

c.　See generally Halper, *People and Property: Use Clauses in Apparel Store Leases,* 6 # 3 Real Est.Rev. 58 (1976); Kane, *Dealing With Assignment, Use and Operating Covenant Lease Clauses,* 2 # 3 Prac.Real Est.Law. 45 (1986).

4.　The validity and enforceability of a restrictive covenant can be challenged in a number of ways.

a.　It may be asserted that a restrictive covenant constitutes an illegal restraint of trade. The test to determine whether an illegal restraint of trade exists is whether the covenant is a reasonable restraint ancillary to the legal relationship between the lessor and lessee, and reasonably limited as to area, businesses prohibited and duration.

1.　The above excerpt indicates that five years is a reasonable duration. The lease executed by a department store or supermarket may have a term of twenty years. Is that too long? Cf. *Sound Ship Building Corp. v. Bethlehem Steel Corp.,* 387 F.Supp. 252 (D.N.J.1975), affirmed, 533 F.2d 96 (3d Cir.1976), cert. denied, 429 U.S. 860, 97 S.Ct. 161, 50 L.Ed.2d 137 (1976). If twenty years is too long a term, how can the restrictive covenant be drafted to give the department store or supermarket the protection it needs?

2.　Is a restrictive covenant necessary to the relationship between a lessor and lessee? "It seems doubtful that all exclusive clauses can properly be justified as essential to the development of speculative shopping centers. Not all centers are constructed in untried areas, and not all tenants require exclusives in their leases. Furthermore, those chain tenants which ordinarily insist on exclusive rights sometimes will enter a desirable center when, because of prior leases or for other reasons, an exclusive cannot be obtained. We cannot know what would happen if exclusive clauses were not available as a means of insulating tenants from competition, but it seems likely that most chain stores and other retail merchants would still join in shopping centers as a means of reaching and serving the vast and growing suburban market.

"Still, if exclusives are not 'absolutely required' for the continued existence and growth of the shopping center movement, their widespread use does indicate that they probably have aided and facilitated the rapid spread of centers in recent years. In some cases an exclusive has proved indispensible to the existence of a center, serving to induce a reluctant key tenant to join the center in a new area where the prospects for success were uncertain. In others, exclusives undoubtedly have encouraged participation by some tenants who find attractive the prospect of entering a new market subject to no competition or only limited competition in the immediate area. The common law has sustained other lease restrictions on land on the ground that they encourage the productive transfer of property. It is thoroughly consistent that courts should now conclude that the contribution of exclusives to the development and growth of shopping centers justifies the competitive restraints such clauses impose." Baum, *Lessors' Covenants Restricting Competition,* 1965 University of Illinois Law Forum 228 at 241–242.

b. A restrictive covenant may also be challenged as a violation of Sections 1 and 2 of the Sherman Antitrust Act, similar state laws, and Section 5 of the Federal Trade Commission Act.

1. Turning to the Sherman Act, is a restrictive covenant "in restraint of trade or commerce among the several states" or is it essentially local in nature? See Note, *Sherman Act Challenges to Shopping Center Leases: Restrictive Covenants as Restraints of Trade Under Section 1*, 7 Ga.L.Rev. 311, 315–327 (1973); Comment, *The Antitrust Implications of Restrictive Covenants in Shopping Center Leases*, 18 Vill.L.Rev. 721, 722–725 (1973); Note, *Jurisdiction Under the Sherman Act: The "Interstate Commerce" Element and the Activities of Local Real Estate Boards and Brokers*, 1979 Duke L.J. 860. In light of the expansive reading given the phrase "substantial effect on interstate commerce" by the Supreme Court in *McLain v. Real Estate Board of New Orleans, Inc.*, 444 U.S. 232, 100 S.Ct. 502, 62 L.Ed.2d 441 (1980), is there much in commercial real estate which is "essentially local in nature"? See generally Note, *Jurisdiction Under the Sherman Act: A Close Look at the Affects Test*, 60 Notre Dame L.Rev. 603 (1985). Does the answer to whether jurisdiction exists under the Sherman Act turn, at least in part, on whether the restrictive covenant is in a lease of space in a regional shopping center, a local shopping center, the business block of a subdivision or in a building devoted to a variety of retail, commercial and, possibly, residential uses?

2. If the Sherman Act applies, does a restrictive covenant create, or tend to create, a monopoly over a market area? "The difficulty with [the] argument [that it does] is that there is no authority for defining the relevant market so narrowly. * * * Although individual shopping centers enjoy some degree of advantage in attracting customers in their trade areas, it is difficult to imagine a case where a center would be the sole practical location for reaching this market. Older shopping areas and other centers are available." Baum, *Lessors' Covenants Restricting Competition*, supra at 247–248. If the market served by a regional shopping center is too narrow, what about the market served by the local center, the business block of a subdivision, or the high-rise multi-use building? See Comment, *Relevant Geographic Market Delineation: The Interchangeability of Standards in Cases Arising Under Section 2 of the Sherman Act and Section 7 of the Clayton Act*, 1979 Duke L.J. 1152. On the other hand, is a restrictive covenant a concerted refusal to deal with competitors of the lessee and unlawful without regard to its impact on competition or injury to the public?

"[V]ertical exclusive arrangements between a single buyer and a single seller are not considered to have the inherent anticompetitive effect or the lack of redeeming virtue that qualifies group boycotts for per se condemnation. Exclusive clauses which are limited in time and area, which are executed as part of a lease, and which may be justified as contributing to the development of shopping centers, seem equally unsuited for per se treatment." Baum, *Lessors' Covenants Restricting Competition*, supra at 249–250.

3. "A third argument against the validity of shopping-center exclusives under the Sherman Act is based on the fact that department and large chain stores play a dominant role in shopping center development. Most centers, particularly large ones, need chain and depart-

ment stores to attract customers to the center; and mortgage financing usually depends upon the developer first obtaining long-term leases from these high credit firms. Until recently, financial institutions seem to have worked from the rule of thumb that from 60 to 75 per cent of the space in a center should be leased to chains. As a result, large chains are sought after as tenants while smaller, independent retailers often find it difficult to obtain shopping center locations.

"The preponderance of chain stores in shopping centers puts the problem of exclusive clauses in new perspective. Up to this point we have analysed the effect of exclusive clauses on competition in one center and the territory surrounding it. Where chain stores are involved, however, it is necessary to look further to appraise the full economic impact of exclusive covenants. If a large chain obtains exclusives in many centers, smaller business competitors may be foreclosed from a substantial part of the retail selling space available in the area of the chain's operations, and the public will be deprived of competitive selling in this space. Furthermore, since other chains may obtain exclusive rights in other centers located in the same area, the parallel actions of several chains may exclude other competitors from shopping centers altogether. * * *

"The analysis here suggested regarding exclusive clauses employed by chain stores is analogous to that which has been used to strike down exclusive-dealing contracts between large manufacturers or other sellers and retail distributors who agree to handle only the sellers' product. Both types of exclusive arrangements may foreclose smaller competitors from outlets they need in order to reach retail markets. But exclusive dealing arrangements in the distribution of goods have been found unlawful not under the Sherman Act but under the more stringent test of section 3 of the Clayton Act, which is specifically designed to ban agreements by buyers not to deal with sellers' competitors where such agreements may have the effect of substantially lessening competition or tending to create a monopoly. Although the standards to be employed in judging exclusive arrangements under section 3 are far from clear, the Supreme Court has indicated that under the Sherman Act more persuasive evidence of actual or potential injury to competition is required. The entire economic setting— including business justifications for the challenged restraint and the strength of remaining competition as well as the percentage of business restrained—is relevant in determining whether the requisite anticompetitive injury has been proved." Baum, *Lessors' Covenants Restricting Competition,* supra at 250–252.

4. Is a restrictive covenant analogous to an agreement between one buyer and one seller, or is it closer, in effect, to an agreement between one buyer and a group of sellers in which event it might be considered a collective boycott? Cf. Note, *The Antitrust Implications of Restrictive Covenants in Shopping Center Leases,* 86 Harv.L.Rev. 1201 (1973).

    a. The effect of a restrictive covenant can be to keep competitive local enterprises out of a shopping plaza. If the plaza is in a developing area, the use of restrictive covenants may result in the area market being dominated by a few national chain stores, and the local competition being eliminated from the market or forced into less desirable locations.

5. A restrictive covenant can be taken one step further by giving the major lessees a veto over prospective lessees. This approach comes quite close to a collective boycott and presents a much weaker case with respect to the reasonableness of the restraint on trade. See Note, *Sherman Act Implications of Major Tenant Veto Powers in Regional Shopping Centers,* 29 Wash. & Lee L.Rev. 67 (1972).

6. The application of Sections 1 and 2 of the Sherman Act, and Section 5 of the Federal Trade Commission Act to restrictive covenants is far from settled. Both the Federal Trade Commission and the Justice Department have attempted to invalidate restrictive covenants, and at times, they have succeeded. See Comment, *The Antitrust Implications of Restrictive Covenants in Shopping Center Leases,* 18 Vill.L.Rev. 721, 745–748 (1973). The position has been taken that certain types of restrictive covenants can, and possibly should, be held illegal per se. See Note, *The Antitrust Implications of Restrictive Covenants in Shopping Center Leases,* 86 Harv.L.Rev. 1201 (1973); Note, *Sherman Act Implications of Major Tenant Veto Powers in Regional Shopping Centers,* 29 Wash. & Lee L.Rev. 67 (1972). This position is particularly applicable to exclusionary covenants, primarily those giving existing lessees a veto with respect to prospective lessees. Other commentary, although not favoring per se treatment, recognizes the possibility of restrictive covenants being invalidated in certain situations under the "rule of reason." See Note, *Sherman Act Challenges to Shopping Center Leases: Restrictive Covenants as Restraints of Trade Under Section 1,* 7 Ga.L.Rev. 311 (1973); Comment, *The Antitrust Implications of Restrictive Covenants in Shopping Center Leases,* 18 Vill.L.Rev. 721 (1973). See generally Halper, *The Antitrust Laws Visit Shopping Center "Use Restrictions",* 4 Real Est.L.J. 3 (1975); Schear and Sheehan, *Restrictive Lease Clauses and the Exclusion of Discounters from Regional Shopping Centers,* 25 Emory L.J. 609 (1976).

c. The Federal Trade Commission, operating under Section 5 of the Federal Trade Commission Act, has had a fair degree of success in challenging restrictive covenants used in regional shopping centers by major retailers. Section 5, which declares unlawful "unfair methods of competition in or affecting commerce," is a rather broad sword in the hands of the Federal Trade Commission. Using this sword, the Federal Trade Commission has obtained consent decrees affecting restrictive covenants in a number of matters. See e.g. *Food Fair Stores, Inc.,* 86 F.T.C. 709 (1975); *The Rouse Co.,* 85 F.T.C. 848 (1975); *Tysons Corner Regional Shopping Center,* CCH Trade Reg.Rep. ¶ 20,532 ('73–'76 Tr.Bin.); *Gimbel Brothers, Inc.,* 83 F.T.C. 1320 (1974); *In re Sears, Roebuck and Co.,* CCH Trade Reg. Rep. ¶ 21,218 ('76–'79 Tr.Bin.); *Strawbridge & Clothier,* 41 Fed.Reg. ¶18,409 (1976). As an example, the consent decree entered against Gimbel Brothers, Inc. requires it, in its capacity as a tenant in a shopping center, to cease and desist from making, carrying out, or enforcing, directly or indirectly, an agreement or provision of any agreement which:

1. grants Gimbel Brothers, Inc. the right to approve or disapprove the entry into a shopping center of any other retailer;

2. grants Gimbel Brothers, Inc. the right to approve or disapprove the amount of floor space that any other retailer may lease or purchase in a shopping center;

3. prohibits the admission into a shopping center of any particular retailer or class of retailers, including, for purposes of illustration: (a) other department stores, (b) junior department stores, (c) discount stores, or (d) catalogue stores;

4. limits the types of merchandise or brands of merchandise or service which any other retailer in a shopping center may offer for sale;

5. specifies that any other retailer in a shopping center shall or shall not sell its merchandise or services at any particular price or within any range of prices;

6. grants Gimbel Brothers, Inc. the right to approve or disapprove the location in a shopping center of any other retailer;

7. specifies or prohibits any type of advertising by other retailers, other than advertising within a shopping center;

8. prohibits price advertising within a shopping center by retailers or controls advertising within a center by retailers in such a way as to make it difficult for customers to discern advertised prices from the common area of such shopping center; or

9. prevents expansion of a shopping center.

The decree also provides that Gimbel Brothers, Inc., in its capacity as a tenant in a shopping center, may not enter into or carry out any conspiracy, combination or arrangement with any other tenant to exclude any tenants from a shopping center or to grant Gimbel Brothers, Inc. or another tenant any control over the admission of other tenants to the shopping center.

Other sections of the decree set out the rights Gimbel Brothers, Inc. specifically retains in its shopping center operations, including the right to withdraw from tenancy if the developer fails to find another acceptable major tenant. In addition, Gimbel Brothers, Inc. retains the right to negotiate with developers or landlords to create, carry out, or enforce agreements:

1. establishing reasonable categories of retailers as tenants adjacent to Gimbel Brothers, Inc. provided there is no specification of price ranges, price lines, trade names, store names, trademarks or brands, or the names of particular retailers, and provided the adjacent store does not exceed certain sizes;

2. maintaining reasonable standards with respect to appearance, signs, maintenance, and housekeeping;

3. prohibiting clearly objectionable types of tenants, including, for purposes of illustration, shops selling pornographic materials;

4. requiring approval of the initial layout of the center, designating the Gimbel Brothers, Inc. store and other buildings, showing parking and common areas, and providing for expansion; and

5. providing for expansion of the center in a manner that does not interfere with auto and foot traffic, the operation of the Gimbel

Brothers, Inc. store, the existing parking ratios and access, and the fulfillment of existing obligations.

d. The consent decree against Tysons Corner Regional Shopping Center and two major tenants of the center, May Department Stores Co. and Woodward and Lathrop, Inc. is similar to the Gimbel Brothers, Inc. decree with respect to the tenants. The shopping center is prohibited by the decree from entering into any lease or enforcing any lease provision which: 1. specifies that any tenant shall or shall not sell merchandise or services at a particular price or within a range of prices; 2. specifies that any tenant shall or shall not sell designated price lines of merchandise; 3. specifies that any tenant shall not be a discounter or sell merchandise or services at discount prices; 4. specifies the content of any advertising by a tenant or prohibits any advertising. Advertising in the center, however, may be regulated, and a tenant may be required to include in its advertising the name of the center; 5. prohibits price advertising within the center or controls advertising in such a way as to make it difficult for consumers in the common area of the center to discern what advertised prices are. The center must also advise the Federal Trade Commission within 60 days of the refusal by a tenant in the center to approve the lease of another tenant or of the approval of such a lease subject to conditions which violate the above prohibitions. The consent decree against Sears, Roebuck and Co. applies to it in its capacity as a major tenant in, and as a developer of, shopping plazas. The terms of the decree with respect to Sears, Roebuck and Co. in its capacity as a tenant are similar to those contained in the decree against Gimbel Brothers, Inc. described above. The terms of the decree with respect to Sears, Roebuck and Co. in its capacity as a developer are similar to those contained in the decree against Tysons Corner Regional Shopping Center described above.

e. The consent decrees obtained by the Federal Trade Commission apply, for the most part, to shopping centers of 200,000 square feet of gross leaseable area or more, of which at least 50,000 square feet is for occupancy by tenants other than the respondent tenant. See Lentzner, *The Antitrust Implications of Radius Clauses in Shopping Center Leases,* 55 U.Det.J.Urb. L. 1 (1977).

f. See generally Halper, *The FTC and Shopping Center Leases,* 10 # 4 Real Est.Rev. 49 (1981).

5. In addition to the type of restrictive covenant discussed above, which is referred to as an exclusive, a lessor may require a lessee to agree that, for a defined period of time, it will not open another establishment within a certain distance from the location to be leased. This is referred to as a radius clause. Obviously, this type of clause raises many of the same concerns discussed above. See *Strawbridge & Clothier,* 41 Fed.Reg. ¶18,409 (1976); *In re Sears, Roebuck and Co.,* CCH Trade Reg.Rep. ¶ 21,218 ('76–'79 Tr.Bin.); Lentzner, *The Antitrust Implications of Radius Clauses in Shopping Center Leases,* 55 U.Det.J.Urb.L. 1 (1977); Comment, *The Shopping Center Radius Clause: Candidate for Antitrust?,* 32 Sw.L.J. 825 (1978); Marsh, *The Federal Antitrust Laws and Radius Clauses in Shopping Center Leases,* 32 Hastings L.J. 839 (1981).

6. Even though the Federal Trade Commission has been successful, under Section 5, with respect to major tenants in regional shopping centers, can a major, minor, local or regional tenant in a local center, or in the business block of a subdivision, or in a multi-use high-rise bargain for or be burdened with a

restrictive covenant? Cf. *Mendell v. Golden–Farley of Hopkinsville, Inc.*, 573 S.W.2d 346 (Ky.App.1978).

7. For the effect of bankruptcy on use restrictions, see Comment, *The Enforceability of Use Restrictions in Assignments of Non–Shopping Center Nonresidential Leases Under Bankruptcy Law*, 57 Temp.L.Q. 821 (1984); Roswick and McEvily, *Use Clauses in Shopping Center Leases: The Effect of the Tenant's Bankruptcy*, 14 Real Est.L.J. 3 (1985).

c. INCOME TAX EFFECTS OF THE LEASING TRANSACTION

(i) LESSEE IMPROVEMENTS

If a lessee constructs improvements on leased premises, the value of the improvements, if they are not in lieu of rent, are not considered income to the lessor. See Section 109 of the Internal Revenue Code. Whether the improvements are in lieu of rent is basically a factual determination made by examining the relationship between the parties, the lease agreement and the overall factual situation. See Reg.Sec. 1.109–1(a) and (b). If the lessee's improvements are not considered income to the lessor, Section 1019 provides that the lessor acquires no basis in the improvements. Section 109 applies to lessee constructed improvements. What are the income tax consequences if a lessor constructs an improvement benefiting a number of lessees in a development, such as a central air conditioning unit, and each lessee pays to the lessor a pro rata portion of the cost of the improvement?

A lessee can depreciate its investment in leasehold improvements. The cost of leasehold improvements made by a lessee must be recovered by the lessee through the use of the cost recovery rules applicable to the improvements regardless of the term of the lease. In the usual case, the lessee will treat the expiration of the lease as a disposition of the improvements and compute gain or loss at that time. See Section 168(i) (8). A lessee can amortize over the term of the lease any leasehold acquisition cost the lessee incurs. When determining the term of a lease for the purpose of amortizing lease acquisition costs, if 75% or more of such costs are attributable to the period of the term of the lease remaining on the date of its acquisition, the renewal period[s] of the lease is not included. See generally the discussion of the income tax treatment of the ground lease in Division III, pages 616 to 628 supra; Stern, *The Tax Impact on the Lessor of the Lessee's Improvements to Real Estate*, 8 J. Real Est.Tax'n 99 (1981); Cain, *Leasehold Improvements by Lessee*, 31 Tul. Tax Inst. 1–15 (1981); Yanowitz and Purcell, *Lessee's Improvements: Making the Most of Planning Opportunities*, 11 J. Real Est.Tax'n 48 (1983); Dalessio and Shenkman, *Improvements to Leased Property: Maximizing the Tax Benefits Regardless of Who Makes Them*, 13 Tax'n Law. 246 (1985).

(ii) LEASE CANCELLATION AND MODIFICATION PAYMENTS

There may come a time when either the lessor, the lessee or both want to cancel or modify the lease prior to its termination. The income tax treatment of payments by the lessee or the lessor to obtain a cancellation or modification of a lease was briefly examined in Division III at pages 622 to 623. A lessor may want to cancel a lease at an early date in order to remodel the premises for a new and more attractive tenant or in order to demolish the premises to construct a new facility. The lessor may pay the lessee a sum of money in consideration of the lessee's agreement to cancel the lease. The payment received by the lessee in consideration of the cancellation of the lease is treated as received in exchange for the lease, and if the leasehold is used in the trade or business of the lessee the amount of the payment in excess of the basis of the lessee in the lease will be treated as capital gains. See Section 1241 and Rev.Rul. 72–85, 1972–1 C.B. 234. Section 1250 or 1245 might require, however, the recapture of some of this gain as ordinary income.

The lessor, in making a payment in consideration of the lessee's agreement to cancel a lease, is incurring a "capital" cost which the lessor may amortize. The problem is determining the period over which the lessor can amortize the cost. The possibilities are numerous. The lessor might demolish the vacated facility and construct a new building for its own use or for lease to a new lessee. In this case the cost of cancellation could be considered a land cost which must be added to the basis of the land and cannot be amortized. See pages 991 to 998 supra. On the other hand, the lessor might take the position that the cancellation cost should be amortized over the remaining term of the canceled lease or over the term of the new lease if the new building is leased or over the life of the new building.

THE MONTGOMERY CO. v. COMMISSIONER
54 T.C. 986 (1970).
[footnotes omitted]

BRUCE, Judge:

*　*　*

Findings of Fact
*　*　*

Petitioner is a corporation organized and existing under the laws of the Commonwealth of Kentucky * * *.

Petitioner was organized on January 26, 1948, under the name Montgomery Auto Company, to engage in the business of retail sale of automobiles and trucks under a franchise from the Chevrolet Motor Division of General Motors Corporation. On May 30, 1952, the corporate name was officially changed to Montgomery Chevrolet, Inc. On

July 15, 1953, petitioner changed its name to The Montgomery Co. and thereafter transferred its operating assets, exclusive of the real estate, plant and buildings, and insurance business, to a new corporation known as Montgomery Chevrolet, Inc., hereinafter sometimes referred to as Chevrolet.

* * *

Petitioner owns and, during the years in issue, did own real estate located on the north and south sides of Liberty Street and on the east side of Second Street in the City of Louisville, Kentucky.

On July 16, 1953, this property was leased to Chevrolet for a term of five years beginning on July 16, 1953, and ending on July 15, 1958, with an option to renew for an additional five years. The monthly rental stated therein was $2,000 per month.

On July 16, 1958, which was the renewal date of the 1953 lease, petitioner and Chevrolet executed a new lease of the same premises for a term of two years, with an option to renew for an additional two years. The monthly rental remained at $2,000.

Again, on July 16, 1960, which was the renewal date of the 1958 lease, the parties executed a new lease agreement for an additional two years with an option of renewal "provided, however, that the tenant must exercise the said option for renewal of this lease for the additional term of two years by giving notice in writing to the landlord of its exercise of the said option at least sixty days (60) in advance of the 15th day of July 1962." The monthly rental remained at $2,000.

On December 26, 1961, The TraveLodge Corporation of San Diego, California, hereinafter sometimes referred to as TraveLodge, made to petitioner an "Offer to Lease" that certain parcel of land then under lease to Chevrolet situated on the *southeast* corner of Second and Liberty Streets, being approximately 48,970 square feet of building area, for a term of 49 years at a rental of $1,000 per month. * * *

This offer was not accepted by petitioner. Petitioner, however, on February 20, 1962, made an "offer to lease" to TraveLodge to be accepted within ten days, which was substantially the same as the offer from TraveLodge, except that the lease was to be for a term of 25 years instead of 49[.] * * *

On February 28, 1962, petitioner * * * received from TraveLodge an "Offer to Lease", to be accepted within [one] day, the said southeastern corner for a term of 25 years with an option to renew for an additional period of 24 years. * * *

On March 20, 1962 * * * an agreement called "AMENDMENT TO AGREEMENT OF LEASE" was entered into between Chevrolet as "first party" and petitioner as "second party." The agreement recited that WHEREAS the parties have heretofore entered into the lease dated July 16, 1960, due to expire on July 15, 1962, and WHEREAS the second party has agreed to lease a portion of the said property covered in the July 16, 1960, lease to TraveLodge, and the first party has agreed to release all of its right in said portion:

NOW, THEREFORE, in consideration of the foregoing * * * the parties hereto have mutually agreed as follows:

(1) The first party will upon ten (10) days notice * * * abandon, and vacate, and surrender, its right, title, interest and possession to the portion of the property * * * being approximately 48,970 square feet of land area.

(2) The first and second parties hereto mutually agree that the Lease Agreement providing for a monthly rental of $2,000.00 and which expires under the terms thereof on July 15, 1962, shall terminate at the expiration of the 10 days notice period as stated in paragraph 1 herein, and the parties agree that a new Lease Agreement shall forthwith be executed by the parties for a period of two years following the date of termination of the present lease with respect to the properties then occupied by the first party and owned by second party under terms and conditions substantially the same as are stated in the present lease, with exception of the amount of the rent which shall be adjusted and reduced to the amount of Fifteen Hundred Dollars ($1,500.00) per month during the two-year term of the new lease.

(3) In consideration of the agreement of the first party to vacate and surrender a portion of the property leased from second party as provided in paragraph (1) herein and in further consideration of the extension of the lease for a period of two years at a rental of $1,500.00 per month by the second party as provided in paragraph (2) herein, *the second party agrees to indemnify and/or reimburse the first party in the sum of $10,000.00 as indemnity for vacating a portion of the property and extending the lease on the remaining property, and to cover the cost and expenses incurred by first party in moving its used cars and other personal property from the vacated premises, and for the expense of removing electric lighting and electric signs from the said premises and the erection of the same at a new location, and for expenses in connection with the expense of removal and reinstallation of a car lift and air compressor.*

[Emphasis added.]

On March 22, 1962, petitioner executed a lease agreement with TraveLodge leasing the *southeast* corner property to TraveLodge for a term of 25 years with an option to renew for an additional 24 years. The rent stated therein was $1,000 per month, plus an annual percentage rent equal to 7½ percent of TraveLodge's gross receipts from the operation of its business on the premises in excess of $160,000 during each lease year. The lease was executed by TraveLodge in the City of San Diego, California, on March 27, 1962.

* * *

On April 20, 1962, petitioner gave notice to Chevrolet to abandon, vacate and surrender its right, title and interest and possession to the portion of the property to be leased to TraveLodge.

On May 1, 1962, petitioner executed an agreement of lease with Chevrolet leasing the property at the *northeast* corner of Second and Liberty Streets comprising about 28,963 square feet of improved property "for a term of two years beginning May 1, 1962, and ending April 30, 1964, with an option of renewal for a period of one year and eight months" at a rental of $1,500 per month.

On May 23, 1962, petitioner paid Chevrolet $10,000. Upon the advice of its accountants, petitioner treated the $10,000 payment to Chevrolet as deferred lease cancellation expense which was to be amortized and deducted over the 2–year term of the new lease with Chevrolet beginning May 1, 1962. * * *

Respondent determined that the $10,000 paid by petitioner to Chevrolet should be deducted over a 25–year period instead of a 2–year period. In the statement attached to the deficiency notice respondent advised petitioner as follows:

> It is held that lease cancellation expense of $10,000.00 paid to Montgomery Chevrolet, Inc., in May 1962 is deductible over the 25–year period of the new lease to the TraveLodge Corporation rather than over the period of the amended lease to Montgomery Chevrolet, Inc. * * *

The payment by petitioner to Chevrolet of the $10,000 was paid to indemnify and reimburse Chevrolet for the expense of removing its property from the southeast corner of Second and Liberty Streets to a new location. It actually cost Chevrolet $11,846.78 to make the move.

* * *

Opinion

* * * [W]e think the respondent's determination should be sustained.

Generally an amount paid by a lessor to a lessee for cancellation of a lease prior to the expiration of its term is a capital expenditure made in order to obtain possession of the premises and is deductible over the unexpired term of the canceled lease. Trustee Corporation, 42 T.C. 482 (1964) and the cases cited at p. 488. But there is a well established exception to the general rule. Business Real Estate Trust of Boston, 25 B.T.A. 191 (1932); Keiler v. United States, 285 F.Supp. 520 (W.D. Kentucky, 1966), affd. per Order 395 F.2d 991 (C.A.6, 1968); cf. Clara Hellman Heller Trust No. 7610, 7 T.C. 556 (1946), reversed sub nom. Wells Fargo B. & U. Trust Co. v. Commissioner, 163 F.2d 521 (C.A.9, 1947), cited by us with approval in *Trustee Corporation,* supra. We think petitioner falls within the exception.

In the *Keiler* case the District Court said:

"The facts of this case are stipulated and it is submitted on the merits.   The record and the briefs of the parties have been considered and it is concluded that the expenditures made by the plaintiffs and their associates to obtain early possession of their leased premises are capital expenditures and are to be amortized over the useful life of the new building which they built to lease to Walgreen.

It is stipulated that the 'sole purpose in acquiring the subleases was to demolish the old building and to erect a new one in its place.'   The facts here, therefore, are similar in all material respects to the facts of Business Real Estate Trust of Boston v. Commissioner, 25 B.T.A. 191 (1932).   At p. 194 it states:

'There is no dispute between the parties that the expenditures in controversy were made solely in order to prepare the way for the new building to be leased to Filene's.   It is equally clear that time was of the essence and that unless immediate possession of the entire property was had the deal could not be put through. * * *   The payments were made to the tenants to obtain immediate possession so that the new building might be erected for lease to Filene's, and for no other purpose.   It is the building that is to produce the income and it seems to us both just and reasonable that these expenditures should be added to the building cost and recovered over its life of 40 years.'

The quoted reasoning of this opinion, both as to the characterization of plaintiffs' expenditures and the method of amortization, is adopted here.   See also Cosmopolitan Corporation v. Commissioner, 18 T.C.M. 542.   [Footnote omitted.]"

Petitioner contends that the so-called "exception" cases noted above are clearly distinguishable in that in those cases the Court either specifically found or it had been stipulated that the "*sole*" purpose of the payment by the taxpayer (here the $10,000) was to acquire a new lease from a third party or to build a new building over the life of which the payments were to be amortized.   Petitioner argues that there was no such stipulation by the parties in the instant case;   that in the amendment to agreement of lease between petitioner and Chevrolet dated March 20, 1962, it is stated that the payment of $10,000 "was at least partly in consideration for the new lease" with Chevrolet;   and that petitioner's accountants treated the $10,000 payment as being attributable to the new lease with Chevrolet.

We are not impressed with petitioner's contention or its supporting argument.   It seems clear to us from the facts stated in our findings that while the July 16, 1960 lease between petitioner and Chevrolet was in effect, petitioner from December 26, 1961 through February 28, 1962, was negotiating with TraveLodge with a view of entering into a much more favorable lease with TraveLodge for the southeast corner of Second and Liberty Streets.   Petitioner and TraveLodge came to an agreement on or about February 28, 1962, but before petitioner could lease the southeast corner to TraveLodge it had to get an agreement from Chevrolet to abandon, vacate and surrender its right, title, interest and possession to the southeast corner, which it accomplished in the agreement with Chevrolet dated March 20, 1962.

We are satisfied that if the negotiations with TraveLodge had not been successful petitioner would not have asked Chevrolet to vacate the southeast corner or have paid the $10,000 to Chevrolet to indemnify and reimburse it for the expense of removing its property from the southeast corner.

We hold the payment of $10,000 to be a capital expenditure amortizable over the 25–year lease with TraveLodge executed on March 22, 1962. *Business Real Estate Trust of Boston,* supra; *Keiler v. United States,* supra. The respondent's determination on this issue is sustained.

* * *

NOTE

1.   Does the court's use of the "but for" test in the above case answer the taxpayer's "sole purpose" argument?

a.   Did the court hold that if the primary purpose of the lease cancellation payment is to secure space to lease to a new tenant that the cost involved in obtaining the cancellation is amortizable over the term of the new lease?

b.   Assume a lease contains a restrictive covenant and the lessee asserts that the business to be engaged in by a new lessee of other space violates the covenant and threatens to enjoin the lessor from executing the new lease. The lessor, to avoid the problem, pays the lessee to obtain a cancellation of the lease. How should the lessor treat, for income tax purposes, the cancellation payment?

c.   In *Handlery Hotels, Inc. v. United States,* 663 F.2d 892 (9th Cir. 1981), the Ninth Circuit Court of Appeals permitted the lessor to amortize over the remaining term of the canceled lease the lessor's lease cancellation cost even though, concurrent with the cancellation, the lessor leased the same space to a new tenant for twenty years on more favorable terms. The court held that the asset acquired by the lessor through the payment of the cancellation cost was the remaining term of the canceled lease. In addition, the court felt that its decision was in line with the majority of decisions on this issue and the Tax Court's decision in *The Montgomery Co.,* 54 T.C. 986 (1970), was an anomaly.

2.   In the case of the demolition of an old building and the construction of a new building to be used by the taxpayer-lessor, lease cancellation costs were required to be amortized over the life of the new building, as opposed to being added to the basis of land or amortized over the remaining term of the canceled leases. See *Houston Chronicle Pub. Co. v. United States,* 339 F.Supp. 1314 (S.D. Tex.1972), affirmed, 481 F.2d 1240 (5th Cir.1973), cert. denied, 414 U.S. 1129, 94 S.Ct. 867, 38 L.Ed.2d 754 (1974); *Third National Bank in Nashville v. United States,* 454 F.2d 689 (6th Cir.1972).

3. A payment by a lessee to a lessor to obtain modification of an existing lease is a capital expenditure to be amortized by the lessee over the remaining term of the lease. Cf. Rev.Rul. 73–176, 1973–1 C.B. 146. Whether the payment is treated as ordinary income or as a return of capital or capital gain by the lessor may turn on the nature of the modification. See Division III, pages 622 to 623; *Boston Fish Market Corp.*, 57 T.C. 884 (1972); *Sirbo Holdings, Inc. v. Comm'r*, 476 F.2d 981 (2d Cir.1973), vacating and remanding, 57 T.C. 530 (1972). The Tax Court, on remand, in *Sirbo Holdings, Inc.*, 61 T.C. 723 (1974), held that the payment to the lessor by the lessee for modification of a provision of the lease was taxable as ordinary income and the Second Circuit Court of Appeals affirmed. See *Sirbo Holdings, Inc. v. Comm'r*, 509 F.2d 1220 (2d Cir.1975). The Court of Appeal's opinion, however, indicates that in the appropriate case such a payment might be treated as a return of capital and capital gain. See Salter and McGowan, *What Sirbo Holdings Decided: A Postscript*, 2 J. Real Est. Tax'n 459 (1975); Note, *Capital Gains Treatment of Restoration Payments: Sirbo Holdings, Inc. v. Commissioner of Internal Revenue*, 7 Conn.L.Rev. 775 (1975).

4. If a lease provides that a lessee, who uses the accrual method of accounting, does not have to actually pay any rent to an unrelated cash method lessor until the last year of the lease and the payment to be made at the end of the last year is equal to a yearly rent times the number of years in the term of the lease plus interest on the deferred rent, can the lessee deduct the rent and interest annually during the term of the lease? Does the lessor recognize any income before the last year of the lease? See Section 467. See generally Wiesner and Massoglia, *Sec. 467 Rental Agreements: Lessors and Lessees Must Watch Their Step*, 16 Tax Adviser 392 (1985); Hamilton and Comi, *The Time Value of Money: Section 467 Rental Agreements Under the Tax Reform Act of 1984*, 63 Taxes 155 (1985); Whitesman, *Section 467: Tax Planning for Deferred–Payment Leases*, 5 Va.Tax Rev. 345 (1985); Shenkman, *Impact of the Deferred Rent Provisions of TRA '84 on Real Estate Leasing*, 13 J. Real Est. Tax'n 51 (1985); Stern and Vogel, *New Rules May Require Inclusion of Payment for Rent or Personal Services Before It is Received*, 14 Tax'n Law. 238 (1986).

5. See Thompson, *Some Tax Problems on Mid–Stream Modifications and Terminations of Leases*, 4 J. Real Est. Tax'n 214 (1977); Note, *The Tax Treatment of the Cost of Terminating a Lease*, 30 Stan.L.Rev. 241 (1977); Levin, *Lease Terminations: Tax Treatment to Landlord and Tenant; Tenant Improvements; Landlord and Tenant Payments for Lease Terminations*, 41 N.Y.U. Inst. Fed. Tax'n 19–1 (1983). See generally Pinner and Kelley, *Planning Opportunities in Structuring Leases of Commercial Real Property*, 64 J. Tax'n 88 (1986).

3. FIRE, CASUALTY AND BUSINESS INTERRUPTION INSURANCE

A major concern of a developer and the developer's mortgagee, when constructing, financing and operating a development, is adequate coverage for losses incurred as a result of fire or other casualty. An uninsured, or a less than fully insured, loss in a high or totally financed development may mean disaster. Therefore, the developer must be knowledgeable with respect to insurance coverage and the effect of the insurance coverage in the event of a loss.

a.   THE MEANING OF ACTUAL CASH VALUE

In general, fire and casualty policies protect the insured "to the extent of the actual cash value of the property at the time of loss, but not exceeding the amount which it would cost to repair or replace the property with material of like kind and quality within a reasonable time after loss." The amount of the insured's recovery in the event of loss depends on the meaning of the phrase "actual cash value."

McANARNEY v. NEWARK FIRE INS. CO.

Court of Appeals of New York, 1928.
247 N.Y. 176, 159 N.E. 902.

* * *

KELLOGG, J. The plaintiff was the vendee of certain real estate purchased in the year 1919 from the defendant Lembeck & Betz Eagle Brewing Company, under written contract, for the sum of $8,000. Seven large buildings, designed for the manufacture of malt, stood upon the premises. Malt had been extensively manufactured therein prior to the year 1918. Owing to the passage of the National Prohibition Act, its manufacture was discontinued in March of that year and thereafter the buildings ceased to be employed for any useful purpose. In January, 1920, policies of insurance insuring the plaintiff and the Lembeck & Betz Eagle Brewing Company, as their interest might appear, against loss of the buildings by fire, in the aggregate sum of $42,750, were taken out. In April, 1920, the buildings were destroyed by fire. Subsequently the plaintiff served proofs of loss wherein he valued the buildings at approximately $60,000 and made claim for the total amount of the insurance. The defendant Newark Fire Insurance Company was one of the insuring companies. It had issued a policy insuring the plaintiff and the defendant Lembeck & Betz Eagle Brewing Company against fire loss in the amount of $2,500. The plaintiff demanded payment from it and, upon its refusal, brought this action to recover the sum of $2,500 promised by its policy. The Lembeck & Betz Eagle Brewing Company had refused to unite with the plaintiff in bringing suit. It was, therefore, made a party defendant. The action was tried before a jury, to which the trial judge submitted the written question: "What was the intrinsic or depreciated structural value of the buildings burned?" The jury returned a verdict specifying the value to have been $55,000. The trial court, having ascertained that the plaintiff had paid to the Lembeck & Betz Eagle Brewing Company the full purchase price for the property, directed judgment in favor of the plaintiff against the Newark Fire Insurance Company for the amount of its policy with interest.

Complaint is made that the trial court in the course of the trial committed a variety of errors in ruling upon the admissibility of proof offered by the defendant. It refused to receive proof that the plaintiff, when a director of the Lembeck & Betz Company, in the year 1919 reported to that company that he had been unable to obtain a purchaser for the property; that in the same year the corporation had directed the plaintiff to erect a sign upon the premises advertising the property for sale for the sum of $12,000. It refused to receive in evidence an affidavit made by the plaintiff in the year 1919 which was filed with the local board of assessors. In this affidavit the plaintiff had stated that the property had no value except for the production of malt; that the production of malt upon the premises had entirely ceased; that the owners would accept for the property the sum of $15,000; that the best offer which had been received was $6,000. To the rulings made, excluding such proof and proof of a similar nature, the defendant duly excepted. Complaint is also made of the court's charge to the jury and of its refusals to charge. The court said to the jury: "Your answer shall not be the market value—shall not be the sum that the buildings would sell for, but what it cost to build them—what it cost to build the structures, less depreciation proven in the case." It charged that the fact that the buildings, because of the passage of the National Prohibition Act, could no longer be used for the manufacture of malt, and the fact that the buildings could no longer be employed for any useful purpose, were wholly immaterial. It further charged that the value of the buildings destroyed was to be measured solely by the cost of replacement less deductions for physical deterioration. The defendant duly excepted to the charges made. It requested the court to charge several propositions of law which were the direct converse of the charges thus made, and, to its refusal, duly excepted.

The policy in suit contained the standard clause, applicable alike to fire losses whether of chattels or buildings, reading as follows: "The Insurance Company does insure * * * to the extent of the actual cash value (ascertained with proper deductions for depreciation) of the property at the time of loss or damage, but not exceeding the amount which it would cost to repair or replace the same with material of like kind and quality within a reasonable time after such loss or damage."

We cannot agree with the defendant that, under this clause, the market value of the buildings destroyed was the exclusive measure of the plaintiff's loss. Insurance is thereby limited to "actual cash value (ascertained with proper deductions for depreciation) of the property at the time of loss or damage." Value ascertained by market price is necessarily expressive of a suitable deduction for depreciation. If "actual cash value" were synonymous with "market value," the words in parenthesis, to have force, would require depreciation to be twice subtracted. No such anomalous result could have been intended. In order that the parenthetical words should have force, therefore, "actual cash value" must be interpreted as having a broader significance than "market value." Moreover, if market value were the rule, property, for which there was no market, would possess no insurable value, a proposition which is clearly untenable. We think it manifest that the clause was not intended to restrict a recovery for this insurance loss to the market value of the insured buildings. We interpret "actual cash value" to have no other significance than "actual value" expressed in terms of money. For methods by which actual value may be ascertained, we must look beyond the terms of the policy to general principles of the law of damages.

No principle, obtaining in the law of damages, requires that the recovery be restricted to the market value of the buildings. * * * "Market value," as an exclusive measure of damages, necessarily involves identity of concept as disclosed by frequency of sale. "Proof of a single sale is not enough to establish a market value." (Sedgwick, sec. 244.) Clearly, where no sales have been made, the opinion of an expert that the property in question "will sell" for a given sum does not establish "market value," in the sense of an exclusive criterion of value. * * * The proposition that "if there be no market, in a restricted sense, yet if the commodity is the subject of sale and there is a selling price, the same rule obtains and proof of cost should be excluded," has not found approval in this court. * * * Self-evidently, the buildings which are the subject of this action had no "market value" in a strict sense. In the first place, buildings, independently of the land upon which they stand, are never the subject of market sales. In the second place, no two buildings are alike in size, proportion, ornamentation, or otherwise. Doubtless no buildings, duplicating those destroyed, could be found the world over. They are incapable of replacement from any market whatsoever. Therefore, the strict rule that market value or market price is an exclusive measure of damage does not apply.

We do not agree with the plaintiff that, under the standard clause, the sole measure of damage was cost of reproduction less physical depreciation. The words "not exceeding the amount which it would cost to repair or replace the same with material of like kind and quality within a reasonable time after such loss or damage," afford no remedy to the assured. They merely express a privilege granted to the insurer. The insurer might, if it so elected, reconstruct the destroyed buildings upon their ancient pattern with materials of like kind and quality, or pay the assured the necessary cost of such reconstruction. If the insurer so elected, it could be allowed nothing for the difference between the value of the old and the new buildings. (Wood on Fire Insurance, sec. 472.) The clause makes no allusion to depreciation, except as it provides for the recovery of "actual cash value" to be "ascertained with proper deductions for depreciation." This provision, while it doubtless comprehends cost of reproduction, does not restrict the field of investigation to such cost or provide that, with depreciation, it shall constitute an exclusive measure of recovery.

Indemnity is the basis and foundation of all insurance law. (Castellain v. Preston, 11 Q.B.D. 380; Richards on Insurance Law, p. 27; Wood on Fire Insurance, sec. 471.) "The contract of the insurer is not that, if the property is burned, he will pay its market value, but that he will indemnify the assured, that is, save him harmless or put him in as good a condition, so far as practicable, as he would have been in if no fire had occurred." (Washington Mills Mfg. Co. v. Weymouth Ins. Co., 135 Mass. 503.) The insurer, in our case, in its contract with the plaintiff stipulated that it "does insure" the plaintiff "to the extent of the actual cash value." Under our interpretation of the phrase, the insurer "does insure" to the limit of actual value. To insure is "to guarantee or secure indemnity for future loss or damage." (The Century Dictionary.) Where insured buildings have been destroyed, the trier of fact may, and should, call to its aid, in order to effectuate complete indemnity, every fact and circumstance which would logically tend to the formation of a correct estimate of the loss. It may consider original cost and cost of reproduction; the opinions upon value given by qualified witnesses; the declarations against interest which may have been made by the assured; the gainful uses to which the buildings might have been put; as well as any other fact reasonably tending to throw light upon the subject. * * *

In the case at bar the trier of fact, in considering cost of reproduction, was required by the policy to make proper "deductions for depreciation." "The word (depreciation) means, by derivation and common usage, 'a fall in value; reduction of worth.'" (N.Y. Life Ins. Co. v. Anderson, 263 F. 527, at 529.) It includes obsolescence. (Nashville, C. & St. L. Ry. Co. v. U.S., 269 F.R. 351, at 355; San Francisco & P.S.S. Co. v. Scott, 253 F.R. 854, at 855.) An obsolete thing is a thing no longer in use. In determining the extent to which these buildings had suffered from depreciation the trier of fact should have been permitted to consider that, owing to the passage of the National Prohibition Act, they were no longer useful for the purposes [for] which they were erected. It should have been permitted to consider their adaptability or inadaptability to other commercial purposes. The law of damages distinguishes between marketable chattels possessed for purposes of sale and chattels possessed for the comfort and well-being of their owner. In the instance of the former it judges their value by the market price. In the instance of the latter it measures their loss, not by their value in a second-hand market, but by the value of their use to the owner who suffers from their deprivation. The latter measure is employed in the case of household furniture, family records, wearing apparel, personal effects and family portraits. (Barker v. Lewis Storage & Transfer Co., 78 Conn. 198, 61 A. 363; Green v. Boston & Lowell R.R. Co., 128 Mass. 221; Lake v. Dye, 232 N.Y. 209, at p. 214, 133 N.E. 448.) Doubtless the law should similarly discriminate between buildings used and usable for commercial purposes and buildings used and usable for residence purposes. "The considerations affecting the value of a family residence and of an apartment house or office building are not entirely the same." (Citizens' Bank v. Fitchburg Fire Ins. Co., [86 Vt. 267].) It might well be held that handsomely carved woodwork or other ornamental features, when found in a private home, have insurable value; whereas, when found in a factory, since they are not useful for factory purposes, they have no such value. However that may be, it is a self-evident proposition that factory buildings peculiarly adapted to the manufacture of malt must have depreciated in value when malt may no longer be manufactured; that buildings useful only for factory purposes have lost value when they are no longer used or usable for such purposes.

The foregoing discussion necessarily establishes that the trial judge committed reversible error in excluding the declarations against interest as to the value of the buildings, made by the plaintiff; in charging the jury that upon the question of value they must consider no other subject than cost of reproduction less depreciation, and in further charging that the obsolesence of the structures or their inutility for commercial or manufacturing purposes might not be considered. Accordingly, the judgment must be reversed.

The judgment should be reversed and a new trial granted, with costs to abide the event.

CARDOZO, Ch. J.; POUND, CRANE, ANDREWS, LEHMAN and O'BRIEN, JJ., concur.

Judgment reversed, etc.

NOTE

1. Why was the seller of the buildings in the above case named in the insurance policies? What was the seller's "insurable interest"? Does a mortgagee have a similar "insurable interest"? What portion of the proceeds paid by the insurance company in the event of loss should be paid to the seller or mortgagee?

2. Some insurance policies contain an eighty percent coinsurance provision. Unless the property is insured for 80% or more of its value, the insured is treated as a coinsurer for the percentage that the property is under-insured. This type of provision only applies to partial losses. If the loss in the above case was a partial loss, the policies contained 80% co-insurance provisions and the plaintiff's valuation of $60,000 for the buildings was accurate, would the plaintiff have collected the face amount of the policies of $42,750, or 86% of $42,750, or some other amount?

3. The court in the above case rejects both market value and reproduction or replacement cost less depreciation as the sole means of measuring or defining actual cash value. If both of these measures are rejected, what is left as a means of defining actual cash value?

    a. The above case is illustrative of what is commonly known as the broad evidence rule—the trier of fact can receive and use any evidence logically tending to show actual cash value. While there are still some jurisdictions which use market value (the amount which would have been arrived at by fair negotiations between a willing buyer and willing seller) and other jurisdictions which use reproduction or replacement cost less depreciation (the amount it would cost to replace the structure using present methods and styles of construction discounted to take account of the age and physical condition of the structure) the current trend is toward the broad evidence rule.

    b. See Hinkle, *The Meaning of "Actual Cash Value"*, 1967 Ins. L.J. 711; Dykes, *"Actual Cash Value": The Magic Words—What Do They Mean?*, 16 Forum 391 (1980); Gilbard, *Actual Cash Value: A Moving Target*, 17 Forum 1346 (1982); Fenner, *About Present Cash Value*, 18

Creighton L.Rev. 305 (1984); Reader, *Modern Day Actual Cash Value: Is It What the Insurers Intend?*, 22 Tort & Ins. L.J. 282 (1987).

4. In rejecting market value as the sole means of determining actual cash value, did the court in the above case hold that the obsolescence of the buildings cannot be considered? Does the court allow consideration of the depreciation of the buildings in determining the amount of recovery under the insurance policies? If so, is this the amount of depreciation shown on the books of the insured, or is depreciation determined in some other manner?

a. While obsolescence and depreciation are proper considerations in determining recovery in a total loss situation such as the above case, should these factors be considered in determining the amount of recovery in a partial loss situation? For example, if a windstorm damages the roof of a building, is the depreciation of the roof taken into account in determining the amount of the recovery?

b. See Williams, *The Determination of the Value of Commercial Real Property: Open Policies*, 1961 Ins. L.J. 300.

5. Assume that the plaintiff in the above case was a lessee who had constructed the buildings under a lease which gave the lessor the right to terminate on 90 days prior notice. On termination the lessee had the right to remove the buildings. Ten days before the fire the lessor gave notice, and at the time of the fire, the lessee intended to demolish the buildings.

a. If the fire was not a quick way for the lessee to accomplish his intent, do the circumstances of the lessor's notice and the lessee's intent have any bearing on the determination of actual cash value under the *McAnarney* test. Are they facts or circumstances "which would logically tend to the formation of a correct estimate of loss"? If the lessor, rather than the lessee, had built the buildings, was the insured, had given the notice to the lessee and intended to demolish, are these circumstances relevant to the determination of the actual cash value of the buildings? See *Knuppel v. American Ins. Co.*, 269 F.2d 163 (7th Cir.1959); *Federowicz v. Potomac Ins. Co. of District of Columbia*, 7 A.D.2d 330, 183 N.Y.S.2d 115 (4th Dept.1959). But cf. *Frost House, Inc. v. Preferred Mutual Ins. Co.*, 15 A.D.2d 741, 223 N.Y.S.2d 875 (1st Dept.1962).

b. Many fire and casualty insurance policies limit recovery under the policy in terms such as "nor in any event for more than the interest of the insured." Do the circumstances described above have a bearing on the determination of the value of the insurable interest of the lessee or the lessor? See Note, *Insurance—Recovery—Extent Under Interest Limitation Clause of the Standard Fire Insurance Policy*, 58 Mich.L.Rev. 592 (1960); *Federowicz v. Potomac Ins. Co. of District of Columbia*, 7 A.D.2d 330, 183 N.Y.S.2d 115 (4th Dept.1959); Birnbaum, *Insurable Interests of Lenders, Tenants, Purchasers and Mixed–Use Occupants*, 17 Real Prop., Prob. & Tr.J. 645 (1982).

c. See generally with respect to the meaning of insurable interest Vukowich, *Insurable Interest: When It Must Exist in Property and Life Insurance*, 7 Willamette L.J. 1 (1971); Fuchs, *The Significance of Insurable Interest*, 47 N.Y.St.B.J. 365 (1975); Pinzur, *Insurable Interest: A Search for Consistency*, 46 Ins.Couns.J. 109 (1979); Fischer, *The Rule of Insurable Interest and the Principle of Indemnity: Are They Measures of Damages in Property Insurance?*, 56 Ind.L.J. 445 (1981).

6.   See generally Cotton, *Insurance Coverage for the Real Estate Venture,* 19 # 3 Prac.Law. 13 (1973).

b.   ALLOCATION OF LOSSES, LIABILITY AND PROCEEDS

In most rental real estate developments there are a number of persons who possess an insurable interest. At the minimum, the lessor, the lessee, and the mortgagee each have an insurable interest. The number of interests in a development requires the allocation of losses, the liability for the losses and the proceeds of the insurance which compensate for the losses. In Division III, see pages 612 to 613 supra, and earlier in this Division, see page 1004 supra, the effect of the provisions of a lease which allocate insurance proceeds among the lessor, lessee and mortgagee was considered. In addition, the lessor and lessee may attempt through provisions in the lease to allocate responsibility for fire and other losses.

NOTE:

ALLOCATING TENANT TORT LIABILITY THROUGH THE FIRE INSURANCE POLICY
33 Indiana Law Journal 397 (1958).
[footnotes omitted]

* * *

[T]he responsibility for fire damage to the premises will be shifted to a negligent tenant, if the real property is subject to lease. If the lease contains a clause clearly exculpating the negligent tenant from liability, responsibility for the risk is then shifted back to the lessor. However, many times the intent of the parties to release the tenant from liability is not clearly expressed. For example, the parties may contract to require the tenant to return the premises in as good condition as when demised, "loss by fire excepted." The courts are divided on the effect of this clause when insurance has been effectuated on the premises, most holding that under these circumstances the clause operates as a release of the tenant's liability for a fire which he negligently caused.

Permissible Alterations in Loss Allocation

New Hampshire is the only state which has consistently adopted the strict view of the illegality of exculpatory clauses. Regardless of how well drafted the exculpatory clause may be, and regardless of how well it expresses the intent of the parties, the New Hampshire courts make it clear that the common law duty to exercise due care may not be contracted away. Exculpatory clauses are claimed to violate New Hampshire's public policy because they induce a want of due care. Several states have at least given token recognition to the New Hampshire view, but the great majority of the states have taken the position that exculpatory clauses can be valid.

In those states recognizing the validity of the exculpatory clause, the courts have explicitly or implicitly sustained the validity of such clauses as a proper exercise of the freedom to contract. However, the same majority of the courts declare that such clauses are not favored and should be strictly construed. Even assuming, however, that the strict construction rule can be of real value in deciding a particular case, its application to the problem at hand is by no means certain. Since the meaning of the "loss by fire excepted" clause is not clear, it might well be construed against the one who drafted the lease or who dominated the negotiations, usually the lessor. * * *

Perhaps the courts construing the "loss by fire excepted" clause as exculpatory can find in the circumstances of the case an "intent" to relieve the tenant. In all of these cases the loss had been paid and an action was brought against the tenant by an insurer, based on the insurer's right of subrogation. In addition, the lessor had either covenanted to carry insurance, or the tenant had contributed to the insurance premiums. Interestingly * * * the older cases in which insurance was not involved did not find similar clauses to be exculpatory. Since intent is nebulous and mainly subjective the courts have some leeway in finding or not finding an "intent" to achieve a certain result. The presence of the insurer as a financially responsible third party could conceivably influence the parties negotiating a lease to exculpate the lessee from his negligent misconduct. On the other hand, the prospect that the lessor would have to bear the entire burden of fire loss where insurance is not carried on the premises, would favor a presumption that the lessor had never intended to exempt the lessee from liability for his negligent acts. Thus the modern trend to find an intent to exculpate the lessee should perhaps be ascribed to the entrance of an insurance company into the picture.

In the * * * cases exculpating the tenant the courts have felt entitled to compare the phrase "loss by fire" in the lease with the same phrase in the insurance policy and to give the clause the same meaning in both contexts. Since the phrase "loss by fire" as used in the insurance policy covers loss resulting from a fire negligently caused, the phrase as used in the lease has been given the same meaning. Such comparison might be justified if the lessor and the lessee were aware of the presence of insurance during the lease negotiations, and especially if the tenant contributed to the premiums. Furthermore, because the action was brought by the insurer in these cases the courts might have been more easily led into viewing the lease and policy in pari materia. Yet, it is also significant that clauses relating to the return of the premises have often been viewed as applicable only to the lessee's duty to make repairs. Even if it is assumed that the courts have properly found an intent to exempt the tenant, and have properly construed the "loss by fire" provisions as applicable to any fire negligently caused, the interests of the insurer as a third party to the transaction remain to be considered.

Exculpatory Clauses and Their Effect on Insurance

The Tenant as a Named Insured

The tenant can have an insurable interest in the demised premises, either because of the presence of improvements on the property or because of an agreement on his part to keep the premises insured against certain perils. Moreover, the tenant has an insurable interest in his own liability for negligence.

Even though the tenant has an insurable interest in the demised premises or in his liability, this should not mean that he is entitled to the advantage of insurance not taken out in his own name. A contract of fire insurance is a personal contract and not a contract *in rem*. It does not insure the property, nor does it even run with the land unless this is expressly stipulated. Unless the policy names the tenant, it does not extend to him even though the lease requires the tenant to keep the buildings insured against fire.

In the cases exculpating the tenant, in which insurance was involved, the tenant could also escape his common law liability for negligence if he could be considered an additional insured under the policy. * * * Perhaps the tenant could be said to be an additional insured in those instances in which he paid the premiums either directly or indirectly by way of rent money or, alternatively, in those instances in which the lessor had covenanted to carry fire insurance. Practically speaking, it would seem that any and all lease agreements could be said to include insurance premiums in the rental whether or not the contracting parties contemplated such an inclusion. However, if an increased rental is given in consideration for an exculpatory clause the intent of the parties is even more clearly expressed and so these cases can be distinguished from those instances in which no such increase has occurred.

Tenant Exculpation and the Insurer's Right of Subrogation

Subrogation is a principle of equity and arises by operation of law. Provided the insurance contract is one of indemnity, it is not mandatory that a subrogation clause be expressed. The principle of subrogation is that the insurer, on payment of the claim to the insured, has a right to recover from a third person who has negligently caused the loss paid under the policy. In the cases exculpating the tenant the insurer had sued him directly. But, because the tenant was exculpated, the insurer's right of subrogation was held to have been destroyed.

Furthermore, in these cases payment was made to the insured, and this operated as a waiver of any possible breach of the subrogation clause in the policy. No doubt the ambiguity in the leases in question contributed to this apparent lack of caution on the part of the insurance companies. Because the policy defense had been waived, the courts did not consider the policy breach problem in more detail.

* * * Under the New York Standard Fire Insurance Policy, which is now in common use, the insurer is subrogated to any "rights" of the insured. Two theories have been advanced as to when the "right" of subrogation vests. One theory is that the right of subrogation vests contingently with the insurer when the loss occurs and the duty to pay the insured has arisen. The other is that the right vests, not upon the duty to pay, but upon the actual act of payment. A close analysis of the problem indicates that although the insurance company may not be able to press for reimbursement against a wrongdoer before it has paid the loss, nevertheless, the courts will protect the carrier before it has made a payment to its insured if a release is executed after the loss has occurred but before payment. Once the loss occurs, a discharge of the wrongdoer by the insured will discharge the insurer "pro tanto."

* * *

NOTE

1. Why would a lessor agree to a provision in a lease exculpating the lessee from responsibility for loss or damage by fire or other casualty caused by the lessee's negligent act? On the other hand, is it not reasonable for the lessee to ask that normal wear and tear and, to some extent, fire and other casualty damage be excepted from the provision obligating it to return the leased premises in the same condition as when leased?

    a. To what extent should fire and other casualty damage be excepted? Should loss or damage from fire or casualty be excepted no matter how caused? Or, only if caused by the lessor or another lessee? Or, only loss or damage *not caused* by the negligence of the lessee, its employees, invitees or customers?

2. The courts appear to have taken the position that if the lease contains a clause exculpating the lessee from responsibility for fire or other casualty damage caused by its negligence, the lessor's insurance company, after it pays the lessor, cannot sue the lessee with respect to a fire the lessee negligently caused. This is because the lessor has no rights against the lessee to which the insurance company can be subrogated. See e.g. *Insurance Co. of North America v. Universal Mortgage Corp. of Wisconsin,* 82 Wis.2d 170, 262 N.W.2d 92 (1978).

    a. There is a possibility, however, that the exculpation or waiver of the lessor's rights against the lessee constitutes a breach of the provisions of the lessor's fire insurance policy, and therefore, the insurance company does not have to pay the lessor.

        1. Assume a lessee and lessor agree to an exculpation clause in a lease. What should be done about the possible breach of the lessor's fire insurance policy? Does a fire and casualty insurance policy protect the insured against losses caused by the insured's negligence?

3. See generally Meyernow, *Exculpatory Provisions in Leases of Commercial Property—A Realistic Appraisal,* 13 New Eng.L.Rev. 739 (1978).

c. BUSINESS INTERRUPTION AND USE AND OCCUPANCY INSURANCE

A fire insurance policy provides the funds for the replacement of the property destroyed. Both a lessor and lessee, however, may suffer a greater loss as a result of the interruption of business resulting from the fire or casualty. While a lessee may terminate a lease on the total or substantial destruction of the leased premises, the lessor's mortgagee may expect the lessor's payments on the mortgage to continue. If the damage is not substantial, the lessee's obligation to pay rent may continue while the lessee cannot conduct business operations on the leased premises for the period needed to restore them. Last, as a result of the casualty both the lessor's and lessee's return from the premises may stop until restoration. The above listed considerations, among others, have resulted in the use of business interruption and use and occupancy insurance by lessors and lessees.

PROBLEM CLAIMS UNDER BUSINESS INTERRUPTION POLICIES

George W. Clarke
4 # 5 Practical Lawyer 64 (1958).

* * *

Fundamentals of Coverage and Routine Adjustments

* * *

The theory of the coverage may be summarized as follows:

Where properties essential to the conduct of the insured's business are damaged or destroyed as the result of a specified hazard, the insured is provided indemnity, subject to certain policy limitations, for loss of income that would otherwise have been received from operations during the period which would be required, by exercise of due diligence, for the restoration of the damage. * * *

[T]he fundamental elements to be determined in the closing of a business interruption loss are:

¶ The length of the suspension period;

¶ The amount of income necessarily lost during and as a result thereof;

¶ The annual business interruption value for use in applying the average clause; and

¶ The applicability of the provisions relative to expediting.

* * *

The Suspension Period

Similar Replacement

* * *

The first question for determination is whether the insured is going to replace the damaged property immediately.

Where the physical damage is great, the insured may have many factors to weigh in making his decision. He may need the proceeds of his basic fire insurance to finance his rebuilding and be loath to commit himself until he has a good idea as to the amount of that adjustment and when the funds will be available. If he had an old plant and did not carry depreciation insurance, the cost of rebuilding may far exceed his physical damage recovery and require arrangements for additional money.

He may wish to expand, retrench or rearrange in such a way as to change completely the physical properties from what they were prior to the fire. He may decide to resume operations elsewhere on premises which he may purchase or lease, or he may quit business entirely.

In many instances the insured may be rather slow in solving these problems and, where replacement is decided upon, it may be some time before it is commenced. Also, in the interim various opportunities for expediting [8] may be lost.

Strictly from a legal proposition, the actual course which the insured decides to take should have no bearing whatsoever on the amount recoverable. Under the policy provisions, the suspension period is fixed as the theoretical time which would be required to restore the property to its previous condition with the exercise of due diligence.

* * *

No Similar Replacement

Where the insured replaces and a controversy results, it is necessary for the company representatives to present and urge a theoretical replacement time against an actuality. When there is no replacement, or one with no similarity to the original premises, both parties must deal in theoreticals.

* * *

At first blush, it would seem that the problem of establishing the time required to replace, by the exercise of due diligence, would be a simple problem of labor and materials, with not much room for divergence of opinion.

It is, however, surprising how wide the range of expert testimony can be as to the time required for even routine construction, and where

---

8. [Expediting involves incurring an expense which is greater than that required for the repair of damages in a routine manner. The expense, however, is less than the amount of the reduction in the insurance claim accomplished thereby. The expense is added to the amount recoverable under the insurance policy.]

either a remote area, unusual construction or specialized machinery is involved, the opportunity for disparity increases greatly.

* * *

Income Prevented

The question of what income was actually prevented is always hypothetical to a degree, regardless of whether or not there is a resumption of business at the original location. As an issue, it is subject to a greater number of collateral issues than any other facet of the problem.

The forms provide that, in making the determination, due consideration shall be given to the experience prior to the fire and the probable experience thereafter.

While previous experience, if available, is used as a guide, it is not regarded as controlling when it appears that other elements, such as a change in market price, general demand or marketability would have produced a different result during the suspension period. See National Union Fire Ins. Co. v. Anderson–Prichard Oil Corp., 141 F.2d 443 (10th Cir.1944); General Ins. Co. of America v. Pathfinder Petroleum Co., 145 F.2d 368 (9th Cir.1944).

The most speculative claims on this issue involve starting businesses that have little or no experience, or businesses that have just completed a substantial change in operation which it is contended would have materially increased their income during the suspension period.

* * *

Where a large amount of coverage is involved, claims of this nature always have potential danger. The obvious argument is, if the companies did not think the insured could make that much income, why did they sell that much insurance. Why do they take the premium and then refuse to pay in full when there is a total suspension!

The answer usually offered is that the insurance coverage is spread among several policies, issued by different companies, each of which has contracts for sale at a specified price per thousand dollars. One of the provisions of these contracts, which a court will instruct is entirely legal and proper, is that in no event can the total recovery under all policies exceed the income which would otherwise have been realized during the suspension period. The individual insurance companies, in the absence of an investigation the cost of which would make the premium prohibitive, have no method of determining what this would be. The amount of insurance to be carried is determined by the insured who has the legal right to buy as much and from as many companies as he pleases, subject to the above limitation.

* * *

Suspensions of Less Than Entire Business

Many suspensions are partial in that operation may continue at a lessened capacity or one step in a progressive series of processing may be completely stopped. Here, the accounting work is accentuated as there must be allocation of cost of materials, overhead, ordinary expense and income, as among the various stages of processing.

Some manufacturers will run material through a series of successive steps of processing in such a way that a market value can be established at the end of each step. While for its own bookkeeping purposes, the owner may treat the entire operation as a single unit for the purpose of ascertaining the proper business interruption claim for damage or destruction to one stage, there must be a segregation as to that stage. In order to be certain that this is properly done, the services of a qualified accountant with basic knowledge of the coverage are indispensable.

* * *

On occasions it may be found that, while the over-all operation was making a profit, the particular processing suspended by the loss was not. Thus, a claim for business interruption loss alleged to have resulted from destruction of a lumber mill owned and operated by an insured, who was using logs from his own logging operation, was successfully defended * * * on the showing that, while he was making some money on the combined operation, his mill was being operated so inefficiently that he would have been money ahead if he had simply sold his logs at market price to other mills instead of running them through his mill and selling the lumber.

* * *

Losses Beyond Scope of Coverage

A complicating and often misunderstood factor is that certain losses of income that the insured may suffer as a result of suspension caused by an insured hazard are beyond the scope of the coverage.

One limitation is that recovery is restricted to loss of income that would otherwise have been earned during the suspension period.

* * * [There may be] a substantial additional but uninsured loss consisting of reduction in income subsequent to the date of full restoration.

* * *

There is, of course, a very obvious reason why this portion of the loss is not insured and coverage must be restricted to the actual suspension period: claims would be opened up to a degree of speculation which would be absurd. It is common knowledge that business interruption for any extended period may, and often does, result in a loss of customers, some for a short period, some for longer periods, and some permanently. Also, an insured may lose key personnel, which would cut down future productivity. There is, however, absolutely no method of determining with any degree of accuracy the amount of such losses or over how long a period they might extend.

*   *   *

On occasions it will be found that key employees, whose salaries have been included as a part of the business interruption claim as necessary continuing expense, have spent a portion of their time on reconstruction work. Such time should, of course, be subtracted from the business interruption claim and, in so holding, the United States Court of Appeals for the 10th Circuit has, in effect, recognized that the two types of coverage may be inter-related by stating: "This item was properly disallowed on the grounds that it had been paid by the insurer as a part of the property loss." National Union Fire Ins. Co. v. Anderson–Prichard Oil Corp., 141 F.2d 443 (10th Cir.1944).

Contribution or Coinsurance Clause

The contribution clause, under the single-item gross earnings form, restricts recovery to that portion of the loss which the insurance carried bears to an agreed percentage of the gross earnings that would have been earned had no loss occurred during the twelve months immediately following the date of the fire. The term "gross earnings" is rather clearly defined in another portion of the form.

Accordingly, aside from the inherent speculativeness already discussed as to what the annual gross earnings would have been had there been no fire, there is usually no particular problem in applying the contribution clause to losses under this form.

*   *   *

NOTE

1. The suspension period is that period of time which would be required to restore the property to its previous condition with the exercise of due diligence and taking account of any expediting which may be feasible. Clearly, reasonable men may differ on the length of the suspension period. What steps can the lessor, lessee and the insurance company take to reduce or eliminate the possibility of controversy with respect to the length of the suspension period?

    a. If replacement or restoration of the destroyed premises is not contemplated, how is the suspension period determined? For example, assume that the parties agree that the suspension period would be a year. A month before the fire, however, the insured makes a decision to terminate business operations within six months and sell the property. On the other hand, the insured may decide to move, and within two months after the fire, the insured may have established business operations at a new location. See *Hawkinson Tread Tire Service Co. v. Indiana Lumbermens Mutual Ins. Co.,* 362 Mo. 823, 245 S.W.2d 24 (1951).

2. Insuring gross earnings less expenses which do not continue through the suspension period or lost net profits plus continuing expenses, as those terms are usually defined in the typical business interruption policy, is not the type of coverage that the typical lessor of rental real estate desires.

a. For accounting and income tax purposes, a development may show a loss or a small profit, while the lessor may receive a substantial return through the cash flow generated by the development. The gross earnings or net profits of a development may not be an accurate measure of the value of the continued operation of the development to the developer.

b. The considerations described above can be taken into account by defining gross earnings to mean net cash flow. There might be, however, a negative cash flow in the years prior to the casualty and, looking toward the years after the point at which the annual amortization of the principal amount of mortgage liability is greater than the annual depreciation deduction, a typical gross earnings or net profit definition might be more desirable.

c. The answer to the concerns described above may be the use of use and occupancy insurance.

1. This type of insurance can take a variety of forms. For example, the policy might provide for recovery of an amount equal to the gross rentals, less saved expenses, which would have been received by the lessor from the premises. How should depreciation during the suspension period be treated under this form of use and occupancy insurance? Can property which has been destroyed by a fire depreciate?

a. A use and occupancy policy may have to have a face amount representing the total insurance protection provided. How does a lessor determine how much insurance to carry since at the time a policy is purchased the extent of the damage and the time required to repair it are not known? This question becomes more significant if the policy contains a coinsurance provision.

2. On the other hand, a policy might provide for a flat per diem or weekly or monthly allowance for the loss of the use of the premises during the suspension period without a limit on the total proceeds.

d. A partial loss will raise many of the same concerns discussed above. A fire in one store in a shopping plaza may have a great or negligible impact on the income of the lessor. The true measure of its effect, however, is in the loss of rental receipts. If a flat rate policy is not used, there may be some problem in allocating expenses to the damaged store, but this is not an insurmountable problem.

3. The suspension period limitation can result in a lessor incurring losses which are not covered by the insurance policy. For example, a lessor may be unable to find a new lessee for restored premises when the damage to the premises was substantial enough to permit the prior lessee to exercise an option to terminate its lease which had a term substantially in excess of the suspension period.

a. Can the lessor, and indirectly the mortgagee, be protected against this type of loss?

4. See generally Miller, *Business Interruption Insurance, A Legal Primer,* 24 Drake L.Rev. 799 (1975); Hecker, *Business Interruption Losses: An Overview,* 12 Forum 629 (1977).

d.   INCOME TAX TREATMENT OF INSURANCE PROCEEDS AND THE DEDUCTIBILITY OF PREMIUMS

THE TAX CONSEQUENCES OF A LOSS

Robert S. Holzman
36 Taxes 49 (1958).

* * *

From the federal income tax point of view, losses or provisions for losses fall into several categories:

(1) The loss is to be claimed as a deduction in the year of incurrence, whether or not that is most convenient taxwise [and whether or not collection has been made on the insurance policy]. Ordinarily a casualty loss is deductible in full [9] (to the extent not compensated for by insurance or otherwise), in accordance with Section 165 of the Internal Revenue Code. However, the amount of the deduction is limited to the adjusted basis of the asset, even though the recovery would be woefully inadequate to purchase a replacement asset at today's prices. * * *

(2) Proceeds of insurance are applied against the loss, and only the excess over the insurance proceeds is deductible. Gain may be capital.

(3) If a business is deprived of property by what Section 1033 of the Code refers to as an involuntary conversion (fire, theft or other casualty), gain on the disposition of business assets held for more than [the required period, under the Code] would be treated as long-term capital gain, [assuming Section[s] 1245 [and] 1250 do not convert some of the gain to ordinary income] while losses would be fully deductible for this purpose. However, gains and losses from involuntary conversions would have to be netted, so that if there were a net gain, a casualty loss would * * * only reduce the amount [of] capital gain.

(4) Reserves for losses or contingencies are not deductible. A reserve set up for self-insurance equal to the estimated premiums that otherwise would be paid to insurance companies is not deductible. * * * A reserve is nondeductible even though insurance is unobtainable, and hence no other provision seems possible. * * *

(5) Repairs are not deductible if they add to the life or usefulness of the property. Instead, the expenditures must be capitalized. * * *

(6) Expenditures to prevent future repair bills or even potential future damage are not currently deductible as repairs. * * *

(7) Use and occupancy insurance proceeds, if in lieu of earnings that would have been taxable, are taxable. * * *

Allowance for most types of insurance premiums is provided for by Section 162 of the Internal Revenue Code, which permits as a deduction "all the ordinary and necessary expenses paid or incurred during the

---

9. [See Section 165(c) for limitations on the deductibility of losses incurred by individuals.]

taxable year in carrying on any trade or business ∗ ∗ ∗." "Among the items included in business expenses," declare the regulations, "are ∗ ∗ ∗ insurance premiums against fire, storm, theft, accident, or similar losses in the case of a business ∗ ∗ ∗." (Regulations Section 1.162–1.)

∗ ∗ ∗ Any [insurance] expense for the business seems to fall within this category of ordinary and necessary expenses, except for the life insurance premiums specifically excluded—and even such premiums have been held to be deductible as a business expense under certain circumstances, as where a creditor takes out a policy on the life of a debtor. (O.D. 38, 1 C.B. 104.)

To be deductible under this heading, the expenditure must be for the purchase of insurance. "Insurance" has been authoritatively defined as follows: "A contract whereby, for an agreed premium, one party undertakes to compensate the other for loss on a specified subject by specified perils." (Bouvier's Law Dictionary, 1946 Edition, page 564.)

As long as the insured is contractually bound to pay premiums to the insurer, it is immaterial that the actual net cost of the insurance is not known in a particular year. ∗ ∗ ∗

Policies, the final net cost of which is not known in the taxable year, are a familiar form of coverage. The retrospective rating plan "gives weight to the loss experience in the current policy year of the individual. ∗ ∗ ∗ The scheme therefore offers an incentive. ∗ ∗ ∗ If the ∗ ∗ ∗ [insured] does accept the retrospective rating plan, the premium for the current policy is adjusted after the termination of the policy period. ∗ ∗ ∗ The premium for the current policy period will be less or more than the premium at standard rates subject to certain limits depending upon the losses developed for the period." (S.B. Ackerman, Insurance (New York, The Ronald Press Company, 1951), pages 670, 672.) That is, if losses have been less than the underwriters expected, a refund of a portion of the premium is made as a reward to the policyholder. If losses prove excessive as compared to the initial expectation of the underwriters, an additional premium or penalty is charged. ∗ ∗ ∗

The tax treatment [is that] ∗ ∗ ∗ the premiums [are] tax deductible in the year of payment [and any] refunds (less loading charges) ∗ ∗ ∗ are included in gross income during the year of receipt.[10] ∗ ∗ ∗

To be deductible, an expenditure must meet the statutory requirements as to its being ordinary and necessary. "The statute contains no express limitation with respect to the reasonableness of the amounts as a condition to deduction, but ∗ ∗ ∗ payments ∗ ∗ ∗ which are excessive in amount, taking into consideration all the facts of the particular case, do not constitute ordinary and necessary business

10. [If the deduction of the premiums did not result in a reduction of tax, a later refund may not have to be included in gross income. See Reg.Sec. 1.111–1(a).]

expenses." * * * Thus *any* amount of premium may not constitute an allowable deduction for tax purposes. Such is the case with certain premiums on factory fire insurance mutuals. Here "members are required to pay premiums in excess of expenses and expected losses. At the end of the year, excess premiums are refunded as dividends, which have been large." * * * In such a case it might be argued that the insured was making a payment that was believed at the time to consist of two elements—part protection and part future dividend. Where, however, the rate is set on a scientific basis under approved actuarial methods on the assumption that the carrier will over a period of years pay out in claims all except loading charges, the amount of the premium could not be said to be unreasonable to any extent. [If the] premium when set in arm's-length bargaining between the insurer and insured [is] such that in the year of payment both parties regarded the payment as one that was exclusively for coverage[, it is deductible]. If, because of retrospective premium adjustment, any amount is to be repaid to the insured, that is of tax concern only in the year of repayment.

An amount accrued and paid in one year as insurance premiums, although refunded in a subsequent year on the cancellation or expiration of the contract, is a proper deduction for tax purposes in the year of accrual and payment. (Louis S. Cohn Company, C.C.H. Dec. 4226, 12 B.T.A. 1281 (1928).) Where a corporation in a taxable period receives refunds of insurance premiums paid and properly deducted in a previous year, they represent taxable income to the corporation when returned to it. (Jamaica Water Supply Company, C.C.H. Dec. 11,256, 42 B.T.A. 359 (1940).) Refunds of premiums on policies of workmen's compensation insurance represent ordinary income and not dividends to an employer. (Houston Chronicle Publishing Company, C.C.H. Dec. 14,101, 3 T.C. 1233 (1944) * * *.

* * *

NOTE

1. If the property damaged by a casualty is used in the trade or business of a taxpayer and is subject to the allowance for depreciation, the excess of insurance proceeds over basis is generally treated as capital gains. Sections 1245 and 1250 may apply to recapture some of the gain at ordinary rates. See Sections 1245(b) and 1250(d).

2. In the event of an involuntary conversion—property destroyed or condemned in whole or in part—Section 1033 permits a taxpayer to avoid recognition of the gain from the receipt of insurance proceeds in excess of the adjusted basis of the property destroyed or condemned, if the insurance or condemnation proceeds are invested in property similar or related in service or use to the property destroyed or condemned within two years after the close of the first taxable year in which any part of the gain is realized. This period can be extended by the Internal Revenue Service on application by the taxpayer. If condemned property is real property held for productive use in trade or business or for investment and the proceeds are invested in property of a like-kind within three years after the close of the first taxable year in which any

part of the gain upon the condemnation is realized. Section 1033 provides for nonrecognition of the gain. See Section 1033(g)(1) and (4).

a. If damaged property is repaired with the use of insurance proceeds, Section 1033 applies. Section 1033 also applies if the insurance proceeds are used to buy stock representing "control" (see Reg.Sec. 1.1033(a)–2(c)(1)) of a corporation owning property similar or related in use to the involuntarily converted property. Does Section 1033 apply if insurance proceeds are used to buy a sixty percent general partnership interest in a limited partnership owning property similar or related in use? See Rev.Rul. 55–351, 1955–1 C.B. 343, and Rev.Rul. 70–144, 1970–1 C.B. 170. Can individual partners replace partnership property, and claim the benefits of Section 1033? See *Mihran Demirjian,* 54 T.C. 1691 (1970), affirmed, 457 F.2d 1 (3d Cir.1972); *Estate of Jerome K. Goldstein,* 35 CCH Tax Ct.Mem. 71 (1976). Cf. Rev.Rul. 66–191, 1966–2 C.B. 300. If property owned by and used in the trade or business of a partnership which property is subject to liabilities in excess of the total amount of the bases of the partners in their partnership interests is condemned, and the partnership elects to and replaces the condemned property with similar property subject to liabilities in the same or a greater amount, do the partners recognize any gain on the transaction despite the application of Section 1033? See Rev.Rul. 81–242, 1981–2 C.B. 147.

b. The basis of the replacement property is its cost decreased by the amount of the gain not recognized. If the replacement property consists of more than one piece of property, the basis, as determined above, is allocated among the replacement properties in proportion to their respective costs. See Rev.Rul. 73–18, 1973–1 C.B. 368.

c. The meaning of the phrase "property similar or related in service or use" is sometimes difficult to determine. If an apartment house owned by a developer is destroyed by fire, can the developer invest the insurance proceeds in an office building and avoid the recognition of gain under Section 1033? See e.g. *Liant Record, Inc. v. Comm'r,* 303 F.2d 326 (2d Cir. 1962); *Clifton Investment Co. v. Comm'r,* 312 F.2d 719 (6th Cir.1963), cert. denied, 373 U.S. 921, 83 S.Ct. 1524, 10 L.Ed.2d 422 (1963); *O.D. Bratton v. J.M. Rountree,* 37 A.F.T.R.2d 76–762 (M.D.Tenn.1976); *Westchester Development Co.,* 63 T.C. 198 (1974), acq. 1975–2 C.B. 2. Revenue Rul. 73–120, 1973–1 C.B. 369, held that the proceeds received from the conversion of a water plant can be invested in an apartment building, under Section 1033. Revenue Rul. 76–319, 1976–2 C.B. 242, held that a billiard center was not similar or related in service or use to a bowling center. In Rev.Rul. 76–390, 1976–2 C.B. 243, and Rev.Rul. 76–391, 1976–2 C.B. 243, a motel and a commercial building leased on a net-lease basis were considered not similar or related in service or use to, nor like-kind replacements of, respectively, a mobile home park and farmland leased to tenant farmers. Apparently, the reason that the properties were not similar or related in service or use or like-kind was that the owner of the mobile home park constructed the motel on land remaining after the involuntary conversion, and the owner of the farm constructed the commercial building on land owned prior to the involuntary conversion of the farmland. Since land had been involuntarily converted, it could not be replaced by a building. The position of the Internal Revenue Service is that the land is not of the same nature or character as a building. See Priv.Ltr.Ruls. 8119029 and 8307007. But see *Davis v. United States,* 589 F.2d 446 (9th Cir.1979); Robinson, *Improve-*

ments Can Qualify as Replacement Property Under Sec. 1033, Says New Decision, 52 J. Tax'n 340 (1980); Ronce, *Land and Improvements Are Definitely Not "Like Kind" (Are They?),* 61 Taxes 382 (1983). In an interesting ruling, the Internal Revenue Service held that an ocean-going seafood processing plant was not similar or related in service or use to a land-based seafood processing plant. See Rev.Rul. 77–192, 1977–1 C.B. 249. On the other hand, Rev.Rul. 78–72, 1978–1 C.B. 258, held that a thirty-year lease of an apartment building was a like-kind replacement for undeveloped real estate held for investment.

3.   If a taxpayer purchases a five-year policy of fire and casualty insurance and pays in full the premium for five years, is the total premium currently deductible? Is the premium treated as a payment for an asset having a life longer than one year which must be amortized over the life of that asset? Does the method of accounting used by the taxpayer make any difference? See *Harold W. Guenther,* 34 CCH Tax Ct.Mem. 834 (1975).

4.   Prior to the 1969 amendments to the Internal Revenue Code, an anomaly existed with respect to losses and gains incurred by a business as a result of a fire or other casualty. If a loss was not insured, it was generally deductible as an ordinary loss under Section 165. If, however, the loss was insured, the amount of the loss, the difference between the adjusted basis of the property and the amount of the insurance proceeds, was treated under Section 1231. Therefore, if in addition to the loss on the insured property there were gains on other Section 1231 property during the taxable year, the amount of the loss would be netted against the capital gains recognized on the other Section 1231 property. On the other hand, if there was a gain as a result of the receipt of insurance proceeds with respect to the destruction of business property, the receipt of insurance proceeds in excess of the adjusted basis of the property, the gain would be treated as capital gain under Section 1231. The amendments to Section 1231 made by the Tax Reform Act of 1969 eliminated this anomaly.

SENATE COMM. ON FINANCE, TAX REFORM ACT OF 1969

S.Rep. No. 552, 91st Cong., 1st Sess. reprinted in 1969 U.S. Code Cong. & Admin. News 2239–2241.

Certain Casualty Losses Under Section 1231 (sec. 516(b) of the bill and sec. 1231(a) of the code)

Present law.—Generally, under present law * * * an uninsured loss on property (held for more than [the holding period required by the Code for long-term capital gain treatment]) resulting from fire, storm, shipwreck, or other casualty, or from theft, is not to be offset against gains treated as capital gains (that is, is not to be classified as a sec. 1231 loss) if the property was used in the taxpayer's trade or business (or was a capital asset held for the production of income). Thus, as a result of the 1958 amendment, these uninsured losses are deductible against ordinary income and are not required to be offset against gains which otherwise are treated as long-term capital gains. In other words, the 1958 amendment provided an exception to the general rule of section 1231 that the overall gain or loss position of the taxpayer under the section determines whether a loss is deductible against ordinary income or whether it must be used to offset what otherwise would be a capital gain.

General reasons for change.—The 1958 amendment was enacted to benefit business taxpayers who self-insure their business properties. Casualty losses on their business properties were excepted from section 1231 (and, thus, are fully deductible against ordinary income) in view of the fact that amounts added to their self-insurance reserves against casualty losses are not deductible although premiums paid to an outside insurance company for the same purpose by business taxpayers who are not self-insurers are deductible.

What may be considered somewhat anomalous results, however, have developed as a result of the 1958 amendment. On the one hand, a business taxpayer with a casualty loss on two similar business properties, one of which is insured and one of which is not, is allowed to deduct the loss on the uninsured property in full against ordinary income and at the same time is allowed to treat the gain on the insured property (the excess of the amount of insurance received over his adjusted basis in the property) as a capital gain. In other words, although this situation would appear to be squarely within the basic concept of section 1231 which requires losses to be netted against gains, such a netting is not required in this situation and, thus the loss rather than reducing the capital gain is deductible in full from ordinary income.

On the other hand, the basic offsetting of gains and losses is required where a business taxpayer only partially insures a business property. Thus, if a business taxpayer has a casualty loss on a business property which is only partially, perhaps 5 percent, insured, the deductibility of the loss against ordinary income is determined by the basic section 1231 rule which looks to the overall gain or loss position of the taxpayer. As indicated, however, if the property had not been insured at all, the loss would have been fully deductible against ordinary income without regard to the taxpayer's overall gain or loss position under section 1231.

The committee agrees with the House that the present distinction under section 1231 between insured and [un]insured casualty losses is unrealistic. Moreover, the committee agrees that it is not appropriate to allow a business taxpayer to deduct an uninsured casualty loss on business property in full from ordinary income when he also has a larger casualty gain on insured business property which is treated as a capital gain. * * *

Explanation of provision.—The House bill and the committee amendments modify the treatment of casualty losses and casualty gains under section 1231 to meet the problems discussed above. Under the bill, casualty (or theft) losses on depreciable property and real estate used in a trade or business and on capital assets held for [the holding period required by the Code for long-term capital gain treatment] are to be consolidated with casualty (or theft) gains on this type of property. If the casualty losses exceed the casualty gains, the net loss, in effect, will be treated as an ordinary loss (without regard to section 1231). On the other hand, if the casualty gains equal or exceed the casualty losses, then the gains and losses will be treated as section 1231 gains and losses which must then be consolidated with other gains and losses under section 1231.

This consolidation rule is to apply whether the casualty property is uninsured, partially insured, or totally insured. In addition, it is to apply in the case of casualty property which is a capital asset held for [the holding period required by the Code for long-term capital gain treatment] whether the property is business property, property held for the production of income or a personal asset. (Although the House clearly intended to include personal capital assets within this consolidation rule, they were inadvertently omitted from the House bill. The committee amendments correct this omission.)

5. The taxation of the proceeds of business interruption and use and occupancy insurance is, in many ways, different than the taxation of the proceeds of fire and casualty insurance.

"It is well settled, and it should come as no surprise to anyone, that a reimbursement for lost profits resulting from the partial or total suspension of a business because of fire is taxable to the recipient as ordinary income and not as capital gain. Moreover taxation is not avoided under the nonrecognition provisions of Section 1033(a) of the Code, even though such proceeds are invested in replacement property similar, or related in service or use, to the property destroyed. This is not true, however, of proceeds received under a valued insurance contract where a flat per-diem (or weekly or monthly) allowance is made for the loss of the use and occupancy of the property destroyed, measured from the date of the occurrence of the fire to the time when the destroyed property can, with due diligence, be replaced and operations be resumed. In such a case the use and occupancy insurance proceeds are added to the ordinary fire insurance proceeds for tax purposes, and their investment in replacement property of similar or related service or use entitles a taxpayer to the nonrecognition of gain benefits of Section 1033(a). This rule has been applied even though a taxpayer's right to the use and occupancy of its plant, for insurance purposes, is treated separately from the physical plant itself and made a distinct object of insurance.

*   *   *

"There is a difference between the language of Section 1033(a), relating to the nonrecognition of gain upon involuntary conversions, and that of Section 1231, which applies special rules to the taxation of recognized gains or losses from involuntary conversions. Section 1033(a) provides that if *property* is compulsorily or involuntarily converted into property similar or related in service or use to the property so converted, or into money which is forthwith in good faith expended in the acquisition of other property similar or related in service or use to the property so converted, no gain shall be recognized.

*   *   *

"*   *   *[T]he term 'property' is used broadly in Section 1033(a), but is restricted in Section 1231 to 'property used in the trade or business,' as defined [in Section 1231(b)(1)]. However, Section 1231 applies not only to the involuntary conversion of property used in the trade or business, but also to the involuntary conversion of 'capital assets held for more than [the holding period required by the Code for long-term capital gain treatment].'

"*   *   *[I]t is arguable that since the destroyed property was itself depreciable property used in a taxpayer's trade or business, the right of use and occupancy of such property, being an 'integral' and 'indispensable' part of such property, must also be depreciable property used in the taxpayer's trade or business, and Section 1231 should be applicable to any gain upon its involuntary conversion.

"The Commissioner might contend that when a building or machinery is constructed or purchased by a taxpayer, the cost of construction or the purchase price relates only to the physical property and not to the intangible right to use and occupancy. Pursuing this, he might continue that while the physical property has a basis for depreciation and may be depreciated, in the ordinary case the right to use and occupancy is not separately paid for and has no basis for depreciation (a zero basis), and is therefore not 'depreciable.' In answer, it may be said that if the right to use and occupancy is an 'integral' and 'indispensable' part of the property destroyed, no dissection of the property can be made so as to claim that one portion is 'depreciable' and another portion is not. Further, if separately paid for, the right to use and occupancy would be property 'of a character which is subject to the allowance for depreciation.' It could be urged with some force that this characterization is not lost because in a particular case no separate payment therefor has been made.

"Even should the Commissioner be able to sustain the contention that the right to use and occupancy is not depreciable property used in a taxpayer's trade or business within the Section 1231 definition, the gain should still qualify as capital gain because Section 1231 also applies to the involuntary conversion of 'capital assets held for more than [the holding period required by the Code for long-term capital gain treatment].' The term 'capital asset' is defined in Section 1221 to mean 'property held by the taxpayer,' with certain exceptions not here applicable. If the right to use and occupancy is a property right, it is 'property' which is 'held' by a taxpayer. Indeed, the Section 1033(a) cases which have held that the involuntary conversion rules are applicable to the proceeds of valued use and occupancy insurance policies are necessarily premised on the right to use and occupancy being 'property.'

* * *

"If the insured right to use and occupancy is treated as separate nondepreciable property with a zero basis to the insured, the entire recovery under the use and occupancy policy would constitute Section 1231 capital gain, if the destroyed property had been held by the taxpayer for more than [the holding period required by the Code for long-term capital gain treatment]. If the right is considered to be an integral part of the physical property itself, the proceeds would be added to the proceeds received by the insured under the direct-damage insurance policies when determining the amount and kind of gain arising out of the insurance settlements, and any gain to the insured arising out of the insurance settlements would be long-term capital gain [11] within the framework of the rules set forth in Section 1231." Merritt, *How the Proceeds of Use and Occupancy, or Business Interruption, Insurance are Taxed,* 36 Taxes 306, 308–315 (1958).

6. The above analysis, which suggests that the proceeds of a flat rate per diem use and occupancy policy are eligible for Section 1033 treatment and possibly subject to treatment as capital gains under Section 1231, may have merit when the insured is a manufacturing or retail concern using the premises for the carrying on of its business. Is the analysis as persuasive, however, when the insured is a real estate developer deriving its income from the use of the premises by others? In Rev.Rul. 73–477, 1973–2 C.B. 302, the Internal Revenue Service indicated that when the proceeds received under a per diem use and occupancy policy depend on the net profits and fixed charges of the insured, the proceeds are considered a reimbursement of the insured's loss of income and are treated as ordinary income. Nonrecognition treatment under Section 1033 is not available. See Reg.Sec. 1.1033(a)–2(c)(8); *Marshall Foods, Inc. v. United States,* 393 F.Supp. 1097 (D.C.Minn.1974), affirmed per curiam, 36 A.F.T.R.2d 75–5095 (8th Cir.1975). Cf. Priv.Ltr.Rul. 8205005. Revenue Rul. 73–477, supra, seems to imply that if the proceeds of a per diem use and occupancy policy are fixed in amount and do not vary according to the insured's

11. [If neither Section 1245 nor 1250 applied to this gain.]

profits, etc., the proceeds can be considered compensation for the loss of a property right, the right to use the property, and nonrecognition treatment under Section 1033 is available. The Internal Revenue Service held in Rev.Rul. 86–12, 1986–1 C.B. 290, that if the coverage of a business interruption policy is based on the profits of the insured, the proceeds derived from the policy are not eligible for treatment under Section 1033 even if the amount of the proceeds paid to the insured does not vary during the suspension period. In Rev.Rul. 74–444, 1974–2 C.B. 272, the Internal Revenue Service, while acknowledging that the proceeds received under a valued use and occupancy policy are received as compensation for the loss of the right to use Section 1231 property, held that the right to the use of the property is not the type of property described in Section 1231(b), that the proceeds received for the loss of the right to use are in the nature of rent, and therefore, the proceeds do not qualify for capital gain treatment under Section 1231. See Priv.Ltr.Rul. 8315007. Cf. *Marshall Foods, Inc. v. United States*, 393 F.Supp. 1097 (D.C.Minn.1974), affirmed per curiam, 36 A.F.T.R.2d 75–5095 (8th Cir.1975).

7. If the proceeds of insurance policies are subject to tax in part or in whole, when are the proceeds subject to tax, and if there is a loss, when is the loss recognized?

    a. If the proceeds of a fire or casualty insurance policy are less than the adjusted basis of the property destroyed, the loss is taken in the year the fire or other casualty occurred reduced by the estimate of the insurance proceeds recoverable. If the amount of insurance proceeds recovered in later years is less or more than estimated, an amended return for the year of the loss is filed.

    b. If the amount of the insurance proceeds to be derived from a fire or casualty policy exceeds the adjusted basis of the property destroyed and "if all the events necessary to fix the direct-damage liability of the fire insurance company occur within the taxable year and if the amount of the liability has become fixed or ascertainable, * * * income, if any, is [recognized] at [that] time. If not, income is [recognized] at the time when the liability does become fixed or ascertainable." Merritt, supra, at 317.

    c. On the other hand, if the proceeds of a business interruption or use and occupancy policy are treated as lost profits, the proceeds may have to be allocated to prior years if the proceeds compensated for profits lost in those years. The proceeds cannot be allocable to years following the year of recovery under the policy, even if the recovery compensated for profits lost in those years because of the "claim of right" doctrine. See Merritt, supra. But cf. *Curtis Electro Lighting, Inc.*, 60 T.C. 633 (1973), vacated and remanded mem., 532 F.2d 756 (7th Cir.1976).

8. See generally Crapo, *Tax Consequences of a Disaster*, 23 # 2 Prac.Law. 51 (1977).

4. WITHDRAWAL OF EARNINGS FROM THE OPERATING ENTITY

No matter how profitable the operation of real estate may be, the direct benefit of its operation is not realized by the participants unless it results in cash in their pockets. There are a number of ways of making an entity's earnings available to the participants while continuing the operation of the entity.

a.   COMPENSATION

A typical method used to make the earnings of an entity available to the participants is the payment of compensation. The word compensation, as used in this section, means more than simply salary. It includes fringe benefits such as stock options, deferred compensation, term life insurance, etc. The payment of compensation, however, can present some difficult problems.

EDITORIAL NOTE
JUDICIAL ATTITUDE TOWARD EXECUTIVE COMPENSATION

29 University of Cincinnati Law Review 245 (1960).
[footnotes omitted]

How much is a man worth? What determines his value? What role is played by the courts of equity in reviewing this determination? The foregoing are just a small sample of the myriad of problems which are inherent in the confused field of compensation paid to corporate executives. Executive compensation programs are so varied, erratic, and complex that despite numerous intensive studies no definite or consistent pattern has as yet been cognizable.

Originally[,] it was presumed that directors were to serve the corporation without pay. They were entitled to no compensation for their services unless there was an express by-law provision, a shareholder's resolution, or a contract for compensation. The courts refused to recognize any implied contractual or quasi-contractual right to compensation, reasoning that the directors' fiduciary capacity precluded remuneration. This presumption was also extended to director-officers. Officers of a corporation, however, who were not directors were not considered to be within this exclusionary rule and were permitted reasonable compensation for their services.

In order to avoid this judicial pronouncement of service without pay, directors began to look for methods of insuring their compensation. The means most commonly used were an express provision in the by-laws or a shareholder resolution delegating to the directors the authority to fix compensation.   *   *   *

Once the management group had overcome the hurdle of nonpayment for their services, new problems as to management compensation immediately sprang forward. These areas of contention initially centered around compensation for past services, quorum requirements for voting compensation payments, and, perhaps the most litigated of all, the problem of judicial review of reasonableness in executive compensation plans.

Generally speaking, the courts were quite quick to strike down any payments to officers or directors for their past services to the corporation. The courts reasoned that such payment would be a misappropriation of corporate funds and a violation of the fiduciary responsibility, absent any type of formal or informal agreement prior to the rendering of the services.

The problems which have been litigated regarding quorum requirements for voting on compensation have left little doubt that in the absence of an express prohibition the directors may compensate themselves, if they follow applicable legal procedures. By far the most litigated issue involved in executive compensation has been the problem of what is reasonable compensation. The term has been defined by courts numerous times, yet it is sometimes still hazardous to predict with any degree of accuracy just how a court will treat a given factual situation.

Directors and officers of a corporation, in addition to their functions as mere agents, occupy a peculiar position of quasi-trustees both to the corporation and to the stockholder which in theory enables the courts of equity to apply their full powers in order to prevent injustice. Thus a court of equity may offer relief to the complaining party in the form of an accounting, injunction, receivership, or even dissolution.

If we assume that the directors have obtained the authority to set their own compensation and if we further assume that they have not violated any quorum requirements nor attempted payments for past services, will a court of equity still review their decision as to the amounts they and the corporate officers are to receive? This has been, and is, one of the most perplexing questions that the practicing corporate attorney must handle. Unquestionably the courts do possess the power to review. However[,] it is well established that courts will not undertake to review the fairness of official salaries in a shareholder's suit attacking them as excessive, unless fraud, bad faith, or abuse of the fiduciary is shown. In dealing with the determination of executive compensation the courts have started by establishing the broad general principle that compensation must be reasonably related to the value of the services rendered. However, the burden of proving misuse or waste is upon the attacking party, and in the absence of a clear showing courts will hesitate to substitute their judgment for the directors.

* * *

The so-called business judgment rule prevented recovery in many of the flurry of cases which were brought after the depression. The courts refused to invade the province allotted to the directors and declined to upset their independent business judgment. * * * A judicial attitude of complacency thus developed toward executive compensation during the 1930's and 1940's. Courts feeling ill-equipped to deal with the problem, permitted the business judgment rule to protect the perhaps excessive plans and refused to lend their aid, save for obvious misappropriations and fraud.

The judicial picture was somewhat different, however, in relation to plans approved by directors of a corporation who were also the recipients of the plans as * * * officer[s] of the corporation. The courts held that in this situation the burden of proving that the salaries voted by directors for themselves as officers are reasonable is upon the directors. A failure to sustain the burden brought judgment for the complaining shareholders and often restitution of the entire salary to the corporation.

* * * [In recent years] stock option plans as well as bonus plans have been adopted by a number of large corporations as a part of their executive compensation program. Bonuses and stock options as a form of executive remuneration are not new. However, their popularity has greatly increased and with the increase has come a somewhat more scrutinizing judicial attitude toward executive compensation at least as to formal matters.

Initially the stock option plan was attacked on the ground that the option constituted a gratuity because the corporation received no consideration for the issuance of the security. The litigations have usually been centered over the problem of whether the consideration received was "good" and sufficient. However, in this connection the courts have quite often placed upon the directors the burden of proving that the consideration is sufficient. This determination of applicable substantive law often disposed of the contest, because of the overwhelming difficulty inherent in sustaining the burden of proof. This crucial hurdle, coupled with the courts' disposition to find spoliation, gift, and waste of corporate assets more readily than in prior cases involving large compensation payments, began a trend of removing compensation decisions from behind the protective veil of the directors' business judgment.

* * *

Conclusion

In the past twenty years the field of executive compensation has been surveyed over and over again both by economic and by legal scholars. Most economic scholars who have published their studies seem to feel that executive compensation is very largely a matter of incentive, and that the corporate directors are the proper evaluators of reasonableness. This view is the position widely held in the business community. A * * * law-and-economic survey * * * suggests that [the] many and erratic deviations between executive remuneration and the magnitude of the executive's job as indicated by the corporations' net income and total assets shows that executive remuneration may not actually, if legally, be fair or reasonable. This law-and-economic survey, although relatively broader, even economically in scope, than many of its predecessors, admittedly does not encompass exhaustively any of the variable economic or the psychological factors which add to an executive's value and worth to his company. Among these are factors such as competition for executives within the industry, and for that matter outside it. Another is the future development of a company which is currently planned and carried out by the present executives, but which will be reflected in profits, sales, or increased assets at a future date. To date no test has been devised which can adequately determine the entire value of an executive.

* * *

NOTE

1. The concern of the stockholders of a corporation with the reasonableness of the compensation of the entity's management personnel is shared by the limited partners of a limited partnership, the beneficiaries of a real estate investment trust, and even the uncompensated nonmanaging general partners of a partnership. Unless a partnership agreement provides otherwise, no partner is entitled to remuneration for acting in the partnership business. See Sec. 18(f) of the Uniform Partnership Act.

> a. Can questions about the compensation of managing participants be avoided by having compensation approved by all the participants in an entity? What can be done about the one dissenter?

2. In the event the reasonableness of compensation is questioned, who has the burden of proof? Is the placement of the burden of proof affected if the compensated personnel are members of the board of directors of the corporation or managing committee of the partnership but do not constitute a majority of the board or of the committee?

> a. How is the question of the "reasonableness" of compensation dealt with in the context of the business judgment rule? Is it possible that compensation can be unreasonable but sustained under the business judgment rule?
>
> > 1. Compare *Berkwitz v. Humphrey*, 163 F.Supp. 78 (N.D.Ohio 1958), with *Lieberman v. Becker*, 38 Del.Ch. 540, 155 A.2d 596 (1959).

3. See generally Schechter, *Executive Compensation*, 47 N.Y.St.B.J. 288 (1975); Vagts, *Challenges to Executive Compensation: For the Markets or the Courts?*, 8 J.Corp.L. 231 (1983).

4. Not only do stockholders, beneficiaries, uncompensated partners, limited partners and creditors have an interest in whether the compensation paid to the managing participants is fair, reasonable, and equitable but since compensation is frequently a deductible business expense, so has the Internal Revenue Service. Section 162(a)(1) has been construed to deny a deduction for other than reasonable compensation. As a result, the business judgment rule has not stood in the way of the Internal Revenue Service contesting the reasonableness of the compensation paid.

PALMETTO PUMP AND IRRIGATION CO. v. TOMLINSON

United States District Court Southern District of Florida, 1962.
9 AFTR 2d 1136, affirmed, 313 F.2d 220 (5th Cir.1963).

McRAE, Jr., District Judge:

Instructions to the Jury

* * *

Under the laws enacted by Congress, a corporation is entitled to certain deductions in computing taxable income, among them being its ordinary and necessary business expenses including a reasonable allowance for salaries or other compensation for personal services actually rendered. A corporation is not entitled to a deduction for dividends paid to its shareholders. The Commissioner of Internal Revenue, or his authorized representative, has the right and the duty under the law to disallow the deduction if the amounts claimed to be compensation for personal services are not in fact compensation or if they are not reasonable in amount. The main purpose of this provision in the law is to prevent a corporation from improperly reducing its corporate taxes by distributing profits to its shareholders disguised as salaries or other compensation.

It is particularly important for you to know that there is no contention by the Government in this case that there was any fraud practiced by the corporation or by any of the individuals involved in determining and paying the amounts involved purportedly as compensation. On the contrary, this case involves a good faith difference of opinion between the plaintiff, as taxpayer, and the Government as to whether the disputed portions of the above-mentioned payments were reasonable under all the circumstances and whether such disputed portions of such payments were as a matter of substance, actually in payment for services tendered or as a distribution of profits because of ownership.

You will be asked to decide whether the payment by the corporation of the amounts disallowed as a deduction by the Commissioner to the recipient stockholders were paid to them because of their ownership in the business rather than because of personal services rendered to the corporation by them as employees.

If the disallowed amounts were paid to them because they were owners of the business, then they are to be treated as dividends or withdrawals of capital even though the payments took the form of compensation.

If you conclude that the payments were in substance, as well as in form, compensation for personal services rendered the corporation, then you will be asked to decide for each of the officers what a reasonable compensation would be for the year involved.

A dividend paid by a corporation to its stockholders is generally paid out of the surplus net profits of the corporation as a return to the stockholders on their investment, that is upon their stockholdings. Money paid out as dividends does not constitute a business expense and cannot be deducted in determining taxable net income for federal income tax purposes. In considering whether the amounts purportedly paid as salaries or other compensation were in part a dividend disguised somewhat as salary or other compensation, you may consider the dividend history of the corporation and all the financial conditions surrounding the payment of or failure to pay dividends. The absence of dividends, coupled with the financial ability to pay them, is some evidence that the purported compensation, in part, constitutes a dividend. In deciding whether the payments were really salaries or whether they were really distributions of earnings or dividends to the owners of the business, you are to consider all the facts and circumstances, not merely the fact as to which there is no dispute that the payments were labeled as salaries and bonuses and that there was no formal declaration of a dividend. In reaching your decision, no single factor is decisive.

* * *

The mere size of the salaries paid is not a matter for your consideration. Your duty is to take the amounts received as salary, view the amounts in light of all the proven facts and decide whether the claimed deduction for 1957 can be treated as a reasonable allowance for salaries or other compensation for personal services actually rendered.

Now, in making your determinations, you may consider, among other matters, the following. These are factors that you take into account, balancing out whether you are to regard this as reasonable or not, and thereby salaries or dividends.

1. Evidence of the amount which would ordinarily be paid for like services by like enterprises under like circumstances.

2. The relationship of the payments to the stockholdings of the recipients.

3. Whether the purported salaries had a reasonable relationship to the gross and net income of the company during the tax year involved; and only the year 1957 is involved

4. Whether part of the amounts paid were year-end distributions at a time when profits of the corporation for the year were known.

5. The dividend history of the corporation and the circumstances existing at the time when dividends were paid or withheld by the corporation in the year involved and prior years.

6. The policy of plaintiff concerning the payment of salary and bonus to its other employees in the year involved and prior years.

7. Whether or not each individual recipient devoted all of his time to the business of the plaintiff corporation, or whether any of them had other time-consuming interests or activities.

8. The quality and quantity of the service actually rendered by each individual recipient, including the amount and the difficulty or simplicity of the work done by each and the responsibilities assumed by each.

9. The professional and business qualifications, experience and background of each individual recipient, including special training and experience and other qualifications.

What may be an ordinary and necessary expense or a reasonable allowance for salaries in a given corporation may vary from year to year, the variance being controlled by the fluctuating conditions of business generally and of the business itself and of management. It also varies in different corporations and sometimes in identical corporations engaged in the same business, located at the same place and practically under the same management, it being in the end largely controlled by the human element involved; that is to say, the capacity, judgment and diligence of those who control its operations.

* * *

Where the issue involves the reasonableness of salaries paid to corporate officers, as here, and all the shares of stock of the corporation are owned by its officers, the reasonableness of the salaries, and whether the payments are in fact payment for services rendered rather than a distribution of the profits based upon ownership, should be looked at more closely by the jury than in a case where outsiders hold some of the shares of stock in order that what is really a distribution of profits may not be passed off as a salary payment.

A bonus, either in a lump sum or a percentage of earnings, paid to a stockholder employee of a corporation at the end of the year, in addition to a fixed salary, does not prevent the total amount paid by the corporation from being reasonable compensation for services; however, the total amount so paid must be reasonable.

But the mere fact, standing alone, that compensation under a bonus compensation plan is larger in a particular successful year than in the immediate preceding years does not make it unreasonable.

It may happen that in any particular locality, no company performing services similar to those of plaintiff, is doing business. Therefore, the fact, alone, that the taxpayer failed to introduce any evidence showing what compensation other companies engaged in the same type of work paid for comparable services during the year in question, should not enter into your deliberations.

* * *

NOTE

1. If the recipient of compensation is not also a participant in the entity paying the compensation, can the compensation be challenged as unreasonable? In such a case the compensation is not a way of distributing the profits of the entity to the participants disguised as salaries. See, however, *Patton v. Commissioner,* 168 F.2d 28 (6th Cir.1948). Section 162(a)(1) makes no distinction between compensation paid to participants in the entity and compensation paid to others, all compensation must be reasonable.

    a. If part or all of an individual's compensation is disallowed as unreasonable and the recipient does not return the amount determined to be unreasonable to the payor under a preexisting agreement, is the unreasonable compensation treated as income to the recipient? If the recipient is a shareholder in the payor corporation or a partner in the payor partnership, and even after disallowing the deduction of the unreasonable amount of compensation, the corporation has no current or accumulated earnings and profits and the partnership still shows a net loss for the year, how does the recipient treat the unreasonable compensation? If the amount of the unreasonable compensation exceeds the basis of the shareholder in his stock or the basis of the partner in his partnership interest, how does the recipient treat the unreasonable compensation? If the recipient is a mere employee with no financial interest in the payor entity, now how does the recipient treat the unreasonable compensation?

b.   See generally Smith, *The Reasonableness of Executive's Compensation in a Closely Held Company,* 50 Taxes 347 (1972); Reimer, *Shareholder–Employee Compensation: How to Minimize Chances of IRS Disallowance,* 5 Tax'n Law. 356 (1977); Hariton and Cassuto, *Executive Compensation for the Closely Held Corporation,* 32 N.Y.U. Inst.Fed. Tax'n 941 (1974); Ford and Page, *Reasonable Compensation: Continuous Controversy,* 5 J.Corp. Tax'n 307 (1979); Rosenbloom, *How to Prove Up an Unreasonable Compensation Case: Methods by Which to Determine Reasonableness,* 60 Taxes 491 (1982).

2.   Since any taxpayer engaged in trade or business is entitled to a deduction for business expenses under Section 162, the question of the reasonableness of compensation can arise in either the incorporated or unincorporated business.

3.   Generally, the income of an S corporation is treated as recognized by its shareholders on a daily basis.   It would appear that the Internal Revenue Service has little reason to challenge the reasonableness of the compensation paid to shareholder-employees of an S corporation.

a.   If, however, some of the shareholders of an S corporation are not active in the business, the salaries of those active in the business can be used as a way of directing the income of the corporation away from high-rate taxpayers and to low-rate taxpayers.   In *Charles Rocco,* 57 T.C. 826 (1972), the Internal Revenue Service asserted that the salary paid the executive officer of an S corporation was unreasonably low.   See Gaffney, Dilley and Laverty, *Inadequate Compensation: An Emerging Issue for Tax–Option Corporations,* 58 Taxes 253 (1980).   Cf. *Gino A. Speca,* 38 CCH Tax Ct.Mem. 544 (1979).

1.   A high-rate active participant in a partnership might attempt to achieve a similar result by gift or transfer of a partnership interest to a low-rate, inactive relative.   Cf. Priv.Ltr.Rul. 8539003.   The income-splitting advantages of this technique, however, have been severely limited by the family partnership provision, Section 704(e). Section 704(b)(2) which denies effect to any provision of a partnership agreement having to do with a partner's distributive share of income, gain, loss, deduction or credit if the provision does not have substantial economic effect also limits the use of the partnership as an income-splitting device.

2.   Section 1366(e) of Subchapter S treats compensation for capital or services furnished by family members in a manner similar to its treatment under Section 704(e).   Section 1366(e) directs the Internal Revenue Service to make such adjustments as are necessary to properly reflect the value of services or capital furnished by a family member to an S corporation which has other family members as shareholders.

4.   In addition to challenging compensation as unreasonable, the Internal Revenue Service has challenged the deductibility of compensation paid during the early days of a real estate venture on the basis that it is a cost of organization, syndication or the cost of an asset.   See e.g. *Estate of W. Burgess Boyd,* 76 T.C. 646 (1981); Rev.Rul. 81–150, 1981–1 C.B. 119; Rev.Rul. 81–153, 1981–1 C.B. 387; Rev.Rul. 81–161, 1981–1 C.B. 313.   Even if the payment of compensation is for ordinary and necessary management functions, the Inter-

nal Revenue Service will attempt to disallow its deduction on the basis that it is a preopening expense. See e.g. *Richard C. Goodwin,* 75 T.C. 424 (1980); Rev. Rul. 81–150, 1981–1 C.B. 119. Preopening expenses, if ordinary and necessary, however, are eligible for amortization over 60 months starting with the commencement of business, as provided by Section 195(b).

5. Section 707(c) of the Internal Revenue Code provides that "guaranteed payments" made to a partner for services, or for the use of capital, are treated as made to one who is not a member of the partnership. One effect of this section is to treat a guaranteed payment made by a partnership to a partner roughly the same as salary or interest, resulting in a deduction to the partnership and income to the recipient partner.

FALCONER v. COMMISSIONER
40 T.C. 1011 (1963).

* * *

DAWSON, Judge: * * *

The issues for decision are:

(1) Whether amounts received by petitioner F.A. Falconer during the calendar years 1957 and 1958 from a partnership were guaranteed payments under the provisions of section 707(c), I.R.C. 1954, and taxable income to petitioners under section 61(a)(1). * * *

On or about September 1, 1957, F.A. Falconer (hereinafter referred to as petitioner) entered into a partnership agreement with Stella Breazeale (sometimes hereinafter referred to as petitioner's partner) to operate an employment agency, doing business under the name of Acme Employment Service (sometimes referred to herein as the partnership). The partnership agreement, dated November 5, 1957, provided in pertinent part, as follows: * * *

"6. As compensation for services to be rendered by the partners, each is to be paid as a salary the sum of $150.00 per week, such salaries to be paid on such date of the week as may be mutually agreed. * * * The salaries so paid insofar as the partners are concerned shall be considered as a part of the operating expense of the business.

"7. It is recognized by the partners that Breazeale has advanced certain sums of money to the partnership and may advance additional sums before the business has attained a sufficient volume of business and attained successful operation so as to pay the operating costs and expenses. It is agreed when the income of the business is sufficient to meet the cost of operations, any and all excess of such income shall be paid monthly to Breazeale until she has been repaid in full all of such advances.

"The ownership of the partnership business shall be on the basis of 50% by Falconer and 50% by Breazeale, and after all advances referred to in the preceding paragraph have been paid to Breazeale, the share of the net profits shall be paid to Falconer as to 50% and paid to Breazeale as to 50%; the division of the net profits and the payment of the same to the respective partners shall be at such time or times as the partners may from time to time mutually agree. In the event of losses accruing to the partnership, each partner shall contribute his or her 50% portion of such loss or losses so that each partner shall bear his or her just portion of such loss and thus avoid the necessity of either partner having to suffer the entire loss. Neither partner shall draw from the business more than his or her respective portion of the net profits without the written consent of the other. * * * "

* * *

The partnership continued in business until May 12, 1958, at which time it was dissolved and was succeeded by a corporation organized under the laws of the State of Texas. It adopted the name of Acme Employment Service, Inc. (sometimes hereinafter referred to as the corporation).

A partnership income tax return of petitioner and Stella Breazeale, doing business as the Acme Employment Service, was initially filed for the partnership for the period commencing September 1, 1957, and ending April 30, 1958, with the district director of internal revenue at Dallas, Tex. This return shows income in the amount of $6,434.80, operating expenses totaling $13,436.62, and a net loss of $7,001.82. It is labeled "First and Final Return."

After filing the first partnership income tax return, an unsigned partnership income tax return of petitioner and Stella Breazeale, doing business as the Acme Employment Service, for the period commencing January 1, 1958, and ending December 31, 1958, was filed with the district director of internal revenue at Dallas, Tex. A loss of $7,292.62 was shown on the return. By letter dated July 10, 1959, addressed to petitioner and Stella Breazeale, the district director advised them that the partnership income tax return had not been executed and requested them to execute a declaration which should have been signed on the return. The declaration was not executed and returned to the district director.

Subsequent to the filing of both of these partnership income tax returns, still another unsigned partnership return of petitioner and Stella Breazeale, doing business as the Acme Employment Service, covering the period commencing September 1, 1957, and ending June 30, 1958, was filed with the district director of internal revenue at Dallas, Tex. A loss of $7,292.62 was shown on this return. Attached thereto is a schedule designated "Withdrawals Made by F.A. Falconer." Such unexecuted return is identical with the return described in the preceding paragraph except that the period in the former return was interlined and another period substituted therefor. Such partnership income tax return has likewise not been executed.

During the calendar year 1957 the petitioner received weekly payments from the partnership under the terms of the partnership agreement aggregating $2,550, which sum was not reported by petitioners as income on their individual income tax return for such year or any other year.

During the period commencing September 1, 1957, and ending June 30, 1958, the petitioner received weekly payments aggregating $6,450, no part of which was reported by petitioner as income on [his] individual income tax return for the calendar year 1957, the calendar year 1958, or any other year.

Of such sum of $6,450, petitioner received income from the partnership under the terms of the partnership agreement in the amount of $2,850 from January 1, 1958 through May 10, 1958. From May 17, 1958, through June 28, 1958, petitioner received $1,050 from the corporation as salary, totaling $3,900 during the calendar year 1958, none of which was reported by petitioner in [his] income tax return for such year. The schedule attached to the last mentioned partnership return reflects the amounts paid by the partnership and the successor corporation and the dates such payments were made.

Petitioner made no contributions to the capital of the partnership. Stella Breazeale contributed all the capital of $19,775. Petitioner executed on May 12, 1958, which was the date the partnership dissolved, a demand promissory note, payable to the order of Stella Breazeale, in the principal sum of $9,862.50.

* * *

Issue 1.   Guaranteed Payments

It is the petitioner's contention that the payments, totaling $5,400, which he received from the partnership in 1957 and 1958 were loaned to him by his partner, Stella Breazeale, and, therefore, created a debt to her, as evidenced by the demand promissory note executed on the date the partnership was dissolved. Respondent, on the other hand, argues that the amounts received constitute guaranteed salary payments under the provisions of section 707(c). We agree with the respondent.

Section 707(c) has no counterpart in the Internal Revenue Code of 1939. It initially appeared in the Internal Revenue Code of 1954. Since we have been unable to locate in our research any court decisions pertaining directly to the issue here presented, we approach the problem as one of first impression. * * * The legislative history of section 707(c) reveals that it was specifically intended to require ordinary income treatment to the partner receiving guaranteed salary payments and to give a deduction at the partnership level.[12]

The touchstone for determining "guaranteed payments" is whether they are payable without regard to partnership income. And, in

12. S.Rep. No. 1622 to accompany H.R. 8300, 83d Cong., 2d Sess., p. 387 (1954), contains the following explanation: "Subsection (c) provides a rule with respect to guaranteed payments to members of a partnership. A partner who renders services to the partnership for a fixed salary, payable without regard to partnership income, shall be treated, to the extent of such amount, as one who is not a partner, and the partnership shall be allowed a deduction for a business expense. The amount of such payment shall be included in the partner's gross income, and shall not be considered a distributive share of partnership income or gain. A partner who is guaranteed a minimum annual amount for his services shall be treated as receiving a fixed payment in that amount."

determining whether in a particular case an amount paid by a partnership to a partner is a "drawing" or a "guaranteed payment," the substance of the transaction, rather than its form, must govern. See sec. 1.707–1(a), Income Tax Regs. These are both factual matters to be judged from all the circumstances.

We are convinced that the facts of this case clearly place the payments made to petitioner within the ambit of the term "guaranteed payments" as used in Section 707(c). Paragraph 6 of the partnership agreement provided that each partner was to receive a salary of $150 per week from the partnership as compensation for services rendered; that the amount of the *compensation* agreed to was subject to change only by mutual agreement of the partners; and that such *salaries* were to be considered a part of the operating expenses of the business. * * * There is no doubt in our minds that these weekly salary payments are made "without regard to the income of the partnership." The partnership was being operated at a loss and, consequently, it was necessary to make the guaranteed salary payments out of the capital Stella Breazeale had contributed. Petitioner's mere characterization of the payments in the partnership returns as "withdrawals" is not persuasive when viewed in connection with the precise provisions of the partnership agreement. This leads us inescapably to the conclusion that the amounts received by petitioner from the partnership under the terms of the agreement are guaranteed payments without regard to the income of the partnership and, as such, are includable in his gross income.

Under the provisions of section 706(a) such payments are characterized as ordinary income to the recipient for his taxable year within or with which ends the partnership taxable year in which the partnership deducted the payments. Hence, the taxable year of the partnership must be first determined.

In view of these rules and the facts herein, this partnership could only adopt a calendar year basis. Since the petitioner reported his income on a calendar year basis during 1957 and 1958, and was a principal partner by virtue of owning a 50–percent interest in the partnership, the partnership was precluded from adopting a fiscal year basis without the prior approval of the Secretary of the Treasury or his delegate. The record not only fails to reveal such approval, but there is no evidence that such approval was ever sought. Thus, the only recourse remaining to the partnership was the adoption of a calendar year which under the specific language of section 1.706–1(b)(1)(ii), Income Tax Regs., does not require the prior approval of the Commissioner. * * * It then follows that the payments, totaling $2,550, made to petitioner during the partnership's taxable year ending December 31, 1957, were includable in his taxable income for the calendar year 1957. Since the partnership's existence terminated [13] upon its dissolution on May 12, 1958, the partnership taxable year was closed on

13. Sec. 708. * * *

that date.[14]   As a result thereof, the guaranteed payments of $2,850 made by the partnership during the taxable year beginning January 1, 1958, and ending May 12, 1958, were includable in petitioner's taxable income for the calendar year 1958.

Petitioner stresses that the "withdrawals by F.A. Falconer, constituted a loan to him and not income." We find no merit in this position. His attempt to cast the relationship between himself and Stella Breazeale as that of debtor and creditor is wholly inconsistent with the express terms of the partnership agreement and contrary to all outward manifestations of their intent. Nor are we swayed by the fact that the petitioner executed a demand note for $9,862.50 to Stella Breazeale on the day the partnership was terminated. We do not even know for what purpose the note was given. The petitioner, who has the burden of proof, offered no evidence regarding it. Consequently, any conclusions we might try to draw with respect to the note and the purpose for it would be purely speculative. Even if we assume, as petitioner would have us do, that the note represented the "withdrawals" by the petitioner from the partnership and "his part of the expenses" paid from the capital account, it cannot serve to convert what was paid as salaries into something else. Certainly the character of such payments cannot be changed retroactively into a loan.

* * *

NOTE

1.   The above case demonstrates the effect of guaranteed payments. If the payments to the taxpayer were considered withdrawals and his basis in his partnership interest was in excess of the amount of the withdrawals plus his share of the losses of the partnership, he would have reported a loss for income tax purposes from the operations of the partnership for the years involved.

2.   Since Section 707(c) refers directly to Section 162(a), the amount of a guaranteed payment with respect to a partner's services must be reasonable compensation in order to be deductible by the partnership. Cf. Rev.Rul. 75–214, 1975–1 C.B. 185; *Jackson E. Cagle, Jr.,* 63 T.C. 86 (1974), affirmed, 539 F.2d 409 (5th Cir.1976); *Sidney Kimmelman,* 72 T.C. 294 (1979). See Sexton, *Guaranteed Payments of a Partnership: Are They Automatically Deductible?,* 41 J.Tax'n 312 (1974); Comment, *Guaranteed Payments of Partnerships: Deductibility Under Section 707(c),* 30 Sw.L.J. 927 (1976). In determining whether a guaranteed payment is deductible, it must meet the same tests, under Section 162(a), as a compensation payment made to a person who is not a member of the partnership and the normal rules of Section 263 (capital expenditures) must be taken into account. Cf. *Parks v. United States,* 434 F.Supp. 206 (N.D.Tex. 1977). See generally Stevenson and Jarchow, *Protecting the Tax Integrity of Partner–Partnership Transactions,* 8 Tax Adviser 82 (1977).

a.   If a payment sought to be deducted as a guaranteed payment is determined with regard to the income of the partnership, Section 707(c) will not apply and the payment will be treated as part of the distributive share of the payee partner. A payment may be said to have been determined with regard to the income of the partnership if it is determined

14.   Sec. 706. * * *

with regard to any amount which is used in the computation of the income of the partnership such as gross or net rent, gross receipts or gross income. See *Edward T. Pratt,* 64 T.C. 203 (1975), affirmed in part, reversed and remanded in part, 550 F.2d 1023 (5th Cir.1977). See Cowan, *Compensating the General Partner: The Pratt Case,* 56 Taxes 10 (1978); Weidner, *Pratt and Deductions for Payments to Partners,* 12 Real Prop., Prob. & Tr.J. 811 (1977). In Rev.Ruls. 81–300, 1981–2 C.B. 143 and 81–301, 1981–2 C.B. 144, the Internal Revenue Service retreated somewhat from the *Pratt* decision. In Rev.Rul. 81–300, management fees, paid to the general partners, of 5% of the gross rentals received by a partnership which owned and operated a shopping plaza, were treated as guaranteed payments under Section 707(c). The fees were paid to the general partners for their management of the partnership and its real estate and were reasonable in light of the services rendered. In Rev.Rul. 81–301, one of the general partners received 10% of the partnership's daily gross income in return for its services advising the partnership with respect to, and managing, the partnership's investments. The general partner's services were substantially the same as services it rendered to third parties in which it did not have an interest, and the amount paid for the services was reasonable in the light of the services rendered. The general partner could be removed as advisor and manager on 60 days notice, and it paid its own expenses connected with the performance of its duties. The 10% of daily gross income was held deductible under Section 707(a).

b. The partnership in the *Pratt* case used the accrual method of accounting while the general partners used the cash method. The partnership accrued but did not pay the management fees to the general partners. If Section 707(a) had applied, the partnership would have been entitled to deduct the fees at the time of the accrual of the fees, but the general partners would not have had to include them in income. Subsequently, Section 267 of the Code was amended to deny a partnership a deduction until the recipient partner takes the fees into income. See Section 267(a) (2). On the other hand, if Section 707(c) had applied, the general partners would have had to include the fees in income since Section 706(a) requires that partners include fees in income in the year in which the partnership deducts them. See generally Hoskins and Bower, *Partner vs. Nonpartner Distinctions After the Deficit Reduction Act of 1984,* 2 J.Ps.Tax'n 99 (1985).

3. Guaranteed payments for a partner's services are considered "compensation for services actually rendered" and therefore, are eligible for exclusion as foreign earned income under Section 911. See *Carey v. United States,* 192 Ct.Cl. 536, 427 F.2d 763 (1970); *A.O. Miller, Jr.,* 52 T.C. 752 (1969), acq. 1972–2 C.B. 2.

4. If guaranteed payments are considered "compensation for services," is the recipient an employee of the partnership for the purposes of the employee benefits sections of the Internal Revenue Code such as, Section 79 (group-term life insurance), Section 101(b) (employee death benefits), Section 105 (amounts received under accident and health plans), Section 106 (contributions by an employer to accident and health plans), Section 119 (meals and lodging) and Section 401 et seq. (employee pension and profit sharing plans)?

a. The Regulations and an early ruling take the position that a partner receiving guaranteed payments is not an employee for the purposes of Section 105(d). See Reg.Sec. 1.707–1(c); Rev.Rul. 56–362, 1956–2 C.B. 100. Cf. *Est. of Thomas J. O'Brien,* 21 CCH Tax Ct.Mem. 944 (1962). The

Fifth Circuit Court of Appeals, however, held that a partnership making guaranteed payments to a partner was the partner's employer for the purposes of Section 119. See *Armstrong v. Phinney*, 394 F.2d 661 (5th Cir. 1968). But see Rev.Rul. 69–184, 1969–1 C.B. 256, which holds that partners receiving guaranteed payments are not employees for F.I.C.A. and F.U.T.A. purposes and Rev.Rul. 72–596, 1972–2 C.B. 395, which holds that premiums paid for workman's compensation insurance on behalf of partners are not deductible by a partnership as amounts paid on behalf of employees even though the partners work alongside the employees.

5. See generally Davis and Vogel, *Guaranteed Payments: Strategies for Avoiding Pitfalls in Their Use*, 2 J.Ps.Tax'n 332 (1986); Postlewaite and Cameron, *Twisting Slowly in the Wind: Guaranteed Payments After the Tax Reform Act of 1984*, 40 Tax Law. 649 (1987); Banoff, *Determining the Character of Guaranteed Payments for Partners' Capital*, 67 J.Tax'n 284 (1987).

b. DISTRIBUTIONS BY A CONTINUING PARTNERSHIP TO PARTNERS—NOT AS SALARY OR GUARANTEED PAYMENTS

As long as a distribution by a partnership to partners is not a fraudulent conveyance and is approved by the partners whose approval is required by the partnership agreement, the distribution can be made and there are very few restrictions imposed on it. At worst, distributions which represent a return of capital must be repaid to the partnership if necessary to pay the creditors of the partnership. See Sec. 17(4) of the U.L.P.A. and Sec. 608 of the Rev.U.L.P.A. In addition, under Sec. 607 of the Rev.U.L.P.A., a partnership may not make a distribution while it is insolvent (liabilities exceed fair value of assets) or make a distribution which causes it to become insolvent. While it is comparatively simple for a partnership to make a distribution to partners, the income tax aspects of a distribution can be quite complex.

PARTNERSHIP DISTRIBUTIONS UNDER THE INTERNAL REVENUE CODE OF 1954

Paul Little
10 Tax Law Review 161 (1954).
[footnotes omitted]

*   *   *

General Principles Governing Distributions

A. *Recognition of Gain or Loss to Distributee*

The announced policy of Congress with respect to the recognition of gain or loss upon the distribution of partnership property is to limit quite narrowly the area in which such gain or loss is recognized. Despite this policy, recognition is, of course, required to the extent that the cash distributed exceeds the total basis to the distributee of his partnership interest, since otherwise the cash in the hands of the distributee would have a basis different from its face amount. Therefore, by the terms of section 731(a)(1) gain is recognized to the distributee only to the extent that "any money" distributed exceeds the partner's basis for his partnership interest immediately before the distribution. This rule applies whether the distribution is a current one received in the normal course of partnership operations or is in liquidation of all or a part of the distributee's partnership interest. However, this provision will prevent the recognition of gain to a distributee to the extent that he receives a distribution in kind.[15]

In furtherance of the stated policy, section 731(a)(2) provides that loss will be recognized only upon a liquidating distribution as a result of which the distributee partner's entire interest in the partnership is terminated, and even here, only when the distribution consists *solely* of money, unrealized receivables, and/or inventory items. * * * In accordance with the * * * legislative policy of limiting recognition of gain or loss on distributions, it is noteworthy that the presence in the distribution of any type of property, other than money, unrealized receivables, or inventory items, will result in the nonrecognition of loss on the distribution. In such a situation the basis of the distributee for his interest in the partnership which exceeds the amount of money and his basis for unrealized receivables and inventory items will then be deemed attributable to the other distributed property, but gain or loss with respect to such other property is postponed until its eventual disposition. By combining these rules with the principle of non-recognition of gain or loss on contributions of property to the partnership, Congress hope[d] to remove the deterrents to the movement of property in and out of partnerships as business reasons dictate.

B. *Recognition of Gain or Loss to Partnership*

Following the Congressional policy of non-recognition of gain or loss to the greatest extent possible on partnership distributions, section 731(b) provides that no gain or loss is recognized to a partnership on a distribution to a partner of property, including money. The term "partnership" as used in this section is apparently intended to include the nondistributee partners also, so that they too will have no recognizable gain or loss. * * *

C. *Nature of Gain or Loss Recognized to Distributee*

The gain or loss which is recognized to the distributee is considered gain or loss from a sale or exchange of the partnership interest of the distributee partner, which interest is considered a capital asset. There is no specific provision governing the holding period to be attributed to the interest in the partnership deemed sold or exchanged. However, under present case law it seems well established that this period begins to run from the date the distributee acquired his interest in the partnership. * * *

---

15. [The rule discussed in the first paragraph will not apply to the extent otherwise provided by section 736 or section 751. See pages 1091 to 1096 infra.]

D.   Basis of Distributed Property in Hands of Distributee

* * * [U]pon the distribution to a partner of money, the distributee's basis for his partnership interest is applied first to such money, dollar for dollar.   Any remaining basis for his partnership interest is then allocated to other assets distributed.   * * * If the distribution is a current distribution or one resulting only in the termination of a portion of the partnership interest, the distributed property takes as its basis in the hands of the distributee the same amount which it had in the hands of the partnership to the extent of the basis of the distributee for his partnership interest, less any cash distributed.   However, if the basis of the distributee's partnership interest is less than the total basis of the distributed assets in the hands of the partnership, the assets may not have a total basis to the distributee in excess of his basis for his partnership interest.   * * *

When there has been a distribution of property in liquidation or a current distribution in which the total basis of the distributee for his interest in the partnership is less than the total partnership basis for the distributed assets, the distributee's basis must be allocated among the various distributed assets.   First, if the distribution consists of any unrealized receivables or inventory items, the distributee's basis for his partnership interest must be allocated to such assets in an amount which will equal the amount of their bases in the hands of the partnership.   If the distributee's basis for his interest is insufficient for this purpose, it must be allocated among these items in proportion to the basis of each in the hands of the partnership.   If his basis is adequate for the purpose, any amount remaining is then allocated to the other distributed assets in proportion to their bases in the hands of the partnership.   On the other hand, if the inventory and receivables consume the entire basis of the distributee's interest in the partnership the basis of these remaining assets will be zero.

E.   Basis of Distributee's Partnership Interest

To the extent that the distribution is not in complete liquidation of the distributee's partnership interest, the * * * Code * * * provides that the basis for that interest shall be reduced by the amount of any money distributed and by the amount of such basis properly allocable to any other distributed property.   However, the basis of the distributee's partnership interest may not be reduced below zero by any distribution.   * * *

F.   Character of Gain or Loss Realized by Distributee on Disposition of Distributed Property

The * * * Code contains nothing specific in the way of a general rule for determining the character of gain or loss which will be realized by a distributee upon the ultimate disposition by him of distributed property.   Therefore, in the absence of some specific provision to the contrary, it seems clear that, * * * the character of such gain or loss will be determined by reference to the character of the asset in the hands of the distributee at the date it is disposed of. However, while this seems to be the general rule under the * * * Code, it is subject to a very important exception, which requires that gain or loss on the ultimate disposition by the distributee partner of unrealized receivables or inventory items distributed to him by a partnership must be considered gain or loss from the sale or exchange of property other than a capital asset. This treatment is mandatory in every case in which the distributed assets consist of unrealized receivables. However, in the case of inventory items, if the sale or exchange by the distributee is not consummated within five years after the distribution, the nature of the gain or loss apparently will depend upon the nature of the assets in his hands at the date of the sale or exchange.

If the assets being disposed of can be considered capital in nature, there shall be included in the period for which they are held the period during which such assets were held by the partnership. The over-all holding period will then be calculated in the usual manner under section 1223. However, the statute contains an exception which prohibits tacking in the case of inventory items, but this should create no hardship since capital gains treatment for such property is not allowed in any event if it is disposed of within five years of its distribution.

G. Optional Adjustment to Partnership Basis for Remaining Undistributed Assets

* * * Congress * * * has * * * authoriz[ed] an increase in partnership basis under certain circumstances when distributed assets take a lower basis in the hands of the distributee and upon the distribution to him of cash in excess of his basis on which gain is recognized. Thus, the basis otherwise lost is restored to the partnership. Nevertheless, such relief is not without its price. Congress has required also that upon a liquidating distribution in the converse situation, i.e., when the distributed assets take a higher basis in the hands of the distributee, partnership basis for the remaining assets shall be decreased. This latter requirement is not, of course, a relief provision since it operates to the detriment of the partnership. In any event, the provision is at least consistent with the relief portion of the statute.

As a prerequisite for making either of such adjustments, the partnership must file an election under section 754. Although the election is a continuing one, which becomes effective upon the filing by the partnership of a statement of election, it may be revoked under [the] regulations * * * upon a showing of a change in the nature of the business. * * *

Exceptions to General Principles Governing Distributions

A.   Adjustment in Basis of Partnership Assets When Distributee Obtains Interest by Transfer

Although the basis of the distributee for his partnership interest is quite distinct from the basis of the partnership for its assets, * * * the basis of assets in the hands of the partnership is used to measure the portion of the distributee's partnership interest which is allocable to each distributed asset. Therefore, any variation or adjustment allowable for his benefit in the basis of partnership assets will directly affect their bases in his hands should they be distributed to him. * * *

Under the * * * Code there are three situations in which an adjustment is authorized in the basis of partnership property, solely on behalf of a distributee who has acquired his interest by sale or exchange or upon the death of a partner, in determining the tax consequences to him of a distribution of partnership assets. The first is upon a distribution to such a person when the general partnership election required by section 754 has been filed. Here, the adjustment is allowed from the date the interest is acquired, even for the purpose of calculating the current distributive share of income and loss of the transferee-partner. Second, even in the absence of such an election, upon a distribution to a partner who has so acquired his interest within two years from the date of such distribution, he may individually elect to make such an adjustment for the purposes of the distribution. Finally, in the absence of an election by either partnership or partner, the Secretary is authorized to require such an adjustment in the basis of partnership property distributed at any time to a partner who acquired his interest by sale or exchange or upon the death of a partner, if the fair market value of any distributed partnership property other than money at the time the partnership interest was acquired by the transferee partner exceeded 110 per cent of its adjusted basis to the partnership.

In each of these cases the adjustment in partnership basis is made only with respect to the distributee acquiring his interest by sale or exchange or upon the death of a partner. As to the amount of the adjustment, the partnership basis for its assets is to be increased or decreased by the difference between the transferee-distributee's basis for his partnership interest and his proportionate share of the adjusted basis of all partnership assets as of the date the interest was acquired. This increase or decrease is then allocated among the individual partnership assets as of that date, generally in the same manner [as] * * * the optional adjustment to partnership basis for remaining undistributed assets. * * *

B. *Disproportionate Distributions of Ordinary Assets or Capital Assets of Partnership*

＊ ＊ ＊ [Section 751(b)] provides that if the partnership holds unrealized receivables or substantially appreciated inventory items (which items are defined broadly enough to include nearly all non-capital assets), and the firm distributes capital assets to a partner in exchange for all or part of his interest in such non-capital assets or vice versa, the transaction, to the extent of this portion of the distribution, shall be considered a sale or exchange of such property between the distributee and the partnership. As will be noted in the ensuing discussion, this has the effect of requiring each partner to account for his share of gain or loss attributable to the assets deemed involved in this portion of the transaction.

1. Nature of Exchange Under Section 751(b)

The first problem encountered in applying this exception to the general principles controlling distributions is that of determining when the distribution of one type of assets is in exchange for an interest of the distributee in the other type. To the extent that the subsection is applicable, it requires the division of the total partnership property generally into non-capital assets (termed "inventory items") which have appreciated 120 per cent over their basis and which exceed 10 per cent of the value of all partnership property, except money, plus unrealized receivables on the one hand, and into capital and section 1231 assets and money, on the other. If the partnership has no such substantially appreciated inventory items and no unrealized receivables, section 751(b) is inapplicable, and the transaction is then treated as any other distribution. However, if the firm holds either appreciated inventory or unrealized receivables, or both, each distribution to a partner must be examined to determine whether it is in exchange for all or part of his interest in property of one type or the other. For convenience in discussion, these inventory items and receivables are hereinafter referred to as group *A* assets, and money, capital assets, and section 1231 assets are referred to as group *B* assets.

The legislative history of section 751(b) indicates that the existence of an exchange must be determined in the light of the proportionate share of the distributee partner in groups *A* and *B*. The clear implication of this background is that the distribution of property from group *A*, for example, to a distributee in excess of his proportionate share of that group will be deemed to have resulted in an exchange in which the distributee receives such excess from the partnership upon his relinquishment of a similar amount in excess of his proportionate share of the assets of group *B*. On the other hand, the receipt of only his proportionate share of either group will normally not result in such exchange. Thus, it appears that a distribution will result in an exchange under section 751(b) only upon the receipt by the distributee of property of one group or the other in excess of his proportionate share thereof, except when some special agreement between the partners specifies that the distribution of only his proportionate share is in cancellation of some part or all of his proportionate share of assets in the other group.

The imposition of a tax upon such an imputed exchange seems to evidence a legislative policy designed primarily to tax each non-distributee partner on his share of the appreciation in inventory and on his share of unrealized receivables as that share leaves the partnership upon a distribution * * *. Similarly, it indicates a policy of taxing the distributee on a part or all of his share of appreciated inventory and unrealized receivables upon a distribution in which he receives in lieu thereof capital assets in excess of his share.

2. Analysis of Nature of Over-all Transaction

Upon section 751(b) being applied to a distribution, although the transaction continues physically to be a distribution, the statute, in effect, requires that it be broken down into three component parts. To the extent of the amount received by the distributee which is in excess of his proportionate share of group *A* assets, for example, this portion of the transaction is considered to have no relationship whatsoever to the remainder. As to this portion, a distribution in effect must be imputed from the partnership to the distributee of a comparable amount of group *B* assets, which constitutes the first component of the transaction. The distributee is then considered to have transferred those assets back to the partnership in exchange for the excessive amount of group *A* assets which he physically receives. This exchange is the second component and is treated as a separate taxable transaction from the standpoint of both the distributee and the partnership. Following the exchange, the remaining component of the complete transaction, the portion recognized as a distribution, may be considered to have taken place. Both the distributee and the partnership will be required to determine the tax consequences of each of these three components of the entire transaction.

3. Nature of Distribution To Which Section Is Applicable

* * *

Determining the application of the provisions of section 751(b) to current partnership distributions, that is, distributions to a partner which do not result in a reduction or termination of his interest in either capital or profits under the terms of the partnership agreement, presents a * * * serious problem. * * *

[T]he statute definitely establishes two different groups of partnership assets, even though such grouping is not recognized by the parties. In addition, the legislative history seems clearly to indicate that at least in the absence of some special type of agreement the existence of an exchange under section 751(b) is to be determined by reference to the proportionate shares of the parties in each of these two groups of assets. In the light of this statutory grouping and attribution to each partner of a proportionate share of each group, it ∗ ∗ ∗ follow[s] axiomatically that a distribution to one partner of assets in excess of his share of one group will cause a reduction in (or relinquishment of) a comparable amount of his share of the assets of the other group.

This construction is consistent with the apparent intention of the legislature, as evidenced by the operation of section 751(b) in other situations, which is to tax non-distributee partners on their share of unrealized receivables and appreciated inventory as such items are distributed, apparently in order to prevent such partners from distributing all of such receivables or inventory to other partners and then [having the gain on the sale of] their own interests [treated as] capital gain. A contrary construction of the section would make it possible to accomplish the proscribed result to a considerable degree, at least, by means of current distributions.

Note also the broad scope of section 751(b). If a current distribution is made to a distributee which consists only of his share of assets of one group, the statutory language clearly would require that the distribution be deemed to result in an exchange if the parties specifically agreed that such distribution would leave the distributee's interest in that type of asset unaffected. This language is so specific that it can hardly be ignored simply because the distribution is a current one.

∗ ∗ ∗

NOTE

1. Section 751, the collapsible partnership provision, applies to the sale of a partnership interest, a distribution in liquidation of an interest in a partnership, a distribution which reduces the interest of a partner but does not eliminate it and a current disproportionate distribution of property. See Reg. Sec. 1.751–1(b). It, however, does not apply to a distribution of money to partners which distribution does not exceed the bases of the partners in their partnership interests and does not have the effect, among the partners and the partnership, of being in exchange for the relinquishment of part or all of a partner's interest in the "751" property of a partnership. See Section 751(b)(1) and Reg.Sec. 1.751–1(b). A current distribution of money to all partners in accord with their proportionate interests in the partnership and not in excess of their bases in their partnership interests is an example of this type of distribution.

Therefore, a current distribution of money by a partnership to its partners is not a taxable transaction if the distribution is in accord with the partners' proportionate interests in the partnership and the amount of the distribution does not exceed the bases of the partners in their partnership interests. The effect of the distribution is to reduce (but not below zero) the partners' bases in their partnership interests. See Section 733. To the extent the money distributed exceeds a partner's basis in the partner's partnership interest, the excess is generally treated as capital gain. See Section 731.

If, however, the partnership owns "751" property, part or all of a proportionate cash distribution which exceeds the bases of the partners in their partnership interests may be treated as ordinary income. See Sections 741 and 751(a).

Revenue Rul. 81–241, 1981–2 C.B. 146, deals with a disproportionate current distribution of money. The revenue ruling indicates that a distribution of money in excess of a partner's basis in his partnership interest, which distribution is an advance against the partner's distributive share of partnership income, is not subject to Section 751(b) and, therefore, not treated as ordinary income. It is only when a distribution of money is in exchange for the partner's interest in other partnership property that Section 751(b) will apply. Revenue Rul. 84–102, 1984–2 C.B. 119, indicates that a constructive cash distribution from a reduction of the partners' shares of partnership liabilities, under Section 752(b), resulting from a new partner joining the partnership, is subject to being treated as ordinary income, under Section 751(b), if the partnership owns "751" property. This result can occur even if the amount of the constructive cash distribution does not exceed the bases of the partners in their partnership interests. See Charyk, *New Problems with Section 751(b)—A Review of Revenue Ruling 84–102,* 12 J. Real Est. Tax'n 166 (1985); Emmons and Fine, *Coping With IRS' Ruling Which Applies Sec. 751 On the Admission of New Partners,* 62 J.Tax'n 160 (1985). Does a shift in the percentages in which the partners share profits and losses which reduces certain partners' shares of the liabilities of a partnership which owns "751" property, result in the recognition of ordinary income, under Section 751(b)? Cf. Note, *Income Tax Treatment of Shifts in Partnership Profit and Loss Interests,* 1984 Duke L.J. 805.

a. Residential, industrial or commercial rental real estate owned by a partnership is not likely to be considered inventory, although such classification is possible if the partnership or partners are considered dealers in that kind of real estate. Although typical unrealized receivables are usually not present in a partnership developing and operating rental real estate, especially a partnership which uses the accrual method of accounting, there is a distinct possibility that the partnership will be subject to potential Sections 1245 and 1250 recapture of depreciation which is considered an unrealized receivable. See Section 751(c).

b. If assets other than money are proportionately distributed by a partnership, the unrealized receivables and inventory assets distributed will produce ordinary income if disposed of at a gain by the distributee within five years of the distribution. If the inventory assets are held for longer than five years, the nature of the gain on the inventory assets will depend on the nature of the assets in the distributee's hands. Regardless when the unrealized receivables are disposed of, ordinary income will result.

2. To illustrate the operation of the distribution rules, Section 751 and the adjustments to basis which may result from a disproportionate distribution, assume Partnership ABC with a balance sheet as follows:

"**Partnership ABC**

	Basis to Partnership of Partnership Property	FMV
Cash	$2,000	$2,000
Land	3,300	4,000
Inventory	2,200	3,000
	$7,500	$9,000

	Basis to Part- ners of Partner- ship Interests	**FMV**
Partner *A*	$2,500	$3,000
Partner *B*	2,500	3,000
Partner *C*	2,500	3,000
	$7,500	$9,000

"Note that the partnership has one ['751' property]—the substantially appreciated inventory—and two ['non–751' properties]—the cash and the land.

"Assume Partner *C* receives all the inventory of the partnership in liquidation of his partnership interest.

"(1) *Treatment of Partner C*

Partner *C* ends up with the one-third share of the inventory to which he was entitled by reason of his one-third partnership interest plus an additional two-thirds share of the inventory. Partner *C* will be deemed to have sold his one-third interest in cash and his one-third interest in land in return for the two-thirds interest in inventory.

(a) *C* gets $666 worth of inventory in lieu of his interest in partnership cash of $666 (one-third of $2,000). Since *C's* basis for his interest in cash is $666 and since *C* receives property equal in value to such interest, he realizes no gain or loss in respect to this aspect of the transaction. (It is part of the common law of federal taxation that the basis of money is face value.)

(b) *C* gets $1,333 worth of inventory in lieu of his interest in partnership land which has a [fair market value (FMV)] of $1,333 (one-third of $4,000), but a basis to *C* of $1,100 (one-third of $3,300). Since *C* receives $1,333 worth of property in exchange for property in which he has a basis of $1,100, he realizes a gain of $233. The gain to him is capital in nature since he will be deemed to have sold a capital asset (the land).

(c) *C* also gets his one-third distributive share of partnership inventory. Although the FMV of this one-third share ($1,000) exceeds its basis to *C* ($733), *C* will not recognize any of this $267 built-in gain because this aspect of the situation does not involve a Section 751(b) exchange.

(d) *C*'s basis in his original one-third interest in inventory will remain at $733. *C*'s basis in the other two-thirds interest in inventory acquired in the transaction will be its 'cost' to *C.* The 'cost' to *C* was the one-third interest in cash he relinquished ($666) plus the one-third interest in the FMV of land he relinquished ($1,333) for a total of $2,000. *C*'s total basis in the inventory is thus $2,733 ($733 + $2,000). Notice that this is equivalent to *C*'s original basis in his partnership interest ($2,500) plus the gain recognized by *C* in the transaction ($233).

"(2) *Treatment of Partnership (remaining Partners A and B).*

(a) The partnership distributed to *C* inventory with a FMV of $666 and a basis of $488 (666/3,000 × 2,200) in exchange for *C*'s interest in cash, worth $666. This is a taxable exchange to the partnership, and since it used property with a basis of $488 to receive property worth $666, it recognizes a gain of $178. This gain will be ordinary income.

(b) The partnership distributed to *C* inventory with a FMV of $1,333 and a basis of $978 (1,333/3,000 × 2,200) in exchange for *C*'s interest in land, worth $1,333. This is a taxable exchange, and since the partnership 'sold' property with a $978 basis to acquire property worth $1,333, it recognizes a $355 gain, [treated] as ordinary income.

(c) The partnership distributed to *C* his one-third interest in inventory. This is not a taxable exchange since it is not a disproportionate property distribution.

(d) The basis to the partnership in its retained cash will in effect remain at $2,000. The basis of the partnership in *C*'s former one-third interest in the land will be its 'cost' to the partnership. The partnership distributed property worth $1,333 to *C* in exchange for the one-third interest in the land. Hence the partnership gets a $1,333 basis in one-third of the land and retains its original $2,200 basis for the remaining two-thirds, for a total basis of $3,533 in the land.

"The Partnership balance sheet at end of the example is as follows:

	Basis	**FMV**
Cash	2,000	2,000
Land	3,533	4,000
Inventory	0	0
	5,533	6,000
Partner *A*	2,766.5	3,000
Partner *B*	2,766.5	3,000
	5,533.0	6,000

"Note that *A* and *B* have each increased their basis in their partnership interests by one-half of the total gain realized by the partnership (one-half of 533 = 266.5)." Sexton, *Cutting a Path Through Section 751—Part Three,* 4 J.Real Est.Tax'n 259, 261–63 (1977).

   a.   See generally Anderson and Bloom, *Collapsible Partnerships: The Complexities of Section 751,* 2 J.Real Est.Tax'n 425 (1975); Applebaum, *Collapsible–Partnership Danger Increases with Use of Partnerships as Tax Shelters,* 42 J.Tax'n 272 (1975); Gutman, *Transactions Between Partners and Partnership: Contributions, Distributions, Basis, Indebtedness,* 31 N.Y.U.Inst.Fed.Tax'n 105 (1973); Sexton, *Cutting a Path Through Section 751—Part One,* 4 J.Real Est.Tax'n 72 (1976); Sexton, *Cutting a Path Through Section 751—Part Two,* 4 J.Real Est.Tax'n 168 (1977); Crumbley and Orbach, *Unraveling a Collapsible Partnership,* 9 Tax Adviser 47 (1978); Drucker and Segal, *Problems and Opportunities in Working with Collapsible Partnerships,* 61 Taxes 110 (1983); Teitelbaum, *Distribution of Partnership Refinancing Proceeds: Nonrecourse Cash Under the Section 704(b) Regulations,* 5 J.Ps.Tax'n 29 (1988); Martin and Jones, *Tax Consequences of a Disproportionate Partnership Distribution,* 20 Tax Adviser 112 (1988).

   b.   With respect to the operation of the optional basis adjustment rules upon a transfer by, or a distribution to, a partner see Snead, *Basis Aspects of a Transfer of a Partnership Interest and Distribution,* 46 Den.L.J. 333 (1969); Caso and Epstein, *An Analysis of the Optional–Basis–Adjustment Rules for Partners and Partnerships,* 42 J.Tax'n 234 (1975); Lawson, *Partnership Optional Basis Adjustment Rules,* 62 A.B.A.J. 1356 (1976); Marchbanks, *Two Elections Concerning Basis Have Most of the Problems in Special Partnership Elections,* 1 J.Ps.Tax'n 230 (1984).

   3.   The income tax effects of a distribution of money in liquidation, or the purchase by the remaining partners, of a retiring or deceased partner's interest

remain to be considered. Assume that the remaining partners do not wish to bring in a new partner. There are two possibilities: (1) The remaining partners can purchase the interest of the retiring or deceased partner; (2) The partnership can liquidate the interest.

a. If the remaining partners decide to purchase the interest, and the transaction is not treated as a partnership liquidation by the Internal Revenue Service, the income tax treatment of a retiring partner and the estate or successor in interest of a deceased partner is governed generally by Section 741. The purchase might be treated as a liquidation if, for example, the partnership agreement provides for liquidation by the partnership and the partnership distributes cash to the remaining partners which they then use to purchase the interest. Cf. *Foxman v. Comm'r*, 352 F.2d 466 (3d Cir.1965); *Bernard D. Spector*, 71 T.C. 1017 (1979), reversed, 641 F.2d 376 (5th Cir.1981), cert. denied, 454 U.S. 868, 102 S.Ct. 334, 70 L.Ed.2d 171 (1981).

1. Section 741 treats any gain or loss recognized by a retiring partner as capital, except to the extent that proceeds are allocated to unrealized receivables and substantially appreciated inventory under Section 751. To the extent the proceeds so allocated exceed the *partnership's* basis for the retiring partner's allocable share of those assets, the retiring partner is treated as recognizing ordinary income. If the retiring partner's basis in his partnership interest is less than his allocable share of the partnership's basis in the assets, the allocable share of his basis in his partnership interest will be used to measure the ordinary income. See Section 751(a); Reg.Sec. 1.751 1(a)(2) and Section 732.

2. The treatment of the estate or successor in interest of a deceased partner will vary from the above as a result of the stepped-up basis in assets, other than "751" property, derived through the application of Sections 742 and 1014. The basis of a deceased partner in his partnership interest which is allocated to non–751 property is equal to the property's fair market value on the date of death or the alternate valuation date, and if no more than fair market value in proceeds is derived from these assets, no gain or loss is recognized. The treatment of unrealized receivables is about the same as that accorded a retiring partner except that Sections 1245 and 1250 recapture becomes zero at the date of death. Therefore, the only Sections 1245 and 1250 recapture included in unrealized receivables is the excess depreciation, if any, taken after the date of death. See Reg.Secs. 1.751–1(c)(6); 1.1250–1(f); 1.1250–3(b) and 1.1245–1(e). In order to achieve this result, the purchase must be made within two years after the date of death, Section 732(d), or an election, under Section 754, providing for an adjustment to the basis of partnership property, under Section 743(b), must be in effect at the date of death or made by the partnership for the year in which the death occurred. It might be further argued that, if the purchase was within two years of the date of death or a 754 election was in effect, no gain or loss is recognized with respect to any of the unrealized receivables, assuming the purchase is at fair market value, since the estate or successor in interest acquires a special partnership basis in all of the unrealized receivables as a result of the application of Sections 1014 and 743(b). This position has been rejected by the Internal Revenue Service and the courts which hold that

unrealized receivables are income in respect of a decedent under Section 691, and therefore, Section 1014(c), which denies a stepped-up basis, applies to the unrealized receivables. As a result, there is no increase in the basis of the estate or successor in interest in the part of the partnership interest allocated to the unrealized receivables, and therefore, there is no adjustment in basis, under Section 743(b). See Rev.Rul. 66–325, 1966–2 C.B. 249; *Woodhall,* 28 CCH Tax Ct.Mem. 1438 (1969), affirmed, 454 F.2d 226 (9th Cir.1972); *Quick's Trust,* 54 T.C. 1336 (1970), affirmed per curiam, 444 F.2d 90 (8th Cir.1971); Balleisen, *How Woodhall, Quick Decisions Will Affect Basis Adjustments to Unrealized Receivables,* 37 J.Tax'n 46 (1972). The suggestion has been made that the foregoing analysis can be extended to include Sections 1245 and 1250 depreciation recapture. See Note, *Death and Taxes: An Analysis of 1014, 743, 236 and The Limited Partnership,* 59 Va.L.Rev. 122, 153–157 (1973). There is still hope that the estate or successor in interest of a deceased partner is entitled to a stepped-up basis in substantially appreciated inventory. See generally Milroy, *Tax Aspects of Partnership Distributions and Transfers of Partnership Interests,* 41 Ind.L.J. 636 (1966).

3. The assumption by the remaining partners of the retiring or deceased partner's share of partnership liabilities is considered part of the purchase price of the partnership interest. See Section 752(d).

4. The remaining partners acquire a cost basis under Section 1012 in the partnership interest purchased. If a Section 754 election is in effect, or elected at the time of the purchase, the remaining partners will acquire a special basis in the partnership assets, under Section 743(b). This section provides that the basis of partnership property shall be increased or decreased by the difference between a transferee's basis in his partnership interest and the proportionate share of the adjusted basis of partnership property. In this case, unrealized receivables and substantially appreciated inventory are included.

b. If it is decided that the partnership will liquidate the retiring or deceased partner's interest, and the transaction is not treated as a purchase by the remaining partners, cf. *William J. Cooney,* 65 T.C. 101 (1975); *A.O. Champlin,* 36 CCH Tax Ct.Mem. 802 (1977), the tax consequences to the retiring partner or the estate or successor in interest of the deceased partner and the remaining partners will depend, in part, on the partnership agreement.

1. In the case of the retiring or deceased partner, with respect to the liquidation proceeds allocated to assets other than unrealized receivables and good will, the consequences will be substantially the same as that discussed with respect to a purchase by the remaining partners. See Section 736(b)(1). The retiring partner recognizes capital gain or loss measured by the difference between the money received, including his share of liabilities "assumed," and the allocable share of the basis of his partnership interest, except to the extent the proceeds are allocated to substantially appreciated inventory. See Section 731(a) and (c). To the extent that proceeds are allocated to substantially appreciated inventory, the gain or loss is ordinary. In the case of a deceased partner, however, the ordinary gain might be avoided by claiming that a stepped-up basis in the substantially appreciated inventory was acquired under Section 1014. See Reg.Sec. 1.736–

1(b)(4). The proceeds allocated to unrealized receivables in excess of the basis allocated to them will be treated as ordinary income in both the retiring and deceased partner situations. See Section 736(a) and (b)(2)(A). The Internal Revenue Service and the courts have clearly rejected a claimed stepped-up basis in the case of the deceased partner. See Section 753; Reg.Sec. 1.753–1(a) and Rev.Rul. 66–325, 1966–2 C.B. 249. The parties can control the taxation of the liquidation proceeds allocated to good will. If the partnership agreement provides for payment with respect to good will, the retiring partner and the estate or successor in interest of the deceased partner is treated as having received the payment under Section 736(b)(1) with capital gain or loss as the result. If, however, the partnership agreement does not provide for payment with respect to good will, the liquidation proceeds allocated to good will in excess of the recipient's basis therein will be treated as ordinary income. See Section 736(a) and (b)(2)(B).

2. An "assumption" by the partnership of the retiring or deceased partner's share of partnership liabilities is treated as a distribution of money by the partnership. See Section 752(b). Cf. Rev.Rul. 74–40, 1974–1 C.B. 159.

3. If a Section 754 election is in effect or made at the time of the liquidation, the partnership can increase or decrease the basis of partnership property by the amount of gain or loss recognized by the retiring partner or the estate or successor in interest of the deceased partner with respect to the payments made by the partnership for the partner's share of partnership property included in Section 736(b)(1) See Section 734(b). If payments are made for unrealized receivables and good will (if the partnership agreement does not provide for a payment with respect to good will) and such payments exceed any basis which the recipient has in these assets, the payments are treated as either a distributive share or guaranteed payments under Section 707(c), depending on the manner of payment. See Section 736(a). In either case, the payments for unrealized receivables and good will have the effect of reducing the taxable income derived by the remaining partners from the partnership. If the partnership is terminated at a time when an obligation to make Section 736(a) guaranteed payments to a retired partner or the estate or successor in interest of a deceased partner exists and the remaining partners individually assume the obligation to make such payments, the amount of such payments paid by each former partner will be deductible by the former partner under Section 162. See Rev.Rul. 75–154, 1975–1 C.B. 186.

c. In general, a retiring partner or the estate or successor in interest of a deceased partner probably will prefer a purchase by the remaining partners or a liquidation pursuant to a partnership agreement providing for a payment with respect to good will, so as to maximize capital gain treatment. On the other hand, the remaining partners probably will prefer a liquidation by the partnership, under Section 736, with no provision made for a payment for good will so as to reduce their distributive shares of income or obtain a deduction under Section 707(c). A liquidation, under Section 736, also will be preferred by the remaining partners if the basis of the retiring partner in his partnership interest is less than his allocable share of the partnership's basis in its property, since a larger adjustment to the basis of partnership property might be possible under

Section 734(b) than under Section 743(b). If, however, the allocable share of the partnership's basis in its property is less than the retiring or deceased partner's basis in his partnership interest, then a purchase by the remaining partners, governed by Section 741, will be preferred (assuming, in the case of a deceased partner, that a Section 754 election was not in effect prior to the purchase and no election is made under Section 732(d)).

d. See generally Solomon, *How Use of Section 736 Enhances Planning in Liquidating Partnership Interests,* 51 J.Tax'n 347 (1979); Cleveland, *Retirement Payments to Partners: Timing of Recognition of Income,* 57 J.Tax'n 86 (1982); Moore, *The Sloan Doctrine—New Twist in the Partnership Interest Sale/Redemption Question?,* 14 Tax Adviser 613 (1983); Morgan and Larason, *Tax Effects of Partner's Departure can be Tailored to Meet Parties' Needs,* 12 Tax'n Law. 132 (1983); Lynch, *Taxation of the Disposition of Partnership Interests: Time to Repeal I.R.C. Section 736,* 65 Neb.L.Rev. 450 (1986); Grossman, *Choosing the Most Advantageous Method for Disposing of a Partnership Interest,* 3 J.Ps.Tax'n 219 (1986); Robinson and Shiff, *Structuring a Partner's Retirement to Achieve the Best Results for Partner and Partnership,* 16 Tax'n Law. 38 (1987); Moore and Patankar, *Secs. 736 and 741 for the Withdrawal of a Partner,* 19 Tax Adviser 307 (1988).

c. CORPORATE DISTRIBUTIONS—NOT AS COMPENSATION NOR IN LIQUIDATION OF THE CORPORATION

The distribution of assets by a corporation to its shareholders, whether in the form of dividends or the repurchase of shares, requires compliance with the applicable provisions of the state statutes governing distributions by corporations. Therefore, in determining whether a distribution can be made by a corporation to its shareholders, the state statutes must be examined and complied with. In all cases, compliance will require, at the minimum, a careful analysis of the corporation's financial statements.

DIVIDENDS—CHANGING PATTERNS
Arthur M. Kreidmann
57 Columbia Law Review 372 (1957).
[footnotes omitted]

* * *

I. Sources of Dividends

* * *

A. *Earned Surplus*

Earned surplus is the fund which is the most common source for the payment of dividends. It exists if there is a residue of net profits remaining with the corporation since it was organized. A more exact and descriptive definition is [as follows]:

"Earned surplus" means the portion of the surplus of a corporation equal to the balance of its net profits, income, gains and losses from the date of incorporation, or from the latest date when a deficit was eliminated by an application of its capital surplus or stated capital or otherwise, after deducting subsequent distributions to shareholders and transfers to stated capital and capital surplus to the extent such distributions and transfers are made out of earned surplus. [Earned surplus shall include also any portion of surplus allocated to earned surplus in mergers, consolidations or acquisitions of all or substantially all of the outstanding shares or of the property and assets of another corporation, domestic or foreign.]

* * *

When the earned surplus standard is employed alone, dividends are not properly payable out of paid-in surplus, capital reduction surplus, or any other kind of surplus fund. Thus, statutes containing such language relatively restrict the source available for dividend payments.

B. Net Profits

The terms "net profits" and "profits" are difficult to define. Most state statutes avoid reference to them. * * * On the basis of a literal interpretation of statutes allowing dividend payments from "net profits," it could be argued that if "net profits" for the current year are realized, dividends may properly be paid therefrom. But in several instances when the construction issue has arisen, courts have held that dividends may not be paid from current profits when there is an impairment of capital. There are, however, authorities to the contrary, supporting the literal interpretation in opinions construing undistributed profits tax statutes.

Some states, by statute, permit payment of dividends out of net profits, even though capital is impaired. But, generally, if the value of the net assets is less than the stated capital represented by all shares having a liquidation preference, dividends may not be paid out of net profits on any shares until the deficiency in such capital has been repaired. * * *

Dividends paid out of net profits when capital is impaired have been termed "nimble" dividends. Actually, such dividends are distributions out of capital, unattended by the requirement of reducing capital pursuant to the applicable statutory procedure. Thus, directors must be "nimble" by declaring dividends out of net profits, usually of the current or preceding fiscal year, before such net profits are closed to the surplus account, i.e., charged against the accumulated deficit. If the statute is not clear as to whether nimble dividends may be declared and decisional law is no guide, directors may avoid risk by effecting a reduction of capital and applying the capital reduction surplus to eliminate the deficit. If this is done, the balance sheet will reflect a condition which permits the payment of dividends out of current net profits.

C. Insolvency

The test of insolvency is not expressly indicative of a dividend source. Rather, it is an admonition which is applicable to all types of dividend statutes and bears an important relation to the statutory scheme.

1. *Nimble dividend statutes.* The nimble dividend statutes sanction the payment of dividends by a corporation which is insolvent in a bankruptcy sense, i.e., net assets are less than stated capital, subject to the condition of non-impairment of capital attributable to shares entitled to a preference on liquidation. But these statutes often couple the provision permitting use of net profits as a source with the cautionary note that directors are liable to creditors if the corporation is insolvent at the time of, or rendered insolvent as a result of, the payment of the dividend. It may be inferred, therefore, that the declaration of a dividend out of net profits at a time when net assets are less than stated capital is subject to the condition that the corporation is not, or will not thereby be, rendered insolvent in the equity sense [(i.e., the corporation cannot pay its debts as they come due)]. * * *

2. *Earned surplus statutes.* In states which limit the source of dividends to earned surplus or "surplus profits arising from the business of the corporation," the test of insolvency in a bankruptcy sense is, of course, inapplicable. But the statutes of many of these states are silent with respect to the standard of insolvency in an equity sense. The possible explanation for such statutory silence is the legislative assumption that a corporation with an earned surplus is necessarily solvent in an equity sense. On the other hand, it is conceivable that a corporation with an earned surplus, in short supply of liquid assets, and with no immediate ability to mortgage properties or convert other assets into cash, would be unable to meet its obligations as they mature.

3. *Other statutes.* In states which neither subscribe to the nimble dividend doctrine nor limit the source of dividends to earned surplus, the statutes frequently prohibit payment of dividends when the corporation is insolvent or would, as a result thereof, be rendered insolvent, or if the payment of the dividend is made when the capital is, or would as a result thereof become, "diminished" (i.e., "impaired"). The tests thus expressed in the disjunctive clearly embrace insolvency both in the equity and in the bankruptcy sense. [The Revised Model Business Corporation Act permits "distributions," which include money or property (other than the corporation's own shares) dividends, share repurchases and similar distributions, to be made by a corporation if, after giving effect to the distribution, a corporation is not insolvent in either the equity or bankruptcy sense and the amount by which its total assets exceed its total liabilities is equal to, or greater than, the maximum amount which would be needed, if the corporation were to be dissolved at the time of the distribution, to satisfy the preferential rights on dissolution of shareholders whose preferential rights are superior to

those shareholders receiving the distribution. Determinations to be made under the bankruptcy insolvency and impairment of preferential rights in liquidation tests can be based upon either the corporate financial statements prepared on the basis of accounting practices and principles which are reasonable in the circumstances or a fair valuation or other method which is reasonable. Section 6.40 of the Revised Model Business Corporation Act, therefore, sanctions the use of unrealized appreciation as a source of dividends where the valuation method used to derive the values was appropriate for the circumstances and, of course, the application of the equity insolvency test permits such distribution to be made.]

* * *

D. Impairment of Capital

This standard requires that, before and after the payment of a dividend, net assets must not be less than stated capital. In most states the test of impairment of capital is applied along with other standards or prescribed sources of dividends. * * * Related to the question of capital impairment are the existence or non-existence of a surplus, the type of surplus from which dividends may be paid, and the kind of dividend payable from a particular type of surplus. The nature of capital and the categories of surplus must, therefore, be analyzed.

II. Capital

Capital is the most elusive factor in the balance sheet equation. Before the enactment of the modern statutes, the essential attribute of capital was defined in terms of a trust fund for the benefit of creditors. The fictional characterization of a balance sheet factor as a "trust fund" invites a confusion between assets, which are things of value, and capital, which connotes merely a dollar amount. The trust fund theory has been criticized as misleading because creditors' claims against a corporation are not limited to an equitable interest in the assets measured by the amount of capital but extend to all assets. Capital must, therefore, be distinguished from assets.

[C]apital [may be defined] as a sum referable to the aggregate of all issued shares having par value plus the aggregate amount of consideration received by the corporation for the issuance of shares without par value plus such amounts as the directors from time to time may transfer thereto. It should be further noted that capital impairment is to be distinguished from capital reduction. Capital is impaired as a result of operational or other losses or a decrease in the value of assets. Capital is reduced only in one way—by compliance with a statutory proceeding to effect a reduction of capital. In brief, capital is a figure that does not reflect the changing element of value as do assets and surplus. Viewed in this light, these balance sheet factors—assets, capital, and surplus—acquire an emphasis in meaning in relation to the law of dividends.

III. Changes in the Treatment of Surplus

In addition to earned surplus there are several other classifications used by accountants to indicate the origin of a particular surplus account. These are: paid-in surplus, capital reduction surplus, donated surplus, dated or reorganization surplus, and revaluation or reappraisal surplus. In recent years the relationship between the different kinds of surplus and the power of a corporation to pay dividends has been re-examined by the legislatures and the courts. The general references to surplus, which did not take cognizance of differences in the origin, have been replaced by the formulations of rules prescribing what kind of surplus constitutes a source for what kind of dividend. The pattern of development sometimes reflects a common approach and at other times indicates a divergence in policy among the several states.

A. *Paid–In Surplus*

Paid-in surplus is the amount in excess of the par value of a corporation's outstanding stock, or in excess of the stated value of no par stock. It may arise at the time of incorporation or at any time thereafter when the holders of newly-issued stock pay an excess amount to equalize their investment with that of stockholders already participating in the corporate enterprise. It is also created by the excess accruing when a corporation sells treasury shares for an amount higher than the capital attributable to them.

As a source of dividends paid-in surplus has been hedged within restricted limits, and its use for such purpose has been tempered with protective measures. Such measures are intended as a safeguard for the investing public against false impressions of prosperity and for the preservation of equities among stockholders *inter se.* [S]tatutes generally prescribe that dividends from this source may be paid only on shares entitled to preferential dividends, and many of them provide that the receiving shareholder be given notice of the source prior to or concurrently with payment.

Notwithstanding the newly imposed restrictive limits upon paid-in surplus as a dividend source, it is, nevertheless, useful as an aid in organizing a new enterprise. During the developmental stage of a business earnings are often negligible or non-existent. At such a time paid-in surplus constitutes a fund for dividends payable to preferred stockholders who bargained for a fixed and continuous return. The creation of a paid-in surplus incidental to the issuance of stock is not an uncommon corporate technique and in some states is expressly sanctioned by statute.

As an accounting guide some of the statutes provide that paid-in surplus may be applied to reduce or eliminate a deficit arising from operations or other losses or from diminution of the value of assets.
*   *   *

B. Capital Reduction Surplus

Capital reduction surplus results when capital is reduced pursuant to statutory proceedings, and is the amount by which capital is reduced. In some states it is no less limited as a dividend source than paid-in surplus. * * * But creating a capital reduction surplus may, concomitantly, create rights of appraisal in preferred stockholders. * * *

It should be noted that stock dividends do not fall within the restrictive scope of those statutes which limit the uses of paid-in or capital reduction surplus as sources of dividends. The only necessary condition for the payment of a stock dividend from such types of surplus is that there be a transfer from surplus to capital account coincidental with the payment of the dividend, subject in some states to a requirement of notice to the shareholders of the source of payment.

C. Donated Surplus

Donated surplus is created when money or property or anything of value is given to a corporation with a resulting increase in the value of assets without any corresponding increase in the capital or any other liability account. It has received the least statutory attention * * *.

D. Revaluation or Reappraisal Surplus

Revaluation or reappraisal surplus results from the unrealized appreciation of assets. It is created when assets are revalued in excess of book value and are carried on the books at the revalued or reappraised amount. On the face of the applicable statute in some states "surplus" appears to be an unqualified source for the payment of dividends. In these and other states where surplus is generally considered as a dividend source, however, revaluation or reappraisal surplus arising from unrealized appreciation of assets is treated in a special way.

The focal starting point in this area of dividend law is the much discussed case of Randall v. Bailey.[16] A trustee in bankruptcy sought to charge directors with liability for paying dividends out of what the trustee alleged was capital. The directors contended that the dividends were properly paid out of revaluation surplus arising out of unrealized appreciation of fixed assets. The New York Court of Appeals precisely framed the issue:

> [M]ay unrealized appreciation in value of fixed assets held for use in carrying on a corporate enterprise be taken into consideration by directors in determining whether a corporate surplus exists from which cash dividends may be paid to stockholders?

The court held that the action of the directors was proper and based its decision on the legislative history of section 58 of the New York Stock Corporation Law and its penal counterpart. These sections signaled a

16. [288 N.Y. 280, 43 N.E.2d 43 (1942).]

departure from the standard of "surplus profits" and replaced it with the criterion of impairment of capital. Thus, the value of assets became the criterion for determining impairment of capital. Accordingly, revaluation surplus accruing from increased values of "fixed assets held for use in carrying on a corporate enterprise" was recognized as a source for dividend payments. * * *

Recognition of this kind of surplus was a challenge to the conventional accounting treatment of assets by which fixed assets are figured at cost less depreciation, and current assets, such as inventories, are carried at the lower of cost or market value. Since *Randall v. Bailey,* several state legislatures have enacted laws to anticipate and demarcate the limits within which its impact would be received. The use of revaluation surplus derived from unrealized appreciation of fixed assets as a dividend source, and of inventories before sale as a cash dividend source is generally restricted, but the use of revaluation surplus derived from unrealized appreciation of any assets as a stock dividend source, is generally permitted. Some states permit the dividend use of revaluation surplus only insofar as it is derived from the unrealized appreciation of marketable securities.

In effect these states have erected legislative barriers to the doctrine of *Randall v. Bailey,* which, on its facts, dealt with a reappraisal of fixed assets, and have extended the bar to the revaluation of current assets with the exception, in certain states, of readily marketable securities. In this respect the * * * laws generally accord with sound accounting practice. The extent to which other states will conform to, or vary from, the approach thus far taken will bear watching. [The Revised Model Business Corporation Act permits the determinations to be made under the bankruptcy insolvency and impairment of preferential rights in liquidation tests to be based upon a fair valuation or other method which is reasonable. Therefore, unrealized appreciation can be used to justify a distribution where the valuation method used to derive the values was appropriate for the circumstances and, of course, the application of the equity insolvency test permitted the distribution to be made.]

* * *

NOTE

1. Section 6.40 of the Revised Model Business Corporation Act permits "distributions," which include money or property (other than the corporation's own shares) dividends, share repurchases and similar distributions, to be made by a corporation if, after giving effect to the distribution, the corporation is not insolvent in either the equity or bankruptcy sense and the amount by which its total assets exceed its total liabilities is equal to, or greater than, the maximum amount which would be needed, if the corporation were to be dissolved at the time of the distribution, to satisfy the preferential rights on dissolution of shareholders whose preferential rights are superior to those shareholders receiving the distribution. Determinations to be made under the bankruptcy insolvency and impairment of preferential rights in liquidation tests can be based upon either the corporate financial statements prepared on the basis of

accounting practices and principles which are reasonable in the circumstances or a fair valuation or other method which is reasonable. Section 6.40, therefore, permits unrealized appreciation to be used in determining whether a corporation can make a distribution in a situation in which the valuation method used to determine the value of the corporation's assets is appropriate for the circumstances and, of course, the application of the equity insolvency test permits the distribution to be made.

2. A real estate corporation developing and operating residential, industrial or commercial rental real estate, which was formed and is doing business in a state in which the statutes provide that dividends and other distributions can only be made out of surplus, frequently faces the question whether distributions to its shareholders can be made out of revaluation or reappraisal surplus. There are at least two points in time when a distribution to shareholders is desired and revaluation or reappraisal surplus may have to be used to support the distribution.

a. Often, a distribution to shareholders is sought to be made at the point of initial financing of a development when the proceeds of the financing exceed the costs of the development. Another time at which the corporation may seek to make a distribution to shareholders is at the point of refinancing after the cross-over point has been reached. See pages 582 to 595 supra.

b. If the corporation is at the point of initial financing, it probably will have no earnings and profits for income tax purposes, assuming Section 312(i) does not apply, and the distribution of the excess proceeds of the financing will be treated, for income tax purposes, as a return of capital and capital gain to the extent the proceeds exceed the recipient shareholders' bases in their stock, assuming Section 341 does not apply. If the corporation is at the refinancing point, the accumulated and current earnings and profits may still be insubstantial and the distribution of the proceeds of the refinancing will be treated, in large measure, as a return of capital and capital gain, again assuming that Sections 312(i) and 341 do not apply.

1. Between the time of initial financing and the time of refinancing, there can be a number of years in which cash flow is substantial, despite the fact that, for accounting and income tax purposes, the corporation shows a loss or a small amount of income. During these years, distributions of some or all of the cash flow may be desired.

c. There are some decisions which permit a distribution out of revaluation or reappraisal surplus. This result has been criticized on the basis that such surplus has not been realized and, therefore, cannot be part of the net profits, gains, etc. which make up earned surplus. See Seward, *Earned Surplus—Its Meaning and Use in the Model Business Corporation Act,* 38 Va.L.Rev. 435 (1952); Gibson, *Surplus, So What?—The Model Act Modernized,* 17 Bus.Law. 476 (1962); Hackney, *The Financial Provisions of the Model Business Corporation Act,* 70 Harv.L.Rev. 1357 (1957); Comment, *Revaluation of Assets as a Source of Cash Dividends,* 2 U.Balt.L.Rev. 57 (1972); Comment, *Appreciated Property as a Source of Dividends: Its Use and Effects in Mississippi,* 48 Miss.L.J. 309 (1977). See generally Kummert, *State Statutory Restrictions on Financial Distributions by Corporations To Shareholders, Part I,* 55 Wash.L.Rev. 359 (1980); *Part II,* 59 Wash. L.Rev. 185 (1984).

1. It might be argued that a form of realization of appreciation takes place at the time of initial financing and at the time of refinancing. The initial financing of the assets based on a value in excess of cost, coupled with the receipt of the proceeds of the financing in excess of cost, arguably represents the realization of appreciation, at least to the extent of the proceeds received in excess of cost. There is a two-pronged argument with respect to realization of appreciation occurring at the time of refinancing. First, to the extent that the value used for refinancing is greater than the present depreciated cost of the assets, the difference has been realized through the depreciation charges against income. Secondly, the receipt of the proceeds of financing in excess of the present depreciated cost of the assets is a form of realization of the appreciation of the property or the lack of actual depreciation. See Fitts, *The Relation of Depreciation to the Determination of Surplus and Earnings Available for Dividends*, 33 Va.L.Rev. 581 (1947).

> a. With respect to a distribution of cash flow at a point in time between initial financing and refinancing, it might be asserted that the amount being distributed, or at least part of it, was realized through depreciation charges against income which reflected a greater amount of depreciation than actually occurred.

d. Under some state statutes, revaluation or reappraisal surplus may constitute part of the capital surplus account. If a corporation's articles of incorporation authorize a distribution out of capital surplus, or a required shareholder vote is obtained, and any other statutory conditions for a distribution out of capital surplus are complied with, a real estate corporation may have a conservative avenue open to it for the distribution to its shareholders of the excess proceeds of the initial financing, cash flow, or the proceeds of a refinancing.

3. Another means of distributing the assets of a corporation to its shareholders is through repurchase of all, or a percentage, of the shares of stock owned by the shareholders. State corporate statutes generally control how and when such a distribution can take place and out of what fund it must be made.

SHARE REPURCHASES UNDER MODERN CORPORATION LAWS

Robert A. Kessler
28 Fordham Law Review 637 (1959–60).
[footnotes omitted]

* * *

* * * [Some state corporate statutes grant] a corporation the right to purchase and deal in its shares out of "unreserved and unrestricted earned surplus," or if the certificate so provides, or [a majority] of the shareholders having voting rights approve, out of its "unreserved and unrestricted capital surplus" as well.

In addition, [in some states], a corporation may also purchase or redeem its shares out of "stated capital" * * * provided no more than the "redemption price"—"call price"—is paid, for its redeemable shares.

No purchase may be made, however, which would result in insolvency in the equity (as opposed to bankruptcy) sense.

* * *

Redeemable Shares

The * * * approval of the purchase of redeemable shares out of capital is qualified [in most states] by [a] limitation * * * which provides:

> No redemption or purchase of redeemable shares shall be made by a corporation when it is insolvent or when such redemption or purchase would render it insolvent, or which would reduce the net assets below the aggregate amount payable to the holders of shares having prior or equal rights to the assets of the corporation upon involuntary dissolution.

The effect of this provision is to protect those senior shareholders who have a liquidation preference in a manner analogous to that protection extended creditors by the bankruptcy insolvency test. It must be conceded that this limitation also affords some protection to creditors. Since the limitation is in terms of the total assets required to satisfy merely the liquidation preference of shareholders, and hence the fund is perhaps not as large as it would be were purchases or calls which reduced assets below liabilities interdicted (it must be recalled that only equity and not bankruptcy insolvency is forbidden), it is true that the asset fund thus frozen would be available to the creditors in priority to the preference shareholders for whom it was ostensibly set up. An additional protection to both creditors and shareholders (whose shares are not purchased) is the proviso * * * that the purchase price may not exceed the price at which the shares may be called.

[A]lthough such purchases may not cause insolvency, they *do* reduce capital, and are, as a result, disadvantageous to creditors. Even if a redeemable shareholder be regarded as a species of corporate creditor, is there any justification for favoring him in preference to the other, and the only legally recognized, creditors * * *? A corporation may be a long way on the road to failure without actually being insolvent (in either the equity or bankruptcy sense). The [redeemable share provisions] allow the directors to "bail out" favored shareholders with no loss, and perhaps even a profit (since the shares may be redeemed at call price when in a failing corporation the market price, and hence cost to the shareholder, may be considerably less), at the possible expense of creditors and junior shareholders. For adequate protection of the latter, purchase of redeemable shares should be allowed only out of earned surplus, and treated as any other share purchase from such source.

* * *

Purchases from Surplus

Contrary to the English rule, most American jurisdictions, apart from express statutory grant, permit a corporation to repurchase its shares where only surplus is used. [M]any modern corporation statutes allow purchases out of "earned surplus" for any purpose, and without limitation, except that these purchases may not be made when insolvency (in the equity sense) is present, or would ensue from such purchases.

[Some of the modern corporation statutes] also permit (with only the same insolvency restriction) such purchases from any type of surplus if a [majority] of the voting shareholders approve, *or* if the articles of incorporation so permit. Since it is customary for corporations to take advantage of any permissive feature of the corporation statutes, it is to be anticipated that all corporations incorporated under these modern statutes will allow such purchases.

It may thus be fairly stated that under [these modern statutes], almost any corporation may repurchase any of its shares out of any type of surplus, no matter how created. Creditors can certainly have no legitimate objection to share repurchases from earned surplus, since their extension of credit is not justifiably made in reliance upon this fund as a security for payment. Purchases * * * which might be undesirable if made from capital cannot be viewed as objectionable from the point of view of creditors where made from earned surplus, the corporation's profit, even though their position would of course be better still with the surplus unexpended.

* * *

As indicated above [some modern statutes] permit share repurchases not only from "earned surplus" but also from "capital surplus," which includes every other type of surplus, since under the * * * definitions [used in many of the modern statutes] capital surplus is that excess of net assets over stated capital which is not earned surplus.

* * *

Under the [modern statutes], [revaluation or reappraisal] surplus [probably would] be available for share repurchases. * * *

The obverse of the asset write-up coin is capital write-down, or a shrinking of assets on which creditors may depend to pay what is owing to them. The situation is especially dangerous for creditors since corporations in good financial circumstances (i.e., which have an unimpaired capital and a substantial *earned* surplus) will not resort to such techniques.

Under [some of the modern statutes], "reduction surplus," the result of a write-down of stated capital, would also be available for share repurchases. [T]he modern statutes * * * are generous in allowing a reduction of "stated capital" in any case by [majority] vote of the affected shareholders * * *, or even * * * by mere majority shareholder vote, where the new stated capital is not below the sum of the aggregate par value of all shares plus the combined liquidation preferences of all shares having such rights. Surplus thus created is expressly made "capital surplus" * * *, and is hence available for share repurchase.

Through use by a corporation of either of these techniques, creditors may discover that what they justifiably considered to be capital has been legally filtered off to their detriment for the benefit of shareholders.

While not sufficient to obviate these problems, at the very least creditors should have the protection that no share purchases will be made if the corporation is insolvent, or would be rendered so by the purchases, in either the equity sense * * * *or* in the bankruptcy sense. This minimal requirement would seem essential to creditors since a dying corporation may still be able to meet its obligations as they fall due (i.e., be technically solvent in the equity sense), although its assets are less than its total debts (insolvency in the bankruptcy sense). Such a requirement is "built-into" [many of the modern statutes], but only in those cases where purchases are permitted solely from surplus, and not in the extraordinary situations where purchases may be from either surplus or capital. Creditors will indeed suffer if a corporation can fritter away its liquid assets through legal share repurchases until the "house of cards" finally collapses in bankruptcy. Fortunately, some states have been foresighted enough to correct this * * * deficiency.

For truly adequate protection, a restriction on share repurchases which retains the asset fund at a level higher than that barely necessary to prevent bankruptcy is requisite. To forestall reduction of the assets to this dangerous level, it is important to restrict such purchases to surplus which has actually been earned, as opposed to allowing such repurchases to be made from a "surplus" which is, in reality, partly (or completely), diverted capital.

Authors usually speak of stated capital requirements as a protection for creditors. They are also a protection for the shareholders. Their effect is obviously to keep the asset fund at a level higher than that which would otherwise be the case. As such, they prevent the dilution of the real value of all shares. Asset disintegration through the subterfuge of artificial creation and distribution of capital surplus is as detrimental to shareholders as it is to creditors, at least to those who are not bought out. Hence, for the protection of both creditors and shareholders, by and large, share repurchases should be limited to actually earned surplus, and not surplus in general, as [many of the modern statutes] in effect allow.

NOTE

1. The repurchase of shares out of earned or capital surplus is subject to substantially the same restrictions, limitations and problems as the making of a dividend distribution from these accounts. See pages 1100 to 1108 supra.

2. Many modern corporation statutes authorize the issuance of redeemable shares. In general, redeemable shares can be repurchased out of stated capital for no more than the redemption price of the shares as long as the corporation is not insolvent, in an equity sense, when the repurchase is made and the repurchase does not cause the corporation to become insolvent or reduce the net assets below the aggregate amount payable to the holders of shares having prior or equal rights to the assets of the corporation upon involuntary dissolution.

    a. Redeemable shares are an effective planning tool in situations in which it is known, on formation of a corporation, that certain shareholders desire the repurchase of their shares at an early point in the life of the corporation.

3. Section 1.40(6) of the Revised Model Business Corporation Act treats share repurchases as "distributions" subject to the same tests as money or property (other than the corporation's own shares) dividends. As a result, under Section 6.40, a corporation may repurchase its shares if such repurchase does not result in either the equity or bankruptcy insolvency of the corporation and does not impair the preferential rights on liquidation of shareholders whose preferential rights are superior to the shareholders whose stock is being repurchased.

The concept of treasury shares has been abandoned by the Revised Model Business Corporation Act. See Section 6.31. In addition, when shares are repurchased for corporate debt the validity of the repurchase under the equity insolvency, bankruptcy insolvency and impairment of preferential rights tests is determined, under Section 6.40(e), at the time of the issuance of the debt and, under Section 6.40(f), such debt is not automatically subordinated to past or future creditors.

4. Since substantially the same restrictions, limitations and problems accompany a repurchase and a dividend, why is one rather than the other chosen for a distribution to shareholders?

    a. If a repurchase is pro rata among all of the shareholders of a corporation or it does not substantially decrease or terminate the proportionate interest of a shareholder or shareholders vis-a-vis the other shareholders, it is treated as a form of dividend distribution for income tax purposes, unless it qualifies as a partial liquidation, no matter what it is called from a corporate standpoint.

    b. If, however, the purpose of the distribution, from the corporate standpoint, is to reduce the interests of the shareholders, it is technically a repurchase in the corporate context. For example, a corporation in two lines of business sells one of the businesses and distributes the proceeds of the sale, repurchasing a proportionate amount of each shareholder's stock in order to reflect in its capital structure the corporation's reduced operations.

(i) INCOME TAX TREATMENT OF DIVIDENDS AND OTHER NONLIQUIDATING DISTRIBUTIONS

Section 301 of the Internal Revenue Code governs the income tax treatment of nonliquidating corporate distributions to shareholders in their capacity as shareholders. Excepted from the coverage of Section 301 are: (1) Distributions in redemption of the stock of shareholders, if treated as a sale or exchange of such stock under Section 302; (2) Redemptions to pay death taxes qualifying under Section 303; (3) Distributions of stock and stock rights qualifying for nonrecognition under Section 305; and (4) Distributions in "partial liquidation" qualifying under Sections 302(b)(4) and 302(e).

If a nonliquidating distribution by a corporation to its shareholders in their capacity as shareholders is not specifically excepted from Section 301, this section determines the "nature" of the distribution. If the distribution is made out of the current or accumulated earnings and profits of a corporation, see Section 316, it is treated as a dividend subject to ordinary income treatment, see Section 301(c)(1). The Internal Revenue Code employs the nimble dividend concept. Even if a corporation has a deficit in accumulated earnings and profits, if a distribution does not exceed current earnings and profits, it is a dividend. Section 316 provides that a distribution is a dividend if made out of accumulated earnings and profits *or* current earnings and profits to the extent thereof and from the most recently accumulated earnings and profits.

If the amount of a distribution exceeds both current and accumulated earnings and profits, the distribution is regarded as a return of capital to the shareholders, reducing the basis of their stock, see Section 301(c)(2), and any excess over basis is treated as capital gain, see Section 301(c)(3)(A), assuming the shareholder is not a dealer and that Section 341 does not apply. Section 316(a) eliminates most tracing problems by specifying that, whenever there are any earnings and profits, a distribution is deemed to be out of the earnings and profits rather than from any other source—and then from the most recent earnings and profits, as noted above.

If a corporation receives a dividend from a domestic corporation, it is entitled to deduct 70% of the dividend received unless the recipient corporation owns at least 20% of the stock of the payor corporation (by vote and by value). If the recipient corporation owns at least 20% of the stock of the payor corporation, the recipient corporation can deduct 80% of the amount received as a dividend from the payor corporation. In addition, members of an "affiliated group," see Section 243(b)(5), of corporations which file separate returns, may, in certain situations, elect to deduct 100% of the dividend.

Treatment of a distribution as a dividend turns on the presence of "earnings and profits," and that concept is not comprehensively defined in the Internal Revenue Code. Earnings and profits are not necessarily the same as cumulative taxable income nor, for that matter, are they necessarily the same as earned surplus or accumulated earnings in an accounting sense. For example, tax exempt income, such as municipal bond interest and life insurance proceeds, is included in earnings and profits, and some deductions, such as the dividends received deduction, are not permitted in computing earnings and profits. The depletion deduction, when used to determine earnings and profits, must be computed using cost rather than percentage. On the other hand, federal income taxes, excess charitable contributions and unreasonable compensation, in some circumstances, are deductible in computing earnings and profits. See Reg. Sec. 1.312–6.

Regulation Sec. 1.312–6 provides that the same method of accounting used in determining taxable income is to be used in determining earnings and profits. Generally, gains and losses are recognized in determining earnings and profits at the same time they are recognized in determining taxable income. Therefore, the tax-free exchange type of transactions, such as provided by Sections 351, 721, 1031 and 1033, are ignored in the determination of earnings and profits. This same concept is employed with respect to cancellation of indebtedness under Section 108, if applied to reduce basis under Section 1017, and lessee improvements, if the improvements are not included in income under Section 109. See Section 312(d).

Section 312 describes the effect of certain transactions on the earnings and profits of a corporation. Among the most important provisions of Section 312, with respect to a real estate corporation, are Sections 312(i), 312(k) and 312(n). Section 312(i) increases the earnings and profits of a corporation in an amount equal to the excess of a loan made, guaranteed or insured by the United States or any agency or instrumentality thereof, over the adjusted basis of the property securing such loan if, while the loan is outstanding, the corporation distributes property with respect to its stock. Immediately after the distribution, the earnings and profits are decreased by the amount of the excess. In determining the earnings and profits of a corporation, Section 312(k) requires that real estate improvements be depreciated using the straight-line method with no salvage value and a useful life of 40 years. Section 312(n) provides for a number of additional adjustments to be made in determining the earnings and profits of a corporation. The most important of these adjustments to a corporation in the real estate business are the following: (1) Construction period carrying charges (interest, property taxes and similar charges) are not currently deductible in determining earnings and profits. They must be added to the basis of the constructed property and will affect earnings and profits as part of the depreciation deduction; (2) The difference between the fair market value of, and the corporation's adjusted basis in, appreciated property distributed to the corporation's shareholders will increase earnings and profits when the property is distributed; and (3) Earnings and profits are increased in the year of sale by the realized gain in an installment sale even though the corporation uses the installment method to report taxable income. See Antognini, *The Impact on Earnings and Profits of Distributions of Appreciated Property,* 14 J. Corp. Tax'n 227 (1987).

See generally Andrews, *"Out of Its Earnings and Profits"; Some Reflections on the Taxation of Dividends,* 69 Harv.L.Rev. 1403 (1956); Albrecht, *"Dividends" and "Earnings or Profits",* 7 Tax L.Rev. 157 (1952); Jacoby, *Earnings and Profits: A Not So Theoretical Concept—*

Some Winds Of Change, 29 N.Y.U.Inst.Fed.Tax'n 649 (1971); Edelstein, *Searching for Some Logic in the Earnings and Profits Rules: Some Recent Developments,* 1974 Tul.Tax Inst. 73; McDaniel, *Earnings and Profits: More than a Cold Accounting Concept: Additions to and Subtractions from,* 32 N.Y.U. Inst.Fed.Tax'n 445 (1974).

In many, but not all, respects the distribution of dividends by an S corporation is subject to the special provisions governing such corporations. See Sections 1361 to 1379. See also Division I, pages 101 to 116 supra, for a discussion of S corporations.

As described above, nonliquidating distributions which qualify for treatment under Section 302 as redemptions or partial liquidation are excepted from the operations of Section 301 and, the gain, if any, recognized by a shareholder is treated as capital gain, unless Section 341 applies.

REDEMPTIONS: LIQUIDATING AND NON–LIQUIDATING; KINDS OF DISTRIBUTIONS

Stephen T. Dean
20 N.Y.U. Institute on Federal Taxation 895 (1962).
[footnotes omitted]

*   *   *

Devious Definition of Partial Liquidation

*   *   *

[If a distribution is one of a series of distributions pursuant to a plan to redeem all of the stock of the distributing corporation, it is treated as received in complete liquidation of the corporation, under Section 331(a), and, as a result, the distribution is treated by the recipient shareholder as a sale or exchange of his stock involving the return of capital and capital gain or loss. See Section 346(a). If the distribution "in partial liquidation" does not qualify for treatment as a sale or exchange under the test described above, such treatment might be achieved, under Section 302(b)(4), if, in general, the distribution is made to a noncorporate shareholder and is "in partial liquidation of the distributing corporation." See Sections 302(b)(4) and 302(e).]

*   *   *

Business Contraction

*   *   *

[Section 302(e) in defining a partial liquidation for the purposes of Section 302(b)(4)] *   *   * includes as a partial liquidation, a distribution which results from the corporation's "ceasing to conduct, or consists of the assets of, a trade or business which has been actively conducted throughout the 5–year period immediately before the distribution," *and* where the distributing corporation thereafter conducts a business it had conducted over the previous five years.

Short Term Liquidation

Additionally, in defining "partial liquidation" [17] Section [302(e)(1)] goes beyond the five-year-two-businesses rule and includes as well a partial redemption distribution which is "not essentially equivalent to a dividend," provided that the redemption is "pursuant to a plan and occurs within the taxable year in which the plan is adopted or within the succeeding taxable year."

The Regulations [defining partial liquidation] give [the following] as an example, * * * [a] corporation abandoned its retinning and soldering operations following a fire which destroyed the top two floors of a seven story building, thereafter distributing the insurance proceeds not required to rehabilitate the building with five stories. * * *

Partial Redemption With Non–Liquidating Characteristics

Section 302 examines the non-liquidating redemption problem under two rules: the general and the specific. The *general* rule is that a redemption will be treated as a "sale or exchange" if it is "*not* essentially equivalent to a dividend." This gets us nowhere at all if we are looking for a statutory solution. Thus it becomes necessary to examine court decisions as to which redemptions are *not* dividend equivalents. * * *

Disproportionate Redemptions [and Complete Terminations of Interest]

The *specific* rule provides certainty by defining certain "disproportionate redemptions" [and "complete terminations of interest"] which automatically achieve a [sale or exchange] result. [These] area[s] of statutory certainty exist where, following the redemption, the redeemed shareholder owns less than 50% of the voting power of all classes of stock entitled to vote, and the retained voting stock is less than 80% of the percentage which the shareholder owned before the redemption [and where the redemption results in a complete termination of the interest in the redeeming corporation owned by the redeemed shareholder].

* * *

Constructive Ownership of Stock

Overriding all of these non-liquidating redemptions is the omnipresent Section 318 which attributes to the redeemed [share]holder the unredeemed shares owned by others who are in a defined relationship to him. Such a [share]holder may find that he is *not* favored by the "disproportion" rules of Section 302(b)(2), or * * * [the Section 302(b) (3) complete termination of interest rules] because he is treated as the

---

17. [Distributions made as part of a "partial liquidation" are regarded as non-liquidating in these materials, since the distributing corporation will remain in existence and operation in "reduced" form.]

constructive owner of shares actually owned by his family or by a partnership, estate, trust or corporation in which he has an interest. Similarly, an estate which has redeemed its stock may be the constructive owner of shares owned by its beneficiaries. Moreover, stock thus constructively owned may be *reattributed* so that the redeemed [share]holder will be deemed to be the constructive owner of shares which are twice or more removed from him.

Limitation Upon Attribution

* * * Section 302(c) * * * [, however,] provides that the *family* attribution rules (initially set in motion by Section 318(a)(1)) will *not* apply if the redeeming [share]holder sells all of the shares actually owned by him *and* he ceases to be an officer, director or employee.

Reduction in Control

However, even though the attribution rules do apply, and even if the redeemed [share]holder cannot claim the benefits of the "disproportion" rule of Section 302(b)(2) [or the "complete termination of interest" rule of Section 302(b)(3)], the redemption still may be argued to be not essentially equivalent to a dividend. * * *

Redemption Related to Stock Purchases

Frequently stock is redeemed by the corporation as an adjunct to agreements [among] the [share]holders. Where a corporation purchases stock from an outgoing [share]holder, the question arises whether the purchase obligation is primarily that of the remaining [share]holders.

Corporation as Agent of [Share]holders

If it is the obligation of the remaining [share]holders, the redemption will constitute a dividend to them, since corporate monies are used to discharge individual obligations of [share]holders. The same dividend result is even more apparent where the remaining [share]holders first purchase the stock of the outgoing [share]holder and, thereafter, the corporation either redeems such stock or pays the purchase obligation.

[Share]holder as Agent for Corporation

However, if the individual [share]holder is acting as agent for the corporation in purchasing and reselling to it the stock of the outgoing [share]holder, he may be free of dividend consequences. Such an agency is not evidenced alone by the fact that corporate redemption was contemplated at the time of the individual purchase of the outgoing [share]holder's stock. In addition, there must be some other indicator of agency, such as a corporate business purpose for the redemption, a temporary lack of corporate funds for the purchase, or a corporate need for the stock, as where it is to be sold to key employees.

Contemporary Redemption and Purchase

There is also potential dividend equivalence where an existing [share]holder disposes of *all* of his stock—part being redeemed by the corporation and the balance being contemporaneously purchased by a new [share]holder. In theory, if the redemption is regarded as *separate* from and *preceding* the sale (when the seller would be the sole [share]holder), the redemption would be a dividend to the seller. If the redemption is regarded as *separate* from and *following* the sale (when the purchaser would be the sole [share]holder), the redemption would be a dividend to the purchaser.

However, the courts have agreed that the *contemporaneous* redemption of part of the seller's stock, as part of a plan to dispose of all of his stock, is not a dividend equivalent. The Treasury Department has concurred, but with the qualification that the transaction "will be closely scrutinized to determine whether the selling [share]holder ceases to be interested in the affairs of the corporation immediately after the redemption."

If the purchaser's acquisition of part of the stock is contemporaneous with the redemption of the balance, and both transactions are part of a single plan, then he should also be free of the danger of dividend equivalence. However, here again, the Treasury Department's concurrence is qualified by reference to *Wall v. United States*[, 164 F.2d 462 (4th Cir.1974),] (which held that there was a dividend where the corporation paid an individual obligation for purchase of stock).

* * *

NOTE

1. Can the "not essentially equivalent to a dividend" language of Section 302(e)(1)(A) be relied on to insure sale or exchange treatment for a partial liquidation?

a. Assume a corporation, because of a reduction in demand for its product, has no further need for a substantial portion of its cash which had been used to provide for its accounts receivable and inventory in times of greater demand. If the corporation distributes the unneeded cash to its shareholders can the individual shareholders claim sale or exchange treatment as a Section 302(b)(4) partial liquidation? See Reg.Sec. 1.346–1(a)(2); Rev.Rul. 60–322, 1960–2 C.B. 118; Rev.Rul. 76–526, 1976–2 C.B. 101. But cf. Rev.Rul. 74–296, 1974–1 C.B. 80; Rev.Rul. 76–289, 1976–2 C.B. 100; Rev. Rul. 78–55, 1978–1 C.B. 88.

b. Does the type of transaction used by the regulations as an example of a partial liquidation qualifying as not essentially equivalent to a dividend differ substantially from the type of transaction incorporated in the "safe harbor" of Section 302(e)(2) which looks to the termination of a business?

c. Cf. Bierman and Fuller, *Not All Business Contractions Qualify as Partial Liquidations Under Section 346*, 42 J. Tax'n 194 (1975); Bierman and Fuller, *Partial Liquidations Under Section 346: Corporate Effects and Special Problems*, 42 J. Tax'n 286 (1975); Witten, *Renting as an Actively Conducted Business Under Secs. 346 and 355: An Economic Concept*, 6 Tax Adviser 404 (1975).

2. When does the "not essentially equivalent to a dividend" language of Section 302(b)(1) provide a means of escaping dividend treatment?

a. If the distribution in redemption does not affect the proportionate interest of the recipient shareholder, but the corporation has a good business reason for the distribution and no intent to distribute a dividend is the recipient shareholder entitled to sale or exchange treatment? See *United States v. Davis*, 397 U.S. 301, 90 S.Ct. 1041, 25 L.Ed.2d 323 (1970); Note, *I.R.C. § 302(b)(1): Dividend Equivalency After United States v. Davis*, 7 Fla.St.U.L.Rev. 505 (1979).

b. Is sale or exchange treatment available if the distribution described above affected the proportionate interest of the recipient shareholders but did not reduce the interest below 50% of the voting power of all classes of stock entitled to vote. Cf. Rev.Rul. 75–502, 1975–2 C.B. 111; Rev. Rul. 76–364, 1976–2 C.B. 91; Rev.Rul. 77–218, 1977–1 C.B. 81; Rev.Rul. 78–104, 1978–2 C.B. 127.

1. If the distribution reduced the recipient shareholder's interest below 50%, but he retained more than 80% of his prior interest, is he now entitled to sale or exchange treatment? See Rev.Rul. 75–502, 1975–2 C.B. 111; Rev.Rul. 75–512, 1975–2 C.B. 112; Rev.Rul. 76–364, 1976–2 C.B. 91; Rev.Rul. 76–385, 1976–2 C.B. 92.

2. See Randall, *Recent Interpretations of the "Meaningful Reduction" Test of I.R.C. Section 302(b)(1)*, 1977 B.Y.U.L.Rev. 253; Zinn and Silverman, *Redemptions of Stock Under Section 302(b)(1)*, 32 Tax Law. 91 (1978); Blumstein, *When Is a Redemption "Not Essentially Equivalent To a Dividend"?*, 7 J.Corp. Tax'n 99 (1980); Kahn, *Stock Redemptions: The Standards for Qualifying as a Purchase Under Section 302(b)*, 50 Fordham L.Rev. 1 (1981).

c. If the reason that the recipient shareholder retained more than 80% of his prior interest or was not reduced below 50% in voting power is because his brother's shares were attributed to him under Section 318, does he stand a chance of succeeding under the "not essentially equivalent to a dividend" provision of Section 302 if he had not spoken to his brother for 20 years because of a serious disagreement which there was no hope of resolving in the future? See *Estate of Arthur H. Squier*, 35 T.C. 950 (1961). But see the Supreme Court's discussion of the application of the attribution rules in *United States v. Davis*, 397 U.S. 301, 90 S.Ct. 1041, 25 L.Ed.2d 323 (1970); and the discussion contained in Rev.Rul. 80–26, 1980–1 C.B. 66. See Randall and Benson, *Family Dissension and the Attribution Rules of Sections 267, 318 and 544*, 53 Taxes 534 (1975); Cathcart, *Section 302 Redemptions: Family Fights and Attribution*, 61 A.B.A.J. 1272 (1975); Note, *The Effect of Family Hostility Upon the Attribution Rules in the "Essentially Equivalent to a Dividend Test"*, 36 Ohio St.L.J. 947 (1975); Note, *Family Hostility Can Mitigate the Application of the Constructive Ownership Rules in Determining Whether a Stock Redemption is Essentially Equivalent to a Dividend*, 7 Tex.Tech.L.Rev. 195 (1975); Englebrecht and

DeCelles, *Family Discord and Section 302 Stock Redemptions: A Review and Analysis,* 58 Taxes 43 (1980); Note, *The "Bad Blood Factor" and § 302 Redemptions: A Retrospective Examination and Analysis,* 85 W.Va.L.Rev. 139 (1982).

3.   If a corporation distributes property rather than cash in redemption or partial liquidation, the corporation will recognize gain equal to the difference between the fair market value of, and its adjusted basis in, the distributed property.

4.   A corporate shareholder will not receive sale or exchange treatment even if the distribution qualifies as a partial liquidation under Section 302(e). See Section 302(b)(4).   A corporate shareholder, however, is entitled to sale or exchange treatment if the distribution qualifies under Sections 302(b)(1) (not essentially equivalent to a dividend), 302(b)(2) (substantially disproportionate redemption), or 302(b)(3) (complete termination of interest).

5.   An entity, such as a partnership, estate, trust or corporation, can have the family attribution rules of Section 318(a)(1) waived in determining whether a redemption results in a complete termination of interest under Section 302(b) (3).   The family attribution rules, however, can only be waived if those persons through whom ownership is attributed to the entity join in the waiver.   See Section 302(c)(2)(C).

6.   The shareholders of an S corporation will be treated similar to the shareholders of a C corporation with regard to a redemption by, or partial liquidation of, the corporation.

d.   REPAYMENT BY THE OPERATING ENTITY OF PARTICIPANTS' LOANS

An entity's cash can be made available to the participants in the entity through repayment of loans made to the entity by the participants.   Loans can be repaid by an entity without the problems involved in complying with the dividend or repurchase provisions of state corporate statutes and the statutory requirements with respect to distributions by a partnership.   Therefore, as opposed to a stock investment, a loan can be repaid without any concern about the existence of a surplus account to support the repayment.   In addition, the part of the participants' contributions to the entity cast as loans, assuming the entity is solvent and the loans are truly loans, generally will share on a par with creditors of the entity rather than being subordinate as equity investments would be.   However, with respect to the order of payment of the liabilities of a partnership upon the distribution of partnership assets in the event of its dissolution and winding-up see Section 40 of the Uniform Partnership Act and Section 23 of the Uniform Limited Partnership Act.   Section 804 of the Revised Uniform Limited Partnership Act draws no distinction between creditors of the partnership who are also partners and third-party creditors in determining the order of the distribution of the assets of a partnership upon dissolution and winding-up, other than with respect to partnership liabilities to partners for distributions under Sections 601 or 604.

The interest paid on loans, if they are treated as loans, is deductible for income tax purposes by a corporation and a partnership, whereas dividends and partnership distributions are not deductible. The repayment of the principal of a loan has none of the tax remifications discussed in the consideration of partnership distributions and redemptions of corporate stock. In general, the repayment of a loan is not taxable to the recipient. It is treated as a return of capital. For the above reasons, the participants in an entity prefer to treat as much as possible of their contributions to it as loans rather than equity investments.

(i) AUTHORIZATION TO BORROW FROM PARTICIPANTS

There is no prohibition against a participant making a loan to an operating entity. Division III, see pages 876 to 882 supra, discusses the authorization of borrowing by an entity. There are, however, limitations present in the Revised Model Business Corporation Act with respect to a corporation *making* loans to its directors. See Section 8.32. Section 13 of the Uniform Limited Partnership Act, while permitting a loan to the partnership by a limited partner, prohibits the receipt or holding of any partnership property as collateral security for the loan and the receipt of any payment with respect to the loan if at the time the assets of the partnership are not sufficient to discharge partnership liabilities to persons not claiming as general or limited partners. The Revised Uniform Limited Partnership Act, in Section 107, permits a partner to lend money to the limited partnership and provides that with respect thereto the partner has the same rights and obligations as a person who is not a partner.

(ii) LOAN OR INVESTMENT

Many corporate statutes prescribe the minimum capitalization of a corporation. Complying with a minimum capitalization provision, however, does not insure that the participants' contributions, in excess of the minimum capitalization, which are cast in the form of loans, will not be challenged as actually constituting an additional equity investment. On the other hand, the failure to provide the minimum capitalization required by a corporate statute may mean in some states that the shareholders are personally liable for the debts of the corporation. In the bankruptcy and common law context, as distinguished from the income tax context, partners' loans to a partnership are not of great concern, since the partners are personally liable for the debts of a partnership. In contrast, loans by limited partners to a limited partnership, especially one with a sole corporate general partner, present many of the same concerns as loans by shareholders to their corporation. Section 13 of the Uniform Limited Partnership Act provides certain limitations on limited partner loans. Section 107 of the Revised Uniform Limited Partnership Act, however, does not restrict the rights of a lender-limited partner in any way.

The primary concern is whether a participant loan is really a loan or, in fact, an equity investment. Participants can make loans to an entity, however, if they are greedy and attempt to cast all or the majority of their investment in the entity as loans, the courts are quick to treat the so-called loans as equity investments. The criteria used by the courts to distinguish loans from equity investments have developed over the years.

SHAREHOLDER ADVANCES: CAPITAL OR LOANS?

Jules S. Cohen
52 American Bankruptcy Law Journal 259 (1978).
[most footnotes omitted]

* * *

The Criteria

Some criteria have to do with the fairness of the shareholder's sharing in dividends with unsecured creditors. These criteria include the adequacy of capital contributed, the ratio of shareholders' loans to shareholders' capital, whether the shareholder took a lien on all assets, the amount of shareholder control, whether the corporation was used for the shareholder's own purposes, and whether the financial failure was caused by undercapitalization.

Most of the criteria have to do with whether the transaction bears the earmarks of an arm's-length bargain. These criteria include the intent of the parties, whether there was an agreement for repayment, provision for interest, a fixed maturity date, a note or other document evidencing the debt, entries of a loan on the parties' books, lack of subordination to other debts, actual partial repayment, restriction on right to enforce collection, use of proceeds to acquire capital assets, loans proportionate to stockholdings, repayment to be made only from earnings, availability of outside financing, and enforcement of collection after default. The more the loans bear these earmarks of an arm's-length transaction, the more likely the courts are to treat the loans as loans and not capital investments.

* * *

Among the criteria considered by the courts in deciding the loan versus capital question, perhaps the paramount criterion is whether the corporation was undercapitalized. Was the amount of equity capital invested in the corporation by the shareholders sufficient in view of its capital requirements to acquire capital assets and have a sufficient amount of working capital on hand to cover pre-opening expenses and initial operational deficits? Courts will consider the testimony of accountants and other expert witnesses as to a reasonable amount of capital for the expected business activity. Courts also use their own judgment as to whether the capital was adequate for the scope of the business. The adequacy of the capitalization of the venture should be judged as of the time of the outset of the venture.[18]

*   *   *

In considering whether corporations were undercapitalized courts have often considered the ratio of the shareholders' loans to their invested capital. This is commonly spoken of as the ratio of debt to equity. Adequate capitalization has been found where the debt to equity ratio was 4 to 1, 6 to 1, 1.8 to 1, 1.7 to 1, 1.5 to 1, and 1.3 to 1. But a low ratio is not conclusive. Because of other circumstances, the advances were treated as capital in cases where the ratios were only 1.4 to 1, 2 to 1, and 1.8 to 1.

Higher ratios of debt to equity have usually resulted in decisions that the advances were capital, not loans.

Another criterion considered by the Courts is the intent of the parties as to whether the advance was a capital investment or loan. But the intent of the parties is not conclusive of the matter.

Other criteria are whether there was an agreement for repayment of the loans, for a fixed maturity date, or for the payment of interest. These are earmarks of an arm's-length transaction and are persuasive that the shareholder has made loans as an outsider might have and that the advances should therefore be treated as loans. Conversely, the absence of these factors indicates the advances were not bona fide arm's-length loans, since the lender did not require an agreement as to such basic elements of a loan transaction as interest and maturity date.

The courts consider whether notes or other debt instruments were executed by the debtor to evidence the debt to the shareholder. If so, this is usually taken as a sign that the transaction was a loan and not an investment of capital. But the existence of debt instruments is not conclusive of the question. In some cases, the courts have held the advance to be a capital investment notwithstanding the existence of debt instruments.   *   *   *

If the shareholder has subordinated his claim to those of other creditors, his claim is usually treated as capital. Lack of subordination has been used as a reason for upholding the transaction as a loan.[19] Normally a bona fide creditor does not subordinate his claim. A shareholder's capital investment is automatically subordinate to creditors' claims. When a creditor-shareholder subordinates, he puts his claim closer to the status of capital and courts are more likely to treat it as capital.

On the other hand, courts sometimes condemn the shareholder's effort to place himself ahead of other creditors by taking liens on assets,[20] and use this as a reason to treat the advance as capital.

---

18. Earle v. W.J. Jones & Son, Inc., 200 F.2d 846 (9 Cir.1952). Contra, In re Fett Roofing and Sheet Metal Co., 438 F.Supp. 726, 730 (E.D.Va.1977).

19. Tomlinson v. The 1661 Corp., 377 F.2d 291 (5 Cir.1967); Contra, In re Lumber, Inc., 12 F.Supp. 302, 308 (D.Or.1954).

20. Braddy v. Randolph, 352 F.2d 80 (4 Cir.1965).

One factor that the courts have remarked on is whether the corporation made any actual repayments on the shareholder's loans. Some cases state that it makes no difference whether repayments were ever made. Others say actual repayment supports a conclusion that the advance was a loan. Conversely, payment of other creditors and no payment to the shareholder-creditor supports treatment as a capital investment, since return of capital is by law postponed to payment of creditors.

In a loan transaction, normally, the creditor may bring action against the debtor upon default. Departure from this norm leads courts to treat shareholders' advances as capital. If the shareholder's loan is fashioned in such a way that there are restrictions on the shareholder's right to enforce payment, the courts have treated the loan as capital * * *. If the shareholder-creditor agrees not to enforce collection, this favors treating the advance as capital.

Use of the funds from the shareholder for acquisition of capital assets is usually taken as a sign of a capital investment, rather than a loan, but not always.

Virtually the only opinion that offers some discussion of this criterion is Arnold v. Phillips.[21] In that case, Arnold formed a corporation to engage in the brewing and bottling business. He put $50,000 capital into the corporation. The corporation began building a plant, and during the first year Arnold advanced an additional $70,000 and received demand notes. The plant cost approximately $115,000. Additional advances were made to begin operations. Approximately one year after the corporation was formed, a new demand note was given to Arnold for $75,000. Two months later a substitute note was given to him for $79,729 secured by a deed of trust on the plant which also stated that it was to secure future indebtedness.

For two years the business prospered. During that time the company paid the interest on Arnold's note and $27,400 of the principal, leaving a principal balance of $52,392. The business then began to lose money. Arnold made additional advances, until his loan stood at $99,379. He foreclosed on the plant and bid it in at the public sale for the amount of his debt. He obtained a deed of the property, but did not record it. On the day of the sale he leased the plant back to the company, which continued to operate there.

Bankruptcy ensued six months later, resulting in total unsecured debts of $66,000 and assets of little value.

The court held that the original $70,000 which he loaned to the corporation was not a loan but a capital investment. The ground for this holding was the fact that the $70,000 loan and the $50,000 capital were used to build the plant. The court said, "although the charter provided for no more capital than $50,000, what it took to build the

21. Arnold v. Phillips, 117 F.2d 497 (5 Cir.1941).

plant and equipment was a permanent investment, in its nature capital."

The court did not ground this holding on any finding or conclusion that the $50,000 admitted capital was inadequate. On the contrary, the court said "it would be hard to say in this case that $50,000 was not a substantial capital. * * *"

The court's conclusion that the $70,000 loan was additional capital because it was used to construct a capital asset seems open to criticism. Had the company acquired a $70,000 permanent mortgage loan from a financing institution and used the proceeds of that loan for the balance of the cost of construction of the plant, no one would contend that the lending institution had contributed $70,000 capital to the corporation.

This criterion involves a consideration of the purpose for which the funds are used. The court implies, without really saying why, that if the funds are used for the acquisition of capital assets, this indicates that the funds are "really" equity capital. If they are used for working capital, apparently, this is an indication that the funds are loans. This idea is at variance with modern business realities. It is common for business enterprises to finance the acquisition of capital assets through an infinite variety of financing arrangements, including equipment leases with or without options to purchase, installment purchase contracts, vehicle financing by dealers or lending institutions, sale-leasebacks, land acquisition and development loans, construction loans, "permanent" mortgage loans, and wrap-around mortgages. It would be a rare enterprise indeed, especially in the case of a new enterprise, where the owners put in a sufficient amount of cash to fully pay for all of the capital assets.

In the face of widespread bona fide arm's-length financing of the acquisition of capital assets by the use of funds advanced by outside lenders, logically the nature of the transaction should not be changed from loan to capital investment solely because the lender is a shareholder.

Looking at the other side of the coin, it is not logical to say that the use of the [proceeds of a shareholder advance] for working capital is a sign that [the shareholder advance is] a loan. There is nothing inherent in the nature of working capital that aids us in categorizing funds used for this purpose as equity capital or loans. In the realities of the business world, sometimes working capital is available by way of the equity capital invested by the shareholders, and sometimes it is made available by borrowing, commonly from commercial banks on the strength of accounts receivable or contract rights. Usually working capital comes from both equity capital and bank borrowings. When a bank loans working capital, no one would contend it has contributed equity capital. Likewise, it is not logical to contend so when the lender is a shareholder.

Where the shareholders make advances to the corporation in proportion to their stock holdings, the courts view this as a sign that the advances are additional capital investments. Conversely, non-proportional advances are more likely to be treated as loans. If non-proportional advances are treated as capital investments, the court seems to be changing the ownership ratios between the shareholders.

Where shareholders gave themselves liens to secure their advances, which put them ahead of other creditors,[22] and then foreclosed their liens to acquire the assets free of the creditors' claims, courts have found the advances to be capital investments.[23] The fact that debentures given shareholders were unsecured has been used as a reason for treating the transaction as capital.[24]

The anticipated source of repayment of the loan is relevant. An agreement that the loan will be repaid from net income after operating expenses is a factor pointing toward capital investment, rather than a loan; similarly, where the advances were not to be repaid in ordinary course as other creditors were paid.

Another criterion considered by the courts is how the transaction was treated on the books of the lender and borrower. If the advance is treated as a loan on the books of both parties, the court is more likely to treat it as a loan.

Another relevant factor is the time when the shareholder advances are made. If the advances are made at or near the time of incorporation, the court is more likely to treat the advance as capital investment. Perhaps that is because that is when capital investments are normally made. If advances are made later to cover unforeseen needs, the court is more likely to treat them as loans.

Another criterion considered by the courts is whether the corporation had the ability to obtain the funds in question from outside lending institutions. The rationale seems to be that if outside financing was available, then the advance was of a type that could have been the subject of an arm's-length loan transaction and should be held to be a loan. The likelihood of payment of the loan by refinancing with an outside lender has been held to be persuasive that sums advanced were loans.[25]

A tax motive in making the advance in the form of a loan is relevant, but this marker points different ways in bankruptcy and tax cases. In a bankruptcy case where an income tax saving motive influenced shareholders to make part of their advances in the form of loans, all of the advances were treated as capital.[26] In tax cases, it has

22. In re Fett Roofing and Sheet Metal Co., 438 F.Supp. 726, 728 (E.D.Va.1977).

23. Braddy v. Randolph, 352 F.2d 80 (4 Cir.1965); Arnold v. Phillips, 117 F.2d 497 (5 Cir.1941); Duberstein v. Werner, 256 F.Supp. 515 (E.D.N.Y.1966) (shareholder-creditor foreclosed his mortgage on the sole asset).

24. Austin Village, Inc. v. United States, 432 F.2d 741 (6 Cir.1970); United States v. Snyder Brothers Co., 367 F.2d 980 (5 Cir.1966); Contra, In re Lumber, Inc., 124 F.Supp. 302, 308 (D.Or.1954).

25. Jaeger Auto Finance Co. v. Nelson, 191 F.Supp. 693 (E.D.Wis.1961).

26. Costello v. Fazio, 256 F.2d 903 (9 Cir.1958); L & M Realty Corp. v. Leo, 249 F.2d 668 (4 Cir.1957).

been stated that the corporation's motive in lessening its income tax did not weigh in favor of treating the advances as capital.[27]

Another criterion is whether there was a failure by the debtor to pay on the due date or whether there was a failure to seek a postponement of payment. But the advance may still be held to be a loan where there is a default in payment of interest or where the shareholder-lender fails to demand payment after default.

Where the shareholder-lender controls the corporation, there is a tendency toward treating the advance as capital; such as where the shareholders could elect four out of seven directors.[28] Conversely, lack of control leads to upholding the loan status of the advance.

If the shareholders have conducted the business in their interest as opposed to the interest of the corporation and its creditors, this has been a factor in courts treating the advances as capital. This has been the result where the shareholders used construction funds to pay personally guaranteed bank notes instead of construction creditors,[29] where a profitable furniture manufacturing business was converted to manufacturing television cabinets for the parent corporation's use,[30] where the loan treatment resulted in favorable tax consequences for the shareholders,[31] and where the subsidiary corporation was used solely to supply the parent corporation with newsprint resulting in losses to the subsidiary.[32]

Where the shareholder has not used the corporation for his own purposes, this favors treatment of the advance as a loan.[33]

One factor considered by some courts in bankruptcy cases is whether the cause of the bankruptcy was related to undercapitalization. If so, the courts tend to treat the advances as capital. The unspoken premise is that had the corporation been adequately capitalized, it would not have failed. If the cause of failure was not undercapitalization, this is a factor in favor of treating the advance as a loan.

* * *

NOTE

1. If a participant's loan is found to be an equity investment, there are a number of possible consequences in the corporate, bankruptcy and common law contexts.

a. The participant may be required to repay any amounts received from the entity in payment of the purported loan. This happens most

27. Campbell v. Carter Foundation Prod. Co., 322 F.2d 829, 832 (5 Cir.1963); Kraft Food Co. v. Commissioner, 232 F.2d 118 (2 Cir.1956).

28. International Tel. & Tel. Corp. v. Holton, 247 F.2d 178 (4 Cir.1957).

29. Braddy v. Randolph, 352 F.2d 80 (4 Cir.1965).

30. International Tel. & Tel. Corp. v. Holton, 247 F.2d 178 (4 Cir.1957).

31. Costello v. Fazio, 256 F.2d 903, 909 (9 Cir.1958).

32. Gannett Co. v. Larry, 21 F.2d 269 (2 Cir.1955).

33. In re Lumber, Inc., 124 F.Supp. 302, 310 (D.Or.1954).

frequently when the participants in a failing entity cause the entity to pay the loans made to it by the participants at the expense of the entity's other creditors.

    b. The participant's claim for the amount of the loan is subordinated to the claims of the entity's general creditors. Actually, this involves a form of practical subordination, once the participant's loan is classified as an equity investment, the participant claim comes after the claims of the entity's general creditors.

    c. In the extreme case and if the minimum capital required by the corporate statute is not provided, the participants may be personally liable for the debts of the entity. Personal liability, if the minimum capital requirements are complied with, would require, in most cases, a finding of fraud, mismanagement or unfair dealings on the part of the participants in addition to their loans being found to be equity investments. Cf. *AMFAC Mechanical Supply Co. v. Federer*, 645 P.2d 73 (Wyo.1982). See Gelb, *Piercing the Corporate Veil—The Undercapitalization Factor*, 59 Chi–Kent L.Rev. 1 (1982).

    2. See generally Loiseaux, *Loans or Capital Contributions to the Close Corporation*, 38 # 1 J.Nat'l A.Ref.Bankr. 4 (1964); Comment, *Limited Liability: A Definitive Judicial Standard for the Inadequate Capitalization Problem*, 47 Temp.L.Q. 321 (1974); Clark, *The Duties of the Corporate Debtor To Its Creditors*, 90 Harv.L.Rev. 505 (1977); Comment, *The Intractable Debt/Equity Problem: A New Structure for Analyzing Shareholder Advances*, 81 Nw.U.L.Rev. 452 (1987).

    3. Because of the income tax advantages of a loan, when compared with an equity investment, the Internal Revenue Service has been one of the most frequent litigants challenging the status of a participant's loan to an entity. This type of litigation can be distinguished from corporate, bankruptcy and common law litigation in several ways.

    a. Apparently, the intent of the participants with respect to whether a loan or equity investment was made is not conclusive on the determination of the status of the investment in the common law, bankruptcy and corporate contexts. In the income tax context, at least some courts have held that intent is all important. See *Gooding Amusement Co., Inc. v. Comm'r*, 23 T.C. 408 (1954), affirmed, 236 F.2d 159 (6th Cir.1956), cert. denied, 352 U.S. 1031, 77 S.Ct. 595, 1 L.Ed.2d 599 (1956).

    1. On the other hand, if intent is determined on the basis of objective facts, such as the subordination of the loan in question to other creditor's claims, is there really a difference?

    b. The burden of proof in the corporate, bankruptcy and common law contexts is generally on the party challenging the status of the loan. The taxpayer has the burden of proof in an income tax setting.

    4. The courts have determined that a number of factors are significant in distinguishing debt from equity in an income tax context.

HARDMAN v. UNITED STATES

United States Court of Appeals, Ninth Circuit, 1987.
827 F.2d 1409.
[footnotes omitted]

TANG, Circuit Judge:

Opinion

* * *

I

Frances Hardman owns twenty-five percent of Hardman, Inc. Together, Mr. and Mrs. Hardman own eighty-nine percent. In February, 1968, Frances Hardman purchased Hale Field, a 100 acre tract of undeveloped land, for $225,000. She made a downpayment and executed a secured promissory note for the remainder of the purchase price. Unable to keep up with the payments, she conveyed the property to Hardman, Inc. in 1972. By this time, Mrs. Hardman had made three annual payments on the promissory note. Hardman, Inc. reimbursed Mrs. Hardman for the three annual payments and the down payment; assumed the promissory note; and executed the following contract:

> In consideration of Frances N. Hardman selling her one hundred (100) acres of Hale Field property to Hardman, Inc. at her cost, Hardman, Inc. hereby agrees to pay Frances N. Hardman one-third of any net profit that Hardman, Inc. may derive from said property.

The contract appeared on corporate stationery, and was signed by Rudolph Hardman as president.

Hardman, Inc. later purchased twenty acres of land adjoining Hale Field. In 1977, the corporation resold the property, including the additional twenty acres, for $600,000. It paid Mrs. Hardman $109,568, one third of the net profit attributable to the 100 acres of Hale Field. The Hardmans reported the payment as gain from the sale of real property * * *. Hardman, Inc. added the payment to its basis in the property and calculated its capital gains accordingly.

The IRS assessed deficiencies against the Hardmans and Hardman, Inc. The taxpayers paid the deficiencies and filed claims for refunds. After the IRS took no action on the claims, the Hardmans and Hardman, Inc. each filed suit in district court. The cases were consolidated and on March 31, 1986, the court entered judgment for the United States.

The district court concluded that the 1972 transaction between Mrs. Hardman and Hardman, Inc. was an equity investment by Mrs. Hardman in the corporation and that the 1977 payment was a dividend taxable as ordinary income. * * * The Hardmans and Hardman, Inc. timely appeal.

II

* * *

Whether the $109,568 payment in 1977 was in satisfaction of an obligation arising from a sale or a dividend cannot be viewed in isolation but must be considered in the context of the overall transaction. The parties agree that the payment correlates to the 1972 property transfer. In this context, characterization of the payment turns on the nature of the property transfer. The Hardmans have characterized this transaction as a sale of property financed in part by a loan to the corporation. Mrs. Hardman's inability to keep up with the payments serves as a valid business reason for transferring the land in exchange for uncertain future profits. * * * If a transfer by a shareholder to her corporation is found to be an equity investment, payments of "interest" or "principal" by the corporation will be treated as constructive dividends or redemptions. See B. Bittker & J. Eustace, Federal Income Taxation of Corporations and Shareholders ¶ 7.05[3] (1979). This is because Congress has chosen to tax distributions to shareholders of corporate earnings and profits [as] ordinary income * * *. We cannot condone taxpayer attempts to bleed off corporate profits [as] capital gains * * *. On the other hand, Congress has chosen to tax gains from the sale of property [as] capital gains * * *. We will not permit the IRS to characterize genuine gains from the sale of property as ordinary income.

This court has identified eleven factors which, to varying degrees, influence resolution of the question of whether a transfer to a corporation by a shareholder is a sale (debt) or a contribution to capital (equity).

(1) the names given to the certificates evidencing the indebtedness;

(2) the presence or absence of a maturity date;

(3) the source of the payments;

(4) the right to enforce payment of principal and interest;

(5) participation and management;

(6) a status equal to or inferior to that of regular corporate creditors;

(7) the intent of the parties;

(8) "thin" or adequate capitalization;

(9) identity of interest between creditor and stockholder;

(10) payment of interest only out of "dividend" money;

(11) the ability of the corporation to obtain loans from outside lending institutions.

Bauer v. CIR, 748 F.2d 1365, 1368 (9th Cir.1984); A.R. Lantz Co. v. United States, 424 F.2d 1330, 1333 (9th Cir.1970); O.H. Kruse Grain & Milling v. CIR, 279 F.2d 123, 125–26 (9th Cir.1960). No one factor is decisive. Bauer, 748 F.2d at 1368. The court must examine the particular circumstances of each case. Id. "The object of the inquiry is not to count factors, but to evaluate them." Id. (quoting Tyler v. Tomlinson, 414 F.2d 844, 848 (9th Cir.1969)).

In upholding the determination of the Commissioner, the district court cited only one of the eleven factors, the absence of a maturity date and other indicia of bona fide indebtedness. * * *

We review for clear error a district court's determination of whether a transaction between a shareholder and her company constitutes a sale or a contribution to capital. Bauer, 748 F.2d at 1367. When a lower court has overemphasized one of the eleven debt-equity factors, "this court has consistently been disposed to reverse." A.R. Lantz Co., 424 F.2d at 1333. However, we will reverse only if, in considering all of the factors, we find that the court clearly erred. Cf. Bauer, 748 F.2d at 1368-71.

1. Names Given to the Certificates Evidencing the Indebtedness. The issuance of a stock certificate indicates an equity contribution and the issuance of a bond, debenture or note indicates a bona fide indebtedness. Estate of Mixon, 464 F.2d 394, 403 (5th Cir.1972). The document executed by Hardman, Inc. lacks a name, but it contains language typical of a promissory note: "[I]n consideration of * * *," "Hardman, Inc. hereby agrees to pay * * *." The document contains no language typical of a stock certificate such as reference to dividend, voting or redemption rights. The factor weighs in favor of a finding that the transaction was a sale.

2. The Presence or Absence of a Maturity Date. The absence of a fixed maturity date indicates that repayment is tied to the fortunes of the business. Id. at 404. The contract contains no fixed maturity date. Furthermore, as the district court pointed out, repayment is not unconditional, nor is the amount of principal and interest stated in a sum certain. These are important factors and the district court concluded that they compelled a finding that the property transfer was a contribution to capital. Although we find merit in the court's finding, we note that the document contains more of the traditional indicia of a debt instrument than that of an equity instrument. Although there is no fixed maturity date, repayment is tied to a fairly certain event—sale of the property—and guarantees payment of an amount relative to the value of the property. An equity instrument, on the other hand, contains no guarantee of dividend payments in any amount at any time.

3. The Source of Payments. If repayment is not dependent upon earnings, the transaction more resembles a sale. Id. at 405. On its face, this factor seems to weigh in favor of a finding of equity because the payment came from corporate profits. However, the payment did not come from the general earnings and profits of the corporation but rather profits from the resale of this particular tract of land. The contract entitled Mrs. Hardman to receive one-third of the profits from resale even if the company suffered a loss in its overall operations. * * * That this payment is tied to the sale of the property, and not the overall fortunes of the corporation, makes it logically distinct from a payment out of earnings and profits. Accordingly, this factor supports a finding that the transaction was in satisfaction of the obligation arising from the original sale rather than a dividend distribution.

4. The Right to Enforce the Payment of Principal and Interest. The presence of an enforceable obligation to pay a share of the profits on resale of the property supports a finding that the transfer was a sale. Id. Mrs. Hardman had an absolute right to enforce the terms of the contract. This feature distinguishes the contract from a stock instrument in which there is no right to enforce payment of dividends. The fact that payment was contingent upon the resale of the property does not make the contract unenforceable. See Restatement (Second) of Contracts §§ 224–226 (1981).

5. Participation in Management. If a stockholder's percentage interest in the corporation or voting rights increase as a result of the transfer, it will contribute to a finding that the transfer was a contribution to capital rather than a sale. Mrs. Hardman's percentage of ownership and control did not change as a result of the transfer.

6. A Status Equal to or Inferior to that of Regular Corporate Creditors. Equity participants take a subordinate position to creditors regarding right to payment upon liquidation. 15A W. Fletcher, Cyclopedia of the Law of Private Corporations § 7481 (rev. perm. ed. 1981). There is no evidence that the parties subordinated Mrs. Hardman's position to those of non-stockholder creditors. Presumably she had an equal right to enforce payment, indicating that the transfer was a sale.

7. The Intent of the Parties. All of the objective evidence points to a conclusion that the parties intended the transaction to be a sale rather than a contribution to capital. The document executed by Hardman, Inc. contains language typical of a promissory note. The written argument and deposition submitted by the Hardmans and Hardman, Inc. indicate that the parties intended the transaction to be a sale. The government argues that the transaction "clearly was designed to improperly convert a subsequent dividend distribution into capital gain" but offers nothing to support this assertion. We note that the purpose of this entire inquiry is to decipher the true intent of the parties. All eleven factors contribute to this evaluation. However, the objective evidence of intent one-sidedly favors the interpretation given by the Hardmans.

8. "Thin" or Adequate Capitalization. Thin capitalization evidences a capital contribution. A high ratio of debt to equity tends to show that the obligation is unrealistic or beyond the corporation's ability to perform. Gyro Eng'g, 417 F.2d at 439. The district court found that the "[c]orporation did not appear to be 'thinly' capitalized but, rather, appeared to be an ongoing, viable corporation with assets other than the property acquired from Mrs. Hardman." This finding supports a conclusion that the transfer was a sale.

9. Identity of Interest Between Creditor and Stockholder. If the property or funds advanced is in proportion to the stockholder's capital interest, it will lend to a finding that the transfer was a contribution to capital. Bauer, 748 F.2d at 1370. Here, only Mrs. Hardman trans-

ferred property to the corporation and the corporation distributed money only to her in connection with the sale of Hale Field. There was no correlation whatsoever between her percentage interest in the corporation and the amount of money distributed to her.

10. Payment of Interest Only Out of "Dividend" Money. This factor is essentially the same as the third factor, "the source of the payments." As we noted earlier, the payment related to profits from the sale of the land not overall earnings and profits. The company was obligated to pay regardless of whether it had accumulated earnings and profits. Therefore, the payment was not from "dividend" money.

11. The Ability of the Corporation to Obtain Loans from Outside Lending Institutions. If a corporation is able to borrow funds from outside sources, the transaction has the appearance of a bona fide indebtedness and indicates that the shareholder acted in the same manner toward the corporation as "ordinary reasonable creditors would have acted." Estate of Mixon, 464 F.2d at 410. If no reasonable creditor would have sold property to the corporation with payments to be made in the future, an inference arises that a reasonable shareholder would not do so either. Id. The district court found that Hardman, Inc. was an ongoing, viable corporation with assets other than the property acquired from Mrs. Hardman. Presumably Hardman, Inc. could easily obtain financing from other sources and the government makes no assertion to the contrary. This factor weighs in favor of a finding that the obligation accompanying the transfer of the property to Hardman, Inc. was a bona fide indebtedness.

III

Our analysis of this transaction in light of these eleven factors leads us to conclude that Mrs. Hardman's transfer of the Hale Field Property to Hardman, Inc. was a sale rather than a contribution to capital. We recognize that the lack of formalities in the instrument executed by Hardman, Inc., raises the suspicion that the transaction was a disguised attempt to extract earnings and profits from the corporation [as] capital gains * * *. However, we find that the trial court erred in relying on this sole factor and neglecting to consider fully the several other factors, all of which point to the opposite conclusion. Accordingly, the decision of the district court is reversed and this case is remanded for a determination of the amount of excess taxes paid by the Hardmans and Hardman, Inc.

Reversed and Remanded.

NOTE

1. If capital gains and ordinary income are taxed at the same rate, would it make any difference in *Hardman v. United States* whether Mrs. Hardman sold or contributed the property to the corporation?

2. Is there a way the Hardmans could have structured the transaction between Mrs. Hardman and the corporation so as to more clearly indicate that

the transaction was a sale for a contingent purchase price rather than a contribution?

3. Are there any factors which the court in *Hardman v. United States* does not list which might be relevant in distinguishing between debt and equity in a different case?

    a. Is whether the purported debtor repaid the debt, or paid installments on the debt, at the required time or times relevant?

    b. Is the purported debtor's use of the proceeds of the debt significant?

    c. See *Mixon v. United States,* 464 F.2d 394 (5th Cir.1972); *Lane v. United States,* 742 F.2d 1311 (11th Cir.1984).

4. Because of the impact the determination whether a loan is, or is not, an equity investment has on a number of sections of the Internal Revenue Code, and the variety of factors examined by the courts in answering this question, Congress acted in this area in 1969.

SENATE COMM. ON FINANCE, TAX REFORM ACT OF 1969

S.Rep. No. 552, 91st Cong., 1st Sess. 137 (1969).
U.S.Code Cong. & Admin.News, 2170–2171.

*   *   *

In view of the uncertainties and difficulties which the distinction between debt and equity has produced in numerous situations *   *   * the committee *   *   * believes that it would be desirable to provide rules for distinguishing debt from equity in the variety of contexts in which this problem can arise. The differing circumstances which characterize these situations, however, would make it difficult for the committee to provide comprehensive and specific statutory rules of universal and equal applicability. In view of this, the committee believes it is appropriate to specifically authorize the Secretary of the Treasury to prescribe the appropriate rules for distinguishing debt from equity in these different situations.

Explanation of provision.—For the above reasons, the committee has added a provision to the House Bill which gives the Secretary of the Treasury or his delegate specific statutory authority to promulgate regulatory guidelines, to the extent necessary or appropriate, for determining whether a corporate obligation constitutes stock or indebtedness. The provision specifies that these guidelines are to set forth factors to be taken into account in determining, with respect to a particular factual situation, whether a debtor-creditor relationship exists or whether a corporation-shareholder relationship exists. The provision also specifies certain factors which may be taken into account in these guidelines. It is not intended that only these factors be included in the guidelines or that, with respect to a particular situation, any of these factors must be included in the guidelines, or that any of the factors which are included by statute must necessarily be given any more weight than other factors added by regulations. The factors specifically listed are as follows:

(1) Whether there is a written unconditional promise to pay on demand or on a specified date a sum certain in money in return for an adequate consideration in money or money's worth and to pay a fixed rate of interest;

(2) Whether there is subordination to or preference over any indebtedness of the corporation;

(3) The ratio of debt to equity of the corporation;

(4) Whether there is convertibility into the stock of the corporation; and

(5) The relationship between holdings of stock in the corporation and holdings of the interest in question.

[T]he guidelines to be promulgated by the Secretary of the Treasury are to be applicable for all purposes of the Internal Revenue Code.

* * *

NOTE

1. Section 385, in effect, gives the Secretary of the Treasury the power to legislate in a substantive area. Other Code sections delegate this duty in procedural matters. Does Section 385 constitute an improper delegation of legislative responsibility?

2. Since Section 385 is specifically limited to the debt of a corporation, what effect does it, and the regulations which may eventually be issued under it, have on a loan made by a partner to a partnership?

3. Both proposed and "final" regulations were issued under Section 385. They, however, were withdrawn and revoked in 1983, and no new regulations have been proposed or issued since then.

    a. The proposed and "final" regulations issued under Section 385 are significant in so far as they provide an indication of the Internal Revenue Service's attitude toward the various factors taken into account in determining whether an instrument is classified as debt or equity.

    1. In general, if an instrument was classified as equity under the regulations, it would be treated as preferred stock for all purposes of the Code, and once so classified, its status could not change. An instrument initially classified as debt, however, could be reclassified as equity under certain circumstances.

    b. The regulations contained separate rules for classifying straight debt instruments (instruments other than hybrid instruments), hybrid instruments (instruments convertible into stock or which provided for contingent payments of principal or interest), cash advances and other unwritten obligations, guaranteed loans and preferred stock. The regulations measured proportionality using a concept described as the "total overlap factor"—the overlap in the ownership of stock which participates in corporate growth and the ownership of the instruments in question. In general, if the total overlap factor with respect to a class of instruments exceeded 50%, the holdings of stock and the instruments were considered substantially proportionate. The total overlap factor was the sum of individual factors, and each individual factor was the lesser of that person's percentage ownership of stock or the class of instruments in question.

Attribution rules, generally those contained in Section 318, were used to determine ownership.

1. Straight debt instruments, if held by an independent creditor, were always classified as debt.

    a. An independent creditor was a creditor who owned (actually and constructively) less than 5% of the corporation's stock and whose percentage ownership of the instruments in question was at least twice as great as the creditor's percentage holdings of stock.

2. Straight debt instruments held by other than independent creditors were classified as debt unless issued proportionately to stock *and* any of the following applied.

    a. The corporation had excessive debt. If the corporation's "outside" debt (all debt except trade accounts payable, accrued operating expenses, taxes and other similar items) to equity ratio was 10:1 or lower, and its "inside" debt (liabilities to independent creditors were excluded) to equity ratio was 3:1 or lower, the corporation's debt would not be considered excessive. (Equity, for these purposes, was computed using the adjusted basis of the corporation's property.)

    b. The instruments were issued for property, they did not state a reasonable rate of interest as of the day of issuance, and they did not give rise to original issue discount or amortizable bond premium. An interest rate was reasonable, if the debt was not nonrecourse, the corporation's "outside" debt to equity ratio was 3:1 or less and the interest rate was equal to any one of the following rates: (1) the rate for income tax deficiencies; (2) the prime rate at a local commercial bank or a rate two points above that rate; (3) a rate determined by reference to U.S. obligations of comparable maturity; (4) the "safe harbor" range of rates under Section 482; or (5) a rate within the range of the rates described above. In addition, a reasonable rate was one which was within the normal range of rates paid to independent creditors on similar instruments by corporations of the same general size and in the same general industry, geographic location and financial condition on the day the determination was made.

    c. The instrument was on demand and did not state a reasonable rate of interest.

    d. Interest was not paid on the instrument within 90 days after the end of the tax year in which it was due and the holder did not pursue normal creditor remedies.

    e. Principal was not paid within 90 days after it was due, the holder did not pursue normal creditor remedies, and the stated interest rate was not reasonable as of the day the principal was due.

3. If straight debt was initially classified as debt and a substantial change was made in its terms such as postponement of the maturity date, a change in the interest rate or subordination and, at that time, the holdings of stock and debt were substantially proportionate, the instrument might then be treated as equity.

4. Hybrid instruments were treated as equity if the ownership of the instruments and the stock of the corporation was substantially proportionate, unless at least 20% of the instruments in question were held by independent creditors.

a. Even if the ownership was not substantially proportionate or 20% of the instruments were held by independent creditors, if the instruments were issued for money and, in general, the equity features accounted for more than 50% of the fair market value of the instruments, they would be classified as equity.

b. If title to one distinct interest in a corporation could not be transferred without transferring title to another interest, i.e., a bond with nondetachable warrants, such "locked interests" were not considered hybrid instruments.

c. Hybrid instruments issued on a nonproportionate basis, and in exchange for property (other than money), were outside of the scope of the regulations.

d. Shortly after the regulations were withdrawn, the Internal Revenue Service ruled on the status of adjustable rate convertible notes the equity features of which would have been valued at less than 50% of the fair market value of the instruments. In Revenue Ruling 83–98, 1983–2 C.B. 40, the Internal Revenue Service considered the status of the notes, each of which was issued for a price equal to the market price of 50 shares of the issuer's common stock. Each note had a 20–year term, and on maturity the holder could elect to receive 60% of the issuance price or 50 shares of the issuer's common stock. Each note was convertible at any time into 50 shares of the issuer's common stock and was callable by the issuer after two years at 60% of the issuance price. Upon the call, however, the holder could convert the notes into the issuer's common stock. The annual interest paid on the notes was equal to the dividends paid on 50 shares of the issuer's stock plus 2% of the issuance price. The interest rate, however, could never be less than 6% nor more than 17.5% based on the issuance price. Lastly, the notes were subordinated to all present and future creditors of the issuer and, in the event of the bankruptcy of the issuer, represented a claim equal to 60% of the issuance price. The Internal Revenue Service treated the notes as equity rather than debt for the following reasons:

(1) The high probability that the notes would be converted into stock—the price of the stock of the corporation would have to fall by more than 40% before a cash redemption or payment would be attractive;

(2) The issuer could force conversion after two years, except in the unlikely event that the price of stock fell by more than 40%;

(3) The guaranteed rate of 6% was unreasonably low when compared to the rate (12%) on notes which were nonconvertible and noncontingent and issued by similar issuers;

(4) More than 65% of the future annual yield of the notes was discretionary with the directors of the issuer, since it was based on the level of dividends paid on the common stock; and

(5) The notes were subordinated to the claims of general creditors.

As a result of this ruling, it is difficult to predict what part of the value of an instrument can be accounted for by its equity features before the instrument will be considered an equity interest rather than debt. It is clear that 40% may be too much. Ten to 20% may be permitted.

e. See generally Comment, *Hybrid Instruments and the Debt–Equity Distinction in Corporate Taxation,* 52 U.Chi.L.Rev. 118 (1985); Willens, *Debt or Equity? Recent Pronouncements Clarify Status of Convertible Debentures,* 16 Tax Adviser 704 (1985); Strasen, *The Taxation of Convertible and Other Equity–Flavored Debt Instruments,* 65 Taxes 937 (1987).

5. Cash advances and other unwritten loans, made by other than an independent creditor, were considered contributions to capital if the corporation had excessive debt and the advances were not repaid within six months after the day they were made.

a. Even if initially classified as debt, cash advances and other unwritten loans would be reclassified as contributions to capital in any year in which the corporation failed to pay interest on them at a reasonable rate.

6. Loans to a corporation guaranteed by its shareholders were treated as loans to, and contributions to capital by, the guaranteeing shareholders if, under existing principles of law (applied without reference to Section 385), the loans were treated as having been made to the guaranteeing shareholders.

4. Subchapter S contains a safe-harbor which, if the requirements thereof are complied with, eliminates the possibility that debt classified as equity might be treated as a second class of stock, thereby terminating the Subchapter S election. For Subchapter S purposes, a straight debt instrument, even if classified as equity for other purposes, will not be treated as a second class of stock. A straight debt instrument is defined as a written unconditional promise to pay a sum certain on demand or on a specified date if in addition: (1) the interest rate and payment dates are not contingent on matters such as corporate profits or corporate discretion; (2) the instrument is not convertible into stock; and (3) the creditor is a person, trust or estate eligible to hold S corporation stock. See Section 1361(c)(5).

5. The "pass through" of an S corporation's net operating losses first reduces the shareholders' bases in their stock and then their bases in the indebtedness owed to them by the corporation. The income of an S corporation taxed to the shareholders first increases their bases in the indebtedness owed them by the corporation to the extent such bases were reduced by the "pass through" of losses and then increases the shareholders' bases in the stock of the corporation. See Section 1367. As a result, if a shareholder's loan is repaid by an S corporation after the shareholder's basis in the loan has been reduced, the repayment will result in income to the shareholder treated, in most circumstances, as capital gains.

6. There are income tax disadvantages to a participant making loans to an entity. If the loans become worthless and the participant is an individual, he, in general, is only entitled to capital loss treatment. See Section 166(d). A partner, in some cases, might be able to treat a debt of the partnership as a

business bad debt. Is the trade or business of a limited partnership, however, attributed to a limited partner?

 a. In most cases, a debt owed by a corporation to one of its individual shareholders is considered a nonbusiness bad debt and, therefore, subject to capital loss treatment. See *Whipple v. Commissioner,* 373 U.S. 193, 83 S.Ct. 1168, 10 L.Ed.2d 288 (1963). If, however, the individual had purchased stock and the loss on the stock qualified for treatment under Section 1244, the individual would be entitled, within certain limits, to treat the loss as an ordinary deduction.

5.   INCORPORATING THE VENTURE

There may be a time in the life of a rental real estate project when the amount of the annual depreciation deduction is less than the amount of the annual amortization of principal of the mortgage on the real estate. If the entity used to operate the real estate is a partnership or another form of unincorporated entity, the partners or proprietors now will be taxed on some of the cash used to make principal payments on the mortgage—not a happy situation! In other instances, the tax advantages of a partnership or proprietorship may be less desirable than the limited liability, free transferability of interests, centralized management, and continuity of life of the corporate form. In either of the above two situations the participants may decide that a viable alternative is to incorporate the venture.

The corporation, rather than the individuals, will pay the income tax on the dollars used to pay the principal of the mortgage. Assuming that the actual depreciation of the improvements does not occur as fast as the amortization of the principal of the mortgage, the increased net value of the real estate of the corporation will be reflected in the value of the shares of stock held by the participants in the corporation.

When incorporating a business entity, what steps must the proprietor or the partners and partnership take to insure that incorporation will result in limited liability for the proprietor and the partners? For example, assume that the proper steps for incorporation under the Revised Model Business Corporation Act are taken. At the time of incorporation, invoices, purchase orders and all other documents are changed to refer to the entity as Real Estate Development Co., Inc., rather than just Real Estate Development Co. Will the partners in the partnership known as Real Estate Development Co., who are now the shareholders of Real Estate Development Co., Inc., be personally liable for the debts of the corporation?

They will be liable for the debts assumed by the corporation which were incurred by the partnership prior to incorporation, unless the creditors agree to release them. Will they be liable for debts incurred by the corporation, after incorporation, to creditors who had done business with the partnership prior to incorporation? Are there any steps, in addition to those required under the Revised Model Business Corporation Act and the changing of the name of the entity on all documents as described above, which the partners should take to avoid personal liability to a continuing creditor? See e.g., Philipp Lithographing v. Babich, 27 Wis.2d 645, 135 N.W.2d 343 (1965); Conner v. Steel, Inc., 28 Colo.App. 1, 470 P.2d 71 (1970); Kingsberry Homes v. Corey, 457 F.2d 181 (7th Cir.1972); Johnston v. Biehl, 7 Wn.App. 757, 502 P.2d 1027 (1972); Custom Equipment Co. v. Young, 564 P.2d 1020 (Okl.App.1976); Ruggles v. Barlow, 577 P.2d 113 (Utah 1978). If, in order to "cut off" personal liability to a continuing creditor, the former partners must demonstrate that the creditor "knew or should have known of the existence of the corporation," how should the continuing creditors be informed of that fact?

Who is a continuing creditor? Is a supplier of window stripping, whose only transaction with the partnership was the sale of some stripping two years prior to incorporation, a continuing creditor? What if the sale was five years or ten years prior to incorporation? Is a creditor who had no transactions with the partnership a continuing creditor if the creditor knew of the existence of the partnership through conversations with others in the trade or if the creditor had been approached, prior to incorporation, for a quotation on certain goods, but no business had been transacted? If all of the above might be considered continuing creditors, how do the former partners, in a commercially feasible manner, inform them of the existence of the corporation and the termination of the partnership? How do the former partners find out about them? Will the type of notice provided for in the Uniform Partnership Act suffice? See Section 35(1)(b)(II). The former partners might lessen their problems by using a completely different name for the corporation. Compare Kingsberry Homes v. Corey, 457 F.2d 181 (7th Cir.1972), with Johnston v. Biehl, 7 Wn.App. 757, 502 P.2d 1027 (1972). The name used by the partnership, however, might be of real value.

Section 351 of the Internal Revenue Code provides that upon incorporation in compliance with the terms of the section neither the transferors nor the corporation will recognize any gain or loss. The income tax concerns of the participants in the unincorporated entity are not solved as simply as the foregoing seems to suggest.

NOTE:

SECTION 351 OF THE INTERNAL REVENUE CODE AND "MID–STREAM" INCORPORATIONS

38 Cincinnati Law Review 96 (1969).

[footnotes omitted]

* * *

Property

Services

Section 351 is not applicable to a transfer unless the transferee corporation receives section 351 property in the exchange. Therefore it is necessary to arrive at a definition of property for section 351 purposes. If the taxpayer transfers something other than section 351 property, the transaction will be outside the application of the section and the change in form will be a taxable event as it was prior to the enactment of the predecessor of section 351. The term property has many different meanings under the Code, but none of them are applicable to section 351. With a few exceptions, the definition which has been gradually formed by the courts includes most of the normal assets of a business—money, patents, trade-names, trade secrets, employment contracts, goodwill, and business know-how. Services, however, are expressly excluded from treatment as property. This does not mean that the issuance of some stock for services will preclude the application of section 351 to afford nonrecognition with regard to the remainder of the stock which is issued for property. Only where less than 80 percent of the stock is issued for property, so that the section 351 control requirement is not met, will the exchange of stock for services prevent section 351 treatment.

What constitutes services has been a continuing source of difficulty. * * * The problem arises when that which is transferred to the corporation is no longer the services themselves, but a right or asset which has been substituted for the services. If a stockholder of a corporation performs services for the corporation, but is not paid for several years, his services have been reduced to an account receivable. Should he later agree to accept additional stock in the corporation in exchange for his account receivable, has he transferred services, or property in the form of a receivable? Services are excluded from section 351 property in order to prevent taxpayers from converting income which would be [treated as] ordinary income * * * into income [treated as] capital gain * * *. Without this exception, a cash basis taxpayer, who realizes no income at the time he performs services but rather defers it until his claim is collected, could avoid recognition of the gain * * * when the services are performed, take a zero basis in the stock he receives for them, and later sell the stock to realize a capital gain. If section 351 applies to his transfer of a claim for services, the result would be the very tax avoidance Congress is presumed to have intended to eliminate. Therefore, the cash basis taxpayer's claim for services should not be afforded section 351 treatment.

* * *

The considerations which apply to a cash basis taxpayer are not present in the case of an accrual basis taxpayer. By employing the accrual method of accounting, the taxpayer has chosen to recognize income when earned and pay tax on it at that time, rather than when received. Because tax has been paid on the claim for services before it is transferred to the corporation, the donation of such a claim to a corporation by an accrual basis taxpayer is the equivalent of his purchase of stock of the corporation with his after-tax earnings. * * * The result in affording him nonrecognition is exactly the same as that achieved by applying the assignment of income doctrine to the cash basis taxpayer. Therefore, there is no reason to deny section 351 treatment to an accrual basis taxpayer who transfers a claim for services in exchange for stock, provided he meets the other requirements of the section.

If the services are not performed for the corporation, but rather for a third person, they are considered to be section 351 property. However, this is not to say that the transaction will be afforded complete nonrecognition. Assume that A performs services for B—a business in a non-corporate form or the owner of such a business. B then owes a debt to A. If B forms C, a corporation, receiving all its stock, this transfer comes within section 351. If B then pays his debt to A with stock in C, this does not take the initial transfer to C outside of section 351; B will still be afforded nonrecognition by the section. [B, however, may recognize gain on the transfer of the C stock to A.] Even if A ultimately receives more than 20 percent of C's stock, the 80–percent control requirement of section 351 will not be defeated. However, the fact that section 351 will afford B nonrecognition on the receipt of the stock does not mean that A's receipt of that stock from B in exchange for services will not be recognized as income. If A is a cash basis taxpayer when he receives the stock, he is being compensated for his services and must recognize ordinary income in an amount equal to the value of the stock received. If A is an accrual basis taxpayer, he recognizes income at the time he performs the services. In that case, his later exchange of his right to compensation should not be taxed again as compensation. Rather, it is merely the equivalent of his receiving cash in payment for his services, paying tax on this receipt, and then purchasing stock with his aftertax earnings.

* * *

Stock or Securities

Another prerequisite to nonrecognition under section 351 is that the transferor must receive stock or securities of the transferee corporation in exchange for the property transferred. Although the terms stock and securities may have established definitions under state corporation and securities laws, these definitions are not determinative for income tax purposes. There appears to be little problem regarding whether that which is received is stock, since the indicia of stock—for example, ownership of the business, voting power, the right to dividends, and the right to share in the assets upon dissolution—provide a good definition. In addition, it must be remembered that if there are sufficient indicia present to raise a fair question whether the instruments are stock, then it is likely that they could meet the test of securities. Whether the instruments are stock as opposed to securities is irrelevant under section 351 since either will meet the statutory requirement and will afford nonrecognition.

The question of what constitutes securities is a more difficult one. Securities in section 351 has been held to mean the same thing as securities in the reorganization sections of the Code. The objective of all the rules governing what constitutes securities is to prevent persons from converting what is in reality a sale for cash into a tax-free transaction by accepting an equivalent of cash in exchange for the property transferred. Under the cases construing the reorganization sections, one of the principal considerations is the term of the instruments received. Bonds, debentures, and notes are generally considered to be securities if their term is a period of 10 years or more; but it is fairly certain that such instruments will not be treated as securities if their term is 5 years or less. It is probable that an average term of over 6½ years will be sufficient to result in a classification as securities.

An additional test which has been developed in the reorganization area is the continuity of interest doctrine. However, since the 80–percent control requirement of section 351 is nothing more than a statutory continuity of interest requirement, this aspect of the definition of a security is not relevant in a section 351 context. ＊ ＊ ＊

Control

Another requirement of section 351 is that the transferor or transferors of the property to the corporation be in control of the corporation *immediately after the exchange.* Control is defined in section 368(c) as ownership of stock of the transferee corporation possessing at least 80 percent of the total combined voting power of all classes of voting stock and of at least 80 percent of the total number of shares of all non-voting classes of stock. The principal problem in this area is the determination of what is meant by "immediately after the exchange." In most "mid-stream" incorporations this requirement will cause no problems because the transferor intends to hold at least 80 percent of the stock of the corporation so that he can continue his established business enterprise in a new form. There are situations, however, in which the transferor is under an obligation to dispose of more than 20 percent of the stock after receiving it from the corporation. In these situations, the control requirement will not be met by a mere momentary possession by the transferor, where his commitment to transfer the stock to a third party is certain to result in the loss of 80–percent control of the corporation. On the other hand, where the transferor's commitment to give up over 20 percent of the shares is subject to some contingency and there is a possibility that the control will not be lost, the momentary possession of the stock by the transferor will satisfy the section 351 control requirement even if the stock is transferred to a third party. Whether there is a contingency in the agreement between the transferor and the third party to dispose of the stock turns upon the essentialness of the agreement to the entire section 351 transaction. If the section 351 transaction could, under no circumstances, have taken place without the agreement to transfer the stock to the third party operating to divest the transferor of control, then the section 351 control requirement is not met because "the legal relations created by one transaction would have been fruitless without a completion of the series" of related transactions. If, however, a transferor voluntarily gives up more than 20 percent of the stock immediately after the transfer, without any prior commitment to do so, no lack of control for purposes of section 351 will result.

In light of existing decisions, under no circumstances should the transferor who wishes his transaction to fall within section 351 allow any of the stock which is due him to be issued directly to a third party by the corporation. In such a case, whether the stock is given up voluntarily or pursuant to an obligation created prior to the section 351 transaction, a loss of control under section 351 may be the consequence.

* * *

Abuses of Section 351

The reason for the enactment of section 351 was to eliminate the artificial economic barriers to a change in the form of a business. In analyzing whether a particular transfer must be afforded nonrecognition in order to effectuate that purpose it is necessary to distinguish between two types of property which may be transferred to the corporation: (1) Property which will be converted into income which the taxpayer would realize in the ordinary course of business without the section 351 transfer, such as receivables, and (2) property which would not be converted into income in the ordinary course of business, such as machinery.

The major obstacle to the incorporation of a going business was the purely artifical realization of income on the transfer of property of the second type, such as plant and equipment used in the business. In the ordinary course of the business in its prior form, such assets would not have been sold or disposed of and no gain would have been realized. They generally are used until they become worthless. However, under the law as it existed prior to the enactment of the predecessor of section 351, a transfer to a corporation was considered to be a taxable event like a sale, and the transferor was forced to recognize and pay tax on the amount of the difference between his basis and the value of the property transferred. Since there was no sale, however, there was no income with which to pay the tax. As a result of this artificial recognition of income, a taxpayer could not incorporate his business unless he had sufficient liquid assets to pay the tax on the artificial gain and desired to use them for such purpose. It was the intent of Congress to eliminate this burden by enacting the predecessor of section 351.

It does not follow, however, that Congress also intended to allow the taxpayer to transfer property belonging in the first category, that is, income *earned* by the business in its previous form which would have been realized in the ordinary course of the business in its previous form * * *. There are two situations under which a taxpayer might attempt to transfer property under section 351 which would have been realized as income in the ordinary course of the business in its prior form. In some transactions, only this type of property is transferred. * * * In such a situation the entire transaction may be disregarded by the Commissioner. If, however, such property is transferred incident to an otherwise legitimate section 351 transaction, the entire transaction should not be set aside, but only that part resulting in tax avoidance. The Commissioner has at his disposal four weapons which he may use to defeat the effect of section 351 when the taxpayer attempts to transfer property which would be converted into income in the ordinary course of the business in its old form. These weapons are discussed below.

A. *Assignment of Income Doctrine*

The assignment of income doctrine is designed to ensure that income is taxed to the person who earns it. * * *

B. *Business Purpose Doctrine*

A second weapon which can be used by the Commissioner to attack a section 351 transfer is the business purpose doctrine. Essentially this doctrine provides that, where a taxpayer engages in a transaction which meets the literal requirements of the Code, the Commissioner may nevertheless disregard it if the taxpayer had no motive for the transaction other than income tax avoidance. * * *

C. *Tax Benefit Doctrine*

Another weapon which the Commissioner may use to counteract the application of section 351 where tax avoidance would result is the tax benefit doctrine. The taxpayer receives a tax benefit when an item of gross income that, in retrospect, should have been included in the taxable income of a prior year was not so included and went untaxed. * * *

D. *Clear Reflection of Income Doctrine*

A fourth weapon available to the Commissioner is his statutory authority to require that the taxpayer's method of accounting clearly reflect his income under sections 446 and 482. These sections may override the application of section 351. * * *

NOTE

1. Is Section 351 applicable, upon incorporation of a partnership, to a partner who receives stock in the corporation for an interest solely in partnership profits which the partner received in return for services? As distinguished from an interest in capital received for services, an interest solely in profits is not generally thought to be subject to income taxation on its receipt. See Pennell, *Current Problems in Partnerships,* U.S.Cal.Tax Inst. 315 (1968); Note, *Taxation of the Service Partner: A Need For Clarification,* 6 Ga.L.Rev. 781 (1972); Reg.Sec. 1.721–1(b). In most cases, the amounts received as a result of an interest in profits will be subject to taxation as ordinary income when received or credited to the partner's account. But see *Sol Diamond,* 56 T.C. 530 (1971), affirmed, 492 F.2d 286 (7th Cir.1974), and Cowan, *Receipt of an Interest in Partnership Profits in Consideration for Services: The Diamond Case,* 27 Tax L.Rev. 161 (1972). The decision of the Tax Court in *Sol Diamond* has been criticized. See Comment, *Taxation of the Service Partner: A Need For Clarification,* supra; Lane, *Sol Diamond: The Tax Court Upsets The Service Partner,* 46 S.Cal.L.Rev. 239 (1973); Comment, *Income Regulation of Future Interests in Partnerships Profits and Losses,* 9 San Diego L.Rev. 373 (1972). The Court of Appeals for the Seventh Circuit, in affirming the Tax Court's *Sol Diamond* decision, held that, while the receipt of a partnership interest solely in profits in return for services can be subject to tax, it is only subject to tax when the value of the partnership interest is not speculative. The value of a partnership interest solely in profits received on formation of a partnership, in most cases, is speculative. While there were some indications that the Internal Revenue Service would not continue to raise the profits interest for services issue, see *GCM Discloses IRS View of Profits Interest for Services,* 57 J.Tax'n 91 (1982), the issue has been raised in recent cases. See *St. John v. United States,* 53 A.F. T.R.2d 84–718 (D.Ill.1983); *Kenroy, Inc.,* 47 CCH Tax Ct.Mem. 1749 (1984); *Kobor v. United States,* 62 A.F.T.R.2d 88–5047, (C.D.Cal.1987).

a. If the receipt of the interest in profits was not subject to tax, the partnership is incorporated and the partner receives 10% of the stock of the corporation for the interest in profits, does the partner now recognize ordinary income in an amount equal to the value of the stock received, despite Section 351? See Pennell, *Current Problems in Partnerships,* supra, and *United States v. Frazell,* 335 F.2d 487 (5th Cir.1964), rehearing denied, 339 F.2d 885 (1964), cert. denied, 380 U.S. 961, 85 S.Ct. 1104, 14 L.Ed.2d 152 (1965). If the partner who transfers the interest in profits receives in return 21% of the voting stock of the corporation, will the other partners be denied nonrecognition treatment under Section 351?

b. A participant in the formation of a corporation, who is to receive 21% of the stock of the corporation primarily in return for services, contributes to the corporation, in partial consideration for the 21% stock interest, property with a value equal to 10% of the value of the stock to be received. Will the other participants, who transfer appreciated property to the corporation, be entitled to Section 351 treatment? See Rev.Proc. 76–22, 1976–1 C.B. 562. Cf. Rev.Rul. 79–194, 1979–1 C.B. 145; Priv.Ltr.Rul. 7915011.

2. If Section 351 applies to the transfer of property to a corporation, will Sections 1245 and 1250 require the recapture of depreciation despite the applicability of Section 351? See Sections 1245(b)(3) and 1250(d)(3). If Section

351 applies to the transfer of property to a corporation, the basis of the corporation in the property transferred generally will be the same as it was in the hands of the transferor subject to certain adjustments. See Section 362(b).

a. If the value of depreciable property to be transferred to the corporation is greatly in excess of the property's adjusted basis in the hands of the transferor, the avoidance of Section 351 may be desirable. For example, the transaction might be cast as a sale rather than an exchange so that the corporation receives a basis in the property equal to the purchase price, rather than a carryover basis. In this situation Sections 1245 and 1250 will apply to the gain recognized.

3. If the transferor uses the cash method of accounting and transfers accounts receivable to the corporation, does Section 351 prevent recognition of the value of the accounts receivable upon transfer? The accounts receivable are probably property, under Section 351. See *Kniffen,* 39 T.C. 553 (1962), acq. 1965–2 C.B. 5. Cf. *Realty Loan Corp.,* 54 T.C. 1083 (1970), affirmed, 478 F.2d 1049 (9th Cir.1973). Since, however, the transferor performed the services necessary to produce the accounts receivable and all that remains is for the accounts receivable to be collected, the transfer of the accounts receivable is arguably an assignment of income. See *H. Lewis Brown,* 40 B.T.A. 565 (1939), affirmed, *Brown v. Comm'r,* 115 F.2d 337 (2d Cir.1940). But see *Thomas W. Briggs,* 15 CCH Tax Ct.Mem. 440 (1956); *Hempt Bros., Inc. v. United States,* 354 F.Supp. 1172 (M.D.Pa.1973), affirmed, 490 F.2d 1172 (3d Cir.1974), cert. denied, 419 U.S. 826, 95 S.Ct. 44, 42 L.Ed.2d 50 (1974); Rev.Rul. 80–198, 1980–2 C.B. 113; Brown, *Incorporating Transfers & Anticipatory Assignments,* 38 U.Pitt.L. Rev. 589 (1977); Keller, *The Midstream Incorporation of a Cash–Basis Taxpayer: An Update,* 38 Md.L.Rev. 480 (1979).

a. Is the reserve for bad debts of a transferor who uses the accrual method of accounting income to the transferor, under the tax benefit doctrine, since the transferor no longer needs the reserve after the transfer of the receivables to the corporation? The Supreme Court in *Nash v. United States,* 398 U.S. 1, 90 S.Ct. 1550, 26 L.Ed.2d 1 (1970), held that accrual method partnerships which transferred accounts receivable at net (face less reserve) in a Section 351 exchange were not taxable on the amount of the reserve.

b. See generally White, *Sleepers that Travel with Section 351 Transfers,* 56 Va.L.Rev. 37 (1970); Comment, *Tax Treatment of Unrealized Receivables: Transfers From an Unincorporated Business to a Controlled Corporation,* 24 Baylor L.Rev. 345 (1972); Frazer, *Organizing a Corporation: Recognizing and Handling the Tax Aspects,* 2 Tax'n Law. 14 (1973); O'Connor, *Tax Problems on Transfers of Assets to Corporations,* 52 Taxes 756 (1974); Burke, *Sec. 351—Problems, Planning and Procedures,* 6 Tax Adviser 103 (1975); Brown, *Incorporating Transfers & Anticipatory Assignments,* 38 U.Pitt.L.Rev. 589 (1977); North, *Organizing the Closely Held Corporation,* 32 N.Y.U.Inst.Fed.Tax'n 697 (1974); Moffett, *The Elusive Definition of Property Under Internal Revenue Code Section 351,* 15 Tulsa L.J. 230 (1979).

4. The transfer of payables by a partnership or proprietorship using the cash method of accounting presented some difficult problems in prior years. Prior to the 1978 Revenue Act, the Internal Revenue Service took the position that cash method payables should be considered liabilities, under Section 357, and the transferor must recognize gain to the extent that the amount of

payables, or amount of the payables in addition to other liabilities transferred, exceeded the adjusted basis of all of the property transferred. See e.g. *Raich,* 46 T.C. 604 (1966); *Testor v. Comm'r,* 327 F.2d 788 (7th Cir.1964); Note, *Section 357(c) and the Cash Basis Taxpayer,* 115 U.Pa.L.Rev. 1154 (1967). The Tax Court agreed with the Internal Revenue Service but was reversed by the Second Circuit Court of Appeals in *Bongiovanni v. Comm'r,* 470 F.2d 921 (2d Cir.1972), and by the Ninth Circuit Court of Appeals in *Wilford Thatcher v. Comm'r,* 533 F.2d 1114 (9th Cir.1976). In *Wilford Thatcher v. Comm'r,* supra, a cash method taxpayer transferred both receivables and payables to a controlled corporation. The Ninth Circuit, reversing the Tax Court, took the position that the "sale," under Section 357(c), was of the receivables in return for the payment of the payables. Therefore, the taxpayer recognized income on the exchange but was entitled to a deduction when the corporation paid the payables. Since the corporation paid the payables during the same tax year the transfer by the taxpayer to the corporation occurred, the deduction for the payment of the payables offset the income recognized under Section 357(c).

a. After being reversed in *Bongiovanni v. Comm'r,* supra, and *Wilford Thatcher v. Comm'r,* supra, the Tax Court reconsidered its position. In *Donald D. Focht,* 68 T.C. 223 (1977), the majority of the Tax Court held that cash method payables are not liabilities for the purposes of Section 357(c) to the extent that the payment of the payables by the transferor would result in deductions. See Note, *Section 357 Liabilities Do Not Include Deductible Liabilities of Cash Method Taxpayers,* 31 Tax Law. 243 (1977).

b. Congress, in the 1978 Revenue Act and the Technical Corrections Act of 1979, laid to rest most of the problems with respect to the transfer of cash method payables. Certain liabilities, including cash method payables, are excluded from treatment as liabilities for the purposes of Section 357(c) if the payment thereof would give rise to deductions and the excluded liabilities did not result in the creation of, or an increase in, the basis of any property. See Section 357(c)(3). In addition, the transferor's basis in the stock and securities of the corporation, received in the Section 351 exchange, is not reduced by the amount of the liabilities excluded under Section 357(c)(3). See Section 358(d)(2). See generally Coven, *Liabilities in Excess of Basis: Focht, Section 357(c)(3) and the Assignment of Income,* 58 Or.L.Rev. 61 (1979). Lastly, the Internal Revenue Service held in Rev.Rul. 80–198, 1980–2 C.B. 113, that a corporation which uses the cash method of accounting can deduct, upon payment, the trade accounts payable assumed by the corporation on the transfer to it, under Section 351, of the assets and liabilities of a cash method sole proprietorship.

5. The combination of constant payment amortization of a mortgage loan used to finance real estate improvements and even straight-line depreciation over a useful life less than the term of the mortgage loan can result in the adjusted basis of the real estate improvements being less than the amount of liabilities to which they are subject upon their transfer to a corporation in a Section 351 exchange. The corporation's taking of the real estate improvements, subject to the liabilities or its assumption of the liabilities in a Section 351 exchange, might be considered the receipt of property by the transferor other than stock or securities, under Section 351(b). Section 357, however, provides that the assumption of, or the taking subject to, the liabilities will not be treated as the receipt of additional property under Section 351(b) if the principal purpose of the assumption of the liabilities, or the acquisition of

property subject to the liabilities, by the corporation was not to avoid Federal income tax, and, if not, was a bona fide business purpose. See Section 357(a). If Section 357(b) applies, the gain on the Section 351 exchange will be recognized to the extent of the liabilities. See Greiner, Behling and Moffett, *Assumption of Liabilities and the Improper Purpose—A Re-examination of Section 357(b),* 32 Tax Law. 111 (1978). If Section 357(b) does not apply, but the liabilities, other than those excluded under Section 357(c)(3), exceed the total of the adjusted bases of all the property transferred, the excess is recognized as income. See Section 357(c). See *F.W. Drybrough v. Comm'r,* 376 F.2d 350 (6th Cir.1967).

6. See generally Jacobs, *Something Simple: A Tax–Free Incorporation,* 37 Tax Law. 133 (1983); Abrams and Kohen, *Planning an Incorporation to Maximize Tax Benefits to Corporation and Its Owners,* 12 Tax'n Law. 74 (1983).

7. Since a partnership is treated as an entity for certain purposes under the Internal Revenue Code, the incorporation of a partnership, under Section 351, presents additional problems. To begin, there are a number of ways in which the partnership assets can be transferred to the corporation.

Revenue Ruling 84–111

1984–2 Cum. Bull. 88.

ISSUE

Does Rev.Rul. 70–239, 1970 C.D. 74, still represent the Service's position with respect to the three situations described therein?

FACTS

The three situations described in Rev.Rul. 70–239 involve partnerships *X, Y,* and *Z,* respectively. Each partnership used the accrual method of accounting and had assets and liabilities consisting of cash, equipment, and accounts payable. The liabilities of each partnership did not exceed the adjusted basis of its assets. The three situations are as follows:

Situation 1

X transferred all of its assets to newly-formed corporation *R* in exchange for all the outstanding stock of *R* and the assumption by *R* of *X*'s liabilities. *X* then terminated by distributing all the stock of *R* to *X*'s partners in proportion to their partnership interests.

Situation 2

Y distributed all of its assets and liabilities to its partners in proportion to their partnership interests in a transaction that constituted a termination of *Y* under section 708(b)(1)(A) of the Code. The partners then transferred all the assets received from *Y* to newly-formed corporation *S* in exchange for all the outstanding stock of *S* and the assumption by *S* of *Y*'s liabilities that had been assumed by the partners.

Situation 3

The partners of Z transferred their partnership interests in Z to newly-formed corporation T in exchange for all the outstanding stock of T. This exchange terminated Z and all of its assets and liabilities became assets and liabilities of T.

In each situation, the steps taken by X, Y, and Z, and the partners of X, Y, and Z, were parts of a plan to transfer the partnership operations to a corporation organized for valid business reasons in exchange for its stock and were not devices to avoid or evade recognition of gain. Rev.Rul. 70–239 holds that because the federal income tax consequences of the three situations are the same, each partnership is considered to have transferred its assets and liabilities to a corporation in exchange for its stock under section 351 of the Internal Revenue Code, followed by a distribution of the stock to the partners in liquidation of the partnership.

LAW AND ANALYSIS

* * *

The premise in Rev.Rul. 70–239 that the federal income tax consequences of the three situations described therein would be the same, without regard to which of the three transactions was entered into, is incorrect. As described below, depending on the format chosen for the transfer to a controlled corporation, the basis and holding periods of the various assets received by the corporation and the basis and holding periods of the stock received by the former partners can vary.

Additionally, Rev.Rul. 70–239 raises questions about potential adverse tax consequences to taxpayers in certain cases involving collapsible corporations defined in section 341 of the Code, personal holding companies described in section 542, small business corporations defined in section 1244, and electing small business corporations defined in section [1361]. Recognition of the three possible methods to incorporate a partnership will enable taxpayers to avoid the above potential pitfalls and will facilitate flexibility with respect to the basis and holding periods of the assets received in the exchange.

HOLDING

Rev.Rul. 70–239 no longer represents the Service's position. The Service's current position is set forth below, and for each situation, the methods described and the underlying assumptions and purposes must be satisfied for the conclusions of this revenue ruling to be applicable.

Situation 1

Under section 351 of the Code, gain or loss is not recognized by X on the transfer by X of all of its assets to R in exchange for R's stock and the assumption by R of X's liabilities.

Under section 362(a) of the Code, R's basis in the assets received from X equals their basis to X immediately before their transfer to R.

Under section 358(a), the basis to X of the stock received from R is the same as the basis to X of the assets transferred to R, reduced by the liabilities assumed by R, which assumption is treated as a payment of money to X under section 358(d). In addition, the assumption by R of X's liabilities decreased each partner's share of the partnership liabilities, thus, decreasing the basis of each partner's partnership interest pursuant to sections 752 and 733.

On distribution of the stock to X's partners, X terminated under section 708(b)(1)(A) of the Code. Pursuant to section 732(b), the basis of the stock distributed to the partners in liquidation of their partnership interests is, with respect to each partner, equal to the adjusted basis of the partner's interest in the partnership.

Under section 1223(1) of the Code, X's holding period for the stock received in the exchange includes its holding period in the capital assets and section 1231 assets transferred (to the extent that the stock was received in exchange for such assets). To the extent the stock was received in exchange for neither capital nor section 1231 assets, X's holding period for such stock begins on the day following the date of the exchange. *See* Rev.Rul. 70–598, 1970–2 C.B. 168. Under section 1223(2), R's holding period in the assets transferred to it includes X's holding period. When X distributed the R stock to its partners, under sections 735(b) and 1223, the partners' holding periods included X's holding period of the stock. Furthermore, such distribution will not violate the control requirement of section 368(c) of the Code.

Situation 2

On the transfer of all of Y's assets to its partners, Y terminated under section 708(b)(1)(A) of the Code, and, pursuant to section 732(b), the basis of the assets (other than money) distributed to the partners in liquidation of their partnership interests in Y was, with respect to each partner, equal to the adjusted basis of the partner's interest in Y, reduced by the money distributed. Under section 752, the decrease in Y's liabilities resulting from the transfer to Y's partners was offset by the partners' corresponding assumption of such liabilities so that the net effect on the basis of each partner's interest in Y, with respect to the liabilities transferred, was zero.

Under section 351 of the Code, gain or loss is not recognized by Y's former partners on the transfer to S in exchange for its stock and the assumption of Y's liabilities, of the assets of Y received by Y's partners in liquidation of Y.

Under section 358(a) of the Code, the basis to the former partners of Y in the stock received from S is the same as the section 732(b) basis to the former partners of Y in the assets received in liquidation of Y and transferred to S, reduced by the liabilities assumed by S, which assumption is treated as a payment of money to the partners under section 358(d).

Under section 362(a) of the Code, S's basis in the assets received from Y's former partners equals their basis to the former partners as determined under section 732(c) immediately before the transfer to S.

Under section 735(b) of the Code, the partners' holding periods for the assets distributed to them by Y includes Y's holding period. Under section 1223(1), the partners' holding periods for the stock received in the exchange includes the partners' holding periods in the capital assets and section 1231 assets transferred to S (to the extent that the stock was received in exchange for such assets). However, to the extent that the stock received was in exchange for neither capital nor section 1231 assets, the holding period of the stock began on the day following the date of the exchange. Under section 1223(2), S's holding period of the Y assets received in the exchange includes the partner's holding periods.

Situation 3

Under section 351 of the Code, gain or loss is not recognized by Z's partners on the transfer of the partnership interests to T in exchange for T stock.

On the transfer of the partnership interests to the corporation, Z terminated under section 708(b)(1)(A) of the Code.

Under section 358(a) of the Code, the basis to the partners of Z of the stock received from T in exchange for their partnership interests equals the basis of their partnership interests transferred to T, reduced by Z's liabilities assumed by T, the release from which is treated as a payment of money to Z's partners under sections 752(d) and 358(d).

T's basis for the assets received in the exchange equals the basis of the partners in their partnership interests allocated in accordance with section 732(c). T's holding period includes Z's holding period in the assets.

Under section 1223(1) of the Code, the holding period of the T stock received by the former partners of Z includes each respective partner's holding period for the partnership interest transferred, except that the holding period of the T stock that was received by the partners of Z in exchange for their interests in section 751 assets of Z that are neither capital assets nor section 1231 assets begins on the day following the date of the exchange.

* * *

NOTE

1. If the assets of a partnership are transferred to a corporation in return for the stock of the corporation and it is desired that the corporation elect S corporation status, since a partnership cannot be a shareholder in an S corporation, the partnership must be liquidated, and the stock of the corporation held by the former individual partners of the partnership. See Section 1361(b)(1)(B).

2. If Situation 1 described in the above revenue ruling is chosen as the way to incorporate a partnership, is the stock of the corporation, in the partners' hands, eligible for Section 1244 treatment? See Reg.Sec. 1.1244(a)–1(b)(2).

     a. If the partnership is not liquidated and continues to hold the stock of the corporation, is the stock eligible for Section 1244 treatment? See Section 1244(a).

3. If the aggregate of the partners' bases in their partnership interests is greater than the aggregate of the partnership's adjusted bases in its assets, which way or ways should be chosen to incorporate the partnership so as to give the corporation the highest possible aggregate adjusted bases in the assets?

     a. What choice should be made if the aggregate of the partnership's adjusted bases in its assets is greater than the aggregate of the partners' bases in their partnership interests?

4. If a partnership's assets include inventory which, under Section 751(d)(1), is not substantially appreciated, which way or ways should be chosen to incorporate the partnership so that the former partners receive the longest possible holding period for all of the stock of the corporation?

5. If the amount of the liabilities of a partnership is greater than the aggregate of the adjusted bases of its assets but less than the aggregate of the bases of the partners in their partnership interests, which way or ways should be chosen to incorporate the partnership in order to avoid recognizing any gain on the transaction?

     a. If the amount of the liabilities is greater than the aggregate of the bases of the partners in their partnership interests but less than the aggregate of the adjusted bases in partnership assets, which way or ways should be chosen?

     b. See Tiller, *Contributing Partnership Interests to a Corporation: "Liabilities" After Smith,* 2 J.Ps.Tax'n 316 (1986).

6. If the continued life of the partnership is desired, which form of incorporation should be chosen?

7. See Bogdanski, *Closely Held Corporations; Vive Les Differences: Revenue Ruling 84–111,* 11 J.Corp.Tax'n 367 (1985); Losey, *New Ruling on Incorporation of Partnership Business,* 1 J.Ps.Tax'n 340 (1985); Feldman and Hotek, *Choices Now Available for a Partnership that Wants to Incorporate Its Operations,* 15 Tax'n Law. 4 (1986); Kramer and Kramer, *Incorporation of a Partnership: IRS's New Position Produces Planning Opportunities and Pitfalls,* 64 Taxes 560 (1986); Barrie and Jones, *Incorporating an Ongoing Partnership: Selecting the Appropriate Method,* 3 J.Ps.Tax'n 335 (1987); Note, *Incorporating a Partnership Under Rev.Rul. 84–111: A New Literal Code Application Approach,* 40 Tax Law. 779 (1987).

6. ACCUMULATED EARNINGS AND PERSONAL HOLDING COMPANIES

If a corporation is used as the operating entity for a rental real estate project, the accumulated earnings and the personal holding company provisions of the Internal Revenue Code present potential concerns. The personal holding company provisions are mechanistic. A corporation either is or is not a personal holding company, under

Sections 541–547. If a corporation's personal holding company income, as defined in Section 543(a), is 60% or more of its adjusted ordinary gross income, as defined in Section 543(b)(2), and the stock ownership requirement of Section 542(a)(2) is met, it is a personal holding company. If either the income or the stock ownership requirement is not met, it is not a personal holding company.

A closely-held corporation operating a rental real estate project generally "lies on the brink" of being a personal holding company. A corporation's adjusted income from rent, as defined in Section 543(b)(3), is not personal holding company income if it constitutes 50% or more of the corporation's adjusted ordinary gross income and the undistributed other personal holding company income of the corporation is less than 10% of its ordinary gross income. If the adjusted income from rent is only 49% of adjusted ordinary gross income, or if the undistributed other personal holding company income is 11% of ordinary gross income, the adjusted income from rent is personal holding company income. Therefore the rental income of the corporation, its other investments, and the income from the investments must be carefully watched and, to the extent possible, controlled.

It may be difficult, however, to determine during the tax year whether the retained income from other investments which produce personal holding company income will exceed the 10% of ordinary gross income. One solution is to distribute to the shareholders of the corporation all of such income received. In addition, Section 563(c) permits dividends paid on or before the 15th day of the third month following the close of the taxable year to be considered as made on the last day of the taxable year.

A fire or just a year with an abnormally high vacancy rate may reduce the rental income of the corporation so that the adjusted income from rents constitutes less than 50% of adjusted ordinary gross income. If the corporation's other income is not personal holding company income, it should have no problems since, in most cases, even if its adjusted income from rent is considered personal holding company income it will not meet the 60% test of Section 542(a)(1). If, however, the corporation's other income is personal holding company income, it will be a personal holding company since the definition of adjusted ordinary gross income does not permit a deduction for dividends paid in arriving at adjusted ordinary gross income.

If the loss of rental income is the result of a fire or other casualty and the corporation receives the proceeds of a business interruption or use and occupancy policy, are the proceeds considered adjusted income from rents? See Section 543(b)(3). If the proceeds are considered ordinary income to the corporation and not rents, they are not personal holding company income and they increase adjusted ordinary gross income. On the other hand, if they are the proceeds of a per diem use and occupancy policy treated under Section 1231, see pages 1069 to 1071 supra, the gain, if any, is not personal holding company income nor is it included in adjusted ordinary gross income. See Section 543(b)(1)(B). For a general discussion of the personal holding company provisions see Division II, pages 552 to 562 supra.

Potential liability for the accumulated earnings tax is frequently present in the operation of a closely-held business in corporate form. As contrasted with the personal holding company provisions, the accumulated earnings tax provisions are far from mechanistic. The accumulated earnings tax provisions, Sections 531–537, do not apply to a personal holding company. They apply when a corporation has been formed or availed of for the purpose of avoiding income tax with respect to its shareholders by permitting earnings and profits to accumulate rather than paying dividends. In *United States v. Donruss*, 393 U.S. 297, 89 S.Ct. 501, 21 L.Ed.2d 495 (1969), the Supreme Court held that the forbidden purpose need not be the sole, dominant, controlling or impelling reason for the accumulation, it is enough if it is just one of many reasons and it does not have to be one of the important reasons. The holding in *United States v. Donruss*, supra, means that justifying an accumulation as required for the reasonable needs, including the reasonably anticipated needs, of a business is the best, if not the only, way of avoiding the imposition of the accumulated earnings tax, unless substantially all of the earnings are paid out as dividends.

WHAT'S NEW UNDER SECTION 531?

Mario P. Borini
19 Tulane Tax Institute 75 (1970).
[most footnotes omitted]

* * *

Unreasonable Accumulation

In general, [the accumulated earnings tax is imposed] on any unreasonable accumulation of taxable income by a corporation which was formed or availed of for the purpose of avoiding income tax with respect to its shareholders. * * *

Because of its factual overtones the question of unreasonable accumulation is unique as to each taxpayer. * * * "Each business has its own history, its own problems and managerial policies." Obviously, an extensive review of the taxpayer's overall plans is necessary before one can determine if indeed there has been an improper retention of earnings and profits. Such a determination is of fundamental importance because this is the key upon which almost all accumulated earnings tax litigation rests and it is the first line of defense in combating the imposition of the penalty tax. Furthermore, the proof of the reasonableness of the accumulation of earnings and profits also serves a two-fold purpose:

1.　It avoids a burden-of-proof problem. If a corporation has accumulated earnings and profits beyond the reasonable needs of its business this will be determinative of the avoidance motive unless by the preponderance of the evidence the corporation can prove the contrary.

2. It bypasses the question of proving the accumulated earnings credit. This amount, which is allowed in computing the penalty tax, is equal to the amount of earnings and profits which is retained for the reasonable needs of the business. The minimum credit is $[250,000]. Thus, corporations normally do not have to worry about the Section 531 tax until accumulated earnings and profits exceed $[250,000].

Under * * * [Section 1561] multiple corporate groups [are] limited to one credit of $[250,000] for all member corporations * * *.

Reasonable Needs of the Business

It should be noted that the term "unreasonable accumulation of earnings and profits" is, by definition, an accumulation beyond the reasonable needs of the business. Obviously, it is therefore incumbent upon the tax practitioner to ascertain what the reasonable needs of the business are when dealing with the Section 531 tax.

The statute and regulations are at best general guides as to what is to be considered reasonable business needs and the extent to which retention of earnings and profits are allowed before a company would be subjected to the Section 531 tax.

Some acceptable grounds for earnings accumulation specifically enumerated in the Regulations are:

1. Amounts required for bona fide business expansion and plant replacement will insulate the corporation from the Section 531 tax.

* * *

2. Money expended in the acquisition of a new business may be a good defense against the penalty tax.

* * *

On the other hand, when a company, through economic factors, can reasonably expect to lose a major part of its business it is incumbent upon management to look for new areas of endeavor. If such a move is contemplated the company should anticipate the ultimate costs involved and accumulate earnings to meet these expenses. * * *

3. Funds required for the retirement of bona fide business indebtedness may be accumulated with impunity.

4. Working capital requirements may be met from accumulation of income. * * *

5. Investments or loans to suppliers or customers necessary for the maintenance of the corporation's business may be financed through retention of earnings.

* * *

Grounds which *may* indicate an accumulation beyond the corporation's reasonable business needs according to the Regulations include the following:

1. Loans to shareholders and expenditures for their personal benefit are not legitimate calls on corporate funds.

* * *

2. Loans having no bona fide corporate business purpose indicate a possible unreasonable accumulation.

* * *

3. Loans between brother-sister corporations are not considered to be reasonable business needs for the accumulation of earnings and profits.

4. Passive investments may be indicative of the proscribed purpose.

* * *

From case law it seems clear that passive investments in and of themselves are not determinative of the proscribed purpose. If one could establish that the reasonably anticipated needs of a business exceeded its retained earnings[,] any passive investments should be considered incidental and standing alone should not subject the corporation to a tax under Section 531.

5. Retentions of earnings to provide against unrealistic hazards may prove detrimental where a taxpayer is defending against the imposition of the Section 531 tax.

* * *

Anticipated Corporate Needs Must Be Reasonable

It is clear from the prior discussion that the question of what are the reasonably anticipated needs of a business is essentially a factual determination. However, according to the regulations there must be an indication that such needs are required through some specific, definite and feasible plan for the use of the accumulation of earnings and profits. This "Indication" should be more than a mere recognition that a problem exists. There must be affirmative action towards accomplishing the objectives for which the corporation has retained its earnings and profits.

Documentary evidence such as corporate minutes, correspondence, and purchase commitments for expansion lend credence to the position that earnings were accumulated for reasonably anticipated future business needs. * * *

Working Capital Needs—Manufacturing Corporations

Working capital requirements of a business have been recognized as a legitimate reason for accumulating income. However, what is to be included in working capital and the amount thereof have caused considerable consternation to taxpayers, the Internal Revenue Service, and the courts. Although no definite answer has been promulgated which would alleviate this problem, the operating cycle approach * * * has been utilized as an objective standard. * * *

It is well settled that the operating cycle of a manufacturing concern consists of that period of time required to convert cash into raw materials, raw materials into an inventory of marketable products, the inventory into sales and accounts receivable and the period required to collect the outstanding accounts. The "operating cycle formula" has been established as a practical guide which produces an amount of earnings and profits necessary for current operations. Basically this mathematical formula * * * generally known as the "Bardahl formula" can be stated as follows:

1. Divide the cost of goods sold by the average inventory to obtain the inventory turnover; convert the result to days.

2. Divide the total sales by average receivables to obtain the receivables turnover; convert the result to days.

3. Add the results, in days, arrived at in Steps 1 and 2 and convert this figure into a percent of a year.

4. Multiply the percentage in Step 3 by the total cost of goods sold plus total operating expenses (excluding depreciation and Federal income taxes). The result will represent the working capital requirements required for one complete operating cycle of the company.

* * *

Working Capital Needs—Nonmanufacturing Corporations

However, * * * the basic formula [may be modified] when applying it to a sales corporation by including the credit terms allowed to the corporation. A reduction is made of the percentage calculated in Step 3 by the percentage of average accounts payable to cost of materials purchased during the year. The effect of this is to reduce the working capital (operating cycle) requirements.

* * *

While in its original and adjusted format the Bardahl formula indicates that *average* inventory and accounts receivable should be used in the calculation of their respective turnovers; the [courts have] approved the more favorable use of *peak* inventories and receivables. Through the utilization of these peak values substantially higher working capital needs are produced. * * *

When a service type corporation is faced with the penalty tax problem a Bardahl computation may not be appropriate. However, this does not necessarily mean that there is no way to adequately establish its working capital needs. The courts will generally consider unusual working capital requirements, circumstances, and normal business conventions when evaluating the reasonableness of the retention of a company's earnings.

* * *

A Critique of the Bardahl Formula

The Bardahl formula has the appeal of simplicity and the aura of preciseness which tends to make it dangerous. In and of itself the formula is not responsive to the realities of the true business needs of a corporation. It uses historical factors as a measure of future costs (needs) without giving due consideration to possible increases of expenses, more intense competition, and the potential growth of a going concern, all of which are subject to inflationary pressures. Oftentimes a corporation having profitable years will, under a Bardahl computation, show a need during these periods for working capital in excess of its net liquid position. Logically the corporation could finance its operations through the use of current and near-term future profits obviating the need to accumulate part of earnings for its "operating cycle" but profits are not considered in the formula. This points up some of the deficiencies of the Bardahl formula and all too often ridiculous results are obtained.

The working capital of a business is normally measured by the excess of current assets over current liabilities. However, inventories could be viewed by a business enterprise as a permanent investment or a base stock, without which the business cannot operate. A more realistic measure of business needs is thus achieved since now the excess of current assets (excluding inventories) over current liabilities would produce the net quick assets available to the corporation. Theoretically these "quick assets" are readily convertible into cash and therefore could be utilized to meet the current operating needs of a business. The working capital requirements, as computed under the Bardahl formula, should therefore be measured against the corporation's net quick assets.[34]

Account should be taken of the economic growth of a company which warrants an accumulation of earnings and profits. The classic economic cycle (depression, recovery, prosperity, recession) has yet to be consistently professed as a proper ground for the retention of earnings and profits. We must recognize that increasing costs, which almost all businesses experience, may not all be passed on to the ultimate consumer. Companies must build their capacity to absorb some of these spiraling expenses which sooner or later may not be recoverable from customers. Moreover, since the purchasing power of a dollar has been [in general] decreasing, the use of historical costs as a measure of future business needs is unrealistic.

A possible solution in arriving at a more meaningful standard would be to convert the amount of the reasonable needs of a business, calculated under a Bardahl-type formula, to current dollar values by the use of an inflation factor. For example, assume that in 19[8]5 a corporation determines that in 19[9]0 it will require a new manufactur-

34. Electric Regulator Corp. v. Commissioner, 336 F.2d 339 (2d Cir.1964); Smoot Sand & Gravel Corp. v. Commissioner, 241 F.2d 197 (4th Cir.1964).

ing facility which in 19[8]5 would cost $1 million. Assume further that the price index in 19[8]5 is 110 and in 19[8]9 it stands at 130, for determining the amount of retained earnings sheltered from the penalty tax in 19[8]9, this need should be stated at $1.2 million.

Purpose and Intent—The Donruss Case

In determining if a corporation comes under the veil of Section 531 a two-pronged test is provided by the statute. There must be:

1. An unreasonable accumulation of earnings and profits, and

2. A tax avoidance purpose for such an accumulation on the part of the shareholders.

Thus far we have dealt with the first prong and now turn our attention to the second.

Prior to *Donruss* one of the major problems in imposing the penalty tax was the degree to which an accumulation must have been motivated by an attempt to avoid income taxes imposed on the shareholders. The question as to whether the proscribed purpose must have been the "sole purpose," the "dominant purpose" or merely "one of the purposes" for the accumulation of earnings, which would cause the penalty tax to be assessed, was in a chaotic state. There was a sharp conflict of authority among the Circuit Courts as to the degree of intent necessary to impose the penalty tax. * * * Presumably the Supreme Court in *Donruss* has clarified and resolved this confusion. It held that, assuming an improper accumulation of earnings, the corporation is subject to the penalty tax if tax avoidance at the shareholder level played any part in the decision not to pay dividends. * * *

It is submitted, however, that this decision has done nothing more than to formalize what tax practitioners have always had uppermost in their minds when defending against a Section 531 tax. That is, the intent test is not of great significance when arguing against the imposition of the penalty tax unless and until there is, in fact, an unjustified amount of accumulated earnings. It has come to pass that this intent test, for practical purposes, has been negated since, as Justice Harlan's dissent infers, it is impossible to show that knowledge of the tax consequences did not play some part, however slight, in the corporation's decision to accumulate earnings.

The Supreme Court's view that tax avoidance need only be one of the purposes creates substantial difficulty in overcoming an assertion that the penalty tax should be imposed due to the existence of the prohibited purpose. The knowledge by the shareholders of the tax ramifications involved is almost a foregone conclusion. Hence, extremely difficult burdens will be placed on the taxpayer when trying to convince a court or jury that despite this knowledge other business reasons, in fact, constituted the ultimate decision to accumulate earnings. Since *no* degree of importance need be established for the tax avoidance purpose the taxpayer's defense has become more cumbersome.

The importance of the Supreme Court's decision is mitigated to some extent by the accumulated earnings tax credit available under Section 535(a), when calculating a company's accumulated taxable income. It is well settled that the taxpayer will be entitled to a credit equal to the amount of earnings and profits retained for the reasonable needs of the business despite the existence of the proscribed purpose. * * * Obviously the best possible grounds for defeating the penalty tax lies in the realm of proving that there was no unreasonable retention of earnings.

Accumulated Taxable Income

It is important to determine the amount, if any, of the accumulated taxable income of a company since this is the base upon which the penalty tax is computed. Basically, Section 535 defines accumulated taxable income as the taxable income of a company adjusted by deducting the following items:

1. Federal income and excess profits taxes accrued or paid during the taxable year, including Sections 531 and 541 taxes, [35]

2. charitable contributions in excess of the [10]% limitation imposed by Section 170(b)(2);

3. [the net capital loss for the taxable year less the amount of net capital gains which has been allowed as a deduction in computing accumulated taxable income for preceding taxable years beginning after July 18, 1984 and has not as yet been used to reduce net capital losses]

                    * * *

4. any excess long-term capital gains over short-term capital losses, excluding any carryover capital losses, net of taxes.

To this result the following is then added:

1. Any net operating loss deduction allowed under Section 172;

2. any special deduction available under Sections 241–247 relating to dividends received by a corporation; and

3. capital loss carryovers as provided under Section 1212.

From the amount so computed there is also deducted the sum of the dividends paid deduction and the accumulated earnings credit. The result is [an] attempt to arrive at the true economic income for the year. * * *

35. An increase in Federal tax liability is deductible for the taxable year under examination in computing accumulated taxable income subject to the accumulated earnings tax. Rev.Rul. 68–632, [1968–2 C.B. 253].

Role of Dividends

In arriving at the base upon which the penalty tax is imposed, namely accumulated taxable income, there is allowed the dividends paid deduction. This deduction is the sum of any dividends paid during the taxable year plus any consent dividends for the taxable year as determined under Section 565. The concept of dividends not only embraces dividends described in Section 316 but also liquidating dividends as long as such distributions are made pro rata.

* * *

Assuming a corporation has no ready cash to pay a dividend; its assets are tied up in inventory and receivables, would it be reasonable to expect the corporation to borrow funds to pay a cash dividend or declare a taxable stock dividend?

The stock dividend argument was specifically rejected in *Faber Cement* where the court stated:

"(I)f we were to accept (the Internal Revenue Service's taxable stock dividend) argument, we doubt that there would ever be a case where, either within its existing capital structure or through appropriate amendment to its charter, a corporate taxpayer would not be able to declare a taxable stock dividend within the specifications of Section 305. We are not prepared to accord respondent such an antimissile missile to overcome proof by taxpayers that accumulated earnings and profits were required by the reasonable needs of the business." [36]

The same rationale should apply to a borrowing-to-pay dividend argument. It is not the monetary size of the accumulation that counts but rather the liquid assets which [are] determinative of the tax.

* * *

NOTE

1. The accumulated earnings tax is imposed on the accumulated taxable income of a corporation formed or availed of for the purpose of avoiding the income tax with respect to its shareholders by permitting earnings and profits to accumulate. See Section 532(a).

    a. Accumulated taxable income equals taxable income for the taxable year, as adjusted pursuant to Section 535(b), minus the sum of the dividends paid deduction and the accumulated earnings credit.

        1. The accumulated earnings credit is the greater of an amount equal to such part of the earnings and profits for the taxable year as are retained for the reasonable needs of the business or $250,000 less the accumulated earnings and profits of the corporation at the close of the preceding taxable year. See Section 535.

36. [50 T.C. 317, 328–329 (1968), acq., 1968–2 C.B. 2.]

2.　In the case of certain personal service corporations, the accumulated earnings credit is reduced to $150,000. See Section 535(c)(2)(B).

b.　The absence of a reasonable business need for an accumulation is presumptive evidence of the purpose to avoid tax with respect to shareholders.　See Section 533(a).

2.　The status of a corporation as a mere holding or investment company is prima facie evidence of the purpose to avoid the income tax with respect to shareholders.　See Section 533(b).　A mere holding or investment company is not entitled to an accumulated earnings credit for earnings and profits accumulated for the reasonable needs of the business.　See Section 535(c)(1).　Section 535(c)(3), however, provides that a mere holding or investment company is entitled to a $250,000 accumulated earnings credit.　Lastly, a mere holding or investment company cannot deduct net capital losses for the purpose of computing accumulated taxable income.　See Section 535(b)(8).　Therefore, for the reasons stated above it is important that a real estate corporation not be classified as a mere holding or investment company.　Regulation Sec. 1.533–1(c) defines a mere holding or investment company as a corporation having practically no activities except holding property and collecting the income therefrom or investing therein.　This definition appears to exclude any active real estate corporations.　Might a corporation which owns a shopping plaza in which all of the tenants have triple net leases be classified as a mere holding or investment company?　See *Starman Investment, Inc. v. United States*, 534 F.2d 834 (9th Cir. 1976); *Empire Land Corporation v. United States*, 473 F.Supp. 1289 (E.D.La. 1979); *H.C. Cockrell Warehouse Corporation*, 71 T.C. 1036 (1979).

3.　The Bardahl formula will not literally apply to a real estate corporation.　How are the working capital needs of a real estate corporation determined?　Can the net quick assets be measured against the current operating expenses of the corporation?　How is the amount of money which the corporation requires for amortization of the principal amount of any mortgage or mortgages taken into account?　Cf. Note, *Section 531: Using the Bardahl Formula to Determine Reasonable Accumulations of Working Capital for a Service Company*, 49 Notre Dame Law. 141 (1973).

4.　If a corporation accumulates earnings to establish a fund out of which shareholders' stock can be redeemed, can the corporation justify the fund as serving a reasonable business need?　See Cuddihy, *Accumulated Earnings and Personal Holding Company Taxes*, 21 N.Y.U.Inst.Fed.Tax'n 401 (1963); *Pelton Steel Castings Co. v. Comm'r*, 251 F.2d 278 (7th Cir.1958), cert. denied, 356 U.S. 958, 78 S.Ct. 995, 2 L.Ed.2d 1066 (1958).　If, instead of accumulating to establish the fund, the corporation accumulates to pay off a note given to a shareholder in redemption of the shareholder's stock, can the corporation now justify the accumulation as serving a reasonable business need?　See Reg. Sec. 1.537–2(b)(3).　Is a note given to a shareholder in redemption of stock a "bona fide indebtedness created in connection with the trade or business"?　Do the reasons for the redemption of the stock of the shareholder make any difference?　See *Mountain State Steel Foundaries, Inc. v. Comm'r*, 284 F.2d 737 (4th Cir.1960).

a.　Is purchasing insurance to provide funds for the redemption of the stock of a shareholder a satisfactory alternative to the corporation's accumulating earnings for this purpose?

5.　See generally Comment, *Reasonable Needs of the Business: The Section 537 Question*, St. Mary's L.J. 444 (1974); Linch, *Defending Against the Accumu-*

lated Earnings Tax, 6 Tax Adviser 518 (1975); Case, *Accumulated Earnings Tax Aspects of Business Expansions and Investments*, 32 Tax L.Rev. 1 (1976); Cunningham, *More Than You Ever Wanted to Know About the Accumulated Earnings Tax*, 6 J.Corp.Tax'n 187 (1979); Horvitz and Hebble, *The Effect of the Section 531 Penalty on Accumulations of Earnings and Profits After TRA '86*, 14 J.Corp.Tax'n 2366 (1987).

INDEX

References are to Pages

†

DATE DUE

W9-AOG-315

C
C

PRINTED IN U.S.A.

GAYLORD

HANDBOOK OF ORIENTAL STUDIES
HANDBUCH DER ORIENTALISTIK

SECTION ONE
THE NEAR AND MIDDLE EAST

EDITED BY

H. ALTENMÜLLER · B. HROUDA · B.A. LEVINE · R.S. O'FAHEY
K.R. VEENHOF · C.H.M. VERSTEEGH

VOLUME SEVENTY-SIX/TWO

CONCISE BIOGRAPHICAL COMPANION TO INDEX ISLAMICUS